FOURTH EDITION

INVESTMENTS

Principles / Practices / Analyses

DOUGLAS H. BELLEMORE, Ph.D.

Professor of Finance
Graduate School of Business Administration
New York University

JOHN C. RITCHIE, JR., Ph.D.

Professor of Finance
Chairman, Department of Finance
School of Business Administration
Temple University

Published by

F42   **SOUTH-WESTERN PUBLISHING CO.**

CINCINNATI   WEST CHICAGO, ILL.   DALLAS   PELHAM MANOR, N.Y.
PALO ALTO, CALIF.   BRIGHTON, ENGLAND

Library of Congress Catalog Card Number: 73-75259
ISBN No.: 0-538-06420-X

1 2 3 4 5 **H** 8 7 6 5 4

Printed in the United States of America

PREFACE

INVESTMENTS—Principles, Practices, Analyses, Fourth Edition, reflects the major changes that have taken place in the securities markets since the Third Edition, especially the fact that institutional investors by 1974 have come to account for 80 percent of the daily trading activity of such markets as the New York Stock Exchange. Also reflected is the fact that in recent years many institutional investors have been stressing short-term (under one year) performance not only in the stock markets but also in the bond markets.

The Fourth Edition consists of 33 chapters organized into an introductory chapter and 9 parts. It provides a logical development of practical investment principles and security analyses as applied by successful practicing financial analysts. It also gives a broad background of completely updated material in the form of many tables and charts. The material is so organized that the instructor who does not wish to use the entire book can logically develop a complete course using only 15 or 19 chapters: a 15-chapter course would consist of Chapters 1, 8-9, 10-12, 13-15, and 28-33; and a 19-chapter course, Chapters 1, 8-9, 10-12, 13-19, and 28-33.

Most of the important writings in professional journals, both before and since the Third Edition of this text, as well as all significant developments in the applied areas of investment, have been considered in the Fourth Edition. These are particularly emphasized in the following chapters:

> Chapter   7—Corporate Financial Policies and the Investor
> Chapter 11—Historical Evolution of Valuation Theories
> Chapter 12—Valuation Procedures Followed by Most Professional Analysts
> Chapter 14—Investment Growth Factors and Projections
> Chapters 28 through 32—These chapters deal with both individual and institutional portfolio policies
> Chapter 33—The Computer in Portfolio Selection

A great deal has been written in the 1960s and early 1970s by theoreticians on valuations that frequently require the use of very long-term projections together with the use of highly complicated mathematical models based on regression analysis. Some investment firms are experimenting with analytical mathematical models in developing valuation models, but experience to date has not proved rewarding; and successful practicing analysts have neither found these models useful nor been convinced that they can be developed. With respect to mathematical models, our views continue to coincide with those of successful analysts as well as those expressed by Professor Douglas A. Hayes (University of Michigan) and Professor David Durand (Massachusetts Institute of Technology), whose writings in the *Financial Analysts Journal* and *The Journal of Finance* have been excerpted in Chapter 11, pages 287 through 289. These comments, however, are in no way to be taken to refer to the use of computers that utilize such data banks as Standard & Poor's Compustat whose tapes are extensively being used by students of the authors, as explained and illustrated in Chapter 33.

The text emphasizes student involvement material at the end of each chapter in the form of questions, work-study problems, and a completely updated suggested readings list of important writings in the field. The instructor will have the use of a comprehensive instructor's manual keyed to this end-of-chapter activity.

The viewpoint of this book reflects the authors' many years of university teaching experience, successful practical portfolio supervisory experience over individual and institutional portfolios, as well as involvement in expert financial testimony in more than one hundred valuation cases heard by United States district courts, the United States Court of Claims, and the United States Supreme Court.

We wish to acknowledge the valuable assistance provided by Reese D. Jones, President, First Valley Bank, Bethlehem, Pennsylvania, in the preparation of Chapter 26, "United States Government Securities," and Chapter 27, "State and Municipal Securities."

In addition, Carolyn Bowers, an economist, engaged in a considerable amount of research necessary for the preparation of the manuscript for the Fourth Edition and provided valuable editorial assistance.

DHB
JCR

CONTENTS

PART SIX   **SPECIAL CLASSES OF SECURITIES**

PART SEVEN   **PUBLIC SECURITIES**

PART EIGHT   **PORTFOLIO POLICIES FOR INDIVIDUALS**

PART NINE   **INSTITUTIONAL PORTFOLIO POLICIES**

1

The Field of Investment

This book is almost entirely concerned with security investments—investments in bonds, private placement notes, equipment obligations, preferred stocks, and common stocks. However, the reader must recognize that savings may be invested in other assets, such as savings accounts, life insurance policies, home ownership, real estate, and private business ownership. The chapters on individual portfolio policies and management will briefly discuss the first two of these other investments. This book does not attempt to cover the fields of investment in real estate and private business ownership because both fields are just as specialized as is the area of security investment, and the old adage that a little knowledge is a dangerous thing can be applied.

ECONOMIC IMPORTANCE OF INVESTMENT

One attribute of the economic system of the United States stands out as being truly remarkable: the ability to produce the great and varied quantity of goods and services necessary to its citizenry. Foreigners seem continually awed with its endowments of factories, natural resources, fine harbors, and so forth. However, being in the midst of this great capacity, the people of the United States too often take this wealth for granted. Because they have been born into it, this fantastic industrial age has become too natural a situation for them. They have lost sight of the groundwork that preceded the building. The emergence of factories came about because of the will, the ambition, and the know-how of men bent on forging the growth of America. But growth also took money! Factories and machines were created only to the extent that the people were, and still are, willing to sacrifice present consumption, to save and invest.

Economic growth is necessary to support a growing population and a rising standard of living. Continued growth and increasingly complex and more efficient production processes require more capital. These capital goods can only be obtained by saving a portion of available current national income and transferring these savings to the hands of those who will use productively the resources represented thereby. A large part of the private capital of society is represented by securities. One important mechanism for transferring the capital represented by savings to productive investors is through the sale of securities. In a private enterprise economy, savings are voluntary rather than forced through state planning as in Eastern (Communist) Europe, Russia, and China. It is important that savings be encouraged and that there be a well-developed and efficient market system for transferring ownership to claims on capital in a private economy.

ROLE OF INVESTMENT: PRODUCTIVE AND UNPRODUCTIVE

Investment's role is indeed crucial. Generally speaking, the greater the production and the employment of capital goods, the greater the capacity to produce goods and services. The economic importance of savings and investment arises from the fact that they are essential to capital formation. The process, moreover, is in part self-generating. A larger stock of capital goods allows greater production, which, in turn, produces a potentially larger surplus for savings and investment in capital goods, and so on through successive periods of capital formation. Historically, this has been the manner in which it has been possible to raise workers' productivity and, as a result, their level of living. Conversely, the problem is just the reverse in under-developed countries that produce little surplus for savings above their minimum needs for consumption. They have difficulty investing in capital goods.

Thus far the discussion of investment has included only those funds saved and invested in capital goods tacitly assumed to be productive. But the broad demand for funds for investment in the capital markets may also be, in part, for unproductive purposes. For example, an individual may buy government bonds with his savings. These funds may be used for unproductive purposes such as defense. On the other hand, the government may channel these funds into such capital projects as roads and schools. If funds are supplied to business, they may be used to replenish depleted working capital, to retire debt, or for other purposes that do not result in net capital formation. Furthermore, all investment in capital goods is not necessarily productive in the economic sense and therefore desirable. In the first place, there may not be sufficient demand for the product; secondly, pollution and/or other damaging aspects to the social environment may outweigh purely economic considerations.

Against this background the role of investment must be modified. But the most important economic aspect of investment is still net capital formation through which an economy increases its productive capacities. Savings and investment are therefore interrelated, and investors should constantly examine and interpret trends in the flow of savings through capital markets.

SECURITY INVESTMENT AND INVESTORS

Security investment is the process of offering money in exchange for securities such as common and preferred stocks, bonds, private placement notes, and equipment trust obligations. Existing claims can be transferred,[1] or new claims can be created and sold. Only the sale of new claims participates directly in net capital formation. The investor in this sense, whether an individual or an institutional investor, offers money in exchange for securities that best suit his particular investment goals, program, and portfolio.

Individual and Institutional Investors

The investor must decide on the proper investment policy to follow. He must ask himself what are his goals and how much risk he is willing and able to assume. Risks, where possible, must be identified and evaluated by the investor. There are several different types of risk faced by the investor, and it is important that he understand and consider all of them. Unfortunately they are all too often ignored by investors. The future is uncertain, and the farther the look into the future, the greater the uncertainty. It is this future uncertainty that is the source of investment risks versus investment rewards.

The question arises as to whether or not the investor should seek interest income, dividend income, capital appreciation, or some combination of these. All investors are concerned with safety of principal, but some place much more stress on this point as an objective than do others. Such investors are mainly interested in preserving their principal; income and capital appreciation are secondary. In this group are individual and institutional investors who desire only the highest-grade investments that are relatively free from the risk of loss for either part or all of their portfolios.

---

[1] The exercise of liquidity preference, in the economist's language.

Of course, if the investor selects this as his primary goal, he must sometimes be willing to accept lower current market yields as a sacrifice for safety. At one extreme are those investors following a policy of buying only short-term United States Government securities. Other investors seek a somewhat higher yield, normally but not always offered by longer-term United States Government securities, for at least part of their portfolios. Next, there are those investors who are willing to accept the somewhat higher risk of various quality municipal and corporate bonds. Other investors who are willing to accept even higher risks may purchase preferred stocks, while still others may be willing to purchase common stocks. Common stocks, of course, have the highest degree of market and financial risk associated with them. The common stockholder is a residual claimant following all other claimants. The two types of risk involved are (1) the risk of dollar capital loss and (2) the risk of dollar income loss. In this respect, securities with the lowest risk are those that are expected to fluctuate the least in market value and to have secure income.

It is important to note that definitely included as investors are those individuals and institutions who purchase common stock. The definition does not exclude those who, after careful analysis and considered evaluation of specific risks in each situation, purchase common stocks mainly to secure long-term capital appreciation. In fact, to exclude this latter group would be to exclude individuals who are subject to high personal income taxes, since their major and often sole purpose in purchasing common stock must be to secure a return in the form of long-term capital appreciation rather than interest or dividend income or short-term capital appreciation. Individuals seeking short-term appreciation are classified as speculators and, if unintelligent speculators, as gamblers. Since the current yield on common stocks has been consistently below that of high-grade bonds since 1958,[2] the major reasons for purchasing common stocks by a person in a high tax bracket would be for capital appreciation.

So far, the approach to investment as opposed to speculation and gambling has been largely from the standpoint of investors' policies and goals. Investment can also be approached from the standpoint of the quality of securities available for purchase. Some securities are definitely of investment quality, and these include not only bonds but also quality preferred and common stocks. Other securities are definitely speculative. Some securities may be so highly speculative that they are little more than a gamble.

At one end of the spectrum of investment values are United States Government securities, followed closely by most state and many local government

---

[2] In 1971 and 1972, yields on common stocks in terms of the averages were less than half the yields on high-grade bonds, averaging approximately 3% versus 7.2%.

securities. These are, in turn, followed by high-grade and medium-grade corporate bonds, by high-grade and medium-grade preferred stocks, and finally by high-grade and medium-grade common stocks. Observation indicates that the graduation between United States Government bonds and the highest-rated corporate bonds has been narrow, thus testifying to investors the less-than-significant corporate financial risks involved because of the relative stability of the economy since 1938. Therefore, there are various degrees of financial risk in investments.

Most investors today expect some capital appreciation from their common stocks. Many investors are interested solely in capital appreciation, while others are interested in wide diversification of their portfolio among bonds and stocks. However, for the portion of common stocks in his portfolio, the investor usually does look forward to long-term capital appreciation. In this respect then, the key phrase for investors, as contrasted to speculators, is long-term capital appreciation. The speculator is not particularly interested in long-term capital appreciation, but he is generally concerned with short-term capital appreciation. Thus the time element, as well as the degree of uncertainty, separates investment from intelligent speculation and the goals of short-term traders.

In recent years, pressures on portfolio managers for performance have tended to shorten the period for expected capital appreciation. This has been especially true in the case of some mutual funds and even some corporate pension funds. To the extent that short-term (under one year) capital gains are being sought, such activity would be classified as short-term speculative trading.[3] The fact that an increasing number of financial institutions gear operations to more speculative objectives has led to concern on the part of some segments of the investment world. There was relatively little performance pressure on portfolio managers in the post-World War II years, 1949-1961. As the Dow Jones Industrial Averages (DJIA) rose from 160 to 735 in December, 1961, stocks rose in price three times as fast as earnings. But with the DJIA reaching a high of about 1,000 in February, 1966, then falling below 850 by 1970, there was mounting pressure on portfolio managers to outperform the averages. The DJIA did rise to approximately 1,050 in 1973, but had fallen to about 900 by May 20, 1973. After 1961, merely holding a cross-section of stocks of major American corporations was far less rewarding than prior to 1962.

Speculation Defined. There can be both intelligent and unintelligent speculation. Investment decisions, by definition, are based on thorough

---

[3] Numerous institutional portfolio managers justify short-term, under-one-year trading as the "new type of investing," but the authors of this book strongly disagree.

analysis of a security to determine its quality and prospects and to evaluate the risks. There must be adequate information available to provide an investor with the facts necessary to make an investment decision. Lack of adequate information can relegate a specific security to the speculative category and, if little or no information is available, to the category of a gamble.

The intelligent speculator also thoroughly analyzes a situation before making a commitment. However, he is willing to operate on the basis of more limited information than the investor and is willing to deliberately assume a higher degree of identifiable risks. The unintelligent speculator makes commitments without investigation. Actually, he closely resembles the gambler and perhaps there is little real distinction here. Those who act on tips provide one example.

There are unknowns and uncertainties in any investment situation, but there are more unknowns and uncertainties in a speculative situation than in an investment situation. The degree of risk assumed provides a most important distinction between the investor and the speculator. Another significant distinction, previously discussed, is the speculator's stress on short-term as opposed to long-term capital appreciation. *Short-term capital appreciation* may be defined as capital appreciation that can be expected in less than a year. The use of a one-year period is somewhat arbitrary, and speculators do make commitments that are expected to take longer to develop. The degree of risk assumed would tend to distinguish such situations from the investment situation. It should be clear that no sharp line separates investment from speculation or separates speculation from gambling. Between the extremes lies a long scale of relative values and risks.

Speculators do make commitments, for speculative purposes, in investment-grade securities. Speculators may speculate in United States Government and other securities of the highest quality seeking short-term capital gains. Often such commitments are highly levered, since borrowed funds are heavily used to purchase the securities. Widespread speculation in new issues of United States Government securities at times illustrates this point.[4]

Gambling Defined. The gambler, as opposed to the speculator, accepts risks with no real desire to identify, appraise, and balance them against the purported opportunities for capital gain. He is unwilling to take the time and to expend the effort to make a thorough investigation and often does not have

---

[4] The reader might find it of value to review the "Treasury-Federal Reserve Study of the Government Securities Market" (Board of Governors of Federal Reserve System and Treasury, February, 1960), Parts I-III, covering the period June, July, and August, 1958, and also to review the price fluctuations from highs to lows of long-term U.S. Government bonds in 1967 and 1968.

the ability and the training to do so. As an individual he is either unintelligent or lazy, and more frequently both. He is apt to appraise the securities markets as air-conditioned racetracks, and usually he will have the same poor record as his counterparts at said places.

In the great majority of these situations, careful appraisal is almost impossible, for there are insufficient facts and the information is unreliable. The gambler purchases the security mainly with the hope of obtaining sizeable capital gains quickly and with little effort. He belongs to the "get rich quick" school. In 1968 such activity was rampant, especially with over-the-counter issues and issues traded on the American Stock Exchange, while blue chip issues were neglected. There was much new issue speculation.

The purchase of securities on so-called "market tips" or on the basis of glamorous scientific name, high-pressure telephone calls, and "penny" Canadian stocks are familiar examples of gambling situations. The hour-by-hour tapereader traders and the day-to-day, week-to-week, nonprofessional market traders are another class of gamblers. The great majority of non-professional short-term traders consider themselves as speculators, but in most cases they are mere gamblers. Little will be said in this book about traders, mainly because their record over the years has been so unsatisfactory compared to the record of intelligent investors and intelligent speculators.[5]

It is interesting to point out that many individuals believe that, while their vocation requires a long period of training, hard work, and experience, investing or intelligent speculation can be accomplished with little training, experience, or ability. It is indeed unfortunate that many people believe this. These individuals may experience some success in the short run, but in the long run most will almost certainly experience a decline in the value of their portfolios. It must be stressed that successful investment and also consistent success in speculation require a degree of technical knowledge, a certain amount of experience, good judgment, and last but not least, diligence in seeking facts. In addition, the successful speculator probably is born with a native flair for speculation that relatively few individuals possess.

Growth in Number of Individual Investors

The amount of disposable personal income in the United States has been increasing for many years. A larger and larger proportion of the people are accumulating funds in excess of their consumption requirements or

---

[5] When Sidney Weinberg, senior partner of Goldman, Sachs, known as Mr. Wall Street, retired in 1967, he stated that he "never traded securities for profit because he never shot craps." He emphasized that he did not believe that one built capital by trading, and Bernard Baruch agreed.

desires. The number of savers and investors has been growing much faster than has the population.

Not only has the number of investors grown substantially, but the average individual today has a keener interest in the market. A decade ago, only one major news broadcast on television gave the DJIA. Today most major news broadcasts and minor broadcasts, both on radio and television, give highlights of the day's happenings in the stock market.

Today it is estimated that there are over 30.8 million individuals in the United States who own common stock. Many are relatively new investors with small portfolios, and many have had little training and experience in investing. Approximately 19 million shareholders held stock portfolios with a market value of less than $10,000 during early 1970.[6] Many have no investment philosophy, no reasonable specific goals, no policy or program. However, the bulk of total savings by individuals annually flows into the capital market through financial intermediaries such as deposit and contractual types of institutions. Individuals in total have been net sellers of common stocks throughout the 1960s and in the early 1970s, although nearly half of their liquid financial asset holdings are still invested in common stocks as a result of the tremendous increase in stock values since 1949 when the DJIA was 160. Individual transactions were at a low level in 1973.

The Investor's Problems

The investor has two major problems: (1) what to buy and (2) when to buy and sell. The problem of what to buy has two aspects: (a) what types of securities are suitable for the investor in the light of his goals and the degree of risk that he is judiciously able and willing to assume (investment policy and program) and the proportion of the various types of securities for his portfolio; and (b) what specific securities are the best relative values of the types selected to meet his requirements (investment selection).

The problem of risk appraisal and selection is the problem of security analysis. A major part of this book, Chapters 8-27, is devoted to the problem of security analysis, security valuation, and finally the selection of various securities. It emphasizes the problem of risks versus rewards.

The problem of when to buy and when to sell is a matter of timing or pricing. The problem of proper pricing in the purchase of specific securities is a distinct part of the process of security analysis. It is the problem of the proper valuation of securities.

---

[6] *Shareownership—1970*, New York Stock Exchange, Census of Shareowners.

At this point it must be emphasized that investment is still as much an art as a science. The assessment of risk cannot be completely reduced to mere mathematical formulas. Scientific methods of research and analysis can and should be used to determine relative security values, although because of the uncertainty involved in forecasts of the future there is no substitute for the judgment and skill of the analyst.[7] Clearly there is much greater uncertainty in some situations than in others, the greatest being with small, new, and untried companies. The farther projections are carried into the future, the greater is the uncertainty. Still, buying stock is buying a share of the future, and success will depend on ability to interpret that future.

It is important to realize that any investment-grade common stock may be overvalued in the market, and sometimes greatly overvalued. It may sell at a price that is composed of two elements—an investment element and a speculative element. The speculative element is the excess value placed on it by the market above its reasonable investment value. In the case of a so-called growth stock, the speculative element may be very large if the stock sells at an extremely high price-earnings ratio that is well above the recommended maximum. Uncertainty makes it difficult to separate these components of price, but a large speculative element creates a very risky situation.

Need for Philosophy, Goals, and Policies

To be successful, it is vital for all investors, both individual and institutional, to develop a philosophy towards investments on which can be based realistic goals and policies to meet their requirements and their legal restrictions if any. Investors must have a philosophy for both bonds and stocks, and they must apply this philosophy consistently.

Various investment policies can lead to success. There is no one right policy that fits each and every individual investor's needs. Various policies and programs that can lead to investment success will be discussed in Chapters 28-32 with the emphasis on common stock investment.

Investors who do formulate policies but then fail to follow them consistently will rarely be successful. The investor must have the courage and the stamina to stay with his policy and program despite the attitude of others operating in the security markets who may disagree with his policy at any particular time. He must learn to distrust his own emotions and he must learn to be unaffected by the emotional actions of others.

---

[7] This point will be examined more thoroughly in Chapters 11 and 12 on valuation and selection of common stocks. In respect to uncertainty, the reading of the following article by the Chief Economist of United States Steel Corporation is suggested: William H. Peterson, "The Future of the Futurists," *Harvard Business Review* (Nov.-Dec. 1967), pp. 168-186.

One investor may consistently follow a policy of selecting only growth stocks, based on reasonable standards; another may follow a policy of choosing a portfolio that is a cross section of American industry; still another may follow a policy of purchasing "out-of-favor" or low price-earnings stocks that he believes will be "comeback" stocks. Other investors may properly combine the above policies in developing and managing a portfolio.

Some investors may follow a policy of "dollar cost averaging" by purchasing stocks at regular intervals regardless of market levels. Others may, through some other method, seek to take advantage automatically of the wide swings that occur in major, or at least intermediate, bear or bull markets.

The records attest to the possibility of successful investing by following any of the policies and programs noted above (and there are others that could be mentioned). The important point is that some logical policy and program must be selected and followed consistently, one that is logical in terms of the particular investor's financial situation, goals, and restrictions, if any. Establishing a portfolio policy and program and following it consistently is essential for success to both institutional and individual investors.

INVESTMENT RISKS

The problem of investment is largely one of deciding on a policy towards risk and then properly evaluating the types and the degrees of risk present in various securities. Investors, of course, are interested in the best possible performance from their portfolios with the least possible risk in attaining objectives. Some compromise between risk and rewards is necessary.

The Problem of Risks

There is no riskless investment. Even keeping cash on hand involves the risk that the purchasing power of the dollar will decline as a result of inflation. The fact that risks exist even in the highest-grade investments can be illustrated by reviewing the record of United States Government bonds. The 3's of 1995 declined from about 107 in 1946 to a low of 59 in 1970. The reason for this decline was rising interest rates. The yields rose from 2.73 percent on this bond in 1946 to 6.23 percent in 1970. The S&P yield and price indexes for selected long-term Treasury issues (maturities in excess of 10 years) dropped from a high price of 111.8 in April, 1946 (yield of 2.08 percent) to a low of 63.73 in August, 1970 (yield of 6.93).[8] By May, 1973, long-term Treasury bonds were yielding approximately 7 percent.

---

[8] June, 1970, represented a historic peak for interest rates and a historic low for corporate bond prices. Practically all bonds were selling at discounts, and bonds issued

The farther one travels down the scale of investments, the higher the degree of risk involved. The investor must realize that, along with the greater risks he assumes, comes often, although not always, the potential for the prospect of greater capital appreciation. Normally, the shorter the time period in which capital appreciation is sought, the greater the risk, although admittedly this is not always the case. Conversely, because of the great uncertainty of the future, the farther ahead one makes projections as a basis for investment commitments, the greater the risks. We suggest that projections be extended only 5 to 6 years into the future or 10 years at the most, with revised projections being made semiannually.

Types of Investment Risks

The most important types of investment risks are:

1. Credit or financial risk—the risk that the issuer's credit will deteriorate. It is also called the *business risk*.
2. Interest rate risk—the risk that interest rates will rise, causing a decline in the market price of limited-income securities (bonds and preferred stocks) and so-called money market or yield stocks (such as electric utility stocks, bank stocks, and many other stocks). It is also called the *money-rate risk*.
3. Purchasing power or inflation risk—the risk that an excessive increase in the money supply may cause the purchasing power of money to decline, seriously affecting the holders of stable value, limited-income investments.
4. Market risk—the risk that the market price of all common stocks or individual stocks will decline substantially and that the investor might be forced to sell, or emotionally does sell, at market lows. Common stocks fluctuate widely in price, although the secular trend is upward. Measures of this risk are constructed in terms of the degree of volatility present in the returns of a given security or portfolio, as discussed in Chapter 11.
5. Psychological risk—the risk that an investor will act emotionally instead of logically in reflecting (a) current waves of great optimism or pessimism that periodically sweep the investment market or (b) current moods of great optimism or pessimism toward certain stock groups or even individual stocks. This risk is closely allied to market risk and the risk of investing in fads.

Credit or Financial Risk. There is always some degree of risk that the credit or financial standing of the issuer of securities will deteriorate in the future. Erstwhile strong central governments have later experienced substantial deterioration in their credit, which has sometimes led to outright defaults, and Penn-Central offers a recent illustration of serious credit risk for stockholders of a large well-known corporation. Great risks are present

---

many years earlier with low-interest-rate coupons were selling at very heavy discounts. High-grade corporate bonds in June, 1970, sold at the highest yields since the post-Civil War period, with AAA corporate utility bonds yielding 8.4%-8.5% and AA corporate utility bonds yielding over 8.6%.

with new and untried ventures. Even when there is no question of integrity, as with projects sponsored by a state government agency, the default of the West Virginia Turnpike Authority in the late 1950s and the Calumet Skyway Authority (Chicago) highlights the risks in any new untried venture based entirely on estimates of future income, with no past record or experience as a guide. There are degrees of risk within the category of new ventures, but as a class they carry the greatest risks. The reader should review the record of new or relatively young companies that "went public" during the post-World War II periods of great investor enthusiasm for new issues, such as 1961. Many were called but few were chosen for success. The younger and smaller the enterprise, the greater the credit, financial, or business risk. But to many unintelligent speculators the lure of small new companies (for example, in 1946, 1953-1954, 1961, and 1967-1968), especially those with scientific names, seemed irresistible.

Interest Rate Risk. Certain investments pay a strictly limited rate of return under their contract with the issuer. Such investments are bonds, private placement notes, equipment trust certificates, other promissory notes, and preferred stocks. When these securities are issued, the contractual rate and the yield to investors are based on the going market yield for securities of equivalent quality and maturity. In tight money periods such as 1966-1969, however, the new issue yields may be well above yields on equivalent quality outstanding issues, making indexes for outstanding bonds misleading.

If, after the date of issue, interest rates rise (such as 1899-1921 and 1946-1973), not only are new issues sold at the higher going market rates, but outstanding issues fall in price to a point where they yield the going market rate for issues of that quality and maturity.

The period from 1946 to 1973 witnessed a long and substantial rise in market interest rates, interrupted at times in recessions by temporary reversals, to the highest bond yields since the Civil War. As interest rates and yields rose, the price of bonds (and preferred stocks) fell so that the yield on outstanding bonds (and preferred stocks) would rise to a level where they were attractive to purchasers.

The bond record from April, 1946, to January, 1973, is indicated in Table 1-1 as shown by Standard & Poor's Indexes for outstanding issues. Rates on *new AA issues* were considerably higher, for example reaching over 8% in June, 1970, and again in 1973.

It is clear from Table 1-1 that investors in bonds in 1946 not only would have accepted a historically low rate of return (after a long decline beginning in 1921), but would have continued to receive this low yield during the years that the bonds were held. In addition, if these securities

TABLE 1-1

Standard & Poor's Indexes

| | | Yields | | | Bond Prices—Indexes | |
Date	U.S. Gov't Long-Term	Corporate High Grade	Municipal High Grade	U.S. Gov't Long-Term	Corporate High Grade	Municipal High Grade
Apr. 1946	2.08%	2.44%	1.45%	111.80	124.6	141.6
Jan. 1960	4.47%	4.62%	4.13%	84.07	92.0	98.3
Aug. 1966	4.84%	5.30%	4.17%	80.56	84.1	98.6
Nov. 1966	4.75%	5.35%	3.93%	81.40	83.5	101.0
Feb. 1967	4.49%	5.09%	3.56%	83.90	86.4	106.3
Dec. 1967	5.44%	6.11%	4.49%	75.18	75.9	93.6
Apr. 1968	5.34%	6.08%	4.41%	76.06	76.2	94.7
Jan. 1969	5.85%	6.48%	4.95%	71.70	72.5	88.0
Dec. 1969	6.86%	7.65%	6.91%	64.21	62.9	68.7
June 1970	7.17%	8.21%	7.06%	62.07	59.0	67.5
Jan. 1973	5.89%	7.25%	5.05%	71.50	66.5	75.9

were sold in intervening years, they would have been sold at a loss. If held until 1973 and if they still had a long period to maturity, the loss would have been in the neighborhood of 36% for long-term United States Government bonds, 47% for high-grade corporate bonds, and 53% for high-grade municipal bonds. Of course, if they were high-quality and matured in 1973, they would have been paid in full at par.

As a group, commercial banks have experienced the greatest problem in this area, as they tend to buy bonds in recessions (periods of low interest rates) and sell bonds in periods of prosperity (high interest rates). However, 85% of issues held have maturities of 5 years or less, reducing the price depreciation risk. But it is clear from the above that the risk was severe for all investors in limited-income securities during the period 1946-1973.

Purchasing Power or Inflation Risk. Throughout the history of the United States, the purchasing power of the dollar has declined. In *all* cases, the inflations that resulted in the major declines in purchasing power in the United States were associated with wars and their aftermath—the Revolutionary War, the Civil War, World Wars I and II, the Korean War, and the Vietnam War.

During the Korean War and the Vietnam War, government borrowing increased the money supply and, especially in the case of Vietnam, an extremely expansive Federal Reserve policy led to increases at a faster

TABLE 1-2

Inflation and Investments—World War II and Aftermath
Money Supply, Consumer Prices, Bond Prices, Bond Yields, Stock Prices, Stock Yields, and Dividends Paid

Year	Total Money Supply ($ Billions)	Index of Consumer Prices 1967=100	Standard & Poor's Index of Bond Prices Corporate AAA	Bond Yields Moody's Corporate AAA%	Standard & Poor's 425 Industrial Prices 1941-43=10			Stock Yields %	Dividends Paid $	Dow Jones Industrial Average			Dividends Paid $
					High	Low	Mean			High	Low	Mean	
1939-41 Av.	46.7	42.8	116.2	2.87	12.04	9.03	10.54	5.49	0.63	148.8	111.2	130.3	6.92
1942	62.9	48.8	117.4	2.83	9.94	7.54	8.74	7.24	0.55	119.7	92.9	106.3	6.40
1943	79.6	51.8	118.3	2.73	12.58	10.00	11.29	4.93	0.58	145.8	119.3	132.5	6.30
1944	90.4	52.7	118.7	2.72	13.18	11.43	12.31	4.86	0.60	152.5	134.2	143.4	6.57
1945	102.3	53.9	121.6	2.62	17.06	12.97	15.02	4.17	0.61	195.8	151.4	173.6	6.69
1946	110.0	58.5	123.4	2.53	18.53	13.64	16.09	3.85	0.66	212.5	163.1	187.8	7.50
1947	115.9	66.9	122.1	2.61	15.83	13.40	14.62	4.93	0.82	186.9	163.2	175.0	9.21
1948	114.3	72.1	118.2	2.82	16.93	13.58	15.26	5.54	0.91	193.2	165.4	179.3	11.50
1949	113.9	71.4	121.0	2.66	16.52	13.23	14.88	6.59	1.14	200.5	161.6	181.1	12.79
1950	119.2	72.1	121.9	2.62	20.60	16.34	18.47	6.57	1.53	235.5	196.8	216.1	16.13
1951	125.8	77.8	117.7	2.86	24.33	20.85	22.59	6.13	1.45	276.4	239.0	257.7	16.34
1952	130.8	79.5	115.8	2.96	26.92	23.30	25.11	5.80	1.44	292.0	256.4	274.2	15.48
1953	132.1	80.1	112.1	3.20	26.99	22.70	24.85	5.80	1.47	293.8	255.5	274.6	16.11
1954	135.6	80.5	117.2	2.90	37.24	24.84	31.04	4.95	1.57	404.4	279.9	342.1	17.47
1955	138.6	80.2	114.4	3.06	49.54	35.61	42.60	4.08	1.68	488.4	388.2	438.3	21.58
1956	140.3	81.4	109.1	3.36	53.28	45.71	49.50	4.09	1.78	521.1	462.4	491.7	29.99
1957	139.3	84.3	101.3	3.89	53.25	41.98	47.62	4.35	1.84	520.8	419.8	470.3	21.61
1958	144.7	86.8	102.9	3.79	58.97	43.20	51.09	3.97	1.79	583.7	436.9	510.3	20.00

TABLE 1-2 (Continued)

Year	Total Money Supply ($ Billions)	Index of Consumer Prices 1967=100	Standard & Poor's Index of Bond Prices Corporate AAA	Bond Yields Moody's Corporate AAA%	Standard & Poor's 425 Industrial Prices 1941-43=10					Dow Jones Industrial Average			
					High	Low	Mean	Stock Yields %	Dividends Paid $	High	Low	Mean	Dividends Paid $
1959	145.6	87.3	95.0	4.38	65.32	57.02	61.17	3.23	1.90	679.4	574.5	626.9	20.74
1960	144.7	88.7	94.6	4.41	65.02	55.34	60.18	3.47	2.00	685.5	566.1	625.8	21.36
1961	149.4	89.6	95.2	4.35	76.69	60.87	68.78	2.98	2.08	734.9	610.3	672.6	22.71
1962	151.6	90.6	96.2	4.33	75.22	54.80	65.01	3.37	2.20	726.0	535.8	630.9	23.30
1963	157.2	91.7	96.8	4.26	79.25	65.48	72.37	3.17	2.38	767.2	646.8	707.0	23.41
1964	160.5	92.9	95.1	4.40	91.29	79.74	85.52	3.01	2.60	891.7	766.1	828.9	31.24
1965	168.0	94.5	93.9	4.49	98.55	86.43	92.49	3.00	2.85	969.3	840.6	904.9	28.61
1966	171.7	97.2	86.1	5.13	100.60	77.89	89.25	3.50	2.98	995.2	744.3	869.7	31.89
1967	183.1	100.0	81.8	5.51	106.15	85.31	95.73	2.86	3.01	943.1	786.4	864.7	30.19
1968 a	197.4	104.2	76.4	6.05	118.03	95.05	106.54	2.81	3.18	985.2	825.1	905.2	31.04 *
1969	203.7	109.8	68.6	6.93	116.24	97.75	106.99	3.22	3.27	968.9	769.9	869.4	33.90
1970	214.8	116.3	64.7	7.19	101.09	95.89	98.49	3.21	3.24	842.0	631.2	736.6	E 32.28
1971	228.2	122.6	66.4	7.16	115.84	99.36	107.60	2.92	3.18	950.8	798.0	874.4	N.A.

* Cash only.

a Bond yields in May, 1968, were the highest since the Civil War, even higher for new issues for the indexes above: old issues, May, 1968, 6.28%; new issues, 6.80%. In May, 1970, interest rates were even higher and bond prices lower. E = estimated. N.A. = Not available.

Source: *Federal Reserve Bulletins, Standard & Poor's Trade and Securities, The Dow Jones Investor's Handbook (1970),* and *Barron's.*

rate than the production of consumer goods. In the case of World War II, the major increase in the money supply was the increase in deposit currency that resulted from the sale of approximately $70 billion of government bonds to the commercial banks and a corresponding increase in the money supply—currency plus demand deposits. Meanwhile, the production of consumer goods was sharply curtailed. The government instituted price controls and rationing to offset the increase in the money supply during World War II so that only about one third of the war-generated inflation was reflected in rising price indexes. The remaining effect was felt after price controls and rationing were removed. *Inflation,* by definition, is an excessive increase in the money supply, relative to increased output of goods and services, which nearly always results in a rise in prices (a decline in the purchasing power of money).

Inflation and Stock Prices in the United States. In the period 1940-1942 to 1957, both the Consumer Price Index and the Wholesale Commodity Price Index approximately doubled. This period included the Korean War and World War II. After previous wars there had always been a depression and a sharp drop in prices, but this did not occur after the Korean War and World War II. Holders of limited-income, stable-value assets, such as bonds, preferred stocks, and bank deposits, continued to receive a limited income during this period, which would purchase less and less. During this same period, as shown in Table 1-2 on pages 14-15, the major stock price indexes quintupled, thereby suggesting an effective offset to inflation.

A well-diversified portfolio, as represented by the Standard & Poor's Industrial Average, approximately tripled in value from 1957 to 1973. During this same period the Consumer Price Index rose more than 50%. Over the entire period 1940-1942 to 1971, the Consumer Price Index just about quadrupled, while the stock indexes rose to about seven times the 1940-1942 level. Over long periods of time, a diversified holding of common stocks has proved to be a good inflation hedge, especially considering the large increases in dividends that occurred during this period.

Earnings and dividends for the stocks in the above indexes rose approximately five times, as shown in Table 1-3.

The investor must realize that, during this particular time of inflation, earnings and dividends approximately quintupled, which is the reason that stocks proved to be a good inflation hedge. Not only did the income from the stocks about quintuple, but the market value rose to a level seven times the 1940-1942 value. Those living on dividend income could have more than

TABLE 1-3

Standard & Poor's and Dow Jones Indexes

Year	Standard & Poor's 500 Composite		Standard & Poor's 425 Industrials		Dow Jones Industrial Index	
	Earnings	Dividends	Earnings	Dividends	Earnings	Dividends
1940	1.05	0.67	1.01	0.63	10.92	7.06
1957	3.37	1.79	3.50	1.84	36.08	21.61
1971	5.42	3.07	5.78	3.18	55.09	30.86

maintained their level of living. In this period, however, the earnings of some stocks not only did not rise but actually declined, and these particular stocks did not prove to be a good inflation hedge. This principle has been true in other countries as well. It is only when corporate earnings and dividends at least keep pace with the general rise in prices in the economy that common stocks prove to be a good hedge against inflation. Common stocks cannot in themselves automatically provide a good inflation hedge.

Inflation and Stock Prices in Europe. An excellent lesson for American investors who view common stocks as a guaranteed hedge against inflation can be found in the European experience in 1962-1966, as shown below.

TABLE 1-4

European Experience, 1962-1966

Country	Cost of Living	Wage Rate	Stock Prices
France	+14%	+30%	Down 35%
Belgium	+15%	+38%	Down 24%
Italy	+21%	+42%	Down 24%
West Germany	+13%	+32%	Down 22%
Netherlands	+26%	+48%	Down 19%

In these countries, business experienced a profits squeeze—profitless prosperity. Regardless of inflation, stocks sell on the basis of earnings and may not rise along with other prices. If the profits squeeze is severe, the securities may actually decline as they did in Europe.

In the United States, also, the stocks of numerous corporations in 1973 were selling below, at, or not much above their 1940-1942 prices because their earnings record from 1940-1973 was poor, although the Consumer Price Index rose over 100%.

The principle to be gleaned from the above is that the prices of stocks will reflect their earnings and dividends records and their estimated earnings and dividends potential. If investors concentrate on an earnings analysis and an earnings projection, and if this record of projections is good overall, their portfolios will do well *whether or not* there is inflation. The stocks whose earnings rise the most will produce the best performance (if their earnings growth is not overdiscounted in their prices), and those whose earnings record is poor will post the worst performance. The investor who carelessly buys stocks because of psychotic fear of inflation rather than on careful and reasonable earnings projections will probably not find that his selections will prove to be a sound inflation hedge. This was especially true of 1966-1973.

Limited-Income Securities in Inflation. The inflation risk is greatest in the area of limited-income securities, debt instruments, and preferred stocks. In the first place, the contract calls for payments at a specified time at a specified rate. Therefore, if the investor has a portfolio consisting exclusively of limited-income securities established in 1940, he would have received the same income each year. But the purchasing power of the fixed income would have declined year by year, with the income in 1957 purchasing only half what it could have purchased in 1940.

If an investor in 1940 had purchased a $1,000 bond due in 1957, he would have been paid back the $1,000 investment in 1957, but the dollars received in 1957 would have purchased only half the quantity of goods that could have been purchased with the $1,000 in 1940. In addition, many bonds were refunded at lower contractual rates, thus causing a decline in actual income received.

In conclusion, during inflation, the owners of debt instruments and preferred stocks will suffer a loss in purchasing power over the years that they hold the fixed-income securities. Therefore, one must realize that debt instruments (excluding convertible bonds and convertible preferreds) expose the investor to serious losses in purchasing power in the event of generally rising prices in the economy.

Market Risk. The major disability and also the source of possible great advantage of common stocks as a class is that they fluctuate widely in price. There are short-term and intermediate-term cycles in stock prices, but more important are the major bear and bull markets. In the pre-World War II markets, major declines were most frequently contained in approximately a 20%-40% range; and in the post-World War II markets, an 18%-30%

range (a 27% decline in 1962 and a 26% decline in 1967). Also, there was the horrendous 89% decline from 1929 to 1932, which signaled and then coincided with the inception and the duration of the Great Depression.

This disability of common stocks as a class is only a disability for investors with diversified portfolios who may be forced to sell common stocks in bear markets or who sell from fear in such bear markets. Therefore, reserve funds should not be invested in common stocks. For both individual investors and institutional investors who maintain diversified holdings and who buy and hold long-term, the result has always been full recovery in the stock market overall and then advance to new historically higher levels. For the long term, the annual capital compounded price appreciation rate of common stocks (DJIA) through 1969 is shown in Table 1-5.

TABLE 1-5

Compound Annual Rate of Growth
of Stock Prices—DJIA

Period	Rate
1897–1962	3.66%
1932–1962	7.06%
1946–1952	5.00%
1952–1962	10.05%
1946–1966	8.75%
1952–January 1966	9.70%
1966–January 1969	7.30%
1968–December 1972	2.20%

Psychological Risk. If an investor is forced to sell common stocks at a loss in a bear market because he needs funds, this is simply a market risk. One cause of forced sales is margin calls. Investors who purchase stocks on margin, partly with borrowed funds, at relatively high prices may later be called on to put up additional margin in stocks, bonds, or cash or be forced to sell the stocks.

However, in many cases individuals act simply out of fear or panic and sell common stocks in bear markets. Such was the case after President Eisenhower's heart attack, the black days of May and June, 1962; after President Kennedy's assassination in 1963; and in the summer and early fall of 1966. Those who did not need to sell, but did sell, later saw the illogic of such action when stocks recovered and rose to new peaks.[9] Therefore, risks may be a combination of psychological and market risks.

---

[9] Standard & Poor's highs and lows since 1966 were as follows:
S&P "500": Oct., 1966 = 73.20; Nov., 1968 = 108.37; May, 1970 = 69.29;
       Jan., 1973 = 135
S&P "425": Oct., 1966 = 77.89; Nov., 1968 = 118.03; May, 1970 = 75.58

In cases of rampant bull markets, such as the new issue market of 1961, investors may be carried along by the extreme optimism of the mass of investors at the moment and might buy stocks at prices that are ridiculously high in terms of any reasonable value standards. Some of this also occurred in 1965 and 1967-1968. Later, as stocks declined, these investors saw the fallacy of their emotional action, particularly if they had purchased the fads of the previous bull market.

The combination of psychological risk and market risk is also illustrated in terms of individual stock groups and even individual stocks. There are fads and fashions in stocks. At times, investors demonstrate extreme optimism towards certain groups of stocks or individual stocks; at other times, extreme pessimism. For example, investors were extremely pessimistic about automobile stocks in 1958 and oil stocks in 1960, but in 1965 they were again very optimistic about such stocks, only to become quite pessimistic again in late 1966. In 1960 and 1961, investors were very optimistic about leisure time stocks such as bowling and boating issues, while in 1963 they were extremely pessimistic about the future of these stocks. In 1959, investors were extremely optimistic about steel stocks, but in 1962 they were extremely pessimistic about them. By January, 1964, a considerable measure of confidence toward steel stocks had returned only to ebb again in 1966-1973. Two of the most "out-of-favor" groups in 1961, because of low earnings or deficits, were the railroads and the airlines; but at the height of the succeeding 1963-early 1966 bull market, investors were strongly optimistic about these two groups, which had outperformed most of the 1961 favorites. Investors in this bull market were also greatly optimistic towards chemical stocks, but in 1967-1968 chemical stocks on the average had declined 50%. Airline stocks also declined 50%. If investors purchase individual stocks or stock groups when optimism is high, then sell these stocks when optimism turns to pessimism, they are bound to have a poor record. To be successful, investors must recognize psychological risks and guard against them.

Defensive Policies Advocated to Combat Risks

The various types of investment risks may be greatly reduced by the application of defensive policies. Defensive policies advocated to combat specific risks are discussed in the following paragraphs.

Combating the Credit or Financial Risk. Careful analysis preceding any investment commitment will greatly reduce the credit or financial risk. In general, it is desirable to avoid small, new, young, and untested enterprises because this risk is especially heavy with such businesses. Intelligent diversification will also considerably reduce the credit or financial risk.

Combating the Interest Rate Risk. The interest rate risk is present because, if interest rates rise after a bond (or other contractual security) is purchased, the market price of the security will decline. The interest rate risk can be combated with spaced maturities and short-term issues.

To the unsophisticated, it might seem sensible to attempt to forecast the trend of interest rates and then to manage a bond portfolio on the basis of these forecasts. However, long experience has convinced most professional bond portfolio managers of the wisdom of following a policy of spaced maturities. In such a portfolio, bonds will come due at regular intervals and funds received can be reinvested in current market yields. Of course, the record of the portfolio will not be as satisfactory as one based on continually correct forecasts of changes in interest rates. But such forecasts have proved extremely difficult and often very costly to the portfolio manager who acted on them, as was shown in the period 1966-1969.

Certain managers of bond accounts handle part of the bond portfolio on the basis of their forecasts of trends of interest rates. It should be explained that the shorter the maturity, the less the interest rate risk will be, and the longer the maturity, the greater the risk will be. There is practically no price risk with short-term treasury bills.

Combating the Purchasing Power or Inflation Risk. The greatest inflation risk lies with limited-income securities. If inflation is in process or is expected, investment in limited-income, stable-value securities should be avoided unless legal or other requirements make such investment mandatory.

To combat the inflation risk, investors should select securities that should rise in price with inflation. These securities could include common stocks, convertible bonds, convertible preferred stocks, real estate, and perhaps such precious assets as diamonds. However, it is not assured that such investments will *per se* provide a hedge against inflation.

If earnings on common stocks and on real estate (commercial) do not rise along with inflation, these assets will not provide a satisfactory inflation hedge. Therefore, in selecting common stocks or real estate as an investment hedge against inflation, the investor must assure himself that earnings will rise at least as fast as prices such as consumer prices.

In the case of diamonds and *objets d'art*, the purchaser must recognize that they produce no income—a serious negative factor—and that the future price will depend solely on the future demand and supply for these assets.

Combating the Market Risk. The market risk is due to the fact that securities fluctuate in market price. This risk is greatest with common stocks and least with high-grade bonds. Therefore, if an investor wishes to combat this risk, he will purchase high-grade debt issues. If he wishes to take virtually no market risk, he will purchase treasury bills. With high-grade debt issues, the only significant market risk is that associated with rising interest rates. As the grade of debt issues goes down, however, the market risk increases. This risk is associated closely with the credit or financial risk. This factor of quality standards for the selection of debt issues will be discussed in Chapters 8 and 9. Certain lower-rated issues may be purchased if the sole reason for their lower rating is the fact that they are subordinated debentures, such as convertibles.

The greatest market risk exists with common stocks, which as a class fluctuate widely. Investors can combat this risk by not investing in common stocks any reserve funds needed for liquidity purposes and thus avoiding forced sales in low markets. Investors can avoid some market risks in specific stocks by careful analysis before purchase and by continuing analytical review, but all common stocks will fluctuate in price.

Combating the Psychological Risk. There is the risk of following the crowd in the case of either the market as a whole or groups of individual stocks. The investor must realize that investors as a whole fluctuate between extremes of optimism and pessimism with regard to the market as a whole, stock groups, and individual stocks. Further, he must realize that there is a tendency to pursue fads in stocks as in other areas.

Investors must learn to act unemotionally and particularly not to let their judgment be influenced by the recurring extremes of optimism and pessimism. Acting on emotional grounds has proved to be a very serious risk.

Balanced Portfolios and the Risk Factor. A balanced portfolio is one that includes both bonds and common stocks and may include preferred stocks as well. The section of a portfolio invested in limited-income, stable-value securities provides a pool of reserve funds that can be used when or if needed, which could be at a time when the stock market is severely depressed. Bonds, as a class, hold a higher quality rating than common stocks because quality bonds fluctuate much less in price than common stocks. Both the credit risk and the market risk are reduced to the extent that there are quality bonds in a portfolio.

Preferred Stocks and Balanced Portfolios. It is generally recognized that there is little place for investment-grade nonconvertible preferred stocks in the investment portfolio of an *individual* (for tax reasons discussed below and in Chapter 3). This also applies to most institutional portfolios, such as pension funds, where there is a free and unlimited choice between bonds and common stocks. It is the reason why few preferred stocks are found in individual portfolios or corporate or other pension funds that are handled with sophistication.[10]

There is a place for investment-grade preferred stocks in the portfolios of life insurance companies and some other corporations. Life insurance companies generally cannot purchase equities in an amount to exceed 5% of total assets except for insured pension fund assets. But they can receive an 85% deduction for dividends on common stocks as well as on preferred stocks. All corporations are entitled to this deduction. For corporate holders, the net yield after taxes from preferred stock considerably exceeds the net yield after taxes from bonds on the basis of relative market yields in the past decade. In recent years, gross market yields on high-grade preferred stocks have been roughly equivalent to gross market yields on high-grade corporate bonds.

Balanced Portfolios and Reserves for Individuals. We have stated that common stock prices fluctuate widely, which is a risk factor to holders of common stocks. Therefore, funds that may be needed suddenly to meet future circumstances, foreseen or unforeseen, cannot judiciously be invested in common stocks. At the very time funds are needed, stock may have fallen to a relatively low level. The size of the reserves depends on many factors (to be discussed in Chapter 28). As a rule of thumb, we suggest that individual investors maintain funds as reserves equivalent to at least one half a year's income. Furthermore, some investors may build temporary reserves during periods when the level of stock prices is unreasonably high in terms of price-earnings ratios, dividend yields, and profit expectations, in order to have reserves available for investment should there be a significant drop in stock prices, as in 1958, 1962, 1966, and 1970. There will always be wide fluctuations in stock prices even though we can expect a long upward secular trend related to the long-term growth of the economy.

For individuals with portfolios of say $100,000 or less, it is recommended that reserves be spread over insured savings accounts (insured up to $20,000

---

[10] One exception to this general principle occurs in periods of peak interest rates, such as 1959-1960 and 1966-1969. At such times individual investors may well be advised to purchase some high-grade *noncallable* preferred stock. While these stocks were not selling at such times to yield more than high-grade bonds, the absence of a call feature permitted investors to lock-in the historically high yields that were not possible with corporate bonds, practically all of which are callable.

in each account) where the interest rate is payable from the date of deposit to the date of withdrawal and the rate is as high or nearly as high as on United States Government securities, even long-term ones. At times (as in 1966, 1967, 1968, and also in 1973), yields on United States Government securities and high-grade corporate bonds may rise so high that it is justifiable to transfer reserve funds from savings accounts to these securities.

For individuals with sizable portfolios and for those in higher-level income tax brackets, above 30% or 33%, there is an important place for tax-exempt securities as reserves. There may be justification for tax-exempt securities for other reasons than simply as reserves. This problem will be discussed in Chapters 26 and 27. For temporary reserves that are being held for later investment in stocks, many investors utilize United States Treasury bills.

In summary, the principle of a balanced individual portfolio, balanced between bonds and common stocks, has been subject to considerable modification in recent years. However, it is still true that the major vehicle for an individual to build capital is through common stocks.

Balanced Portfolios and Institutional Investors. Certain institutional portfolios such as those of commercial banks, mutual savings banks, savings and loan associations, and life insurance companies by law must be largely or entirely invested in debt instruments and not in equity securities (stocks). The principle is that financial institutions have fixed dollar claims that must be met and that these claims should be balanced by stable-value fixed-income investments, especially when there is a need for liquidity and when the financial institutions are heavily leveraged.

One large and growing group of financial intermediaries are corporate pension funds, which are not limited to investment in debt instruments. They follow a policy of a portfolio balanced between bonds and common stocks, with only a negligible amount of preferred stocks. In 1971, corporate pension funds had at market values approximately 63% of their funds (assets) invested in common stocks and about 30% in bonds (as discussed in Chapter 32), with increasing preference for common stocks in the 1960s.

Again, this balance reduces both the credit risk and the market risk. However, the market risk in the case of a diversified portfolio of common stocks is negligible for institutional investors, except perhaps property and casualty insurance companies. There is no necessity for liquidating securities, especially the common stock segment of the portfolio, at any particular time (for example, during bear markets). Actually, in the case of pension funds for major corporations, there is little foreseeable need for liquidating any of their portfolios. This is also true of state pension funds.

Combating Risks by Careful Selection Based on Thorough Analysis. No investment commitment should be made until a situation has been thoroughly investigated. While investment is still as much an art as a science, and while judgment and skill are vital, proper judgment cannot be made unless facts are gathered and interpreted. Since the enactment of the federal securities legislation in the 1930s and later amendments (including the 1964 legislation affecting over-the-counter securities), analysts do have information on which to base decisions, although lack of uniformity in corporate reporting still gives rise to many problems and there are still important factual and statistical gaps to an ideal analysis, as for example conglomerate companies. An important part of this book is devoted to proper methods of security analysis and security evaluation as performed by professional security analysts.

The risks of making investments without investigation are so basic that it would seem unnecessary to stress this point. However, the records prove that millions of investors have, at times at least, failed to investigate properly before investing. They cannot very well appraise risks if they do not gather and interpret the necessary information and identify their risks or if they do not act on the advice of professionals whose recommendations are based on careful security analysis.

Reducing Risk by Intelligent Diversification. The principle of diversification is basic in investment. Wide diversification reduces risks to a minimum. Wide diversification, combined with careful selection, will almost assure reasonable investment success over the long term. Diversification is the basis of mutual fund investment policies and other institutional portfolios, such as private pension funds and insurance company portfolios. Success in following a policy of diversification does not imply spectacular success. Those seeking unusual success cannot practice wide diversification, for diversification limits capital appreciation. On the other hand, investors and speculators who do not diversify incur much heavier risks and *few* manage to achieve spectacular success over lengthy periods. Innate flair and skill are necessary for successful speculation in a limited number of securities.

Proper Timing. Proper timing means proper pricing of purchases and proper determination of when to sell. It might be noted that the timing of sales is considered by many professionals to be even more difficult than the timing of purchases. Poor timing means purchasing securities at high prices and then witnessing a subsequent substantial price decline, or failure to sell distinctly overvalued securities, or selling securities too soon.

There are various aspects of timing: timing in respect to the market as a whole, timing in respect to security groups, and timing in respect to individual stocks. These aspects will be discussed in later chapters. Security analysis to determine sound values and reasonable prices to pay for securities should reduce considerably the timing risk.

All that has been said about psychological risks is pertinent to timing. Emotional rather than logical judgment results in poor timing. To an important extent, proper timing often means actions contrary to the "crowd."

Need for Sound Portfolio Management

The process of making and carrying out a decision to invest in securities is called *portfolio management*. Investment risks are reduced by proper portfolio management. The last two parts of this book (Chapters 28 to 33) are devoted to both individual and institutional portfolio management. Portfolio management has become a profession for thousands of individuals as investment counsel for both individual and institutional portfolio managers.

Management of a portfolio of significant size is a time-consuming and painstaking job. Success requires training, experience, and, above all, sound judgment and emotional stability. It is curious how many individuals believe that individual portfolio management does not require much knowledge, training, and experience and that successful management does not consume much time and effort.

Investment decisions should be made only after their effect on the portfolio as a whole is determined. The first consideration is the need and the financial circumstances. The second consideration is reasonable and rational goals for the individual or the institution. For individuals, the investment program must be considered as only part of the financial program. The funds available may be so small in relation to the financial need that all funds should be channeled into life insurance and reserves and none will be available for investment. In any case, required insurance and reserves should be adequately met before an investment program is initiated.

Investment management must be knowledgeable. Not only does successful investment management depend on proper security analysis of each situation, but also this analysis must be based on a sound knowledge and understanding of the basic forces in the economy that affect security values. Therefore, the following knowledge is essential for sound investment management:

1. Knowledge of past and current trends of the economy as evidenced by Gross National Product and its component elements, and judgments as to future trends.

2. Knowledge of the major factors in business cycles and current information on business cycle developments—leading, coincident, and lagging indicators and future expectations.

3. Knowledge of the flow of savings through the capital markets, the supply of credit, the Federal Reserve policy, the United States Treasury fiscal policy, and the absolute and relative role of financial intermediaries and individuals in the capital markets.

4. Knowledge of the history of the security markets as indicated by the record of:

   a. Stock price indexes such as:

      Standard & Poor's 500 composite.
      Standard & Poor's 425 industrials.
      Dow Jones Industrial Average.
      New York Stock Exchange, American Stock Exchange, and over-the-counter indexes.
      Special indexes of security and industry groups.

   b. Price-earnings ratios.
   c. Earnings yields.
   d. Dividend yields of common stocks.
   e. Dividend yields of preferred stocks.
   f. Bond yields.
   g. Bond yields in relation to stock dividend yields and stock earnings yields, that is, the spread between these yields currently and historically.

QUESTIONS

1. Discuss the crucial role played by investment in the American economy. Distinguish between real investment and security investment in your answer.

2. One writer has said that "the word *investment* is used with such a variety of meanings that it poses a minor problem in semantics." Discuss this statement in the light of various possible meanings that might be attached to the word *investments*.

3. Define investment as opposed to speculation, and define speculation as opposed to gambling.

4. Distinguish between the various types of risks faced by investors and indicate techniques useful in combating each type of risk.

5. (a) Why do highest-grade corporate bonds, at times, yield very little more than government bonds?
   (b) Which types of bonds should the individual purchase?

6. Why is an investment philosophy necessary for the success of either the individual or the institutional investor?

7. Explain the advantages of the diversification approach to investments as contrasted with a highly selective nondiversified approach.

8. (a) What is meant by a "balanced portfolio"?
   (b) In view of the purchasing power risk, would it not be wiser for an individual to invest in common stocks all funds not currently needed? Discuss.
9. (a) Are there fashions in stocks? If so, name one stock currently in vogue.
   (b) What is an out-of-favor, low price-earnings situation? Give an example of an industry or a stock.

10. (a) Are common stocks a good hedge against inflation? Discuss.
    (b) Are bonds a hedge against inflation? Discuss.

WORK-STUDY PROBLEM

List one bond and three stocks that might be classified in each of the following categories and defend your classification:

(a) An investment.
(b) A speculation.
(c) A gamble.

Discuss the risks that might be attached to each category.

SUGGESTED READINGS

Beja, Abraham. "On Systematic and Unsystematic Components of Financial Risk." *The Journal of Finance* (March, 1972), pp. 37-45.

Carter, E. Eugene. "What Are the Risks in Risk Analysis?" *Harvard Business Review* (July-August, 1972), pp. 72-82.

Francis, Jack Clark. *Investment Analysis and Management.* New York: McGraw Hill Book Company, 1972. Part IV, Chapter 13.

Fredrikson, E. Bruce. *Frontiers of Investment Analysis,* 2d ed. Scranton, Pa.: Intext Educational Publishers, 1971. Chapters 1-3.

Helfert, Erich A. *Techniques of Financial Analysis,* 3d ed. Homewood, Illinois: Richard D. Irwin, Inc., 1972. Chapter 6.

Levy, Haim, and Marshall Sarnat. *Investment and Portfolio Analysis.* New York: John Wiley & Sons, Inc., 1972. Chapter 6.

Smith, Adam. *Supermoney.* New York: Random House, Inc., 1972.

Williamson, J. Peter. *Investments.* New York: Praeger Publishers, 1971.

Wu, Hsiu-Kwang, and Alan J. Zakon. *Elements of Investments,* 2d ed. New York: Holt, Rinehart and Winston, Inc., 1972. Chapters 20, 25.

Zinbarg, Edward D. "Modern Approach to Investment Risk." *Financial Executive* (February, 1973), pp. 44-61.

THE
CAPITAL
MARKET

2

The Securities Markets

This chapter deals with the investment banker, whose primary function is to bring together the buyers and sellers of securities, and with the types of markets where the trading of securities takes place. The trading of securities may exist in an informally organized over-the-counter market or a formally organized security exchange.

THE INVESTMENT BANKER

Essentially a merchandising middleman, the investment banker accomplishes the function of bringing together the suppliers and the users of long-term investment funds by means of any of the following:

1. Purchasing (*underwriting*) entire new security issues and re-offering them to investors.
2. Agreeing to use his best efforts to sell the issue without committing himself to an underwriting agreement.
3. Guaranteeing to subscribe to and resell any portion of a new issue not already subscribed to by the existing securityholders of that issue (*standby underwritings*)
4. Acting as *finder* for a fee in the case of probably at least 75 percent of issues sold directly by issuers to investors (*private placements*).

Other Functions of the Investment Banker

In his role as a merchandising middleman of securities, the investment banker performs other related functions which are described in the first four paragraphs on page 32.

Wholesaler and Retailer. Investment bankers act both as wholesalers and as retailers. Their wholesaler's function consists of selling the issue they have underwritten to other investment firms that are primarily retailers. Most underwriters, however, also form and manage a purchase group to buy an issue, in which case they are also acting in the capacity of retailer. The larger underwriters do only a small amount of retailing.

Advisory Service to Issuer. Investment bankers have knowledge of the objectives of the various classes of investors and can therefore offer to the issuing corporations advice as to the type of securities to be issued, size of the issue, timing, maturity, callable features, protective clauses in the contract, and other provisions.

Investigation of the Issuer. The investment banker's reputation and integrity are his greatest assets. He must scrutinize proposed issues carefully. If the investment banker has not dealt with the issuer, he may make a preliminary investigation of the industry, the company, and its position in the industry. If the preliminary study is favorable for the issue, priority for the proposed underwriting will be requested and a more thorough study will be undertaken.

This subsequent investigation is designed to furnish the investment banker with information on which to base his final decision as to whether to underwrite. It provides most, if not all, of the material needed for the registration statement and the prospectus that must be filed with the Securities and Exchange Commission (SEC) under the provisions of the Securities Act of 1933. The final report is prepared by the investment banker's buying department, based on the reports of outside accountants, engineers, lawyers, and other experts as well as the department's own report. If the final recommendation submitted for the firm's approval is favorable and is accepted by the firm, the financial condition of the capital markets is checked to determine whether the issue will be well received. If the market is deemed satisfactory, the investment banker accepts the underwriting along with the agreement by other participants in the underwriting group.

Origination of New Security Issues

The issues that investment bankers purchase and resell to investors are obtained either by *private negotiation* with the issuer or by successful bidding against other investment bankers in *competitive bidding*. Table 2-1 shows the types and the amounts of new securities offered for cash in the United States and Table 2-2 shows the net change in corporate securities outstanding for the period 1968-1972.

Prior to the 1930s and the federal Securities Acts, all new issues (except a few offered directly by issuers to individual investors) were underwritten by investment bankers. Beginning in the 1930s, issuers began to sell securities directly to institutional investors by private placements. In general, however, issuers use investment bankers as finders to place the issue with financial institutions for a fee. By the mid-1960s, private placements accounted for 50%-60% of all new debt issues, but by the early 1970s the percentage had declined to 22% because of conditions in the capital markets. The percentage for common stock issues was about 3%; for preferred stock issues, about 5%.

TABLE 2-1

New Securities Offered for Cash in the U.S. by Type of Security
(Estimated Gross Proceeds in Billions of Dollars)

Year	All Types of Securities			Bonds, Debentures, Notes			Preferred Stock	Common Stock
	All Issues	Non-Corp.	Corp.	All Issues	Non-Corp.	Corp.		
1968	65.6	43.6	22.0	61.0	43.6	17.4	.637	3.946
1969	52.7	26.0	26.7	44.3	26.0	18.3	.682	7.714
1970	88.7	49.7	38.9	80.0	49.7	30.3	1.390	7.240
1971	106.4	60.4	46.0	92.3	60.4	31.9	3.683	10.459
1972	94.9	54.3	40.7	82.0	54.3	27.7	3.270	9.685

Note: Statistics for preferred and common stocks are carried to 3 decimals to indicate annual fluctuations.

TABLE 2-2

Net Changes in Corporate Securities Outstanding, 1968-1972

Year	Stocks		Debt		
	New Issues	Net Change in Outstanding	Total	New Issues Convertible	Net Change in Outstanding
1972	15,242	13,018	27,065	2,286	19,062
1971	14,769	13,452	31,917	3,607	23,728
1970	9,213	6,801	29,495	2,656	22,825
1969	9,318	4,272	19,523	4,041	13,755
1968	6,057	—900	19,381	3,281	13,962

Source: *SEC Statistical Bulletins* (February and March, 1973).

Underwriting Contracts. Most underwriting contracts are firm underwriting contracts as discussed below. At times when an issue is quite speculative, underwriters (usually small investment banking firms) may accept such issues as best-efforts deals, meaning that they will be committed to use their best efforts to sell the issue rather than make a firm commitment to buy the entire issue. In cases where a corporation has issued rights to a new issue, the corporation will usually also sign a standby-underwriting agreement with the investment bankers, which is a firm underwriting contract for a fee [1] to purchase all securities not purchased by those exercising the rights to the new issue.

Under *firm underwriting,* the most common form, a group of investment bankers agrees to purchase an entire issue, contracting to pay the full purchase price on a specified date. The investment banker expects to resell the entire issue within a very brief period. Commonly, the risk is spread among a large number of investment bankers. The underwriting agreement may include escape clauses that permit the cancellation of the contract before the sale. However, most bond underwriting contracts allow very few "outs" for either party. But in the case of highly speculative issues, the escape clause may be so broad as to make a mockery of the phrase "firm underwriting" and result in essence in a "best-efforts" agreement.

Purchase Group. When the issue is of considerable size, the originating underwriters will form a purchase group to join in the purchase contract in order to spread the risk. Each member of the purchase group, by signing the purchase group agreement, authorizes the originating investment banker as syndicate manager to act for the members in signing the underwriting agreement with the issuer. As syndicate manager he is then responsible for allocating the appropriate number of shares to each member and for determining which sales are to be allowed specified concessions below the offering price. The syndicate manager may engage in transactions aimed at stabilizing the market for the security during the underwriting as provided for in the federal Securities Acts. Each underwriter agrees to purchase a stipulated

---

[1] The fee typically consists of a certain amount for each share of stock so underwritten plus an additional amount for each share the investment banker is obliged to purchase. The cost of the issue is essentially an insurance that the entire issue will be sold regardless of its acceptance and regardless of any sudden adverse developments in the capital markets. During the underwriting period the investment banker will support the rights by purchasing rights in the market if necessary and then a few times during the period selling the rights in a "lay-off procedure." An excellent discussion of the lay-off of rights during the subscription period to minimize the risk of unsubscribed stock to the investment banker can be found in M. H. Waterman, *Investment Banking Functions* (Ann Arbor, Mich.: Bureau of Business Research, University of Michigan, 1958), pp. 136-140.

amount of the new issue, to abide by the rules governing the sale of the securities to the public, and to make settlement on the final date.[2]

Content of the Purchase Agreement. The underwriters agree to purchase and the issuer agrees to sell the securities as described. Customarily, the issuer agrees to assume all the expenses of preparing the issue for sale, including the cost of preparing and printing the necessary copies of the registration and prospectus. The issuer also furnishes the investment banker with sufficient copies of the preliminary prospectus, the "red herring," [3] as well as all amendments and the final prospectus.[4] The offering price, spread, industry discounts and commissions, net proceeds to the issuer, and settlement date are also included in the final agreement. The underwriters agree to proceed with a public offering as soon as the registration statement is effective or at some other specified date thereafter.

Underwriting Spreads. The *spread* is the difference between the price paid the issuer for the securities and the price at which they are sold to the public. It varies considerably among different issues. It may be less than 1¼% of the par value of high-grade bonds and as much as 10-25% of the cost of smaller, unseasoned, speculative common stock issues.

Members of the purchase group are entitled to the full spread on securities they buy and retail. A discount from the public offering price is allowed on the part of the issue that is wholesaled to the selling group, thus reducing the spread on such portions as are wholesaled. This discount is the selling

---

[2] Typically, the issuer's securities are delivered to the underwriter against cash payment about 7 to 10 days after the public offering date. The investment banker can have a substantial unsold inventory that requires financing on his part after this date if the issue does not sell well.

[3] A preliminary prospectus circulated during the registration period but in advance of the effective date of the registration statement and bearing a red-ink legend that it is to be used for information only and is not deemed an offer to sell or a solicitation of an offer to buy.

[4] The underwriters require the following guarantees from the issuer in the purchase agreement: (a) that he file a registration statement and any amendments required by the SEC and otherwise comply with all the stipulations of the Securities Act of 1933; (b) that the registration statement and prospectus contain no untrue or misleading information, that the financial statements therein have been prepared by independent certified public accountants, that they reflect the true financial state of the issuer, and that no material changes in the financial condition of the issuer have occurred since the date of the latest statement; (c) that any lawsuits in process or pending have been accurately described in the registration statement; (d) that the issuer will use the funds obtained from the sale of the issue only for the purposes stated; (e) that the issuer will use his best efforts to assure that the issue complies with all state security laws in the states where the underwriters intend to make distribution of the issue; (f) that the issuer will endeavor to secure the listing of the issue on any exchange to which he has agreed to apply; and (g) that the issuer will indemnify the underwriters for any liability that they incur because of omissions of material facts or untrue or misleading statements in the registration statement or prospectus, provided the underwriters were not responsible for the data.

group's compensation. The remainder of the spread on securities retailed by the selling group accrues to the purchase group.

The underwriting spread actually consists of three elements: (1) payment for the expenses of origination and distribution of the issue; (2) the risk involved in underwriting the issue; and (3) the equivalent of a commission for selling the issue.

Selling Group. While the purchase group is being organized, a selling group is also being formed. Estimates of the potential market from the new members added by the selling group must be obtained before the purchase group members can determine whether or not they can handle the issue. The selling group must be ready to start distributing the securities as soon as the purchase contract is signed and the registration is cleared with the SEC and becomes effective. Members of the purchase group ordinarily will also be members of the selling group. Both must be members of the National Association of Securities Dealers.

In one type of selling group, the dealers are offered a specified share of the new issue and may subscribe for the full amount or a smaller amount. If the dealer subscribes for the full amount and may be sure that he receives this amount, he has a *firm* commitment. Additional subscriptions may be made subject to allotment by the manager. In another type of selling group, the dealer may subscribe for as large an amount as he desires, all subject to the allotment of the manager. Inasmuch as the full amount or a lesser amount may be received, the dealer may be tempted to oversubscribe. Members of the selling group, who have tentatively and informally estimated the amount of securities that they are willing to take, may not legally make final commitments prior to the effective date of the registration statement.

No member may offer securities below the public offering price during the life of the selling group, which may be terminated on a specified date or on such earlier or later date as may be determined. When the issue has been distributed to the group, members may deal among themselves or with other members of the National Association of Securities Dealers at the public offering price less the approved selling group discount. Once the selling group is dissolved, the issue may be sold without restriction.

Advertising the Issue. While the Securities Act of 1933 prohibits any public offering except by means of the final prospectus, the SEC not only has officially encouraged the use of the preliminary *red herring* prospectus but also has recognized the necessity for the public advertising of issues in journals and newspapers. It has approved two types of advertising. The *tombstone prospectus,* often published in newspapers on the public offering date or immediately thereafter, is an extremely brief advertisement giving a few specific facts about the issue and listing the syndicate members. It specifically states that it is "not an offer to sell or solicitation of an offer to buy." The *newspaper prospectus* presents the more important facts about the issue in abbreviated form, and the SEC approves the omission from this advertisement of many details that must appear in the red herring prospectus and in the final prospectus.

Public Offering of the Securities. The public offering commences when the selling group manager officially "opens the books," entering the approved subscriptions from the members of the selling group and from any other dealers who may participate in the distribution. If dealers oversubscribe the issue, the books are no sooner opened than they are closed and the issue is said to have "gone out the window." If the issue is not selling well, it is "sticky" and the books remain open for a considerable time. The books may actually never be formally closed if the entire issue is not placed, and any unsold portion must then be distributed among the members of the purchase group and the syndicate is closed.

Competitive Bidding. While most new security offerings are originated by direct negotiation between the investment banker and the issuer, competitive bidding has assumed importance in certain regulated issues. Competitive bidding is firmly established in state and municipal finance because tax exemption and standardization minimize the importance of banking connections, because it helps to escape criticism of political favoritism, and generally because statutes require it. The United States Treasury, as well as agencies of the Federal Government, have always used competitive bidding. The Securities and Exchange Commission, as authorized by the Public Utility Holding Company Act of 1935, moreover, requires competitive bidding in the case of issues of registered public utility holding companies and their subsidiaries. The Federal Power Commission has also required competitive bidding for utilities subject to regulation under the Federal Power Act, and state commissions have done likewise.[5] The Interstate Commerce Commission, which regulates financing by railroads, has long required competitive bidding on almost all railroad securities, although in recent years it has approved private placements of some equipment issues. Under this method of financing, bids are submitted to the issuer who awards the issue to the highest bidder. It rarely happens that no bids are received or that all of the bids received are rejected, although such occurrences have been more frequent since 1966 because of historically high bond yields.

---

[5] These commissions may make certain exceptions to the requirements for competitive bidding if they deem the exception is in the public's interest.

Private Placements. Investment bankers may be bypassed in several ways by corporations seeking new funds. The two most common ways are for the corporate issuer (1) to sell the issue directly to present stockholders or (2) to obtain by negotiation private placement with one or a few institutional investors. Life insurance companies as a group are the largest direct placement lenders and together with corporate pension funds absorb most private placements, which are usually debt issues. The size of the average placement is smaller (70% under $3,000,000) than that of public issues, but there are also many very large private placements totaling $100,000,000 or more. As shown in Table 2-3, private placements approximated 55-65% of all debt issues during the years 1963-1965 and then declined sharply in the tight capital markets to 17% in 1970, then rose to 32% in 1972.

TABLE 2-3

Private Placement of Securities as a Percent of Total Corporate Issues Offered for Cash in the U.S.

	Percent of			Percent of			Percent of	
Year	All Issues	Debt Issues	Year	All Issues	Debt Issues	Year	All Issues	Debt Issues
1945	17.0	20.7	1954	38.5	46.5	1963	52.4	56.6
1946	27.8	38.2	1955	34.0	44.5	1964	53.0	66.7
1947	34.0	42.6	1956	35.5	47.2	1965	53.1	59.4
1948	43.6	50.4	1957	30.5	38.6	1966	43.0	48.4
1949	41.3	50.2	1958	27.4	30.7	1967	28.9	31.7
1950	42.1	52.0	1959	38.3	52.0	1968	31.7	40.1
1951	44.1	5 .4	1960	34.4	43.3	1969	22.5	32.8
1952	42.0	5 .1	1961	38.1	50.1	1970	13.2	16.9
1953	37.3	45.6	1962	43.3	50.5	1971	17.0	23.9
						1972	25.7	31.7

Sources: Annual Reports of Securities and Exchange Commission; January and February, 1973 issues of the *SEC Statistical Bulletin.*

Private placements are probably somewhat cheaper for the small and medium-sized issues than any other method of selling securities, although this is certainly not always the case. In any event, this is usually not the chief reason for private placement. Private placement avoids many of the delays, legal complications, and costs coincident with public issues. Private placements are not subject to the registration provisions of the Securities Act of 1933, while public offerings, with some exceptions, must be registered. Also, private placements are accomplished by negotiation. The contract provisions are therefore tailormade and flexible to a degree not possible with public issues. Renegotiation between issuer and lender is quite feasible if at any time difficulties arise and it seems advisable to rewrite some terms of the agreement. Private placement negotiations can be carried on privately, leaving the borrower at liberty to disclose confidential information that he is not desirous of making public. Finally, the direct placement may be consummated with a speed that is not possible where securities are publicly issued.

The major disadvantage of private placements lies in their narrow distribution. A large number of securityholders creates a pool of potential buyers for the issuer's products and can act as an important aid in selling additional securities at some future date.

Investment bankers and commercial bankers serve as finders for most private placements, receiving a finder's fee for this service. Frequently they aid the issuers in preparing the papers necessary to submit the proposal to potential institutional investors.

OVER-THE-COUNTER MARKET

The over-the-counter (OTC) market is the broadest of all markets for securities. Trading in this market exists outside the organized exchanges. While data regarding the volume of trading are not available, it is usually acknowledged that the total volume of business transacted in the over-the-counter market exceeds that of all organized exchanges by a wide margin, if trading in both bond and stock issues is included.[6]

Though without a central marketplace where business may be transacted, the over-the-counter market is well organized in its operations. Dealers trade directly with each other and with brokers and customers using the current bid-and-asked prices provided by a computerized communications network known as NASDAQ (National Association of Securities Dealers Automated Quotations System). This automatic quotation system ties together 1,000 brokerage houses nationwide. It not only quotes the bid and asked prices of the unlisted securities, but it also includes some of those securities listed on the stock exchanges that are traded over-the-counter.

By its very nature, the over-the-counter market is far more flexible in its operations than are the organized exchanges. There are no specified units of trading, and trading hours are not fixed. Business is generally transacted

---

[6] Frank Reilly, "First Look at O-T-C Volume," *Financial Analysts Journal* (January-February, 1969).

from 10:00 a.m. to 4:30 p.m. on weekdays. The only exception is transactions in United States Government securities, which must take place between 10:00 a.m. and 4:00 p.m. on Monday to Friday.

Issues Traded

The over-the-counter market serves to facilitate the distribution of new issues of securities as well as secondary distributions of outstanding securities held by individuals, estates, or financial institutions. This market offers the investor a significantly greater selection of issues than do the listed markets with respect to the number of issues offered and in terms of quality, ranging from the most stable, conservative, and seasoned high-grade securities to the most speculative of issues. The securities traded over-the-counter are of national, regional, and local importance. They include the bond issues of most corporations, domestic and foreign governments, states and their municipal subdivisions, railroads, utilities, all open-end mutual fund shares, most insurance company stock issues, virtually all bank stocks, and a rather broad list of common equities. By the late 1960s this market broadened substantially for equities and became extremely active, including a broad speculative market for individuals and institutions.

Trading in the Market

Firms making up the over-the-counter market are investment bankers, brokers, and dealers. It is the dealers, however, who constitute the backbone of this market. While there are thousands of dealers, a large proportion in dollar amount of business tends to be concentrated in a relatively small number of firms, and many dealers are highly specialized in particular issues. The dealers buy or sell for their own accounts or sell directly to their customers. New York Stock Exchange member firms became extremely active in the over-the-counter market by the late 1960s. Dealers may operate in the over-the-counter market in one of two ways: (1) they try to avoid taking a position in an issue by keeping the volume of buying and selling in each issue in balance, or (2) they take a position in an issue for trading purposes by buying more than they sell, or vice versa.

Unlike the organized exchanges, the over-the-counter market is a negotiated market. Dealers create and maintain markets for given issues. Prices are bid and asked offers, and these prices or quotes form the basis of negotiation, not the actual price at which the issue has been bought or sold. The differential or spread is the dealer's gross profit margin.

Regulation

The over-the-counter market is subject to regulation designed to protect the investor. In addition to regulation by the Securities and Exchange Commission and various state-enforced requirements, over-the-counter dealers are self-regulated by the National Association of Securities Dealers (NASD), a nonprofit organization set up in 1939 by the Maloney Act of 1938, which amended the Securities Exchange Act of 1934. The organization establishes and enforces fair rules of business conduct for its members and promotes ethical trade practices. Most firms of any importance in the investment banking business are members of the NASD and are subject to its rules. Violations may result in a member's suspension or expulsion from the Association and are regarded as serious because of the loss of reputation as well as preferential member trading privileges. Disciplinary action by the Association is subject to review by the SEC.

In 1964, Congress amended the Securities Exchange Act of 1934 to subject firms with $1,000,000 in assets and 500 or more stockholders to the same disclosure, proxy, and other regulations as are required for listed companies. This was a tremendous help to those seeking to analyze and evaluate over-the-counter securities.

ORGANIZED SECURITY EXCHANGES

Organized security exchanges provide an established location where brokers buy and sell securities in a formal market during established hours on designated days. Organized markets are found in many of the nation's larger cities, as follows:

Registered Exchanges

American Stock Exchange	National Stock Exchange, Inc.
Boston Stock Exchange	New York Stock Exchange, Inc.
Chicago Board of Trade	Pacific Coast Stock Exchange
Cincinnati Stock Exchange	PBW Stock Exchange
Detroit Stock Exchange	Salt Lake Stock Exchange
Midwest Stock Exchange	Spokane Stock Exchange

Exempt Exchanges (Nonregistered)

Honolulu Stock Exchange
Richmond Stock Exchange

The New York Stock Exchange (NYSE) is the largest and best known of the national exchanges. The American Stock Exchange (ASE) is the second largest nationally. The volume of all exchanges reached all-time peaks in 1968 [7] and again in 1971-1972, but declined sharply in 1973.

The largest regional exchanges are the Midwest Stock Exchange, the Pacific Coast Stock Exchange, and the Philadelphia-Baltimore-Washington Stock Exchange, all formed by the merger of several smaller exchanges. The regional exchanges account for a very small proportion of total trading in securities in terms of both share and dollar volume. Their primary function is to maintain an organized market for regional issues not qualified for listing on national exchanges. But considerable business in NYSE-listed issues is transacted on the Pacific Coast Stock Exchange. Within the framework of the entire market for securities, the regional exchanges appear to provide some transition between the over-the-counter market and listing on the national exchanges.

Although trading procedures and practices differ to some extent among the exchanges, national as well as regional, their organization and operations, especially those of the American Stock Exchange, resemble those of the New York Stock Exchange.

Purpose of Security Exchanges

Any mechanism that aids the flow of capital funds aids the entire economy. Herein lies one basic economic value of security markets. New issues of securities are not handled through the facilities of the exchanges, which are markets for trading in securities already issued. While not directly involved in the sale of new securities, nevertheless the exchanges promote the saving-investment process by providing a place where liquidity preference may be exercised. Many individuals would be reluctant to invest their cash savings by purchasing securities unless a convenient market existed where these securities could be readily converted into cash. The security markets perform this function by maintaining a continuous market for securities. By providing markets in rights to new issues, the exchanges aid in the sale and distribution of new issues.

A security is highly *marketable* if it can be sold quickly at close to its current market quotation. Marketability and liquidity are not synonymous. *Liquidity* implies the ability to convert to cash with little or no money loss

---

[7] Volume increased so substantially in 1968 that both the New York Stock Exchange and the American Stock Exchange had to close one day a week in mid-1968 in order to attempt to catch up on "fails" to deliver on date required. It was then decided to be open each day in 1969, but only from 10 a.m. to 2 p.m.

in relation to the price at which the security was acquired. A security may be highly marketable (small changes in price between transactions), but its price may fluctuate widely from month-to-month or year-to-year. Many investors in at least part of their portfolio require only limited marketability. Furthermore, a security or private placement could have a high degree of safety of principal and yet lack marketability or liquidity.

Distinguishing Features of Security Exchanges

Special features that distinguish the organized security exchanges from the over-the-counter market are discussed in the next four paragraphs.

Exchange Markets as Auction Markets. Security exchanges are of the two-sided, auction type. A broker representing a buyer and a broker representing a seller consummate a transaction by bidding competitively against other brokers on the floor of the exchange. The highest bidder purchases the security from the seller offering to sell at the lowest price. Market prices then are determined by the demand of the investing public for the limited supply of security issues. It is a rule of the exchanges that the initial bid or offer at a given price has priority over any other. Priority is established in the order in which offers to buy and sell are received on the floor of the exchange. The exchange itself does not buy or sell securities, nor does it fix prices at which they are sold. It provides the marketplace.

Exchange Trading in Seasoned Securities. Exchanges, and particularly the New York Stock Exchange, deal primarily in "seasoned" securities that have been outstanding for some time rather than in newly issued securities. The American Stock Exchange [8] and especially the regional exchanges provide markets for the newer, "unseasoned" issues prior to their graduation to the New York Stock Exchange. While institutions have come to account for the majority of transactions on the NYSE, individuals account for 80% of the ASE volume.

Trade in Listed Securities. The securities traded on the exchanges are primarily "listed" securities of companies that have applied for listing, have complied with certain requirements of the exchange, and have had their applications accepted by the exchange. For many years there has been no trading in unlisted securities on the New York Stock Exchange. The American Stock Exchange still does some business in unlisted securities. Of the

---

[8] Included in the issues listed on the American Stock Exchange are some issues of large, seasoned corporations, but these issues are in the minority.

1,391 securities traded on the American Stock Exchange, only 67 (4.8%) are unlisted.[9]

Unit of Trading. The regular trading unit on the exchanges is called a *round lot*, 100 shares of stock for most securities. In a few cases, the unit of trading has been established at 10 shares. Orders for less than 100 shares or the established unit of trading are called *odd lots*.

Membership in the New York Stock Exchange [10]

The New York Stock Exchange is a voluntary association with membership limited to a maximum of 1,375. Individuals acquire membership by the purchase of a "seat" from an existing member or from the estate of a deceased member. Formal application for admittance must be made to the Department on Members. Each applicant must be an American citizen, at least 21 years of age, and sponsored by two members of the Exchange. The price of a seat is arrived at by private negotiation or by auction and is determined primarily by the profitability of the membership, which is largely a function of the volume of trading. The highest price ever paid was $625,000 in 1929. In 1968 and again in 1969, a seat sold for $515,000, the highest since 1929.[11] But prices fell to around $90,000 in 1973.

Trading on the floor of the Exchange is carried on exclusively by members. These are either partners or voting stockholders of member firms, or in a few cases they are members not associated with any firm. There are 1,366 Exchange members and 572 Exchange member organizations, including 353 partnerships and 219 corporations. Member firms have about 3,636 branch offices in over 1,000 cities in 50 states, the District of Columbia, Puerto Rico, and 24 foreign countries. In addition, member firms are connected by direct wire with about as many nonmember firms here and abroad.

Board of Governors. Exchange policy and regulations governing the conduct of members and allied members are established by a Board of Governors consisting of 10 brokers, 10 public members, and a Chairman of the Board.

---

[9] *American Stock Exchange Fact Book,* 1971 Edition.

[10] *New York Stock Exchange Fact Book,* 1971 edition.

[11] The 1968 and 1969 membership price of $515,000 was really equivalent to the 1929 previous high of $625,000 because the latter price represented a right to 1¼ "seats." The low price was $17,000 in 1942. The American Stock Exchange high was $254,000 in 1929 and $350,000 in 1969; the ASE low was $650 in 1942.

Exchange Members. Members of the Exchange are classified as commission brokers, specialists, odd-lot dealers, floor traders, or bond traders. These names indicate the function that the members perform, as discussed in the following paragraphs.

Commission Brokers. Acting as agents for the customers of their firms, these brokers execute orders, both regular and odd-lot. As remuneration for their services, they receive an established commission set by the Exchange. They are the most numerous of all the members operating on the floor of the Exchange.

Specialists. Specialists may act both as brokers and as dealers. A specialist specializes in one or more securities traded at a single post on the floor of the Exchange. When he is on the floor, he stays at this post. He is permitted to operate either for himself as a principal or for his customer as an agent, but he may not act as a broker and a dealer in the same transaction. He must always give precedence to an order other than his own.

Commission brokers generally allow specialists to execute on the brokers' behalf any customers' market orders and limit or stop orders that by their nature may not be immediately executed. With 1,330 common and 510 preferred stock issues of 1,351 corporations listed on the Exchange (January, 1971), commission brokers would find it prohibitively expensive, and in fact physically impossible, to follow all of their customers' limit or stop orders and to execute them efficiently. Specialists record on their books all limit and stop orders to sell or buy either above or below market. Orders on the specialist's book do give him a select, though incomplete, picture of the market in which he specializes, which is a much better viewpoint than that of everyone else. For this reason, the specialist acting for his own account as a principal often has been criticized. However, as he performs a useful function in "making a market" as well as in maintaining orderly markets by purchasing stock at a higher price than anyone else is willing to pay, it is generally agreed that the advantages of his operation more than offset the disadvantages. Specialists' operations are very strictly regulated and supervised.

Under existing rules the specialist may not disclose any information concerning orders on his book, except to authorized members of the SEC or to executives of the Exchange in the course of their official duties. There must be a specialist approved by the Board of Governors for each listed stock. A specialist is almost always a specialist in several stocks. Except in the case of a few large-volume stocks, there is only one specialist for each stock.

Odd-Lot Dealers. Odd-lot dealers and brokers deal principally in odd-lot orders, that is, transactions involving less than 100 shares. There is only one major odd-lot firm with whom most member firms of the NYSE deal.

Floor Traders. Those members who act exclusively for their own accounts as speculators seeking quick profits are known as floor traders. They do not act either for the public or for other members. Because they are purely speculators, they have been subject to considerable criticism since the passage of the Securities Exchange Act of 1934. As a result of the restrictions on their activities, the number of members primarily engaged in floor trading has dwindled until there are now less than 20.

Bond Traders. Certain members of the Exchange trade only in bonds, either as brokers or as dealers. The bond market is also an auction market. The trading takes place on a special floor area connected with the main trading floor of the Exchange. The total number of bond issues listed on the Exchange in 1971 was 1,729 with a par value of $135 billion. Even in the case of listed bonds, most of the trading in bonds is in the over-the-counter markets. In recent years, the volume of bond trading on the Exchange has not been very significant.

Listing of Securities

Initiative for listing securities comes from the issuing corporation, often with the support and the encouragement of a member of the Exchange. The corporation's listing application places at the disposal of the Exchange information necessary to determine the suitability of the security for trading on the Exchange and provides the public with information necessary to appraise the investment merits of the security. If the company satisfies the standards of the Exchange and agrees to the terms of the listing arrangement, the securities are approved for listing. At this point a certificate is sent to the Securities and Exchange Commission stating that the Exchange has approved for listing the specified securities. Registration with the Commission ordinarily becomes effective 30 days after it receives the Exchange certification. The securities are officially listed and trading begins on the floor of the Exchange on the effective date for the registration statement.

Department of Stock List. When a corporation applies for listing, the Exchange's Department of Stock List conducts a thorough investigation of the company's history, financial structure, size, and volume of business, as well as the degree of public interest in its business and securities, whether local or national in scope.[12]

Eligibility for Listing. In determining eligibility for listing, the Department of Stock List is particularly concerned with the degree of national interest in the company, its relative position and stability in its industry, and whether it is engaged in an expanding industry with prospects of at least maintaining its position. While each case is decided on its own merits, there are certain minimum standards.[13]

When an application has been approved, the applicant signs certain listing agreements under which the corporation agrees to abide by the rules of the Exchange and the Securities and Exchange Commission. Listing information filed by an applicant to conform with New York Stock Exchange and Securities and Exchange Commission requirements must be kept up to date. Corporations meet this requirement by filing annually with the Exchange copies of their published certified financial statements and other supplemental information required by the New York Stock Exchange and the Securities and Exchange Commission. The issuer is required to maintain a transfer agent and a registrar in New York City. The company pays

---

[12] The application for original listing requires data under the following major headings:

1. Heading	12. Stockholder Relations
2. Description of Transaction	13. Dividend Record
3. Authority for Issuance	14. Options, Warrants, Conversion Rights, etc.
4. History and Business	
5. Property Description	15. Litigation
6. Affiliated Companies	16. Business, Financial and Accounting Policies
7. Management	
8. Capitalization	17. Financial Statements
9. Funded Debt	18. Opinion of Counsel
10. Stock Provisions	19. General Information
11. Employees-Labor Relations	20. Signature
	21. Exhibits

[13] The minimum standards are as follows:

Number of stockholders
Holders of 100 shares or more 2,000
    (The number of beneficial holders of stock held in the name of NYSE member organizations will be considered in addition to holders of record. NYSE will make any necessary check of such holdings.)

Number of shares
Publicly held 1,000,000
Market value publicly-held shares $16,000,000
    (While greater emphasis is placed on market value, an additional measure of size is $16 million minimum net tangible assets.)

Demonstrated earning power before federal income taxes and under competitive conditions
Latest fiscal year · . . . . $ 2,500,000
Each of preceding two years . . . . $ 2,000,000

the Exchange's initial listing fee and, in addition, pays an annual fee for continued listing privilege.

Delisting. The Exchange has the right to delist a security or suspend dealings in it at any time it judges such action advisable, but with the prior approval of the SEC. A security may be delisted if it becomes inactive and is likely to remain so, or if the issuing corporation contracts in size to the point where it no longer meets initial listing standards.

Trading on the Exchange

Once a security is listed, it is assigned to a "post" or U-shaped station on the floor; all trading in that security is done at that location. The customer's order is relayed by telephone to the company's clerk in the firm's booth on the trading floor, who in turn transfers it to the NYSE member representing the firm on the floor. As soon as the member picks up the order, he goes as rapidly as possible to the post where the stock is being traded to enter the bidding or to give the order to the specialist in the stock. Once the transaction has been completed, the brokers who participated notify their firms and the customer receives confirmation of the order's execution. The transaction is reported on the ticker tape by the New York Quotations Company, a subsidiary corporation of the Exchange.[14]

Cash Purchase. A purchase on the Exchange may be made on a 100% cash basis. The buyer may take possession of the stock certificate, or leave it with his broker for safekeeping, or have the broker retain it in the firm's name as a "street certificate" to facilitate its transfer at some later date without the necessity of endorsing the certificate.

Margin Buying. Buying on margin permits the buyer to purchase securities without paying the full price with his funds. In effect, he obtains the amount of the margin as a loan from his broker, who retains the securities purchased as collateral for the loan. Although the certificate is in a "street name" (broker's name), the customer as beneficial owner of the stock is entitled to receive any dividends and to vote the stock through his broker. Margin requirements are initially determined by the Federal Reserve Board under authority provided by the Securities Exchange Act of 1934. In 1973 the margin requirement was set at 65% for stocks, 50% for convertible bonds, and 65% for short sales.

---

[14] Most member firms now use one of several types of reporting machines based on computer operations that provide not only current price quotations, etc., but also dividend yields and price-earnings ratios.

If a customer's equity falls below 25% of the market value of the securities, the broker must request additional margin or sell the securities to protect himself against loss. Most brokers require that the equity be at least 33%. A broker may also re-hypothecate the certificate with a bank, and most brokers do so in order to obtain the loanable funds.

Delivery and Settlement. Transactions in stocks and bonds are normally made in one of three ways:

1. *Regular way,* requiring settlement on the fifth business day following the day of the contract. (The bulk of transactions are "regular way.")

2. *Cash,* requiring delivery of the securities and payment for them on the day of the contract.

3. *Seller's option,* requiring delivery on the day of the expiration of the option, or at the option of the seller on any prior business day upon one day's written notice, provided such notice is not given before 4:00 p.m. nor before the day when delivery would be due in the "regular way."

In 1968 the number of "fails" to deliver as required reached a peak and became a very serious problem for many firms. The total was over $3 billion. But since then, "fails" have declined substantially as volume declined.

Market and Limit Orders. Generally, market orders (to be executed "at the market") are more satisfactory for securities with good marketability, whereas limit orders (to be executed only at specified prices) are more advantageous in securities of limited marketability with a wide spread between bid and asked prices. Orders to buy and sell "at the market" are to be executed as soon as possible at the best price obtainable by the broker on the trading floor. The "best price" is the lowest price for a buy order and the highest price for a sell order. The obvious advantage of a market order is its rapid execution, which can be a particularly important factor when the market is rising or declining sharply. The basic disadvantage of a market order is that the "best price available" may be quite unsatisfactory. It is best to be cautious with respect to market orders in inactive stocks or in issues performing erratically and fluctuating over a wide range. If considerable time has elapsed since the last quotation, it is advisable to ask for a "bid and ask" quotation before placing an order.

Unlike a market order, which may be executed without limitations as to price, a limit order instructs the broker to execute the order within certain price limits set by the customer, no higher than the limit price in a buy order and no lower than the limit price in a sell order. Under existing Exchange rules, once a stock is ex-dividend, all limit orders in the stock are adjusted for the amount of the dividend. The primary disadvantage of the limit order is that the order may never be executed and the investor may have "missed the market" only by a small margin.

Stop-Loss Order. A stop-loss order is a special type of limit order. Once the stock on the Exchange has sold at or beyond the stop-loss price, the stop order becomes a market order. The difficulty with stop-loss orders, in fact with all limit orders, is that the customer may forget that he has placed them, with the result that they may be executed at a time when he no longer wants them executed. Technically, selecting the points at which stop-loss orders will be placed is a difficult problem and depends largely on the chart action of the stock. A small price decline often can launch a wave of stop-loss selling that may appreciably accelerate the price drop in the stock. Stop-loss orders are used defensively to minimize or prevent losses automatically if the market suddenly changes direction. In numerous cases, when a specialist notifies a member of the Board of Governors that the current price of a stock is close to the stop price on a large volume of orders, the Exchange will bar all stop orders on the stock until the congestion is cleared away.[15]

Day Orders and Open Orders. A day order is one that automatically expires at the close of the day it is placed if not executed by that time. Orders are usually considered as day orders unless otherwise specified. Open orders, however, may be entered for some limited period, such as a week or a month, or may remain effective until executed or canceled, known as "good-'til-canceled" or G.T.C. orders. Under New York Stock Exchange rules, all G.T.C. orders outstanding must be confirmed or renewed with the floor specialist at six-month intervals, on the last day of April and of October. Brokerage firms also may check their orders with the customers at least once a month and usually do.

Odd-Lot Orders. An order for the purchase or the sale of less than the unit of trading is an odd-lot order. An odd-lot transaction depends upon prior execution of a round lot, and the odd-lot may be executed only at the

---

[15] The New York Stock Exchange in recent years has ordered cancellation of all stop orders on certain stocks when the volume of such orders has created a potential situation detrimental to an orderly market. The American Stock Exchange also has followed the same policy.

odd-lot differential of ⅛ of a point for a stock selling below $55 and of ¼ of a point for a stock selling at $55 or above. The odd-lot differential is the odd-lot dealer's compensation and is in addition to the broker's commission. The differential increases the cost in the purchase of stock and decreases the proceeds from the sale of stock. If, for example, the next round-lot sale is at 61, the price to the seller of an odd lot is 60¾ and the price to the buyer of an odd lot is 61¼.

Short Selling. A short sale is the sale of stock by a seller who borrows the stock in order to make delivery and later returns the stock to the lender. There are several reasons why individuals may wish to sell short. The primary purpose is to speculate on the anticipation of a price decline in the stock. The short seller hopes to acquire the stock to "cover" the sale at a lower price in the future, realizing a profit measured by the difference between the selling price and the later purchase price after commissions and other expenses. There is no limit to the short seller's loss if the market rises and he does not "buy in." To prevent "bear raiding" and demoralization of the markets by short sellers deliberately depressing the market, the Securities and Exchange Commission has ruled that a short sale must be so designated when the order is placed and may not be executed at a price below the last preceding regular sale. A short sale must be made on an "up tick" or may be made at the price of the last regular trade only if the previous price change was upward. If the last price change was downward, the short sale must be made above the last price, on an "up tick."

When a customer sells short, his broker loans him the stock or borrows the stock from another customer or broker. Dividends declared to stockholders of record during the time a short sale is in effect belong to the lender of the stock.[16] To provide security for the loan of stock, the borrowing broker deposits with the lending broker the market price of the borrowed shares obtained from the short sale transaction.

Puts and Calls.[17] Options to sell or buy a designated number of shares (usually 100) of a given security at a fixed price within a stated time at an agreed premium are called "puts and calls." A "straddle" or a "spread" is a combination of a put-and-call option to sell or buy a particular stock at the same price or at different prices. Options may be for 30, 60, or 90 days

---

[16] The member firm involved pays the dividend to the lender of the stock and charges the short seller the amount of the dividend.

[17] See Herbert Filers, *Understanding Put and Call Operations* (New York: Crown Publishers, Inc.).

or 6 months. Options are primarily speculative commitments, although they do offer possibilities for hedging and limiting losses. The major advantage of options is that the maximum loss which may be incurred is limited to the cost of the option. Options are expensive to purchase and to maintain, however, and the investor must renew the option at its expiration if he is to continue his protection. The fact that most options are never exercised indicates the risk involved. Much of the business in puts and calls is transacted in New York City by members of the Put and Call Brokers and Dealers Association. Options must be guaranteed by members of the New York Stock Exchange for the protection of buyers. The public in the 1960s and early 1970s became quite interested in options and the volume in these transactions increased very substantially. And in 1972 the Chicago Board of Trade established the Chicago Board Options Exchange.

Commissions and Transfer Taxes. Stock exchanges legislate a schedule of minimum commission rates. In 1968 the NYSE, under pressure from the SEC, adopted an "Interim Fee—Reform Plan" which was accepted by the SEC. This new schedule provides for a volume discount to nonmember customers on certain larger stock transactions, reduction in floor brokerage and clearance charges between exchange members, and prohibition of customer-directed "give-ups" of parts of commissions earned by brokers executing transactions to other brokers as directed by the principal—usually a mutual fund desiring to compensate the other broker for his services to the fund, particularly the services of selling the fund's shares.

Another major change in the rate structure effective as of April, 1972, was the abandonment of a fixed commission schedule for trades in excess of $300,000. Fees for transactions of this magnitude are now negotiated.

The investor should be familiar with the various components comprising his total cost in purchasing securities and his net proceeds in selling securities. It is particularly important that these values be computed accurately when reporting gains and losses from security transactions for income tax purposes. To illustrate, the purchaser of 100 shares of stock selling at $40 per share on the New York Stock Exchange would pay $4,058 for his stock, including the price of $4,000 plus the broker's commission of $58 as per the rates currently effective on New York Stock Exchange transactions. The net proceeds to the seller of the stock is the price minus the broker's commission, the New York State transfer tax, and the SEC registration fee. The seller of 100 shares of stock selling at $40 would therefore receive $3,938.67, computed as shown at the top of page 53.

```
Price: 100 shares at 40 ...............................  $4,000.00
Less:
        Commission: ½ of $40 + $38 .............  $58.00
        New York State transfer tax:
        $0.0325 per share * .....................    3.25
        SEC registration fee: 1¢ for each $500 or frac-
        tion thereof ...........................    0.08     61.33
Net proceeds to seller .................................  $3,938.67
```

* Rate in effect from July 1, 1972, through June 30, 1973.

The Third Market

The "third market" is the over-the-counter market in listed securities. This market has developed fairly recently in response to the institutional investors' dissatisfaction over not being given a volume discount for large block trading on the organized exchanges, and it exists to serve the needs of this group of investors. As the volume of business of institutional investors (mutual funds, insurance companies, and pension funds) has markedly increased in recent years, the "third market" business has increased also. This has obviously effected a decline in the volume of block trading transacted on the New York Stock Exchange and resulted in the creation of competitive markets for those securities.[18] This has been especially true since mid-1972, at which time NASDAQ began quoting the more active "listed" stocks, making their prices immediately available to over-the-counter dealers and brokers.

The Market System of the Future

Because of the rise in institutional investing, the New York Stock Exchange, which is organized primarily to serve the individual trader, is now structurally anachronistic. NASDAQ with its growing number of "listed" securities is making the "third market" a real threat to the Exchange's once monopolistic position. For this reason various plans for reorganization of the entire securities market are now under discussion. A computerized nationwide market disclosure system involving a consolidated ticker tape is

---

[18] Morris Mendelson, *From Automated Quotes to Automated Trading: Restructuring the Stock Market in the U.S.,* New York University, Graduate School of Business Administration, March, 1972. "In 1961, institutional off-the-floor trading in listed stock was little more than 10 percent. In the third quarter of 1970, total off-the-floor trading, which is mostly institutional, was estimated to be in excess of 20 percent. The off-the-floor shares of trading grew by over 25 percent between mid-1968 and late 1970."

currently being developed to report all prices and trading that would take place in a newly proposed central securities market. This central market system as presently conceived would be controlled not only by regulations, but also by the inevitable forces of competition. It would be able to execute matched buy and sell orders and also to constitute a vehicle for integrating block and retail trading. It would serve the institutional investor without denying certain priorities to the individual trader. And it would provide for the most efficient execution of trades, while still preserving the most equitable participation of the traders. There will undoubtedly be a major overhaul in the securities industry along with the necessary sweeping legislative changes in the near future, but the actual realization of a central securities market system will surely evolve slowly.

QUESTIONS

1. (a) State the primary function of an investment banker.
   (b) Name three other functions performed by investment bankers.
2. Discuss briefly the purpose of the investigation of an issuing company by an investment banker.
3. (a) Describe the type of agreement entered into in a "best-efforts" underwriting. Under what circumstances will an investment banker usually insist upon this form of agreement?
   (b) Define a "firm underwriting." Is a standby underwriting a firm underwriting? Discuss.
4. (a) Describe briefly the nature and the content of a purchase agreement between the underwriting group and the issuing corporation.
   (b) Describe the basic function of the purchase group in an underwriting.
5. (a) Define the term "underwriters' spread."
   (b) What are the usual spreads in bond issues, preferred stock issues, and common stock issues? Account for the differences in spread.
6. Name three criteria of a successful underwriting.
7. Discuss briefly the investment bankers' responsibility to the investing public.
8. (a) Compare competitive bidding and "origination by negotiation."
   (b) Name the types of securities usually sold by each method.
9. Discuss briefly the significance of private placements as a means of selling new issues. Indicate the importance of such issues relative to public issues in recent years.
10. (a) Distinguish between primary and secondary markets.
    (b) What is the economic function of these markets? How does each contribute to the basic economic function?
    (c) How do the organized security markets differ from the over-the-counter market?

11. (a) Distinguish between marketability and liquidity. Give an example of a financial instrument having marketability but not liquidity.
    (b) Is marketability synonymous with safety of principal? Could an instrument have safety of principal and yet lack marketability? Discuss.

12. (a) Differentiate between a broker and a dealer and indicate how each derives his compensation.
    (b) Name the categories into which active members of the New York Stock Exchange are placed. Differentiate as to the role played by each category.
    (c) Discuss briefly the functions of a specialist on the Exchange.

13. (a) Who can trade on the floor of the exchanges?
    (b) Of what significance to the investor is the fact that a company he is considering investing in is listed on the New York Stock Exchange?
    (c) What information, of value to a prospective investor, could be found in a New York Stock Exchange listing statement?
    (d) Why does the Exchange refuse to list nonvoting stock?
    (e) What special listing requirements are required of a preferred stock on the Exchange?

14. (a) Distinguish between a limit order and a stop-loss order. When would each be used?
    (b) What are the advantages and the disadvantages of placing a market order?
    (c) What are the advantages and the major risks of buying stock on margin?

15. Define a short sale. What are the regulations governing short sales?

16. What is the "third market"?

17. Define "fails" to deliver and discuss the problem.

18. Why must the securities market be reorganized, and what kind of system is currently being proposed?

WORK-STUDY PROBLEMS

1. Describe the activities of a large investment banking firm, covering in particular the following:
    (a) The types of security issues normally originated by competitive bidding and the types of security issues normally originated by negotiated deal.
    (b) The four categories normally covered in a thorough investigation of an issuing company by an investment banking firm.
    (c) The spread.
    (d) The agreement among the underwriters.
    (e) The underwriting agreement.

(f) The advantages and the disadvantages of private placement and the role of the investment banking houses in private placement.

2. Write a short paper giving the reasons why an industrial concern:
   (a) Would seek to have its securities listed on the New York Stock Exchange.
   (b) Would prefer to have its securities traded over-the-counter.

SUGGESTED READINGS

Baker, Guthrie. "Blueprint for Constructive Reform." *Financial Analysts Journal* (November-December, 1971), pp. 20-22,62.

Black, Fisher. "Toward a Fully Computerized Stock Exchange." *Financial Analysts Journal* (November-December, 1971), pp. 24-28, 86-87.

Cary, William L., and Walter Werner. "Outlook for Securities Markets." *Harvard Business Review* (July-August, 1971), pp. 16-18, 22-25, 160.

Crouch, Robert L. "The Volume of Transactions and Price Changes on the New York Stock Exchange." *Financial Analysts Journal* (July-August, 1970), pp. 104-109.

Fanning, James E. "A Four-Indicator System for Forecasting the Market." *Financial Analysts Journal* (September-October, 1971), pp. 49-56.

Feuerstein, Donald M. "Toward a National System of Securities Exchanges: The Third and Fourth Markets." *Financial Analysts Journal* (July-August, 1972), pp. 57-59, 82-86.

Granger, G. W. J., and O. Morgenstern. *The Predictability of Stock Market Prices*. Lexington, Mass.: D. C. Heath & Co., 1970.

Hayes, Samuel L. III. "Investment Banking: Power Structure in Flux." *Harvard Business Review* (March-April, 1971), pp. 136-152.

Homa, Kenneth E., and Dwight M. Jaffee. "The Supply of Money and Common Stock Prices." *The Journal of Finance* (December, 1971), pp. 1045-1066.

Latané, Henry A., Donald L. Tuttle, and William E. Young. "Market Indexes and Their Implications for Portfolio Management." *Financial Analysts Journal* (September-October, 1971), pp. 75-85.

McDonald, J. G., and A. K. Fisher. "New Issue Stock Price Behavior." *The Journal of Finance* (March, 1972), pp. 97-102.

Reilly, Frank K. "Price Changes in NYSE, AMEX, & OTC Stocks Compared." *Financial Analysts Journal* (March-April, 1971), pp. 54-59.

Smidt, Seymour. "Which Road to an Efficient Stock Market?" *Financial Analysts Journal* (September-October, 1971), pp. 18-20, 64-69.

Stern, Walter P., and William C. Norby. "Investment Research and Market Structure—Today and Tomorrow." *Financial Analysts Journal* (January-February, 1972), pp. 24-28, 85-87.

West, Richard R. "Institutional Trading and the Changing Stock Market." *Financial Analysts Journal* (May-June, 1971), pp. 17-24, 71-72, 78.

Historical Behavior of Markets for Limited-Income Securities

Economists state that, in any country, what is produced minus what is consumed equals *savings* and that savings equal investment. This chapter attempts to describe the nature and extent of savings in our economy, how these funds flow into the capital markets as long-term securities or investments, and how interest rates in the capital markets fluctuate in relation to the supply and demand of investment funds.

SAVINGS IN THE UNITED STATES

The term savings may be described as gross or net, depending on whether or not deductions or allowances are made for certain items. Savings may also be classified according to who accumulates them: individuals, business firms, or governments.

Gross Savings

Gross savings means gross with no deductions for consumption of capital; it represents gross investment with no allowances for such items as actual depreciation or decline in the value of assets. The sources of gross savings are: (1) personal savings, (2) corporate savings (undistributed corporate profits), and (3) corporate and noncorporate capital consumption allowances charged off as expenses on income statements but not representing actual cash outlays. Table 3-1 shows sources (those who supply the funds) and uses (those who furnish the demand for funds) of gross savings in the U.S.

TABLE 3-1

Sources and Uses of Gross Savings, 1960-1970 (Billions of Dollars)

Source or Use	1960	1964	1965	1966	1967	1968	1969	1970	1971	1972
Gross Private Savings	119.5	126.8	127.7	119.5	129.3	135.2	135.8	153.4	170.3	178.4
Personal savings	29.8	34.6	38.8	29.8	38.7	38.4	37.6	54.1	60.9	54.8
Undistributed corporate profits	27.8	28.2	24.2	27.8	24.7	26.7	25.9	16.2	20.5	26.1
Corporate inventory valuation adjustments	—1.6	—.7	—.8	—1.6	—1.2	—3.2	—5.6	—4.5	—4.7	—6.0
Corporate capital consumption allowances	39.0	39.8	40.3	39.0	41.4	45.9	49.1	56.2	60.3	67.7
Noncorporate capital consumption allowances	24.5	24.9	25.2	24.5	25.7	27.4	28.8	31.4	33.5	36.0
Wage accruals less disbursements	.0	.0	.0	.0	.0	.0	.0	.0	.4	—0.3
Government Surplus or Deficit (—), National Income and Product Accounts	3.2	—.3	—10.9	3.2	—12.4	—6.7	8.9	—13.1	—16.9	—5.9
Federal	.3	—3.3	—11.9	.3	—12.5	—5.2	9.5	—13.6	—21.7	—18.5
State and local	2.9	3.0	1.0	2.9	.1	—1.5	—.6	.5	4.8	12.6
Gross Investment	120.2	124.0	112.9	120.2	114.0	125.9	138.8	136.6	149.9	173.3
Gross private domestic investment	118.0	122.2	110.4	118.0	112.2	126.2	139.4	135.3	152.0	180.4
Net foreign investment	2.2	1.8	2.5	2.2	1.8	—.3	—.6	1.3	—2.1	—7.1
Statistical discrepancy	—2.6	—3.8	—4.0	—2.6	—3.0	—2.5	—5.9	—4.5	—4.8	0.1

Source: U.S. Department of Commerce, *Survey of Current Business* (various issues).

Gross business savings consist of undistributed corporate profits (retained earnings) and capital consumption allowances (largely depreciation) charged to expense but not representing outlays of cash. These funds are invested in the business either as working capital or as fixed investments. To the extent that these funds are available, they reduce the demands for funds by business in the capital markets. However, it must be noted that if profits decline and dividends remain essentially unchanged, then undistributed profits decline. This condition may cause business confidence to decline and business demands on the capital markets to decline accordingly. In general, however, as was shown in 1967 and again in 1969-1970, business today takes the long look, and probably only a long (two- or three-year recession) and very sharp and protracted decline in profits will cause business to substantially defer capital investment plans and reduce demands on the capital markets for funds. Thus, as in 1970, a decline in undistributed profits may be reflected in an actual increased demand for funds in the capital markets in order to continue capital programs as planned.

Net Savings and Investment Funds

Net savings for the economy flow from two sources: (1) undistributed profits of business firms and (2) personal savings of individuals. Net savings of business (undistributed profits) do not flow into the capital markets for investment but are invested directly by the business concerned. As noted before, undistributed profits, to the extent available, reduce the demand for funds by business in the capital markets.

The sources and the uses of funds of nonfinancial corporate business from 1965 to 1973 are presented in Table 3-2. It can be noted for 1972 that, of the total sources of funds of $132.1 billion, $81.0 billion was provided internally, represented by undistributed profits of $20.0 billion and by capital consumption allowances (largely depreciation) of $64.5 billion. Therefore, internal sources provided about 61 percent of the total sources, and capital consumption allowances provided more than two thirds of these internal sources. The relative importance of internal financing fell a bit during the 1960s. While the total amount of funds raised has consistently grown (except for 1970), undistributed profits fell off sharply after 1967. Rising capital consumption allowances were not sufficient to maintain the relative importance of internal financing in the face of the sharp drop in undistributed profits. These internal sources are after dividends.

External sources of $51.1 billion therefore represented about 39 percent of the total sources of corporation funds. Of these external sources, the sale of securities supplied $25.3 billion ($12.9 billion in bonds plus $12.4 billion

TABLE 3-2

Sources and Uses of Funds, Nonfinancial Corporations, 1965-1973 (Billions of Dollars)

Sources of Funds	1965	1966	1967	1968	1969	1970	1971	1972	1973
Internal Sources									
Undistributed profits	23.1	24.7	21.1	19.9	16.0	10.8	14.5	20.0	25.8
Corporate inventory valuation adjustment	-1.7	-1.8	-1.1	-3.3	-5.1	-4.4	-4.7	-6.0	-6.0
Capital consumption allowances	35.2	38.2	41.5	45.1	49.9	52.7	57.3	64.5	71.5
Profit tax liability	2.2	.2	-4.7	2.9	-3.3	-2.7	4.0	2.5	2.0
Total	58.8	61.4	56.8	64.6	57.5	56.4	71.1	81.0	93.3
Long-Term Funds									
Net new bond issues	5.4	10.2	14.7	12.9	12.1	20.3	18.7	12.9	14.0
Net new stock issues	.....	1.2	2.3	-.9	3.4	5.8	12.6	12.4	11.5
Total net new issues	5.4	11.4	17.0	12.0	15.5	26.1	31.3	25.3	25.5
Mortgages	3.9	4.2	4.5	5.8	4.8	5.3	11.2	10.5	11.5
Term bank loans	4.3	2.6	2.8	4.4	5.8	2.0	2.0	3.7	4.5
Total	13.6	18.2	24.3	22.2	26.1	33.4	44.5	39.5	41.5
Short-Term Funds									
Open market paper	-.3	1.0	1.5	1.6	2.7	2.6	-1.5	1.0	1.5
Short-term bank loans	6.4	5.6	4.0	4.9	6.3	.3	1.3	5.3	7.0
Finance company loans	.6	.....	-.3	1.8	4.2	2.3	2.0	1.8	2.0
Bank loans held by nonbank investors	.....	.....	.....	.....	.6	-.1	-.1	-.1	-.1
Total	6.7	6.6	5.2	8.3	13.8	5.1	1.7	8.0	10.4
Other Short-Term Sources									
Payables to U.S. Government	.4	1.2	1.5	.6	.9	-.8	-1.7	-.5	.....
Other liabilities	3.2	3.6	5.1	4.3	4.3	3.8	3.9	4.1	4.0
Total	3.6	4.8	6.6	4.9	5.2	3.0	2.2	3.6	4.0
Total sources	82.7	91.0	92.9	100.0	102.6	97.9	119.5	132.1	149.2

TABLE 3-2 (Continued)

Uses of Funds	1965	1966	1967	1968	1969	1970	1971	1972	1973
State and Local Government Securities	.9	—1.0	—.3	.5	—1.0	—.6	1.0	1.0	.5
Short-Term Funds									
Trade credit	12.5	10.6	7.0	14.8	17.6	6.8	6.0	15.5	14.0
Less: Trade debt	11.7	9.3	6.0	9.8	14.3	3.6	5.1	10.5	8.0
Net trade credit	.8	1.3	1.0	5.0	3.3	3.2	.9	5.0	6.0
Open market paper	.5	—.2	3.8	2.5	2.7	.6	1.8	1.2	1.5
Consumer credit	1.2	1.2	1.0	.8	1.3	1.4	.7	1.2	1.3
Total	2.5	2.3	5.8	8.3	7.3	5.2	3.4	7.4	8.8
U.S. Government and Agency Securities									
U.S. Government securities	—1.8	—1.8	—.8	.1	—1.8	—3.0	2.6	—2.2	—
Federal agency securities	.4	.4	—1.4	.8	.5	.1	.1	......	......
Total	—1.4	—1.4	—2.3	.9	—1.3	—2.9	2.7	—2.2	—.5
Total funds	2.0	—.1	3.2	9.7	5.0	1.7	7.1	6.2	8.8
Physical Assets									
Plant and equipment	52.8	61.6	62.5	67.4	74.3	76.5	78.8	91.3	104.5
Residential structures	2.0	1.1	2.3	2.3	3.0	3.4	5.3	6.5	6.0
Inventories	7.9	14.4	7.3	6.4	6.7	4.8	1.1	5.0	10.0
Total	62.7	77.1	72.1	76.2	84.0	84.6	85.2	102.8	120.5
Cash Assets									
Demand deposits and currency	.3	.3	1.5	1.1	1.5	.3	4.5	2.0	.5
Time deposits	2.3	—1.4	2.1	.4	—2.4	1.7	.6	2.5	1.5
Total	2.6	—1.1	3.6	1.5	—.9	2.0	5.1	4.5	2.0
Other Assets									
Receivables from U.S. Government	.5	.7	.6	......	—.3	—.6	—.7	—.2	—.5
Foreign investments	3.3	3.0	2.7	1.1	2.2	3.6	3.4	3.5	3.9
Miscellaneous assets	.1	.7	.8	1.3	.8	.7	1.7	1.5	1.3
Total	3.9	4.4	4.1	2.4	2.7	3.7	4.4	4.8	4.7
Total uses	71.2	80.3	83.0	89.8	90.8	92.0	101.8	118.3	136.0
Discrepancy—sources less uses	11.5	10.7	9.9	10.2	11.8	5.9	17.7	13.8	13.2

Source: *Bankers Trust Investment Outlook for 1973.*

in stocks) and mortgage funds supplied $10.5 billion. Stock prices rose rather generally during the early 1960s, reaching a peak during 1966 and supported by large amounts of funds flowing into the market and limited new issues of stock. This pattern changed markedly in 1969. New common stock issues rose to $3.4 billion in 1969 from $—.9 billion in 1968 and $2.3 billion in 1967. Note the sharply increased importance of stocks as an external source of funds in Table 3-2 for 1970, 1971, and 1972. Some fear a continued relatively high level of new stock issues during the 1970s that could hold down stock prices even though profits are rising because of the increased supply factor.[1]

Of the total funds (uses) of $118.3 billion demanded by corporations in 1972, 87 percent was used to increase holdings of physical assets (83 percent invested in fixed assets and 4 percent in inventories). Increase in working capital, including inventories noted above, represented about 12 percent of total uses of funds.

Government Savings and Dissavings

When the federal government (or state and local governments) operates at a surplus, this surplus contributes to savings; when it operates at a deficit, this deficit represents dissavings. During the post-World War II period to 1969, state and local governments in total increased their debts from $14 billion to $130 billion by borrowing in the capital markets. However, in terms of the *national income accounts* for the calendar years 1950-1967, the federal government had accumulated net deficits (dissavings) of $30 billion. In terms of potential demands on the capital markets, the federal government had an excess of payments to the public over receipts from the public in *most* post-World War II years beginning with 1950 as shown in Table 3–3. But deficits resulted in an increase in the federal debt from $257 billion on December 31, 1949 (down from $279 billion in 1945) to $345 billion in January, 1968, or potential net demands on the capital markets of $88 billion. However, the Federal Reserve banks purchased $30 billion and U.S. investor accounts purchased $37 billion, or a total of $67 billion, leaving only $21 billion of the $88 billion increase in the federal debt from 1949-1968 as a demand on the capital markets to be purchased by the public. The federal debt was $398 billion on June 30, 1971.

---

[1] For example, see the following *Wall Street Journal* articles: "New Offerings Seen Depressing Prices More Even if Money Eases," February 6, 1970, p. 1; "Heard on the Street," October 19, 1971, p. 43; "Market's Scary Days May Be Near an End, Most Analysts Believe," November 5, 1971, p. 21.

TABLE 3-3

Federal Government Cash Receipts from and Payments to the Public,
Excess of Receipts or of Payments (—) for Fiscal Years 1950-1971
(Millions of Dollars)

Year	Excess	Year	Excess	Year	Excess	Year	Excess
1950	—$2,207	1956	$ 4,542	1962	—$5,797	1968	—$19,131
1951	7,593	1957	2,099	1963	— 4,012	1969	4,712
1952	49	1958	— 1,580	1964	— 4,802	1970	— 714
1953	— 5,274	1959	—13,092	1965	— 2,696	1971	—21,916
1954	— 232	1960	2,750	1966	— 3,347		
1955	—$2,702	1961	— 2,300	1967	— 1,546		

Source: Federal Reserve bulletins and Treasury bulletins (various issues).

Personal Savings

Personal savings represent a source of funds in the market for investments. Table 3-4 itemizes savings of individuals in the United States. Items
(a)-(f) inclusive show the net increase in holdings of *private* financial assets,
and the total of these increases ($51.3 billion in 1964, $56.0 billion in 1965,
$54.4 billion in 1966, and $74.6 billion in 1970) represents gross financial
savings. When increases in debt are deducted from gross savings, net financial
savings ($15.4 billion in 1964, and $45.7 billion in 1970) are obtained.

Most of the gross increase in financial asset holdings of individuals flows
into the capital markets through financial institutions. In 1970, of the $74.6
billion gross increase in financial assets, $37.0 billion or 49.4% flowed
into cash and deposit-type savings institutions and $23.5 billion or 31.5%
flowed into contractual-type institutions (insurance and pension reserves).
Only $8.4 billion or 11.2% flowed directly into securities investments. In
the exceptional year 1969, $16.3 billion was attracted into securities by high
interest rates. Of this $16.3 billion increase in holdings of securities, $14.7
billion flowed into United States Government securities and $5.4 billion into
corporate and foreign bonds for a total of $20.1 billion. Corporate stock
was sold on balance by individuals.

What is highly important to note in Table 3-4 is that individuals *in
total* have been net sellers of stocks. It is true that millions of additional
individuals have become owners of stocks in recent years and other millions
have added to their stock holdings; but, in total, individuals have been net
sellers of stocks for many years—net sellers to the institutional investors.

TABLE 3-4

Savings by Individuals, 1946-1971 [1] (Billions of Dollars)

Year or Quarter	Total	Increase in Financial Assets							Net Investment in			Less: Increase in Debt		
		Total [2]	Currency and Demand Deposits (a)	Savings Accounts (b)	Securities			Insurance and Pension Reserves [5] (f)	Non-farm Homes	Con-sumer Durables	Non-corporate Business Assets	Mort-gage Debt on Non-farm Homes	Con-sumer Credit	Other Debts [6]
					Govern-ment Bonds [3] (c)	Corpo-rate and Foreign Bonds (d)	Corpo-rate Stock [4] (e)							
1946	25.4	18.4	4.8	6.3	—1.2	—0.9	1.1	5.3	4.2	5.8	3.3	3.8	2.7	—0.2
1947	20.7	13.3	—.5	3.4	2.3	—.8	1.1	5.4	6.9	7.5	3.2	4.3	3.2	2.6
1948	23.6	9.2	—2.5	2.3	1.2	.2	1.0	5.3	10.5	7.1	7.4	5.0	2.8	2.6
1949	19.2	10.0	—1.9	2.6	1.8	.4	.7	5.5	9.0	7.0	2.4	4.1	2.9	2.4
1950	27.3	13.7	2.2	2.5	.4	.8	.7	6.9	13.7	10.2	6.4	7.4	4.1	5.2
1951	30.3	18.0	4.6	4.5	.5	.2	1.6	6.2	13.5	5.5	4.5	7.1	1.2	2.8
1952	26.3	21.4	1.7	7.7	.8	.0	1.6	7.6	12.8	3.6	2.5	6.4	4.8	2.9
1953	29.9	22.1	.5	8.3	2.4	.0	.9	7.9	13.5	6.4	1.6	7.7	3.9	2.1
1954	27.9	22.3	1.9	9.2	.9	—.4	.7	7.9	13.7	4.9	2.7	8.6	1.1	6.0
1955	33.6	27.9	.8	8.8	5.9	1.1	1.1	8.4	17.7	9.9	3.5	12.2	6.4	6.8
1956	34.9	28.9	1.2	9.5	3.4	.9	2.0	9.6	16.4	5.9	1.9	11.2	3.5	3.5
1957	33.5	28.0	—.5	12.1	1.9	1.0	1.5	9.5	13.8	4.9	2.4	8.8	2.6	4.2
1958	32.5	31.1	3.3	14.0	—1.9	1.1	1.5	10.1	12.7	.6	3.3	8.8	.2	6.2
1959	33.2	34.9	.4	11.4	8.1	.3	.6	11.5	16.5	5.5	3.2	12.6	6.4	7.9
1960	28.7	27.7	—1.9	12.4	2.9	.2	—.4	11.7	14.5	5.1	2.1	10.8	4.6	5.4
1961	31.3	34.9	1.3	17.4	.7	.3	.4	12.2	12.0	2.9	3.2	10.9	1.8	8.8
1962	37.3	39.3	2.9	23.4	.8	—.6	—2.1	12.8	12.8	6.7	5.6	12.7	5.8	8.5
1963	38.9	44.9	5.5	23.0	4.3	—.6	—2.8	13.9	12.6	8.9	6.9	14.8	7.9	11.9
1964	45.2	51.3	6.5	23.9	4.2	.5	.0	15.3	12.5	11.2	6.2	16.0	8.5	11.4

TABLE 3-4 (Continued)

Year or Quarter	Total	Increase in Financial Assets — Total²	Currency and Demand Deposits (a)	Savings Accounts (b)	Securities — Government Bonds³ (c)	Corporate and Foreign Bonds (d)	Corporate Stock (e)	Insurance and Pension Reserves⁵ (f)	Net Investment in — Nonfarm Homes	Consumer Durables	Noncorporate Business Assets	Less: Increase in Debt — Mortgage Debt on Nonfarm Homes	Consumer Credit	Other Debts⁶
1965	52.5	56.0	7.3	26.4	4.4	.7	−1.9	17.2	12.0	14.8	9.0	15.2	10.0	13.9
1966	56.1	54.4	3.1	19.1	9.5	2.0	−1.0	18.0	11.5	15.2	7.2	12.3	7.2	12.7
1967	62.0	65.9	9.5	33.7	−.4	3.6	−4.1	18.9	9.2	12.4	8.2	10.5	4.6	18.6
1968	63.5	69.6	11.3	28.6	6.2	5.4	−7.5	19.8	12.8	16.7	7.7	14.9	11.1	17.4
1969	56.1	60.9	6.0	13.3	14.7	5.4	−3.8	20.2	12.8	15.5	8.0	16.2	9.3	15.5
1970	71.4	74.6	4.8	32.2	−1.2	12.2	−2.6	23.5	9.7	8.4	7.7	12.5	4.3	12.1
Seasonally adjusted annual rates														
1970: I	61.3	57.4	5.5	5.0	16.0	12.3	−6.7	20.1	10.6	10.4	7.3	11.0	4.8	8.5
II	77.3	75.3	7.5	30.7	−3.7	10.2	−.1	26.2	10.2	10.7	7.9	12.2	6.1	8.5
III	73.5	84.9	5.1	44.2	−5.4	11.3	.7	21.6	8.0	9.2	8.5	13.7	6.2	17.2
IV	73.7	80.7	1.1	49.1	−11.8	14.9	−4.3	25.8	9.9	3.1	7.2	13.0	.2	13.9
1971: I	87.7	90.4	10.9	97.9	−49.9	9.5	−12.8	27.5	12.0	15.1	12.6	13.1	4.0	25.2
II	99.6	114.4	15.7	67.8	−5.9	7.8	−3.2	28.4	15.2	17.5	10.0	22.7	9.0	25.8
III	82.8	97.3	4.6	57.6	−.1	6.1	−5.1	26.6	16.7	20.8	12.2	27.1	12.6	24.5

¹ Individuals' saving sector includes households, private trust funds, nonprofit institutions, farms, and other noncorporate businesses.
² Includes miscellaneous financial assets, not shown separately.
³ U.S. Government and agency securities and State and local obligations.
⁴ Includes investment company shares.
⁵ Private life insurance reserves, private insured and noninsured pension reserves, and government insurance and pension reserves.
⁶ Security credit, policy loans, noncorporate business debt, and other debt.

Source: *Economic Report of the President, January, 1972, p. 217.*

This is so even after allowance is made for the net increase by individuals in their holdings of investment company shares. Therefore, in spite of the widespread talk of inflation and of the individual's fear of inflation, investors in total have still been net sellers of common stocks as savings flow into financial institutions.

Financial Asset Holdings of Individuals

Table 3-5 lists the financial assets and liabilities of individuals. It has just been stated that overwhelmingly in most years the bulk of the annual savings of individuals flows into investment indirectly through financial intermediaries, largely deposit-type and contractual-type institutions; that individuals invest annually only a small proportion of savings through direct investment in securities; and finally that individuals, in total, have been net sellers of equity securities for quite a number of years, while the institutional investors have annually been net purchasers of equities. However, Table 3-5 shows that in the year 1971, for example, $1,182 billion or 52.7% of individuals' financial assets listed at current market values were invested in securities and that $975 billion or 43.5% of total financial assets were invested

TABLE 3-5

Financial Assets of Individuals in the United States, 1966-1971, Selected Years (Billions of Dollars)

Type of Asset	1966	1967	1970	1971
Currency and Demand Deposits	110	100	141	132
Time Deposits and Savings Shares	297	340	407	493
U.S. Government, State, and Municipal Bonds ..	124	215	134	207
Corporate and Foreign Bonds	12	17	40	48
Mortgages and Commercial Paper *		37		48
Common and Preferred Stock	594	755	748	879
Life Insurance Reserves *		115		137
Pension Fund Reserves *	207	185	270	268
Government Insurance and Pension Reserves * ..	65		92	
Security Credit *		3		2
Miscellaneous Financial Assets *	70	20	92	29
Total	1,479	1,787	1,924	2,243

* Reporting procedures were revised in 1971 to increase coverage, and only the year 1967 was restated in terms of the 1971 format. Government insurance and pension reserves were no longer reported separately.

Source: *New York Stock Exchange Fact Book* (various issues).

in corporate securities and $879 billion or 39.2% in common and preferred stocks (largely, common).

The reason for the apparent discrepancy between the *annual investment* in financial asset figures and the *financial asset holdings* figures is not difficult to uncover—it is the tremendous rise in stock prices in the post-World War II years. For example, if the DJIA were to decline from the high of 950 in 1971 to the 160 level where it was at one time in each of the years 1946-49 inclusive, the total market values of equities held by individuals would decline 86.8% from about $879 billion to about $116 billion and the total financial asset holdings would decline from $2.2 trillion to $1.4 trillion. At that figure, equity holdings of individuals would amount to only 8% of the financial asset holdings instead of the 38.8% recorded in 1971. Therefore, it is the great increase in the level of stock prices since 1949 that resulted in the fact that over 50% of the financial assets were invested in securities and 38.8% in stocks in spite of the fact that individuals have been net sellers of stocks for many years.

FLOW OF FUNDS

Investment markets bring together those who supply the funds (sources of funds) and those who furnish the demand for funds (uses of funds). An effective picture of the financial markets is provided in the Federal Reserve Board's flow of funds statistics, which are designed to account for sources and uses of funds in the economy and which appear monthly in the *Federal Reserve Bulletin.*

The Two Major Investment Markets

There are two major money markets: (1) the market for short-term funds and (2) the market for long-term or investment funds (the capital market). This textbook is primarily concerned with the long-term or investment market for funds. However, while most funds seeking investments flow into the long-term capital markets, some investment funds are more fluid and do shift at times from the long-term and the intermediate-term markets to the short-term market. A picture of the short-term market for funds is presented in Table 3-6.

Sources and Uses of Investment Funds

It has been stated that savings equal investment in any nation. The savings of individuals flowing into the capital markets have been analyzed in the

TABLE 3-6

Summary of Financing—Short-Term Funds (Billions of Dollars)

	1964	1965	1966	1967	1968	1969	1970	1971 (est.)	1972 (proj.)
USES (FUNDS RAISED)									
Open market paper	.6	— .4	1.0	2.1	1.5	3.3	3.7	.1	2.0
Consumer credit	8.5	10.0	7.2	4.6	11.1	9.3	4.3	10.0	12.5
Policy loans	.5	.5	1.4	.9	1.2	2.5	2.2	1.0	1.5
Loans and discounts of nonbudget agencies	.1	.2	1.0	1.3	.8	1.2	.8	.9	2.2
Bank loans on securities	.5	.1	.5	1.5	1.3	—1.1	1.3	— .9	1.0
Bank short-term loans to nonfinancial business									
Held by banks and affiliates	3.2	8.0	7.5	5.0	6.2	7.6	1.2	4.7	8.7
Held by nonbank investors	...	...	...	...	...	.6	.1	.1	.1
Total	3.2	8.0	7.5	5.0	6.2	8.2	1.1	4.6	8.6
Other bank loans									
Held by banks and affiliates	2.4	1.7	.6	2.1	3.1	2.5	.7	4.2	2.5
Held by nonbank investors *	...	...	...	...	...	.6	.8	.2	.1
Total	2.4	1.7	.6	2.1	3.1	3.1	1.5	4.0	2.4
Other business credit									
Net trade credit of nonfinancial corporations	4.9	5.9	4.0	3.7	4.4	—1.2	.5	7.5	8.5
Finance company loans	1.4	2.0	1.2	— .4	2.2	4.8	2.1	2.3	2.5
Total	6.3	7.9	5.2	3.3	6.6	3.6	2.6	9.8	11.0
Total uses	22.1	28.1	24.4	20.8	31.8	30.1	17.6	29.5	41.2
SOURCES (FUNDS SUPPLIED)									
Savings institutions—contractual-type									
Life insurance companies	.4	.6	1.5	1.0	1.2	3.4	3.0	1.9	2.3
Private noninsured pension funds	...	...	...	.1	.1	.1	...	...	...
Total	.4	.6	1.5	1.1	1.3	3.5	3.0	1.9	2.3

TABLE 3-6 (Continued)

	1964	1965	1966	1967	1968	1969	1970	1971 (est.)	1972 (proj.)
Savings institutions—deposit-type									
Savings and loan associations	.1	.1	.1	...	.1	...	.4	.9	.2
Mutual savings banks	.1	.1	.1	...	.2	.2	.3	.3	.3
Credit unions	.8	1.0	.9	.7	1.2	1.4	.9	1.7	1.9
Total	1.0	1.2	1.0	.7	1.5	1.6	1.6	2.9	2.4
Mutual funds	—.1	.3	.5	...	.3	1.2	—.4	—.6	...
Total savings institutions	1.3	2.1	3.0	1.8	3.1	6.3	4.2	4.2	4.7
Commercial banks **	10.6	13.9	12.8	12.8	14.4	12.8	7.2	13.6	18.4
Nonfinancial corporations	7.8	7.6	7.2	6.1	10.5	8.7	.4	5.7	11.8
Financial corporations	3.5	4.6	3.0	.2	4.6	7.4	1.5	3.2	4.2
Government									
Federal Reserve banks	—.1	.1	...	...	—.1	...	...	.2	.1
Nonbudget agencies	.1	.2	1.0	1.3	.8	1.2	.8	.9	2.2
Total	...	.3	1.0	1.2	.7	1.2	.8	1.1	2.3
Other investor groups									
Noncorporate business	.3	.4	.5	.5	.7	.5	.5	.5	.6
Foreign investors	.2	.4	.3	.2	.6	1.0	.5	.4	.5
Total	.5	.8	.8	.7	1.3	1.5	1.0	.9	1.1
Residual: Individuals and others ***	—.1	—.1	—.1	—.3	—.1	1.1	.6	—.3	—.2
Total gross sources	23.6	29.1	27.8	22.6	34.3	39.0	15.6	28.4	42.3
Less: Open market paper raised by financial intermediaries	1.5	1.0	3.4	1.8	2.5	8.9	—2.0	—1.1	1.1
Total net sources	22.1	28.1	24.4	20.8	31.8	30.1	17.6	29.5	41.2

* May include some long-term loans.
** Includes affiliates.
*** Includes bank loans held by nonbank investors.

Source: *The Investment Outlook*, Bankers Trust Company, New York, 1972.

TABLE 3-7

Sources and Uses of Long-Term Investment Funds, 1965-1973 (Billions of Dollars)

	1965	1966	1967	1968	1969	1970	1971	1972 (est.)	1973 (proj.)
USES (FUNDS RAISED)									
Real estate mortgages	25.7	21.3	22.9	27.4	27.8	26.7	48.6	64.0	61.0
Corporate securities									
Bonds	5.4	10.2	14.7	12.9	12.1	20.3	18.7	12.9	14.0
Stocks	...	1.2	2.3	−.9	3.4	5.8	12.6	12.4	11.5
Total	5.4	11.4	17.0	12.0	15.5	26.1	31.3	25.3	25.5
State and local government securities	7.6	6.4	8.5	10.4	8.7	13.9	20.6	15.0	13.5
Foreign securities	1.0	.7	1.3	1.7	1.5	.9	.9	.6	1.0
Term loans									
Commercial banks	4.5	2.3	2.5	3.9	5.4	1.9	2.6	4.9	5.9
Banks for cooperatives	.1	.1	.1	.1	.1	.2	...	.1	.1
Total	4.6	2.4	2.6	4.0	5.5	2.1	2.6	5.0	6.0
Total uses	44.3	42.2	52.3	55.5	59.0	69.7	104.1	109.9	107.0
SOURCES (FUNDS SUPPLIED)									
Contractual-type savings institutions									
Life insurance companies	8.2	6.8	7.7	7.7	5.5	5.9	10.6	11.7	12.3
Private noninsured pension funds	5.4	6.1	5.9	5.4	6.2	6.7	7.6	6.0	6.5
State and local government retirement funds	2.9	3.7	4.5	4.2	5.4	6.5	7.7	7.9	8.8
Fire and casualty insurance companies	1.2	1.9	3.0	2.6	2.6	3.9	6.3	6.8	5.7
Total	17.7	18.5	21.0	20.0	19.6	23.0	32.2	32.4	33.3

TABLE 3-7 (Continued)

	1965	1966	1967	1968	1969	1970	1971	1972 (est.)	1973 (proj.)
Deposit-type savings institutions									
Savings and loan associations	9.0	3.8	7.5	9.4	9.6	10.5	25.5	32.5	28.6
Mutual savings banks	4.1	3.0	5.4	4.4	3.1	3.6	8.7	9.4	8.6
Credit unions	.1	.1	...	.1	-.1	.2	.5	.4	.4
Total	13.1	6.8	12.9	13.9	12.6	14.2	34.7	42.3	37.6
Mutual funds	1.6	1.4	1.5	1.9	2.7	1.8	.6	-2.0	.3
Total savings institutions	32.4	26.7	35.4	35.8	34.9	39.1	67.5	72.7	71.2
Commercial banks	15.3	9.4	16.4	19.5	11.0	15.9	26.5	28.1	24.4
Nonfinancial corporations	.9	-1.0	-.3	.5	-1.0	-.6	1.0	1.0	.5
Financial corporations	.5	-.6	.4	.7	1.0	2.2	2.8	3.8	4.0
Government									
U.S. Government	.2	1.4	1.1	1.4	1.4	.4	.7	.3	.4
Nonbudget agencies	1.2	2.7	1.9	2.3	4.5	5.6	3.7	3.8	4.3
State and local general funds	.1	...	.1	.3	.2	.5	1.4	1.8	2.5
Total	1.5	4.1	3.1	4.0	6.1	6.5	5.8	5.9	7.2
Foreign investors	-.1	-.4	.4	2.3	1.7	1.0	1.0	1.9	2.8
Residual: Individuals and others	-3.6	4.9	-1.8	-6.2	7.9	9.3	5.4	2.4	1.4
Total gross sources	46.9	43.1	53.6	56.6	61.6	73.3	110.0	115.8	111.5
Less: Investment funds raised by financial intermediaries									
Bonds	2.7	.9	1.3	1.1	1.7	2.6	5.0	5.3	4.0
Stocks	-.1	...	...	...	.9	1.0	.9	.6	.5
Total	2.6	.9	1.3	1.1	2.6	3.6	5.9	5.9	4.5
Total net sources	44.3	42.2	52.3	55.5	59.0	69.7	104.1	109.9	107.0

Source: *Bankers Trust Investment Outlook for 1973.*

preceding section. Table 3-7 presents the sources and uses of long-term investment funds. The sources figures confirm previous statements that savings of individuals flow into the capital markets largely through indirect investment through financial intermediaries and not through direct investment in securities. The figures represent *net,* not *gross,* increases. For example, the figures for mortgages, corporate securities, and state and local government securities are *net* of retirements.

There are three major demands for investment funds (uses of funds or funds raised) on the capital markets: (1) real estate mortgages; (2) corporate securities—debt issues and equities; and (3) state and local government securities. Each year, even when mortgage markets are disrupted by highly competitive rates in the capital markets (1966-1969), the mortgage demand is consistently the highest satisfied demand for investment funds in the capital markets. Corporate issues take second place, with the bulk of such issues being debt securities and only a relatively small amount being equity securities.[2] The relative importance of equity securities increased sharply in 1971 and was expected to again be historically high in 1972 and 1973. The issues of state and local governments satisfy the balance of the demand, except in years of significant federal deficits.

Investments by Financial Institutions in Equities

It has been stated that the savings of individuals flow into the capital markets and into investment largely through financial intermediaries and that these financial intermediaries, except for investment companies and corporate noninsured pension funds, invest mainly in debt instruments. The extent to which financial institutions do invest in equities is indicated in Table 3-8. At the end of World War II, financial institutions owned stock having a value equal to about 10% of the total value of all stocks listed on the New York Stock Exchange. By the end of 1971, these holdings had risen to about $210 billion and were equal to about 28.3% of the total value of all stocks listed on the New York Stock Exchange. Of course, financial institutions also hold large amounts of other equities as well.

Inasmuch as the total value of all stocks listed on the New York Stock Exchange was in the neighborhood of $742 billion in 1971 and since only about $60 billion net of equities had been issued since World War II, the force of this institutional demand on stock prices, price-earnings ratios, and yields can be seen. Institutions were willing to increase their holdings of stocks year by year in the face of sharply rising stock prices—from a base

---

[2] See Table 2-1 (New Securities Offered for Cash in the United States by Type of Security) on page 33.

TABLE 3-8

Estimated Holdings of NYSE-Listed Stocks by Financial Institutions (Billions of Dollars)

Type of Institution	1949	1956	1960	1961	1962	1963	1964	1965	1966	1967	1968	1969	1970p
Insurance companies:													
Life	1.1	2.3	3.2	4.0	4.1	4.6	5.3	6.4	6.2	7.4	9.3	9.7	10.9
Nonlife	1.7	4.5	6.0	7.7	7.1	8.2	9.5	10.1	9.2	11.4	12.8	11.7	12.2
Investment companies:													
Open-end	1.4	7.1	12.4	17.2	15.4	18.6	21.8	26.5	25.4	33.0	43.9	39.8	39.4
Closed-end	1.6	4.0	4.2	5.6	5.3	5.7	6.6	5.6	4.0	4.6	5.5	4.1	4.4
Noninsured pension funds:													
Corporate	0.5	5.3	13.5	18.7	17.9	22.6	27.5	32.5	31.4	43.0	49.2	46.9	51.7
Other private	*	0.4	0.8	1.1	1.0	1.3	1.6	1.9	2.0	2.7	3.0	2.8	3.0
State and local government	*	0.2	0.5	0.7	0.8	1.0	1.5	2.0	2.2	3.2	3.2	4.6	5.0
Nonprofit institutions:													
College and university endowments	1.1	2.4	2.9	3.7	3.3	4.0	4.5	5.4	4.9	6.0	7.6	6.8	7.1
Foundations	1.1	4.1	5.3	7.2	6.7	8.1	9.5	11.0	9.7	11.9	13.5	13.9	14.1
Other	1.0	3.1	4.4	5.6	5.0	5.9	6.8	7.7	6.9	8.7	9.8	8.9	9.0
Common trust funds	*	1.0	1.4	1.9	1.7	2.4	2.6	3.2	2.9	3.8	4.3	4.1	4.2
Mutual savings banks	0.2	0.2	0.2	0.3	0.4	0.4	0.4	0.5	0.5	0.6	0.7	0.8	0.9
TOTAL	9.7	34.6	54.8	73.7	68.7	82.8	97.6	112.8	105.3	136.3	162.8	154.1	161.9
Market value of ALL NYSE-listed stock	76.3	219.2	307.0	387.8	345.8	411.3	474.3	537.5	482.5	605.8	692.3	629.5	636.4
Estimated percent held by above institutions	12.7	15.8	17.9	19.0	19.9	20.1	20.6	21.0	21.8	22.5	23.5	24.5	25.4

* Less than $50 million. p= preliminary estimates.

Source: *New York Stock Exchange Fact Book* (various issues).

of 160 DJIA in *each* of the years 1946-1949 inclusive to a high of 1001 in 1966 and to the 890 level at December 31, 1971. Stock prices in the years 1949-1966 rose three times as fast as earnings, and price-earnings multipliers rose from 6-7 times to 20-21 times while dividend yields fell from 6-7% to 3%. Individuals owned 90% of the stock in 1946, and institutions held about 10%. Institutions were able to raise the percentage to 22.5% in 1967 by purchasing stocks at higher and higher prices, higher and higher price-earnings ratios, and lower and lower dividend yields.

The influence of institutional investments on the New York Stock Exchange market is even greater than would be implied by their ownership of 28% of the value of all listed stocks. A New York Stock Exchange "Public Transactions Study" covering the total number of shares traded during 1969 disclosed that institutions accounted for 42% of the shares traded and 46% of the dollar value of transactions; public individuals, 34% and 28%; and New York Stock Exchange members, 24% and 26%. In other words, individuals accounted for 28% of the value of transactions; and the remainder, or 72%, was accounted for by institutions (46%) and New York Stock Exchange members (26%).

Supply and Demand for Funds

The flow of the supply of funds into the capital markets is the flow of personal savings into investment, largely through financial intermediaries, and is reflected in the holdings of financial assets of individuals. On the demand side, the major demands are supplied by those seeking mortgage funds, by business, and by state and local governments. In addition, the federal government may, at times, as the result of budget deficits, furnish a significant demand for funds. This demand becomes important in years of war, such as World War II, the Korean War, and the war in Vietnam, causing high federal deficits.

On the supply side, the flow of savings into the capital markets could be characterized in the postwar years as being fairly stable and rising along with prosperity and the upward trend of disposable personal income. On the demand side, the mortgage demand and the demands from state and local governments have also been fairly steady and rising in the post-World War II years. The fluctuating segments of demand for funds have been the demands by business and the demands of the federal government, though the effective demand for mortgage funds did rise sharply in 1971, 1972, and 1973; however, it was not matched on the supply side in 1973.

INTEREST RATES

Interest rates in the capital markets represent the price paid for funds as evidenced by yields on securities, and such rates reflect the relationship of the supply of funds (sources) and the demand for funds (uses).

Interest Rates and Stock Yields

As most funds flow into capital markets through financial intermediaries and as the great majority of the funds flow into debt instruments, the fluctuation in demand and supply of funds is largely reflected in the trend of interest rates. In addition, debt instruments do compete with equity investments. As interest rates rise, debt instruments and preferred stocks become more competitive with common stock investments for investors who are yield conscious. As interest rates decline, debt instruments and preferred stocks become less competitive with common stocks.

It is true, however, that investors in common stocks have been increasingly willing in the post-World War II years to accept lower and lower yields on common stocks. In the 1960s they accepted about half the yield (3%) that they were willing to accept in the years 1946-1949 (6.7%). Furthermore, for the first time since 1929, investors since 1959 have been willing to purchase common stocks on the average at yields considerably below yields on high-grade corporate bonds, until by 1967-1969 yields on common stocks were only half (or less) of yields on high-grade corporate bonds, that is 3% versus 6%-7%. Common stock investors have thought in terms of "overall rates of return," including realized and/or expected capital appreciation, rather than dividend yields alone.

Yields in the form of interest or dividends are quite important to some investors, especially institutional investors. They are less important to other investors. At some point, as the yield spread in favor of bonds and preferred stocks widens, certain classes of investors may shift investment policy to favor bonds and preferred stocks. In 1967 and 1968, the yield spread between bonds and common stocks (in favor of bonds) was the widest in history. But for all stocks, dividend yields act as a floor on prices.

Table 3-9 shows bond yields and interest rates from 1939-1971 and Table 3-10 shows common stock prices, earnings, and yields from 1939-1971. A comparison of these two tables will disclose the pattern of the year-to-year change in yield spread between bond interest and dividend yield.

TABLE 3-9

Bond Yields and Interest Rates, 1939-1971 (Percent per Annum)

| Year or Month | U.S. Government Securities | | | | Corporate Bonds (Moody's) | | High-grade municipal bonds (Standard & Poor's) | Average rate on short-term bank loans to business— selected cities | Prime commercial paper, 4-6 months | Federal Reserve Bank discount rate | FHA new home mortgage yields[5] |
	3-month Treasury bills[1]	9-12 month issues[2]	3-5 year issues[3]	Taxable bonds[4]	AAA	BBB					
1939	.023	...	.59	...	3.01	4.96	2.76	2.1	.59	1.00	...
1940	.014	...	.50	...	2.84	4.75	2.50	2.1	.56	1.00	...
1941	.103	...	.73	...	2.77	4.33	2.10	2.0	.53	1.00	...
1942	.326	...	1.46	2.46	2.83	4.28	2.36	2.2	.66[6]	1.00	...
1943	.373	0.75	1.34	2.47	2.73	3.91	2.06	2.6	.69[6]	1.00	...
1944	.375	.79	1.33	2.48	2.72	3.61	1.86	2.4	.73[6]	1.00	...
1945	.375	.81	1.18	2.37	2.62	3.29	1.67	2.2	.75[6]	1.00	...
1946	.375	.82	1.16	2.19	2.53	3.05	1.64	2.1	.81[6]	1.00	...
1947	.594	.88	1.32	2.25	2.61	3.24	2.01	2.1	1.03	1.00	...
1948	1.040	1.14	1.62	2.44	2.82	3.47	2.40	2.5	1.44	1.34	...
1949	1.102	1.14	1.43	2.31	2.66	3.42	2.21	2.68	1.49	1.50	4.34
1950	1.218	1.26	1.50	2.32	2.62	3.24	1.98	2.69	1.45	1.59	4.17
1951	1.552	1.73	1.93	2.57	2.86	3.41	2.00	3.11	2.16	1.75	4.21
1952	1.766	1.81	2.13	2.68	2.96	3.52	2.19	3.49	2.33	1.75	4.29
1953	1.931	2.07	2.56	2.94	3.20	3.74	2.72	3.69	2.52	1.99	4.61
1954	.953	.92	1.82	2.55	2.90	3.51	2.37	3.61	1.58	1.60	4.62
1955	1.753	1.89	2.50	2.84	3.06	3.53	2.53	3.70	2.18	1.89	4.64
1956	2.658	2.83	3.12	3.08	3.36	3.88	2.93	4.20	3.31	2.77	4.79
1957	3.267	3.53	3.62	3.47	3.89	4.71	3.60	4.62	3.81	3.12	5.42
1958	1.839	2.09	2.90	3.43	3.79	4.73	3.56	4.34	2.46	2.15	5.49
1959	3.405	4.11	4.33	4.08	4.38	5.05	3.95[7]	5.00	3.97	3.36	5.71
1960	2.928	3.55	3.99	4.02	4.41	5.19	3.73	5.16	3.85	3.53	6.18
1961	2.378	2.91	3.60	3.90	4.35	5.08	3.46	4.97	2.97	3.00	5.80
1962	2.778	3.02	3.57	3.95	4.33	5.02	3.18	5.00	3.26	3.00	5.61

TABLE 3-9 (Continued)

| Year or Month | U.S. Government Securities | | | | Corporate Bonds (Moody's) | | High-grade municipal bonds (Standard & Poor's) | Average rate on short-term bank loans to business—selected cities | Prime commercial paper, 4-6 months | Federal Reserve Bank discount rate | FHA new home mortgage yields [5] |
	3-month Treasury bills [1]	9-12 month issues [2]	3-5 year issues [3]	Taxable bonds [4]	AAA	BBB					
1963	3.157	3.28	3.72	4.00	4.26	4.86	3.23	5.01	3.55	3.23	5.47
1964	3.549	3.76	4.06	4.15	4.40	4.83	3.22	4.99	3.97	3.55	5.45
1965	3.954	4.09	4.22	4.21	4.49	4.87	3.27	5.06	4.38	4.04	5.46
1966	4.881	5.17	5.16	4.65	5.13	5.67	3.82	6.00	5.55	4.50	6.29
1967	4.321	4.84	5.07	4.85	5.51	6.23	3.98 [7]	6.00	5.10	4.19	6.55
1968	5.339	5.62	5.59	5.26	6.18	6.94	4.51	6.68	5.90	5.17	7.13
1969	6.677	7.06	6.85	6.12	7.03	7.81	5.81	8.21	7.83	5.87	8.19
1970	6.458	6.90	7.37	6.58	8.04	9.11	6.51	8.48	7.72	5.95	9.05
1971	4.348	4.75	5.77	5.74	7.39	8.56	5.70	6.32	5.11	4.88	7.78

[1] Rate on new issues within period: First issued in December 1929 and issued irregularly in 1930. Bills were tax exempt prior to March 1, 1941, and fully taxable thereafter. For 1934-37, series includes issues with maturities of more than 3 months.

[2] Certificates of indebtedness and selected note and bond issues (fully taxable).

[3] Selected note and bond issues. Issues were partially tax exempt prior to 1941, and fully taxable thereafter.

[4] First issued in 1941. Series includes bonds which are neither due nor callable before a given number of years as follows: April 1953 to date, 10 years; April 1952, March 1953, 12 years; October 1941-March 1952, 15 years.

[5] Data for first of the month, based on the maximum permissible interest rate (7 percent beginning February 18, 1971). Through July 1961, computed on 25-year mortgages paid in 12 years and thereafter, 30-year mortgages prepaid in 15 years.

[6] From October 30, 1942, to April 24, 1946, a preferential rate of 0.50 percent was in effect for advances secured by Government securities maturing in 1 year or less.

[7] Series revised. Not strictly comparable with earlier data.

Note.—Yields and rates computed for New York City except for short-term bank loans.

Source: *Economic Report of the President*, January, 1972, p. 262.

TABLE 3-10

Common Stock Prices, Earnings and Yields, and Stock Market Credit, 1939-1971

Year or Month	Standard & Poor's Common Stock Data						Stock Market Credit			
	Price Indexes [1] (1941-43 = 10)				Dividend yield [2] (percent)	Price/ earnings ratio [3]	Customer credit (excluding U.S. Government securities)			Bank loans to brokers and dealers [6]
	Total (500 stocks)	Industrials (425 stocks)	Public utilities (55 stocks)	Railroads (20 stocks)			Total	Net debit balances [4]	Bank loans to "others" [5]	
							Millions of dollars			
1939	12.06	11.77	16.34	9.82	4.05	13.80	....	....	....	715
1940	11.02	10.69	15.05	9.41	5.59	10.25	....	....	....	584
1941	9.82	9.72	10.93	9.39	6.82	8.27	....	....	....	535
1942	8.67	8.78	7.74	8.81	7.23	8.80	....	....	....	850
1943	11.50	11.49	11.34	11.81	4.93	12.84	....	....	....	1,328
1944	12.47	12.34	12.81	13.47	4.86	13.66	....	....	....	2,137
1945	15.16	14.72	16.84	18.21	4.17	16.33	1,374	942	353	2,782
1946	17.08	16.48	20.76	19.09	3.85	17.69	976	473	432	1,471
1947	15.17	14.85	18.01	14.02	4.93	9.36	1,032	517	503	784
1948	15.53	15.34	16.77	15.27	5.54	6.91	968	499	469	1,331
1949	15.23	15.00	17.87	12.83	6.59	6.64	1,249	821	428	1,608
1950	18.40	18.33	19.96	15.53	6.57	6.63	1,798	1,237	561	1,742
1951	22.34	22.68	20.59	19.91	6.13	9.27	1,826	1,253	573	1,419
1952	24.50	24.78	22.86	22.49	5.80	10.47	1,980	1,332	648	2,002
1953	24.73	24.84	24.03	22.60	5.80	9.69	2,445	1,665	780	2,248
1954	29.69	30.25	27.57	23.96	4.95	11.25	3,436	2,388	1,048	2,688
1955	40.49	42.40	31.37	32.94	4.08	11.51	4,080	2,791	1,239	2,852
1956	46.62	49.80	32.25	33.65	4.09	14.05	3,984	2,823	1,161	2,214
1957	44.38	47.63	32.19	28.11	4.35	12.89	3,576	2,482	1,094	2,190
1958	46.24	49.36	37.22	27.05	3.97	16.64	4,537	3,285	1,252	2,569
1959	57.38	61.45	44.15	35.09	3.23	17.05	4,461	3,280	1,181	2,584
1960	55.85	59.43	46.86	30.31	3.47	17.09	4,415	3,222	1,193	2,614

TABLE 3-10 (Continued)

Year or Month	Standard & Poor's Common Stock Data						Stock Market Credit			
	Price Indexes [1]				Dividend yield [2] (percent)	Price/earnings ratio [3]	Customer credit (excluding U.S. Government securities)			Bank loans to brokers and dealers [6]
	Total (500 stocks)	Industrials (425 stocks)	Public utilities (55 stocks)	Railroads (20 stocks)			Total	Net debit balances [4]	Bank loans to "others" [5]	
	1941-43 = 10						Millions of dollars			
1961	66.27	69.99	60.20	32.83	2.98	21.06	5,602	4,259	1,343	3,398
1962	62.38	65.54	59.16	30.56	3.37	16.68	5,494	4,125	1,369	4,352
1963	69.87	73.39	64.99	37.58	3.17	17.62	7,242	5,515	4,727	4,754
1964	81.37	86.19	69.91	45.46	3.01	18.08	7,053	5,079	1,974	4,631
1965	88.17	93.48	76.08	46.78	3.00	17.08	7,770	5,521 [5]	2,249 [6]	4,277
1966	85.26	91.08	68.21	46.34	3.40	14.92	7,444	5,329	2,115	4,501
1967	91.93	99.18	68.10	46.72	3.20	17.52	10,347	7,883	2,464	5,082
1968	98.70	107.49	66.42	48.84	3.07	17.20	12,488	9,790	2,698	5,796
1969	97.84	107.13	62.64	45.95	3.24	16.57	10,010	7,445 [7]	2,565 [7]	5,141
1970	83.22	91.29	54.48	32.13	3.83	15.91	....	(8)	2,350	6,088
1971 p	98.29	108.35	59.33	41.94	3.14	....	....	(8)	2,438	6,264

[1] Monthly data are averages of daily figures and annual data are averages of monthly figures.

[2] Aggregate cash dividends (based on latest known annual rate) divided by the aggregate market value of the stocks in the group based on Wednesday closing prices. Monthly data are averages of the four or five weekly figures and annual data are averages of monthly figures.

[3] Ratio of quarterly earnings (seasonally adjusted annual rate) to price index for last day in quarter. Annual ratios are averages of quarterly data.

[4] As reported by member firms of the New York Stock Exchange carrying margin accounts. Balances secured by U.S. Government obligations are excluded through 1967 and included thereafter. Data are for end of period.

[5] Loans by weekly reporting member banks (weekly reporting large commercial banks beginning 1965) to other than brokers and dealers for purchasing or carrying securities except U.S. Government obligations. Data are for last Wednesday.

[6] Loans by weekly reporting member banks (weekly reporting large commercial banks beginning 1965) for purchasing of carrying securities, including U.S. Government obligations. Data are for last Wednesday.

[7] Revised series beginning June 1969; not strictly comparable with earlier data.

[8] Series discontinued beginning July 1970.

Source: *Economic Report of the President*, January, 1972, p. 287.

The Structure of Interest Rates

In the financial community and among investors, the comment is frequently heard that the interest rate is rising or falling. However, there is not one interest rate but rather a structure of interest rates consisting of short-term rates, intermediate-term rates, and long-term rates. Figure 3-1 shows the yield fluctuations in different maturity categories for 1965-1967.

Two generalities may be made, but they are not always true. Generally, all interest rates move in the same direction, either up or down together, although short-term rates proportionately move over a wider range. Generally, the longer the maturity, the higher the rate becomes; the farther into the future, the greater the uncertainty. However, interest rates representing different maturity categories do not always move together, and sometimes short-term rates will exceed intermediate-term rates and at times will exceed long-term rates. Finally, within maturity categories there are quality ratings for specific securities and groups. Within any one maturity category, the higher the quality grade of issues, the lower the rate; the lower the quality grade, the higher the rate. It might seem that tax-exempt securities have higher quality ratings than United States Government securities since the tax-exempts sell at lower market yields; but for those who make the market for tax-exempts (those who buy and sell them) the net yields must be higher for tax-exempts than the net yields after taxes on United States Government securities if their purchase of tax-exempts is to be justified.

Interest rates reflect the demand and supply factors at work in the markets. The greater the intensity of demand relative to the intensity of supply, the higher the rates, and vice versa. The intensity of demand fluctuates more than the supply of funds and is, in this respect, more important in establishing rates. In addition to the normal economic demand and supply factors, entry of the Federal Reserve into the market on either the demand or the supply side also affects interest rates, especially in the short-term markets. Normally, in periods of business expansion, demand becomes larger relative to supply and therefore interest rates rise (as in the expansion period of 1961-1969), especially if the federal government is adding to the total demand for funds. Conversely, in periods of recession, supply becomes larger relative to demand and therefore interest rates decline.

The reason why interest rates for different maturity categories do not always move in the same direction or the reason why short-term rates sometimes exceed long-term rates is that there are different demand and supply forces for each category. A large segment of the flow of funds into the capital markets or of funds already invested does not move freely from one maturity category to another, for example from short-term maturities to long-term maturities, and vice versa. Furthermore, the Federal Reserve,

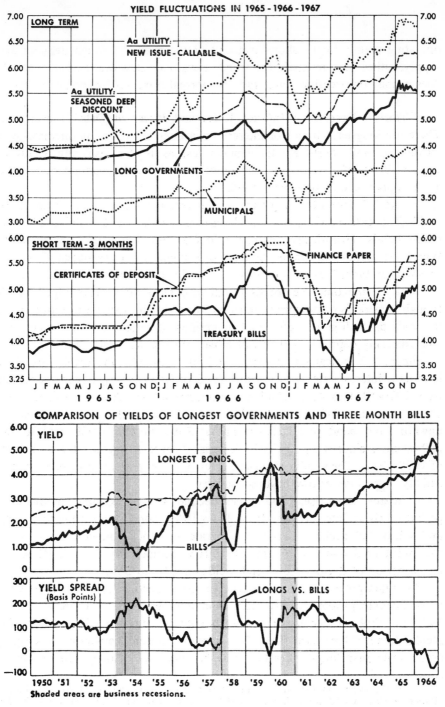

FIGURE 3-1

Source: Sidney Homer, *The Anatomy of the Bear Bond Market, 1965-1966-1967*
(New York: Salomon Brothers & Hutzler, January, 1968).

operating mainly in the short-term end of the market through demand and supply, either may intensify the trend upward or downward as it generally does or may on occasion counteract the normal trend set by economic forces.

Historical Records of Interest Rates and Prices of Debt Instruments.[3] There are long-term trends of interest rates interrupted by intermediate-term movements and short-term movements just as is the case with yields of equities. Prices of debt instruments and of preferred and common stocks move in the opposite direction from yields.

Figure 3-2 shows the long-term secular trend of interest rates from 1800-1967. The data used on all very long-term charts are for high-grade corporate bonds. Historically, before World War II and especially before World War I the amount of United States Government securities outstanding was so small at times [4] as not to provide significant indications of rate trends.

Most of the time the trends of all long-term rates move together, although in periods of prosperity rates on lower-quality issues will move closer to yields on high-grade issues and in periods of serious business recessions and especially depressions they will move much wider apart.

Figure 3-2 indicates that from 1900 to 1920-1921 the secular trend of long-term interest rates was upward (and of bond prices, downward); that from 1920-1921 to April, 1946, the secular trend was downward (and bond prices, upward); and that from 1946 to 1969 the secular trend was sharply upward (and bond prices, downward). Rates in 1967-1969 rose to the highest rates since the post-Civil War period, even surpassing the high level of 1920-1921. The secular trend was interrupted in periods of peak economic activity or periods of low business activity.

If interest rates rise, bond prices decline; so, for example, in the long period of rising interest rates from 1946-1969, bond prices showed a long and substantial decline. This was a period in which common stock prices rose substantially—from 160 to 995 DJIA (temporarily 1011 in 1966)—and a period of declining dividend yields—6-7% to 3%.

As stated previously, all rates tend to move together, although short-term rates fluctuate proportionately more than long-term rates. Therefore, from 1900 to 1969 the secular trend of short-term rates tended to follow the secular trend of long-term rates. The spread between short-term rates (generally lower than long-term rates) may be very wide at times (for example,

---

[3] For the most complete history of interest rates the reader is referred to Sidney Homer, *A History of Interest Rates—2000 B.C. to the Present* (New Brunswick, N. J.: Rutgers University Press, 1963), a study financed by a grant from the Ford Foundation; and also to B. G. Malkiel, *The Term Structure of Interest Rates—Expectations and Behavior Patterns* (Princeton, N. J.: Princeton University Press, 1963).

[4] At times there was none outstanding, for example before World War I.

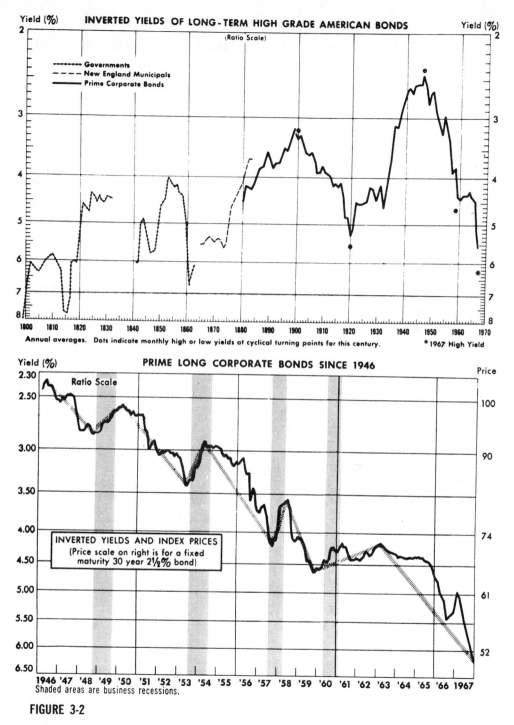

FIGURE 3-2

Source: *The Bear Bond Market of 1965-1966—The Recovery* (New York: Salomon Brothers & Hutzler).

CHAPTER 3 *Historical Behavior of Markets for Limited-Income Securities* **83**

during the 1930s and World War II) and quite narrow at other times (for example, 1959 and 1966-1969).

In the 1930s most investment funds were seeking security and tended to crowd into short-term investments, especially United States Treasury bills. This, combined with the fact that commercial banks had huge excessive idle reserves (around $5 billion), caused yields on United States Treasury bills to fall to nearly a zero yield (twice, temporarily, actually to a negative yield, for special temporary reasons).

Yields on United States Treasury bills reached their lows, therefore, in the late 1930s before World War II, while yields on long-term securities did not reach their lows until April, 1946. During World War II, yields on United States Treasury bills were pegged at ⅜ of 1% and United States long-term bonds at gradually declining yields until a low of around 2.12% was reached in April, 1946, for the longest term issues.

The Federal Reserve (commonly referred to as the FED) actually pegged prices, and therefore yields, not only during World War II but until the Spring of 1951—the time of the "Treasury-Federal Reserve Accord" reached during the first 12 months of the Korean War, with sharp inflationary forces in evidence. As a result of the "Accord," the FED returned to a policy of fostering an orderly rather than a pegged market for United States Government securities, thus freeing its hand to restrain credit when it considered such a policy necessary to combat too rapid expansion resulting in inflationary price increases especially in the level of consumer prices.

The Federal Reserve and Interest Rates. The Federal Reserve acts to control credit, and thereby interest rates, mainly through its operations in the open market in United States Government securities and largely in the short-term end of this market.[5] Its policy is generally to aid the government in fostering economic growth and employment by providing sufficient bank reserves to finance this growth without significant inflation and by strengthening credit and reducing the cost of money in recessions to encourage economic recovery. The fractional reserve system compounds the effects.

Generally, the FED acted in this manner in the post-World War II years. It let credit tighten as expansion became very strong and eased credit

---

[5] When the FED purchases securities in the open market, it pays with a check drawn on the Federal Reserve Bank of New York, which eventually is credited to the reserve account of some commercial bank member of the Federal Reserve System, thus increasing this bank's ability to expand loans and investments. When the FED sells securities in the open market, the eventual result is the reduction of the reserves of member banks as their reserve accounts with the FED are charged with the check received by the FED drawn on these banks. In this case the reserves of commercial banks are reduced and likewise their ability to increase loans and investments.

substantially in recessions. But in the 1966-1969 business expansion (the longest on record), while stating its desire to prevent inflation and while asking for fiscal restraints in late 1965 and 1966-1968, the FED continued to expand credit most of the time (except temporarily in 1966) at an unusually rapid rate, thus contributing to inflation in an environment of rising federal deficits. For a short time in 1966 (June-October) the Federal Reserve did let credit tighten. The results, in the light of monetary demands for funds for all segments of the economy and from rising federal deficits, was a serious "credit crunch" or liquidity crisis. After November, 1966, through late 1968, the Federal Reserve reversed its policy and expanded credit at an annual rate of around 8%-10%. While business did recede somewhat in the first half of 1967, the demand for funds continued to rise. In spite of a FED "easy credit policy," long-term interest rates rose sharply after February to the highest levels since the Civil War by late November-December, 1967, and short-term rates held down by the FED policy until June also rose substantially thereafter. The major additional demand force was caused by the rising federal deficit. In early 1969, interest rates made new historical peaks since the post-Civil War period.

While the FED continually reiterated its position against inflation and called for fiscal restraint (higher taxes and lower federal spending in 1967-1969), it continued to increase the money supply at a rate of 8% a year in spite of a rise in consumer prices at a rate of 4% a year.[6] Its actions were contrary to its stated "philosophy." It was encouraging inflation while speaking out against the forces of inflation. Finally, in June, 1968, Congress acted and passed the surtax bill, which included required reductions in proposed spending for fiscal 1969. Almost immediately the FED eased credit.

In recent years the FED generally went along in actions, if not in "philosophy," with the Administration, which followed the credo of the "New Economics" that the government could foster sustained and substantial economic growth—even with a war in Vietnam—without significant inflation. However, the FED perhaps learned in 1968 that a long-continued and easy credit and monetary policy might not bring low interest rates but might in the long run actually result in higher interest rates. An easy money policy places more funds in the hands of consumers and businessmen, who use these funds to bid for goods and services. This can contribute to higher prices, including higher prices for "funds" or money—in other words, high interest rates. Professor Milton Friedman, of the University of Chicago, had stated this probability, and in late 1967 and early 1968 he was joined in this

---

[6] When this is contrasted with a long-term rate of 2.4%, it certainly adds to inflationary pressures that threaten the economy.

thinking by other economists from some of the largest commercial banks and even one of the twelve Federal Reserve banks itself. Because of the Administration's policy in the 1960s to try to force economic growth regardless of consequences, in 1968 many economists and Wall Street experts were forecasting the continuation of a high level for long-term interest rates indefinitely into the future, that is, a level somewhat equivalent to the mean of the 1966-1968 level.

An economic downturn coupled with continued and rising inflationary pressures led to wage and price controls in 1971. Interest rates did drop sharply in late 1971, but were beginning to rise again by March, 1972. Inflationary pressures and large government deficits were still with us. Both factors suggest relatively high interest rates tending in upward direction through 1973.

Brief Summary of Trends of Interest Rates and Bond Prices [7]

Since 1900 there have been three major secular trends in interest rates and bond prices:
1. From 1900-1920, a secular rise in interest rates and decline in bond prices.
2. From 1920-1946, a secular decline in interest rates and rise in bond prices.
3. From 1946-1973, a secular rise in interest rates and decline in bond prices.

The period 1900-1920 was a period of secular rise in interest rates and secular decline in bond prices. Prior to the 1930s, the absolute low for bond yields in the United States was reached in 1899 when the average yield of municipal bonds (New England) and prime corporate bonds reached the 3.07%-3.20% level. From 1899 to 1920 bond yields rose substantially. The 1900-1920 bear market period for bonds can be subdivided into three major periods of rising yields and bond price declines, interrupted by two temporary and short periods of declining interest rates and rising bond prices. For the period, bond yields rose from a 3.20% level in 1899 to 5.56% in May, 1920.

The period 1920-1946 was a period of secular decline in interest rates and secular rise in bond prices. This period can be subdivided into three periods of major declines in yields and major rises in bond prices, interrupted temporarily by two important but short reversals of the secular trend. The two interruptions in the secular decline of interest rates and the secular rise in bond prices were January, 1928, to September, 1929, and May, 1931, to January, 1932. During this long secular decline in interest rates, yields of

---

[7] Sidney Homer, *A History of Interest Rates—2000 B.C. to the Present* (New Brunswick, N.J.: Rutgers University Press, 1963), Chap. xvii.

prime corporate bonds declined from 5.50% in May, 1930, to 2.37% in April, 1946.

The period 1946-1973 was a period of secular rise in interest rates and secular decline in bond prices, interrupted only temporarily during the several recessions experienced during the period. Interest rates finally surpassed the highs of 1920 and then rose so that in 1967 and 1968 the yields on prime corporate bonds and treasuries and municipals were at the highest levels since the post-Civil War period. By January, 1969, yields on the high AAA grade corporate bonds had risen from 2.3% in April, 1946, to 6.45%, and a utility "AAA" rated issue sold to cost the issuer 7.10 and to yield over 7%. Barron's high-grade corporate bond index rose to 6.69%. Yields on the longest term United States Government bonds rose from an absolute low of 2.08% in April, 1946, to a high of 5.8% for longest term government issues. Yields on United States Government issues with 5-10 year maturities rose to 6.5%. Yields on three-month Treasury bills rose to 6.3%. Barron's yield on municipals rose from a low of 0.90% in 1946 to 4.8%. In periods of historically high yields, the yields on new issues of bonds are usually significantly higher than the yields on outstanding issues as reflected in yields on the bond indexes. This was true, for example, in 1967, 1968, and 1969.

Brief Historical Records of Preferred Stocks, Preferred Stock Yields, and Bond Yields

Because preferred stocks are limited-income securities, their yields and prices tend to move in the same direction as interest rates and bond prices. However, in a period of very serious business decline, as in the depression of the 1930s, preferred stocks may decline in price substantially and their yields may rise significantly even though there is little decline in the price and little increase in the yield of high-grade bonds. For example, as shown in Table 3-11, in 1929 the yield for Standard & Poor's High-Grade Bond Index was 5.10% and the high average monthly yield on the S&P Preferred Stock Index was only 5.18%. However, in June, 1932, the yield on the preferred stock index reached a monthly average peak of 6.88% while the S&P's High-Grade Bond Index was yielding only 5.35% versus a peak of 5.10% in 1929.

In 1946 the yield on the S&P High-Grade Corporate Bond Index was 2.40%. As interest rates and bond yields rose and bond prices declined from 1946 to 1971, the yield on preferred stocks rose from 3.42% to 6.81% while the index for high-grade utility bonds rose to 7.34%. Therefore, the yield on outstanding preferred stocks was .53 basic points lower in December, 1971 than the yield on the high-grade corporate utility bond index.

TABLE 3-11

Yields on Preferred Stocks and High-Grade Corporate Bonds—Listed Issues,
Standard & Poor's Indexes

			Spread	
Year	Preferred Stock Yields	High-Grade Corporate Bond Yields—Public Utilities	In Favor of Bonds	In Favor of Preferred Stocks
1929 Peak	5.18%	5.10%		.08
1932 Peak	6.88%	5.35%		1.53
1946 Low	3.42%	2.40%		1.02
1965 Average	4.33%	4.60%	.27	
1966 Average	4.97%	5.36%	.39	
1967 Average	5.34%	5.81%	.47	
1969 January	6.02%	6.95%	.93	
1971 December	6.81%	7.34%	.53	

While the yield on preferred stocks historically was always above the yield on the bond index, gradually in the years 1946-1971 the spread between the yields narrowed and finally the yields on preferred stocks actually declined significantly below the bond yields. It would seem that this implies that the preferred stocks are of higher quality than the bonds. This is not a correct conclusion. The answer lies in the tax situation for the major purchasers of preferred stocks in recent years, that is, corporate investors. For corporate investors, the interest received on debt securities is fully taxable at current corporate tax rates, but the tax on dividends received on either common stocks or preferred stocks is restricted to 15% of dividends received. The situation that would have held in 1968 for corporate investors is shown in Table 3-12.

TABLE 3-12

Income Received by Corporate Investors from Interest Income
and from Dividend Income, May, 1968

Income		Applicable Tax Rate	Net Return After Taxes
Interest income on high-grade outstanding bonds:			
6.54%	June, 1968	48.0% = 3.14%	3.40%
6.54%	July, 1968	52.8% = 3.45%	3.09%
Dividend income on preferred stock:			
5.91%	June, 1968	48.0% × 15% = 7.2% = .426%	5.48%
5.91%	July, 1968	52.8% × 15% = 7.9% = .467%	5.44%

It can be seen from Table 3-12 that the actual yield for corporate investors is much higher on preferred stocks than on bonds. This situation is not true for individual investors who pay the same tax rate on dividend income as on bond interest. Therefore, individual investors should not compete with corporate investors for straight preferred stocks unless there is a yield differential for preferred stocks of at least 1%, which has not been the situation for over two decades. The bonds are higher quality and in 1969 would actually give approximately 9/10 of 1% higher yield.

QUESTIONS

1. (a) What are the major demands for funds?
   (b) List the basic components of the demand for funds by businessmen.
2. (a) Distinguish between gross capital formation and net capital formation.
   (b) How does the Department of Commerce definition of internal sources of funds differ from the one commonly used by financial analysts?
3. Distinguish between net savings and gross savings. What are the sources of net savings?
4. (a) Since the early 1950s, depreciation and amortization allowances have been listed by many financial writers as representing a greater proportion of internally generated funds then retained earnings. Is depreciation a source of funds? Discuss.
   (b) Are corporate debt issues or stock issues of greater importance as external source of funds? Why?
5. (a) Discuss the commercial banks as a source of funds for government, consumers, and business in recent years.
   (b) Indicate the relative importance of life insurance companies and pension funds in the capital market.
6. (a) What is the function of the money markets? In what ways are the money markets significant to investors?
   (b) Distinguish between the market for short-term funds and the market for long-term funds.
7. (a) Of what significance are the actions of the Federal Reserve System to the investing public?
   (b) How does the Federal Reserve operate to influence the economy?
   (c) Does the Federal Reserve ever come into conflict with the Treasury Department? If so, give examples of such conflict.
8. (a) What is meant by the structure of interest rates?
   (b) Do short-term and long-term interest rates always move in the same direction? If not, explain under what conditions opposite movements might occur.

9. During the money crunch of 1968-1969, high-grade bonds fell in price while low-grade issues often maintained or even rose in price. How do you explain this?

10. Should individual investors have been purchasing high-grade preferred stocks in recent years? Why or why not?

WORK-STUDY PROBLEM

Using the *Economic Report of the President* for the most recent year (and for prior years if necessary), tabulate for the years 1969, 1970, 1971, and 1972 (and for more recent years as available) the most important sources of supply and demand for funds. Account for any deficits.

(a) Set up the tabulations as follows:

Supply of Funds

Personal

Savings Accounts
Securities
Insurance and Pension Reserves
Currency and Demand Deposits
Total Personal

Business

Retained Earnings
Capital Consumption Allowance
Total Business

Total Private Supply

Demand for Funds

Personal

Residential Building
Consumer Durables
Total Personal

Business

Total Uses of Funds

Government

Federal
Municipal
Total Government

Total Demand
Deficit

Deficit Met by Personal Borrowing
>Increase in Consumer Debt
>Increase in Mortgage Debt
>Increase in Farm Debt
>Total Personal

Deficit Met by Corporate Business Borrowing

Deficit Met by Government Borrowing
>Increase in Federal Debt
>Increase in State Debt
>Total Government

Total Borrowing

(b) Comment on significant changes during the past four years and illustrate how these changes might have affected money rates.

(c) Discuss possible additions to the above tabulations that might make the comparison more meaningful.

SUGGESTED READINGS

Bierwag, G. O., and M. A. Grove. "A Model of the Structure of Prices of Marketable U.S. Treasury Securities." *Journal of Money, Credit and Banking* (August, 1971), pp. 605-629.

Cohen, Jacob. "Interpreting the Real and Financial Via the Linkage of Financial Flow." *The Journal of Finance* (March, 1968).

Cohen, Jacob, and Richard K. Miller. "A Flow of Funds Model of the Stock Market." *Journal of Economics and Business,* Temple University, Vol. 25, No. 2 (Winter, 1973), pp. 71-82.

Christian, J. W. "A Further Analysis of the Objectives of American Monetary Policy." *The Journal of Finance* (June, 1968).

Federal Reserve Bulletin. Monthly issues.

Goldsmith, Raymond W. *The Flow of Capital Funds in the Postwar Economy.* New York: National Bureau of Economic Research, 1965.

Graham, Benjamin, David L. Dodd, and C. Sidney Cottle. *Security Analysis,* 4th ed. New York: McGraw-Hill Book Company, 1962. Parts 3 and 5.

Hart, Albert G. "Connecting Links Between Monetary Policy and Fixed Investment." *Issues in Banking and Monetary Analysis.* New York: Holt, Rinehart and Winston, Inc., 1967. Chapter 4.

Homer, Sidney. *A History of Interest Rates—2000 B.C. to the Present.* New Brunswick, N. J.: Rutgers University Press, 1963. Parts III and IV.

Hyman, D. N. "A Behavioral Model for Financial Intermediation." *Economic Business Bulletin* (Spring-Summer, 1972), pp. 9-17.

Malkiel, B. G. *The Term Structure of Interest Rates—Expectations and Behavior Patterns.* Princeton, N. J.: Princeton University Press, 1963.

Ott, D. J., and A. F. Ott. "Monetary and Fiscal Policy, Goals and Choice of Instruments." *Quarterly Journal of Economics* (May, 1968).

Sargen, T. J. "Anticipated Inflation and Nominal Interest." *Quarterly Journal of Economics* (May, 1972), pp. 212-225.

Soldofsky, Robert M., and Roger L. Miller. "Risk-Premium Curves for Different Classes of Long-Term Securities, 1950-1966." *The Journal of Finance* (June, 1969), pp. 429-445.

Taylor, J. H. "Debt Management and the Term Structure of Interest Rates." *Journal of Money, Credit and Banking* (August, 1971), pp. 702-708.

Historical Behavior of Markets for Common Stocks

Stocks fluctuate in price for two major reasons: (1) because of fluctuations in earnings and dividends, both actual and expected; and (2) because of the psychology or emotions of investors, that is, recurring waves of pessimism and optimism towards stocks in general and individual stocks. The objective of this chapter is to explain: how stock prices are measured and what stock market trends are; what bull and bear market cycles are and how they may be forecasted; what the market trends are for industries as well as individual stocks; and, finally, how the investor may benefit from not only the upswing but also the downswing of the stock market.

MEASURING TRENDS IN STOCK PRICES

Periods of economic expansion and contraction have and will continue to be reflected in the stock market. Stock prices generally fluctuate in the direction of the trend and the expected trend of corporate earnings, both for individual corporations and in total. The negative effects of these fluctuations are concurrent with the liquidity requirements of the investors concerned.

Significance of Fluctuations in Stock Prices to the Investor

For institutional investors with little or no liquidity problems, these fluctuations are of negligible significance, as will be described later in the chapter. The problem of liquidity, however, is a recognizable fact to some investors. Requirements for certain institutions entail a ready reserve in bonds and/or short-term governments, while individuals' reserves are kept in insured savings accounts and United States Treasury bills and bonds. Large and wealthy individual investors in medium and high tax brackets should have the major portion of their reserve funds either in tax-exempt securities or, for short-term reserves, in United States Treasury bills. It is of paramount importance, then, that investors do not maneuver themselves into such a position that they are forced to sell their stocks. Removal of this risk eliminates the major disadvantage of common stock portfolios as long-term investments. For well-diversified portfolios of common stocks, dividend income has experienced minor declines only in about four years since 1938 and dividend income has risen about four times since 1937.

Stock Price Indexes

Stock price indexes or averages are prepared by a number of sources to serve as market barometers. These indexes or averages give information about fluctuations in the securities markets and provide a basis of historical continuity of security price movements. The most important price indexes [1] are discussed in the following paragraphs.

Dow Jones Stock Price Indexes. Dow Jones & Co., Inc. publishes four stock indexes: (1) an index comprising 30 industrial common stocks, (2) an index comprising 20 railroad common stocks, (3) an index comprising 15 utility common stocks, and (4) a composite index including all 65 stocks mentioned. The most important of these indexes is the first one—the Dow Jones Industrial Average (DJIA). The DJIA, which is made up of 30 blue chip industrial common stocks, is published each day by Dow Jones & Co., Inc., in *The Wall Street Journal* in points and in percentages. The published percentage figures reflect more accurately than any others just how the market for the 30 stocks moves from day to day. Computers now continuously calculate and quote the DJIA during market hours. The DJIA is the most widely quoted and most extensively used stock price index, although it does not offer the most accurate portrayal of the total stock market.[2] Historical statistics for the DJIA are shown in Table 4-1.

The Dow Jones Industrial Average, the majority of whose earlier stocks were railroad companies, originated in 1885. Beginning in 1896, the DJIA

---

[1] Other stock price indexes are the American Stock Exchange (AMEX) Average, the Associated Press Stock Averages, and the New York Times Index. (See articles on stock indexes in the May-June, 1967, issue of the *Financial Analysts Journal.*)

[2] The Dow Jones sample of stocks represents only about one fourth of 1 percent of the total stocks listed on the NYSE (30/1300). Also, small and new firms are not represented in the sample.

TABLE 4-1

Dow Jones Industrial Average—Annual Data

Year	BK. VAL.	DAILY CLOSING PRICES						EARNS. PER SHARE $	DIVIDENDS PER SHARE		PRICE-EARNINGS RATIO				DIVIDEND YIELD REPORTED				DIVIDEND YIELD CASH			
		High Date	High Pr.	Low Date	Low Pr.	Last	Mean		Rptd. $	Cash* $	High x	Low x	Last x	Mean x	High %	Low %	Last %	Mean %	High %	Low %	Last %	Mean %
1947	149	7/24	187	5/17	163	181	175	18.80	9.21	9.21	9.9	8.7	9.6	9.3	4.9	5.6	5.1	5.3	4.9	5.6	5.1	5.3
48	160	6/15	193	3/16	165	177	179	23.07	11.50	10.47	8.4	7.2	7.7	7.8	6.0	7.0	6.5	6.4	5.4	6.3	5.9	5.8
49	170	12/30	201	6/13	162	200	181	23.54	12.79	11.78	8.5	6.9	8.5	7.7	6.4	7.9	6.4	7.1	5.9	7.3	5.9	6.5
1950	194	11/24	235	1/13	197	235	216	30.70	16.13	15.62	7.7	6.4	7.7	7.0	6.9	8.2	6.9	7.5	6.6	7.9	6.6	7.2
51	203	9/13	276	1/3	239	269	258	26.59	16.14	15.22	10.4	9.0	10.1	9.7	5.9	6.8	6.1	6.3	5.5	6.4	5.7	5.9
52	213	12/30	292	5/1	256	292	274	24.78	15.43	15.23	11.8	10.4	11.8	11.1	5.3	6.0	5.3	5.7	5.2	5.9	5.2	5.6
53	224	1/5	294	9/14	255	281	275	27.23	16.11	15.28	10.8	9.4	10.3	10.1	5.5	6.3	5.7	5.9	5.2	6.0	5.4	5.6
54	249	12/31	404	1/11	280	404	342	28.18	17.47	16.96	14.4	9.9	14.4	12.1	4.3	6.2	4.3	5.1	4.2	6.1	4.2	5.0
1955	272	12/30	488	1/17	388	488	438	35.78	21.58	18.80	13.7	10.8	13.7	12.2	4.4	5.6	4.4	4.9	3.8	4.8	3.8	4.3
56	285	4/6	521	1/23	462	499	492	33.34	22.99	20.09	15.6	13.9	15.0	14.7	4.4	5.0	4.6	4.7	3.9	4.3	4.0	4.1
57	299	7/12	521	10/22	420	436	470	36.08	21.61	20.34	14.4	11.6	12.1	13.0	4.2	5.2	5.0	4.6	3.9	4.8	4.7	4.3
58	311	12/31	584	2/25	437	584	510	27.95	20.00	19.03	20.9	15.6	20.9	18.3	3.4	4.6	3.4	3.9	3.3	4.4	3.3	3.7
59	339	12/31	679	2/9	574	679	627	34.41	20.74	19.38	19.8	16.7	19.8	18.3	3.1	3.6	3.1	3.3	2.9	3.4	2.9	3.1
1960	347	1/5	685	10/25	566	616	626	32.21	21.36	20.46	21.3	17.6	19.1	19.4	3.1	3.8	3.5	3.4	3.0	3.6	3.3	3.3
61	365	12/13	735	1/3	610	731	673	31.91	22.71	21.28	23.0	19.1	22.9	21.1	3.1	3.7	3.1	3.4	2.9	3.5	2.9	3.2
62	401	1/3	726	6/26	536	652	631	36.43	23.30	22.09	19.9	14.7	17.9	17.3	3.2	4.3	3.6	3.7	3.0	4.1	3.4	3.5
63	426	12/18	767	1/2	647	763	707	41.21	23.41	23.20	18.6	15.7	18.5	17.2	3.2	3.6	3.1	3.3	3.0	3.6	3.0	3.3
64	417	11/18	892	1/2	766	874	829	46.43	31.24	25.38	19.2	16.5	18.8	17.9	3.5	4.1	3.6	3.8	2.8	3.3	2.9	3.1
1965	453	12/31	969	6/28	841	969	905	53.67	28.61	28.17	18.1	15.7	18.1	16.9	3.0	3.4	3.0	3.2	2.9	3.3	2.9	3.1
66	476	2/9	995	10/7	744	786	870	57.67	31.89	30.12	17.3	12.9	13.6	15.1	3.2	4.3	4.1	3.7	3.0	4.0	3.8	3.5
67	477	9/25	943	1/3	786	905	965	53.87	30.19	29.84	17.5	14.6	16.8	16.1	3.2	3.8	3.3	3.5	3.2	3.8	3.3	3.4
68	521	12/3	985	3/21	825	944	905	57.93	31.34	31.34	17.0	14.2	16.3	15.3	3.2	3.8	3.3	3.5	3.2	3.8	3.3	3.5
69	542	5/14	969	12/17	770	800	870	57.02	33.90	32.29	17.0	13.5	14.0	15.3	3.5	4.4	4.2	3.9	3.3	4.2	4.0	3.7
1970	573	12/29	842	5/26	631	839	737	51.02	31.53	31.53	16.5	12.4	16.4	14.4	3.7	5.0	3.8	4.3	3.7	5.0	3.8	4.3
71	608	4/28	951	11/23	798	890	875	55.09	30.86	30.86	17.3	14.5	16.2	15.9	3.2	3.9	3.5	3.5	3.2	3.9	3.5	3.5
72	NA	12/11	1036	1/26	889	1020	981	67.13	32.27	32.27	15.4	13.2	15.2	14.6	3.1	3.6	3.2	3.3	3.1	3.6	3.2	3.3

* Compiled by BTCo. prior to 1958, thereafter by Barron's.   NA = Not available.

was completely changed so that it was composed of 12 industrial stocks. In 1916 the list was increased to 20 stocks, and at that time the new average was worked back to 1914. Then, on October 1, 1928, the list grew to 30 stocks, where it has remained since, although numerous substitutions have been made among the component stocks periodically.

Substitutions for stocks included in the DJIA are made: (1) when a stock becomes considerably less active; (2) when its movements, because of an unusually low price, become so small that they have little effect on the average; or (3) when, for some other reason, the stocks cease to be representative of a substantial sector of American industry.

The 30 common stocks included in the DJIA as of 1971 are listed below. The composition of the 30 stocks has not changed since 1959.

Allied Chemical Corp.	International Nickel Co. of
Aluminum Co. of America	Canada,(Ltd.
American Brands, Inc.	International Paper Co.
American Can Co.	Johns-Manville Corp.
American Telephone &	Owens-Illinois, Inc.
Telegraph Co.	Procter & Gamble Co.
Anaconda Co.	Sears, Roebuck & Co.
Bethlehem Steel Corp.	Standard Oil Co. of California
Chrysler Corp.	Standard Oil Co. of New Jersey
DuPont (E. I.) de Nemours & Co.	Swift & Co.
Eastman Kodak Co.	Texaco Incorporated
General Electric Co.	Union Carbide Corp.
General Foods Corp.	United Aircraft Corp.
General Motors Corp.	United States Steel Corp.
Goodyear Tire & Rubber Co.	Westinghouse Electric Corp.
International Harvester Co.	Woolworth (F. W.) Co.

Originally the DJIA was computed by determining the simple arithmetical average (mean) of the prices of the number of stocks in the index. When there were 12 stocks, the prices of the 12 were added together and the total was divided by 12. When there were 20 stocks, the sum of the 20 individual prices was divided by 20. However, when some corporations whose stocks were included in the list began splitting shares, this system produced distortions. To correct the distortion, Dow Jones adopted a solution that has been in effect since 1928: they changed the divisor to reflect the splits or the substitutions made in stocks composing the average. Each split in the 30-stock group lowered the divisor over the years. As of January 1, 1969, when the DJIA is computed, the total market price of the 30 stocks is divided, not by 30, but by 2.011.[3]

---

[3] The weighting system has been criticized on the grounds that the weights now used do not relate to any relevant market proportions or market opportunities.

Standard & Poor's Stock Price Indexes.[4] Standard & Poor's Corporation publishes four stock indexes: (1) an index comprising 425 industrial common stocks, (2) an index comprising 25 rail stocks, (3) an index comprising 50 utility stocks, and (4) an index including all 500 stocks mentioned. All of the above indexes are adjusted to the same base, 1941-1943 = 10.

Standard & Poor's 500 Composite Stock Price Index represents approximately 90% of the market value of all common stocks listed on the New York Stock Exchange. This composite index is calculated at the opening and the closing of the market as well as each hour that the market is open. S&P's 425 Industrial Stock Price Index comprises a great portion of the 500 Index and therefore gives a general portrayal of the 500 Index. In both of these indexes, the major companies are heavily weighted, because the price of each share is multiplied by the number of shares outstanding in calculating the total market value. Both of these indexes closely paralleled the DJIA until 1966. From 1966 to January, 1969, however, the S&P indexes suggested superior stock market performance.

The 500 Index was linked to the old Standard & Poor's Composite Index of 90 stocks extending back to 1926. This 1926-1957 record was then linked to the Cowles Commission Index, extending the record back to 1871. Therefore, the history of Standard & Poor's Composite Index so adjusted extends from 1871 to the present day. Historical statistics for the S&P 500 Index and the S&P 425 Index are shown in Tables 4-2 and 4-3 respectively.

New York Stock Exchange Stock Price Index. The most important stock price index published by the New York Stock Exchange is the NYSE Common Stock Index. It is a composite index including all the equity issues listed on the NYSE. It takes into consideration the total market value of every common stock traded on the NYSE and reflects each transaction in every stock. The index number expresses the relationship between total current market value and the base market value as of December 31, 1965. The NYSE Common Stock Index is computed each half hour throughout the trading day. Historical statistics for this index are shown in Table 4-4.

Comparison of Stock Price Indexes. Table 4-5 presents a comparison of the yearly index figures for the DJIA and for the S&P 425. At least since 1929 and up to 1966, the DJIA has presented a reasonably reliable picture of the trend and the level of stock prices, closely paralleling the record of

---

[4] Standard & Poor's Trade and Securities Statistics, *Security Price Record,* 1969 edition.

TABLE 4-2

Standard & Poor's 500 Stocks Composite Index (1941-1943 = 10)—Annual Data

Year	DAILY CLOSING PRICES						EARNS. PER SHARE	DIVS. PER SHARE	PRICE-EARNINGS RATIO				DIVIDEND YIELD			
	High		Low		Last	Mean			High	Low	Last	Mean	High	Low	Last	Mean
	Date	Price	Date	Price			$	$	x	x	x	x	%	%	%	%
1947	2/8	16.20	5/17	13.71	15.30	14.96	1.61	0.84	10.1	8.5	9.5	9.3	5.2	6.1	5.5	5.6
48	6/15	17.06	2/14	13.84	15.20	15.45	2.29	0.93	7.4	6.0	6.6	6.7	5.5	6.7	6.1	6.0
49	12/30	16.79	6/13	13.55	16.76	15.17	2.32	1.14	7.2	5.8	7.2	6.5	6.8	8.4	6.8	7.5
1950	12/29	20.43	1/14	16.65	20.41	18.54	2.84	1.47	7.2	5.9	7.2	6.5	7.2	8.8	7.2	7.9
51	10/15	23.85	1/3	20.69	23.77	22.27	2.44	1.41	9.8	8.5	9.7	9.1	5.9	6.8	5.9	6.3
52	12/30	26.59	2/20	23.09	26.57	24.84	2.40	1.41	11.1	9.6	11.1	10.4	5.3	6.1	5.3	5.7
53	1/5	26.66	9/14	22.71	24.81	24.69	2.51	1.45	10.6	9.0	9.9	9.8	5.4	6.4	5.8	5.9
54	12/31	35.98	1/11	24.80	35.98	30.39	2.77	1.54	13.0	9.0	13.0	11.0	4.3	6.2	4.3	5.1
1955	11/14	46.41	1/17	34.58	45.48	40.50	3.62	1.64	12.8	9.6	12.6	11.2	3.5	4.7	3.6	4.0
56	8/2	49.74	1/23	43.11	46.67	46.43	3.41	1.74	14.6	12.6	13.7	13.6	3.5	4.0	3.7	3.7
57	7/15	49.13	10/22	38.98	39.99	44.06	3.37	1.79	14.6	11.6	11.9	13.1	3.6	4.6	4.5	4.1
58	12/31	55.21	1/2	40.33	55.21	47.77	2.89	1.75	19.1	14.0	19.1	16.5	3.2	4.3	3.2	3.7
59	8/3	60.71	2/9	53.58	59.89	57.15	3.39	1.83	17.9	15.8	17.7	16.9	3.0	3.4	3.1	3.2
1960	1/5	60.39	10/25	52.30	58.11	56.35	3.27	1.95	18.5	16.0	17.8	17.2	3.2	3.7	3.4	3.5
61	12/12	72.64	1/3	57.57	71.55	65.11	3.19	2.02	22.8	18.0	22.4	20.4	2.8	3.5	2.8	3.1
62	1/3	71.13	6/26	52.32	63.10	61.73	3.67	2.13	19.4	14.3	17.2	16.8	3.0	4.1	3.4	3.5
63	12/31	75.02	1/2	62.69	75.02	68.86	4.02	2.28	18.7	15.6	18.7	17.1	3.0	3.6	3.0	3.3
64	11/20	86.28	1/2	75.43	84.75	80.86	4.55	2.50	19.0	16.6	18.6	17.8	2.9	3.3	2.9	3.1
1965	11/15	92.63	6/28	81.60	92.43	87.12	5.19	2.72	17.8	15.7	17.8	16.8	2.9	3.3	2.9	3.1
66	2/9	94.06	10/7	73.20	80.33	83.63	5.55	2.87	16.9	13.2	14.5	15.1	3.1	3.9	3.6	3.4
67	9/25	97.59	1/3	80.38	96.47	88.99	5.33	2.92	18.3	15.4	18.1	16.7	3.0	3.6	3.0	3.3
68	11/29	108.37	3/5	87.72	103.86	98.05	5.76	3.07	18.8	15.2	18.0	17.0	2.8	3.5	3.0	3.1
69	5/14	106.16	12/17	89.20	92.06	97.68	5.78	3.16	18.4	15.4	15.9	16.9	3.0	3.5	3.4	3.2
1970	1/5	93.46	5/26	69.29	92.15	81.38	5.13	3.14	18.2	13.5	18.0	15.9	3.4	4.5	3.4	3.9
71	4/28	104.77	11/23	90.16	102.09	97.47	5.70	3.07	18.4	15.8	17.9	17.1	2.9	3.4	3.0	3.1
72	12/11	119.12	1/3	101.67	118.05	112.95	6.37 e	3.15	18.7	16.0	18.5	17.7	2.6	3.1	2.7	2.8

e — Estimated by S&P.

TABLE 4-3

Standard & Poor's 425 Industrial Stock Index (1941-1943 = 10)—Annual Data

Year	BOOK VALUE Yr.-End	DAILY CLOSING PRICE High Date	High Price	Low Date	Low Price	Last	Mean	EARNS. PER SHARE	DIVS. PER SHARE	P-E RATIO High	Low	Last	Mean	DIV. YIELD High	Low	Last	Mean
			$					$	$	x	x	x	x	%	%	%	%
1947	12.49*	7/24	15.83	5/17	13.40	15.18	14.62	1.59	0.82	10.0	8.4	9.5	9.2	5.2	6.1	5.4	5.6
48	14.53	6/15	16.93	3/16	13.58	15.12	15.26	2.33	0.91	7.3	5.8	6.5	6.5	5.4	6.7	6.0	6.0
49	15.17	12/30	16.52	6/13	13.23	16.49	14.88	2.42	1.14	6.8	5.5	6.8	6.1	6.9	8.6	6.9	7.7
1950	16.77	11/24	20.60	1/14	16.34	20.57	18.47	2.93	1.53	7.0	5.6	7.0	6.3	7.4	9.4	7.4	8.3
51	18.66	10/15	24.33	1/3	20.85	24.24	22.59	2.55	1.45	9.5	8.2	9.5	8.9	6.0	7.0	6.0	6.4
52	20.15	12/30	26.92	2/29	23.30	26.89	25.11	2.46	1.44	10.9	9.5	10.9	10.2	5.3	6.2	5.4	5.7
53	20.76	1/5	26.99	9/14	22.70	24.87	24.85	2.59	1.47	10.4	8.8	9.6	9.6	5.4	6.5	5.9	5.9
54	22.09	12/31	37.34	1/11	24.84	37.24	31.04	2.89	1.57	12.9	8.6	12.9	10.7	4.2	6.3	4.2	5.1
1955	25.09	11/14	49.54	1/17	35.66	48.44	42.60	3.78	1.68	13.1	9.4	12.8	11.3	3.4	4.7	3.5	3.9
56	26.35	8/2	52.28	1/23	45.71	50.08	49.50	3.53	1.78	15.1	12.9	14.2	14.0	3.3	3.9	3.6	3.6
57	29.44	7/15	53.25	10/22	41.98	42.86	47.62	3.50	1.84	15.2	12.0	12.2	13.6	3.5	4.4	4.3	3.9
58	30.66	12/31	58.97	1/10	43.20	58.97	51.09	2.95	1.79	20.0	14.6	20.0	17.3	3.0	4.1	3.0	3.5
59	32.26	8/3	65.32	2/9	57.02	64.50	61.17	3.53	1.90	18.5	16.2	18.3	17.3	2.9	3.3	2.9	3.1
1960	33.74	1/5	65.02	10/25	55.34	61.49	60.18	3.39	2.00	19.2	16.3	18.1	17.8	3.1	3.6	3.3	3.3
61	34.85	12/12	76.69	1/3	60.87	75.72	68.78	3.37	2.08	22.8	18.1	22.5	20.4	2.7	3.4	2.7	3.0
62	36.37	1/2	75.22	6/26	54.80	66.00	65.01	3.87	2.20	19.4	14.2	17.1	16.8	2.9	4.0	3.3	3.4
63	38.17	12/31	79.25	1/2	65.48	79.25	72.37	4.24	2.38	18.7	15.4	18.7	17.1	3.0	3.6	3.0	3.3
64	40.23	11/20	91.29	1/2	79.74	89.62	85.52	4.83	2.60	18.9	16.5	18.6	17.7	2.8	3.3	2.9	3.0
1965	43.50	11/15	98.55	6/28	86.43	98.47	92.49	5.51	2.85	17.9	15.7	17.9	16.8	2.9	3.3	2.9	3.1
66	45.59	2/9	100.60	10/7	77.89	85.24	89.25	5.89	2.98	17.1	13.2	14.5	15.2	3.0	3.8	3.5	3.3
67	47.78	10/9	106.15	1/3	85.31	104.90	95.73	5.66	3.01	18.8	15.1	18.5	16.9	2.8	3.5	2.9	3.1
68	50.21	11/29	118.03	3/5	95.05	113.02	106.54	6.15	3.18	19.2	15.4	18.3	17.3	2.7	3.3	2.8	3.0
69	51.70	5/14	116.24	7/29	97.75	101.49	107.00	6.17	3.27	18.8	15.8	16.4	17.3	2.8	3.3	3.2	3.1
1970	52.65	1/5	102.87	5/26	75.58	100.90	89.23	5.43	3.24	18.9	13.9	18.6	16.4	3.1	4.3	3.2	3.6
71	55.28	4/28	115.84	11/23	99.36	112.72	107.60	6.02	3.18	19.2	16.5	18.7	17.9	2.7	3.2	2.8	3.0
72	NA	12/11	132.95	1/3	112.19	131.87	125.67	6.74ᵉ	3.22	19.7	16.6	19.6	18.6	2.4	2.9	2.4	2.6

* Restated to exclude reserve for deferred income taxes.   NA = Not available.
e = Estimated by S&P.

TABLE 4-4

NYSE Common Stock Index—Annual Data (12/31/65 = 50.00)

Year	High Date	High Price	Low Date	Low Price	Last	Mean
1939	10/21	7.64	4/8	6.06	7.38	6.85
1940	4/6	7.56	5/25	5.66	6.43	6.61
1941	1/11	6.61	12/27	5.27	5.27	5.94
1942	12/26	5.93	4/25	4.64	5.93	5.29
1943	7/17	7.64	1/2	5.99	7.14	6.82
1944	12/16	8.14	2/5	7.11	8.14	7.63
1945	12/8	10.86	1/20	8.22	10.67	9.54
1946	6/3	11.89	11/23	8.85	9.44	10.37
1947	2/8	9.91	5/17	8.33	9.25	9.12
1948	6/11	10.25	2/14	8.46	8.99	9.36
1949	12/31	9.91	6/10	8.22	9.91	9.07
1950	12/30	12.01	1/14	9.85	12.01	10.93
1951	9/14	13.89	1/6	12.28	13.60	13.09
1952	12/26	14.49	10/24	13.31	14.49	13.90
1953	1/2	14.65	9/18	12.62	13.60	13.64
1954	12/31	19.40	1/8	13.70	19.40	16.55
1955	12/9	23.71	1/7	19.05	23.71	21.38
1956	8/3	25.90	1/20	22.55	24.35	24.23
1957	7/12	26.30	12/20	20.92	21.11	23.61
1958	12/24	28.85	1/10	21.45	28.85	25.15
1959	7/31	32.39	2/6	28.94	31.67	30.67
1960	1/8	31.99	10/21	28.38	30.94	30.19
1961	12/8	38.60	1/6	31.17	38.39	34.89
1962	3/16	38.02	6/22	28.20	33.81	33.11
1963	12/27	39.92	1/4	34.41	39.92	37.17
1964	11/18	46.49	1/3	40.47	45.65	43.48
1965	12/31	50.00	6/28	43.64	50.00	46.82
1966	2/9	51.06	10/7	39.37	43.72	45.22
1967	9/29	54.18	1/3	43.74	53.83	48.96
1968	11/29	61.27	3/5	48.70	58.90	54.99
1969	5/14	59.32	7/29	49.31	51.53	54.31
1970	1/5	52.36	5/26	37.69	50.23	45.03

Note: Index not calculated prior to 1939. Based on weekly data 1/7/39-5/28/64 and daily thereafter.

Source: New York Stock Exchange.

the S&P 425 Industrial Stock Price Index. After the 25% market decline in 1966, the S&P indexes and the NYSE Index recovered and made new highs in 1967 and 1968, but the DJIA lagged well behind. The broader indexes portrayed a much more bullish picture in 1967 and 1968 than did the DJIA, which only recovered to its 1966 high in December, 1968.

An examination of Table 4-5 readily reveals the long upward secular trend of stock prices. Of course there were times when this trend was interrupted; but in spite of declines or horizontal movements in the stock market, the secular trend has definitely been strongly upward, paralleling roughly the growth of the economy. From 1950 to 1966, the S&P 425 rose

TABLE 4-5

Comparative Record
Standard & Poor's 425 Industrial Stock Price Index and Dow Jones Industrial Average

	Prices									Earnings Per Share		
	High			Low			Mean					
	S&P 425		DJIA	S&P 425		DJIA	S&P 425		DJIA	S&P 425		DJIA
	Actual	Actual x 10	Actual	Actual	Actual x 10	Actual	Actual	Actual x 10	Actual	Actual	Actual x 10	Actual
1947	15.83	158.3	186.9	13.40	134.0	163.2	14.62	146.2	175.0	1.59	15.90	18.80
1948	16.93	169.3	193.2	13.58	135.8	165.4	15.26	152.6	179.3	2.33	23.30	23.07
1949	16.52	165.2	200.5	13.23	132.3	161.6	14.88	148.8	181.0	2.42	24.20	23.54
1950	20.60	206.0	235.5	16.34	163.4	196.8	18.47	184.7	216.1	2.93	29.30	30.70
1951	24.33	243.3	276.4	20.85	208.5	239.0	22.59	225.9	257.7	2.55	25.50	26.59
1952	26.92	269.2	292.0	23.30	233.0	256.4	25.11	251.1	274.2	2.46	24.60	24.76
1953	26.99	270.0	293.8	22.70	227.0	255.5	24.85	248.5	274.6	2.59	25.90	27.23
1954 ¹	37.24	372.4	404.4	24.84	248.4	279.9	31.04	310.4	342.1	2.89	28.90	28.40
1955	49.54	495.4	488.4	35.66	356.6	388.2	42.60	426.0	438.3	3.78	37.80	35.78
1956	53.28	532.8	521.1	45.71	457.1	462.4	49.50	495.0	491.7	3.53	35.30	33.34
1957 ²	53.25	532.5	520.8	41.98	419.8	419.8	47.62	476.2	470.3	3.50	35.00	36.08
1958	58.97	569.7	583.7	43.20	432.0	436.9	51.09	510.9	510.0	2.95	29.50	27.95
1959	65.32	653.2	679.4	57.02	570.2	574.5	61.17	611.7	626.9	3.53	35.30	34.31
1960	65.02	650.2	635.5	55.34	553.4	566.1	60.18	601.8	625.8	3.39	33.90	32.21
1961	76.69	766.9	734.4	60.87	608.7	610.3	68.78	687.8	672.6	3.37	33.70	31.91
1962	75.22	752.2	726.0	54.80	548.0	535.8	65.01	650.1	630.9	3.87	36.70	36.43
1963	79.25	792.5	767.2	65.48	654.8	646.8	72.37	723.7	707.0	4.24	42.40	41.21
1964	91.29	912.9	891.7	79.74	797.4	766.1	85.52	855.2	828.9	4.83	48.30	46.43
1965	98.55	985.5	969.3	86.43	864.3	840.6	92.49	924.9	904.9	5.51	55.10	53.67
1966	100.60	1006.0	995.2	77.89	778.9	744.3	89.25	892.5	869.7	5.89	58.90	57.67
1967	106.15	1061.5	943.1	85.31	853.1	786.4	95.73	957.3	864.8	5.66	56.60	53.87
1968	118.03	1180.3	985.0	95.09	950.5	825.0	106.54	1065.4	905.0	6.16	61.60	57.93
1969	116.24	1162.4	969.0	97.75	977.5	770.0	107.00	1070.0	870.0	6.17	61.70	57.02
1970	102.87	1028.7	842.0	75.58	755.8	631.0	89.23	892.3	737.0	5.40	54.00	51.02

¹ By 1954 both the DJIA and S&P Indexes had finally recovered to and surpassed 1929 high.
² By 1957 the Consumer Price Index had risen from approximately 50 (1940-41) to 100, but the DJIA and the S&P 425 Index were about 5 times the 1941 level.

from 16.34 to 100.60, or a gain of over 500%, and the DJIA rose from 197 to 995, or also roughly 500%. In both cases the prices of stocks as measured by these indexes rose three times as fast as earnings. In December, 1968, the S&P 425 reached 118 while the DJIA recovered to 985, but the highs reached in 1970 were only 103 and 842 respectively.

Stock Market Trends

There are basically four types of stock market trends: (1) the long-term secular trends in stock prices; (2) the primary or bull and bear market trends (trends that have shown a definite correlation with the cycles of both business and profits); (3) the secondary trends that are within bull and bear markets; and (4) the day-to-day, week-to-week, and month-to-month trends. This book is mainly concerned with the long-term trends correlated with the growth of earnings and dividends. The long secular rise of earnings, dividends, and stock disclosed by these trends has provided the major justification for investment in common stocks.

Compound Annual Growth Rate of Stock Prices. There has been a long-term secular growth of stock prices. In certain periods stock prices have risen faster than gross national product (GNP) and at other times at a slower rate. For certain periods the growth rate was negative. After 1929, it took stock averages until 1953-1954 to regain their 1929 level. The compound annual growth rate of stock prices, earnings, and dividends for selected years is shown in Table 4-6 below.

The long-run compound annual growth rate for stock prices has been 4.3% per year; for earnings, about 3.8% per year; and for dividends, 3.6% per year. The higher rate for stock prices reflects the unusual rise in stock

TABLE 4-6

Compound Annual Growth Rate
Standard & Poor's 500 Composite Stock Price Index

Years	Stock Prices S&P 500	Earnings S&P 500	Dividends S&P 500
1900-1929	6.3%	4.6%	4.4%
1900-1961	4.3%	3.3%	3.4%
1900-1966	4.3%	3.8%	3.6%
1929-1954	0.5%	2.2%	1.9%
1929-1961	2.6%	2.2%	2.4%
1929-1966	3.0%	3.4%	3.0%
1946-1961	9.3%	7.8%	7.4%
1946-1966	8.3%	8.7%	7.2%

prices from 1949-1966. Within the period 1960-1966 there was a phenomenal increase in earnings, but the 1967-1971 record indicates that it would be unwise to predict continuation of earnings and dividends at the 1960-1966 rate. Over the years it is probable that stock prices, earnings, and dividends will do well to increase as fast as the growth rate for GNP rather than faster, as was the case in 1960-1966. Historically, except for the 1960-1966 years, they grew at a slower rate than GNP. Therefore, if one projected a growth in GNP in actual dollars of 5%-6% per year, the projection for stock earnings, dividends, and prices would probably be at a little slower rate or at best the same rate.

In the years 1949-1961 inclusive, the prices of common stocks rose over three times as fast as earnings: from price-earnings ratios of 5.5 to 6.8 in 1949 to ratios of 18.1 to 24 in December, 1961. In other words, investors were willing to pay three times as much for a dollar of earnings in December, 1961, as in 1949. Specifically, if a stock earned $5 per share in 1949, investors were willing to pay $27 to $35 per share for this stock; whereas if a stock earned $5 per share in December, 1961, investors were willing to pay $90 to $115 per share. It will be granted that the quality of earnings improved significantly during the period, because the reported earnings were after deduction of substantially heavier charges for depreciation, especially after 1954. Investors in late 1961 were purchasing stocks at dividend yields of 2.88%. In January, 1969, yields were about 2.88% and price-earnings ratios were 17 to 19.

From 1960 through 1966, corporate earnings rose about 80% (All U.S. Corporations and DJIA), but stock prices rose only from a 685 DJIA peak in 1960 and a 735 DJIA peak in 1961 to 995 in 1966, or a rise of only 45% from the 1960 peak and 35% from the 1961 peak. The range of the DJIA in 1966 was 744 to 995 and in 1967 was 786 to 943.

Common stocks grew rapidly in popularity among all classes of investors, institutional and individual, through 1968; and the odds strongly favor a continuation of this long-term trend. Furthermore, there has been a relative scarcity of common stocks, and stock sales of major corporations have been extremely few since large corporations have generally acquired funds in the capital market by the sale of debt issues rather than equity issues, though stock issues expanded markedly in 1970 and 1971. In fact, only about $45 billion of equity securities were sold net 1946 through 1968. Only major changes in our tax laws bringing the cost of equity issues more in line with the cost of debt issues would be likely to alter greatly the scarcity factor of common stocks. But such a development appears extremely unlikely. Therefore, because of this scarcity factor and the expected growth in earnings, the compound annual growth rate for common stock prices can be anticipated at a minimum of 4% and perhaps closer to 5%. The same growth rate for dividends can also be expected. This would, of course, be much lower than the post-World War II growth up to 1969, because in that period stock prices grew three times as fast as earnings.

Primary and Short-Term Market Trends. There is no serious area of disagreement on the subject of the really long-term future trend of stock prices. Stock prices are rather universally expected to demonstrate a compound annual growth rate somewhat equivalent to the long-term growth rate experienced in the past. As in the past, this rate in the future can be expected to correlate with the long-term compound annual growth rate of corporate earnings and dividends for common stock investments.

There are, however, primary trends that are usually designated as the bull and bear market trends. Within these primary bear and bull market trends there are intermediate trends that temporarily reverse the primary trend and make it very difficult to identify the primary trends while they are in progress. Finally, there are very short hour-to-hour, day-to-day, week-to-week, and month-to-month trends within the intermediate trend, which in turn act to confuse investors' attempts to identify the primary trend. Only in retrospect is identification easy. The authors of this book subscribe to the random walk theory and suggest that readers review the bibliography of the theory at the end of this chapter.

THE PRIMARY OR BULL AND BEAR MARKET TREND

The long-term secular trend of stock prices is interrupted by intervening bear and bull markets. Major bear and bull markets are generally correlated with the rise and fall of corporate profits, which in turn are associated with business cycles.

Bull and Bear Market Cycles

Eleven business cycle peaks and troughs have been identified from 1920 to 1972. The correlation of business cycles with stock market cycles is shown in Table 4-7.

The major bear markets, based on the Dow Jones Industrial Average, are shown in Table 4-8. In general, the major bear markets have been correlated with declines in business. Major exceptions are the declines in 1941-1942 that correlated with World War II, the declines in 1946-1948 that correlated with fear of war with Russia and fear of a postwar depression, and the declines in 1949, 1953-1954, and 1957-1958. So far as the 27%

TABLE 4-7

Major Stock Market Cycles and Business Cycles

Stock Market Peaks	Business Cycle Peaks	Stock Market Lows	Business Cycle Troughs
January 3, 1920	January, 1920	August 24, 1920	July, 1921
March 20, 1923	May, 1923	October 27, 1923	July, 1924
August 14, 1926	October, 1926	January 25, 1927	November, 1927
October 9, 1929	August, 1929	July 4, 1932	March, 1933
March 10, 1937	May, 1937	March 31, 1938	June, 1938
*	February, 1945	*	October, 1945
June 15, 1948	November, 1948	June 13, 1949	October, 1949
January 5, 1953	July, 1953	September 14, 1953	August, 1954
July 12, 1957	July, 1957	October 22, 1957	April, 1958
January 5, 1960	May, 1960	October 25, 1960	February, 1961
December 2, 1969	November, 1969	May 26, 1970	November, 1970

* No peak until May 29, 1946, in stock market; 1961 economic expansion carried into 1969.

decline in 1962 was concerned, the only explanation would appear to be the very great speculation in the stock market in 1961 and a possible fear of a recession in 1962 or 1963. Actually, there was only a hesitancy of business in 1962. The 26% decline in 1966 forecast the decline in earnings in 1967, although in retrospect it overdiscounted the decline. The 29% decline during the 1969-1970 bear market represents the sharpest decline on record since World War II, and it did forecast a particularly sharp decline in corporate profits before taxes.

Forecasting Bull and Bear Markets by Forecasting Changes in the Trend of Business

A study of statistics of bear and bull market cycles would indicate that if investors had successfully forecast the peak of business cycles they could have profited by selling stocks prior to the peak of the business cycle and then purchasing them prior to the start of each recovery. The stock market, in most cases, discounted both the beginning of the recession and the beginning of the recovery. Even when its appears that the stock market decline did not begin until just at the outset of the recession, it must be remembered that the date identified as the beginning of the recession was not actually established by economists until some months after the recession had actually begun. This has also been true of economic recessions.

In order to forecast trends in stock prices and, most important, changes in direction of the long-term trend, the investor must accurately ascertain changes in the direction of economic activity and overall corporate profits.

TABLE 4-8

Major Bear Markets—Dow Jones Industrial Average 1920-1966

Period	High	Low	Point Decline	Percentage Decline From High	Business Cycle Peaks
1/3/20 to 8/24/21	109.88	70.31	39.57	36.0	January, 1920
3/20/23 to 10/27/23	105.38	85.76	19.62	18.6	May, 1923
9/9/29 to 11/13/29	381.17	198.69	182.48	47.9	August, 1929
4/17/30 to 12/16/30	294.07	157.51	136.56	46.4	
2/24/31 to 12/17/31	194.36	73.79	120.57	62.0*	
3/8/32 to 7/8/32	88.78	41.22	47.56	53.6*	
9/9/29 to 7/8/32	381.17	41.22	339.95	89.2*	Low—March, 1933
2/5/34 to 7/26/34	110.74	85.51	55.23	49.9	
3/10/37 to 3/31/38	194.40	98.95	95.45	49.1	May, 1937
1/3/40 to 4/28/42	152.80	92.92	59.88	39.2	
5/29/46 to 10/9/46	212.50	163.12	49.38	23.2	February, 1945
Lows—1946, 1947, 1948, and 1949		162-165	....	....	November, 1948
6/15/48 to 6/13/49	193.16	161.60			
1/5/53 to 9/14/53	293.79	255.49	38.30	13.0	July, 1953
7/12/57 to 10/22/57	520.77	419.79	100.98	19.4	July, 1957
12/31/59 to 10/25/60	685.47	566.03	119.44	17.4	May, 1960
12/13/61 to 6/26/62	734.91	535.76	199.15	27.1	
2/9/66 to 10/7/66	995.15	744.32	250.83	25.2	
9/26/67 to 3/22/68	951.57	817.61	133.96	14.1	
12/2/68 to 5/26/70	994.65	627.46	367.19	36.9	November, 1969
4/28/71 to 11/23/71	958.12	790.67	167.45	17.5	

    * All of these declines are part of the major decline from the 1929 peak to the 1932 depression low. In the 27 years from 1940-1966, all declines were in the 13%-30% range, with most in the 19%-27% range.

But even if a change in business activity and corporate profits is correctly foretold, in order to profit the investor must discount the change in advance of the occurrence in order to buy or sell before investors in general become aware of the change in market direction; otherwise the profitable opportunities are lost. Finally, despite the improvement in techniques of business forecasting over the past 30 years, forecasting is still partly an art as well as a science. There is a strong temptation to extrapolate going trends.

If the investor feels that he is accurate enough as an economic forecaster to act to take advantage of these cycles, he may attempt to do so.[5] However,

---

    [5] For those who would examine this area more deeply, a study of the following is suggested: (a) *Signals of Recessions and Recovery*, National Bureau of Economic

most professionals, including institutional investors, have learned by experience that it is too difficult for most investors to do so and they therefore ignore these seeming opportunities to benefit from bull and bear market cycles. Again, it is emphasized that the authors subscribe to the random walk theory.

Forecasting Bull and Bear Markets by Technical Methods

Because of the poor record of most of those who have attempted to forecast stock price trends on the basis of economic forecasting, many investors have for years attempted to use technical methods for forecasting stock market trends. A few of these technical methods are briefly discussed in the following paragraphs. A wide review of empirical evidence and the judgment of most successful investors—those who have built up substantial capital over the years—leads to the comment that the technical methods for forecasting have not proved very rewarding.

The Dow Theory. This is the oldest of the technical theories. The theory was first developed in an editorial in *The Wall Street Journal* by Charles H. Dow and W. P. Hamilton around the turn of the century.[6] The theory assumes that investors can profit through taking advantage of primary market trends by not attempting to buck the trend. It does not attempt to forecast the beginning of primary trends but is purposely late. It attempts to identify primary trends once they are established. Identification of trends is purposely late in order to avoid mistaking short-term trends for primary trends.

It is assumed that in a primary uptrend (bull market) each succeeding cycle will produce a peak higher than the last preceding one and also a trough in declines higher than the preceding one. Conversely, in a primary downtrend (bear market), each secondary peak will be lower than the last

---

Research (Princeton, N. J.: Princeton University Press, 1961); (b) *Business Conditions Digest,* a monthly publication of the United States Department of Commerce. The latter brings together many of the available economic indications in convenient form for analysis and interpretation. The presentation and the classification of series and the business cycle turning dates are those designated by the National Bureau of Economic Research (NBER), which has been the leader in this field of investigation. One of the most important of the leading indicators is the trend of stock prices, which adds to the difficulty of the investor in attempting to forecast changes in stock prices on the basis of economic forecasting.

[6] See (a) Robert Rhea, "The Dow Theory," *Barron's* (1932), reprints of a series of editorials by Charles H. Dow and W. P. Hamilton; (b) Richard L. Russell, "Dow Theory Revisited," *Barron's* (December 1, 1958), p. 9. See also "The Money Men" (the later disciples of Dow, especially John McGee), *Forbes* (December 15, 1968), p. 66.

preceding peak and each secondary trough lower than the last preceding one. If this is true, once a new peak exceeds the last peak and the succeeding low is above the last trough, then a bull market signal has been given. Also, when a peak is below the last preceding peak and the subsequent trough is below the last preceding trough, a bear market signal has been presented.

Many Dow theorists still believe that the action of the Dow Jones Rail Average must confirm the action of the Dow Jones Industrial Average before a true bull or bear market signal has been posted. Others believe that the use of the rail average in this respect has lost much of its validity.

Some critics of the theory point to a period such as 1946-1949 or January, 1956, to mid-1957, when the trend was horizontal, to prove that those following the Dow theory, being purposely late, entered the market just before it was to take a major downtrend and exited just before there was a major uptrend. Another valid criticism is that many Dow theorists frequently disagree in identifying the secondary peaks and troughs to be used as signals. They even disagree as to whether the Dow Jones figures can be rounded in determining a signal or whether the figure must be carried to the second decimal point.

While many analysts have written advising the use of the Dow theory, few if any have published their "successful results" from following the theory to prove that their portfolios so managed have outperformed over the long-term investors who have purchased sound values and held for the long term. Until such proof is available, the "claims" of the Dow theorists cannot be accepted. Some investors argue that the Dow theory has many followers, who, by their actions, make the theory work to some extent; but empirical evidence, certainly in recent years, gives little support for those who claim that it has been a successful working theory.

Other Technical Theories. The more publicized of the other technical theories are commented on only briefly in the following paragraphs, largely because of lack of faith in the technical approach to forecasting turning points in bull and bear markets. Their proponents may well state that these theories are not fully interpreted in these brief comments.

Resistance Points. Certain investors argue that, for stocks as a whole or for individual stocks, resistance points can be calculated in the same manner as for the Dow averages, the previous low or high points. If market prices go through these resistance points, it is an indication of a downward or an upward trend. Volume figures are also considered important. If volume is rising in a rising market, this is a bullish indication; but if volume dries up in a rising market, this is an indication that the trend is slowing down or may be reversed. These much-heralded resistance points fell like kingpins in the 1966 and 1969 bear markets. Still, such points as previous bull market highs or lows appear to present some value as resistance points or reference points in later markets, but by no means infallible reference-resistance points. In the case of individual stocks, previous bear market lows and bull market highs have quite frequently proved worthwhile resistance points.

Odd-Lot Index. Another technique used by technical market analysts rests on the study of daily odd-lot statistics. The interpretation of these statistics rests on the "theory of contrary opinion." Odd-lot trading is considered to reflect the investment decisions of small investors. The collective decisions of small investors are usually wrong according to this theory, and investment success may be achieved by consistently acting contrary to the odd-lot figures. Some investors simply argue that the odd-lot figures are useful indicators of popular opinion and that when such opinion becomes "too uniform" one should take an opposite position in the market.

The absolute levels of odd-lot buying and selling are of less significance than the ratio of odd-lot sales to purchases—the *odd-lot index.* The odd-lot index is calculated daily and is plotted against a stock price index such as the DJIA. The analyst looks for differences in the directions of the odd-lot index and the stock price index.

Investors do tend to shift from waves of optimism to waves of pessimism and they generally overdo it at both extremes, but the difficulty is in pinpointing the turning point. An examination of the period from 1960 through 1969 suggests that utilization of the odd-lot technique would have resulted in poor timing results. The odd-lot index and other such approaches are too simple to be really effective. Mechanistic approaches will never replace good judgment on the part of the investor in any aspect of investing.

Volume. If a market is rising on rising volume, many traders consider this a strong plus sign and they apply the same reasoning to individual stocks. Conversely, they argue that declining volume on the downside is a signal that the market, while temporarily declining, is basically sound and that a new uptrend can be expected. However, a downward volume trend is considered negative and an upward volume trend is considered positive.

While there is certainly some merit in this thinking, the fact is that the greatest optimism will bring out the greatest volume at or near market peaks; conversely, the greatest pessimism will generate the greatest volume at or near market lows—a selling climax. This is the great weakness of the theory. The theory is applied both to individual stocks and to the market.

Year-End Tax Selling. There is always some tax selling to establish tax losses for the calendar year. However, relatively large amounts of tax selling occur in years when the market is relatively low in the last quarter.

In years when the market is depressed during the last quarter of the year, it frequently has a significant recovery in the first quarter of the following year as indicated in Table 4-9. Therefore, in years when the market makes its low for the year in the last four months of the year, there has frequently been an opportunity to obtain capital gains by buying in that quarter compared to the first quarter of the following year.

Short Selling. While short selling has been severely restricted under the Securities Exchange Act of 1934, it can still attain material importance. Some traders assume that if the short interest is especially high, the shorts are usually wrong. They also assume that the short interest provides a cushion for a market decline at some point as the shorts cover. In the case of individual stocks, some traders calculate the ratio of stock that is short to one day's normal volume for that stock. If the short interest is equal to two or more days' volume, they consider that the downside risk is significantly reduced—that the shorts will cover any weakness in the stock.

Breadth of the Market. It is certainly true that the more stocks there are participating in a market trend, the more indication there is of a unanimity of opinion. More stocks participating is indicative of an upsurge. Conversely, if the number of stocks participating in a rally, especially the number making new highs, decreases, the rally is considered to be weakening. If fewer and fewer stocks make new lows, the decline may be coming to an end.

Horizontal Channels for Specific Stocks. If a stock moves horizontally for some time, it is said to form a channel and, sooner or later, there should be a breakout from this channel. While it appears, from empirical evidence, that the odds favor such an action on the upside, it is more a question of interesting odds than certainty in predicting whether a stock has actually broken out of its channel from an established base.

MARKET TRENDS FOR INDUSTRIES AND INDIVIDUAL STOCKS

There is a tendency for most stocks to follow the averages of the popular indexes. Individual corporate earnings, however, are still the key factor in the situation. The important question is whether the earnings in an industry or a company are rising as fast as or faster than earnings for

TABLE 4-9

DJIA—Potentials in Loss Years

	Quarterly High—1st Quarter				%		Quarterly High—1st Quarter				%
	Monthly Low		Following Year				Monthly Low		Following Year		
Year	Month	DJIA	Month	DJIA	Increase	Year	Month	DJIA	Month	DJIA	Increase
1971	Nov.	798	Mar.	941	+18						
1966	Oct.	744	Jan.	850	+14	1953	Sept.	256	Feb.	304	+19
1960	Oct.	567	March	674	+22	1946	Oct.	163	Feb.	185	+13
1957	Oct.	420	Oct.	459	+ 9	1937	Nov.	114	Jan.	134	+18

corporations overall or whether they are trending horizontally or in the opposite direction. For example, from the first quarter of 1961 through 1966 overall corporate profits rose at a compounded annual rate of nearly 15% per year. Industries and companies whose rate of growth was noticeably slower, however, performed worse than the averages in the market. Specifically, earnings of electric utilities continued to rise at a compounded rate of 6½%-7½% per year (the long-term trend rate); but as this was noticeably slower than for "all U.S. corporations" or for the DJIA, electric utilities fell out of favor with investors. They continued out of favor in 1966 and 1967 largely because of competing high yields from public utility bonds (6%-7%) and also from the belief that electric utilities have to enter the capital markets frequently for funds and would be penalized by the high cost of capital. After mid-1968 they began to return to favor.

Price Trends of Different Industries

At any point of time the stocks of an industry may be either out of favor or strongly in favor with investors. For industries that are out of favor with investors, the price trend of their stocks will either clearly run counter to the trend of the market if it is rising or at least will show a relatively smaller appreciation, and they will sell at relatively low price-earnings ratios. Conversely, for industries that are strongly in favor with investors at the moment, the stocks will show a greater price appreciation than the average.

For example, in the period from December, 1961, to February, 1966, the DJIA rose 35% from 735 to 995, but the stock price indexes for the following industries actually declined:

Banks	192 to 175		Packaging	48 to 46
Building Materials	245 to 180		Packing	50 to 46
Electric Utilities	100 to 98		Paper	170 to 155
Grocery Chains	300 to 280		Steel and Iron	330 to 290
Installment Financing	230 to 200		Tobacco	200 to 125

In other words, while the market averages rose 35%, stocks in these industries did not participate in the rise but actually declined.

Conversely, the stock price indexes of the following industries did much better than the averages during the period.

Aircraft	160 to 416	Electrical Equipment	300 to 500
Air Freight	90 to 330	Foods	190 to 260
Automobile Equipment	105 to 130	Farm Equipment	180 to 430
Automobiles	80 to 200	Gold Mining	45 to 135
Drugs	350 to 600		

The industries whose stocks rose the most in the bull markets of 1961-1966 were those that showed a marked growth in earnings; conversely, those showing a mediocre or poor earnings record demonstrated the worst market performance. This was also true in the late 1966 through 1968 recovery.

Major industries move in and out of favor with investors and such trends often offer very real capital gains potential for those truly long-term investors who can see beyond temporary difficulties. Such stocks sell at definitely lower price-earnings ratios than the price-earnings ratios of the averages.

Price Trends of Individual Stocks

In general, the price trend of a stock will follow that of other stocks in the same industry. But the quality of earnings, the rate of earnings growth, and the stability of earnings are of paramount importance. The quality stocks in an industry may act relatively better than the other stocks in that industry when the industry is falling out of favor with investors. The stock of companies whose earnings are growing most rapidly and that also demonstrate recession-resistance characteristics (continued growth in a recession) will be most attractive to investors and will post the best record in the market. Conversely, those stocks whose earnings growth is slow or is nil, whose earnings are declining, or whose earnings record is cyclical will generally post the poorest market performance.

The most important factor in the price of a stock is the anticipation of future profits. This anticipation is strongly influenced by the current trend and the past record, especially the record of the recent past.

The factors listed below are always mentioned as influencing the price action of a stock, but they are generally the result of investor thinking in regard to prospective earnings over the next year or two.

1. *Market sponsorship.* When institutional investors (such as mutual funds and pension funds), major brokerage firms, and national advisory services are recommending the purchase or the sale of a stock, market action reflects this advice. Recommended sales have a negative effect.

2. *Financial public relations.* Financial public relations help to bring to the attention of investors favorable developments for a company.

3. *Wide investor stamp of quality.* A long, satisfactory record that results in a company's joining the "blue chip" class builds strong investor confidence and causes stocks to act better than otherwise would be the case if industry problems develop. This is also true of "little blue chips."

4. *Accumulation or disposal of large blocks of stock.* Such action, especially by institutional investors or by certain individuals or groups, will strongly affect stock market action.

5. *Fast growth in earnings.* Fast growth in earnings quarter by quarter with relatively small capitalization and a relatively small floating supply of stocks were what many investors were seeking in the 1967-1969 stock market. This was especially true of the "performance" mutual funds.

BENEFITING FROM MAJOR MARKET SWINGS

In view of the historical behavior of stock markets which has been described heretofore, the wise investor would do well to look into the various means by which he could, in the long run, turn the tides of the stock market in his favor. The rest of this chapter deals with several ways to profit from the major market swings or to reduce if not avoid the possible losses that may result therefrom.

Dollar-Cost Averaging

Dollar-cost averaging is a method of accumulating a capital fund. Today, it is common practice by many individuals, mutual funds, insurance companies, and trustees for pension funds, profit-sharing funds, and labor union funds to purchase regularly on a dollar-cost-averaging basis securities that represent sound value as long-term holdings. A dollar-cost-averaging program is based on the premise that a rather steady flow of funds will be available each year for regular periodic investment. The investor selects the stocks he will include in his portfolio and then buys equal dollar amounts of stock at equal time intervals, regardless of the level of the market. The stock selection problem, however, is not avoided by a dollar-averaging plan, except in mutual funds.

It has been stated that the price paid (obtaining a sound value per dollar invested) is the most important element in an investment decision. Dollar-cost averaging is a method of purchasing securities at reasonable prices *on the average.* Even if the program is initiated near the top of a bull market as in 1927, 1928, and 1929, costs will be averaged down in subsequent years as in the 1930s. The investor can be reasonably certain that his program will work out satisfactorily over a period of time. The investor must be able to continue the plan to a successful conclusion. He should be sure that he will not be forced to liquidate his holdings when the stock market is depressed, but rather that he will be able to continue to accumulate stocks at the lower prices then available.

Inasmuch as the investor over any reasonably long period of time will purchase shares at different times at different prices, there will always be a variation between the average price per share and the average cost per share of shares purchased under a dollar-cost averaging plan. The *average price* is calculated by totaling the market price per share paid for each transaction and dividing by the number of transactions. The *average cost* is calculated by totaling the amounts invested and dividing by the number of shares owned. *The average cost will always be the lower of the two figures* because over the years more than half the number of shares will be purchased at less than the average price. This assumes that a stock will trend in cycles and not merely continue a decline indefinitely with no noticeable recovery.

Examples of Dollar-Cost Averaging. Assume that an investor actually initiated dollar-cost averaging when the Dow Jones Industrial Average was historically high. Assume also that he purchased regularly every three months through a subsequent decline and through a recovery until the market recovered 20% from its bottom. The market might still be 30% below the average of all the prices that he had paid; but the market value of his portfolio would be about equal to the total cost of all shares purchased. As the market declined, the investor would receive *more shares for the same amount of dollars*. This accounts for the satisfactory result. Simple arithmetic shows that $100 would buy only 4 shares at $25 per share but would buy 10 shares at $10 per share or 20 shares at $5 per share. Over the period of investment, more than half the number of shares would be purchased at less than the average of all prices paid.

The principles and the advantages of dollar-cost averaging are developed in Table 4-10. It is assumed that an individual invests $1,000 annually in the DJIA, beginning with 1925 and ending with 1966. About the same results would have been obtained with a well-diversified mutual fund. The example selected the worst possible time for beginning a dollar-cost averaging program (1925), purchasing as the market rose to a historic peak during the next four years only to be followed by the Great Depression. Certain facts are evident from this table:

1. In the 7th through 11th years, the market value would have been below cost; in the 12th year, it would again have been above cost.
2. In the 14th, 16th, 17th, and 18th years the market value would again have been below cost. This did not happen again in the entire 42 years of the program.

TABLE 4-10

Dollar-Cost Averaging with the Dow Jones Industrial Average

Year	DJIA	Amount Invested	Shares Purchased	Cumulative Shares	Cumulative Cost	Market Value
1925	137	$1,000	7.30	7.30	$ 1,000	$ 1,000
1926	151	1,000	6.62	13.92	2,000	2,102
1927	178	1,000	5.62	19.54	3,000	3,478
1928	246	1,000	4.07	23.61	4,000	5,808
1929	290*	1,000	3.45	27.06	5,000	7,847
1930	226	1,000	4.42	31.48	6,000	7,114
1931	134	1,000	7.46	38.94	7,000	D 5,218
1932	65	1,000	15.38	54.32	8,000	D 3,531
1933	79	1,000	12.66	66.98	9,000	D 5,291
1934	98	1,000	10.20	77.18	10,000	D 7,564
1935	123	1,000	8.13	85.31	11,000	D10,493
1936	164	1,000	6.10	91.41	12,000	14,991
1937	154	1,000	6.49	97.90	13,000	15,077
1938	129	1,000	7.75	105.65	14,000	D13,629
1939	139	1,000	7.19	112.84	15,000	15,685
1940	132	1,000	7.58	120.42	16,000	D15,895
1941	120	1,000	8.33	128.75	17,000	D15,454
1942	106	1,000	9.43	138.18	18,000	D14,647
1943	133	1,000	7.52	145.70	19,000	19,378
1944	143	1,000	6.99	152.69	20,000	21,835
1945	174	1,000	5.75	158.44	21,000	27,569
1946	188	1,000	5.32	163.76	22,000	30,787
1947	175	1,000	5.71	169.47	23,000	29,657
1948	179	1,000	5.59	175.06	24,000	31,336
1949	181	1,000	5.52	180.58	25,000	32,685
1950	216	1,000	4.63	185.21	26,000	40,005
1951	258	$1,000	3.88	189.09	$27,000	$48,785
1952	274	1,000	3.65	192.74	28,000	52,811
1953	275	1,000	3.64	196.38	29,000	54,005
1954	342*	1,000	2.92	199.30	30,000	68,161
1955	438	1,000	2.28	201.58	31,000	88,292
1956	492	1,000	2.03	203.61	32,000	100,176
1957	470	1,000	2.13	205.74	33,000	96,698
1958	510	1,000	1.96	207.70	34,000	109,927
1959	627	1,000	1.59	209.29	35,000	131,225
1960	626	1,000	1.60	210.89	36,000	132,017
1961	673	1,000	1.49	212.38	37,000	142,932
1962	631	1,000	1.58	213.96	38,000	135,009
1963	707	1,000	1.41	215.37	39,000	152,267
1964	829	1,000	1.21	216.58	40,000	179,545
1965	905	1,000	1.10	217.68	41,000	197,000
1966	870	1,000	1.15	218.83	42,000	190,038
1967	865	1,000	1.16	219.99	43,000	190,291
1968	905	1,000	1.10	221.09	44,000	200,086
1969	870	1,000	1.15	222.24	45,000	193,349
1970	737	1,000	1.36	223.60	46,000	164,793
1971	874	1,000	1.14	224.74	47,000	196,423
1972—						
Jan., 1973	968	1,000	1.03	225.77	48,000	218,545
Jan. 1973—						
High	1047			225.77	48,000	236,381
Peak						
1966	995			218.83	42,000	217,735

Note: The above figures assume that an individual invested $1,000 per year from 1925 to 1966 (a total of $42,000) at the arithmetic mean average of prices for the DJIA for each year. At the peak of the DJIA in 1966, the market value of the portfolio would have been $217,735.

* 1953 is the year the DJIA finally reached and surpassed the 1929 peak.   D—Decrease.

3. The DJIA did not return to its 1929 peak until 1954, but from 1943 on the market value of the portfolio would always have exceeded cost. In 1954, the accumulated cost was $30,000 but the market value was $68,161.
4. In 1966, the accumulated cost of the portfolio was $42,000, but the market value was $190,038 at the mean for the year and $217,735 at the peak for the year.

Summary of Dollar-Cost Averaging. In summary, a dollar-cost averaging program has the following advantages:

1. It substitutes a mechanical objective plan for a subjective determination of when to buy. Also, the plan may be modified to provide for taking profits when the market price of the stock held shows a predetermined capital gain above average cost. Most investors do poorly on timing their transactions objectively.
2. It does not matter at what point in the market the plan is initiated as long as it is followed consistently as a long-range plan of capital accumulation. Admittedly, success would take longer if the plan were begun just before a rapid rise in stock prices since average cost would rise rapidly and any decline in stock prices occurring later when the fund is larger would reduce average costs less rapidly.
3. At times the market value of the portfolio may decline below its cost; but the longer the plan is followed, the less likely this will happen. The investor with the true long-range viewpoint will ignore, as temporary, declines below cost unless he logically believes the selections of stocks were poor.

Formula Timing [7]

Formula timing is a method of handling a capital fund already accumulated. It provides a mechanical method for automatically selling stocks as the market rises beyond a predetermined level and for automatically purchasing stocks when the market declines below a certain level. It recognizes that the market will fluctuate and it eliminates the emotional factor. It takes advantage of market fluctuations by selling in rising markets and purchasing in falling markets.

Formula timing not only assumes that the market will fluctuate, but it also makes the assumption that the future channels in which the market will fluctuate can be predicted, giving acknowledgment to the long, secular uptrend. This channel must be projected. If the market rises above the channel or falls below the channel and stays there, then the operation of most formula timing plans will be unsatisfactory.

---

[7] C. Sidney Cottle and W. Tate Whitman, *Investment Timing—The Formula Plan Approach* (New York: McGraw-Hill Book Company, 1953); and Lucile Tomlinson, *Practical Formulas for Successful Investing* (New York: Wilfred Funk, Inc., 1953).

Formula timing plans enjoyed their greatest vogue from 1944-1954, although statistics on just how many institutional investors actually used them are impossible to secure. In the period 1945-1949 inclusive, the market moved rather horizontally, in a channel of about 160 to 200, and numerous professionals assumed that by following a formula plan they could benefit by the major fluctuations. However, as the market moved higher and higher in the 1950s it rose above and stayed above most channels that had been projected for formula timing. By 1954, the DJIA had risen above its 1929 peak and never again fell below this peak. As a result, users of such formulas became more and more disillusioned with plans that had forced them out of the market and kept them out. Even for those plans that permitted retention of some common stocks, the recognition that stocks had been sold at what proved to be low levels caused the discontinuance of the use of formulas. It is doubtful if any, or certainly more than a few, formula timing plans were in operation by the late 1960s.

The two major types of formula timing plans are discussed briefly in the following paragraphs. There are many other variations.

Constant Ratio Plan. The constant ratio plan is one of the simplest of the formula plans. The portfolio is divided into an aggressive side represented by common stocks and a defensive side represented by high-grade bonds. For example, a total portfolio of $40,000 might be held half in common stocks and half in high-grade bonds. The aim of the plan is to keep the aggressive side at $20,000. If stock prices fall, bonds will be sold and sufficient stock will be purchased to keep the total stock value at $20,000. If stock prices rise, stocks will be sold and bonds will be purchased to keep the total stock value at $20,000. The user of such a plan must know when to adjust his portfolio periodically or when specified percentage levels of advance or decline have been exceeded in terms of market action.

Variable Ratio Plan. A lower and lower proportion of stocks relative to bonds will be held as the market rises and a larger and larger proportion will be held as the market declines. The proportion of stocks may, for example, be allowed to fluctuate between 30% and 70%, with 50% of the funds invested in stocks in the middle of the projected channel. Any other range suitable for the individual account may be adopted.

Capital Gains and Losses

Income tax benefits can often be gained from balancing capital gains against capital losses. It is common practice for investors near the end of each year to examine their capital gains and losses for the year to date and then to look over their portfolios to see if sales of additional stock at either a profit or a loss would be beneficial in reducing income taxes.

Capital Assets. Capital gains and losses (gains or losses on the sale of capital assets such as securities) are accorded separate treatment from other types of income. For tax purposes, capital assets are defined as any property held by the taxpayer except:

1. Stock in trade or other property properly included in inventory; for example, merchandise.
2. Property held primarily for sale to customers in the ordinary course of business; for example, stocks and bonds of a dealer in securities.
3. Federal, state, and municipal obligations issued on or after March 1, 1941, on a discount basis and payable without interest at a fixed maturity not exceeding one year from date of issue.
4. Real and/or depreciable property used in a trade or business. But if the net effect of all transactions in real and depreciable business property held over 6 months is a gain, then such property falls into the category of capital assets.

Long-Term and Short-Term Gains and Losses. The income tax law divides capital gains and losses into long-term and short-term transactions according to the holding period of the securities sold or exchanged. Gains or losses incurred in the sale of securities held for 6 months or less are classed as short-term, while those held for over 6 months are classed as long-term. While *all* capital gains and losses, whether short-term or long-term, are recognized 100%, only 50% of net long-term capital gains are taken into account for income tax purposes as indicated in the problems below. The terms *net* short-term and *net* long-term capital gains or losses refer to the *excess* of either gains over losses or losses over gains, taking into account 100% of gains and losses of each *class*. Long-term gains are first matched against long-term losses and short-term gains against short-term losses.

Tax Treatment of Capital Gains and Losses. The tax treatment of capital gains and losses depends on whether there are net capital gains or net capital losses and whether these gains or losses are short-term or long-term.

Capital Gains Exceeding Losses. If capital gains exceed losses, the tax treatment depends on whether these gains are *net* short-term gains or *net* long-term gains.

(a) If the *net* short-term gain exceeds the *net* long-term loss, the *excess* is added to ordinary income and therefore is taxed as ordinary income.

Assume a $6,000 net short-term gain and a $3,000 net long-term loss.

100% of *net* short-term gain $6,000
100% of *net* long-term loss 3,000

Net short-term capital gain $3,000

This $3,000 short-term capital gain would be added to ordinary income.

(b) If the *net* long-term gain exceeds the *net* short-term loss, 50 percent of the *excess* is added to ordinary income or an alternative tax treatment is used.

Assume a $6,000 net long-term gain and a $3,000 net short-term loss.

100% of *net* long-term gain $6,000
100% of *net* short-term loss 3,000

Difference $3,000
50% of difference 1,500

Net long-term capital gain taxable at regular normal and surtax rates $1,500

The alternative tax method can be used if there is an excess of long-term gains over either long-term losses or short-term losses or if there is a long-term gain only. Under this method the net long-term gain is omitted from taxable income and a partial tax is computed on the reduced taxable income. A capital gains tax of 25% of the first $50,000 of gain and 50% of the taxpayer's top bracket rate on the excess above $50,000 is added to the partial tax to determine the total tax due for the year 1972 and thereafter. The alternative tax method should be used at a $32,000 taxable income level for an unmarried individual or a married person filing separately; $38,000 income level for a head of household; and $44,000 for married persons filing jointly and for a surviving spouse.

Capital Gains Only. If there are both *net* short-term gains and *net* long-term gains, the net short-term gains are taxed as ordinary income but only 50% of the net long-terms gains are taken into account (or the alternative method is used where applicable).

Net Capital Losses. If there is a *net* capital loss, either short-term or long-term, it is fully deductible against a *net* capital gain in its class, short-term or long-term. If all capital losses exceed all capital gains, the net loss is deductible as follows:

1. The excess of capital losses over capital gains may be deducted from ordinary income up to the extent of $1,000 in the year in which the loss is realized.

2. Any remaining unused net loss above this $1,000 may be carried forward and applied in succeeding years as a deduction from capital gains in those years and as a deduction from ordinary income up to the extent of $1,000 in each year for an unlimited number of years.

QUESTIONS

1. (a) Common stock prices have fluctuated widely in the past and can be expected to continue to do so in the future. Discuss the major underlying reasons for variations in stock prices.
   (b) Discuss liquidity needs of investors in terms of long-term investment goals.

2. (a) Contrast the stock indexes published by Dow Jones & Co. with those published by Standard & Poor's Corporation and by the New York Stock Exchange.
   (b) Are movements of the Dow Jones indexes and those of the Standard & Poor's indexes correlated?
   (c) Which indexes do you feel are preferable? Why?

3. (a) Distinguish between the four basic types of stock market trends.
   (b) Which are of most significance to the investor? Why?

4. (a) What have been the compounded annual growth rates of stock prices, earnings, and dividends and of GNP:
   (1) From 1900 to the present?
   (2) From 1961 to the present?
   (b) Do you feel that the growth rate in stock prices from 1961 to the present serves as a sound basis for predicting future growth in stock prices? Why or why not?

5. It has been said that investment management implicitly involves business and economic forecasting. Why?

6. In January, 1969, common stock yields were less than half of bond yields. How can this be justified on the basis of relative risk factors?

7. Are technical market analysis and security analysis contradictory? Can both be used simultaneously? Discuss.

8. (a) What is the theory of contrary opinion?
   (b) How does this theory relate to the odd-lot theory?

9. (a) Is dollar-cost averaging a formula plan? Why or why not?
   (b) Why does one anticipate that average cost per share will be lower than average market price per share for a portfolio constructed through the use of the dollar-cost averaging technique?

10. (a) What is meant by mechanical timing? Give some illustrations and define the methods.
    (b) What limitations are inherent in formula planning? Distinguish between the various formula plans in answering this question.

11. (a) Assume a popular political figure is assassinated during a prolonged bear market. Would past history suggest that this would likely affect stock prices? Why or why not?
    (b) If the stock market seemed hardly to react to such startling bad news, what implications might this suggest to investors?

WORK-STUDY PROBLEMS

1. (a) Discuss the trend of price-earnings ratios during the late 1950s and up to early 1962 as compared with the trend in the late 1920s.
   (b) In what way did general investment psychology in the late 1950s and early 1960s resemble that of the late 1920s?
   (c) What has happened to price-earnings ratios since 1966?
   (d) Does investment psychology currently resemble that of the 1920s?

2. From *The Wall Street Journal* and/or other sources, chart the Dow Jones average of 30 industrial stocks and the Dow Jones average of 20 railroads on a monthly basis for the past ten years. Then determine on the basis of the Dow theory:
   (a) If the long-term trend is upward or downward.
   (b) If the railroad average seems to confirm the trend noted in (a).
   (c) If resistance points have been violated.
   (d) According to the Dow theory, are we currently in a bull or bear market? Explain.

SUGGESTED READINGS

Cootner, Paul H. (ed.). *The Random Character of Stock Market Prices.* Cambridge, Mass.: MIT Press, 1964. (This is *must* reading.)

Cottle, C. Sidney, and W. Tate Whitman. *Investment Timing—The Formula Plan Approach.* New York: McGraw-Hill Book Company, 1953.

Edwards, R. D., and John Magee, Jr. *Technical Analysis of Stock Trends,* 5th ed. Springfield, Mass.: J. Magee, Inc., 1968.

Eiteman, D. K, C. A. Dice, and W. J. Eiteman. *The Stock Market,* 4th ed. New York: McGraw-Hill Book Company, 1966. Chapter 5.

Financial Analysts Journal. Articles as listed below.
   Random walk theories of stock prices:
      Jensen, Michael C. "Random Walks (A Comment)." (Nov.-Dec., 1967), pp. 77-86.
      Kewley, Thomas J., and Richard A. Stevenson. "The Odd-Lot Theory for Individual Stocks: A Reply." (Jan.-Feb., 1969), pp. 99-104.
      Levy, Robert A. "Random Walks: Reality or Myth." (Nov.-Dec., 1967), pp. 69-76.
      Levy, Robert A. "Random Walks: Reality or Myth (Reply)." (Jan.-Feb., 1968), pp. 129-132.
      Molodovsky, Nicholas. "Stock Values and Stock Prices." (Nov.-Dec., 1968), pp. 134-148.
      Renshaw, Edward F. "The Random Walk Hypothesis, Performance Management, and Portfolio Theory." (Mar.-Apr., 1968), pp. 114-119.
      Smith, Randall D. "Short Interest and Stock Market Prices." (Nov.-Dec., 1968), pp. 151-154.

Van Horne, J. C. and George G. C. Parker. "An Empirical Test." (Nov.-Dec., 1967), pp. 87-94.

Wallich, Henry. "What Does the Random Walk Hypothesis Mean to Security Analysts?" (Mar.-Apr., 1968), pp. 159-162.

Fisher, Lawrence, and James H. Lorie. "Rates of Return on Investments in Common Stock: The Year-by-Year Record, 1926-65." *Journal of Business,* Vol. XLI, No. 3 (July, 1968).

——————. "Some Studies of Variability of Returns on Investments in Common Stocks." *Journal of Business,* Vol. XLIII, No. 2 (April, 1970).

Freund, W. C. "Will Demand for Stocks Exceed Supply?" *Financial Analysts Journal* (July-August, 1971), pp. 37-44.

Jensen, Michael C., and George A. Bennington. "Random Walks and Technical Theories: Some Additional Evidence." *The Journal of Finance,* Vol. XXV, No. 2 (May, 1970).

Lorie, James H., and Mary T. Hamilton. "Stock Market Indexes," in *Modern Developments in Investment Management,* edited by Lorie and Brealey. New York: Praeger Publishers, 1972.

Malkiel, B. G., and R. Quandt. *Strategies and Rational Decisions in the Securities Option Market.* Cambridge, Mass.: The M.I.T. Press, 1969.

Morgenstern, Oscar, and Clive W. J. Granger. *The Predictability of Stock Market Prices.* Lexington, Mass.: D. C. Heath & Company, 1970.

Rolo, Charles J., and George J. Nelson (eds.). *The Anatomy of Wall Street.* Philadelphia: J. B. Lippincott Co., 1968. Chapters 12 and 13.

Schultz, Harry D., and Samson Coslow. *A Theory of Wall Street Wisdom.* Palisades Park, N. J.: Investors Press, Inc., 1966.

Security Prices, Graduate School of Business of the University of Chicago. A supplement to *The Journal of Business.* Articles by J. H. Lorie, L. Fisher, B. F. King, E. F. Fama and M. E. Blume, and B. Mandelbrot.

Shiskin, Julius. "Signals of Recession and Recovery," Occasional Paper No. 77. New York, N. Y.: National Bureau of Economic Research, 1961.

——————. "Systematic Aspects of Stock Price Fluctuations," in *Modern Developments in Investment Management,* edited by Lorie and Brealey. New York: Praeger Publishers, 1972.

Smidt, Seymour. "A New Look at the Random Walk Hypothesis." *Journal of Financial and Quantitative Analysis,* September, 1968.

Smith, Adam (Goodman, G. J. W.). *The Money Game.* New York: Random House, 1967.

Sprinkel, Beryl W. *Money and Stock Prices.* Homewood, Ill.: Richard D. Irwin, Inc., 1964.

Tomlinson, Lucile. *Practical Formulas for Successful Investing.* New York: Wilfred Funk, Inc., 1953.

Zweig, Martin E. "An Investor Expectations Stock Price Predictive Model Using Closed-End Fund Premiums." *The Journal of Finance* (March, 1973), pp. 67-78.

CORPORATE
SECURITIES
AND
FINANCIAL
POLICIES

Common Stocks and
Preferred Stocks

A prospective investor in corporate securities should have a basic knowledge of the corporate form of business organization and the types of securities offered by a corporation, including the rights and privileges attached thereto. Corporate securities are divided into two major classes: stocks and bonds. Stocks, both common and preferred, are the subject of this chapter. Bonds, which include debt instruments such as private placement notes and equipment obligations, are the subject of Chapter 6.

CORPORATIONS

The advantages of the corporate form of business organization are so important that, one by one, most major fields of economic activity have come under the domination of corporations. In the United States today, about 80% of gross receipts and about 67% of net profits of business are generated by corporations, yet there are only about 1.5 million corporations while there are about 10 million single proprietorships and about 1 million partnerships. Furthermore, the 500 largest industrial corporations (.037% of the total number) account for about 45% of all corporate profits after taxes.

The total of private corporate securities at market value in 1971 was over $1 trillion, four fifths of which represented corporate stocks and approximately $681 billion of which represented the market value of stocks listed on the New York Stock Exchange. This amount is about four times the $317 billion of United States Government *marketable* securities, over one third of which are held by United States Government agencies and trust funds, Federal Reserve banks, and state and local government funds. State and local government issues totaled $166 billion at the end of 1971.

In the case of individuals, 84% of their security holdings at market value consist of corporate securities. In the case of private pension funds, 67% of their assets, at market value, consist of corporate securities. In the case of life insurance companies, approximately 50% of their assets are invested in securities, of which corporates represent 46.5% of assets.

Legal Restrictions on a Corporation

The traditional definition of a corporation dates to the Dartmouth College case of 1819.[1] This Supreme Court decision, read by Chief Justice Marshall, described the corporation as an artificial entity, created, empowered, and restricted by charter. The charter is, in effect, a contract between the state, the corporation, and the stockholders. Today charters are granted almost automatically when legal requirements are met.

Corporate restrictions vary among states, but all state statutes govern such matters as stockholders' rights, dividends, and the right of the directors to create corporate debt. Small companies usually incorporate in the state in which they operate, but large companies may choose states that are more liberal in the powers and flexibility granted to directors.

There are special incorporation statutes for special classes of corporations such as public utilities, banks, and insurance companies. In the case of federal charters for national banks and state charters for public utilities, banks, and insurance companies, statutes usually specify in detail the requirements for the charter. In these cases, granting of a charter must have the approval of the state commissions concerned, such as the public utility commission, insurance commission, banking commission, or their equivalent.

---

[1] "A corporation is an artificial being, invisible, intangible and existing only in contemplation of law. Being the mere creation of law, it possesses only those properties, which the character of its creation confers upon it, either expressly or as incidental to its very existence. These are such as are supposed best calculated to effect the object for which it was created. Among the most important are immortality, and if the expression may be allowed, individuality; properties by which a perpetual succession of many persons are considered as the same, and may act as a single individual. They enable a corporation to manage its own affairs and to hold property without the perplexing intricacies, the hazardous and endless necessity of perpetual conveyance for the purpose of transmitting it from hand to hand. It is chiefly for the purpose of clothing bodies of men, in succession, with these qualities and capabilities, that corporations were invented, and are in use. By these means, a perpetual succession of individuals are capable of acting for the promotion of the particular object, like an immortal being." *Trustees of Dartmouth College* v. *Woodward*, 4 Wheat (U.S.) 518, 643, and 659 (1819).

Because the powers of the corporation are limited by the charter, there is a tendency to have the articles written in a form to convey broad powers. Any activities outside the express and implied powers are *ultra vires* and can result in legal action. At the time of incorporation, the charter is filed with the Secretary of State in the state in which the business is incorporated.

It sometimes becomes necessary for the directors to amend the articles of incorporation, for instance to increase the number of authorized shares or to effect a merger. However, stockholders must vote to approve any amendments. In most states, the preferred stockholder, who usually has no vote, must approve any changes in the charter that affect his rights. Also, many state statutes require that compensation be made available to dissenting stockholders in the case of a merger, often in the form of payment to them of the appraised value of their shares.

Nature of Corporate Stock

The ownership of a corporation is represented by shares of stock. There may be only one class of stock (common stock) or there may be additional classes of stock with various preferences (preferred stock). Each share of stock represents a fractional ownership in the total stock of the corporation, and each share has the same rights and limitations as every other share of the same class. A stock certificate is issued to each owner as evidence of the number of shares of each class of stock he owns.

Issuance and Transfer of Stock

The classes of stock and the total number of shares of each class authorized to be issued by a corporation are stated in the original or amended corporate charter as approved by stockholders. The directors then provide for its sale and issuance. Once issuance has been approved, the stock certificate is completed and an entry is made in the stock ledger of the corporation. A stock certificate issued by a corporation bears the stockholder's name, his address, and the number of shares he owns. This information is recorded in the stockholders record book kept by the corporation; or in the case of large corporations, by the transfer department of a bank acting as transfer agent for the corporation, and is constantly maintained up to date. The stock certificate is generally engraved or lithographed and on its face shows the name of the corporation, the class of stock, the state of incorporation, and certain basic information about the stock and the corporation. The signatures of company officers and the transfer agent and registrar also appear, as does the owner's name.

If a stockholder wishes to sell stock that is registered in his name, he assigns it to the purchaser by endorsing his name in the space provided on the back of the stock certificate. Instead of this endorsement, he may attach to the certificate a signed stock power of attorney or assignment. If a stockholder wishes to maintain the ownership of stock but uses it as collateral for a loan, he can attach a stock power of attorney to the certificate, which will then be accepted as collateral. If a stockholder wishes to sell and assign only a part of the holdings represented by his certificate, he will indicate this on his assignment. Two new certificates will then be issued, one to the former owner and one to the new owner.

The actual transfer work is usually accomplished by a trust company. The stock certificate is sent to the transfer agent. If the stock is listed on the New York Stock Exchange, an independent transfer agent and also an independent registrar are required. The registrar checks to make certain that no more than the authorized stock is issued. Because the transfer agent cannot recognize the authority of the stockholder's signature, it is usually required that the signature be guaranteed by a securities dealer, bank, or trust company. Then the certificate is received by the transfer agent, who will cancel the old certificate, revise the records to show the correct owner, and issue the new certificate.

When stock is purchased on margin, the stock is generally kept in the broker's name. This is called a *street certificate*. When the stockholder sells such stock, the broker endorses it and sends it for transfer.

If a stock certificate is lost or stolen, the corporation will issue a new certificate but the stockholder must post a surety bond. This is done to protect the corporation in case the "lost or stolen" certificate is presented to it by a person who can prove that he is a true and rightful owner.

Stockholders of corporations under both common law and state statutes have the right to a list of all stockholders so that they may communicate with them. Originally this meant that they had the right to inspect the actual stockholders record book, but now it is generally interpreted as a right to be furnished (at their own expense) with the information contained in the stockholders ledger.

Fundamental Difference Between Stockholders and Bondholders

Stockholders are owners of a corporation; bondholders are creditors of a corporation. Creditors such as bondholders can sue if their claims for interest and principal are not met when due. But stockholders, common or preferred, are entitled to dividends only when dividends are declared by the corporation's board of directors. Preferred stock is a limited-return security, and the preferred stockholder occupies a strictly delineated ownership position. Common stockholders are the *residual claimants* entitled to the ownership of what is left after all expenses and all claims of creditors are met as well as the preferences of preferred stockholders. The more profitable the corporation's activities, the more valuable is the common stockholder's equity because of his residual position.

Volume of Corporate Debt Issues and Stock Issues

Except during the great stock market boom of the late 1920s, the annual dollar value of new corporate debt issues has always greatly exceeded the dollar value of stock issues. It should be noted that all noncorporate security issues are debt issues. Table 5-1 shows new security offerings for cash in 1964-1971, Table 5-2 shows new convertible bonds offered for cash in 1956-1971, and Table 5-3 shows changes in corporate securities outstanding from 1940-1971.

It can be seen from Table 5-3 that corporate debt issues, both gross and net after retirement, exceed stock issues by a wide margin and that retirements of securities each year are substantial for both debt and equity issues. Some writers, such as Sidney Homer of Salomon Brothers, suggest that the marked increase in equity issues after 1967 may suggest different supply-demand relationships for corporate stocks in the 1970s that could tend to curb potential bull markets.

TABLE 5-1

New Security Offerings for Cash (Billions of Dollars)

	1964	1967	1968	1969	1970	1971
All offerings	37.2	68.5	65.6	52.7	88.6	105.2
Noncorporate—all civil debt issues	23.2	43.7	43.6	26.0	49.7	60.1
Corporate	14.0	24.8	22.0	26.7	38.9	45.1
Total corporate	14.0	24.8	22.0	26.7	38.9	45.1
Bonds (including private placements and equipment obligations)	10.9	22.0	17.4	18.3	30.3	32.1
Publicly offered	3.6	15.0	10.7	12.7	25.4	24.8
Privately placed	7.2	7.0	6.7	5.6	4.9	7.4
Preferred stock	.4	.9	.6	.7	1.4	3.7
Common stock (excluding investment companies) ...	2.0	2.0	3.9	7.7	7.2	9.3

Source: Securities and Exchange Commission, *Statistical Bulletins.*

TABLE 5-2

New Convertible Bonds Offered for Cash (Billions of Dollars)

1956	0.93	1960	0.46	1964	0.43	1968	3.28
1957	1.06	1961	0.71	1965	1.26	1969	4.04
1958	1.15	1962	0.45	1966	1.87	1970	2.66
1959	0.63	1963	0.36	1967	4.48	1971	3.61

Source: Securities and Exchange Commission, *Statistical Bulletins.*

TABLE 5-3

Changes in Corporate Securities Outstanding—Cash Transactions Only
(Billions of Dollars)

Year	All Types			Bonds and Notes			Stocks		
	New Issues	Retirements	Net Change	New Issues	Retirements	Net Change	New Issues	Retirements	Net Change
1940	2.8	3.0	— .3	2.5	2.8	— .3	.3	.2	+ .1
1945	6.1	6.7	— .6	4.9	5.9	— 1.0	1.2	.8	+ .5
1950	6.7	3.2	+ 3.5	4.8	2.8	+ 2.0	1.9	.4	+ 1.5
1955	11.1	5.1	+ 6.1	7.6	3.4	+ 4.2	3.6	1.7	+ 1.9
1960	10.8	4.1	+ 6.7	8.1	3.1	+ 5.0	2.7	1.0	+ 1.7
1961	13.6	5.8	+ 7.8	9.2	4.0	+ 5.2	4.5	1.8	+ 2.7
1962	10.9	5.3	+ 5.6	8.6	3.7	+ 4.9	2.3	1.6	+ .7
1963	12.5	7.2	+ 5.3	10.6	5.0	+ 5.6	1.9	2.2	— .2
1964	14.5	6.4	+ 8.1	10.7	4.1	+ 6.6	3.7	2.3	+ 1.4
1965	16.0	7.6	+ 8.4	12.7	4.6	+ 8.1	3.2	3.0	+ .2
1966	19.8	7.5	+12.3	15.6	4.5	+11.1	4.2	3.0	+ 1.2
1967	26.0	7.7	+18.2	21.3	5.3	+16.0	4.7	2.4	+ 2.3
1968	25.4	12.4	+13.1	19.4	5.4	+14.0	6.1	7.0	— 0.9
1969	28.8	10.8	+18.0	19.5	5.8	+13.8	9.3	5.0	+ 4.3
1970	38.7	9.1	+29.6	29.5	6.7	+22.8	9.2	2.4	+ 6.8
1971	46.7	9.5	+37.2	31.9	8.2	+23.7	14.8	1.3	+13.5

Source: Securities and Exchange Commission, *Statistical Bulletins.*

COMMON STOCKS

Common stock is an equity security that represents residual ownership in a corporation. It carries the greatest risks and ordinarily it shares in profits to the greatest extent. Usually common stock holds the basic voting contract to elect directors and to vote on amendments to the corporate charter.

Dividends

The discussion of dividends here will deal only with technicalities; financial policies regarding dividends will be discussed in Chapter 7. Dividends are usually disbursed in cash, but frequently corporations pay dividends in stock and occasionally in property.

Cash Dividends. Cash dividends are declared by the board of directors to be paid by check on a certain future date to stockholders of record as of a certain date, the record date being between the declaration date and the payment date.[2] For example, a corporation may declare a dividend on November 15 payable on December 15 to stockholders of record on December 1.

The great majority of corporations declare and pay cash dividends quarterly, although a few pay dividends monthly, semiannually, or even annually. The ordinary cash dividend is paid out of earnings and is fully taxable to the recipient except when the stockholder is notified that it is partly or totally a return of capital.

Stock Dividends. Stock dividends are payments to stockholders in shares of stock and are usually designated, for example, as a 2%, 5%, 10%, 20%, or 100% stock dividend. Stock dividends are pro rata dividends. If a 2% stock dividend is declared, a stockholder with 100 shares would receive 2 additional shares; for a 100% stock dividend, a stockholder with 100 shares would receive 100 additional shares. After a stock dividend, the stockholders have more shares, but these shares represent exactly the same equity value in the corporation. The basic balance sheet formula (assets minus liabilities equals total owners' equity or claim on the assets) does not change with stock dividends even though the number of shares outstanding has been increased.

For example, after a corporation with 1,000,000 shares outstanding declares and pays a 100% stock dividend, the corporation will have 2,000,000 shares outstanding representing the identical equity value. If earnings per share for the year are $2 before the 100% stock dividend, the earnings per share after the dividend will be $1 per share. The stockholder has received nothing more of value but now simply has 2 shares representing the same equity value and the same earnings as when he had 1 share.

---

[2] At the present time, larger trust companies with modern accounting machines can take off stockholders lists as of 3:30 p.m. of the date of record. The records are then ready for new stock transfers the next day. If a stock is listed on an exchange, the date for which transactions on the exchange go ex-dividend is set by the exchange. The ex-dividend date precedes the record date sufficiently to permit stock purchased before the ex-dividend date to be recorded in the name of the purchaser and for him to be listed as a recipient of the dividend.

Because the equity value for each stockholder does not change by reason of a stock dividend, the stock dividend is not taxable to the recipient for income tax purposes. The general rule is that any distribution by a corporation of its own stock (including treasury stock) as a stock dividend is tax free unless the distribution of stock is considered in lieu of a distribution of money or other properties or changes the equity position of the recipient. Also, since the stockholder has received nothing more of value than he already possessed, restrictions in bond and note indentures as to the payment of dividends are not usually applicable to stock dividends.

It is true, however, that the market value of the 2 shares in the above example may rise in total above the market value of 1 share. Assume that the old share had a market value of $100 and that, therefore, the value of each share after a 100% stock dividend should be $50. However, because more investors may be willing to purchase a stock in the $50 range, the stock may rise to $60, reflecting a greater demand and better marketability.

Furthermore, as a practical matter, the dividend is often raised after a 100% stock dividend, in this case possibly from $5 on the old shares to $2.60 on the new shares ($5.20 on the basis of the old stock). The market value of the shares will tend to rise, reflecting the higher dividend. Of course, earnings do not change because of the stock dividend, and the cash dividend could just as well have been raised to $5.20 on the old shares.

When a stock dividend is anything less than 100%, it may result in the issuance of rights that entitle the purchaser to fractional shares. For example, if a stock dividend of 2% is declared, the owner of 40 shares would receive $8/10$ of a share of new stock. Corporations will usually provide either for the stockholder to buy an additional fraction (in this case $2/10$ of a share) or for the corporation to sell, at the stockholder's request, the fractional shares.

If the stockholder sells the stock he received as a dividend, he has sold a part of his share in the assets, voting, and earning power of the company. In other words, he has diluted his equity. Unfortunately, this fact is not understood by many investors who believe that a stock dividend is something extra and that its sale does not reduce the stockholder's proportionate equity in the corporation.

From an accounting standpoint, when a stock dividend is declared and paid, the corporation must charge the retained earnings account and credit the capital stock account for an equivalent amount.[3] Under some state laws,

---

[3] The New York Stock Exchange requires, for listed corporations, that the minimum amount a company charges to retained earnings be equivalent to the pro rata market value of the stock dividend and that this be explained in a memorandum to stockholders. For example, if the market value of the shares is $50 and a 10% stock dividend is declared, there should be a charge to the retained earnings account of $5

a corporation may charge the stock dividend to the "capital stock in excess of par or stated value" (capital surplus) account rather than to the "retained earnings" account. Therefore, a corporation in these states could theoretically pay a stock dividend even if it had no current earnings or no amount in the retained earnings account. This is an objectionable practice, for stock dividends should represent a stated amount of recent earnings that have been reinvested in the business so that the added capital can lead to increased future profits.

Table 5-4 shows statistics on the number and the percentage amount of stock dividends declared and paid in recent years.

TABLE 5-4

Stock Dividends and Splits

Year	Less than 25%	25% to 49%	50% to 99%	2-for-1 to 2½-for-1	3-for-1 to 3½-for-1	4-for-1	Over 4-for-1	Total
1970	108	1	11	20	6	—	1	147
1969	111	3	37	101	7	1	1	261
1968	115	10	26	100	11	—	—	262
1967	142	7	17	62	6	—	—	234
1966	148	6	20	105	9	—	—	288
1965	154	9	18	82	2	2	2	269
1964	155	12	15	63	13	—	1	259
1963	168	11	10	38	5	—	—	232
1962	188	4	5	44	11	4	2	258
1961	170	5	8	34	17	2	—	236

Note: Includes common and preferred issues. Data based on effective dates.

Source: *New York Stock Exchange 1970 Fact Book.*

Property Dividends. Property dividends represent a distribution of the assets of the corporation. If these dividends take the form of a liquidating dividend, stockholders must approve the distribution. Property dividends may take one of three forms:

1. Payment in the form of securities of other corporations owned by the distributing company. These securities may represent securities of affiliates or subsidiaries or simply a security investment. One example would be distribution to duPont stockholders of shares in General Motors Corporation. Another example is the distribution by public utility holding

---

per share based on the original number of shares outstanding and a credit to the capital stock account of $5 per share. This ruling tends to protect a corporation that, for example, is earning $4 per share, paying a stock dividend of 10% with a market value of $5, but then charging the retained earnings account with only $4, that is, payment of a stock dividend with a market value in excess of earnings.

companies of shares of subsidiaries of which they were forced to divest themselves under the provision of the Public Utility Holding Company Act of 1935. Such distributions of securities are frequently described as *spin-offs.*

2. Payment in the form of merchandise. Such payments are unusual, but they may be made in products produced and sold by the corporation in lieu of cash dividends.

3. Payment in the form of other securities of the same corporation, such as preferred stock or bonds.

The tax status to the stockholder receiving such a dividend may be complicated. In most cases, the distributing corporation will obtain a tax ruling from federal income tax authorities and will then notify the stockholders of the ruling and the required tax accounting treatment on the stockholder's own records. If the property dividend is clearly a liquidating dividend approved as such by the stockholders, the dividend is considered to be a return of capital and as such is nontaxable. However, such nontaxable dividends representing a return of capital must be shown on the shareowner's own records as a deduction from original cost, thereby establishing a new cost basis for tax purposes.

Stock Splits

When a corporation splits its stock, it gives the stockholders additional shares of stock in proportion to their current holdings. In the case of a 2-for-1 split, the stockholder receives 2 shares in exchange for his 1 old share. Some corporations may simply have him retain his old share and then send him an additional share. A stock split may be set at any ratio, as for example 3-for-2 (3 new shares for each 2 old shares).

In the case of a *stock dividend*, the corporation in its books will *debit* the retained earnings account for the total dollar amount, reducing that account accordingly, and *credit* the capital stock account for the same amount, thus increasing the total dollar amount of the capital stock account. But in the case of a *stock split*, there is no dollar charge—debit or credit—to any account. The total dollar amount of all capital accounts remains unchanged; only the par value or stated value per share is reduced. For example, with a 2-for-1 split of a $100 par stock, the par value of each share is reduced to $50.

In periods of rising stock markets, such as the long-term upward trend from 1949 (DJIA 160) to 1969 (DJIA 995), stock splits occur frequently, usually for the purpose of bringing the market price of a stock down to a price range considered to be attractive to a majority of investors, thus broadening the share ownership of the stock. As in the case with stock dividends, the stockholder has only received additional pieces of paper, with the result that the total number of shares he now owns have the same identical claim to assets and earning power as the old share. But stockholders generally favor stock splits. Part of the reason for this is that, more often than not, directors take the occasion of a stock split to raise the dividend so that the total paid on the new shares plus the old shares is greater than the total that had been paid on the old shares before the split. Of course, the dividend could have been simply raised without splitting the stock. Also, as mentioned in connection with stock dividends, the lower price tends to broaden the market, which may result in greater demand for the company's stock and greater market value for the stockholders.

For tax purposes, a stock split is considered as only a division of the old shares into a greater number of new shares. However, the stockholder must reduce the cost basis of the company stock on his books. For example, if the stockholder has purchased 100 shares at $100 per share and if there is a 2-for-1 stock split, he must reduce the cost basis for each of the 200 shares to $50; if it were a 3-for-1 split, he would reduce his cost basis on 300 shares to $33.33.

Subscription Rights to New Stock Issues

When a corporation wishes to sell additional common stock, the directors must approve the issue and the corporation must have sufficient authorized and unissued stock available to cover the requirements of the new issue. If sufficient authorized stock is not available, stockholders must vote to approve an increase in the number of authorized shares.

Usually new stock issues are offered to existing stockholders by means of subscription rights. If the additional shares were sold directly to the public, the proportionate interest of each original stockholder would be reduced. A subscription right gives the stockholder the privilege of purchasing new securities at a stipulated price. The subscription price is usually sufficiently below the current market price to induce the stockholders to buy the additional shares. Because subscription rights expire in a few weeks, they have no value if the market price falls to or below the subscription price.

Preemptive Right. The right of a stockholder to subscribe to a new issue of stock is sometimes called the preemptive right. The preemptive right is a matter of common law doctrine rather than of statutory law. Some states, such as Indiana and California, set aside the common law doctrine by providing specifically that no stockholder shall have a preemptive right unless such a right is reserved in the corporate charter. When the pre-emptive right is recognized, it is usually denied to preferred stock and reserved solely for common stock.

Information in Rights Announcement. An announcement of rights by a corporation involves the record date, the basis of the subscription, the sub-scription price, and the expiration date. For example, a company may announce rights on September 15 whereby stockholders of record on September 20 may, at a subscription price of $42 a share, subscribe until October 20 to 1 new share of stock for each 5 shares then owned.

Form of Rights. A right accrues to each share of old stock. A stock-holder, therefore, has as many rights as he has shares of old stock; and when issued, they are in the form of negotiable stock purchase warrants. A *warrant* is a certificate that indicates the amount of new stock to which the holder is entitled to subscribe, the subscription price, the terms of pay-ment, and the expiration date. Two forms are provided on the back of the warrant. One is to be filled out and signed if the stockholder exercises the subscription privilege, while the other is an assignment form to be used if the stockholder wants to sell the privilege.

The market price of the stock before the record date includes the right to participate in the new issue, and the stock is therefore said to sell "cum rights." After the record date, other things being equal, the stock drops proportionately in value and is said to be "ex-rights." This will happen if the market in general is not moving up or down and/or if no other material factor affecting the company's position comes to the attention of investors making them more or less willing to purchase the company's securities. These are, of course, large "ifs."

Market for Rights. A regular market arises in rights. If a stockholder needs 10 rights in order to subscribe to 1 new share but owns only 5 shares of old stock, he may either sell the 5 rights accruing to him or buy an additional 5 rights in the market to obtain sufficient rights to subscribe to 1 new share. The value of a right depends upon the market price of the old stock, the subscription price of the new stock, and the number of rights needed to subscribe to 1 new share. The last two of these factors remain constant, but the market price is variable.

Calculation of Value of Rights. The following example illustrates the calculation of the value of a right. If a share of stock to which a right is attached sells at the market for 66, its price as a unit of ownership is 66 minus the value of 1 right. Assume that the subscription price has been fixed at 44, enabling an existing stockholder to buy an additional share for 44 instead of the current market price. The exercise of this privilege will create a saving that is measured by the difference between the price of the stock itself (66 minus the value of 1 right) and the subscription price of 44. This can be expressed as:

$$66 - 1 \text{ right} - 44$$

If it is assumed that 10 rights are necessary to purchase 1 share of the new stock, the amount computed above represents the value of 10 rights. This can be stated algebraically as follows:

$$10 \text{ rights} = 66 - 1 \text{ right} - 44$$
$$11 \text{ rights} = 66 - 44$$
$$1 \text{ right} = \frac{66 - 44}{11}$$
$$1 \text{ right} = \$2$$

Thus the value of a right with a stock selling "cum rights" is often calculated directly by the formula:

$$\text{Value of 1 right} = \frac{P}{R + 1}$$

where P represents the premium (market price minus the subscription price) and R represents the number of rights needed to subscribe to 1 share of new stock. This problem can be worked out directly as follows:

$$\text{Value of 1 right} = \frac{22}{10 + 1} = \$2$$

After the record date, the stock goes "ex-rights"; the buyer of the stock is not entitled to the right, which remains with the seller. The market price of the stock in this case no longer includes the value of a right. If the assumed market price is now 64, with the subscription price remaining the same, the saving gained upon subscribing for a new share is expressed as 64-44. As before, this saving represents the value of 10 rights, so that:

$$1 \text{ right} = \frac{64 - 44}{10}$$
$$1 \text{ right} = \$2$$

The direct formula for this computation is usually written:

$$\text{Value of 1 right} = \frac{P}{R}$$

In reality, the value of the right to existing stockholders should merely be considered as payment to them for loss in value of their old shares. However, many stockholders who receive these rights sell them and consider the cash received as sort of an additional bonus. They justify such thinking with the assumption that if per-share earnings are not diluted and if the dividend remains the same, while the stock may decline after it goes "ex-rights," it will soon rise again to its old price. Subsequent market action will often seem to justify this belief. The real question is whether or not the dividend might have been raised and the stock actually have sold at a higher price if it had not been for the rights offering.

Stock Purchase Option Warrants

Stock rights as discussed above, which accrue to existing stockholders only, should not be confused with what are known as *stock purchase option warrants*. Some companies issue long-term option warrants allowing purchase of their common stock at specified prices, usually considerably above the market value of the stock at the time. This gives the option contract a speculative flavor in that it is a long-term call on the stock, which may achieve considerable value if the stock should rise in price. The value of these warrants is not determined by any formula but reflects the opinion of speculators as to future profits that may be made on the stock by exercising the warrants based on expected future stock prices.

Specifically, the value of a warrant depends upon: (1) the terms of the contract, that is, the option price and the life of the warrant (its duration); (2) the current market price of the stock; (3) the ratio of the number of outstanding warrants to the number of shares of common stock outstanding; and (4) an estimate of the future price trend of the common stock and therefore its future price level.

If the common stock is selling above the option price of the warrant, the warrant has at least a mathematical value. If a warrant has an option price of $20 and the stock is selling at $25, the mathematical value of the warrant is $5. If the common stock is selling below the option price, the value of the warrant is overwritten and it has no mathematical value other than the present value of the expected differential between the option price and the future price of the common stock.

PREFERRED STOCKS

Preferred stock is exactly what the term indicates: an equity security that enjoys certain preferences or priorities over common stock. Specifically, these priorities are: (1) preferences as to dividends and (2) usually preferences as to assets ahead of common stock in case of liquidation. No dividend may be paid on the common stock before the stated dividend is paid on the preferred stock. In liquidation, assets equal to an amount stated in the preferred stock contract must be distributed to the preferred stockholders before any distribution is made to the common stockholders in most cases. Investors in preferred stock typically accept a limited income in exchange for their priority protection ahead of the common stockholders. Very few preferred stocks are granted the privilege of participation in income beyond their stated dividend.

Comparing Preferred Stock with Creditor Security

Preferred stock is *like* a creditor security in that the rate of return paid is strictly *limited* to the amount of the contract regardless of the prosperity of the issuer. But it is distinctly *unlike* a creditor security in that the dividend is not a liability and is not "owed" until it is declared by the board of directors, while interest on a debt is a legal claim when due that is enforceable in the courts. The preferred contract is distinctly inferior to a creditor contract of a bond or other debt instrument. The principal paid is never due, although under a "call" feature the issuer may decide to redeem the preferred stock.

Comparing Preferred Stock with Equity Security

Preferred stock is *like* a common stock in that it is an equity security and the dividend is paid at the full discretion of the directors, who declare such a dividend only if they believe conditions warrant it. It is *unlike* a common stock in that, because of the strictly limited nature of the dividend, it does not participate in any increasing prosperity of the corporation, for all benefits of such increasing prosperity accrue to the residual common stock. It is true that the quality of a preferred stock may improve as the financial status of a corporation improves. The corporation may have several issues of preferred stock outstanding with their own order of priority indicated by their designation such as first, second, and third preferred stock issues.

Variety of Preferred Stock Provisions

The exact priorities enjoyed by a preferred stock vary considerably by issues, and the investor can be sure of the nature of the preference only if he examines the articles of incorporation. Because the articles of incorporation are not easily accessible, investors and financial analysts usually rely on the summary of the contractual provisions contained on the stock certificates and in the material furnished by the statistical services such as Standard & Poor's and Moody's.

In the great majority of cases, the preferred stock enjoys priority as to dividends and as to assets in liquidation. However, there may or may not be other provisions for voting, cumulative, callable, participating, convertible, and sinking fund privileges.

Voting Provisions. Since the 1930s it has been increasingly common for corporations to grant voting power to preferred stock, but many preferred stocks are still outstanding without normal voting power. However, even a nonvoting preferred stock may have the power to vote on corporate actions that affect its rights or priorities, such as the issuance of new preferred stocks or bonds, changes in the preferences, mergers, or major changes in the character of the business.

Many preferred stock contracts call for automatic voting power if dividends are in arrears for a stated period. The number of preferred shares is usually so small in comparison with the common shares, however, that the preferred stocks often have relatively little power. Moreover, the power is generally handled ineffectually. The NYSE requires that preferred stock be given voting power when dividends are in arrears for a stated period. So long as there is adequate earnings coverage for dividends, the preferred stockholder need not be concerned with the provisions for voting power of his stock.

Cumulative and Noncumulative Provisions. Preferred stock may be cumulative or noncumulative. If it is cumulative, any dividends not paid when due are in arrears and no dividends may be paid on the common stock until all past arrears have been paid.

Noncumulative preferred stock invites an obvious abuse: directors could refuse to pay dividends on the preferred stock for a number of years, even if earned, and then they might pay one dividend on the preferred and pay the rest of the accumulated earnings to the common stockholders if funds were available. The United States Supreme Court [4] has held that if the preferred contract states that the stock is noncumulative, there is no requirement to pay past preferred dividends regardless of the amount of the corporation's profits during the years when dividends were not declared.

---

[4] *Barclay* v. *Wabash Railway*, 2280 U. S. 197 (1930).

Callable Provisions. Most preferred contracts provide that the issuer may, on proper notice, call in the preferred stock, paying the price stated in the contract, which is usually at a premium stated at $5 to $10 above par but may be as high as $25 above par. If stock is noncallable, the corporation may make a tender offer of a specific amount, but acceptance is voluntary. The call feature must be considered a negative feature by the investor as it will usually be exercised at a time when the going interest rates (yields) on preferred stocks and bonds are lower than the contractual rates on the outstanding issues. The issuer has calculated that it will save funds by virtue of the refunding even after payment of the premium. Conversely, the investor must lose income if he either accepts the new issue or reinvests the payment received in an issue of the same quality at the current market yields.

Participating Provisions. There are relatively few participating preferred stocks outstanding, although in the period after 1964 a number of new issues did appear on the market. The contract for a participating preferred stock provides that the preferred stock shall receive a stated dividend before the common stock receives any dividend. Then, usually the common stock receives a matching dividend based on book value or some other agreeable amount; but if the common stock is to receive any excess over this amount, the preferred stock will share with the common stock in the excess earnings in proportion to the book value of the two classes of stock. Normally, common stockholders rarely agree to give the preferred stockholders priority both to dividends and to a share in the growth of the company.

Convertible Provisions.[5] Numerous preferred stocks enjoy provisions under the articles of incorporation that permit the holder at his option to convert into common stock at a stated ratio. The ratio is the number of common shares that will be received if the preferred stock is submitted to the corporation for conversion. A considerable amount of convertible stock was issued over the past 30 years, especially in periods when investors were particularly inflation conscious but still desired the protection of a limited-income security. Many were issued in mergers in the 1960s. If earnings of a corporation rise along with inflation (which is by no means certain),[6] the common shares rise in price and therefore the preferred stock, which is convertible into common stock, will also rise in market value.

---

[5] Calculations pertinent to the appraisal of convertible securities are covered in relation to bonds in Chapter 9.

[6] See the topic entitled "Inflation and Stock Prices in the United States" in Chapter 1, pp. 16-17.

The issuer can usually sell a convertible preferred stock at a lower rate than a straight preferred stock and frequently at a lower cost than if it sold common stock. The issuer can also assume that over the years much or all of the preferred stock will be converted into common stock. Dividends will rise to a point where the dividend on the common stock will be received on conversion and will exceed the dividend on the preferred stock.

If the number of outstanding common shares is increased, the conversion ratio is usually adjusted automatically (by a provision of the preferred contract) so that the stockholder is protected from dilution of his conversion privilege.

Some corporations, instead of issuing convertible preferreds, have sold preferreds with purchase option warrants attached. The warrant may be detached and, together with a stipulated amount of cash, may be exchanged for a given number of shares of common stock.

Sinking Fund Provisions. In the years after World War II, an increasing number of preferred stocks have enjoyed the added protection of sinking funds. Under a sinking fund agreement, the issuer is obligated to retire, through purchase, an amount of preferred stock annually. The annual dollar amount to be used to retire the shares may be fixed (as is the case under many bond sinking fund agreements) or it may fluctuate with earnings or with sales (as is also the case under some bond sinking fund agreements). The quality of the outstanding issues should improve as the amount outstanding is progressively reduced.

Some investment men have sought, usually as a sales device, to designate preferred stocks with sinking funds as "junior bonds" because of the sinking fund. However, the inclusion of a sinking fund provision in the contract in no way changes the equity nature of the preferred stock to a creditor relationship, even though it does strengthen the contract.

Other Protective Provisions. Preferred stock is frequently protected by certain restrictive covenants in the contract. In general, these parallel some of the restrictions used in bond and private placement note indentures to protect creditors. For instance, restrictions may limit the payment of common stock dividends if earnings and working capital are below a certain level.

The preferred contract usually contains a provision preventing the issue of new securities having priority ahead of the preferred stock, such as secured obligations. On the other hand, few preferred contracts contain provisions regarding the maintenance of net working capital at a certain minimum level or, in fact, limiting the amount of unsecured debt. It should be clear that to exclude such provisions provides the corporation with the latitude to severely undermine the position of the preferred stock.

Preferred Stock Outstanding

It is likely that the total amount of preferred stock outstanding in the current decade is not much, if any, higher than in 1929 because of the fact that retirements have tended to balance new issues. Preferred issues represented about 6% of all new corporate security issues (debt and stock) from 1945 to 1967. In 1970 there were approximately 700 preferred issues traded on the national securities exchanges with a market in the neighborhood of $27 billion, which is equivalent to 4.13% of the value of common issues traded on the exchanges and 3.97% of the total value of common and preferred issues combined.[7]

The case of convertible preferred stock, however, is somewhat different. It is estimated that in 1971 there were over 200 convertible preferred stocks on the market against only a few dozen a decade earlier. In 1966 alone, 44 new convertible preferred issues were admitted to NYSE trading, contrasted to 15 in 1965 and 10 in 1964. On the American Stock Exchange, there were 8 applications for listing in 1966, contrasted to 1 in 1965 and 2 in 1964. Convertible preferred stocks are favored by investors as limited-income securities that can provide a hedge against inflation. They may be favored by corporate management in periods of bear stock markets when management wishes to sell an equity security but hesitates to do so with the common stock selling at a relatively low price. They are popular in mergers.

QUESTIONS

1. Corporations are often described as "entities" or "personalities." What is meant by this? Of what significance is an understanding of this concept to investors?

2. (a) Distinguish between the two basic contractual forms of investment securities.
   (b) Explain the legal and investment position of a common stockholder relative to holders of other classes of securities in a corporation.

3. Discuss the basic rights of the common stockholder, noting any limitations that may be present in relation to these rights.

4. (a) What is the significance of the record date in relation to a declared dividend?
   (b) Distinguish between a stock dividend and a stock split and discuss the significance of each to stockholders.
   (c) What is the tax status to the recipient of a stock dividend? of a property dividend?
   (d) Define the term "ex-dividend."

---

[7] Annual Reports of the SEC.

5. Describe the conditions under which a corporation might prefer to issue a stock dividend rather than pay a cash dividend. Under what conditions would you as a stockholder prefer stock dividends to payment of cash dividends?

6. XYZ Corporation announced on May 1 that rights will be mailed on June 1 to stockholders of record as of May 15. May 12th was announced as the final date allowing sufficient time to become a stockholder of record on May 15 in the event one purchased the stock after May 1. The holder of five rights would be entitled to purchase one new share at a cost of $50. What was the theoretical value of a right on May 9th if XYZ stock was then priced at $100 a share in the stock market?

7. How are the rights of the preferred stockholder determined? What rights is he usually given?

8. Define each of the following terms in relation to preferred stock:
   (a) Cumulative.
   (b) Callable.
   (c) Participating.
   (d) Convertible.

9. Explain the significance of a call feature in a preferred stock from the standpoint of both the issuing corporation and the investor.

WORK-STUDY PROBLEMS

1. In early 1961 the American Telephone & Telegraph Company announced a rights offering. Each holder of 20 shares of AT&T common stock on February 23, 1961, was entitled to subscribe to 1 additional share at $86. Just prior to the announcement, the stock was selling for about $113 per share. The subscription period expired on April 14, 1961.

   (a) What would you expect to happen to the price of the stock after the announcement? Why?

   (b) Calculate the theoretical price of the stock during the rights-on period. How is this related to the theoretical value of a right during the rights-on period?

   (c) When will the investor in AT&T stock be able to sell his rights in the market (give dates)? What price should theoretically prevail for a right?

   (d) Determine the price movements of the stock and the rights from the date of announcement to the expiration date from published sources. How do they compare with the theoretical prices you calculated? Explain any differences.

2. Refer to the latest issue of the Securities and Exchange Commission Statistical Bulletin. Derive figures on new security offerings and corporate securities outstanding. Contrast this information with Table 5-1, Table 5-2, and Table 5-3 and comment on the patterns you observe.

SUGGESTED READINGS

Brigham, Eugene F. "An Analysis of Convertible Debentures," *The Journal of Finance.* Vol. XXI (March, 1966), pp. 35-54.

Brittain, John A. *Corporate Dividend Policy,* Studies of Government Finance. Washington, D. C.: The Brookings Institution, 1966.

Donaldson, Gordon. "In Defense of Preferred Stock," *Readings in Finance.* New York: Appleton-Century-Crofts, 1966. Pages 251-274.

Elton, E. J., and M. J. Gruber. "The Cost of Retained Earnings—Implications of Share Repurchase." *Industrial Management Review* (Spring, 1968), pp. 87-104.

——————. "The Effect of Share Repurchases on the Value of the Firm." *The Journal of Finance* (March, 1968), pp. 135-150.

Financial Analysts Journal. Articles as listed below.

    Guthart, Leo A. "Why Companies Buy Their Own Stock." (Mar.-Apr., 1967), pp. 105-112.

    Kassouf, Sheen T. "Warrant Price Behavior, 1945 to 1964." (Jan.-Feb., 1968), pp. 123-128.

    Schwartz, W. "Warrants: A Form of Equity Capital." (September-October 1970), pp. 87-101.

    Sharpe, William F., and Guy M. Cooper. "Risk-Return Classes of New York Stock Exchange Common Stocks." (March-April, 1972).

    Shelton, John P. "Warrant Stock—Price Relations." Part I (May-June, 1967), pp. 143-151. Part II (July-Aug., 1967), pp. 88-100.

    Snyder, G. L. "A Look at Options." (Jan.-Feb., 1967), pp. 100-103.

    Soldofsky, R. M., and Craig R. Johnson. "Rights Timing." (July-Aug., 1967), pp. 101-106.

    Stevenson, Richard A. "The Variability of Common Stock Quality Ratings." (Nov.-Dec., 1966), pp. 97-102.

    Young, Allan. "Common Stocks After Repurchase." (Sept.-Oct., 1967), pp. 117-122.

Fisher, D. E., and F. A. Wilt, Jr. "Non-Convertible Preferred Stock as a Financing Instrument 1950-1965." *The Journal of Finance.* (September, 1968), p. 611.

Graham, Benjamin, David L. Dodd, and C. Sidney Cottle. *Security Analysis,* 4th ed. New York: McGraw-Hill Book Company, 1962. Chapters 28 and 29.

Furst, Richard W. "Does Listing Increase the Market Price of Common Stocks?" *Journal of Business* (April, 1970), pp. 174-180.

Johnson, K. B. "Stocks Splits and Price Change." *The Journal of Finance* (December, 1966), pp. 675-686.

McDonald, J. G., and A. K. Fisher. "New Issue Stock Price Behavior." *The Journal of Finance* (March, 1972), pp. 97-102.

Pinches, G. E. "Financing with Convertible Preferred Stocks, 1960-1967." *The Journal of Finance* (March, 1970), pp. 53-64.

Van Horne, J. C. "New Listings and Their Price Behavior." *The Journal of Finance* (September, 1970), pp. 783-794.

Weston, J. F., and E. F. Brigham. *Managerial Finance,* 4th ed. New York: Holt, Rinehart, and Winston, Inc., 1972. Chapters 14-15.

Debt Instruments

At the time of incorporation, a business must sell stock in order to come into being. Some corporations may never again seek long-term external funds by the sale of securities; their growth in assets stems entirely from the increase in equity represented by the reinvestment of earnings. But most corporations later sell additional securities—stocks or debt instruments. Stocks were discussed in Chapter 5. In this chapter the general characteristics of debt instruments are presented before going into a detailed discussion of bonds.

CHARACTERISTICS OF CORPORATE DEBT INSTRUMENTS

The major forms of debt instruments used by corporations for external long-term debt financing are bonds, notes, private placement notes, equipment obligations, and commercial bank term loans. Until the passage of the Securities Act of 1933 and the Securities and Exchange Act of 1934, most long-term corporate debt financing took the form of bond issues plus the sale of equipment obligations by the railroads. In the 1930s corporations began to borrow by issuing private placement notes to financial intermediaries. These issues are sold privately to one or a few financial intermediaries and there is no public sale. By the late 1930s one third of all corporate debt issues annually were in the form of private placements, by the mid-1960s the percentage had risen to 55%-60%, but in 1967 the percentage fell back to 31% and fell further to 23% in 1971 due to capital market conditions.

The discussion in Chapters 8 and 9 of the analysis of corporate debt issues by investors will note that the standards proposed for the quality, valuation, and selection of debt instruments generally apply to all types.

Most corporate debt securities are bought and held by financial intermediaries, the majority being bought and held by insurance companies and pension funds. All corporate private placement notes are purchased by financial intermediaries. Most utility issues and most railroad equipment issues must be sold publicly at competitive bidding, although at times permission is granted by the regulatory commissions for negotiated underwriting or private placements. State, municipal, and revenue bond issues must be sold at competitive bidding. On the other hand, a large majority of industrial issues are not sold as public issues but are privately placed.

At the end of 1971, the total of the financial asset holdings of individuals was $2.24 trillion and their net equity in financial assets after deductions for mortgage debt, consumer debt, and security loans was $1.11 trillion. Of the total financial assets of $2.24 trillion, only $48 billion was in the form of corporate bonds, notes, and commercial paper. Thus, individuals' holdings of corporate debt issues represented only 2.1% of their total financial assets and 23% of their holdings of all debt securities (refer to Table 3-5 in Chapter 3).

Creating Debtor-Creditor Relationships

The major difference between stocks and bonds rests in the debtor-creditor relationship of the latter. When a corporation borrows, it incurs a liability for the principal amount borrowed as well as for the periodic interest payments. Failure to pay either the principal or the interest when due constitutes a legal default, and court proceedings can be instituted to enforce the contract. Creditors have a prior legal claim over common and preferred stockholders as to both the income and the assets of the corporation for the principal due them and interest. In times of poor business, the prior claim of bondholders becomes very significant. In case of default, if income and assets prove insufficient to meet the prior claims of creditors, the creditors may take over the corporation and the stockholders may find their investments completely liquidated and their stock valueless.

Trading on the Equity and Leverage

When a corporation borrows (or issues preferred stock), it is *trading on the stockholders' equity*. This means that certain investors are willing to advance funds to the corporation at a fixed rate of return because of the equity cushion of safety provided by the investment of the owners and because their claims precede those of the owners.

When corporations trade on their stockholders' equity, they introduce *leverage* into their capitalization. If the *rate of return* earned on total capitalization increases, the rate of return on the stockholders' equity will rise at a faster rate because of the fixed rate paid to the creditors. Conversely, if the rate of return on total capitalization declines, it will decline faster on the stockholders' equity and may even disappear while the creditors receive their full contractual rate. Of course, the rate of return on total capitalization may decline to a point where a default of debtors' claims will occur.

BONDS

Bonds are certificates of indebtedness issued under the seal of a corporation or issued by governments or their subdivisions and agencies. A bond contains the promise of the issuer to pay a certain sum of money at a specified date, usually at a minimum of 5 years from the date of issue, plus a promise to pay interest on the principal of the loan at a specified rate (stated percentage of par or principal value) on specified dates (usually semi-annually) during the period of the loan.

General Description of Bonds

Individual bonds are part of a large debt issue and are in total protected by a detailed bond contract known as an *indenture*. The total of the individual bonds must not exceed the total issue authorized. Both the trustees of the issue and the registrar check to make certain of compliance with the contract in this and all other respects. When the individual bonds, certificates, or notes have been signed by the proper officials of the corporation and authorized by the trustees and registrar, they are delivered to the investors. Frequently, *interim certificates* are issued at the time of sale of a bond issue, later being replaced by bonds when they have been printed.

Individual bonds usually have a minimum denomination of $1,000, but some issues have denominations as high as $100,000, and a very few have a par of $100. United States Government savings bonds have a par value as low as $25. Bonds of small denominations (under $1,000 par value) are frequently spoken of as *baby bonds*. Corporations believe that the expense incidental to the issuance of baby bonds prohibits their use, and bond investors as a class are not interested in such bonds. One firm on Wall Street specializes in such issues. The government's situation is unique since it can and does sell to small individual investors, with quasi-governmental and nongovernmental agencies absorbing much of the selling expense.

The rate of interest on prime corporate bonds over their long history has seldom been less than 2½% and for most domestic bond issues has seldom been over 6%. In 1899 and again in 1946, the low rates were reached; in 1920-1921 and 1966-1973 the highest rates (7%+) prevailed, reaching the highest levels since the post-Civil War period. The difference in yield of different issues of the same maturity at time of sale and in market yield after the bonds are outstanding represents the difference in risk as estimated by the financial community.

Because borrowers and investors are free to make any type of contract with any terms they mutually agree upon, there are a wide variety of provisions in existing issues. For example, there is great variety in the maturity of issues, in provisions as to whether they can be called before maturity, in the type of security pledged to protect the issue, and in restricting clauses contained to protect the investor. As is the case with preferred stock, some bond issues may be convertible into common stock. They may or may not have sinking funds. Most post-World War II new issues have had sinking funds. Finally, there is a wide range in quality.

Bond Indenture

As previously stated, the contract between the issuer and the lenders (bondholders or private placement noteholders or other noteholders) is known as the indenture, and the terms of the agreement are stated in minute detail in this generally lengthy document.[1] The three parties to the contract are the issuer, the trustees for the bondholders, and the bondholders.

The indenture provisions include a promise of the borrower to pay principal and interest when due, to maintain the property adequately, and to operate the corporation judiciously. The borrower generally agrees not to change its business materially through merger or sale of property except under certain conditions. There usually are agreements included to make payments to a sinking fund, to provide for annual debt amortization in the case of private placements, to limit indebtedness, and to subject dividend payments to certain restrictions. Other sections of the indenture state:

1. Any limitations on the total amount of bonds to be issued under the indenture unless the amount is unlimited. If the original sale represents all that can be issued, it is a *closed indenture*. If permission is granted to later issue additional bonds with equal standing, it is an *open indenture*.

---

[1] Federal, state, and municipal issues do not use indentures, but revenue bonds do.

The modern practice is to use *open indentures,* which permit the corporation to secure additional funds for expansion but also protect the present bondholders by restrictions governing new issues. An *unlimited indenture* does not place any limit on the size of future issues under this indenture.

2. Any limitation regarding the payment of dividends, such as if working capital or earnings decline below stated standards.
3. Requirements as to the purpose for which additional bonds may be issued.
4. Characteristics of the real property (real estate) or personal property (securities) that are to be pledged as security, if any.
5. Details regarding interest and principal payments and regarding bond regulations and authentications.
6. Call provisions, sinking fund agreements, and other special features.
7. Conversion options, if any.
8. Methods of registration and details concerning principal payments and interest payments.

Inasmuch as there are usually many bondholders, each holding a certificate of participation in the indenture, a trustee is appointed to protect their interests at all times. The trustee has a number of functions such as:

1. Authenticating the bonds by countersigning them at the time of issue to prevent the issue of bonds above the authorized limit.
2. Holding the mortgage on real property (real estate), or acting as custodian of the personal property (stocks or bonds) in the case of collateral obligations.
3. Receiving both interest and principal payments from the debtor when due and distributing them to the bondholders.
4. Ascertaining that all provisions laid down in the indenture, which are obligations of the debtor, are complied with.
5. Taking action against the debtor if the latter fails to fulfill his obligations, especially if he is in default either as to interest or to principal.

The Trust Indenture Act of 1939 was passed to provide protection for bondholders. The provisions of the act exclude any personal financial interest in the issue by the trustees and require the issuer to send semiannual financial reports through the trustee to the bondholders. Other requirements provide that the trustee receive lists of original bondholders, financial statements, and evidence that the provisions of the bond indenture are being fulfilled. Until these provisions are complied with, registration under the Securities Act of 1933 is impossible. In general, the act provides a statute embodying the provisions of common law, which were not strictly enforced prior to the passage of the act.

Classification of Bonds

Bonds may be classified in a number of ways. Since these classifications are useful in bond analysis, the principal methods of classification and the various types of bonds will be discussed briefly. There are five main categories: (1) bonds classified by issuing agency; (2) bonds classified by purpose of issue; (3) bonds classified by method of interest payment; (4) bonds classified by method of repayment; and (5) bonds classified by assets pledged as security.

Bonds Classified by Issuing Agency. This classification needs little comment. A grouping of bonds by issuing agencies is extremely useful in bond analysis and is the usual classification followed by the statistical services. Examples are: industrial bonds, railroad bonds, utility bonds, and civil bonds—federal, state, municipal, and revenue.

Bonds Classified by Purpose of Issue. Most bond titles in this classification are self-explanatory. It is fairly obvious that at least the major part of the proceeds from a bridge bond issue, for example, will be used to construct a bridge. A bond title often serves as a statement of the intended purpose of the funds raised by the bond sale, although sometimes the title of a particular bond may be misleading. Special-purpose bonds are discussed in the following paragraphs.

Prior-Lien Bonds and Receivers' Certificates. The corporation may issue securities with a prior lien ahead of outstanding mortgage bonds in times of financial difficulties such as receivership. When they are issued with the consent of the first-mortgage bondholders, they are called *prior-lien bonds.* If they are issued by court decree during a receivership, they are called *receivers' certificates.*

Mortgage bondholders subordinate their interests when the corporation is in financial difficulty in the hope that an injection of new funds will enable the corporation to operate successfully again. Without the injection of new funds, the corporation might be forced to liquidate its assets. The sacrifices of the bondholders in liquidation would frequently be greater than the loss of their prior lien.

Refunding Bonds. A *refunding bond* is issued to replace an outstanding issue that has come due or to replace a higher coupon rate bond with a lower coupon rate bond during a time of low market bond yields.

Adjustment Bonds. *Adjustment bonds* are issued during a reorganization of a corporation in exchange for securities outstanding.

Bonds Classified by Method of Interest Payment. The three most common types are discussed in the following paragraphs.

Coupon Bonds or Bearer Bonds. The majority of bonds outstanding are probably coupon bonds or bearer bonds, although quite a number may be exchanged at the holders' option into registered bonds. A *coupon bond* is a bond to which is attached, at the time of issue, one coupon for each interest payment. The holder clips the respective coupon on each interest date and deposits it with his bank for collection. The owner's name does not appear on the bond and the issuer does not keep a record of the owners. Since coupon bonds are transferred simply by delivering the bonds, they are also called *bearer bonds*, meaning that whoever lawfully has possession is the owner and entitled to all interest payments and principal when due. Because transfer is made not by endorsement but by simple delivery, unusual care should be exercised to prevent coupon or bearer bonds from being lost or stolen. Each bond does have a number, and this number should be recorded by all bondholders. A record of the number should accompany all transfers.

Registered Bonds. A *registered bond* differs from a coupon or bearer bond in that the owner's name appears on the bond. The corporation records it, thereby making it transferable only through endorsement by the owner, as is the case with stocks. There are, however, two classes of registered bonds: (1) fully registered bonds and (2) bonds registered as to principal only. In the case of fully registered bonds, interest is paid by check on interest dates to the owner whose name appears on the corporation record, just as is the case with dividends. But if a bond is registered as to principal only, coupons are attached for each interest payment, which are clipped and deposited for collection as is the case with coupon bonds.

Because the great majority of all bonds are owned by financial institutions, it would be preferable for them to hold registered bonds and to receive interest by checks instead of having to clip coupons. In recent years, therefore, there has been pressure on corporations to issue registered bonds rather than coupon bonds. This pressure has begun to have a real effect.

Income Bonds. The distinguishing feature of *income bonds* is that interest must be paid only to the extent that it is earned. Furthermore, interest not paid usually accrues only for a limited number of payments. In some cases a portion of the interest payment is mandatory and the remainder is contingent on earnings. Income bonds resemble stocks more than bonds in their claim to earnings, although they hold a priority to stocks of the same issuer.

Income bonds often arise in exchange for other securities in readjustments and reorganizations in order to reduce the burden of fixed charges to manageable proportions. Most have been issued in reorganizations of railroads and construction companies. A few companies have issued income bonds to replace preferred stocks because the interest paid is tax deductible and the net cost is less than preferred dividends, which are paid *after* taxes are calculated. Recently, income bonds have been offered and sold as new financing. Trans World Airlines successfully issued 6½% subordinated income debentures.

Investors in income bonds should be sure that the contract under which the income bonds are issued specifies in great detail exactly how the income available to pay the interest is to be calculated. Without satisfactory provisions, the management would be able to manipulate expenses so that no income would be indicated as available to pay interest on the bonds. Because a corporation in financial difficulties often has underdepreciated and poorly maintained property, there is a strong temptation for management to report no income available for income bonds for some years.

Bonds Classified by Method of Repayment. The most common types are discussed in the following paragraphs.

Callable Bonds. Bond issues that may be redeemed before maturity at the option of the issuer are designated *callable* or *redeemable.* The callable feature in a bond is undesirable from the investor's standpoint. Such bonds will be called only if it is advantageous to the corporation. This means that it is generally disadvantageous to the investor, since the most frequent reason for calling bonds is to refund at a lower interest rate. This is why in recent years, when funds were relatively tight and interest rates were relatively high, institutional investors pressed for noncallable bonds. But usually lenders settled for bonds that were not callable for at least 5 years, or in some cases not callable for 10 years. Insurance companies made many noncallable private placement loans during the high-interest years 1966-1969.

Usually the call price starts high, say at 110, and declines gradually by steps as the maturity date approaches. There are actually two call prices: (1) the first or lower price is for calls by lot for the sinking fund; (2) the second or higher price is for the redemption of the entire issue. The latter call prices usually decline periodically. The nearer to maturity, the less the corporation may save by refunding at a lower interest rate and, of course, the less the investor has to lose by surrendering the bond when it is called in periods of interest rate declines.

Sinking Fund Bonds. A *sinking fund provision* requires that the corporation set aside, periodically, a specific sum for the purpose of retiring all, or a substantial portion, of its outstanding bonds before or at maturity. Provisions vary widely and the value of a sinking fund can be determined only by specific analysis of the actual sinking fund in question. It has been estimated that less than 35% of all outstanding bonds are protected by sinking funds. However, most new bonds sold include sinking fund provisions.

The fact that a bond is "protected" by sinking fund provisions in the indenture does not change what would otherwise be a speculative bond into a high-grade investment. In any case, the bondholder does not wish annual sinking fund requirements to be so large that they will cause difficulty or financial stringency for the corporation.

Payments to the sinking fund may be specific amounts annually, or they may sometimes be fixed as a certain percentage of sales or earnings in order that the payments will not financially embarrass the debtor in times of poor business. The purpose of the sinking fund is to reduce the debt faster than the property behind the security depreciates, as well as to retire all or most of the debt by maturity. Some contracts permit corporations to add new property as security behind the bonds instead of reducing the debt by calling bonds under sinking fund requirements. Most utility mortgage bond indentures include this provision. Sinking fund provisions are usually more flexible than serial bond requirements and not so often the cause of defaults. If interest payments are made, bondholders often waive sinking fund requirements rather than force the issuer into reorganization or bankruptcy.

Serial Bonds. A corporation or government body may sell a large issue consisting of bonds that mature on successive dates as specified by the serial numbers on the bonds. *Most serial issues, except for equipment trust issues, are municipal issues.* Most private placement issues include in their indentures amortization requirements that make the issue in effect a serial issue. The serial feature provides a means for paying off the funded debt periodically in installments and is a substitute for sinking funds, accomplishing the same purpose, only more directly. Interest rates are adjusted for the various maturities, from the shortest to the longest, by varying the coupon rate or by varying the selling price at the time of issue. Many investors favor such securities as a convenient means of staggering the maturity dates of their investments over a determined schedule.

Convertible Bonds.[2] The conversion feature of a bond relates to its transfer into another type of security, usually common stocks, at the option of the owner for a given period of time. This period may vary from one with an unrestricted time limit to one of very short duration. The conversion ratio often becomes less favorable to the investor with the passage of time.

---

[2] Calculations useful in appraising convertible bonds are discussed in Chapter 8.

The conversion feature offers the benefits of both a fixed income and a hedge against inflation. Nonconvertible bonds fluctuate in price in accordance with changes in overall market yield patterns. A convertible provision will disturb this pattern when the total value of the stock into which the bond is convertible exceeds the straight investment value of the bond. At this point, a further rise in the price of the common stock into which the bond is convertible will cause at least a parallel rise in the price of the bond. For example, assume a $1,000 bond convertible into common stock at $50 a share (convertible into 20 shares). Like any other bond, it may sell at a price based solely on the coupon rate, the maturity, and the credit standing of the issuer if the market sees no advantage in the conversion privilege. If, however, the stock were selling at $60 a share, the bond would sell for at least 20 times $60, or $1,200. A convertible bond will usually sell at some premium over conversion value since the opportunity to speculate on rises in the value of the stock generally has some appeal. Traders may anticipate a continuing rise in the value of the stock and desire to acquire a speculative call on the common stock.

The convertible bond indenture must be specific on certain points: the terms of conversion, the period in which conversion can take place if there is a time limit, the ratio at which each bond can be converted into stock (the conversion price), and the provisions protecting against the dilution of the conversion privilege if additional stock is issued by the corporation. If there were no provisions against dilution of the conversion privilege, the convertible bondholder would be at a disadvantage when the corporation issued additional stock. For example, if the corporation paid a 100% stock dividend or split its stock 2-for-1, the value of the conversion privilege, if not protected, would be cut in half.

If the convertible bond has a call provision, as most do, the issuer can force conversion by calling the bond at a time when the investor will receive more in stock value than in accepting the call price. American Telephone and Telegraph Company has frequently followed this procedure.

Perpetual Bonds. In the United States, bonds are always given a definite maturity date. The British and Canadian governments have issued some perpetual bonds that never come due. In the United States, a few bonds have been issued that have such long maturities that they might as well be designated as perpetual. In 1967, *Standard & Poor's Bond Guide* gave facts on approximately 6,660 issues,[3] all of which are corporate issues except for

---

[3] Two of the bonds listed by Standard & Poor's have such long maturities that they are the same as perpetual issues:
  (1) Elmira and Williamsport Railroad—5's due 2862.
  (2) West Shore Railroad—1st 4's due 2361.

a relatively few issues of foreign governments or their political subdivisions. In 1967, only 108 of the 6,660 issues listed had maturities in the year 2000 or beyond.

Bonds Classified by Assets Pledged as Security. This classification requires considerable explanation, for security provisions and the type of security pledged vary widely.

Unsecured Bonds—Debentures. Unsecured bonds or debentures are secured only by the general credit of the issuer. The unsecured bondholder is a creditor, having a position equal but not superior to all other general creditors. Many outstanding unsecured industrial debenture issues enjoy high investment rating and compare favorably in yield to high-grade first-mortgage bonds, since bond quality in the final analysis depends not on asset liens but on what the company can earn and its cash flow. The key to all investment values is earning power, related ability to pay, and cash flow.

Discernible differences between unsecured and secured bonds arise with the question of investor protection. In the case of default of either interest or principal, the corporation can be sued for the debt by the bondholder or the private placement note holder, but debenture bondholders hold no claim to specific assets and only share with other unsecured creditors in reorganization or liquidation. Secured bonds, on the other hand, are protected by a specific lien against either real or personal property, giving them a prior claim to the proceeds generated by such assets. Debenture bonds generally are not preceded by secured issues with prior claims, and frequently the indenture contains a covenant that the debentures will become secured obligations on a par with any new mortgage if one is subsequently placed on the property. Occasionally, a security designated as a debenture may not be a bond at all. The investor must always look behind the title of a security to determine the true nature of the contract.

Subordinated debentures. In recent years, a considerable number of *subordinated debentures* have been issued. These bonds are subordinated to other debentures, to mortgage bonds outstanding, or in some cases to mortgage bonds that may be issued later subject to stated restrictive measures. In the majority of cases, these debentures have been made acceptable to

---

In addition, the listings included 13 other railroad issues with maturities from 2029 to 2056, and two issues of public service electric and gas due in 2037. Of the 6,660 issues listed by Standard & Poor's in 1967, 108 had maturities in 2000 or beyond, and 54 of those were railroad issues, 31 were telephone issues, 8 were public utility issues, and 13 were Brazilian issues. There were only 1 industrial issue and only 2 financial company issues with such long maturities.

investors by carrying a conversion feature (into common stock). In most cases these bonds have received ratings of BBB, BB, or B. Some examples of such issues are given below. Many private placement notes are also subordinated notes.

TABLE 6-1

Examples of Subordinated Convertible Debentures

Issuer	Type			S&P Rating 1967
Air Reduction Co.	CV Sub Deb	3⅞'s	'87	BBB
Aluminum Company of America	CV Sub Deb	5¼'s	'91	BBB
American Airlines, Inc.	CV Sub Deb	5½'s	'91	BB
Boeing Co.	CV Sub Deb	5½'s	'91	BB
Celanese Corp.	CV Sub Deb	4's	'90	BB
General Telephone & Electronics Corp.	CV Sub Deb	4's	'90	BB
Grace (W. R.) & Co.	CV Sub Deb	4¼'s	'90	BB
Olin Corp.	CV Sub Deb	5½'s	'82	BB
Pan American World Airways, Inc.	CV Sub Deb	4½'s	'86	BB
Sinclair Oil Corp.	CV Sub Deb	4⅜'s	'86	BBB
Stauffer Chemical Co.	CV Sub Deb	4½'s	'91	BBB
Stevens (J. P.) & Company	CV Sub Deb	4's	'90	BB
United Air Lines, Inc.	CV Sub Deb	5's	'91	BB
United Aircraft Corp.	CV Sub Deb	5⅜'s	'91	BB

Government bonds. Bonds of federal, state, local, and foreign governments are unsecured. The protection behind such bonds is the general credit and taxing power of the issuing governments. There are exceptions to these full-faith and obligation securities: certain bonds issued by governmental agencies or their instrumentalities are sold to provide funds for constructing revenue-producing public works, such as turnpike, tunnel, or bridge bonds. The revenue and the specific assets of the project are pledged under an indenture to secure the bonds, but they are not full-faith and credit obligations of the government that established the agency, instrumentality, or authority. If there is a default, the investor can look only to the revenues and the assets of the project for his protection. These revenue bonds are discussed in Chapter 27.

Secured Bonds—Mortgage Bonds. Secured bonds developed naturally years ago from the practice of making secured loans on homes and business properties. Such loans are secured by mortgages, that is, pledges of real estate. At an early date, corporations began using this device to secure loans.

Most bonds outstanding, other than government bonds, are secured by mortgages on real property (real estate). For example, practically all bonds issued by utility and railroad corporations are mortgage bonds. First-mortgage bonds are known as *senior* or *underlying issues*; second mortgage bonds are known as *junior issues*. However, industrial bonds issued in recent years have generally been debenture bonds, especially top-grade bonds.

After-acquired clause. Corporations issuing mortgage bonds pledge specific assets, which are listed in great detail in the mortgage and in the bond indenture, as security for the payment of interest and principal. The assets so pledged may include not only all the assets currently owned by the corporation but also could include all assets that may be acquired in the future. Such provision is called an *after-acquired clause.* This clause was frequently used prior to 1900 and then went out of favor. In recent years, however, as corporations have issued open-end mortgage bonds, the after-acquired clause has again frequently been included.

Types of mortgages. Mortgages may be either open, closed, open-end, or limited open-end. The *open mortgage*, which is the most liberal, allows the corporation to issue unlimited amounts of bonds, all with an equal first-mortgage claim, but it offers no protection to the original bondholders. The poor investment position of original holders would create marketing difficulties, and therefore such bonds are rarely issued.

A *closed mortgage* requires secondary issues to maintain a junior position to the original issue. Rather than affording the investor maximum protection, the provisional rigidity could limit corporate expansion and the acquisition of needed funds.

A compromise between these extremes of liberality and rigidity lies in the *open-end mortgage.* While the issuance of secondary issues on an equal status with the original issue is permissible, certain protective investor provisions are included. For example, the corporation may be permitted to issue additional bonds under the original mortgage up to 75% of the value of the assets acquired if the interest charges on the total indebtedness of the corporation, including the new issue, can be earned at least a stated number of times, as evidenced by corporate expected earnings over the past 3-5 years. Provisions to be met under such an issue are varied in actual practice, and the above example is illustrative rather than comprehensive.

A *limited open-end mortgage* allows for financial growth by permitting bonds to be issued up to an authorized amount, considerably in excess of the initial issue. However, it places a definite limit on the maximum amount of first-mortgage bonds that can be issued, thereby providing protection for the original bondholders. The mortgage should also contain safeguards similar to those in open-end mortgages, such as an earnings-coverage restriction.

Leasehold mortgage bonds. These bonds were issued in rather large amounts in the 1920s; then, because of a poor record, they became rather uncommon until the post-World War II years. These bonds are issued to finance the construction of buildings such as apartment houses, hotels, office buildings, or shopping centers on leased land. The corporation issuing the bonds has previously leased the land on which the building is to be erected. The lease generally requires that all taxes on the land be paid plus a fixed annual rental. The lease, plus the buildings constructed, is pledged as security for the leasehold mortgage bonds. The bondholder must recognize that income from the building must be sufficient to meet all taxes, the leased rental, and all operating and maintenance expenses before any part of it is available for the leasehold mortgage bonds. The bondholders should recognize the junior nature of their claims with regard to leasehold charges on the total indebtedness of the corporation, including the mortgage bonds.

Priority of the mortgage. The bond mortgage may be a senior or first mortgage or a second, third, or some other order of junior mortgage, the number indicating the priority of its claim against the assets pledged.

The more bond issues a corporation has outstanding, the more difficult the problem of analysis becomes.[4] A corporation with a complex capital structure may have a first-mortgage bond that enjoys a first claim on only a small part of the assets of the company. When a bond is in fact a second-, third-, or fourth-mortgage bond, the title usually does not disclose this fact. Rather than calling them second- or third-mortgage bonds, a superficial but noncommittal title is given to such bonds. The investor should determine the exact position that each issue holds in the capital structure of the corporation before he buys the bond. The position of subordinated debentures should be carefully analyzed.

Action in default. If a corporation defaults on its contract under a mortgage, it is the duty of the trustee for the bondholders to bring legal action in the courts to secure payment. This action may take the form of instituting foreclosure proceedings against the pledged assets. These assets may be held under court supervision to satisfy the claims of the bondholders, but usually the bondholders decide by agreement to reorganize the corporation, taking into account the priority of claims of creditors. The bankruptcy

---

[4] See Chapter 9 for recommended methods of analysis.

statutes, revised in the 1930s, emphasize reorganization rather than liquidation. In case of default in any part of the contract, the entire debt usually becomes due automatically and is in default (acceleration clause).

In case of reorganization or liquidation, the order of the creditors' priority of claim will determine the distribution of the new securities of the reorganized corporation or the liquidation payments. The United States Supreme Court has repeatedly reiterated the doctrine of absolute priority. In essence the doctrine states that in case of financial difficulties, all claims must be satisfied in the strict order of their priority. No claim, junior in priority to a senior claim, can be compensated until the senior claim has been fully satisfied. Of course, the claimants with senior claims may waive wholly or partially their rights if they desire to do so. In cases of financial difficulties, the value of secured claims over unsecured claims becomes vitally important. The secured claimants may receive all the value obtained in reorganization or liquidation, leaving nothing for the unsecured creditors.

Secured Bonds—Collateral Trust Bonds and Notes. Collateral trust bonds or collateral trust notes are secured by the stocks and the bonds of other corporations (personal property),[5] which are pledged with the trustees. Occasionally the issuer pledges certain of its own senior issues as security. This type of bond constitutes only a relatively small percentage of all bond issues today. If the collateral trust bonds are issued by a parent holding company, as is usually the case, the pledged securities are generally securities of subsidiaries.

The most relevant factors in determining the worth of a collateral trust bond are the strength and the credit of the issuing corporation, apart from the pledged collateral, and the value and the nature of the collateral. In some cases, the only assets owned by the company issuing the collateral trust bonds are those securities pledged as collateral to secure the bond. It follows in such a case that the credit of the issuing company is itself based entirely on the value of these securities.

Before an investor purchases collateral trust securities, a careful analysis should be made of the pledged securities. It is frequently difficult, however, to secure adequate financial reports of the companies whose securities make up the collateral. If these securities are preceded by prior claims, or if (as is usually the case) they are principally the securities of the issuing corporation's subsidiaries, the collateral trust bondholder may be in a very weak position, although there is nothing inherently unsound about the device. The revenue from securities protecting the bondholder is easier to determine if the underlying companies do not have any securities outstanding other than

---

[5] Personal property as opposed to real estate, the latter being legally designated as real property.

those pledged to secure the collateral trust bonds and if all the securities pledged have a first claim on the earnings of their respective companies. The record of many of the collateral trust securities issued in the 1920s, the period of their greatest popularity, left much to be desired.

The investor should ascertain whether substitution of collateral is permitted, and if so, what the restrictions and the safeguards are. If substitution is permitted, specific safeguards should be laid down in order that adequate security be maintained at all times. The indenture provisions protecting collateral trust bonds are extremely important, for they indicate the action to be followed by the trustee in case of default of interest or principal.

Guaranteed Bonds. Guaranteed bonds almost always have been railroad bonds. It has occasionally been advantageous or necessary for a railroad company to guarantee the securities of another when it has leased the road of the other company. The securityholders of the leased road usually require some definite assurance of income in exchange for relinquishing control over the railroad.

The guaranteed securities, which usually include not only the bonds but also the preferred and common stock of the leased road, may be stamped "guaranteed," endorsed by the guaranteeing railroad, and signed by a legal representative of the railroad providing the guarantee. When securities are guaranteed, they become in effect a debenture bond of the guarantor. If the company providing the guarantee is financially stronger than the railroad whose securities are being guaranteed, the value of the securities is increased.

Assumed Bonds. When the assets of one corporation are acquired by another, either by purchase, merger, or consolidation, the corporation that has acquired the assets must also assume all of the obligations, even though the obligations may continue to bear their original title. These securities are also found most commonly in the railroad field.

Equipment Certificates and Notes.[6] Equipment trust certificates are issued principally to finance the purchase of railroad equipment, buses, trucks, and aircraft. Such certificates are retired annually, according to a specified time schedule, usually over a 10-year period. Investors can select those certificates due at the times that best fit the maturity requirements of their investment schedules. The certificates are repaid at a rate faster than the equipment depreciates in order to protect the investor by maintaining sufficient asset

---

[6] Donald MacQueen Street, *Railroad Equipment Financing* (New York: Columbia University Press, 1959).

value behind the outstanding certificates. These certificates are customarily issued up to a maximum of 85% of the value of the new equipment, although in the last decade a few have been issued up to nearly 100%.

These certificates are issued under two plans: the Philadelphia (Lease) Plan, or the New York (Conditional Bill of Sale) Plan. From the investor's standpoint, it does not make much difference which plan is followed. Under the Lease Plan, the trustees sell participation certificates against the equipment to investors and lease the equipment to the railroad. Under the Conditional Bill of Sale Plan, equipment is sold to the railroads under a conditional bill of sale with possession passing to the buyer but title remaining with the seller until payments have been completed.

The investment standing of these securities, as a class, is high because of their generally excellent record both economically and in litigation. Particular issues vary in credit rating, depending upon the credit standing of the issuing corporation.[7] The excellent history of equipment trust obligations in general is based on a number of factors, namely:

1. The issuer, even in financial difficulty, wishes to keep its newest and most efficient equipment, which is essential to its operation, and this new equipment will be well maintained.

2. Even in reorganizations, the courts usually will permit the continued payment of interest on equipment trust securities, even though all other securities of the issuer may be in default.

3. The asset value behind the equipment trust debt is constantly increasing because the debt is paid off faster than the equipment depreciates.

4. Generally, there has been a good secondhand market for this mobile equipment if the trustees decide to repossess it. The situation is somewhat analogous to the good secondhand market that exists for automobiles. Repossession is generally not too difficult.

Bonds of Nonprofit Corporations

Securities are also issued by nonprofit organizations. Nonprofit organizations comprise a branch of the capital market which supplies funds for churches, hospitals, colleges, and other institutions.

Church bonds, which range in issue from several hundred thousand dollars to over $2 million, are rated highly by rating services, usually as "AA" or "A." If the issuer is a public institution, such as a state university, the bonds will be revenue bonds with the tax-exempt advantage.

Most investors hold these bonds until maturity or until they are retired. Bonds issued by churches have had a favorable experience, and for over a

---

[7] But even the equipment trust certificates of the New York, New Haven Railroad, in reorganization, were rated BBB in 1968, the lowest ratings of any issues.

quarter of a century there have been no defaults. During the depression of the 1930s, adjustments were made on a few issues by lowering the coupon rate. In 1968 a few such issues were considered of questionable quality.

Under SEC regulations, registration is not required for offerings issued by nonprofit organizations.

Bond Prices and Accrued Interest on Bonds

The market price of a bond is expressed as a percentage of its face value, which is customarily $1,000. Therefore, a quotation of 97⅛ for a corporate bond indicates a price of $971.25, or 97⅛% of $1,000. United States Treasury bonds are quoted in thirty-seconds of a point. A quotation of 106.17 on this type of bond indicates a price of $1,065.31.

Bonds may be quoted "flat" or on an "and interest" basis. "Flat" quotations are normally used for bonds that are in default in the payment of interest and, in the case of income bonds, where the payment of interest is contingent upon earnings. When quoted on an "and interest" basis, the buyer pays to the seller not only the agreed price, but also accrued interest. Since accrued interest for the full interest period will be paid to the buyer on the next interest date, or to whomever is the holder of the bond on that date, the buyer is expected to pay the seller the amount of accrued interest since the preceding interest date.

Accrued interest on bonds is normally computed on the basis of a 30-day month and a 360-day year except in the case of United States Government securities where the actual numbers of days is used. The seller is entitled to accrued interest up to, but not including, the day of delivery. Table 6-2 is one of many tables that are available for calculating interest.

To illustrate, assume a 6% bond, par $1,000, with interest payment dates on January 1 and July 1, is sold on Monday, June 12, for delivery on Friday, June 16, at a price of 105. The total cost to the buyer of such a bond would be $1,082.50 (this includes the price of $1,050, the accrued interest of $27.50, and the commission of $5). The seller would receive $1,072.47 which is computed as follows:

Quoted Price : 1 bond at 105		$1,050.00
Accrued Interest: 5 months and 15 days at 6% per year ..		27.50
Total Price		$1,077.50
Less: Commission, 1 bond (price over 100)....	$5.00	
SEC registration fee (calculated at 1¢ for each $500 or fraction thereof of money invested)	.03	5.03
Net Proceeds to Seller		$1,072.47

TABLE 6-2

Accrued Interest on $1,000 (360-Day Basis)

Days	5%	6%	Days	5%	6%	Months	5%	6%
1	.1389	.1667	16	2.2222	2.6667	1 mo.	4.1667	5.0000
2	.2778	.3333	17	2.3611	2.8333	2 mo.	8.3333	10.0000
3	.4167	.5000	18	2.5000	3.0000	3 mo.	12.5000	15.0000
4	.5556	.6667	19	2.6389	3.1667	4 mo.	16.6667	20.0000
5	.6944	.8333	20	2.7778	3.3333	5 mo.	20.8333	25.0000
6	.8333	1.0000	21	2.9167	3.5000	6 mo.	25.0000	30.0000
7	.9722	1.1667	22	3.0556	3.6667	7 mo.	29.1667	35.0000
8	1.1111	1.3333	23	3.1944	3.8333	8 mo.	33.3333	40.0000
9	1.2500	1.5000	24	3.3333	4.0000	9 mo.	37.5000	45.0000
10	1.3889	1.6667	25	3.4722	4.1667	10 mo.	41.6667	50.0000
11	1.5278	1.8333	26	3.6111	4.3333	11 mo.	45.8333	55.0000
12	1.6667	2.0000	27	3.7500	4.5000	12 mo.	50.0000	60.0000
13	1.8056	2.1667	28	3.8889	4.6667			
14	1.9444	2.3333	29	4.0278	4.8333			
15	2.0833	2.5000	30	4.1667	5.0000			

Bond Yield

The price of a bond reflects current thinking as to the appropriate yield for that particular security dependent upon the market's evaluation of its investment quality at that moment and its maturity. The yield does not result from the fact that a bond is selling at a certain price. Rather, the bond is selling at a price to give it the resultant yield required by investors at that particular time. The bond price alone has little meaning because the investor is primarily interested in the rate of yield return that he receives on the bond.

The yield that an investor receives from a bond is mathematically a function of three factors: (1) its price; (2) its nominal or coupon rate of interest; and (3) the length of time to maturity.

Current Yield. Current yield on bonds is calculated by dividing the annual interest received in dollars by the cash price of the bond. Though sometimes referred to as the "stock yield," it is really quite different since the interest is contractually fixed while dividends are not.

The yield on bonds is usually calculated to maturity rather than on a current basis. However, most investors and statistical services calculate current yield rather than yield to maturity in the case of very speculative bonds. Also, current yield could be of interest to an investor who depends heavily on his portfolio for current income.

TABLE 6-3

Coupon Yield Tables 4.50% (4.50 Coupon)

Maturity Yield	17½ Years	18 Years	18½ Years	19 Years	19½ Years	20 Years	20½ Years	21 Years
2.00	136.7607	137.6344	138.4994	139.3558	140.2038	141.0434	141.8746	142.6976
2.25	132.3993	133.1513	133.8950	134.6304	135.3576	136.0768	136.7879	137.4911
2.50	128.2079	128.8473	129.4788	130.1025	130.7185	131.3269	131.9278	132.5213
2.78	124.1793	124.7145	125.2424	125.7631	126.2768	126.7835	127.2834	127.7765
2.80	123.3925	123.9078	124.4160	124.9171	125.4114	125.8988	126.3795	126.8535
2.85	122.6119	123.1076	123.5964	124.0783	124.5534	125.0218	125.4837	125.9390
2.90	121.8374	122.3139	122.7835	123.2464	123.7028	124.1525	124.5959	125.0329
2.95	121.0691	121.5265	121.9774	122.4216	122.8595	123.2909	123.7161	124.1351
3.00	120.3067	120.7455	121.1778	121.6038	122.0234	122.4369	122.8442	123.2455
3.05	119.5503	119.9708	120.3849	120.7928	121.1946	121.5903	121.9801	122.3641
3.10	118.7999	119.2022	119.5985	119.9886	120.3729	120.7512	121.1238	121.4907
3.15	118.0553	118.4399	118.8185	119.1912	119.5582	119.9194	120.2751	120.6253
3.20	117.3165	117.6836	118.0449	118.4005	118.7505	119.0949	119.4340	119.7677
3.25	116.5836	116.9334	117.2776	117.6164	117.9497	118.2777	118.6004	118.9180
3.30	115.8563	116.1892	116.5167	116.8388	117.1558	117.4675	117.7743	118.0760
3.35	115.1347	115.4509	115.7619	116.0678	116.3686	116.6645	116.9555	117.2417
3.40	114.4188	114.7186	115.0134	115.3032	115.5882	115.8684	116.1440	116.4149
3.45	113.7084	113.9921	114.2709	114.5450	114.8145	115.0793	115.3397	115.5957
3.50	113.0036	113.2714	113.5345	113.7931	114.0473	114.2971	114.5426	114.7839
3.55	112.3043	112.5564	112.8041	113.0475	113.2867	113.5217	113.7526	113.9795
3.60	111.6104	111.8471	112.0797	112.3082	112.5326	112.7530	112.9696	113.1823
3.65	110.9219	111.1435	111.3612	111.5749	111.7849	111.9910	112.1935	112.3923
3.70	110.2387	110.4455	110.6485	110.8478	111.0435	111.2357	111.4243	111.6095
3.75	109.5609	109.7530	109.9416	110.1267	110.3085	110.4868	110.6619	110.8338
3.80	108.8883	109.0661	109.2405	109.4117	109.5796	109.7445	109.9063	110.0650
3.85	108.2209	108.3845	108.5450	108.7025	108.8570	109.0086	109.1573	109.3032
3.90	107.5587	107.7084	107.8552	107.9993	108.1405	108.2791	108.4150	108.5483
3.95	106.9017	107.0377	107.1710	107.3018	107.4301	107.5558	107.6792	107.8001
4.00	106.2497	106.3722	106.4924	106.6102	106.7256	106.8389	106.9499	107.0587
4.05	105.6027	105.7120	105.8192	105.9242	106.0272	106.1281	106.2270	106.3239

TABLE 6-3 (Continued)

Maturity Yield	17½ Years	18 Years	18½ Years	19 Years	19½ Years	20 Years	20½ Years	21 Years
4.10	104.9607	105.0571	105.1515	105.2440	105.3346	105.4234	105.5105	105.5957
4.15	104.3237	104.4073	104.4891	104.5693	104.6479	104.7248	104.8002	104.8741
4.20	103.6917	103.7626	103.8322	103.9003	103.9669	104.0323	104.0962	104.1589
4.25	103.0644	103.1231	103.1805	103.2367	103.2918	103.3457	103.3984	103.4501
4.30	102.4420	102.4885	102.5341	102.5786	102.6222	102.6649	102.7068	102.7477
4.35	101.8245	101.8590	101.8928	101.9260	101.9584	101.9901	102.0211	102.0515
4.40	101.2116	101.2344	101.2568	101.2787	101.3001	101.3210	101.3415	101.3615
4.45	100.6035	100.6148	100.6259	100.6367	100.6473	100.6577	100.6678	100.6777
4.50	100.0000	100.0000	100.0000	100.0000	100.0000	100.0000	100.0000	100.0000
4.55	99.4012	99.3900	99.3792	99.3685	99.3581	99.3480	99.3380	99.3283
4.60	98.8069	98.7849	98.7633	98.7422	98.7216	98.7015	98.6818	98.6626
4.65	98.2172	98.1844	98.1524	98.1211	98.0905	98.0606	98.0313	98.0028
4.70	97.6321	97.5887	97.5464	97.5050	97.4646	97.4251	97.3865	97.3488
4.75	97.0514	96.9977	96.9452	96.8940	96.8439	96.7951	96.7473	96.7007
4.80	96.4751	96.4112	96.3489	96.2879	96.2285	96.1704	96.1136	96.0582
4.85	95.9032	95.8294	95.7573	95.6869	95.6181	95.5510	95.4855	95.4215
4.90	95.3357	95.2521	95.1704	95.0907	95.0129	94.9369	94.8628	94.7904
4.95	94.7726	94.6793	94.5882	94.4994	94.4126	94.3280	94.2454	94.1649
5.00	94.2137	94.1109	94.0107	93.9128	93.8174	93.7243	93.6335	93.5448
5.05	93.6591	93.5470	93.4377	93.3311	93.2271	93.1257	93.0268	92.9303
5.10	93.1087	92.9875	92.8694	92.7541	92.6418	92.5322	92.4253	92.3212
5.15	92.5625	92.4324	92.3055	92.1818	92.0612	91.9437	91.8291	91.7174
5.20	92.0204	91.8815	91.7461	91.6142	91.4855	91.3602	91.2380	91.1189
5.25	91.4825	91.3350	91.1912	91.0511	90.9146	90.7816	90.6520	90.5257
5.30	90.9486	90.7926	90.6407	90.4926	90.3484	90.2079	90.0710	89.9376
5.40	89.8930	89.7206	89.5526	89.3891	89.2299	89.0749	88.9240	88.7770
5.50	88.8533	88.6650	88.4848	88.3034	88.1299	87.9609	87.7965	87.6365
5.60	87.8293	87.6258	87.4278	87.2352	87.0479	86.8656	86.6884	86.5159
5.70	86.8207	86.6025	86.3904	86.1841	85.9836	85.7886	85.5990	85.4147
5.75	86.3220	86.0967	85.8778	85.6645	85.4580	85.2568	85.0613	84.8713
5.80	85.8272	85.5949	85.3692	85.1499	84.9367	84.7295	84.5282	84.3326
6.00	83.8846	83.6258	83.3746	83.1307	82.8938	82.6639	82.4407	82.2240
6.25	81.5372	81.2482	80.9679	80.6962	80.4326	80.1771	79.9293	79.6890
6.50	79.2761	78.9599	78.6537	78.3571	78.0698	77.7916	77.5221	77.2611
7.00	74.9992	74.6369	74.2868	73.9486	73.6219	73.3062	73.0011	72.7064

Source: Financial Publishing Company, Boston, Massachusetts.

Net Yield to Maturity. The net yield to maturity relates the annual income and the accumulation or amortization, as the case may be, to the funds invested in the bond, allowing for the time horizon of the bond. If a bond is purchased at 95 ($950), the investor will receive at maturity the face value of $1,000, which is $50 more than he invested. This increase in value of $50 is called accumulation and must be considered, along with the interest, when calculating yield. When a bond is purchased above par, the premium is called amortization; and this reduces the yield calculated on the basis of annual interest (the current yield). The *net yield to maturity* may be defined as the interest rate that equates the present value of the annual interest payments and the final payment of principal at maturity with the current cost of the bond. Bond tables, showing net yields to maturity for varying interest rates and varying maturities, are calculated on this basis.

To illustrate, assume the purchase of a 4½% bond, due in 20 years, at 98 ($980). The net yield to maturity can be found by consulting a bond table like the portion shown in Table 6-3. In the column headed 20 years the amount that is nearest to the purchase price of 98 (98.0606) is located, and the net yield to maturity of 4.65% is found in the extreme column to the left on a line with the price closest to 98.

Alternatively one can determine the maximum price he would pay to receive a desired yield to maturity for a bond. Assume the investor wants a yield to maturity of at least 6.25% and is considering the purchase of a 4½% coupon bond maturing in 19½ years. Then he should pay no more than 80.4326 or $804.32, assuming the bond has a par of $1,000.

Approximating the Net Yield to Maturity. The net yield to maturity can be approximated for the 4½% bond, due in 20 years, purchased at 98 ($980), by appropriately adjusting the annual income received and the amount invested to allow for the accumulation present. The accumulation of $20 ($1,000 par minus the $980 cost) occurs during the life of the bond at an average yearly rate of $1. This figure, added to the yearly interest, gives an approximate annual return of $46. But since the investor has not actually received the additional $1, it is as though the bondholder's total investment is increasing each year from $980 to $999 in the final or twentieth year. The average annual investment would be $980 + $999 ÷ 2, or $989.50. Thus, there is an average annual return of $46 on an average annual investment of $989.50, or an approximate net yield to maturity of 4.65%. While the true net yield to maturity is approximated very accurately in this instance, the same will not necessarily hold true for other cases. Only bond tables, or present value calculations, allow for the time pattern in which the funds are actually received.

Present Value and Bond Yield Tables. A dollar received today is clearly worth more than a dollar received one year from now. Two justifications can be offered for this statement: (1) The risk that the dollar will not be forthcoming a year from now is avoided; and (2) The currently received dollar can earn a return during the year. The investor therefore would not relinquish dollars he holds for a promise of future repayment, unless he also received adequate payment for the use of that money. If he felt he could earn 10% in alternative uses of equivalent risk, he would not invest $1 today unless he expected to receive $1.10 a year from now. We could reverse this statement and say that the present value of $1.10 received a year from now is $1 when discounted at 10%.

In general terms, the future value of any amount at compound interest is

$$F = P \ (1 + r)^n$$

where n is the number of years in the time horizon, P the beginning amount or principal, F the future amount, and r the interest rate. When we attempt to find the present value of a future amount, we merely solve for P rather than F and the equation becomes as follows:

$$P = \frac{F}{(1 + r)^n}$$

When discussing a bond, P is the amount invested, F the principal received at maturity, n the number of years to maturity, and r the net yield to maturity that one must determine. Fortunately bond tables have done the arithmetic for us, though the calculations could be made by using more detailed present value tables than Tables 6-4 and 6-5 on pages 170-171.

Effect of Discount Municipal Bonds. Discount municipal bonds pose an additional problem since capital gains are subject to tax at capital gains rates, while interest received on municipal bonds is not taxable to the investor. In order to reflect the effect of the capital gains tax on the yield to maturity, it is often assumed that this yield should be reduced by an amount equal to the capital gains rate applicable to the investor times the difference between the yield to maturity and the coupon rate. This method is not exact; in some test calculations it has been as much as 10 basic points off, but can give reasonably good approximations.

QUESTIONS

1. (a) What is a corporate private placement note?
   (b) Who purchases such instruments?

TABLE 6-4

Present Value of $1 Received at the End of Year

Years Hence	1%	2%	4%	6%	8%	10%	12%	14%	15%	16%	18%	20%	22%	24%	25%	26%	28%	30%	35%	40%	45%	50%
1	0.990	0.980	0.962	0.943	0.926	0.909	0.893	0.877	0.870	0.862	0.847	0.833	0.820	0.806	0.800	0.794	0.781	0.769	0.741	0.714	0.690	0.607
2	0.980	0.961	0.925	0.890	0.857	0.826	0.797	0.769	0.756	0.743	0.718	0.694	0.672	0.650	0.640	0.630	0.610	0.592	0.549	0.510	0.476	0.444
3	0.971	0.942	0.889	0.840	0.794	0.751	0.712	0.675	0.658	0.641	0.609	0.579	0.551	0.524	0.512	0.500	0.477	0.455	0.406	0.364	0.328	0.290
4	0.961	0.924	0.855	0.792	0.735	0.683	0.636	0.592	0.572	0.552	0.516	0.482	0.451	0.423	0.410	0.397	0.373	0.350	0.301	0.260	0.226	0.198
5	0.951	0.906	0.822	0.747	0.681	0.621	0.567	0.519	0.497	0.476	0.437	0.402	0.370	0.341	0.328	0.315	0.291	0.269	0.223	0.186	0.156	0.132
6	0.942	0.888	0.790	0.705	0.630	0.564	0.507	0.456	0.432	0.410	0.370	0.335	0.303	0.275	0.262	0.250	0.227	0.207	0.165	0.133	0.108	0.088
7	0.933	0.871	0.760	0.665	0.583	0.513	0.452	0.400	0.376	0.354	0.314	0.279	0.249	0.222	0.210	0.198	0.178	0.159	0.122	0.095	0.074	0.059
8	0.923	0.853	0.731	0.627	0.540	0.467	0.404	0.351	0.327	0.305	0.266	0.233	0.204	0.179	0.168	0.157	0.139	0.123	0.091	0.068	0.051	0.039
9	0.914	0.837	0.703	0.592	0.500	0.424	0.361	0.308	0.284	0.263	0.225	0.194	0.167	0.144	0.134	0.125	0.108	0.094	0.067	0.048	0.035	0.026
10	0.905	0.820	0.676	0.558	0.463	0.386	0.322	0.270	0.247	0.227	0.191	0.162	0.137	0.116	0.107	0.099	0.085	0.073	0.050	0.035	0.024	0.017
11	0.896	0.804	0.650	0.527	0.429	0.350	0.287	0.237	0.215	0.195	0.162	0.135	0.112	0.094	0.086	0.079	0.066	0.056	0.037	0.025	0.017	0.012
12	0.887	0.788	0.625	0.497	0.397	0.319	0.257	0.208	0.187	0.168	0.137	0.112	0.092	0.076	0.069	0.062	0.052	0.043	0.027	0.018	0.012	0.008
13	0.879	0.773	0.601	0.469	0.368	0.290	0.229	0.182	0.163	0.145	0.116	0.093	0.075	0.061	0.055	0.050	0.040	0.033	0.020	0.013	0.008	0.005
14	0.870	0.758	0.577	0.442	0.340	0.263	0.205	0.160	0.141	0.125	0.099	0.078	0.062	0.049	0.044	0.039	0.032	0.025	0.015	0.009	0.006	0.003
15	0.861	0.743	0.555	0.417	0.315	0.239	0.183	0.140	0.123	0.108	0.084	0.065	0.051	0.040	0.035	0.031	0.025	0.020	0.011	0.006	0.004	0.002
16	0.853	0.728	0.534	0.394	0.292	0.218	0.163	0.123	0.107	0.093	0.071	0.054	0.042	0.032	0.028	0.025	0.019	0.015	0.008	0.005	0.003	0.002
17	0.844	0.714	0.513	0.371	0.270	0.198	0.146	0.108	0.093	0.080	0.060	0.045	0.034	0.026	0.023	0.020	0.015	0.012	0.006	0.003	0.002	0.001
18	0.836	0.700	0.494	0.350	0.250	0.180	0.130	0.095	0.081	0.069	0.051	0.038	0.028	0.021	0.018	0.016	0.012	0.009	0.005	0.002	0.001	0.001
19	0.828	0.686	0.475	0.331	0.232	0.164	0.116	0.083	0.070	0.060	0.043	0.031	0.023	0.017	0.014	0.012	0.009	0.007	0.003	0.002	0.001	
20	0.820	0.673	0.456	0.312	0.215	0.149	0.104	0.073	0.061	0.051	0.037	0.026	0.019	0.014	0.012	0.010	0.007	0.005	0.002	0.001		
21	0.811	0.660	0.439	0.294	0.199	0.135	0.093	0.064	0.053	0.044	0.031	0.022	0.015	0.011	0.009	0.008	0.006	0.004	0.002	0.001		
22	0.803	0.647	0.422	0.278	0.184	0.123	0.083	0.056	0.046	0.038	0.026	0.018	0.013	0.009	0.007	0.006	0.004	0.003	0.001	0.001		
23	0.795	0.634	0.406	0.262	0.170	0.112	0.074	0.049	0.040	0.033	0.022	0.015	0.010	0.007	0.006	0.005	0.003	0.002	0.001			
24	0.788	0.622	0.390	0.247	0.158	0.102	0.066	0.043	0.035	0.028	0.019	0.013	0.008	0.006	0.005	0.004	0.003	0.002	0.001			
25	0.780	0.610	0.375	0.233	0.146	0.092	0.059	0.038	0.030	0.024	0.016	0.010	0.007	0.005	0.004	0.003	0.002	0.001	0.001			
26	0.772	0.598	0.361	0.220	0.135	0.084	0.053	0.033	0.026	0.021	0.014	0.009	0.006	0.004	0.003	0.002	0.002	0.001				
27	0.764	0.586	0.347	0.207	0.125	0.076	0.047	0.029	0.023	0.018	0.011	0.007	0.005	0.003	0.002	0.002	0.001	0.001				
28	0.757	0.574	0.333	0.196	0.116	0.069	0.042	0.026	0.020	0.016	0.010	0.006	0.004	0.002	0.002	0.002	0.001	0.001				
29	0.749	0.563	0.321	0.185	0.107	0.063	0.037	0.022	0.017	0.014	0.008	0.005	0.003	0.002	0.002	0.001	0.001					
30	0.742	0.552	0.308	0.174	0.099	0.057	0.033	0.020	0.015	0.012	0.007	0.004		0.002	0.001	0.001						
40	0.672	0.453	0.208	0.097	0.046	0.022	0.011	0.005	0.004	0.003	0.001	0.001										
50	0.608	0.372	0.141	0.054	0.021	0.009	0.003	0.001	0.001	0.001												

Source: R. N. Anthony, *Management Accounting: Text and Cases* (Homewood, Ill.: Richard D. Irwin, Inc., 1970), Appendix, Table A.

TABLE 6-5

Present Value of $1 Received Annually at the End of Each Year for N Years

Years (N)	1%	2%	4%	6%	8%	10%	12%	14%	15%	16%	18%	20%	22%	24%	25%	26%	28%	30%	35%	40%	45%	50%
1	0.990	0.980	0.962	0.943	0.926	0.909	0.893	0.877	0.870	0.862	0.847	0.833	0.820	0.806	0.800	0.794	0.781	0.769	0.741	0.714	0.690	0.667
2	1.970	1.942	1.886	1.833	1.783	1.736	1.690	1.647	1.626	1.605	1.566	1.528	1.492	1.457	1.440	1.424	1.392	1.361	1.289	1.224	1.165	1.111
3	2.941	2.884	2.775	2.673	2.577	2.487	2.402	2.322	2.283	2.246	2.174	2.106	2.042	1.981	1.952	1.923	1.868	1.816	1.696	1.589	1.493	1.407
4	3.902	3.808	3.630	3.465	3.312	3.170	3.037	2.914	2.855	2.798	2.690	2.589	2.494	2.404	2.362	2.320	2.241	2.166	1.997	1.849	1.720	1.605
5	4.853	4.713	4.452	4.212	3.993	3.791	3.605	3.433	3.352	3.274	3.127	2.991	2.864	2.745	2.689	2.635	2.532	2.436	2.220	2.035	1.876	1.737
6	5.795	5.601	5.242	4.917	4.623	4.355	4.111	3.889	3.784	3.685	3.498	3.326	3.167	3.020	2.951	2.885	2.759	2.643	2.385	2.168	1.983	1.824
7	6.728	6.472	6.002	5.582	5.206	4.868	4.564	4.288	4.160	4.039	3.812	3.605	3.416	3.242	3.161	3.083	2.937	2.802	2.508	2.263	2.057	1.883
8	7.652	7.325	6.733	6.210	5.747	5.335	4.968	4.639	4.487	4.344	4.078	3.837	3.619	3.421	3.329	3.241	3.076	2.925	2.598	2.331	2.108	1.922
9	8.566	8.162	7.435	6.802	6.247	5.759	5.328	4.946	4.772	4.607	4.303	4.031	3.786	3.566	3.463	3.366	3.184	3.019	2.665	2.379	2.144	1.948
10	9.471	8.983	8.111	7.360	6.710	6.145	5.650	5.216	5.019	4.833	4.494	4.192	3.923	3.682	3.571	3.465	3.269	3.092	2.715	2.414	2.168	1.965
11	10.368	9.787	8.760	7.887	7.139	6.495	5.988	5.453	5.234	5.029	4.656	4.327	4.035	3.776	3.656	3.544	3.335	3.147	2.752	2.438	2.185	1.977
12	11.255	10.575	9.385	8.384	7.536	6.814	6.194	5.660	5.421	5.197	4.793	4.439	4.127	3.851	3.725	3.606	3.387	3.190	2.779	2.456	2.196	1.985
13	12.134	11.343	9.986	8.853	7.904	7.103	6.424	5.842	5.583	5.342	4.910	4.533	4.203	3.912	3.780	3.656	3.427	3.223	2.799	2.468	2.204	1.990
14	13.004	12.106	10.563	9.295	8.244	7.367	6.628	6.002	5.724	5.468	5.008	4.611	4.265	3.962	3.824	3.695	3.459	3.249	2.814	2.477	2.210	1.993
15	13.865	12.849	11.118	9.712	8.559	7.606	6.811	6.142	5.847	5.575	5.092	4.675	4.315	4.001	3.859	3.726	3.483	3.268	2.825	2.484	2.214	1.995
16	14.718	13.578	11.652	10.106	8.851	7.824	6.974	6.265	5.954	5.669	5.162	4.730	4.357	4.033	3.887	3.751	3.503	3.283	2.834	2.489	2.216	1.997
17	15.562	14.292	12.166	10.477	9.122	8.022	7.120	6.373	6.047	5.749	5.222	4.775	4.391	4.059	3.910	3.771	3.518	3.295	2.840	2.492	2.218	1.998
18	16.398	14.992	12.659	10.828	9.372	8.201	7.250	6.467	6.128	5.818	5.273	4.812	4.419	4.080	3.928	3.786	3.529	3.304	2.844	2.494	2.219	1.999
19	17.226	15.678	13.134	11.158	9.604	8.365	7.366	6.550	6.198	5.877	5.316	4.844	4.442	4.097	3.942	3.799	3.539	3.311	2.848	2.496	2.220	1.999
20	18.046	16.351	13.590	11.470	9.818	8.514	7.469	6.623	6.259	5.929	5.353	4.870	4.460	4.110	3.954	3.808	3.546	3.316	2.850	2.497	2.221	1.999
21	18.857	17.011	14.029	11.764	10.017	8.649	7.562	6.687	6.312	5.973	5.384	4.891	4.476	4.121	3.963	3.816	3.551	3.320	2.852	2.498	2.221	2.000
22	19.660	17.658	14.451	12.042	10.201	8.772	7.645	6.743	6.359	6.011	5.410	4.909	4.488	4.130	3.970	3.822	3.556	3.323	2.853	2.498	2.222	2.000
23	20.456	18.292	14.857	12.303	10.371	8.883	7.718	6.792	6.399	6.044	5.432	4.925	4.499	4.137	3.976	3.827	3.559	3.325	2.854	2.499	2.222	2.000
24	21.243	18.914	15.247	12.550	10.529	8.985	7.784	6.835	6.434	6.073	5.451	4.937	4.507	4.143	3.981	3.831	3.562	3.327	2.855	2.499	2.222	2.000
25	22.023	19.523	15.622	12.783	10.675	9.077	7.843	6.873	6.464	6.097	5.467	4.948	4.514	4.147	3.985	3.834	3.564	3.329	2.856	2.499	2.222	2.000
26	22.795	20.121	15.983	13.003	10.810	9.161	7.896	6.906	6.491	6.118	5.480	4.956	4.520	4.151	3.988	3.837	3.566	3.330	2.856	2.500	2.222	2.000
27	23.500	20.707	16.330	13.211	10.935	9.237	7.943	6.935	6.514	6.136	5.492	4.964	4.524	4.154	3.990	3.839	3.567	3.331	2.856	2.500	2.222	2.000
28	24.316	21.281	16.663	13.406	11.051	9.307	7.984	6.961	6.534	6.152	5.502	4.970	4.528	4.157	3.992	3.840	3.568	3.331	2.857	2.500	2.222	2.000
29	25.066	21.844	16.984	13.591	11.158	9.370	8.022	6.983	6.551	6.166	5.510	4.975	4.531	4.159	3.994	3.841	3.569	3.332	2.857	2.500	2.222	2.000
30	25.808	22.396	17.292	13.765	11.258	9.427	8.055	7.003	6.566	6.177	5.517	4.979	4.534	4.160	3.995	3.842	3.569	3.332	2.857	2.500	2.222	2.000
40	32.835	27.355	19.793	15.040	11.925	9.779	8.244	7.105	6.642	6.234	5.548	4.997	4.544	4.166	3.999	3.846	3.571	3.333	2.857	2.500	2.222	2.000
50	39.196	31.424	21.482	15.762	12.234	9.915	8.304	7.133	6.661	6.246	5.554	4.999	4.545	4.167	4.000	3.846	3.571	3.333	2.857	2.500	2.222	2.000

Source: R. N. Anthony, *Management Accounting: Text and Cases* (Homewood, Ill.: Richard D. Irwin, Inc., 1970), Appendix, Table B.

2. (a) Define trading on the equity and illustrate the concept by means of assumed figures. Explain leverage.
   (b) Of what significance to investors is the degree of trading on the equity practiced by a corporation?

3. Would you be using financial leverage if you bought a car or a home on credit terms? Why or why not?

4. (a) Define a bond indenture and describe its usual provisions.
   (b) Discuss the importance to investors of the Trust Indenture Act of 1939.

5. (a) Why do financial intermediaries prefer registered bonds to coupon bonds?
   (b) Which type of bond do you believe is preferable for individual investors? Why?

6. (a) Are callable bonds desirable from the investor's standpoint?
   (b) What protection does a sinking fund offer the investor? What are its limitations?

7. (a) Why are most high-grade industrial bonds usually debenture bonds?
   (b) How should the safety of a bond be evaluated? Should a lien on assets receive major consideration from a bond analyst? Discuss.
   (c) What is a subordinated debenture?

8. (a) Distinguish between a convertible bond and a bond with detachable warrants.
   (b) How would one calculate the possible dilution effect of each type while the bond is outstanding?

9. Discuss the nature of preferred stocks as compared with bonds. Indicate the differences and the performance of both historically.

10. (a) Is yield for a bond usually quoted in the same way as yield for a stock? Are they equally significant to an investor? Discuss.
    (b) Calculate the net yield to maturity for each of the following bonds by means of the approximate method: (1) a 20-year, 8¼% bond offered at $1,020, par $1,000; and (2) a 30-year, 4½% bond offered at $700, par $1,000.
    (c) Prove by use of present value tables that a $1,000 par bond carrying a coupon rate of 4½% with 18 years to go until maturity, quoted at 83.6258, will yield 6% to maturity.

WORK-STUDY PROBLEMS

1. Summarize and give a critique of the findings reported in W. Braddock Hickman's *Corporate Bond Quality and Investor Experience* (New York: National Bureau of Economic Research, 1958).

2. Select two investment grade convertible bonds and determine the following information:
   (a) Exact name, description, and current price.
   (b) Call price (and date, if significant).
   (c) Yield to maturity.
   (d) The terms of conversion, duration of the conversion privilege, and possible limitations on the conversion privilege.
   (e) The conversion value of the bond in terms of the stock into which it is convertible. If this value is different from the current market price of the bond, suggest a possible explanation for the difference.
   (f) The nature of the security supporting the bond issue.

SUGGESTED READINGS

Atkinson, Thomas R. *Trends in Corporate Bond Quality,* National Bureau of Economic Research. New York: Columbia University Press, 1967.

Brand, Louis. *Investing for Profit in Convertible Bonds,* Rev. ed. New York: Standard & Poor's Corporation, 1964.

Donaldson, Gordon. *Corporate Bond Capacity.* Boston, Mass.: Harvard Graduate School of Business Administration, 1961.

Financial Analysts Journal. Articles as listed below.

  Ascher, Leonard W. "Selected Bonds for Capital Gains." (March-April, 1971), pp. 74-79.
  Barges, Alexander. "Growth Rates and Debt Capacity." (Jan.-Feb., 1968), pp. 100-104.
  Baskin, Elba F., and Gary M. Crooch. "Historical Rates of Return on Investments." (Nov.-Dec., 1968), pp. 95-97.
  Harris, John T. "A Comparison of Long-Term Deep Discount and Current Coupon Bonds." (July-Aug., 1968), pp. 81-85.
  Jen, Frank C., and James E. Wert. "Sinking Funds and Bond Yields." (Mar.-Apr., 1967), pp. 125-133.
  Johanneson, Richard I., Jr. "The Effect of Coupon on Bond Price Fluctuations." (Sept.-Oct., 1968), pp. 89-92.
  Johnson, Robert L. "The Value of the Call Privilege." (Mar.-Apr., 1967), pp. 134-140.
  Schwartz, William. "Convertibles Get Realistic Image." (July-Aug., 1967), pp. 55-58.
  Soldofsky, Robert M. "Performance of Convertibles." (March-April, 1971), pp. 61-65.

Fisher, Lawrence. "Determinants of Risk Premiums on Corporate Bonds," *The Journal of Political Economy.* Vol. LXVII, No. 3 (June, 1959), pp. 217-237.

Graham, Benjamin, David D. Dodd, and Sidney Cottle. *Security Analysis,* 4th ed. New York: McGraw-Hill Book Company, 1962. Parts 3 and 5.

Hayes, Douglas H. *Investments: Analysis & Management,* 2d. ed. New York: The MacMillan Company, 1966. Chapter 12.

Hickman, W. Braddock. *Corporate Bond Quality and Investor Experience.* New York: National Bureau of Economic Research, 1958.

Jen, Frank C., and James E. Wert. "The Effects of Call Risk on Corporate Bond Yields." *The Journal of Finance* (December, 1967), pp. 637-652.

——————. "The Preferred Call Provision and Corporate Bond Yields." *Journal of Financial and Quantitative Analysis* (June, 1968), pp. 157-169.

Johnson, Ramon E. "Term Structures of Corporate Bond Yields as a Function of Risk of Default." *The Journal of Finance* (May, 1967), pp. 313-345.

McEnally, Richard W. "Risk-Premium Curves for Different Classes of Long-Term Securities, 1950-1966: Comment." *The Journal of Finance* (September, 1972), pp. 933-939. (Also see reply, pp. 940-945).

Morgan, B. W. "Corporate Debt and Stockholder Portfolio Selection." *Yale Economic Essays,* 7 (Fall, 1967), pp. 201-259.

Pogue, Thomas F., and Robert M. Soldofsky. "What's in a Bond Rating?" *Journal of Financial and Quantitative Analysis* (June, 1969), pp. 201-228.

Soldofsky, Robert M., and Roger L. Miller. "Risk-Premium Curves for Different Classes of Long-Term Securities, 1950-1966." *The Journal of Finance* (June, 1969), pp. 429-445.

Weston, Fred J., and Eugene E. Brigham. *Managerial Finance,* 4th ed. New York: Holt, Rinehart and Winston, Inc., 1972, Chapters 15 and 17.

7

Corporate Financial Policies and the Investor

This chapter examines financial policies of corporations and the necessity of seeking external sources of funds to meet corporate objectives. It discusses financial policies affecting the decision as to whether or not external sources of funds are to be used, and if so, the form of securities to be sold in order to provide these funds, that is, the problems of trading on the equity and leverage. The investor engaged in the valuation and the selection of securities must understand the financial policies that are so important to corporate financial results, that is, the sources, uses, and control of funds.

CORPORATE FINANCIAL MANAGEMENT

The stockholders are the owners of the corporation and they elect the directors who establish overall corporate policies, including financial policies. The directors, in turn, select the operating management. It should be the major goal of the corporate directors and management to maximize the investment standing of the corporation's stock and the quality of its credit.[1]

---

[1] While there are a very considerable number of writings stating that this should be the goal of corporate management, numerous broad research studies in depth have shown that salaries of officers have a much closer correlation to sales volume and asset size of companies than to earnings. Certainly corporate officers are aware of this fact and may emphasize asset and sales growth more than earnings growth, which wou'ₐ¹ therefore tend not to maximize the value of the corporation's shares in the market. The great merger movement may reflect this thinking (example—conglomerates).

Goals of Corporate Financial Management

The major goal of the private business corporation is to produce a satisfactory profit and to obtain an adequate rate of growth of profits as the result of additional investment and the improvement of operating efficiencies. It is also true that expansion may result from mergers and acquisitions. The major tests of the success of corporate management are the rate of return on sales and the rate of return on total capital invested, on total assets, and on stockholders' equity. If the corporation does not trade on its equity by issuing limited-income securities or arranging short-term loans, the latter two ratios will be equal. In measuring the success and the quality of management, the corporation's rate of return on investment is compared with that for all corporations and for competing corporations in the same industry or industries in which the corporation operates.

Dividends must be paid from earnings and cash flow, and the amount and the growth rate of dividends depends upon the amount and the growth of earnings and cash flow as well as corporate financial policy. The major protection for limited-income securities is also earnings and cash flow. No investor would logically purchase a common stock if it was expected that earnings, cash flow, and dividends would show no growth in the future, making it a *de facto* limited-income security without the contractual advantages of a true fixed-income security. The investor would be wiser in such cases to purchase a limited-income security such as a bond. This was particularly true in the past decade when yields on high-grade bonds were consistently higher than average yields on stocks (6%-8% vs. 3%-4%).

Functions of Corporate Financial Management

Corporate financial management is a segment of the overall administrative function. Traditionally, it has been mainly concerned with the flow of funds into and through the organization. Funds must be available—either from internal generation or from external sources or both—to satisfactorily fulfill the corporate objectives and to meet all the corporate obligations when due while maintaining a reasonable margin of safety at all times. The corporate objectives are ultimately focused on a goal of higher earnings from rising corporate investments and a high rate of return on invested capital and equity.

In the past, corporate financial management has been mainly preoccupied with two major areas: (1) management of short-term fluctuating needs, which involves liquidity and short-term financial strength; and (2) management of long-term funds, which is at the heart of development and expansion. In recent years, however, it has come to be recognized that a clearly related function to the two major functions noted above is that of short-term and long-term *profit planning*. It is somewhat surprising that for years profit planning occupied a relatively minor role in corporate financial management in spite of the fact that the final test of corporate performance is the profits test and the rate of return on invested capital and owners' equity.

Corporate financial management is therefore concerned with the volume of business done and projected, the expenses necessary to support the volume of business, the break-even point for operations, the profit margins, and the return on invested capital. The *break-even point* is an analytical tool that relates volume, costs, and profits. Important in this concept is the relationship of variable and fixed costs to volume and to total costs.

MANAGEMENT OF SHORT-TERM FLUCTUATING FINANCIAL NEEDS

Analysis of short-term financial needs is concerned with the adequacy of working capital and cash flow patterns. The sources and uses of funds statement provides historical perspective for this analysis, and planning efforts are summarized in the cash budget.

Working Capital

The *working capital* of a corporation consists of its current assets, the major components of which are cash and cash items (U.S. Treasury bills, certificates of deposit, and commercial paper), receivables, and inventories. The management of working capital is a continuous process that exercises control over the daily ebb and flow of the corporate financial resources that are constantly circulating through the business in one form or another. The so-called natural cycle of activity will vary according to the nature of the business, as for example:

1. Financial corporations: cash, to debtors, to cash.
2. Retail merchandising corporations: cash, to merchandise inventories, to sales, to receivables, to cash.
3. Manufacturing corporations: cash, to raw materials inventories, to work in process inventories, to finished goods inventories, to sales, to receivables, to cash.

The term *net working capital* refers to current assets minus current liabilities. The major components of current liabilities are bank loans; other short-term borrowing, such as trade accounts and notes payable; wages, salaries, and taxes accrued; and dividends declared but not yet paid.

Common stockholders and the owners of debt instruments are both vitally interested in the proper management of working capital. Working capital is the source of corporate short-term liquidity. Sufficient working capital is necessary to meet debt obligations such as interest payments, debt amortization, and sinking fund requirements and to pay cash dividends.

Corporate financial management desires sufficient working capital, but it may be just as poor policy to have excess working capital as to have too little working capital. The major factors that affect working capital are sales volume, costs, price level changes, depreciation policy, operating efficiency, profit margins, debt requirements, dividend policy, and cash requirements under the capital budgeting program. Techniques useful in analyzing the adequacy of working capital are discussed in Chapters 17-19.

Corporations should avoid excessive working capital above a margin of reasonable safety and liquidity. Excessive working capital may result in a low rate of return and it may reflect and encourage management inefficiency and even speculation. Unnecessary expenses may be encouraged, and dividend policy may become more liberal than is justified considering sound investment opportunities that may be available. A policy of constantly maintaining excessive working capital may result in the deferment or the rejection of profitable investment opportunities. Conversely, if working capital is insufficient, the business may face the risk of failure to meet its obligations, imaginative executives may find it difficult or impossible to implement their plans, the corporation's credit rating both in the trade and in the capital markets may be jeopardized, it may be impossible to take advantage of discounts for prepayments, and dividend policies may be affected adversely. Idle funds are generally kept in Treasury bills or certificates of deposit.

In the 1960s, especially after 1965, corporate liquidity continued to decline to the lowest level since the 1930s, reflecting the high cost of borrowed funds and great pressure to keep working capital at a minimum and to maintain a high circulation as a factor in increasing profits. Some financial analysts became concerned that the pressure for "efficiency" in handling working capital was unduly jeopardizing corporate liquidity and ability to meet commitments when due. Corporate liquidity in 1969 was at the lowest level since the 1930s. Funding of short-term debt in the bond market during 1972 did improve corporate liquidity positions.

Cash Budget

The sales department should provide management with a projection of sales volume, and then the accounting department should prepare an operating budget based on the sales budget. In many companies, corporate financial management will prepare three budgets: one based on the sales volume projected by the sales department and two others based on estimates of sales volume, one somewhat lower and one somewhat higher.

In preparing a cash budget, corporate financial management will estimate the minimum cash balance that should be maintained. It will then estimate, within a time schedule, the inflow from collections and the outflow for payments. It will include all funds that flow down from sales which are not drained off by actual cash expenditures. It will estimate the cash needs for such items as dividends, amortization of debt, repurchases of corporate securities, and additions to plant and equipment. It will then also determine the extent, if any, of the need for external sources of funds because of insufficient internal sources.

Normally, the financial analyst will not have access to these cash budgets, but the bank loan office making a term loan and the financial intermediary making a private placement loan may require, and often receive, such budgets along with sources and uses of funds statements.

Sources and Uses of Funds Statement

The *sources and uses of funds statement* [2] supplies a picture of changes in working capital. As presented in the corporation's annual report, it reflects changes in balance sheet assets over a fiscal period adjusted by necessary information obtained from the income statement. An increase in an asset represents a use of funds and a decrease in an asset represents a source of funds. An increase in a liability or in the equity accounts represents a source of funds; a decrease, a use of funds. Major sources and uses (or applications) of funds are listed at the top of page 180.

The *sources and uses of funds statement* is an essential tool for control required by corporate financial management.[3] In recent years there has been a growing recognition by outside financial analysts that they too should have such statements available for security analysis. Pressures by financial analysts, the New York Stock Exchange, and the American Institute of Certified Public Accountants (AICPA) have combined rather effectively in encouraging corporations to supply such statements in their annual reports. In fact, there has been rather general criticism of corporate management that uses cash flow figures in annual reports unsupported by sources and

---

[2] The sources and uses of funds statement is frequently called the source and application of funds statement or merely the funds statement. The Accounting Principles Board of the AICPA in its Opinion No. 19 recommended that the title of this statement be "Statement of Changes in Financial Position."

[3] If internal sources of funds start with retained earnings after dividends, then dividends do not appear as a use of funds (vs. U. S. Dept. of Commerce reporting).

Sources and Uses of Funds

Major Sources of Funds	*Major Uses of Funds*
Internal:	Gross additions to plant & equipment
Net income after taxes	Net increases in current assets:
Depreciation and depletion	Cash and cash items
External:	Temporary investment in market-
Accounts payable	able securities
Notes payable	Time certificates of deposit
Other current liabilities	Commercial paper
Sale of securities	Receivables
Common stock	Inventories
Preferred stock	Dividends
Long-term debt instruments	Investments in affiliates
Increase in minority interests	Increases in other assets
	Repurchase of corporation's outstand-
	ing debt or equity securities

uses of funds statements. Criticism is particularly severe if such managements stress "cash flow per share" rather than "earnings per share" figures or use the term "cash flow earnings." [4] Common stockholders and creditors alike place considerable stress on an analysis of the sources and uses of funds statement and the cash flow in determining protection of investments.

Cash Flow

Cash flow may be defined as the total of net income after taxes plus all nonfund or noncash items deducted from income in the income statement less all noncash credit items added in the income statement before determination of net profit. It is, therefore, similar to working capital flow (funds) from operations and is not likely to provide a completely accurate measure of the actual flow of cash in the business.

Since the late 1950s, the cash flow concept has assumed greater importance in common stock analysis. Cash-flow-per-share figures appear in company annual reports and in analyses by advisory services and brokerage firms. Proper interpretation of cash flow is useful in analysis.

The explicit statement of and emphasis on cash-flow-per-share figures raise questions as to the significance of such figures. Have new operating or financial conditions justified a shift of emphasis from earnings after depreciation as opposed to those before depreciation? Are cash-flow-per-share

---

[4] For example, see William A. Paton, "The 'Cash-Flow' Illusion," *Accounting Review*, Vol. XXXVIII, No. 2 (April, 1963), pp. 243-251.

figures superior to after-tax earnings per share as an indicator for judging the ability of the firm to pay dividends, finance additional assets, or repay debt? Some analysts seem to believe so, on the grounds that a far greater amount of internal funds are available for the above purposes than might be inferred from the earnings analysis. Graham, Dodd, and Cottle [5] offer evidence to dispute this view. They point out that while depreciation, depletion, and amortization charges for all corporations rose from $4.3 billion in 1946 to $22.8 billion in 1960, suggesting liberal and even possibly excessive charges, the percentage rise in depreciation has kept in line, more or less, with the rise in plant and equipment expenditures during this period. Evidence suggests that current rates are geared to an overall life span of 20 years, which hardly appears too short. Depreciation is an expense, *not* income similar to reported profits. It represents the consumption of capital,. and the above data do not suggest that any hidden reserves capable of expanding the asset base are being provided in current depreciation charges.

Cash flow figures should be used, along with an analysis of a sources and uses of funds statement, only as a *supplement* to earnings per share and not as a substitute for earnings per share. Such figures are of value in comparative analysis in view of the markedly different accounting techniques and life estimates that may be applied by different firms in calculating depreciation charges and depletion charges.

A review of the list of sources and uses of funds will identify the uses for cash flow. The working capital position of a company is linked to its cash flow, and the cash flow provides the funds for dividend payments and is the best test of corporate debt capacity [6] available to the borrower or the investor because it provides the funds to meet total financial charges—interest plus debt amortization or sinking fund requirements. For a more complete understanding of cash flow, the reader should consult Chapter 17.

In 1961 because of the frequent misuse of cash flow figures in company annual reports, brokerage house reports, and other reports and in order to encourage a sounder understanding of cash flow, the American Institute of Certified Public Accountants published a 98-page research report, " 'Cash Flow' Analysis and the Funds Statement." [7]

---

[5] B. Graham, D. Dodd, and S. Cottle, *Security Analysis* (4th ed.; New York: McGraw-Hill Book Company, Inc., 1962), p. 158.

[6] Gordon Donaldson, *Corporate Debt Capacity* (Boston, Mass.: Division of Research, Graduate School of Business Administration, Harvard University, 1961).

[7] Perry Mason, " 'Cash Flow' Analysis and the Funds Statement," *Accounting Research Study No. 2* (New York: American Institute of Certified Public Accountants, 1961).

LONG-TERM FINANCING

Corporate financial policy regarding long-term financing is policy respecting the corporation's *capitalization structure,* a term used to refer to the ratio of debt, preferred stock, and common stock equity to the total capitalization of a firm. If the goal of corporate management is to maximize the investment standing of its common stock in the market and the quality of its credit, the decision as to capitalization structure should be based on policies that will accomplish this goal.

Variations in Capitalization Structure

Any variation in the amount of debt, preferred stock, or common stock equity of a corporation changes its capital structure.[8] Corporate financial management must judge the effect of such variations on the earnings per share, the stockholders' equity, and the market price of the stock. The relative cost of capital, depending on sources, is very important.

It is clear that certain managements have decided against any use of limited-income securities regardless of any beneficial effect that their use might have on earnings on the common stock equity and therefore on the market price of the corporation's stock. Clearly the investment quality of some of these corporations is so high that a policy of not issuing any debt could not have been based on the opinion that investors would not purchase the debt issues or would purchase them only at competitive rates quite high in comparison to the rate for top quality equity issues. It can only be assumed that such managements did not want any long-term debt and made no attempt to determine the cost of capital on an equity cost versus a debt cost basis. They might characterize this policy as conservative, although a judgment by outside financial experts might characterize it as ultra-conservative to say the least.[9] Many of these companies have grown to great size merely by the reinvestment of retained earnings after dividend payments, or alternatively by selling additional common stock. Here it can be noted that relatively few of our really major industrial corporations have sold common stock for cash since 1929. When they have sold securities,

---

[8] As will be indicated later, a number of corporations introduce leverage into their "capitalization" by leasing assets instead of issuing debt instruments to obtain funds with which to purchase the assets. None capitalize leases on the balance sheet.

[9] Such managements have at least implied that they did not use debt finances because of the risk. But this attitude without attempting to measure the degree of risk is illogical because the risk would be only one of many risks that business must face. A company cannot be in business without assuming risks. See Gordon Donaldson, *Corporate Debt Capacity* (Boston, Mass.: Division of Research, Graduate School of Business Administration, Harvard University, 1961), pp. 94-95.

the securities have been largely debt instruments, so that not many corporations fall into the class of ultraconservative management mentioned above.

Directors of some of the debt-free corporations might have stated that the lower the percentage of debt, the higher the corporation's quality of credit with the ultimate implication that a corporation with no debt would have the highest quality of credit, but this certainly is not so. One has only to cite the quality of credit of many utility companies and many oil companies to refute this assumption.

Only an extremely small number of large publicly owned companies have completely debt-free capitalization, although quite a number do have relatively small debt ratios. In an analysis of approximately 1,000 publicly owned corporations listed in the January, 1968, *Standard & Poor's Stock Guide,* only about 3% had completely debt-free capital structures.

Postulates of Long-Term Financing

Generally, corporate earnings grow over time as a result of additional earnings generated from additional investments, although for a period increased efficiency can produce rising earnings from better profit margins.

Corporate financial management in its handling of long-term funds should consider certain postulates of long-term financing that have come to be rather generally accepted. Investors should also understand these postulates.

1. The need for funds should be projected from sources and uses of funds statements and cash budgets rather than from income statements. Financial requirements, including debt repayment schedules, should then be budgeted.
2. If a firm issues limited-income securities in addition to common stock, it is trading on its equity. This introduces leverage into its capitalization, which magnifies the profits and losses for the common stockholder and may reduce the cost of capital versus equity financing.[10]
3. The type of external financing is affected by the character of the firm's assets on the general assumption that long-term liabilities should be created only to acquire long-term assets such as plant and equipment.
4. The test that should constantly be applied when long-term external financing is being considered is whether or not, and to what extent, per share earnings will be increased as a result of the investment of the funds acquired. Therefore, the relative cost of capital is highly important.
5. Large firms tend to have a larger proportion of assets invested in fixed assets and tend to use external long-term financing to a greater extent than smaller firms. This is partly due to the availability of long-term

---

[10] Some writers have disputed this claim, stating that, except for the tax advantage of debt financing, the cost of capital and the total value of all the corporation's securities combined is unaffected by the form of the corporation capitalization structure. This subject is discussed later in the chapter.

credit for large firms versus small firms. Many small and medium-size firms encounter considerable difficulty in arranging long-term debt financing.

6. The older the firm and the larger its equity base, the greater the availability of long-term external credit.

7. Except for very rapidly growing firms, investors tend to place a higher value on a dollar of dividends than a dollar of retained earnings, and they prefer stable dividends rather than fluctuating dividends. These factors will be reflected in the price level of the corporation's stock in the market. Investors never expect a 100% payout of earnings, and for most companies dividend payments in the 45%-60% range are acceptable.[11]

8. Financing and capitalization plans should provide for flexibility to meet future financial needs. As a corollary, corporate financial management should constantly be awake to the possibilities of refunding long-term obligations when conditions in the financial markets would make this economically advisable or to otherwise readjust capital structures.

Capital Budgeting

In almost all cases, if a corporation is to increase its earnings over any period of years, it must increase its investment in assets. This generally means an increase in its fixed assets. However, when fixed assets are increased to enable the firm to increase production and sales, working capital must also be increased. Additional capital investments therefore furnish the basis for an expanding company and expanding earnings. The future of most companies essentially rests on the capital budgeting decisions of management,[12] which makes these decisions of vital importance to the investor in seeking and determining earnings growth.

It is rather generally agreed that a company cannot have too many potentially worthwhile projects to consider because failure to consider a project may result in failure to participate in a profitable area. When a large array of potential projects is available, management must decide on "which projects." This is probably the most important decision for management. The analysis of potential projects requires a wide range of professional and technical ability encompassing the areas of product research, market research, economic analysis, accounting management in such areas as costs and depreciation, and financial analysis.

One must guard against accepting the simple theory that increases in capital expenditures (capital inputs) for a nation or a company will increase productivity, giving little attention to the fact that to be *economically*

---

[11] This matter is examined in detail later in the chapter.

[12] Of course, expansion may be obtained through mergers and acquisitions, which may involve the expenditure of funds, but usually it is accomplished by the exchange of securities, in most cases by the exchange of common stock or the issuance of convertible securities or preferred stock.

productive the output must satisfy the demands of consumers. Great emphasis must be placed on the decision-making process as to "which projects" and the highly valuable management and technical knowledge required for such successful decision making. The future is always uncertain, management foresight of a high caliber is a scarce commodity, and the necessary decision process is highly complex. Successful capital budgeting and the management of capital expenditures assumes that management intends to maximize the long-run return on the common stockholders' equity, to increase the company's gross income, and to maintain satisfactory corporate liquidity at all times, keeping the corporation's credit position one of high quality. Some managements use a 5-year planning horizon, while others extend the planning horizon to 10 or more years.

Various methods have been proposed or used to select projects for investment. The three major methods are:

1. Postponability method—the effect of postponement of the project.
2. Payback period method—how long it will take to recover the investment.
3. Discounted cash flow (DCF) rate of return method.[13]

The postponability method is not advisable because it would constantly require the flow of funds into projects that appear necessary at the moment, ignoring the long-range advantages of other projects. The payback period method is often rejected because it favors the projects that will recover the investment first even though they will not be the most profitable in the long run. However, because of the relatively short time horizon of many (perhaps most) investors, including an increasing number of institutional investors, a majority of the managements of large corporations have more recently tended mainly to emphasize projects that will yield the highest returns over the next 4-6 years (rather than those that will yield the highest return over the longer term) or the payback approach.[14]

---

[13] There are other rate of return methods, but the discounted cash flow method is preferred by the authors of this book, who, however, recognize investor pressure to select projects yielding the highest return in the short 4-6 year period, as well as a steady growth in earnings. (See footnote 14 below.)

[14] Eugene M. Lerner and Alfred Rappaport, "Capital Budgeting and Reported Earnings to Shareholders," *Financial Executive* (January, 1969). (From a paper delivered at annual meeting of American Accounting Association, August, 1968.)

Over the past ten or fifteen years we have witnessed a constant stream of articles, speeches, and conferences urging firms to adopt a discounted cash flow (DCF) approach for making their capital budgeting decisions. At the same time, widespread educational programs have been carried on by business schools, trade associations, and consulting firms to explain the advantages of DCF. Despite all of this activity, a recent study indicates that less than one-half of 163 firms selected from the *Fortune* list of 500 companies employ the DCF approach. [Alexander A. Robichek and John G. McDonald, *Financial Management in Transition* (Menlo Park, Calif.: Stanford Research Institute), p. 7.]

The *discounted cash flow (DCF) method* relates the calculated investment requirements for the project to the estimated net cash inflow from the project over its entire life. Properly used, the calculated rate of return considers all the following: the time pattern of investment and earnings, depreciation allowances, and the effect of taxes. Compound interest tables are used to calculate the interest rates that will make the *present value* of the total anticipated cash inflow equivalent to the original cost of the project. The same method of calculation is used as is done when determining the yield on a bond or an annuity. By taking cash flow for each year as a separate unit and discounting each unit back to the present, the discounted cash flow method recognizes that distant earnings have less value than early earnings. The relative desirability of projects can then be assessed and selection made in terms of the cost of raising the funds necessary to undertake the projects under consideration.

Financing Capital Projects—Cost of Capital Controversy

Corporate financial management is faced with the decision as to how projects can be financed: whether from internal or external funds; if from external funds, whether by the issuance of debt or equity securities; and if from equity securities, whether by preferred stock or by common stock.

The traditional argument is that by "trading on the equity" and issuing fixed-income securities, leverage is introduced into capitalization, the cost of capital is reduced, and the rate of return on stockholders' equity is increased in relation to new equity financing. The excess earned on funds supplied by bondholders over payment to bondholders accrues to the stockholders. Corporations should develop a balanced capital structure, but the decision as to the proportion of debt to equity should rest on the degree of uncertainty inherent in that particular industry and firm. The argument assumes that the total value of all the corporation's securities will be increased

---

Many writers noting the relatively slow acceptance of DCF attribute this to a lack of understanding or a feeling of futility about projecting cash flows more than a few years into the future. A second reason frequently cited is that payback benchmarks are often an important consideration to risk-conscious decision makers with strong liquidity preferences. For a given firm, both of these factors may well discourage the use of DCF. We believe that a third, but largely overlooked, reason for the failure of DCF to gain wider acceptance is that management has found that it does not successfully come to grips with the vital consideration of what earnings it reports to shareholders. If the application of a DCF criterion results in an erratic earnings pattern, and if managers prefer to report a pattern of orderly and sustained earnings growth, then it is reasonable to suggest that this fact may account for some of the reluctance to adopt the DCF approach for capital budgeting decisions.

The importance of earnings per share is generally linked by management to its broad objective of creating increasing value for the benefit of shareholders.

and the cost of capital decreased as leverage is increased, but only to an *optimum point*. Beyond that point any further increase in trading on the equity (the debt-to-equity ratio) is unwise, creating risks related to the uncertain characteristics of that particular industry and business, and such further use will increase the corporation's cost of capital.

In this assumption, the point of *optimum leverage* for any particular corporation will vary according to the corporation's and the investors' assessments of the business uncertainty for the firm. Numerous writings have taken issue with this stand. Durand[15] has argued that the total risk or uncertainty that must be assumed by all securityholders as a group cannot be altered by the manner in which this total risk is distributed among various classes of securityholders, that is, by manipulation of the capital structure of the corporation. He argues that differences in capital structure only shift the *manner* in which earnings and uncertainty of earnings are distributed among stockholders and bondholders, but that there can be no change in total amount of uncertainty. He concluded that total corporate value should not be affected by capital structure but actually is by the imperfections in capital markets (hence modified traditionalists' viewpoints). It therefore followed from this reasoning that any advantage to stockholders (an increase in the rate of return on equity) that does result empirically from an increase in the proportion of debt in capitalization is solely the result of the tax-deductible nature of interest costs on debt. Traditionally, however, most corporate directors (and the authors of this book) believe that, even without the tax advantage, stockholders would benefit from a capitalization levered up to an optimum point.

Modigliani and Miller[16] also hold that the cost of capital function of a firm will be unaffected by the degree of leverage employed by the firm. Their assumptions are quite different from Durand's modified view. They assume that equity cost will rise (the price-earnings multiplier will fall) by exactly the amount required to keep the average cost of capital of the firm unchanged as debt is increased. This assumes *perfect securities markets* in which arbitrage or swapping of securities brings about the necessary changes, as investors may use their own leverage by buying on margin. This is unreal.

Modigliani and Miller do recognize the tax-saving aspects of debt financing. When allowing for taxes, their model seems to say that cost of

---

[15] David Durand, *The Cost of Debt and Equity Funds for Business: Trends and Problems of Measurement* (New York: National Bureau of Economic Research, Inc., 1952). Relative costs of alternative financing methods are very important.

[16] F. Modigliani and M. H. Miller, "The Cost of Capital, Corporation Finance and the Theory of Investment," *American Economic Review* (June, 1958). A major revision of the 1958 article appeared in Modigliani and Miller's article "Cost of Capital to the Electric Utility Industry," *American Economic Review* (June, 1966).

capital would continue to decrease as leverage was increased right up to the point of 99.9% of debt. They, unlike the authors of this text and corporate directors and investors, seem to see no optimum point of leverage up to the 99.9% figure. But in 1966 Modigliani and Miller said that this is not a logical implication of their static equilibrium theory.

The fundamental differences between the two schools of thought have been aptly set forth by David Durand. Durand points out that the proponents of the second (or entity) approach "argue that the totality of risk incurred by all securityholders of a given company cannot be altered by merely changing the capitalization proportions. Such a change could only alter the proportion of the total risk borne by each class of securityholder." In regard to the first (or optimal) approach he states: "Those who adhere strictly to this method contend: first, that *conservative* increases in bonded debt do not increase the risk borne by the common stockholders; second, that a package of securities containing a conservative proportion of bonds will justifiably command a higher market price than a package of common stock alone." This assumes an optimum point of leverage beyond which conservative policy would not add debt because of an increase in risk and therefore in cost.

Empirical Evidence in the Capital Markets

Empirical evidence is that management will generally retain as large an amount of earnings as is deemed advisable considering capital and dividend requirements (thus building equity internally) and then will rely heavily on debt financing when obtaining funds externally as shown by SEC figures. (See Table 2-1 in Chapter 2.)

This book is most concerned with empirical evidence as to how corporate financial management and the capital markets actually function and not with mere theories unsupported by empirical evidence. Empirical evidence seems to support the theory that for many corporations, probably for most, there is a broad range of leverage levels in which the cost of equity is little affected by variations in capital structure and that, therefore, use of leverage to this extent is advantageous to stockholders. This means that generally there seems to be little difference in the cost of capital between companies with varying degrees of leverage operating in the same industry. Those who hold to the position that there is an *optimum point for leverage* tend to rest their case on the proposition that corporate management is well aware that there is an optimum point of leverage and in actual practice usually make sure that they do not push debt above this level. In this they are supported by policies of the lenders, largely financial intermediaries. On the other hand, those whose articles would seem to imply that there is no limit (no optimum point) for leverage claim that empirical evidence does not disclose rising costs of capital with rising leverage. The first group thinks that corporate management, by not, in fact, pushing beyond an optimum point or perhaps by staying well below such a point, fails to provide cases that would specifically disprove the theory.

In any case, business does not operate and will not operate in a tax-free world, and certainly under the tax laws that exist the tax advantage of deducting interest on debt *does* increase the rate of return on stockholders' equity based on after-tax earnings for a levered corporation versus an un-levered corporation. The cost of capital does fall as leverage is increased to the optimum point, and stockholders do benefit when corporations lever their capitalization by trading on their equity. The optimum point for a given firm would depend on many factors, most important of which is probably the level of income generated and the stability or lack of stability of that income and the amount and stability of cash flow.

Although it is admittedly difficult to prove, there would come a point when increases in the debt capitalization rate would offset the tax savings for debt financing. While lenders would, in most cases, probably refuse to lend beyond the optimum point when the leverage adds undue risk, in cases where they would lend beyond this point they would certainly increase the cost of capital. The use of leverage beyond the optimum point acceptable to lenders may reduce the total value of all the corporation's securities and raise the cost of capital above what the cost would have been if leverage had been used more wisely.

Mergers and Acquisitions

Corporations can and do expand through mergers as well as through capital expenditures and acquisitions. The period since World War II has witnessed the greatest number of mergers and acquisitions in history, especially the late 1960s.[17] There are various ways of accomplishing mergers and acquisitions, but in this book an exhaustive review of such methods is not necessary. The two most commonly used methods are: (1) purchase for cash, either from funds on hand or from funds obtained by the sale of securities; and (2) the exchange of stock of the acquiring company

---

[17] W. W. Alberts and J. E. Segall, *The Corporate Merger* (Chicago, Illinois: The University of Chicago Press, 1966).

for the stock of the company being acquired. The latter method is the most common one, supplemented by the use of convertible securities.

If earnings are properly adjusted (accounting adjustments) to be comparable for both companies, then if the stocks are exchanged on their price-earnings ratio basis, there is no dilution of earnings for the acquiring company. For example, if earnings per share for Company A (the acquiring company) are $5 per share and for Company B (the company being acquired) are $2.50 per share, an exchange of 1 share of Company A stock for 2 shares of Company B stock would result in no dilution of earnings for the acquiring company, assuming that the growth rate for earnings was identical. However, the acquiring company has frequently been so anxious to acquire the other company, whose earnings may be rising at a rapid rate, that frequently it will issue more of its stock than would be required on a purely equivalent current earnings ratio basis. The justification is that while *initially* there will be a dilution, the rapid growth of earnings of the company being acquired will eliminate this disability in a few years. The use of convertibles initially may obscure dilution.

CORPORATE DIVIDEND POLICIES

Corporation directors in determining dividend policies must weigh many factors and must establish a compromise between factors that are conflicting. In any one year they may decide to declare cash dividends only, or cash dividends plus stock dividends, or stock dividends only, or none at all. The goal should be to maximize the investment status of the stock.

Cash Dividends

Cash dividends, preferred or common, are never a liability of the corporation until declared by the directors,[18] who have the sole power to determine dividend policy.

Bases for Directors' Decisions on Dividends. The major factors considered by directors in deciding on dividend payments at the dividend meeting are:

1. *Availability of cash.* Cash flow provides the funds to pay dividends, to meet requirements for additional working capital as the volume of business expands, to pay for replacement of and additions to plant and

---

[18] See J. A. Brittain, *Corporate Dividend Policy* (Washington, D.C.: The Brookings Institution, 1966) and R. S. Holzman, *Tax on Accumulated Earnings* (New York: The Ronald Press Co., 1956).

equipment, to meet debt amortization and other repayment requirements, and to provide funds for the repurchase of outstanding securities. Directors must allow for all these factors when deciding the amount available for dividends. The sources and uses of funds statement, the cash budget, and the capital budget offer the necessary data and projections for sound analysis of the availability of cash. Directors must carefully analyze past, current, and projected earnings that underlie the budgets. The volatility as well as the amount of earnings is important.

2. *Legal and tax factors.* Legally, under most state statutes, the directors must charge cash dividends to the retained earnings account, which, with the addition of earnings for the current fiscal period, must be sufficient to absorb the amount charged for dividends declared. Furthermore, many debt indentures restrict part of all of the retained earnings account from charges for dividends. Such restrictions should appear in notes to the financial statements in annual reports. Under the Internal Revenue Code, Sections 531-537, the Treasury Department may assess a penalty tax for the unreasonable retention of earnings. Therefore, at each dividend meeting directors should review current working capital, cash budgets, and capital budgets, as well as any requirements for corporate securities to be reacquired. If such a review justifies the need of the business for the retention of earnings in terms of the planned level of operations, the directors can feel assured that the corporation will not later be assessed a penalty for unreasonable retention of earnings.

3. *Restrictions,* if any, imposed by regulatory commissions.

4. *Desires of stockholders for dividends.* The attitude of stockholders in general towards current dividend policy is reflected in the market price of the company's stock and the resulting price-earnings ratio relative to the market averages and to the stock of competing companies in the same industry. If the major goal of management should be, and generally is, to maximize the investment status of its stock and the quality of its credit in the capital markets, directors must consider the desire of the stockholders for dividends. While recognizing that the tax burden on dividend payments is very severe for stockholders in the high tax brackets, directors cannot establish dividend policy to favor large minority stockholders against the desire of other stockholders for dividends. An analysis of the stockholder list should be made to determine classes of stockholders, such as institutional holders, large holders, medium-sized holders, and small holders. An attempt should then be made to analyze the attitudes of these groups toward dividend payments as opposed to internal growth. The higher the growth rate of earnings, the less important are dividends to the investor. But Sections 531-537 of the IRC cannot be ignored.

It should be clear from the above that directors may face conflicting factors—a clear need for funds equal to entire net earnings versus a desire of stockholders for dividends. Fortunately, the choice is not necessarily between not paying dividends and not meeting the corporation's needs. Rather, it is a choice between internal and external sources of funds. The excess of corporate needs over retained earnings can and is usually met from external sources. In all cases, relative costs of capital are vital.

TABLE 7-1

Historical Record of Earnings, Dividends, Cash Flow, and Payout Ratios

	All U. S. Corporations						Dow Jones Industrial Average			Standard & Poor's 500 Composite Average		
Year	Profits After Taxes	Capital Consumption Allowances	Cash Flow Net Profits After Taxes Plus Cap. Cons. Allowances	Dividends	Div. As % of Net Profits	Div. As % of Cash Flow	Earn. Per Sh.	Div.* Per Sh.	Payout Ratio	Earn. Per Sh.	Div. Per Sh.	Payout Ratio
	($ Bil.)	($ Bil.)	($ Bil.)	($ Bil.)	%	%	$	$	%	$	$	%
1926	N.A.	N.A.	N.A.	N.A.	N.A.	N.A.	14.97	7.42	50	1.24	0.69	56
1927	N.A.	N.A.	N.A.	N.A.	N.A.	N.A.	12.39	8.29	67	1.11	0.77	69
1928	N.A.	N.A.	N.A.	N.A.	N.A.	N.A.	16.64	9.76	59	1.38	0.85	62
1929	8.6	4.2	12.8	5.8	67	45	19.94	12.25	61	1.61	0.97	60
1926-29	N.A.	N.A.	N.A.	N.A.	N.A.	N.A.	63.94	37.72	59	5.34	3.28	61
1930R	2.9	4.3	7.2	5.5	190	76	11.02	9.63	87	0.97	0.98	101
1931R	-.9	4.3	5.2	4.1	…	79	4.09	7.50	183	0.61	0.82	134
1932D	-2.7	4.0	6.7	2.5	…	37	d 0.51	4.62		0.49	0.50	102
1933D	.4	3.8	4.2	2.0	500	48	2.11	3.20	152	0.44	0.44	100
1934	1.6	3.6	5.2	2.6	163	50	3.91	3.66	94	0.49	0.45	92
1935	2.6	3.6	6.2	2.8	108	45	6.34	4.55	72	0.77	0.47	61
1936	4.9	3.6	8.5	4.5	92	53	10.07	7.05	70	1.03	0.72	70
1930-36	8.8	27.2	43.2	24.0	273	56	37.03	40.21	109	4.80	4.38	91
1937	5.3	3.6	8.9	4.7	89	53	11.49	8.78	76	1.19	0.80	67
1938R	2.9	3.7	6.6	3.2	110	48	6.01	4.84	81	0.63	0.51	81
1939	5.6	3.7	9.3	3.8	68	41	9.11	6.00	66	0.87	0.62	71
1937-39	13.8	11.0	24.8	11.7	85	47	26.61	19.62	74	2.69	1.93	72
1930-38	17.0**	34.5	58.7	31.9	188	54	54.53#	53.83	99	6.62	5.69	86
1930-39	22.6	38.2	68.0	35.7	158	53	63.64	59.83	94	7.79	6.31	84
1940W	7.2	3.8	11.0	4.0	56	36	10.92	7.06	65	1.06	0.67	63
1941W	10.1	4.3	14.4	4.4	44	31	11.64	7.59	65	1.18	0.71	60
1942WW	10.1	5.0	15.1	4.3	43	28	9.22	6.40	69	1.00	0.59	59
1943WW	11.1	5.4	16.5	4.4	40	27	9.74	6.30	65	0.93	0.61	66
1944WW	11.2	6.1	17.3	4.6	41	27	10.07	6.57	63	0.94	0.64	68
1945WW	9.0	6.4	15.4	4.6	51	31	10.56	6.69	65	0.98	0.66	68
1940-45WW	58.7	31.0	89.7	26.3								

TABLE 7-1 (Continued)

Year												
1946	15.5	4.7	20.2	5.6	36	28	13.63	7.50	55	1.03	0.71	69
1947	20.2	5.8	26.0	6.3	31	24	18.80	9.21	49	1.63	0.84	52
1948	22.7	7.0	29.7	7.0	31	24	23.07	10.47	45	2.28	0.93	41
1949R	18.5	7.9	26.4	7.2	39	27	23.54	11.78	50	2.32	1.14	49
1950	24.9	8.8	33.7	8.8	35	26	30.70	15.62	51	2.83	1.47	52
1946-50	101.8	34.2	136.0	34.9	34	26	109.80	54.58	50	10.09	5.09	50
1951	21.6	10.3	31.9	8.6	40	27	26.59	15.22	57	2.44	1.41	58
1952	19.6	11.5	31.1	8.6	44	28	24.78	15.23	61	2.40	1.41	59
1953	20.4	13.2	33.6	8.9	44	26	27.23	15.28	56	2.51	1.45	58
1954	20.6	15.0	35.6	9.3	45	26	28.40	16.96	60	2.77	1.54	56
1955	27.0	17.4	44.4	10.5	39	24	35.78	18.80	53	3.62	1.64	45
1956	27.2	18.9	46.1	11.3	42	25	33.34	20.09	60	3.41	1.74	51
1957	26.0	20.8	46.8	11.7	45	25	36.08	20.34	56	3.37	1.79	53
1958R	22.3	22.0	44.3	11.6	52	26	27.94	19.03	68	2.89	1.75	61
1959	28.5	23.5	52.0	12.6	44	24	34.31	19.38	56	3.39	1.83	54
1951-59	213.2	152.6	365.8	93.1	44	25	274.44	160.33	58	26.80	14.56	54
1960R	26.7	24.9	51.6	13.4	50	26	32.21	20.46	64	3.31	1.95	59
1961	27.2	26.2	53.5	13.8	51	26	31.91	21.28	67	3.19	2.02	63
1962	31.2	30.1	61.3	15.2	49	25	36.43	22.09	61	3.67	2.13	58
1963	33.1	31.8	64.8	16.5	49	25	41.21	23.20	56	4.02	2.28	57
1964	38.4	33.9	72.3	17.8	46	25	46.43	25.38	55	4.55	2.50	55
1965	46.5	36.4	82.9	19.8	44	24	53.67	28.17	52	5.19	2.72	52
1966	49.9	39.5	89.5	20.8	41	23	57.67	30.12	52	5.55	2.87	52
1960-66	253.0	223.7	473.2	117.3	46	24	299.53	170.70	57	29.48	16.47	56
1951-66	466.2	376.3	842.2	210.4	45	24	573.85	331.02	58	56.28	31.03	55
1937-66	640.5	452.5	1092.7	283.3	44	25	772.41	445.83	58	75.15	41.93	56
1929-66	657.9	483.7	1148.7	313.1	47	27	829.38	498.29	60	81.56	47.28	58
1926-66	N.A.	N.A.	N.A.	N.A.	N.A.	N.A.	873.38	523.76	60	85.29	49.59	58
1937-66: % Inc.	813%	983%	882%	349%			401%	242%		364%	259%	
1966 vs. 1937	9.1x	10.8x	9.9x	4.5x			5.0x	3.4x		4.6x	3.6x	
1967‡	46.6	43.0	89.6	21.4	45	23	53.87	29.84	55	5.33	2.92	55
1968	47.8	46.8	94.6	23.6	49	24	57.89	31.34	54	5.76	3.07	53
1969	44.8	51.9	95.8	24.3	54	25	57.02	33.90	59	5.78	3.16	55
1970	40.2	55.2	95.4	24.8	61	25	51.02	31.53	62	5.13	3.14	62
1971	45.9	60.3	106.2	25.4	55	23	55.09	30.86	56	5.70	3.07	54

D—Depression; N.A.—Not available; P—Preliminary; R—Recession; W—War in Europe; WW—World War II; d—Deficit; x—times; *—Cash dividend only; **—Net of losses, 1931-32; #—Net of loss in 1932; ‡—1967 mini-recession.

Source: U. S. Department of Commerce, *Survey of Current Business*, various issues; *Standard & Poor's Analysts Handbook*; and the *Dow Jones Investor's Handbook*.

Empirical Evidence of Dividend Policies. Before the voluminous literature on dividend policy is considered and interpreted, it is desirable to review some *empirical evidence* for companies as a whole as furnished by statistics in Table 7-1 for (1) all U.S. corporations, (2) the Dow Jones Industrial Average, and (3) the Standard & Poor's 500 Composite Average. It must be kept constantly in mind that there is a rather wide range of policy in terms of dividend payment versus earnings retention between industries and also between companies within an industry. However, a large percentage of companies do fall within the range indicated by statistics for the DJIA and the S&P 500 and for All U. S. Corporations.[19]

The usual analysis and discussion of payout policy is in terms of the proportion of earnings paid out as dividends. Because the highly significant ratio of dividends to cash flow is often overlooked, Table 7-1 shows for all U.S. corporations a column headed "Dividends As % of Cash Flow."

The empirical evidence for three distinct time periods is reviewed because corporate dividend policy was greatly affected by the radically different economic environments of each of these three periods: (1) the depressed 1930s, (2) the World War II period and its immediate aftermath, and (3) the post-World War II period to 1971. The record for the entire period 1926-1971 appears in Table 7-1.

Dividend Policy in the Depressed 1930s. Corporate dividend policy in the 1930s was established in an environment of low earnings or actual deficits in which investment opportunities did not appear too promising. It was difficult to think in terms of expansion when operations were well below capacity and rate of return on current investment was very low or nonexistent.

An examination of the total for the years 1930-1938 inclusive shows that the payout of dividends to earnings ratio was 188% for all U.S. corporations, 99% for the DJIA, and 86% for the S&P 500. If the year 1939 is included, the payouts were 158%, 94%, and 84% respectively. Furthermore, while dividends were reduced sharply, they still represented heavy payments for the group in the years of net deficits. Corporate policy certainly gave strong support to the argument that directors believe that stockholders desire dividends even in years of a great depression. Every effort was made to make such payments over a considerable period of time, even if dividends exceeded earnings for as long a period as a decade.

Immediately the question arises as to how dividends can be paid in excess of earnings over an extended period of time. It is true that the

---

[19] Refer to Chapter 4 for tables on the 1929-1968 dividend record of the DJIA and the S&P 500 and 425 indexes.

retained earnings account (earned surplus) must be sufficient to absorb the portion of the *accounting charges* for the amount of the dividend. But this is purely accounting. The American Institute of Certified Public Accountants has campaigned against the use of the term "earned surplus account" because *surplus* has a "money in the bank sound" even though in fact a corporation with a large "earned surplus" account may, in fact, have no cash. The account reflects past earnings that have been reinvested in the business in the assets, and to a large extent for most companies in fixed assets. Clearly, no funds as such are available for dividends if they are permanently invested in the business.

This brings out the great importance of cash flow, which is at least as important in dividend policy as is earnings. The column in Table 7-1 headed "Dividends as % of Cash Flow" indicates that never in the 1930s did dividends exceed cash flow. Earnings are reported after deductions for depreciation; but depreciation, while a very real expense, does not as such drain off funds flowing down from sales or gross income. The funds that flow down can be used for investment in assets, for dividend payments, or for other purposes. This is *how* corporations were able to pay dividends in excess of earnings. But, of course, to the extent that dividends exceed earnings, funds are used that otherwise would be utilized to replace depreciated assets. To the extent that part of the dividends exceeds earnings, the payout of capital constitutes corporate *dissavings* as opposed to retention and reinvestment of part or all of the earnings that represent corporate savings. Table 7-2 shows the amount of corporate dissavings in the 1930s.

TABLE 7-2

Corporate Dissavings in the 1930s (Millions of Dollars) ($+ =$ Savings)

1930	+$ 647	1935	−$ 424
1931	− 2,522	1936	− 330
1932	− 4,191	1937	+ 592
1933	− 3,746	1938	+ 737
1934	− 1,590	1939	+ 1,120

Total net dissavings for the decade of the 1930s was $9.2 billion. Fixed business capital in the U. S.: 1929, $7 billion; 1939, $6 billion; 1965, $57 billion. Figures are for net stock (fixed business capital) after depreciation.

Dividend Policy During World War II and Through 1948. In the 1930s dividends paid had greatly exceeded net income, resulting in corporate dissavings and in depreciated plant and equipment with a much lower value in

1939 than in 1929 because plant and equipment replacement was less than the depreciation. During World War II, however, as profits after taxes rose sharply, dividend payouts relative to net profits declined sharply. Dividends as a percentage of net profits fell to 45% for the years 1940-1945 inclusive and fell even lower in the immediate post-war years to 31% in 1947 and 1948. Thereafter the payout ratios rose to more normal levels, averaging 45% in the years 1951-1966 inclusive and somewhat higher at the end of the period.

Dividend Policy in the Post-World War II Years. The years 1946-1948 were adjustment years. The significant years were 1949-1971 as far as payout ratios to net earnings after taxes were concerned. In terms of dividends to cash flow for all U.S. corporations, the ratio fell to 24% in 1947 and ranged between 23% and 27% for all years except 1952 when it rose to 28%.

In terms of the ratio of dividends to net after taxes, the median figure for all U.S. corporations was 45.0% and the mean was 46.3%. It was somewhat higher for the DJIA and for the S&P 500 as shown in Table 7-3 below.

TABLE 7-3

Payout Ratios, Post-World War II Years, 1949-1966

	All U. S. Corporations		DJIA	S&P 500
	Dividends to Cash Flow	Dividends to Net After Taxes	Dividends to Net After Taxes	Dividends to Net After Taxes
Median	25.0%	45.0%	56.0%	55.0%
Mean	25.1	46.3	57.5	55.3

The depression and war years were very abnormal years. Prior to the 1930s corporations tended to pay out about two thirds of their earnings as dividends. In the post-World War II years, the ratio (DJIA and S&P 500) has tended to be about 10% lower, or 55%-56%, for two reasons: (1) directors considered opportunities for reinvestment of earnings especially profitable, and (2) investors seemed to agree, as indicated by the rising price-earnings ratios and the declining dividend yields at which they were willing to purchase stocks in the market. They were willing to accept lower dividend yields (lower than bond yields) and lower payout ratios than in previous years and they were willing to pay more (higher P/E's) for each dollar of earnings. In the 1960s dividend yields were usually around 3%.

The period 1961-1966 was a most exceptional period for corporate profits. The 1960-1961 recession ended in the first quarter of 1961. From the first quarter of 1961 to the entire year of 1966, net profits of all U.S. corporations rose from $24.4 billion to $51.0 billion, or a doubling in 5 years at an annual compound rate of growth of 14.81% per year. Taking total profits of $26.7 billion in 1960 as a base, corporate profits rose to $51.0 billion in 1966, or an increase of 91.0%, for a compound annual rate of about 11.4% per year. It is clear from Table 7-1 (DJIA and S&P 500) that corporate directors permitted the payout ratio to decline to 52% in 1965 and 1966. Investors showed growing enthusiasm for stocks in 1961-1966 (when the DJIA ranged from 735 to 995) and obviously did not take a negative attitude toward the declining payout ratios. It is true that after February, 1966, stocks declined 25%; but this was a reflection of anticipation of lower earnings in 1967, not of dissatisfaction with payout ratios of 52%. By December, 1968, the DJIA had recovered to its 1966 high, the S&P 500 index was 108 versus its peak of 94 in 1966, and the S&P 425 index was 118 versus its peak of 100 in 1966. The S&P dividend yield in December, 1968, was only 2.87% as compared with 3.01% in February, 1966. In early 1969 stock prices declined 10% and dividend yields rose. The sharp rise in the proportion of after-tax profits paid out by all U.S. corporations during the years 1969-1971 appears to have been caused by a decline in profits rather than a change in dividend policy.

Dividends *vs.* Bond Interest. One final comment may be made on corporate dividends, and this is relative to bond interest. One strong argument for bond investment versus common stock investment historically has been that interest is fixed and stable but dividends fluctuate considerably. And yet a strong argument for common stocks over the past three decades (1938-1939 to 1971) has been their great stability for diversified portfolios in addition to their very substantial increase in dividends as shown in Table 7-4. In December, 1972, dividend yields (S&P) averaged only 2.7% vs. 7.01% for outstanding top-grade corporate bond issues.

Stock Dividends

Many corporations pay regular stock dividends either instead of or as a supplement to cash dividends. Other corporations pay occasional stock dividends. The major justification for a regular stock dividend policy is that the stock dividend represents earnings retained in the business to be used for additional investments that the directors believe will be sufficiently profitable

TABLE 7-4

Cash Dividends—All U.S. Corporations, DJIA, and S&P 500 Composite

Years	All U. S. Corporations ($ Billions)	DJIA	S&P 500
1938	3.2	$ 4.84	$0.51
1939	3.8	6.00	0.62
1966	21.1	30.11	2.87
1968	24.6	31.34	3.07
1971	25.4	30.86	3.07
Increase %	694%	538%	502%
Decline	Only Years In Which Dividends Declined		
1941 to 1942	$ 4.4 to 4.3	$ 7.59 to $ 6.40	$0.71 to 0.59
1942 to 1943		6.40 to 6.30	0.59 to 0.61
1950 to 1951	8.8 to 8.6	15.62 to 15.22	1.47 to 1.41
1957 to 1958	11.7 to 11.6	20.34 to 19.03	1.79 to 1.75
Increases	Total Increases		
1966 vs. 1937	4.5x	3.6x	3.4x
1966 vs. 1939	5.6x	5.0x	4.6x
1971 vs. 1939	6.7x	5.1x	4.6x

to be justifiable. The stockholders receive a tangible piece of paper, although the new total of all shares held will have no higher basic earning power or asset value than before the stock dividend. But, as opposed to a cash dividend, the stockholder will pay no tax on the stock dividend.

For example, assume a 100% stock dividend. On the books of account, the stock dividend will be charged to retained earnings (a reduction) and credited to the capital stock account (an increase). However, the total of the capital accounts (assets—liabilities = capital) will remain the same. Each stockholder's total equity will not change and his *proportionate* share in past, current, and future earnings will not change. He now has 2 shares of stock having exactly the same basic value as 1 share held previously. The total economic value of his shares on the market should not change because there are no more assets and no more earning power behind his total holdings than before the 100% stock dividend. However, in this case, as in the case of a stock split, if the market price of the old shares was high, the effect of the 100% dividend may be to reduce the price to a range attractive to more buyers, which may increase demand and therefore create a higher total value in the market for all shares than before the stock dividend. Furthermore, as in the case of a stock split, the dividend is usually raised, which tends to raise the price of the stock.

If a corporation pays a stock dividend regularly instead of a cash dividend, supposedly the directors prefer to reinvest earnings rather than to pay out cash, but they desire to give a tangible recognition to the retained earnings in the form of a stock dividend. Theoretically, if earnings rise 10% a year, a 10% stock dividend could be paid each year. Actually, however, assume that the stock is selling at $45 and earning $3 per year but that a 10% stock dividend is valued by investors at $4.50 even though earnings are only $3. This condition existed in the late 1920s as corporations paid out stock having a market value considerably in excess of their earnings, lifting themselves up by their bootstraps. Specifically, when stock selling at $45 paid a stock dividend of 10% that investors valued at $4.50, it was reasoned that a stock paying $4.50 (even though it was earning only $3) should sell higher than $45. The stock would rise in value and the next year it might sell at $60. It might even earn $3.50 that year, but a 10% stock dividend would be valued at $6, and so the process continued. To avoid such distributions, the New York Stock Exchange will not permit a corporation to pay a stock dividend with a market value in excess of the amount that is to be charged to retained earnings, which amount should not exceed earnings.

As long as income continues to rise, the policy of retaining earnings and paying a regular stock dividend proportionate to the earnings increase is satisfactory. However, numerous corporations have maintained a policy of regular small stock dividends in addition to cash dividends in spite of a mediocre earnings record, so that the effect of stock dividends has not been satisfactory for stockholders. For example, International Paper Company regularly paid a 2% stock dividend for the years 1958-1963 inclusive, which meant that the number of shares of its stock outstanding, taking 1957 as 100, rose to 112 as a result of stock dividends. The amount of stock outstanding rose 12.62%. Net earnings per share on stock outstanding were $2.51 in 1955, $2.35 in 1956, $2.06 in 1959, $1.48 in 1963, $2.40 in 1966, and $2.08 in 1967. The stock sold at highs of $48 in 1956 but only $35 in 1966 (when the DJIA rose from a high of 521 to a high of 995). The stock's high in 1967 was $32, and the price range in 1968 was 26-40. The additional stock and the resulting lower reported earnings per share had a depressing influence on the market price. Many similar cases could be cited. On the other hand, in the case of electric utility companies, which constantly expand and frequently sell additional stock by rights issues, a strong case could be made for a regular stock dividend instead of a cash dividend. However, stockholders' desires for cash dividends have so far precluded such policies not only for electric utilities but for many other corporations.[20]

---

[20] A large utility company announced in 1968 its intention to pay part of its dividend in stock, but stockholder reaction was so negative that the decision was rescinded.

QUESTIONS

1. (a) What should be the major goal of corporate directors and corporate management?
   (b) How would you judge whether an individual corporation was fulfilling its stated goal?

2. (a) What are the dangers to a business of maintaining inadequate working capital?
   (b) Why should investors in a corporation be concerned if an above-average amount of working capital is maintained?

3. What has been happening to corporate net working capital in the 1960s? Do you feel the trend noted is favorable or unfavorable? Discuss.

4. How can effective cash budgeting aid the financial manager in maximizing profits for the business?

5. What estimates must be made in preparing the cash budget?

6. (a) Discuss the significance of cash-flow-per-share figures.
   (b) In what ways might such figures be misleading?

7. What is the significance to the investor of financial leverage?

8. (a) Does the degree of leverage utilized by a firm affect the cost of capital of that firm? Discuss.
   (b) What empirical evidence is available concerning the above question?

9. Explain the pros and cons of various methods used in capital budgeting for selection of new projects for investment.

10. (a) Is the following statement true or false? "Other things being equal, firms with relatively stable sales patterns through time can and should incur relatively high debt ratios." Explain your answer.
    (b) What is the likely effect on the degree of financial leverage and the capital structure of the firm of each of the following occurrences?
       (1) The firm repurchases 20% of its outstanding preferred stock (6% dividend requirement) by means of funds raised through the sale of common stock. Common stock is presently receiving a 6% dividend.
       (2) The firm repurchases 20% of its outstanding preferred stock (6% dividend requirement) by means of funds raised through the sale of 8% bonds.
       (3) An issue of convertible bonds is converted.
       (4) The firm retains 70 percent of its annual earnings recorded for the year just ended.

WORK-STUDY PROBLEMS

1. Assume that a corporation reports earnings in the current fiscal year of $50,000. The following estimates of net profits after taxes are those that

could be obtained in the long run by retaining various amounts of earn-- ings. Assume that stockholders could earn 7% after taxes through alternative investments of equivalent risk.

Retained Earnings	Estimated Net Profit after Taxes
$10,000	$1,500
20,000	2,400
30,000	3,000
40,000	3,200
50,000	3,300

(a) Ignoring personal income taxes, what amount should be paid out in dividends if the stockholders wish to maximize the amount earned on their total investment?

(b) If the stockholders face a personal income tax rate mean, median, and mode of 25% on marginal income, how should this affect dividend policy?

2. Prepare a table covering a 10-year period showing the following data for A.T. & T. Corporation and I.B.M. Corporation:

Year	Earnings Per Share	Dividends Per Share	Price Range; Common Stock	Percent of Earnings Paid In Dividends	Dividend Yield

On the basis of these data answer the following questions:

(a) What differences do you find in dividend policy?

(b) What explanations would you advance for these differences? Do you believe each policy is justified? Why?

(c) What effect do you believe changes in the current dividend policies of each company would have on current market price of their stock? Explain your answer.

SUGGESTED READINGS

Aharoni, Yair. *The Foreign Investment Decision Process*. Boston, Mass.: Graduate School of Business Administration, Harvard University, 1966.

Barges, Alexander. *The Effect of Capital Structure on the Cost of Capital*. Englewood Cliffs, N.J.: Prentice-Hall, Inc., 1963.

Bierman, Harold, Jr. "Risk and the Addition of Debt to the Capital Structure." *Journal of Financial and Quantitative Analysis* (December, 1968), pp. 415-426.

Brigham, Eugene F., and Myron J. Gordon. "Leverage, Dividend Policy and the Cost of Capital." *The Journal of Finance* (March, 1968), pp. 85-104.

——————. "A Reply to Leverage, Dividend Policy and the Cost of Capital: A Comment." *The Journal of Finance* (September, 1970), pp. 904-908.

Brittain, John A. *Corporate Dividend Policy*. Washington, D.C.: The Brookings Institution, 1966.

Budd, A. P., and Litzenberger. "Changes in the Supply of Money, the Firm's Market Value and Cost of Capital." *The Journal of Finance* (March, 1973), pp. 49-57.

Davenport, Michael. "Leverage, Dividend Policy and the Cost of Capital: A Comment." *The Journal of Finance* (September, 1970), pp. 893-897.

Durand, David. *The Cost of Debt and Equity Funds for Business: Trends and Problems of Measurement*. New York: National Bureau of Economic Research, Inc., 1952.

Fama, Eugene F., and Harvey Babiak. "Dividend Policy: An Empirical Analysis." *Journal of the American Statistical Association* (December, 1968) pp. 1132-1161.

Friend, Irwin, and Marshall Packett. "Dividends and Stock Prices." *American Economic Review* (September, 1964), pp. 656-82.

Gordon, M. J. *The Investment, Financing and Valuation of the Corporation*. Homewood, Illinois: Richard D. Irwin, Inc., 1962.

Haslem, John A. "Leverage Effects on Corporate Earnings." *Arizona Business Review* (March, 1970), pp. 7-11.

Lerner, Eugene M., and Alfred Rappaport. "Capital Budgeting and Reported Earnings to Shareholders." A paper presented at the annual meeting of the American Accounting Association, August, 1968.

Loomis, C. J. "A Case for Dropping Dividends." *Fortune* (June, 1968), pp. 181-185ff.

MacDougal, G. E. "Investing in a Dividend Boost." *Harvard Business Review* (July-August, 1967), pp. 87-92.

Mendelson, Morris. "Leverage, Dividend Policy and the Cost of Capital: A Comment." *The Journal of Finance* (September, 1970), pp. 898-903.

Modigliani, F., and M. H. Miller. "The Cost of Capital, Corporation Finance and the Theory of Investment," *American Economic Review*. (June, 1958), pp. 261-297.

——————. "Cost of Capital to the Electric Utility Industry," *American Economic Review*. June, 1966. (This is a major revision of the 1958 article.)

Rubinstein, Mark E. "A Mean-Variance Synthesis of Corporate Financial Theory." *The Journal of Finance* (March, 1973), pp. 167-181.

Sarma, L.V.L.N., and K.S.H. Rao. "Leverage and the Value of the Firm." *The Journal of Finance* (September, 1969), pp. 673-678.

Stapleton, Richard C. "Portfolio Analysis, Stock Valuation and Capital Budgeting Decision Rules for Risky Projects." *The Journal of Finance* (March, 1971), pp. 95-118.

Tepper, Irwin. "Revealed Preference Methods and the Pure Theory of the Cost of Capital." *The Journal of Finance* (March, 1973), pp. 35-48.

Walter, James E. *Dividend Policy and Enterprise Valuation*. Belmont, California: Wadsworth Publishing Company, Inc., 1967.

PART THREE

INVESTMENT IN LIMITED-INCOME SECURITIES

Investment Strategies for Limited-Income Securities

Bonds may be purchased for investment or for speculation. Bonds are purchased for investment by those seeking relative stability of income and stability of capital investment. Bond speculators, on the other hand, are concerned with potential capital appreciation, not relatively high interest yields. Selection of limited-income securities for capital appreciation closely resembles common stock speculation and should be considered in that context except for speculation in changes in the level of interest rates by professionals.

This chapter concentrates on investment grade limited-income securities because it is felt that limited-income *investors,* especially individuals, are usually best served with quality instruments. Investment grade debt securities include not only bonds, but also private placement notes and other debt instruments. At the end of this chapter is a discussion of the strategies for investment in preferred stocks since they are purchased for the same purposes as bonds although they are equity, not creditor, issues.

INVESTMENT GRADE LIMITED-INCOME SECURITIES

The investor should consider several factors before deciding to purchase investment grade limited-income securities. In other words, what would he gain, as well as give up, by investing in bonds rather than in common stocks, for example. Further, he should know what forms of protection are available to him as an investor in limited-income securities.

Major Advantages of Limited-Income Securities

For investment grade debt instruments the advantages claimed are relatively *stable value* and *stable income*. Their market value should fluctuate only with changes in interest rates. By comparison, investment grade common stocks will fluctuate much more in price than investment grade bonds.

A major advantage of bonds over stocks is that, since 1958, bonds have steadily yielded more than the current dividend yield on common stocks (DJIA, S&P, etc.); and in the 1970s, twice the yield on common stocks. Therefore, since 1958 the decision to purchase common stocks versus bonds has had to assume an overall rate of return of dividend yield *plus expected capital appreciation* in excess of bond yields by a significant margin.

It is a truism that if the debt security (or preferred stock) is really investment grade, the safety of the income from the security is assured beyond any reasonable doubt. Even in the years without major recessions, 1938-1973, the dividends of a few major companies have been reduced.[1] But for well-diversified common stock portfolios since 1938, the stability of dividend income has been nearly equivalent to the stability of bond interest; and in addition, dividend income has risen over 5 times since 1938.

Sacrifices Made by the Bond Investor

The purchaser of limited-income securities does make some real sacrifices in his attempt to maintain the dollar amount of his capital and the dollar amount of his income, especially in periods of rising prices. His four real sacrifices in the case of bonds and notes are:

1. He agrees to accept a fixed dollar return on his investment regardless of the amount of profits generated by the issuer.

2. He agrees to accept repayment at a future date of the same number of dollars that he loaned regardless of the purchasing power of these dollars at the time of repayment or the success of the issuer, which may lead to large increases in the value of the common stock of the issuer.

3. He will witness a decline in the market value of the bond, which may be substantial, when interest rates rise above the level existing at the time he purchased the bond.[2] (Example: 1946-1970.)

4. Capital appreciation during the life of the bond (except in the case of convertible bonds) can occur only if interest rates decline or if the credit rating of the issuer rises.

---

[1] Reduction in dividends from 1969 to 1970 were: Chrysler, $2 to $0.80; General Motors, $4.30 to $3.40; General Dynamics, $0.125 to $0.50. Reduction for duPont from 1968 to 1970 was $5.50 to $5.25 to $5.00. These are a few examples.

[2] This risk has certainly been evident since 1946 as indicated in Chapter 3.

Since capital appreciation is not a likely potential in an investment grade bond or preferred stock (except as a reflection of declining interest rates) and income will never increase, the investor in such securities should ascertain beyond any reasonable doubt that he will not suffer loss of expected income. At least he wants to be assured of receiving what is promised, as he can never receive any more. Quality and security must compensate the investor for the sacrifices he accepts by investing in investment grade limited-income securities.

A speculator who buys bonds in default or close to default can enjoy substantial capital appreciation if the issuer succeeds in solving its financial problems and in improving its credit rating. Certainly, then, all bonds are not absolutely fixed-income securities. The risks assumed by the speculator are high and parallel those assumed in purchasing speculative common stocks, although judicious selection may afford large capital gains for both.

The investor desires protection of principal and strong assurance of income when he purchases limited-income securities. For the individual investor there are many issues of the higher grades (A rating and above) from which to choose. He should reject those about which he has the slightest question and choose from the many top-quality issues available. The investor who rejects a bond that later proves to have been a good investment loses little by this rejection. He has not lost the opportunity for a substantial capital gain, as can be true with investment grade as well as other common stocks. Later, evidence will be offered to indicate that yield spreads usually are not wide enough to compensate for the risks involved in reaching for relatively high yields of bonds below a BBB grade. This is especially true if stability of market price is desired.

Protection of Fixed-Income Securities Investments

Protection of capital invested in fixed-income securities and of the income from such securities is provided in varying degrees by the factors discussed in the following paragraphs.

Contract Protection. The contract covering fixed-income securities provides some protection for the investment, but it does not provide the major protection. Fixed-income securities have advantages over common stocks because of the nature of their contracts, and bonds have advantages over equity securities (preferred or common) because of the *creditor* nature of the debt contracts. If a debt contract to pay interest and principal when due is not fulfilled, the corporation is in legal default; therefore, every effort will be made to fulfill this contract. On the other hand, dividends, common or preferred, are discretionary with the directors, and nonpayment of fixed-income preferred stock dividends is not a legal default.

Ability of Corporation to Meet Legal Claims. The major protection of investments in fixed-income securities is not the contract but the corporation's ability to meet *all* its legal claims. This means not only the specific claims of bondholders, but also the claims of all creditors at all times. If a corporation defaults on *any* of the legal claims against it, then, at the very least, all its bondholders will witness a severe decline in the market value of these securities. Safety of a fixed-income securities investment therefore depends chiefly on the earning power of the issuer and its cash flow.

Asset Values and Asset Liens. Before the 1930s, the investment community tended to emphasize the asset values behind fixed-income securities as providing the major protection for bondholders on the assumption that, even in the case of defaults on contracts, the bondholders were protected by their claim against the assets. However, the experience of the investor holding defaulted bonds in the 1930s provided sufficient evidence that this approach is disillusioning. High book-value asset "protection" did not prevent default. On defaults or near defaults, the market value of bonds (including mortgage bonds) declined drastically, and in many cases major losses were suffered as a result of reorganization or liquidation. Even in cases where financial reorganization plans provided a new security of equal par value to the bondholder's initial investment before default, during the intervening period the bondholders experienced a major decline in market value in addition to the loss of interest during this period.

In case of defaults, the legal difficulties are time-consuming and costly, and in the final settlements asset values often prove quite insufficient to protect the interest of bondholders.[3] The conclusion is, therefore, that investors in fixed-income securities should concentrate on rigorous analysis to determine if claims can be expected to be met when due beyond any reasonable doubt, and they should not rely on asset values and on asset liens. The emphasis should be on avoidance of potential trouble.

---

[3] The case of equipment obligations is an exception to the rule. Asset values are important in this instance. The equipment represents the newest and best equipment of the corporation, the debt has been reduced faster than the equipment has depreciated, and the marketability of the equipment is excellent. Finally, the legal history of special treatment for equipment obligations in periods of difficulty all contribute to the generally high or excellent ratings. In fact, even in the case of railroads in receivership, such as the New York, New Haven and Hartford, their equipment obligations were rated above their mortgage obligations that were in default.

Protection for the bondholders is predicated on the ability of the company in question to meet its obligations.[4] All AAA rated industrial debenture bonds are ranked AAA because of their specific ability to pay and not because of their asset values. Today, particularly in the industrial field, there is a keen realization that earning power and adequate cash flow afford the chief protection of bondholders and that the absence of liens is generally not important. Many debenture bonds (unsecured promises to pay) receive the very highest ratings. Actually, of industrial issues with the highest ratings, debenture issues constitute the majority.[5]

Debenture bondholders should be concerned with answers to the following:

1. Are there any existing creditors enjoying a prior claim?
2. If senior claims exist, what are the terms of their contracts with the corporation?
3. Can the corporation in the future issue other securities with a senior claim without the consent of the debenture bondholders?
4. If senior securities can be issued in the future, what can be the extent and the kind of such claims?

The answers to these questions, together with an analysis of the margin of safety (times fixed charges earned) and the cash flow protection, determine whether or not the debenture bond is a satisfactory investment medium.

Mortgage bonds do have a specific lien against assets that entitles the bondholders to prior claim in default. Railroad bonds are usually mortgage bonds. The highest ranked of these are protected by the highest income per mile of road and per dollar of mortgage bonds. Earnings power is their real protection, not asset liens.

The absence of specific claims against assets is not in itself a negative factor, but any doubt concerning a corporation's ability to meet all of its obligations should eliminate it from consideration for investment bond portfolios. Normally the senior obligations of an issuer should be recommended; but if a significant yield spread between bonds of the same issuer exists, the higher-yielding bond should be purchased if any are available.

---

[4] Relatively few industrial bonds receive a AAA rating. Examples of AAA rated industrial bonds are: Texaco S.F. Debs. 5¾ 1997; General Electric S.F. Debs. 5.30 1992; General Motors Corp. Debs. 3¼ 1979; Gulf Oil Corp. S.F. Debs. 5.35 1991; National Dairy Products Debs. 4⅜ 1992. A very considerable number of electric utility bonds are rated AAA.

Some examples of AA rated industrial bonds are: Anchor Hocking Glass S.F. Deb. 5½ 1991; Bethlehem Steel Corp. S.F. Deb. 3¼ 1992; Borden Co. S.F. Deb. 4⅜ 1991; Corn Products Co. Sub. Deb. 4⅝ 1983; Dow Chemical S.F. Deb. 4¾ 1981; Firestone Tire & Rubber Deb. 4¼ 1988; General Motors Corp. Deb. 3¼ 1979; B. F. Goodrich Co. S.F. Deb. 4⅝ 1985. These are all debentures (unsecured promises to pay) resting only on the general credit standing of the issuer.

[5] Note that all AAA rated industrial bonds listed in footnote 4 were debenture bonds.

Stability of Earnings Record and Margin of Safety

A safe, fixed income investment is one that will be well-protected in periods of business recessions and depressions as well as in periods of prosperity. Sufficiency and stability of earning power and cash flow are the major tests. The *margin of safety* should be wide enough so that no doubt exists as to the company's ability to meet its debts, no matter what the economic circumstances. The earning power of the issuer and its cash flow in previous years of poor business should be reviewed and weighed against the general financial and debt situation of the issuer. The record of the industry as well as that of the company should be reviewed and projected.

The margin of safety required will vary with the industry and the company. Utilities, for example, require a lower margin of safety than cyclical industries such as steel, as shown later in this chapter.[6]

It is a widely accepted premise among most investors, as well as many economists, that major depressions are a thing of the past and that recessions in the future will continue to be of the mild character experienced since 1938.[7] However, even if this should be the case, it does not follow that investors can ignore the dangers of adverse turns in the economy in selecting fixed-income securities. In the first place, the greater stability of the economy as measured by fluctuations in GNP has not prevented large fluctuations in overall corporate profits and cash flows. In addition, certain major industries continue to exhibit greater fluctuations in earnings than are reflected in the total picture for all corporate profits. Furthermore, profits have become more sensitive to economic recession in the post-World War II period. Finally, individual companies within an industry will exhibit wider fluctuations in earnings than the industry average.

BOND INVESTMENT PHILOSOPHIES AND STRATEGIES

One possible investment approach would be to avoid fixed-income securities in the more cyclical industries. This approach, however, implies that certain other industries are recession proof and ignores coverage leading to safety in adversity and stability in relation to price. It is more judicious to analyze each company carefully to determine the degree of fluctuation in its gross revenues and net earnings, as well as industry factors.

---

[6] For a discussion of the proper techniques to be utilized in calculating this measure and suggested standards, see Chapter 9.

[7] For an excellent statement of this position and supporting reasons for such beliefs, see A. F. Burns, "Progress Towards Economic Stability," *American Economic Review*, Vol. I, No. 1 (March, 1960), pp. 1-19.

Stability of Industrial Companies

Increased competition in any industry may pare profits drastically in spite of increases in sales volume and may well affect some companies in that industry more severely than others. If an industry has considerable instability in earnings, this may sometimes be compensated for by insisting on higher margins of safety. This concept should also be applied to industrial companies that demonstrate greater fluctuations in earnings than do other companies in the same industry. But dangers of relying on heavy coverage are highlighted by Acme Steel's drop from a coverage of 18.62x in 1956 to 1.93x in 1961.

The Hickman Study

A study published in 1958 under the sponsorship of the National Bureau of Economic Research concluded that within the period 1900-1943 large investors who purchased a large portfolio of well-diversified, higher-yielding bonds, below the top grades, would have had satisfactory results *if they kept the bonds through all difficulties experienced until the bonds were finally paid off.* The yield on the entire portfolio, after allowing for losses, would have exceeded the yield on a high-grade portfolio. However, the psychological risk must not be ignored, for even institutional investment committees will be sorely tempted to sell bonds at a loss when the issuer encounters serious financial difficulty. Furthermore, while in the long run such bonds may work out satisfactorily, they will sell at low prices if the issuer experiences financial difficulty, and this will result in substantial losses if the issue must be or is liquidated.

If investors are convinced that they will hold bonds until maturity regardless of the issuers' financial difficulties, then the conclusions of the National Bureau of Economic Research are pertinent.[8] For speculators, however, a better program might be to aim at purchasing such bonds when the issuers are experiencing difficulties. After all, if a diversified portfolio of such securities will work out satisfactorily, those who purchase in time of trouble when the securities are undervalued will obviously fare much better than those who purchase the securities when issued and hold them through all difficulties. The National Bureau of Economic Research study included the record of the Great Depression.

---

[8] W. Braddock Hickman, *Corporate Bond Quality and Investor Experience,* National Bureau of Economic Research (Princeton, N. J.: Princeton University Press, 1958). A summary was published by the Bureau as "Corporate Bonds, Quality and Investment Performance," Occasional Paper 59. This study was partially updated in Thomas R. Atkinson, *Trends in Corporate Bond Quality,* National Bureau of Economic Research (New York: Columbia University Press, 1967).

The study should be at least as helpful to speculators as to investors, and it is likely to be more useful as a guide to the former than the latter because of the psychological factors involved. A few of the principal conclusions of this study, which covered the period 1900-1943, are given below.[9]

1. Life-span yields realized on the aggregate of bonds studied equaled yields promised at offerings so that the net loss rate, measured in current dollars, was zero.

2. Capital gains and capital losses were substantial on bonds offered and extinguished in different periods and on outstandings held over different assumed chronological investment periods.

3. Although the overall record of straight corporate bonds was excellent, capital losses were large on bonds bought during the buoyant twenties that were still outstanding in the thirties and thus subject to the heavy default risks of the Great Depression.

4. Agency ratings, market ratings, legal lists, and other selected indicators of prospective bond quality proved to be useful guides in ranking bond offerings and outstanding in the order of risk of subsequent default.

5. The comprehensive record indicates that the principal advantages of high-grade corporate bond portfolios are a low default risk and loss rate and comparative stability of prices. The disadvantages are low promised yields and, over long investment periods, low realized rates of return.

6. The principal advantages of a low-grade bond portfolio are high promised yields and, if the list is large, well-diversified, and held over a long period, high realized yields. The disadvantages are high default and loss rates and price instability.

7. For small investors and those seeking liquidity in the bond account, the advantages of a high-grade portfolio frequently outweighed the disadvantages. For very large permanent investors holding well-diversified portfolios, the reverse frequently proved to be the case.

8. Comparisons of the performance of bonds classified by the various measures of prospective quality indicate that a list meeting a fixed market-rating standard was less stable than lists selected by agency ratings or legal status. The obverse of the coin is that over short periods the market rating was more sensitive to impending defaults than agency ratings or legal lists.

9. Corporate bonds were typically undervalued in the market at or near the date of default. As a result, investors selling at that time suffered large losses, while those purchasing obtained correspondingly large gains.

10. Because of the price instability of low-grade issues, realized returns were usually lower on low grades than on high grades when purchased at offering and sold at default, and loss rates were correspondingly higher. Conversely, under most rating systems, realized returns were higher on low grades than on high grades when purchased at default and held to extinguishment.

11. Although life-span loss rates on defaulted bonds were higher for low grades than for high grades, yields promised at offering were also higher so that the realized yields obtained on the various quality groups of defaulted bonds were about the same.

---

[9] Ibid.

PART THREE *Investment in Limited-Income Securities*

12. The quality of corporate bond offerings and outstandings, considered both prospectively and retrospectively, was subject to secular and cyclical swings of substantial amplitude, perhaps partly because of the behavior of corporate earnings and partly because of changes in investor confidence.

13. Judged by the differential behavior of selected groups of bonds over selected periods, the errors in rating corporate bonds can be traced principally to the business cycle and to the difficulty of forecasting.

14. Typical patterns of behavior, such as those outlined above, emerge only when corporate bonds are viewed in broad aggregates and over long investment periods. Wide disparity of performance was the rule for minor groupings and for bonds held over short investment periods.

Market Yields and Quality

The daily quotations for bonds (and therefore yields) in the marketplace are evidence of the investment market's quality classification of bonds. This market rating is the yield spread or algebraic difference between the yield to maturity on a particular security on a certain date and the yield to maturity of the highest-grade corporate bond with the same maturity on that date.

In periods of prosperity, especially after a long period of *relative* economic stability as from 1938 to 1973, the yield spread between AAA and BBB bonds will gradually narrow to 50-75 base points or even less (refer to Table 3-10 in Chapter 3). As the spread narrows, BBB bonds become increasingly less attractive. At times, as in the 1932 depression, the yield of the BBB bond index may be twice that for AAA bonds. While this might appear to justify the purchase of BBB bonds, the real justification would be the capital gains potential for the BBB bonds. If these bonds are held and continue to pay interest, and if the yield and price gap later narrows in subsequent periods of prosperity, the buyer may receive a 100% capital gain. Therefore, he would not purchase such bonds because of the high yield, but because of the large potential capital appreciation. These mathematical gradations of risk are somewhat illusory—although perhaps necessary for the practical operations of the bond market.

It might be argued that *if* the market actually did correctly calculate risk potential and that if there was one portfolio consisting entirely of AAA bonds and another consisting entirely of BBB bonds, the net yields over a long period of years for both portfolios would be identical. The losses on the BBB portfolio would absorb all the higher promised yields for that portfolio.

Strategies for Large Institutional Investors

Up to this point, the strategies for bond investment emphasized analysis that would provide for the selection of bonds whose principal and interest payments were assured beyond any reasonable doubt even in years of poor business. These strategies applied to individual investors and also to relatively small institutional investors or those requiring stability and liquidity. Individuals have become heavy buyers of bonds in recent years.

On the other hand, institutional investors own a major percentage of all corporate long-term debt issues. A large proportion of this total is owned by the very large financial intermediaries (large life insurance companies and pension funds) who have very large permanent portfolios with minimal liquidity problems. These investors can, and do, follow strategies that are thoroughly justified for their portfolios but that are distinctly not suitable for portfolios of individuals. Specifically, they can properly purchase lower quality debt issues than should individuals or other small investors or those with liquidity problems. Many such investments are private placement notes not rated by the agencies.

Empirical Evidence Supporting Strategies for Large Portfolios. Selection of investment strategy for individual portfolios, as indicated in the Hickman Study,[10] reflects personal preferences as well as practicality, the latter having been determined by the totality of financial resources available. Large investors, through their ability to average capital gains and *act as self-insurers,* are less concerned with the risk of individual investments. Concern in this case is determined by restrictions resulting from self-imposed constraints designed to avoid areas of excessively high default risks and legal constraints.

The study noted that some investors require liquidity and seek salability and price stability. Others, such as life insurance companies and corporate pension funds (by far the largest holders of corporate long-term debt issues), may have little interest in liquidity per se.

In the private placement area, insurance and pension funds enjoy more practical leeway. They also aid the financing of business firms that might find it difficult and costly to sell debt issues publicly. Furthermore, these private placements do not carry ratings by the statistical agencies. Finally, if a private placement runs into difficulty, the insurance company or the pension fund would have considerably more difficulty in selling it than would be the case for a marketable bond. They are constrained to work out the difficulties with the issuer.

In conclusion, institutions such as life insurance companies and pension funds properly can and do follow in some segments of their portfolio, such as private placements, a bond investment policy that reflects the conclusions of the Hickman Study. These portfolios are largely permanent and well-diversified. These institutional investors successfully act as self-insurers of

---

10 *Ibid.*

their investments. The compounding of the high yield on issues below high grade will absorb any losses and provide a net yield higher than if overall portfolios consisted solely of high-grade bonds. Furthermore, many private placements have stock warrants attached, which, when finally liquidated, may add substantially to the net return on the private placement note.

The Atkinson Study.[11] The postwar years have been so free of bond defaults that one might conclude that no quality problem exists. In an attempt to update the Hickman Study, Atkinson found that U.S. corporate bonds defaulting in the period 1945-1965 averaged less than 0.1 percent of the volume outstanding compared to 1.7 percent of the outstanding bonds that defaulted in 1900-1943. The postwar defaults were concentrated in railroad bonds. Although the Hickman Study warned that investor confidence engendered by extended periods of prosperity appears to generate security issues of less than prime quality, defaults in the postwar period were not concentrated in a particular cycle phase because the recessions were not severe. However, those defaulting were largely offered in years of business peaks or one year before the cycle peak. In each major industry group directly placed issues had lower coverage than public offerings.

Therefore, if we consider the Atkinson study together with the tremendous amount of issues since 1944, as well as the substantial decline in corporate liquidity, the factor of debt quality may well give rise to serious concern on the part of investors.

Purchase of Speculative Bonds. When a bond is purchased for speculative purposes, the purchase is usually made when the corporation is in the process of reorganization (or at least when its securities are near default) and the bonds are selling far below par. Between the late 1930s and the early 1940s, speculators with faith in the railroads and ability to analyze their bonds reaped tremendous profits by purchasing the bonds of roads that were in reorganization and then selling them as railroad income revived during World War II. Purchasers of defaulted bonds had faith in a depressed industry when the great bulk of investors were not interested. A few such opportunities also existed in the case of certain Eastern railroads in the 1970s.

CONVERTIBLE BONDS AND PREFERRED STOCKS

The privilege of convertibility into stock adds a speculative feature to bonds. The investor buying a convertible bond supposedly receives the

---

[11] Atkinson, *op. cit.*

advantages of a bond—safety of principal, income stability, and senior protection—and in addition the advantage that if the stock of the issuer rises in the market, the bond will enjoy corresponding appreciation. However, if the stock falls, the bond is expected to decline in price only to the point where it will still yield a satisfactory return on its investment or straight-bond value and no further. Most convertibles are rated below the A grade.

This double-hedge thinking can be and was dangerous in certain years after World War II, as 1966-1970. Many convertible bonds were bought on margin.[12] When interest rates rose, bond prices fell, and some of these bondholders experienced margin calls they could not meet. The bonds were sold, depressing the market below a price the convertible bondholders had thought possible based on their estimate as to the price floor at which they should sell on a purely yield or straight investment bond basis.

Convertible bonds should be judged on their qualifications as investment grade bonds or should be contrasted to and compared on a similar basis with common stocks.

Special Advantages of Convertible Bonds

Convertible bonds do have special advantages for certain financial institutions, notably commercial banks. One advantage, not legally available to them in investment media, is the possibility of capital gains through participation in corporate earnings growth. In addition, when bond prices

---

[12] Under Federal Reserve margin requirements, all listed bonds until 1968 were subject to the regular margin requirements and unlisted bonds could not be purchased through brokers on margin. However, up to 1968 commercial banks could lend on the security of convertible bonds as high an amount as they deemed reasonable, often as high as 75% of market value (25% margin). In 1967 the Federal Reserve Board brought such lending transactions under special margin regulations.

On February 1, 1968, the Federal Reserve Bank of New York in Circular No. 6108, "Changes in Margin Regulation, No. 2," imposed a new margin requirement "on loans made by banks for the purpose of purchasing or carrying securities convertible into registered stock. This requirement will be set independently of the margin requirement for loans to purchase or carry registered stock, and is fixed initially at 50%. The same requirement applies to loans by brokers and dealers on registered convertible securities, instead of the present 70%, but margin requirements are removed from loans they make on nonconvertible bonds (not subject only to house rules of the brokers themselves). In consequence, banks, brokers, and dealers will be on substantially the same footing in these respects."

Changes in requirements through January 1, 1973, were as follows:

	On Margin Stocks	On Conv. Bond	On Short Sales
1968	70%	50%	70%
1970	80%	60%	80%
1971	65%	50%	65%
1972	55%	50%	55%
1973	65%	50%	65%

are declining, convertible bonds are the only group of bonds whose prices can rise. Convertible bonds have good marketability, as shown by active trading in larger issues on the New York Stock Exchange, whereas non-convertible corporate issues of similar quality are sometimes difficult to follow since they are traded over-the-counter. There are purchase restrictions, imposed on certain investors such as commercial banks, prescribed by the Comptroller of the Currency. In 1957, approval was given for the purchase of eligible convertible issues if the yield obtained is reasonably similar to nonconvertible issues of similar quality and maturity. These restrictions have created an aura of uncertainty with regard to banks assuming the risks of convertible bonds. For these reasons and others discussed in Chapter 31, commercial banks hold relatively few convertibles.

The potential advantages noted for convertibles make them attractive to many investors and they often sell at substantial premiums over their straight investment bond value. But convertible bonds have not always lived up to the great promises held for them. Prices of convertibles rose to very high levels in 1965; but in 1966, when both stock and bond markets declined, many convertible issues declined even more than the stocks into which they were convertible. Still, largely because of inflation fears, an exceptionally large quantity of new convertible bond issues were successfully marketed in the years 1966-1969, especially by conglomerates. Then in 1969 and 1970 severe declines resulted in heavy losses.

Calculations for Convertible Securities

The key step in convertible bond selection is calculation of the straight investment value of the bond and then the premium over this investment value in the market price of the bond. The next significant step is to project the expected price of the common stock, and finally to determine the amount of premium over the investment value that appears justified in the light of the expected increase in the market value of the stock.

Known Factors. The factors about a convertible bond issue that are usually known are:

1. Its coupon rate.
2. Its maturity date.
3. Its quality rating by rating agencies.
4. The conversion price stated in the bond contract or the stated number of common shares that will be received on conversion. Frequently the conversion price will change during the life of the bond, usually rising in stages. The original contract states the scale of the conversion price,

the dates on which the conversion price changes, and the new prices on those dates.

5. The market price.

Unknown Factors. The factors about a convertible bond issue that must be calculated by investors are:

1. Actual number of shares obtained by conversion.
2. Conversion premium over parity price.
3. Bond yield.
4. Straight bond or investment value vs. market price.
5. Premium over investment value in the market price.

The calculation of these unknown factors is discussed below.

Actual Number of Shares Obtained by Conversion. The actual number of shares that will be obtained by conversion is found by dividing the par value of the bond by the currently applicable contractual conversion price.

Conversion Premium over Parity Price. The *conversion premium* is the excess of the cost per share of stock if obtained by conversion (with the bond valued at its current market price) over the cost per share if the stock is purchased in the market at its current market price per share. The *parity price* is the market price at which an equal exchange of value would result from execution of the conversion privilege. The parity price may be expressed mathematically as follows:

$$\frac{\text{Bond Par}}{\text{Conversion Price}} = \frac{\text{Bond Price (market)}}{\text{Stock Price (market)}}$$

In conversion, the bondholder loses accrued interest on the bonds but gains accrued dividends on the stock.

There is usually, although not always, some conversion premium; that is, it will usually be more expensive to obtain the stock through buying the bond and converting to stock than through purchasing the stock directly. Rarely, if ever, can investors locate a situation where stock can actually be obtained more cheaply by buying the bond and then converting to stock rather than by buying the stock directly. This is because professional arbitragers are constantly looking for such situations and, if they find one, would immediately buy the bond and concurrently sell the stock short, later covering the short sale by delivery of stock obtained by converting the bond.

Bond Yield. The yield to maturity and the current or stock yield can be calculated as described on pages 165-169 in Chapter 6.

Straight Bond or Investment Value vs. Market Price of Bond. The calculation of the premium of the bond's current market price over investment value is the key to convertible bond investments.

The *straight bond or investment value* is the calculated value at which the bond should sell in the market, exclusive of the convertible feature (assuming that it was not a convertible bond). To effect this calculation, the investor must first determine the bond's quality and then determine the yield at which straight nonconvertible bonds of that quality and maturity are selling in the current market. A straight nonconvertible bond should sell at full yield. For example, if a bond is classed as of "A" quality and it is the bond of an oil company, then the investor determines the yield at which "A" bonds of oil companies *with the same maturity* are currently selling. If the answer is 5.75%, then by the use of a bond table the investor calculates the price at which the convertible bond in question would need to sell in order to yield 5.75%. This amount would be its straight bond or investment value.

Premium over Investment Value. The *premium over investment value* is the excess of the current market price over the calculated investment value of the bond if it were simply a straight nonconvertible bond. This premium over investment value represents the points of risk. For example, if the market value of the convertible bond is 150 ($1,500) and the calculated investment value of the bond is 105 ($1,050), then the points at risk are 45 ($450). This means that if the price of the stock into which the bond is converted should decline substantially, the bond should not decline below the investment value that was calculated to be 105 simply as a straight bond. If the investment value was properly calculated for that quality bond with that maturity *and if the interest rates do not rise* from the time of calculation, then 105 should be the price below which the bond will not fall. However, if interest rates do rise, the investment value will decline and must be recalculated on the basis of the current level of bond yields of that quality bond and at that maturity.

Dilution of Conversion Privileges

In the case of a common split or a large stock dividend, the conversion privilege of a bond or a preferred stock may be diluted or destroyed. Normally the conversion privilege of a convertible security is protected by a provision in the bond indenture or certificate of incorporation providing for a pro rata adjustment of the conversion price, correcting the price so that there is no dilution of the conversion privilege.

Analysis Techniques for Preferred Stocks

Straight preferred stocks are limited-income equity securities purchased for the same reason as all other limited-income securities such as bonds. However, the preferred contract is distinctly inferior to that of bonds because it reflects equity rather than creditor status. Nevertheless, the same techniques of analysis should be applied to preferred stocks as are applied to debt instruments because, like bonds, their income will never rise and they cannot experience capital appreciation (except from declines in overall interest rates). The only changes that can occur are reduction or elimination of the dividend and/or declines in market price. Therefore, the emphasis should be on analysis techniques that give maximum assurance (1) that dividends will be paid in years of poor business as well as good business beyond any reasonable doubt and (2) that the coverage of dividends (calculated on an overall basis) will be sufficient to prevent any doubt about payment of dividends to arise in investors in the market.

Preferred stocks are a hybrid security, having the disadvantages of bonds and common stock without their advantages. The disadvantages are that dividends may be passed simply by decision of the directors, and that dividends, like interest payments, will never be increased. The contractual advantage of a bondholder as a creditor is not possessed by the preferred stockholder. In addition, the common stock advantages of potential increases in dividends and potential capital appreciation are not possessed by preferred stock. For these reasons, the standards for investment grade preferred stocks should be even more rigorous than the standards for bonds. Relatively few preferred stocks can meet such tests. (Standards for selection of limited-income securities are discussed in Chapter 9.)

The most serious and the most recent disadvantage of preferred stocks is that lately the market yields of high-grade preferred stocks have been no higher than (and sometimes not as high as) the market yields of high-grade utility bonds. For individual investors who would in fact receive the same net yield after taxes, whichever security is purchased (high-grade preferred stocks or high-grade bonds), there is little if any justification for the purchase of straight investment grade preferred stocks. For corporate investors the philosophy is different because they pay a tax on only 15% of dividends received versus the full corporate tax on bond interest received, resulting in a much higher net yield from preferreds than from bonds.

The average preferred stock is of lower quality than would meet investment standards because such stocks do not have a margin of protection that will assure continuance of the dividend beyond any reasonable doubt. Analysis of preferred stocks tends to concentrate on the distinction between the *exceptional* preferred stock and the *average* preferred stock.

QUESTIONS

1. What are the essential disadvantages accruing to the purchaser of fixed-income securities? the major advantages?

2. Why are fixed-income securities often referred to as limited-income securities?

3. (a) When should an investor purchase bonds for investment and when for speculation? What type of bonds would you recommend for speculative purchases?
   (b) Is it possible to speculate in high-grade bonds? Discuss.

4. Determine the trend of the Consumer Price Index over the last ten years. Of what significance are your findings to an investor in limited-income securities?

5. (a) What advantages does a lien on assets offer to the investor?
   (b) Should such a lien receive major consideration from a bond analyst? Discuss.

6. (a) How does the investor measure stability of earning power?
   (b) Should the bond investor confine his investment to the most stable industries? Discuss.

7. Should individual investors follow the same strategies for bond investment as the large institutional investors? Carefully explain your answer.

8. (a) Discuss the pros and cons of convertible bonds from the standpoint of (1) an individual investor and (2) a financial institution.
   (b) Define "conversion premium" and "parity price" as related to convertible bonds. Of what significance are these concepts to the investor?
   (c) Define "premium over investment value" in relation to a convertible bond and discuss its significance to the bond analyst.

9. It can be said that the market price of a convertible is a reflection of either the quality of its straight debt instruments or its common stock. Explain the circumstances under which each of the two factors mentioned is likely to predominate in determining market price of the convertible bond.

10. (a) Discuss the statement "Preferred stocks are a hybrid security, having the disadvantages of bonds and common stocks without their advantages."
    (b) Are preferred stocks a good investment for individual investors? Carefully explain your position versus corporate investors.

WORK-STUDY PROBLEMS

1. (a) Why are so many debenture bonds rated so highly? Find at least three examples among bonds currently traded and show how they support this thesis.

(b) Select ten investment grade debenture bond issues and determine whether or not they are callable and the degree of call protection offered the investor. In terms of the yields offered on these bonds, is call protection particularly significant to the investor? Discuss.

2. Select two currently outstanding convertible bonds and determine the following information for these bonds:

> Coupon rate for each bond.
> Maturity date for each bond.
> S & P quality rating for each bond.
> Yield on straight bonds of similar quality to each issue.
> The conversion price and ratio for each bond.
> The current market price of the convertible bonds.
> The current market price of the common stock of the issuing companies.
> The currently applicable call price of the bonds, if any, and the date at which changes will occur in the call price if they are not constant until maturity of the bonds.
> The current dividend yield on the common stock of the issuing companies.

(a) Utilize the above information to calculate the following for each of the bonds you selected:

> The conversion premium for each bond.
> The yield to maturity for each bond.
> The current straight bond value and the potential downside risk suggested.
> The call risk, if any, present in each bond.
> The relative advantage or disadvantage present, in terms of current yield, by being a holder of the bond rather than a holder of the common stock.

(b) Based on the information you have now developed on each bond, which appears to be the more desirable purchase?

(c) What additional information would you need to properly evaluate the desirability of purchasing either bond?

(d) If the market price of the common stock for the issuing company of each bond were to increase 30% over the next two years, what would you expect to be the minimum price at which each convertible bond would sell? Explain your answer.

SUGGESTED READINGS

Beja, Abraham. "On Systematic and Unsystematic Components of Financial Risk." *The Journal of Finance* (March, 1972), pp. 37-45.

Ellis, Charles D. "Bonds for Long-Term Investors." *Financial Analysts Journal* (March-April, 1970), pp. 81-85.

Lindlow, Wesley. *Inside the Money Market.* New York: Random House, 1972.

Nelson, Charles R. *The Term Structure of Interest Rates.* New York: Basic Books, 1972.

Williamson, J. Peter. "Computerized Approaches to Bond Switching." *Financial Analysts Journal* (July-August, 1970), pp. 65-72.

Standards for Selection
of Limited-Income Securities

Some general standards and protective provisions for bond investment, including the authors' conclusions regarding them, are presented in this chapter. Following these general standards are specific quantitative tests for the selection of bonds and preferred stocks.

GENERAL STANDARDS AND PROTECTIVE PROVISIONS

Investors can logically be much more rigid in establishing standards for limited-income securities (debt issues and straight preferred stocks) than for common stocks. This is because rejection of a limited-income security, even if it later proves to have been high grade, does not carry with it the same potential penalty that is present when a common stock is rejected. If a common stock is rejected, a significant capital gains potential may be lost, which is not true with investment grade bonds or preferred stocks where capital gains potentials do not exist (except in periods of declining interest rates). The post-World War II years have been relatively default free for bonds after the rather serious defaults of the 1930s.

Bond Ratings

To assist in determining the quality of bonds, there are bond ratings supplied by agencies, legal lists, and market quality ratings.

Bond Rating Agencies. The published reports of statistical agencies (Standard & Poor's Corporation and Moody's Investor Service, Inc.) suggest that agency ratings represent an attempt to rank issues in the order of the probable risk of default and the possible magnitude of default loss.[1] The rating of A and higher signifies investment grade bonds; BBB, medium grade, on the borderline of investment grade; BB, lower medium grade; B, speculative; CCC and CC, outright speculative; C, income bonds on which no interest is being paid; and DDD and below, bonds in default. However, the agencies do warn against the use of their ratings as a guide to the *relative* attractiveness of an issue, that is, the probable actual realized yield for an investor. The Hickman Study [2] indicated that "the record of the agencies over the period studied (1900-1943) was remarkably good insofar as their ratings pertain to the risk of default." [3] It would appear that defaults and losses were, on the whole, larger for issues rated low grade than for issues rated high grade so that a program of purchasing only upper medium to high grade issues would have worked out better for most small investors. Theoretically, the reverse was possible for large investors since they were in a position to average out the definitely higher risks on the lower grade issues. However, in practice many large institutional investors are prevented from acquiring a broadly diversified list of low-grade issues by regulatory authority or company policy.[4] But especially in the case of private placements (not

---

[1] Comparative ratings of the rating agencies are:

Standard & Poor's				Moody's			
AAA	BBB	CCC	DDD	Aaa	Baa	Caa	Daa
AA	BB	CC	DD	Aa	Ba	Ca	Da
A	B	C	D	A	B	C	D

[2] W. Braddock Hickman, *Corporate Bond Quality and Investor Experience,* National Bureau of Economic Research (Princeton, N. J.; Princeton University Press, 1958). Note that the study covered the worst period of defaults in history—the Great Depression. The study did find that, as opposed to the universe of bonds, "the agencies appear to have been less successful in predicting relative default experience for offerings between major industry groups." This study was partially updated in Thomas R. Atkinson, *Trends in Corporate Bond Quality,* National Bureau of Economic Research (New York: Columbia University Press, 1967). Defaults in 1945-1965 were 0.1% versus 1.7% in 1900-1943.

[3] *Ibid,* p. 10. Although mistakes were made, those issues rated high grade at offering and at the beginning of assumed chronological investment periods had lower default rates than those rated low grade, summarized as follows:

Rating Category	Default Rate (% of Par Value)
I (AAA)	5.9
II (AA)	6.0
III (A)	13.4
IV (BBB)	19.1
V-IX (BB and below)	42.4
No Rating	28.6

[4] *Ibid.,* p. 201. In addition, capital losses as measured by the difference between par value and market price at default were consistently smaller for the higher grades that went into default than for the low grades. Furthermore, as issues neared the years

agency rated), the issues of insurance companies and pension funds may go down in quality.

It was found that the agencies rated bonds up in expansions and down in contractions, following business cycles and reflecting the instability of corporate earnings, which vitiates somewhat the claim to consideration of long-term factors only. Certainly the shifting of bond ratings causes problems for commercial banks and other regulated financial intermediaries.

Regulatory Restrictions and the Legal Lists.[5] Even though state statutes establishing legal lists for savings banks have been criticized as outmoded, 12 of the 17 states in which savings banks are located still have such statutes. The statutes establish elaborate tests in respect to assets, earnings, dividends, prior default record, and so forth. While the agencies included about 75% of corporate bonds as high grade, the legal lists of Massachusetts, New York, and Maine included only about one third.[6] While the default record of bonds on the legal lists was considerably lower than that of nonlegal bonds as a class, it was also true that the funds concentrating in the legal list issues found their yields noticeably below those on the average for other bonds rated the same by the rating agencies.[7] Both promised yields and realized yields proved to be definitely lower on legal lists than on nonlegal bonds.[8]

---

in which they actually defaulted, the agencies had a good record of reducing the ratings during the years preceding the default. Also important is the extremely small default rate on the two highest ratings (AAA and AA), only 6%, and the rapid rise in the default rate as one moves to lower grade issues.

[5] While the statutes for rated bonds no longer specifically state that bonds rated in the top four categories are considered eligible investment for national banks by the Comptroller of the Currency, it is generally assumed that this is so. Also, the Secretary of the Treasury, the Board of Governors of the Federal Reserve System, the Directors of the Federal Deposit Insurance Corporation, and the Comptroller of the Currency in a joint resolution stated that securities in Group I (obligations in the four highest grades and unrated securities of equivalent investment values) are to be carried at book value (amortized cost). Securities failing to meet this test are valued at the market price, and 50% of the net depreciation is deducted in computing net capital. Similar valuation practices are imposed upon insurance companies by the National Association of Insurance Commissioners.

[6] Hickman, *op. cit.*, pp. 211-212.

[7] *Ibid.*, pp. 212–214.

[8] *Ibid.*, p. 345. "Comparisons as to default and yield experience between legal bonds and equally inclusive lists constructed from agency ratings show only minor differences that are generally not statistically significant. So far as the record goes, it suggests that the agency ratings were perhaps slightly more sensitive to impending defaults than the legal lists. Promised yields and loss rates on legal bonds were usually higher than on the agency-rating equivalents, so that realized yields were about the same, but neither of these two rating systems was markedly superior to the other, either in these or in other respects."

Market Ratings. The market is constantly rating bonds in terms of their market yields graded down from the lowest yields to the highest yields, thus expressing risk premiums. By their nature, market ratings are much more volatile than agency ratings. The Hickman Study concluded that "the market's appraisal of the quality of an issue at offering is a fairly good indicator of its probable quality at extinguishment." [9]

Conclusion on Ratings. Individual and other relatively small investors should concentrate bond holdings in issues rated in the top four or even top three rating categories.[10] Large institutional investors, on the other hand, have the protection of self-insurance through well-diversified portfolios, since the risk of default on certain issues is recompensed by the higher realized yields on the remaining issues held. They can compound the higher yields on issues that have a satisfactory history, which will more than offset losses.

Size of Obligor and Size of Issue [11]

As might be expected, there is a strong positive correlation between the asset size of an obligor and the size of issues, although the correlation is not perfect. The Hickman Study found that the percent of the par amount of offerings of the combined industries that subsequently went into default declined as the size scale moved up from issues under $5 million to issues of

---

[9] *Ibid.*, p. 305. "The proportion of the par-amount total of offerings rated I-IV (BBB-AAA) at extinguishment moves inversely, and quite systematically, with the size of the yield spread at offering—moves directly, that is, with the market's original estimate of quality. The same is true within each of the major industry groups, with the single exception of industrials with market ratings of under ½ percent, where, because of the sizable volume not rated by the agencies at extinguishment, the proportion rated I-IV was slightly under that of offerings with market ratings of ½ to 1 percent. . . . We conclude that the quality of an issue at offering as determined by the market rating provides a fairly reliable forecast of its quality at extinguishment."

[10] Two exceptions to this requirement may be made: (1) if an issuer has two or more issues outstanding and one or more are rated above BBB, and if the yield between these issues is significant, the BBB issue may be purchased under the reasoning that none should be purchased unless all are of sufficient quality to justify investment; (2) in the case of convertible issues, most of which are rated BBB or lower. If the rating simply reflects the fact that the issue is a subordinated debenture but other bonds of the same issue are rated A or higher, the BBB convertible issue may be purchased under the same thinking as was developed above.

[11] In examining defaults, especially as related to size of obligor and size of issue, we must isolate the railroads as an exception to the general experience because of the very bad record of the railroads in the 1930s with nearly one third of Class I railroad mileage (also the Eastern Railroads in 1969-1973) in the hands of receivers.

$50 million and over. Total public utilities and industrials show the same pattern, but railroads and street railways present a different picture.[12]

Industry Groups [13]

The industrial bonds that had the highest promised yields (large risk provisions) at date of issue tended to post a higher default rate than the industrial bonds that had lower promised yields and losses. Those industries that over the years had the strongest growth rates had better records, especially as compared to those of declining industries. The Hickman Study stated the following:

> For rapidly growing industries, the actual loss rates observed depended largely upon the investment quality of the individual issues floated by the members of the group, i.e., upon their profit margins, *cash flows,* and myriads of other factors relating to the risk of default. Examples are petroleum and coal products, which had the highest growth rate of any industry in the manufacturing group over the period 1899-1937, and had a low default rate and loss rate; and transportation equipment (automobiles plus transportation equipment except automobiles), which had the second highest growth rate, but a high default and loss rate [because intense competition caused a heavy mortality among the companies and only a few major companies survived].
>
> Greater regularity (in default rates) is to be observed among industries that suffered substantial declines in output . . . and among industries that were retarded by competition of other products or services. Most issues of

---

[12] Hickman, *op. cit.,* p. 494.

Proportions of Offerings 1900-1943 in Given Size-of-Issue Classes That Went into Default Before 1944

All Regular Offerings	Under $5 Million	$5-19 Million	$20-49 Million	$50 Million And Over
Proportion of Total	24.9%	19.0%	16.4%	16.3%
Railroads	20.6	26.2	33.1	24.5
Street Railways	67.1	47.7	71.9	82.0
Public Utilities	13.2	9.1	4.3	5.2
Industrials	33.7	23.3	7.5	12.1

Proportion of Offerings 1900-1943 in Given Size-of-Obligor Classes at Offering That Went into Default Before 1944

All Regular Offerings	All Sizes Of Obligors	Under $5 Million	$5–99 Million	$100–199 Million	$200 Million And Over	Information Lacking
Proportion of Total .	19.1%	23.6%	18.8%	17.0%	16.4%	30.4%
Railroads	27.3	18.5	26.6	37.2	27.0	20.6
Street Railways ..	65.2	64.5	60.8	60.5	73.4	69.5
Public Utilities ..	8.0	13.7	7.2	3.4	6.2	20.7
Industrials	19.6	38.0	25.3	17.2	3.4	34.3

[13] *Ibid.,* p. 89.

such industries had low earnings protection, so that default rates and loss rates were high.[14]

Definitely cyclical industries and companies will suffer serious declines in earnings in recessions and depressions. A company in such industries tends to have a relatively low debt capacity. Some should have no long-term debt and others a debt that is only a small proportion of total capitalization so that fixed charges including debt amortization will be covered by a satisfactory margin in cyclical downturns.

Terms of the Issue and Standards for Bond Investment

The major distinguishing feature of bonds, private placement notes, and other notes as contrasted to equity securities is the legal nature (creditor-debtor relationship) of the debt contract. This legal priority is the base for the superior investment rating as a class. However, with debt instruments as with equity securities the protection of the investment rests principally on the ability of the issuer to produce adequate earnings and cash flow.

Provisions Protecting Senior Issues. A senior obligation enjoys a priority of claims over other securities of the same issuer. For such securities the investor wants reasonable provisions in the contract to protect his priority financial position and to prevent the issuer from actions that will impair his financial position. Further, if unforeseen, unexpected developments do occur, it is desirable that the contract provide for adequate remedies to protect, to the greatest extent possible, the investor's position.

Provisions Regarding Issuance of an Additional Amount of the Same Issue. Most modern contracts permit the later issuance of additional amounts of bonds under the same issue but subject to two major requirements: (1) that fixed charges on a pro forma basis, including the additional bonds, will be met beyond a reasonable doubt; (2) that the additional obligation will not exceed say 75% of the value of the new property being acquired (railroad equipment) and 60% in the case of public utilities.

Provisions Regarding Subsequent Issues with Prior Liens. Most indentures protecting senior issues provide that no subsequent issues will be given a prior lien over that of the original issue.

---

[14] *Ibid.*, p. 99.

Equal and Ratable Provisions. If a security is a debenture issue, the indenture usually provides that the issue will share "equally and ratably" in any mortgage liens that may subsequently be placed on the issuer's property.

Provisions Regarding Reduction of Debt Principal. The creditors' position is weakened if only interest payments are made while the debt principal remains intact. For this reason, three common methods are used to reduce the debt principal during the life of the issues: (1) sinking funds for publicly issued bonds,[15] (2) amortization for term loans and private placements, and (3) serial maturities for equipment obligations and municipal issues. All debt issues should be protected in one of these three ways.

Provisions Regarding Working Capital. While provisions regarding working capital are rather common in contracts protecting private placements, they are still rather unusual in bond indentures and even then are found only in industrial issues. Working capital is not considered a problem area for utilities, which do not have either inventory or receivables problems. Working capital protection provisions, when they are used in private placements with institutions, should require that net working capital be maintained at a level at least equal to total funded debt. This requirement is more severe than is usual when such clauses appear, but it is reasonable. Other provisions frequently found restrict the payment of dividends if working capital falls below a designated level such as noted above. In the case of smaller companies, private placements and term loan agreements frequently include restrictions on officers' salaries if working capital declines below a specified level.

Provisions for Subordinated Convertible Debentures. Since World War II, and especially in the late 1960s, corporations have issued a substantial amount of subordinated convertible debentures. These are usually specifically subordinated to commercial bank term loans and also other senior issues. To make the subordinated issues acceptable to buyers and, especially in the late 1960s, to enable them to be sold at significantly lower yields than current levels of straight bond yields, these issues have been made convertible into common stock of the issuer. This also makes the debt issues attractive to

---

[15] In the case of many public utility issues the indenture provides that, instead of placing funds in a sinking fund to retire the issue, funds may be used to acquire new assets. Most utilities are regularly expanding. Protection is provided by requiring that substitution of new property for sinking fund payments will be limited to say 75% of the value of the property and that charges on a pro forma basis will be covered by a required minimum. Average utility plant and capitalization double about every 10 years.

investors (individuals and mutual funds), who ordinarily do not buy corporate bonds to any significant extent. An inflation psychology also aids in their sale. Investors calculate that if earnings of the corporation rise measurably, the conversion feature will be profitable and the effective overall yield will eventually rise significantly above the contract rate on the issue.

Call Provisions. Most debt issues carry two call provisions, one covering the call of the entire issue and the other covering calls for the sinking fund. The price quoted for sinking fund calls is the lower of the two. The call price covering the entire issue will be noticeably higher but usually will decline in steps as the period to maturity decreases.

The call provisions are a negative factor for the investor, as the issuers will not call the entire issue except in periods when market yields are below the contract yield on the issue. In periods of tight money, as in 1966-1969, lenders for new issues will attempt to have the first call date extended to a minimum of 5 years from date of issue. Some borrowers will secure lower interest costs at such times by providing 10-year call protection clauses. At such times, the lower the quality of the issue and the smaller the size of the corporation, the more likely that the private placement contract will provide that the issuer has no redemption privileges.

Provisions for Leasebacks and Other Leases. The senior issues should be reasonably protected from the burden of the fixed charges of leases (interest payments and related costs) just as they should be protected from the burdens of long-term debt issues for which leases are usually a substitute. Therefore, all that has been said heretofore about protection in the case of subordinated debt issues is equally applicable in the case of leases.

Obligor's Dividend Record

One of the bases for evaluating the investment quality of an issuer and its securities has been the long-term dividend record. Provisions regarding this record are common in statutes governing legal investment. A long-term dividend record is certainly a plus factor. However, a corporation may have maintained such a record, especially in recent years, at the expense of a sound financial policy. On the other side of the coin, a rapidly growing company in a rapidly growing industry may have followed a "no dividend" or "low dividend" policy in order to conserve funds for reinvestment. Therefore, each case must be examined on its own merits. It can be stated, however, that most well-established companies whose bonds have met other tests for fixed-income securities and especially the fixed coverage test have had a long, uninterrupted dividend record and that this has also been true in the case of most investment grade common stocks. For the reasons discussed, it does not seem necessary to provide a separate dividend payment test as such. It would be quite unusual, except in the case of clearly growth companies, for a corporation to meet satisfactorily the fixed charge coverage test and yet not to have had a long, uninterrupted dividend record.

Lien Position

It has repeatedly been stated that the protection for limited-income securities is the ability of the obligor to meet all its debt obligations at all times (not only interest but debt amortization) and by a sufficient margin to avoid any doubts arising as to this ability.

Asset Values and Funded Debt. While asset value tests were at one time important, the experience of the 1930s proved that asset value tests as opposed to fixed charge coverage tests were illusory. An exception to this principle would be the case of equipment obligations where the asset values are significant.[16]

It is true that in almost all cases long-term debt should be incurred only to finance the purchase of fixed assets, and therefore a relationship of the cost of fixed assets to long-term debt would appear justifiable. However, again it would be most exceptional to find a situation where other tests, including the overriding fixed coverage tests (interest and also amortization), would be met satisfactorily but an asset coverage test would not be met. It has been suggested by some writers that an asset test should be applied to public utility bonds, but such a test is quite unnecessary.

Equipment Obligations. The lowest rating given to railroad equipment obligations (even if the railroad is in receivership) is usually BBB. The reasons for this are: (1) the mobility of the rolling stock and the attitude of the courts on receivership towards payment of these obligations, (2) the paying off of equipment obligations serially at a rate that exceeds their depreciation, and (3) the value of equipment when new, usually 25%-33% above the amount of the equipment obligations. Once more it must be emphasized that without the equipment, which is usually the newest and the most serviceable, the railroad (including one in receivership) will be at an extreme disadvantage; therefore the issuer will make every attempt to meet the interest

---

[16] There might also be an exception in the case of quality investment grade securities, especially high-grade bonds collateralizing a collateral trust bond.

payments on equipment obligations when they become due. Realistically speaking, they have no choice. In summary then, the overall record of equipment obligations has been good and their ratings of BBB or better in most cases are certainly merited by their record.

Real Estate Mortgage Bonds. In the 1920s large numbers of bonds were issued secured by various real estate properties. These were not bond issues of an industrial, utility, or railroad corporation with the entire issue sold by the obligor and backed by property owned and used by one corporation; rather, these bonds were issued usually by a real estate company and generally secured by a wide diversity of properties. A large proportion of such issues went into default in the 1930s, again emphasizing that protection for bondholders rests on ability to pay (income) and not asset lien.[17] As in the case of residential mortgages issued in the 1920s, most did not provide for regular amortization of the debt. Those issued in the post-World War II period, as with residential mortgages, almost always provide for regular debt amortization, which improves their quality over those issued in the 1920s.

Actually, a large majority of the real estate bonds issued since 1945 have been the Public Housing Administration bonds. The distinguishing feature of such bonds is that they enjoy the equivalent of a United States Government guarantee, and therefore the investor need not be concerned with the net income coverage or the asset security behind the bond. Not only do these bonds enjoy the equivalent of a United States Government guarantee, but also the interest received is exempt from federal income taxes and generally also from state income taxes in the state of issuance.

Stock Equity Test for Long-Term Debt

One of the reasons why corporations are able to trade on their equity (sell debt issues) is that creditors rely heavily on the fact that the owners (stockholders) have invested a specified amount in the company and this amount acts as a cushion of protection for the debtors who are in a priority position with any loss absorbed first by the stockholders. While the basic principle is sound, reliance on the equity figure as shown on the balance sheet may be dangerous, for the asset figures that appear on the balance sheet may be highly inflated in terms of earning power value. Therefore, an "equity at market" test is preferable to a book equity test.

The *equity at market test* is based on the market value that investors place on the ownership value of the enterprise, which in turn is based largely

---

[17] Many of these bonds declined so substantially in price that they fell far below the economic values of the real estate behind the bonds, making them attractive purchases at those prices.

on their judgment of the earning power of the corporation (the amount and the quality of the earning power in terms of growth and volatility). The market's evaluation of the equity of the corporation can be calculated by multiplying the current market price of the company's stock by the number of shares outstanding. If there is preferred stock outstanding, its total market value (or par or liquidity value) is added to the market value of the common stock, resulting in the market's evaluation of the equity cushion behind the debt. To this amount is added the par value of long-term debt to arrive at the market value of the corporation's capitalization. The proportion of the capitalization in debt and in equity can then be determined. These proportions can be compared to those in the company's book capitalization, and the amount of financial leverage can be calculated on both bases.

The importance of the equity at market test as compared with the debt test can best be illustrated as follows:

	Book Capitalization			Capitalization Equity At Market	
Bonds (par value)	$10,000,000	42%		$10,000,000	59%
Preferred Stock (par)	2,000,000	8%		2,000,000	12%
Common Stock Equity (1,000,000 shares)	12,000,000	50%	(@$5)	5,000,000	29%
Total	$24,000,000	100%		$17,000,000	100%

On the basis of book value, it appears that the common stock equity represents 50% of capitalization and that the debt represents only 42% of capitalization. In an industry with reasonable earnings stability, if coverage under the fixed-charge coverage test is adequate, the equity would appear to be satisfactory. However, using the equity at market test, the debt appears as 59% of capitalization and the common equity cushion as only 29%. Furthermore, the debt is $10 million against a common equity cushion of only $5 million. The debt-to-common-equity rate is 2 to 1, or $2 of debt for every $1 of common equity. Investors are saying that the equity cushion is far less than is indicated on the books. In this case, the investor is on notice that the market considers the equity cushion relatively small and the financial leverage relatively large, and he is warned accordingly.

This type of test is particularly applicable in the case of railroads and industrials. Railroads have a very heavy debt and very large fixed assets, but in most cases their book capitalization indicates a satisfactory equity cushion. However, the market value of most common stocks of railroads in 1973 showed that the equity cushion was very small—only a fraction of the equity cushion based on book figures. This small equity cushion was to an important degree also true of airlines in 1969-1970 and again in 1973.

Recognition must be given to the argument that, because the market value of stocks fluctuates so widely, the equity at market test will also fluctuate widely and is therefore not a reasonable test. Even after giving recognition to the problems involved, it must be concluded that the equity at market test is significant. Unless the trend of the prices of common stock has been downward for some time, the investor may take the average price of the security for a period of the past several years or may multiply earnings for the most recent 12-month period by the average price-earnings ratio at which the stock has sold in the past several years. Such modifications should satisfy most of the criticism aimed at this test.

Conclusions on Protective Features of Bonds, Private Placement Notes, and Preferred Stock Contracts

In spite of the rather detailed discussion of the nature and the importance of protection provisions, our major thesis is that investment in limited-income securities is in essence a negative one of analysis and rejection until a satisfactory issue is found. This is so because the investor will never receive any higher income than is promised or any capital appreciation other than that provided by declining interest rates. Even in the latter case, this advantage is frequently lost by exercise of the call feature by the issuer. On this basis, no security should be selected unless there is every reasonable assurance that the corporation will meet all its obligations.

However, as previously noted, large institutional investors with permanent, well-diversified portfolios and little or no liquidity problems can and do act as self-insurers and select lower quality issues, accepting greater risks than do individuals and small institutional investors or those with liquidity problems.

SPECIFIC QUANTITATIVE TESTS

In the analysis of all securities, the quantitative standards applied to the *past record* are pertinent even though it is the future record that will determine the soundness of the judgment to purchase a security. However, in the case of bonds and preferred stocks, the past record is much more important than it is in the case of common stocks. If the corporation's past record is not excellent, bonds or preferred stocks should not be purchased. In the case of common stocks, the analyst may decide that the issuer's character has changed and that a capital appreciation potential exists. Common stock analysis includes qualitative factors and heavily stresses earnings projections.

The greatest risk is in new enterprises, even when they are sponsored by government agencies.[18] In general, debt or preferred issues of new enterprises should be avoided because they have not gone through a testing period. All judgments rest on estimates of the future with little allowance for miscalculation and no potential for capital gains for bondholders or preferred stockholders to offset the risks that estimates may be wrong.

A Brief Empirical Review of the Basis for Agency Ratings

The rating agencies in establishing ratings for bonds in the 1970s give consideration to the record all the way back through the 1930s to the last major depression. The record of industries and companies in the 1930s in terms of their cyclical characteristics is evaluated. Specifically, the railroad industry's very poor record in the 1930s (when one third of Class I mileage was in receivership) together with its cyclical record after World War II is a major reason why only a handful of railroad bonds receive either an AA or AAA rating and not too many an A rating. The post-World War II bond defaults (only .1% of volume outstanding) were concentrated in railroad bonds. This total default record compares with the 1900-1943 default record of 1.7% of all outstanding bonds.

Cyclical Rate of Return on Investment
All Class I Railroads

1929 — 5.30%	1961 — 1.97%	1969 — 2.36%
1932 — 1.37%	1966 — 3.90%	1970 — 1.73%
1953 — 4.19%	1967 — 2.45%	1971 — 2.47%
1958 — 2.76%	1968 — 2.44%	1972 — 2.95%

Coverage of Fixed Charges

The most important test that is applied to limited-income securities by most investors has always been the margin by which the amount available for fixed charges (and in the case of preferred stocks, fixed charges plus preferred dividends) exceeds the requirements. This test, properly calculated and properly applied, has generally proved to be a satisfactory test in the selection of limited-income securities. It has continued to be the major test used by most investors, although certain institutional investors in recent years have supplemented this test by a cash flow test (to be discussed on pages 241-244).

---

[18] Examples are West Virginia Turnpike Bonds and Calumet Skyway Bonds.

Calculation of Coverage of Fixed Charges. There are two schools of thought regarding the calculation of coverage of fixed charges in order to protect holders of limited-income securities:

(1) One school believes that coverage of fixed charges should be calculated on the basis of the amount available *before* income taxes because fixed charges (interest) are a deductible expense before calculation of profits for income taxes. If there is no profit after deduction of interest, no taxes are due. Furthermore, this school believes that the payment of taxes clearly does not impair the *current* ability of the corporation to pay interest, although the use of cash for taxes may impair ability to pay succeeding payments of fixed charges.

(2) The other school believes that coverage of fixed charges should be calculated on the amount available *after* income taxes on the assumption that (granted that interest is payable before taxes) if the concern is to continue as a going concern, it must pay these taxes and this payment will affect its financial strength, reducing its cash by an equivalent amount.

In corporate reporting to stockholders, it has been customary to show the amount available for interest *after* the deduction of taxes. Of course, the analyst can always add back the taxes and then calculate the amount of coverage *before* taxes. The financial services uniformly show coverage *after* taxes, although in addition they normally also report coverage *before* taxes.[19]

If a company has an income bond outstanding, the interest on this bond is not legally a fixed charge; therefore, in reporting coverage for fixed-income obligations, the interest on income bonds is not included by the services. However, most analysts believe that the test should be to meet all obligations, including interest on income bonds.

If a 50% income tax rate for earnings of corporations is assumed, standards for coverage after taxes could be set and then be multiplied by 2 for standards on a before-tax basis, or standards for coverage before taxes could be set and then be divided by 2 to obtain standards on an after-tax basis. There are difficulties, however, in establishing a standard of coverage and then arbitrarily doubling it or reducing it by half. If a company has had the advantage of tax credits or tax refunds for the fiscal period in question, the taxes paid will be lower than would normally be the case based on its income, and the coverage after fixed charges will reflect this. If tax credits or refunds are not expected after the current year, the analyst must adjust his coverage figure accordingly. Furthermore, if the company has an income bond outstanding and if the interest charges were paid, the fixed charge coverage for the company's fixed-income bonds is usually calculated without including the interest charges on the income bond, and the taxes will have

---

[19] In Standard & Poor's bond guide, coverage is on an after-tax basis.

been reduced by that payment. Again, the coverage figure will appear higher than it really is.

Several actual methods of calculating coverage of fixed charges can be used. The most important of these methods are discussed below.

Prior Deductions Method. Under this method, the prior charges ahead of any issue are first deducted to obtain the amount available for a junior issue and then the coverage is calculated on this balance.

Illustration:

First-mortgage 5% bonds	$5,000,000
Second-mortgage 6% bonds	1,000,000
Third-mortgage 6% bonds	500,000

Earnings available to pay all fixed charges	$1,000,000	
Interest on first-mortgage bonds (5% $\times$ $5,000,000) ...	250,000	
Coverage for first-mortgage bonds (1,000,000 $\div$ 250,000)		4x
Balance available for second-mortgage bonds	$ 750,000	
Interest on second-mortgage bonds (6% $\times$ $1,000,000).	60,000	
Coverage for second-mortgage bonds (750,000 $\div$ 60,000)		12.5x
Balance available for third-mortgage bonds	$ 690,000	
Interest on third-mortgage bonds (6% $\times$ $500,000)	30,000	
Coverage for third-mortgage bonds (690,000 $\div$ 30,000) .		23x

Under this method, it appears that the second-mortgage bond with a coverage of 12.5x is better protected than the first-mortgage bond with a prior claim but coverage of only 4x. Quite obviously, the second-mortgage bond cannot be better protected than the first-mortgage bond. In the case of the third-mortgage bond, it appears exceptionally well protected with a coverage of 23x. Again, it is quite illogical that the third-mortgage bond is better protected than the first- and second-mortgage bonds.

While it is quite clear as between the three bonds, if an investor simply used this method for the second- or third-mortgage bond and then compared the coverage to bonds of another corporation, he could really assume a nonexistent relationship for those bonds superior to the first-mortgage bonds of the other company. *The prior deduction method is indefensible and should never be used.*

Cumulative Deductions Method. Under this method, the coverage for the first-mortgage bond is calculated in the same manner as was done under the prior deduction method and coverage will again be shown as 4x. However, from that point on, this method differs. For each secondary junior lien, the total amount of interest for the issue in question is added to all interest on all prior issues and then the total is related to the amount available for all issues.

Illustration:

First-mortgage 5% bonds	$5,000,000
Second-mortgage 6% bonds	1,000,000
Third-mortgage 6% bonds	500,000

Earnings available to pay all fixed charges	$1,000,000	
Interest on first-mortgage bonds (5% $\times$ $5,000,000) ...	$ 250,000	
Coverage for first-mortgage bonds (1,000,000 $\div$ 250,000)		4x
Interest on second-mortgage bonds (6% $\times$ $1,000,000) .	60,000	
Cumulative interest on first- and second-mortgage bonds	$ 310,000	
Coverage for second-mortgage bonds (1,000,000 $\div$ 310,000)		3.2x
Interest on third-mortgage bonds (6% $\times$ $500,000)	30,000	
Cumulative interest on all three bond issues	$ 340,000	
Coverage for third-mortgage bonds (1,000,000 $\div$ 340,000)		2.9x

Clearly, this method is logical. All junior issues show a lower coverage than the senior issues above them. Wall Street generally uses this method.

Historical Record of Coverage of Fixed Charges. An analysis of ratings of railroad bonds by the agencies indicates that the record of coverage of fixed charges must have been quite satisfactory in the 1930s (and subsequently) for a bond to receive either an AAA or AA rating in the 1970s. In fact, only two or three railroad bonds (such as Union Pacific Ref. C 2½'s of 1991) received an AAA rating, and only a handful (such as Norfolk and Western 1st Con. 4's of 1996 and a few terminal and belt line bonds guaranteed by several railroads) received an AA rating. Only a few others received an A rating. The latter usually had not covered their fixed charges in the worst years of the 1930s but had reduced their debts considerably since that time and had a satisfactory coverage record (2.65x to 5.00x) in the post-World War II years.

In the case of industrial bonds, there is wide range of quality. Again the record of the 1930s was considered by the agencies in establishing their ratings in the 1970s. The relatively few industrial bonds that received an AAA rating were those of industries whose bonds had had a satisfactory coverage in the 1930s and an excellent record since that time (such as bonds of some of the top petroleum companies). An important number of industrial bonds are rated AA, but here again the record of the companies was satisfactory in the 1930s and they have had a very good coverage record since that time. Industrial bonds rated AA have shown a range of coverage in the post-World War II years of 8.00x to 20.00x. Even for industrial bonds rated A, the long-term record has had to be good, and in the post-World War II years the coverage for such bonds has ranged from 3.50x to 9.75x. Bonds rated BBB have had a good coverage in the post-World War II years, but their coverage in the worst years of the 1930s did fall into the 1.00x to 2.00x range. There are a large number of industrial bonds rated BBB (medium-grade with some speculative element) and BB (lower medium-grade with only minimum investment characteristics). There are also a large number of industrial bonds rated B (definitely speculative) and CCC (outright speculative). The years after World War II have been relatively default free.

The public utility industry has a long record of stability of earnings that was well demonstrated for operating companies in the 1930s [20] and that has been a major consideration in the overall high rating of public utility bonds. There are quite a number of electric utility bonds rated AAA, and all of them showed coverage of no less than 2.75x in the worst years of the early 1930s. In the post-World War II years their coverage ranged between 3.50x and 5.00x, considerably less than for the very few AAA rated industrial bonds but ample justification for the rating because of the excellent stability of the industry and the companies' earnings. The many electric utility bonds receiving an AA rating in the 1970s had good coverage in the 1930s, although a little lower than for AAA rated bonds. In the post-war years their range of coverage was 2.80x to 4.20x, or somewhat less than the range of coverage for AAA rated utility bonds.

Almost all electric utility bonds are rated A or higher. A very few are rated only BBB, and the range of coverage for the latter has been 2.10x to 3.50x in recent years. The bonds of one company that is partly utility and partly industrial—General Telephone & Electronics—are also rated BBB. Their coverage in the post-World War II years has ranged between 2.50x and 3.16x. All of the electric utility bonds are rated BBB or higher and the majority are rated A or above. There appear to be no electric utility bonds rated below BBB.

What Should Be Included in Fixed Charges. Interest on debt is a fixed charge. For the owner of income bonds and preferred stock, both the interest and the dividends received should be considered fixed charges. Requirements representing sinking funds and amortization of debt principal are not usually included as fixed charges and will be covered when cash flow is discussed. The noninclusion of such items in fixed charges is usually justified by pointing out (1) that creditors are usually willing to waive sinking fund payments for a year or two if a company is temporarily embarrassed

---

[20] In the 1930s a number of the large public utility holding companies with highly leveraged overcapitalized capital strength collapsed and losses of investors were heavy, but this was not true of operating companies.

but still able to meet interest requirements and (2) that sinking fund payments are presumed to be covered by depreciation charges, which are not included in the numerator of the normal fixed-coverage ratio. However, if the indenture calls for mandatory sinking fund payments, the trustee for bondholders may be constrained to enforce the contract. These payments should then be included in fixed charges.

There is disagreement among financial analysts as to the proportion of annual lease charges that should be included in fixed charges in calculating fixed-charge coverage. A company that leases an important part of the assets it uses may be working with the same amount of fixed assets and producing the same profits after lease rentals as a company that borrows funds to acquire assets, but the former will show significantly lower debt and interest charges in its financial statements. The fixed-charge coverage ratio and the asset coverage (over debt) of the company leasing assets would appear superior when actually the cash flow requirements of the two companies may be relatively similar.

Some analysts feel that it is not appropriate to include the entire rental payment among fixed charges. The portion of the lease representing depreciation on the landlord's property, as opposed to that portion representing interest and profit to the landlord, is akin to principal payments on debt and could be thought of as reducing the lease obligation. Analysts believe that only the portion representing interest should appropriately be included in fixed charges. In order to test the sureness of cash flow covering required payments, however, the entire fixed portion of the rental should be included in the fixed-charge ratio since it cannot be avoided as can depreciation charges. Of course, earnings before interest charges, lease payments, and taxes should then be used as the numerator. The importance of breaking the rental payment down into the part representing interest and profit and the part representing depreciation on property is significant for purposes of stating *on a comparable basis* the assets and the liabilities of companies that do and do not lease.[21]

For a holding company, besides interest payments on its own debt, there is the question of interest charges and dividend payments of its subsidiaries. The subsidiary cannot pay common dividends until it has met both its debt and preferred stock obligations. Therefore, the stockholders of the holding company should realize that fixed charges include not only the direct charges

---

[21] A good discussion of the problems involved in properly relating leases to financial statements is found in J. H. Myers, *Reporting of Leases in Financial Statements* (New York: American Institute of Certified Public Accountants, 1962). The reader is also directed to A. T. Nelson, *The Impact of Leases on Financial Analysis* (East Lansing, Mich.: Michigan State University, 1963).

of the parent company's debt, but also the interest charges and the preferred dividend payments of the subsidiaries.

Standards for Minimum Coverage of Fixed Charges. On the basis of the preceding discussion of the actual coverage of fixed charges typical in the top four agency rating classifications, the following minimum coverage requirements can be established:

1. First Test—Average Earnings for Past Eight Years:

	Public Utilities	Industrials	Railroads
Before taxes	5.30x	7.70x	5.75x
After taxes	2.75x	4.00x	3.00x
Actual annual average after taxes for companies with BBB ratings, 1958-1967	2.83x	6.12x	1.69x

The after-tax standard assumes a 48% tax rate with the figures rounded to a practical standard for ease of reference.

2. Second Test—Minimum Coverage in Worst Year Since World War II:

	Public Utilities	Industrials	Railroads
Before taxes	3.85x	5.75x	4.80x
After taxes	2.00x	3.00x	2.50x
Actual worst years after taxes for companies with BBB ratings, 1958-1967	2.09x	2.97x	deficit
Since 1929 (in 1930s)	1.55x	1.10x	deficit

Cash Flow Protection for Limited-Income Securities

Cash flow analysis, although still not in wide use, is nevertheless a necessary yardstick to be used by corporate financial management as well as by investors in corporate debt securities to determine *corporate debt capacity.* Investor protection can be impaired by inability of the issuer to meet sinking fund or amortization requirements since these also are legal obligations. Therefore, the analyst should make some determination of the issuer's capacity to cover total requirements, including both interest payments and annual debt reduction. Coverage of both is essential.

Undoubtedly, time and use will increase the importance of cash flow analysis (discussed in detail in Chapter 17). However, for the present, because of its underdeveloped and relatively untested nature, cash flow analysis to determine cash adequacy should be used as a supplementary tool in conjunction with the standard earnings coverage tests in determining the quality of publicly issued bonds.

It is certainly true that the majority of investors and analysts in determining the quality of publicly issued bonds will still be guided largely by the standards of coverage previously described because they will argue that they have worked. However, internal management of companies and private placement lenders are certainly engaging more and more in cash flow analysis to determine corporate debt capacity, and this approach will probably gradually garner adherents from other investing groups.

Professor Donaldson [22] has stated:

> The earnings coverage form of debt capacity is generally intended as a crude approximation of risk measurement in cash flow terms—the higher the risk, the higher the required cushion of "normal" net earnings available for debt servicing in excess of debt servicing charges. In this sense, the flow of earnings is assumed to be the rough equivalent of a flow of cash of comparable size. By subtracting the amount of the debt servicing from a net earnings figure which is some multiple thereof, the remainder presumably represents the anticipated shortage in annual cash inflow which would result under recession conditions. In theory, such a standard, if properly defined, would provide absolute protection against the risk of cash insolvency from debt since the assumption is that the earnings (cash) available for debt servicing would not go below a 1:1 relationship under recession conditions. It was pointed out that while such a standard may be adequate for creditors' (investors') loan portfolios, it is inadequate from the borrowers' point of view. Net earnings as is described by the conventional income statement (even adjusted for noncash charges such as depreciation) does not provide a reliable measure of net cash inflow, particularly in periods of substantial changes in the scale of operations, and the potential shrinkage in cash flows during a recession can only be assumed by taking the behavior of all major determinants of cash flow into consideration. . . .[23]
> . . . It is therefore essential to look behind the historical record of variations in the elements of cash flow, if the full potential of recession cash flow behavior is to be described [and cash adequacy or inadequacy determined].[24]

Professor Donaldson also stated:

> In general, the common practices with respect to debt standards have been described . . . as unnecessarily crude and at times meaningless and misleading. This is a harsh comment on the financial practices of many well-managed and obviously successful businesses. . . . There appear to be four main . . . reasons why this situation exists in industry today.
> (1) The debt concepts of public utility finance developed in an earlier era have been uncritically adopted in an area of business activity and in a

---

[22] Gordon Donaldson, *Corporate Debt Capacity,* Division of Research, Graduate School of Business Administration (Boston, Mass.: Harvard University, 1961) pp. 161-162.

[23] Cash flow, sources and uses of funds analysis, and working capital management were discussed previously in Chapter 7. These items are now included in many annual reports.

[24] Donaldson, *op. cit.,* p. 166.

debt framework where they do not apply (i.e., where there is far less stability than in public utilities).

(2) The corporate financial officer has all too frequently sought his standards in those of the creditor and investor where crude criteria may not only be adequate but necessary due to time and *data limitations*.[25]

(3) Many corporate financial people have not been stimulated to think through the full implications of risk associated with fixed obligations.

(4) Many who are aware of the job to be done and have the data to do it believe that the cost of such an analysis would outweigh the possible gains in refinement.[26]

Net earnings as reported in typical accounting income statements (even adjusted for noncash charges) do not provide a reliable measure for predicting future net cash flows for purposes of judging safety of fixed-income securities. Companies undergo substantial changes in the scale of operations through time; therefore significant variations in cash flow can take place from year-to-year. The ultimate concern of the analyst is with the probability that net cash balances will be so reduced during some future recession period that default will become a likely event. The potential shrinkage in cash flow can only be assessed by studying carefully the behavior of all major determinants and the likelihood of that behavior being repeated in the future. The analyst will examine the extent of decline in sales, the reasons underlying that decline, the variations in the balance of receivables, and cost behavior in various depressed phases of the business cycle. He will compile a historical record showing the percentage change of each major cash flow component during years of adversity. He must then estimate the probable sales declines (expressed as a probability distribution in terms of a drop that is serious) and the probable cost behavior likely to be associated with the estimated possible sales declines. For example, one could estimate for a given company that a sales decline of 50% has only a 10% chance of occurring, that one of 25%-40% has a 15% chance of occurring, that one of 10%-25% has a 25% chance of occurring, and that a 10% decline in sales has a 50% chance of occurring. Appropriate cost estimates could be related to each sales assumption to generate a probability distribution of cash flows during periods of adversity.

Unfortunately, as previously noted, the information at the analyst's disposal is inadequate for such complete analysis unless he represents a private placement or bank lender. To the extent that data are available, the analyst should attempt to determine the likely sales declines that will be associated with periods of adversity and the probable effects on cash flow.

---

[25] This identifies the problems of the external financial security analyst in cash flow analysis.

[26] Donaldson, *op. cit.,* p. 155. Also see Thomas R. Atkinson, *op. cit.*

More and more pressure is being brought to bear on corporations to have them publish complete sources and uses of funds statements and related information to aid the analyst in cash flow analysis, and many are doing so.

Standards for Selection of Preferred Stocks

In discussing the calculation of coverage for bonds, the prior deduction method for junior bonds was rejected. For the same reasons, the prior deduction method for preferred stock is rejected. In many cases, the coverage for preferred stock would appear to be much better than for bonds, which have a prior claim. This would be clearly illogical and misleading.

While the cumulative deduction method may be and is being generally used, the total deductions method is preferable for all issues on the principle that, unless all issues are protected, none deserves a high investment rating.

In the case of preferred stock, the total deduction method should be used, although when there is only one issue of preferred stock the cumulative deduction method will give exactly the same results for the preferreds as the total deduction method.

Logically, to qualify as an investment-grade preferred stock, not only must the security meet the requirements for an investment-grade bond, but also the standards applied should exceed those for high-grade bonds because of the inferior contract of preferreds. The margin of safety for the preferred stock must be so wide that all dividend payments are assured beyond any reasonable doubt.

While logic would dictate *higher standards* for preferred stocks than for bonds, to require higher standards than those listed for investment-grade bonds on a cumulative basis (including preferred dividends) could exclude an important proportion of preferred stocks ranked by the market as high grade. If, therefore, the *same standards* are used in any particular case, it will mean that for the preferreds to just qualify, *the margin of protection for the bonds must exceed minimum standards.* To put it another way, if the corporation has a bond issue or a serial bond issue that just meets minimum standards by the cumulative deductions method, then by applying the *same* standards it would be found that the preferred stock could not qualify.

When the coverage for preferred stocks is being calculated on the basis of earnings available *before* taxes, the problem is not quite as simple as would be the case if the issue was not a preferred stock but say a third-mortgage bond. All bond interest is deductible for tax purposes, but preferred stock dividends are payable from net income remaining *after* income taxes. If a third-mortgage bond is assumed instead of a preferred stock issue, the required earnings available for all issues to provide a certain specific coverage would be less than if the third issue were preferred stock.

Two methods of calculating the coverage for preferred stocks are illustrated and discussed on the following pages. Table 9-1 is based on earnings available *after* taxes. Table 9-2 is based on earnings available *before* taxes.

It can be noted in Table 9-1 that on an *after-tax basis* the coverage for the *third*-mortgage bond is 2.94x, which would also be the coverage on a *total deduction basis* for the *first*-mortgage bond. On a *cumulative deduction basis* the coverage for the *first*-mortgage bond is 4.00x. The coverage for the

---

TABLE 9-1

Coverage for Bond Interest and Preferred Stock Dividends
Based on After-Tax Earnings

	Corporations with Three Bond Issues and No Preferred Stock	Corporations with Two Bond Issues and One Freferred Stock
First-mortgage 5% bonds	$5,000,000	$5,000,000
Second-mortgage 6% bonds	1,000,000	1,000,000
Third-mortgage 6% bonds	500,000	
Preferred stock, 6%, (10,000 shares, $50 par)	———	500,000
Earnings available *after* taxes for all issues	1,000,000	1,000,000
Interest on first-mortgage bonds	250,000	250,000
Coverage for first-mortgage bonds ..	$\dfrac{1,000,000}{250,000} = 4.00\text{x}$	$\dfrac{1,000,000}{250,000} = 4.00\text{x}$
Interest on first- and second-mortgage bonds ($250,000 + $60,000)	310,000	310,000
Coverage for second-mortgage bonds	$\dfrac{1,000,000}{310,000} = 3.23\text{x}$	$\dfrac{1,000,000}{310,000} = 3.23\text{x}$
Interest on first-, second-, and third-mortgage bonds ($250,000 + $60,000 + $30,000)	340,000	
Coverage for third-mortgage bonds ..	$\dfrac{1,000,000}{340,000} = 2.94\text{x}$	
Interest on first- and second-mortgage bonds and preferred stock ($250,000 + $60,000 + $30,000)		340,000
Coverage for preferred stock		$\dfrac{1,000,000}{340,000} = 2.94\text{x}$

TABLE 9-2

Coverage for Bond Interest and Preferred Stock Dividends
Based on Before-Tax Earnings

	Corporations with Three Bond Issues and No Preferred Stock	Corporations with Two Bond Issues and One Preferred Stock
First-mortgage 5% bonds	$5,000,000	$5,000,000
Second-mortgage 6% bonds	1,000,000	1,000,000
Third-mortgage 6% bonds	500,000	
Preferred stock, 6% (10,000 shares, $50 par)		500,000
Earnings available *before* taxes for all issues	1,000,000	1,000,000
Interest on first-mortgage bonds	250,000	250,000
Coverage for first-mortgage bonds ..	$\dfrac{1,000,000}{250,000} = 4.00x$	$\dfrac{1,000,000}{250,000} = 4.00x$
Interest on first- and second-mortgage bonds ($250,000 + $60,000) ...	310,000	310,000
Coverage for second-mortgage bonds	$\dfrac{1,000,000}{310,000} = 3.23x$	$\dfrac{1,000,000}{310,000} = 3.23x$
Interest on first-, second-, and third-mortgage bonds ($250,000 + $60,000 + $30,000)	340,000	
Coverage for third-mortgage bonds ..	$\dfrac{1,000,000}{340,000} = 2.94x$	
Balance available for preferred stock before taxes ($1,000,000 — $310,000)		690,000
Federal income tax at 48%		331,200
Coverage for preferred stock on total deduction basis ($250,000 + $60,000 + $331,200 + $30,000)		$\dfrac{1,000,000}{671,200} = 1.49x$
Earnings per share on preferred stock		$35.88

third-mortgage bond in Table 9-1 is the same as the coverage for the preferred stock; however, this is only because the earnings available for *both* corporations are $1,000,000 *after* taxes. If there is only *one* corporation with a choice of either a *third*-mortgage bond *or* a preferred stock, the coverage will always be higher if the bond is used because the interest on the bond would be tax deductible while the dividend on the preferred stock would be paid *after* taxes had been deducted. The amount of income available after taxes to pay the preferred stock dividend would therefore be less than that available to pay interest on the third-mortgage bond. It is improper to assume that each would have the same earnings available after taxes as was done in the illustration. Calculations of the number of times charges are covered must be made as shown in Table 9-2 in order to give recognition to the effect of taxes. It can clearly be noted in Table 9-2 that under the *cumulative deduction method* the coverage for preferred stock is only 1.49x.

Table 9-2 assumes that a corporation is considering a choice. In the first column, it issues a *third*-mortgage bond, while in the second-column it issues preferred stock instead of a *third*-mortgage bond. Assuming that earnings available for all issues *before taxes* are $1,000,000, then the coverage for the third-mortgage bond on a before-tax basis would be 2.94x. If preferred stock is issued, the coverage for preferred stock dividends will be only 1.49x. This is due to the fact that interest is tax deductible while preferred dividends are not. In calculating the coverage for the preferred stock, the tax is added to the bond interest and then related to the amount available for the preferred stock.

Given the tax rate, a computation can be used to approximately reconcile the coverage on a preferred issue with a bond issue. The tax rate is simply divided by 1 less the tax rate. Table 9-2 uses a tax rate of 48%, therefore:

$$\frac{.48}{1.00 - .48} = \frac{48}{52} = 0.92$$

The coverage for the *third*-mortgage bond with interest charges totaling the same amount as the preferred stock dividend would therefore be .92 times greater than the coverage for the preferred stock. Multiplying 1.92 by 1.49 gives 2.86, which is reasonably close to the 2.94 shown in the table as coverage for the *third*-mortgage bonds.

QUESTIONS

1. (a) Discuss the validity of agency ratings of bonds from the standpoint of judging quality.
   (b) Have bond yields on new offerings, as determined in the market, been well related to the quality of bonds at maturity? Discuss.

2. What are legal lists? Are they a good guide for the individual investor in bonds?

3. (a) Explain the significance of restrictive covenants in long-term debt contracts.
   (b) What type of restrictive covenants might be found?

4. Discuss the significance of a call provision to the investor if:

   (a) A decline in interest rates is expected.

   (b) A rise in interest rates is expected.

5. Why do equipment obligations of railroads have such high standing in the capital markets?

6. (a) What is a market value of equity test? In what ways is it superior to capitalization ratios calculated at book value?

   (b) How significant are capitalization ratios in judging bond quality?

7. What ratio or ratios indicate the stability or lack of stability of the protection for bondholders and preferred stockholders? Discuss the calculations of these ratios in terms of assessing stability of protection through time.

8. What would you study to judge the relative investment attractiveness of two bonds? Rate the criteria suggested by you in the order of relative importance for selection purposes and defend your position.

9. (a) If you had the Income Statement and the Balance Sheet for a given company, how would you determine the proper figures to use as the numerator and denominator in an interest coverage ratio? Clearly specify where the information would be located for both numerator and denominator if more than one issue were involved.

   (b) How does a fixed-charges coverage ratio differ from an interest coverage ratio? Be specific.

10. Professor Donaldson has stated that "the earnings coverage form of debt capacity is generally intended as a crude approximation of risk measurement in cash flow terms."

    (a) What faults lie in earnings coverage measures?

    (b) What practical difficulties stand in the way of developing a more adequate cash flow analysis for the purpose of judging the debt capacity?

WORK-STUDY PROBLEMS

1. (a) Contrast the time-fixed-charges covered figures over the last few years for debt issues of manufacturing concerns, electric utilities, and railroads. What differences do you find?

   (b) How are the differences noted by you reflected in agency ratings for debt issues in each of the three areas? Contrast a selected manufacturing company, electric utility, and railroad security, each rated AA by S&P.

   (c) Can the differences noted by you be justified? Discuss.

2. A balance sheet and an income statement for the XYZ Manufacturing Corporation are given on page 249.

XYZ Manufacturing Corporation
Balance Sheet
December 31, 19 - -

Cash	$ 75,000	Accounts Payable	$110,000
Accounts Receivable	250,000	Notes Payable—Bank, 6%	30,000
Inventories	180,000	Other Current Liabilities ..	30,000
Property and		First-Mortgage Bonds, 4%,	
Equipment $695,000		due 1985	150,000
Less Accumulated		Second-Mortgage Bonds,	
Depreciation ... 290,000		5%, due 1995	50,000
	$405,000	Preferred Stock, 5%,	
		$100 Par	100,000
		Common Stock, $100 Par..	250,000
		Retained Earnings	190,000
		Total Liabilities and	
Total Assets	$910,000	Capital	$910,000

XYZ Manufacturing Corporation
Income Statement
For the Year Ended December 31, 19 - -

Net Sales	$1,235,000
Less Cost of Sales	860,000
Gross Profit	$ 375,000
Less Selling and Administrative Expenses	320,000
Net Operating Income	$ 55,000
Interest Expense	10,300
Net Income Before Federal Income Taxes	$ 44,700
Federal Income Taxes	16,956
Net Income After Federal Income Taxes	$ 27,744

(a) Calculate the times-interest-covered ratio for the first-mortgage bonds.

(b) Calculate the times-interest-covered ratio for the second-mortgage bonds.

(c) What would be the times-interest-covered ratio for this firm if a total deductions method were used?

(d) Would you consider any or all of this corporation's bonds to be investment-grade? If the information given is inadequate for purposes of rating these bonds, what additional information would you require?

(e) If you had decided to buy the bonds of this corporation (assuming that both first- and second-mortgage bonds were selling at par), which would you buy? Why?

SUGGESTED READINGS

Atkinson, Thomas R. *Trends in Corporate Bond Quality*. National Bureau of Economic Research. New York: Columbia University Press, 1967.

Donaldson, Gordon. *Corporate Debt Capacity.* Boston, Mass.: Harvard University, Graduate School of Business Administration, 1961. Part 2.

Fisher, Lawrence. "Determinants of Risk Premiums on Corporate Bonds." *Journal of Political Economy* (June, 1959), pp. 217-237.

Francis, Jack Clark. *Investment Analysis and Management.* New York: McGraw Hill Book Company, 1972. Chapter 8.

Fredrickson, E. Bruce. *Frontiers of Investment Analysis,* 2d ed. Scranton, Pa.: Intext Educational Publishers, 1971. Chapters 14-15, 19-20.

Groth, Stephen C. "The Trouble with Convertibles." *Financial Analysts Journal* (November-December, 1972), pp. 92-95.

Harris, John T. "A Comparison of Long-Term Debt Discount and Current Coupon Bonds." *Financial Analysts Journal* (July-August, 1968).

Hoffland, David L. "The Price-Rating Structure of the Municipal Bond Market." *Financial Analysts Journal* (March-April, 1972), pp. 65-70.

Homer, Sidney. "2000 B.C. to the Present," *A History of Interest Rates.* New Brunswick, N.J.: Rutgers University Press, 1963.

Levy, Haim, and Marshall Sarnat. *Investment and Portfolio Analysis.* New York: John Wiley & Sons, Inc., 1972. Chapter IV.

Soldofsky, Robert M. "Yield-Risk Performance of Convertible Securities." *Financial Analysts Journal* (March-April, 1971), pp. 61-65, 79.

Terrell, William T., and William J. Frazer, Jr. "Interest Rates, Portfolio Behavior and Marketable Government Securities." *The Journal of Finance* (March, 1972), pp. 1-35.

Wu, Hsiu-Kwang, and Alan J. Zakon. *Elements of Investing,* 2d ed. New York: Holt, Rinehart and Winston, Inc., 1972. Chapters 16, 19.

PART
FOUR

INVESTMENT IN COMMON STOCKS

Investment Strategies
for Common Stocks

Common stocks may have value for two possible reasons. First, the security confers residual claim to the corporation's net income, which is the basis for dividends. Second, corporate success is reflected in growth in earnings and dividends and capital gains through rises in the price of the stock, reflecting and in the *long run* correlating closely with increases in earnings and dividends. The basic premises of security analysis are that careful analysis can lead to useful estimates of earnings growth and therefore of future earnings and dividend trends, and that it can provide a basis for meaningful comparative appraisal of common stock values.[1]

This chapter is concerned with *strategies* used in the acquisition and sale of common stocks by investors as opposed to traders. Traders generally make no pretense that they are buying and selling common stocks as a result of careful *valuation* by security analysis in depth. In fact, it often seems that the less there is known about a security, the greater is its appeal to non-professional traders, who simply want an interesting story or emphasize technical factors rather than economic fundamentals.

SHORT-TERM APPROACH

The anticipation of either short-period or cyclical market movements is the basis of the short-term approach to investment in common stocks. Chapter 4, "Historical Behavior of Markets for Common Stocks," discussed

---

[1] Chapters 13-25 discuss the application of valuation techniques in the field of security analysis.

various methods used by traders to anticipate market movements for the market as a whole, particular groups of securities, or particular stocks.[2]

Trader Selection

There are two important reasons for stating that nonprofessional investors should not attempt to build capital or to manage capital funds on the basis of the anticipation of market movements. First, successful professionals are practically unanimous in stating that the great majority of traders have a very poor record over any long period of time. Traders rarely build substantial capital by such activity over the years. A few, of course, do have a successful record. Most would have had a far better record of accumulating capital or increasing capital if they had acted as investors rather than as traders. The great majority of those who have accumulated capital through common stock ownership over their working years have done so by following the canons of investment instead of trading.

The activities of nonprofessional traders in 1967-1968 and 1972 were no different from that of traders 30 years ago when the following interpretation of traders' operations was published: ". . . more zeal and energy, more fanatical hope, and more intense anguish have been expended over the past century in efforts to 'forecast' the stock market than in almost any other single line of human action."

In spite of the very poor record of nonprofessional traders over the years, a large number of individuals, including professional managers of so-called performance funds, act as traders while calling themselves investors. One has simply to analyze the records of 1961, 1965, 1967-1969, and 1973 to recognize the extent and the intensity of nonprofessionals' activity as well as the activity of the "performance" funds.

The second reason for rejecting the trading approach to common stock investing is the scientific analyses that have been published on the futility of attempting to forecast market movements, especially short-term.

An article in the *Financial Analysts Journal* by the former editor, Nicholas Molodovsky,[3] summarized a study published by Princeton scholars.[4]

---

[2] A review of Chapter 4 at this point will be helpful.

[3] Nicholas Molodovsky, "Lessons from the Recent Past," *Financial Analysts Journal* (January-February, 1964). Also see Adam Smith (pseudonym of George J. W. Goodman, editor of *The Institutional Investor*), *The Money Game* (New York: Random House, Inc., 1968).

[4] A paper by Godfrey, Granger, and Morgenstein released in the fall of 1963 by Princeton University's Econometric Research Program. Others have argued against the "random walk" theory.

Readings suggesting that stock prices do not follow a "random walk" include the

Molodovsky commented that "whatever its merits, the results reached by the Princetonians are quite similar to those of other academic explorers of the stock market. They argue that stock prices (in general) perform a 'random walk'—which implies that the next move is independent of all past moves or events." We agree that this is true in the short run.

Cyclical Timing

In general, stock prices for particular groups of stocks and for particular individual stocks reflect anticipations of future company earnings, but the *degree* of discounting and the *timing* of discounting cannot be reduced to any standard pattern.

One difficulty in attempting to profit by *cyclical timing* as opposed to anticipation of shorter market investments is that stock price trends are one of the most consistent of the "leading indicators" used by economists in forecasting changes in the business cycle. An investor attempting to take advantage of cyclical timing must *anticipate* changes in the business cycle and in business profits well ahead of the forecasts by business economists. This has been a formidable if not an impossible task for most investors. This is why many of the large, old, and well-respected investment counsel firms make little or no attempt to profit from cyclical timing; in fact, they emphasize that they do not do so. Profiting from cyclical timing is difficult

---

following from *The Random Character of Stock Market Prices* (Cambridge, Mass.: The M.I.T. Press, 1964):

Sidney S. Alexander, "Price Movements in Speculative Markets," pp. 199-218; "Trends on Random Walk," pp. 338-372.

Paul H. Cootner, "Stock Prices; Random vs. Systematic Changes," pp. 221-252. (Cootner distinguishes between random walk over time, which he believes price trends do follow, and the fact that there are trends. A price move once initiated tends to persist.)

William Steiger, "A Test of Nonrandomness in Stock Price Changes," pp. 253-261.

Also see Henry C. Wallich, "Random Walk and Security Analysts," *Financial Analysts Journal* (March-April, 1968), for an excellent article on random walk theory with which the authors of this book are in general agreement as far as any short-term forecasting is concerned. Professor Wallich's major points are: "Random walk theory . . . in its *narrow version* . . . says that the *next move* of the market or a stock cannot be predicted from any past behavior . . . warning . . . addressed mainly to chartists. . . . A broader version . . . says that in a well functioning (economic) market known information has already been fully discounted. The next move of the market will reflect information not yet known. But the latter is an idealization of even so good a market as the New York Stock Exchange. News does not travel instantaneously, it is not acted upon immediately; some people have inside information. Prophecies can be self-fulfilling . . . follow a leader. Moreover a few rare individuals may genuinely be able to see farther ahead than the rest. Thus the broader version of the random walk probably is only approximately accurate."

at best and profiting from short-term timing trading is even more difficult over any extended period of time. However, every four years there were bear market lows, as in 1953, 1957-1958, 1962, 1966, and 1970.

Anticipation of Stock Prices for the Next Twelve Months

A large proportion of recommendations to purchase emanating from brokerage firms have always been based on the anticipation and the hope that the stocks recommended will do well—better than the averages—over the following year.[5] The reason for this emphasis on relatively short-term performance is that registered representatives have found that an important percentage of their customers really expect or hope for this type of performance and do not have the *patience* to be long-term investors. Usually the smaller the investor's portfolio, the more emphasis he places on short-term capital appreciation.

Increased Performance Pressure Since 1966

The rise in stock prices from the 1946-1949 base (DJIA approximately 160 in each year) to 735 in December, 1961 and to 1,000 in February, 1966 ($160,000 to $1,000,000) provided a market environment that made it difficult not to generate an excellent portfolio performance during this period, especially in a diversified portfolio of major blue chip companies. The majority of investors were pleased with the performance of their portfolios, whether they were individual investors, professionals, owners of stocks in mutual funds, or those responsible for selecting the professionals to manage corporate pension funds.

However, after February, 1966 (DJIA—995 and S&P—100) the permance of the general market of diversified portfolios of major companies was far poorer than the 1946-1966 period. In the six-year period (February, 1966 to February, 1972) the DJIA had in only two months (November-December, 1968) managed to revert to its February, 1966 level. The S&P 425 did rise from 100 in 1966 to 118 in December, 1968, and finally again to 118 in February, 1972, with the DJIA at 930. The high for the S&P 425 was 133 in 1972; for the DJIA, 1036. All indexes made new all time highs in January, 1973: DJIA, 1067; S&P "425," 135; and S&P "500," 120.

---

[5] Furthermore, recommendations to sell (or switch) are usually based on the premise that the stock suggested for sale will not perform particularly well over the near term. Wall Street has traditionally issued relatively few negative company reports. See John T. Lyons, "Wall Street's Hatchet Men—The Growing Influence of the Negative Report," *The Institutional Investor* (January, 1969), p. 29.

The 1966 to 1973 record of the general market, of course, reflected the horizontal channel of corporate profits, 1966 to 1972, as shown in Table 10-1. The market value of a stock and stock indexes reflect the current and, more important, the expected level of corporate earnings.

The 1949-1966 performance record had not prepared investors for the mediocre 1966-1973 record of a diversified portfolio of major stocks in major industries. They could not understand why the professional managers had done so well for them during 1949-1966 and then had posted such a relatively mediocre record during 1966-1972. Individual investors, mutual fund investors, and those selecting the managers of corporate pension funds were all demanding better performance. Investment managers and individual investors both strove for better short-term (up to one year) performance, and after February, 1966, came the adoption of new terms such as "performance investors," "performance mutual funds," and "go-go funds." The pressure for better performance mounted as some professionals did post spectacular one-year records.[6] After 1969 the "go-go" became "no-go" funds.

From 1966-1973, the type of fund that did succeed in securing an exceptional performance either tended to concentrate on important companies that had and were continuing to post an exceptional rate of earnings growth (such as Avon Products, IBM, Polaroid, and Xerox) or selected much smaller and lesser known companies that were currently showing a rapid growth in earnings, especially those with relatively small capitalizations and a relatively small floating supply of stock in the market. In many instances (although not all) the performance-minded professionals paid little attention to standards of value and were willing to pay very high price-earnings ratios for current rapid growth. They especially analyzed recent (last year or so) quarterly rates of earnings growth and concentrated on companies with the best recent record. They wanted companies with a "story." Consequently, stocks showing the fastest growth in earnings and corporations with small capitalizations rose spectacularly in price in 1966-1972, irrespective of poor DJIA and mediocre S&P index performance. Stock prices for the favored stocks were not indicative of any determined basic value but relied rather on investor faith, possibly a "follow-the-leader" type of psychology.

---

[6] For example, the managers of the Enterprise Fund secured a 113.7% rise in 1967 and a 36% rise in 1968 in net assets per share. Mr. Carr of Enterprise Fund stated that "management of money used to be synonymous with a predominance of blue chip names in the portfolio." He was highly critical of a policy of simply "buying and holding the blue chips." Many professionals decided that they had to try and emulate the performance record of the Enterprise Fund. But what about the record of the Manhattan Fund, launched with such glamorous hopes of spectacular performance? See Chapter 25, "Investment Company Stocks," for an elaboration of mutual fund performance in the late 1960s.

TABLE 10-1

Brief Record of Corporate Profits, 1961-1972

Year	Net Corporate Profits After Taxes All U.S. Corporations ($ Billions)	Earnings Per Share DJIA	Earnings Per Share S&P 425	Stock Prices DJIA	Stock Prices S&P 425
1960	$26.7	$32.21	$3.39	H 685	H 65.02
1961—1st Q.	A 24.4	A 22.80	A 2.96	H 679	H 67.72
1961	27.2	31.91	3.37	H 735	H 76.69
1966	49.9	57.68	5.89	....	
1966				H $\frac{}{995}$ L $\frac{}{744}$	H $\frac{}{100.60}$ L $\frac{}{77.89}$

Range—1967-1972

Year	Net Corporate Profits	EPS DJIA	EPS S&P 425	DJIA First	DJIA High	DJIA Low	DJIA Last	S&P "425" First	S&P "425" High	S&P "425" Low	S&P "425" Last
1967	46.6	53.87	5.66	786	943	786	905	86.66	106.15	85.31	104.80
1968	47.8	57.89	6.16	907	985	825	944	104.61	118.03	95.05	113.02
1969	44.8	57.02	6.17	948	969	770	800	113.14	116.24	97.75	107.00
1970	40.2	51.02	5.36	809	842	631	839	102.87	116.24	75.58	100.90
1971	45.9	55.09	5.73	839	951	798	890	100.91	116.75	98.44	109.67
1972	53.1	67.11	6.74	889	1036	889	1020	111.74	132.95	111.74	131.87

H—High; L—Low; A—Quarterly at Annual Rate.
The indexes declined 12-16% by mid-1973.

As others joined the performance school, the more gains resulted. As institutional investors became dominant, major stocks on the NYSE did not do well unless they were being acquired by institutions.

However, when the time to sell does come (when earnings growth slows down), only a limited proportion of such "investors" in these popular stocks, especially medium-sized or small companies, can realize a profit. Many investors, including funds, will be locked in and unable to shift to other stocks. Only the very skillful and fleet of foot can profit. Only time can tell whether or not short-term performance-oriented "investors" as a group (as opposed to those who are long-term, value-oriented) can really have a superior long-term performance. But certainly as more investors and funds join the "performance school," it will be more difficult to secure exceptional performance. Concentration on medium-sized or smaller companies with relatively little floating stock outstanding can result in spectacular increases, but it can also lead to disastrous declines when liquidation sets in.

The cause of performance pressures has been the relatively mediocre record of a diversified portfolio of major American corporations in 1966-1972, as reflected in the record of the DJIA during this period when corporate profits rose 80% from a 1959-1960 base. We have previously made estimates that corporate profits overall, for the DJIA and for the S&P indexes (500 and 425), will rise only at approximately a 5% rate or at best at the rate of growth for GNP, possibly 6% in the period 1975-1980. If that is the case, diversified portfolios of major corporations as reflected in the DJIA and the S&P 425 Industrials will probably rise only at about the same rate. Thus, the pressures for performance that developed in the 1960s can be expected to continue. Furthermore, as major industries and their stocks go in and out of favor, a well-diversified portfolio would negatively reflect this fact, that is, broad diversification would mirror the averages.

Under these assumptions, portfolio managers would have the following two major methods of securing better portfolio performance than this record as projected to 1980:

1. Purchase growth stocks whose future performance has not been over-discounted in their market price, especially of very young, smaller companies.

2. Take advantage of bear markets, as in 1953, 1957-1958, 1962, 1966, 1970, and 1973.

3. Emphasize the purchase of stocks of major companies in major industries when they are temporarily out-of-favor and selling at low price-earnings ratios relative to the DJIA and the S&P "425" and "500" indexes.

VALUATION APPROACH

The valuation approach to acquiring common stocks may take several forms. Four variations that are discussed below are: to buy and hold, to diversify, to select sound-value companies only, and to select only the faster-growing industries.

Buy-and-Hold Approach

The strategy that has probably provided the base for the accumulation of substantial capital over many years by more investors than any other strategy—at least up to 1966—is the "buy-and-hold" approach. When an analysis is made of many large capital funds that have been accumulated by individual investors during their lifetime, one is always impressed by the important proportion of the common stock portfolios that represent securities bought and held continuously from the time of acquisition. When the buy-and-hold approach has been combined with dollar-cost averaging (discussed in Chapter 4 and illustrated in Table 4-10), the record has been especially good.

One type of buy-and-hold approach that has produced especially fine results is that of company stock purchase plans such as those in operation for many years at Sears Roebuck, J. C. Penney, and many other firms.

The buy-and-hold approach is *not* often advocated by brokers, who generally wish to see selling as well as buying activity in accounts. Therefore, there has developed on Wall Street such cliches as "Don't go to sleep with stocks" and "Does your portfolio contain stocks that have changed their character and should be weeded out?" Such statements or questions are followed by examples of companies that once had a good following and have since had a poor record or have been eliminated in reorganizations.

It is certainly true that portfolios should be reviewed regularly to ascertain if the fundamentals have so changed or are so much in the process of change that they should be eliminated. However, the investor may be hounded by brokers to sell quality stocks that are *temporarily out-of-favor* (such as chemicals in 1968-1970) in order to switch into favorites of the moment. Such a policy will bring poor results. Brokers are not likely to point out the long-term record of well-diversified portfolios including major industrial companies, insurance companies, and banks that represent a cross section of American industry. For example, a portfolio purchased in the 1920s, 1930s, 1940s, or 1950s consisting of the 10 largest American industrial companies in 10 major industries, 5 operating electric utilities, and 5 major insurance companies would have a good record. This would have been especially true if the buy-and-hold policy had been associated with a dollar-cost averaging program. Also, if in the 1920s a portfolio had been invested entirely in the 30 DJIA stocks and changes had been made only when changes were made in the composite of the DJIA,[7] the portfolio would have had an excellent record. However, as noted above, while the buy-and-hold opportunities gave excellent results in 1949-1966 and also for much longer periods, it produced only mediocre results in 1966-1973 and probably in the period 1974-1980 may provide a compounded rate of price appreciation of only 6% or less. From 1949 to 1966 price-earnings ratios for the DJIA rose from 6x-7x to 18x as stock prices rose three times as fast as earnings. It cannot be expected that a similar proportionate increase in price-earnings ratios will take place in the foreseeable future.

Cross-Section-of-American-Industry Approach

This strategy of diversification, combined with the buy-and-hold approach, embodies the insurance principle of reducing risk by diversification. It is based on the premise that a common stock portfolio that represents a cross section of American industry will produce a record of stability and growth paralleling the stability and growth of the economy. Few if any of the managements of mutual investment funds, corporate pension funds, or other institutional funds admit to following such a policy. But an analysis of many such large portfolios is clear evidence that in fact—in spite of considerable portfolio turnover—the real policy has been to have a diversified cross section of major American industries. Therefore, most large mutual fund portfolios, in spite of their turnovers, have a record closely paralleling the record of the DJIA and of the S&P 500 Composite or 425 Industrials.

The cross-section-of-American-industry approach substitutes diversification for selectivity, at least to some extent. Because selectivity is the product of security analysis as a basis for portfolio management, it should be obvious why portfolio managements do not like to advertise that they are, in fact, following a diversified cross-section-of-industry approach. They must seek to justify payment for management services. They sell "professional" management (for example, the mutual funds).

Selectivity, however, can be combined with a cross-section-of-American-industry approach to provide a better performance while still following a

---

[7] No substitutes have been made in the DJIA 30 stocks since 1959 when Anaconda replaced American Smelting, Swift & Co. replaced Corn Products, Aluminum Company of America replaced National Steel, and Owens-Illinois replaced National Distillers.

policy of diversification with respect to portfolios in which additional funds are being invested annually. Specifically, each year there are *different* industries and companies that offer especially sound long-term values. By emphasizing purchases in such groups, a portfolio can be accumulated that is a cross section of industry but that still has been purchased on the basis of security analysis—selectivity based on value. It must be admitted, however, that a combination of a cross-section approach and a sound-value approach would often mean the purchase of temporarily out-of-favor, low price-earnings ratio stocks, and most investors (including institutional investors) are not temperamentally suited to purchasing out-of-favor securities. This is why most institutional portfolios have a record that parallels, but is not better than, the record of the DJIA or the S&P indexes. Without exception, institutional or individual portfolios that manage to outperform these indexes employ selectivity, even though they may have a reasonably diversified portfolio. However, it should be acknowledged that a record significantly outperforming the DJIA *requires a great deal of skill and a high level of judgment,* that the portfolio cannot be broadly diversified, and that higher risks will be taken.

Another variation of the cross-section approach is to purchase a cross section of what the American economy is expected to be some years hence on projection of the gradually changing nature of the economy. Looking ahead to after 1973, the annual compound rate of growth for such portfolios may average only about 5%-6% per year, which is the expected rate of corporate earnings growth.

Sound-Value Approach

Perhaps the most reasonable approach to security valuation and selection from the standpoint of the professional security analyst is the sound-value approach. This approach is based on the premise that no common stock should be purchased unless a careful industry and company analysis has been made, unless the security represents a sound value based on a careful projection of earnings and dividends for the next 3-6 years, and unless tested standards of value have been applied to these projections of earnings and dividends. This approach does assume that careful analysis can determine reasonable values for securities and can recognize undervaluation in the marketplace and attractive relative values as well as overvaluation.

The procedure of sound-value analysis is stressed in Chapter 11 as well as in Chapters 15-25 inclusive. This very important approach will therefore not be discussed further in this chapter. But in no way should this be taken to imply that this approach does not deserve the most serious consideration, for it is at the heart of security analysis.

Growth Stock Approach

In the mid-1920s the concept became accepted that common stocks provided the best form of investment because earnings, dividends, and market prices would, on the average, parallel the economy's growth, which was expected to be excellent. Nurtured by this idea, the birth of the growth stock approach ensued, first in the late 1920s and then again after World War II. This approach was predicated on the premise that the investor should put his money in the faster-growing industries. Investors who identified such growth companies (Avon Products, IBM, Polaroid, and Xerox) before there was any major public recognition of their potential have had spectacular portfolio performance, and even those who came in later have had an excellent performance record. Those who purchased early and held for a long period profited from their skill and judgment in purchasing these growth issues at reasonable prices. Those who came in later profited by the growing enthusiasm for these stocks when earnings continued to grow at an exceptional rate and when price-earnings ratios continued to be high relative to the averages.

An important question is whether a growth stock policy can be recommended as a strategy to be followed by *individual* investors *in general* or by *institutional* investors *in general*. An increasing number of individual and institutional investors each year have joined the group seeking to concentrate an important segment of their portfolios in growth stocks, especially after the mediocre period of major blue chip stocks in 1966-1973. The best investment record in the 1960s and early 1970s was in institutional-type growth stocks.

It is obviously a truism that large groups of investors cannot properly identify true growth companies before investors in general make such identifications. The more investors who attempt to follow this strategy, the more unlikely it is that many can purchase the stocks before the market places a very high price tag on rapid growth and future earnings. With so many professionals and others seeking growth stocks, few such stocks remain unidentified very long. But the stress is on young, small companies.

Confronted with the problem of identifying true growth companies, the investor is faced with the dilemma of identifying a company as a growth company after only a very few years of rapid earnings growth, which may prove to be the entire period of rapid growth. On the other hand, if the investor waits until a long-term record of rapid growth clearly identifies a company as a growth company, the period of continuing high growth may be coming to a close or future growth may be overdiscounted in market price.

The investor considering the growth stock strategy should be well aware of the awesome mathematical function of compounding as shown in Table

10-2. To meet the qualifications of a growth company, it is assumed that earnings will at least double every 5 or 6 years, that is, will increase at a compounded annual rate of 12.2% to 14.8% per year.

The tremendous effect of compounding should obviously cause investors to pause in any long-term projections of sales and earnings for growth companies. Xerox, with sales of approximately $740 million in 1967, doubled sales in the next two years and reached $2.4 billion sales in 1972.

TABLE 10-2

Results of Compounding Annual Growth Rates [8]
Growth of $1 at Individual Growth Rates Per Year

Growth Rate	12.2%	14.8%	18.9%	26%	42%	100%
Year						
1						2.000
2					2.016	4.000
3				2.000		
4			1.999		4.066	
5		1.994				
6	1.995			4.002		
7						
8			3.994			
9						
10		3.941				
11						
12	3.980					

---

[8] The following simple formula may be used to obtain the approximate number of years required to double an investment at a required growth rate: divide the number 72 by the growth rate desired. The accuracy of the calculation is shown in the following figures comparing the approximate results with the actual results:

Approximate Growth Rate	Approximate Number of Years	Actual Number of Years
3%	24.0 years	24.0 years
4	18.0	18.0
5	14.4	14.4
6	12.0	12.0
7	10.3	10.3
8	9.0	9.0
9	8.0	8.0
10	7.2	7.2
11	6.5	6.5
12	6.0	6.1
13	5.6	5.6
14	5.0	5.3
15	4.8	5.0
16	4.5	4.8
17	4.2	4.5
18	4.0	4.2
19	3.8	4.0
20	3.6	3.8

PART FOUR *Investment in Common Stocks*

At a compounded rate of 15% for 20 years, sales by 1992 would be 16.4 × $2.4 billion, or $39.4 billion. If the rate of compounding should continue for 50 years, sales would be 1,084 × $2.4 billion, or $2.6 trillion. Such effects of compounding obviously indicate that at some stage the compounding growth rate must decrease to the level of growth of the average company and industry.

The historical record of most successful companies indicates that after some years of rapid growth, the growth rate diminishes. Eventually the company reaches maturity with a growth paralleling the growth of earnings for "All U.S. Corporations." In the great majority of cases, the longer the record of exceptionally high growth, the nearer the company is to its stage of maturity. There have been few Avon's, IBM's, Xerox's and Polaroid's. As institutional investors have become dominant and individual investors less important, NYSE-listed stocks of major companies that have done well usually are those stocks that have been acquired by institutions.

Ingredients of Growth.[9] In almost all industries and companies that have demonstrated exceptionally high rates of growth, the major catalyst has been research and development. The drug, office machine, electronics, aerospace, oceanography, and new anti-pollution industries are only a few of the examples. Research and development has often resulted in new products and processes and in radically improved products or exceptional marketing techniques.

The investor seeking growth companies will tend to concentrate on research-oriented companies. But large expenditures for research staffs and facilities do not by themselves guarantee a rapid growth in sales and earnings. The *quality* of research cannot be measured by funds spent, facilities owned, or scientists employed. The *quality* of research can be measured only by the value of the research output.

Sales Growth Versus Earnings Growth. It is earnings growth that is being sought by the investor seeking growth stocks. In almost all cases, a sustained and rapid growth in earnings is correlated with a sustained and rapid growth in sales, but there have been instances where a rapid, sustained, and substantial growth in gross revenues has not resulted in an equivalent growth in earnings.

Many cases can be cited where gross revenues have grown, especially as a result of mergers and acquisitions, but earnings have shown only a mediocre or below-average increase because of dilution (for example, the case of conglomerates).

---

[9] See Chapter 14 for detailed discussion of growth ingredients.

Price Paid for Growth Stocks. Once a company has been identified as a growth company whose projected earnings are estimated to grow at a rapid pace, its shares have more value in terms of price-earnings ratios than the shares of a company whose earnings are growing only in line with over-all corporate earnings.

Capitalization Rate for Growth Stocks. In general, on Wall Street the capitalization of earnings is the most important basis for investment decisions relative to common stocks, although numerous academicians have attacked this approach. The quality of earnings determines the capitalization rate, with quality a function of the stability and growth rate of earnings. For growth companies, the dividend paid, if any, is not significant. Capitalization of earnings as it applies to growth companies is discussed briefly here; a more detailed discussion will be given in later chapters.

In determining the capitalization rate to be used for a company whose earnings are expected to grow at the same rate as the DJIA or the S&P 425 Industrials, the investor must first determine the expected range of price-earnings ratios for these averages over the next 5 or 6 years. In this book the assumption is made that most of the time over the next 5 or 6 years these averages will sell in a range of 15x to 20x their current earnings [10] and that earnings will grow at an annual compound rate of growth of 4½% to 6% per year. On this basis, stocks with average earnings growth will be expected to have a record parallel to that of the averages and also to sell within the range of price-earnings ratios of the averages. It will be necessary to pay a higher price-earnings ratio for all issues of clearly identified growth stocks than for average stocks. Investors should therefore be willing to pay a maximum of 35x or perhaps 40x current earnings for quality growth stocks (for example, a leading company in an important industry) when earnings are expected to grow at a rate of at least 12% to 14% per year. It is advisable to set a maximum price-earnings ratio of 35x or 40x because, if earnings of the growth stock selected do double in 5 or 6 years, the price-earnings ratio (based on cost) 5 or 6 years hence will have declined from 35x to 17½x current earnings or from 40x to 20x current earnings.

Advocates of growth stocks say that high price-earnings ratios are illusory because rapid growth in earnings will soon bring these ratios—based on cost—to a reasonable figure. If the maximum is limited to 40x earnings, then that thesis can be accepted. To go any higher would be to discount earnings growth so far in advance that the risks of such distant projections

---

[10] Every few years we expect bear markets, as in 1957-1958, 1962, 1966, and 1969-1970, to temporarily reduce P/E ratios to the 12-14 level for the S&P "425" and "500" averages below the more "normal" 16-18 P/E range.

PART FOUR *Investment in Common Stocks*

would outweigh the potential profit advantages from such stocks. Even at 40x earnings, the risks are significant, especially with little dividend yield.

To set a maximum price-earnings ratio as shown above will eliminate at any point of time many of the most popular growth stocks of the moment. However, it will also avoid the purchase of stocks at very high prices that would subject the investor to the major risk of very sharp price declines. Furthermore, even for Avon Products, IBM, Polaroid, and Xerox, by steadfastly adhering to this standard maximum, the investor has witnessed periods in recent years when the stocks of these companies did decline to an acceptable price-earnings range.

What is questionable at this point is just what the owner of a growth stock should do when he sees the price-earnings ratio continue to increase. Should he sell his security and realize a capital gain or should he hold it? This is a difficult question to answer generally, since the course of action taken will be determined by the circumstances. If the company appears to have a high expected growth rate for the next 5 or 6 years and it is currently selling at 35x to 45x its current earnings, the security should certainly be held. However, if the investor is still going to have any standards as a guide, there often comes a point when the sale of the stock is justified, as for example if it rises to 60x to 80x earnings. Admittedly, this is contrary to the general thinking on Wall Street, for the highest price-earnings ratios (for example, Avon and International Flavors & Fragrances) indicate the greatest optimism.

LOW PRICE-EARNINGS, OUT-OF-FAVOR APPROACH

The authors have had very considerable experience with the low P/E approach over a long period of years and therefore recommend some consideration of this approach for the relatively few investors who have the emotional stamina to go against the crowd and to exercise the usual analysis and patience required for success in following this strategy.

Cyclical Undervaluation of Securities

The undervalued strategy may be used to describe a cyclical approach to common stock investments. Chapter 4 discussed the record of major bull and bear markets and the frequent discounting in these markets of general business conditions. During business recessions *the market, in general, is undervalued* in terms of any norm related to the long upward secular trend. Also, at such times some groups and many individual stocks, frequently representing major companies in major industries, decline more than the averages. The strategy could be to wait and buy in bear markets and to sell in top areas of bull markets. Such an approach has been dismissed for most investors because the record has shown that the application of this aspect of theory is extremely difficult to accomplish. Interestingly, major bear market lows have tended to occur approximately every four years— 1953, 1957-1958, 1962, 1966, and 1970. Of course, there is no assurance that this record will be repeated in the future. The past record can simply represent a series of coincidences, but is generally related to a discounting of an expected economic recession. Many major stocks were at low P/E's in 1973.

Undervalued Out-of-Favor, Low P/E Stocks

It is true that the greatest number of undervaluations will be at the bottom of bear markets, but in any year there are some undervaluations of major companies in major industries as well as numerous undervaluations of other companies. The undervaluation strategist will often buy in periods of bear markets, but he is *not* influenced by market psychology and, unlike the cyclical strategist, he will not postpone buying to wait for bear markets. He can also buy in bull markets, as some low price-earnings, out-of-favor industries and companies are *always* available regardless of market levels.

Investors do not need to be encouraged to follow a growth stock policy because it appears very logical to them. Just the reverse is true with the low price-earnings, out-of-favor strategy. Not only does it mean going against the crowd and exercising unusual patience, but also it appears to fly in the face of logic. It seems logical to buy stocks in corporations that have had and currently have a good earnings record, while it appears quite illogical to purchase stocks in industries and companies (the airlines in 1969-1970) whose problems are obvious to all. However, a little thought should raise questions concerning a policy that would buy stocks when they are popular (suggesting high demand and price peaks) and sell them when they are unpopular (suggesting low demand and price troughs), although this is just what a good many investors regularly do. Most brokers advocate waiting for an actual turnaround to be evidenced, but this is very difficult timing before prices reflect the turnaround.

Assumptions for Low Price-Earnings, Out-of-Favor Strategy

There are two basic assumptions for the low price-earnings, out-of-favor strategy. The first assumption is that the record shows that most major industries have fluctuated between periods in which they did quite well, followed by periods when they faced problems of various degrees of severity, followed by periods of renewed prosperity as problems were solved. The result is that industries are at times popular with investors (when they are doing well) and at other times unpopular or relatively unpopular with investors (when they have problems and especially if the results are an actual decline in earnings). This same problem may at times affect companies even when their industry is experiencing prosperity (for example, Chrysler in 1961 and 1970). All three major auto stocks were at low P/E's in 1973.

The second basic assumption is that investors in the market tend to exaggerate either prosperity or high growth factors and likewise to exaggerate the problems that may beset a company or an industry. This exaggeration often places the price of growth stocks far above any level justified by a reasonable expectation for the future so that a heavy speculative element is included in the price. Conversely, exaggeration often forces down the price of a problem out-of-favor stock, as much from lack of buying interest as from selling pressures, until on any reasonable basis the stock becomes heavily undervalued on the premise (very frequently erroneous) that the problems are unsolvable and permanent. The latter exaggeration results in even greater unpopularity than might otherwise occur. The market is making no allowance for a potential recovery of earnings. This was true of the chemical and airline stocks in 1967 and 1970 as well as relatively true of the utilities stocks for the entire period 1965-1973.

One reason for the exaggeration of the problem in the low price-earnings, out-of-favor groups is the acceptance of the life-cycle theory. It is assumed that industries and companies follow a life-cycle pattern similar to that of human life; they are born, grow rapidly, have a limited period of maturity, and then decline to their inevitable demise. Most major industries and companies do experience a relatively brief initial period of rapid growth. But there the similarity ends. They usually enter *a very long period* of maturity without showing much evidence of a serious continuous decline and demise.

The long period of maturity faced by most industries proves an ideal working ground for the out-of-favor stocks because, during maturity, the industry experiences recurring waves of popularity and unpopularity. The low price-earnings, out-of-favor strategists will take advantage of these cycles by purchasing the securities when they are out-of-favor and selling them in subsequent periods of popularity.

There is one other factor that should be mentioned because of its increasing importance. As more and more investors, both individual and institutional, have become "one-year-performance" minded, they not only will not buy but will sell stocks of companies whose earnings prospects are poor or mediocre for the next year in order to buy stocks with better earnings prospects. This policy has resulted in additional pressure on the low price-earnings, out-of-favor group that has lowered their prices to even greater undervaluations and therefore provided even greater 3-4 year capital gains potentials. Again, many major stocks were at low P/E's in 1973.

The low price-earnings, out-of-favor strategist must be convinced that at least there will be a reasonable recovery of earning power. This assumption is based on careful analysis of the industry and the company concerned *and confidence that a recovery of earning power will lead to substantial capital gains*. Most successful experiments in this strategy have tended to reduce risks by concentrating on major companies in major industries.

Large Investments in Low Price-Earnings, Out-of-Favor Stocks by Sophisticated Groups

The low price-earnings, out-of-favor strategists should always be awake to situations in which large amounts of sophisticated money are flowing into certain out-of-favor stocks. They should consider that such information is considerably more valuable than the offhand recommendations that are so frequent on Wall Street, especially in bull markets. And yet this type of public information is usually ignored by most professionals and laymen. If sophisticated investors are backing their judgment with millions of dollars, it is perhaps worthwhile to make an analysis of such out-of-favor stocks.

Selectivity in Out-of-Favor Stocks

Selectivity is the *sine qua non* of security analysis and is just as important whether one is using the low price-earnings, out-of-favor strategy or the growth stock strategy. Because selectivity is as important here as elsewhere, the low price-earnings, out-of-favor strategists can be content to work with a *very few* industries and companies—sometimes only one and usually a maximum of five situations. *They can therefore confine their investments at any point of time to a few major companies in important industries*. There are always such situations available, so it is never necessary to take the higher risks usually associated with lesser companies and industries.

Low Downside Price Risks for Out-of-Favor Companies

Consideration of downside price risks is equally important with consideration of upside capital appreciation for common stock investments. The downside risk is usually quite limited, and frequently this is indicated by its horizontal trend line on a price chart. The stock has usually declined to a level where the price-earnings ratio is below (often well below) the price-earnings ratio for the "averages," and the yield is often well above the yield on the "averages" (sometimes as high as twice the yield on the "averages"). This situation reduces the downside price risk. Frequently, such stocks can be bought by dividend-yield-conscious investors as well as by strongly capital-appreciation-oriented investors. In such cases, the yield-oriented investor can enjoy, in addition to the current satisfactory dividend yield, an important capital gains potential (example, chemicals in 1969-1970).

Those working with low price-earnings, out-of-favor stocks have developed certain techniques for locating out-of-favor stocks of important companies in important industries as an aid to increasing the capital gains potential. It is recommended that no low price-earnings, out-of-favor stocks be purchased unless they have declined at least 45%-50% from their highs in the past few years. A 50% decline, which is frequently the situation, would provide a capital gains potential of 100%. Of course, no stock should be purchased simply on this basis, but only after careful analysis and projection of earnings for the next 5 or 6 years in order to justify the expected capital gains.

In conclusion, it should be emphasized that when the low price-earnings, out-of-favor approach is used, the portfolio should be largely invested in stocks of important companies in important industries.

QUESTIONS

1. What factors underlie the value of a common stock?

2. (a) What is the "random walk" hypothesis?
   (b) Relate the "random walk" hypothesis to the activities of traders.
   (c) Would you recommend short-term trading as a means of building capital for the average investor? Why or why not?

3. Would you recommend the use of cyclical timing as a means of purchasing stock? Defend your answer.

4. (a) Why was it relatively easy for most investment consulting firms to show good results during the period 1946-1961? Did they do as well during the period 1961-1966? 1966-1972?
   (b) What approach or approaches would you suggest as appropriate for aggressive investors during the 1970s?

5. (a) What is the difference between the buy-and-hold approach and the trading approach?
   (b) Which approach would you expect brokerage firms to advocate? Why?
   (c) Evaluate the success of a buy-and-hold approach since the Second World War.

6. (a) Why does the performance record of many institutional investors parallel the record of the DJIA or S&P indexes?
   (b) Relate selectivity to the cross-section-of-American-industry approach.

7. (a) How does one identify a growth stock?
   (b) What problems are inherent in attempting to profit from following a growth stock strategy?
   (c) How does one go about determining a proper price-earnings ratio for a growth stock?

8. (a) Why is the out-of-favor approach psychologically difficult for an investor to follow?
   (b) How would you identify an out-of-favor stock?
   (c) Is the low price-earnings, out-of-favor stock approach consistent with (1) a properly diversified portfolio and (2) a cross-section-of-American-industry approach? Discuss.

WORK-STUDY PROBLEMS

1. (a) Based on a study of relevant factors, suggest two attractive under-valued situations today. Be prepared to defend your choices.
   (b) What are the advantages of the low price-earnings, out-of-favor approach to investments?

2. Review the portfolio of a few selected mutual funds over the last 10 years. What investment approach is suggested?

SUGGESTED READINGS

Agmon, Tamir. "The Relations Among Equity Markets: A Study of Share Price Co-Movements in the United States, United Kingdom, Germany and Japan." *The Journal of Finance* (September, 1972), pp. 839-855.

Ambachtsheer, Keith. "Portfolio Theory and Security Analyst." *Financial Analysts Journal* (November-December, 1972), pp. 53-57.

Andrews, John R., Jr. "The Fundamental Case for Investing in Growth." *Financial Analysts Journal* (November-December, 1970), pp. 55-64.

Babcock, Guilford. "The Concept of Sustainable Growth." *Financial Analysts Journal* (May-June, 1970), pp. 108-114.

Bellemore, Douglas H. *The Strategic Investor.* New York: Simmons-Broadman Publishing Co., 1963.

Bleakley, Fred. "Burt Dorsett: For CREF, A Continuing Faith in Growth." *Institutional Investor* (January, 1971), pp. 57-60, 86-88.

Cheng, Paol, and M. King Deets. "Portfolio Returns and the Random Walk Theory." *The Journal of Finance* (March, 1971), pp. 11-30.

Cootner, Paul H. (Ed.). *The Random Character of Stock Market Prices.* Cambridge, Mass.: The MIT Press, 1964.

Diefenbach, R. N. "How Good Is Institutional Research?" *Financial Analysts Journal* (January-February, 1972), pp. 54-60.

Ellis, C. D. "Will Success Spoil Performance Investing?" *Financial Analysts Journal* (September-October, 1968).

Foster, Earl M. "Price-Earnings Ratio and Corporate Growth." *Financial Analysts Journal* (July-August, 1970), pp. 115-118.

Francis, Jack Clark, and Stephen H. Archer. *Portfolio Analysis.* Englewood Cliffs, N.J.: Prentice Hall, 1971. Chapter 9.

Fredrikson, E. Bruce. *Frontiers of Investment Analysis,* 2nd ed. Scranton, Pa.: Intext Educational Publishers, 1971. Chapters 3, 4, 5, 16-18.

Good, Walter R. "Valuing Quality Growth Stocks." *Financial Analysts Journal* (September-October, 1972), pp. 47-56.

Graham, Benjamin, David L. Dodd, C. Sidney Cottle, and Charles Tatham. *Security Analysis, Principles and Techniques.* New York: McGraw Hill Book Company, 1962. Part I.

Grubel, Herbert C., and Kenneth Fadner. "The Interdependence of International Equity Markets." *The Journal of Finance* (March, 1971), pp. 89-94.

Hodges, Stewart, and Richard Brealey. "Portfolio Selection in a Dynamic and Uncertain World." *Financial Analysts Journal* (November-December, 1972), pp. 58-69.

Homa, Kenneth E., and Dwight M. Jaffee. "The Supply of Money and Common Stock Prices." *The Journal of Finance* (December, 1971), pp. 1045-1066.

Levin, Jesse. "Growth Rates—The Bigger They Come, the Harder They Fall." *Financial Analysts Journal* (November-December, 1972), pp. 71-77.

Malkiel, Burton C., and Richard E. Quandt. "The Supply of Money and Common Stock Prices: Comment." *The Journal of Finance* (September, 1972), pp. 921-926.

McDonald, J. C., and A. K. Fisher. "New-Issue Stock Price Behavior." *The Journal of Finance* (March, 1972), pp. 97-102.

Niederhoffer, Victor, and Patrick J. Regan. "Earnings Changes, Analysts' Forecasts and Stock Prices." *Financial Analysts Journal* (May-June, 1972), pp. 65-71.

Reilly, Frank K. "Evidence Regarding a Segmented Stock Market." *The Journal of Finance* (June, 1972), pp. 607-625.

Robichek, Alexander A., and Marcus C. Bogue. "A Note on the Behavior of Expected Price/Earnings Ratios over Time." *The Journal of Finance* (June, 1971), pp. 731-735.

Rudolph, J. Allan. "The Money Supply and Common Stock Prices." *Financial Analysts Journal* (March-April, 1972), pp. 19-25.

Sauvain, Harry. *Investment Management,* 5th ed. Englewood Cliffs, N.J.: Prentice Hall, Inc., 1973. Part II.

Sharpe, William F. "Risk, Market Sensitivity and Diversification." *Financial Analysts Journal* (January-February, 1972), pp. 74-78.

——————. "Simple Strategies for Portfolio Diversification: Comment." *The Journal of Finance* (March, 1972), pp. 127-129.

Smith, Adam. *Supermoney*. New York: Random House, Inc., 1972.

——————. *The Money Game*. New York: Random House, Inc., 1968.

Smith, R.G.E. "Uncertainty, Information and Investment Decisions." *The Journal of Finance* (March, 1971), pp. 67-82.

Sprinkil, Beryl Wayne. *Money and Markets*. Homewood, Ill.: Dow Jones-Irwin, Inc., 1971.

Stern, Walter P., and William C. Norby. "Investment Research and Market Structure—Today and Tomorrow." *Financial Analysts Journal* (January-February, 1972), pp. 24-28, 85-87.

Van Horne, James C., and William F. Glassmire, Jr. "The Impact of Unanticipated Changes in Inflation on the Value of Common Stocks." *The Journal of Finance* (December, 1972), pp. 1081-1092.

Williamson, Peter J. *Investments—New Analytical Techniques*. New York: Praeger Publishers, 1971.

11

Historical Evolution of Valuation Theories

The premise for all theories for the valuation of common stocks, either for the market as a whole (DJIA or S&P 500 or 425 Indexes) or for individual stocks, is that an absolute, intrinsic or investment value or value range may be determined apart from the current market price for individual stocks.[1] It assumes that at least significant overvaluation or undervaluation in the market can be identified accordingly and relative values determined.

VALUATION OF COMMON STOCKS

Until 1930, little or no attempt was made to develop or expound on any valuation theory for common stocks. It was accepted by most investors that a common stock, like any economic good, was worth what it would bring in the market, that is, its current market price. Certainly up to the 1920s at least, the purchase and the sale of common stock was considered by most investors to be a speculative activity and not an investment operation. Gradually, however, some common stocks of companies with a long record of success (a long and satisfactory earnings and dividend record) came to be accepted as investments. The relatively few stocks deserving an investment rating were looked upon as something like junior bonds and were selected on somewhat the same basis as bonds—largely a balance sheet analysis of asset values. To qualify, they had to have a market price somewhat closely related to par or asset values (on the balance sheet) supported

---

[1] In many court cases, such as merger cases in which one of the authors of this book has testified, the essential problem is to establish an investment value for the stocks involved.

by a long record of success in terms of their satisfactory earnings and dividend record. Few stocks qualified under these constraints—only long-established companies such as duPont and General Electric qualified.

Attitudes Toward Valuation of Common Stocks in the 1920s

In 1924, a study published by Edgar Lawrence Smith [2] showed that a well-diversified, representative list of common stocks (of important companies) had consistently outperformed a bond portfolio in any 10-year period since the Civil War, including periods of deflation as well as inflation, taking into consideration capital appreciation and any capital losses as well as dividend or interest income. He concluded that there had, and probably would continue to be, a long-term secular uptrend in the portfolio value of a representative list of common stocks of important companies.

By the end of the 1920s, great enthusiasm for, and speculation in, common stocks became the order of the day on the theory that common stocks as a class could be accepted as investments and would have an excellent long-term growth record in earnings, dividends, and capital appreciation. Perpetual prosperity for the economy was projected. A "growth stock" cult developed which assumed that if common stocks, as a class, would perform well, the stocks of growth companies would do even better. The price paid was assumed to be of little significance, as before very long the growth in earnings would justify any current price no matter how high and no matter how low the current yield. Up to the 1930s little or no attention was paid to the problem of establishing an absolute, intrinsic or investment value or value range for common stocks (or a particular common stock) apart from their current market price. Even today, many actual investors and many professional analysts—perhaps most—either make no attempt to determine an intrinsic or investment value or value range of a stock or make only a fairly unsophisticated attempt to arrive at some intrinsic value. They fail to do this in spite of the publication of many articles by academicians which present methods of arriving at the intrinsic investment value of a common stock and show the need to establish investment values independent of market prices in many court cases.

Valuation Methods Suggested in the 1930s

Probably as a result of the crash of common stocks in 1929, which by 1932 culminated in a 90% decline in common stock prices, a reappraisal of

_____
[2] Edgar Lawrence Smith, *Common Stocks as Long-Term Investments* (New York: The Macmillan Co., 1924).

investment techniques was made to ascertain "what had gone wrong." This naturally led to an attempt to determine whether some method could be found to arrive at an intrinsic or investment value for stocks and especially to identify such gross overvaluations as had occurred in 1929.

What Samuel Eliot Guild said in 1931 would still be quite pertinent today. He stated: "One of the anomalies of the science of investment today is the tremendous amount of money and labor which is put into research work as contrasted with the comparatively inaccurate and unintelligent manner in which its results, in terms of a stock's estimated prospects for the future, are applied to the current price of the stock in order to determine the investment return which may reasonably be expected from it over any given period on the basis of any given estimate." [3]

To illustrate that investment analysis contributed little or nothing satisfactory in the area of valuation in 1929 or even by 1938, J. B. Williams stated in 1938: "That investment analysis until now has been altogether unequal to the demands put upon it should be clear from the tremendous fluctuations in stock prices that have occurred in recent years. As will be shown . . . proper canons of evaluation, generally accepted as authoritative, should have helped to check these price swings somewhat." [4]

Major Factors Considered in the Valuation of Common Stocks

The major factors considered in the valuation of common stocks either in the case of formalized methods of valuation based on well-defined theories of valuation or quite informal and unsophisticated methods of valuation are:

1. *Asset values.* These values were considered highly important in quality ratings for stocks and bonds in the period before the 1920s but gradually have been considered less and less important by most investors since that time except, to a degree, for specific areas such as financial companies, utilities, and natural resource companies; even here, earnings are the key.

2. *Estimated future earnings and dividends.* The length of time of projections varies widely among investors and analysts, some making formal estimates for the next 12 months only, and others making projections of earnings

---

[3] Samuel Eliot Guild, *Stock Growth and Discount Tables* (Boston: Financial Publishing Co., 1931), p. 23.

In the 1962 edition of Graham, Dodd, and Cottle's *Security Analysis,* 4th ed. (New York: McGraw-Hill Book Company, 1962), on page 434 the authors state: ". . . Wall Street . . . too many studies of individual companies which do not provide an adequate basis for investment decision . . . usually such studies do not arrive at a carefully calculated value or value range." On page 441 they state: "The appraisal approach is still too new to permit us to be dogmatic about its value, either absolutely or relatively to the methods of analysis."

[4] J. B. Williams, *The Theory of Investment Value (1938),* (Reprint; Amsterdam, The Netherlands: North Holland Publishing Company, 1964).

extending for many years into the future. Many practicing financial analysts base their recommendations on projections of earnings for the next 4-6 years and in some cases for a maximum of 8-10 years.

3. *Expected future dividends.* This is the basis for most present-worth theories suggested by academicians.

4. *Capitalization rate.* This is the multiplier to be applied to earnings or dividends, that is, the price-earnings ratio or the price-dividends ratio to be applied to estimates of earnings or dividends or to current earnings *as a result of an assessment* of the quality, expected growth rate, and volatility of future earnings and dividends.

The relative importance of each of these factors in actual stock valuations by professionals will be discussed in the next chapter. In this chapter they will be discussed only as they pertain specifically to valuation theories developed after 1929 and through the late 1960s. Capitalization theories and practices of professional financial analysts are excluded in this chapter.

PRESENT WORTH VALUATION THEORIES

In 1930 Robert F. Wiese stated that "the proper price of any security, *whether a stock or a bond,* is the sum of all the future income payments discounted at the current rate of interest in order to arrive at the present value." [5] It is believed that this was the first statement of the present value theory applied to common stocks. However, the present value theory had been in use for many years prior to 1930 as the basis for the construction of bond tables, furnishing yields to maturity or to the first call date for bonds and the present value of future interest payments and payment of principal at maturity.

Then in 1931 Samuel Eliot Guild published a book entitled *Stock Growth and Discount Tables.* This was the *initial step* in the development of measures of intrinsic value, although the author did not develop a theory of intrinsic or investment value for a stock. The Guild tables and their application will be discussed later in this chapter.

John Burr Williams' Present Worth Theory

In 1938 John Burr Williams published his book, *The Theory of Investment Value.* [6] He used essentially the same definition of investment value as had Robert F. Wiese in 1930. Williams stated:

---

[5] Robert F. Wiese, "Investing for True Value," *Barron's* (September 8, 1930), p. 5. Most theories of valuation developed later by academicians since 1930 have rested on this premise.

[6] Williams, *op. cit.* Between S. E. Guild's book and J. B. Williams' book, G. A. D. Preinreich published a book, *The Nature of Dividends,* which contained an appendix

Let us define investment value of a stock as the present worth of all dividends to be paid upon it. . . . To appraise the investment value then it is necessary to estimate the future payments. The annuity of payments, adjusted for changes in the value of money itself, may then be discounted at the *pure interest* rate demanded by the investor. . . .

This definition of investment value can be expressed by the following equations:

$$V_0 = \sum_{t=1}^{t=\infty} \pi_t v^t = \pi_1 v + \pi_2 v^2 + \pi_3 v^3 + \cdots$$

Actually $\sum_{t=1}^{t=\infty}$ is not a factor to be multiplied by the other factors

π_t and v^t but is only an operational sign applied to these two factors taken together.

Two ways of denoting an infinite series are:

$$\pi_1 v + \pi_2 v^2 + \pi_3 v^3 + \cdots$$

or

$$\sum_{t=1}^{t=\infty} \pi_1 v^t$$

Therefore, $v_0 = \pi_1 v + \pi_2 v^2 + \pi_3 v^3 \cdots$

V_0 = investment value at the start; π_1 = dividends in year one; V_t = discount factor to state expected dividends in present value terms

or

V = present worth of future income streams
c_1 = cash dividend income in period one
i = discount rate demand applied by investor
n = life of the investment
c_n = income, not only dividends but also liquidity proceeds from a stock, if any, in final year for which stock is held

$$V = \frac{c_1}{1+i} + \frac{c_2}{(1+i)^2} + \cdots + \frac{c_n}{(1+i)^n} \quad {}^{7}$$

Defense for Discounting Dividends Instead of Earnings.[8] As a defense for discounting dividends instead of earnings, Williams[9] stated:

---

that extended some of Guild's thinking and the Guild tables. Williams was the first to introduce a formula for the calculation of present value of a stock.

[7] *Ibid.,* p. 50.

[8] At the time of the publication of Williams' book as well as currently in terms of newer variations of the present worth theories, critics argue that the formulas should be based on the present worth of future earnings and not dividends. Williams' defense of using dividends is essentially the same defense of the method as that given today. Lerner and Carleton in 1966 used dividends, not earnings, in their model discussed later in this chapter.

[9] Williams, *op. cit.,* pp. 57-58.

Most people will object at once to the foregoing *formula* for stocks by saying that it should use the present worth of future *earnings,* not future *dividends.* But should not earnings and dividends give the same answer under the implicit assumptions of our critics? If earnings, not paid out in dividends, are all successfully reinvested at compound interest for the benefit of the stockholder, as the critics imply, then these earnings should produce dividends . . . then our *formula* will take account of them when it takes account of all future dividends; but if they will not, then our *formula* will rightly refrain from including them in any discounted annuity of benefits.

Earnings are only a means to an end, and the means should not be mistaken for the end. Therefore, we must say that a stock derives its value from its dividends, not its earnings. In short, a stock is worth only *what you can get out of it.*

In saying that dividends, not earnings, determine value, we seem to be reversing the usual rule that is drilled into every beginner's head when he starts to trade in the market; namely, that earnings, not dividends, make prices. The apparent contradiction is easily explained, however, for we are discussing *permanent investment not speculative trading,* and dividends *for years to come,* not income for the moment only. Of course it is true that low earnings together with a high dividend for the time being should be looked at askance, but likewise it is true that these low earnings mean low dividends *in the long run.* On analysis, therefore, it will be seen that no contradiction really exists between our formula using dividends and the common precept regarding earnings.

How to estimate the future dividends for use in our formula is, of course, the difficulty.[10]

In applying the foregoing formulas, each investor should use his own rate of interest (discount). If one investor demands 10 percent and another 2 percent as minimum wages of abstinence (saving and investing instead of spending) then the same stock . . . will be accorded a lower value by one than the other. The only case in which the market rate of interest should be applied is when the analyst is speaking *not* for himself *personally* but for investors in general. Then he should use the pure interest rate as it is expected to be found in the open market in the years to come.[11]

---

[10] This is not only "the difficulty," but such long-term projections as are required by the present worth approach are so uncertain as to be of little practical value in attempting to determine the value of a stock in the judgment of successful, practicing financial analysts generally. Frank J. Heinemeyer, Executive Vice-President of Prudential Insurance Company of America, has said: "In our security analysis at Prudential whether we are analyzing debt or equity securities, 90% of our investigation is on earning power. We are interested in the past level of earnings, the current level, and the trend of earnings so that we can arrive at an estimate of earnings over the four or five years in the future." *Journal of Accountancy* (December, 1967), p. 33.

Again see our footnote 13 in Chapter 7. Eugene M. Lerner, in a paper delivered before the American Accounting Association in August, 1968, recognized as a result of an empirical study why corporate management in selecting projects for investment did not use the discounted cash flow approach to capital budgeting. The reason was that investors in the market emphasized the up-to-five-years approach rather than the longer-term approach in market valuation and selection.

[11] But we must note here that short-term interest rates fluctuate much more than earnings.

Compound Interest at a Changing Rate. On the subject of a changing rate of interest, Williams [12] said:

In the usual discussion of compound interest, it is always assumed that the rate of interest stays the same throughout the period in question. The assumption of a changing rate is never discussed and apparently the possibility of such a thing is not even considered.[13] Yet in theory, a changing rate is conceivable, and so provision for it, when it occurs, should be made in our formula thus: $V_o = \pi + V_1 V_2 \ldots V_t$ where

$$V_1 = \frac{1}{1 + i_1} \; ; V_2 = \frac{1}{1 + i_2} \; ; \text{ etc.}$$

and

i_1 = interest rate in first year

i_2 = interest rate in second year

i = interest rate in (t) th year

The interest rate i_t in every case is that for one-year loans made at the beginning of the year t, and paid at the end of it.

The meaning of the equation can be shown by an example. Suppose that investors think that the interest rate *for one-year loans,* as determined by the equilibrium of the demand and supply for new savings, will be:

i_1 = ½% in 1937

i_2 = 1% in 1938

i_3 = 1½% in 1939

i_4 = 2% in 1940

i_5 = 2½% in 1941

i_6 = 3% in 1942

Then the present worth of π dollars payable

at the end of 1937 will be $\dfrac{\pi}{(100\frac{1}{2}\%)}$

at the end of 1938 will be $\dfrac{\pi}{(100\frac{1}{2}\%)\ (101\%)}$

at the end of 1939 will be $\dfrac{\pi}{(100\frac{1}{2}\%)\ (101\%)\ (101\frac{1}{2}\%)}$

and at the end of t years will be $\pi + V_1 V_2 \ldots V_t$

Williams [14] also stated:

Marketability, or salability, or liquidity, is an attribute of an investment to which many buyers of necessity attach great importance. Yet it would

---

[12] Williams, *op. cit.,* pp. 58-60.

[13] Selecting the discount rate based on changing estimates ignores the great uncertainty in such estimates of future interest rates, for example, 1946, 1950, 1961, and 1968.

[14] Williams, *op. cit.,* p. 74.

not be helpful to amend our definition of investment value in such a way as to make it take cognizance of marketability . . . inclusion would only lead to confusion. Better to treat intrinsic value as one thing, salability as another.

> . . . To divorce liquidity, or salability, or marketability, from the concept of investment value is in conformity, moreover, with accepted usage outside the field of investment.

Lerner and Carleton's Present Worth Theory

The most recent full-blown development of the present worth approach is in a book by Lerner and Carleton.[15] Their definition of a stock's value is essentially the same as that given by Wiese in 1930 and Williams in 1938. The basic assumption on which the entire book rests is as follows: *"The price of each stock is defined as the capitalized value of the future stream of dividends."* The authors proceed to state:[16]

> Today analysts are primarily interested in estimating the future earnings of the company. . . . Linking projected earnings to projected security prices, however, remains a more elusive problem. Two different approaches have been utilized.
>
> Some analysts capitalize a corporation's estimated earnings by means of an historical multiple . . . this approach enjoys wide use but it is difficult to accept because the theoretical rationale for including some variables and rejecting others does not seem to have been carefully developed in most cases.[17]. . . *In this text the price of a share of stock will be treated not as a multiple of earnings but as a constrained function of dividends.* To be explicit, *the price of each stock is defined as the capitalized value of the future stream of dividends.* The future stream of dividends is then limited or constrained by two factors. First, dividends are limited by the prevailing competitive conditions in the product market in which the firm sells its output and the factor market in which it purchases its inputs. Secondly, the future stream of dividends is constrained by conditions in the financial market. If lenders are reluctant to advance funds in the quantities desired at prevailing interest rates, for example, the likelihood of a high dividend growth rate is reduced.
>
> The rate of discount, or *capitalization rate,* that investors will apply to the future stream of dividends is postulated as a function of two variables; the alternative investment opportunities open to shareholders, and the riskiness of the firm in question. The dividend capitalization equation and the two constraints can be combined into a system of equations. Thus, the price of a stock can be represented as:

---

[15] Eugene M. Lerner and Willard T. Carleton, *A Theory of Financial Analysis* (New York: Harcourt, Brace & World, Inc., 1966). While this theory was to an important extent developed from the Harry M. Markowitz model, Lerner and Carleton stated that "practical application of the Markowitz quantitative programing approach to portfolio selection has not been particularly successful up to now." (Still valid in 1973.)

[16] *Ibid.,* pp. 10-11.

[17] Practicing financial analysts and the authors of this book generally use some variation of the approach that capitalizes a corporation's earnings.

$$P = P\left(\frac{r,\ b,\ i,\ \dfrac{L}{E}} {} \right)$$

where r = average rate of return on assets, b = average corporate retention rate, i = average interest rate paid on borrowed funds, and L/E = ratio of total liabilities to total equity. The constraint imposed by the product and factor markets can be represented as:

$$LC\left(r,\ b,\ i,\ \frac{L}{E} \right) = O$$

while the constraint imposed by the financial market can be represented as:

$$FC\left(i,\ \frac{L}{E} \right) = O$$

When the two constraints are substituted into the price equation, two of the four variables are eliminated. By observing the values of the other two variables and the price of the stock, the analyst can determine what the market implies the following parameters to be:

1. The change in the rate of return that will arise as a result of a change in the rate of growth of national income.
2. The change in the rate of return that will result from a change in the corporation's growth rate.
3. The change in the rate of discount that will arise from a change in the variance of the corporation's growth rate.

Moreover, once these parameters are known, the analytical process can be reversed and answers can be found to questions such as: Given the parameters associated with income and growth, what rate of growth does the market believe the corporation will achieve? What rate of discount is the market currently applying to the future stream of dividends?

In discussing their dividend capitalization model, Lerner and Carleton [18] said:

> The price that an investor is willing to pay for the shares of a corporation *may be defined simply as the present value of the future stream of income that he expects to receive.* [In a footnote the authors state that "the present value approach to security valuation given above discounts all future dividends from the present to infinity."]
> . . . Although the empirical problem of determining the expected growth rate of dividends is quite difficult,[19] the formal problem of stock valuation

---

[18] Lerner and Carleton, *op. cit.*, pp. 107-108.

[19] This is a real understatement of the problem. As previously noted, most practicing financial analysts reject all "present worth of *all* future dividends" and "present worth of *all* future earnings" valuation theories for the good reason that they recognize that, when such long-term projections are required, the uncertainties are so great that the estimates are not meaningful in any practical sense. Corporate management itself has little faith in its own projections beyond 5 years, although it must make them and use them; but corporate management is certainly not going to provide its long-term estimates to outside analysts, especially in the case of industrial companies. The authors, Lerner and Carleton, dismiss this impossible problem by simply stating that analysts must obtain the needed information for their model by acting like

itself is not so formidable a problem as it may at first appear. For even though investors know that a corporation's growth will vary over time, shareholders can be thought of as formulating a subjective *probability distribution* of future growth rates at a *moment in time*. *The mean of this distribution—the expected normal growth rate—can then be treated as 'fixed' or steady value.*

If the expected rate of growth in a security's dividend is g percent a year, and if investors want a return on their investment of k percent a year, what is today's price (the present value) of the security?

The answer can be found directly. The price of a stock, P_o, is defined as the present value of its future stream of revenue:

$$P_o = \frac{R_o}{1 + k} + \frac{R_o (1 + g)}{(1 + k)^2} + \frac{R_o (1 + g)^2}{(1 + k)^3} + \cdots + \frac{R_o (1 + g)^{n-1}}{(1 + k)^n} \quad [7.1]$$

where R_o = the revenue that investors expect to receive at the end of the first period, $R_o (1 + g)$ = the revenue expected at the end of the second period, and so on up to period n.

Multiplying both sides of equation 7.1 by $(1 + k)/(1 + g)$ and subtracting equation 7.1 from the resulting expression, we get

$$\frac{P_o (1 + k)}{(1 + g)} - P_o = \frac{R_o}{(1 + g)} - \frac{R_o (1 + g)^{n-1}}{(1 + k)^n} \quad [7.2]$$

Notice that if k is greater than g, indicating that the rate of discount is greater than the rate of growth, $(1 + g)/(1 + k)$ will be less than one. The second number of the right-hand portion of equation 7.2 will therefore approach zero after a sufficient number of years have passed and thus it can be ignored when n is sufficiently large. If, on the other hand, $g > k$, then the term would become infinitely large. But in terms of equation 7.1 this would mean that the price of the stock would approach infinity. Since no stock has ever sold at an infinite price, this situation is clearly impossible. In more formal terms we can therefore say that a necessary condition for valuing a stock is that $k > g$.

Equation 7.2 can be used to develop an even simpler expression for the price of a stock, given the assumption n is very large. In that case,

$$\frac{P_o (1 + k)}{(1 + g)} - P_o = \frac{R_o}{(1 + g)}$$

$$P_o (1 + k - 1 - .g) = R_o$$

$$P_o = \frac{R_o}{(k - g)} \quad [7.3]$$

---

detectives. Since corporate managements must invest for the long term, they may act on long-term capital projections in their capital budgeting and investment decisions, but many managements emphasize projects returning the most in 5 years. Investors are not forced to invest for such long terms and therefore need not accept the great risks of acting on very long-term projections for 20, 30, 40, or 50 years. Again see our footnote 13 in Chapter 7. It relates this reasoning to Eugene M. Lerner and Willard T. Carleton, "The Integration of Capital Budgeting and Stock Valuation," *American Economic Review* (September, 1964).

Therefore, if one estimates a perpetual 5% growth rate and an 8% discount rate for a given stock or stock grouping (such as the S&P Index), the value for each dollar of current dividends applicable can be calculated as

$$\frac{1}{k - g} = \frac{1}{.08 - .05} = \frac{1}{.03} = \$33.33$$

If limited time horizons are taken, the growth and discount rates must be applied year-by-year to get the present value of each projected year's dividends and the final anticipated market value of the stock discounted to present value. The arithmetic becomes burdensome for an extended period, and, as previously noted, very difficult assumptions must be made.

An additional problem in applying present value theory is choosing an appropriate discount rate (k) to be used to discount future dividends back to their present value. Table 11-1 shows that $1 fifty years hence, discounted at 5% has a present value of only about 9 cents; discounted at 8%, only 2 cents; and discounted at 16%, only 1 cent. Furthermore, at an 8% discount rate, $1 thirty years hence has a value of only 9 cents. The effect of discounting, therefore, eliminates the practical use of a discount rate of higher than 8%. Most theorists have used discount rates ranging from 5% to 8% when discounting an assumed stream of dividends.

The key to the attitude of Lerner and Carleton is obvious in the following statement:

> The contents of this book admittedly are *theoretical*. What we are interested in constructing, as the title suggests, is the *theory* of financial analysis, a frame of reference . . . we *leave* the level of *application* to the reader. We hope, however, that the ideas developed in this book will stimulate him to meaningful and empirical work in financial analysis. Otherwise, we will not have realized our basic goal in this undertaking.[20]

Critiques of All Present Worth Valuation Theories

The major reason why present worth theories of common stock valuation, which state that the value of a stock is the discounted value of the future stream of dividends (or earnings), have not been generally used by successful practicing financial analysts is simple. They realize from experience that such long-term projections of earnings and dividends as are required by these theories do not produce figures that have enough reasonable accuracy to be of any practical value. The contribution of such theoretical work lies in suggesting the relationships between factors underlying the variables. To date in published reports, only a few professionals have suggested that they

---

[20] Lerner and Carleton, *A Theory of Financial Analysis, op. cit.,* Summary, p. 11.

TABLE 11-1

Present Value of $1 to be Received in Indicated Number of Years Hence, Discounted at Indicated Rate—%

Years Hence	4%	5%	6%	8%	10%	12%	14%	16%	18%	20%	22%	24%	25%
10	0.676	0.614	0.558	0.463	0.386	0.322	0.270	0.227	0.191	0.162	0.137	0.116	0.107
15	0.555	0.481	0.417	0.315	0.239	0.183	0.140	0.108	0.084	0.065	0.051	0.040	0.035
20	0.456	0.377	0.312	0.215	0.149	0.104	0.073	0.051	0.037	0.026	0.019	0.014	0.012
25	0.375	0.295	0.233	0.146	0.092	0.059	0.038	0.024	0.016	0.010	0.007	0.005	0.004
30	0.308	0.231	0.174	0.099	0.057	0.033	0.020	0.012	0.007	0.004	0.003	0.002	0.001
35	0.253	0.181	0.130	0.063	0.036	0.019	0.010	0.006	0.003	0.002	0.001	0.001	—
40	0.208	0.142	0.097	0.046	0.022	0.011	0.005	0.003	0.001	0.001	—	—	—
45	0.171	0.111	0.073	0.031	0.014	0.006	0.003	0.001	0.001	—	—	—	—
50	0.141	0.087	0.054	0.021	0.009	0.003	0.001	0.001	—	—	—	—	—

For a complete set of common stock present value tables, see Eugene F. Brigham and James L. Pappas, *Common Stock Present Value Tables* (Los Angeles: Bureau of Business and Economic Research. University of California, June, 1966), 95 pages.

apply the procedures of the theorists and none have reported doing so successfully for any long period of time such as 10, 15, or 20 years. But, of course, such a possibility cannot be ruled out in the future.

An effective critique of present worth valuation theories is given in the appraisal of valuation theories by Ralph A. Bing.[21] Bing suggests "the good old price/earnings multiplier" as "eminently adaptable to our limited foresight" and very flexible.

An effective critique of Lerner and Carleton's present worth theory is found in the critical review by Douglas A. Hayes. The following comments by Hayes deserve particular emphasis:

> It might be noted that considerable controversy currently exists in this area as to the usefulness of computer programs to suggest and delineate the characteristics of efficient or optimum portfolios. It is my tentative opinion that existing models for portfolio structure are likely to be of *very limited practical use* as they seem to involve some highly questionable assumptions in order to obtain required qualifications, such as that the entire spectrum of risk factors can be adequately measured by the relative price volatility of individual issues.
>
> Although the concept that investment results are likely to be heavily related to corporate performance in a long-term sense is generally accepted, some recent contributions to the field have *alleged* that the implementation methodology should be completely revolutionized. For example, Lerner and Carleton *allege* (1) that a critical investigation of the past financial statements to reveal potential problems of consistency and comparability of reported income and balance sheet data can be largely discarded because accounting and disclosure standards have improved to the point where the underlying data require no critical review. Moreover, they *allege* that financial risk factors no longer require appraisal because of the greatly improved stability features of the economy; in lieu thereof, they suggest elegant mathematical techniques to develop the theoretical effects of assumed patterns of various management decisions and economic data on security values.
>
> However, the *empirical evidence* would suggest that these allegations are seriously in error. . . . a strong case can be made that the reported income of many, if not most, corporations have become subject to *increased problems* of consistency and comparability *rather than less*. Again, while there is no doubt that general economic stability has been greatly improved through the development and vigorous application of modern fiscal and monetary concepts, individual industries and companies continue to record wide variations in revenues and net income.
>
> In a dynamic and highly competitive private economy, it is entirely possible for a condition of general stability and growth on a macro-economic basis to be accompanied by wide fluctuations and divergent trends on a micro-basis. Therefore, *the position* that techniques designed to estimate potential risks arising from potential earnings instability are entirely obsolete because severe general depression conditions are highly unlikely *appears open to serious question.*

---

[21] Ralph A. Bing, "Appraising Our Methods of Stock Appraisal," *Financial Analysts Journal* (May-June, 1964), pp. 118-124.

In short, the argument that a large portion of conventional analysis techniques should be discarded *in favor of elaborate mathematical models does not appear convincing for practical purposes* in the present stage of the arts. [See 1968 David Durand quotation in footnote 22.]

It is doubtful if they will completely replace orthodox techniques because of the necessity to introduce highly simplifying assumptions in order to reduce the models to manageable proportions.

A second area of conflict relates to the usefulness of present-value theory and related techniques in determining common stock values. One group holds that such techniques are highly desirable to provide a more rigorous framework for making selection decisions and that their use may also sharpen greatly comparative value estimates. On the other side, it is argued that because of recurrent dynamic changes within the economy and individual industries, the *long-term earnings forecasts required under the present-value approach have little actual validity. As a consequence it is concluded that what appears to be a scientific and precise method of valuation is merely a theoretical exercise at best and misleading at worst.*[22]

RISK CONSIDERATIONS

Chapter 1 noted that investment is largely a problem of deciding on a policy toward risk and then properly evaluating the types and degrees of risk present in various available investment alternatives. A foundation of economic theory is that investors must expect to be compensated with higher returns if they are to assume greater risks. In other words, rational investors seek assets that expose them to minimum risk for the level of expected return; conversely, they seek the maximum expected return for a given risk-class of assets.

Variations in Risk

Present value theorists initially seemed to assume that variations in risk among alternative investment opportunities would be handled through variations in the discount rate utilized in the valuation process. Practicing analysts typically do attempt to make allowance for risk by varying the capitalization rate used. An extensive research effort has been devoted to the problem of

---

[22] Douglas A. Hayes, "The Dimension of Analysis, A Critical Review," *Financial Analysts Journal* (September-October, 1966).

See also David Durand, "State of the Finance Field: Further Comment," *The Journal of Finance* (December, 1968), p. 853, "New Finance vs. Traditional Finance." This article by Professor Durand, of Massachusetts Institute of Technology, is largely a critique of an article by Gordon Pye that appeared in the December, 1967, issue of *The Journal of Finance,* but it is also broader in its criticism of the New Finance and the academic writers using mathematical approaches in this field. We agree with the criticism and quote from Professor Durand's article as follows:

measuring the degree of risk in individual securities and portfolios and to constructing an integrated, risk-reward approach to selecting securities.

A landmark work in the area of risk analysis was that of Harry Markowitz, who first clearly defined the concept of diversification in a measurable way and showed the extent to which diversification could reduce portfolio risks.[23] He introduced the idea of quantifying risk by measuring variability in rate of return. The variability of returns could be measured in terms of an objective probability distribution formed by historical data or a subjective probability distribution of the analyst's expected future returns. Historical data would only be useful if the probability distribution of rates of return were fairly stationary through time.

The quantitative approach is anything but new in finance; in the hands of the actuaries, it dates back to the eighteenth century. What, then, is the difference?

Weston provided some clarification by listing these specific subjects: mathematical models, statistical testing of hypotheses, techniques of operations research, and programming. But even these do not define the difference clearly. . . .

The difference . . . is the effectiveness with which quantitative methods are used. The actuaries have managed to keep at least one foot on the ground by addressing themselves to workaday problems requiring mathematical solutions; and although these problems may seem dull and uninteresting to the new finance men, they are at least tractable, and usable solutions are forthcoming. *The new finance men, on the other hand,* have lost virtually all contact with terra firma. On the whole, they seem to be more interested in demonstrating their mathematical prowess than in solving genuine problems; often they seem to be playing mathematical games. Perhaps Sauvain had something of the sort in mind when he wrote: "Some of these bright young men spent so much time studying mathematics and theory that they learned too little about finance. Once in a while one of my quantitative colleagues comes to me with a question about some instrument or institution that reveals abysmal ignorance."

Sauvain might have added that some of these same young men spent so much time studying statistical theory and formal methodology that they learned too little about practical data handling, sources of data, or the need for critical appraisal of data. When they build models, they often become so infatuated with the product that they will plug in any data, no matter how inappropriate, just to obtain numerical results. . . . The idea of adapting their analytical approach to the limitations of available data hardly ever occurs to them. . . .

. . . Speaking in generalities, one can easily argue that the new finance is good because it has provided us with a kit of powerful new tools for the solution of problems. But regardless of how powerful these tools may be under ideal conditions, they will be virtually impotent under operating conditions unless: (a) appropriate data are available, (b) the investigator knows how to obtain and use the data, (c) the tool itself is appropriate to the problem at hand. . . .

If the powerful new tools are used as ineffectively as they seem to be— Pye's paper is hardly exceptional—then the future of the new finance and the finance field in general is black. Meltzer's prediction (quoted by Weston . . .) that the textbooks five or six years hence will look much like the professional journals of the past few years is pessimistic indeed. It suggests that coming generations of business school graduates will embark on their business careers well indoctrinated in the ineffective use of quantitative methods and abysmally ignorant of finance. Is this what we really want?

[23] Harry Markowitz, "Portfolio Selection," *The Journal of Finance* (March, 1952).

Systematic and Unsystematic Risk

Total risk, defined as the total variability in the return of an asset, has been divided in modern literature into two parts: systematic and unsystematic risk. *Systematic risk* represents that portion of total risk caused by factors that affect the prices of all marketable securities, resulting from changes in the economic, political, and sociological environment that underlie security markets in general. Systematic risk is evidenced by the drop in price of a stock in sympathy with stocks in general. Stocks whose price movements are highly correlated with a broad market index, such as the Standard & Poor's 500 or the New York Stock Exchange Index, would suggest high systematic risk. Marshall Blume has estimated that, on the average, 30 percent of the variation in a stock's price can be explained by variation in a market index.[24] What we previously described as market risk, psychological risk, and purchasing power risk are largely forms of systematic risk though unsystematic risk is certainly present in the psychological and purchasing power risks.

Unsystematic risk represents the portion of total risk that is unique to the firm or industry. Technological change, shifts in consumer tastes, and poor management (generally related to financial risk) are some of the factors that can bring about unsystematic variability in future returns from an investment. Note that such factors relate to a given firm or situation and do not affect other situations or the security markets in general.

The Concept of the Characteristic Line and the Beta Coefficient

The standard deviation (σ) or the coefficient of variation (σ/mean of the probability distribution) of the probability distribution of expected returns is generally suggested as an appropriate quantitative indicator of total risk for a given security. Treynor has suggested studying the nature of systematic and unsystematic risk by drawing a characteristic line for each individual security under study or for a comparison of portfolios.[25] The action of the stock market is plotted on the X axis of a graph in terms of rate of return for different market periods,[26] while the rates of return for the investment

---

[24] Marshall E. Blume, "On the Assessment of Risk," *The Journal of Finance* (March, 1971), p. 4.

[25] Jack L. Treynor, "How to Rate Management of Investment Funds," *Harvard Business Review* (January-February, 1965), pp. 63-75.

[26] $r_{mt} = \dfrac{S\&P_{500t+1} - S\&P_{500t}}{S\&P_{500t}}$ if measured in terms of the Standard & Poor 500 index for a period of one year or less.

asset or portfolio under study in equivalent periods [27] are plotted on the Y axis. Then a line of best relationship is fitted to the points either by hand or by using the least-squares regression method. The line so fitted is called the characteristic line.

If the stock tends to magnify movements of the market, the line will be sharply sloped as in Figure 11-1A on page 292; if the stock moves very closely with changes in the market index, the line will appear as in Figure 11-1B; finally, if the stock is defensive in nature (does not tend to drop as rapidly as the market in general or move up as rapidly), the line will appear as in Figure 11-1C. Mutual funds rather than individual stocks were contrasted in the diagrams, but the interpretation is the same.

Note that the diagrams refer to high, medium, and low betas. If the least-squares regression method were used to fit a straight line to the plotted observations for investment μ, the equation of such a line would take the general form $\alpha\mu + b_\mu r_{mt}$ where r_{mt} refers to the market return for a given period. The $\alpha\mu$ is called the alpha coefficient for security μ and would be the estimate of the return for investment when the market return is zero. The beta coefficient (b_μ) represents the slope of the characteristic line and is an index of systematic risk (not total risk). When the beta coefficient is larger than one, the distribution of returns for that security is more volatile than the market as a whole and therefore offers the potential of outperforming the market when the market is rising, but also suggests greater risk when the market is falling. Such an asset would best be included in the portfolio of an aggressive investor. A beta of less than one suggests a defensive security in the sense that it is less volatile than the market in general.

Risk and Return

Academicians and practitioners have argued that investors should focus on undiversifiable systematic risk when attempting to minimize risk exposure for any given level of expected return. This does assume a reasonably well diversified portfolio since unsystematic risk can be offset to a large extent through adequate diversification.[28] Merrill Lynch states: "In a typical, diversified investment porfolio of thirty or more common stocks . . . diversification eliminates so much of the unsystematic risk that roughly 85 to 95 percent

---

[27] $r_{st} = \dfrac{D_t + P_{t+1} - P_t}{P_t}$ for a stock if measured for periods of one year or less.

[28] See Merrill Lynch, Pierce, Fenner & Smith, Inc., *Security Risk Evaluation— Beta Coefficients,* New York, New York, October, 1971; or Jack C. Francis, *Investment Analysis and Management* (New York: McGraw-Hill Book Company, 1972), pp. 272-276.

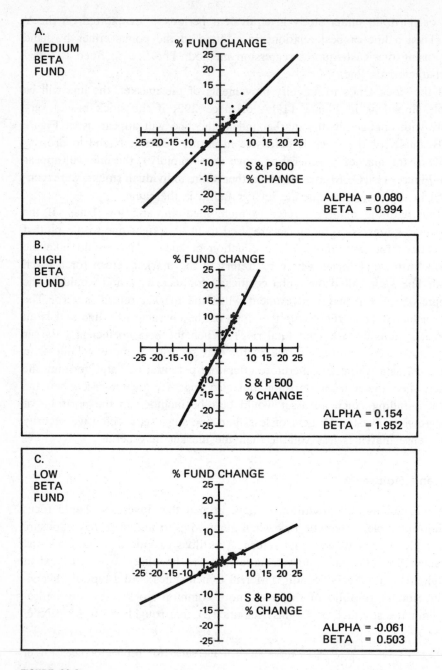

FIGURE 11-1

Source: *Security Risk Evaluation: Beta Coefficients,* Computer Research and Applications Department, Merrill Lynch, Pierce, Fenner & Smith, Inc., New York, New York, October, 1971.

of all risk is market risk and only 5 to 15 percent is unsystematic risk." Betas can be used to suggest the market sensitivity of a portfolio and to indicate the effects on volatility of contemplated changes in the portfolios. Also, the risk portion of the discount rate used in valuing a given security might well be expressed as a function of the various betas of the securities under consideration, with an additional allowance for unsystematic risk that could vary markedly from security to security.

GROWTH YIELD FORMULAS AND TABLES

Although there is an unwillingness on the part of some investors to project earnings for any given period of time, *many professional and other investors do estimate a projection rate of growth for earnings and dividends for whatever span of figures they consider reasonable.* They do this by determining the minimum rate of return benefit that they are willing to receive. They then ask the question: Given certain present market prices for stocks, what future results in terms of earnings and dividend growth rates will they need to develop in order to produce their required rate of return?

Largely as a result of the 1929-1931 and 1932 stock market debacle, Samuel Eliot Guild appears to be the first to have asked the above question and attempted to supply the answer in his book *Stock Growth and Discount Tables.*[29] His assumptions and recommendations are as sound today as in 1931. Guild's thesis and those of the others of the "school" (Soldofsky, Murphy, Bauman, Molodovsky, May, and Chottiner) will not be discussed.

Samuel Eliot Guild's Tables

Guild [30] stated the problem as follows:

The primary motive which impels us to put our money to work (to invest) is to obtain an adequate return from it and yet at the same time we wish to find a reasonable assurance with regard to the safety of principal.[31] . . . We will conclude that common stocks are bought by the true long-term investor upon the basis of a gradually increasing income with a consequent appreciation of principal over a period of time. . . . *The question*

---

[29] Guild, *op. cit.* It is true that Irving Fisher did express some of these fundamentals earlier in his *The Nature of Capital and Interest.*

[30] *Ibid.,* pp. 14-15. Collaborators were R. G. Wiese, Stephen Herd, T. H. Brown, and others.

[31] Current theorists who advocate the use of highly complicated mathematical formulas and computers should give considerable thought to Guild's emphasis on the word "tool" and the limitation of a "tool." This is especially true for those who provide the tool and then blithely leave the development of figures to be placed in their formulas up to the professionals as if this presented no particular problem when, in fact, it *is* the problem with such theories. To be specific, it is the actual long-term projections of earnings and dividends that they leave to the unwilling analysts. (Again see footnote 13 in Chapter 7.)

of how long he must wait, therefore, in order to receive any given return on his investment is of considerable importance to him.

The average investor is often too content to buy a stock which appeals to him, regardless of its price, in the vague hope that it will eventually prove to be of some *undefined* benefit to him within some *unspecified* time. He usually fails completely to balance his current price against his idea of any definite benefit he may hope to derive from its ownership within any given number of years.[32] [This is still true in 1973 for many investors.]

Regarding his tables, Guild stated:

. . . The present book of tables is a tool . . . a new *tool* for all investors in stocks. Being no more than a *tool*, it will not be supposed to be an Aladdin's Lamp, which when rubbed, will in some way reveal the stock which is to show the greatest increase in market value over the coming twelve-months. When you buy a bond table, you don't expect therewith to have obtained a sure means of picking out the best bond on the market. On the contrary you expect to find a collection of columns of numbers expressing certain numerical relationships between coupon rate, yield rate, price and date of maturity. Yet even these figures are based on certain fundamental assumptions that the bond will be redeemed at maturity, and will be held until maturity.[33] [And also will pay its regular interest during its life.]

. . . We must now make our estimate of what may reasonably be expected of the company (future earnings and interest) [34] and apply them to the current price of the stock . . . the value of each investor's estimate varies, of course, with his ability and his resources, and the most successful investor will, over a sufficient period of time, usually be the one who has the best information and the greatest ability to use it intelligently. However, there is no reason that each investor should not apply such estimates as he may have to the current price of his stock in terms which mean something to him. He may use as conservative or as optimistic estimates as he chooses, but he should at least know what those estimates mean as applied to the price he must pay for his stock.

"A . . . logical application of such estimates would be to ascertain the period required before total dividends received would reach the equivalent of an average income of a period of (say) 5% per annum in order to compare it with the income which would have been obtained for a 5% bond, or with the equivalent income from another stock. *This question involves the present worth of future payments on a 5% basis.*

. . . These tables . . . will immediately combine *with mathematical accuracy* the various factors entering into each (investment) problem to give a complete picture of the final results obtained *on the basis of each investor's estimate of the future. The alternative is to combine these factors mentally, which is obviously impossible, or else to go through a long and laborious calculation in each instance.*[35]

[32] Looking back at 1929, Guild in 1931 contended that "stocks gave neither an adequate current return nor any immediate assurance as to the safety of the principal involved."

[33] Guild, *op. cit.,* p. 27.

[34] Guild was not necessarily requiring actual projection of earnings or dividends but only the expected rate of growth for each.

[35] Guild, *op. cit.,* pp. 15-16.

Basic Tables. Guild has seven basic tables in his book, the first four of which are the most important. They are:

Table I—Current Yield. "This is the familiar table of stock yields, which gives the current percentage yield when the price and dividend are known."

Table II—Future Yield. "Table II is applicable when dividends are presumed to be increasing over a period of years and it is desired to find what the yield would be at some future time on the present price of the stock. It is evident that three more elements given to those in Table I will have to be added. One element is the rate of increase; the second is the future yield desired; the third is the period required to reach a given or desired yield."

Table III—Equivalent Yield. "Table III is designed to meet the same case as Table II, i.e., when dividends are presumed to be increasing over a period of years, *but* here the factor to be sought is the yield which would be equivalent to an average yield over the period instead of the yield at the end of the period. Table III consequently adds one more element to those given in Table II. Here, again, when all but one element are known, the remaining element can be discovered from the Table."

Table IV—Equivalent Total Returns. This is Guild's most important table and he uses 16 variations of it in his book. The variations represent various examples for use of Table IV using different rates of return from 5% through 25%.

Guild gives fourteen illustrations for the use of his tables, as follows:

1. To find the *period required* for the *dividend* from a stock to reach a *given yield on the present price* of the stock when dividends are presumed to be increasing annually at a given rate.
2. To find *the yield at the end of some specified period on the present price of the stock* when dividends are presumed to be increasing annually at a certain rate.
3. To find *the annual rate of increase in dividends required* for the dividend from the stock to reach a *given yield on its present price* within a specified period of time.
4. To find *the price at which a stock would have to be purchased* to give a certain *dividend yield* by the end of a given period if dividends are to increase annually at some specified rate.
5. To find *the period required* for *dividends* from a stock to reach the *equivalent of a given annual return for the period on its present price* (instead of merely a given return at the end of the period) when dividends are presumed to be increasing at a given rate.
6. To find *the annual rate of return on the present price of a stock* which would be equivalent to the *dividends received* during a given period when dividends are presumed to be increasing at a certain rate annually.
7. To find *the annual rate of increase in dividends required* to receive the *equivalent of a given annual return on the purchase price* of the stock within a specified period of time.
8. To find *the price at which a stock should be purchased* to give the *equivalent of a certain annual return on its purchase price* within a specified time if dividends are to increase annually at a given rate.

9. To find *the period required* for the *total investment return* from the stock to be *equivalent to a given annual return on its present price* for the period if certain assumptions are made with regard to its future performance.

10. To find *the annual rate of return on the present price of a stock* for a given period which would be equivalent to the *total investment return* received during the period if certain assumptions are made with regard to its future performance.

11. To find *the present price at which a stock would have to be purchased* to give a *total investment return* over a given period which would be equivalent to a certain annual return on its purchase price for the period if certain assumptions are made with regard to its future performance.

12. To find *the trend of growth required* to receive a total investment return over a given period which would be equivalent to a certain annual return for the period if certain assumptions are made with regard to future performance.

13. To find *the price-earnings ratio at which a stock would have to sell at* the end of a certain period of time if the total investment return from it over the period is to be equivalent to a given annual return of a period if certain assumptions are made with regard to its future performance.

14. Certain broader and more general applications of Table IV. [There are 116 applications of Table IV in Guild's book.]

Six factors underlie Table IV as prepared by Guild. They are:

1. Equivalent total returns (the return the investor desires or the discount rate deemed appropriate by the investor).
2. Average growth rate in earnings that is anticipated.
3. The dividend pay-out ratio assumed.
4. Price-earnings (P/E) ratio assumed at time of sale.
5. Number of years of growth assumed. (Found on left side of table and identified as years required.)
6. Price-earnings ratio at which the stock is selling now.

If the investor has some ideas or estimates about five of the six factors, he can determine the numerical value of the remaining factor simply by referring to the appropriate table.

For purposes of illustration, assume that an investor is considering buying a certain stock and makes the following estimates:

1. Company's earnings will grow at an average rate of 5% per year.
2. Dividend pay-out ratio is estimated at 60%.
3. Growth period estimated for 10 years.
4. Assumed P/E ratio for stock 10 years from now is 16.67.
5. Investor desires a total return of 6% (considers 6% an appropriate rate of discount).

The question is, at what price is the stock deemed to correspond to its real value, or, in other words, what is an appropriate current P/E ratio?

Guild's Table IV—For Equivalent Total Returns of 6% (illustrated in Table 11-2), consistent with the other assumptions made suggests the stock is worth about 20.86 times its current earnings. The tables then offer a way of quantifying many varied assumptions and suggesting at a minimum needed growth rates and future P/E ratios to justify given current P/E multipliers.

Table III can be used to estimate the required number of years to reach an equivalent yield when the current price and dividend of the stock are known. For example, Guild suggests the comparison of General Electric stock, selling at $400 a share in 1929 and paying a dividend of $6, with

---

TABLE 11-2

For Equivalent Total Return of 6%

When it is estimated that

The trend of growth in earnings during the period will be at an annual rate of   5%

and

The proportion of earnings to be paid out in dividends during the period will be   60%

and

The stock will sell at the end of the period at a ratio of—

	3.0%	3.6%	4.2%	4.8%	5.4%	6.0%	7.2%	8.4%
(a) Dividend to Market Price (Dividend Yield) ..	3.0%	3.6%	4.2%	4.8%	5.4%	6.0%	7.2%	8.4%
or								
(b) Earnings to Market Price......	5%	6%	7%	8%	9%	10%	12%	14%
or								
(c) Market Price to Earnings	20.00	16.67	14.29	12.50	11.11	10.00	8.33	7.14

Years Required:

1	20.41	17.11	14.74	12.97	11.60	10.50	8.85	7.67
2	20.81	17.54	15.20	13.45	12.09	10.99	9.36	8.20
3	21.21	17.97	15.65	13.92	12.56	11.49	9.87	8.71
4	21.60	18.39	16.10	14.38	13.04	11.97	10.37	9.23
5	22.00	18.81	16.54	14.84	13.51	12.45	10.87	9.73
6	22.38	19.23	16.98	15.29	13.98	12.93	11.36	10.23
7	22.76	19.64	17.42	15.75	14.44	13.40	11.84	10.73
8	23.14	20.05	17.84	16.19	14.90	13.87	12.33	11.22
9	23.52	20.45	18.27	16.63	15.36	14.33	12.80	11.72
10	23.89	20.86	13.69	17.07	15.80	14.79	13.28	12.19
15	25.70	22.81	20.74	19.19	17.98	17.03	15.58	14.55
20	27.43	24.67	22.70	21.22	20.07	19.15	17.78	16.79

The figures in the body of this table are the number of times its earnings per share at which a stock is selling at present.

Source: S. E. Guild, *Stock Growth and Discount Tables,* 1931, p. 132.

---

a bond yielding 5% in 1929.[36] The bond then paid the equivalent of $20 in annual interest on $400 of capital.

Guild further stated:

> In order to compare the two anticipated incomes, it is necessary to reduce them both to a present worth basis. . . . We now find . . . that with a trend of growth at the rate of 15 percent per annum, it will be approximately 15 years before *total cash dividends received* (for the period) will reach the equivalent of an *average annual income for the period of 5 percent;* with a trend of growth at the rate of 10 percent, approximately 25 years; and at the rate of 7½% percent, approximately 35 years.
>
> It must constantly be borne in mind, however, that at certain times our optimism has a tendency to place so great a handicap upon many of our best stocks by bidding them up to such relatively high prices that they must show extraordinary gains to justify such prices in terms of adequate return within a reasonable period of time. It is futile to argue that our estimates of future earnings or earnings-to-price ratios are necessarily inexact, and that it is, therefore, useless to know what they mean as applied to current prices. Whether we reduce these estimates, such as they may be, accurately to definite terms, or whether we simply allow them inaccurately, through some vague mental process, to resolve themselves into an indefinite "hunch," we are *obviously forced to depend,* consciously or subconsciously, *upon our estimates of the future* in making any decision with *regard to the purchase,* sale, or even retention of any common stock for investment purposes.[37]

Summary. Guild provided a set of tables that would enable the investor to calculate the rate of return he would receive on a given stock at either its current market price or at some other selected price. The investor would decide first *on the number of years into the future for which he was willing to make his projections.* He would then estimate the rate of growth of future earnings, future dividends and future payout ratios, and the future price of the stock, the latter based on his estimate of earnings (derived from application of his estimated growth rate) on a terminal date and the estimated price-earnings ratio in the market on that date. The investor would then calculate, from the table, the actual rate of return on his investment at the current market price or designated price. *The investor should establish the minimum rate of return that is acceptable to him on such an investment; then from the table, using the above estimates, he could calculate the number of years it would take for him to receive his required rate of return at the rate of growth of earnings and dividends that he had used as the basis for his projections.* Finally, by making these calculations for a number of stocks, the investor could calculate which stock offered the best relative value at the moment. He could do this at any level for the market.

---

36 *Ibid.,* p. 17.
37 *Ibid.,* pp. 22-23.

The procedure advocated by Guild did not attempt to determine the present value of a stock for *all* investors—its intrinsic or investment value range. It simply enabled the investor to determine what rate of return he would receive *if* a stock was purchased at its current market price or any other specified price and held for a given number of years, *or* how many years it would need to be held in order to provide the rate of return required by that investor.

Of course, given the estimated market price of the stock in the terminal years of the estimates (the estimated earnings in that year times the estimated P/E rate), the investor using a rate of discount he deemed appropriate could then discount to the present time the terminal value of the stock, thus arriving at its present worth.

The Guild approach has much validity today and still provides a very reasonable approach to common stock selections, not excluding a present worth approach as defined in the paragraph above.

Soldofsky and Murphy's Tables [38]

Among the recent expansions of Guild's theory and tables are the tables developed by Soldofsky and Murphy that were published in 1961 and revised in 1964. The tables consist of one-step and two-step growth yield tables. The one-step tables assume a continuous growth period with a constant dividend growth rate. The two-step tables assume two growth periods with a different but constant growth rate for each. Unlike Guild's tables, these tables are based on *dividend*—not *earnings*—growth rates. The figures in the body of the tables are, therefore, *price-dividend* ratios rather than *price-earnings* ratios. The scope of these tables is broader than the scope of Guild's tables and improves their usefulness for practical application.

The use of the two-step tables can be illustrated by assuming that the dividend on IBM will grow at a constant 15% a year for the next 10 years, will then decline to a constant 10% for another 10 years, and subsequently will stay at the level reached. The appropriate discount rate is assumed to be 6½%. The problem is the reasonable current price for such a stock. The answer to this question can be found in the portion of the Soldofsky and Murphy table shown in Table 11-3. The present worth for the stock would be 87 times the current dividend of $4.40; therefore, IBM stock would be worth about $383 per share.

---

[38] R. M. Soldofsky and James T. Murphy, *Growth Yields on Common Stocks: Theory and Tables* (Rev. ed.; Iowa City, Iowa: Bureau of Business and Economic Research, State University of Iowa, 1964).

TABLE 11-3

Dividend Growth Yield

First Growth Period	Second Growth Period	Total Years	Dividend Growth Rates 15%, 10% Discount Rate		
			6½%	6.75%	7%
5	5	10	40.89	39.13	37.51
10	10	20	87.00	82.20	77.77
15	10	25	133.90	125.42	117.67
20	15	35	254.56	234.54	216.49

Source: Soldofsky and Murphy, *Growth Yields on Common Stocks,* p. 118.

Soldofsky and Murphy noted that their two-step tables were built on the tables contributed by Guild and were adopted for use in a comparable program. They also stated: [39]

> . . . Guild's . . . tables are quite brief, and in our opinion, they are considerably more difficult to use than ours (even though they are flexible).
> . . . Two of the problems from the investors' point of view are how to determine *which* stock to choose among stocks whose earnings and dividends are *growing at different rates,* and how to rate the return on alternative investment opportunities in such a way as to facilitate the comparison of the alternatives. . . . Other major problems (ones not covered in this book) are the projection of earnings and dividends per share, the timing of purchases and sales of shares relative to short-run price fluctuations, diversification of share-ownership and portfolio management.
> . . . The major purposes of this book are to assist the investor in the selection of shares whose earnings and dividends are growing at different rates, and to help him to state the *probable* rate of return from such investment opportunities. The Growth Yield Tables presented are *not* a device to reduce the uncertainty about the future of a business unit or the stock market in general. . . . The second part of the Chapter [Chapter 2] is a criticism of the customary method of calculating the yield on a stock [current dividends divided by current prices]. In Chapter 3 the growth yield concept is developed and its advantages and limitations are discussed.
> . . . The rate of growth of dividends depends upon both the rate of earnings on book value [equity investment capital] and on payout ratio . . . the rate of growth of total assets may be quite different from the rate of growth of book value per share. . . . One major cause is the dilution of book value per share that occurs when additional common stock is issued at a price below the present book value per share. . . . Under the typical conditions of rising dividend payments, . . . traditional method of computing dividend yield . . . understates the true dividend yield . . . because

---

[39] *Ibid.,* pp. iii and 1-7.

it takes a higher discount rate to equate the *rising* dividend stream with the market price. That part of the dividend stream which is above the payment at the beginning of the period is not—cannot be—included in the determination of the yield by the almost universally accepted rule-of-thumb method.

Soldofsky and Murphy accept the proposition that "given the nature of the problem considered in the book, growth yield probably will be of little interest to individuals who think in terms of purchase and disposition of stocks at substantial gains in periods of less than five years." Throughout their book, therefore, major arguments for long-term projections are given using 20 to 25 years in terms of the growth of the earnings, profits, etc., but not giving recognition to the uncertainties in long-term projections for individual companies. They point out that many companies make and act on long-term projections, but they do not mention that corporate management may do this while the individual need not commit his funds permanently for 20 years or more and they do not mention that corporate officers and directors generally do not have too much faith in their own projections beyond 5 or 6 years and certainly not beyond 10 years. Finally, they ignore the increased pressures for portfolio performance in those managing not only individuals' portfolios but also institutional portfolios such as mutual funds and pension funds. They argue that the investor can be a very long-term holder and should, therefore, think and project in terms of the very long term. But this does not mitigate the tremendous uncertainties of such long-term projections—the Achilles' heel of the present worth theorists.

The major criticism of the assumption on which Soldofsky and Murphy's tables are based is that they assume that investors are interested only in the total and *average* rate of return received over a very long period of time and not on actual current yields received initially or at any point of time during the period. This may be true for some investors, but certainly is not true for many others. Investors' time horizons are usually 1-3 years.

W. Scott Bauman's Tables [40]

The variable rate tables in Bauman's 1963 monograph, like the tables of Soldofsky and Murphy, are in terms of *price-dividend* ratios, but there are two differences between the Bauman tables and those of Soldofsky and Murphy and of Guild.

---

[40] W. Scott Bauman, *Estimating the Present Value of Common Stocks by the Variable Rate Method,* Monograph (Ann Arbor, Mich.: Bureau of Business Research, The University of Michigan, 1963).

First, Bauman correctly recognizes that an abnormally high growth rate can exist for only a limited period. He therefore included a transitional period during which a high rate is assumed to decline evenly and gradually to the eventual growth rate of an average company, which might be approximately 4%-5% per year.[41]

Second, Bauman states that "since the dividend estimate is subject to greater uncertainty for each succeeding future year, it follows that the future discount rate which is applied to each year's dividend should be higher than the rate applied to the dividend expected in the preceding year." [42]

Bauman uses a variable rate of discount that increases with time. He accepts the basic present value theory. The subtitle of his book is "A Study of the Present Value Theory and a Practical Solution to the Problem of Common Stock Valuation." [43] Bauman states (as would Lerner and Carleton):

> In the last several years, attention has focused increasingly on the "present value theory," as a means of properly appraising the worth of common stock investment. Present value has gained wide acceptance as a concept; *however the development of a sound and practical method of applying this theory to actual investment situations presents a major problem.*[44]

All of the present value theorists make this assumption, but none of them submits proof of "wide acceptance" by practicing analysts and application of the theory in published studies. Our own experience in the financial community has not disclosed any "wide acceptance." In fact, only a few professionals appear to have attempted to apply the theory. One of the practicing analysts who was a present value theorist was the late Nicholas Molodovsky, a prolific writer and the editor of the *Financial Analysts Journal*.

---

[41] This is the rate that we are now using for our projection of corporate profits overall or on the averages for 1968-1975.

[42] Bauman, *op. cit.,* p. 12.

[43] The foreword by Dr. Wilford J. Eiteman, of the University of Michigan, states that until now, "application of the theory to present practical situations has been hampered by the fact that existing present value tables require their users to assume a *constant rate of growth* that will continue indefinitely. . . . In the monograph, Dr. Bauman presents a series of variable rate tables which permit users to assume finite growth periods as short as *two* years or as long as *thirty* years. . . . The availability of these new tables frees present value analysts from the unrealistic assumptions heretofore involved in practical applications of their theory." [The relatively unrealistic assumption made by nonanalysts is that analysts can realistically project earnings with any reasonable degree of assurance for as long periods as the present value theorists generally assume.]

[44] Bauman, *op. cit.,* Preface.

Molodovsky, May, and Chottiner's Tables [45]

These authors in 1965 presented another variation in the application of the present worth theory. They stated quite simply:

> The theoretical structure of our Tables rests on the foundation that the value of a common stock is the "present worth" of its future stream of dividends.
>
> Mathematically, value (v) is:
>
> $$V = D_o + \frac{D}{1 + k} + \frac{D}{(1 + k)^2} + \cdots + \frac{D_n}{(1 + k)^n} + \cdots$$
>
> The model assumes dividend projection taken out to infinity. Fortunately, economic infinity is not as forbidding as it may sound. This is because the discount factor becomes so large in the distant future that contributions to value become negligible.[46]
>
> . . . To make the model operational, as well as theoretically sound, a relationship between dividends and earnings had to be found to make the latter become the basic input for the model. Such a link exists. . . . The relative mix is primarily a function of the investment opportunities of the firm. . . . Our tables are computed by using the hypothesis that the payout ratio is a function of earnings growth. [We agree].
>
> . . . This statistical transformation having been performed, it became possible to use *earnings growth rates* in a basic dividend model. Earnings growth projections should be made by the user, the usual statement by present value theorists. But the corresponding entries in the tables show the present worth *not* of earnings, but of dividends which correlation analysis allocates to the *earnings growth rates* in question.[47]

There are three distinguishing features of Molodovsky, May, and Chottiner's approach:

1. While their calculations were based on a price-earnings ratio like Guild's, they eliminated Guild's explicit assumption of the dividend payout ratio and inserted a built-in relationship between the growth rate and the dividend payout ratio that they had found through correlation analysis. They stated:

---

[45] Nicholas Molodovsky, Catherine May, and Sherman Chottiner, "Common Stock Valuation: Theory and Tables," *Financial Analysts Journal* (March-April, 1965), pp. pp. 104-112.

[46] We are not concerned with projections to infinity, but we are concerned with projections for even a period up to 20 years because we do not consider them realistic enough to be practically useful. We will need to see satisfactory, empirical evidence on a rather wide basis to change our thinking in this respect. (See footnote 13, Chapter 7.)

[47] Therefore, the major emphasis is not on projecting specific earnings and dividends as such by economic methods discussed in the following chapter, but by establishing and projecting *earnings growth rates*.

Corporate earnings can either be paid out as dividends or reinvested in the company. The relative mix is primarily a function of the investment opportunities of the firm.

Low dividend payouts are a result of high investment return which, in turn, causes high earnings growth. High dividend payouts are a result of low investment return which, in turn, causes low earnings growth. Our tables are computed by using the hypothesis that the payout ratio is a function of earnings growth. An equation was applied to the Cowles Commission data and the Standard and Poor's "500" for the period 1871 to 1962. Using the least squares criterion, a multiple regression was obtained expressing the relation between payout ratios and current and lagged earnings growth rates.[18]

2. The growth pattern resembles to some extent Bauman's thesis. These authors construct their tables on the basis of the following growth pattern:

a. A high but constant growth rate for the growth period.
b. A transitional period during which the growth rate declines to zero growth rate.
c. Zero growth rate is extended indefinitely.

3. The price-earnings ratios in the body of the tables are price-*normal* earning ratios, *not* price-*current* earnings ratios. They state:

Normal earnings are not a precise figure. They may be found by trend-line analysis, using the least squares criterion. Even so, judgment must enter into the selection of trend periods. A less satisfactory but still acceptable approach is to determine normal earnings by averaging last year's earnings with the current level of earnings and next year's expected earnings.[19]

REGRESSION ANALYSIS AND INTRINSIC VALUE

Numerous attempts have been made to apply regression analysis to the problem of developing models that would predict intrinsic value for a stock. The experience with such models has not been highly favorable to date, but analysts and institutions continue to use regression itself and experiment with valuation models based on the results of regression analysis.

Meader's Multiple Correlation Techniques [50]

Meader used multiple correlation techniques to develop the following formula for the year 1933: $\hat{P} = 1.7 + 1.35^S + .12B + .20W + 3.0E + 8.40D$ when $\hat{P}$ is the estimated mean price of the stock in 1933, S is the

---

[48] Molodovsky, May, and Chottiner, *op. cit.,* p. 105.
[49] *Ibid.*
[50] J. W. Meader, "A Formula for Determining Basic Values Underlying Common Stock Prices," *The Annalist,* Vol. 46 (November 29, 1935), p. 749.

1933 transactions in millions of shares, B is book value, W is net working capital, E is earnings per share, and D is dividends per share. Tests comparing the actual mean prices for the stocks listed on the NYSE in 1933 with their prices as calculated by the above formula did indicate some extreme deviations, but Meader felt these were readily explainable; and in terms of the results for the great number of stocks tested he felt he had developed a significantly useful tool. His regressions were cross-section analyses (as opposed to time series analyses) run across many companies in the time period for which the equation was developed. High correlation was indicated for the initial regressions and in regressions run in later years. Unfortunately, however, the regression coefficients varied widely from year to year. This means that the weighting system which minimizes the squared deviations in prices in one period is not a valuable weighting system for predicting prices in later periods.

Whitbeck-Kisor's Normalized Price/Earnings Ratio [51]

Whitbeck-Kisor also used a cross-section multiple regression analysis to develop a model based on 135 selected stocks using data for June of 1962. They attempted to determine a stock "normalized" price/earnings ratio, defined as the ratio of current share price to the level of earnings per share, that would prevail if the economy were experiencing mid-cyclical business conditions. Based on data current as of June 8, 1962, the following equation was developed:

Theoretical P/E ratio = 8.2 + 1.5 (projected growth rate in earnings per share) + 6.7 (dividend payout ratio) — 0.2 (standard error of earnings per share about its trend).

After developing a similar equation from current historical data, the user would plug in his estimates of the three independent variables for the stocks he was valuing. He would then multiply the resulting estimated normalized price/earnings ratio for each stock by his estimate of that stock's normalized earnings to produce a justified price for each stock. If the ratio of actual to justified price is less than .85, Whitbeck-Kisor results suggest that the stock should be bought or held because it is underpriced; while if the ratio of actual to justified price exceeds 1.15, the stock should be sold or sold short. Again, when the model was rerun in later periods using the same sample of stocks, the weights shifted markedly. In other words, later runs produced an entirely different estimated normalized P/E ratio for a stock

---

[51] V. S. Whitbeck and M. Kisor, Jr., "A New Tool in Investment Decision Making," *Financial Analysts Journal*, Vol. 19 (May-June, 1963), pp. 55-62.

whose growth factor, standard error of the estimate, and dividend payout ratio values had not changed.

Malkiel and Cragg's Predictive Equation [52]

Malkiel and Cragg developed a predictive equation of the following general form:

$$P/E = a + b_1 g_i + b_2 (d/e)_i - b_3 B_i$$

where P/E = the ith firm's price-earnings multiplier
g_i = historical growth rate in the ith firm's earnings (as measured from its cash flows)
$(d/e)_i$ = the average dividend payout ratio of the ith firm
b_i = the beta coefficient of the ith firm

Multiple regression analysis was used to develop equations for each of the years from 1961 through 1965, using a sample of over 150 firms. Correlation coefficients ranged from .66 to .80 suggesting reasonable predictability. However, the regression coefficients again changed markedly through time. Malkiel and Cragg suggest reestimating the regression coefficients at least annually so as to keep the model current and useful for predicting. However, the absolute amount of yearly change in the weights suggested by the data for the years 1961-1965 makes us question the usefulness in a predicting sense of even annual equations.

SUMMARY OF EVOLUTION OF VALUATION THEORIES

Prior to 1930 there was little attempt to even propose any theory or method of common stock valuation. In economics, *objective* value is established whenever the *subjective* values of potential buyers and sellers meet in a market transaction. Objective values (the current market price) for stocks were generally accepted as their investment values. If other values were considered, they were vaguely conceived and not developed on the basis of any well-established theories or methods. Most investors assumed that most stocks would rise in price over the years, interrupted by only temporary setbacks, and that some stocks would rise at a greater rate than the "average stocks."

The stock market debacle in 1929 and the eventual 89% decline in the market averages (including a decline in a stock such as American Telephone and Telegraph from 315 to 75 despite the fact that it maintained a $9

---

[52] B. G. Malkiel and J. G. Cragg, "Expectations and the Structure of Share Prices," *American Economic Review*, Vol. LX, No. 4 (September, 1970).

dividend) shocked all investors. It caused some to ask whether it was possible to establish an intrinsic or investment value separate and apart from the current market price in order to avoid a major decline in market price after the purchase of stock.

A few investors, financial writers, and academicians gave the problem some serious attention, and theories of common stock valuation began to be developed and published in the 1930s, notably those of R. F. Wiese in 1930, S. E. Guild in 1931, and J. B. Williams in 1938. The most important of these theories, including the most important developed and published through 1973, have been discussed in detail.

In essence, the valuation theories discussed here were variations (and, according to their advocates, "improvements and refinements") of the theory as first proposed by R. F. Wiese in an article in *Barron's* in 1930,[53] and subsequently refined and expanded by a series of theorists, ending up with the highly involved mathematical procedures and models advocated by numerous academicians. Like David Durand, we are highly skeptical.

QUESTIONS

1. How would you explain the lack of valuation theories of common stock before 1930?

2. Discuss the significance of the study published by Edgar Lawrence Smith in 1924.

3. What was Guild's contribution to the science of investments?

4. (a) Discuss the significance of the major factors considered to influence the value of common stocks.
   (b) Which of these factors is most important in the approach to valuation suggested by J. B. Williams?

5. Should dividends or earnings be used as the basis for the determination of common stock values? Discuss.

6. What practical difficulties are encountered in applying present value theory to common stock valuation?

7. (a) Describe the Lerner-Carleton model for the valuation of a common stock.
   (b) How do they handle the effects of marketability and the impact of taxes in their valuation model?
   (c) Why must $k > g$ in their model? Is this condition likely to hold in the real world?

---

[53] Wiese, *op. cit.*, "The proper price of any security, whether a stock or a bond, is the sum of all the future income payments discounted at the rate of interest in order to arrive at the present value."

8. Discuss the criticisms made by Douglas Hayes and David Durand of the use of highly mathematical models by the New Finance academicians.

9. (a) Distinguish between systematic and unsystematic risk. Does diversification tend to lessen total risk or one particular type of risk? Discuss.

   (b) What is meant by a characteristic line for a stock or a mutual fund? How does the characteristic line relate to the concept of the beta coefficient?

   (c) Is the beta coefficient a measure of total risk for an individual stock? For the portfolio of a mutual fund? Discuss.

   (d) How might an investor use betas to help in selecting stocks?

10. Discuss the contributions of:
    (a) Soldofsky and Murphy.
    (b) W. Scott Bauman.
    (c) Molodovsky, May, and Chottiner.

11. Most analysts agree that the value of common stock is dependent on earnings. Why then do the common stocks of companies showing losses still have market value?

12. (a) What measure of earnings variability is used by Whitbeck and Kisor in their article entitled "A New Tool in Investment Decision Making?" Why might a coefficient of variation be a better measure when comparing two stocks?

    (b) What is meant by "normalized earnings" in Whitbeck and Kisor's article?

    (c) Differentiate between a cross-section approach and a time series approach in a multiple correlation study. Which approach was used by Whitbeck and Kisor? What limitations are inherent in the approach they used?

    (d) How would an investor use the approach suggested by Whitbeck and Kisor to select stocks?

WORK-STUDY PROBLEMS

1. (a) If one assumes a growth rate in perpetuity of 4% and a discount rate of 8%, what is the present value of $1 of current dividends?

   (b) What are some of the practical difficulties encountered in applying present value calculations to the evaluation of common stocks?

   (c) What considerations are important in choosing an appropriate discount rate in present value calculations?

2. (a) What is the basic purpose or purposes of the Soldofsky-Murphy tables?

   (b) What two critical estimates are required of the investor who wishes to utilize the Soldofsky-Murphy tables? What important factor underlies these estimates but is not explicitly stated?

(c) What criticisms would you make of the Soldofsky-Murphy tables?

(d) Assume that an investor required a 9% rate of return for the risk he associated with XYZ stock. Further assume that the stock pays a current dividend of $3 per share and that he expects dividends to grow at a 15% rate for the next 5 years, 6% for the following 45 years, and not at all after that. What is the maximum price the investor could pay currently for XYZ stock according to the two-step Soldofsky-Murphy tables?

SUGGESTED READINGS

Bauman, W. Scott. *Estimating the Present Value of Common Stocks by the Variable Rate Method,* Monograph. Ann Arbor, Mich.: Bureau of Business Research, Graduate School of Business Administration, The University of Michigan, 1963.

Beja, Avraham. "On Systematic and Unsystematic Components of Financial Risk." *The Journal of Finance* (March, 1972), pp. 37-45.

Bing, Ralph A. "Appraising Our Methods of Stock Appraisal." *Financial Analysts Journal* (May-June, 1964), pp. 118-124.

——————. "Scientific Investment Analysis." *Financial Analysts Journal* (May-June, 1967).

Blume, Marshall E. "On the Assessment of Risk." *The Journal of Finance* (March, 1971).

Bower, Richard S., and Dorothy H. Bower. "Risk and the Valuation of Common Stock." *Journal of Political Economy* (June, 1969), pp. 349-362.

Brealey, Richard A. *An Introduction to Risk and Return from Common Stocks.* Cambridge, Massachusetts: The M.I.T. Press, 1969.

Carter, E. Eugene. "What Are the Risks in Risk Analysis?" *Harvard Business Review* (July-August, 1972), pp. 72-82.

Durand, David. "State of the Finance Field: Further Comment." *The Journal of Finance* (December, 1968).

Foster, Earl M. "The Price-Earnings Ratio and Growth." *Financial Analysts Journal* (January-February, 1970), pp. 96-103.

Francis, Jack C. *Investment Analysis and Management.* New York: McGraw-Hill Book Company, 1972. Part IV, Chapter 13.

Gruber, Dean E. "Real and Illusory Earnings Growth." *Financial Analysts Journal* (March-April, 1969).

Guild, Samuel E. *Stock Growth and Discount Tables.* Boston: Financial Publishing Company, 1931. This book is out of print.

Hayes, Douglas A. "The Dimensions of Analysis, A Critical Review." *Financial Analysts Journal* (September-October, 1966), pp. 81-84.

Latané, Henry A., and Donald L. Tuttle. *Security Analysis and Portfolio Management.* New York: The Ronald Press Company, 1970. Chapters 8, 9 and 23.

Levy, Robert A. "Stationarity of Beta Coefficients." *Financial Analysts Journal* (November-December, 1971), pp. 55-62.

Malkiel, Burton G., and J. G. Cragg. "Expectations and the Structure of Share Prices," *American Economic Review,* Vol. LX, No. 4 (September, 1970).

Margoskes, Sanford L. "Modified Present Value Profile." *Financial Analysts Journal* (March-April, 1968).

Mennis, Edmund A. "New Tools for Profits Analysis." *Financial Analysts Journal* (January-February, 1969).

Molodovsky, Nicholas. "Stock Values and Stock Prices." *Financial Analysts Journal* (November-December, 1968).

Molodovsky, N., C. May, and S. Chottiner. "Common Stock Valuation: Theory and Tables." *Financial Analysts Journal* (March-April, 1965), pp. 104-112.

Moog, Joseph S., William T. Carleton, and Eugene M. Lerner. "Defining the Finance Function—A Model Systems Approach." *The Journal of Finance* (December, 1967).

Murphy, J. E., and Nelson J. Russell. "Stability of P/E Ratios." *Financial Analysts Journal* (March-April, 1969).

Nichols, Alan. "A Note on the Lerner-Carleton Analysis." *The Journal of Finance* (December, 1968).

Peterson, William H. "The Future and the Futurists (Uncertainties of the Future)." *Harvard Business Review* (November-December, 1967).

Renshaw, Edward F. "Return on S&P Industrials." *Financial Analysts Journal* (January-February, 1969).

Sauvain, Harry. "Comment (on the State of the Finance Field)." *The Journal of Finance* (December, 1967).

Smith, Edgar L. *Common Stocks as Long-Term Investments.* New York: The Macmillan Company, 1924.

Soldofsky, R. M., and James T. Murphy. *Growth Yields on Common Stocks: Theory and Tables,* Rev. ed. Iowa City, Iowa: Bureau of Business and Economic Research, State University of Iowa, 1964.

Tepper, Irwin. "Revealed Preference Methods and the Pure Theory of the Cost of Capital." *The Journal of Finance* (March, 1973), pp. 35-48.

Treynor, Jack L. "How to Rate Management of Investment Funds." *Harvard Business Review* (January-February, 1965), pp. 63-75.

Weston, J. Fred. "The State of the Finance Field." *The Journal of Finance* (December, 1967).

Whitbeck, Volkert S., and Manown Kisor, Jr. "A New Tool in Investment Decision-Making." *Financial Analysts Journal* (May-June, 1963), pp. 55-62.

Wiese, Robert F. "Investing for True Value." *Barron's* (September 8, 1930), p. 5.

Williams, J. B. *The Theory of Investment Value (1938),* Reprint. Amsterdam, The Netherlands: North Holland Publishing Company, 1964.

12

Valuation Procedures Followed by Most Professional Analysts

Professional analysts, investors, and portfolio managers (not traders) recognize that they can do a better professional job in their recommendations and commitments to buy, sell, or hold common stocks if they can calculate an intrinsic or investment value for a common stock, separate and distinct from its current market price, and then compare this investment value with the current market price. Still, many individuals and professional investors make no such attempt, or at least no sophisticated attempt, because of the great difficulty in determining such values even in terms of earnings and dividend projections for a period of from 4 to 10 years. Many investors, including professionals, simply attempt in a rather general way to assign a qualitative rating and price-earnings ratio to a stock without basing their selection on any sophisticated projections of quantitative data. However, a growing number of financial analysts are making sophisticated valuations.

VALUATION APPROACH FOR COMMON STOCKS

Professional analysts recognize that certain stocks lend themselves better to the valuation technique than others and that some stocks are completely unsuitable for valuation procedures. Valuation procedures must rest on projections of earnings and dividends for a number of years into the future based on either growth rate projections or detailed economic projections of the financial statements. The longer the record and the greater the stability of industry sales, past earnings, and dividends, the more suitable are the issues for the determination of an intrinsic or investment value.

Conversely, the newer a company and industry or the more volatility in its gross revenues and earnings in the past, the less suitable are the issues for the valuation process. In fact, it is doubtful that valuation can be applied at all to most new companies, as for example Comstat in the 1960s.

It is important to emphasize that an issue that is not suitable for the valuation technique because of the degree of uncertainty regarding future earnings and dividends is not suitable for appraisal *per se*. If a stock cannot be appraised with any reasonable degree of assurance, it cannot be classed as an investment commitment. At best, it must be classified as highly speculative, and at worst, as a mere gamble.

Margin of Safety Required

At this juncture the position of the analyst should be to require a margin of safety in the purchase of common stocks. This margin of safety can only represent a spread in favor of the intrinsic or investment value in relation to the market price at which the common stock is currently available. Conversely, to the extent that the current market price exceeds a determined intrinsic value or value range, the excess must be considered a speculative factor. The greater the excess, the greater the degree of speculation and risk in such a commitment. However, because the future is always uncertain to a degree and because investment valuations are established largely on the basis of projected earnings and dividends, the purchase at or below estimated intrinsic value is no *absolute guarantee* against future loss from a possible decline in market price and a sale or liquidation at the lower market price. The investor and the analyst are always attempting to locate the best relative values at any point of time, based on their estimates of probabilities.

Legal Investment Values Required

Those analysts who do attempt to develop investment values separate and distinct from market prices recognize that such an approach has, for years, been used where legal investment values have been required, and many themselves have often been the "experts" who have prepared those legal valuations.[1] Up to the late 1960s, most *published* valuations for common stocks have come from legal court cases. Professional analysts

---

[1] For example, one of the authors of this text has been called upon to make such legal valuations, including the valuation in the Texas Gulf Sulphur and SEC case; the valuation for the defendants in the Great Western Sugar Co. and Colorado Milling and Elevator Co. case; the valuation in the Conde Nast and Patriot Nast Publications Co. case; and RKO-General, Martin Marietta Corp., and Susquehanna Corp. cases.

have been loathe to publish valuations that would require disclosure of their "long-term" (generally 5 to 10 years) earnings and dividend projections. Legal valuations (appraisals) are often required in the case of closed corporations (not publicly owned) and have been very frequent in merger cases.

Professional analysts believe that uncertainties of projections of earnings and dividends in closed corporation cases are ordinarily much greater than the uncertainties surrounding medium- and long-range projections for publicly owned corporations. Electric utility companies, however, are especially well suited to the valuation procedures because the factor of uncertainty in projecting their future earnings and dividends is considerably less than is the case for most industrial companies. In fact, for electric utilities the uncertainty rests largely on the possible change in the regulatory climate in which the utilities operate [2] and secondly on the level and projection of the level of interest rates, as was emphasized in 1967-1973.

Up until the 1930s, most valuations (and they were largely in the legal area) were based on asset values and the record of past earnings and dividends. However, as in the Texas Gulf Sulphur case mentioned in footnote 1, legal valuations, as well as valuations by professionals on Wall Street and also by the present value theorists, have tended to place most of the emphasis on "projected earnings" (or dividends) or on the rate of earnings (or dividends) growth rather than on asset values. This has also been true in many cases of corporate reorganization. The Supreme Court decisions as well as the SEC decisions have supported this emphasis on projected earnings in valuation cases,[3] as have the terms of exchange for the multitude of mergers in the 1960s.

FORECASTING MAJOR TRENDS FOR THE ECONOMY AS A WHOLE AND FOR CORPORATE PROFITS

Before the analyst attempts to project earnings and dividends and/or growth rates for earnings and dividends for a particular industry or company, he must first project the economic environment in which industries and companies must operate, that is, GNP and industry components.

---

[2] As a result of the "divestiture clause" in the Public Utility Holding Company Act of 1935, many legal valuations were required, and these provide an excellent source of information on valuation procedures. It is recommended that the reader review some of these cases. The SEC itself, which is responsible for the implementation of the rules and regulations under the Public Utility Holding Company Act, has published much information on valuation techniques used and approved in this field. Divestiture required that holding companies divest themselves of all nonutility subsidiaries and all subsidiaries not operating in contiguous territory.

[3] See Chelcie C. Bosland, *Valuation Theories and Decisions of the Securities and Exchange Commission* (New York: Simmons-Boardman Publishing Corp., 1964).

It is generally accepted that our economic environment in the future will probably reflect the same type of stability that it has exhibited since 1938 and in the post-World War II years—a growing economy interrupted by only minor recessions. However, as noted earlier, "All U. S. Corporations" profits have declined 20% or more in each of the mild post-war recessions (quarterly peaks to quarterly lows), and in the case of particular industries and companies, the profit declines were much greater. In the mini-recession of 1967 the annual decline was about 5% but for manufacturing corporations was closer to 9% and for the DJIA was 6.6%, high quarter to low.

In projections for GNP and its major components, the analyst should be guided by the long-term secular trend. The larger the projected segment, such as GNP, the more the analyst can feel confident in extrapolating the long-term trend. However, as the large component (such as GNP) is broken down into smaller components, especially for industries and even more so for companies, extrapolation entails greater and greater risks. Also, the shorter the going trend, especially if it is out of line with the longer-term secular trend, the greater the risk of extrapolation in all areas. In all cases, the analyst must realize that he is working with probabilities and not even reasonable certainties. He hopes to be reasonably close 75% of the time.

Table 12-1 below shows the growth rate for "All U. S. Corporations," the DJIA, and the S&P 500 Composite.

TABLE 12-1

Compound Annual Growth Rate of Corporate Profits

Period	All U.S. Corporations	DJIA	S&P 500
1909-1929	4.5%	4.5%	4.6%
1929-1959	4.2	1.8	2.6
1929-1966	4.9	2.9	3.4
1947-1961	2.1	3.9	4.9
1947-1966	4.7	6.1	6.5
1959-1966	7.9	7.7	7.1
1966-1968 (2 yrs.)*	0.0	1.3	1.8
1966-1971 **	0.0	0.0	0.5

* Profits declined in 1967.

** Profits declined during this period, except as reported per share for the S&P 500. Profits rose substantially in 1971 and to new peaks in 1972 and again in 1973.

Profits growth rate for "All U. S. Corporations," for the DJIA, and for the S&P 500 was quite close in the period 1909-1929 and averaged about 1.3% less than the growth rate for GNP. But it is clear from the table above that the growth rate for "All U. S. Corporations" for 1929-1959 exceeded by a wide margin the growth rates of the DJIA and the S&P 500. The corporate profits for "All U. S. Corporations" regained and surpassed their 1929 level some years before this was the case for the DJIA and the S&P 500. However, once the DJIA and the S&P 500 earnings reached and surpassed their 1929 level, their growth and earnings were substantially faster than this growth for "All U. S. Corporations" until 1959. In the 1959-1966 period the rate of growth for profits for "All U. S. Corporations" exceeded the rate for the two averages but not by a really significant amount. Profits actually declined during the 1966-1971 period for all but the S&P 500 group where growth was insignificant. Growth resumed in 1972 and 1973.

We are going to assume that the growth and earnings for the DJIA and the S&P 500 will average about the same as our projections for "All U. S. Corporations." We place the latter growth rate in the future at 4.5% to 5.3% (the 1947-1966 rate was 4.7%). We will, therefore, project earnings for the DJIA and S&P 500 at between 4.5% and 5.3% per year compounded. We appreciate that the spread between these percentages can result in significantly different earnings over an extended period; but we still believe that if they come at all near the mark, they will be helpful in other projections of corporate earnings for industries and individual companies. Again, of course, there will be differences of opinion on growth rates, and each analyst may select the rate that he deems reasonable, including the inflation factor. We certainly make no claim to being omnipotent on such matters and realize that we are dealing only with probabilities. Our main emphasis here is that such projections should be made to establish a framework for the projections for industries and individual companies.

COMPONENTS IN THE VALUATION PROCEDURE FOR COMMON STOCKS

The four basic *quantitative* factors that may be considered in the valuation of common stocks are: (1) the asset value factor, (2) the earnings factor, (3) the dividend factor, and (4) the capitalization rate factor.

While these major valuation factors are all quantitative, they are certainly affected by qualitative factors [4] such as the character of the industry, management capabilities, and research and development.

---

[4] Many investors make commitments solely or largely on the basis of qualitative factors rather than applying judgments to a careful analysis of quantitative factors as well. Also, once quantitative factors are analyzed, projections themselves are qualitative.

Each of these factors will be discussed in the above order, which, however, does not imply the relative importance of the separate factors. Earnings are by far the most important factor, and from earnings flow dividends, and stock prices are correlated to earnings and dividends.

The Asset Value Factor [5]

Before the 1920s, asset values (balance sheet figures) were the major basis for selection of bonds and of the relatively few common stocks that were admitted to the selective group of investment equities. However, in the 1920s, especially in the later 1920s, investors began to downgrade asset values in the selection of common equities, preferring to concentrate on earnings. In the 1930s, investors became very disenchanted with the supposed asset safety factor for bonds. It became clear that the safety factor for corporate bonds was the sufficiency and stability of corporate earnings and cash flow and that, when earnings protection disappeared, assets in terms of book figures proved to be scant protection for the bondholder.

For many years, therefore, asset values have been more and more ignored for common stock analysis and bond analysis, except in a few limited areas such as mergers and acquisitions and in the area of financial, utility, and natural resource companies. It is in the area of financial companies, public utilities, and natural resource companies that investors believe asset values deserve consideration in establishing investment values.

Historically, asset book values of financial companies have received more attention by investors than any other area. In theory at least, the assets of financial companies consist of assets considered both to be highly liquid and also to have an economic, marketable value reasonably close to their book figures. In the case of U. S. Government securities, tax-exempt securities, and other marketable securities, this assumption is reasonable, except that in periods of substantial rise in interest rates (such as in 1967-1970) it should be noted that market values declined significantly. In the case of loans to business and consumers, including mortgage loans, management policy as to the quality of loans accepted determines the relationship of true value to book figures. Failures of commercial banks and finance companies and numerous problems for savings and loan holding companies in the 1960s stress the importance of qualitative factors. In the 1930s many fire and casualty companies invested heavily in common stocks, and the 89% decline in stock market values caused serious problems and some failures.

---

[5] Chapter 18 will explain why balance sheet asset figures are not valuations and why accountants repeatedly emphasize this point. For example, for fixed assets the figures are costs less amortization of the costs, and the result may have little relationship to economic values such as earning power or realized market values.

Investors are familiar with the situation of open-end investment companies (mutual funds) where new stock is sold at net asset values and, in a majority of cases, plus a sales charge ranging from 6% to 9%. Furthermore, mutual funds redeem their shares at net asset value calculated at the daily closing value. Shares of closed-end companies since 1929 usually have been priced at varying degrees of discount from their net asset values, the degree of discount representing the appraisal of investors as to the quality of investment management as demonstrated by the funds' performance records. Shares of a number of the newer "dual funds" developed and sold in the late 1960s have also tended to sell at a discount from their net asset values.

Historically, the market price of shares of commercial banks and insurance companies (other than life insurance companies) tended to bear some relationship to book value. Those having a relatively excellent earnings growth record sold at considerably above book value (over 100% in a few cases) in recent years, while others with a poor earnings growth record sold near or occasionally somewhat below book value. But clearly the earnings record and projections have largely determined market prices. This factor will be examined in some detail in the chapters on bank stocks and insurance stocks. All statistical reviews of bank stocks and insurance stocks indicate the relationship between book value (liquidating value for insurance companies) and market price. In general, investors in bank stocks are only interested in the 50 or at most the 100 largest banks.[6]

---

[6] In a comparative statistical compilation for 52 banks in 1958 and 59 banks in 1966 issued by the First Boston Corporation (issued annually), the "market price as a percentage of book value" is given. The 59 banks are classified in percentage groups in the table below. One of the firms specializing in bank stocks states that book value is of relatively little significance in its analysis and valuation. This firm stresses earnings.

1966—59 Bank Stocks

Market Price As % of Book Value

No. of Banks	Market To Book Value %	No. of Banks	Market To Book Value %
1	97.0%	3	160-169
8	100-109	1	170-179
12	110-119	1	180-189
12	120-129	1	190-199
Total 33	97-129	Total 6	160-199
9	130-139	1	200-209*
5	140-149	1	210-219*
4	150-159	Total 2	200-219
Total (51)	(97-159)	(8)	(160-219)
Grand Total		59	

1958—52 Bank Stocks

Market Price As % of Book Value

No. of Banks	Market To Book Value %	No. of Banks	Market To Book Value %
2	92-98	3	160-169
5	100-109		
4	110-119	1	180-189
11	120-129	1	190-199
22	92-129	5	160-199
10	130-139	1	218
8	140-149	2	242-244*
4	150-159		
(44)	(92-159)	(8)	(160-244)
Grand Total		52	

* The three banks having the fastest earnings growth record:
Valley National Bank—Phoenix, Arizona.
Wachovia Bank and Trust Co.—Winston Salem, North Carolina.
Citizens and Southern Bank of Atlanta, Georgia.

* The banks having the fastest earnings growth record:
Valley National Bank—Phoenix, Arizona.
Republic National Bank—Dallas, Texas.
(This last bank stock was selling at only 162% of book value in 1966, and it still is in the next to the highest group.)

In one year, for the 45 largest fire and casualty insurance companies the arithmetic mean of market price to liquidating value (adjusted book or asset value) was 71.7%. There were 4 companies where the percentage was over 100% and 4 cases where the percentage was below 50%. One year, for the 29 largest companies the arithmetic mean was 71.2% and there were 2 companies where the percentage was over 100% and 2 companies where the percentage was below 50%. Also in one year, for 21 life insurance companies the percentage of market to liquidating value was below 90% for 2 companies, between 90% and 99% for 5 companies, between 100% and 125% for 8 companies, between 135% and 139% for 2 companies, 157% for 2 companies, 199% for 1 company, and 294% for 1 company. The latter 2 companies have shown the fastest growth.

It has been argued that the asset valuation for natural resource companies is an important component of valuation. However, the wide fluctuation in prices of natural resource stocks during the 100% price inflation in 1941-1957 and also the 1965-1973 inflation indicated clearly that the earnings (and dividends) of all industrial companies (*including* natural resource companies) largely determined their value—the earning power of their assets determined the value of their assets. If natural resources cannot be removed, processed, and sold at a reasonable profit, this is reflected strongly in their market prices regardless of cost or replacement values of natural resources owned.

Utility companies are entitled legally (but not guaranteed) to earn a "fair rate of return" on the fair value of their assets used in the public service. The utility commissions determine the asset "rate base," which usually represents over 90% of total balance sheet assets. Because of this fact, asset book values are of importance to the investor to the extent that these book figures are included in the rate base.

In the case of other types of companies not discussed above, asset book values receive very little attention from professional analysts. However, in cases where asset book values are low in relation to market value, the investors are recognizing exceptional earnings and earnings growth and are valuing management and usually research highly. Conversely, asset book values in excess of market values reflect relatively poor earning power. The analyst in the latter case (for example, railroads and airlines in 1970) may project a recovery in earning power and on this basis calculate serious undervaluations in the market.

The Earnings Factor

The detailed procedure suggested for the projection of earnings and dividends for particular groups of stocks will be reserved for discussion in the section of the book on security analysis as well as in the chapters covering security analysis of special classes of securities. In addition, consideration is given to this problem in Chapter 14. In all honesty, it must be explained that in actual practice projections of earnings in each instance are based on a considerable number of variables that are constantly shifting in terms of facts, character, and absolute and relative importance.[7] As a result, it is not practical to develop in a text or even in lectures any highly refined techniques for projections for each type of company as students of investment would, no doubt, desire. The judgment and the skill of the professional analyst are of paramount importance. Techniques for a surgeon or a doctor can, to a certain extent, be learned; but *skill* in both medical and investment analysis is the final result of a combination of intelligence, ability, and experience, culminating in the analyst's final judgment.

It is true that most published studies (professional analyses) recommending the purchase or the retention (in a relatively few cases such studies recommend the sale) of stocks generally include earnings and dividend projections for only the next year or much less frequently the next 2 years. Numerous published studies also include projections of a rate of growth for earnings and dividends. However, more and more professional analysts include in their *unpublished analyses*, on which the judgment in *published* studies are based, projections of earnings and dividends and growth rates for a longer period, as for example for the next 5 years and occasionally for as long as 10 years. Sometimes this simply means a projection of earnings for the target year 5-6 years hence, and perhaps a range of earnings for the intervening years and an average of earnings or earnings for a midpoint year. It is also not unusual for internal studies to correlate the projections to the analyst's projections for the DJIA and/or the S&P 500 Composite and 425 Industrials by methods suggested later in this chapter. For large investment departments of trust companies and insurance companies, these projections are standard procedure.

There is the well-known law of physics that a body in motion tends to continue in the same direction. This also applies in the investment field, either to stocks in general or to individual stocks. The odds do favor a continuation of the earnings trend and the growth rates—upward, horizontal, or downward, as the case may be. For this reason (plus the great difficulty and uncertainties involved in earnings projections), many analysts in fact, although not admitting it, tend largely to extrapolate the going trend of

---

[7] While natural forces tend to cause past (through current) trends to continue, perhaps the most important job of the analyst is to ascertain if, in his judgment, the past and current trend should be accepted or rejected. Many investors, after rather cursory analysis, tend simply to project past and current trends, good or poor.

earnings and dividends, correlating this with their quality classification of the company, and then to use these factors as a basis for selecting a capitalization rate for earnings (the price/earnings multiplier). However, the really successful investors and professional analysts *are not* those who largely extrapolate going trends, especially for those stocks and industries that are most popular at the moment.[8] On the contrary, the most important successes of investors and analysts rest on their ability to anticipate a change in the trend of earnings for industries and companies and the rate of growth of earnings *before* such a change is anticipated by the market in general (for example, the railroads and the airlines in 1961, the chemical and automobile industries in 1971 and 1972, and the airlines in 1971-1972).

Valuation Based on Earnings. Because so many of Wall Street's recommendations are based on current earnings and dividends, or on projections of earnings for the next year, or on average earnings or dividends, or on a combination of these factors related to an assigned quality rating for the issue, valuation based on current earnings and dividends will be discussed briefly before valuation based on projection of earnings is discussed.

Valuation Based on Current Earnings and Dividends. Current earnings and dividends or projections for the next twelve months are probably used more frequently on Wall Street than any other data as an indication of relative attractiveness of stocks. While we disagree strongly with this approach, there must be some reason for this method of analysis to be used so widely. Certainly, current and recent past earnings do reflect the earning power of the enterprise that has been realized and the actual results of past management policy.[9] Furthermore, because it is realized that directors recognize that stockholders do not relish dividend reductions, current dividends do usually represent the amount of dividends that directors believe the corporation can sustain in periods of business downturns as well as in periods of normal business and boom business. For example, corporate profits grew at a spectacular rate in the long 1961-1966 expansion, but dividends grew at a lesser rate, probably because directors viewed earnings

---

[8] Traders may find that most of the time they must follow this procedure, but most traders are not successful and this book is not concerned with trading or trading techniques. Admittedly, numerous professional managers of performance portfolios were following variations of this trading technique in the late 1960s.

[9] Of course they may also represent a combination of favorable or unfavorable temporary factors. The investor must determine the probability that factors underlying past performance will be the most significant determinants of future performance and will continue to influence results as they have in the past. Where he anticipates basic changes in underlying factors, past results will not serve as an adequate projection of the future. (See A. Zeikel, *Financial Analysts Journal,* March-April, 1969, p. 119.)

growth in this period as being abnormal, especially after the relatively poor earnings record in the period 1948-1961. The 1967-1970 earnings record proved that their skepticism was warranted.

Furthermore, current earnings and dividends and current price-earnings ratios, price-dividend ratios, and dividend yield give at least some tentative indications of the *relative* attractiveness of common stocks as determined by investors in general, including the important institutional investors and the professional analysts who advise these investors.

The investor can also compare the price-earnings ratio and the price-dividend ratio of a given stock with current price-earnings ratios and price-dividend ratios for the "averages" and with his projections for the averages. Certainly, *if* in a given environment investors are willing to select common stocks at current market levels that are considered reasonable and acceptable, relative values and even quantitative values for certain stocks may be determined on the basis of current earnings and dividends after a review of a company's past record. Specifically, perhaps some justification for using current earnings and dividends can be made: (1) if the past record of a company indicates that it deserves a quality or investment rating because of a long, consistent record of earnings and dividends, stability and growth superior to that of the averages, and stability in periods of general business declines; and (2) if the price-earnings ratio and the price-dividend ratio for the company are generally in line with those of the averages.

However, even in such cases, if this simple approach is to be used, the investor should have determined on the basis of both quantitative and qualitative information that the stock is of long-term investment quality and that the stock will fill overall portfolio objectives of that particular investor. In essence, of course, the investor is accepting the current market level, which is what the majority of investors, including institutional investors, do in many cases. This acceptance does imply that the investor currently has numerous alternate choices all the time at all market levels.

Valuation Based on Average Earnings. Using an average of *past* earnings as an indication of value also has some justification in certain cases, but mainly as opposed to using ·*only* current earnings and dividends as an indication of value. In cases where the past record indicates somewhat volatile earnings over the business cycle, it should be obvious that average earnings are more important than current earnings, especially if current earnings reflect the prosperity of years such as 1966, 1968, and 1973. Taking average earnings and dividends (instead of current earnings and dividends) and current price, if the resultant price-earnings and price-dividend ratios calculated on current market price are significantly below the price-earnings and price-dividend ratios for the "averages," this could be used as some indication of value. Unless the dividend yield is estimated to be satisfactory and protected, even in years of poor business, the stock should be rejected. Finally, as in the case of current earnings and dividends, the analysis of both quantitative and qualitative factors including quality of capital investment and financial policies should give assurance of satisfactory long-term investment prospects. One weakness in using average earnings is that it gives no indication of the growth factor in the past or as a probability factor for the future. Another is the fact that perhaps the most important job of the analyst is to question the continuation of the past trends to determine if conditions really justify the assumption that the strong probability is that past trends will continue.

Valuation Based on Projections of Earnings and Dividends. Most sophisticated valuation procedures that attempt to place a value or value range on a common stock, as opposed to procedures that attempt to indicate comparative overvaluation or undervaluation or merely to indicate value as previously discussed, base their valuation on projections of earnings and/or dividends or at the very least on projections of the growth rate for earnings and dividends. It has been noted that the present worth theorists generally base their formulas on dividend projections far into the future, 20 years at least and often 30, 40, or 50 years hence. We rejected such theories on the premise that such long-term projections are so uncertain as to be practically useless. When professional and other investors do value stocks on projections of earnings and dividends beyond 1 year, they usually select periods of from 4 to 6 years and to a maximum of 10 years.[10] Even here, uncertainties are large.

Valuation Based on Projections of Earnings for Individual Companies. Projections of the major aggregates of the GNP and of profits for "All U. S. Corporations," the DJIA, and the S&P 500 Composite in terms of expected rates of growth have been discussed previously. Projections of earnings for individual companies will now be discussed. Again it must be emphasized that the uncertainties in respect to projection of earnings for individual companies are much greater and the probabilities of reasonable accuracy much less than the uncertainties in projecting the major aggregates such as GNP and total corporate profits. The record of published earnings projections for individual companies gives ample evidence of the difficulties in projecting earnings for individual companies, and the farther out the projections, the greater the uncertainties. It is, of course, true that the degree

---

[10] See footnote 10 in Chapter 11 quoting from a statement by the senior investment officer of the Prudential Insurance Company of America.

of uncertainty regarding future earnings of individual companies varies widely between companies and industries. These uncertainties, for example, are much less in the area of projections for electric utility companies than of projections for industrial companies; they are less in the case of certain industrial companies selling consumers' nondurable goods, such as food and soft drinks, than in industries producing and selling durable products and consumers' durable goods; and they are also less than in the case of new companies. For new companies there is no record, only future expectations.

Certainly, an important task of common stock analysts is to determine procedures to estimate the potential *growth rate* for industrial companies. The analyst will examine the course of past earnings growth to determine whether those elements that produced satisfactory, average, or excellent results in the past can be expected to operate on the same side in the future. In determining earnings growth rates, the investor will work from certain base years or period indexes to isolate interim fluctuations from long-term growth trends. For example, he may work from a previous business boom year. The period used should be long enough to encompass a full business cycle. The use of approximately a 10-year period is suggested.

Past results are pertinent only to the extent that they can reasonably be expected to indicate a future range of *probability*. The investor must realize that few companies have demonstrated a continuous rate of growth uninterrupted by interim fluctuations. What is asked for in a company to deserve a quality industrial rating is reasonable stability in business downturns and a satisfactory long-term growth rate of earnings and dividends.

The best type of growth record is one in which all the important elements of growth have risen at somewhat the same rate: invested capital, sales, and net earnings, with the profit margin remaining constant or perhaps improving. The most important cause of earnings growth is growth in assets and a comparative growth in sales. However, there may be a growth in sales without a growth in profits. Earnings growth can also result from improvement in profit margins, such as normally occurs for many companies in the earlier years of an expansion but which was experienced by most companies from 1961 through 1966. However, there is a limit beyond which companies can significantly improve profit margins. In some cases sales growth can be substantial enough to offset at least a slight decline in profit margins. A relatively few companies, classed as "growth companies," show a very fast growth in earnings; but the tremendous process of compounding must at some point result in a slowdown, especially from high growth rates, because of the limitations of the market and inroads by competition. Therefore, the investor should be careful in projecting exceptionally high past and current growth rates for long periods into the future.

In any case the investor should realize that he is working with *prob-abilities* and that is all. Regardless of quality, more serious risks are associated even with investment-grade individual common stocks as opposed to investment-grade bonds. The common stocks are residual claimants, and therefore errors in projection of earnings have a more serious effect on valuations of common stock than on valuation of bonds. Furthermore, the fact that some stocks are classified as speculative is based on the relative difficulty of projecting future earnings and dividends with any reasonable degree of assurance.

In spite of the uncertainties in the projection of future earnings and dividends, or at least growth rates for all common stock, security analysis is still premised on the assumption that it is more judicious to attempt to estimate a value range for a common stock on the basis of an estimate of future earnings and dividends than simply to purchase stocks regardless of price on the basis of a mere hope for some "undefined benefits over some unspecified period of time." The future earnings and the current value probably should be expressed in a range rather than in a single specific figure, because the latter implies a precision that is not possible. Any such figure or range is merely a probability.

The two basic *economic* methods for estimating future earnings and dividends,[11] which can be used separately or in conjunction with one another, are:

1. Projection of the income statement—sales and other major items, final net profit margin, and net profit.
2. Projection of total invested capital and rate of return on invested capital and therefore the net profits.

The first approach has more adherents than the second approach and will therefore be discussed first.

Projection of the Income Statement. The net earnings of the company are the result of deducting business costs from the gross revenue of the business. Therefore, if an investor can project company income statements for a reasonable number of years (5-6 years, with a review of these estimates each year in the future) with reasonable assurance that the figures are meaningful, then he has a sound basis for placing a value on a particular common stock.

The first step in the projection of the income statement would entail projections of sales (or gross revenue). There are a number of ways in

---

[11] It is suggested that at this point the reader review Chapter 7, "Corporate Financial Policies and the Investor," because much of the material in that chapter is highly pertinent to the following discussion. Also Chapters 10 and 14 should be reviewed, especially the discussion of growth in Chapter 14.

which the investor can proceed to project sales. He may first study industry trends and then project industry volume, industry competition, and industry pricing practices—a demand-supply-price economic analysis.[12]

The investor may project the company's volume based on projected industry volume and the expected proportion of industry volume to be garnered by the company being analyzed.[13] Also, taking projections for industry prices as a guide, he can project company prices and by multiplying expected unit sales volume times expected selling prices he can arrive at the expected dollar amount of sales. Next he can project major items of expenses and the operating ratio (operating expenses to operating revenues), or he can simply apply projections of the operating ratio to gross income. Finally he can apply projections of the net profit ratio to gross revenue. If major expenses are to be projected, they should include material costs, labor costs, depreciation, and overhead. To project the income statement in detail gives rise to so many problems, such as intimate knowledge of the company, that many financial analysts will not attempt the detailed procedure in respect to projections of the income statement. However, for certain industries (such as utilities) the procedure is rather commonplace.

The investor must also project nonoperating income and nonoperating expenses of a recurring nature, including such major items as financial expenses (interest on debts, term rental payments, etc.) Finally, the analyst will arrive at projections for net profits. In projecting pre-tax profits, the investor is in essence projecting pre-tax profit margins. In this respect, he may simply project sales and then use a predetermined pre-tax profit margin based on past averages for selected periods deemed significant and reasonable in the light of future expectations. Taxes and an after-tax profit must also be projected. He may also make two sets of projections, one on the optimistic side and one on the conservative side, providing a range of earnings. Much

---

[12] In many cases the investor will discover a reasonably good correlation between revenue and some components of GNP such as disposable personal income. If this is the case, he has numerous sophisticated projections of the latter available to which he can correlate projections of industry and company sales. There are numerous methods of projecting sales that generally are based on the expectation of a continuation of past growth rates and similar records. These can be classed as follows: (1) projection by simple past averages, (2) projection by least squares method, (3) projection by correlation analysis with other variables, (4) projection by semilog plot, and (5) projection by multiple base averages. Explanations of these technical approaches are outside the scope of this book, but the reader who is interested can consult a good book on statistics for the details of such methods, such as John R. Stockton, *Introduction to Business and Economic Statistics* (4th ed.; Cincinnati, Ohio: South-Western Publishing Co., 1971).

[13] See Clopper Almon, Jr., *The American Economy to 1975, An Inter-Industry Forecast* (New York: Harper & Row, 1966). This book develops the first long-range input-output table forecasts of the American economy using fully what is known about supply correlations among the industries of the nation. The whole economy is divided into 90 industries. Other sources of information are discussed in Chapter 13.

can be said for this method because of the realization that in any case he is dealing only with *probabilities*.

In using both this approach and the rate of return on investment approach, the analyst will usually need additional facts not supplied by published company annual and interim reports, reports filed with regulatory groups such as the SEC, reports of the major statistical services, and industry reports by trade associations, the government, etc.[14] The analyst will need to go behind the published information in order to glean information concerning trends and expected results associated with capital budgeting projections from research and development, potential improvement in production efficiency, competitive problems, changes in manufacturing, and industry conditions including competitive factors. The growing importance of research and technical changes and the effect on company trends makes such additional information not only valuable but usually essential for proper analysis. Changes resulting from such factors can materially alter a company's past record of earnings growth rates in terms of future operation.

Professional analysts seek this type of information from field trips, visitations with corporate officers, and attendance at meetings of financial analysts' societies addressed by corporate officers and followed by question periods. The pronounced trend toward diversification in industrial America and the rise of many conglomerates have greatly increased the analyst's problems and provide a strong reason for seeking assistance from management since published reports often give so-little help in this vital area of analysis. More and more industrial companies break down sales and profits by product line, subsidiaries, or affiliates. The SEC requirements and the Financial Executives Institute have been increasing pressure for disclosure of such material.

The smaller the size of the company, the more important are personal contacts and interviews. But professional analysts attempting to do a thorough job of analysis never complete and finalize reports until they have secured as much missing information as possible from interviews with corporate officers—ideally, the sum total of data needed for decision making.

The end result of the entire analysis is to project the future earnings of the company either year by year for a period of 4 to 10 years or for a target year 4 to 10 years hence, or at least to project a rate of growth for earnings and dividends.

Rate of Return on Investment Method of Projecting Earnings. Much can be said in favor of the rate of return on investment method of projecting

---

[14] The decision as to the proportion of industry sales to assign to a particular company can often be a very difficult assignment. Many corporate managements do a fairly good job of projecting total industry sales, but then they overestimate the proportion that will be garnered by their own company.

earnings. A corporation is primarily in business to earn a profit on its invested capital. The best test of management performance is the rate of return on invested capital. The best method to use in comparative analysis between companies is a comparison of rates of return on *total invested capital*, although many use only *equity capital*. The return on both total invested capital and equity capital should be calculated and projected. Investors normally will not wish to make a long-term investment in a corporation if they do not expect that its earnings will grow *at least* in line with growth of earnings for the leading averages.

Perhaps the most vital function of corporate management is the capital budget function described in detail in Chapter 7. Corporate officers realize that growth in earnings will generally flow only from additional profitable investment and, therefore, they expend considerable time and effort in preparing capital budgeting programs in order to select those projects that will yield the largest net return on capital investment.[15]

For all these reasons, the most reliable forecast of future earnings will probably be based on projections of the future earning power of the business as a whole, which in essence will mean the total dollars invested and especially the rate of return on investment. Furthermore, while the investor in common stocks is most concerned with earnings per share, it is considered advisable to derive such estimates by first estimating earnings on total invested capital. Total invested capital will be the same as capital invested by the common stockholder only if the capitalization structure contains no noncurrent debt or preferred stock and if assets have been acquired from the sale of equity securities or through the retention of earnings. Some analysts prefer to analyze rate of return on assets.

It should also be noted that, by using total invested capital, comparisons with other companies having different capital structures are more meaningful. Also in comparing prior years for a particular company, the rate of return on total capital is a more satisfactory vehicle if there have been changes in the capital structure of the company.

The important factor is the *rate* of return on total capital and not merely the dollar amount earned, because efficiency of management is measured not by dollars earned but by *rate* of earnings to total invested capital.

In determining a rate of return to be applied to total capital that is *expected to be invested in the future span of years* selected for projection, the investor may use one of several approaches. He may accept the past

---

[15] Of course, improving profit margins on the existing sales level or maintaining the same margin with sales growth within the limits of existing capacity can at least for a time bring about earnings growth. But over an extended period, higher earnings usually flow from profitable utilization of larger investments in assets. Corporate management may stress projects that will provide the highest yields over the next 5 years because of investors' interest in such records as opposed to a very long period.

rate of return if it has shown reasonable stability and has not been declining. Or better still, the investor may decide to examine carefully the factors that contributed to the past rate of return. Such an investigation will center around the rate of return on sales (profit margin) and the rate of turnover of capital invested as indicated by the ratio of capital investment to sales (total capital investment divided by sales).

In determining the expected total or average capital that the firm will have invested in the future, the investor may examine carefully past capital budgeting plans and the results of implementation of such plans as well as the financial policies that determine the relationship of internal sources (retained earnings) to external sources of funds (sale of securities) as sources of funds for capital investment.

In cases where major reliance has been placed on retained earnings, the analyst may decide that it is necessary to combine the projection of the income statement approach with the rate of return on investment approach. From the projection of the income statement combined with the use of the corporation's normal payout policy, an estimate can be obtained of probable future retained earnings as a source of funds for capital investment. *A good argument can be made for using both the projection of the income statement approach and the rate of return on investment approach to establish future earnings so that the results of one can act as a check on the other.*

Present Worth Valuation. A present worth valuation based on a 5-6 year projection of earnings might be used, but not one based on projections of 20 or more years into the future. If earnings are projected for 6 years hence, however, a capitalization rate can be applied to the earnings to establish a probable market price for the stock 6 years hence. The present worth of that stock can then be calculated by applying a discount rate representing the investor's opportunity cost to the market price 6 years hence and adding the present value of the expected dividend stream discounted at the same rate.

The Dividend Factor [16]

The value of a business is its earning power, especially the quality of earning power as evidenced by its stability and growth. A tremendous amount has been written concerning the relative importance of retained earnings and dividends in the valuation of common stocks. The professionals and investors in general have considered earnings much more important than dividends, especially the rate of growth of earnings, while the theorists have

---

[16] John A. Brittain, *Corporate Dividend Policy,* Studies of Government Finance (Washington, D. C.: The Brookings Institution, 1966 and 1968).

tended to emphasize the dividends. The answer is probably a compromise—"it all depends." In any case, amount and rate of growth of dividends are dependent on amount, stability, and growth rate of earnings and of cash flow. The faster the growth rate, the less important are dividends.

Basically, corporate financial management and investors *in general take the same approach to dividends and retained earnings.* In essence, this approach is that the greater the opportunities for growth as implied in the *rate* of growth of earnings, the more management is inclined to retain earnings to finance the expansion of assets and future growth in earnings. Conversely, the fewer the opportunities for profitable investment and therefore the slower the rate of growth of earnings, the less incentive there is to retain earnings and the higher the payout ratio is.

The faster the growth rate of earnings, the less desirous investors are for dividends and dividend yields; in fact, they are willing to accept a zero dividend yield on the fastest growing companies. Conversely, the slower the growth rate of earnings (and also the less stable the earnings), the more investors insist on a dividend yield. Investors would not logically purchase a common stock if they believed that its earnings would not grow at all or would not recover if it has been depressed; they would prefer a bond. Therefore, the significant factors are the stability of earnings and the *rate* of expected growth of earnings. Dividends become of increasing significance in the valuation of common stock and in market valuation only as the rate of earnings growth declines or levels off. If a company that has enjoyed a rapid growth in earnings enters a period where the rate of growth slows down considerably, then investors will demand a significant yield relative to the yield posted by the market averages.

Roughly, the great majority of corporations can be divided into three groups: (1) a relatively small group of companies whose earnings are growing at a very rapid rate; (2) a very large group of relatively mature companies whose earnings grow at about the same rate as the averages for all U. S. corporations or at least within a reasonable range; and (3) a group of companies that have demonstrated a very low rate of earnings growth or little if any earnings growth at least in recent years as well as volatility in earnings and dividends. In the first group, management may decide to retain all or almost all of earnings. In the middle group, the payout ratios may range between 40% and 60%.[17] In the third group, the payout will be high, based on "average" earnings. Because most companies belong in the

---

[17] See Table 8-1 in Chapter 8 covering payout ratios. A review of the discussion in Chapter 8 of corporate financial policy and especially dividend policy should be helpful at this point. Also refer to the numerous journal articles in the bibliography for Chapter 11.

large middle group with earnings growing at a moderate pace, dividend yields are highly important for this group as for the third group.

However, even when dividend yields are important, common stock investors since the end of World War II have been willing to accept lower and lower dividend yields as indicated by dividend yields on the "averages." Dividend yields have declined from 6%-7% in the 1947-1949 period [18] to a low of 2.88% in 1961 and have averaged in the 3%-3.5% range ever since. Furthermore, since 1957 common stock yields have ranged from about 1% below to only ½% of high-grade bond yields. Prior to 1928-1929, current dividend yields on common stocks were always above high-grade bond yields, and after 1929 they were also always above high-grade bond yields until 1957. Since 1957 they have been below high-grade bond yields, and in 1967-1973 the spread in favor of bond yields was the widest in history. For example, in 1969 there was a yield of 3.0% for common stocks in the average versus 7.4% for AAA grade corporate bonds and 7.4% plus for A utility bonds. These bond yields refer to new issue yields, not index yields. An "AA" utility bond in 1970 yielded 9.2%; in 1973, 8.0%.

In summary, earnings and their corresponding growth rate are more important than dividends in the valuation of stock. Stock prices reflect investor expectation of earnings and earnings growth. But dividend yield increases in importance in the situation of two companies with comparable earnings growth. Furthermore, it is a truism that most companies will experience a growth rate of earnings paralleling that of the economy, and in these cases the dividend yield will be of significant importance. The firm with the higher payout ratio in its earnings growth group will tend to sell at a higher market price. This is especially true for average growth firms.

The Capitalization Rate Factor

The final procedure in establishing the valuation of common stocks is the determination of a capitalization rate (what investors are willing to pay for $1 of earnings). This rate is the multiplier that is to be applied to current earnings, or an average of past earnings, or an average of future

---

[18] In general, the higher the growth rate for earnings, the less interest investors have in dividends and dividend yields; the slower the growth rate, the more importance is placed on dividend yields. Specifically, if earnings are expected to grow at 25% per year compounded, no dividend yield is expected; if the growth rate is projected at 15% per year, perhaps a 1%-2% dividend yield is expected; if the growth rate is estimated at 5%-7%, then perhaps a 3% dividend yield is expected; and if the growth rate is estimated to be less than a 5%-7% rate, an even higher dividend yield rate is demanded.

projections for a future "target" year, or earnings for a midpoint year in terms of the years for which projections are made. The capitalization rate is the most significant factor in any decision in stock valuation by either professional analysts or lay investors.

The capitalization rate or price-earnings ratio of a stock shown by the market price of that stock reflects a composite of investor expectation of the rate of earnings growth and the volatility of earnings. Table 12-2 presents examples of price-earnings (P/E) ratios and yields for certain stock groups.

TABLE 12-2
Examples of Capitalization Rates and Yields for Certain Stock Groups *

	1966 New High Bull Market		1966 Bear Market Low		40% Recovery From Bear Market Low March, 1967		Dec. 1971	
	P/E	Yield	P/E	Yield	P/E	Yield	P/E	Yield
DJIA	18.7	3.0	14.0	3.9	15.3	3.5	16.2	3.4
500 Stock Composite	17.6	2.9	14.1	3.7	17.8	3.0	17.9	3.0
Industrial Composite	17.7	2.9	13.9	3.8	18.2	2.9	18.7	2.8
Office Equipment	29.8	1.3	20.7	1.4	29.0	1.1	35.5	1.4
Drugs	28.1	1.8	18.8	2.6	24.7	2.1	29.6	1.8
Electronics	26.3	0.8	17.6	1.0	27.2	0.6	30.5	0.9
Aluminum	19.8	2.0	10.7	2.6	14.9	2.2	19.7	4.2
Chemicals	19.2	2.7	11.7	4.1	14.8	3.5	18.1	3.6
Containers—Glass	17.4	2.4	14.3	2.6	15.1	2.5	13.8	3.7
Department Stores	15.7	2.8	11.4	3.8	12.6	3.6	21.0	3.1
Food Chains	14.6	3.7	10.3	5.0	11.5	4.8	15.5	3.9
Automobiles	12.8	3.2	8.1	4.6	9.3	4.2	12.1	4.0
Cigarettes	12.8	5.0	9.7	6.1	11.5	5.3	12.2	3.8
Beet Sugar	9.4	4.8	7.8	5.8	10.0	4.8	10.5	4.3

* Again in bear markets of 1970 and 1973, P/E ratios fell and dividend yields rose.

The basic question with regard to the capitalization rate (multiplier) is the question of what earnings are to be used in the equation. In the market, the published P/E's and dividend yields are rates based on current earnings— latest 12 months or estimates for the current year and current dividends.

The investor may properly apply the multiplier to current earnings only *after* he has projected future earnings in terms of the stability and *rate* of growth. He is applying a capitalization rate to current earnings, but the rate that he will use in any particular case will be based on his assumption as to the quality of earnings. A large proportion of buyers of common stocks set a capitalization rate that they will apply to current earnings on the basis of a *vague, undefined* expectation of what future earnings and dividends are expected to be in the undefined future. Of course, the investor can apply the multiplier to the average of his projected earnings for say the next 5 years or the midpoint of earnings in that period, or he may apply it to a target year. Whatever capitalization rate he uses will reflect capitalization rates in the current market as given in Table 12-2 and also what he expects the capitalization rate to be for the averages and their components in the future, including his target year.

Expectations as to capitalization rates over the next 5 to 6 years will now be developed. Of course, the investor is at liberty to set his own capitalization rates at whatever level he chooses. The investor should first review past capitalization rates for the averages. It has been noted that P/E ratios rose from 1946-1949 to 1961 when stock prices rose twice as fast as earnings. The P/E ratios rose from 6x-7x to a peak of 24x-25x in 1961, while dividend yields fell from 6%-7% to 2.9%. Price-earnings ratios then fell to 14x in June of 1962 (bear market) and again to 13x in October of 1966 (bear market). In the years since 1961, the P/E for the DJIA fluctuated between 13x and 19x. It is reasonable to assume that in the future, the next 5-6 years, the P/E for the leading averages will fluctuate between 13x and 20x and that most of the time it will range between 15x and 20x. P/E ratios (averages) fell to 12.4-13.5 in 1970, and yields rose to 4.5-5.0%.

The DJIA represents major corporations, most of which are classified as blue chips. Therefore, for major corporations where earnings and dividends are expected to grow at the same rate as earnings for the DJIA, a basic capitalization rate (multiplier) for the averages of 15x-17x applied to current earnings can be used. Earlier in this chapter it was estimated that earnings for the DJIA would grow at a rate of from 4.5% to 5.3%. This book will work with an expected growth rate of 5%. A growth rate of 5% per year will cause earnings to rise from $1 to $1.28 in 5 years, to $1.34 (or one third) in 6 years, to $1.48 (an increase of approximately 50%) in 8 years, and to $1.63 (or approximately two thirds) in 10 years. In 14 years, earnings would about double from $1 to $1.98. Therefore, if projections for a particular company show an annual growth rate of earnings of 5% a year for the next 5-6 years or 5-10 years, a capitalization multiplier or basic multiplier of 15x-17x would be used. Acceptance of the basic multiplier of 15x-17x for the averages means acceptance as sound of a higher multiplier than the 10x that was considered normal in the immediate post-war years. On the other hand, multipliers of 21x-25x that temporarily occurred in some of the post-World War II markets are being rejected as abnormally high.

Another way of interpreting the 15x-17x multiplier is that this produces an earnings yield of 5.9% (P/E 17x) to 6.7% (P/E 15x). It is assumed that payout ratios for companies such as are represented in the averages will range from 55%-60%. It is further assumed this will produce current dividend yields of about 3.25% to 4.00%, which has been the range most of the time for the past decade and which is accepted as normal for the foreseeable future. The expected 5% per year growth is for years after 1973.

If stocks of companies identified in the market as growth companies are to be purchased, it will be necessary to pay a considerably higher multiplier of current earnings than for stocks of companies whose earnings are expected to grow at only 5% per year, which is the expectancy for the DJIA or for the S&P 500 Composite or 425 Industrials. However, a maximum multiplier should be set. For this purpose the definition of a growth company will be one that, on the basis of projected earnings, will double its earnings in 5 to 6 years or at a compound annual rate of 12.2% to 15%. To qualify for the *maximum* multiplier for a growth company (35x-40x current earnings), the company must be a leader in an important industry—a quality company with a good record. A high growth rate for an unseasoned company will not qualify it for the maximum multiplier. The base for establishing this maximum is that if earnings actually do rise as projected and at least double in 5 to 6 years, then a price-earnings ratio that was 35x-40x on the purchase date will decline to 17½x-20x on the cost base in 5 to 6 years, which is where the averages are expected to sell at that time if it is a "normal" market year. The downside risk in purchasing growth stocks has therefore been limited. Adhering to this strategy will prevent the purchase of numerous growth stocks at specific times when the market is exceptionally enthusiastic about their prospects. But it has also been found that numerous times in recurring bear markets such stocks do come down in price so that they are within the 30x-40x maximum range. For example, this standard prevented the purchase of IBM in 1960 and 1961 but permitted its purchase in 1962, 1966, 1970, and 1973. It prevented the purchase of Xerox in 1964 but permitted its purchase in 1966 and 1970. The major advantage of the standard is that if it prevents the purchase of 10 stocks, it is probably true that the investor is fortunate that he did not purchase at least 8 or 9 of the 10. It is also true that the other 1 or 2 stocks might have proved to be a worthwhile purchase even at higher P/E's than the standard. Of course, if the investor has the luck or the skill to select with some consistency the 1 or 2 stocks out of the 10 that may properly be purchased above the standard, then he does not need the standard. But individuals with such skill are very rare.

Stocks in the below-average group that sell at P/E ratios below 13x in normal markets and usually with yields of 5% and higher are almost always currently out of favor with investors. Some of these stocks are deservedly out of favor and quite correctly may remain in this classification rather indefinitely. On the other hand, numerous instances occur when major companies temporarily have problems and experience a sharp decline, or at best a leveling off of earnings. If the investor in such cases has made a careful projection of earnings for the next 4 or 6 years and if those projections indicate a recovery in earning power, these stocks often offer interesting commitment opportunities both for the long-term investor and for the aggressive investor seeking significant capital gains over the next 4 or 6 years. These stocks frequently sell at relatively high dividend yields, and often the dividends are well protected even at the lower level of earnings currently being experienced. In such cases, for example, as chemical, automobile, and tobacco stocks in 1966 and 1970, the investor found them available at 9x-12x earnings and with well-protected dividend yields of 4%-5% and sometimes higher. Stocks in this classification should not be purchased at higher multiples than 9x-12x current earnings, and risk is considerably lessened if they are major companies in major industries. However, if earnings have been rather suddenly and sharply depressed, the investor may properly use an average of earnings for the past 5 years instead of current earnings. In such cases, however, he must be reasonably assured of the *probability* of recovery in earnings, that is, that the earnings decline or leveling off is temporary in terms of 1 to 3 years.

QUESTIONS

1. What is the basic purpose of an analyst's examination?

2. (a) What is meant by intrinsic value of a common stock?
   (b) What type of stocks lend themselves best to determining intrinsic value? Why?

3. Would asset value as reflected in the corporate balance sheet be a significant valuation factor for (1) natural resource companies and (2) utilities? Define asset values in the balance sheet.

4. (a) How is book value per share calculated?
   (b) How do you explain the fact that the market price per share for many closed-end funds and industrial companies has often been higher than the book value per share?

5. (a) Is extrapolation of trends a valid method for projecting the GNP long-term? Is this technique equally valid for projecting earnings of an individual company? Discuss.

(b) Project the GNP for 10 years by some means acceptable to you and justify your technique.

6. "Current earnings and dividends or projections for the next 12 months are probably used more frequently on Wall Street than any other data as an indication of relative attractiveness of stocks."
   (a) What possible justification can you offer for this procedure?
   (b) What dangers do you see in such an approach?

7. (a) Assume that you are going to make an earnings forecast for Philadelphia Electric Company. What factors would you take into consideration?
   (b) What type of stocks would offer the most difficulties in making earnings projections? Why?

8. What are the two methods used in projecting earnings for an individual company?

9. Under what conditions would you expect a high proportional retention of earnings (low dividend payout ratio) to (1) benefit the price of a stock and (2) have adverse effects on the price of a stock?

10. (a) What is a capitalization rate? Explain earnings yield.
    (b) Why do stocks have different capitalization rates in the market?

WORK-STUDY PROBLEMS

1. Assume that Corporation A presently earns $7 per share and pays a $4 dividend per share. Further assume that earnings per share and dividends are expected to grow at a 5% annual compounded rate for the next 5 years, that the stock is expected to sell at a price-earnings ratio of 16 after 5 years, and that the risk associated with the stock justifies a before-tax discount factor of 8%.
   (a) According to present value theory, what is the intrinsic value of this stock?
   (b) What limitations, if any, are created by using a before-tax discount rate?

2. (a) Compute the intrinsic value for a share of common stock, utilizing present value techniques and the following assumptions:
    (1) The investor is taxed at 50% on ordinary income and 25% on capital gains.
    (2) The stock is expected to pay a $2 dividend at the end of the first annual holding period, and dividends are expected to grow at a 10% compounded annual rate thereafter.

(3) Earnings per share are currently $4.50 and expected to grow at a compound annual rate of 20% for each year during which the investor holds the stock.

(4) The investor expects to sell the stock at the end of the third holding period, and expects a P/E ratio of 25 to apply to the stock at that time.

(5) The investor believes he can earn 14% on investments of equivalent risk.

(6) The stock is currently selling for $81.00 per share.

(b) Would the above appear to be an attractive investment opportunity? Explain your answer in terms of the percentage margin available to cover forecasting errors.

3. (a) Forecast the sales, profits, and earnings per share for a company, selected by you, for the next 5 years. Carefully identify the assumptions underlying your forecast for both the industry and the company.

(b) Using the above forecast as a basis, value the stock by means of the present value approach. Explain your choice of a discount rate. Assume that at the end of the fifth year you sold the stock at a price equal to expected EPS at that time multiplied by the expected price-earnings ratio at that time.

(c) Value your stock by means of a capitalization rate you feel is appropriate. Justify your choice of an appropriate capitalization rate and the earnings per share figure you use.

SUGGESTED READINGS

Bauman, W. Scott. *Estimating the Present Value of Common Stocks by the Variable Rate Method*, Monograph. Ann Arbor, Mich.: Bureau of Business Research, The University of Michigan, 1963.

Bauman, W. Scott, and Thomas A. Klein. *Investment Profit Correlation*. Ann Arbor, Mich.: Bureau of Business Research, The University of Michigan, 1968.

Beidleman, Carl R. "Pitfalls of the Price-Earnings Ratio." *Financial Analysts Journal* (September-October, 1971), pp. 86-91.

Bing, Ralph A. "Appraising Our Methods of Stock Appraisal." *Financial Analysts Journal* (May-June, 1964), pp. 118-124.

—————. "Survey of Practitioners' Stock Evaluation Methods." *Financial Analysts Journal* (May-June, 1971), pp. 55-60.

Brittain, John A. *Corporate Dividend Policy*, Studies of Government Finance. Washington, D. C.: The Brookings Institution, 1966 and 1968.

Budd, A. P., and R. H. Litzenberger. "Changes in the Supply of Money, the Firm's Market Value and Cost of Capital." *The Journal of Finance* (March, 1973), pp. 49-57.

Buff, J. H., G. G. Bigger, and J. G. Burkhead. "The Application of New Decision Analysis Techniques to Investment Research." *Financial Analysts Journal* (November-December, 1968).

Durand, David. "State of the Finance Field: Further Comment." *The Journal of Finance* (December, 1968).

Foster, Earl M. "The Price-Earnings Ratio and Growth." *Financial Analysts Journal* (January-February, 1970), pp. 96-103.

Gordon, Myron J. *The Investment, Financing and Valuation of the Corporation*. Homewood, Illinois: Richard D. Irwin, Inc., 1962.

Guild, Samuel E. *Stock Growth and Discount Tables*. Boston: Financial Publishing Company, 1931. This book is out of print.

Hayes, Douglas A. "The Dimensions of Analysis, A Critical Review." *Financial Analysts Journal* (September-October, 1966), pp. 81-84.

Kantor, Michael. "Market Sensitivities." *Financial Analysts Journal* (January-February, 1971), pp. 64-68.

Latané, Henry A., and Donald L. Tuttle. *Security Analysis and Portfolio Management*. New York: The Ronald Press Company, 1970. Chapters 8, 9 and 23.

Lerner, Eugene M., and Willard T. Carleton. *A Theory of Financial Analysis*. New York: Harcourt, Brace & World, Inc., 1966.

Lerner, Eugene M., and Alfred Rappaport. "Capital Budgeting and Reported Earnings to Shareholders." A paper delivered at the annual meeting of the American Accounting Association, August, 1968.

Molodovsky, N., C. May, and S. Chottiner. "Common Stock Valuation: Theory and Tables." *Financial Analysts Journal* (March-April, 1965), pp. 104-112.

Reilly, Frank K. "The Misdirected Emphasis in Security Valuation." *Financial Analysts Journal* (January-February, 1973), pp. 54ff.

Smith, Edgar L. *Common Stocks as Long-Term Investments*. New York: The Macmillan Company, 1924.

Smith, Keith V., and Maurice B. Goudzwaari. "Survey of Investment Management Teaching Versus Practice." *The Journal of Finance* (May, 1970), pp. 329-339.

Soldofsky, R. M., and James T. Murphy. *Growth Yields on Common Stocks: Theory and Tables*, Rev. ed. Iowa City, Iowa: Bureau of Business and Economic Research, State University of Iowa, 1964.

Treynor, Jack L., *et. al.* "Using Portfolio Composition to Estimate Risk." *Financial Analysts Journal* (September-October, 1968), pp. 93-100.

Wendt, Paul F. "Current Growth Stock Valuation Methods." *Financial Analysts Journal* (March-April, 1965), pp. 91-101.

Wiese, Robert F. "Investing for True Value." *Barron's* (September 8, 1930), p. 5.

Williams, J. B. *The Theory of Investment Value (1938),* Reprint. Amsterdam, The Netherland: North Holland Publishing Company, 1964.

Zinbarg, Edward D. "A Modern Approach to Investment Risk." *Financial Executive* (February, 1973), pp. 44-61.

PART
FIVE

SECURITY ANALYSIS

Sources of Information and Protection for the Investor

The subjects of sources of information and protection for the investor are closely interrelated. The federal securities legislation has two purposes: (1) to furnish investors with practical, reliable, and accurate information on securities to enable them to make decisions and (2) to provide fair and equitable trading markets (markets without manipulation) for investors.

SOURCES OF INFORMATION

Investors may obtain information from a variety of sources. In gathering information for intelligent decisions as to the relative attractiveness of securities, investors must choose those sources most essential to their purposes. They should be well informed on economic and security market trends and knowledgeable about industry and company developments. Sources of information include financial news periodicals, statistical services, government publications, trade journals and industry publications, company annual and interim reports and offering prospectuses, and significant literature furnished by brokers. Investors may also seek the advice of brokers or investment counselors, taking care to choose firms with an excellent reputation. Given the facts, investors must rely upon their judgment in making investment decisions unless they rely entirely on investment advisers.

General Economic and Background Information

Investors should understand the fundamental economic factors underlying security valuations and affecting company earnings and they should have some knowledge of technical market factors. Current general economic and background information is available from many sources.

Financial News Sources. Many investors obtain most of their *daily* financial information by reading the financial pages of newspapers. These pages have developed into general business sections. Company earnings reports and items on new products and manufacturing processes, mergers, acquisitions, proxy contests, and current business and industry trends are featured. Financial sections of newspapers include statistics and indexes of general business activity; complete transactions and prices for securities listed on major exchanges, and bid and asked prices for securities traded over-the-counter; the well-known and much quoted Dow Jones and Standard & Poor's market averages; and conditions in the money market. Among the most useful daily publications are the *New York Times, The Wall Street Journal*, and the *Journal of Commerce*; among the weekly publications, the *Commercial and Financial Chronicle* and *Barron's National Business & Financial Weekly*. Also, a number of financial magazines cover current business news, discuss various companies, or forecast market trends and recommend attractive investments. Of these, *Business Week, Forbes, Financial World, Fortune, Nation's Business*, and *The Magazine of Wall Street* are most representative. In addition, many investors read the letters and reports issued by brokerage firms, the advisory letters and publications issued by the various financial services, and monthly reviews or bank letters on economic conditions released periodically by many of the nation's leading commercial banks [1] and the Federal Reserve banks. An additional source of "spot news" is the Dow Jones financial news ticker, the only one of its kind in the country.[2]

Perhaps the best known and most widely used services are Moody's large investment manuals and Standard & Poor's *Corporation Records*. Moody's manuals contain descriptive matter on industries and financial statements on a wide variety of companies, issues, and institutions. Annual Moody's manuals are available for *Municipals and Governments, Banks and Finance Companies, Industrials, Public Utilities,* and *Transportation.*

Though not nearly so specialized as Moody's volumes, Standard & Poor's *Corporation Records* also is a basic book of information and provides comprehensive coverage of almost all important corporate issuers of securities,

---

[1] The Monthly Economic Letters of The First National City Bank of New York; Morgan Guaranty Trust Co., New York; and Cleveland Trust Co. are all excellent.

[2] The ticker is a printing telegraph that operates continuously throughout the day, enabling investors to immediately evaluate the impact of economic, political, or financial factors and developments on the markets.

PART FIVE *Security Analysis*

both listed and unlisted issues. The next most extensive Standard & Poor's services are the loose-leaf *Standard Listed Stock Reports* and *Standard Bond Reports*. Each of these services consists of a set of several hundred advisory reports on important and active securities, and these reports are revised frequently. Stock reports contain statistical data on sales, earnings, dividends, market history, and so forth, and a general description of the issuer's business together with some appraisal of future prospects.[3] Bond reports contain Standard & Poor's bond ratings and quantitative and qualitative data necessary to a quick evaluation of bond quality.

Other widely used Standard & Poor's publications include the *Outlook*, designed as a weekly investment advisory service and stock market publication; the *Analysts Handbook*, an annual statistical service supplemented by monthly issues, providing comparative data on earnings, dividends, yields, and similar data by industry; the *Dividend Record*, containing annual and current data on dividend payments and declaration dates; and the *Register of Directors and Executives*, an annual publication listing officers and their principal business affiliations and addresses. Moody's also issues many publications comparable to Standard & Poor's services, for example Moody's *Stock Survey*, which is issued weekly with comment and opinions on the bond and stock markets and also containing Moody's security recommendations. Finally, almost all registered representatives and many investors keep readily available Standard & Poor's *Stock Guide* and Standard & Poor's *Bond Guide* in booklet form containing the most pertinent information on a large number of securities, including earnings, dividends, price ranges, and capitalization. Standard & Poor's biannual *Trade and Statistics* and the bimonthly and monthly issues supply historical statistics on securities markets and important industries.

Industry Surveys and Publications. No proper valuation of a security either in absolute terms or relative to other securities can be made prior to an analysis and judgment of the nature and prospects of the industry or industries (if a conglomerate) in which the company operates. There are many sources of industry information. The sources most frequently used are Standard & Poor's *Industry Surveys—Basic Analysis*, issued approximately once a year and supplemented during the year by a briefer survey updating the most important information in the industry surveys. These surveys contain lengthy discussions of the forces affecting developments within an industry as well as statistical data pertinent to an analysis in depth

---

[3] Standard & Poor's Compustat Tapes are used by most large brokerage firms to supply quite complete financial information back to 1946 on all listed securities and on important unlisted securities. Using their own computers and these tapes, the brokerage firms can quickly analyze past records.

of an industry's prospects, stability, profits, and growth. (Figure 13-1 lists the data found in a Standard & Poor's survey.) There are also many industry publications. Probably two thirds of price changes for a stock reflect industry factors and only one third reflect specific company characteristics.

U. S. Government Publications. The Federal Government and its agencies, as well as the Board of Governors of the Federal Reserve System, regularly prepare and release numerous bulletins, publications, and studies on the nation's business as well as statistical studies and information on particular industries. The annual *Statistical Abstract of the United States* provides economic and statistical information on many industries and indicates more complete government publications issued by government bureaus and agencies. The U.S. Department of Commerce publications are the most generally used sources and are the bases for most of the material included and interpreted by private business services and publications. The major publications of the U. S. Department of Commerce are:

1. *Survey of Current Business.* A monthly publication that is largely a tabulation of monthly economic statistics, covering Gross National Product and its subdivisions, general business indicators, prices, corporate profits before and after taxes, corporate dividends and retained earnings, corporate sales and employment by industry, and similar data.
2. *Business Statistics.* A biennial supplement to the *Survey of Current Business* issued in odd-numbered years.
3. *U. S. Industrial Outlook.* Issued annually and contains forecasts for the following year for major industries.
4. *The National Income and Product Accounts of the United States.* Includes statistical tables covering all major industries.
5. *Business Conditions Digest.* Issued monthly and contains charts and statistical data on the U.S. economy. A *must* as a basis for any forecasting.

Company Information

The basic information for company analysis comes from the company either directly in the form of annual, semiannual, and quarterly reports and intermittent news releases or indirectly through a regulatory body (in the latter case, to a large extent, material filed with the SEC). However, for quick reference the Standard & Poor's *Stock Reports* and *Industry Surveys* together with Moody's reports receive the most use.

Company Reports to Stockholders. As a result of pressure from the securities exchanges, from professional analysts, from the American Institute of Certified Public Accountants, and from institutional investors and other

1. Long-Term Outlook
2. Construction Activity
3. Construction Costs—Construction Expenditures (Table)
   Table—10-Yr. Record by 43 Major Groups
4. Residential Construction—Demand
   Non-Farm Dwelling Units Started
   Mortgage Analysis
       10-Yr. Consumer and Mortgage Debt Comparisons
   Population Data—Table 10 years
       No. Household & Family Units
       No. Mortgages, Housing Vacancy Statistics—10 years
   Federal Activities
   Low-Cost Housing
5. Non-Residential Construction
6. Farm Construction
7. Utility Construction
8. Public Construction
   Urban Renewal
   Highways
   Sewer and Water
   Educational
9. Maintenance and Repairs
   10-Yr. Record by 25 Major Groupings
10. Supply Trades
    10-Yr. Record by 40 Major Materials, Air Conditioning & Heating
    Asbestos—10-yr. Record
    Asphalt—10-yr. Record
    Cement—10-yr. Record
    Elevators and Escalators
    Fiber Glass
    Flat Glass
    Gypsum & Wallboard
    Hardboard

Lumber & Plywood—10-yr. Record
Paint
Plumbing, Piping
Tile & Clay
11. Composite Industry Data—8-yr. Record—Cement, Roofing & Wallboard, Heating, Air Conditioning, Plumbing
12. Comparative Company Analyses —10-yr. Analyses
13. Plant and Equipment Outlays— 10-yr. Record by Companies and by Major Materials
    Capital Expenditures as a Percentage of Gross Plant —By Companies and by Major Materials
14. Sales Record
    By Companies and by Major Materials
15. Profit Margins
    By Companies and by Major Materials
16. Net Income Record
    By Companies and by Major Materials
17. Dividend Policies
    Companies of Major Groupings vs. "425" Industrials
    Common Dividends as a Percentage of Earnings—By Companies and by Major Materials
18. Market Action of Building Stocks —10-yr. Analyses
    Composite Price-Earnings Ratios—by Companies and by Major Materials
19. Relative Yield Performance
    By Companies and by Major Materials
20. Preferred Stocks—Major Items by Companies
21. Statistical Data—5 pages
    For Companies—10 Items

FIGURE 13-1

Outline of Standard & Poor's 40-Page Building Industry Survey—Basic Analysis

investors, company annual reports have shown a marked improvement over the years and the trend is fortunately continuing. From the standpoint of disclosure, great progress has been made, but there is still a long way to go to improve the uniformity of corporate financial reporting. Investors should read the text of the annual reports completely to determine company policy and goals, research, new products, labor relations, and so forth. By studying a series of reports covering a period of years, they may determine the extent to which policies were advocated and goals were realized. The financial information must be studied, ratios calculated, and results analyzed. Company semiannual and quarterly reports bring some of the most important financial information up-to-date. Finally, intermittent news releases inform the investor of major current happenings affecting the company.

Reports Filed with the SEC. Today, most companies that the analyst will wish to study must file reports with the SEC. In 1964 the Securities Exchange Act of 1934 was amended, providing under a new Section (12g) for the registration of securities traded *over-the-counter* whose issues have total assets in excess of $1 million and a class of equity securities held of record by at least 500 persons.[4] However, there have been amendments since 1964.

The information filed with the SEC and available to the general public is filed under the following forms:

Registration Statement—Form S-1 (1933 Act).[5] This is the most commonly used form under the Securities Act of 1933. Part I of Form S-1 is for the prospectus (a summary of the registration statement) and Part II lists other information required in the registration statement but not in the prospectus. The "red herring" is the preliminary prospectus issued before the final prospectus is issued and while the issue is in negotiation.

Part I of Form S-1

Information required in the prospectus: [6]

---

[4] *The Report of the Special Study of Securities Markets of the SEC* (Washington, D. C.: U. S. Government Printing Office, 1963), Chapter IX, p. 60, stated: "With disclosure being the cornerstone of Federal Securities regulations, the great safeguard that governs the conduct of corporate managements in many of their activities and the great bulwark against reckless corporate publicity and irresponsible recommendations and sale of securities, it seems wholly indefensible that most investors in over-the-counter securities should be afforded less protection than is provided for investors in exchange listed securities through the insider reports, proxy, prospectus, and annual reports required by the Exchange Act." The 1964 Amendments were the result.

[5] For a complete description of all forms used by registrants and for accounting requirements under federal securities legislation, see Louis H. Rappaport, *SEC Accounting Practice and Procedure* (3d ed.; New York: The Ronald Press Co., 1972).

[6] *Ibid.* In 1971 and 1972 the SEC was urging that reports be more understandable to laymen.

Item 1. Offering price information.
Item 2. Plan of distribution and nature of the underwriters' obligation.
Item 3. Use of proceeds by registrant.
Item 4. Sales of securities otherwise than for cash.
Item 5. Capital structure.
Item 6. Summary of earnings.
Item 7. State and date of incorporation and type of organization of the registrant.
Item 8. Parents of the registrant.
Item 9. Description of the business and its development during the past five years.
Item 10. Description and location of principal plants, mines, and other physical properties.
Item 11. If organized within five years, names of and transactions with promoters.
Item 12. Pending legal proceedings.
Item 13, 14, and 15. Information as to capital stock, funded debt, or other securities being registered.
Item 16. Names of directors and executive officers.
Item 17. Remuneration of directors and officers.
Item 18. Outstanding options to purchase securities from the registrant or subsidiaries.
Item 19. Principal holders of registrant's securities.
Item 20. Interest of directors, officers, and certain other persons in certain transactions.
Item 21. Financial statements.

Part II of Form S-1

Information not required in the prospectus—examples:
Item 22. Arrangements limiting, restricting, or stabilizing the market for securities being offered.
Item 23. Expenses of the issue.
Item 24. Relationship of registrant to experts named in the registration statement (including accountants).
Item 25. Sales of securities to special parties.
Item 26. Recent sales of unregistered securities.
Item 27. List of subsidiaries of the registrant.
Item 28. Franchises or concessions held by the registrar.
Item 29. Indemnification arrangements for officers and directors.
Item 30. Accounting for proceeds from sale of capital stock being registered.
Item 31. List of financial statements and exhibits.

Registration Statement—Form 10 (1934 Act). This is the principal form used for registration of securities under the 1934 Act. The information required generally falls under the following subject headings:[7]

1. Financial statements of the registrant.
2. Consolidated financial statements.

---

[7] *Ibid.*

3. Financial statements of unconsolidated subsidiaries and 50% owned companies.
4. Financial statements of affiliates whose securities are pledged as collateral.
5. Special provisions in connection with reorganization of registrant.
6. Special provisions in connection with succession by the registrant to other businesses.
7. Special provisions in connection with acquisition of other businesses.
8. Special provisions for financial statements of banks and insurance companies.
9. Registrants not in the production stage.
10. Historical financial information.
11. Filing of other statements in certain cases.

Annual Report—Form 10-K (1934 Act). This is the annual report to update registration statements. Most companies must file this annual Form 10-K report, which includes financial statistics and supplementary statements. Briefly, the annual report must contain:[8]

Item 1. Names of securities exchanges on which company's securities are registered.
Item 2. Number of stockholders.
Item 3. List of parents and subsidiaries.
Item 4. Important changes during the year in the business.
Item 5. Principal holders of voting securities.
Item 6. Directors of the registrant.
Item 7. Remuneration of directors and officers.
Item 8. Options to purchase securities from the registrant or its subsidiaries granted to, or exercised by, directors and officers during the year.
Item 9. Interest of management and others in certain transactions.
Item 10. Financial statements and exhibits—often in more detail than appears in company annual reports.

This Form 10-K report must be filed within 120 days after the close of the company's fiscal year.

Interim Reports—Form 8-K (1934 Act). This so-called current report must be filed only when certain significant events occur, such as changes in control of registrant, acquisition or disposition of a significant amount of assets otherwise used in the ordinary course of the business, material legal proceedings, changes in registered securities, changes in collateral for registered securities, material defaults on senior securities, material increases in amounts of registrant's outstanding securities, granting or extension of options to purchase securities of registrant or subsidiaries, revaluation of assets of registrant or significant subsidiaries or material restatement of registrant's capital accounts, and information as to matters submitted to vote

---

[8] *Ibid.*

of security holders. Form 8-K must be filed within ten days after the end of any month during which any of the events covered occur.

Semiannual Reports—Form 9-K (1934 Act). A semiannual report on Form 9-K must be filed by registered companies with the exception of banks and bank holding companies, investment companies, insurance companies, public utilities, and transportation companies that must file with ICC, FPC, or FCC; and companies in seasonal production, foreign issuers, and promotional or development companies.

SEC Reports and Investors. The statistical services extract the most important information from the SEC filings and make the data readily available to investors. However, if the analyst is making a study in depth of a company, he should inspect the SEC filings directly at the exchanges or the offices of the SEC because important data is included in them that do not appear in annual reports or reports of statistical services.[9]

Reports Filed with Regulatory Commissions Other than the SEC. When an industry is regulated, prescribed accounting methods and a fair degree of standardization in reporting is the rule. While much of the data on file with regulatory agencies is available to the public, much information is available only through secondary sources.

Reports filed with regulatory bodies provide a wealth of material for financial analysis. The major regulatory authorities other than the SEC with which reports must be filed are as follows:

1. Interstate Commerce Commission (ICC)
2. Civil Aeronautics Board (CAB)
3. Federal Power Commission (FPC)
4. State public utility commissions
5. State insurance commissions
6. Federal Reserve Board
7. Federal Deposit Insurance Corporation (FDIC)
8. Comptroller of the Currency
9. State banking commissions

Information Obtained Directly from the Company. Analysts frequently seek to obtain additional information not published by the company by direct interviews with officers of the company. The professional analysts— members of the Financial Analysts Federation—have over the years placed considerable pressure on management to disclose pertinent information that

---

[9] The SEC intends to require in prospectuses more simplified data for laymen, followed by more detailed data for professional analysts.

is often not obtainable in published reports. Figure 13-2 shows the type of questions that a professional analyst usually asks when visiting companies on a "field trip." [10]

PROTECTION FOR THE INVESTOR

A comprehensive national legal framework to regulate all aspects of securities transactions did not exist prior to the enactment of the various federal acts that will be described in this section. However, both prior to the enactment of federal legislation and subsequent to it, there has been state regulation of securities transactions which has proved by itself quite inadequate because of the national scope of the securities markets. State legislation takes the form of registration of securities and security dealers; in some states, such as New York, Connecticut, Delaware, and Maryland, it takes the form of antifraud legislation.

Securities Act of 1933

Congress passed the Securities Act of 1933 "to provide full and fair disclosure of the character of securities sold in interstate and foreign commerce and through the mails and to prevent fraud in the sale thereof, and for other purposes." The act requires that, with certain specific exceptions as to type and size of issue, before new corporate securities may be sold or offered for sale, a registration statement and prospectus must be filed with the SEC.

Registration Statement. A registration statement must be submitted and signed by the principal executive and the financial officers of the issuing company and by a majority of its board of directors. Information required in the statement is outlined in Schedule A of the act.[11]

---

[10] Also see, *How to Interview Corporate Executives* (New York: The New York Society of Security Analysts, August 7, 1972).

[11] The most important information required in Schedule A is as follows: (1) purpose of the issue; (2) price at which the issue is to be publicly offered; (3) price at which the issue is to be offered to any special group; (4) disclosure of any purchase option agreements; (5) underwriters' commissions or discounts; (6) promotion expenses; (7) net proceeds of the issue to the company; (8) remuneration of directors and officers receiving over $25,000 per year; (9) disclosure of any special contracts as management profit-sharing plans; (10) complete capitalization statement; (11) detailed balance sheet; (12) detailed earnings statements for last three years; (13) names and addresses of directors, officers, and underwriters; (14) names and addresses of stockholders owning more than 10% of any class of stocks or of outstanding stock; (15) a copy of the underwriting agreement; (16) a copy of legal opinions; (17) a copy of articles of incorporation; (18) copies of all underlying agreements or indentures affecting the new issues to be offered. (See SEC Annual Report on the subject.)

Sales

1. Percentage gain or loss, year to date vs. year before.
2. Estimates for full year:
    (a) Units and dollars.
    (b) Identical store sales (retailing).
3. Explanation of sales changes, either way.
4. Sales breakdowns (year to date):
    (a) By divisions.
    (b) By major product groups.
    (c) By major consuming markets.
5. Explanation of sales trends above or below the industry average.
6. Demand prospects: near, intermediate, and longer term.
7. Inventory status of company, its distributors, ultimate users.
8. Price levels vs. year ago—impact on unit and dollar sales.
9. Outlook for selling price: firm, up, or down. Why?
10. Company's percent of industry sales (i.e., "trade position").
11. Foreign sales aspects:
    (a) Percent of export sales.
    (b) Percent contributed by foreign branches.
    (c) Outlook abroad by countries.
12. Percent of sales derived from Government business—type of work.

Selling and Distribution

1. Methods used: direct to users, via wholesalers, retailers, branch warehouses, or combination of these.
2. Percent of selling costs to total sales.
3. Methods of compensation to selling forces: number of salesmen employed.
4. Advertising and promotional efforts, use of TV and other publicity media, with actual costs of this type of expense.
5. Extent of geographic coverage of the nation; plans, if any, to extend marketing areas, add new distributors, etc.
6. Economic radius of distribution from individual points; importance of freight rates.

Competition

1. What concerns are viewed as chief competitors?
2. Few or many competitors?
3. Is competition cutthroat or live-and-let-live type?
4. Are competitors strongly or weakly financed units?
5. In what way do company's products and services have an advantage, if any, over competition?
6. Is new competition entering field?
7. Where does company rank in its field or fields?
8. Importance of brand names, trade marks, patents, or servicing methods.

FIGURE 13-2

Types of Questions That Analysts Ask When Visiting Companies

Source: Joseph M. Galanis, "A Primer for Field Contact Work," *Financial Analysts Journal* (August, 1956).

Patent Aspects
1. Importance re sales and prices.
2. Expiration dates of basic or supplementary patents; expected impact on sales, price structure, profit margins, etc., upon expirations.

Production
1. Rate of operations to date vs. year ago; prospective rates of operation over foreseeable future.
2. Basis of operations; 1-2-3 shift, 7-8 hour day, or continous operations?
3. Overtime premium pay?
4. Number of plants and character of their construction; multistory or single-story (modern)?
5. Status of equipment: new, modernized, or obsolete?
6. Does company rate as a low-cost, high-cost, or average-cost producer?
7. Steps, if any, being taken to improve production methods and to increase productive efficiency.

Raw Materials
1. Major raw materials used; sources, domestic and foreign. Ample supplies or storage?
2. Price history of raw materials used. Volatility?
3. Extent of integration.
4. Is LIFO method of inventory valuation used?

Expansion
1. Details of program: plant locations, additions, product lines to be added.
2. Capital outlays involved; methods of financing, if any, contemplated.
3. Percent to be added to plant capacity on a square foot basis, or in physical units, or in dollar sales volume.
4. Any certificates of necessity or fast amortization of new facilities involved?
5. Any new acquisitions in mind?
6. Costs of new construction and equipment per unit of added production vs. one to five years ago.
7. Expected sales per $1 of new plant account investment vs. other years.

Research
1. Amounts, or percent, of sales spent annually on research.
2. Number employed and number possessing advanced degrees.
3. Record of recent patents granted as result of research.
4. New products on the fire and their prospects.
5. Percent of current sales from new products traceable to research over the past five to fifteen years. (This is the most important factor in evaluating research.)

Management
1. Does management show continuity or frequent changes?
2. Average age of top management officials.
3. Is the company a one-man outfit?
4. Methods of recruiting and training executives.
5. Is management centralized or decentralized?

FIGURE 13-2 (continued)

Employee Relations

1. Long-term strike record.
2. Percent of employees unionized—which plants?
3. Management policies on labor relations.
4. Chief employee benefits.
5. Labor turnover rates.

Financial

1. Most recent capitalization and changes.
2. Any current bank loans outstanding? Explanation.
3. Adequacy of working capital in relation to current and anticipated sales, compared with earlier years.
4. Near term maturities? Refundings? Retirements? Comment on ability to meet these obligations.
5. Any new financing in offing? Kind.
6. Insured, replacement, or appraisal value of fixed assets (especially natural resources) vs. book value.

Dividend Policies and Prospects

1. Payout policy, percent of earnings, percent of cash flow.
2. Prospect for extras.
3. Prospect for stock dividends.
4. Chances for increase (or decrease) in regular annual rate.

Earnings

1. Trend of labor and materials costs, percent of each to sales.
2. Ability to adjust selling prices to higher costs.
3. Cost savings programs, and comments.
4. Profit margins vs. year ago.
5. Trend of earnings to date vs. year ago.
6. Per share earnings for full year.
7. Nonrecurring items. Explanation.
8. Nonoperating sources of income vs. year ago.

Miscellaneous Topics

During the average interview, the analyst will think of spur-of-the-moment questions induced by information or comments of the contact. In addition, it may prove advisable to request comment on such individual topics as:

1. Status of current litigation.
2. Impact of Government Consent Decree.
3. Status of particular long-term sales contracts.
4. Problems arising as result of a current strike or aftermath of one settled.
5. Extent of insurance coverage in connection with floods or other disasters.

FIGURE 13-2 (concluded)

The Prospectus. Realizing that a registration statement is too time-consuming for most to read, Congress provided for the filing of a prospectus that summarizes the information in the registration statement. It must be offered to every person solicited and to all who purchase or indicate an interest in the securities at or before the actual offering. Its purpose is to provide the investor with the data required to analyze the value of an issue. Originally the required prospectus was very voluminous. Later the SEC approved smaller pocket-sized prospectuses now in use for many years. Since the time span between actual public announcement of an offering and selling of new securities is often only a matter of hours, the SEC has permitted a relaxation of the regulations to give prospective buyers information on the issue *during* the registration period but prior to the sale by allowing the distribution of a preliminary prospectus referred to as a "red herring." [12]

Liabilities for False Registration Under the Act of 1933. A large number of persons can be liable for false and misleading statements in the registration statement or prospectuses and may be sued for damages under civil law. Persons who *willfully* violate any of the provisions of the act or rules and regulations, or who *willfully* make a false statement or omit a material fact in a registration statement, may be held *criminally* liable and subject to fine, imprisonment, or both. If any part of an effective registration statement makes a false statement of a material fact or has omissions of essential data, the issuer, underwriters, and responsible parties may be sued by any purchaser of the security offered.[13] The primary value of the provisions has been their preventive function.

---

[12] In 1972 the SEC stated in its 37th Annual Report (p. 31): "Many prospectuses are still lengthy and complex . . . they may be accurate and complete and useful for financial analysts and sophisticated investors, they may be unintelligible to the average investor and thus fail to achieve their statutory purpose of providing full and fair disclosure to investors. Accordingly, the Commission . . . invited comments and suggestions . . . with respect to reasonable measures which might be taken to improve the readability and informativeness of prospectuses and other documents the purpose of which is to inform investors or securityholders."

[13] In addition to all persons who sign the registration statement, these individuals are liable: (1) every person who was a director or a partner in the issuing firm at the time of filing of the part of the registration statement under question; (2) every person who, with his consent, is named in the registration statement as a director or a partner; (3) every accountant, engineer, appraiser, or other person whose profession gives authority to his statements and who, with his consent, has been named as having prepared or certified any part of the registration, but liability attaches only to those portions actually prepared or certified by the individuals; (4) every underwriter of the security. Liability was becoming more of a problem for accountants in the early 1970s, and also for lawyers.

Securities Exchange Act of 1934

The passage of this act brought national security exchanges under federal control "to insure the maintenance of a fair and honest market in such transactions." Voluntary regulations by the exchanges, nevertheless, continue to govern much of stock exchange procedure, and self-regulation by the National Association of Security Dealers governs much of the operations of the over-the-counter securities markets in accordance with the significance attached to the concept of industry self-regulation.

The principal objectives of the act may be summarized as follows:

1. To provide the public with reliable information about securities listed on national security exchanges.
2. To eliminate manipulation, fraud, and dissemination of false information in the securities markets.
3. To insure just and equitable trading in the security markets.
4. To regulate the use of credit for the purpose of security trading.
5. To regulate trading by insiders in the security markets.
6. To regulate the use of proxies by corporate officials.

Furthermore, the act makes provision for *both* civil and criminal liabilities for those who violate its requirements.

Provisions Controlling and Regulating Security Trading. The 1934 Act provides comprehensive regulation of security trading and the prevention of manipulation in any form. To establish a fair and equitable market, certain practices are prohibited and others are controlled. The following are among the more important practices specifically prohibited:

1. Creating a misleading appearance of active trading through wash sales (an order to buy and an order to sell given at the same time), matched orders, or pool operation.
2. Creating trading activity to raise or depress the price of a registered security for the purpose of inducing buying or selling by others.
3. Disseminating information for the purpose of creating a change in price.
4. Making false and misleading statements regarding a security to create market activity or to induce buying or selling by others.
5. Pegging (fixing or stabilizing prices) except by investment bankers during underwriting.

Regulation of Corporate "Insiders." Officers, directors, and beneficial owners of 10% or more of a company's voting securities are generally known as "insiders." By virtue of their relationship with the corporation, they occupy a more favored position than other investors when they trade in the corporation's securities. To discourage "insiders" from capitalizing on confidential information, the SEC requires such owners of 10% or more of a company's equity securities (common and preferred stocks, convertible bonds, and bonds with stock warrants) to file a monthly statement of their transactions in the securities. To prevent unfair use of information by "insiders," the law requires that any profits realized from security transactions within a 6-month period must be forfeited to the corporation. A suit to recover short-term profits may be instituted by the corporation or any stockholder. The SEC was very active in this area in the 1968-1973 period.[14]

Regulation of Proxies. Regulation X-14 issued by the SEC requires a proxy solicitation to contain: a statement of the stockholder's rights concerning revocation and the right of dissension; the identity of those who will pay the cost of solicitation; a statement concerning on whose behalf the solicitation is being made and the interests of the party in the corporation; and complete information with respect to voting rights, classes of stock outstanding, directors and officers and their remuneration, candidates for election, and the specific types of action to be undertaken for the corporation.[15]

Regulation of the Over-the-Counter Markets. The over-the-counter markets are subject to federal regulation under Section 15 of the Securities

---

[14] Two SEC landmark "insider" cases are: *Securities and Exchange Commission* v. *Texas Gulf Sulphur Co.*, 258 F Supp. 262 (1966), 401 F2d 833 (1968); and *Newmark* v. *RKO General, Inc.*, 425 F2d 348 (1970). A co-author of this text, Douglas H. Bellemore, was the financial expert witness in the two cases that went to trial as well as over 40 other federal court valuation cases. The Texas Gulf Sulphur Case was a ruling of the U. S. Court of Appeals reversing most of the judgment order in favor of TGS and its officials rendered by the U. S. District Court for Southern New York in 1966. The case dealt directly with "claimed" misuse of insider information not made available to the public. The SEC "claimed" the TGS officers and directors used inside information to their profit in security transactions. The Appeals Court in TGS stated that "anyone in possession of material inside information is an insider and must refrain from telling anyone or refrain from trading in or recommending the securities concerned while such information remains undisclosed." The Newmark-RKO case extended the theory of "insiders" to include "corporate insiders" (RKO) as well as individuals.

[15] *Rule 10b-5, Employment of manipulative and deceptive devices.* Numerous lawsuits were being instituted in the late 1960s by the SEC and by stockholders (especially in regard to *proxies,* prospectuses, and registration statements) under this rule. In 1969 the SEC ruled that this section and *tender* offers of the 1934 act also covered *proxies* issued in *mergers* and tender offers.

   Rule—"It shall be unlawful for any person, directly or indirectly, by the use of any means or instrumentality of interstate commerce, or of the mails, or of any facility of any national securities exchange, (1) to employ any device, scheme, or artifice to defraud, (2) to make any untrue statement of a material fact or to omit to state a material fact necessary in order to make the statements made, in the light of the circumstances under which they were made, not misleading, or (3) to engage in any act, practice, or course of business which operates or would operate as a fraud or deceit upon any person in connection with the purchase or sale of any security." [See Alan R.

Exchange Act of 1934 and under the Maloney Act of 1938 that amended the legislation by the addition of Section 15a to the act. The 1964 Amendments to the Securities Exchange Act for the first time extended the registration, periodic reporting, proxy solicitation, and insider reporting and trading provisions to issuers of securities traded over-the-counter having total assets of $1,000,000 and a class of equity security held of record initially by 500 or more persons, if the issuer is engaged in interstate commerce or its securities are traded by means of the instruments of interstate commerce. The required registration statement that must be filed under new Section 12(g) of the act is similar to that required on an exchange.

Public Utility Holding Company Act of 1935

In administering the Public Utility Holding Company Act, the SEC regulates *interstate* public utility holding company systems and their operating company subsidiaries engaged in the electric utility business and/or in the retail distribution of gas. A holding company is defined by the act as one that directly or indirectly owns, controls, or holds with power to vote 10% or more of the outstanding voting stock. All such holding companies are required by law to register and file annual reports with the Commission.

Trust Indenture Act of 1939

The contract (indenture) between the issuer of corporate securities and the bondholders sets forth the relationship of the trustee to the issuer and the bondholders. The act applies to securities required to be registered under the Securities Act of 1933 and securities issued in exchange for other securities of the same corporation or under a reorganization plan approved by a court, which may not be required to be registered.

The major purpose of the act is to continue the theory of full disclosure first developed in the Securities Act of 1933. The issuer is required by the act to send periodic reports through the trustee to the bondholders, and the corporate trustee is required to maintain bondholder lists to provide a method of communication between the bondholders and the issuers in accordance with the provisions of the indentures.

Investment Company Act of 1940

This legislation had two main purposes: (1) full disclosure and (2)

Bromberg, *Securities Law—Fraud—SEC Rule 10b-5* (New York: McGraw-Hill Book Company).]

the prevention of the speculative abuses and management manipulation characteristic of the late 1920s. The act was broadly amended in 1970.[16]

> The Investment Company Act of 1940 provides for the registration and regulation of companies primarily engaged in the business of investing, reinvesting, owning, holding, or trading in securities. The Act, among other things, requires disclosure of the financial condition and investment policies of such companies; prohibits changing the nature of their business or their investment policies without shareholders' approval; regulates the means of custody of the companies' assets; requires management contracts to be submitted to security holders for approval; prohibits underwriters, investment bankers, and brokers from constituting more than a minority of the directors of such companies; and prohibits transactions between such companies and their officers, directors, and affiliates except with approval of the Commission. The Act also regulates the issuance of senior securities. . . . The Companies must issue prospectuses when offering new stock, which must be periodically updated to conform to SEC requirements.[17]

Investment Advisers Act of 1940

> . . . The Act requires persons engaged for compensation in the business of advising others with respect to securities to register with the Commission and to conform to statutory standards designed to protect the public interest. The Act prohibits fraudulent, deceptive or manipulative acts or practices. . . . Advisers are also required to make, keep or preserve books and records in accordance with the Commission's rules and the Commission is empowered to conduct inspection of such books and records.[18]

SEC Accounting Regulations

By virtue of authority granted by the Securities Act of 1933, the SEC has defined accounting terms and prescribed the form in which required financial statements must be presented, stipulating the method to be used in the determination of depreciation and depletion, in the valuation of assets

---

[16] Major 1970 amendments provided the following: "(a) Investment advisers . . . have a fiduciary duty with respect to the receipt of compensation for services or payments of a material nature paid . . . to the adviser or an affiliate of the adviser; (b) the NASD may by rule prohibit . . . offering such shares at a price which includes an excessive sales load; and (c) "front-end-load sales charges on contractual plans may be imposed under either of two alternative methods: (1) "spread load" alternative —the sales load is restricted to not more than 20 percent of any payment and not more than an average of 16 percent over the first 4 years of the plan, or (2) periodic payment plan certificates may still be sold with a 50 percent front-end-load, but plan sponsors must refund to any investor surrendering his certificate within the first 18 months . . . that portion of the sales charges which exceeds 15 percent of the gross payments made as well as pay him the value of his account."

[17] From the 32nd Annual Report, p. 98.
[18] From the 32nd Annual Report, p. 109.

and liabilities, in the treatment of recurring and nonrecurring charges or profits, and in the manner in which operating income is to be segregated from income obtained from other sources and other matters. The SEC has adhered quite closely to sound accounting principles as generally understood by the accounting profession. SEC rulings are published in the form of Accounting Series Releases. The Commission generally has not attempted to impose its ideas on the accounting profession, but instead has chosen to cooperate closely with it, first submitting any proposed regulation to the American Institute of Certified Public Accountants. The SEC generally has assigned full responsibility for adequate disclosure in financial reports filed with it to management, not to the accountants certifying the statements. In recent years, however, there have been a rising number of suits against accounting firms.

In late 1971 Congress, for the first time setting itself above the SEC and the AICPA, passed legislation stating that "no taxpayer shall be required without his consent to use any particular method of accounting for the (investment) credit." On Dec. 9 the AICPA-APB issued an unanimous denunciation of Congressional involvement in this accounting principle, as well as indicated disapproval of Congress overriding the AICPA and SEC.

Major Problems for Regulatory Agencies

In each of its Annual Reports, the SEC reviews industry problems and the viewpoint of the Commission in respect to these problems. The major areas covered in the SEC 37th Annual Report issued in 1972 for the fiscal year ended June 30, 1971, are discussed in the remainder of this chapter.

Investor Protection—Market Structure. The Commission has taken steps to improve procedures for detecting and monitoring financial and operational problems at firms. In August, 1971 (fully effective in mid-1972), the Commission dropped the maximum permissible ratio of aggregate indebtedness (of brokerage firms) from 20 to 1 to 15 to 1 and also instituted a requirement for the contraction or liquidation of a firm when its net capital ratio exceeds 12 to 1. By August, 1972, the net capital rule will be largely in force. In June, 1971, Chairman Casey pointed out the need to develop a sound industry-wide operational system which would satisfy the need for the prompt consummation of securities transactions and resolve the diverse settlement practices of the various securities markets.

Structure and Level of NYSE Commission Rates. This subject was discussed in Chapter 2 of this text. In 1971 the SEC approved new commission rate schedules for the New York Stock Exchange. The SEC authorized competitive regulation rates for portions of orders above a level not higher than $500,000. In 1972 the $500,000 level was reduced to $300,000. New minimum rate schedules were also adopted.

Automated Quotations Systems. For very many years brokers and the public have had available automated quotation systems for securities traded on exchanges. On February 8, 1971, the National Association of Security Dealers formally commenced public operations of the NASDAQ automated quotations system with approximately 2,300 over-the-counter securities. In May, 1972, the New York Stock Exchange suggested that a "composite tape" to serve the securities market of the future be jointly developed by the member stock exchanges. It told the SEC that such a tape could be activated within 40 weeks after approval by all exchanges. The next step, of course, is the integration of the automated quotation systems of the exchanges with the NASD automated quotations system.

Institutional Investor Performance. The Institutional Investor Study Report of the SEC, dated March 10, 1971, contained the following initial conclusions of the Commission with respect to institutional investors:

1. Although institutions have increased their share of outstanding equity securities, the increase has been relatively slow-paced over time. Institutions have tended to concentrate their purchases and holdings in the more stable securities of larger corporations while individual investors have sought and obtained higher returns on more risky securities.
2. Competitive pressures on institutional portfolio managers for improved investment performance have led to the rapid growth of relatively exotic, aggressively managed investment vehicles—and to increased willingness on the part of many institutions to adopt more aggressive investment strategies and trading practices.
3. The study's data indicated that institutional trading was associated with relatively few of the large price changes that occur in the securities markets.
4. Although it appears that limited numbers of institutions, particularly banks, have the potential economic power—were they to act together—to exercise control or influence over a number of portfolio companies, the study found that except in the case of takeover situations, institutions generally report that they do not participate in decision making.

Securities Industry. Two studies on the securities industry have been published by the Senate. The first study, dated October, 1971, contained two parts: Part I dealt with commission rates and institutional membership, and Part II dealt with financial and operational problems.

The second study, dated February, 1972, contained the following major headings: (1) Operational breakdown within brokerage firms in the late

1970s; (2) Continuing evolution of the marketplace; (3) Changes in the economics of the industry; and (4) Regulatory structure of the securities industry. This report includes recommendations with respect to operational problems, market structure, commission rates, and institutional membership. The recommendations include giving the SEC control over organized agencies in clearance and settlement methods, encouraging of competition in the markets and among market makers as a foundation for a truly national system under SEC leadership, and eliminating fixed commission rates on institutional size transactions. Fixed rates were raised in September, 1973.

Restricted (Letter) Stock. *Restricted securities* represent securities acquired from issuers in transactions not involving public offerings. There has been filed with the SEC a "letter" stating that the purchase was instituted as an investment and not for the purpose of resale. The SEC states that this is one of the most difficult areas of securities law. Related to this problem is the problem of securities held by persons in a control relationship with the issuer. The following rules regarding restricted stock were included in the 37th Annual Report:

1. *Rule 144.* This rule replaces the old *subjective* tests of "state of mind" and "change of circumstances." The rule substitutes certain clear-cut *objective* standards: a two-year holding period and the availability of information to the general public. The rule also permits holders of restricted securities and persons in a control relationship with the issuer to sell, after a two-year holding period designed to assure that the seller has held the securities at risk, limited amounts of securities through brokers without registration, provided adequate information about the issuer is available. A companion rule would require that the annual and quarterly report forms state whether all required filings within the preceding 90 days had been made so that sellers will know whether Rule 144 is available for their use. To prevent substantial blocks from coming into the market at one time, which may result in wide swings in the market price, the revised rule permits the sale of a maximum of 1 percent of the outstanding stock of an issuer in any six-month period.

2. *Rule 237.* This rule recognizes that noncontrolling persons owning restricted securities of issuers which do not satisfy all of the conditions of Rule 144 might have difficulty in selling those securities due to circumstances beyond their control. Rule 237 was designed to avoid unduly restricting the liquidity of such investments. Any person satisfying the conditions of the rule is permitted to offer securities up to 1 percent of the amount of the class outstanding, or $50,000—whichever is less— during any 12-month period, reduced by the amount of any other sales pursuant to an exemption under Section 3(b) of the act or Rule 144 during the period. The conditions are: (1) The seller has owned and fully paid for the securities for at least five years; (2) The issuer is a domestic organization actively engaged in business as a going concern for at least five years; (3) The securities are sold in negotiated transactions otherwise than through a broker or dealer; and (4) The seller must file a notice of intention to sell securities under the rule.

QUESTIONS

1. What sources of information would you suggest to a prospective investor wishing to study the textile industry?

2. (a) What type of information might one find in a Form 10-K report filed with the Securities and Exchange Commission?

   (b) How does a Form 10-K report differ from a Form 8-K report?

3. (a) Explain briefly the reasons for the passage of federal statutes regulating the securities business.

   (b) Did the passage of federal statutes eliminate the need for state blue-sky laws?

4. (a) What is the purpose of the Securities Act of 1933?

   (b) To what branch of the securities business does the Securities Act of 1933 apply?

   (c) Name at least four classes of securities that are exempted from the provisions of the Securities Act of 1933. Why were they exempted?

5. (a) Distinguish between a registration statement and a prospectus.

   (b) What is the purpose of a prospectus?

   (c) What is a red herring? Why is it issued?

6. (a) Discuss the determination, purpose, and significance of the registration statement.

   (b) Discuss the issuance of stop orders by the SEC.

7. Discuss briefly the liabilities arising from false registration under the Securities Act of 1933. Compare these to liabilities under the Securities Act of 1934.

8. (a) What are the basic objectives of the Securities Exchange Act of 1934?

   (b) What is a wash sale and why is it prohibited under the Act of 1934?

   (c) Under what circumstances is pegging or price stabilizing permitted?

9. (a) Discuss the regulation of corporate officers and "insiders" under the Securities Exchange Act of 1934.

   (b) What was the significance of the charges brought during 1968 against Merrill Lynch, Pierce, Fenner and Smith, Inc. by the SEC?

   (c) What is a proxy?

10. (a) Discuss regulation of the over-the-counter markets.

    (b) What is the NASD? What are its rules of fair practice and its uniform practice code?

    (c) What are the two main purposes of the Investment Company Act of 1940?

11. (a) What is the NASDAQ automated quotation system?
   (b) What are "restricted securities"?
   (c) Outline the conditions under which restricted securities may be resold to the public without registration with the SEC.

WORK-STUDY PROBLEMS

1. Explain whether the following actions or lack of actions would be considered violations subject to possible penalty by the Securities and Exchange Commission. Explain the rules involved in each case.
   (a) After the Securities and Exchange Commission has allowed the registration statement for a security to become effective and it is being sold, the salesman may verbally, but not in writing, tell a prospective customer that the Securities and Exchange Commission has approved the issue.
   (b) The bonds of a company with investment rating of A or better can be sold a few days after registration without waiting for the 20-day waiting period.
   (c) The issuer may withdraw on written notice, without penalty, the registration of a security filed with the SEC.
      (1) After the effective date of registration.
      (2) Before the effective date of registration.
   (d) It is not necessary for a company to disclose that it is being sued for a large amount of money for a patent infringement if the company has legal advice that the claim is probably groundless.
   (e) A company that fails to mention that goodwill is carried at $1 might be subject to a severe penalty.
   (f) Failure to register a new issue with New York State officials in Albany, New York, would subject the issuer to penalties for securities sold in New York State.
   (g) Registration is not necessary for the sale of securities of (1) the Bank for Reconstruction and Development; (2) the Port of New York Authority; (3) the First National City Bank of New York; (4) the Consolidated Edison Company of New York, Inc.; (5) The Mack Trucks, Inc.; and (6) the Chesapeake and Ohio Railway Co.
   (h) An individual owning 9% of the common stock of a company listed on the New York Stock Exchange would be liable to penalties if he sold any or all of this stock without reporting the transaction to the Securities and Exchange Commission.
   (i) Disclosure by the Securities and Exchange Commission of information filed by an issuer is a cause of action against the Securities and Exchange Commission.
   (j) A company did not include a copy of its Form 10-K report in the annual report sent to shareholders.

2. (a) What is the Securities Investors Protection Corporation? How is it funded?
   (b) What is the basic protection afforded a customer by SIPC?
   (c) How is a customer's claim for securities valued?

SUGGESTED READINGS

Backer, Morton. "Financial Reporting and Security Investment Decisions." *Financial Analysts Journal* (March-April, 1971), pp. 67-72, 79.

Brown, R. Gene. "Ethical and Other Problems in Publishing Financial Forecasts." *Financial Analysts Journal* (March-April, 1972), pp. 38-45, 86-87.

Burton, John C. "Ethics in Corporate Financial Disclosure." *Financial Analysts Journal* (January-February, 1972), pp. 49-53.

Damant, David C. "Financial Forecasting by Companies." *Financial Analysts Journal* (September-October, 1972), pp. 44-46, 59.

Farrar, Donald E. "The Coming Reform on Wall Street." *Harvard Business Review* (September-October, 1972), pp. 108-117.

Feuerstein, Donald M. "Toward a National System of Securities Exchanges: The Third and Fourth Markets." *Financial Analysts Journal* (July-August, 1972), pp. 57-59, 82-86.

Fritz, David. "Whatever Happened to the Other Institutional Study?" *The Institutional Investor* (May, 1972), pp. 58-59, 82, 86-87, 90-93, 106-112.

Gray, Daniel H. "Standards of Corporate Responsibility Are Changing." *Financial Analysts Journal* (September-October, 1971), pp. 28-29, 73-74.

Herman, Edward S., and Carl F. Safanda. "Allocating Investment Information." *Financial Analysts Journal* (January-February, 1973), pp. 23-28, 88-91.

"Loomis on Inside Information" (Editorial interview). *Financial Analysts Journal* (May-June, 1972), pp. 20-25, 82-88.

Nelson, Harry L., Jr. "Let's Make Investment Advisers Accountable." *Financial Analysts Journal* (January-February, 1973), pp. 19-22.

New York Society of Security Analysts. "How To Interview a Corporate Executive." Training Program for Junior Analysts, 1972.

Owens, Hugh F. "Investment Adviser Regulation." *Financial Analysts Journal* (January-February, 1973), pp. 12-18.

Rappaport, Alfred, and Eugene Lerner. "Public Reporting by Diversified Companies." *Financial Analysts Journal* (January-February, 1970), pp. 54-64.

Rappaport, Louis H. *SEC Accounting Practices and Procedures,* 3d ed. New York: The Ronald Press, 1972.

Securities Law—Fraud—SEC Rule 10b-5, Vol. 1 & 2. New York: McGraw-Hill Book Company, 1971.

Singhvi, Surendra. "Corporate Management's Inclination to Disclose Financial Information." *Financial Analysts Journal* (July-August, 1972), pp. 66-73.

Investment Growth Factors and Projections

Since 1946, the government has been most concerned with attempting to foster economic growth sufficient to keep or push unemployment to a minimum and at the same time to raise the level of consumption of the "average American" with special emphasis on the "underprivileged." While the goals are creditable, it must be recognized that too great an emphasis on growth, where the rate of growth pursued exceeds current capacity of capital equipment and skilled manpower, results in maladjustments within the economy and, more specifically, may foster inflationary forces. There is a danger of establishing impractical and unrealizable goals for growth, and in the 1970s many ecologists, scientists, and others warned of the perils of economic and population growth.[1]

LONG-TERM ECONOMIC GROWTH

Our economy has maintained a long-term upward secular growth, only temporarily interrupted by recessions and depressions, including the extremely severe and extended depression of the 1930s and the much milder recessions experienced since 1938 and in the post-World War II years. It is the expectation of practically all economists of any stature that a continuation of the long-term secular growth of the economy can be projected. There is, however, debate on what is a reasonable rate of projection for this growth,[2]

---

[1] Symposium on Perils of Economic and Population Growth, Smithsonian Institute, "Warnings on Perils of Growth," *New York Times,* March 3, 1972, p. 41.

[2] "The Economic Accounts of the U.S.—Retrospect and Prospect," *Survey of Current Business,* Anniversary Issue, Vol. 51, No. 7 (July, 1971).

especially "real" growth. The tables and charts in this chapter represent projections by the National Industrial Conference Board.

Common Stock Growth

The major justification for investment in common stocks is the long-term record of growth of corporate gross revenues, earnings, dividends, and stock prices. If earnings did not grow, it would be unlikely that dividends would grow for any significant period or that there would be a significant growth in the market price of a stock, and these are the only two justifications for the purchase of common stock. Furthermore, it is questionable if a bond or a preferred stock should receive a quality rating if the earnings of the issuer are not expected to rise. Business history provides few cases where earnings of an industry or a company have shown a horizontal trend for many years. They have either risen or declined; they did not move sidewise.

In terms of all common stocks or a widely diversified portfolio of common stocks, the long-term record of growth of earnings, dividends, and stock prices shows a somewhat slower growth than the long-term growth of the economy. Admittedly, while earning power of a broad spectrum of stocks such as those represented by the S&P 500 index may be expected to grow at approximately the same rate as or slightly slower than the economy, individual stocks will show quite varied patterns. In the final analysis, the problem of valuation and selection of common stocks depends upon a projection of future earnings and dividends for individual stocks and then a determination of a reasonable price to pay for the projected growth potential and volatility—an appropriate capitalization rate applied to current earnings.

Growth Rates for Gross National Product

Any attempt at projections must rest first on an historical analysis. The best source is the 255-page study, "Long-Term Economic Growth 1860-1965."[3] Table 14-1 is taken from that study. It gives compound growth rates based on three different statistical methods. The growth rate of GNP from 1966 to 1972 and for corporate profits is given in Table 14-2.

There cannot be a growth of corporate profits without a growth of GNP. The importance of "real" growth in constant dollars as opposed to mere growth in "current dollars," which includes inflation (price level increases),

---

[3] U.S. Department of Commerce, Bureau of the Census, "Long-Term Economic Growth 1860-1965, A Statistical Compendium" (Washington, D.C.: U.S. Government Printing Office, October, 1966). See especially pages 106-113 of this study for charts on growth rate triangles.

TABLE 14-1

Alternative "Real" Growth Rate Formulas for U.S. Gross National Product [4]
(Compound Annual Growth Rates)

	1890 to 1907	1907 to 1929	1929 to 1965
All figures are for "real" growth calculated by:			
1. Compound interest rate formula with initial and terminal years of annual data as selected points ...	4.4%	2.7%	3.1%
2. Fitting linear equation to logarithms of annual data	4.5	2.7	3.9
3. Fitting exponential equation to annual data (Pesek Method)	4.6	2.8	3.7

	1948 to 1957	1948 to 1965	1957 to 1965
1. Type 1 above	3.8%	3.8%	3.9%
2. Type 2 above	4.0	3.5	4.0
3. Type 3 above	3.9	3.5	4.1
4. Compound interest rate formula with initial and terminal business cycle averages as selected points	3.7	3.3	3.9

is clearly indicated (for those who accept the theory that common stocks per se are an inflation hedge) by reviewing Table 14-2. In the period 1957-1965 (in Table 14-1) there was only a very slow rate of inflation; in fact, the GNP deflator only rose from 100 in 1958 to 110.86 for 1965, or a compounded rate of inflation of only 1.5% per year. In that period "Corporate Profits After Taxes" (see Table 14-3) for "All U.S. Corporations" rose from $26.0 billion in 1957 and $26.7 billion in 1960 to $49.9 billion for 1966. On the other hand, with the much greater inflation in 1966-1972, corporate profits after taxes reached a peak in 1966 and then moved up and down in a broad horizontal channel not surpassing the 1966 peak until 1972.

Corporate Profits and GNP. The historical growth rate of corporate profits has been considerably more irregular and volatile than the growth rate of GNP. Business cycles are reflected in an exaggerated degree in the record of corporate profits, and this in turn has been reflected in the record of dividends and stock prices, especially fluctuations in stock prices.

---

[4] The method of "Selected Points" is not influenced by cyclical patterns between initial and terminal years. The linear trend fitted by least squares to the logarithms of the data is influenced by cyclical patterns.

TABLE 14-2

Growth Rate of GNP and Corporate Profits, 1966 to 1973 (Billions of Dollars)

Year	GNP Current Dollars	Price Deflator for GNP 1958 = 100	%	GNP in 1958 Dollars	Growth Rate GNP Current Dollars %	1958 Dollars %	After-Tax Profits All U.S. Corp. $	Dow Jones Industrial Average (Share)	S&P "500" Composite (Share)
1965	684.9	110.86		617.8			46.5	53.67	5.19
1966	749.9	113.94	+2.77	658.1	+9.45	+6.52	49.9	57.68	5.55
1967	793.9	117.59	+3.20	675.2	+5.86	+2.60	46.6	53.87	5.33
1968	864.2	122.30	+4.00	706.6	+8.86	+4.65	47.8	57.89	5.76
1969	930.3	128.20	+4.83	725.6	+7.51	+2.56	44.8	57.02	5.78
1970	977.1	135.23	+5.52	722.5	+4.84	−0.05	39.3	51.02	5.09
1971	1055.5	141.61	+4.64	745.4	+7.46	+2.69	47.6	55.09	5.41
1972	1155.2	146.10	+3.02	790.7	+9.65	+6.44	55.4	67.11	6.42
1966-69					+7.45	+3.31			
1966-70					+6.80	+3.15			
1966-71					+7.00	+3.05			
1966-72					+7.45	+3.10			
1973E							70.0E	82.75E	7.68E

TABLE 14-3

Corporate Profits in Dollars and as a Percentage of GNP (Billions of Dollars)

Year	GNP Current $'s	GNP 1958 $'s	Corporate Profits All U.S. Corporations Before Taxes $	Before Taxes % GNP	After Taxes $	After Taxes % GNP
1929	103	204	10.5	10.2	8.6	8.3
1930	90	184	7.0	7.8	2.9	3.2
1931	76	169	2.0	2.6	−.9	—
1932	58	144	−1.3	—	−2.7	—
1933	56	142	−1.2	—	.4	0.7
1934	65	154	1.7	2.6	1.6	2.5
1935	72	170	3.4	4.6	2.6	3.6
1936	83	193	5.6	6.7	4.9	5.9
1937	90	203	6.8	7.6	5.3	5.9
1938	85	193	4.9	5.8	2.9	3.4
1939	91	209	6.3	6.9	5.6	6.2
1940	100	227	9.8	9.8	7.2	7.2
1941	125	264	15.2	12.2	10.1	8.1
1942	158	298	20.3	12.8	10.1	6.4
1943	192	337	24.4	12.7	11.1	5.8
1944	210	361	23.8	11.3	11.2	5.3
1945	212	355	19.2	9.1	9.0	4.2
1946	209	313	19.3	9.2	15.5	7.4
1947	221	310	25.6	11.6	20.2	9.1
1948	258	324	33.0	12.8	22.7	8.8
1949	257	324	30.8	12.0	18.5	7.2
1950	285	355	37.7	13.2	24.9	8.7
1951	328	383	42.7	13.0	21.6	6.6
1952	346	395	39.9	11.5	19.6	5.7
1953	365	413	39.6	10.8	20.4	5.6
1954	365	407	38.0	10.4	20.6	5.6
1955	398	438	46.9	11.8	27.0	6.8
1956	419	446	46.1	11.0	27.2	6.5
1957	441	453	45.6	10.3	26.0	5.9
1958	447	447	41.1	9.2	22.3	5.0
1959	484	676	52.1	10.8	28.5	5.9
1960	504	438	49.7	9.9	26.7	5.3
1961	550	497	50.3	9.7	27.2	5.2
1962	560	530	55.4	9.9	31.2	5.6
1963	591	551	59.4	10.1	33.1	5.6
1964	632	581	66.8	10.6	38.4	6.1
1965	685	618	77.8	11.4	46.5	6.8
1966	750	658	84.2	11.4	49.9	6.7
1967	794	675	79.8	10.5	46.6	5.9
1968	864	707	87.6	10.1	47.8	5.5
1969	930	726	84.9	9.1	44.8	4.8
1970	977	723	74.0	7.6	39.3	4.0
1971	1056	745	85.1	8.1	47.6	4.5
1972	1155	791	98.0	8.5	55.4	4.8

Another way to examine the growth record of corporate profits is to examine corporate profits as a percentage of GNP. Unfortunately, there are *no satisfactory* statistics for "all corporate profits" before 1929, although there are earnings statistics for the DJIA and for the Standard & Poor's indexes for a much longer period, in the latter case linked to earlier estimates of the Cowles Common Stock Indexes.

The relation of corporate profits to GNP is shown in Table 14-3. As a practical matter, only the record since World War II is significant to investors. The 1930s seem significant only to indicate that in depression (and recession) profits decline more than GNP. The cyclical upturns in 1936-1937 and 1939 show how rapidly profits regained their position relative to GNP during recovery periods. The 1940s and even the early 1950s reflect the effects of war and its immediate aftermath and the very rapid rise in depreciation charges that occurred during and after 1954. Independent studies suggest that depreciation charges were too low for an inflationary economy from 1946 through 1954,[5] and reported profits were exaggerated. The low ratio of profits to GNP, 4.0% in 1970 and 4.8% in 1972, is noted.

Growth Rates for Major Components of GNP. Expenditures in the private sector of the economy are the major force for growth in the economy, and consumer expenditures (personal consumption expenditures) dominate the private sector because they constitute 63-65% of GNP. Total government purchases of goods and services amounted to about 22% of GNP, and gross private domestic investment the remaining 13-14%. Equipment for producing consumer products or services represents a derived demand from the final demand by consumers for goods and services. Thus, the consumer is king in our economy; and most projections for GNP and its components start with projections of consumer demand and then utilize these data in the analyses of various industries, investment, and employment.[6]

Projections for GNP to 1980 (NICB). The National Industrial Conference Board has published its projections for GNP and its major components to 1980 in "Economic Growth in the Seventies."[7] We accept these projections as reliable as any that are available at this writing. The highlights of this report for the periods 1929-1968, 1975, and 1980 are presented in Figures 14-1, 14-2, 14-3, and Tables 14-4, 14-5, 14-6, and 14-7.

---

[5] See M. Brown, "Depreciation and Corporate Profits," *Survey of Current Business* (October, 1963), and *Survey of Current Business* (May, 1968).

[6] As a source of projections of the economy, the reader is referred to "Economic Growth in the Seventies," a report from the National Industrial Conference Board which is available to educators for $3 per copy.

[7] *Ibid.*

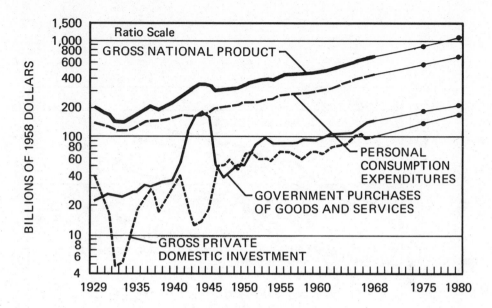

FIGURE 14-1

Constant Dollar Gross National Product and Components,
1929-1968, 1975, and 1980

   Source: National Industrial Conference Board, *Economic Growth in the Seventies,*
p. 44.

The analyst should examine the tables mentioned above and then, in
making projections for security analysis, should use these or similar projections by recognized research groups as a base for analysis and valuation
of industries and companies.

The reader should pay particular attention to Table 14-7, Rates of
Change in Gross National Product and Components. It can be noted that
from 1947 to 1968 GNP grew at a compound annual rate of 6.4% in
current dollars and 4.0% in real terms. Projections from 1968 to 1975 are
for growth in current dollars of 7.4% per year and in real dollars, 4.1%
(the latter about equal to the 1947-1968 rate). The rates for 1975-1980
are approximately the same, but include slightly less inflation and slightly
more real growth. Financial analysts should also study projections carefully
for the major components of GNP as these will influence projections for
various industries and, therefore, companies within these industries.

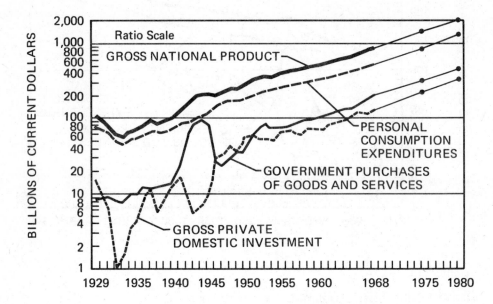

FIGURE 14-2

Current Dollar Gross National Product and Components,
1929-1968, 1975, and 1980

Source: National Industrial Conference Board, *Economic Growth in the Seventies,*
p. 45.

Industry Growth

Some writers, notably the late Julius Grodinsky, have drawn a rough parallel between industry and the human life cycle. They point out correctly that when new industries are born, there is often a rush by many companies to enter the field in the period of initial and usually rapid growth. This is generally followed by a shakeout period with only a relatively few survivors and by a continuing period of strong growth, although the rate of growth is slower than in the initial period. Grodinsky described these periods as the (1) pioneering stage and (2) expansion stage. This concept is sound, but there are many problems to be recognized in the rest of the stages as defined

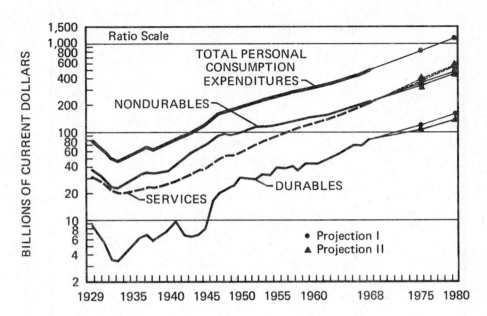

FIGURE 14-3

Current Dollar Personal Consumption Expenditure, 1929-1968,
and Alternative Projections to 1975 and 1980

Source: National Industrial Conference Board, *Economic Growth in the Seventies,*
p. 45.

by Grodinsky, who stated: "The industrial life cycle—with its four stages of
pioneering, expansion, stagnation, and decay—is minutely analyzed in order
to point up the principle that an expanding company in an expanding industry in an expanding economy is the touchdown of investment success." [8]
He also stated: "Investors in choosing an industry will be wise in selecting
one characterized by rapid growth. Though not all industries characterized
by slow growth or slight declines eventually lose their earning power, the
tendency is in that direction." [9] A large number of investors accept this
thesis. In fact, investing by institutions stresses this approach.

___

[8] Julius Grodinsky, *Investments* (New York: The Ronald Press Co., 1953), p. v.
Part II of the book, "Appraisal of the Industry," has three subdivisions: (1) Expansion
and Decline; (2) Industrial Life Cycle; (3) Signs of Growth and Decay.
[9] *Ibid.,* p. 87.

TABLE 14-4

Projection of Real GNP from Inputs

	1965	1968	1975	1980	Percent Annual Average Change		
					1965-75	1968-75	1975-80
Private Sector							
Farm							
Employment (thousands)	4,338	3,823	3,110	2,620	—3.4	—3.0	—3.5
Hours worked per week	45.7	44.8	43.5	42.4	—0.3	—0.4	—0.5
Output per man-hour (1958 constant dollars)	$ 2.30	$ 2.62	$ 4.09	$ 5.47	5.9	6.6	6.0
Output	$ 23.7	$ 23.3	$ 28.8	$ 31.6	2.0	3.1	1.9
Nonfarm							
Employment (thousands)	61,357	66,535	76,020	82,670	2.2	1.9	1.7
Hours worked per week	39.1	38.1	37.4	36.8	—0.5	—0.3	—0.3
Output per man-hour (1958 constant dollars)	$ 4.36	$ 4.73	$ 5.67	$ 6.55	2.6	2.6	2.9
Output	$ 543.3	$ 624.6	$ 839.3	$1,036.0	4.4	4.3	4.3
Total private sector							
Output	$ 567.0	$ 647.9	$ 868.1	$1,067.6	4.4	4.3	4.2
Government							
Employment (thousands)	12,110	14,246	16,600	18,500	3.2	2.2	2.2
Output per man-year	$4,194	$4,190	$4,200	$4,200	—	—	—
Output	$ 50.8	$ 59.7	$ 69.7	$ 77.7	3.2	2.2	2.2
Total							
Output	$ 617.8	$ 707.6	$ 937.8	$1,145.3	4.3	4.1	4.1

Source: National Industrial Conference Board, *Economic Growth in the Seventies*, p. 34.

TABLE 14-5

Gross National Product and Components (Billions of 1958 Constant Dollars)

	1968	1975	1980	Distribution		
				1968	1975	1980
Gross national product	$707.6	$937.8	$1,145.3	100.00%	100.00%	100.00%
Personal consumption expenditures	452.6	605.3	746.5	63.96	64.52	65.18
Durables	80.7	nse	nse	11.40	—	—
Nondurables	196.9	nse	nse	27.83	—	—
Services	175.0	nse	nse	24.73	—	—
Gross private domestic investment	105.7	144.9	179.8	14.94	15.45	15.70
Fixed investment	99.1	135.9	168.8	14.00	14.49	14.74
Nonresidential	75.8	103.1	128.3	10.71	10.99	11.20
Structures	22.7	32.8	40.1	3.21	3.50	3.50
Producers' durable equipment	53.2	70.3	88.2	7.52	7.50	7.70
Residential	23.3	32.8	40.5	3.29	3.50	3.54
Nonfarm	22.8	32.4	40.0	3.22	3.45	3.49
Change in business inventories	6.6	9.0	11.0	0.93	1.00	0.96
Net exports	0.9	1.4	1.5	—	0.15	0.13
Government expenditures	148.4	186.3	217.5	20.97	19.86	18.99
Federal	78.9	86.5	96.2	11.15	9.22	8.40
Defense	nse	nse	nse	—	—	—
Other	nse	nse	nse	—	—	—
State and local	69.5	99.8	121.3	9.82	10.64	10.59

nse = Not separately estimated.

Source: National Industrial Conference Board, *Economic Growth in the Seventies*, p. 34.

TABLE 14-6

Gross National Product and Components (Billions of Current Dollars)

	1968	1975	1980	Distribution		
				1968	1975	1980
Gross national product	$865.7	$1,429.2	$1,992.8	100.00%	100.00%	100.00%
Personal consumption expenditures	536.6	876.0	1,209.9	61.98	61.29	60.72
Durables	83.3	a	a	9.62	—	—
Nondurables	230.6	a	a	26.64	—	—
Services	222.8	a	a	25.73	—	—
Gross private domestic investment	126.3	228.9	333.5	14.59	16.02	16.74
Fixed investment	119.0	214.7	315.4	13.75	15.02	15.83
Nonresidential	88.8	153.1	219.7	10.26	10.71	11.02
Structures	29.3	59.4	90.5	3.38	4.16	4.54
Producers' durable equipment	59.5	93.7	129.2	6.87	6.56	6.48
Residential	30.2	61.6	95.7	3.49	4.31	4.80
Nonfarm	29.6	60.8	94.5	3.42	4.25	4.74
Change in business inventories	7.3	14.2	18.1	0.84	0.99	0.91
Net exports	2.5	3.0	1.9	0.29	0.21	0.10
Government expenditures	200.3	321.3	447.5	23.14	22.48	22.46
Federal	99.5	134.1	169.3	11.49	9.38	8.50
Defense	78.0	96.5	114.3	9.01	6.75	5.74
Other	21.5	37.6	55.0	2.48	2.63	2.76
State and local	100.7	187.2	278.2	11.64	13.10	13.96

a = Not projected.

Source: National Industrial Conference Board, *Economic Growth in the Seventies,* p. 35.

TABLE 14-7

Rates of Change in Gross National Product and Components (Percent)

	1947-1968			1968-1975			1975-1980		
	Rate of Growth in Current $	Rate of Growth in = Real Terms	Rate of Growth Deflator	Rate of Growth in Current $	Rate of Growth in = Real Terms	Rate of Growth Deflator	Rate of Growth in Current $	Rate of Growth in = Real Terms	Rate of Growth Deflator
Gross national product	6.4%	4.0%	2.4%	7.4%	4.1%	3.2%	6.9%	4.1%	2.7%
Personal consumption expenditure	5.9	3.8	2.1	7.2	4.2	2.9	6.7	4.3	2.3
Durables	6.9	5.8	1.1	—	—	—	—	—	—
Nondurables	4.5	2.9	1.6	—	—	—	—	—	—
Services	7.3	4.2	3.1	—	—	—	—	—	—
Gross private domestic investment	—	—	—	—	—	—	—	—	—
Fixed income	6.1	3.2	2.9	8.8	4.6	4.0	8.0	4.4	3.4
Nonresidential	6.6	3.7	2.9	8.1	4.5	3.5	7.5	4.5	2.7
Structures	6.7	3.2	3.5	10.6	5.4	5.0	8.8	4.1	4.5
Producers' durable equipment	6.6	3.8	2.8	6.7	4.1	2.5	6.6	4.7	2.0
Residential	4.8	2.0	2.8	10.7	5.0	5.4	9.2	4.3	4.7
Nonfarm	5.1	2.1	3.0	10.8	5.2	5.4	9.2	4.3	4.7
Change in business inventories	—	—	—	—	—	—	—	—	—
Net exports	—	—	—	—	—	—	—	—	—
Government expenditures	10.3	6.5	3.8	7.0	3.3	3.6	6.8	3.1	3.6
Federal	10.4	7.0	3.4	4.4	1.3	2.9	4.8	2.2	2.6
Defense	10.8	—	—	3.1	—	—	3.4	—	—
Other	8.9	—	—	8.3	—	—	7.9	—	—
State and local	10.2	6.0	4.2	9.2	5.3	3.9	8.2	4.0	4.1

Source: National Industrial Conference Board, *Economic Growth in the Seventies*, p. 35.

Grodinsky pointed out the great risks in selecting stocks of companies in the pioneering stage prior to the first shakeout and survival of the few.[10] Those with luck or skill, or a combination of both, who have selected the few survivors may have done well, but the difficulties of such selection in the pioneering stage have been very great. Security analysis, valuation, and selection require adequate information. If there is little or no past record, there is little to guide future projections; therefore, security analysis and valuation of new companies in new industries are extremely difficult if not impossible to accomplish—and many tried this method in the late 1960s.

The life-cycle theory at least implies, even where not explicitly stated by proponents, that investors should only purchase securities of companies whose earnings have grown and are expected to grow at a significantly faster rate than earnings of corporations overall. Thus, it in fact becomes the "growth" theory of investment that so many investors have adopted. But, by definition, only an extremely small proportion of all stocks can meet the test. If an important proportion of investment funds attempts to crowd into this small select group, the prices of the stocks can and very frequently do get pushed up to extremely high prices (high price-earnings ratios). Conversely, other stocks may be relatively neglected by institutions.

Most companies must, by definition, be in industries in the maturity stage, still growing but only at about the same rate as the economy (or a slightly higher or slightly lower rate). Other companies must be in industries growing at a significantly slower rate, while a relatively few industries and companies may be showing a definite secular downturn. Under the life-cycle or growth-stock thesis, all of these companies should be avoided regardless of the prices at which their securities sell on the market. This would preclude a portfolio that was a cross-section of the American economy, which would grow only with the economy. It could also eliminate investment in industries and companies that were experiencing temporary periods of decline in earnings even though it may be projected that they will experience an earnings recovery. The decline in earnings may be interpreted as suggesting the entry

---

[10] Numerous studies confirm the great risk in purchasing stocks of new companies. Examples are:

(1) Federal Reserve Bank of New York, *Monthly Review*, April, 1969.

(2) "Report of Special Study of Securities Markets of the SEC" (House Document No. 95, Part I, 1963), p. 551. A sample of 504 newly organized companies during the period 1952-1962 was studied. At the end of 1962, 55% either could not be located or were inactive, liquidated, dissolved, or in receivership or reorganization. Another 25% were reporting operating losses. Only 25% were operating profitably or had merged with other companies.

(3) Irwin Friend, *Investment Banking and the New Issue Market,* Summary Volume (Philadelphia: University of Pennsylvania Press), pp. 78-85. The study indicated a strong tendency for the rate of return on new industrial corporate issues to be below the rates of return on seasoned issues.

into the mature stage. The fact that the securities may then sell at very low prices in relation to projected earnings is not considered to make them attractive. Mature companies are excluded from consideration at any price by the growth-stock investors, especially many institutional investors.

There are investors who believe that price should be the final determinant of the stock selected (not recognized by life-cycle or growth-stock theory investors) and that substantial capital gains can be made by investing in major companies in major industries when it is determined that they are significantly undervalued at their current market at low P/E ratios.

While the history of some companies and industries does fit rather neatly into the complete life-cycle framework, many exceptions in the latter two stages are found. Industries and companies are not necessarily characterized by permanent stagnation as they mature. Furthermore, many modern companies operate in more than one industry and quite often change their product lines. It can often be quite difficult to define an "industry" in a meaningful sense for investment purposes, let alone classify companies within given industries according to the life-cycle stages.

Forecasting End-Use Demand Through Input-Output Tables

Above-average growth for a company is usually predicated on expected rapid growth of the industry in which the company operates. However, a company may accomplish above-average growth by gaining an increased share of total industry demand. Forecasting end-use demand is therefore important to the analyst, although quite difficult to accomplish.

Historically, analysts would simply obtain from industry and company sources the major end-uses of the products produced, would then forecast the demand for each of these end-uses, and would include these forecasts in final total industry demand projections. This process started with the past end-use demand statistics and the historical patterns found. The analyst then tried to forecast future trends and shifts in demand leading to estimates of new potential end-use demand. The problem of substitutes and competing products, of course, had to be considered in such forecasts. In many industries this involved an analysis of foreign as well as domestic demand and supply. Such analysis is still in its initial stages.

The heart of any really sophisticated system of forecasting that includes demand and supply analysis will eventually rest on input-output tables. However, such tables were not used in the past and are not generally used at present, but they could be used in the future for industry analyses.

Input-output tables indicate how much each industry requires of the production of each other industry in order to produce each dollar of its own output. The various industrial subdivisions are listed both vertically and horizontally, similar to an intercity mileage chart on a road map. The individual inputs into a given industry are read vertically, while the industry's dollar sales to other specific industries are read horizontally. This is called an *input-output flow table,* as it shows the flow of dollar sales from each industry to other industries. Another table is prepared that is based on the flow table but that divides each column in the flow table by the *output* of the using industry. This table effectively presents the requirements of an industry for each dollar of its output and therefore is called an *input-output coefficient table.* Reductions to company bases are still some time off.

Input-output analysis has a variety of applications, including evaluating an individual firm's sales potential and probing the implications of broad economic programs. But such company forecasts are still some years off.

ANALYZING GROWTH

After the analyst has projections for GNP and its components and for specific industries, he will proceed to analyze past growth of the company, current factors, and then make his projections for that company.

Charting as an Aid in Analyzing Growth

In analyzing growth, the analyst will find it helpful to chart certain data from available statistics in areas such as sales, by-products, net income, cash flow, and earnings per share. He can do this comparative analysis for a period of years for the same company, and he should also compare the data with past records and projections for competing companies.

In such charting it is helpful to use semilogarithmic chart paper. Arithmetically ruled paper can give misleading results, as equal space on the chart reflects *equal absolute quantities,* not rates of growth. On the other hand, with semilogarithmic chart paper, equal space changes represent *equal percentage* changes, and thus changes in rates of growth are highlighted. With index numbers, a base year or period is shown, and the resulting index numbers for each year clearly show the relative percentage changes from the base year. Semilogarithmic paper serves the same purpose. The slope of a line and the changing character of the slope on semilogarithmic paper indicate the stability or the accelerating or decelerating nature of the rate of growth. Mere extrapolation of the future is never justified.

Growth in Sales or Gross Revenues

While growth in earnings and especially in earnings per share is what the investor is most concerned with because this provides the basis for increased future earnings, dividends, and higher stock prices, it will be exceptional for earnings to increase for any extended period of time if this increase is not the result of a growth in sales (or gross revenues). Therefore, the analyst first concentrates on the record of sales growth and a projection of sales. Furthermore, there must be a growth in demand to make possible a growth in sales. All such analysis begins with a review of the past record, in effect a demand-supply-price analysis for the industry and the company.

The analyst tabulates past sales growth for a period of years, at least 5 and preferably 10 years. He calculates the compounded rate of growth and the regularity or the irregularity of the rate of growth. The resistance of company sales to general economic recessions is of interest, as well as the trend in sales. In this respect, it is often useful to plot the long-term secular trend on a chart and to analyze the variability and persistence of that trend. The analyst should compare the sales record and rate of growth with those of competing industries to the extent that such comparisons are meaningful. For example: aluminum vs. copper; glass containers vs. tin, aluminum, and paper containers; and synthetic fibers vs. natural fibers. Finally, the sales record should be compared with the record of GNP and any major components of GNP that provide meaningful comparison; for example, sales of department stores or drug companies might best be correlated with disposable personal income since their products are consumer goods. A true "growth" situation will show a more rapid growth than the economy as a whole and the major components of GNP to which it is related.

An analysis of total sales dollars of a company may give a misleading impression of growth. During an inflationary period, especially a temporary period of fairly rapid inflation, a company may well report rising dollar sales that do not represent growth in underlying demand for the company's output but merely rising prices with a constant or declining number of units being sold. A rapid-growth company, on the other hand, could report a similar rate of growth in dollar sales but be experiencing a much more rapid real rate of growth. It may not be raising prices (or decreasing them) as it realizes the benefits of economies of scale in a growing market, but the number of units sold may be expanding rapidly. Recent SEC requirements for publication of sales breakdowns and profits breakdowns by levels of business have been very helpful for analysts.[11]

---

[11] See the discussion of SEC requirements in Chapters 13, 15, and 16.

Unit sales should be analyzed as well as dollar sales. In most cases, unfortunately, the analyst can only obtain units produced rather than sold. Production may be going into inventory, as in the case of steel in the first six months of 1968, rather than representing sales. Later sales may draw not only on production but also on inventory. However, over any extended period in a well-managed company, unit production must correlate closely with unit sales.

The analyst can secure unit production data from numerous sources. The U. S. Government's yearly *Statistical Abstract of the United States* furnishes a great amount of data on this subject. Current data can be obtained from the *Survey of Current Business,* trade periodicals, and industry associations. In addition, the *Federal Reserve Bulletin* furnishes the Index of Industrial Production monthly in total and subdivided into many industry comparisons. In the latter case, indexes are shown rather than actual production units; but for the purpose of analyzing growth, they serve the same purpose as actual unit production figures and could even be converted to units for approximations. Industry trade associations also provide data.

Industry price data must also be analyzed. The dollar sales figures for industries and companies are the result of multiplying unit sales by the price of these sales. The price level in any industry is the result of the meeting of demand and supply forces in the marketplace. There is a strong tendency in industries in the pioneering stage for prices to be relatively high, and then this is usually followed by a declining price trend as the advantages of large-scale production are evidenced and as the industry reaches out for larger markets. Furthermore, increasing competition is encountered in the expansion stage, and the desire to utilize unused capacity often spurs price reductions. Finally, industrial companies may not come in line evenly as markets expand but in large fits and spurts that are not always synchronized with demand. There is also a problem if inflationary forces are strong in the nation as in 1941-1957 and 1969-1973. Under such conditions, the cost of labor and materials rises and industries attempt to raise prices to maintain profit margins. For various reasons, some industries do not have a demand situation that will support raising prices sufficiently to offset rising costs, and government controls may restrict price increases as in 1972-1973.

The analyst should review the past price record and the current situation relative to general and more specialized price indexes and relative to the record of prices of competing products. The price record is one good indication of the strength and the growth of demand. Grodinsky felt that a relative rise in prices compared with a competitive industry or the general price level was one danger signal suggesting approaching maturity and/or decline.

Price data and price indexes can often be used to reduce industry and company dollar sales to a unit equivalent basis to analyze the growth of unit sales where physical unit statistics are not available.

In the final analysis, the analyst must ascertain the determinants of the sales record he is studying. He is attempting to forecast *future* sales trends, and he must decide whether the sales pattern that existed in the past will persist in the future. If changes seem likely, he must determine the estimated extent and nature of the changes. Mere extrapolation is never wise.

Growth in Earnings

The investment value of a stock and its market price over any period of time are determined by its earnings and by its expected earnings and dividends. Gross revenues (mainly sales) are the basic source of funds; gross revenues less expenses result in corporate earnings. There may be sales or revenue growth over the years without a correlated growth in earnings, or in fact the sales growth may be accompanied by a decrease in earnings. Earnings growth provides both an important part of the funds as well as the incentive to increase sales capacity. On the negative side, exceptionally high profits may attract entry of other firms and, therefore, more competition into the field.

Investors, in the final analysis, are interested not in growth in total corporate net earnings as such, but in growth in earnings per share. There can be growth in total net earnings, but a slower or even negative growth in earnings per share because of an increase in the number of shares outstanding (earnings dilution). Growth in earnings per share can be the result of either growth in the rate of return on the stockholders' equity or growth in the total equity per share, or both. Volatility is also very significant.

Over any extended period of time there usually must be an increase in total invested capital and in stockholders' equity to provide increases in earnings per share. It would be unusual simply to have an increased rate of return on a more or less stable equity base. A growth in stockholders' equity and in equity per share is the result of either earnings retention (the payment in dividends of less than 100% of earnings) or the sale of additional stock at prices in excess of book value. The most important source of the growth of assets of industrial corporations has been retained earnings, and for some corporations this has been the sole source of growth.

For other corporations the source of growth of assets has been a combination of retained earnings, the sale of debt instruments or other increases in liabilities (such as increases in liability "reserves" of insurance companies or deposits in banks), and the sale of common and preferred stock.

An increase in assets resulting from an increase in liabilities does not increase the stockholders' equity at the time of the increase in liabilities but only if earnings on the additional assets exceed the cost of capital, that is, the cost of the increased liabilities. It results from financial leverage.

As a result of retaining earnings (and for all corporations over any extended period the payout of the earnings ratio is less than 100%),[12] the rate of growth of earnings per share is the product of the rate of return on equity times the rate of earnings retained. In calculating the annual rate of return on equity, it is more meaningful to use as the equity base an average of the equity at the beginning and the end of the fiscal period, thus allowing for the flow of retained earnings into investment and into equity during the year.

If corporations overall or in terms of the DJIA or the Standard & Poor's indexes retain 45% of earnings (as was the case generally in the 1960s) and if they earn pre-tax 10%-13% (average 11½%) on their total equity, then the annual compound rate of growth of earnings per share can be calculated at 11½% x 45%, or 5.18% per year. With a 13% rate of return, the percentage is 13% x 45%, or 5.85% per year earnings growth. It may be estimated that the GNP will grow at a rate of 5%-6½% per year (allowing for a rate of inflation of 1½% per year) and at 6-7½% per year (allowing for a rate of inflation of 3½% per year). The expected corporate earnings growth rate would tend to parallel the growth rate for the GNP but probably over time at a slightly slower rate. In the *exceptional* period 1960-1966, the growth rate was much higher; but long-term, the growth rate for profits was a little lower than GNP and a declining ratio to GNP.

Rate of Return on Sales and on Equity

The analyst is interested not only in the historical rate of return on equity but also in the reason for this rate of return on equity. The net rate of return on sales is one source of the rate of return on equity. The investor is also interested in both the turnover rate of total invested capital (sales to invested capital) and the turnover rate of equity capital (sales to equity capital). Given a stated rate of return on sales, the higher the turnover rate of stockholders' equity, the higher the rate of return on this equity. Table 14-8 shows the effect of changes in the turnover rate of stockholders' equity and in the rate of return on sales. Table 14-9 shows the historical record of these ratios for major durable and nondurable industries.

---

[12] The 1930s was an exception, as corporations in total during the 1930s did pay out over 100% of net profits after taxes, although in no year did they pay out more than 75% of cash flow.

TABLE 14-8

Rate of Equity Turnover, Net Profit Margin on Sales, and
Rate of Return on Stockholders' Equity

Rate of Equity Turnover	×	Net Profit Margin on Sales	=	Rate of Return on Stockholders' Equity	Rate of Equity Turnover	×	Net Profit Margin on Sales	=	Rate of Return on Stockholders' Equity
1	×	1%	=	1%	1	×	4%	=	4%
2	×	1%	=	2%	2	×	4%	=	8%
3	×	1%	=	3%	3	×	4%	=	12%
1	×	2%	=	2%	1	×	5%	=	5%
2	×	2%	=	4%	2	×	5%	=	10%
3	×	2%	=	6%	3	×	5%	=	15%
1	×	3%	=	3%	1	×	6%	=	6%
2	×	3%	=	6%	2	×	6%	=	12%
3	×	3%	=	9%	3	×	6%	=	18%

It is clear from Table 14-8 that the rate of return on stockholders' equity can grow either as the result of an increase in the rate of equity turnover or an increase in the rate of return on sales, or both.

Tables 14-8, 14-9, and 14-10 simply present the income statement rates of return using the final net profit margins on sales. In addition, the analyst may also calculate other ratios such as:

1. Ratio of operating income (before taxes) to sales.
2. Ratio of nonoperating income (before taxes) to sales.
3. Ratio of net income (before taxes) to sales.
4. Ratio of net income (after taxes) to sales. (Most important.)

The analyst can then multiply each of the ratios shown above by the turnover rate of stockholders' equity to arrive at the rate of return on stockholders' equity in terms of (1) operating income, (2) net income before or after taxes, and (3) nonoperating income. In the case of non-operating income ratios, these nonoperating income figures also include nonoperating expense items, and the ratio of nonoperating income to sales may be negative. Adjustments for extraordinary items must be made.

The equity turnover component of profits growth can be subjected to more critical analysis. For example, the asset turnover (the ratio of sales to operating assets) can be calculated. This ratio is especially useful in comparing different companies in the same industry, indicating the extent to which each dollar of operating assets produces a dollar of sales or the management's efficiency in utilizing the assets.

TABLE 14-9

Relation of Profits After Taxes to Stockholders' Equity and to Sales, All Manufacturing Corporations, by Industry Group, (1950-72)

Year or quarter	All manufacturing corporations [1]	Total durable [2]	Motor vehicles and equipment	Aircraft and parts	Electrical machinery, equipment, and supplies	Machinery (except electrical)	Fabricated metal products	Primary iron and steel industries	Primary nonferrous metal industries	Stone, clay, and glass products	Furniture and fixtures	Lumber and wood products (except furniture)	Instruments and related products	Miscellaneous manufacturing (including ordnance)
						Durable goods industries								
Ratio of profits after Federal income taxes (annual rate) to stockholders' equity—percent [3]														
1950	15.4	16.9	25.3	...	20.9	14.1	16.0	14.3	15.1	17.7	15.2	17.5	16.7	12.3
1951	12.1	13.0	14.3	...	14.0	13.0	13.4	12.3	13.8	14.2	11.3	11.9	13.2	9.7
1952	10.3	11.1	13.9	...	13.7	11.3	10.1	8.5	11.6	11.7	8.6	8.5	11.6	7.0
1953	10.5	11.1	13.9	...	13.1	9.8	9.8	10.7	11.1	11.8	8.2	7.1	11.4	8.2
1954	9.9	10.3	14.1	...	12.4	8.6	7.6	8.1	10.4	12.5	6.0	6.3	12.3	7.5
1955	12.6	13.8	21.7	...	12.3	10.3	10.0	13.5	15.5	15.6	9.2	11.1	12.5	8.5
1956	12.3	12.8	13.1	...	11.4	12.6	10.7	12.7	16.4	14.9	11.6	8.7	12.4	11.6
1957	10.9	11.3	14.2	17.7	12.5	10.7	9.3	11.4	9.3	12.4	8.5	4.7	12.0	7.7
1958	8.6	8.0	8.2	13.2	10.2	6.9	7.3	7.2	6.0	10.2	6.3	5.7	10.6	8.2
1959	10.4	10.4	14.5	8.1	12.5	9.7	8.0	8.0	7.9	12.7	8.9	9.4	13.1	9.3
1960	9.2	8.5	13.5	7.3	9.5	7.5	5.6	7.2	7.1	9.9	6.5	3.6	11.6	9.2
1961	8.9	8.1	11.4	9.8	8.9	7.8	5.9	6.1	7.1	8.9	4.9	4.1	10.6	9.9
1962	9.8	9.6	16.3	12.7	10.0	9.1	7.9	5.4	7.5	8.9	7.9	5.6	12.0	9.4
1963	10.3	10.1	16.7	11.3	10.1	9.6	8.3	7.0	7.6	8.7	8.3	8.2	12.1	8.8
1964	11.6	11.7	16.9	12.2	11.2	12.5	10.1	8.8	9.8	9.6	10.1	9.9	14.4	9.5
1965	13.0	13.8	19.5	15.2	13.5	14.1	13.2	9.8	11.9	10.3	13.4	10.1	17.5	10.7
1966	13.4	14.2	15.9	14.4	14.8	15.0	14.7	10.2	14.8	9.9	14.2	10.0	20.9	15.4
1967	11.7	11.7	11.7	12.9	12.8	12.9	12.7	7.7	10.9	8.2	12.1	8.6	18.0	13.1
1968	12.1	12.2	15.1	14.2	12.2	12.3	11.7	7.6	10.8	9.2	12.2	14.6	16.6	12.4
1969	11.5	11.4	12.6	10.6	11.1	12.2	11.3	7.6	12.2	9.2	12.6	13.0	15.6	11.6
1970	9.3	8.3	6.1	6.8	9.1	9.8	8.5	4.3	10.6	6.9	7.9	5.6	14.3	10.0
1971	9.7	9.0	13.1	5.8	9.5	8.7	8.3	4.5	5.1	9.2	9.5	11.4	13.6	9.0
1971: I	8.9	8.0	14.8	5.4	8.0	7.5	7.1	5.0	6.7	3.1	4.9	6.7	10.2	8.6
II	10.7	10.8	15.6	6.7	9.7	9.3	10.2	8.5	8.1	12.5	10.5	12.4	14.2	10.6
III	9.3	8.1	7.0	6.5	9.4	8.4	9.4	.5	2.1	12.1	11.5	14.0	15.0	10.3
IV	9.8	9.3	14.7	4.4	10.8	9.6	6.4	4.1	3.3	8.8	11.0	12.2	14.7	6.3
1972: I	9.5	9.3	16.2	6.4	8.5	9.5	9.4	4.0	5.7	5.0	9.8	12.3	12.8	8.1
II	11.3	12.4	18.7	9.1	11.1	12.0	12.3	7.5	7.5	12.7	14.3	18.6	14.2	11.0
III	10.1	9.6	5.5	6.8	10.2	11.3	12.0	5.0	4.9	13.4	13.2	18.7	15.1	9.9
Profits after Federal income taxes per dollar of sales—cents														
1950	7.1	7.7	8.3	...	7.2	7.3	6.8	7.9	10.2	10.1	5.1	9.4	8.6	5.6
1951	4.8	5.3	4.7	...	5.0	5.5	5.0	5.8	7.8	7.1	3.4	5.5	6.1	3.7
1952	4.3	4.5	4.7	...	4.5	4.8	4.0	4.7	6.7	6.6	2.7	4.1	4.8	2.7
1953	4.3	4.2	3.9	...	4.1	4.2	3.6	5.3	6.3	6.5	2.6	3.5	4.6	2.9
1954	4.5	4.6	5.1	...	4.5	4.4	3.1	5.3	6.6	7.4	2.1	3.4	5.5	2.8
1955	5.4	5.7	6.9	...	4.4	5.1	3.8	7.2	8.3	8.6	2.9	5.4	6.0	3.1
1956	5.3	5.2	5.2	...	3.8	5.4	4.0	6.7	9.3	8.2	3.4	3.9	5.8	3.6
1957	4.8	4.8	5.4	2.9	4.2	4.8	3.6	6.6	6.6	7.5	2.6	2.3	5.7	2.5
1958	4.2	3.9	4.0	2.4	3.8	3.7	3.1	5.4	4.7	6.8	2.0	2.8	5.4	3.0
1959	4.8	4.8	6.3	1.6	4.4	4.8	3.2	5.4	5.8	7.9	2.7	4.2	6.5	3.5
1960	4.4	4.0	5.9	1.4	3.5	3.9	2.4	5.1	5.4	6.6	2.1	1.7	5.9	3.5
1961	4.3	3.9	5.5	1.8	3.5	4.1	2.5	4.6	5.3	5.8	1.6	1.9	5.4	3.6
1962	4.5	4.4	6.9	2.4	3.7	4.5	3.1	3.9	5.5	5.6	2.3	2.5	5.9	3.4
1963	4.7	4.5	6.9	2.3	3.8	4.7	3.2	4.8	5.3	5.3	2.4	3.3	6.0	3.3
1964	5.2	5.1	7.0	2.6	4.2	5.8	3.7	5.6	6.5	5.6	2.9	3.9	7.2	3.6
1965	5.6	5.7	7.2	3.3	4.8	6.2	4.5	5.7	7.3	5.9	3.7	4.0	8.6	3.8
1966	5.6	5.6	6.2	3.0	4.8	6.4	4.9	5.8	8.2	5.6	3.9	3.8	9.5	4.9
1967	5.0	4.8	4.9	2.7	4.4	5.7	4.5	4.8	6.8	4.8	3.5	3.4	8.5	4.2
1968	5.1	4.8	5.7	3.2	4.3	5.5	4.1	4.6	6.2	5.2	3.4	5.3	8.1	4.0
1969	4.8	4.6	4.7	3.0	3.9	5.4	3.8	4.4	6.6	4.7	3.5	4.8	7.8	3.8
1970	4.0	3.5	2.6	2.0	3.3	4.6	3.0	2.5	6.2	3.6	2.5	2.5	7.3	3.4
1971	4.1	3.8	4.6	1.8	3.5	4.2	2.9	2.6	3.3	4.5	3.0	4.4	7.2	3.2
1971: I	3.9	3.5	5.2	1.7	3.1	3.8	2.6	2.9	4.4	1.8	1.7	3.0	5.7	3.3
II	4.5	4.3	5.4	1.9	3.7	4.3	3.5	4.1	4.8	5.8	3.3	4.7	7.4	3.8
III	4.1	3.5	2.8	2.2	3.6	4.1	3.3	.3	1.4	5.4	3.6	5.2	8.0	3.7
IV	4.1	3.8	4.9	1.4	3.8	4.6	2.1	2.5	2.3	4.3	3.3	4.5	7.7	1.9
1972: I	4.0	3.9	5.4	2.1	3.2	4.7	3.1	2.3	3.7	2.7	3.0	4.4	7.3	2.8
II	4.5	4.7	5.8	2.9	4.0	5.4	3.8	3.7	4.5	5.8	3.9	5.8	7.6	3.5
III	4.2	4.0	2.1	2.3	3.8	5.3	3.9	2.6	3.2	5.9	3.6	5.7	8.0	3.2

Nondurable goods industries

Year or quarter	Total nondurable [1][2]	Food and kindred products	Tobacco manufactures	Textile mill products	Apparel and related products	Paper and allied products	Printing and publishing [1]	Chemicals and allied products	Petroleum refining	Rubber and miscellaneous plastic products	Leather and leather products
Ratio of profits after Federal income taxes (annual rate) to stockholders' equity—percent											
1950	14.1	12.3	11.5	12.7	10.1	16.2	11.5	17.8		16.9	10.9
1951	11.2	8.1	9.5	8.2	2.9	13.9	10.3	12.2	15.2	14.8	2.1
1952	9.7	7.6	8.4	4.2	4.4	10.5	9.1	10.9	13.3	11.1	5.8
1953	9.9	8.1	9.4	4.6	5.1	10.1	9.4	10.7	13.4	11.3	6.0
1954	9.6	8.1	10.2	1.8	4.5	9.9	9.2	11.6	12.7	10.6	5.9
1955	11.4	8.9	11.4	5.7	6.1	11.5	10.2	14.7	13.4	13.2	8.5
1956	11.8	9.3	11.7	5.8	8.1	11.6	13.0	14.2	13.9	12.2	7.2
1957	10.6	8.7	12.5	4.2	6.3	8.9	11.7	13.3	12.5	11.1	7.0
1958	9.2	8.7	13.5	3.5	4.9	8.1	9.0	11.4	10.0	9.1	5.7
1959	10.4	9.3	13.4	7.5	8.6	9.5	11.4	13.7	9.8	11.0	8.5
1960	9.8	8.7	13.4	5.8	7.7	8.5	10.6	12.2	10.1	9.1	6.3
1961	9.6	8.9	13.6	5.0	7.2	7.9	8.5	11.8	10.3	9.3	4.4
1962	9.9	8.8	13.1	6.2	9.3	8.1	10.3	12.4	10.1	9.6	6.9
1963	10.4	9.0	13.4	6.1	7.7	8.1	9.2	12.9	11.3	9.2	6.9
1964	11.5	10.0	13.4	8.5	11.7	9.3	12.6	14.4	11.4	10.6	10.5
1965	12.2	10.7	13.5	10.9	12.7	9.4	14.2	15.2	11.8	11.7	11.6
1966	12.7	11.2	14.1	10.1	13.3	10.6	15.6	15.1	12.4	12.2	12.9
1967	11.8	10.8	14.4	7.6	12.0	9.1	13.0	13.1	12.5	10.3	11.9
1968	11.9	10.8	14.4	8.8	13.0	9.7	12.5	13.3	12.3	12.3	13.0
1969	11.5	10.9	14.5	7.9	11.9	10.1	12.6	12.8	11.7	10.3	9.3
1970	10.3	10.8	15.7	5.1	9.3	7.0	11.2	11.4	11.0	7.1	9.4
1971	10.3	11.0	15.8	6.7	11.2	4.8	10.7	11.8	10.3	9.6	8.2
1971: I	9.8	10.2	14.8	4.6	5.5	4.9	7.9	11.7	11.0	7.6	8.3
II	10.6	11.5	15.7	7.2	10.9	5.9	10.8	12.8	9.9	10.9	8.1
III	10.6	11.7	17.1	6.5	12.5	5.3	10.4	11.8	10.6	9.3	7.9
IV	10.2	10.6	15.3	8.2	15.1	2.9	13.6	11.0	9.8	10.5	8.3
1972: I	9.8	10.1	15.1	6.4	10.9	6.5	7.6	12.8	8.8	10.2	
II	10.2	11.7	15.9	7.3	9.3	10.5	12.6	12.9	7.4	12.1	6.3
III	10.5	11.4	15.3	7.3	12.4	8.6	12.6	12.9	8.6	10.0	10.6
Profits after Federal income taxes per dollar of sales—cents											
1950	6.5	3.4	4.9	5.8	2.8	8.8	4.5	10.3	L	5.8	3.7
1951	4.5	2.0	3.8	3.4	.6	6.6	3.7	6.5	11.1	4.5	.6
1952	4.1	1.9	3.2	1.9	1.0	5.7	3.3	6.1	10.1	3.6	1.8
1953	4.3	2.0	3.7	2.2	1.2	5.4	3.4	6.1	10.4	3.8	1.8
1954	4.4	2.1	4.2	1.0	1.1	5.6	3.4	6.8	10.6	4.0	1.9
1955	5.1	2.3	4.8	2.6	1.3	6.1	3.6	8.3	11.1	4.4	2.5
1956	5.3	2.4	5.0	2.6	1.6	6.1	4.2	8.0	11.6	4.4	2.1
1957	4.9	2.2	5.2	1.9	1.3	5.0	3.7	7.6	10.6	4.2	2.0
1958	4.4	2.2	5.4	1.6	1.0	4.7	3.1	7.0	9.5	3.5	1.7
1959	4.9	2.4	5.4	3.0	1.5	5.2	4.0	7.9	9.5	4.0	2.2
1960	4.8	2.3	5.5	2.5	1.4	5.0	3.6	7.5	9.9	3.6	1.6
1961	4.7	2.3	5.7	2.1	1.3	4.7	2.8	7.3	10.3	3.8	1.1
1962	4.7	2.3	5.7	2.4	1.6	4.6	3.4	7.4	9.7	3.7	1.8
1963	4.9	2.4	5.9	2.3	1.4	4.5	3.2	7.5	10.8	3.6	1.8
1964	5.4	2.7	5.9	3.1	2.1	5.1	4.3	7.9	10.9	4.1	2.6
1965	5.5	2.7	5.9	3.8	2.3	4.9	4.8	7.9	11.1	4.3	2.8
1966	5.6	2.7	5.9	3.6	2.4	5.4	5.1	7.8	11.2	4.4	3.0
1967	5.3	2.6	5.9	2.9	2.3	4.7	4.4	6.9	11.0	3.9	3.0
1968	5.2	2.6	5.5	3.1	2.4	4.7	4.1	6.8	10.7	4.5	3.3
1969	5.0	2.6	5.2	2.9	2.3	4.8	4.7	6.5	10.1	3.8	2.6
1970	4.5	2.5	5.8	1.9	1.9	3.4	4.2	5.9	9.3	2.7	2.5
1971	4.5	2.6	6.1	2.4	2.4	2.3	4.1	6.1	8.3	3.6	2.2
1971: I	4.4	2.5	6.0	1.7	1.3	2.5	3.1	6.2	8.9	3.1	2.3
II	4.6	2.7	6.0	2.6	2.4	2.8	4.1	6.4	8.0	3.9	2.3
III	4.6	2.8	6.5	2.4	2.6	2.5	4.0	6.1	8.7	3.5	2.1
IV	4.3	2.5	6.0	2.9	3.0	1.4	5.0	5.7	7.5	3.9	2.2
1972: I	4.2	2.4	5.9	2.3	2.3	3.0	3.0	6.4	6.8	4.0	2.8
II	4.3	2.7	6.2	2.5	2.0	4.6	4.8	6.3	5.8	4.3	1.7
III	4.4	2.6	6.0	2.6	2.3	3.8	4.9	6.5	6.8	3.7	2.8

[1] Includes newspapers beginning 1969.
[2] Includes certain industries not shown separately.
[3] Annual ratios based on average equity for the year (using four end-of-quarter figures). Quarterly ratios based on equity at end of quarter only.

Note.—For explanatory notes concerning compilation of the series, see "Quarterly Financial Report for Manufacturing Corporations," Federal Trade Commission.

Source: Federal Trade Commission.

TABLE 14-10

Effect of Capitalization (Financial) Leverage—Five-Year Period

	Return on Total Capital	Return on Equity
Coastal States Gas Producing Co. (utility)	9.9%	28.8%
Continental Telephone Corp.	8.2	20.4
Panhandle Eastern Pipe Line Co.	7.6	19.1
General Telephone & Electronics Corp.	7.2	13.8
Texas Utilities Co.	7.3	14.4
RCA Corporation	13.4	20.3
Trans World Airlines, Inc.	8.4	19.9
Beneficial Corp.	7.1	19.0
General Dynamics Corp.	11.2	18.6
American Airlines, Inc.	7.4	18.3
Eastern Air Lines, Inc.	5.0	18.0
Crown Cork & Seal Company, Inc.	10.9	16.8
Georgia-Pacific Corp.	8.4	13.8
C.I.T. Financial Corp.	5.6	13.5
Celanese Corp.	7.1	13.0
Owens-Illinois Inc.	7.4	12.8
Pittston Co.	7.9	12.6
General American Transportation Corp.	6.1	12.4
Tenneco Inc.	5.8	12.2
Airco Inc.	7.4	11.6
Kaiser Aluminum & Chemical Corp.	6.5	11.4
Uniroyal, Inc.	6.9	10.1
Aluminum Company of America	6.5	10.0
Reynolds Metals Co.	5.5	8.8

Chapter 9 discussed leverage as indicated by capitalization ratios, including the advantages and the disadvantages (risks) of leverage for stockholders. The ratio of operating assets to stockholders' equity can also be calculated. This ratio indicates the number of dollars of assets working for each dollar of stockholders' equity. This is a way of measuring the extent to which the corporation is using other-than-equity capital to acquire assets.

As with all other ratios, the analyst is interested in reviewing the trends over a period of years for the ratios discussed in this section. If the ratio of sales to operating assets is increasing, it may at first glance be assumed that the corporation is using its assets more efficiently by securing a growing amount of sales for each dollar invested in assets; *but it may also* indicate a need for more investment in assets. Conversely, if the ratio is declining, either it may indicate declining utilization of assets or it may indicate that the industry has increased its capital to a point substantially exceeding current demand and that this has resulted in declining sales prices reflecting more competitive pricing.

There is one other factor that may influence the ratio of sales to operating assets. There has been an increased use of leased assets as opposed to purchased assets in many industries. Sales may be increased because of the increased use of leased assets, but the leased assets do not appear on the balance sheet. If the effect of leasing is not recognized, incorrect conclusions may be drawn from the trend of the ratio of sales to operating assets.

The conclusion of any investment analysis of a corporation is the projected rate of growth of earnings and the actual projected earnings and dividends that will result from this rate of growth and their volatility.

Corporations are in business to make a profit, and the major tests of corporate management are the rates of return earned on sales, on total capital invested, and on stockholders' equity. The difference between the latter two ratios indicates the effect of leverage. Table 14-10 shows the effect of capitalization leverage over a 5-year period for selected companies.

Management and Earnings Growth

Management has the responsibility of generating sales (or gross revenues) and the responsibility of controlling costs with the aim of obtaining the maximum proportion of revenues to net profit. Finally, it has the responsibility of maintaining the rate of return on total capital invested in assets and the rate of return on stockholders' equity. The record in these respects indicates the quality of management. Superior management will earn the highest rate of return on total invested capital and on stockholders' equity. Financial success is the result of high-quality management and failure is the result of poor management. Rate of return *and* its volatility are important.

It is very difficult to measure the quality of management other than as indicated above, but professional analysts are constantly attempting to make such qualitative judgments in their financial reports to companies. They attempt to learn as much as possible concerning management policies and the direction of these policies. However, they will have more faith in stated management policies and the direction in which management says it is headed if past statements of management policies have actually resulted in the realization of the stated goals as shown by the quantitative record.

The financial analyst visiting with management and attempting to reconcile stated policies with actual results will attempt to assess the intensity of management's desire for the company to grow rather than the desire to rest on its laurels. In this respect, the age of management is often quite important. As management ages, there can be a tendency to slow down. This tendency can be offset by the regular influx of younger blood into top management as shown by a policy of mandatory retirements and the training and development of junior management for positions of responsibility. The analyst must be aware of one negative factor disclosed by numerous studies. These studies have shown in many cases a much closer correlation between the size of a business (sales and assets) and management compensation than between net profits and management compensation. Therefore, the analyst must determine if the company places emphasis on growth in profits and not merely growth in total assets and sales. Still, the investor wants a management dedicated to sales growth, because without growth in revenue there cannot for any extended period be a growth in earnings, dividends, and stock prices.

In analyzing management and management policies and goals, the investor must realize that our economy is in a constant state of change, in some areas gradual change and in others revolutionary change. Sales growth will usually result from product and marketing research. Management must therefore follow policies that will anticipate and contribute to change in its products and product mix in competition within the industry and with other industries. Markets may be broadened not only by innovations but also by means taken to reduce costs and therefore reach larger markets by lowering sales prices.

Research and Development

In analyzing research and development, the emphasis should be not on the amounts spent *per se* but on the results of research in terms of sales and profits. Because management realizes the importance placed on research and development, there is a tendency for some managements to inflate reported expenditures on research and development by expense items that really do not properly belong in this category. The analyst can avoid this trap by concentrating on an analysis of the results of research and development. In numerous cases, management goes to the other extreme and does not report research and development expenditures separately; but because it is results that count, this policy is not as much of a handicap to analysis as some analysts would imply. In any case, the diligent analyst can get some help in determining the amounts spent by checking the companies' registration statements under both the SEC Act of 1933 and the SEC Act of 1934, now required for over-the-counter securities as well as for securities listed on exchanges.

In analyzing company research and development, some companies provide assistance to the analyst by dividing research and development expenses into three headings: (1) basic research, (2) product-oriented research, and (3) specialized research, the latter usually under contract with the government. While contract research for the government does not directly and immediately help the company's civilian business knowledge and experience, gains are often transferable to civilian products.

Most companies do not spend an important part of research and development expenditures on basic research, although the hope of such research is that some of it will produce some practical results in the long run. Usually, it is only very large and profitable companies that believe they can justify significant expenditures for basic research. Outstanding examples are American Telephone & Telegraph Company and RCA Corporation. Most companies stress mainly product research.

On the other side of the research and development problem is the record of many new companies started by engineers and scientists to capitalize on their research ideas. In many cases, the results have been unsatisfactory since innovators have often lacked practical business know-how and have been long on imagination but short on the requirements of the marketplace and the necessity to be profit-oriented. But there have been numerous spectacular successes which have caused this type of "investment" to be attractive to many investors.

Innovation involves risk, and success is usually the result of a balance between fostering innovation without accepting exceptionally large risks requiring large amounts of capital. On the other hand, management that overemphasizes the risk aspect will be deterred from obtaining exceptional growth. Exceptional profit growth will usually be the result of accepting above-normal risk. Again the age of top-level management is a factor. Older management, in general, is usually less willing to take important risks.

The size of a company also enters into the risk picture. Large companies (such as RCA Corporation and International Business Machines) can accept substantial dollar amounts of risk that cannot be assumed or even financed by smaller companies. In respect to size, the marketing aspect of converting innovations into sales and profits is as important as innovation itself and most of the time exceeds substantially the research and development expenses.

Size provides both the funds and the opportunity to successfully promote new products. However, there have been numerous exceptions.

Growth Through Mergers

The post-World War II years have witnessed the largest and by far the greatest merger movements in our history. Mergers provide the fastest method of corporate growth. One of the major problems involved in mergers of successful companies is the problem of the management of the companies involved. Top management of the constituent company being absorbed now finds that it is no longer the top management but subservient to other top management. This can interfere with the successful operations of the companies in the merged enterprise. Historically, the major justification for mergers has been the argument that the merged companies can operate more efficiently and with lower overhead. The advantages of economy of size include lower operating costs and smaller financial costs. In recent years it appears that numerous mergers have placed undue emphasis on the financial aspect of the merger, rather than on opportunities for higher profits for the constituent companies as compared to their results when they were separate entities. Specifically, in the conglomerate field, management may take advantage of the relative popularity of such companies with investors and the resulting relatively high price-earnings ratios at which their stock sells in the market. For example, assume that a parent-conglomerate whose stock is selling at 20x P/E acquires, on an exchange-of-stock basis, companies selling at 10x P/E. As a result of a continuing series of such acquisitions, the parent-conglomerate may show a "growth in earnings" even though the constituent companies are showing very little earnings growth. Furthermore, if the parent builds a capital structure using convertible securities, leverage may also result in "earnings growth" superior to the actual earnings growth of the constituents. In analyzing management aspects of mergers, the analyst will wish to carefully analyze management policies in these respects, seeking real and not illusory growth in earnings.

As a company grows, the problems of top management in handling the larger company also increase. In the case of conglomerates, the problems may multiply sharply. Managements that were successful in managing companies of a given size and in only one industry may prove to be less successful in meeting the problems of rapidly expanding companies. The analyst must constantly measure the performance of management as a company grows, particularly if the growth is spectacular as a result of mergers and heavily diversified.

Historically, management has usually been faced with a period of digestion as it has acquired companies of any significant size. This has been a period of adjustment before the expected economies are effected. One seeming phenomenon of the merger movement of the 1960s was the apparent ability of management to escape the difficulties of such an adjustment period. But the record of 1969-1973 brought out the major weakness in many of the former popular conglomerates, and drastic declines in the stock prices resulted.

QUESTIONS

1. It has been said that "growth" is the normal characteristic of the American economy. What is the significance of this statement to investors? What investment philosophy is suggested?

2. (a) What has been the long-term growth rate in GNP in our economy?
   (b) Has the recent growth rate in GNP been higher or lower than the long-term growth rate? How does inflation affect the statistics?
   (c) Of what significance are growth rates of GNP to investors?

3. What are the most important underlying factors to study in attempting to project consumer expenditures in the future?

4. (a) What are input-output tables? In your answer distinguish between the input-output flow table and the input-output coefficient table.
   (b) Of what use might such tables be to investment analysts?

5. Explain the concept of a life cycle of an industry.

6. Discuss the usefulness and the limitations of the "industrial life cycle" concept from the standpoint of investment analysis.

7. Discuss the charts you would draw to aid in analyzing sales growth of a company and what you would specifically look for in the analysis of those charts. Note specifically the data you would include in the charts, the time period you would study, and the scale you would use in constructing the charts.

8. (a) Why should the analyst carefully study unit-sales data as well as dollar-sales data?
   (b) Of what significance is the product price record of a company?

9. (a) What are the two basic factors underlying growth in earnings per share? Why is volatility as important as growth?
   (b) How would you assess the likely effect of earnings retention on future earnings per share?
   (c) Carefully explain the relationship between profit margins and rate of return on equity capital and on total capital for a given company.

10. (a) How would a security analyst attempt to determine whether or not management had a sufficiently broad conception of its market?
    (b) What factors would you study in evaluating the management of a company? Do analysts often rely on their intuition in this respect?

WORK-STUDY PROBLEMS

1. Select three industries you believe will outperform the economy over the next five years and justify your choices.
2. (a) Select two companies in the same industry, with quite different price-earnings ratios, and prepare charts that you feel would be helpful in studying their growth trends in sales and earnings and their volatility.
   (b) Prepare sales and earnings projections for these companies for the next five years, carefully noting the assumptions underlying your projections.
   (c) What factors underline differences in growth rates and volatility of earnings of the two companies as observed by you?

SUGGESTED READINGS

Andrews, John R., Jr. "The Fundamental Case for Investing in Growth." *Financial Analysts Journal* (November-December, 1970), pp. 55-64.

Babcock, Guilford C. "The Concept of Sustainable Growth." *Financial Analysts Journal* (May-June, 1970), pp. 108-114.

Bellemore, Douglas H. *The Strategic Investor.* New York: Simmons-Boardman Publishing Company, 1963.

Bleakley, Fred. "Burt Dorsett: For CREF, A Continuing Faith in Growth." *The Institutional Investor* (January, 1971), pp. 57-60, 86-88.

———————. "How Persistence Has Paid Off for T. Rowe Price." *The Institutional Investor* (April, 1972), pp. 60-62, 106-118.

Bolton, Steven E. *Security Analysis and Portfolio Management.* New York: Holt, Rinehart and Winston, 1972. Chapter 5.

Fredrikson, E. Bruce. *Frontiers of Investment Analysis,* 2d ed. Scranton, Pa.: Intext Educational Publishers, 1971. Chapters 28-30.

Good, Walter R. "Valuing Quality Growth Stocks." *Financial Analysts Journal* (September-October, 1972), pp. 47-56.

Levy, Haim, and Marshall Sarnat. *Investment and Portfolio Analysis.* New York: John Wiley & Sons, Inc., 1972. Chapter V, Sec. 7.

McDonald, J. G., and A. K. Fisher. "New Issue Stock Price Behavior." *The Journal of Finance* (March, 1972), pp. 97-102.

Robichek, A. A., and M. C. Bogue. "A Note on the Behavior of Expected Price/Earnings Ratios Over Time." *The Journal of Finance* (June, 1971), pp. 731-735.

Schulkin, Peter A. "Real Estate Investment Trusts." *Financial Analysts Journal* (May-June, 1971), pp. 33-39, 74-78.

Wallich, Henry C. "Does the Volatility of Growth Stocks Demonstrate Irrational Behavior?" *The Institutional Investor* (January, 1970), pp. 36-49.

15

Major Problems in
Security Analysis

The goal of security analysis is the selection of securities best suited for each type of portfolio—securities that offer the best relative values among the literally thousands of issues available. *Security analysis* may be defined as the analysis of the economic and financial record of industries and the particular companies (and their securities) operating in those industries for the practical purpose of determining the probabilities in terms of expected future income, quality, estimated value, and price of a particular security relative to other available securities. *Future income* to the investor—the overall rate of return expected—consists of interest income from debt securities, dividend income from stocks, plus capital appreciation or minus capital losses. To the investor the future income from a security will be determined by the future income of the issuer of a security, i.e., the rate of growth and stability of future earnings of the security. In order to project the future record which determines the value of a security, the past record and current characteristics of that security must be analyzed.

FUNCTIONS AND EXTENT OF SECURITY ANALYSIS

Listed below are several functions of the security analyst. To execute these functions properly, the security analyst will need a sound training in economics, accounting, corporate finance, and money and banking, as well as in the historical behavior of the securities markets as discussed in Chapters 3 and 4.

1. Obtaining the facts—to gather the pertinent facts on industries and companies and other issues, past and current, as a basis for projections of sales and earnings.

2. Analyzing and interpreting the facts—with special attention to financial facts and adjustment, when necessary, of reported financial data to ascertain the recurring earning power of the corporation (for noncorporate issues, the income available from specific securities) and to obtain a basis for reasonable projections of earnings and financial strength and quality of securities of an issuer.

3. Projecting industry and company sales and earnings and valuation of securities.

4. Selecting—to determine the relative attractiveness of a security, compared to alternative investments, at its current price or at some other stipulated price level in terms of its calculated investment value, the latter based largely on a projection for common stock of the rate of growth and stability of future earnings.

5. Advising—to prepare recommendations to buy, hold, sell, or exchange specific issues for specific types of portfolios based on sound principles and pertinent portfolio characteristics and to consider future probabilities for the security developed in the analysis. This involves balancing risks *vs.* probable rewards in terms of expected overall rate of return.

The extent of an analysis varies with its purpose; the complexity of the problem; the characteristics of the industry involved; and the data, time, and funds available. In the text we develop procedures for an in-depth analysis of the type prepared for financial institutions and for regulatory statements and prospectuses. In the latter case, of course, the analyst has the full cooperation of management to a greater extent than is the situation for analysts employed by investment banking and brokerage firms, trust departments of commercial banks, and corporate pension funds. On the other hand, analysts in some brokerage firms are pressured to produce a large output of reports, and such reports are often superficial and of little value. In Chapter 13 we reviewed the major types of source information available to financial analysts and investors. The quality of an analysis depends upon the time and effort expended and the analyst's judgment. A large number of securities are scanned to select those to be analyzed.

FACTORS UNDERLYING SECURITY ANALYSIS

In making an analysis of securities, both qualitative and quantitative factors must be considered. A general discussion of these factors follows.

Qualitative Factors

Qualitative factors such as industry characteristics, the quality of management, and the quality of research and development are rather *subjective* as is also to a large extent the factor of projections (trends) of *quantitative data* such as earnings and dividends. Qualitative factors are considerably more difficult to evaluate than actual quantitative data relating to past or current experience. The *quantitative* factors are those largely contained in the company's financial exhibits: the balance sheets, income statements, and supplementary schedules such as sources and application of funds statements and related cash flow figures. The quantitative factors include assets, liabilities, capitalization, sales and expense breakdowns, earnings, dividends, and similar data. These appear to be quite objective, although as will be seen the determination of exactly what figures to report and the manner in which they are reported does depend on numerous subjective judgment decisions. In the analysis of a specific company, the major *quantitative* factors can be analyzed with considerably more confidence than the *qualitative* factors taken separately, although the *quantitative* factors are the end result of the *qualitative* factors.

The major qualitative factors are: (1) determination of the characteristics of the industry and the company, especially the expected future stability or volatility of industry and company sales and earnings; (2) estimation of the future *trend* of industry and company sales and earnings and *rate of growth* of each; (3) interpretation of the quality of research and development in terms of past, current, and expected future results; and (4) rating the overall quality of management separately from the quantitative results to the extent that this is practically possible.

Of course, qualitative factors are reflected in statistical results; but their analysis, independent of income statement and balance sheet figures, is a difficult and complicated task. Nevertheless, judgment on qualitative factors is an indispensable part of any complete study of a security. Unfortunately, after reading many published analyses, one is frequently left with the impression that the judgment of qualitative factors is far easier than is in fact the case. Sometimes some of the qualitative factors are expressed in quantitative terms. The qualitative factors are inherently *subjective* in nature, and expressing them in quantitative terms does not make them *objective* factors. The fact that they are only probabilities should be emphasized.

Theoretically, in some cases a bond of a company might deserve a quality rating while the common stock does not, because investors assume that the past record implies great future stability in sales, earnings, and cash flow and a satisfactory margin of safety over fixed charges and debt amortization, even though significant growth is not anticipated. On the other hand, investors are usually not willing to accept the risk position of a common stockholder *if* there can be no reasonable probability of growth in earnings at least to the growth in earnings for corporations taken as a whole. If there is little or no expected growth, rarely will investors rate a common stock as being high quality. If no growth of recovery in earnings is expected, the investor should prefer a bond investment, but not bond investment in a company where the projection is for no growth in sales and earnings.

All *trend* projections are based on subjective, qualitative factors, including the vital projections of the growth rate for earnings and dividends as well as projected earnings and dividends themselves. Trend projections must be recognized for what they are, an exercise in *probabilities*.[1] However, because of the exact mathematical figures produced, trend projections are often given the stature of a preciseness that is not possible; at most, all that is obtained is a *range of probabilities*. This is one of the dangers of the newer highly mathematical approaches that tend to imply an element of preciseness that is impossible to attain.

This does not mean that future projections, because they are qualitative and quite subjective and require a high level of judgment by the analyst, are not worthwhile and in fact essential; it merely emphasizes the uncertainties and the factor of probability. Because of these factors, investors tend to favor those situations where they believe the uncertainties appear at a minimum. The same cannot be said for speculators, many of whom would pose as investors. Furthermore, the analyst tends to select those commitments where he believes the uncertainties are offset by a large margin of safety and that he considers to possess inherent factors of stability. Many investors and analysts tend to favor those industries and companies that appear to have the best prospects, hoping that the exceptionally good prospects visualized will overbalance ever-present factors of uncertainty. However, if there is a rather general agreement among investors as to the bright prospects for a particular industry and company, the price of the stock of such companies often reflects this to such an extent that there is, in fact, no margin of safety to offset uncertainties. All favorable factors are fully discounted and unfavorable factors are ignored. Finally, the further into the future the projections, the greater the uncertainty and the risks recognized by the analyst.

Qualitative factors, such as excellent management and research and development, are too often given exaggerated priority with respect to the company and the stock involved. What is expected of management and research is to produce an above-normal rate of return on investment. Since this factor, if present, will be clearly evident in quantitative figures, both actual and projected, policy should be initiated to avoid "double counting," that is, paying twice for the same factors. A price-earnings ratio higher than is deserved should not be applied to expected abnormally high earnings growth simply because of excellent management, which in fact is responsible for

---

[1] The student should be familiar with probability theory as developed in such books as W. C. Guenther, *Concepts of Probability* (New York: McGraw-Hill Book Co., 1968).

the exceptionally high rate of earnings growth that has already entered into the high capitalization rate. Management's goal is to maximize earnings.

Quantitative Factors

Most of the succeeding chapters through Chapter 27 are devoted to an analysis of quantitative factors—factors that are measurable in quantitative terms—although qualitative factors will also be discussed. As noted in earlier chapters, the quality and the process of selection should rest largely on the determination of the margin of safety factors. In the case of bonds, the margin of safety is the margin of earnings and cash flow above debt and preferred stock requirements, including sinking fund and amortization requirements. In the case of common stocks, the margin of safety is the margin of value above the market price at which a common stock is available. In the latter case, in a negative sense there should at least not be any significant margin of risk measured by any overvaluation of the market price compared to the estimated range of value for the stock. The success of the investor's choice of common stocks will rest on the corporation's future earnings record. The emphasis in analysis should be to determine the *probabilities* that a corporation's future record will improve, continue its established trend, or possibly deteriorate. The quantitative figures and the qualitative factors are interpreted by the analyst's judgment, and both will be weighed in the final determination regarding an investment commitment.

PROBLEMS OF THE FINANCIAL ANALYST

A preliminary screening should have selected specific securities deserving further consideration.[2] The standards used to select specific securities for further study from the thousands available are the usual indicators of value such as earnings and dividends; quality ratings judged by such factors as expected earnings and stability and growth of earnings; standard tests of financial strength such as liquidity, capitalization, and profitability ratios; and the past market price record and its volatility. Only those securities selected in the preliminary screening warrant further and extensive analysis.

The Problem of Quality Grading

The problems of grading the quality and determining the value of securities have been discussed at some length in Chapters 9 to 14 of this book.

---

[2] The computer is proving to be an excellent tool in the initial scanning process.

In the case of debt instruments and straight-investment preferred stocks, the problem is almost entirely one of determining the quality of securities based on standards developed from past experience. The major emphasis is on ability to meet all obligations in years of poor business by a sufficient margin of safety so that at all times investors in general will have no doubt about the company's ability to meet its obligations. These standards are largely based on an analysis of one type of risk—the financial risk or quality of the issuer's credit. It is readily acknowledged that the purchaser of a nonconvertible limited-income security accepts knowingly the interest rate and purchasing power risks inherent in such securities.

In the case of the lower-grade bonds and preferred stocks, the requirements for analysis tend to take on the aspects of common stock analysis. Standards and principles are not, and probably cannot be, as well standardized as is the case for investment-grade bonds, private placements, and investment-grade preferred stocks. In the case of common stocks, there is not only the problem of quality gradation, but also the much more difficult and necessary subsequent step of valuation in both the absolute sense and relative to other investment opportunities.

The problem of *quality grading* common stocks is not essentially different from the process of grading bonds and preferred stocks. In fact, it is difficult to think in terms of a quality bond or a quality stock if the other securities of the issuer do not also deserve a quality rating. As previously noted, the *quality* identification procedure rests largely on the past record and the current financial credit of the issuer and is largely an *objective* procedure. In fact, for a large proportion of common stocks, the job of quality identification and gradation has been done satisfactorily in the market itself, reflecting the opinions of thousands of professional analysts and the investors whom they advise. In most cases, a company that an investor would, after careful analysis, select as the quality company in a particular industry has also been so selected by the professional analysts and reflected in the "market" where it sells at the highest price-earnings ratio and the lowest yield of any stock in its industry. To a lesser but important extent (except perhaps in the elusive area of stock currently designated as high-growth stock), the market has also done a fairly good job of relative quality selection among all stocks in terms of price-earnings ratios and yield.

The Valuation Problem

With common stocks, the *valuation problem* is of supreme importance and rests more on the future prospects for the company than on its past record. The very best quality common stocks may be so overpriced in the market in terms of any reasonable valuation that their price reflects, in part, a heavy speculative element. While the quality grading procedure is largely *objective,* the valuation procedure for common stocks contains a very strong *subjective* element—the investor's judgment as to probabilities for future earnings and dividends, the rate of growth of earnings and dividends and the stability of such growth, and finally the capitalization rate to be applied to earnings. The *probabilities* are in a wider range than in the case of quality gradation because so much depends on the uncertainties of the future. The further one attempts to project, the greater the uncertainties.

In the area of valuation and selection of common stocks, specialization has been as important as in other professional areas, such as law and medicine, because of the complexities of our economic world. Therefore, there are utility analysts, railroad analysts, bank stock analysts, insurance stock analysts, and specialists in chemicals, drugs, autos, steel, and so forth.

In earlier discussions it has been noted that some investors select and buy common stocks merely because they "expect" them to "do well" over the coming months or year—"doing well" meaning outperforming the general market. This is the "anticipation" approach. Unfortunately, many institutional investors, especially mutual funds, as well as individuals, had been lured into this "one-year performance" category in the late 1960s. Many suffered heavy losses in 1969-1970. But a growing number of professional analysts attempt to determine either *absolute* or *relative values* for common stocks and on this basis recommend the best values available at any stage of the market. This approach can be described as an attempt to develop an "appraisal value" or "investment value" for a stock.

In the latter case, the valuation appraisal depends largely on projections of earnings and dividends to determine a *probability range* for earnings and dividends and thus a range of value for a stock. As pointed out previously, many academicians advocate the "present value" approach based on very long-range projections of earnings and/or dividends or the growth rate for the latter. The professional analysts have rarely accepted this challenge because they believe that such very long-term projections cannot develop estimates of sufficient probability to be of practical value. *On the other hand, the professionals as well as lay investors do,* to a large extent, use the "capitalization approach" to common stock valuation and selection, with earnings and dividends projected for from 3 to 6 years, or in a few cases up to a maximum of 10 years. The capitalization rate used is based on the expected capitalization rate for the DJIA and the S&P indexes over the next 3 or 6 years and at the end of the period and on an estimate of the market's capitalization rate for the industry and company concerned. The latter is based on the past capitalization rate related to the market indicators and the expected rate of growth and stability of earnings and dividends for the company in question, also related to expectations for the market indexes. Such procedures may also encompass the present value of the expected price of the stock 3 or 6 years hence, the latter based on the expected earnings and dividends for that target year and the expected price-earnings ratio for the stock in that target year based on expected earnings growth and earnings. This present value technique is quite different from that of the J. B. Williams through Lerner and Carleton present value school, which advocates very long-term projections of dividends (and in some cases earnings).

The Problem of Projecting Earnings and Cash Flow

The financial analyst must project earnings and cash flow of issuers of securities. But historically, as well as currently, nonfinancial analysts have tended to be quite critical of valuations of financial analysts based on the projections of future earnings even though pure logic must support the premise that the value of a security of a business must rest on the future, not the past. Even when valuations are prepared, based solely on the past record, these must imply at the very least that the past can be merely extrapolated into the future—a dangerous assumption. Unless one wishes merely to extrapolate the past, financial analysis must terminate with a projection of the future earnings and the valuation of the securities of the issuer.

There has been intelligent recognition that the value of a business and its common stock rests on expected earnings for a long period of time. Years ago Mr. Justice Holmes stated, "The commercial value of property consists of the expectation of income from it." While criticism of the procedure of determining the value of common stock on the basis of projected earnings has continued to the present time, more recently there has been recognition of the realities of this procedure in the securities markets by the following groups that have had the major impact in the determination of accepted accounting principles: the AICPA, the SEC, and the Financial Analysts Federation.[3]

View of the AICPA. Two studies of the American Institute of Certified Public Accountants are cited in this section. In Accounting Research Study

---

[3] Congress in 1971 for the first time injected its judgment into "accepted accounting principles" by legislation: ". . . no taxpayer shall be required to use any particular method of accounting for the investment credit in reports subject to any federal agency." Further, Congress injected the Treasury Department (rather than the SEC) into the area by requiring consistency in the use of the accounting method selected for reporting the investment credit unless the Treasury Department consents to a change.

No. 2 (1962), "Cash Flow Analysis and the Funds Statement," Items 13-14 read as follows:

> The security analyst is primarily concerned with two problems:
> (1) The earnings trend in relation to the securities of a particular company—here he is concerned with the past and current earnings and financial strength in order to project earnings.
> (2) The investment features of one company as compared to another—he compares the potential earnings and the financial strength of various companies.

In a report on "Symposium on Ethics in Corporate Fnancial Reporting," *The Journal of Accountancy* (January, 1972), the section on Published Forecasts and Financial Reporting read as follows:

> Another major subject considered at some length in the symposium was whether or not the publication of historical financial statements constituted sufficient financial disclosure by corporations. . . .
>
> While it was apparent from the discussion that total agreement was far from being reached on the subject of published forecasts, there was considerably greater feeling in favor of some form of forecasting than had existed three years before—there was general agreement that one logical step was to pursue the forecasting issue in a systematic fashion at a subsequent meeting of the four sponsoring organizations.

At this symposium Commissioner James Needham of the SEC commented that the SEC was rethinking its historical opposition to the publication of forecasts in registration statements and other published documents.[4]

View of the SEC. Statements made by SEC Chairman William J. Casey which were cited in two articles of *The Journal of Accountancy* follow:

> . . . the SEC should "re-examine" its policy of neither requiring nor permitting the inclusion of predictions in securities filings. . . . The time has come to take a broader view of *what is pertinent to investment values* and the obligation to convey *economic reality* as management knows it to stockholders and investors.[5]

---

[4] "Symposium on Ethics in Corporate Financial Reporting," *The Journal of Accountancy* (January, 1972), p. 48. This symposium, held on November 18-19, 1971, was sponsored by the American Institute of Certified Public Accountants, the Financial Analysts Federation, the Financial Executives Institute, and the Robert Morris Associates at Seaview Country Club, Absecon, New Jersey. In three years (1971 versus 1968) a significant change in viewpoint could be detected. Among the participants the financial analysts seemed generally in agreement that public forecasting was an idea whose time had come while corporate executives, although not agreeing that regular published forecasts were the right answer, did concur that financial management had a responsibility to avoid surprises and that regular published forecasts was one of the ways of meeting this responsibility. Several executives, however, preferred the approach of giving assistance to analysts so that their forecasts were not too far away from reality as currently perceived by the corporations.

[5] "SEC Taking New Look at Profit Forecasting Policy," *The Journal of Accountancy* (January, 1972).

Mr. Casey pointed out that *his belief in the need for predictions* of business activity was at variance with an SEC study done a scant three years ago. He said that it seemed irregular to him that projections of sales and income, deemed to be relevant for trading market purposes, were traditionally not required in prospectuses.

In the other article, Chairman Casey declared that the SEC is "pushing as hard as we know how the principle that if forecasts are put out at all, they should be made available to everyone." He said that some forecasts are "pivotal to today's trading market and, since they are in fact being used so widely, perhaps they should be permitted in disclosure documents." Further, he stated that "the securities markets are essentially markets for discounting future incomes and that investors are future oriented." But the disclosure system, which is supposed to help investors, blocks out "any reference to the matters in which investors are most keenly interested," namely, projections of future earnings and market values of assets carried at depreciated historical cost.[6]

The Problem of Financial Reporting to Outsiders

The federal securities acts had three major goals as far as financial information was concerned: (1) the prevention of dissemination of fraudulent and purposely misleading financial information; (2) the requirement for full disclosure of material information necessary to make investment decisions; and (3) the maintenance of fair and equitable trading markets and the prevention of manipulation in these markets (the 1934 Act deals in this area). The first of these goals—the prevention of dissemination of fraudulent and purposely misleading information—has to an important extent been accomplished. However, the requirement that financial information should be sufficiently *uniform* as between companies to meet the needs of analysts and investors has certainly not been satisfactorily accomplished, but progress in this area is constantly being made.

Fraudulent and Purposely Misleading Reports. Since the passage of the federal securities legislation in the early 1930s as discussed in Chapter 14, those who use published financial statements have had little to criticize in the sense of fraudulent or purposely misleading statements. The enforcement agency, the SEC, has to a large extent successfully prevented the dissemination of fraudulent and misleading financial reports. Until the 1964 Amendments, this legislation covered only new issues registered under the Securities

---

[6] "SEC Pressing for Forecasts, Chairman Casey Announces," *The Journal of Accountancy* (March, 1972).

Act of 1933 and securities registered on national exchanges. As a result of the 1964 Amendments, the legislation now also applies to over-the-counter securities, where the issuer has total assets in excess of $1,000,000 and a class of equity securities "held of record by 500 or more persons." Therefore, to an important extent the war against *fraudulent and purposely misleading* statements has been largely won.

Inadequate Disclosure vs. Lack of Uniformity.[7] For some years a battle has raged over whether the information problem is largely one of "inadequate disclosure" or one of "lack of uniformity" in corporate reporting. At the outset it should be stated that this book is largely on the side of those who have stressed lack of uniformity in corporate reporting as the *main* problem, which, however, does not imply that there are not some disclosure problems. The SEC has placed most of its efforts on the requirement of full, accurate, and adequate disclosure of material information while lately stressing clarity for investors and more material for analysts.

---

[7] The reader should review the article by Leonard Spacek, "Are Double Standards Good Enough?" *Financial Analysts Journal* (March-April, 1965), pp. 17-21 and 23-26, an address before the New York Society of Security Analysts, on September 30, 1964 by Mr. Spacek of Arthur Andersen and Co., one of the largest and most respected accounting firms. In this article he stated: "The Securities and Exchange Commission has a responsibility only to Congress for its supervision of accounting and financial reporting. It has no responsibility to the investor. The SEC, like you and the stock exchange, relies upon the financial information presented by the corporation on the basis that it has been double checked . . . by the public accountant . . . and therefore must be appropriate for public consumption. . . . SEC's 29th Annual Report (stated) . . . The Commission's principal means of providing investor protection from inadequate reporting, fraudulent practice and overreaching by management is by requiring a certificate by an independent public accountant . . . an opinion . . . that the financial statements are presented fairly, in conformity with accounting principles and practices which are recognized as sound and which have attained general acceptance." Mr. Spacek adds: "Our profession has concluded that accounting practices need not be the same among companies, if there is 'authoritative support' for alternate practices . . . practices followed by other companies, or it may be expressed in a text book . . . (However) consistency in reporting among companies in the same industry would be helpful for investors. The result is that we have double-standard accounting . . . double standards which result in several methods of providing for depreciation, in several methods of accounting for goodwill, and in the omission of certain types of liabilities from the balance sheet.

"An illustration of the effect . . . (in) recent losses to the public . . . (in) savings and loan stock. Deferred taxes aggregating up to one half of reported income had not been accrued . . . and the bad debt reserves were usually classified as capital. . . . While deferred taxes represent a source of interest-free capital, they do not constitute income in any year until the deferred tax is eliminated. . . . The savings and loan stocks were sold as growth stocks, and the amounts shown in earnings in place of the low earnings which would have been reported under methods followed by other industries, were undoubtedly used by public investors as an indicator of future prospects. It is fortunate that usually only one industry at a time comes face to face with some of the consequences of this type of accounting. When the investor becomes aware of inadequate accounting in several industries at *one* time, we will have another 1932."

The disclosure school states that "given sufficient disclosure, the investor or analyst can make whatever adjustments are necessary to arrive at the uniformity he desires." Even if this is true, which is doubtful, why should the investor or the analyst be required to spend this time and effort, as for example in searching through SEC filings? Why should there not be more consistency within industries to make figures from annual reports more comparable and useful on their face? Should not the statements be prepared for the *user* rather than only in terms of what the accountants have traditionally advocated and managements desired? *Users* desire statements that are reliable and informative for their needs in appraising the company and in making intercompany comparisons. Some have claimed that investors have asked for fish and received a serpent. *Users* of statements are not so much interested in a past accounting of stewardship as in learning the current financial standing of an enterprise and its profitability and earning power to serve as a base for projections of earnings and dividends. For example, the balance sheet "values" offsetting liabilities and capital used in determining solvency are merely (fixed asset) cost figures less amortization of costs and not values in any economic sense. The economic values of assets are capitalized earning values.

No reasonable investor or analyst seeks absolute uniformity, which would eliminate any flexibility that may justifiably be required because of the complex and varied nature of business operations. But investors and analysts do seek considerably more uniformity for companies within major industry groups so that there can be comparability.[8]

---

[8] In *Accounting Research Bulletin No. 43* (New York: American Institute of Certified Public Accountants, 1961), Ch. 2, Sec. A, p. 15, the following statement concerning comparative financial statement analysis is made:

1. The presentation of comparative financial statements in annual and other reports enhances the usefulness of such reports and brings out more clearly the nature and trends of current changes affecting the enterprise. Such presentation emphasizes the fact that statements for a series of periods are far more significant than those for a single period and that the accounts for one period are but an installment of what is essentially a continuous history.

2. In any one year it is ordinarily desirable that the balance sheet, the income statement, and the surplus statement be given for one or more preceding years as well as for the current year. Footnotes, explanations, and accountants' qualifications which appeared on the statements for the preceding years should be repeated, or at least referred to, in the comparative statements to the extent that they continue to be of significance. If, because of reclassifications or for other reasons, changes have occurred in the manner of or basis for presenting corresponding items for two or more periods, information should be furnished which will explain the change. This procedure is in conformity with the well recognized principle that any change in practice which affects comparability should be disclosed.

3. It is necessary that prior-year figures shown for comparative purposes be in

The fact that the published statements are certified by CPA's as being in accordance with "generally accepted accounting principles" still gives wide latitude to management in the manner in which items are reported. Quite different results can be effected by using one acceptable method as opposed to another. This complicates considerably analysts' problems in making comparisons between companies. Accountants and management need to balance the advantages of uniformity against any *necessity* for flexibility. The greater the uniformity that can reasonably be justified, the more the statements will meet the need of the *users* for comparability. In the meantime, the analyst's job is further complicated by the lack of uniformity and he must be well aware of the deficiencies in all comparative analysis.

One question that should be asked is what would meet the disclosure requirements of financial statement users. Certainly the answer is not greater and greater disclosure *per se,* but rather the disclosure of *material* information necessary for the proper evaluation of a corporation's securities. There is no advantage in simply pouring out more and more figures of an inconsequential and immaterial nature. A mere proliferation of details may only make it more difficult to sift out the really material information. As G. K. Chesterton pointed out, "the best place to hide a leaf is in a forest." It is not the quantity of information alone, even where computers are available, that leads to more effective evaluation of a corporation and its stock, but rather the significance and the materiality of the data available and the clarity of presentation.

To a large extent then, the question is one of *materiality* of disclosure and not complete disclosure.[9] Accountants and corporate management should be encouraged to publish only information that financial analysts and other users of the data indicate they consider useful and not what accountants consider to be essential.

---

fact comparable with those shown for the most recent period, or that any exceptions to comparability be clearly brought out.

If the investor finds that statements for prior-years or between companies are not comparable, he must make adjustments so that they will, in fact, be comparable to the extent that information is available. Otherwise, he cannot establish relative values or a range of absolute values.

[9] See William Holmes, "Materiality—Through the Looking Glass," *Journal of Accountancy* (February, 1972), pp. 44-49.

Under SEC regulations, S-X-Rule 1-02 states: "The term 'materiality' when used to qualify a requirement for the furnishing of information as to any subject, *limits* the information required to those matters as to which an average prudent investor ought reasonably to be informed before purchasing the security registered." Rule-3-06 goes beyond this to say: "The information required with respect to any statement should be furnished as a minimum requirement to which should be added such further material information as is necessary to make the required statements, in the light of the circumstances under which they are made, not 'misleading.' Certainly, materiality cannot be determined only on the basis of the percentage of an item to net income or other factors. Also important is the nature of the item."

Perhaps the crux of the argument between the "disclosure" advocates and the "uniformity" advocates rests on the following point. The disclosure advocates claim to be not too concerned with the form and the arrangement of financial data in the manner desired by financial analysts, but rather that the information required by analysts appear "somewhere in the annual report," perhaps in the footnotes. This rests on the premise that if the information is disclosed, the analysts can make any adjustments in the financial statements that they deem necessary to meet their requirements.

While the "oversimplified language" approach to terminology and form is not advocated, there would seem to be no purpose (except to confuse and aggravate) in presenting material in such a manner that the job of the financial analyst, to say nothing of the reasonably knowledgeable investor, is made more demanding and time consuming than is necessary. *Accountants and management should diligently inquire* into the users' reasonable and practical requirements and then do all in their power to satisfy those needs. Reports should not be so prepared that only the very experienced professional can dig out, rearrange, and adjust the published figures by interpretation of notes to financial statements and other supplementary information elsewhere in the text of annual reports, as is necessary to arrive at an accurate appraisal of the quality of a company's securities and the value of its stock, when more effective methods of presenting the data could have been used. There is a middle ground between the "oversimplified language approach" and the "disclosure approach," and accountants and management should work it out as a "game of skill approach." *The only purpose for making the analysts' or investors' job more difficult than it is would seem to be to try to make it difficult to arrive at a true picture of the financial condition and the earnings prospects of the enterprise. The chief criticism of the preparers of published financial statements is that all too frequently they do not provide in a satisfactory form the information necessary for a proper appraisal of the enterprise.* This is still a real problem for the analyst and the investor, although constant progress is being made.

QUESTIONS

1. (a) Define the term "security analysis." What is the basic purpose of security analysis?
   (b) Outline the view of S.E.C. Chairman, William J. Casey, as suggested by his comments concerning profit forecasts during the year 1972. Do accountants generally agree with this view? Do you believe profit forecasts should be an integral part of the annual report published by business corporations? Support your position.

2. (a) What are the five functions performed by a security analyst?
   (b) What determines the proper depth and detail that should be included in a security analysis?

3. What standards would you use in preliminary screening to select those securities worthy of further in-depth study from the thousands available?

4. (a) Distinguish between the grading and the valuation of stocks.
   (b) Is a high-grade stock always a good purchase? Discuss.
   (c) Under what conditions might a bond be considered high grade while the common stock of the same company might not deserve a quality rating? Find an example of this situation in the market today.

5. (a) Differentiate between quantitative and qualitative factors to be considered in security analysis.
   (b) What is meant by "double counting" in reference to qualitative factors and management?

6. What are the shortcomings of relying on either quantitative analysis or qualitative analysis exclusively?

7. What constitutes the margin of safety for a common stock? for bonds and preferred stocks?

8. What are the major goals of the federal securities acts as far as financial information is concerned?

9. Why must the values of securities established through security analysis be relative and not absolute?

10. "Given sufficient disclosure, the investor or analyst can make whatever adjustments are necessary to arrive at the uniformity he desires." Discuss this statement in terms of your agreement or disagreement with the basic idea expressed.

11. (a) What would be appropriate guidelines for reporting if corporations are required to publish breakdowns of sales and income by major divisions so that the data published will meet the disclosure requirements of financial statement users? Discuss the SEC 10% of income basis.
    (b) What is meant by "materiality of disclosure?"
    (c) Is lack of "full disclosure" the main problem facing analysts today? Discuss.

12. What problems are created for the financial analyst by reporting techniques used by accountants in handling company pension plans?

WORK-STUDY PROBLEMS

1. Review company annual reports or Moody's manuals in order to find at least one example of a disclosure problem and one example of a problem in uniformity of corporate reporting. Describe and discuss each example.

2. (a) How do the accountants define "materiality"? Could their definition lead to reported profit results that could mislead an analyst? Discuss.
   (b) What is meant by the so-called big bath accounting by corporations? In what way or ways could such accounting mislead an analyst?

3. Select five large corporations at random. What kind of product line data was included in their last annual reports? Is the SEC likely to have different product line data than that you found in the annual reports? Do you believe the reports are adequate? Discuss.

SUGGESTED READINGS

Anderson, Arthur, & Co. *Objective of Financial Statements for Business Enterprises.* Chicago, Illinois: Arthur Andersen & Co., 1972.

Briloff, Abraham J. *Unaccountable Accounting.* New York: Harper & Rowe, 1973.

Carmichael, D. R. "Reporting on Forecasts—A U.K. Perspective." *The Journal of Accountancy* (January, 1973), pp. 36-47.

Casey, William J. "Disclosure and Form 10K." *The Journal of Accountancy* (October, 1972), p. 73.

——————. "Toward Common Accounting Standards" (Address). *The Journal of Accountancy* (October, 1972), p. 70-73.

Friend, Edward H. "A 1972 Critique on Funding Media For Pension Plans." *The Journal of Accountancy* (August, 1972), pp. 29-40.

Hagerman, R. L., Thomas F. Keller, and Russell J. Petersen. "Accounting Research and Accounting Principles" (New AICPA Financial Accounting Standards Board). *The Journal of Accountancy* (March, 1973), pp. 52-55.

Kaplan, Robert, and Richard Roll. "Accounting Changes and Stock Prices." *Financial Analysts Journal* (January-February, 1973), pp. 48-53.

Norby, William C., and Frances G. Stone. "Objectives of Financial Accounting and Reporting from the Viewpoint of the Financial Analyst." *Financial Analysts Journal* (July-August, 1972), pp. 39-45, 76-81.

Olsen, Wallace E. "Trial Period Suggested for Publication of Forecasts." *The Journal of Accountancy* (January, 1973), p. 10.

SEC Accounting Practices and Procedures, 3d ed. New York: The Ronald Press Co., 1972.

"SEC Calls for Cash Budget Forecasts for New Issues." *The Journal of Accountancy* (September, 1972), pp. 12-14.

Shank, John K. "Case of the Disclosure Debate." *Harvard Business Review* (January-February, 1972), pp. 142-158.

Woolsey, S. M. "Approach to Solving Materiality Problems" (relevance of any item included or omitted in financial statements). *The Journal Of Accountancy* (March, 1973), pp. 47-50.

Analysis of the
Income Statement

While at one time the balance sheet was considered the most important statement in the analysis process, for many years major emphasis has been placed on the income statement—not only in the case of common stock analysis, but also in the case of bonds, private placements, and preferred stock analysis. Projected earnings (and dividends) determine a stock's value.

The margin of safety for bondholders and other long-term creditors and for preferred stockholders is provided by a corporation's earnings *and* cash flow. The value of a business (of its invested capital) is the amount that can be earned on the invested capital. Therefore, the analyst must determine the hard-core earning power of the business and, especially for the common stock investor, must secure an earnings base of true recurring earnings from which he may project growth and volatility of earnings and dividends. All a common stockholder can receive from his investment is dividends and/or capital appreciation, and both are dependent upon future earnings (and expectations by investors of these future earnings and dividends).

PREPARATION OF INCOME STATEMENTS

The most fundamental accounting principle applied to the income statement is that which requires the matching of revenues and expenses. Usually annual reports and those filed with the SEC include statements from previous years and, if these are to be in fact comparable, there must be consistency in the accounting principles followed for the entire period.

Reporting Accounting Changes

The AICPA issued "APB Opinion No. 20: Accounting Changes" in July, 1971, which stated among other things:

1. A change in accounting . . . may significantly affect the presentation of both financial position and results of operations for an accounting period and the trends shown in comparative financial statements and historical summaries. The change should therefore be reported in a manner which will facilitate analysis and understanding of the financial statements.

15. . . . there is a presumption that an accounting principle once adopted should not be changed. . . . Consistent use of accounting principles from one accounting period to another enhances the utility of financial statements to users by facilitating analysis and understanding of comparative accounting data.

16. The presumption . . . may be overcome only if the enterprise justifies the use of an alternative acceptable accounting principle on the basis that it is preferable. . . .

17. The nature of and justification for a change in accounting principle and its effect on income should be disclosed in the financial statements of the period in which the change is made. The justification for the change should explain clearly why the newly adopted accounting principle is preferable.[1]

Forms to Use

There are two major forms of income statement. The first is the *current operating performance statement* or clean income statement (ordinary, recurring annual items); the second is the *all-inclusive income statement,* an example of which is shown in Table 16-1.

In December, 1966, the AICPA-APB issued Opinion No. 9, "Reporting the Result of Operations," which stated:

---

[1] "APB Opinion No. 20: Accounting Changes," *The Journal of Accountancy* (October, 1971), pp. 63-72. "This Opinion defines various types of accounting changes and establishes guides for determining the manner of reporting each type. It also covers reporting a correction of an error in previously issued financial statements. . . . The guides . . . may be appropriate in presenting financial information in other forms or for special purposes. . . . The term *accounting change* . . . means a change in (a) an accounting principle, (b) an accounting estimate, or (c) the reporting entity (which is a special type of change in accounting principle classified separately for purposes of this Opinion). A change in accounting principle results from adoption of a generally accepted accounting principle different from the one used previously for reporting purposes. The term *accounting principle* includes 'not only accounting principles and practices but also the methods of applying them.' . . . . Changes in accounting principle are numerous and varied. They include . . . a change in the method of inventory pricing, . . . a change in depreciation method for previously recorded assets, . . . a change in the method of accounting for long-term construction-type contracts, . . . and a change in accounting for research and development expenditures, . . . and . . . a change in accounting principle to effect a change in estimate."

TABLE 16-1

All-Inclusive Income Statement

Major Divisions	Comments
Gross Sales or Revenues	Usually not given.
Sales Returns and Allowances and Cash Discount	Usually not given.
Net Sales or Revenues	Usually the first item in the income statement. SEC requires a breakdown of sales (and profits) by line of business.
Other Income	Listed here in the AICPA recommended form; but if it is material, analysts prefer that it be listed below where indicated.
Cost of Goods Sold	Rarely broken down into its components.
Gross Profit	Net sales less cost of goods sold.
Gross Profit Margin	Percent of gross profit to sales calculated by analyst.
Selling Expenses	Promotion, selling, and distribution expenses.
General Administrative Expenses	Salaries, wages, office supplies, insurance, taxes other than income taxes, etc.
Profit from Operations	
Profit from Operations—Margin	Percent of sales; operating profit margin calculated by analyst.
Other Income	Nonoperating income such as dividends and interest income. When it is regular and recurring in nature, the AICPA recommends showing it separately under net sales; but if the item is substantial, analysts prefer that it be located here in the statement.
Other Expenses	Nonoperating expenses such as bond interest, note interest, amortization and bond discount.
Income Before Income Taxes	
Income Taxes	Federal and foreign income taxes.
Income Before Extraordinary Items	
Extraordinary Income and Extraordinary Expenses	Nonrecurring items of material amount, net of applicable income tax. Major items should be explained.
Net Income	
Net Income—Profit Margin	Net profit on sales calculated by analyst.
Retained Earnings at Beginning of Year	
Cash Dividends on Common Stock	(Also preferred dividends if any.)
Cash Dividends as a Percentage of Net Income	Payout ratio calculated by analyst.
Retained Earnings at End of Year	

Per Share of Common Stock:
  Income Before Extraordinary Items
  Extraordinary Items Net of Taxes
  Final Net Income
  Dividends	

The Board has concluded that *net income should reflect all items of profit and loss recognized during the period* (the all-inclusive income statement) with the sole exception of the prior period adjustments described (paragraphs 23 and 25). Extraordinary items should be segregated from the results of ordinary operations and shown separately in the income statement (at the bottom) with disclosure of the nature and amounts thereof. . . .

The principal advantages are: (a) inclusion of all operating items related to the current period, with segregation and disclosure of extraordinary items; (b) a reporting of current income from operations free from distortions resulting from material items directly related to prior periods; and (c) proper retroactive reflection in comparative financial statements of material adjustments relating directly to prior periods. . . .

Earnings per share should be disclosed in the statement of income—especially if per share data should disclose amounts for (a) income before extraordinary items; (b) extraordinary items, if any (less applicable income tax); and (c) net income, the total of (a) and (b) . . . this format will help to eliminate the tendency of many users to place undue emphasis on one amount reported as earnings per share." [2]

The analyst should prepare a spread sheet of the company's income statement for the number of years that he considers necessary, for example for 5 or 10 years. In this respect the analyst can obtain printouts from Standard & Poor's Compustat tapes which will produce all the data he needs and, in addition, contain all the ratios required including 100% statement breakdowns. It is especially important (1) that extraordinary and nonrecurring items be listed, as recommended by the AICPA, at the bottom of the income statement after net income *before* extraordinary items has been calculated and (2) that earnings per share be shown both before extraordinary nonrecurring items and after such items. The analyst in determining true recurring earnings should also add back to income any deductions for arbitrary and contingency reserves. He will adjust income tax deductions where a significant variation between reported earnings and earnings for tax purposes has been noted so as to derive a meaningful income figure for comparative and projection purposes. Finally, for comparative analysis with other companies, the analyst must recognize the lack of uniformity in reporting (as, for example, different methods used for reporting depreciation and inventory) and must make such adjustments as will provide for comparability between different companies being analyzed.

Presentation of Data

The presentation of data on all-inclusive income statements can be made in two forms: the multiple-step form and the single-step form. In the

----

[2] APB Opinion No. 13 states that the Opinion No. 9 requirement for all-inclusive income statements also applies to reporting by commercial banks.

conventional *multiple-step form*, a series of deductions and intermediate income figures are presented before arriving at the final figure for net income for the year. In the *single-step form*, the total of all expenses is deducted from the total of all income to arrive at the final figure for net income after income taxes. A comparison of the two forms is presented in Table 16-2. The multiple-step form is favored by analysts because it presents more information. The single-step form is favored by those who believe that the

---

TABLE 16-2

Income Statement Form [3]

Multiple-Step Form (Favored by Analysts)	Single-Step Form (With Other Income at Top of Statement)
Gross Sales	
Deduct Sales Returns and Allowances	
Net Sales	Sales, less Returns and Allowances
	Other Income
Deduct Cost of Goods Sold	Costs and Expenses:
	Cost of Goods Sold
Gross Profit on Sales	
Deduct Operating Expenses:	Selling Expenses
Selling, General, and Administrative	General and Administrative Expenses
	Other Expenses
Net Operating Income	
Add or Deduct Other Income and Other Expenses	
Net Income Before Income Taxes	
Deduct Income Taxes	Income Taxes
Net Income Before Extraordinary Items (net of related income taxes)	Net Income Before Extraordinary Items
Add or Deduct Extraordinary Items (net of related income taxes)	Add or Deduct Extraordinary Items (net of related income taxes)
Net Income for the Year	Net Income for the Year

---

[3] Paul Grady, "Inventory of Generally Accepted Accounting Principles for Business Enterprises," *Accounting Research Study No. 7* (New York: American Institute of Certified Public Accountants, 1965), Chapter 8, pp. 301-302.

multiple-step form is subject to misinterpretation since users of the form may gain the impression that some costs take precedence over others and that the intermediate profit or income figures represent some form of significant earning power.

Accounting for Consolidated Statements

Practically all large corporations are holding companies with subsidiaries and frequently with affiliates. A *subsidiary* is a corporation controlled by a parent company, the latter owning at least 50% of the voting stock of the subsidiary. In practice, an important proportion of subsidiaries are 100% owned. To file a consolidated tax return, the parent must own at least 80% of the voting and nonvoting stock of the subsidiary, but not including preferred stock. The definition of an *affiliate* is not so precise. It includes corporations that are effectively controlled even though there is less than a 50% ownership.

Noting the Extent of Consolidation. The first "note" to the financial statements in an annual report indicates whether they are consolidated statements and the extent of consolidation. It may state that "all subsidiaries are consolidated," or "all subsidiaries are consolidated except 'X' financial subsidiary," or "all domestic subsidiaries are consolidated but not foreign subsidiaries." The reason why the company's financial subsidiary is not consolidated is that such corporations have a very large debt-to-equity ratio, which would, if consolidated, significantly raise the consolidated debt-to-equity ratio on the consolidated balance sheet. It is assumed that a finance company, because of the liquid nature of its assets, can safely carry a higher debt-to-equity ratio; but if consolidated, its relatively large debt would have a negative effect on the parent's consolidated statement.

Consolidated statements combine all the companies involved into one corporation. Intercompany transactions are eliminated to prevent double counting. All assets and liabilities are consolidated; and all earnings and losses are consolidated in one final net income or net loss figure. Consolidation of earnings should be measured comparably against the previous record of the company to allow both the investor and the analyst a basis for analysis of company earnings and growth in earnings. Again, if a corporation consolidates when it did not do so previously, adjustments should be made in reports for previous years to make them comparable.

Equity Method vs. Cost Method of Accounting. When a corporation consolidates its 50%-or-more-owned subsidiary, it consolidates the assets and liabilities of the subsidiary into the assets and liabilities of the consolidated balance sheet (eliminating intercompany transactions) and consolidates the income or losses of the subsidiary into the consolidated statement of income. As in the past, it has frequently been the practice, where less than 50% of the stock of another corporation is owned, not to use the equity method of accounting but to merely report in the balance sheet the initial "cost" of the investment with no reflection of subsequent equity in retained earnings of the investee; and in the consolidated income account, to report only actual dividends, if any received, and not to reflect in the income statement any equity in the earnings of the less-than-50%-owned company, except when dividends are paid from those earnings.

However, in March, 1971, the AICPA issued Opinion No. 18, "The Equity Method of Accounting for Investments in Common Stock," [4] which requires that the *equity method,* rather than the *cost method*, be applied both in consolidated financial statements and in parent company statements prepared for issuance to stockholders as the financial statement of the primary reporting entry to account for investment in voting stock of:

1. Unconsolidated subsidiaries (where at least 20% of the voting stock is owned).
2. Incorporated joint ventures.
3. Other companies, 50% or less owned, over whose operating and financial policies the investor (parent company) is able to exercise "significant influence."

ANALYSIS OF ITEMS ON THE INCOME STATEMENT

The remainder of this chapter is devoted to an analysis of the major divisions that appear on an all-inclusive income statement, including the items that may be listed under each division.

---

[4] See: "APB Opinion No. 18: The Equity Method of Accounting for Investments in Common Stock," *The Journal of Accountancy* (June, 1971), pp. 63-69; and "Applying APB Opinion No. 18: The Equity Method," *The Journal of Accountancy* (September, 1971), pp. 54-62. Under the equity method the investment is initially recorded at cost. The carrying amount is adjusted to recognize the investor's share of the earnings or losses of the investee subsequent to the date of investment, with the amount of the adjustment included in the determination of the investor's net income. Dividends received reduce the carrying amount of the investment. Opinion No. 18 requires that in applying the equity method, any difference between the cost of an investment and the investor's equity in the net assets of the investee at the date of investment be accounted for as if the investee were a consolidated subsidiary. Accordingly, the cost of the investment would first be allocated to the investor's share of the investee's net identified assets and liabilities on the basis of the fair value. Only excess of the cost of the investment over the sum of the amounts so allocated should be considered to be goodwill. Such goodwill should be amortized over a period not to exceed 40 years as a reduction of the amount recognized each period by the investor as its equity in the earnings or losses of the investee.

Net Sales or Revenue

The major purpose of a business corporation is to produce sales, or revenues, and to earn a profit on these revenues. Therefore, the analyst has a major concern with the size, trend, and composition of these revenues. He reviews the level of sales over the past 5-10 years and, by using the 100% statement analysis, determines the percentage that each major income statement item bears to sales, ending with the percent that after-tax profit in operations bears to sales. Until 1970 the major difficulty found in analyzing the revenues of nonregulated enterprises was, in most cases, the inability to obtain a breakdown of sales by line of business and by product line. The more diversified the business, the more serious was the problem.

On July 14, 1969, the SEC published Securities Act Release No. 4988 which provided for amendments to Forms S-1, S-7 (for registration of securities issued under the Securities Act of 1933), and Form 10 required for registration of outstanding securities (Securities Exchange Act of 1934). A member of the American Accounting Association's Committee of Accounting Theory Construction and Verification observed that:

> These amendments require disclosure of the nature of business done and intended to be done by the registrant and its subsidiaries with respect to sales and profit information by lines of business . . . they are not binding as reporting standards for annual reports to shareholders. As a practical matter . . . they may be viewed as applying to annual reports to shareholders. . . . There seems little advantage, therefore, for companies not to disclose sales and profit data by segments in annual reports to shareholders when such information is included in reports filed with the SEC.[5]

The analyst's job, after reviewing the past and latest current figures that are available, is to project revenues for the next 3, 5, and perhaps even 10 years by analyzing industry and company product and services *demand* as well as *supply* and *price* factors and then by projecting company income statements, including net profit margins and net profits. The projection of costs is, of course, also a problem. Some analysts merely project sales and

---

[5] K. Fred Skousen, "Standards for Reporting by Lines of Business," *The Journal of Accountancy* (February, 1970), pp. 39-46. Skousen adds that: "There is also reason to believe that the above amendments will apply to all corporations required to file Form 10-K—the annual report filed by a corporation with the SEC under the 1934 Act. . . . Some will continue to argue that the extended disclosure requirements are too stringent, that the potential dangers of such disclosures are greater than the potential benefits which may be derived; others will assert that the requirements are too flexible, that they do not go far enough. Another group . . . a majority in the opinion of the author, will view the reporting standards as useful guidelines for providing relevant and necessary information for the investing public. . . . It can only be hoped that such extensive, unified and dedicated efforts accomplish their intended purpose of providing financial information in the interest and for the protection of the investing public. . . ."

profit margins, then project profits from estimated revenues on this basis. (See Chapter 12.)

Registered corporations are required by federal securities legislation to make interim reports. Investors in reviewing quarterly, semiannual, and nine-month published income figures must recognize the seasonal nature, if any, of certain corporate incomes. For example, in such cases the investor can be greatly misled if he multiplies quarterly figures by four- or six-month figures by 2. Instead, when there is an important seasonal element, the investor should review the quarterly and semiannual results of previous years, calculate the seasonal factor, and interpret current interim reports in the light of the past year's figures. Furthermore, the investor must realize that it is usual for corporations to make final-year adjustments in the final quarter of the year—adjustments that have not been reflected in quarterly, semi-annual, or nine-month reports. Again, reference to adjustments in the final quarter of previous years may aid the investor in his estimate of earnings for the current fiscal year, although this method cannot be assumed to be a complete answer since major differences may appear in different years.

Cost of Goods Sold

The major items in cost of goods sold are inventory costs. At the same moment that income is increased by revenues derived from the sale of a product sold, it is also decreased by the cost of that product in modern accounting. In actual practice, accountants usually determine the cost of goods sold by adding the value of inventory on hand at the beginning of a period to that acquired during the period, thereby determining the cost of goods available for sale. The value of the goods on hand at the end of the period is subtracted from the total cost of goods available for sale to determine the cost of goods sold figure used in the income statement. This figure should never be combined with selling and administrative expenses, as the details are needed to facilitate effective analysis. Unfortunately, however, many companies do not report these items separately.

Determining the appropriate cost to apply to the goods remaining in the ending inventory when price levels are changing requires choosing a costing method that assumes the order in which units of production will be sold. Most important in this respect are the *first-in, first-out* (Fifo) method and the *last-in, first-out* (Lifo) method of costing inventories.

Fifo and Lifo Inventory Accounting. Traditionally inventories were carried on the Fifo basis, which assumed that the cost flow was first-in, first-out. This is consistent with the actual physical practice of using the goods received first. However, during the period since 1941, inflation has been a "way of life." Many companies have shifted to the Lifo method—last-in, first-out. This assumes, for accounting purposes, that the goods last acquired are the first sold. In a period of rising prices, the use of Fifo results in inventory profits that inflate total profits; and if reporting for tax purposes is on this basis, it results in higher taxes. The items "first in" "cost of goods sold" are the lowest cost items, and yet sales are on a current price basis. On the other hand, the use of Lifo results in the last or higher cost items being used in "cost of goods sold"; therefore, a lower profit is reported than if Fifo is used. In a period of rising prices, Lifo will result in lower profits in the income statement and therefore lower income taxes; it will also result in a lower inventory figure in the balance sheet and a lower net worth figure because the higher cost figures have been removed from inventory. Finally, because Fifo accounting incorporates inventory gains and losses, profits usually appear to be more volatile during the course of the business cycle than under Lifo.

Rules Governing the Use of Lifo. The tax laws permit the use of Lifo by *all* companies who choose to do so, but they must comply with certain requirements. The inventories must be reported on a cost basis. Furthermore, *the taxpayer who uses the Lifo method for tax purposes must also use the Lifo method in all published financial statements.* However, if sound accounting practice dictates that inventories be marked down to market, which is below cost, this procedure may be followed in the company's annual published financial statement, but the amount of the reduction is not available as a tax deduction.

A corporation may change to Lifo simply by notifying the Treasury Department, giving the details of the type of inventories carried and the exact method to be used in valuing additions to inventories. The Treasury Department will then affirm or disapprove the specific details of the Lifo method that the company intends to use. Once the Lifo method is approved and is used, the corporation *must* continue to use the method until the Internal Revenue Service approves a request for change.[6] The company may not shift back and forth to benefit taxwise.

---

[6] Sometimes, erroneously, Lifo is assumed to be a method of adjusting for overall or general changes in the price level. In "Reporting the Financial Effects of Price-Level Changes," *Accounting Research Study No. 6* (New York: American Institute of Certified Public Accountants, 1963), on page 40 the following statement is made:

. . . If the most recent purchase prices are used in calculating the Lifo cost of materials used or Lifo cost of goods sold, they will in most cases correspond closely to the replacement costs in the market at the end of the current period. Except by coincidence, these specific replacement costs [for specific products], whether taken

The analyst can use any of the following ratios in analyzing inventories: (1) inventories to net working capital; (2) current debt to inventories; (3) cost of goods sold to inventories [7] (inventory turnover); and (4) inventory to sales. Trends for "unfilled orders" are also analyzed.

Gross Profit and Gross Profit Margin

Net sales minus cost of goods sold yields gross profit on sales, which taken as a percentage of sales produces the gross profit margin. This is a useful tool for comparison of different years for the same company and for comparison between companies assuming that the figures used are comparable, that is, that inventory accounting policies are similar and that the components of "cost of goods sold" are similar, which is not always the case. As noted above, if inventory methods have been changed, adjustments must be made if possible to make the past years' figures comparable. For a particular company, a comparison of gross profit margins for a period of years may disclose that (a) sales prices are rising or falling in relation to the cost of goods sold or (b) there has been a change in the product mix.

Selling Expenses and General Administrative Expenses

These two items are sometimes combined and sometimes shown separately. Even if both figures are shown separately, they furnish only overall information except for the very important calculation of operating profit margin or operating ratio. This ratio of operating expenses to sales is a

---

directly from market data or approximated by the use of indexes of specific goods, *will not* coincide with the movement of prices in general as measured by an index of the general price level. Thus the general price level could be stable, while the Lifo index moved up or down; the Lifo index could be stable, while prices in general were falling or rising.

Furthermore, Lifo makes no adjustment at all for inventories on the balance sheet. The more the general price level moves, up or down, the further removed is a Lifo inventory from even approximating an inventory adjusted for changes in the general price level. Lifo is a method for excluding changes in the replacement costs of specific commodities from "realized profits"; it is not intended to and cannot cope with the measurement problem created by a change in the general purchasing power of money as measured by an "all-commodity" index.

[7] If net sales is used as the numerator rather than cost of goods sold, variations in the inventory turnover could result either from changes in the turnover of inventory or from changes in the gross margin. It would not be possible to determine the origin of change without further investigation. Cost of goods sold, on the other hand, is calculated on the same basis as inventory, and changes will represent changes in the turnover of inventory, which is what the analysts are trying to isolate. Dun and Bradstreet do relate net sales to inventory in their publications, though cost of goods sold is superior from a logical standpoint.

very important ratio because it indicates the efficiency of operations. In most cases companies report selling and administrative expenses "exclusive of items listed below." Examples of items that may be listed "separately below" are depreciation and rapid amortization, depletion, maintenance and repair, research and development expenses, rental expenses, exploratory expenses, and employee compensation and benefit payments (mainly pension costs). The analyst should calculate each of these items as a percentage of sales and should note the trends in this regard over the period of years under review.

Depreciation, Rapid Amortization, and Depletion. This item, which is a noncash and nonfund item, is of major importance—so important that the next chapter is largely devoted to it. There is considerable lack of uniformity in corporate reporting of depreciation and the related investment credit although the AICPA recommends deferred tax accounting.

Research and Development. Rapid growth of sales and earnings can be attributed largely to *quality* research and development (or mergers). Total expenditures in this area would best be analyzed by comparison with previous years and other companies, and by using this figure as a percentage of sales. Furthermore, the real test is the percentage of sales and profits that results from the company's previous research and development expenditures —what research has produced.

Another question arises in the analysis of research and development. Instead of expensing the items annually as they occur, some companies capitalize these items by debiting them to an asset account. This results in two problems:

1. The problem of meaningful comparisons between two companies or with past years. For meaningful comparisons, an adjustment must be made to place the statements on a comparable basis. This would generally mean constructing a new statement on which the items that were previously capitalized are now treated as expenses.
2. The problem of whether any research and development expense should be capitalized at all. When such items are capitalized instead of expensed, the expenses of the company are lower and the profits are higher.

The argument for capitalizing research and development items is that expenditures are being made currently but that benefits will be received for a number of years into the future. The argument for expensing these items (as with advertising and promotional expense) is that they are a necessary annual expense in our highly competitive economy and that consequently most companies expense them, which means that comparisons between companies are not possible until statements are placed on a comparative basis.

It is also true that a company which has been expensing these items may suddenly decide to capitalize them, or vice versa. This would eliminate comparability unless adjustments are made by the company in its 5- or 10-year review summary of financial reports or by the analyst. Finally, to capitalize these items is to assume future benefits that may be quite uncertain.

Rental Expenses. Today we find a large number of corporations leasing instead of owning assets. Thus lease rentals become very important expenses, as they always have been for many railroads. This important item should be, and often is, shown as a separate item in the income statement. As noted earlier, information on the details regarding lease agreements should be furnished; but such information is often presented in a sketchy and unsatisfactory manner. These are at least to an important extent equivalent to fixed charges on debt for which the lease is a substitute, and the fixed charge element of the lease rental can force a company into financial difficulties just as readily as can fixed charges on funded debt or other debt. This topic will be discussed in detail in Chapter 18.

Exploratory Expenses, Including Intangible, Drilling, and Development Costs. In the case of oil, gas, and mining companies, this classification is a major expense item. Therefore, it is important to consider it in comparative analysis between companies and for the same company in past years. Most oil and natural gas companies desire to maintain their positions in "reserves owned" relative to other companies, and this figure provides an indication of efforts in this respect. The problem is that many companies expense this item fully in published reports as is allowed for tax purposes, while others capitalize these expenses in the balance sheet and amortize them, usually over the life of the asset or the leasehold. When the analyst is making a comparative analysis between companies, he must make adjustments if possible to place the companies on a comparable basis. The company that is expensing all such items will report lower profits than the company that capitalizes them. This, at times, is important in explaining markedly different price-earnings ratios for oil companies.

Employee Compensations. This item is usually not shown separately in the income statement but is spread out over other expense items as applicable. However, the labor cost factor is highly important, and frequently the information will be presented separately from the income statement elsewhere in annual reports. Professional analysts are generally able to obtain this vital information from company sources.

Pension Costs and Other Employee Benefits. This item is, of course, an additional wage and salary cost and has been of rapidly increasing importance in the total labor cost picture. It is helpful for the analyst to have this figure for comparative analysis. Not only will the trend of higher pension costs persist, but the pressures to vest pension rights can add substantially to these costs if such vesting becomes a requirement.[8]

On the subject of accounting for the cost of pension plans, the AICPA published its recommendations and conclusions in 1966. It stated:

> Pension cost can vary significantly, depending on the actuarial cost method selected; furthermore, there are many variations in the application of the methods, in the necessary actuarial assumptions concerning employee turnover, mortality, compensation levels, pension fund earnings, etc., and in the treatment of actuarial gains and losses. . . .
>
> 23. To be acceptable for determining cost for accounting purposes, an actuarial cost method should be rational and systematic and should be consistently applied so that it results in a reasonable measure of pension cost from year to year. Therefore, in applying an actuarial cost method that separately assigns a portion of cost as past or prior service cost, any amortization of such portion should be based on a rational and systematic plan and generally should result in reasonably stable annual amounts. The equivalent of interest on the unfunded portion may be stated separately or it may be included in the amortization. . .[9]

Profit from Operations and Operating Ratio

The profit from operations is the result of deducting all operating expenses, including the cost of goods sold, from net sales. It indicates the operating efficiency of the management. The operating ratio (total operating costs as a percentage of sales) is especially useful in comparative analysis of the efficiency of competing companies and of the same company over a period of years. One should be careful that the turnover of operating assets (net sales divided by total operating assets) is similar when comparing the operating ratio of different companies. To be meaningful, the composition of operating expenses must be presented in a consistent accounting manner.

Other Income

In the past, other income, if shown separately, was usually entered in the income statement following profit from operations. If the item is

---

[8] In 1972 President Nixon sent proposed pension plan legislation to Congress, and the House Ways and Means Committee held hearings. In essence the plan involves the "rule of 50" which provides that an employee's right to pension benefits becomes vested, that is, becomes irrevocable, after his combined age and length of service with an employer totals 50 years.

[9] "Accounting for the Cost of Pension Plans," *Opinions of the Accounting Principles Board No. 8* (New York: American Institute of Certified PPublic Accountants, 1966).

substantial, it usually follows operating income and expenses but prior to extraordinary income and expenses, as shown in the form presented in Table 16-1 earlier in this chapter.

Other Expenses

In the past, other expense items directly related to other income items were deducted with general expenses, and therefore other income as reported was gross of associated expenses; but the other income now is generally reported net of expenses directly associated with such other income reported. Therefore, other expenses as now reported in the income statement generally consist only of regularly recurring other expenses that are not associated with other income, for example such items as bond interest, note interest, and amortization of bond discount.

Income Before Income Taxes

This item represents income calculated by deducting all reported expenses from all reported income. The ratio of income *before* income taxes to sales is an important ratio in analyzing and determining the corporation's earning power and in comparative statement analysis.

Income Taxes

Current accounting practice requires that the income tax expense reported in the income statement be computed on book income, not taxable income. When there are differences between book and taxable income, an allocation of tax expense between reporting periods may be necessary; there may be either charges or credits to the expense account accompanied by entries to deferred accounts on the balance sheet, i.e., deferred tax accounting.

Current practice also requires that, where appropriate, income taxes be separately computed on (and reported with) income from ordinary operations and on income from extraordinary items.

The analyst should calculate the percentage of taxes applicable to income before taxes. If the percentage is about 50%, the analyst can assume that the corporation's book income from ordinary sources is about the same as that reported for tax purposes. However, if the percentage is significantly different, he should attempt to determine reasons for the disparity. Some of the reasons why a company may show differences between book and taxable income are discussed below.

Depreciation and Investment Credit. Accounting for depreciation and for the investment credit for tax purposes is often different from the reporting in published reports as discussed in Chapter 17.

Depletion. Depletion accounting for natural resource companies is different from cost depreciation accounting because most companies use "percentage depletion" accounting for tax purposes rather than "cost depreciation," which almost always results in a much lower tax rate than the effective rate for companies not in industries with wasting assets. While the analyst may use this depletion figure for comparative purposes and in calculating cash flow, he has no opportunity to check on its validity as to the particular company under analysis.

Tax-Exempt Income. If the company has invested in tax-exempt securities, it will include income from such securities but will pay no tax on this income. If such investments are substantial, they will account for a significantly lower effective tax rate on income than the current corporate tax rate. This is also true to the extent that any income received from subsidiaries or affiliates is considered a return of capital for tax purposes.

Dividends Received from Domestic Corporations. The dividends received from domestic corporations on both preferred stock and common stock are subject to the corporate income tax only to the extent of 15% of such dividends received; 85% of such dividends are not included in income for tax purposes. Therefore, assuming a corporate tax rate of 48%, the effective rate on dividends received is only 48% x 15% or 7.2%. If a corporation has a large dividend income, such as is the case with fire and casualty companies or some holding companies, this could account for a much lower effective tax rate than the 48% rate.

Long-Term Capital Gains on Sale of Capital Assets. As with individuals, if capital assets are held more than 6 months, they are subject to a maximum capital gains tax of only 25%. Capital assets consist in the main of real property or securities. Any net *loss* on sales of capital assets may be deducted from ordinary income. Except for corporations whose main business is dealing (purchases and sales) in capital assets, capital gains or losses should be entered in the extraordinary income and expense section of the income statement following income taxes.

Capitalized Items and Deferred Expense Items. There are numerous items that a corporation may expense in its tax return but capitalize in its published balance sheet. This procedure was discussed previously in connection with research and development expenses. Numerous companies have followed a similar procedure in regard to advertising and promotional expenses. Analysts generally disagree with capitalization and deferral of certain expense items.[10]

Other items that are sometimes capitalized in annual reports although expensed in tax returns are intangible drilling costs of oil and natural gas producers and exploration and development expenses of mining companies. These all raise a problem for the analyst attempting to place different companies on a comparable base.

Another item that must be mentioned is interest charged to construction credit, which is capitalized by public utility companies in their published statements but is expensed in their income tax reports. This item will be examined in detail in Chapter 21.

One further item should be mentioned because it is often capitalized in published balance sheets while being expensed in tax reports to the Internal Revenue Service. This is the item of cost applicable to "start-up" and related expenses for new plants. The analyst may decide that, if the company is regularly expanding, it is justifiable to capitalize such expenses as is done in the company's published reports. This item will almost always be expensed in the tax report. The reverse item is cost of plant closing, which should also be entered in the extraordinary items section.

Installment Sales. Many companies report the full effect of installment sales when the sales are made, thus reporting the full profit in that fiscal year. However, for tax purposes they report only actual income as payment is received. Therefore, reported taxes in published income statements will be at a rate lower than the regular corporate rate because higher profits are being reported to stockholders than to the Internal Revenue Service. Because the taxes are deferred, the published report should include an estimate of deferred taxes applied to the sales reported in the published statement and should also provide sufficiently for estimated bad debts.[11]

---

[10] When companies defer items that more properly should be currently expensed, the result is higher reported profit. For 1968 United Air Lines cushioned its decline in profits by deferring to later years the costs of training pilots, mechanics, and ground crews to handle new equipment. It was estimated that such deferrals of expenses amounted to $9-$10 million. The analyst must make adjustments increasing reported expenses and decreasing reported profits for these and similar expense items that he believes should be expensed in the current year rather than deferred to later years.

[11] The Internal Revenue Code has been amended in respect to rates for taxable years beginning with 1970. The capital gains which does not qualify for the 25% rate is subject to a 29½% rate for taxable years beginning in 1970; and for years beginning with 1971 the rate is 32½%, but in effect it will create a maximum rate of 35%.

Goodwill. The item of goodwill, once so important in corporate balance sheets, became relatively unimportant until the great acquisitions movement of the post-World War II years. In recent years, costs of acquisitions have often been well in excess of the book value of the assets acquired and a balancing item of goodwill has had to be added in the balance sheet unless this excess is charged off immediately and in total to the capital account.[12] The AICPA requires that the item of goodwill be amortized annually as a charge against income over a period of not more than 40 years.

Net Operating Loss. Such losses sustained in any fiscal year may be applied to reduce previously reported profits, first in the 3 preceding years and then, if there is still an amount remaining, in the 5 succeeding years. As applied to the 3 preceding years, this requires a recalculation of reported income previously filed with the Internal Revenue Service. Under this procedure, when the reported profits are reduced by the loss, the lower recalculated profits will result in a lower tax than was required when the original report was filed and therefore a tax refund or tax credit will be secured. The result of the tax refund is to reduce the effect of the tax loss by approximately one half. Thus, in effect, the federal government has absorbed approximately one half of the tax loss. As noted above, the remaining portion of the loss not absorbed in the 3 preceding years may be carried forward for 5 years, reducing the tax that would otherwise be required against realized profits. While the tax saving is certainly real, it results from operating losses in previous years and has nothing to do with current and future operations and true earnings. Unfortunately, many companies simply reduce taxes in the income statement and report net income and earnings per share only after such lower taxes without disclosing the actual tax adjustments.

Just as in the case of capital gains and losses, a tax credit item for previous losses carried forward should appear as a separate item in the extraordinary items section of the income statement following income taxes. As recommended by the AICPA, the earnings per share of common stock should be shown at the bottom of the income statement for (a) income per share before extraordinary items, (b) extraordinary items per share net of taxes, (c) final net income per share, and (d) dividends per share.

Acquisition of Companies Having Net Loss Carry-Forward Items. If such a company is acquired, the acquiring company can use this carry-forward loss

---

[12] In August, 1970, the AICPA-APB issued Opinion No. 16, "Business Combinations," resulting in the acceptance in practice of two methods of accounting for business combinations: "purchase," and "pooling of interests." The reader should see Chapter 18 for an explanation and references on this Opinion.

to reduce future taxes even though the acquiring company had no loss itself in previous years. To avoid having corporations acquire such loss companies for the main or sole reason of the tax benefit, such acquisitions must be for business reasons, that is, continuation of the company's business or combining the company's business with that of the acquiring company. If the acquiring company cannot justify the acquisition on this "business purpose" basis, it loses the advantage of the tax carry-forward. In any case, if the tax carry-forward is used, it should appear in the extraordinary items section of the income statement.

Other Tax Privileges. Federal legislation provides tax privileges for the following:

1. Shipping lines, which receive subsidies from the federal government and are governed by legislation that both requires in some instances and permits in others the transfer of earnings, tax free, to reserve funds that may or may not later be subject to tax.
2. Life insurance companies, which receive favorable tax treatment. While the present legislation is less favorable than heretofore, it still provides a lower tax base than for ordinary corporations.
3. Savings and loan associations, which are required by law to build up substantial reserves by the annual transfer of earnings, tax free, to their reserve accounts. Legislation requires that reserves be built up to 12% of the total of insured savings accounts and then be maintained at this level as the total of insured accounts increases. Annually 10% of net earnings *before* interest on savings accounts must be transferred to reserves until the requirement is met. Congress has placed an overall limitation for tax purposes on the accumulation of reserves, such accumulations being generally limited to 12% of withdrawable accounts.

Income Before Extraordinary Items

The income figure after taxes but before extraordinary items should be shown separately on the income statement.

Extraordinary Items

These are items of an extraordinary and *nonrecurring* nature. It is recommended by the AICPA that these items, if material, should be shown separately and properly identified at the bottom of the income statement *following* the heading "Income Before Extraordinary Items." There are numerous items of this type. The most important of these items were discussed previously and are reviewed in the following paragraphs.

The analyst is attempting to determine the true annual earning power of the corporation in order to establish a base from which to project future earnings and dividends. Items that are not of a recurring nature should be eliminated from the income statement for any particular year in order to calculate the normal recurring earning power of the business. If the analyst feels that such items have been included in the income statement and have not been placed in a special extraordinary items section at the bottom, he should restate the income statement in the form recommended by the AICPA (see Table 16-1 earlier in this chapter). He should then show income per share before extraordinary nonrecurring items and then net income per share including such items. The true recurring earning power of a company is shown by the income per share before extraordinary non-recurring items, and the analyst in making projections will work from that base figure.

Classification of Nonrecurring Items. Such items represent transactions that are not part of the regular normal course of a particular year's operation. These nonrecurring items fall into two categories: (1) they reflect events that occurred in previous years or (2) they represent items that did occur within the fiscal year under review but that do not represent normal recurrent operations and are, instead, items of an exceptional nature. Category (1) includes such items as tax adjustments covering previous years' operations (additional tax payments or refunds relating to past years), the settlement of claims such as lawsuits or government renegotiation claims that have been carried forward from previous years, and adjustments of depreciation charges made in past years. Category (2) includes such items as adjustments in the book value of investments, profits or losses resulting from the sale of investments (except of financial companies), the sale of other assets above or below their book value, the receipt of exceptional dividends from subsidiaries, and profits from bond retirements. If extraordinary items of a nonrecurring nature appear in the income statement, they should be identified as nonrecurrent, should be segregated, and should be entered in the bottom section of the income statement.

Adjustments for Material Amounts. In line with the general principles regarding adjustments, the analyst in determining true recurring earnings as a base for projecting earnings need not make any adjustments if the amount involved would not materially affect the final result. If the amount is material, however, the analyst must determine whether or not these nonrecurring items have been reported to stockholders in a manner that properly presents true earnings for the year in question.

Eliminations That Should Be Made. In determining true recurring earnings as a base for earnings projections, adjustments should be made to eliminate the following items if they represent material amounts and if they have been included in regular income: refundable taxes for past years; adjustments for depreciation charged against income in previous years, as well as for the taxes incident thereto; profits from the sale of assets, including related taxes; adjustments in the retained earnings account incidental to a merger, if such items have been included in the income account; the elimination or reduction of reserves established by charges to income in previous years, such as reserves for contingencies, reserves for possible declines in inventories, and adjustments to change inventory from Fifo to Lifo or vice versa; and adjustments for declines in the value of security investments (for nonfinancial companies) or in provisions for possible losses from foreign exchange or foreign assets. These adjustments are made in order to arrive at the true recurring income for the year as a base for projections.

QUESTIONS

1. Explain briefly the significance of consolidated financial statements from the standpoint of the security analyst.

2. (a) Distinguish between the equity method and the cost method in preparing consolidated statements. When is the equity method required?
   (b) When would "goodwill" be properly recorded in relation to an acquisition if the equity method were used? How should the goodwill account be handled over time?

3. (a) Distinguish between a subsidiary and an affiliate.
   (b) In what ways does the growing importance of foreign operations for many U.S. corporations make more difficult the analysis of the income statements of such corporations?
   (c) Defend the lack of inclusion of a company's financial subsidiary in a consolidated statement.

4. Ajax Company owns a 50% interest in a nonconsolidated subsidiary, which reported earnings for the year of $400,000. There are 100,000 shares of Ajax Company stock outstanding, and Ajax reports earnings per share for the year of $3.60, including dividends of $100,000 received on the stock of the nonconsolidated subsidiary.
   (a) Discuss the significance of the reported $3.60 per share earnings of Ajax Company and what adjustments should be made by the analyst to reflect "true earnings" per share for Ajax Company shareholders.
   (b) Would it make any difference if the nonconsolidated subsidiary were a foreign operation rather than a domestic operation? Discuss.

5. (a) Should extraordinary items such as a substantial gain (or loss) on the sale of fixed assets no longer needed in the business be reflected in the income statement or should they be treated as direct credits or

debits to the retained earnings account? How would you as an analyst handle such items? Discuss.

(b) How should nonrecurring items be treated by the analyst?

6. Distinguish between a "clean income statement" and an "all-inclusive income statement." Which would you, as an analyst, prefer? Support your position.

7. The SEC, with the full approval of security analysts and investors, has been requiring registrants under the 1933 Securities Act to furnish an "appropriate disclosure" when the contribution of a line of business or products to net income differs substantially from its contribution to net sales.

(a) What possible objections could companies have to providing divisional or product sales and profit breakdowns in their income statements?

(b) Evaluate the recommendations of the Financial Executives Institute for dealing with this problem. (Articles in *Financial Executive,* 1967-1968.)

8. What problems exist in the interpretation of interim reports?

9. Discuss briefly the effect on both the balance sheet and the income statement of using the Lifo method rather than the Fifo method of accounting for inventory during a period of rising prices.

10. What types of items are normally responsible for differences between net income for tax purposes and net income as reported to stockholders? Discuss the problems raised by at least five of these items.

WORK-STUDY PROBLEMS

1. Examine the inventory valuation methods (see *Moody's Industrial Manual* and/or company annual reports) used by the following companies and report on these inventory valuation methods in the light of each company's financial condition, nature of the business, and the general business outlook.

(a) Continental Oil Company.
(b) Ford Motor Company.
(c) General Foods Corporation.
(d) Goodyear Tire & Rubber Co.
(e) Phelps Dodge Corporation.
(f) Reynolds Metals Company.
(g) Reynolds (R. J.) Industries.

2. (a) Using a *Federal Reserve Bulletin* (the latest available, which contains the table, "Sales, Profits, and Dividends of Large Corporations"), calculate for the past 5 years the annual compound rate of growth of sales, net profits after taxes, and dividends:

(1) Of the total of 170 corporations.
(2) Of each of the industry groups.

(b) Calculate the ratio of net profits after taxes to sales (revenues) and the payout ratio of dividends to net profits after taxes for 5 years for:

  (1) The total of 170 corporations.

  (2) Each of the industry groups.

(c) Discuss the differences in trends and in actual ratios between each of the industry groups as calculated in (a) and (b).

(d) Compare the ratio of net profits after taxes to sales for the industries in the *Federal Reserve Bulletin* table to those in the last April issue of the Monthly Letter of the First National City Bank of New York and in the SEC-FTC Quarterly Financial Report for Manufacturing Corporations.

(e) Choose one company in a field you select from those listed in the *Federal Reserve Bulletin* table and tabulate the sales and the net income of that company for 10 years and the ratio of net income to sales for each year. Compare the trends of your company with the trends of its industry.

(f) Calculate the compound annual rate of growth of sales and net income for your company based on (e) above for 5 years. Compare the growth rates:

  (1) Of your company with the total of 170 corporations.

  (2) Of your company with its industry.

3. (a) Reynolds Tobacco Company changed from using a Fifo costing system for inventory to a Lifo costing system in 1957. How should this have been handled in their annual reports, according to modern accounting principles?

(b) Review the 1957 annual report for Reynolds Tobacco Company. Did they handle the change in accordance with said accounting principles? Discuss.

(c) Did the change affect the price of Reynolds stock when the report was issued? (See *Wall Street Journal* article dated February 3, 1958.) What problem, if any, was created for investors?

SUGGESTED READINGS

Accounting Trends and Techniques (Annual). New York: American Institute of Certified Public Accountants.

Ball, Ray. "Risk, Return & Disequilibrium: An Application to Change in Accounting Techniques." *The Journal of Finance* (May, 1972), pp. 343-354.

Ball, Ray, and Ross Watts. "Some Time Series Properties of Accounting Income." *The Journal of Finance* (June, 1972), pp. 663-681.

Barrett, M. Edgar, and Gerald J. Holtz. "The Case Against One Set of Books for Financial and Tax Accounting." *Financial Executive* (September, 1972), pp. 30-42.

Bernstein, Leopold A. "Extraordinary Gains and Losses—Their Significance to the Financial Analyst." *Financial Analysts Journal* (November-December, 1972), pp. 49-52, 88-90.

Bernstein, Peter L. "Advice to Managers: Watch Earnings, Not Ticker Tape." *Harvard Business Review* (January-February, 1973), pp. 63-69.

Bissell, George S. "A Professional Investor Looks at Earnings Forecasts." *Financial Analysts Journal* (May-June, 1972), pp. 73-78.

Blackie, William. "The Quality of Earnings." *Financial Executive* (July, 1972), pp. 24-27.

Brown, R. Gene. "Ethical and Other Problems in Publishing Financial Forecasts." *Financial Analysts Journal* (March-April, 1972), pp. 38-45, 86-87.

Carmichael, D. R. "Reporting on Forecasts: A U.K. Perspective." *The Journal of Accountancy* (January, 1973), pp. 36-45.

Chambers, John C., Satinder K. Mullick, and Donald D. Smith. "How to Choose the Right Forecasting Technique." *Harvard Business Review* (July-August, 1971), pp. 45-74.

Davidson, Sidney, and T. Carter Hagaman. "Should Companies Be Required to Publish Their Earnings Forecasts—A Debate?" *The Institutional Investor* (April, 1972), pp. 56-59.

Gray, William S., III. "Proposal for Systematic Disclosure of Corporate Forecasts." *Financial Analysts Journal* (January-February, 1973), pp. 64-71. (Also see in the same issue, "Corporate Forecasts—Legal Aspects and Corporate Forecast," pp. 72-76.)

"How Accurate Are Forecasts?" (Editorial). *Financial Executive* (March, 1973), pp. 26-32.

Kapnick, Harvey E. "Will Financial Forecasts Really Help Investors?" *Financial Executive* (August, 1972), pp. 50-54.

Lipay, R. J. "Exploring the Extraordinary Item." *Financial Executive* (March, 1973), pp. 20-25.

Mattlin, Everett. "Are the Days of the Numbers Game Numbered?" *The Institutional Investor* (November, 1971), pp. 41, 68-71.

——————. "The Hunt for the Corporate Nuance." *The Institutional Investor* (November, 1971), pp. 38.

Niederhoffer, Victor, and Patrick J. Regan. "Earnings Changes, Analysts' Forecasts and Stock Prices." *Financial Analysts Journal* (May-June, 1972), pp. 65-71.

Pivar, Samuel. "Implementation of APB Opinions Nos. 16 and 17 (Business Combinations, Pooling or Purchase)." *The Journal of Accountancy* (November, 1972), pp. 58-65.

Reego, William A. "Reflecting Historical Cost and Current Values in Financial Reporting." *Financial Executive* (March, 1973), pp. 50-58.

Treynor, Jack L. "The Trouble With Earnings." *Financial Analysts Journal* (September-October, 1972), pp. 41-43.

17

Noncash Charges and Cash Flow

Some expenses that are deducted in the income account represent an accounting charge but not a corresponding cash outlay, thereby affecting a company's cash flow. Examples of major noncash items that will be discussed below are depreciation, depletion, and the amortization of intangibles. Investment credit, another item to be considered in cash flow analysis, is included at the end of this chapter.

DEPRECIATION

"Depreciation accounting is a system of accounting which aims to distribute the cost . . . of tangible capital assets, less salvage (if any) over the estimated useful life of the unit (which may be a group of assets) in a systematic and rational manner. It is a process of allocation [of cost], not of valuation. *Depreciation for the year* is the portion of the total charge under such a system that is allocated to the year. Although the allocation may properly take into account occurrences during the year, it is not intended to be a measurement of the effect of all such occurrences."

Because the accounting charge for depreciation does not represent a corresponding outlay of cash, some investors and analysts have at least implied that depreciation is not a real expense by using the terms "cash earnings per share" or "cash flow earnings per share" and have even substituted these terms for "net earnings per share." Strong criticism of this position by the AICPA, the NYSE, and the Financial Analysts Federation has sharply reduced the use of these terms in brokerage houses and annual corporate reports.

Because fixed assets, particularly plant and equipment, represent such a substantial outlay, it would be impractical to write them off entirely as an expense charged against the income of the year in which they are purchased, especially since benefits from their use will be received over an extended period. Furthermore, as soon as it is purchased, a fixed asset begins to depreciate. To ignore this fact would be to experience a gradual loss of capital without any reflection of the fact on the books of account. Accountants consider the original cost of a fixed asset to be a prepaid expense that must be amortized during the service life of the asset by regular periodic charges to the depreciation expense account. After deduction of the annual charge, the remaining amount is the *unamortized cost;* but in no way, except by coincidence, does this amount represent the *economic value* of the asset at that time. Accountants never "certify" to balance sheet *values.*

Basis for Depreciation—Replacement Value vs. Original Cost

The inflation that was experienced in 1941-1957 as the result of World War II and the Korean War and in 1965-1973 as the result of the Vietnam War has led many to advocate a policy of substituting replacement cost for original cost as the basis for determining depreciation charges in the income statement. Corporate management has been especially vocal in this regard. The basic function of depreciation charges, as seen by accountants, is to amortize the cost of a capital asset over its useful life. Management is concerned with a second function: providing the funds needed for replacement of assets after they have worn out or become technologically obsolete. Depreciation charges do not in and of themselves provide a company with cash. However, they do not represent a corresponding outlay of cash and, to the extent that they are tax deductible, they do protect cash generated by sales operations from the burden of taxes.

When replacement costs have risen far above original cost, prudent business management must recognize this capital erosion and set aside the additional funds necessary to continue a business in operation. Such funds must presently be provided from retained earnings because the income tax laws do not recognize the inflation situation. In other words, income taxes must be paid on the capital lost through inflation, which makes the problem of maintaining a company's capital doubly difficult.

It is interesting to note that other countries (for example, The Netherlands, Chile, and Brazil), with more rapid inflation than the United States, have changed their tax laws in various ways to prevent the gradual liquidation of capital investment through payment of income taxes on capital eroded by inflation; asset values are raised yearly and depreciated on the new values.

The accounting profession is quite strong in its stand that depreciation charges should be based on values shown in the balance sheet and that these values should be original cost. A change to replacement cost would fundamentally change concepts of accounting, since it would represent a breaking away from the basic idea that balance sheet and expense accounts are based on monetary cost and not on economic values. The cost basis of measurement has the advantages of (1) uniformity of interpretation on the values to be entered in the balance sheet, (2) acting as a basis for determining expense charges, and (3) objectivity. Accountants question whether a system based on an attempt to measure replacement values, with its loss of objectivity, has additional advantages that more than offset the advantages of the cost basis. Additional questions are raised, such as whether the assets are replaced with like assets or superior ones that justify part of the higher cost, whether the assets will in fact be replaced as technology changes, and whether current or future customers should pay for the replaced equipment.[1]

In June, 1969, the AICPA issued "Statement of the APB No. 3: Financial Statement Restated for General Price Level Changes." This statement, which still holds as the AICPA thinking at this writing, is quoted in part as follows:

> The Board believes that general price-level financial statements or pertinent information extracted from them present useful information not available from basic historical-dollar financial statements. General price-level information may be presented in addition to the basic historical statement but should not be presented as the basic statements. The Board believes that general price-level information is not required at this time for fair presentation of financial position and results of operations in conformity with general accepted principles in the United States. The GNP deflator is the most comprehensive indicator of the general price level in the United States. Consequently, it should normally be used to prepare general price-level statements in the United States.[2]

This view was reiterated by the AICPA in its "Fundamental Statement" published in October, 1970.

Professor Solomon Fabricant disagrees with the position of the AICPA and expressed his disagreement when he concluded that:

> . . . general price-level information is required at this time for a fair presentation of the financial position of business enterprises—if not in the basic statement, then at least in supplementary statements. . . . A major objective of financial accounting is to present information useful in making economic decisions. For accountants to avow this, and then in effect to stop

---

[1] See *Accounting Research Bulletin No. 43,* published in 1953, for both the majority view and the dissenting view of a special committee appointed by the AICPA to study this question.

[2] "Statement of the APB No. 3: Financial Statement Restated for General Price-Level Changes," *The Journal of Accountancy* (September, 1969), pp. 62-68.

short of doing what needs to be done to reach the objective, is to expose themselves to the charge of nonfeasance. . . . APB Statement No. 3 presents a useful guide to the preparation of 'general price-level financial statements.' Accountants should begin to use this guide to prepare and present this information. The forward of this Statement emphasizes that 'presentation of such information is not mandatory.' But I see no good reason for not presenting such information; I can see many good reasons for doing so.[3]

Magnitude of Depreciation

The two major reasons why investors and analysts need to devote so much attention to depreciation are: (1) the magnitude of depreciation and (2) the leeway that management can exercise in reporting depreciation because it is a noncash expense, that is, the lack of uniformity in reporting depreciation in published reports. The magnitude of depreciation is evident when it is related to corporate profits as is done in Table 17-1. It can be seen from this table that depreciation in absolute terms has risen from $4.7 billion annually in 1946 to $43.0 billion in 1967 and an estimated $61.7 billion for 1972. Furthermore, in relative terms, depreciation as a percentage of Cash Flow I (depreciation plus net profits) ranged between 41% and 47% in the 1960s, and depreciation as a percentage of Cash Flow II (depreciation plus undistributed profits after dividends) ranged between 58% and 72% in the same period.[4] Cash flow, as discussed in Chapter 7, provides the cash for corporate purposes. The major uses of cash flow are: (1) corporate dividends and debt amortization, including sinking fund payments; (2) required increases in working capital; and (3) internal sources of funds for capital budget programs, repurchase of company securities, etc. In broad terms, cash flow (of which net profits are a component) represents the protection for all investors for both dividends and debt service requirements, including sinking funds and amortization but excluding interest.

Methods of Reporting Depreciation

While corporate laws and accounting principles require that corporations make some charge for depreciation (usually based on cost), corporate

---

[3] Solomon Fabricant, "Inflation and Current Accountancy Practices—An Economist's View," *The Journal of Accountancy* (December, 1971).

[4] The U. S. Department of Commerce in its monthly *Survey of Current Business* adds all capital consumption allowances to net profits after taxes to get Cash Flow I and adds capital consumption allowances to net profits after taxes and dividends to get Cash Flow II. Capital consumption allowances in the late 1960s averaged $4-$5 billion higher than depreciation alone. This represented depreciation plus the Department's estimates of capital items charged to expense instead of being capitalized plus accidental damages.

TABLE 17-1

All U.S. Corporations, 1946-1972, Absolute Importance of Depreciation and Relative Importance to Cash Flow (Millions of Dollars)

	1	2	3	4	5	6	7	8
Year	Capital Consumption Allowances (Depreciation)	Profits Before Taxes	Profits Tax	Tax Profits After Taxes	Total Cash Flow I Capital Consumption Allowances Plus Net Profits After Taxes (Col. 1 + 4)	Undistributed Profits (Profits After Dividends)	Net Cash Flow II Capital Consumption Allowances Plus Undistributed Profits (Col. 1 + 6)	Capital Consumption Allowances As % Of Cash Flow II (Col. 1 ÷ Col. 7)
1946	4.7	24.6	9.1	15.5	20.2	9.9	14.6	32.2
1947	5.8	31.5	11.5	20.2	26.0	13.9	19.7	29.4
1948	7.0	35.2	12.5	22.7	29.7	15.6	22.6	31.0
1949	7.9	28.9	10.4	18.5	26.4	11.3	19.2	41.4
1950	8.8	42.6	17.8	24.9	33.7	16.0	24.8	35.5
1951	10.3	43.9	22.3	21.6	31.9	13.0	23.3	44.2
1952	11.5	38.9	19.4	19.6	31.1	11.0	22.5	51.1
1953	13.2	40.6	20.3	20.4	33.6	11.5	24.7	53.4
1954	15.0	38.3	17.7	20.6	35.6	11.3	26.3	57.0
1955	17.4	48.6	21.6	27.0	44.4	16.5	33.9	51.3
1956	18.9	48.8	21.7	27.2	46.1	15.9	34.8	54.3
1957	20.8	47.2	21.2	26.0	46.8	14.2	35.0	59.4
1958	22.0	41.4	19.0	22.3	44.3	10.8	32.8	67.1
1959	23.5	52.1	27.7	28.5	52.0	15.9	39.4	59.6
1960	24.9	49.7	23.0	26.7	51.6	13.2	38.1	65.4
1961	26.2	50.3	23.1	27.2	53.4	13.5	39.7	66.0
1962	30.1	55.4	24.2	31.2	61.3	16.0	46.1	65.3
1963	31.8	59.4	26.3	33.1	64.9	16.6	48.4	65.7
1964	33.9	66.8	28.3	38.4	72.3	20.6	54.5	62.2
1965	36.4	77.8	31.3	46.5	82.9	26.7	63.1	57.7
1966	39.5	84.2	34.3	49.9	89.4	29.1	68.6	57.6
1967	43.0	79.8	33.2	46.6	89.6	25.3	68.3	62.9
1968	46.8	87.6	39.9	47.8	94.6	24.2	71.0	66.0
1969 R	51.9	84.9	40.1	44.8	96.8	20.5	72.4	71.7
1970 R	55.2	74.3	34.1	40.2	95.3	15.4	70.6	78.2
1971 R	60.3	83.3	37.3	45.9	106.2	20.5	80.8	74.6
1972 R	67.7	93.7	41.0	52.6	120.3	26.3	94.0	72.0

R = Revised in 1973.

management is permitted numerous alternatives in the manner in which it amortizes the cost of fixed assets over their useful life on its books and in published reports. Prior to 1954 (the Internal Revenue Code permitted new methods beginning in 1954), corporations were required to use straight-line depreciation for tax purposes except when certificates of necessity had been issued for defense projects permitting rapid amortization. The management of corporations also used straight-line depreciation in their books and in published reports.

The *straight-line method* provides for the regular distribution of the original cost of fixed assets, less their estimated salvage value, over their estimated service lives. In addition to the straight-line method of depreciation, the Internal Revenue Code permits two other depreciation methods: the declining-balance method and the sum-of-the-years-digits method.

The *declining-balance method* permits a taxpayer to use a rate of depreciation, not exceeding twice the straight-line rate, on the original cost (unadjusted for salvage value) less accumulated depreciation. It should be noted that the Code permits a taxpayer to change at any time from the declining-balance method to the straight-line method, since it is arithmetically impossible to charge all original cost as depreciation under the declining-balance method. The straight-line rate would be based on a realistic estimate of the remaining life of the property at the time of the switch.

The *sum-of-the-years-digits method* is somewhat more complicated. The annual depreciation deduction is calculated by applying a changing fraction to the original cost of the property less the estimated salvage value. The numerator of the fraction is the number of useful years of life remaining for the property, what it will be in the first year, in the second year, etc. The denominator is the factorial sum of the estimated useful life of the property. For a fixed asset with an estimated life of 5 years, the fractions used would be 5/15, 4/15, 3/15, 2/15, and 1/15.

The annual depreciation charges under the three depreciation methods are contrasted in Table 17-2.

Asset Depreciation Range (ADR) System. In June, 1971, the Treasury Department adopted the Asset Depreciation Range System (ADR). When this system was adopted, the Department announced that taxpayers not electing it would be able to elect the depreciation guidelines without the reserve ratio test. Congress gave the President authority to prescribe a *class life system,* which is a combination of both ADR and the guidelines for property placed in service after 1970. Thus, taxpayers are able to compute depreciation either under the new class life system or under the general rules using estimated useful lives (old Bulletin F). Many of the elements of the

TABLE 17-2

Annual Depreciation Charge (For a fixed asset costing $1,000 with no expected salvage value and with an estimated useful life of 5 years)

Year	Straight-Line Method	Declining-Balance Method	Sum-of-the-Years-Digits Method
1	$200	$400	$333.33
2	200	240	266.67
3	200	144	200.00
4	200	108*	133.33
5	200	108*	66.67

* It is assumed that the taxpayer availed himself of his option to switch to straight-line depreciation in the fourth year.

ADR system (including the repeat of the reserve ratio test) are designed to achieve a simpler administration of the depreciation rules. It is expected that the new class life system will retain these elements of ADR. The ADR system is summarized as follows:

> The ADR System is based on broad industry classes of assets. For each guideline class, a range of years (called 'asset depreciation range') is given. For each asset in an asset guideline class, the taxpayer may select a depreciation period within the asset depreciation range prescribed for that class. This depreciation period is then used to compute the depreciation deduction.
>
> A taxpayer using ADR does not have to justify his retirement and replacement policies. A depreciation period selected for an asset cannot be changed by either the taxpayer or the IRS during the remaining period of use of the asset.
>
> The ADR election is an annual one. It applies to assets first placed in service after 1970.[5]

Flow-Through Method and Normalizing Method of Reporting Depreciation. Since 1954 most corporations, while taking advantage of the rapid amortization permitted under the Code for tax purposes, have reported publicly on a straight-line basis to stockholders. Until fiscal 1968, income statements in annual reports of numerous corporations reported depreciation by the *flow-through method,* which annually flows through the full tax savings (resulting from rapid amortization for tax reporting) down to net income. But other corporations reported depreciation by the *normalizing method,* making a charge in the income account equivalent to the tax savings and thus washing out the benefits of the tax savings as far as final net income in their published income statements. In published statements the charge

---

[5] *1972 U.S. Master Tax Guide,* published by Commercial Clearing House, Inc., p. 410.

for deferred taxes is usually included in the total item entitled "Federal Income Taxes."

In December, 1967, the AICPA stated categorically that the *deferred method* of tax allocation should be followed.[6] An exception to insistence on the deferred method would be in cases of regulated companies like public utilities where particular regulatory authorities may require the use of *flow-through* accounting.

Those who favor *normalizing* state that the use of rapid amortization for tax purposes will result in lower taxes being paid in the earlier years of the life of the assets than under the straight-line method because of higher depreciation charges, but that in later years depreciation will be less than straight-line rates and taxes will therefore be higher than in the earlier years. Total taxes for the entire life of the assets should be the same under either straight-line for tax purposes or rapid amortization for tax purposes. Therefore, tax savings are merely temporary and deferred until later years of lower depreciation charges. Those holding this viewpoint, including the AICPA and the SEC, therefore wish to eliminate any effect of tax savings on net income in the earlier years of the assets' life.

Those who have advocated the *flow-through* method, including numerous state public utility commissions (not the SEC), have argued that as long as a company is rather regularly expanding and purchasing fixed assets, the new assets will have the advantage of rapid amortization, therefore offsetting the declining depreciation on older assets. The lower taxes paid in the earlier years, therefore, are not merely deferred to later years but will never be paid. Therefore, there will be a constantly increasing "deferred taxes" account on the balance sheet.

As previously noted,[7] although depreciation is a true expense, it does not involve an outlay of cash in the period charged; therefore, the sales revenues allocated to the depreciation charges do represent a tax-protected source of funds to the business enterprise. Although the total depreciation charged over the life of the asset is not affected by the method used, the greater amounts of revenues protected in early years by the declining-balance method and the sum-of-the-years-digits method have a higher present value than funds that might be protected in later years.

Rapid amortization is similar to an interest-free loan from the Treasury Department. Generally, firms do not have access to other sources of funds with no greater risk or cost than the funds provided by depreciation. Therefore, acquiring an increased amount of funds through depreciation tends to lower the cost of capital to the firm.

---

[6] "Accounting for Income Taxes," *Opinions of the Accounting Principles Board No. 11* (New York: American Institute of Certified Public Accountants, 1967).

[7] See the discussion of cash flow in Chapter 7.

DEPLETION

The depletion allowance, for tax purposes, represents recognition of the fact that operations of companies with wasting assets result in a decrease in the value of their natural resources as these are used up. *Depletion* is the accounting term applied to the amortization of the cost of exhaustible natural resources, such as oil pools, mineral resources, and standing timber.

Wasting Asset Companies

The majority of wasting asset companies, such as oil and mining companies, depreciate their *fixed assets* through cost depreciation charges to a depreciation expense account. However, for their *wasting assets* they use percentage depletion accounting. Also, these wasting asset companies have large expenditure and development costs. A comparative cash flow analysis, because of heavy depletion charges and encompassing special tax treatment for these development costs, is as essential as net income analysis for wasting asset companies and has been used for such companies for many years.[8]

Percentage Depletion Method [9]

This method differs from normal depreciation methods, and therefore from the cost amortization method, in that allowable depletion charges are based on *gross income* instead of on the cost of reserves. "Gross income" in this context is not gross income as used elsewhere in the Code, as explained in the following paragraphs.

Percentage depletion is calculated by multiplying the allowable percentage for the particular mineral in question by the *gross income* from the

---

[8] On the companies' own books and for public reporting purposes on charges for depletion, they deduct that percentage of the cost of the natural resource property which the mineral (or the resource) extracted bears to the total resource content. This is known as the "units-of-production" method. This method is also applied to calculate the depreciation on wells and other equipment, such as cars, where their service life is governed by the same factors.

[9] *Sec. 613, Percentage Depletion—Internal Revenue Code*

General Rule—In the case of mines, wells, and other natural deposits listed in subsection (b) the allowance for depletion under Section 611 shall be the percentage, specified in subsection (b), of the gross income from the property, excluding from such gross income an amount equal to any rents or royalties paid or incurred by the taxpayer in respect of the property. Such allowances shall not exceed 50 percent of the taxpayer's taxable income from the property computed without allowance for depletion. In no case shall the allowance for depletion under Section 611 be less than if computed without reference to this section (i.e., not less than the cost method.)

property, but it is limited to 50% of the taxable or net income from the property. The *gross income* under Treasury regulations is not the same as the *gross income* of the taxpayer as defined in other sections of the Internal Revenue Code. Rather, according to the Treasury, it must be calculated separately. It is the amount for which the mineral is sold if the sale takes place in the vicinity of the property in the form in which the mineral is customarily sold by basic producers; or it is the calculated value at the *basic stage* of production in case it is sold later at a more advanced stage, for example, after processing. Any gas or oil or coal used by the producer itself for fuel may not be included in calculating the *gross income* from oil, gas, or coal properties.

The determination of *gross income* for purposes of depletion allowances is frequently more difficult in the case of mines than in the case of oil or gas properties because of the wide variation in the grade and frequently the lack of posted prices, and also because ore is generally not sold in the crude form as first extracted but normally only after some refinement.

Exploration and Related Costs

Under the Internal Revenue Code, *the taxpayer has the choice* of accounting for exploration costs not in excess of $400,000 by either (1) charging them off currently as incurred or (2) considering them as a deferred charge to be deducted proportionately as the extracted minerals that result from the exploration are sold. All such expenditures *may be* capitalized. Any excess exploration costs *must be* capitalized. Such deductions are in addition to depletion allowances, but they must be considered when the taxpayer is calculating net income to determine the 50% limitation for percentage depletion.

Mine Development Costs. The present Code permits the taxpayer *either* to deduct currently *or* to defer costs of mine development sustained in either the development or the production stage, and the amount deductible in any one year is unlimited. Such deduction is in addition to depletion allowances. However, these deductions must be taken into consideration when the taxpayer is calculating net income to determine the 50% limitation for percentage depletion.

Intangible Drilling and Development Costs—Gas and Oil. The Code permits the taxpayer to elect *either* to deduct intangible drilling and development costs as incurred *or* to capitalize them as additional leasehold costs. The amortization of current costs, if capitalized, is treated as depletion and thus differs from the treatment of such capitalized costs for mine exploration and related costs. In the case of gas and oil properties, when the percentage depletion method is used, it is in effect in lieu of the amortization of the capitalized costs.

Exploration Costs—Gas and Oil. All of the geological and related costs incurred to determine the existence, location, extent, or quality of gas or oil deposits can normally be added to costs of leases retained or acquired as a result of such explorations. Also, expenses of determining the location of test wells and the actual drilling of these wells are considered intangible drilling costs that the taxpayer may either capitalize or deduct in the year incurred, in accordance with his normal accounting procedure for such intangible costs. This results in substantial tax savings for oil companies.

Depletion and Depreciation Reserves Distributed to Stockholders

Unfortunately, the income tax regulations confuse the status of depreciation and depletion reserves that are accumulated. These regulations state that "a distribution made from (charged to) a depletion or depreciation reserve based upon the cost or other basis of the property, instead of being charged to retained earnings, will not be considered as having been paid out of the earnings of the property." Therefore, such distributions to stockholders are not taxable as ordinary dividends. However, the regulation clearly states that such reserves are "not a part of surplus out of which *ordinary dividends* may be paid." The intention is clear that such distributions are considered to be *liquidating dividends* because they represent a return of capital and not a distribution of earnings. Numerous tax-exempt dividends result, and this prior to 1972 was the major reason for the tax-exempt status to the recipient of a portion of dividends paid by many public utility companies.

AMORTIZATION OF INTANGIBLES

In addition to the major noncash charges for depreciation and depletion in the income statement, the amortization of intangibles such as goodwill, patents, and trademarks represents noncash charges in the income account.

Intangible Assets

The following statements are pertinent to the classification and amortization of intangible assets:

Intangible assets are classified in *ARB No. 43*, Chapter 5, par. 2 as follows:

(a) Those having a term of existence limited by law, regulation, or agreement, or by their nature (such as patents, copyrights, *leases, licenses, franchises for a fixed term, and goodwill as to which there is evidence of limited duration*);

(b) Those having no such limited term of existence and as to which there is, at the time of acquisition, no indication of limited life (such as goodwill generally, going value, trade names, secret processes, subcription lists, perpetual franchises, and organization costs).[10]

When a corporation decides that a type (b) intangible may not continue to have value during the entire life of the enterprise, it may amortize the cost of such intangible by systematic charges against income despite the fact that there are no present indications of limited existence or loss of value which would indicate that it has become type (a) and despite the fact that expenditures are being made to maintain its value.[11]

The accounting for a particular business enterprise ordinarily does not recognize the total value of the enterprise, and it is not the purpose of accounting to determine or measure that value. Accounting and the resulting financial statements present information about financial position and results of operations (including net income) which, with innumerable other factors affecting investor decisions, enter into the investors' determination of the value of a business enterprise—as evidenced by the market price of its stock. Consequently, only by coincidence does the total value of an enterprise equal the total amount of net assets shown in its balance sheet.[12]

. . . The market price of the stock of a business represents, in effect, a composite opinion of many investors as to the quality of a business' earning power.[13]

The decisions of investors and creditors involve the process of choice. . . . Therefore, the financial information about a business [financial statements] will be useful to investors and creditors only if that information provides a basis for *comparing* the performance of that business with others.[14]

. . . Regardless of the quality of investor judgment and the myriad factors which mold his opinions on stock values, the appraisal of a business enterprise's prospects for future profits (earning power) primarily governs, in the long run, the prices at which shares of stock in the business are traded. Future profits provide the basis for both dividends and investment growth. . . .[15]

---

[10] "Inventory of Generally Accepted Accounting Principles for Business Enterprises," *Accounting Research Study No. 7* (New York: American Institute of Certified Public Accountants, 1965), p. 154.

[11] *Ibid.*, p. 155.

[12] "Accounting for Goodwill," *Accounting Research Study No. 10* (New York: American Institute of Certified Public Accountants, 1968), p. 5.

[13] *Ibid.*, p. 14.

[14] *Ibid.*, p. 23.

[15] *Ibid.*, pp. 24-25.

Goodwill in Business Combinations

As previously noted, there has been a tremendous merger movement in the post-World War II years. Under the *purchase of assets method* of accounting as opposed to the *pooling of interests method* of accounting for mergers, substantial amounts of *goodwill* are frequently added to the balance sheet of the acquiring company when it acquires assets in excess of the book value of the company being acquired.

Pertinent paragraphs in "APB Opinion No. 16: Business Combinations" issued by the AICPA in August, 1970, are quoted below.

1. A business combination occurs when a corporation and one or more incorporated or unincorporated businesses are brought together into one accounting entity. The single entity carries on the activities of the previously separate, independent enterprises.

2. Two methods of accounting for business combinations—'purchase' and 'pooling of interests'—have been accepted in practice and supported in pronouncements of the Board and its predecessor, the committee on accounting procedure. The accounting treatment of a combination may affect significantly the reported financial position and net income of the combined corporation for prior, current, and future periods.[16]

Under the "purchase of assets" method of accounting, the net assets acquired are recorded at cost and are measured in cash on the fair value of securities or other property turned over, or for the fair value of the property acquired, whichever seems more reasonable. Under the pooling of interests method of accounting, the combined financial position of the constituent companies is in effect the same as though they had previously been affiliated and therefore *no goodwill* results. (See Chapter 18, p. 467.)

APB Opinion No. 16 continues:

8. The Board concludes that the purchase method and the pooling of interests method are both acceptable in accounting for business combinations, although not as alternatives in accounting for the same business combination. A business combination which meets specified conditions requires accounting by the pooling of interests method. . . . All other business combinations should be accounted for as an acquisition of one or more companies by a corporation. . . . The cost should then be allocated to the identifiable individual assets acquired and liabilities assumed based on their fair values; the unallocated cost should be recorded as goodwill.

15. The pooling of interests method of accounting is applied only to business combinations effected by an exchange of stock and not to those involving primarily cash, other assets, or liabilities. . . .[17]

---

[16] "APB Opinion No. 16: Business Combinations," *The Journal of Accountancy* (October, 1970), pp. 69-85.

[17] *Ibid.*

As a result of Opinion No. 16, the use of the pooling of interests method has been severely restricted since 1970.

In the same month (August, 1970) that the AICPA issued APB Opinion No. 16, it also issued the related "APB Opinion No. 17: Intangible Assets" which stated among other things:

27. The Board believes that the value of intangible assets at any one date eventually disappears and that the recorded costs of intangible assets should be amortized by systematic charges to income over the periods estimated to be benefited. . . .

28. . . . . A reasonable estimate of the useful life may often be based on upper and lower limits even though a fixed existence is not determinable.

29. The period of amortization should not, however, exceed forty years. . . .[18]

CASH FLOW AND FINANCIAL ANALYSIS [19]

Cash flow is not a new concept, but prior to the 1950s it was usually emphasized only in the analysis of wasting asset industries, such as oil companies, for purposes of comparative analysis between companies.

Differing Concepts of Cash Flow

Cash flow is used on Wall Street to designate net earnings after taxes, depreciation, and depletion, with depreciation and depletion added back. This could be designated as "net earnings after taxes but before depreciation." Another concept (retained earnings plus depreciation) implies that dividends are in essence almost like a fixed charge, and those of this opinion think of cash flow as retained earnings plus depreciation. Analysts reject the latter concept because all empirical evidence indicates that, before determining dividend payments, directors analyze the corporate cash flow and the sources and uses of funds statements—current and projected. However, it is true that once a dividend rate is established, directors will make every effort to maintain it. The ratio of dividends to cash flow is far more stable than the ratio of dividends to earnings.

The most important point to emphasize is that depreciation (and depletion) is a very real expense just as important as other operating costs. Any

---

[18] "APB Opinion No. 17: Intangible Assets," *The Journal of Accountancy* (October, 1970), pp. 85-89.

[19] The U.S. Department of Commerce in its *Survey of Current Business* presents two cash flow figures: (1) net profits after taxes, gross of dividends plus capital consumption allowances, and (2) net profits after taxes, net of dividends plus capital consumption allowances. Capital consumption allowances represent depreciation *plus* capital items charged to current expense and accidental damages. This *excess* over depreciation averages between $4 and $6 billion per year.

attempt to downgrade the importance of depreciation (or depletion) as an expense can produce an erroneous conception of true corporate earnings power. In most cases, when annual reports shifted to emphasis on cash flow earnings, it was usually an attempt to shift attention from a poor or mediocre earnings record.

In situations where an investor purchases common stock at a price significantly lower than book value, for example at net current asset book value, and therefore has not in effect paid anything for fixed assets, it can be argued that inasmuch as he paid nothing for the fixed assets, depreciation or depletion is not a real cost *to him.* It is claimed, therefore, that he can ignore the factor of depreciation and think in terms of earnings on his cost, that is, in terms of cash flow earnings whether reinvested in property or paid out as dividends. While there is some merit in this argument, this thinking can be dangerous, for inability to generate adequate earnings after depreciation may lead to serious financial problems and inability to replace assets as they depreciate.

Depreciation or depletion can only be considered a source of funds in the sense that funds generated by sales are not siphoned off by depreciation or depletion because these are noncash expenses in the income account. Therefore, funds flow down through the statement and are not diverted by these accounting charges. But a situation where there is no profit before depreciation, or where there is a loss before depreciation, clearly emphasizes that depreciation by and of itself is not a source of funds.

Statement of Changes in Financial Position

In March, 1971, the AICPA issued "APB Opinion No. 19: Reporting Changes in Financial Position," some important paragraphs of which are cited below:

1. In 1963 the Accounting Principles Board issued Opinion No. 3, "The Statement of Source and Application of Funds." Support of that Opinion by the principal stock exchanges and its acceptance by the business community have resulted in a significant increase in the number of companies that present a statement of sources and uses of funds (funds statement) in annual financial reports to shareholders. Several regulatory agencies have acted recently to require funds statements in certain reports filed with them.

2. APB Opinion No. 3 encouraged but did not require presentation of a funds statement. In view of the present widespread recognition of the usefulness of information on sources and uses of funds, the Board has considered whether presentation of such a statement should be required to complement the income statement and the balance sheet. . . .

3. This Opinion sets forth the Board's conclusions and supersedes APB Opinion No. 3. . . .

7. The Board concludes that information concerning the financing and investing activities of a business enterprise and the changes in its financial position for a period is essential for financial statement users, particularly owners and creditors, in making economic decisions. When financial statements purporting to present both financial position (balance sheet) and results of operations (statement of income and retained earnings) are issued, a statement summarizing changes in financial position should also be presented as a basic financial statement for each period for which an income statement is presented. These conclusions apply to all profit-oriented business entities, whether or not the reporting entity normally classifies its assets and liabilities as current and non-current.

16. This Opinion shall be effective for fiscal periods ending after September 30, 1971. . . .[20]

Only one member of the APB dissented to Opinion No. 19.

INVESTMENT CREDIT [21]

In order to encourage plant modernization and expansion and the purchase of equipment, Congress in 1962 amended the Internal Revenue Code to apply up to 7% of the cost of certain property, new and used, in the year of purchase as a direct offset to the taxpayer's tax liability. In general, the *full 7%* credit is available only for the purchase of *tangible personal property* and other tangible property with a useful life of 7 years or more. If credits available in any one year are in excess of the taxes that would otherwise be due in that year, carry-backs and carry-forwards are allowed.

If the useful life of qualified property is 7 years or more, 100% qualifies; if its useful life is at least 5 years but less than 7 years, 66⅔% qualifies; and if its useful life is at least 3 years but less than 5 years, 33⅓% qualifies. Restrictions on public utility property effectively reduce the 7% credit to 4%. This credit was originally introduced in 1962, suspended between October

---

[20] "APB Opinion No. 19: Reporting Changes in Financial Position," *The Journal of Accountancy* (June, 1971), pp. 69-73. Because of the broadened concepts of the "Funds Statement," the APB recommended that the title "Statement of Source and Application of Funds" be changed to "Statement of Changes in Financial Position."

[21] The investment credit is available for only "Section 38 property" (new or used) and must meet all of the tests:

    (1) It is tangible *personal* property (other than inventories) or is nonpersonal tangible property meeting certain qualifications.

    (2) It is subject to the allowance for depreciation (or amortized in lieu of depreciation, such as leasehold improvements amortized over the remaining

10, 1966 and March 9, 1967, and repealed generally on April 18, 1969. It was restored as of January, 1971.

Amendments to the Internal Revenue Code

Under the 1962 law, when the tax credit was taken it also had to be used to reduce the amount of the cost of the asset that could be depreciated, that is, from 100% to 93%. Specifically, the taxpayer received an immediate credit equivalent to 7% and could then depreciate 93% under its usual method of depreciation.

However, the taxpayer can now receive the advantage of the 7% tax credit in the year of purchase of the depreciable asset, but *in addition* can then depreciate 100% of the cost of the asset rather than the previous 93%. Assuming a tax rate of 50%, a corporation is in effect given the right to depreciate 114% of the cost of the asset.

Accounting Treatment for the Investment Credit

After the enactment of the 1962 Amendment to the Internal Revenue Code that established the 7% investment credit, the American Institute of Certified Public Accountants issued Opinion No. 2 [22] in which the Accounting Principles Board concluded that the investment credit "should be reflected in net income [in financial records and published reports] over the productive life of acquired property and *not* in the year in which it is placed in service" and therefore the year in which the entire tax credit is actually allowed.

In late 1971 the AICPA had decided to require that investment credit be amortized over the useful life of the asset and the SEC had agreed, while the U.S. Treasury Department said it was neutral. Then Congress, for the first time setting itself above the SEC and the AICPA, passed legislation stating that "no taxpayer shall be required without his consent to use any particular method of accounting for the (investment) credit." On December 9 the AICPA-APB issued an unanimous denunciation of Congressional involvement in this accounting principle and indicated disapproval of Congress overriding the AICPA and the SEC.

---

term of the lease, when the useful life is longer).
(3) It has a useful life of 3 years or more measured from the time it is placed in service.

[22] "Accounting for the 'Investment Credit,'" *Opinions of the Accounting Principles Board No. 2* (New York: American Institute of Certified Public Accountants, 1962), par. 13, p. 7.

QUESTIONS

1. What are the two basic causes of depreciation of an asset?

2. Since the depreciation charges of a given period do not represent corresponding cash outlays in that period, are they a real expense of that period? Discuss carefully.

3. "It is well known that since World War II internal equity finance—the reinvestment of retained earnings and depreciation funds—has provided a huge proportion of total corporate funds and that external equity finance . . . has played a relatively small role." (Arnold W. Sametz, "Trends in the Volume and Composition of Equity Finance," *The Journal of Finance,* September, 1964, p. 450.) Is depreciation a source of funds? Explain carefully.

4. (a) Should depreciation be based on replacement costs? Justify your position.

   (b) Describe briefly the attitude of the accounting profession regarding the proper basis for depreciation. Do you agree with this position? Why or why not?

5. (a) How would "general price level financial statements" differ from those typically included in corporate annual reports?

   (b) What is the position of the AICPA concerning such statements? As a financial analyst, would you support the position taken by AICPA? Discuss.

6. Generally accepted accounting principles require that the cost of fixed assets be spread over their useful life in such a way as to allocate it as equitably as possible to periods during which services are obtained from the use of the facilities (a paraphrasing of a statement by the Accounting Principles Board).

   (a) What flexibility does the corporation have in determining the annual depreciation charge?

   (b) Of what significance is this flexibility to investment analysts?

   (c) Discuss the merits and shortcomings of the accelerated depreciation techniques. As a stockholder, under what circumstances would you prefer that your company (1) use the methods, and (2) not use such methods?

   (d) Can the accelerated methods reduce the impact of price-level changes on the firm? Explain.

7. What is the maximum rate at which assets can be written off under the three depreciation methods?

8. (a) What is meant by "normalizing" in reference to accelerated depreciation methods and tax consequences?

   (b) Do you feel the flow-through technique or the normalizing technique should be used in preparing corporate income statements? Justify your position. What is the stand of the AICPA? of the SEC?

9. In 1971 the APB proposed that the 7% investment credit, then being reestablished for business corporations by the Nixon administration, be

deferred over the anticipated life of the equipment purchased for accounting purposes.

(a) What is the investment credit?

(b) Discuss the significance of the position taken by the APB for investors.

10. Describe how depletion is calculated under the cost method. How does this differ from the percentage depletion method?

11. How are exploration costs for oil and gas normally accounted for? Of what significance is this to investors?

12. Are there any conditions under which a wasting asset company would be justified in not providing for depletion?

13. Discuss goodwill under "pooling of interests" vs. "purchase of assets."

WORK-STUDY PROBLEMS

1. (a) Calculate the cash flow of General Motors Corporation for the past 5 years, submitting with your solution the actual calculations.

(b) Project the cash flow of General Motors for the next 5 years.

(c) Examine the source and application of funds statements of General Motors Corporation for the past 5 years and present an interpretation of the figures.

2. Assume that Companies A and B each have sales of $100,000,000, expenses other than depreciation of $60,000,000, and 5,000,000 shares of common stock outstanding.

(a) Calculate the first year's depreciation on assets of $100,000,000 that have a 10-year life:

(1) For Company A on the straight-line basis.

(2) For Company B on the double declining-balance basis.

(b) Assume that the tax rate applicable to both companies is 48% and that Company B uses the flow-through technique.

(1) Prepare an income statement for each company.

(2) Calculate the net income and the net earnings per share for each company.

(c) Assume that Company B uses the normalizing technique.

(1) Prepare the income statement for Company B.

(2) Calculate the net income and the net earnings per share.

SUGGESTED READINGS

APB Statement No. 4. "Basic Concepts and Accounting Principles Underlying Financial Statements of Business Enterprises." New York: American Institute of Certified Public Accountants, October, 1970.

Accounting Trends and Techniques (annual). New York: American Institute of Certified Public Accountants.

AICPA-APB Opinions. New York: American Institute of Certified Public Accountants.

  Opinion No.   3—"The Statement of Source and Application of Funds." October, 1963.

  Opinion No. 11—"Accounting for Income Taxes" (Includes Deferred Taxes). December, 1967.

  Opinion No. 12—"Omnibus Opinion" (Includes Disclosure of Depreciation). December, 1967.

  Opinion No. 19—"Reporting Changes in Financial Position." March, 1971.

  Opinion No. 20—"Accounting Changes." July, 1971.

  Opinion No. 22—"Disclosure of Accounting Policies." April, 1972. (Also see Paul Pacte, "Some Comment on Applying APB Opinion No. 22." *The Journal of Accountancy* (December, 1972), pp. 60-61.)

Backer, Morton. "Valuation Reporting in the Netherlands: A Real-Life Example," *Financial Executive* (January, 1973), pp. 40-50.

Barbatelli, Ettore. "How Business Can Take Maximum Advantage of Investment Tax Credit." *Financial Executive* (June, 1972), pp. 56-63.

Barrett, M. Edgar. "Proposed Bases for Asset Valuation." *Financial Executive* (January, 1973), pp. 12-17.

Editor's Notebook. "The Investment Tax Credit." *The Journal of Accountancy* (February, 1972), pp. 29.

Kapnick, Harvey. "Accounting for Tax Incentives—Reconsideration of Objectives Required." (APB Opinion No. 11, based on a compromised method—straight-line depreciation—accelerated depreciation—deferred taxes) *The Journal of Accountancy* (August, 1972), pp. 71-76.

Lamden, Charles W. "Depreciation—A Reliability Gap." *The Journal of Accountancy* (April, 1972), pp. 67-70.

Mautz, Robert K. "A Few Words for Historical Cost." *Financial Executive* (January, 1973), pp. 23-27, 64.

Reego, William A. "Reflecting Historical Cost and Current Values in Financial Reporting." *Financial Executive* (March, 1973), pp. 50-58.

Roberts, Aubrey C., and David R. L. Gabhart. "Statement of Funds: A Glimpse of the Future?" *The Journal of Accountancy* (April, 1972), pp. 54-59.

Rosenfield, Paul. "The Confusion Between General Price-Level Restatement and Current Value Accounting." *The Journal of Accountancy* (October, 1972), pp. 63-68.

"Some Further Comments" (Editorial). *Financial Executive* (January, 1973), pp. 52-59.

Staubus, George J. "An Analysis of APB Statement No. 4." *The Journal of Accountancy* (February, 1972), pp. 36-43.

Trienens, Howard J. "Legal Aspects of Fair Value Accounting." *Financial Executive* (January, 1973), pp. 30-35.

Analysis of the Balance Sheet

At one time the balance sheet was considered the key to investment analysis for fixed income securities, for preferred stock, and also for the relatively few common stocks that could be accepted into the family of investment securities. The protection for an investment-grade security was assumed to rest largely on an adequate asset backing of (1) mortgages secured by sufficient real property and (2) book value (or par value) of equity securities backed by sufficient assets.

In the 1930s, fixed income investors found that assumed asset protection often turned out to be a disastrous illusion, while fixed income securities protected by adequate earning power weathered the storm. This caused the attention of investors to shift to income statement analysis. Investors learned that if earnings and cash flow proved insufficient to meet fixed charges, assumed asset protection usually just melted away. When assets were taken over, their liquidation value proved far lower than book value—on the average only 10 cents on the dollar in bankruptcy cases.

It came to be realized that depreciation is only a method of amortizing the cost of fixed assets and that, as far as fixed assets are involved, net asset book value is simply cost less amortization of cost. It was recognized that such unamortized cost could only coincidently represent economically realizable values and this was true of most other asset figures.

In terms of common stocks, it has long been recognized that for most corporations there frequently is little correlation between the earning power value of a stock and its book value and, therefore, between the economic value of stock and the economic value of assets and their book value. Most investors and analysts pay little attention to book value, except in the case of

(1) financial corporations whose asset values are assumed to be close to realized market values, (2) public utilities because they are entitled (although not guaranteed) to earn a fair return on the fair value of assets used in the public service, and (3) on occasion, natural resources companies.

As the years have passed, less and less attention has been paid to balance sheet analysis, and in many cases analysis has rested almost solely on income statement analysis. While it is true that the value of a business and particularly of the owner's equity rests largely on earning power and on dividend paying ability dependent on earning power, this does not preclude balance sheet analysis—especially as the liquidity of corporations in the United States today is lower than at any time since the early 1930s in terms of cash.

BALANCE SHEET DISCLOSURE

Investors must be clear in their minds as to what balance sheets purport to show as opposed to what they often believe is presented. The investor examines the balance sheet to determine the company's current financial position, the amount and the nature of invested capital and the sources of invested capital, and the proportionate division of corporate capitalization.

Balance Sheet Values

Accountants report fixed assets on the balance sheet only as presenting their original cost and the amortization of that cost over the useful life of the asset. And yet many investors and analysts tend to view the asset figures on the balance sheet as asset "values."

Unfortunately, many of the users of financial statements are not cognizant of the accounting usage of the word *value*; this usage is discussed in the following quotation:

VALUE AND ITS DERIVATIVES

Value is a word of many meanings. Just as beauty is said to lie in the eye of the beholder, so worth may lie in the mind of the appraiser. There is no unique standard of worth which is both realistic and objectively applicable. . . . But apart from the difficulty of measuring *value* when the word is used to connote *worth,* it is evident that in the literature of business, economics, and accounting, *value* is used in varying significances, not all of which have any definite connotation of worth. The word is commonly employed in accounting to describe the figure at which an asset or liability is carried in the accounts, even though the amount may be determined by a process which is not one of valuation in any ordinary sense.

Since accounting is predominantly based on cost, the proper uses of the word *value* in accounting are largely restricted to the statement of items at cost, or at modifications of cost. In accounting, the term *market value* is used in senses differing somewhat from those attaching to the expression in law. As applied to securities, it means a sum computed on the assumption that value is measurable by market quotations; as applied to inventories, it is compiled from a variety of considerations, including market quotations, cost of replacement, and probable sales price. In the case of so-called fixed assets the *value* shown in accounts is the balance of their cost (actual or modified) after deducting recorded depreciation. Thus the following definition would seem to be appropriate:

> *Value* as used in accounts signifies the amount at which an item is stated, in accordance with the accounting principles related to that item. Using the word *value* in this sense, it may be said that balance-sheet values generally represent cost to the accounting unit or some modification thereof; but sometimes they are determined in other ways, as for instance on the basis of market values or cost of replacement, in which cases the basis should be indicated in financial statements.

The word *value* should seldom if ever be used in accounting statements without a qualifying adjective.

BOOK VALUE

The term *book value* is one of several widely used expressions in which the word *value* appears with a particular qualifying adjective to denote a particular concept of value. *Book value* is to be distinguished from such terms as fair or market value or liquidating value, in that it refers to amounts reflected on accounting records and in financial statements.

The term *book value* is seldom if ever used in the body of financial statements, either as an indication of the basis of stating an item therein or in connection with owners' equities. To do so would involve a pointless truism and such use is therefore not recommended.

. . .

This use of the word value does not involve the concept of current worth, but rather refers to a particular method of quantitative determination.

. . .

Book value signifies the amount at which an item is stated in accordance with the accounting principles related to the item.

. . . More specific terms . . . can be used in describing the kind of value at which individual items are stated; as, for example, *cost less depreciation, lower of cost or current replacement cost,* or *lower of cost or selling price.* Similarly, the term *ledger balance* or a term such as the *amount shown in published financial statements* would more clearly and accurately convey an exact meaning. The committee believes that any reference to a quantitative determination of a specific item can be more clearly and specifically described by terms other than the general and relatively vague term *book value.*

Recommendations: The committee recommends that the use of the term *book value* in referring to amounts at which individual items are stated in books of account or in financial statements, be avoided, and that, instead, the basis of amounts intended to apply to individual items be described specifically and precisely.

Owners' equity

The committee recognizes that the term *book value* is also used in various business arrangements . . .

When the intent of the parties is not clear as to the use of the term *book value* in reference to owners' equity, the committee suggests the following definition:

> *Book value* is the amount shown on accounting records or related financial statements at or as of the date when the determination is made, after adjustments necessary to reflect (1) corrections of errors, and (2) the application of accounting practices which have been consistently followed.

> *Recommendations:* In view of the fact that the intent of the parties to arrangements involving sale or transfer of business interests should govern, and the foregoing definition may not reflect such intent, the committee recommends that the term *book value* be avoided. Instead of this term it is recommended that any agreement involving the general concept of book value should contain a clearly defined understanding in specific and detailed terms, particularly as to such matters as are referred to under "owners' equity." [1]

Balance Sheet Information Sought by Analysts

The balance sheet describes the financial position of the corporation to the extent that it lists the amount (debits or credits) shown on the books in the asset, liability, and capital accounts. The difference between the total amount of the asset accounts and the total amount of the liability accounts is the total of the capital or equity accounts, the common and preferred equity.

"Balance sheet" is a distinctly technical accounting term. "In this view, a balance sheet may be defined as: A tabular statement or summary of balances (debit and credit) carried forward after an actual or constructive closing of books of account kept according to principles of accounting." [2] This is as far as accountants are willing to go in accepting responsibility for what a balance sheet purports to report. So, the investor must expect neither more nor less than this and should not infer that it purports otherwise in any analysis. Certainly it does not purport to list economic or investment values.

The major types of information that the analyst seeks from the balance sheet are:

---

[1] "Inventory of Generally Accepted Accounting Principles for Business Enterprises," *Accounting Research Study No. 7* (New York: American Institute of Certified Public Accountants, 1965), pp. 229-232. See also Paul M. Foster, "Asset Disclosure for Stockholder Decision," *Financial Executive* (January, 1967), and Solomon Fabricant, "Inflation and Current Accounting Practice," *The Journal of Accountancy* (December, 1971), pp. 39-44.

[2] *Accounting Research Study No. 7, op. cit.,* p. 226.

1. The sources of funds that have been used to acquire the corporate assets:
   (a) The long-term funds invested by creditors (bondholders, private placement noteholders, equipment trust noteholders, etc.), by preferred stockholders, and by common stockholders. In the case of common stockholders, it includes earnings retained in the business (not paid out as dividends) and capital in excess of par.
   (b) The short-term funds supplied by banks, commercial paper houses, factors and trade creditors, etc.

   On the basis of the above information, the investor can calculate the proportion of invested capital contributed by creditors, preferred stockholders and common stockholders and can determine such ratios as long-term debt to stockholders' equity. It is often worthwhile for the investor to calculate the market value of the corporation's securities and the ratios of each component to the total capitalization so calculated. In this calculation, par value is often used for bonds and preferred stock, but market value is used for common stock; hence the term "total capitalization with common at market" (number of shares times market value).

2. The strength of the corporation's working capital position as indicated by the various working capital ratios (discussed in the next chapter). These ratios indicate the corporation's assumed ability to meet current liabilities, which are expected to be paid with current assets.

3. The assets of the corporation, which indicate the sources of the corporation's income and the manner in which capital was invested.

4. Data for an analysis of the balance sheet combined with an analysis of the income statements to indicate:
   (a) The amount and the rate of return on total long-term capitalization (an excellent test of corporate management).
   (b) The rate of return on total assets.
   (c) The rate of return on the stockholders' equity.
   (d) A check of the retained earnings account in the balance sheet with the earnings reported over a period of years in the income statement. (Retained earnings at the beginning of the period plus earnings for the entire period less dividends paid should give the total in the retained earnings account at the end of the period, except for charges or credits made directly to the retained earnings account that may not have been recorded in any income statement but that should have been disclosed in annual reports.)

5. The AICPA recommends that a "Funds Statement" also be provided.

Problems of Balance Sheet Analysis

Most of the problems of balance sheet analysis are contained on the asset side of the balance sheet with especial attention to fixed assets and intangibles. The current assets are generally stated at amounts that represent a figure close to their economic value: securities at market; inventories at cost or market, whichever is lower; and receivables less estimated doubtful accounts. In the case of fixed assets and intangibles, however, the amounts stated are cost less accumulated amortization of cost, and the net book amounts may be far from any economic values. In fact, the *true economic values* are largely capitalization values based on current or normal earning power.

In the balance sheet, the total of the liability and capital accounts is balanced by the total of the asset accounts. The extent to which these claims against assets are balanced by equivalent amounts depends on the economic value of the assets rather than on the balance sheet figures, which merely represent book figures, and in the case of fixed assets and intangibles, cost less amortization.

In total the liabilities and capital must be balanced by an equivalent total of assets so that the balance sheet figures will balance. The basic accounting formula is: Assets — Liabilities = Capital or Net Worth. If the dollar amount of assets on the balance sheet exactly equals the dollar amount of liabilities, there is no capital equity or ownership value. If the dollar amount of liabilities on the balance sheet exceeds the dollar amount of assets as reported on the balance sheet, then the corporation is insolvent—it has a capital deficit.

ASSETS SECTION OF THE BALANCE SHEET

In considering assets in the balance sheet as offsets to the liabilities and capital, it is very important that the analyst recognize what asset figures really mean and not have the illusion that these offsets to liabilities and capital represent reliable estimates of economic value, except to some extent in the case of current assets; and even in this case book figures may be far removed from economic values, especially in the case of inventories.

A well-regarded statement on accounting for assets follows:

> *Objective C.* Account for the assets invested in the enterprise by stock-holders (through property contributed or retained earnings) and creditors, in a meaningful manner, so that when considered with the liabilities and equity capital of stockholders there will be a fair presentation of the financial position of the enterprise both at the beginning and end of the period. It should be understood that financial position or balance sheet statements do not purport to show either present values of assets to the enterprise or values which might be realized in liquidation. They are going-concern figures.[3]

Current Assets—Working Capital

Current assets of a business (also called circulating assets or working assets) represent its *working capital*. The American Institute of Certified

---

[3] *Ibid.*, p. 62.

Public Accountants defines and discusses working capital and current assets as follows:

The working capital of a borrower has always been of prime interest to grantors of credit; and bond indentures, credit agreements, and preferred stock agreements commonly contain provisions restricting corporate actions which would effect a reduction or impairment of working capital [and would impair ability to satisfy debt requirements]. . . . Considerable variation and inconsistency exist, however, with respect to their [current assets and current liabilities] classification and display in financial statements.

. . . In the past, definitions of current assets have tended to be overly concerned with whether the assets may be *immediately* realizable. The discussion which follows takes cognizance of the tendency for creditors to rely more upon the ability of debtors to pay their obligations out of the proceeds of current operations and less upon the debtor's ability to pay in case of liquidation. It should be emphasized that financial statements of a going concern are prepared on the assumption that the company will continue in business. Accordingly, the views expressed in this section represent a departure from any narrow definition or strict *one-year* interpretation of either current assets or current liabilities; the objective is to relate the criteria developed to the operating cycle of a business.

. . . *Net working capital* is represented by the excess of current assets over current liabilities and identifies the relatively liquid portion of total enterprise capital which constitutes a margin or buffer for meeting obligations within the ordinary operating cycle of the business. [Frequently the term *working capital* is used to mean *net working capital*.]

For accounting purposes, the term *current assets* is used to designate cash and other assets or resources commonly identified as those which are reasonably expected to be realized in cash or sold or consumed during the normal operating cycle of the business. Thus the term comprehends in general such resources as (a) cash available for current operations and items which are the equivalent of cash; (b) inventories of merchandise, raw materials, goods in process, finished goods, operating supplies, and ordinary maintenance material and parts; (c) trade accounts, notes, and acceptances receivable; (d) receivables from officers, employees, affiliates, and others, if collectible in the ordinary course of business within a year; (e) instalment or deferred accounts and notes receivable if they conform generally to normal trade practices and terms within the business; (f) marketable securities representing the investment of cash available for current operations; and (g) prepaid expenses such as insurance, interest, rents, taxes, unused royalties, current paid advertising service not yet received, and operating supplies. Prepaid expenses are not current assets in the sense that they will be converted into cash but in the sense that, if not paid in advance, they would require the use of current assets during the operating cycle.

The ordinary operations of a business involve a circulation of capital within the current asset group. Cash is expended for materials, finished parts, operating supplies, labor, and other factory services, and such expenditures are accumulated as inventory cost. Inventory costs, upon sale of the products to which such costs attach, are converted into trade receivables and ultimately into cash again. The average time intervening between the acquisition of materials or services entering this process and the final cash realization constitutes an *operating cycle*. A one-year time period is to be used as a basis for the segregation of current assets in cases where there are several operating cycles occurring within a year. However, where the period of the operating cycle is more than twelve months, as in, for instance, the tobacco, distillery, and lumber businesses, the longer period should be used. Where a particular business has no clearly defined operating cycle, the one-year rule should govern.

This concept of the nature of current assets contemplates the exclusion from that classification of such resources as: (a) cash and claims to cash which are restricted as to withdrawal or use for other than current operations, are designated for expenditure in the acquisition or construction of non-current assets, or are segregated for the liquidation of long-term debts; (b) investments in securities (whether marketable or not) or advances which have been made for the purposes of control, affiliation, or other continuing business advantage; (c) receivables arising from unusual transactions (such as the sale of capital assets, or loans or advances to affiliates, officers, or employees) which are not expected to be collected within twelve months; (d) cash surrender value of life insurance policies; (e) land and other natural resources; (f) depreciable assets; and (g) long-term prepayments which are fairly chargeable to the operations of several years, or deferred charges such as unamortized debt discount and expense, bonus payments under a long-term lease, costs of rearrangement of factory layout or removal to a new location, and certain types of research and development costs.[4]

Current Liabilities

Because of the nature of working capital and the necessity of relating current liabilities to current assets, current liabilities are discussed here in connection with current assets. Current assets represent those items that will be used to pay current liabilities; the amount and the quality should be such that the margin of safety is sufficient.

The American Institute of Certified Public Accountants defines and discusses current liabilities as follows:

> The term *current liabilities* is used principally to designate obligations whose liquidation is reasonably expected to require the use of existing resources properly classifiable as current assets, or the creation of other current liabilities. As a balance-sheet category, the classification is intended to include obligations for items which have entered into the operating cycle, such as payables incurred in the acquisition of materials and supplies to be used in the production of goods or in providing services to be offered for sale; collections received in advance of the delivery of goods or performance of services; and debts which arise from operations directly related to the operating cycle, such as accruals for wages, salaries, commissions, rentals, royalties, and income and other taxes. Other liabilities whose regular and ordinary liquidation is expected to occur within a relatively short period of

---

[4] "Restatement and Revision of Accounting Research Bulletins," *Accounting Research Bulletin No. 43* (New York: American Institute of Certified Public Accountants, 1953), Ch. 3, Sec. A, pp. 19-21.

time, usually twelve months, are also intended for inclusion such as short-term debts arising from the acquisition of capital assets, serial maturities of long-term obligations, amounts required to be expended within one year under sinking fund provisions, and agency obligations arising from the collection or acceptance of cash or other assets for the account of third persons.

This concept of current liabilities would include estimated or accrued amounts which are expected to be required to cover expenditures within the year for known obligations (a) the amount of which can be determined only approximately (as in the case of provisions for accruing bonus payments) or (b) where the specific person or persons to whom payments will be made cannot as yet be designated (as in the case of estimated costs to be incurred in connection with guaranteed servicing or repair of products already sold). The current liability classification, however, is not intended to include a contractual obligation falling due at an early date which is expected to be refunded, or debts to be liquidated by funds which have been accumulated in accounts of a type not properly classified as current assets, or long-term obligations incurred to provide increased amounts of working capital for long periods. When the amounts of the periodic payments of an obligation are, by contract, measured by current transactions, as for example by rents (leases) or revenues received in the case of equipment trust certificates or by the depletion of natural resources in the case of property obligations, the portion of the total obligation to be included as a current liability should be that representing the amount accrued at the balance-sheet date.[5]

Cash and Cash Equivalent Items [6]

Sometimes cash and cash equivalent items are arbitrarily segregated and not included in current assets. If such segregated items have been arbitrarily excluded from current assets and if these items are, in fact, subject to the full control of management and not required to be segregated by regulations or contract agreements, the analyst should add them back to the current assets.

Receivables

In examining receivables, the analyst must consider the nature of the receivables in terms of the characteristics of the industry and the company's business. He must determine whether they are proportionately larger than normal in respect to current assets for the type of business and whether the deductions for "estimated doubtful accounts" are reasonable and in line with industry averages. To the extent possible, the analyst determines the quality of the receivables, considering the nature of the business. Any information on the average age of receivables and trends in this respect is significant. The

---

[5] *Ibid.*, pp. 21-23.

[6] See Paul F. Anderson and Harmon R. D. Boyd, "The Management of Excess Corporate Cash," *Financial Executive* (October, 1964).

receivables turnover figure in relation to the industry average is an important analytical tool (as described in Chapter 19).

Installment Sales and Receivables

Various methods are used in accounting for installment sales. The two most important methods are:

1. Consider each collection on installment sales as both a recovery of cost and a return of profit to the same extent as the ratio of cost and profit at the time the sale was consummated. Such installment sales are only taken up as income and considered as income for tax purposes in the period in which the receivables are *actually collected*.

2. Consider the full amount of installment sales as ordinary sales for the period in which the sales are first consummated, although income taxes will not be paid until the receivables are actually collected. In such cases the analyst should make an estimate of the income taxes to be paid when the receivables are collected and should deduct these taxes from the receivables on the balance sheet.

It is important that the estimate for doubtful or uncollectible accounts be reasonable in relation to receivables in the case of installment sales, and this is especially true if profits on installment sales are taken into income in the period that the sales are accomplished rather than when receivables are collected. If a corporation sells its installment notes to banks or finance companies, it should note whether they have been sold outright or on a "recourse basis." In the latter case the corporation has a contingent liability, which is usually not shown in the balance sheet but is included only as a footnote. The analyst must consider the size of these contingent liabilities and the likelihood of the contingency materializing in the light of the industry and company experience and the character of the receivables.

Inventories

The analyst should, where possible, calculate inventory turnover. Unfortunately a definitive ratio can usually be achieved only through an examination in terms of annual figures, dividing cost of goods sold by average inventory. Ideally, with respect to seasonal businesses, monthly sales at cost would be the most relevant, but annual figures are often the only ones available to investors.

Recessions, generally characterized as inventory recessions, result from excessive inventories following expansion and require working down. Wide fluctuation in the price structure has heretofore caused severe inventory problems; but the advent of computer controls combined with economic and market analysis has measurably reduced the inventory problem as opposed to what it was prior to 1945. Still, in certain industries, excessive inventories and inventory price fluctuations can cause serious financial problems.

The analyst must also consider all the applications of Fifo and Lifo inventory accounting as applied to analysis between companies and over a period of years for the same company if company reports do not provide actual figures over a period during which inventory accounting was changed from Fifo to Lifo or vice versa.[7]

Long-Term Investments—Noncurrent Assets

A basic accounting position on the reporting of long-term investments and noncurrent assets is quoted below.

> *Long-term investments in securities ordinarily should be carried at cost. When market quotations are available, the aggregate quoted amounts should be disclosed. Investments in affiliates should be segregated from other investments.*
>
> One of the noncurrent classifications applicable to assets is that of investments. Common investments owned by business enterprises include shares of stock, bonds, and other securities, mortgages and contracts receivable, life insurance policies on the lives of officers that designate the company as beneficiary, and special funds to finance plant expansion or to retire long-term debt. Temporary investments are classed as current assets; only long-term holdings of securities are classified as investments.
>
> The [balance sheet] value of investment securities is not normally affected by fluctuation in the market value. Adjustments to the initial valuation are normally made only when there is evidence of a permanent decline in value, such as default of bond interest or principal.[8]

The reader should review the discussion in Chapter 17 as well as AICPA-APB Opinion No. 18.[9]

Fixed Assets

Fixed assets consist of land, plant, and equipment. Unlike current assets, which in most cases are reported in the balance sheet at amounts reasonably close to their economic or realizable value, fixed assets are simply reported at cost less amortization of cost, that is, fixed assets at cost less accumulated depreciation. Depreciation was examined in some detail (in Chapter 17), and

---

[7] See Chapter 17 and APB Opinion No. 20 in *The Journal of Accountancy* (October, 1971), pp. 63-72.

[8] *Accounting Research Study No. 7, op. cit.,* pp. 259-260; and APB Opinion No. 18.

[9] See *The Journal of Accountancy* (June, 1971), pp. 63-75; and (September, 1971), pp. 54-62.

it was emphasized that the process of depreciation is the process of amortization of cost over the estimated life of the asset and in no sense a process of valuation.

The economic value of fixed assets is their earning power, which bears no necessary relationship to the amount at which they are carried in the books. However, in most cases the going-concern value and the replacement value of fixed assets in recent years are usually well in excess of the amount at which the fixed assets are recorded in the company's books of account. This is especially true if rapid tax depreciation is also reflected in the books. The other important factor has been inflation. However, in spite of these factors, if the assets under present management and perhaps under any management do not have satisfactory earning power in relation to the amount at which they are recorded on the books, then they are in fact overvalued on the books, often seriously overvalued.

Wasting Assets

Natural resources are wasting assets. They are physically exhausted through extraction and, except for timber, they are irreplaceable. Until these resources are extracted from the land, they are classified as fixed assets; once they have been extracted, they are classified as inventories until sold.

Accepted practice in accounting for natural resources is as follows:

> . . . When the presence of a natural resource is discovered *subsequent* to acquisition of the property, or when the extent of the deposit is determined to be materially more extensive than previously assessed, it is accepted practice to reconsider previous allocations of aggregate cost.
>
> The search for new resources is a continuing endeavor . . . This endeavor necessitates large outlays for exploration, options, lease bonuses, advance royalties, abstract and recording fees, geological and geophysical staff expenses, and so forth. Even when the most advanced geological and geophysical technology is used to predict reserves, there is no assurance that resource deposits in paying quantities will be located, or that once located, the original estimates of the deposit will hold up. The uncertainty characteristic of extractive industries presents difficult problems of cost determination and allocation. It is accepted practice either to capitalize or expense the outlays mentioned above; but the majority practice is to capitalize the costs that are readily identifiable with the successful acquisition of specific resources in paying quantities and to expense the others.[10]

Intangibles

Intangibles that appear in the balance sheet come from two sources:

---

[10] *Accounting Research Study, No. 7, op. cit.,* p. 258. The subject of depletion was discussed in some depth in Chapter 17.

(1) intangible assets purchased outright and (2) intangible assets developed initially in the regular course of business.

Intangibles purchased outright are intangibles (such as goodwill) that have been acquired in exchange for an issue of securities, for cash, or for other considerations. These intangibles have been acquired separately but usually are part of a total acquisition. Initial intangibles should be recorded at cost, as with all assets, which may be the fair value of consideration given. The AICPA stated in APB Opinion No. 17 (1970) that the costs of *all* intangible assets, including goodwill arising from a "purchase" type of business combination, should be recorded as assets and should be amortized by systematic charges to income over estimated benefit periods, the period of amortization not to exceed 40 years.[11]

Intangible items have been extremely important in recent years as the result of the multitude of mergers and other acquisitions that have taken place. It is quite common for the acquiring corporation to pay more than the book value of the assets acquired and the difference is considered to be goodwill under the *purchase of assets method*.

Those intangibles whose life is definitely limited by law or agreement or regulation (patents, copyrights, leases, licenses, franchises for a fixed term, and goodwill as to which there is evidence of limited duration) should be amortized by a systematic charge to the income account. In the case of intangibles for which there cannot be assigned any definite limited life (goodwill generally, going value, trade names, secret processes, subscription lists, perpetual franchises, and organization costs), when it becomes reasonably evident that a meaningful term of existence is limited and that the intangibles, therefore, have become like the other intangibles mentioned above, the cost should be amortized over the estimated period of usefulness. But if the period of usefulness is relatively short so that the income account might be unduly burdened by amortization and give a misleading picture of income, then the intangible may be charged off directly to retained earnings.

There may be intangible assets developed in the regular course of the business, for example as the result of research and development or of advertising and promotion. With respect to research and development, the author of an AICPA-published study has stated that "the most practical treatment is to charge these expenditures to expense currently, for it is usually difficult to determine in advance the benefit that may result in future periods."[12] With respect to advertising costs incident to developing consumer preference for trademarks, trade names, brand names, and brands, this author has also

[11] Also see Dean S. Eiteman, "Critical Problems in Accounting for Goodwill," *The Journal of Accountancy* (March, 1971), pp. 46-50.

[12] *Accounting Research Study No. 7, op. cit.*, pp. 265-266.

stated: "It is, however, impossible to delineate the portion of advertising costs that have expired in the production of current revenue from the portion that may be applicable to the future. Treatment as current expense is, therefore, accepted practice." [13]

The above costs developed in the regular course of the business are normal business expenses in our highly competitive economy and therefore they should be expensed rather than capitalized. It may be argued that occasionally such expenses are exceptionally large in any one year and therefore should be capitalized and amortized over a period of years. However, situations where this is justified are the exception.

LIABILITIES AND CAPITAL SECTIONS OF THE BALANCE SHEET

As stated on page 462, the account "current liabilities" was discussed therein following the topic on "current assets—working capital" because of the inherent relationship between these two accounts.

Capitalization of the Corporation [14]

The balance sheet furnishes reliable information on the amount of capital that has been invested in the business (including retained earnings) and also how the capital invested has been divided between the various sources of capital. Investors should analyze the capitalization of the corporation by the use of ratios (discussed in Chapter 19) to indicate the degree to which the corporation is trading on its equity and the resultant degree of financial leverage and rates of return on capitalization. They should also calculate capitalization with common at market.

Long-Term Debt

This consists of long-term obligations such as bonds, private placement notes, equipment obligations, and term and time bank loans, the latter generally with maturities of 1 to 8 years. The amounts that appear on the balance sheet can generally be assumed to state accurately the amount of long-term obligations currently outstanding. Notes to financial statements

---

[13] *Ibid.,* p. 266.

[14] For discussions of long-term debt, trading on the equity, and financial leverage, the reader should review Chapter 5, "Common Stocks and Preferred Stocks"; Chapter 6, "Debt Instruments"; Chapter 7, "Corporate Financial Policies and the Investor"; Chapter 8, "Investment Strategies for Limited-Income Securities"; and Chapter 9, "Standards for Selection of Limited-Income Securities."

will furnish additional information about the debt contracts, such as restrictive clauses against retained earnings for dividends and officers' salaries.

The balance sheet itself will not reveal so-called off balance sheet liabilities, such as obligations for long-term leases and unfunded pension liabilities, which are only noted in footnotes to the financial statement. These obligations are real, although accountants do not consider them to be liabilities of the type to be recorded on the balance sheet. The investor must give careful attention to these "off balance sheet" liabilities and often must seek information from SEC registration statements in addition to the usually meager information appearing in the footnotes to the financial statements.

Leases

In the post-World War II period, leasing has become a major method of financing the use of property and equipment, and annual rentals under leases run into billions of dollars. Leasing differs in technique (although often not in substance) from conventional purchase of assets. Because of the relatively new use of leases in many areas, basic principles and practices for accounting for leases in published financial statements have not been clearly defined. Specifically, they do not appear as liabilities on the balance sheet but only as footnotes, and the disclosure in the footnotes is usually meager. In most cases, lease financing is a substitute for straight-debt financing, which must appear on the balance sheet. The AICPA has been pressured by creditors and financial analysts to recommend more complete information and uniform reporting for leases in financial statements. The result has been the AICPA Research Study No. 4 (1962), Opinion No. 5 (1964), Opinion No. 7 (1966), and Opinion No. 27.[15] Opinion No. 5 recognized the desirability of capitalizing leases on the balance sheet, but not all leases. Opinion No. 7 was inconsistent with Opinion No. 5. In October, 1973, the SEC issued a new rule effective for all reports filed subsequent to December 1, 1973, requiring that corporations disclose the financial impact of lease commitments including impact of lease costs on income and the capitalized value of certain long-term leases.

Many analysts consider a lease obligation a real liability and therefore agree with the resolution universally passed on June 1, 1966, at a meeting of

---

[15] The full titles of these publications by the American Institute of Certified Public Accountants are:

(a) "Reporting of Leases in Financial Statements," *Accounting Research Study No. 4* (1962), p. 140.
(b) "Reporting of Leases in Financial Statements of Lessee," *Opinions of the Accounting Principles Board No. 5* (1964).
(c) "Accounting for Leases in Financial Statements of Lessors," *Opinions of the Accounting Principles Board No. 7* (1966)
(d) "Accounting for Lease Transactions by Manufacturers or Dealer Lessors," *Opinion of the Accounting Principles Board No. 27* (November, 1972).

the Board of Directors of Robert Morris Associates (a national organization of bank lending officers) as follows:

> Whereas lease obligations of companies are often material and irrevocable liabilities and represent a significant method of financing property and equipment used by many companies, and
>
> Whereas the AICPA published an excellent research study on this subject of the reporting of leases in financial statements (Accounting Research Study No. 4 by John H. Myers) and
>
> Whereas the manner of showing leases in the financial statements of lessees requires improvement to properly reflect the economic and accounting facts, therefore, be it
>
> Resolved that Robert Morris Associates suggest to the Accounting Principles Board of the AICPA that its Opinion No. 5 on "Reporting of Leases in Financial Statements of Lessee" be revised to more nearly conform to the conclusions of Accounting Research Study No. 4 and to require that all financing leases totaling a material amount *be reflected in balance sheets as obligations of the lessee companies.* (Note: Agrees with 1973 SEC ruling.)

It has been stated that a lease may be a liability for one user of financial statements but not for another, which appears to be specious reasoning. The lease is a receivable to the lessor and a liability to the lessee.

The basis for capitalizing of leases is that they are in effect "installment purchases" of property and that the costs should be amortized. It can be agreed that some leases should be capitalized as installment purchases of property and some as leases.

The financial analyst should consider a lease for the installment purchase of property as a liability and only a substitute for a debt obligation. If the corporation does not capitalize it on the balance sheet (as few, if any, do), the analyst should prepare his own balance sheet capitalizing the lease and then analyze the balance sheet on this basis. However, in many cases (perhaps a majority), not all of the lease payment is an actual fixed charge. Part of the periodic lease payment may be contingent on sales. Therefore, only the fixed portion of the lease rental should be capitalized and an appropriate rate determined by the analyst preparing his own revised balance sheet of the company under review.

Unfunded Pension Reserves—Past Service Cost

When a corporation establishes a pension fund, it accepts two costs: (1) past service costs that have not been funded and (2) current pension costs based on current payrolls. Accounting for pension costs and especially legislation to require vesting of pensions was discussed in Chapter 16.

The problem as far as the balance sheet is concerned is that of past service costs—the unfunded pension costs covering the period prior to the inauguration of the pension plan. These funds were not set aside previously but would have been funded if a pension plan had been in effect. The amount of these unfunded pension costs is often very substantial and in the case of large corporations may amount to several hundred million dollars. These unfunded pension costs are a liability of the corporation. However, many (perhaps most) pension fund agreements provide that annual payments to amortize unfunded pension costs may be skipped in years of poor earnings, sometimes for as many as three consecutive years. Probably because of this flexibility in liability payments, the unfunded premium liability is not considered to be a liability of the nature that must be stated on the balance sheet but only as a footnote to the financial statement.

However, the Accounting Principles Board of the AICPA stated that a major objective of Opinion No. 8 was to eliminate inappropriate fluctuation in recorded pension costs. It stated that "costs should not be limited to the amounts for which the company has a *legal* liability." The principles involved are that the pension cost accounting method should be *applied consistently from year to year* and that the amount recognized for past pension service costs *should be relatively stable from year to year*.[16] Opinion No. 8 does not require that certified statements disclose the amount of unfunded or otherwise unprovided for past or prior service costs. However, the SEC does require such disclosure.

It is certainly true that the unfunded cost is to a degree a fluctuating type of liability and therefore it need not be a requirement to incorporate it as a liability on the balance sheet proper. However, the requirement by the AICPA that the amount of the annual past pension service cost (amortized) should be *reasonably stable* from year to year should place the analyst on notice that the liability for past service costs is a liability that should be amortized in a relatively stable manner.

Preferred Stock Equity

If the corporation has preferred stock outstanding, the balance sheet will disclose the number of shares, the par or stated value per share, and the total dollar amount of the preferred stock. In the balance sheet, preferred stock

---

[16] Julius W. Phoenix, Jr. and William D. Bosse, "Accounting for the Cost of Pension Plans—More Information on APB No. 8, *The Journal of Accountancy* (October, 1967); and "Pension Reform," *The Journal of Accountancy* (May, 1972), p. 76.

is listed in the capital section along with the common stock. It is true that it is largely an equity security, but it is a strictly limited equity security.

The preferred stock is senior to the common stock. The amount shown on the balance sheet should represent the claim of preferred stock coming ahead of the common stock, but this is not always the manner in which it is reported on the balance sheet. If the preferred stock has a par value or a stated value relatively close to its legal claim (for example, liquidating value) ahead of the common stock, then the balance sheet closely reflects the actual situation. However, if the stated value is only a nominal amount and is not close to the claim of the preferred stock, then the preferred stock on the balance sheet (number of shares of preferred stock times the stated value) does not reflect the true situation. In addition, there may be dividend arrears, which, while they are not liabilities of the corporation, do represent a claim senior to the common stock. However, such arrearages are usually not shown on the balance sheet but are disclosed only as a footnote thereto.

In summary, if the balance sheet does not properly reflect the preferred stock's claim ahead of the common stock, the analyst should reconstruct the balance sheet so that it properly reflects the preferred claims that are senior to the common stock.

Common Stock Equity

Because the common stock is the residual claimant to the assets and the earnings of the corporation, the common stock section of the balance sheet is divided into three separate accounts: capital stock, retained earnings (formerly earned surplus), and capital paid-in in excess of par (or stated) value (formerly capital surplus).

There is considerable lack of uniformity in the manner in which common stock (and preferred stock) is reported in the balance sheet. Analysts feel that the trend in recent years towards highly condensed statements supported by notes to financial statements has gone too far—for example, giving only one summary figure for capital stock. Furthermore, in spite of the opinion [17] that the term "surplus" should not be used because it has a "money in the bank" connotation that is quite misleading, a few major corporations are still using the term on their balance sheets.

---

[17] *Accounting Research Study No. 7, op. cit.,* pp. 188-190, states:

67. While the terms *capital surplus* and *earned surplus* have been widely used, they are open to serious objection.

(1) The term *surplus* has a connotation of excess, overplus, residue, or "that

An authoritative writer [18] on accounting has suggested the following breakdown of the capital section of the balance sheet, although stating that "the detail breakdown . . . is not ordinarily shown in financial statements." This would be an ideal breakdown, assuming always that the preferred claim was adequately disclosed. "In case there are two or more classes of stock, account for the equity capital invested for each and disclose the rights and preferences to dividends and to principal in liquidation."

Stockholders' Equity in Capital Invested:

Capital Stock:

Preferred stock—5% cumulative; par value $100; authorized_____shares; issued_____shares   . . . . .

Class A preferred stock—$2.00 cumulative; no par value, redeemable value $30; authorized and issued _____shares   . . . . .

Common stock—no par value; stated value $10; authorized_____shares; issued_____shares of which_____are in treasury   . . . . .

  . . . . .

---

which remains when use or need is satisfied" (Webster), whereas no such meaning is intended where the term is used in accounting.

(2) The terms *capital* and *surplus* have established meanings in other fields, such as economics and law, which are not in accordance with the concepts the accountant seeks to express in using those terms.

(3) The use of the term *capital surplus* (or, as it is sometimes called, *paid-in surplus*) gives rise to confusion. If the word *surplus* is intended to indicate capital accumulated by the retention of earnings, i.e., retained income, it is not properly used in the term *capital surplus;* and if it is intended to indicate a portion of the capital, there is an element of redundancy in the term *capital surplus.*

(4) If the term *capital stock* (and in some states the term *capital surplus*) be used to indicate capital which, in the legal sense, is restricted as to withdrawal, there is an implication in the terms *surplus* or *earned surplus* of availability for dividends. This is unfortunate because the status of corporate assets may well be such that they are not, as a practical matter, or as a matter of prudent management, available for dividends.

68. In seeking terms more nearly connotative of the ideas sought to be expressed, consideration should be given primarily to the *sources* from which the proprietary capital was derived. . . .

69. In view of the foregoing the committee in 1949 . . . recommending that, in the balance-sheet presentation of stockholders' equity:

(1) The use of the term *surplus* (whether standing alone or in such combinations as *capital surplus, paid-in surplus, earned surplus, appraisal surplus,* etc.) be discontinued. . . .

(3) The term *earned surplus* be replaced by terms which will indicate source, such as *retained income, retained earnings, accumulated earnings,* or *earnings retained for use in the business.* In the case of a deficit, the amount would be shown as a deduction from contributed capital with appropriate description.

[18] *Ibid.,* pp. 191-192.

Capital Paid-in in Excess of Par, Redemption and Stated
  Values of Capital Stocks:
    Premium on preferred stock . . . . .
    Arising from treasury stock transactions . . . . .
    Paid-in on common stock . . . . .
    Retained earnings capitalized on stock dividends . . . .

Retained Earnings:
    Appropriated in amount equal to restriction under
      bank loan as to payment of dividends . . . . .
    Unappropriated . . . .

    Total . . . . .

    Deduct Cost of_____Shares of Treasury Stock . . . . .

    Stockholder Equity . . . . .

QUESTIONS

1. Discuss briefly what the balance sheet reveals regarding a corporation.

2. "Depreciation is only a method of amortizing the cost of fixed assets . . . net asset book value is simply cost less amortization of cost." Discuss the significance of this statement for investment analysts in terms of analyzing the balance sheet.

3. (a) What type of assets would likely show book values similar to economic net worth? Why might the values of many assets on the balance sheet be far, far different from economic worth?
   (b) Give several illustrations of ways in which asset values, as expressed in the balance sheet, might mislead investors.

4. Distinguish carefully between book value, market value, liquidating value, and "true economic value."

5. (a) Define the term "operating cycle" of a corporation in respect to working capital.
   (b) How might the length of the operating cycle affect the amount of working capital required in a business? Explain carefully.

6. Are prepaid items properly current assets? Should an analyst include them as current assets? Discuss.

7. Describe the normal effects of a moderate business recession on the liquidity of corporations.

8. How are current liabilities defined by accountants?

9. (a) What are the more desirable methods of accounting for installment sales?
   (b) Would a liability account appear in the balance sheet of a corporation if it sold its installment notes to banks or finance companies? Should a liability account appear? Discuss.

10. (a) Are all securities owned by a corporation properly classified as current assets? Should any be classified as current assets? Discuss.
    (b) How are securities valued in the balance sheet?
11. (a) What is an intangible asset? Give examples.
    (b) How might an intangible asset arise in a merger? Discuss the proper accounting for such an intangible asset. Contrast "purchase of assets" with "pooling of interests."
    (c) How should the accountant handle research and development costs? Justify your position.
12. What is an "off balance sheet" liability? Where might an analyst gain information about such liabilities?
13. What is the significance of the way leased assets are handled accounting-wise for investment analysts?

WORK-STUDY PROBLEMS

1. The balance sheet items for two years of a manufacturer of office equipment are given below:
   (a) Arrange the balance sheet in proper order, paying particular attention to arrangement of the current assets and the current liabilities.
   (b) Explain, using at least two ratios for the two years, why the stock of this company might decline on release of the figures for the second year.

Balance Sheet, December 31

	First Year	Following Year
	(000)	
Cash	$ 1,208	$ 700
Plant	9,219	12,410
Short-Term Notes Payable	—	2,095
Accounts Receivable	4,368	5,455
Inventories	5,300	8,208
Plant Depreciation	2,569	2,788
Miscellaneous Liabilities	1,924	1,734
Taxes Payable	1,622	638
Investments in Subsidiaries	1,044	951
Surplus	9,950	10,016
Accounts Payable	2,116	4,351
Miscellaneous Assets	174	540
Net Property	6,650	9,622
Capital Stock	3,132	3,142
Bonded Debt	—	3,500
	$18,744	$25,476

2. Critically examine an annual report of a well-known company with reference to the adequacy of the data presented. Particular attention might be given to the following:

   (a) Description of the products.
   (b) Breakdown of sales by products, customers, and geographic areas.
   (c) Affiliations of directors.
   (d) Comparative balance sheets and income accounts with details as to inventory and depreciation policies.
   (e) Capital expenditures.
   (f) Labor costs.
   (g) Research progress and expenditures.
   (h) Lease arrangements and handling of pension costs.
   (i) Comments on competition, industry problems, and outlook.

3. Calculate the capitalization ratios for each of the following and comment on the record:

   (a) For a major electric utility.
   (b) For a major airline.
   (c) For a major railroad.
   (d) For one of the largest steel companies.
   (e) For each of the major automobile companies.

   (Calculate the capitalization ratios based on book capitalization and also based on capitalization using common equity at market value.)

SUGGESTED READINGS

Black, Fischer, and Myron Scholes. "The Valuation of Option Contracts and a Test of Market Efficiency." *The Journal of Finance* (May, 1972), pp. 399-417.

Cretien, Paul D., Jr. "Premiums on Convertible Bonds: Comment." *The Journal of Finance* (September, 1970), pp. 917-922.

Elton, Edwin J., and Martin J. Gruber. "The Economic Value of the Call Option." *The Journal of Finance* (September, 1972), pp. 891-901.

Johnson, R. W., and W. G. Lewellen. "Analysis of the Lease-Or-Buy Decision." *The Journal of Finance* (September, 1972), pp. 815-823.

Litzenberger, R. H., and Charles P. Jones. "The Capital Structure and the Cost of Capital: Comment." *The Journal of Finance* (June, 1970), pp. 669-673.

Reego, W. A. "Reflecting Historical Cost and Current Values in Financial Reporting." *Financial Executive* (March, 1973), pp. 50-58.

Rogers, Donald R., and R. W. Schattke. "Buy-Outs of Stock Options: Compensation or Capital?" *Journal of Accountancy* (August, 1972), pp. 55-59.

Ratio Analysis of Statements

The major function of statement analysis is to disclose those significant *relationships* demonstrated by the past and recent record of a company so that the trends and the current financial condition of the company may be determined and a meaningful projection of the company's future performance *probabilities* in respect to earnings and dividends may be estimated. Statement analysis must recognize the necessity of analyzing the balance sheet, the income statement, and the funds statement.

This chapter deals with ratio analysis of financial statements. It must be recognized that any actual ratios considered satisfactory will vary, often widely, depending upon the nature and the record of the industry and the company; therefore, no overall, all-inclusive standards can be fully meaningful. In this respect the analyst will find helpful the industry ratios provided in the Standard & Poor's industry surveys, those published by the SEC-FTC *Quarterly Financial Report for Manufacturing Corporations,* and the long-term annual figures in the *Economic Report of the President.*

The use of computers and especially of the Standard & Poor's Compustat Tape greatly simplifies the analyst's work, providing him with a wide variety of ratios that would not be feasible in most cases if the ratios had to be determined by hand calculations, as was the case before computers came into wide use in the financial community. In fact, there are more significant ratios on the tape than analysts customarily utilize.

BALANCE SHEET RATIO ANALYSIS

The purpose of balance sheet ratio analysis is to determine to the extent possible the financial position of the company, especially its ability to meet its obligations when due, the appropriateness of the capital structure, the degree of financial leverage in the capital structure, and the weakness (if any) in the structure as related to the stability or the lack of stability of industry and company earnings. Activity ratios, using data from both the balance sheet and the income statement, are useful in assessing the soundness of current assets and in assessing the effectiveness with which the firm is employing its resources, including rates of return on assets, total capital, and equity. The analysis must be supplemented by a "funds statement" analysis which is really a *working capital* analysis.

Liquidity and Related Ratios

The balance sheet ratios most commonly used in analyzing the liquidity and the related current positions of a company are discussed in the following paragraphs.

Working Capital Position. Current assets represent the working capital or circulating capital, and *net* working capital is the difference between current assets and current liabilities. The major tests applied to working capital are intended to determine (1) the company's ability to meet current liabilities when due and the margin of safety in this respect, and (2) management's efficiency in its use of working capital. Investors, both in equities and in debt obligations, are vitally interested in measures of the adequacy of a firm's working capital. A complete analysis of working capital requires a thorough analysis of cash flows, the "funds statement," and especially forecasts of funds flows in future periods. Ratios relating certain components of current assets to current liabilities and ratios relating to certain activities provide the usual tests used by financial analysts outside the company as opposed to internal management analysis.

Current Ratio. The simplest test is the current ratio—that of current assets to current liabilities. It indicates the company's ability to pay all current liabilities if all current assets were to be converted into cash. For many years it has been rather loosely stated that as a general rule this ratio should be in the neighborhood of 2 to 1—two dollars of current assets for each dollar of current liabilities. For all U.S. corporations in recent years the ratio has fallen well below 2 to 1. A general standard fails to recognize that an appropriate current ratio is a function of the nature of a company's business and varies in different companies and industries. Tests of the *composition* of the current assets are much more important than the overall ratio. For example, if the current ratio was only 1.5 to 1 but the ratio of cash and cash items to current liabilities was 1 to 1, there would be no problem in meeting the current obligations. In the case of public utility companies where there is no inventory problem and relatively no receivables collection problem, a current ratio of 1.1 or 1.2 to 1 has generally proved satisfactory. Conversely, if the current ratio for an industrial company was 3 to 1 but slow-moving inventories represented 90% of current assets and the ratio of other current assets to current liabilities was therefore only 0.3 to 1, the company would be in a weak financial position. The current ratio analysis must be supplemented by other working capital ratios, as well as a careful analysis of the "funds statement."

Acid-Test (Quick) Ratio. Because the problem in meeting current liabilities may rest on slowness or even inability to convert inventories into cash to meet current obligations, the acid-test (quick) ratio is frequently used. This is the ratio of current assets minus inventories (and also usually minus accruals and prepaid expenses) to current liabilities. In effect this is the ratio of cash and cash items plus receivables (sometimes called *quick assets*) to current liabilities. Of course, in some situations receivables may include a substantial amount of accounts that are overdue, raising questions as to their quality. The acid-test ratio assumes that receivables are of good quality and will, in the normal operating cycle, be converted into cash. When receivables are assumed by the past record to be liquid, this ratio provides an excellent test of ability to pay current debts. For many industries, the acid-test ratio should be about 1 to 1. The analyst should make a comparison of the ratios for the company being analyzed with industry ratios over the years and should study the trend in the company's ratios.

Cash Ratio. The cash ratio, which is the ratio of cash and cash items [1] to current liabilities, is the strictest of all tests. Quite obviously, if the cash ratio is 1 to 1, the company can have no problem in meeting its short-term obligations when due. For most companies, the ratio will rarely be this high. The analyst may find that for the industry and the company under review a cash ratio as low as 0.3 or 0.4 or 0.5 to 1 has proved quite satisfactory. For all U. S. corporations, the ratio in recent years has averaged close to 0.25 to 1.

Working Capital Turnover. As sales volume increases, the investment in inventories and receivables increases, suggesting a close relationship between sales and net working capital. The working capital turnover is computed

---

[1] Cash items usually consist of short-term governments or certificates of deposit, but they may also include commercial paper and bankers' acceptances.

by dividing net sales by net working capital. It is included among the "Fourteen Important Ratios" of Dun & Bradstreet, and it is recommended by Roy A. Foulke [2] as a sensitive indicator of undertrading or overtrading in relation to the firm's resources. Too low a turnover of working capital indicates inefficient use of current assets, and too high a turnover makes a firm vulnerable to minor reductions in sales. The working capital turnover ratio is a more sensitive indicator than an inventory turnover ratio. [3] Rises or declines in sales may well be accompanied by corresponding movements of inventory so that inventory turnover may remain unchanged. Such inventory changes are usually accompanied by equivalent changes in current liabilities, thus maintaining a stable net working capital. Therefore, while the inventory turnover ratio might remain constant, the working capital turnover ratio would rise with a rise in sales, suggesting more quickly the possibility of overtrading.

The working capital turnover ratio shows wide difference from one industry to another, and the proper ratio to be maintained varies with different lines of business activity. No obvious overall standard exists. The analyst should determine the trend of this ratio for the firm being studied and should contrast the firm's ratio and trend to S&P industry averages.

Accounts Receivable Turnover. Analysis of working capital can include the determination of the time taken to translate receivables into cash. This accounts receivable turnover can be obtained by dividing the net credit sales by the average balances of accounts receivable outstanding. This turnover may be converted into the number of days' sales outstanding by dividing the turnover figure into 365. One would usually expect the accounts receivable turnover to be relatively in line with the firm's terms of sale. Any serious delay in converting receivables into cash may impair the ability to meet current debts. On the other side of the coin, a high receivables turnover rate would tend to offset a low current ratio.

Inventory Turnover. The inventory turnover is computed by dividing the cost of materials used during the year by the average investment in inventories. A low rate indicates that probably the investment in inventory is too high for the output and the sales capacity of the business. A high rate may indicate that the inventories maintained are too low. The finished

---

[2] Roy A. Foulke, *Practical Financial Statement Analysis* (New York: McGraw-Hill Book Company, Inc., 1961), Chapter 15.

[3] Nathaniel Jackendoff, *A Study of Published Industry Financial and Operating Ratios* (Philadelphia: Bureau of Economic and Business Research, Temple University, 1962), p. 12.

goods turnover is computed by dividing the cost of goods sold by the average finished goods inventory. The number of days' sales represented by current inventory holdings can be expressed by dividing the turnover figure into 365. The gross profit per inventory turnover is calculated by dividing the gross profit by the inventory turnover ratio.

The average days' sales outstanding in receivables and in inventory can be combined to obtain an "average age of conversion" of noncash current assets into cash. These figures are useful in the attempt to project cash flows.

Capitalization Ratios [4]

In addition to liquidity ratios, analysts calculate capitalization ratios to determine the extent to which the corporation is trading on its equity and the resulting financial leverage. The analyst relates these capitalization ratios to the stability or the lack of stability of industry and company earnings as shown by the past records. It is generally assumed that the greater the stability of industry and company earnings and cash flow, the more the company can trade on its equity and the higher is the allowable ratio of debt to total capitalization or debt to equity.

In the case of new and unseasoned companies or companies in highly cyclical industries, it may be financially unsound to have much if any long-term debt. Some analysts argue that for certain companies in highly cyclical industries long-term debt may be a sound financial policy if fixed charges for servicing the debt, including debt amortization, are covered by a satisfactory earnings and cash flow margin, even in years of seriously depressed business. In essence, a high proportion of debt in the capital structure means heavy fixed charges, including debt amortization or sinking fund requirements that can be a serious burden in highly cyclical industries.

For companies where earnings stability justifies a levered capital structure, the common stockholders can benefit by trading on the equity, with the excess of earnings on funds above the after-tax cost of capital obtained by selling debt obligations (or preferred stock) flowing down through to the income statement. But for those companies whose lack of earnings stability suggests that it is unwise to use significant amounts of long-term debt, a levered capital structure can be detrimental to the interests of the equity investors. The railroad and air transport industries illustrate the problem.

Speculative and Leveraged Capital Structure. If highly levered capital structures have had serious financial consequences, as for example the

---

[4] The reader should review Chapter 9, "Standards for Selection of Limited-Income Securities."

railroads and the airlines in 1960-1961 and 1970-1971, this will be reflected in exceptionally low prices for the securities of such companies during the period of financial difficulties. However, if the speculative-minded investor believes that the worst has been experienced and that a decided improvement in earning power can be expected, the commitment in these securities, especially equities such as railroad and airline equities in 1970, can be very rewarding in succeeding years. Of course, such actions by speculative or aggressive investors fit into a general out-of-favor, low price-earnings industry approach for common stock investors. It appears that in the case of many railroad stocks in 1965 and early 1966 and possibly all airline stocks at this time, the financial leverage factor, considered so negative in 1961, was either being completely ignored or simply being accepted as a strong positive factor by many investors who viewed the result of leverage in the 1961-1965 period. But the negative effects of financial leverage, as well as the negative effect of operating leverage, were again being recognized for the airlines in 1968-1970; in 1971 the effects were positive and in 1973, negative.

Percentage of Each Component to Total Capitalization. The capitalization ratios can be calculated in various ways. Perhaps the most usual way is to calculate the proportion of total capitalization represented by long-term debt, preferred stock, and common stock equity. The common stock equity is the total of capital stock plus retained earnings plus the excess of capital stock over par or stated value. It was suggested earlier that the investor frequently may wish to calculate capitalization ratios at market as well as on a book basis. In this case, unless long-term debt obligations are in default or preferred dividends are in arrears, the figures used for the long-term debt or preferred stock may simply be the par values, but the common equity is calculated by multiplying the number of outstanding shares (less any treasury stock) by the current market price. Such a calculation may indicate considerably more or considerably less financial leverage than that calculated on a strictly book basis. It reflects the market's evaluation of what the enterprise is worth, and the investor is purchasing on the basis of market prices, not book figures. Ratios of debt to equity are often used.

INCOME STATEMENT RATIO ANALYSIS

As explained in earlier chapters, the value of an enterprise (and its divisional units of equity—shares of common stock) is essentially based on its hard core of earning power (projected) and on the dividends that can be and are paid from these earnings. Furthermore, the key tests of corporate management are the ratio of these earnings to total capital invested in the business and also the rate earned on equity capital and on assets.

Methods of Analyzing Income Statements

In discussing the analysis of the income statement, it is assumed that the analyst has made all the adjustments that he deems necessary in order that the income statement reflects the true earnings power, excluding extraordinary items, of the corporation, thus providing a sound base for projections.

The 100% Income Statement. One method of analyzing income statements for a period of years is to take net sales as 100% and then to calculate the percentage that the major items in the income statement bear to net sales. Such items as cost of goods sold, operating expenses, depreciation, maintenance, labor costs, net operating income, other income, other expenses, and finally net income are then placed on a comparable percentage basis. An inspection of these 100% income statements on spread sheets for a period of years shows clearly the trends of the ratios of important items to net sales.

Base Period Analysis. Another method of income statement analysis for a period of years is to establish a base year (or a base period of several years) and to use this base year (or the average of the years in the base period) as equal to 100%. The analyst can then calculate the relationship of the major items in the income statements for each year to the base year.[5] This comparison will indicate the growth (or the decline) of these items year by year and for the entire period under review. Having calculated the percentage increase from the base year or base period, the analyst can then (through the use of compound interest tables) calculate the compound rates of annual growth for the period. The more regular the growth, the more significant is the compound annual growth rate.

The analyst can thus compare the trends of related items to judge whether favorable or unfavorable tendencies are reflected by the data. Certainly, one would expect operating costs to rise with increases in sales; but costs that increase at a faster rate than sales are a negative factor. The percentage increase in sales over a given time span can be contrasted against the percentage increase in GNP (or if more pertinent, one of its components such as disposable personal income, or personal consumption expenditures, or consumption

---

[5] In selecting a base year or years, the analyst will find it advantageous to use a base year or a base period that also serves as a base for U.S. Department of Commerce figures, which he may want to use for comparative purposes. The Union Carbide Corporation furnishes an excellent booklet for calculating compound growth rates.

expenditures for durable goods) over the same period to determine if the company is growing as fast as the economy or a major component of the economy. The percentage increase in sales can also be compared with industry sales to determine if the company is maintaining its share of the market. The rate of growth of sales can also be meaningfully contrasted with the rate of growth of operating assets.

Most Significant Income Statement Ratios

The most significant ratios used in analyzing the income statement are discussed in the following paragraphs.

Gross Profit Ratio. This is the ratio of gross profit to net sales. It can be analyzed in terms of the trend over a period of years for the same company, but just as important is its relationship to other companies in the same industry. As noted earlier, the method of inventory valuation used (for example, Lifo versus Fifo) is quite important, and the analyst must be sure that the figures used for comparison between companies and also for the same company are in fact comparable over a period of years.

Operating Expense Ratio. This is the ratio of total operating expenses to net sales. The operating expenses are the expenses of operating the business, including cost of goods sold. This ratio indicates the operating efficiency of the management.

In addition to calculating the operating expense ratio, the analyst should also calculate (if data are available) the ratio of major components of operating expenses to net sales: depreciation, maintenance or repairs (especially for railroads), total labor costs, pension costs, and research and development and other expenses that, because of the nature of the industry and the company, are significant.

Net Operating Margin. This is the ratio of net operating income to net sales. It is the complement of the operating expense ratio, since the two when added always equal 100%.

The net operating margin indicates the percentage of sales available to meet fixed charges, pay taxes, and provide for dividends. In determining the quality of debt obligations, many analysts consider this percentage of equal importance with the number of times fixed charges are earned. In considering the amount of income remaining after operating expenses (the amount available to meet fixed charges), see the discussion of fixed charge coverage in Chapter 9. Tests may be on an after-tax or a before-tax basis.

The coverage test based on the amount available calculated as sales minus operating expenses is the coverage test on a before-tax basis. As indicated in Chapter 9, the statistical services give priority to the coverage test based on the amount available *after* taxes rather than *before* taxes. If this latter test is used, the analyst must take the amount of net income *after* taxes and add back fixed charges to this figure to obtain the total available to meet fixed charges after payment of taxes.

Other Income and Other Expense as Percentages of Sales. If these items are material, their source and their regularity or lack of regularity over the years should be analyzed. The ratio to net sales and also to final net income should be calculated.

Net Income Before Taxes as a Percentage of Sales. Net income before taxes as a percentage of sales is an intermediate determinant of the final rate of return on invested capital. It is very important for comparisons of companies in the same industry. Comparison is not meaningful for companies in different industries with quite different asset turnover ratios. Industry statistics for profits per dollar of sales, before and after taxes, are given in Table 19-1 and Table 19-2.

The ratio of net income before taxes to sales is the percentage of sales brought down to pre-tax net profit for the common stockholder. This percentage may be very low; but if inventory turnover and capital investment turnover (capital investment to sales, or cost of goods sold to sales) is high, the rate of return on investment may still be high.[6] Conversely, if the net income before taxes as a percentage of sales is high but inventory and capital investment turnover are low, the rate of return on investment may be low. The investor is concerned, in the final analysis, with the return on capital investment. This ratio in conjunction with the asset turnover ratio offers the best indication of the operating efficiency of the firm.

Income Tax Percentages. The percentage of income taxes to net sales and especially the percentage of income taxes to net income before income taxes should be calculated and variations in the trend should be determined. Chapter 16 discussed reasons why the percentage of income taxes to net income before income taxes may vary from the current effective tax rate. The ratio of net income after taxes but before extraordinary items to net sales should also be examined.

---

[6] Return on asset investment equals the operating margin times the turnover of asset investment.

TABLE 19-1

Profits per Dollar of Sales, by Industry (Cents)

Industry	Before federal income taxes					After taxes				
	3Q 1971	4Q 1971	1Q 1972[2]	2Q 1972	3Q 1972	3Q 1971	4Q 1971	1Q 1972	2Q 1972	3Q 1972
All manufacturing corporations ..	6.9	6.9	7.1	7.8	7.2	4.1	4.1	4.0	4.5	4.2
Durable goods	6.3	7.0	7.3	8.6	7.1	3.5	3.8	3.9	4.7	4.0
Transportation equipment ...	4.7	7.7	8.3	9.3	4.2	2.7	3.9	4.3	4.9	2.2
Motor vehicles and equipment [1]	4.8	9.8	10.4	11.0	4.0	2.8	4.9	5.4	5.8	2.1
Aircraft and parts [1]	4.0	2.6	3.9	5.1	4.3	2.2	1.4	2.1	2.9	2.3
Electrical machinery, equipment, and supplies	6.6	6.7	6.4	7.1	7.1	3.6	3.8	3.2	4.0	3.8
Other machinery	8.0	8.8	8.8	10.0	9.7	4.1	4.6	4.7	5.4	5.3
Metalworking machinery and equipment [1]	3.8	3.5	4.6	7.0	6.5	1.3	1.7	1.9	4.0	3.5
Other fabricated metal products	6.3	4.5	5.9	7.2	6.9	3.3	2.1	3.1	3.8	3.9
Primary metal industries	0.8	3.1	4.6	6.2	4.3	0.8	2.4	2.8	4.0	2.8
Primary iron and steel [1] ..	0.2	3.0	4.0	5.9	4.1	0.3	2.5	2.3	3.7	2.6
Primary nonferrous metals [1]	1.7	3.4	5.7	6.8	4.6	1.4	2.3	3.7	4.5	3.2
Stone, clay, and glass products	9.3	6.9	5.6	9.6	9.5	5.4	4.3	2.7	5.8	5.9
Furniture and fixtures	6.7	6.5	5.8	7.2	6.8	3.6	3.3	3.0	3.9	3.6
Lumber and wood products, except furniture	7.9	6.7	7.0	9.1	9.0	5.2	4.5	4.4	5.8	5.7
Instruments and related products	14.7	13.6	13.0	14.0	14.6	8.0	7.7	7.3	7.6	8.0
Miscellaneous manufacturing and ordnance	7.1	4.6	5.2	7.0	6.7	3.7	1.9	2.8	3.5	3.2
Nondurable goods	7.5	6.7	6.8	7.0	7.3	4.6	4.3	4.2	4.3	4.4
Food and kindred products ..	5.2	4.6	4.4	4.9	4.8	2.8	2.5	2.4	2.7	2.6
Dairy products [1]	4.7	3.7	3.5	3.7	3.8	2.6	2.1	1.9	2.1	2.0
Bakery products [1]	4.1	4.8	4.6	4.6	4.4	2.0	2.4	2.4	2.4	2.2
Alcoholic beverages [1]	9.2	7.7	6.8	8.0	9.0	4.8	4.2	3.6	4.3	4.9
Tobacco manufactures	12.1	11.2	11.0	11.5	11.5	6.5	6.0	5.9	6.2	6.0
Textile mill products	4.7	5.2	4.5	4.6	4.8	2.4	2.9	2.3	2.5	2.6
Apparel and other finished products	4.8	5.1	4.2	3.8	4.4	2.6	3.0	2.3	2.0	2.3
Paper and allied products ...	4.5	3.2	5.4	7.6	6.5	2.5	1.4	3.0	4.6	3.8
Printing and publishing	8.0	9.0	6.3	8.9	9.1	4.0	5.0	3.0	4.8	4.9
Chemicals and allied products	11.1	9.9	11.6	11.1	11.5	6.1	5.7	6.4	6.3	6.5
Basic chemicals [1]	8.5	6.5	9.6	10.3	9.0	4.8	3.8	5.6	6.0	5.3
Drugs [1]	17.4	17.5	19.0	17.2	19.0	9.4	10.3	10.4	9.7	10.7
Petroleum refining and related industries	10.2	8.1	7.9	7.0	8.6	8.6	7.5	6.7	5.7	6.8
Petroleum refining [1]	10.2	8.1	7.9	7.0	8.6	8.7	7.5	6.8	5.8	6.8
Rubber and miscellaneous plastics products	6.5	6.8	7.3	8.0	6.9	3.5	3.9	4.0	4.3	3.7
Leather and leather products	4.6	5.2	5.7	4.3	5.3	2.1	2.2	2.8	1.7	2.8

[1] Included in major industry above.
[2] Revised.

Source: Federal Trade Commission, *Quarterly Financial Report for Manufacturing Corporations,* Third Quarter, 1972 (Washington, D.C.: U.S. Government Printing Office), p. 8. See similar tables in *Economic Report of the President* (issued annually).

TABLE 19-2

Profits per Dollar of Sales, by Asset Size and Industry Group (Cents)

Asset size	Before federal income taxes					After taxes				
	3Q 1971	4Q 1971	1Q 1972[1]	2Q 1972	3Q 1972	3Q 1971	4Q 1971	1Q 1972	2Q 1972	3Q 1972
All manufacturing corporations ..	6.9	6.9	7.1	7.8	7.2	4.1	4.1	4.0	4.5	4.2
Under $1 million	3.3	2.6	3.5	4.6	5.0	1.7	1.1	2.1	2.9	3.3
$ 1 million to $ 5 million	5.2	4.3	4.6	5.6	5.2	2.7	2.2	2.2	3.0	2.7
$ 5 million to $ 10 million	6.5	6.8	5.6	6.5	6.4	3.1	3.4	2.8	3.2	3.2
$ 10 million to $ 25 million	6.5	5.7	5.7	7.3	6.7	3.1	2.7	2.7	3.7	3.4
$ 25 million to $ 50 million	5.9	5.8	5.9	7.1	6.3	2.9	2.8	2.9	3.6	3.2
$ 50 million to $ 100 million	7.1	7.2	6.7	7.8	7.6	3.6	3.8	3.5	4.1	4.0
$ 100 million to $ 250 million	7.6	6.7	6.3	7.6	7.4	4.0	3.8	3.4	4.1	4.6
$ 250 million to $1,000 million	7.3	7.8	7.2	8.0	7.7	4.0	4.5	3.8	4.5	4.3
$1,000 million and over	7.9	8.2	8.8	9.2	8.0	5.2	5.3	5.4	5.5	5.0
Durable goods	6.3	7.0	7.3	8.6	7.1	3.5	3.8	3.0	4.7	4.0
Under $5 million	4.7	3.5	4.7	6.3	6.2	2.4	1.5	2.5	3.7	3.7
$ 5 million to $ 10 million	7.6	7.6	6.5	8.2	7.9	3.7	3.6	3.1	4.0	4.0
$ 10 million to $ 25 million	7.0	6.0	6.7	8.3	7.5	3.3	2.8	3.3	4.2	3.9
$ 25 million to $ 50 million	6.5	6.4	6.7	8.3	7.2	3.2	3.1	3.3	4.3	3.7
$ 50 million to $ 100 million	6.7	6.7	6.6	8.2	7.8	3.3	3.3	3.4	4.2	4.2
$ 100 million to $ 250 million	7.2	5.9	6.1	7.8	7.5	3.8	3.2	3.3	4.2	4.1
$ 250 million to $1,000 million	6.2	6.8	6.2	7.7	6.9	3.4	3.8	2.9	4.2	3.8
$1,000 million and over	6.6	8.6	9.0	9.8	7.2	3.9	4.9	4.9	5.5	4.1
Nondurable goods	7.5	6.7	6.8	7.0	7.3	4.6	4.3	4.2	4.3	4.4
Under $5 million	3.8	3.3	3.5	4.0	4.1	1.9	1.7	1.8	2.2	2.3
$ 5 million to $ 10 million	5.7	6.2	4.9	5.0	4.9	2.7	3.3	2.5	2.4	2.5
$ 10 million to $ 25 million	6.0	5.5	4.8	6.3	6.0	-3.0	2.7	2.2	3.2	3.0
$ 25 million to $ 50 million	5.4	5.2	5.2	5.9	5.4	2.6	2.5	2.6	2.9	2.8
$ 50 million to $ 100 million	7.5	7.8	6.9	7.3	7.3	3.9	4.4	3.7	4.0	3.8
$ 100 million to $ 250 million	7.9	7.4	6.5	7.3	7.3	4.2	4.2	3.5	4.0	3.9
$ 250 million to $1,000 million	8.2	8.7	8.0	8.3	8.3	4.5	5.0	4.4	4.8	4.7
$1,000 million and over	9.5	7.6	8.5	8.2	9.0	6.9	5.9	6.0	5.6	6.1

[1] Revised.

Source: Federal Trade Commission, *Quarterly Financial Report for Manufacturing Corporations*, Third Quarter, 1972 (Washington, D.C.: U.S. Government Printing Office), p. 9. See similar tables in *Economic Report of the President* (issued annually).

Extraordinary Item Percentages. If the item is material, it should be calculated as a percentage of net sales and also as a percentage of net income *after* extraordinary items. Variations in the relative importance of extraordinary nonrecurring items should be carefully analyzed.

Net Income After Extraordinary Items as a Percentage of Sales. If extraordinary nonrecurring items are material, the net income after extraordinary items (net profit margin) should be calculated as a percentage of sales. There will be three net income figures before taxes and three after taxes if the "all-inclusive statement" recommended by the AICPA is used.

Earnings Per Share

As indicated in Chapter 16, the AICPA favors the all-inclusive income statement, which presents near the bottom of the statement both net earnings per share *before* extraordinary (nonrecurring) items and also earnings per share *after* extraordinary items. If it is assumed that the analyst has previously made all necessary adjustments in the income account before the determination of the earnings per share figure before extraordinary items, then this is the figure that is the key to his final valuation for a common stock. An evaluation of the current earnings per share and the past record along with the volatility and growth rate provides a base for projection of future earnings (and dividends). The volatility and the growth of earnings per share from a base year or base period should be calculated. The methods for projecting earnings per share were discussed in earlier chapters.

On Wall Street, by far the most significant figure used in reference to a common stock is its earnings per share, along with its correlated ratio of market price to earnings per share (the P/E ratio). Because of the interest in earnings per share, considerable emphasis is placed on this figure by the statistical services. The AICPA and others have criticized the undue emphasis on earnings per share, especially where *only* this figure is presented unsupported by the full income statement. From the investor's standpoint, the earnings per share figure is significant only if it represents "true recurring earnings per share" after the income statement has been carefully analyzed and adjusted if necessary and after the business as a whole has been analyzed.

The two major criticisms of the use of the earnings per share figure by itself are: (1) without correlation with an income statement review and analysis, it can lead to erroneous conclusions; and (2) it concentrates the investor's attention on a single figure without reference to the corporation as a whole, as a going concern, and as an economic operation, which would provide information on the sources and the nature of income and provide some basis for a reasonable projection of earnings and dividends.[7]

---

[7] APB Opinion No. 15 (May, 1969). See also, "Suggested Refinements of Procedures in Determining Earnings per Share," *The Journal of Accountancy* (January, 1970). Also read APB Opinion No. 9, "Reporting the Results of Operations."

"Earnings per share data are used in evaluating the past operating performance of a business in forming an opinion as to its potential and in making investment decisions . . . presented in prospectuses, proxy material, and reports to stockholders. . . . It is important that such data be computed on a consistent basis and presented in the most meaningful manner. . . . Computational guidelines . . . are contained in Appendix A. . . . The Board has concluded that earnings per share or net loss per share data *should be shown* on the face of the income statement (consistent with paragraph 20 of APB Opinion No. 9). Earnings per share amounts should therefore be presented for (a) income *before* extraordinary items and (b) net income (after extraordinary items). It may also be desirable to present earnings per share amounts for extraordinary items.

Dividends Per Share

The stability and the growth of dividends from a base year or a base period should be calculated. Explanations should be sought for significant changes in dividend payout policy as well as for the relation of the payout to overall financial policy. For most corporations, dividend yield is important. Only in the case of very rapid growth companies is it ignored.

Payout Ratio as a Percentage of Dividends to Earnings. Having adjusted (or accepted) the reported earnings per share, the analyst can calculate the ratio of dividends per share to earnings per share. Assuming that the directors follow a fairly well-defined dividend policy, this policy is indicated by a review of the payout ratio for a period of years and may be projected.

Dividends as a Percentage of Cash Flow. Cash flow provides protection for dividends, and directors do not like to cut dividends. As previously noted, for the entire period of the 1930s, dividends exceeded earnings for all U.S. corporations but did not exceed cash flow. In no year did dividends exceed 75% of cash flow. This ratio has varied little for many years.

COMBINED STATEMENT RATIO ANALYSIS

The first test of profitability—net profit as a percentage of sales—has already been discussed. However, that is only an intermediate test of profitability and not a final test. The final tests are rates of return on assets, on

---

"The capital structures of many corporations are relatively simple—that is, they either consist of only common stock or include no potentially dilutive convertible securities, options, warrants, or other rights that upon conversion or exercise could in the aggregate dilute earnings per share.

"Corporations with capital structures other than those described in the preceding paragraph should present two types of earnings per share data (dual presentation) with equal prominence on the face of the income statement. The first . . . is based on the outstanding shares and those securities that are in substance equivalent to common shares and have a dilutive effect. The second is pro-forma . . . which reflects the dilution of earnings per share that would have occurred if *all* contingent issuances of common stock that would individually reduce earnings per share had taken place at the beginning of the period (or time of issuance of the convertible security, etc., if later).

". . . The dual presentation . . . should be made for *all* periods presented . . . (and) will give . . . an understanding of the extent and trend of the potential dilution. When results of operations of a prior period included in the statement of income or summary of earnings have been restated as a result of a prior period adjustment, earnings per share data . . . should be restated. The effect of the restatement, expressed in per share terms, should be disclosed in the year of restatement.

". . . financial statements should include a description, in summary form, sufficient to explain the . . . rights and privileges of the various securities outstanding."

capital, and on common equity, as well as the past and expected growth rate of earnings.

Net Income Before Extraordinary Items as a Percentage of Total Invested Capital

The purpose of the invested capital is to earn an adequate profit. The rate of return on invested capital is therefore a key measure of management performance. The capital invested is the total capital supplied by all investors, creditors, preferred stockholders, and common stockholders.

Net Income Before Extraordinary Items as a Percentage of Equity Capital

The stockholders supply the equity capital and they are the residual claimants to the profits generated. If there is preferred stock outstanding, the amount paid in preferred dividends is deducted from the net income after taxes available for all equity investors and the remainder is calculated as a percentage of the common stockholders' total equity.

If the capitalization is levered, the difference between the rate of return on total capital invested and the rate of return on the common stockholders' equity clearly indicates the effect of trading on the equity. Where favorable leverage exists, the rate of return on the common stockholders' equity will exceed the rate earned on total invested capital.

The relationship between the rate of return on common stockholders' equity and the rate earned on total invested capital can be expressed in the following equation:

$$\frac{\text{Net Profit}}{\text{Assets}} \times \frac{\text{Assets}}{\text{Owners' Equity}} = \frac{\text{Net Profit}}{\text{Owners' Equity}}$$

As previously noted, the proportion of assets financed by creditors, as expressed in a capitalization ratio, is an indication of the degree of financial leverage present.

Industry statistics on annual rates of profit on stockholders' equity, before and after federal income taxes, are presented in Table 19-3 and in Table 19-4.

Sales Per Dollar of Total Capital Funds Ratio

In connection with the discussion of capital funds, this is another ratio that affects profitability although it is not itself a profit ratio. This is the

PART FIVE *Security Analysis*

ratio of sales per dollar of total capital funds, and it indicates the rate of turnover of invested capital. If $10 million represents total capital invested

TABLE 19-3

Annual Rates of Profit on Stockholders' Equity, by Industry, All Manufacturing Corporations (Percent)

Industry	Before federal income taxes					After taxes				
	4Q 1970	1Q 1971	2Q 1971	3Q 1971	4Q 1971	4Q 1970	1Q 1971	2Q 1971	3Q 1971	4Q 1971
All manufacturing corporations ..	13.8	15.4	18.2	15.9	16.5	8.7	8.9	10.7	9.3	9.8
Durable goods	11.5	15.1	19.4	14.5	17.1	7.1	8.0	10.8	8.1	9.3
Transportation equipment ...	0.0	22.7	24.7	12.8	23.2	2.7	12.1	13.6	7.4	11.7
Motor vehicles and equipment [1]	-3.7	27.7	28.4	12.1	29.0	1.7	14.8	15.6	7.0	14.7
Aircraft and parts [1]	9.4	9.8	12.0	11.6	8.3	5.7	5.4	6.7	6.5	4.4
Electrical machinery, equipment, and supplies	17.9	15.1	17.3	17.1	19.3	10.1	8.0	9.7	9.4	10.4
Other machinery	17.7	15.1	18.1	16.5	18.4	9.0	7.5	9.3	8.4	9.6
Metalworking machinery and equipment [1]	9.7	8.7	11.9	8.3	7.1	4.5	3.5	5.4	2.7	3.4
Other fabricated metal products	11.7	14.0	19.3	17.9	13.7	5.9	7.1	10.2	9.4	6.4
Primary metal industries	5.9	8.8	13.6	1.3	4.8	4.9	5.8	8.3	1.2	3.8
Primary iron and steel [1] ..	2.5	8.2	15.2	0.3	4.8	2.8	5.0	8.5	0.5	4.1
Primary nonferrous metals [1]	10.3	9.6	11.5	2.5	4.8	7.6	6.7	8.1	2.1	3.3
Stone, clay, and glass products	11.6	7.0	21.1	21.0	14.4	6.9	3.1	12.5	12.1	8.8
Furniture and fixtures	15.8	11.4	19.1	21.2	21.6	7.8	4.9	10.5	11.5	11.0
Lumber and wood products, except furniture	8.1	10.8	19.3	21.5	18.3	4.3	6.7	12.4	14.0	12.2
Instruments and related products	27.4	19.9	26.0	27.6	25.9	15.5	10.2	14.2	15.0	14.7
Miscellaneous manufacturing and ordnance	21.3	16.2	19.7	19.7	15.2	11.7	8.6	10.6	10.3	6.3
Nondurable goods	16.0	15.7	17.0	17.2	16.0	10.3	9.8	10.6	10.6	10.2
Food and kindred products ..	20.2	19.3	21.3	21.9	19.5	11.0	10.2	11.5	11.7	10.6
Dairy products [1]	17.0	18.7	21.2	22.7	18.3	9.6	9.8	11.5	12.3	10.6
Bakery products [1]	21.2	21.0	23.4	19.5	23.0	10.4	9.8	12.2	9.4	11.3
Alcoholic beverages [1]	20.4	15.7	19.8	22.7	21.5	11.3	8.4	10.4	12.0	11.6
Tobacco manufactures	31.5	27.3	31.0	32.1	28.8	16.6	14.8	15.7	17.1	15.3
Textile mill products	10.2	9.5	13.7	12.8	14.8	4.8	4.6	7.2	6.5	8.2
Apparel and other finished products	15.8	12.6	19.3	23.0	26.3	7.3	5.5	10.9	12.5	15.1
Paper and allied products ...	8.6	8.8	10.7	9.8	6.9	5.3	4.9	5.9	5.3	2.9
Printing and publishing	22.4	15.7	20.6	20.7	24.2	11.5	7.9	10.8	10.4	13.6
Chemicals and allied products	18.1	20.6	22.5	21.5	19.3	10.5	11.7	12.8	11.8	11.0
Basic chemicals [1]	9.8	15.3	18.3	14.8	11.1	6.3	9.0	10.7	8.4	6.5
Drugs [1]	30.4	32.4	30.0	32.9	32.5	17.5	18.0	16.6	17.9	19.1
Petroleum refining and related industries	13.9	13.2	11.6	12.6	10.6	11.9	10.9	10.0	10.6	9.8
Petroleum refining [1]	13.9	13.3	11.5	12.5	10.5	11.9	11.0	9.9	10.6	9.8
Rubber and miscellaneous plastics products	9.1	13.8	20.3	17.3	18.2	4.8	7.6	10.9	9.3	10.5
Leather and leather products	18.2	17.7	16.4	16.9	19.8	9.0	8.3	8.1	7.9	8.3

[1] Included in major industry above.

Source: *Quarterly Financial Report for Manufacturing Corporations*, Fourth Quarter, 1971, p. 10. Also see the annual *Economic Report of the President*.

and if sales total $20 million, the capital turnover ratio is 2 to 1. Although this ratio is often used, the asset turnover ratio is preferable. There is little additional insight provided by this ratio compared to the asset to sales turnover ratio.

Sales Per Dollar of Common Equity at the Market

Analysts frequently calculate the ratio of sales to total common stock equity at its market value and then convert it into a per-share basis. They can then determine the dollar amount of sales for each dollar of common stock market value. Some analysts simply calculate the net sales per share

TABLE 19-4

Annual Rates of Profit on Stockholders' Equity, by Asset Size and Industry Group (Percent)

Asset size	Before federal income taxes					After taxes				
	4Q 1970	1Q 1971	2Q 1971	3Q 1971	4Q 1971	4Q 1970	1Q 1971	2Q 1971	3Q 1971	4Q 1971
All manufacturing corporations ..	13.8	15.4	18.2	15.9	16.5	8.7	8.9	10.7	9.3	9.8
Under $1 million	5.9	9.1	21.2	16.2	13.4	0.4	2.9	12.5	8.5	5.6
$ 1 million to $ 5 million	15.4	12.9	19.6	19.9	17.1	6.9	5.4	10.1	10.2	8.6
$ 5 million to $ 10 million	15.2	13.4	18.9	18.1	20.9	6.8	6.0	9.0	9.2	10.6
$ 10 million to $ 25 million	14.1	13.8	18.2	17.6	15.7	6.7	6.6	9.1	8.6	7.5
$ 25 million to $ 50 million	14.0	11.8	19.6	16.1	16.0	7.1	5.7	10.0	7.9	7.7
$ 50 million to $ 100 million	13.7	12.0	16.9	17.6	17.8	7.3	5.8	8.8	8.9	9.4
$ 100 million to $ 250 million	16.1	14.6	18.1	19.0	17.1	9.2	7.8	9.7	10.0	9.6
$ 250 million to $1,000 million	17.7	16.2	18.4	17.4	18.7	10.3	8.9	10.3	9.5	10.7
$1,000 million and over	12.3	16.7	17.7	14.0	15.6	9.3	10.7	11.3	9.3	10.2
Durable goods	11.5	15.1	19.4	14.5	17.1	7.1	8.0	10.8	8.1	9.3
Under $5 million	10.4	8.8	18.8	16.5	13.2	3.6	2.3	10.3	8.7	5.5
$ 5 million to $ 10 million	13.8	12.5	18.9	17.6	18.8	5.9	5.3	9.2	8.6	9.0
$ 10 million to $ 25 million	13.4	11.0	17.9	17.1	14.5	6.3	4.9	8.6	8.2	6.7
$ 25 million to $ 50 million	11.7	9.4	19.4	16.0	15.9	5.8	4.1	9.8	7.9	7.7
$ 50 million to $ 100 million	9.5	9.7	16.4	16.1	16.1	4.7	4.3	8.5	7.9	8.0
$ 100 million to $ 250 million	12.0	11.8	16.0	16.8	13.5	7.0	6.1	8.4	8.8	7.4
$ 250 million to $1,000 million	13.1	13.6	16.9	14.0	15.5	7.6	7.4	9.5	7.6	8.8
$1,000 million and over	11.0	18.8	21.2	13.3	19.3	8.1	10.8	12.2	7.9	11.0
Nondurable goods	16.0	15.7	17.0	17.2	16.0	10.3	9.8	10.6	10.6	10.2
Under $5 million	12.0	14.3	22.4	20.1	18.0	4.5	6.8	12.4	10.3	9.3
$ 5 million to $ 10 million	16.7	14.4	18.7	21.1	23.4	8.0	6.8	8.9	10.0	12.4
$ 10 million to $ 25 million	15.0	17.0	18.5	18.2	16.9	7.2	8.6	9.7	9.0	8.4
$ 25 million to $ 50 million	16.6	14.8	19.7	16.2	16.2	8.5	7.8	10.3	7.9	7.7
$ 50 million to $ 100 million	18.7	15.0	17.6	19.6	19.8	10.2	7.7	9.1	10.2	11.1
$ 100 million to $ 250 million	20.5	17.4	20.1	21.1	20.2	11.6	9.4	11.0	11.2	11.6
$ 250 million to $1,000 million	21.6	18.5	19.8	20.3	21.6	12.6	10.2	11.1	11.1	12.4
$1,000 million and over	13.5	14.7	14.3	14.7	12.2	10.5	10.6	10.3	10.6	9.4

Source: *Quarterly Financial Report for Manufacturing Corporations,* Fourth Quarter, 1971. See similar tables in the annual *Economic Report of the President.*

of common stock. However, the investor is concerned with the profit earned on his capital, not simply the volume of sales generated by his capital.

GROWTH AND STABILITY RATIOS AND MEASUREMENTS

The quality of a common stock and its relative attractiveness, and therefore the capitalization rate (P/E ratio) that investors in the market are willing to apply to current earnings, is based on (1) investors' estimates of the growth rate for earnings and (2) the stability or the volatility of earnings reflecting recessions for the economy or that particular industry or other factors. It would not be logical to purchase a common stock if its earnings (and therefore its dividends) were not expected to grow. In such a case, a limited-income security would be preferable to a nongrowth stock; but it must be a limited-income security of another company, for it is not considered advisable to purchase even limited-income securities of a company where no growth in earnings is projected because earnings for a company will rarely move horizontally for any extended period. The higher the growth rate and the less the volatility of earnings, the higher the P/E investors pay.

If earnings are expected to grow at approximately the same rate as earnings for the indexes (DJIA and S&P indexes) and if they are expected to exhibit stability equal to those of the indexes, investors will be willing to capitalize earnings at the same rate as the current and expected range of P/E ratios for these indexes, say for example 14x to 20x earnings. If the earnings growth is expected to be at a noticeably slower rate, and especially if earnings are expected to be volatile, investors will only accept a lower P/E ratio, especially if it is to be compounded by less earnings and dividend stability, say perhaps 8x to 12x the P/E multiples. If the earnings growth is expected to be significantly greater than for the indexes, say 12% to 14% per year compounded, many investors will be willing to accept a P/E ratio higher than for the averages, say 25x to 40x earnings. For those relatively few companies where the earnings growth is expected to be substantially higher than 12% to 14% per year, at least some investors will be willing to apply a P/E ratio even higher than 40x earnings. A compound annual earnings growth of 12% to 14% per year will result in a doubling of earnings in 5 or 6 years.

Growth Characteristic Measurements

Tests that may be applied to measure the growth characteristics of a company are discussed in the next three paragraphs.

Record of Sales Growth. Sales growth is usually calculated on a compound annual basis from a base year or a base period. To the extent that growth has been relatively steady, a meaningful past rate of growth and a compound rate of annual growth can be determined. Usually, in order to post a good growth record for earnings, a company must have experienced a good growth in sales. Sometimes a company and/or an industry has posted a good record of sales growth but only a mediocre record of earnings growth and sometimes no earnings growth. Therefore, the analyst must determine the reason for the growth in sales—for example, mergers. Sometimes the advantages of mergers are not carried through to net income, at least during what may be a long period of digestion of the companies acquired. In other cases an industry may demonstrate a good revenue growth but a poor net earnings record. The SEC has urged publication of sales-order backlogs.[8]

Growth of Net Profits Available for All Capital Funds. The figure for net profits is the total of net income after taxes plus fixed charges added back if the company has long-term debt outstanding. This test is one of the most important tests of management. However, if the company has issued a considerable amount of new common stock during the period, for example in the case of an acquisition, the record of growth of total net profits for all capital funds might appear satisfactory; *but* when it is carried down to net per share, there may have been dilution, resulting in a poor or mediocre growth record for earnings per share.

Growth of Earnings per Share. This test is, of course, the most crucial test for the common stockholder. Common stock will sell on the basis of the expected growth and volatility of earnings per share (and dividends per share), and considerable emphasis will be placed on the past record of growth, especially the recent period. What the analyst calculates is the compound annual growth rate and the stability of the growth rate, and then he projects a growth rate for the future. The performance school in 1967-1969 and 1972-1973 was concentrating on quarterly earnings growth rates. The stability of the above variables should also be analyzed.

Market Price Ratios

Ratios based on market price offer investors important measurements of growth and earnings stability.

---

[8] J. S. McCosker, "Backlog Reporting," *The Journal of Accountancy* (May, 1969), pp. 53-60.

Price-Earnings Ratio. The P/E ratio may be the current price divided by (1) the latest available 12 months' earnings, or (2) earnings projected for the next 12 months, or (3) the average or midpoint of projected earnings for the next 5 or 6 years, or (4) the earnings expectation in a target year 3 to 6 years hence. On Wall Street the price-earnings ratio is the most commonly used method of determining relative values of various stocks. While the P/E ratio used and quoted on Wall Street is usually based on the latest available 12 months' earnings or on estimated earnings for the current fiscal year *or* the next 12 months, the process is not quite as indefensible as it might seem. While the earnings used are current earnings, the actual capitalization rate applied to the earnings for specific stocks reflects investors' estimates of future earnings for a period of years into the future (the higher the growth rate and the less volatility, the higher the P/E).

Risk increases to the extent that projections are extended farther and farther into the future. The range of the price-earnings ratio for a stock for a period of the past 5 to 10 years and for the stocks in its industry should be analyzed and related to the range for the DJIA or the S&P 500 and 425 for the same years, that is, as a percentage of the P/E ratios for these averages.[9]

Earnings Yield. Surprisingly enough, this highly important ratio is not used very frequently on Wall Street. It is the reciprocal of the price-earnings ratio. The earnings yield may be calculated (1) by dividing one year's earnings by the current market price or (2) by dividing 100 by the price-earnings ratio.

If all earnings were paid out as cash dividends, the earnings yield and the dividend yield would be identical. Dividends would be equal to 100% of earnings. This, of course, is rarely the case. The earnings yield also represents the rate of return that the company is earning based on the current price of its stock or the current rate of return that would be earned if the total stock of the company were purchased at its current market price.

Table 19-5 on page 496 indicates the correlation of the earnings yield with the price-earnings ratio.

Dividend Yield. The dividend yield is calculated by dividing the current annual dividend by the current market price. It is most meaningful in industries and companies that have demonstrated stability of earnings and

---

[9] A study of time horizons of investors found that it tends to range between 1 and 3 years. See "An Estimate of the Time Horizons and Expected Yield for a Selected Group of Common Shares 1935-1955," *International Economic Review* (May, 1961), pp. 179-198. For many "performance investors," including numerous institutional "investors," in the late 1960s and 1970s the time horizon was shortened to 1 year.

TABLE 19-5

Examples of Earnings Yields for Selected Price-Earnings Ratios

Market Price	Annual Earnings	Price-Earnings Ratio	Earnings Yield	Market Price	Annual Earnings	Price-Earnings Ratio	Earnings Yield
$600	$6.00	100x	1.00%	$90	$6.00	15x	6.6%
450	6.00	75x	1.13	84	6.00	14x	7.14
300	6.00	50x	2.00	78	6.00	13x	7.69
240	6.00	40x	2.50	72	6.00	12x	8.33
198	6.00	33x	3.00	66	6.00	11x	9.09
150	6.00	25x	4.00	60	6.00	10x	10.00
120	6.00	20x	5.00	54	6.00	9x	11.11
114	6.00	19x	5.26	48	6.00	8x	12.50
108	6.00	18x	5.56	42	6.00	7x	14.29
102	6.00	17x	5.88	36	6.00	6x	16.67
96	6.00	16x	6.25	30	6.00	5x	20.00

consistent growth. However, since 1938 a well-diversified portfolio of common stocks would have demonstrated excellent dividend stability and, in addition, substantial dividend growth. This was true of most large, well-diversified mutual funds as well as for the market averages. Therefore, overall dividend yield is a much more significant figure than it was prior to 1938 for well-diversified portfolios.[10]

Price Range of Stock. The price range of the stock—high, low, and mean—should be tabulated for the past 5 to 10 years or longer. The prices should be adjusted for stock splits and stock dividends. Price charts should be examined.

Other Per-Share Figures

Several additional per-share calculations are used to measure the growth and the stability of a company. The most important are:

Equity per Share as a Percentage of Market Value. This ratio is calculated by deducting total liabilities (plus the par or liquidating value of all issues senior to the common stock) from the total assets (usually less intangibles) and dividing the result by the number of outstanding shares (less treasury stock).[11] Equity per share of common stock therefore consists of

---

[10] See Table 7-1 in Chapter 7.

[11] Goodwill was discussed previously, but it should be noted again that in recent years goodwill has become an important item on numerous balance sheets as a result of acquisition costs in excess of the book value of the assets of the acquired companies where the purchase of assets method rather than the pooling of interests method is used.

the common stock equity on the balance sheet divided by the number of outstanding shares of common stock. It is then expressed as a percentage of market price.

For most companies, exclusive of financial companies and utility companies, Wall Street does not consider equity per share (in reality net asset value) as significant because:

1. Asset figures on the balance sheet only represent cost (usually adjusted to market value if that is lower than cost) for current assets and represent cost less amortization for fixed assets and intangibles. As was explained in Chapter 18, there is no basis for assuming that such book figures represent current economic value.
2. The value of most assets is their earning power, not their book figures. This is essentially true also for banks, insurance companies, and utilities.

Market prices of common stocks in general bear little relationship to equity per share because the market value of common stocks is based on their earning power performance, projected earnings, and dividends expected to be paid from projected earnings. At any time, investors can find many common stocks selling well below their equity per share because of poor earnings or actual losses; conversely, many common stocks can be found selling far in excess of equity per share because of their high rate of past, current, and projected earnings growth.

Net Working Capital or Net Current Asset Book Value per Share. This ratio is not actually based on net working capital or net current asset book value per share because it is calculated (1) by deducting *all liabilities* (short-term and long-term) from current assets, not just *current liabilities,* and (2) then dividing the result by the number of outstanding shares (less treasury stock).

It is always possible to find numerous common stocks selling at market prices below the stock's net current asset book value because of a poor earnings record and currently poor earnings or actual losses. The fact that these stocks are selling below net current asset book value should not imply to the investor that they therefore represent interesting values. Only if the investor can reasonably expect a *change* can he decide that an interesting capital gains potential exists. Such a change could be a new management that would revitalize earning power, or acquisition by another company that will at least pay the equivalent of net current asset value for the stock, or liquidation that would end in an expected payout to common stockholders of a sum in excess of the current market price.

Net Cash Book Value of Common Stock as a Percentage of Market Price. The net cash book value of a common stock is the total of cash and cash items less *all liabilities* and less the par or liquidating value of all other senior securities divided by the number of outstanding shares. It is quite unusual to find the market value of a stock significantly below the net cash book value, although such situations were not uncommon in 1932-1933.

Cash Flow per Share. The importance of cash flow and its proper use as well as misuse by investors has been discussed earlier at some length. Cash flow per share should not be used as a substitute for earnings per share. Cash flow figures can be properly interpreted only if the interpretation is accompanied by an analysis of sources and applications of funds statements. In comparative analysis, cash flow per share adjusts for varying depreciation and depletion policies between competing companies in the same industry (for example, the petroleum industry).

Depreciation per Share. Because for many companies depreciation is such a major item and because the depreciation policies of various companies differ significantly in their results, the figure for depreciation per share is useful for comparative analysis, especially when it is related to net earnings per share and cash flow per share.[12] (Depletion per share is also useful.)

Other Depreciation Ratios. Depreciation is such an important item that two additional depreciation ratios may be used: (1) depreciation to gross plant and (2) depreciation to net plant.

Physical Data Ratios

In addition to the statement ratios discussed in this chapter, analysts frequently use certain physical data ratios and often reduce them to a per-share basis.

Physical Reserves. Reserves are of utmost importance to companies dependent on wasting assets for their operations. Reported reserves of major companies normally provide a conservative representation of such assets. The analyst should note carefully the quality or grade of reserves as well as the quantity, with special attention to changes in grade from year to year since these are largely indicative of current mining policy and possible "high-grading" (mining primarily the highest grade ores in the deposit) in any given year.

Reserves of oil and gas, normally stated in terms of millions of barrels and billions of cubic feet respectively, are frequently reported on a per-share

---

[12] See Chapter 17 for a discussion of depreciation.

basis. The estimated value of reserves can be computed by multiplying the number of units in reserve by the going market price per unit.

Capacity. Producers and processors of various materials normally have specific productive or fabricating capacity that may be expressed in terms of physical units. Data of physical capacity are particularly valuable in determining the relative position of individual companies within an industry. These data can be reduced to a per-share or a per-employee basis for comparison between companies. Trends for a period of years may be significant. Capacity can also be related to order backlogs for units and dollars.

Production. Production data in units are of considerable interest to the analyst. Related to capacity figures, they provide an indication of the level of operations within a company, which in turn can be compared to industry figures. In companies concentrating primarily on one type of product (for example, crude oil, ingot steel, or copper), production data in units can be used to calculate selling prices, production costs, and profits per unit. Such data also enable the analyst to determine the effects of changes in costs and selling prices on the profit margins of the company.

Freight Volume. Detailed information relative to volume, product composition, and geographical distribution of freight carried is especially valuable to the analyst in appraising the outlook for a transportation company such as a railroad, airline, trucking service, or barge line.

Changes in the Capital Stock Account

Various adjustments that the security analyst must make in examining the financial statements of a corporation have been discussed in some detail in other sections of this book. In addition to these, he may find it necessary to recompute per-share figures as reported to reflect changes in the capital stock account. In many instances, corporations report per-share data adjusted for changes in the capitalization during a period of 5, 10, or more years in the past. Some adjustments may be required to establish a similar base between different companies for comparative purposes or to facilitate year-to-year comparisons for a given company.

The analyst should examine closely any changes in the total number of shares outstanding. The major factors responsible for such changes are stock split-ups, stock dividends, new common stock financing, the issuance of stock to effect a merger, and the conversion of outstanding convertible senior securities. The number of common shares outstanding may also be increased through the issuance of stock under company bonus or incentive plans or under employee stock purchase programs, or it may be decreased when stock is repurchased by the company itself. These latter factors are usually of rather nominal importance.

Stock Split-Ups. A stock split results in increasing the number of outstanding shares. In the case of *either* a stock split or a stock dividend, *the total amount* of all capital accounts *combined* is not affected. In the case of a stock split, the dollar amount in each of these accounts also remains unchanged. Only the par or stated value per share is reduced, and the number of shares is increased in relation to the split ratio, that is, 2 for 1, 3 for 1, etc. However, in the case of a stock dividend, the retained earnings account is charged with the amount of the dividend and the capital stock account is credited for the same amount. Adjustments for split-ups merely involve dividing all per-share data for years prior to the effective date of the split by the appropriate figure. It is standard practice for corporations to make this adjustment themselves in their reports to stockholders. The statistical services also generally make these prior-year adjustments when reporting results for a period of past years.

Stock Dividends. A stock dividend increases the number of shares outstanding by the percentage paid, that is, 3%, 5%, 10%, etc. It does not involve any change in par or stated value per share, but rather it transfers a portion of the retained earnings account to the capital stock account. Some investors consider that the payment of a stock dividend instead of a cash dividend or as a supplement to a conservative cash disbursement is quite similar to the sale of new common stock. The corporation management retains cash earnings in the business, normally to finance expansion and for working capital requirements, and issues stock to the shareholders instead of a cash return on their investment. In effect, from the corporation's standpoint, additional capital is being raised from existing shareholders as opposed to paying out earnings in the form of cash dividends and then selling additional stock. On this premise, stock dividends should be regarded as an addition to both the capital account and the actual capital invested in the business on which the corporation should reasonably be expected to earn some margin of profit. It is on this basis that the analyst must determine whether or not an adjustment in reported figures is necessary.

In calculating the rate of return on stockholders' equity, the analyst will calculate the percentage on total owners' equity, that is, the capital stock account plus the retained earnings account plus the capital stock in excess of par or stated value account. Assuming that Corporation X, which did not pay any stock dividends, retained the same amount of earnings as

Corporation Y, which did pay stock dividends, the rate of return on total stockholders' equity would be the same for the two corporations. The retained earnings account of Corporation X would be larger and the capital stock account would be smaller than in the case of Corporation Y; but the total of all capital accounts would be the same in both cases. From the standpoint of economic value, the stockholder has more pieces of paper after receiving either a stock dividend or a stock split, but the value of his total holdings does not change.

It may not be necessary to account for fairly small stock dividends, say 3% or 4%, when comparing data for only two preceding years, since the changes in capitalization are fairly negligible for analysis purposes. But the cumulative effect of numerous stock dividends paid over a period of years can result in a very significant distortion of the earnings record if no adjustments are made. Most corporations adjust *prior* year per-share figures to reflect stock dividends, since their earnings records normally are correctly enhanced as a result.

Mergers. In order to maintain an adequate basis for comparison of financial data over a period of several years, reported earnings for years prior to any merger effected by a company should be adjusted to reflect the earning power of the merged unit or units during those *past years*. Most corporations restate prior years' data to show on a pro forma basis the effects of a merger on both balance sheet and income account items. This represents proper procedure and significantly facilitates the work of the analyst in evaluating the relative industry position of the parent enterprise compared to other existing units. It should be pointed out, however, that most mergers are undertaken because the merging units believe that certain operating or competitive advantages will be obtained from combined operation, even though it will often take several years to integrate the merged units and effect the efficiencies.[13] The analyst should bear in mind that possible savings incident to a merger in the form of improved efficiency, the elimination of duplications, or stronger overall management cannot be reflected in adjusted past data. Thus, if past results are used as a basis for

---

[13] In the 1960s it appeared that many conglomerates were able to escape this digestion period and report year-by-year rising earnings per share in spite of many acquisitions. However, some analysts had some doubts about this "new era" phenomenon. Furthermore, conglomerates offer few of the economic advantages usually available to other types of mergers. In 1969-1972, investors viewed conglomerates negatively.

Some conglomerates have compared sales and earnings of the total companies acquired during a particular year with sales and earnings exclusive of their newly acquired company in preceding years, thus giving the illusion of an increase in sales and earnings that had not really occurred. See Abraham J. Briloff, "Dirty Pooling— How To Succeed in Business Without Really Trying," *Barron's* (July 15, 1968), p. 1.

projecting future earning power, some allowance should be made for the potential improvement resulting from combined operations. Of course, this factor will vary widely among different companies, depending primarily on the nature of the industry and the characteristics of the individual units merged and most of all on the quality of management.

Corporations sometimes do not adjust past data to reflect the effect of a merger. This is not acceptable practice in that, for comparative purposes, prior years' earnings are understated relative to those for the year in which the merger was consummated and subsequent years. In such cases, the analyst should make the necessary adjustment by adding to income in the years preceding the merger the income reported by the absorbed units and recomputing per-share figures on this combined basis. Otherwise, earnings growth will be exaggerated.

Sale of New Stock. The analyst should expect common stock financing to be justified by adequate earnings (rate of return) on the new funds in the future. This factor seldom poses any adjustment problem in security analysis, as it is accepted practice *not* to adjust prior years' earnings to reflect a broader capitalization resulting from the sale of new common stock. The new stock enters into the computation of per-share figures only in the year during which it is issued and in subsequent fiscal periods. To make prior-year adjustments for this additional stock, as if it had been outstanding in previous years, would not be justified because the funds now obtained from the sale of the additional stock were not available as earning assets prior to the year received.

The AICPA in APB Opinion No. 9, and reaffirmed in Opinion No. 15, stated: "The computation of earnings per share should be based on the weighted average number of shares outstanding during the period."

Conversion of Convertible Senior Securities and Warrants. The number of shares of common stock that a corporation has outstanding can be increased significantly as a result of the conversion of outstanding senior issues and warrants.

In May, 1969, the AICPA [14] ruled that audited statements in annual reports must give earnings per share which reflect potential dilution of these earnings through warrants and options as well as through convertible securities. This rule could lessen the use of these securities, especially in corporate acquisitions.

---

[14] See footnote 7 on page 488 which summarizes the most important factors in Opinion No. 15.

QUESTIONS

1. Why are ratios utilized in the analysis of financial statements?

2. What ratios would you suggest be studied to analyze short-term liquidity of a business? Support your choices and state the components of each ratio.

3. Which of the following changes in stated ratios indicate (1) favorable and (2) unfavorable developments for a company? Carefully support your answer, indicating possible conditions that should lead to a different conclusion.

   (a) An increase in the current ratio.
   (b) An increase in the inventory turnover ratio.
   (c) A decrease in the receivable turnover ratio.
   (d) A decrease in the asset turnover ratio (net sales divided by total assets).
   (e) A decrease in the operating margin (net operating income divided by net sales).

4. (a) Why might a working capital turnover ratio be a more sensitive indicator of overtrading than an inventory turnover ratio?
   (b) What is meant by "average age of conversion"? How can this concept be used by the analyst?

5. (a) Define capitalization ratios and discuss the various ways in which they can be calculated. Explain financial leverage.
   (b) In what industries would you expect to find high debt capitalization ratios? low debt capitalization ratios? Discuss these ratios for airlines.

6. What is the significance of each of the following ratios and what relationships exist between the ratios?

   (a) Net income after taxes divided by net sales.
   (b) Net income after taxes divided by total assets.
   (c) Net income after taxes divided by owners' investment.

7. What factors would you study in analyzing the record of sales growth of a company?

8. (a) Compare the significance of the dividend-price ratio and the earnings-price ratio. What relationship do these ratios have to the price-earnings ratio, if any?
   (b) How do you calculate a price-earnings ratio? an earnings yield?

9. Why are physical data ratios reduced to a per-share figure?

10. (a) Distinguish between a stock split and a stock dividend accounting.
    (b) Why must the analyst adjust past data for stock dividends or stock splits of significant amounts?

11. How might the fact that convertible securities are outstanding affect the interpretation of reported earnings per share figures through time? What

adjustments, if any, should an analyst make when convertible securities are outstanding? Assume whatever figures are necessary to illustrate the problem and the adjustments you suggest.

12. What problems arise for analysts in mergers, especially conglomerates?

WORK-STUDY PROBLEMS

1. The income accounts and the balance sheets of the XYZ Chemical Company for two years are summarized below.

Income Account, December 31
($ millions)

	First Year	Second Year
Net sales	$1,578	$1,587
Cost of goods sold	1,001	1,016
Selling and administrative expenses	142	147
Depreciation	129	144
Interest on debt	17	18
Provision for income taxes	131	120
Net income	158	142
Dividends	108	108

Number of shares in both years, 29,800,000

Balance Sheet, December 31
($ millions)

	First Year	Second Year
Assets:		
Current assets:		
Cash items	$ 125	$ 120
Accounts receivable	208	230
Inventories	355	340
Total current assets	$ 688	$ 690
Plant and equipment	$2,176	$2,301
Less accumulated depreciation	1,206	1,315
	$ 970	$ 986
Other assets	$ 54	$ 58
Total assets	$1,712	$1,734
Liabilities and stockholders' equity:		
Current liabilities:		
Accounts payable	$ 66	$ 64
Taxes	120	120
Other current liabilities	60	61
Total current liabilities	$ 246	$ 245
Long-term debt	484	470
Common stock	248	248
Retained earnings	734	771
Total liabilities and stockholders' equity	$1,712	$1,734

(a) From the data given above, calculate the following for both years:

    (1) The gross profit as a percentage of net sales.
    (2) The net operating income as a percentage of net sales.
    (3) Depreciation as a percentage of sales.
    (4) Coverage of interest before and after taxes.
    (5) Net income as a percentage of net sales.
    (6) Net income to total capital funds.
    (7) Net income to stockholders' equity.
    (8) Payout ratio.
    (9) Per-share earnings of common stock.
   (10) Dividend per share of common stock.
   (11) Current ratio.
   (12) Working capital to debt ratio.
   (13) Age of accounts receivable.
   (14) Turnover of inventory.
   (15) On the basis of an assumed market price of 102 on the stock, determine:

        (a) The current dividend yield and earnings yield.
        (b) The price-earnings ratio.
        (c) The price-cash flow ratio.

(b) Comment on any changes that are of interest.

2. The following ratios were calculated from the income statements for the year ended December 31, 1972 for Texaco and AT&T.

	Texaco	AT&T
Net operating margin	19.3%	36.7%
After-tax margin	9.9%	11.9%

(a) What is a margin? Do these figures indicate that AT&T operates more efficiently than Texaco? Explain your position carefully.

(b) Which company earned a higher return on total assets? owners' capital? Are your findings here similar to those suggested by their reported margins? Explain any differences found and be as explicit as you can about underlying relationships.

(c) Does either company make effective use of financial leverage? Support your answer with appropriate calculations from the statements.

SUGGESTED READINGS

Accounting Trends and Techniques (Annual). New York: American Institute of Certified Public Accountants.

Almanac of Business and Industrial Financial Ratios, 1973 edition. Englewood Cliffs, N.J.: Prentice-Hall, Inc., 1973.

Bierman, Harold J., Jr. "ROI as a Measure of Managerial Performance." *Financial Executive* (March, 1973), pp. 40-46.

"Comparative Rate of Return on Sales and on Stockholders' Equity for Preceding Two Years for Leading Industries (Annual)." *Monthly Economic Letter.* New York: First National City Bank of New York.

Forbes Annual Report on American Industry. New York: Forbes.

Fortune (Annual report). "500 Largest U.S. Corporations," and "200 Largest Industrials Outside the U.S." Chicago, Ill.: Time, Inc.

Latané, Henry A., Donald L. Tuttle, and Charles P. Jones. "P/E Ratio vs. Changes in Earnings in Forecasting Future Price Changes." *Financial Analysts Journal* (January-February, 1969), pp. 117-120.

Mennis, Edmund A. "New Tools for Profit Analysis." *Financial Analysts Journal* (January-February, 1969), pp. 25-53.

Murphy, Joseph E., Jr., and J. Russell Nelson. "Five Principles of Financial Relationships." *Financial Analysts Journal* (March-April, 1971), pp. 38-52.

Standard & Poor's Basic Industry Survey (Annual for each major industry). New York: Standard & Poor's Corporation.

U.S. Federal Trade Commission. *Economic Report of the President* (Annual). See tables on relation of profit after taxes to stockholder equity and to sales for "All Manufacturing by Industry" group. See also *Quarterly Financial Report for Manufacturing Corporations.* Washington, D.C.: Superintendent of Documents.

SPECIAL CLASSES
OF SECURITIES

Industrial Securities

Companies included in the industrial group present a large and dissimilar array to investors. The wide variety and differences make the problem of security analysis difficult. Generalizations are less useful here, for example, than they are in the public utility field where both the industry and the companies within the industry have much in common, including standardization of accounts and stability of operations, revenues, and earnings.

Industrial companies include all those not fitting in the specialized classifications discussed in Chapters 21-25. In Table 20-1, which shows net income, return on net worth, and margin of sales for leading corporations, the industries through and including "trade" are industrials. The largest group in the industrial class is manufacturing companies, which account for nearly three quarters of the net income generated by all industrial companies. The growth rate of industries varies widely.[1]

Industrial companies may suffer severely from competition or, on the other hand, may earn high rates of return on their investments if they enjoy industry leadership, particularly in research and patents in a growth industry (for example, IBM, Merck, Xerox, and Avon Products). Some industrial companies evidence strong cyclical characteristics, while others are quite non-cyclical. The reward for top management, as well as the penalty for mediocre or poor management, is especially great in the field of industrials.

---

[1] The reader should review the following U. S. Department of Commerce publications: *U. S. Industrial Outlook* (latest annual issue) and *Long-Term Economic Growth 1866-1965*.

TABLE 20-1

Net Income of Leading Corporations for the Years 1970 and 1971 (Dollar Figures in Millions)

No. of Cos.	Industrial Groups	Reported Net Income After Taxes 1970	1971	Percent Change	Net Worth Beginning of 1971 (a)	% Return on Net Worth (a) 1970	1971	% Change in Sales (b)	% Margin on Sales (c) 1970	1971
15	Baking	74.1	85.1	+15	688.7	11.0	12.4	+15	2.5	2.5
13	Dairy products	275.7	305.8	+11	2,434.0	12.0	12.6	+10	3.1	3.1
35	Meatpacking	93.9	121.3	+29	1,495.5	6.6	8.1	+3	0.9	1.1
13	Sugar	52.1	74.9	+44	716.9	7.5	10.4	+10	2.9	3.6
81	Other food products	813.1	854.3	+5	6,813.3	12.8	12.5	+8	3.7	3.6
19	Soft drinks	249.7	288.4	+16	1,257.0	22.7	22.9	+10	6.8	7.1
11	Brewing	130.6	146.7	+12	902.9	16.0	16.2	+12	5.7	5.8
11	Distilling	179.6	185.8	+3	1,885.5	10.1	9.9	+6	4.1	4.0
86	Tobacco products	438.7	506.3	+15	3,001.6	16.4	16.9	+8	5.4	5.7
11	Textile products	254.1	250.7	−1	4,066.4	6.4	6.2	+8	2.5	2.3
97	Clothing and apparel	202.3	213.6	+6	2,049.8	10.7	10.4	+8	3.0	2.9
28	Shoes, leather, etc.	104.7	112.0	+7	1,034.7	10.6	10.8	+5	3.0	3.0
59	Rubber and allied products	353.7	471.6	+33	4,818.7	7.6	9.8	+7	3.1	3.8
25	Lumber and wood products	283.7	321.6	+13	2,944.3	10.2	10.9	+15	5.1	5.0
37	Furniture and fixtures	46.4	61.8	+33	582.8	8.4	10.6	+10	3.3	4.0
62	Paper and allied products	588.8	453.6	−23	8,127.5	7.4	5.6	+5	3.9	2.9
96	Printing and publishing	395.8	401.8	+2	3,396.8	12.5	11.8	+5	5.6	5.4
76	Chemical products	1,470.2	1,578.2	+7	15,958.8	9.5	9.9	+5	5.3	5.4
27	Paint and allied products	68.5	80.4	+17	1,108.0	6.2	7.3	+5	2.6	2.8
41	Drugs and medicines	1,084.0	1,231.6	+14	6,450.1	18.8	19.1	+10	9.1	9.5
34	Soap and cosmetics	491.2	546.3	+11	2,920.3	18.7	18.7	+8	6.6	6.8
96	Petroleum prod. and refining	5,937.5	6,419.2	+8	57,079.3	11.0	11.2	+11	7.3	7.1
18	Cement	73.8	94.8	+29	1,218.8	6.1	7.8	+14	5.1	5.7
11	Glass products	201.8	254.8	+26	2,285.3	9.0	11.1	+10	4.8	5.5
41	Other stone and clay products	192.5	249.0	+29	2,836.6	7.0	8.8	+11	4.0	4.7
65	Iron and steel	626.6	609.4	−3	13,581.1	4.6	4.5	+4	2.9	2.7
56	Nonferrous metals	1,002.1	515.7	−49	9,898.5	10.6	5.2	+3	6.8	3.6
35	Hardware and tools	152.8	157.9	+3	1,281.6	12.5	12.3	+3	5.4	5.4
52	Building, heat., plumb. equip.	127.0	166.5	+31	1,878.2	7.0	8.9	+4	2.2	2.6
69	Other metal products	267.4	241.1	−10	2,723.3	10.4	8.8	+4	3.8	3.3
44	Farm. constr., mat.-hdlg. equip.	425.3	420.9	−1	4,804.5	9.3	8.8	+6	4.0	3.7
62	Office equipment, computers	1,210.2	1,295.1	+7	9,746.3	13.9	13.3	+6	8.1	7.9
170	Other machinery	743.0	722.2	−3	7,415.8	10.5	9.7	+3	4.3	4.0
331	Electrical equip. & electronics	1,856.3	2,044.4	+10	19,574.1	11.9	10.4	+4	3.6	3.3
18	Household appliances	255.0	265.7	+4	2,289.3	11.9	11.6	+4	3.9	3.9
10	Autos and trucks	1,042.1	2,696.0	+159	17,974.4	5.8	15.0	+28	2.4	4.9
48	Automotive parts	240.8	292.3	+21	2,809.2	8.9	10.4	+6	3.4	3.9
7	Railway equipment	72.5	74.4	+3	809.0	9.4	9.2	+3	4.6	4.5
47	Aerospace	446.6	619.4	+39	6,822.5	6.7	9.1	+7	1.7	2.5
148	Instruments, photo. goods, etc.	1,186.5	1,308.4	+10	8,288.5	15.8	15.8	+7	7.9	8.2
114	Misc. manufacturing	189.8	232.1	+22	2,614.0	8.5	8.9	+12	3.1	3.4
2,319	**Total manufacturing**	**23,900.8**	**26,971.3**	**+13**	**248,583.7**	**10.1**	**10.8**	**+8**	**4.5**	**4.7**

No. of Cos.	Industrial Groups	Reported Net Income After Taxes			Net Worth Beginning of 1971 (a)	% Return on Net Worth (a)		% Change in Sales (b)	% Margin on Sales (c)	
		1970	1971	Percent Change		1970	1971		1970	1971
22	Metal mining (d)	168.0	144.4	− 14	1,435.1	12.4	10.1	− 1	9.7	9.5
7	Coal mining (d)	44.9	30.9	− 31	366.7	14.4	8.4	− 3	6.9	4.4
6	Other mining, quarrying (d)	69.5	34.9	− 50	779.6	9.4	4.5	− 1	13.6	6.8
35	**Total mining (d)**	**282.4**	**210.2**	**− 26**	**2,581.4**	**11.7**	**8.1**	**− 1**	**10.4**	**7.7**
62	Food chains	420.5	426.4	+ 1	3,770.5	12.0	11.3	+ 7	1.1	1.0
120	Variety chains	443.6	504.2	+ 14	3,977.2	12.3	12.8	+ 12	2.3	2.4
76	Department and specialty	470.2	535.7	+ 14	4,803.9	10.5	11.2	+ 16	2.6	2.6
8	Mail order	536.7	626.8	+ 17	4,665.2	12.3	13.4	+ 8	4.3	4.6
215	Wholesale and misc.	624.3	525.4	− 16	5,165.3	13.4	10.2	+ 10	2.8	2.1
481	**Total trade**	**2,495.3**	**2,618.5**	**+ 5**	**22,382.1**	**12.1**	**11.7**	**+ 10**	**2.3**	**2.2**
68	Class I railroads (e, f)	229.0	358.9	+ 57	17,323.3	1.3	2.1	+ 5	1.9	2.8
38	Common carrier trucking (e)	70.3	153.5	+ 118	788.3	9.6	19.5	+ 18	2.3	4.2
32	Air transport (e)	D-87.4	66.9	#	3,377.4	#	2.0	+ 9	#	0.7
18	Misc. transportation (e)	119.4	120.0	+ 1	988.4	13.3	12.1	+ 5	3.1	3.4
156	**Total transportation (e)**	**331.3**	**699.3**	**+111**	**22,477.5**	**1.5**	**3.1**	**+ 6**	**1.2**	**2.3**
186	Electric power and gas (e)	4,168.9	4,646.0	+ 11	41,519.3	11.3	11.2	+ 12	12.3	12.2
16	Telephone and telegraph (e)	2,590.4	2,689.1	+ 4	28,322.3	9.5	9.5	+ 10	11.6	11.0
202	**Total public utilities (e)**	**6,759.4**	**7,335.1**	**+ 9**	**69,841.5**	**10.5**	**10.5**	**+ 11**	**12.0**	**11.7**
45	Amusements and hotels	83.8	95.0	+ 13	1,217.4	7.9	7.8	+ 5	3.4	3.6
74	Restaurants and hotels	182.9	183.5	*	1,577.3	13.6	11.6	+ 14	4.2	3.7
329	Other business services	413.7	525.5	+ 27	4,455.3	10.3	11.8	+ 9	3.3	3.9
47	Construction	116.7	150.8	+ 29	1,586.3	8.1	9.5	+ 17	2.2	2.4
495	**Total services**	**797.1**	**954.8**	**+ 20**	**8,836.3**	**10.1**	**10.8**	**+ 11**	**3.2**	**3.5**
3,688	**Total nonfinancial**	**34,566.3**	**38,789.1**	**+ 12**	**374,702.6**	**9.8**	**10.4**	**+ 9**	**4.6**	**4.7**
50	Commercial bank holding cos.	1,599.6	1,771.1	+ 11	13,685.1	12.4	12.9	....	....	....
828	Property & liability insurance (g)	987.1	1,750.0	+ 77	14,144.5	6.9	12.4	....	....	....
223	Investment funds (h)	1,347.0	1,272.4	− 6	41,875.7	2.9	3.0	....	....	....
45	Sales finance	476.2	568.1	+ 19	5,384.2	9.5	10.6	....	....	....
63	Real estate	96.4	127.0	+ 32	887.1	13.0	14.3	....	....	....
1,209	**Total financial**	**4,506.2**	**5,488.6**	**+ 22**	**75,976.6**	**5.7**	**7.2**	....	....	....
4,897	**Grand total**	**39,072.6**	**44,277.7**	**+ 13**	**450,679.2**	**9.0**	**9.8**	....	....	....

* Less than 0.5%. # Not calculated because of deficit. D Deficit.
(a) Net worth is equivalent to shareholders' equity or "book net assets" or capital and surplus. (b) About 1% of nonfinancial firms with 5% of the income do not report sales or revenues. Data include income from investments and other sources as well as from sales. (c) Profit margins are computed for all companies sales or gross revenue figures. (d) Net income is reported before depletion charges in some cases. (e) Due to the large proportion of capital investment in the form of funded debt, rate of return on total property investment would be lower than that shown net worth only. (f) Association of American Railroads tabulation; Penn Central partly estimated. (g) Estimated by A. M. Best Co. for all stock companies on an adjusted basis. (h) Income in most cases excludes capital gains or losses on investments.

Source: First National City Bank, April, 1972.

INDUSTRY ANALYSIS

The record and the success of a company will depend to a great extent on the fortunes of the industry (or industries) in which it operates. Therefore, no sound judgment as to whether to buy, hold, or sell the securities of a particular company can be made until a judgment on its industry (or industries) has been made. But all too frequently, judgments on a stock are made that have *not* been preceded by careful appraisal of an industry and its prospects and thus are merely an indefinite projection of the current trends of an industry, i.e., average, below average, or excellent growth.

Industry Categories

Investors tend to place industries in one of the three major categories discussed in the following paragraphs.

Average Industries. These are industries that in the past have had a record roughly paralleling the record of GNP or the economy as a whole and that in the future are expected to continue this record. These industries and the companies within them are expected to grow at roughly the same rate as the economy and also to reflect cyclical fluctuations of the economy. Some industries will still experience greater cyclical characteristics than others. These will, to a great extent, be industries producing consumers' and producers' postponable durable goods (or their raw materials or components) or producing goods or services that do not fall into the classification of necessities. Extractive industries, for example, have been particularly vulnerable to cyclical recessions. Necessities, admittedly, are not easy to define in the light of our highly affluent society. Business recessions have been mild since 1938. Mature industries are average-growth industries.

Growth Industries. Many investors are eager to buy stocks in growth industries, which are termed "growth stocks" when exceptional growth performance is anticipated. Investments in such industries as business machines, photography, science, aerospace, oceanography and, more recently, drugs and anti-pollution have provided high performance for many investors. However, over the long pull, the majority of investors cannot concentrate on such issues. Those who consistently purchase such stocks *regardless of their price* will have a poor record. Growth stocks are by nature exceptional and there are not enough "to go around" for the great majority of investors, individual and institutional. In 1973 institutional investors accounted for 80% of market trading in heavily favored, major growth stocks.

It is human nature for investors to desire to get in on the ground floor of what seems to be a potentially fast-growing industry. However, most stocks classified as growth stocks have not enjoyed this rating long-term, and new companies have taken their place. The higher the projected growth rate above the average growth for all industries and the longer the projections, the greater the risk that such projections will not be realized. Most growth stocks have enjoyed a relatively short period of exceptionally rapid growth. In many cases, the termination of such a growth period is painfully abrupt and stock market prices drop drastically. For an investor to accomplish exceptional capital gains, he must be adept in judgment both as to when to *buy* and when to *sell* most growth issues. There have been very few IBM's, Polaroid's, and Xerox's. *However, it is still true and probably it will continue to be true that the majority of investors who do post the most successful and exceptional portfolio growth records will be those who skillfully and shrewdly use the vehicle of growth stocks.* To deserve the designation "growth industry," Wall Street generally requires:

1. That the threat of obsolescence from technological developments or other changes does not presently appear significant for the industry as a whole.
2. That the demand for the industry's product is growing at a significantly faster rate than the growth of GNP, and competing industries if such exist.
3. That as sales increase, mass production techniques will reduce costs and permit a reduction in sales prices to stimulate additional demands, but not enough to reduce profits, thus prolonging the period of rapid growth.
4. That relatively few companies dominate the industry.
5. That the industry has emerged from its initial stages into a period where the observable growth rate in sales and earnings is significantly higher than that of industries in general and supposedly can be projected for some years. Earnings are expected to grow at least 12% per year.

Industries with a Poorer-Than-Average Record or a Recent Sharp Decline. There have always been industries and companies that have, at least for some period of time, posted a record in terms of gross revenues and net profits that is inferior to that of the growth of the economy as a whole and to "all U.S. corporations" and the stock averages. Others have also grown at a slower rate than GNP and have in addition demonstrated highly cyclical characteristics. Still others have only recently encountered some serious problems that have adversely affected earnings. This may be temporary. Institutional investors tend to reject such stocks.

Industries with a Long Mediocre or Poor Record. Within this classification are some industries that have had a poor record and have been "out-of-favor" for some years. In the case of those with a long poor-to-mediocre record, there are some industries that may be expected to do little better in the future than in the past. However, in some cases, after a long record of deterioration, a revival has provided interesting opportunities for investors who projected a significant recovery for a long out-of-favor industry (for example, the railroads and the airlines in 1961 and their subsequent recovery in 1962-1966, followed by another period of losses in 1970-1971).

Industries That Have Recently Shown a Sharp Decline. Wall Street places so much emphasis on the recent or current record that it frequently demonstrates great dissatisfaction in terms of market prices and P/E ratios with industries posting a currently poor record even though the long-term record has paralleled the growth of GNP or has perhaps been superior to the record for GNP. The chemicals in 1968-1971 are an excellent illustration. The favorable reversal in investment attitudes towards airline stocks in 1962-1966 and the unfavorable reversal in 1967-1971, then favorable again in 1972, shows how quickly investor attitudes can change.

Industries with Difficulties Exaggerated by Performance Pressures. When industries have problems and are out of favor, performance pressures have often been so strong that many investors, including many professional investors and portfolio managers, will not even take the time to make an industry analysis in depth to determine objectively and unemotionally the longer-term industry prospects—say for the next 3 or 6 years. There has been so much emphasis by Wall Street in recent years on short-term performance (even monthly and quarterly) that industries suffering even a temporary setback tend to be sold and ignored, that is, they tend to be neglected in terms of any really objective analysis in depth to determine the longer-term prospects. The pressure for short-term performance on portfolio managers as well as on brokers, including those directing policies of mutual funds and pension funds, has been as strong in the 1970s as the 1960s.

Industries out of Favor Because of Current Trend Projections. There is a great tendency on Wall Street to project the current trend, no matter how short its duration, in the case of either a rapid growth or a sharp decline.[2]

---

[2] The investor should review this factor in selection of stocks in 1967-1970 when this approach was strikingly prevalent. Examples of such situations, followed later by renewed investor acceptance, were the automobile industry in 1958, 1966, and 1970; the international oils in 1959-1960; the electric equipment industry in 1960-1962; and the airlines and railroads in 1961-1962. The chemical and airline industries in 1970 were providing such a potential. In any year, the astute investor can locate major companies in major industries whose stocks are selling at 45%-50% and below their previous highs. Careful unemotional analysis can always discover among such industries and companies sound values and significant long-term (3 to 5 years) capital gains potentials based on reasonable, unemotional projections of a *recovery in earning power*.

At any point of time, those industries that are currently out of favor with investors include some that correctly deserve this judgment of Wall Street, but also within this group are those that do not deserve the very low rating they are currently receiving. If an investor is willing to make a careful industry appraisal in depth, he can always locate at least one major industry (and major companies in that industry) where, in his judgment, the current difficulties are only temporary. He may decide that, over the longer term, their *long-term* satisfactory record will continue and that therefore they are distinctly undervalued in the market, offering relatively safe and substantial capital gains potentials. These stocks are usually available at low P/E ratios and high yields.

Major Emphasis in Industry Analysis

The major emphasis in industry analysis should be on an objective, economic analysis of the demand and supply factors for the industry, including a careful analysis of potential competition and the price prospects for the industry's products or services. It is the reasonable accuracy of projections that gives success.

Industry Analysis in Depth. Although the investor is led to believe that the buy, sell, or hold recommendations of professionals are premised on a thorough investigation of the industry in question, such is often not the case. But industry analysis should be an essential part of any analysis of a particular industrial company—a supply-demand-price economic analysis.

It should be noted at this point that even though an industry is posting a good or excellent record, some of the components of the industry may not be. Examples of this failure of a company to share in an industry's profitability in the past were Chrysler in 1955-1962 and Montgomery Ward in 1946-1967. Later, significant favorable reversals in trends occurred and both companies received strong investment approval, for example in 1968-1972, only to fall again into disfavor in 1973.

Qualified Industry Specialists. While industry analysis is often ignored, competent specialists have developed among financial analysts for the large

---

In such cases, the downside risk in stock prices (especially where there are relatively high, well-protected dividend yields) may be very small compared to the upside potential over the next 3 to 5 years. This discussion refers to major industries. It should be emphasized that most of our major industries (and major companies in these industries) are mature industries; therefore, in the light of continuing substantial performance pressures, good results from investing in these industries can probably be obtained only by application of the out-of-favor, low P/E investment philosophy and policy—not buy and hold.

brokerage firms and institutional investors. There are utility, chemical, drug, aerospace, automobile, steel, paper, and many other industry specialists. Many of these specialists are highly competent. Of course, it must be emphasized that in the final analysis it is the *judgment* of the analyst applied to the facts that is the crucial ingredient for success. Techniques in analysis may be taught and learned, but judgment to project accurately is the result of a combination of knowledge, experience, skill, and native ability.

There is also one other factor that must be mentioned. Industry specialists among the financial analysts tend to have a "constitutional weakness" always, or generally to favor their industry and its prospects, or at most to be neutral rather than negative. Few chemical industry specialists publicly expressed negative opinions in 1965 and early 1966, few specialists in life insurance stocks publicly expressed negative views about industry and company prospects in 1964 in light of the extremely high price-earnings ratios, and few airline analysts forecasted the 1968-1969 and 1973 airline problems.

While the industry specialist should be mainly concerned with the long-term outlook for the industry, he should also be knowledgeable on the development of major problems that could adversely affect industry sales and profits over the next 1 or 2 years and therefore stock prices over the short term as well as the intermediate and long term.

The investor should use the industry specialist's facts and also his interpretation of the facts. Then, realizing the tendency of industry specialists to favor their industry, the investor should make his own interpretation and judgment. All of the above indicates some of the problems in utilizing the industry analyses of professionals. But to ignore industry analysis never establishes a basis for long-term success in portfolio management. Decision making in this area is one of the most difficult faced by the investor, but it is crucial. Correct demand-supply-price projections are vital for success.

Demand-Supply-Price Analysis. An industry analysis should be an economic analysis based on a study of the demand and supply forces in the industry and their relation to the prices of the industry products and services and the competitive factors. The best way to illustrate this fact is to present an outline of a thorough institutional type of analysis of an industry in general and a company in particular. Economic analysis is the key factor.

Illustrative Industry Analysis

Part I of the report on "General Motors Corporation in the World Automobile Market" provides an excellent example of an industry analysis. This

**General Motors Corporation
In the World Automobile Market**

An Investment Analysis

Part I. The World Automobile and Commercial Vehicle Markets

  A. Future Domestic Automobile Demand

   1. Domestic Demography
        Growth
        Age Structure and Household Formations
        Dispersion

   2. Economic Growth and Living Standards
        Gross National Product
        Personal Disposable Income

   3. Future Modes of Surface Transportation
        The Private Automobile and the Common Carrier
        Highway Improvement

   4. Annual New Car Demand
        New Demand plus Replacement Demand
        Projections of Demand

  B. Future Domestic Commercial Vehicle Markets—Demand

   1. The Freight Industry
        Regulated Motor Carriers
        Unregulated Motor Carriers
        Projections

  C. Future Foreign Vehicle Markets

   1. Foreign Automobile Demand
        West Germany
        France
        Italy
        Benelux
        United Kingdom
        Sweden
        EFTA—Excluding the U. K. and Sweden
        Canada
        Australia
        Japan
        Overseas Sterling Area
        South America and the Rest of the Free World
        Total Foreign Passenger Car Demand

   2. Foreign Truck Demand
        European Economic Community
        European Free Trade Association
        Canada
        Australia
        Japan
        Overseas Sterling Area
        South America and the Rest of the Free World
        Total Foreign Truck Demand

industry analysis, outlined on page 517, covers the demand side of the automobile industry for both domestic and foreign markets. (The supply side of the industry is given in Part II of this report, outlined on page 521.)

Part I of the outline of the automobile industry analysis presented here is useful as an illustration of a professional, institutional type of industry analysis and as the basis for a discussion of demand-supply-price analysis.[3]

Demand-Supply Analysis. In the case of the automobile industry, in the demand-supply analysis the major emphasis is on demand analysis, that is, industry projections of domestic and worldwide demand for automobiles and trucks.[4] While emphasis on demand is usually the case in most industries, it is especially true in the automobile industry where about 95% of domestic sales by U.S. manufacturers are made by only three manufacturers: General Motors with about 52% of industry sales, Ford with about 27%, and Chrysler (after a decline from 18% to 6-7% and then a recovery) with about 16-17% in 1968. In the case of worldwide sales, General Motors has accounted for about 30%, Ford about 20%, and Chrysler about 10%. The other major world automobile manufacturers have been Volkswagen, Fiat,

---

[3] "General Motors Corporation in the World Automobile Market," a professional industrial report consisting of 107 printed pages of relatively small print and included in a Staff Analysis, Subcommittee on Domestic Finance, Committee on Banking and Currency, House of Representatives, 88th Congress, 2nd Session (Washington: U.S. Government Printing Office, 1966).

[4] In the report on General Motors, the following industry projections of unit demand and sales were made:

New Car Sales Projections Future Rate of Growth 4%		Projected Annual Truck Demand Future Rate of Growth 3.5%	
Annual Unit Sales		Unit Demand	
1965	7,525,000 [1]	1965	1,210,000 [1]
	7,900,000 [2]		1,277,000 [2]
	8,274,000 [3] *		1,348,000 [3]
1970	9,155,000 [1]	1970	1,432,000 [1]
	9,611,000 [2]		1,417,000 [2]
	10,067,000 [3]		1,601,000 [3]

[1] Assume scrappage rate of 6.2% of rejected autos   [1] Assuming 5.1% scrappage rate
[2] Assume scrappage rate of 6.7% of rejected autos   [2] Assuming 5.6% scrappage rate
[3] Assume scrappage rate of 7.2% of rejected autos   [3] Assuming 6.1% scrappage rate

	Industry (cars)	G.M. (cars)	G.M.%
Actual 1965 unit sales (millions)	9.3	4.9	53.0%
Actual 1966 unit sales (millions)	8.5	4.4	51.8%
Actual 1967 unit sales (millions)	7.5	4.1	54.7%
Actual 1968 unit sales (millions)	8.6	4.5	52.3%
Actual 1969 unit sales (millions)	8.5	4.4	51.8%
Actual 1970 unit sales (millions)	7.1	3.3	46.5%
Actual 1971 unit sales (millions)	8.7	4.7	54.0%
Actual 1972 unit sales (millions)	9.3	4.8	51.7%

Renault, BMC units, Citroen, Peugeot, and Simca. By 1968, Japan had surpassed West Germany and had become the number two country in world automobile production, exporting significantly to the United States. Its major output has been in Toyota and Datsun cars.

The supply segment of an industry analysis includes an analysis of the competitive and cost aspects of the industry. In the General Motors report, the supply analysis consisted of comparative sales of General Motors with two of its competitors—domestic and worldwide. In other industries, such as steel, the supply side of the analysis is more difficult because of the relatively large numbers of suppliers, both domestic and foreign, and also because of the importance of foreign imports or exports in the supply picture. In still other industries the sources of raw materials and their amount, location, and control are very important. Other factors also complicate supply analysis.

Price Analysis. After completing the supply and demand study, the analyst must determine the past, current, and future price trends for the industry's products and services. While these prices are usually the result of the interaction of the demand and supply schedules, the factor of government intervention in pricing is also of concern. This was demonstrated in the United States in the case of the steel, aluminum, copper, and drug industries in the 1960s and of the overall government controls in 1971-1973. Foreign cartel operations approved by foreign governments are also a case in point. Taking all factors into consideration, the analyst must project industry product prices (or at least a price range) as well as volume in order to arrive at projections for industry and company dollar sales that will be the result of multiplying projected volume by projected price. The out-of-favor aspects of the aluminum, paper, airline, steel, and food chain industries all reflect pricing problems.

COMPANY ANALYSIS

The illustration of a company analysis given below is useful as the basis for a discussion of various aspects of a company analysis that follows a thorough demand-supply-price industry analysis.

Illustrative Company Analysis

Parts II and III of the report on "General Motors Corporation in the World Automobile Market," outlined on page 521, provide a good illustration of a detailed company analysis. The report includes the supply side of the industry by showing General Motors' position in the industry. It was prepared for institutional investors. The report also includes financial data about the company's capitalization, actual earnings, and projected earnings, as well as the market evaluation of General Motors stock. The financial data indicate the types of information that an analyst should require and analyze in a thorough institutional type of company analysis.

Brief History. Most analysts present a brief history of the company to set the stage for an understanding of the company's current operations and its industry prospects. In this case, the company history covers a long span and accounts for 1½ pages of the 107-page printed report.

Product or Sales Breakdown. The product or sales breakdown was covered in about 5 printed pages of text in the General Motors report. The report also presented a tabular breakdown as shown below. The text of

Estimated Breakdown of Sales ($)

U. S. Passenger Cars:	30.7%
Chevrolet	7.2
Pontiac	6.9
Oldsmobile	6.1
Buick	5.7
Cadillac	
Total U. S. Passenger Cars (over the years 48%-56%) ..	56.6%
U. S. Trucks (Chevrolet and GMC)	8.8
Other U. S. Automobile Parts, etc.	2.8
Total U. S. Automotive	68.2%
Canadian Automotive	4.1
Overseas Operations (including Nonautomotive)	14.5
Nonautomotive (Domestic)	10.1
Defense Sales	3.1
Total	100.0%

the report included one paragraph on each category in the estimated breakdown, except that there were five paragraphs on overseas operations: one each for Germany, Great Britain, Australia, South American Group, and Miscellaneous Overseas and Distribution Facilities.

Sales breakdowns by products, divisions, and subsidiaries are important, but many companies still do not provide sufficient breakdowns in their annual reports and analysts then must attempt to secure the information directly from the company. Assistance is being provided in this area—especially in the case of conglomerates.[5] Of course, what the analysts would

---

[5] The SEC requires disclosure by divisions or subsidiaries (in its filings) that account for at least 10% of sales revenues.

General Motors Corporation
In the World Automobile Market

An Investment Analysis—Concluded

Part II. General Motors Corporation

    A. A Brief History

    B. Product Breakdown
1. Chevrolet
2. Buick—Oldsmobile—Pontiac
3. Cadillac
4. Fisher Body
5. Other Accessory Divisions
6. United Motor Service
7. General Motors of Canada and McKinnon Industries
8. Overseas Operations
    German—Adam Opel A.G.
    Great Britain—Vauxhall Motors Limited
    Australia—General Motors Holden Pty. Ltd.
    South American Group
    Miscellaneous Overseas Assembly and Distribution Facilities
9. Nonautomotive Business
10. Defense Sales

    C. Financial
1. General Motors Operating Record
2. Return on Net Worth and Return on Total Capitalization
3. Capital Expenditures and Sources of Internal Funds
4. Capital Expenditures for Special Tools
5. Earnings of Nonconsolidated Subsidiaries
6. Earnings from Operations Outside the U. S. and Canada

    D. Long-Term Earnings Projections

    E. Industry Position—Supply Situation in the Industry

    F. Research and Development

    G. Organization, Management, and Operating Philosophy
1. Operating Divisions
2. Staff Functions
3. Policy Formulation
4. The Central Office
5. Labor Relations

    H. Distribution Organization and Policies

    I. Antitrust—(potential problems for General Motors)

Part III. Market Evaluation of General Motors Common Stock

    A. Stock Price, Earnings, and Price/Earnings Comparisons

    B. Comparative Valuations—(comparison with other automobile companies and the DJIA)

like (but rarely obtain) is not only a breakdown of sales but a breakdown of costs and net income by products, divisions, and subsidiaries. Pressure is building up for corporations to provide this information to stockholders. The more information that an analyst can obtain in this area, the more reliable are his analysis and his projections. The rate of growth in sales over a reasonably long time period, the persistence of that growth currently, and the causes provide the basis for sales and earnings projections.

Capital Expenditures—Past, Current, and Planned.[6] In order to secure growth in earnings, corporations must usually increase their total invested capital and their revenues. Therefore, perhaps the most important job of corporate management is the determination under its capital budgeting program of the size and the direction of its capital expenditures. For many companies, corporate capital expenditures are simply aimed at maintaining the corporation's position in its industry, rather than toward finding the most profitable investment opportunities. In any case, the analyst must review past capital expenditures and the rate of return accomplished, especially company policies in this respect and the trend. Then he must secure as much information as possible on capital budgeting plans and expected rate of return on proposed projects. Admittedly, such information (especially long-term projections) is difficult to obtain, but at least the security analyst should make every reasonable effort to secure it. This type of information does help in assessing the ability of management to meet changing market demands.

Industry Position. In the case of General Motors, the company has had a dominant position in its industry for many years, with sales representing about 50% of industry sales. IBM has for many years enjoyed an even more dominant position in its industry, and Xerox and Polaroid have also enjoyed extremely dominant positions. In other industries, a major company may have had a declining dominance; for example, U. S. Steel at one time accounted for 33% of sales, but in recent years only 22% to 23%. DuPont gradually lost its prominent position in the chemical industry and its stock in 1968-1970 was distinctly unpopular until 1971.

In any case, the analyst should determine the company's relative position in its industry. It is important to determine the trends of the relative position of the companies being analyzed as well as that of other major corporations. In the General Motors report, about 1 page of text and 2 pages of tables were devoted to the company's relative industry position. This subject came under the heading of supply analysis and competitive analysis.

---

[6] The reader should review Chapter 7, "Corporate Financial Policies and the Investor," and Chapter 14, "Investment Growth Factors and Projections."

Research and Development. Research and development expenditures are necessary (1) to develop and produce new and improved products and services and (2) simply to maintain a company's competitive position within its own industry, as well as cost efficiencies needed to maintain its industry's position relative to competitive industries' products, processes, and services. Generally, an investor will not invest in an industry unless he expects its growth to at least parallel the growth in GNP,[7] and, as noted earlier, many investors tend to favor the fastest growing industries and companies. Normally, the growth of an industry, especially rapid growth, is closely associated with research and development. Research and development expenditures vary widely by industry in absolute amounts and relative to gross revenues. However, the key factor in research and development is not the amount spent or the number of employees in research or research facilities, but the results of research in terms of added revenues. Therefore, the analyst will seek to determine what percentage of current sales have resulted from company research and development and also, if possible, the direction and the potential of current research expenditures. This is the real test of research and also of superior management.

In the case of the automobile industry, the major efforts of research and development are aimed at maintaining or improving industry position by improving the product by operating efficiencies, and by meeting government safety and anti-pollution requirements by 1975-1977. However, in other industries such as electronics and drugs, research and development expenses are, to an important extent, aimed at developing completely new, or at least significantly different, products. The industries that have demonstrated the greatest growth have usually done so as a result of research and development. Therefore, this area cannot be overemphasized.

Research and Development in the Financial Statements. Research and development in the financial statements of companies should represent research oriented toward technological innovation, not market research or product testing. Unfortunately, management may be tempted to include the cost of such research in reported "research and development." The analyst must try to determine the nature of the charges in order to provide a judgment as to likely future results. He should try to obtain a detailed breakdown.

Technological Forecasting. Technological forecasts as a direction for research is an organized way of predicting future scientific and engineering progress based on past developments. Of course, additional research will

_____

[7] Some investors seeking mainly capital gains may invest in companies and industries on the basis of an expectation of a substantial recovery in earning power.

continue to develop brand-new sciences based on key new discoveries that have not been forecast, such as the transistor, integrated circuitry, the laser, desalting of seawater, and photo (TV type) telephone communications.

A panel on research and innovation headed by Robert A. Charpie, president of the Carbide Electronics Division of the Union Carbide Corporation, submitted a report to the government. Some conclusions in this report were:

1. "Even a casual reading of the business history of this country makes it clear that these innovative enterprises are an important part of the process that differentiates our rate of progress from that of the rest of the world."
2. The panel selected three technological industries and measured their impact on the economy. "In 1945 . . . the television, jet travel, and digital computer industries were commercially nonexistent. In 1965, these industries contributed more than $13 billion to GNP and an estimated 900,000 jobs and, very important, affected the quality of our lives."
3. The report demonstrated that research and development expenditures were by no means synonymous with innovation. Research and development typically represented less than 10% of the total innovative costs of a new product.
4. The panel noted that a handful of large companies (having 5,000 or more employees) *performed almost all of the research and development* conducted in the nation, although *that was not necessarily indicative of innovative performance.* For example, "of 61 important innovations of the twentieth century, over half of them stemmed from independent inventors or small companies. If, however, innovations come from individuals or small companies, the chief problem is first in attracting venture capital, and then in managing the business as it grows and in marketing the product.
5. "The challenge is to explore new ways for large companies to work with small technological based companies to develop within themselves sub-environments that foster the enthusiasm and entrepreneurial spirit of the small firm while benefiting from the overall resources of the total corporate environment."

Certain other factors have come out in studies of innovation. The most important are:

1. It is a continuous process that appears to evolve from the relatively slow accumulation of pertinent facts.
2. It is most often achieved by scientists engaged actively in solving specific research problems.
3. It frequently requires a decade or more to produce 70%-90% of research that results in a radical innovation and then only a relatively short time to obtain the final results.[8]

---

[8] The reader is referred to the following studies on innovation and research:

(1) Department of Defense, *Project Hindsight* (Washington: U. S. Government Printing Office, 1967).
(2) National Association of Manufacturers, *Review of 500 Industry Innovations and How They Came About* (New York: National Association of Manufacturers, 1967).

Organization, Management, and Operating Philosophy. Any report should at least briefly describe the company's organization and then should analyze the quality of management and its operating philosophy. In the General Motors report there are five subdivisions of this area: (1) operating divisions, (2) staff functions, (3) policy formulation, (4) the central office, and (5) labor relations.

The Board of Directors sets company policy, and the operating management executes the policy. Obviously, correct policy is highly important to success. In the case of General Motors, while some emphasis has been placed on product diversification outside the automobile industry, overall the company's policy has been to place heavy emphasis on the automobile business, which produces the major proportion of the company's profits.

The key to nearly any successful business is the management responsible for operating the company. This is especially important for industrial companies. The reason for General Motors' success can be traced directly to its ability to obtain outstanding administrative talents and to place them in an organizational environment conducive to effective operation. In respect to management, the following quotations from GM's report indicate very clearly what analysts should look for as evidence of excellent management.

> When duPont made its investment in GM in the early 1920s, the organizational structure was changed. . . . Alfred P. Sloan, Jr. . . . was elected president. He observed that too much time was being wasted in solving detailed administrative problems and in meeting critical daily situations which were constantly arising. This not only placed an overwhelming burden on a small number of executives and limited initiative, but was time consuming and expensive and left little opportunity for management to do any long-range planning.

> In order to overcome these management inefficiencies, Mr. Sloan reorganized GM on a foundation of *centralized* policy and *decentralized* administration. He realized that concentration at the policy-making levels of a company makes possible directional control and coordination. Decentralization on the operating levels, when properly established, develops initiative and responsibility, creating a balanced distribution of decisions on all executive personnel.

> Mr. Sloan's concept of the management of a great industrial organization, expressed in his own words, is "to divide it into as many parts as consistently can be done, place in charge of each part the most capable executive that can be found, develop a system of coordination so that each part may strengthen and support each other part, thus not only welding all parts together in the common interest of a joint enterprise, but also importantly developing ability and initiative through the instrumentalities of responsibility and ambition—developing men and giving them an opportunity to exercise their talents, both in their own interests as well as in that of the business.

(3) Jacob Schmookler, *Invention and Economic Growth* (Cambridge, Mass.: Harvard University Press, 1967).

The above principles have continued in GM and other companies. A study of management policies of IBM, Xerox, Polaroid, Merck, and Eastman Kodak will prove enlightening.

Tests of Corporate Management. The professional analyst should advise the investor objectively as to the quality of corporate management in the particular company under consideration. This can be done through an examination of the company's record of performance (the percentage of net profit on sales and the rate of return on total capital invested, on stockholders' equity, and on assets), especially the trends in this respect.

The quality of management is difficult to analyze in qualitative terms. Motivation is often as important as competence. The analyst must determine if existing management has a strong desire to excel, to make the company grow at least as fast as the economy, and to stress earnings growth.

In making the final tests, comparisons must largely rest on comparisons with other companies in the same industry. Of course, the industry itself may have such a poor potential that the investor does not wish to make a commitment in that industry. However, there may be some excellent managements in the industry that still find it impossible to earn a satisfactory rate of return on investment.

Comparative Analysis of Management Performance. The major tests of corporate management that are best for comparative tests of competing companies in the same industry are the rate of return on investment and the growth rate of earnings per share. While growth of revenues and total earnings are important, the key factor that discloses any dilution is earnings per share. The analyst must always adjust reported earnings where necessary to determine true earning power.[9]

Labor Relations. There are really two major problems in the area of labor: (1) favorable labor relations as evidenced by few (if any) strikes, minimal labor turnover, the ability to attract and keep efficient employees, and the ability to post a strong and increasing labor productivity record; (2) ability to reduce the ratio of labor costs to revenues, or at least to maintain the ratio at a steady level. After an excellent record in the latter respect from 1961 through 1966, American industry found this to be a major problem. Some improvements occurred in 1971-1973.

---

[9] Numerous studies in recent years have shown that, in many cases, salaries of corporate management show a much greater correlation with volume of sales and size of business than with profits and rate of return on investments. The investor should, however, favor those companies where management clearly by the financial record puts most stress on rate of return on investments. At this point the reader should review Chapter 7, "Corporate Financial Policies and the Investor."

For U. S. corporations as a whole, corporate net profits reached a post-World War II peak in 1959 of $28.5 billion and then declined slightly in 1960 and 1961 ($26.7 and $27.2 billion respectively), reaching a quarterly low at annual rate of $24.4 billion for the first quarter of 1961. They then rose to a peak of $49.9 billion for 1966, or an increase of 75% (1959-1966).[10] There was a 105% increase from the first quarter of 1961 ($24.4 billion) to the entire year of 1966 ($49.9 billion). During this period, weekly earnings in manufacturing industries rose only from $88.26 in 1959 to $110.00 in January, 1966, or $111.92 for the year 1966. This represented a rise of only 27%. Labor cost per *unit* of output (1957-1959 = 100) was 99.9 in February, 1966, and the ratio of price (of product sales) to unit labor costs was 105.0 in the first quarter of 1966 (1957-1959 = 100). Labor costs began to rise more rapidly than productivity in 1967-1970.

Most corporations, therefore, in the period 1959-1966 enjoyed a favorable ratio of labor cost to sales. The result was a spectacular increase in profits. But the 1966-1970 record was only horizontal. Then in 1971-1973 rapidly rising volume, increased labor productivity, and lower unit labor costs caused profits to rise to new all-time peaks in 1972 and 1973. The analyst can use such ratios as are indicated above to check on the relative performance of a company within its industry and for comparison with industries in general. The better the company's labor relations, the less the company will be subject to costly interruptions in its operation schedule. But some strikes are inevitable.

Capitalization and Actual Earnings. These financial data about the corporation are presented in the following form:

Capitalization. The data given below are broken down in detail in a more complete table:

	Book Capitalization [11]
Long-Term Debt	5.7%
Capital Stock:	
Preferred	4.4
Common	89.9
Total	100.0%

[10] Using the 1959-1960 average as a base (1959 boom year and 1960 recession year), corporate profits after taxes for "All U.S. Corporations" rose 91% to the 1966 level ($26.95 billion to $49.9 billion). Then profits were in a horizontal channel: $46.6 billion in 1967, $47.8 billion in 1968, $44.8 billion in 1969, $40.2 billion in 1970, $45.9 billion n 1971, and finally a new high of $52.6 billion in 1972. In 1972 earnings per share of DJIA and S&P indexes were at new historic highs versus previous highs in 1968.

[11] As suggested in the chapters on financial statement analysis, these percentages should also be shown on the basis of market values, that is, capitalization with common at market value and debt and preferred stock at book figures.

Operating Record. The data are presented in the form of a ten-year table with the following headings:

Year	Sales	Net Income	Net Income as % of Sales	Net Income Per Share	Dividends Per Share	Price Range	Average P/E Ratio

Return on Net Worth. The data are presented in the form of a ten-year table with the following headings:

General Motors	Automobile Industry	U. S. Industry Average

Capital Expenditures and Sources of Internal Funds. The data are presented in the form of a ten-year table with the following headings:

Year	Capital Expenditures	Depreciation, Depletion, and Amortization	Retained Earnings	Total Internal Funds	Excess (Deficit) Internal Funds To Capital Expenditures	Net Working Capital

Capital Expenditures for Special Tools. The data are presented in the form of a six-year table with the following headings:

Year	Expenditures for Special Tools	Amortization of Special Tools	Unamortized Tools

Equity in Earnings of Subsidiaries Not Consolidated. The data are presented in a six-year table with the following headings:

Year	Total	Per Share

Earnings from Operations Outside the U.S. and Canada. The data are presented in a ten-year table with the following headings:

Year	GM's Total Investment Outside U. S. and Canada	Less General Reserve Applicable to Foreign Operations	Net Investments Outside U. S. and Canada	Foreign Income	% of GM's Total Net Income	Per 1960 Common Share

Long-Term Earnings Projections. On the subject of long-term earnings projections, the General Motors report states:

It is well recognized that realistic analysis requires more than a modest degree of caution in preparing future projections. Any long-term appraisal of General Motors' earnings per share is dependent upon a magnitude of assumptions which make any result so tenuous as to seriously question its validity. Nevertheless, this report attempts to establish some determining industry criteria in the form of demographic estimates, income projections, highway construction plans, and scrappage rates. This form of projection then establishes an expected business environment for the world vehicle industry. Utilizing this industry base, a projected participating range for

General Motors is superimposed thereon, which provides high, medium, and low sales projections. Each of these three projections is then subject to a high and low profit margin estimate and a final net income per share range is derived. These results are conceived as *normal earnings* power ranges providing a median range for 1965 of between $4.75 and $5.00 per share.[12] It should be emphasized that cyclical effects have not been considered and no attempt has been made to project the timing or shape of future business cycles. Future estimates have been predicated upon the same assumptions as were those for 1965. The tables providing for the above earnings estimates are presented below.

Earnings Projections
Based on Assumptions As to Total Industry Sales

	Low Sales Projection		Medium Sales Projection		High Sales Projection	
	GM % of Market	I $000,000	GM % of Market	II $000,000	GM % of Market	III $000,000
U. S. Auto	45%	$ 8,544	50%	$ 9,480	55%	$ 10,440
U. S. Trucks	37.5	1,110	40	1,209	42.5	1,285
Foreign	12.5	2,185	15	2,622	17.5	3,059
Sub-Total		11,848		13,311		14,784
Other U. S. Auto		400		500		600
Sub-Total		12,248		13,811		15,384
Non-Auto 10%		1,225		1,381		1,538
Sub-Total		13,473		15,192		16,922
Defense		500		750		1,000
Total Sales		13,973		15,942		17,922

	Low	High	Low	High	Low	Low
Profit Margin	16%	17%	18%	19%	19%	20%
Pre-Tax Profit	2,235.7	2,375.4	2,870.0	3,029.0	3,215.2	3,384.4
Net Income	1,073.1	1,140.2	1,378.0	1,453.9	1,543.3	1,624.5
Per Share	$3.70	$3.93	$4.75	$5.01	$5.00	$5.32

Note: Derived industry production levels:

U. S. Automobiles	7.7 million units
U. S. Trucks	1.3 million units
Foreign (cars & trucks)	10.1 million units

Market Evaluation of Common Stock. Part III of the General Motors report presents comparative data concerning stock price, earnings, and price-earnings ratios. In addition to the financial ratios used in Parts II and III of the General Motors report, most of the financial ratios suggested in Chapter 19 should be included for comprehensive coverage.

---

[12] Actual earnings for General Motors were:

1962	1963	1964	1965	1966	1967	1968
$5.09	$5.55	$6.04	$7.40	$6.23	$5.66	$6.02

1969	1970	1971	1972	1973
$5.95	$2.09	$6.72	$7.51	$9.00 E

The Problem of Conglomerates [13]

While the investor analyzing industrial companies has always been faced with the problem that many companies do business in a number of industries through divisions and subsidiaries, the problem assumed major proportions in the late 1960s. The SEC took recognition of the fact in requirements for corporations to furnish breakdowns by divisions or subsidiaries where sales breakdowns were considered material in registered statements. The Financial Executives Institute in 1968 in a report to the SEC had pressured the SEC. To some extent in the 1960s the rush to conglomerates appeared to be somewhat of a fad. Heavy cash flow realized by many companies plus a new breed of innovation-growth-minded managements led to the trend.

Conglomerates are multi-industry companies. By 1970, 24 major multi-industry companies had developed, some of the best known of which were Olin Mathieson, W. R. Grace, International Telephone & Telegraph, Litton Industries, Textron, Gulf & Western Industries, Houdaille Industries, and Ling-Temco-Vought. Investors in 1966-1969 were demonstrating an almost feverish desire to own these stocks, paying little attention to the severe problem of analysis and especially to the accounting problems involved in determining net income and its sources. Actually, not many appreciate that General Electric, by itself, covered to varying degrees most of the industries served by the companies named above. In 1968-1970 it appeared that these stocks were losing their glamour for investors, particularly as a result of SEC pressure for more informative corporate reporting and also as a result of the Justice Department's statement of intentions to study the area in terms of antitrust. The conglomerate stocks declined much more than the market indexes in 1969-1970. [14]

---

[13] The reader should review the previous discussion of conglomerates in Chapters 15 and 16.

[14] Several developments negatively affected the conglomerate stocks in 1969-1970. Chairman Mills of the tax-writing House Ways and Means Committee stated that conglomerates "substantially decrease competition, whether or not the mergers occur in similar lines of business, because of the consolidation of financial power that results." Mr. Mills questions the wisdom of tax laws that make the use of convertible debentures (interest is tax deductible) highly attractive both to the conglomerate and the acquired company. Chairman Mills proposed that interest on such convertibles be excluded as a tax-deductible expense. Mills' other target was a then-current provision in the tax law that permits capital gains taxes on such exchanges to be deferred until the convertible debentures are paid off, perhaps in 20 years. Thus the tax deferral is equivalent to an interest-free loan from the Treasury. At the same time the antitrust economists in the Federal Trade Commission in 1969 argued that conglomerates actually decrease competition because profits from some divisions can be used to subsidize losses of others and drive out competition in those industries. The entry of conglomerates into an industry tends to discourage other entrants. They also implied that conglomerates obtain a position to demand reciprocal tie-in sales. In March, 1969, the FTC announced its intention to file an antitrust suit against the acquisition of the Allis-

While management is highly important in any industrial company, the demands on management reach their zenith with multi-industry companies. On the positive side, top management skills can be applied cross-industry; but on the negative side, if problems develop simultaneously in several industries in which a conglomerate is engaged, this may overtax even the highest quality of management. Investors seemed to assume in the late 1960s up to 1970 that the success of conglomerates was assured just by the nature of the phenomena as they "reported" rapid earnings growth.

Investors should appreciate that, as the development of multi-industry companies progressed, there emerged three types:

1. Really homogeneous multi-industry types such as Eastman Kodak, General Precision Equipment, Air Reduction, Rexall, and Chemetron. The distinguishing feature of these amalgamations is that, while they are multi-industry, the extension into other industries appeared as logical branches of existing business and was usually accomplished by the parent constructing and closely controlling plants to serve the additional industry to be included. These companies appear to be the most logical forms and the ones that are relatively less difficult to appraise, although lack of financial information on the separate divisions does cause problems.

   General Electric, National Distillers, Pittsburgh Plate Glass, and Olin Mathieson should probably be included in the homogeneous category because they have all emphasized interexpansion much more than acquisitions, but some analysts class them differently because of their rather broad extension into varied industries.

2. Multi-industry companies that have extended as the result of scientific and technological development of the group as a whole where there is some correlation between the parts. Examples of this type are Litton, Ling-Temco-Vought, and Lear Siegler. Again the process appears to have developed logically, and the closeness of technical and scientific developments and controls justifies the multi-industry company.

3. The true conglomerates consist of multi-industry firms where the parent merely or largely limits its activity to financial control and support and very broad policy decisions. The relationship between the separate units of the conglomerates is tenuous to say the least. Examples of this type of multi-industry company are Textron, Ogden Corporation, Automatic Sprinkler, and Gulf & Western Industries.

Chalmers Manufacturing Company by White Consolidated Industries, Inc. The suit was based in part on the legally novel ground that the merger would *increase the concentration in manufacturing generally.* At the same time new SEC Chairman Budge and Finance Chairman Cohen recommended legal requirements that those making take-over bids disclose their identities, source of funds, and corporate intentions. Finally, also at this time the president of the NYSE stated that, in the case of two listed convertible debentures of two conglomerates, there was a serious question as to whether the interest on the debt was covered by present or future earnings. These conglomerate convertibles were largely acquired by individuals, and the question is raised as to whether they simply accepted the convertibles in their general enthusiasm for conglomerates or had carefully analyzed the coverage of interest as should be done for all debt issues.

In the middle and late 1960s some of the multi-industry companies grew so fast through rapid acquisition that even competent analysts found it highly difficult, if not impossible, to develop accurate earnings projections for these groups, especially because of the lack of divisional reporting. In such cases, how could the "average" investor hope to cope with the problem? The answer was that he simply bought on faith—faith in a vogue.[15]

Suggested Outline for an Analysis of an Industrial Company

Below is a suggested outline for a comprehensive analysis of an industrial company, including both an industry and a company analysis:

---

[15] One very competent analyst on Wall Street had the following comment on the problem of analyzing conglomerates:

> Under such volatile conditions it is virtually impossible for investors or even trained security analysts to make accurate earnings projections. At the same time, most of these companies do not fit logically into any one specific industry, thus making "normal" P/E ratio ranges unattainable. A less orthodox approach, therefore, must be used in appraising the prospects of many conglomerate companies.
>
> It narrows down to an evaluation of management—the ability of those executives to continue making favorable acquisitions and to control and develop all existing operations, regardless of how diverse. Subjective assessments of management become the determining factors in setting price/earnings ratios, which in turn reflect profit growth rates which are anticipated.
>
> Some of the factors to be considered in an evaluation of management include:
>
> 1. What has been their track record? That is, how many acquisitions have been made that have not worked out?
> 2. What financing methods have been employed in making acquisitions? Have expansion benefits been watered down by equity dilution?
> 3. Is growth primarily dependent on continuing acquisitions? What percent of sales are contributed by acquisitions made in the past five years?
> 4. In what direction and how quickly are expansion programs moving?
> 5. How susceptible is the company's expansion policy to the possible loss of a key executive?
> 6. Are immediate earnings per share benefits required in acquisitions or is management willing to wait for profits by building up promising but currently unprofitable situations?

Furthermore, corporate reporting practices of many of the conglomerates left a great deal to be desired. See Abraham J. Briloff, "Dirty Pooling—How To Succeed in Business," *Barron's* (July 15, 1968), and also the suggested readings at the end of this chapter.

It came to be realized by many investors that the rise in earnings of many conglomerates was partly an illusion resulting from the fact that if a conglomerate's stock sold say at a 20 P/E multiple and it could keep acquiring stocks selling at 10 P/E multiples, the parent's earnings could rise at a faster rate than that of company operations, and partly that the rate of growth had been further accelerated by the use of convertible financing, without disclosing before 1968 the potential dilution inherent in the use of convertibles. Until SEC regulations in 1968 and 1969 required financial reports to disclose the effect of potential dilution from conversion of convertibles, such dilution was largely ignored. This was also true of divisional reporting.

ANALYSIS OF AN INDUSTRIAL COMPANY

Part I—Industry Analysis

A. Economic Importance and Characteristics of Industry
   Stage and Development of Industry, Its Life-Cycle Position
   Degree of Fluctuation in Industry—Sales, Profits, and Earnings per
      Share in Relation to Economic Cycles and Life Cycles
   Regulation and Control of Industry by Government
   Labor Problems in Industry, History of Labor Strife, and Costs
   Other Industry Problems—Major and Minor

B. Demand Factors
   Nature of Demand for Industry's Products
   Past Record of Demand—Correlation with GNP, Disposable Personal
      Income, and Other GNP Components As Have Proved Relevant
   Current Demand
   Estimated Future Demand—1 year, 3 years, 5 years, 10 years
   Foreign Sales Demand if Pertinent

C. Supply Factors
   Nature of Supply and Competition
   Concentration of Supply—Breakdown of Supply by Companies
   Estimated Present Industry Capacity—Projection of Industry Capacity
   Foreign Competition—Importance and Nature of Imports—Current
      and Projected
   Foreign Competition—Tariffs and Quotas
   Patents and Trademarks of Major or Minor Importance

D. Price Factors
   Past Relationship of Supply and Demand Factors and Prices and
      Government Intervention if Any—Types and Degree of Price
      Competition
   Relationship of Demand to Capacity and to Pricing
   Importance of Raw Material Costs
   Importance of Labor Costs
   Current Pricing Situation
   Estimated Future Pricing Situations Considering Supply and Demand
      Factors for Next 1, 3, 5, and 10 Years

Part II—Company Analysis

(Comparison with at Least Two Competing Companies in Industry)

A. Economic Analysis
   1. History and Business of Company
   2. Relative Position of Company in Industry—Trend in this Regard vs.
      Major Competition
   3. Breakdown of Company Sales by Divisions, Subsidiaries, and Affili-
      ates
   4. Management—Senior Level, Second Level, and Junior Level—
      Executive Development Programs
   5. Labor Problems—History of Labor Strife
   6. Research and Development—New Products—Direction
   7. Capital Expenditures (Past and Projected) and Their Nature
   8. Any Special Problems of Company

B. Financial Analysis—Comparative Statement Analysis for Past 10 Years
 1. Balance Sheet Analysis—Determination of Financial Strength
    a. Working Capital Analysis
    b. Analysis of Other Assets—Fixed Assets—Investments
    c. Analysis of Capitalization—At Book and Common at Market
    d. Off-Balance Sheet Liabilities—Leases, Unfunded Pensions, and Other Similar Liabilities
    e. Book Value—Increase for Past 10 Years, Past 5 Years

 2. Income Statement Analysis—All-Inclusive Statement Preferred
    a. Sales Breakdown by Products, Divisions, and Subsidiaries
    b. Percent Net Increase in Sales—Trends (Since Base Year)
    c. Sales/Gross Plant—Trend Index (Base Year = 100%)
    d. Capital Expenditures/Sales—Growth Index (Base Year = 100%)
    e. Pretax Operating Profit/Sales—Trends (After Depreciation)
    f. Wages and Salaries/Sales—Index (Base Year = 100%)
    g. Research and Development Expenditures/Sales
    h. Depreciation (Depletion) and Rapid Amortization
    i. Cash Flow and Sources and Uses of Funds Analysis
    j. Interest Coverage on Debt—Actual and Trends From Base Year
    k. Adjustment of Reported Earnings For Nonrecurring Earnings—Per-Share Adjusted Earnings—Growth Record (Base Year = 100%)
    l. Cash Flow Per Share—Growth Record (Base Year = 100%)
    m. Projection of Earnings for Next 1, 3, and 5 Years—Estimated Range, High and Low

 3. Balance Sheet Ratios [16]
    a. Working Capital
       (1) Current Ratio
       (2) Quick Ratio
       (3) Cash and Cash Items to Current Liabilities
       (4) Net Working Capital Per Dollar of Sales—Actual and Trends vs. Base Year
    b. Capitalization
       (1) Book Capitalization and Market Capitalization
       (2) Extent of Trading on Equity and Leverage—Effect

 4. Income Statement Ratios
    a. Growth Ratios from Base Year or Period
       (1) Dollar Net Sales—Compound Annual % Rate of Growth
       (2) Dollar Net Profit—Compound Annual % Rate of Growth
       (3) Dollar Earnings Per Share—Compound Annual % Rate of Growth
    b. Stability Ratios—Record in Poor Business Years—Volatility
       (1) Dollar Net Sales—Decline %
       (2) Dollar Net Profit—Decline %
       (3) Earnings Per Share—Decline %

---

[16] Refer to Chapter 19 for complete balance sheet and income statement ratios to be used.

      (4) Fixed Charge Coverage on Debt—Actual and Decline % in Years of Poor Business

      (5) Preferred Stock Coverage—Overall Basis—Actual and Decline % in Years of Poor Business

    c. Profit Ratios

      (1) Net Profit After Taxes As Percent of Sales—Actual and Trend

      (2) Net Profit on Total Capital Funds—Actual and Trend

      (3) Net Profit on Stockholders' Equity—Actual and Trend

    d. Payout Ratios

      (1) Dividends Per Share—% of Net Income

      (2) Dividends Per Share—% of Cash Flow

    e. Price/Earnings Ratios—Trend vs. Industry and DJIA or S&P 425

    f. Dividend Yields—Trend vs. Industry and DJIA or S&P 425

    g. Earnings Yield—Trend vs. Industry and DJIA or S&P 425

  5. Market Price of Shares—Annual Range Past 10 Years Adjusted for Stock Splits and Stock Dividends and the Effect on Reported Earnings

---

QUESTIONS

1. (a) How are industrial securities defined?
   (b) What are the major groups of industrial securities?
   (c) Relatively, how important are manufacturing corporations in the industrial group?

2. (a) Define a growth industry.
   (b) Could a growth industry possibly be an out-of-favor industry? Discuss.

3. What dangers does an investor face when he concentrates on purchasing securities of companies classified as being in rapid-growth industries in the securities markets?

4. (a) Discuss opportunities in low price-earnings ratios in out-of-favor industries.
   (b) Why is the current stress on performance by institutional managers likely to create additional opportunities for the alert investor?

5. (a) Explain the importance of industry demand and supply forces for the security analyst.
   (b) How are these related to industry prices and profits?

6. Discuss the likely effect of a sharp dip in the economy on sales, profits, and the market price of common shares of:
   (a) A tobacco company.
   (b) A sugar company.
   (c) A machine tool producer, automobile producer, or steel producer.
   (d) A public utility.

7. (a) What should the analyst attempt to learn about the management team?

(b) How can an analyst evaluate management?

8. (a) How important are research and development expenditures in American industry?

(b) What are some of the analyst's problems in this area?

(c) What items in the area of research expenditures should be investigated by the analyst?

9. What factors should the analyst consider in reviewing the labor factor, the labor problems, and the productivity trends of various industries?

10. What special problems do conglomerates pose for the analyst?

WORK-STUDY PROBLEMS

1. (a) Select a company showing a growth trend of earnings noticeably higher than the average for all corporations (at least twice the average growth rate).

(b) Tabulate the earnings of this company on a *per-share basis* over the last 10 years. Be sure these earnings are properly adjusted to reflect true recurring earnings.

(c) Tabulate the following actual annual per-share earnings of Standard & Poor's 425 industrial companies. (Bring the illustrative figures up to date).

Year	Per Share	Year	Per Share	Year	Per Share
1955	12.65	1960	18.92	1965	17.65
1956	3.70	1961	3.67	1966	5.77
1957	3.32	1962	4.19	1967	5.91
1958	3.33	1963	4.48	1968	6.13E
1959	3.26	1964	4.78		

(d) Calculate the percentage of the earnings of your company in each year to the per-share earnings of Standard & Poor's 425 companies and plot these figures on semilog paper.

(e) Obtain the price-earnings ratio of your company, using year-end prices. See the "Commercial and Financial Chronicle" or "Bank and Quotation Record" for each year.

(f) Divide the price-earnings ratio of your company by the price-earnings ratio of Standard & Poor's 425 companies and plot the results on 3- or 4-cycle semilog paper for each year. The following are the price-earnings ratios of Standard & Poor's 425 companies on the basis of year-end prices (update the illustrative figures):

Year	P/E Ratio	Year	P/E Ratio	Year	P/E Ratio
1955	12.65	1960	18.92	1965	17.65
1956	13.54	1961	20.63	1966	14.77
1957	12.91	1962	15.75	1967	17.79
1958	17.71	1963	17.69	1968	17.88
1959	19.79	1964	18.75		

(g) Observe and comment on the record.

2. Assume that you, as a securities broker, are approached by L. W. Jones and asked to buy stock in Jones Food Systems, Inc., which he describes to you as follows:

Jones Food Systems, Inc. will be a new company organized to manufacture and sell precooked meals. These meals will be prepared on disposable plates and will be sold at retail for $1 per plate. A variety of foods has been tested for consumer acceptance, including the following:

Swiss Steak, Gravy
Filet Mignon, Bordelaise Sauce
Roast Lamb, Gravy
Chicken a la King, Sauce

The above plates are ready to serve by heating for a short time. It is planned to sell these precooked meals to airlines, railroads, hotels, restaurants, bus lines, and even institutional buyers. In addition, it is believed that housewives will constitute an enormous market.

Extensive experiments have been made, and six chemists or food technologists have been employed. The company plans to lease quarters from the Ranger Packing Company at Newark, New Jersey. This location will have the advantage of assuring the supplies of vegetables. The meats will be purchased in the open market.

It is estimated that $4,000,000 will be needed to start this business, as follows:

Plant	$ 700,000
Equipment	700,000
Working capital to finance inventories (including 6 months' supply of vegetables and 43 days' supply of meats), payroll, and other requirements in initial stage of operation	2,000,000
Research, advertising, and sales promotion	600,000
	$4,000,000

To raise this money, it is proposed to sell 400,000 shares of stock at $10 a share. The promoter, L. W. Jones, is to have 50,000 shares for his services to the company.

The management of this enterprise is to be headed by Jones, who is about 46 years old, an electrical engineer, and a graduate of the United States Naval Academy. In 1949 he founded his own company to manufacture a pressure gauge he had invented. His company also manufactures electrical combines and power drives. L. W. Jones & Company's stock was initially sold at $5 a share by well-known investment bankers and is now worth $45 a share and earning $2.03 a share. He desires to expand his interest by manufacturing food processing machines and selling them to Jones Food Systems, Inc. He will be president of this new concern and will receive a $40,000 salary per annum.

Jones will be assisted by Frederick W. Smith as vice-president and director. Smith is at present vice-president and general manager of a camera company. He will receive a salary of $35,000. Harriet Holt, who is now treasurer of L. W. Jones & Company, will be treasurer and secretary of the new company. The directors will include Gordon A.

Stuffer of Stuffer Restaurant Co.; Thomas J. Henderson, a banker; and John Peters, a hotel manager. William Grimes, another director, is a friend of Jones.

(a) Assuming that you or your client can afford to put money into such a venture, list the reasons for and against participating in its financing on the basis of the above description.

(b) What additional information would you require?

(c) How would you obtain this information?

3. (a) Calculate the growth rate of the net income of the following chemical companies for a 10-year period.
   Airco Inc.
   Diamond Shamrock Corp. (formerly Diamond Alkali Co.)
   Dow Chemical Co.
   E. I. du Pont de Nemours & Co.
   Hercules, Inc.
   Union Carbide Corp.

(b) Calculate the price-earnings (most recent earnings) ratios of the companies.

(c) Chart the growth rate and the price-earnings ratio to determine the correlation.

Note: Correlation may be determined roughly by drawing a line through the dots, or by the following equations:

$$\Sigma(Y) = Na + b\Sigma(X)$$
$$\Sigma(XY) = a\Sigma X + b\Sigma(X)^2$$

If the equations are used to determine the estimating equation, the degree of relationship can be measured by determining the coefficient of correlation (r^2).

SUGGESTED READINGS

Accounting Trends and Techniques (Annual). New York: American Institute of Certified Public Accountants.

Analysts' Handbook (A Guide to Industry Publications for Securities Analysts). New York: The New York Society of Security Analysts, Inc., 1972, pp. 67. (A *must* source).

Financial Analysts Journal (Bimonthly). New York: The Financial Analysts Federation, 1972.

Forbes (Twice monthly). New York: Forbes, Inc.

Moody's Industrial Manual (Annual). New York: Moody's Investors Service. Registration Statements and Prospectuses.

Standard & Poor's, Basic Industry Surveys (Annual for each major industry). New York: Standard & Poor's Corporation.

Value Line Investment Service. New York: Arnold Bernhard & Co.

21

Public Utility Securities

The general legal and economic classification of public utilities includes, among others: (a) electric light and power companies; (b) companies supplying natural or manufactured gas, either pipeline companies or direct operating companies; (c) railroad and other transportation companies; (d) telephone, telegraph, and other companies supplying communication services; and (e) companies supplying water.

In the financial community railroads are placed in a separate classification for separate analysis, and accordingly they will be discussed in a separate chapter. Because electric utilities represent by far the major segment of investor interest in public utilities, they will be concentrated on in this chapter. Space limitations do not permit separate coverage in this book of other types of utilities, such as gas and communication companies, that are of significant importance in the investment field.

THE PUBLIC UTILITY INDUSTRY

Public utility companies are required to meet the demands for service of all users, irrespective of fluctuation in that demand. This, of course, does require maintenance of capacity to meet peak loads, with certain amounts of idle capacity at other times. The Federal Power Commission favors a 20% reserve margin.

Characteristics of Public Utility Companies

Public utility companies can be identified by the following salient features:

1. They are affected with a public interest. Their service is a necessity for most people, and public utilities must meet public demand.

2. They operate under conditions where direct competition is not practical, although there may be competition between services, such as electric service versus gas service for heating.

3. Because of the above factors, they are subject to broad regulation (especially rate regulation) by one or more governmental bodies or agencies.

4. Production of services is simultaneous with customer use and, unlike industrial companies, there is no inventory problem and a minimum of "receivables" problem.

Investment Status of Electric Utilities

For a number of years, securities of electric utility companies have enjoyed a quality rating because of their steady earnings and growth. During the 1930s the collapse of the highly overcapitalized holding companies followed by required divestiture of many operating companies under the Holding Company Act of 1935, largely accomplished in the 1950s, cast a shadow over the industries' common stocks. However, these stocks subsequently regained their investment status as quality issues and developed broad investor appeal although the latter was lost after 1965.

The great majority of the bonds of electric utilities have enjoyed AA and A ratings (with a few enjoying an AAA rating). In recent years they have been selling at close to market yields of the companies' bonds. Utility common stocks have also enjoyed a quality rating for many years. The major factors in the purchase of these common stocks have been their yield and the expectation that correlated to the growth of gross revenues and capacity. Earnings and dividends would double about every 10 years; and if the price/earnings ratio remained stable, the investor could expect the price of these stocks to increase with earnings.

Utility common stocks must compete on a yield basis with bonds although stocks have the added advantage that their yields, based on costs, can be expected to rise with the growth of earnings and dividends. Gross revenues and capacities of utilities doubled (7-8% growth rate) in 1961-1972.

Relative Decline in Investor Preference for Utility Companies

Electric utility common stock must not only compete with bonds on a yield basis, but also compete with other groups such as industrial, bank, and insurance common stocks. The P/E ratio at which stocks of industry groups sell in the market is the best indication of relative investor preference.

In the post-World War II years, electric utility common stocks reached their peak of popularity relative to industrials in 1949, when the P/E ratio of the Dow Jones Utility Index was at P/E 12, about 150% of the Dow Jones Industrial Average of P/E 7.6. But thereafter this investor preference, reflected in relative P/E's, steadily deteriorated until the P/E ratio of the utility group fell to the area of only 89% of the DJIA P/E in the years 1958-1961, rose slightly to over 100% in 1962-1966, but then fell back to the 87% area in the years 1967-1972. In early 1973 electric utility common stocks were selling well below their absolute peak prices established in 1965 and at 11-12 P/E's versus 16-17 for the DJIA.

As noted earlier, electric utility common stocks are purchased because of their well-protected dividend yield and their expected growth in earnings and dividends, resulting in higher yields on cost and capital appreciation. However, because of the regulated nature of their business (regulation of rates), their earnings (even for growth area utilities) cannot be expected to enjoy very rapid rates of growth as is a potential for numerous industrials.

The principal factors that have had a negative effect on investor preferences for these stocks during the years 1949-1973 were (1) rising interest rates in the capital market for bonds, and (2) inflation.

Rising Interest Rates. Long-term corporate AAA bonds had market yields of 2.50% in 1946 and 2.60% in 1949. These rates rose to 4.38% in 1959, 4.41% in 1960, 5.13% in 1966, and an average of 8.04% in 1970 (peak for AAA was 8.50% and for AA, over 9%). The reader should review charts or prices of utility common stocks in 1958-1973 and prices of corporate bonds during the same period and note that prices of utility stocks parallel the related long downward trend of bond prices and reflect, of course, the significant upward trend of interest rates. In 1973 many utility stocks were yielding 7% plus versus 7.5% for utility AA bonds.

Standard & Poor's Index of high-grade bonds declined from a peak of 124 in 1946 and 122-123 in 1949 to 103 in 1958 and a low of 59 in 1970, reflecting the long rise in interest rates in 1946-1970 (64 in 1973).

High and rising interest rates for bonds make utility common stocks relatively less attractive. In addition, utilities are capital intensive; that is, they are regularly selling their securities, including bonds, in the capital markets. Utilities generally double their capacity every 10 years; therefore, higher interest rates increase their costs of capital, and there can be a considerable lag before higher costs are passed on to customers in the form of higher rates approved by regulatory authorities.

Inflation. The implicit price deflator for GNP approximately doubled from 60 in 1945 to 122 in 1968 and 156 in January, 1973. There are two decidedly negative effects of inflation for utility common stocks. First, inflation reduces the relative attractiveness of common stock purchased largely for its dividend yield. The dividend dollar has a declining value. Second, inflation raises the cost of capital equipment and operating costs. There may be a long lag and squeezed earnings before these costs can be passed on in the form of higher rates.

Further Problems of Electric Utilities

Projections made in 1960 as to the proportion of electric power generated by nuclear plants have not been realized, and costs of new plants and their operation have been significantly higher than anticipated. Environmentalists have been successful in preventing the approval of plant sites for many proposed nuclear as well as conventional plants. Furthermore, breakdowns of nuclear plants have considerably exceeded estimates, and the expenses resulting from downtime and the number of workers required for repairs have significantly exceeded similar expenditures for conventional plants. Nuclear plants represented only 2.2% of generating capacity in 1971 although 7% of plants under construction were nuclear. The cost-price squeeze in the 1960s restricted their earnings growth—the effect of inflation on operating and construction costs. The impact on capital costs of the rapid rise of wages and other construction costs and the higher interest rates paid to borrowers caused many investors to become deeply concerned about the future financial health of electric utilities. The DJ utility stock average fell back to its 1963 level in mid-1973.

Regulation of Public Utility Industry

An analysis of utility companies should begin with an analysis of the regulatory climate followed by an economic analysis of the territory served and an economic and financial analysis of the company. Unless the regulatory climate is satisfactory, the analyst should not proceed further. To a major extent, earnings of electric utility companies are actually determined by regulatory authorities who must approve all rate changes. This is true of all classes of public utilities.

Because utility companies are natural monopolies that supply a necessary service to the public, it is universally recognized that they must be subject to government regulation. Electric utility companies are domiciled in the state in which they operate and are subject to regulation by state public utility commissions. These regulations embrace practically all aspects of operations, including accounting procedures and financial operations. In addition to state regulation, some utilities are subject to regulation by the Federal Power Commission (if they operate interstate or use waterpower from "navigable streams" to generate electricity). Furthermore, the Securities and Exchange Commission regulates public utility holding companies under the Public Utility Holding Company Act of 1935. Since most electric companies operate in intrastate rather than interstate areas, state regulation by public utility commissions is generally more important than federal regulation. An exception would be holding companies and interstate gas pipelines.

Regulation covers a broad area, the most important part being rates; but it also includes service rendered, purchase and sale of assets, issuance of securities, and uniform accounting systems. Utilities are required to conform to the uniform system of accounts to which most state utility commissions have subscribed. An excellent utility will make every effort to maintain good relations with its regulatory commission. However, at some point it may find it necessary to apply to the courts for approval of rate increases if the commission refuses to sanction equitable rates that would yield a fair return on the fair value of the property and that would provide sufficient income to maintain the financial standing of the company's securities in the capital markets. The United States Supreme Court has the final decision in rate cases involving the question of fair return.

The National Association of Railroad and Utility Commissions adopted a revised uniform system of accounts for electric and gas utilities in 1961, and the Federal Power Commission requires essentially the same system for hydroelectric companies and utility companies that come under its jurisdiction. Other types of utility companies are also required to use a uniform system of accounting. It is certainly true that this uniform accounting is a real aid to financial analysis of utility companies because the analyst can assume that accounts identified by similar names represent identical items as between utilities. However, it must be noted that while there is uniform accounting, there is a considerable divergence in actual accounting practices and published reports, for example, flow-through versus normalizing for depreciation methods.

Importance of Regulation to Investors. It has been noted that the regulatory climate in which a utility must operate is of vital importance to the investor, especially because of the effect of regulation on rates and service standards and on rate of return on investment. The rates charged must be approved by the regulatory commission, and the rates charged times the units sold determine the gross income of the utility. The utility has control over its costs but not its revenues. An electric utility company is permitted (not guaranteed) to earn a fair return on the fair value of its property used in the public service.[1] This was the major emphasis up until 1940.

The Hope Natural Gas decision by the U.S. Supreme Court in 1944[2] has been interpreted as releasing the regulatory commissions from the necessity of adhering to any specific method of determining the rate base. The *method* used by a commission in determining utility rate base valuation is no longer subject to judicial (U. S. Supreme Court) review. Rather, the overall effect of the rates charged on the company's credit standing in the capital markets became the crucial issue. As most utilities are rather frequently in the capital markets to secure funds for expansion, the ability to secure their funds at a reasonable competitive cost is crucial and was so recognized by the Court (the cost-of-capital approach).

Methods of determining a fair rate of return vary widely. Some commissions use the accounting and statistical approach; others have considered the rising cost of new money (1946-1973). There is also evidence in some decisions of the recognition of "attrition" in earnings resulting from inflation (or the effect of inflation on the rate base). Rate of return has also been allowed based on a test-year rate base. The latter is limited, however, because of the constantly increasing costs of new facilities.

Rate of Return on Rate Base. Utilities are permitted to charge rates that will produce the rate of return on their asset rate base approved by the

---

[1] (a) *Smyth* vs. *Ames,* U.S. Supreme Court—1898: "What the company is entitled *to ask* is a fair return upon the value of that which it employs for the public's convenience. On the other hand, what the public is entitled to demand is that no more be exacted from it . . . than the services rendered . . . are reasonably worth."

(b) Bluefield Water Works, U. S. Supreme Court—1928: "A public utility is entitled to such rates as will permit it to earn a return on the value of its property which it employs for the convenience of the public equal to that generally being made at the same time and in the same general part of the country on investments in other business undertakings which are attended by corresponding risks and uncertainties.

"The return should be reasonably sufficient to assure confidence in the financial soundness of the utility, and should be adequate, under efficient and economical management, to maintain and support its credit and enable it to raise the money necessary for the proper discharge of its public duties."

[2] *Federal Power Commission* vs. *Hope Natural Gas Company,* 320 U.S. 603, 1944. "From the investor or company point of view it is important that there be enough revenue not only for operating expenses, but also for the capital costs of the business. These include service on the debt and dividends on the stock. By that standard the return to the equity owner should be commensurate with returns on investments in other enterprises having commensurate risks. That return, moreover, should be sufficient to assure confidence in the financial integrity of the enterprise, so as to maintain its credit and to attract capital."

regulatory commission. The allowed rate of return varies among states. In general, the spread ranges from a low in some states of 5% to a high in some states of 10%.

The relatively few so-called growth utilities have had two major factors that contributed to growth in earnings greater than that of the industry overall: (1) a favorable regulatory climate—average rate of return of 7.3%— on their rate base and (2) the advantage of operating in a rapidly growing economic area, such as Florida and Texas. Both factors had to be present. For example, in spite of the exceptionally rapid population and economic growth in California after World War II, the regulatory climate was not very satisfactory, as the rate of return on the rate base tended to be held to an annual 5½%; therefore, California electric utility companies did not demonstrate nearly as high an earnings growth rate as did the Florida and Texas utilities in the post-World War II years, as reflected in stock prices.

In economic growth areas, utilities must expand their plants rapidly, which means frequent trips to the capital markets for relatively large sums of capital. Regulatory commissions in states like Florida and Texas wanted to be sure that utilities under their jurisdiction would meet an excellent response to their demands for funds in the capital markets at relatively low costs; therefore, they tended to permit relatively high rates of return on the utility rate base.

It is important for the investor to know the rate of return permitted in the state where the utility under analysis operates, as well as whether there has been a trend up or down.[3] The investor should also be familiar with the political climate in the state in regard to the utility commission or the probability of a change in the regulatory climate as a result of a changed political environment.

Of course, the rate base is as important as the allowed rate of return on the rate base. The investor should, therefore, know the principle on which the commission calculates the rate base. For example, a rate base estimated on cost would be much lower than one based on reproduction cost or one that recognized the effect of inflation on property value.

---

[3] "Public Utility Reports" (Washington: Public Utility Reports, Inc.), published semimonthly. Percent of utilities earning a given rate of return in 1971 were as follows:

Rate	% of Utilities	Rate	% of Utilities
Less than 5.00%	5.2	6.00 to 7.99%	65.3
5.00 to 5.99%	6.2	8.00 to 8.99%	16.6
6.00 to 6.99%	30.6	9.00 to 9.99%	6.2
7.00 to 7.99%	34.7	10.00% and over	0.5
		weighted average	7.3

Finally, earnings and reported earnings are affected both by the accounting policies required by the commission and by the company's reporting policies. This is especially true in respect to depreciation accounting.

Economic Environment for Public Utilities

Each utility company is limited to the economy of the area in which it has been granted exclusive operating rights. The investor should study the area served to determine the type and number of customers (especially the type of industries that the utility serves), the state of economic development in the area, and the relative cost conditions that exist for utility firms in different sections of the country. A firm serving industrial, commercial, and residential customers is less vulnerable to cyclical changes in the volume of business than a firm serving primarily industrial firms. The investor desires balanced business, with not too much concentration on cyclical industrial business. The effect of these factors on the operations of a public utility will be integrated in the discussion of utility income statement analysis.

FINANCIAL ANALYSIS OF PUBLIC UTILITY SECURITIES

The remainder of this chapter consists of an analysis of public utility securities based on balance sheet items, income statement items, selected ratios, physical factors, projection of earnings, and future cost problems.

Balance Sheet Analysis [4]

A discussion of the analysis of important items on the balance sheets of public utility companies is presented in the following paragraphs.

Working Capital. Current assets of electric utilities include no inventories, and their receivables are sound and do not include any significant amount of past-due accounts. The threat to suspend service is enough to keep the receivables current. For these reasons, utilities, unlike industrials, do not maintain any substantial *net* working capital.

A utility is allowed to earn a fair return on the fair value of the property used in the public service. The current assets of the company form part

---

[4] Throughout the following discussion, the reader should refer to the illustrated financial statements and revenue analyses of the Pacific Gas and Electric Company that appear on pages 548-552.

of the rate base. But regulatory authorities do place a strict limit on the amount of current assets that may be added to the company's fixed assets in arriving at a rate base. Utilities are allowed to earn on assets that are *required* to enable the utility to properly service its customers. Any excess over this amount would not be allowed to be included in the rate base. Usually, a company will not consistently maintain excess current assets that it is not permitted to include in the rate base. However, when funds are obtained for construction purposes by the sale of securities, they do remain in current assets until expended. While such funds are not added to the rate base, special accounting rules for utilities do permit a special income account designated "Interest charged to construction—credit." This item will be discussed later in this chapter. In effect, this interest is capitalized.

The regulatory authorities will definitely limit the amount of working capital required to meet operating expenses, frequently to an amount sufficient for a period of a month and a half. For these purposes, depreciation and taxes are excluded from the operating expenses. In determining the amount of working capital that can be considered a part of the company's rate base, regulatory commissions may request that federal tax accruals be eliminated from consideration in determining the amount of working capital in excess of requirements.

Utility Plant. The great majority of a utility company's assets are fixed assets—plant and equipment. Fixed assets allowed in the rate base will generally represent over 90% of total assets. One of the ratios suggested for industrial companies was the ratio of invested capital to sales, or capital turnover. In the case of utility plants, the company's plant and equipment will amount to several years' gross operating revenues. Because utility companies must be ready at all times to serve customer needs, they must keep sufficient capacity on hand to meet peak needs. Much of the time, some of the capacity will be idle (30% to 40%). The analyst should study the system load factor as an indication of efficiency in utilization of the plant. This ratio is discussed later in this chapter.

If one company provides more than one service (for example, electricity and gas), the balance sheet should provide a breakdown of the plant account into the components providing the different services. The investor will use such a breakdown in relating the components to the specific revenues generated by each as reported in the income statement. Without the plant breakdown, it would be impossible to determine the rate of return on invested assets earned by each of the components.

Under the uniform system of accounts, the plant account is carried at original cost. When the analyst is making a determination of the economic

TABLE 21-1

Balance Sheet, Pacific Gas and Electric Company, December 31, 1972 and 1971

	Thousands	
	1972	1971
ASSETS		
UTILITY PLANT—At Original Cost:		
Electric	$4,073,748	$3,796,512
Gas	1,218,016	1,155,013
Other Departments and Common	334,273	322,966
Construction Work in Progress	607,764	459,855
Total Utility Plant	6,233,801	5,734,346
Accumulated Depreciation	1,518,239	1,403,462
UTILITY PLANT—NET	4,715,562	4,330,884
INVESTMENTS:		
Subsidiaries	39,123	31,969
Nonutility Property and Other—at cost	4,112	4,083
TOTAL INVESTMENTS	43,235	36,052
CURRENT ASSETS:		
Cash	25,604	25,464
Temporary Cash Investments—at cost	—	46,812
Accounts Receivable (less allowance for uncollectible accounts: 1972, $2,567; 1971, $2,188)	122,997	109,325
Materials and Supplies—at average cost	25,680	27,375
Fuel Oil—at average cost	14,711	9,643
Gas Stored Underground—at average cost	23,863	23,663
Prepayments	14,702	14,221
TOTAL CURRENT ASSETS	227,557	256,503
DEFERRED DEBITS:		
Unamortized Bond Expense	5,527	6,140
Other	1,213	1,246
TOTAL DEFERRED DEBITS	6,740	7,386
TOTAL	$4,993,094	$4,630,825
LIABILITIES		
CAPITALIZATION:		
Common Stock	$ 610,861	$ 610,861
Excess of Premiums Over Discounts and Expenses on Outstanding Shares	208,704	200,216
Reinvested Earnings	790,460	710,450
Common Stock Equity	1,610,025	1,521,527
Preferred Stock	564,951	464,951
Total	2,174,976	1,986,478
Mortgage Bonds	2,389,973	2,301,043
TOTAL CAPITALIZATION	4,564,949	4,287,521
CURRENT LIABILITIES:		
Short-term Notes	54,000	—
Accounts Payable	90,279	76,908
Taxes Accrued	41,018	46,297
Dividends Payable	26,267	25,045
Mortgage Bonds—current portion	14,720	11,021
Other	37,312	34,851
TOTAL CURRENT LIABILITIES	263,596	194,122
CUSTOMER ADVANCES FOR CONSTRUCTION	31,442	24,980
RESERVES AND DEFERRED CREDITS	10,100	7,352
CONTRIBUTIONS IN AID OF CONSTRUCTION	73,744	64,641
ACCUMULATED DEFERRED TAXES ON INCOME— Accelerated Amortization	49,263	52,209
TOTAL	$4,993,094	$4,630,825

TABLE 21-2

Statement of Income, Pacific Gas and Electric Company
For the Years Ended December 31, 1972 and 1971

	Thousands	
	1972	1971
OPERATING REVENUES:		
Electric	$ 854,446	$ 790,046
Gas	493,789	467,963
Other	2,378	2,336
TOTAL	1,350,613	1,260,345
OPERATING EXPENSES:		
Operation:		
Natural Gas Purchased	373,528	337,675
Power Purchased	52,007	49,171
Other Production	40,323	30,602
Transmission	15,627	14,471
Distribution	60,415	54,611
Customer Accounts	46,719	42,848
Marketing	10,282	10,474
Administrative and General	69,922	60,615
Total	668,823	600,467
Maintenance	66,913	62,980
Depreciation	142,461	131,326
Federal Income Taxes	60,905	75,637
State Income Taxes	12,869	8,136
Other Taxes	117,731	114,886
TOTAL	1,069,702	993,432
OPERATING INCOME	280,911	266,913
OTHER INCOME AND INCOME DEDUCTIONS:		
Allowance for Funds Used During Construction	38,084	25,888
Gain on Bonds Purchased for Sinking Fund	9,819	9,767
Other—net	16,452	7,241
TOTAL	64,355	42,896
INCOME BEFORE INTEREST CHARGES	345,266	309,809
INTEREST CHARGES:		
Interest on Mortgage Bonds	127,633	114,898
Miscellaneous Interest and Amortization of Bond Discount, Premium and Expense	2,289	1,797
TOTAL	129,922	116,695
NET INCOME	215,344	193,114
PREFERRED DIVIDEND REQUIREMENTS	31,109	25,399
EARNINGS AVAILABLE FOR COMMON	$ 184,235	$ 167,715
AVERAGE COMMON SHARES OUTSTANDING (Thousands)	61,086	61,086
EARNINGS PER COMMON SHARE	$3.02	$2.75
DIVIDENDS DECLARED PER COMMON SHARE	$1.72	$1.64

value of the plant, he will relate the book value to the gross operating revenues generated. In the case of electric companies whose plants are primarily steam generating plants, he will expect a rate of plant to revenues of about 4 to 1; in the case of plants primarily hydroelectric, he will expect a rate of approximately 7 to 1. The latter indicates the much higher cost of hydroelectric plants. If ratios are much higher than this, the analyst will probably decide that the amount for plant on the books represents an over-valuation. The analyst's best check will be to compare the book value with the allowable rate base value. In recent years the figures generally have been close.

TABLE 21-3

Revenues and Sales, Pacific Gas and Electric Company

	Thousands		Increase (Decrease)	
	1972	1971	Amount	Percent
ELECTRIC DEPARTMENT				
REVENUES:				
Residential	$ 321,692	$ 297,784	$ 23,908	8.0 %
Commercial	304,537	278,541	25,996	9.3
Industrial (1000 KW demand or over)	120,743	107,293	13,450	12.5
Agricultural Power	63,197	56,427	6,770	12.0
Public Street and Highway Lighting .	14,896	13,892	1,004	7.2
Other Electric Utilities	11,695	20,077	(8,382)	(41.7)
Miscellaneous	17,686	16,032	1,654	10.3
TOTAL	$ 854,446	$ 790,046	$ 64,400	8.2 %
SALES—KWH:				
Residential	14,574,577	13,700,235	874,342	6.4 %
Commercial	15,265,100	14,066,023	1,199,077	8.5
Industrial (1000 KW demand or over)	12,581,962	10,993,780	1,588,182	14.4
Agricultural Power	4,125,328	3,670,930	454,398	12.4
Public Street and Highway Lighting .	381,453	360,372	21,081	5.8
Other Electric Utilities	1,426,603	3,186,852	(1,760,249)	(55.2)
Total Sales to Customers	48,355,023	45,978,192	2,376,831	5.2
Delivered for the Account of Others .	5,130,406	4,879,495	250,911	5.1
TOTAL	53,485,429	50,857,687	2,627,742	5.2 %
GAS DEPARTMENT				
REVENUES:				
Residential	$ 236,698	$ 229,755	$ 6,943	3.0 %
Commercial	60,987	59,088	1,899	3.2
Industrial	169,761	155,253	14,508	9.3
Other Gas Utilities	25,861	23,640	2,221	9.4
Miscellaneous	482	227	255	112.3
TOTAL	$ 493,789	$ 467,963	$ 25,826	5.5 %
SALES—MCF:				
Residential	253,631	259,130	(5,499)	(2.1)%
Commercial	78,558	79,952	(1,394)	(1.7)
Industrial	353,270	350,216	3,054	0.9
Other Gas Utilities	50,777	56,621	(5,844)	(10.3)
Total Sales to Customers	736,236	745,919	(9,683)	(1.3)
Company Use (Electric generation) .	255,500	215,942	39,558	18.3
TOTAL	991,736	961,861	29,875	3.1 %

TABLE 21-4

Statement of Reinvested Earnings, Pacific Gas and Electric Company
For the Years Ended December 31, 1972 and 1971

| | ——Thousands—— | |
	1972	1971
BALANCE, JANUARY 1	$710,450	$641,515
NET INCOME	215,344	193,114
TOTAL	925,794	834,629
DIVIDENDS DECLARED ON CAPITAL STOCK—CASH:		
Preferred	30,266	23,998
Common	105,068	100,181
TOTAL	135,334	124,179
BALANCE, DECEMBER 31	$790,460	$710,450

TABLE 21-5

Statement of Changes in Financial Position, Pacific Gas and Electric Company
For the Years Ended December 31, 1972 and 1971

| FUNDS PROVIDED: | ——Thousands—— | |
	1972	1971
Funds Derived from Operations:		
Net Income	$215,344	$193,114
Non-fund Items in Net Income:		
Depreciation (including charges to other accounts)	150,855	139,070
Gain on Bonds Purchased for Sinking Fund	(9,819)	(9,767)
Other—net	(8,674)	(2,354)
Total Funds Derived from Operations*	347,706	320,063
Preferred Stock Sold—net	108,488	104,077
Mortgage Bonds Sold—net	123,610	273,353
Utility Plant Sold and Salvaged	17,193	18,214
Increase in Short-term Borrowing	54,000	—
Decrease in Other Working Capital Items	40,721	—
Other Changes—net	8,473	2,690
TOTAL	$700,191	$718,397
FUNDS APPLIED:		
Capital Expenditures*	$543,640	$451,851
Mortgage Bonds Retired (at cost)	21,217	44,246
Dividends—preferred and common stocks	135,334	124,179
Decrease in Short-term Borrowing	—	63,550
Increase in Other Working Capital Items	—	34,571
TOTAL	$700,191	$718,397

* Includes allowance for funds used during construction.
( ) Denotes deduction.

TABLE 21-6

Comparative Statistics, Pacific Gas and Electric Company

PER COMMON SHARE:	1972	1971	1970	1969
Earnings	$ 3.02	$ 2.75	$ 2.47	$ 2.58
Dividends Declared	$ 1.72	$ 1.64	$ 1.50	$ 1.50
Dividend Payout Ratio	57.0%	59.7%	60.9%	58.2%
Book Value (End of Year)	$26.36	$24.91	$23.66	$22.79
Market Price—High	33⅜	36⅜	35	39½
Market Price—Low	26⅜	28⅜	22½	29½
Market Price—Close	32⅝	32⅜	34⅝	32¾
CAPITAL EXPENDITURES (Thousands):				
Electric Department	$432,781	$355,242	$297,930	$240,468
Gas Department	71,345	60,432	68,320	61,428
Other	39,514	36,177	49,081	38,094
TOTAL	$543,640	$451,851	$415,331	$339,990
ELECTRIC STATISTICS:				
Net System Output (Millions of KWH)	59,124	54,665	51,277	48,885
Net System Output—Percent				
Hydroelectric Plants	19.8%	25.6%	26.9%	31.4%
Thermal Electric Plants	52.7	46.5	48.6	45.2
Other Producers	27.5	27.9	24.5	23.4
Total	100.0%	100.0%	100.0%	100.0%
System Capability—KW				
Hydroelectric Plants	2,529,300	2,514,300	2,514,300	2,514,300
Thermal Electric Plants	7,888,000	7,062,000	6,942,400	6,962,400
Other Producers	2,540,600	2,444,400	2,110,800	1,551,600
Total	12,957,900	12,020,700	11,567,500	11,028,300
Net System Peak Demand—KW	10,469,800	9,713,000	8,807,700	8,227,100
Average Annual Residential Consumption—KWH	6,213	6,048	5,697	5,545
Total Customers (End of Year)	2,767,978	2,675,942	2,597,314	2,536,703
Customers Per Mile of Distribution Line	36.0	35.4	34.8	34.5
GAS STATISTICS:				
Gas Purchased (Thousands of MCF)	1,015,319	1,004,547	950,652	878,484
Sources of Gas Purchased—Percent				
From California	23.5%	24.8%	25.2%	25.2%
From Other States	40.3	41.2	43.7	45.3
From Canada	36.2	34.0	31.1	29.5
Total	100.0%	100.0%	100.0%	100.0%
Average Cost of Gas Purchased—MCF				
From California	33.7¢	31.7¢	30.2¢	29.9¢
From Other States (at Calif.-Ariz. border)	39.4	37.5	33.9	31.4
From Canada (at Calif.-Ore. border)	36.9	32.7	30.4	28.2
Average	37.2¢	34.3¢	31.9¢	30.1¢
Peak Day Sendout—MCF	3,918,844	3,798,462	3,633,341	3,445,626
Average Annual Residential Consumption—MCF	115.7	121.7	107.7	116.2
Total Customers (End of Year)	2,383,609	2,317,686	2,258,285	2,208,046
Customers Per Mile of Distribution Main	95.6	95.0	94.1	94.0

Accumulated Depreciation. As with other industries, this figure is shown separately as a deduction from the plant at cost. Under the uniform system of accounts, a charge must be made monthly for depreciation. In most cases, the straight-line method of depreciation is used in the books of accounts and in reports to stockholders; liberalized depreciation, for tax purposes.[5]

Deferred Taxes Account. Many utility companies, inasmuch as they use rapid amortization for tax purposes, charge a deferred taxes account in the income statement and credit a deferred taxes account in the balance sheet, as was discussed in Chapter 17. Some utilities have in the past included this balance sheet account under "capitalization" as part of the common equity. The SEC, however, believes that classifying this item as a component part of common stock equity is misleading for financial statement purposes.[6] This account should not appear as part of common equity, but rather as a liability. Since 1968 the AICPA rules have required the deferred tax method.

Capitalization Ratios. Previous chapters have discussed the importance of trading on the equity, financial leverage, and capitalization ratios. It was noted that utility companies and others with very stable earnings could probably have substantial leverage in their capitalization. It is quite general to find the following capitalization ratios for electric and gas utilities:

Bonds and Preferred Stock	65%
Common Stock Equity	35
Total	100%

The SEC, under Public Utility Holding Company Act releases, has always held that a 25% common stock equity is the absolute minimum, but not a satisfactory minimum.[7] However, as a matter of practice, a 30-35% equity ratio tends to be the average for most of the industry, because institutional investors who are still holders of utility equities generally resist anything much below that level.

---

[5] In some cases, utilities use the sinking fund method. Under this method the amount charged each year will accumulate at a compound rate of interest to an amount sufficient to equal the original cost less salvage value at the end of service life.

[6] Release No. 14173, Securities Act of 1934 (also similar releases under the 1933 Investment Company Act and Holding Company Act) states: "So far as this Commission is concerned, since it believes that classifying this item (deferred taxes) as a component part of common stock equity is misleading for financial statement purposes, it does not intend to consider the item as part of common stock equity for analytical purposes, although it may give consideration to the item as one of a number of relevant factors in appraising the overall financial condition of a company."

[7] SEC Opinion under Public Utility Holding Company Act states: "We have never regarded a 25% common stock ratio as being anything other than a floor below which existing common stock equity ratios should not drop, or to which existing lower ratios should, as a minimum, increase. We have continuously striven to have common stock equity ratios maintained at, or increased to, levels substantially above 25% of capitalization and surplus."

The real question, therefore, is the division of the 65% between bonds and preferred stock. Many officials in the industry, many public utility commissions, and many financial analysts agree that, because of the great earnings stability in the industry and the tax advantages accruing to debt financing, it is perfectly proper to have 65% debt and 35% common equity with no preferred stock. Because the interest on bonds is fully tax deductible while preferred dividends are payable *after* calculation of federal income taxes, utility preferred stock, which in recent years sold in the market at approximately the same yields as utility bonds, is a more expensive method of financing. If the debt is 65% of total capitalization, it will represent about 72% of net plant account if the latter represents 90% of total assets.

In the 1940s the industry average tended to be:

Bonds	50%
Preferred Stock	15%
Common Stock Equity	35%
Total	100%

However, many utility companies, with the approval of utility commissions, have let the preferred ratio decline so that by 1971 the industry ratio tended to be more like:

Bonds	54.8%
Preferred Stock	9.8%
Common Stock Equity	35.4%
Total	100%

In 1961 the SEC, in the American Electric Power Case,[8] stated that it would not institute any adverse action if capitalization ratios, after the completion of a financing operation, were not higher in respect to debt than the following:

	Total Capitalization and Surplus
Long-term debt, including long-term bank loans, not in excess of	65% [9]
Common stock equity not less than	30%

The SEC noted that, in calculating the above ratios, total capitalization should not include "any deferred tax" account representing the accumulation of tax deductions that represent charges made currently against income as a result of accelerated amortization (under certificates of necessity) or

---

[8] SEC Holding Company Act, Release No. 14753.
[9] If the total of mortgage debt included in long-term debt did not exceed 60% of total capitalization and surplus.

liberalized depreciation for federal income tax purposes. It appears that in this case the SEC was establishing the maximum debt to capitalization ratio that it would approve. The SEC ruling has encouraged more debt financing and less preferred stock financing, which is desirable.

The Federal Power Commission has stated that it favors a capitalization of 60% debt and 40% common and preferred equity.

Income Statement Analysis

Because of the uniform system of accounting, utility income statements generally provide the investor with the information he needs in the form he desires and usually with sufficient disclosure. However, a few reservations must be noted, some of which are unique to utility statement analysis.

Revenue Breakdown Analysis.[10] Utility companies do supply a breakdown by divisions, not only where different types of utility services are provided (for example gas and electric) but also by commercial, industrial, and residential sales, and sales to governmental bodies. The breakdown supplied by electric utilities is not only by revenues but also by kilowatt hours sold to various classes of customers. Unfortunately, usually no similar breakdown of expenses is furnished. It should be clear that if only a breakdown of revenues is furnished but no breakdown of expenses, the analyst will find it difficult, if not impossible, to determine accurately the profitability of the various types of services. Typical regulatory procedure commonly requires that each service be self-supporting, and the analyst must satisfy himself that a department showing poor earnings is not being temporarily supported by one showing excessive earnings.

A utility company is to a large extent the prisoner of its geographic and economic environment. Its service is limited to its functional territory except to the extent that it may make sales to other utilities. The utilities that have shown the fastest growth in revenues have quite naturally been those that are located in the fastest growing economic areas, such as Florida and Texas.

Aggressive management may attract business to its area and increase sales by proper promotional rates. The investor should make a study of the economy of the area served, its growth rate, its major industries, and its population growth in order to project the future of the economy of the area and thus the future growth of revenues for the utility.

---

[10] On the average, two thirds of KWH sales go to industrial and commercial users.

The analyst will want to examine the rate schedules for different types of services, including step and promotional rates. Of course, he can calculate average rates for each type of customer if he has revenue and unit figures.

Residential Load. Historically, the residential load has demonstrated great stability and sustained growth, little affected by economic downturns, especially of the type experienced since 1938. It is important for the analyst to compare residential rates and the average monthly electric bill with those of other utilities in the general area or in equivalent areas, to compare the average residential load with that for the country and similar areas, and to examine promotional rate schedules. The higher the rates, the more risk there is for adverse political action and pressure on rates. A sound promotional residential rate structure and a trend of rising residential load can imply a progressive management. In addition to the growth of the residential load for lighting and increased use of appliances, in many areas the air-conditioning load has grown so fast that utilities often have two peak periods—one around Christmas and the other in the summer. The electric heating load is also growing significantly in some areas. The electric utility companies over the years and under pressure from consumers were able gradually to reduce rates as a result of increased usage per customer, increased efficiency of production and distribution, and also automation. But in the 1970s higher operating and capital costs have resulted in general rate increases.

In addition to the importance of rates themselves, another measure used for comparative purposes is the average residential bill developed from composite electric utility industry figures. In making comparisons, it must be realized that cost factors can cause differentials between utilities, making it impossible for some utilities to lower rates to the level of utilities in other areas. However, a higher rate of use and low rates are a strong plus factor. In analyzing the average monthly residential bill, a correlation must be made between the amount of kilowatt hours of service provided and the charges made. (U.S. average residential rate per KWH is 2.22¢.)

Commercial Load—Commercial Lighting and Small Power. The commercial load has demonstrated about as much stability as the residential load. However, in a deep depression such as the 1930s, such loads have been subject to significant declines.

Customer classification includes stores, restaurants, filling stations, garages, hotels, drugstores, theaters, hardware stores, and retail establishments in general. The commercial load consists of lighting, small power, and airconditioners. Overall it has experienced a growth somewhat less than residential loads. The growing use of airconditioners has been an important factor of growth in many areas. (U.S. average rate is 2.08¢.)

Industrial Load—Large Power and Light. The industrial load is more vulnerable to business cycle developments than other segments of the utility company's business. This is especially true in industrial areas producing largely durable goods, either capital goods or consumer durables. The more diversified the industrial load, the greater its stability. While the commercial rates are lower than the residential rates, the really low rates are for the industrial load. It quite obviously costs less to supply large loads to a specific customer, and the utility must offer competitive rates to keep and attract industry and to keep large users from installing their own generating equipment.[11] One advantage of the industrial load is that usually, except in two- and three-shift operations, the demand is off-peak or at different periods from the residential peak load, which is usually at night. (Average rate is 1.02¢.)

Street and Highway Lighting. This lighting can be a significant factor in many cases. This load is as stable as the residential load, but political pressures on rates can be serious.

Sales to Other Companies for Resale. Utilities have built up a wide network of intercommunications both for emergency purposes and also for frequent normal sale at the time of off-peak loads. In some cases such sales are significant, and the analyst must analyze their stability or lack of stability and their contribution to earnings.

Operating Expenses.[12] Operating income statements of utility companies based on the uniform system of accounting frequently give only the following items separately: maintenance, depreciation, other taxes, and federal income taxes. They group the remaining expenses under "other expenses." Some also make a practice of disclosing expenses for purchased gas or electricity.

An operating ratio calculated on the basis of this presentation (ratio of total operating expense to operating revenues) is not very revealing, nor does it offer a satisfactory basis for comparison with other companies. Federal taxes are included in the operating ratios published by the statistical services; but since they are not subject to management control, it would be more appropriate to exclude them from a ratio whose major purpose is to measure the efficiency of a company. Actually, management efficiency can be better tested by studying its control of fixed costs (efficiency of production equipment), labor costs, fuel costs, purchased fuel if any, and

---

[11] The latter was becoming competitive in some areas in the late 1960s.

[12] Again, a review of the Pacific Gas and Electric Company statements found earlier in this chapter is suggested. Overall operating expenses excluding maintenance, depreciation, and taxes represent 42% of revenues; including depreciation and maintenance, 60%; and including all taxes, 77.5%.

maintenance costs. The analyst should calculate the rate of these major expenses to operating revenues to obtain net operating income.

Based on the Composite Income Account for Privately Owned Class A and Class B Electric Utilities in the United States for the year ended December 31, 1970,[13] operating expenses were 39.5%, maintenance was 6.6%, depreciation and amortization were 11.1%, taxes other than income taxes were 10.5%, federal income taxes were 8.0%, and net operating revenues were 22.9% of electric utility operating income. Depreciation to gross utility plants was 2.2%.

It should be fairly obvious that if power is generated largely or solely from hydroelectric plants, then there will be little or no fuel costs and also the labor cost factor will be somewhat lower than in the case of steam generating plants. This will result in lower *operating expenses* and a higher *operating profit* for hydroelectric companies than for steam generating companies. However, since the hydroelectric plants are several times as expensive to build, capital costs for depreciation and for the cost of capital funds will therefore be considerably higher, thus frequently offsetting the savings on fuel and labor cost over the steam plants.

Special Nonoperating Charges That Reduce Income Taxes. At times, utility companies as well as other companies may make in their income accounts *special* charges that are not *ordinary* operating expenses but that are allowed as expenses for income tax purposes and that therefore reduce taxes. There are a variety of such charges, including special write-downs of property, expenses related to the refunding of bond issues (such as write-offs of bond premiums), and the charge-off of unamortized bond discount and expense.

Utility companies handle this special classification in different ways in their published statements. They are actually paying less taxes than they normally would be paying on their regular income if it were not for the special "one-shot" charge against income. Corporations regularly report in their income statements their estimate of income taxes accrued. The SEC has stated that this item should reflect the actual taxes that the company expects to pay and that the items should not be increased (even if shown separately) by an amount equivalent to what the corporation would have paid if it were not for this special charge. The SEC, however, will approve the inclusion of a special charge (equivalent to the additional tax that would have been paid) if this item is reported as a special charge deductible from gross income (that is, deductible from the amount available for fixed charges),

---

[13] Federal Power Commission; *Statistics of Electric Utilities in the United States, Privately Owned* (Washington: U.S. Government Printing Office, 1973). This is an annual publication, but there is a 2-year lag.

but this item must clearly identify and specify the nature of the charge and the exact amount involved. Most utilities, therefore, report special charges in this manner.

Financial analysts, however, argue that if this charge is included in the income statement, it should more properly be considered as an addition to taxes and should therefore be deducted *before* arriving at the gross income figure or the balance available for fixed charges, rather than being deducted from gross income *after* it has been calculated in the manner required by the SEC.

Maintenance Expense. Utility plants are practically always well maintained, and the analyst therefore does not need to worry about problems of undermaintenance. While material and supplies are used in maintenance, the bulk of maintenance expenses is for labor and this will be included in the total labor cost to revenue analysis suggested earlier (6.9% of revenues).

Book Depreciation and Published Reported Depreciation. Generally depreciation charges are based on service life studies developed by the company concerned and also are related to industry experience, with most companies using straight-line depreciation for books of account and published statements but liberalized depreciation for tax purposes. On the average, depreciation charges for electric utilities with steam generating plants average about 2.3% of gross plant. In the case of hydroelectric plants where the property has a longer life, the average is nearer 2% of plant or sometimes slightly lower. (Depreciation is 11.2% of revenues.)

Depreciation for Federal Income Tax Purposes.[14] Prior to 1961, utility companies could receive certificates of necessity permitting rapid amortization of plants over a 5-year period, but they are no longer eligible for these certificates. However, as for all other companies, they can use "liberalized depreciation" for tax purposes under the 1954 Code provided that the new material or property was acquired after December 31, 1953.

The Securities and Exchange Commission and the Federal Power Commission favor the normalizing or deferred tax method of reporting depreciation.[15] Unfortunately, there is no uniformity in the state commissions'

---

[14] The reader should review Chapter 17 on depreciation, especially the section on flow-through and normalizing.

[15] In the case of companies that are using liberalized depreciation (and in the past, accelerated amortization under certificates of necessity) the SEC stated:

In a year in which costs are deducted for tax purposes in amounts greater than those used for financial statement purposes, then, unless corrected, there is a failure to properly match costs and revenues in the financial statements by the recommended or required accounting for depreciation by companies using "liberalized depreciation for tax purposes." Some commissions require that the companies "normalize" and some require that they "flow through." The AICPA recommends normalizing by all companies including utilities.

In reports to stockholders some companies will use the flow-through method and other companies will use the normalizing method. In the case of two companies under identical conditions, the one using the flow-through method will report higher earnings in the earlier years than the one using the normalizing method, simply as a result of the difference in accounting treatment. If a company shifts from normalizing to flow-through, it will immediately report higher earnings, everything else remaining the same. Utility analysts have pointed out that investors frequently do not appear to differentiate between a company using the flow-through method and a company using the normalizing method but simply apply the same price-earnings ratio to both companies. If possible, the investor should make an adjustment to bring both companies into line, although this is admittedly difficult to do on the basis of the information generally available. At the very least, however, the investor should realize that he is paying a higher price-earnings ratio for true operating earnings in the case of a company using the flow-

---

amount of the tax effect of the cost differential. To correct the resultant distortion in periodic net income after taxes, it is therefore necessary to charge income in earlier years with an amount equal to the tax reduction and to return this amount to income in subsequent years when the amount charged for financial statement purposes exceeds the amount deducted for tax purposes. It is our understanding that such deferred tax accounting is in accordance with generally accepted accounting principles. [In 1968 the AICPA required this method.]

. . . acceleration of tax deductions in earlier years results in deferring to later years the payment of taxes on an amount equivalent to the cost differential. Because of the interrelationship between income taxes and depreciation, the Commission is of the view that in the earlier years the charge equivalent to the tax reduction should be treated either (1) as a provision for future taxes in the income statement with a corresponding credit in the balance sheet to a non-equity caption such as a "deferred tax credit," or (2) as additional depreciation in the income statement with a corresponding addition to the "accumulated provision for depreciation" in the balance sheet. In the Commission's view it is improper to charge income with an item required for the proper determination of net income and concurrently to credit earned surplus.

For the foregoing reasons, on and after the effective date of this statement (April 30, 1960) of administrative policy, any financial statement filed with this Commission which designates as earned surplus (or its equivalent) or in any manner as part of equity capital (even though accompanied by words of limitation such as "restricted" or "appropriated") the accumulated credit arising from accounting for reductions in income taxes resulting from deducting costs for income tax purposes at a more rapid rate than for financial statement purposes will be presumed by the Commission to be misleading or inaccurate despite disclosure contained in the certificate of the accountant or in footnotes to the statements, provided the amounts involved are material.

through method than in the case of a company that is normalizing if both companies are selling at the same "reported earnings" P/E ratio.

Gross Income. This item is the balance remaining after operating expenses have been deducted from *gross revenues*. It is the amount available to cover the fixed charges and is the basis for calculating the coverage or margin of safety for the bonds.

Fixed Charges. Fixed charges are deducted from the gross income available for fixed charges to arrive at the amount available for dividends—preferred and common. The fixed charges items shown separately in public utility income statements are generally in conformance with those found in income statements of nonutility companies, but in addition there is another item peculiar to utility accounting. This is the item "interest charged to construction credit." The regular items found in all income statements are: (1) interest on long-term debt, (2) other interest charges; (3) amortization of debt discount, premiums, and expenses; (4) taxes assumed by the company on interest received by creditors (bondholders), either paid to the bondholders or paid directly to the government on their behalf; and finally, (5) other income deductions representing charges to income and not deducted elsewhere. (Times earned in 1972 = 2.8x; in 1966 = 3.6x.)

Interest Charged to Construction Credit. This item is peculiar to public utility accounting. It arises from the fact that when a utility sells a security issue and receives the proceeds, these funds temporarily become part of current assets until they are actually paid out for construction of new plant and installation of new equipment. As noted earlier, utilities are strictly limited as to the amount of current assets (working capital) that can be included in their rate base on which they are permitted to earn a fair rate of return. These funds for construction must be excluded from the rate base or the earnings base. If the matter were left at that point, the utilities would be paying the cost for the funds but would not be permitted to earn on these funds as part of their rate base. Therefore, they are permitted to capitalize the interest cost of these funds prior to the time that these funds are actually invested in fixed assets. The item ceases as soon as the funds are actually invested in fixed assets and added to the rate base.

The investor must realize that the interest charged to construction credit item is temporary in nature and will disappear as soon as the funds are invested in fixed assets. Ideally, as soon as this occurs the company will begin to earn a fair return on the additional plant and equipment, and the additional earnings will replace the amount that was previously added to earnings for interest charged to construction credit. If it actually works out this way, there is no problem. However, if there is a lag between the time that the interest charged to construction credit ceases and the additional earnings flow from the new plant, there is a problem. It is a noncash item.

Assume that the item was equal to $0.25 per share this year as part of total reported earnings of $2.25, so that earnings without this item are $2.00 per share. Next year the item is lost. If earnings on the old property (exclusive of the new property) rise by say 8%, earnings on the old property would rise from $2.00 to $2.16. If no additional earnings next year flow from the new property, the earnings will be reported next year at $2.16 versus $2.25 for this year. If earnings on the new property next year are $0.09 per share, the earnings on the old property of $2.16 plus the $0.09 on the new property will give total earnings for next year of $2.25 per share versus $2.25 this year. Of course, earnings on the new property could immediately be equal to $0.25, which would result in earnings of $2.16 plus $0.25 or a total of $2.41 for next year. The point to emphasize is that in projecting future earnings for the next year and thereafter, the investor must make allowances for any reduction in earnings that will result when the interest charged to construction credit is eliminated. If the item is material on a per-share basis, the analyst must give special attention to it.

The uniform system of accounts provides that the item "interest charged to construction" appear as a "credit" in the "gross income deductions" section of the income statement. This results in its being a deduction credit from the charges for interest, amortization of debt discount, and so forth. The final result of showing the item as a *credit* against gross income deductions, of course, is the same as if the item were merely added to gross income. However, from the standpoint of financial analysis, it is more logical to add the item to gross income rather than to handle it as required under the uniform system of accounting. For all private electric utilities, this item rose from $127,480,000 or 2.6% of construction costs in 1966 to $588,406,000 or 5.9% of construction costs in 1970.

Fixed Charge Coverage and Interest Charged to Construction Credit. If interest charged to construction is handled as required under the uniform system of accounts, the coverage test will be lower than if the analyst removes it as a credit in the gross income deductions section and then adds it to gross income available for fixed charges. The latter treatment is justified because in effect the company is capitalizing the item, legitimately adding it to the cost of construction. The analyst thus properly arrives at a higher coverage ratio.

Coverage for Preferred Dividends on Overall Basis and Interest Charged to Construction Credit. As noted earlier, coverage for preferred dividends should be calculated on an overall basis (preferred dividends plus all prior charges). Therefore, as in the paragraph above, if the analyst adds interest charged to construction to gross income, he will obtain a higher coverage rate than if the item is left as a credit in the gross income deductions section as required under the uniform system of accounts.

Earnings Available for Common and Interest Charged to Construction Credit. As far as the earnings available for the common stock are concerned, it does not make any difference which way the interest charged to construction is handled. The amount available for the common in either case will reflect the *addition* of the item, either as an addition to gross income or as a credit to income deductions.

Selected Ratios

The following ratios permit a quick appraisal of the overall results of the privately owned electric utility companies' operations in 1966-1970.

	1970	1969	1968	1967	1966
Long-term debt:					
Percent of total capitalization	54.8	54.6	53.8	53.0	52.3
Percent of net utility plant ..	52.5	51.9	51.6	51.1	50.6
Times interest charges earned (after taxes)	2.8	2.9	3.1	3.4	3.6
Net income percent of revenues	14.7	15.2	15.4	16.2	16.2
Return on common equity— percent	11.8	12.2	12.3	12.8	12.8
Common dividend payout rate— percent	70.9	69.6	70.7	68.4	67.9
Electric operations percent of total operations (revenue basis)	85.6	85.5	85.2	84.9	84.7
Gross electric plant per dollar electric revenue	$4.71	$4.64	$4.60	$4.57	$4.46
Electric operating expenses percent of electric operating revenues—(operating ratio)	77.4	77.1	77.3	76.7	76.9
Electric operating income percent of net electric plant plus working capital	7.3	7.4	7.3	7.4	7.4

Source: *Federal Power Commission Statistics of Electric Utilities in the United States, Privately Owned* (Washington, D.C.: U.S. Government Printing Office, 1973).

Physical Factors and Ratios

The following ratios based on physical factors are important in a thorough analysis of a public utility company.

System Peak Load to Capacity. The bulk of the capital invested in a utility company is invested in plant and equipment, and this provides the company's output capacity. It would, of course, be ideal if output was generally close to capacity most of the time with only an allowance for a certain reserve leeway. However, the demand for the service will vary considerably during the year, and a company must be prepared to meet all demands at all times. Sometimes, of course, part of a heavy peak demand is met with purchased power.

The *system peak* is usually calculated at the peak load for any full hour during the year. It is stated in kilowatts for one hour. This system peak is a measure of the capacity needed without any additional allowance for reserves at peak periods. As noted earlier, many utilities now have two peaks—one in December and one in the summer, the latter caused by the air-conditioning load.[16]

System Load Factor. This is the relation of the average system load to the system peak load, usually calculated on an annual basis.

Specifically, there are 365 days in a year with 24 hours in each day, a total of 8,760 hours in a year. The total amount of kilowatts (kw) provided in a year is divided by the number of hours in a year.

Assume: 1,000,000,000 kw output per year, and peak load of 200,000 kw.

Then: $\dfrac{1,000,000,000 \text{ kw}}{8,760 \text{ hours}} = 114,150$ kw output per hour

And: $\dfrac{114,150 \text{ kw (output per hour)}}{200,000 \text{ kw (peak load)}} = 57\%$ load factor

The load factor is 57% of capacity. The higher the load factor, the more efficient is the utility's operation. It definitely should not be below 50%, and usually it will not be over 66% of capacity.

---

[16] Most of the electric systems in the U.S. now experience peak seasons during the summer, but four regions that still are winter-peak are New England; the Tennessee Valley Authority area; Pensacola, Florida; and the Pacific Northwest. The Federal Power Commission believes that the utilities should have minimum power reserves of 20%—meaning reserves in terms of generating capacity to peak loads. In 1962 the FPC estimated reserves in the West at 21%, but in the Southeast at only 16%. Utilities in recent years have encountered increasing difficulty in securing public approval for the location of new plants resulting from pressures from environmental groups and the atomic plants from safety-concerned groups.

Output of Kilowatts per Unit of Fuel Consumption. One measure of the efficiency of the generating plant is the amount of fuel required to generate 1 kw of electricity. In the early 1920s, 3.5 pounds of coal were required to generate 1 kw. The industry average today is around 0.85 pounds of coal, with the newest and most efficient plant generating 1 kw with as little as 0.60-0.65 pounds of coal. Another measurement, because both gas and coal are used and because coal varies considerably in BTU content, is the number of BTU's required to generate 1 kw of electricity. The most modern generating plant can generate 1 kw with only 8,500 BTU's, and the industry average is roughly 10,880 BTU's to generate 1 kw.

Projection of Earnings

Earlier chapters in this book discussed the principles of earnings projections for (1) projection of revenues and net profit on revenues and (2) projection of invested capital and rate of return on invested capital. Both methods can be used effectively in the projection of electric utilities earnings. Furthermore, except for changes in the regulatory climate, including regulatory changes and effects of inflation, the trend line of earnings tends to rise at a fairly steady rate commensurate at least with the recent past.

Future Cost Problems

Over the next decade gas and electric companies will be faced with two major additional cost factors. First, antipollution costs will be significantly greater if the companies are to comply with federal and state antipollution standards. Second, worldwide costs of energy sources will probably rise substantially because of rising demand in relation to available supplies. Regulation of the gas and electric utility industry will result in a lag between these rising costs and rate increases.

QUESTIONS

1. What are the major characteristics of a public utility?
2. (a) What is the current investment status of electric utility stocks?
   (b) What caused the change in investment status for electric utility stocks that occurred after 1949?
   (c) Is an inflationary environment favorable for utility common stocks? Preferred stocks? Explain.
3. Discuss the importance of the Hope Natural Gas Company Case to investors.

4. Rapid growth in population is the factor necessary to identify a growth utility stock. Is this true or false? Explain your answer.

5. (a) "The National Association of Railroad and Utility Commissions adopted a revised uniform system of accounts for electric and gas utilities in 1961. . . ." Does this insure completed comparable accounting reports for electric utility companies? Discuss.

   (b) Distinguish between (1) original cost, (2) replacement cost, and (3) fair value as public utility rate bases. Which base is used by the commission in your state?

6. Would a current ratio be a particularly significant factor in an analysis of an electric utility security? Discuss. What is the industry median?

7. (a) Why does an analyst desire a breakdown of the plant account into components providing different services by the utility (for example, electric and gas)?

   (b) How does the fact that a company's plants are primarily steam-generating plants as opposed to hydroelectric plants affect the analyst's determination of the economic value of the plant?

8. (a) Why are measures of plant utilization so significant in analyses of electric utilities securities?

   (b) What physical ratios are used to analyze plant utilization and efficiency of utilization of plant?

9. Discuss the capitalization ratios generally considered desirable in the electric utility industry. Relate this to cost of capitalization analysis.

10. In what ways might customer composition for a given electric utility affect the cyclical stability of the utility's revenues?

11. (a) What are the main breakdowns of utility operating costs that should be studied by the analyst?

    (b) Criticize the breakdown usually given under the uniform system of accounts used by public utilities.

12. (a) What is the meaning of the account "accrued deferred taxes"?

    (b) What significance might the finding of such an account in the balance sheet have for the price-earnings ratio?

WORK-STUDY PROBLEMS

1. The data at the top of page 567 provide the principal important statistics of two public electric utility companies.

   (a) Calculate the following for each company:
      (1) Depreciation ratio.
      (2) Maintenance ratio.
      (3) Interest coverage before and after taxes.
      (4) Net operating revenue to net plant.

	Company A	Company B
	(In thousands)	
Operating Revenue	$ 91,468	$133,126
Operating Expenses	31,361	56,910
Maintenance	5,411	8,026
Depreciation	11,385	13,447
Taxes	20,367	35,340
Miscellaneous	532	0
Operating Revenue Deduction	69,056	113,723
Net Operating Revenue	22,412	19,403
Interest	6,366	4,465
Net Income	16,046	14,938
Preferred Dividend	2,416	1,960
Common Dividend	10,373	8,961
Plant	498,500	492,558
Depreciation	76,591	139,820
Net Plant	421,909	352,738

	Company A	Company B
Debt	$211,675	$147,889
Preferred	52,500	43,000
Common	88,828	74,676
Surplus	43,636	84,532

		Company A	Company B
Number of Shares of Common (100)		10,373	7,467
Customers	1965	227,000	474,000
Customers	1972	295,000	487,000
Capacity	1972	1,340,000	1,051,000
Peak Load	1972	1,108,000	1,041,000
Load Factor	1972	68.0	58.0
Average Residential Use	1972	4,081	2,430
Average Residential Rate	1972 (cents per kw)	2.70	3.91

(5) Operating ratio.

(6) Ratio of debt to capitalization.

(7) Overall coverage of preferred dividend.

(8) Per share earned on common.

(9) Per-share dividend on common.

(10) Reserve margin.

(b) Comment on the stocks of these two companies, assuming that Company A is selling at 33 and Company B at 38. Take into consideration the above calculations compared with the average for the industry as well as the growth of the customers served, the load factor, the average use, the yield, and the price-earnings ratio.

2. (a) What has been the record of utility companies in your state in securing rate increases since 1950? How does this record compare with that of other states?

(b) What rate of return is permitted for electric utilities in your state? How is it calculated? Do you believe the method used and the rate allowed would be relatively desirable to investors? Discuss.

SUGGESTED READINGS

American Gas Association. *Annual Report*. Arlington, Va.: American Gas Association.

Edison Electric Institute. New York: Edison Electric Institute.
  (1) *Annual Report* (Industry projections).
  (2) *Statistical Yearbook*.
  (3) Weekly and monthly statistical releases.

Electrical World (Annual statistical report, Parts I & II). New York: McGraw-Hill Book Company.

Gordon, Myron J., J. S. McCollum, and Michael J. Brennan. "Valuation and the Cost of Capital for Regulated Utilities—Comment." *The Journal of Finance* (December, 1972), pp. 1150-1155.

Moody's Public Utility Manual (Annual). New York: Moody's Investors Service, Inc.

Public Utilities (Fortnightly). Washington, D.C.: Public Utilities Reports, Inc.

Standard & Poor's, Basic Industry Surveys—Electric Public Utilities. New York: Standard & Poor's Corporation.

U.S. Federal Power Commission. Washington, D.C.: U.S. Superintendent of Documents.
  (1) *Annual Report*.
  (2) *Annual Statistics of Electric Utilities in the U.S. (Privately owned)*.
  (3) *FPC Weekly Newsletter* (No charge).
  (4) *Electric Power Statistics* (Monthly bulletin).
  (5) *National Electric Rate Book* (Annual).

Transportation Securities

The three major components of the transportation industry that will be discussed in this chapter are the railroad industry, the trucking industry, and the airline industry. Because the railroad industry is the most complicated and has had the most problems and the poorest record, the major part of this chapter will be devoted to it. Statistics presented here are for Class I railroads which account for 98% of industry revenues and over 95% of all railroad mileage.

In a broad context all three industries mentioned above are public utilities subject to federal regulatory authorities. The airlines are subject to Civil Aeronautics Board (CAB) regulations; railroads, motor carriers, and operators of internal waterways and oil pipelines come under the jurisdiction of the Interstate Commerce Commission (ICC) which was established in 1887. Many amendments to the initial legislation and many court cases have considerably broadened the jurisdiction of the ICC. While the ICC has very broad powers including accounting (unification of accounts), security issues, and construction, its most vital areas of control are the regulation of rates, mergers and consolidations, and abandonments of rail services. As a result of railroad regulations,[1] the financial analyst has available

---

[1] See *Historical Review of Railroad Regulations to 1958.* The following provide a brief historical review of railroad legislation and court cases:

[a] 1887—Establishment of the ICC.

[b] 1898—It was ruled in *Smith* vs. *Ames* that rates must not be confiscating and must allow "a fair return on the fair value of the property" used in the public service.

[c] 1910—The Mann-Elkins Act shifted the burden of proof as to the reasonableness of rates from ICC to the railroads.

[d] 1933—The Transportation Act of 1920 intended to restore financial and physical health to the railroads, but the premise of this act was that all that was needed was

information on financial and physical data in minute detail. Because of the nature of the railroad industry, railroad rates are established on a group basis (as against a company basis for electric utilities) for those railroads serving the same general territory. The more efficient members of the group can therefore be more profitable than other members of the group charging identical rates.

PROBLEMS OF THE RAILROAD INDUSTRY

Historically the railroad industry has received the bulk of its gross operating revenues and practically all of its net operating revenues from freight traffic (see Table 22-1). Passenger revenues were at one time significant, but since World War II passenger business has been consistently unprofitable. The industry has a very heavy capital investment ($28 billion in 1972) largely financed by debt issues rather than equity. Capital turnover is low compared to most industries except electric utilities. For example, railroads have a turnover of capital invested of only 0.45 per year.

Passenger Service Deficit

The railroads showed a deficit for all passenger and allied services in every year after 1945. Finally, beginning May 1, 1971, all intercity passenger train operations (except for four railroads which elected not to participate and except for commuter trains) were assumed by the National Railroad Passenger Corporation (more popularly known as Amtrak) under the terms of the Railroad Passenger Service Act of 1970. The passenger service deficit, except for extraordinary charges relating to the take-over, was therefore substantially reduced except for commuter lines not taken over.

Declining Freight Revenues

Until the Great Depression of the 1930s, the securities of railroad bonds, preferred stock, and common stock had enjoyed considerable investment

---

permission to raise rates high enough to permit a fair return. It ignored the factor of competition and did nothing to encourage mergers to eliminate excess railroad mileage.

e 1933—The Emergency Transportation Act of 1933 recognized the extremely serious nature of the financial plight of the railroads but did not effectively change the rules and permit mergers which were necessary to eliminate excessive railroad mileage. Neither did this act provide the basis for railroads to effectively compete for transportation business.

f 1958—The Transportation Act of 1958 at long last provided effective machinery for mergers and in effect also permitted railroads to pass along their efficiencies in the form of lower rates regardless of the effect on competing forms of transportation.

TABLE 22-1

Railroad Revenues (Millions of Dollars)

Year	Total Operating Revenues	Freight Revenues		Passenger Revenues		Passenger Commutation	
		Total	As % of Operating Revenues	Total	As % of Operating Revenues	Total	As % of Passenger Revenues
1929	6,279.5	4,825.6	76.8	873.6	13.9	72.2	8.3
1944	9,436.8*	6,998.6	74.2	1,790.3	19.0	57.0	3.2
1947	8,684.9	7,041.2	81.1	963.3	11.1	67.4	7.0
1955	10,106.3	8,538.3	84.5	742.9	7.4	101.4	13.6
1965	10,207.9	8,836.0	86.6	533.1	5.2	136.4	25.6
1970	11,991.7	10,926.8	91.1	420.5	3.5	172.3	41.0
1971	12,688.9	11,785.9	92.9	294.1**	2.3**	173.6**	59.0**
1972	13,411.1	12,571.7	93.7	257.1	1.9	174.1	67.7

* World War II.
** Amtrak took over all long haul traffic except for four railroads as of May 1, 1971.

status and represented a significant portion of the portfolios of both institutions and individuals. But from 1929 to 1933 railroad freight revenues declined 50% and passenger revenues, 62%. In 1932 Class I railroads earned a mere 1.37% overall on the investment, and this rate of return is the relationship of net railway operating income (the remainder of operating income after deducting operating expenses, taxes, and lease rentals of equipment and joint facilities, but *before* recording nonoperating income and deducting fixed charges, such as interest on debt and rents for leased lines) to railway investment. Therefore, the 1.37% on investment did not cover fixed charges. Thus, in the 1930s over one third of railroad mileage went into receivership and another third was close to the brink of receivership.

Because competition from trucks, buses, and the airlines was reduced by wartime restrictions, the railroads enjoyed reasonable prosperity during World War II. The railroads also did fairly well in 1946-1955 and 1963-1966. But in only one year since 1946 has the rate of return on investment been over 4% (4.22% in 1955). Since 1957, the rate of return on investment was over 3% only in the years 1963-1966. Furthermore, in the recession years of 1961 and 1970 the rate fell to 1.97% and 1.79%, respectively, versus 1.37% in the Great Depression year of 1932.

The collapse of the railroads in the Great Depression and the very poor and highly cyclical nature of the record since World War II have removed most railroad securities (except for equipment trust issues) from the classification of quality investment securities and, hence, largely from the portfolios of institutional and individual investors. However, the securities of seven railroads (see page 575) do have some investor attention.

Those who purchased rail securities in the post-World War II years and have had success had to have been particularly thorough and judicious in their analysis, as well as very careful in their timing of purchases *and* sales. In general, success has meant purchasing in down economic cycles and, just as important, selling in recovery cycles. A buy-and-hold strategy has given poor results.

Competition for Freight. The major problem for the railroads has been their competitive loss of freight traffic as shown in Table 22-2. Excluding oil pipelines, the railroad carried nearly 80% of all intercity freight traffic tonnage in both 1929 and during World War II. After the war this percentage declined to 64% in 1950, 53% in 1960, and only 50% by 1972. Conversely, trucks increased their percentage from about 3% in 1929 to 11% in 1939, a decline to 6% during the war, and then an increase to just under 20% by 1950 and just under 30% by 1972. In addition, traffic handled on the rivers and canals increased from 1.5% in 1929 to 5.5% in 1950, 11% in 1960, and about 14% in 1972.

Competition for Intercity Freight. The record of competition for intercity freight tonnage is also shown in Table 22-2.

TABLE 22-2

Intercity Freight, Freight Ton Miles (In Millions, % Excludes Oil and Pipelines)

	(1)	(2) Total Excluding Pipe Lines	(3) Railroads		(4) Trucks		(5) Rivers & Canals		(6) Great Lakes	
Year	Total		Total	% of Col. 2	Total	% of Col. 2	Total	% of Col. 2	Total	% of Col. 2
1929	607,375	580,475	454,800	78.3	19,689	3.4	8,661	1.5	97,322	16.8
1939	543,534	487,932	338,850	69.4	52,821	10.8	19,937	4.1	76,312	15.6
1944	1,088,266	955,402	746,912	78.2	58,264	6.1	31,380	3.3	118,769	12.4
1950	1,062,637	933,462	596,540	63.9	172,860	18.5	51,657	5.5	111,687	12.0
1960	1,314,270	1,085,644	579,130	53.3	285,483	26.3	120,785	11.1	99,468	9.2
1970	1,935,960	1,504,960	771,000	51.2	412,000	27.4	204,085	13.6	114,475	7.6
1971	1,938,430	1,494,000	746,000	50.0	430,000	28.8	210,003	14.1	105,027	7.0
1972	2,015,800	1,558,800	785,000	50.4	445,000	28.5	218,000	14.0	107,000	6.9

The above figures, moreover, do not present the full impact of the competitive losses to the railroads. The trucks tend to take over the cream of the high-revenue traffic, leaving the heavier, relatively low-value tonnage, such as coal and steel, for the railroads to carry. As a result, while trucks carried only about 27% of intercity freight tonnage in 1968 compared to 50% for the railroads, annual truck gross revenues by 1968 were exceeding railroad gross revenues; and this trend has continued in the 1970s.

TABLE 22-3

The Financial Record of the Railroads (Cyclical), Selected Years (Millions of Dollars)

Year	Operating Revenues	Freight Revenues	Operating Expenses	Maintenance Ways & Structures	Maintenance Equipment	Transportation Expenses	Taxes	Net Railway Oper. Inc.	Rate of Return	Net Income	Earn.* DJ Rails Aver.
1929	6,279.5	4,825.6	4,506.1	855.4	1202.9	2,080.0	396.7	1251.7	5.30	896.8	N.A.
1939	3,995.0	3,251.1	2,918.2	466.8	765.9	1,417.8	355.7	588.7	2.56	93.2	2.04
1944	9,436.8	6,998.6	6,282.1	1263.3	1587.5	2,973.9	1846.0	1106.3	4.70	667.2	10.00
1947	8,685.0	7,041.2	6,797.3	1212.1	1558.0	3,476.4	936.4	780.7	3.44	478.9	8.53
1948	9,671.7	7,976.3	7,472.0	1348.0	1702.9	4,421.1	1028.5	1002.0	4.31	698.1	13.89
1951	10,390.6	8,634.1	8,041.3	1478.8	1945.0	3,974.5	1203.3	942.5	3.76	693.2	14.87
1955	10,106.3	8,538.3	7,646.4	1387.5	1787.7	3,769.9	1080.4	1128.0	4.22	927.1	19.79
1956	10,550.9	8,951.4	8,108.4	1405.0	1892.6	4,043.5	1121.3	1068.2	3.95	876.3	19.52
1957	10,491.4	8,928.5	8,227.5	1430.5	1913.0	4,094.8	1068.4	922.3	3.36	737.4	15.55
1958	9,564.6	8,070.8	7,543.8	1223.4	1720.4	3,834.3	957.2	762.3	2.76	601.7	12.35
1959	9,825.1	8,312.2	7,704.8	1236.5	1797.9	3,887.7	1047.6	747.7	2.72	577.7	11.11
1960	9,514.3	8,025.4	7,565.3	1191.7	1759.8	3,832.9	998.8	584.0	2.13	444.6	6.70
1961	9,189.1	7,739.0	7,274.3	1117.7	1683.4	3,710.8	991.1	537.8	1.97	382.4	4.89
1962	9,439.9	7,991.1	7,418.6	1154.8	1743.6	3,755.1	905.0	725.7	2.74	571.0	9.38
1963	9,559.5	8,146.1	7,451.6	1182.5	1731.7	3,771.3	886.4	805.7	3.12	651.6	12.69
1964	9,856.5	8,455.5	7,737.8	1225.8	1763.8	3,920.6	870.6	818.2	3.16	698.2	14.49
1965	10,207.9	8,836.0	7,849.8	1235.8	1774.9	4,020.2	916.5	961.5	3.69	814.6	19.35
1966	10,654.7	9,280.6	8,117.7	1303.7	1843.6	4,139.3	968.4	1045.9	3.90	903.8	20.90
1967	10,366.0	9,130.2	8,204.5	1287.8	1867.8	4,186.0	910.2	676.4	2.46	553.8	12.80
1968	10,854.7	9,749.8	8,581.0	1405.1	1914.3	4,354.7	946.3	677.6	2.44	569.4	17.59
1969	11,456.3	10,346.3	9,066.5	1503.0	2002.3	4,595.6	1029.1	654.7	2.36	514.2	15.39
1970	11,991.7	10,921.8	9,650.0	1612.6	2165.3	4,873.3	1068.5	485.9	1.73	226.6	8.52
1971R	12,689.0	11,786.1	10,055.3	1813.1	2350.9	4,889.8	1089.7	695.5	2.47	347.1	15.25
1972	13,411.1	12,571.7	10,549.9	1917.6	2392.9	5,208.7	1143.1	835.1	2.95	499.9	18.75

* Became Dow Jones Transportation Average, January 1, 1970.

Highly Cyclical Nature

A review of Table 22-3 highlights certain factors. In spite of the growth of GNP from $258 billion in 1948 to $1,152 billion in 1972 or a quadrupling, operating revenues of the railroads were in a horizontal channel as the railroads lost to competitive modes of transportation. Operating revenues were $9.7 billion in 1948, $9.6 billion in 1958, and only $10.9 billion in 1968. Not until 1969 and 1970 were they above $11 billion. Taxes in 1970, 1971, and 1972 were only slightly above $1.0 billion.

Net railway operating income proved very cyclical: $1.0 billion in 1948, $922 million in 1957, but only $538 million in 1961; then it rose to $1.05 billion in 1966 and fell to $486 million in 1970. The record of net income was $698 million in 1948, a post-World War II peak of $927 million in 1955, and then a low of $383 million in 1961 and a postwar low of $227 million in 1970.

The rate of return on investment was 4.31% in 1948 and 4.22% in 1955 (peaks for the postwar years), and it fell to 1.97% in 1961 and 1.73% in 1970 (the latter not much higher than the 1.37% in the depression year of 1932 and only 2.95% in 1972). The financial record therefore shows a very poor overall history plus very severe cyclical declines. Hence, the industry as such must be given a speculative, not an investment, rating.

Area Differences Within the Railroad Industry. The statistics in Table 22-3 show the poor record and highly cyclical nature of the industry but obscure some more favorable factors shown in Table 22-4.

The peak net income for the industry after World War II was obtained in 1955. But while the Eastern District showed deficits in 1970-1972, the net income of the Southern District was 16.4%—higher in 1971 than in 1955—while the net income for the Western District had recovered in 1971 to essentially the same peak as 1955. The latter were both higher in 1972.

TABLE 22-4

Net Income of Class I Railroads (Millions of Dollars)

Year	United States	Eastern District	Southern District	Western District
1955	927.1	349.3	153.8	424.0
1961	382.4	2.7 Def.	84.0	301.1
1966	903.8	285.1	141.4	477.3
1967	553.8	94.1	126.1	333.6
1970	226.6	276.3 Def.	159.5	343.4
1971	354.5	243.0 Def.	179.1	418.4
1972	499.9	157.1 Def.	207.7	449.3

The railroads which have managed to do much better than the industry have been either the long haul roads with significant nonrailroad income, such as the Atchison, Topeka & Santa Fe Railroad, and the coal roads such as the Chesapeake & Ohio and the Norfolk & Western.

The investment community considers seven railroads to be representative of considerably higher quality than the industry overall. These are: (1) the Atchison, Topeka & Santa Fe (Santa Fe Industries Holding Company), (2) Burlington, (3) Chesapeake & Ohio, (4) Norfolk & Western, (5) Southern, (6) Southern Pacific, and (7) Union Pacific. Their earnings records, compared to the Dow Jones Transportation Index (Rail Index prior to January 1, 1970), are given in Table 22-5. The reader should review these railroads to determine major factors for their relatively good showing, including long hauls (or coal roads) and nonrailroad income. In addition, these railroads generally reflect the success of mergers as compared to the merger debacle of the largest system, the Penn-Central (Pennsylvania Railroad and New York Central).

TABLE 22-5

Earnings per Share of Seven Higher Quality Railroads, 1966-1972

	1972	1971	1970	1969	1968	1967	1966
Santa Fe Industries	3.50	2.66*	1.96*	2.43	1.81	1.72	3.12
Burlington	3.90	2.74*	2.01	3.09	3.75*	2.73	5.67
Chesapeake & Ohio	6.75	3.25*	6.09*	6.05	6.21	6.02	7.61
Norfolk & Western	9.00	7.18*	6.14	8.60	8.07	8.01	10.61
Southern	6.10	4.87	3.78	3.16	2.99	2.80	2.72
Southern Pacific	4.10	3.81	2.86	3.41	3.27	2.71	3.47
Union Pacific	4.75	4.03	3.56	3.70	3.39	3.57	3.84
DJ Transportation Index ..	18.75	15.25	8.52	15.39	17.59	12.80	20.90
Class I Railroads ($Mil.)							
Net Income	5.00	347	226	514	569	554	904

* Excludes significant extraordinary items in these years.

Taxes. The heavy burden of taxes, especially payroll taxes, and its relation to operating revenues and to net income is shown in Table 22-6. In the three years 1967-1969 inclusive, net income averaged only about 5% of operating revenues while tax accruals approximated nearly 9%. In the three years 1970-1972, net income averaged only about 3% of operating revenues but tax accruals averaged about 8.6%. Payroll taxes represented somewhat over 54% of total tax accruals and about 85% of federal taxes. State and local taxes represented nearly 40% of all tax accruals. While the income taxes for railroads have traditionally been relatively low, the other taxes have been (and will continue to be) a heavy burden for railroads.

TABLE 22-6

Railroad Tax Accruals (Millions of Dollars)

Year	Operating Revenues	Net Income % of Oper. Rev.	Net Income $	Total Railway Tax Accruals $	Total Railway Tax Accruals % of Oper. Rev.	Total	Federal Taxes Payroll Total	Federal Taxes % of Total Accruals	% of Fed.	Inc.	Other State & Local	Foreign
1966	10,655	8.5	904	968	9.1	626	439	45.4	70.1	186	339	2.9
1967	10,366	5.3	554	910	8.8	544	477	52.4	87.7	66	363	2.8
1968	10,855	5.2	569	946	8.7	580	513	54.2	88.4	66	364	3.1
1969	11,450	4.5	514	1,029	9.0	640	533	51.8	83.3	106	386	3.5
1970	11,992	1.9	227	1,068	8.9	665	576	53.9	86.5	88	399	3.8
1971	12,689	2.8	347	1,088	8.6	686	578	53.1	84.3	106	398	4.0
1972	13,411	3.7	500	1,143	8.5	736	622	54.4	84.5	114	403	4.0

"**Other Income.**" For some railroads "other income" is a significant factor and quite important in the valuation of their securities. However, the analyst must first analyze railroad operations because, if these are not reasonably profitable, they may largely nullify the benefits of "other income." In some cases "other income" does cushion the effects of recession declines in railway operating income.[2]

Labor Factor. The labor factor, combined with extremely serious competition from trucks, the highly cyclical nature of operations, and heavy fixed charges, represents the major negative factor for the railroad industry. It is not widely appreciated that the railroads have managed to increase labor productivity to the extent that the number of employees has been reduced from about 1,400,000 in 1944 and at the end of World War II to 1,058,216 in 1953 and 526,091 in 1972, while at the same time carrying 785,000 million ton miles of freight in 1972 versus 737,246 million ton miles in 1944. Productivity of employees doubled as a result of large capital expenditures such as converting from steam to diesel, increasing average freight train speed, increasing the size of freight cars, etc.

However, the negative factor is that, with only half as many employees in 1972 as in 1946, compensation in 1972 was $6.4 billion or 46.4%

---

[2] Santa Fe Industries has substantial "other income" derived from oil and lumber operations. Burlington has substantial "other income" from timber, oil and gas, and real estate rentals. Southern Pacific has substantial "other income" from truck routes; pipelines; oil, gas, and mineral rights; and 3.85 million acres of nontransportation land. Union Pacific's "other income" is substantial from oil and gas profits. Therefore, of the seven better quality railroads, only the Chesapeake & Ohio, the Norfolk & Western, and Southern Pacific do not have relatively substantial "other income."

of gross revenues (52% including health and welfare)[3] and 48% higher than compensation of $4.0 billion at the end of World War II, when essentially wages accounted for slightly under 50% of gross revenues. Average earnings per year of employees were quadrupled from $3,218 in 1947 to $12,213 in 1972. All the benefits of the capital expenditures and higher production were absorbed by the employees with little or no benefit for securityholders, with the rate of return on investment of 1.75% in 1970 and 2.95% in 1971, versus 3.44% in 1947 and 4.31% in 1948. And related to the labor factor is the fact that payroll taxes in 1972 ($622 million) represent 54% of all tax accruals and compare to total net income of $500 million.

RAILROAD FINANCIAL ANALYSIS

The first part of this chapter examined the railroad industry as a whole and its problems. The investor must next examine the particular railroad company, whose security he contemplates purchasing, and compare its record and prospects with that of other railroads as well as with other investment opportunities.

Financial analysis of a railroad company centers on an examination of its income statement and its balance sheet, with main emphasis on the former. The uniform accounting system required of railroads offers relatively comparable financial and operating data. The great mass of data offered, due to ICC requirements, requires a high degree of selectivity on the part of the analyst in order to avoid unnecessary analysis of minute details. There are significant differences between industrial and railroad financial statements that the analyst must give special attention to.

Railroad Income Statement Analysis

A general form for analysis of railroad income statements is suggested in Table 22-7.[4]

"Revenues" in railroad accounting terminology always means gross income before deduction of expenses. "Income" on railroad statements is

---

[3] Labor factor, in cents per dollar of gross revenues, for 1970:

Labor (salaries and wages)	45.0
Health and welfare	2.2
Payroll taxes	4.8
Total	52.0

[4] Significant railroad income account data as percentages of gross revenues for selected railroads in 1965 are contained in Tables 22-12 and 22-13.

TABLE 22-7

Railroad Income Statement Analysis

Railroad Income Statement Items	Ratios	Analysis Ratios Company Ratio 100%	Industry Average 100%
Gross Operating Revenues		100%	100%
Passenger Revenues [5]	Ratio to Gross Operating Revenues		
Maintenance Expenses—Total	Ratio to Gross Operating Revenues		
Maintenance of Ways and Structures	Ratio to Gross Operating Revenues		
Maintenance of Equipment			
Transportation Expenses	Ratio to Gross Operating Revenues		
Total Operating Expenses—Operating	Ratio to Gross Operating Revenues		
Ratio	Ratio to Gross Operating Revenues		
Taxes: Federal Income; Ratio to Gross			
Revenues and	Ratio to Net Income Before Taxes		
Taxes: Other than Federal Income	Ratio to Gross Revenues		
Jt. Facility & Equipment Rentals	Ratio to Gross Revenues		
Net Railway Operating Income	Ratio to Gross Revenues		
Gross Profit Margin	Ratio to Gross Revenues		
Other Income Less Other Deductions *	Ratio to Gross Revenues		
Available for Fixed Charges	Ratio to Gross Revenues		
Fixed Charges	Ratio to Gross Revenues		
Times Fixed Charges Earned	Coverage		
Contingent Interest	Ratio to Gross Revenues		
Contingent Interest Plus Fixed Charges	Ratio to Gross Revenues		
Times Charges Overall Earned	Coverage		
Net Income	Ratio to Gross Revenues		
Preferred Dividend Requirements	Ratio to Gross Revenues		
Times Earned, Overall Including Preferred Dividends	Coverage		
Available for Common	Ratio to Gross Revenues		
Available Per Share of Common			
Depreciation	Ratio to Gross Revenues		
Depreciation as a % of Fixed Charges	Also Cash Flow to Fixed Charges		
Working Capital			
Coverage of Fixed Charges by Working Capital			

* "Other outside income" if significant must be charged.

synonymous with "net income" as used in industrial accounting. Also, while federal income taxes are deducted from net income on industrial company statements, they are included in the same category as property and excise taxes in railroad accounting. Federal income taxes, therefore, reduce reported net railway operating income, while they would not affect reported net operating income of an industrial company.

Railroad Operating Revenues—Traffic Analysis. The analysis of operating revenues should include an examination of the following: (1) sources of revenue and trends of major components of gross revenue; (2) trend of gross revenue—carloading and tonnage analysis; (3) strategic position of traffic; (4) trend of traffic between competing systems; (5) trend of traffic density—volume of ton miles carried by railroads; (6) length of average haul; (7) stability of traffic for an entire business cycle; (8) review of the

---

[5] The passenger deficit (total including allocated costs and "solely related") and the passenger operating ratio must be examined and their relative importance determined.

trend of revenues shown by analysis of operating revenues—analyst's estimate of future annual normal revenues, range of normal future revenues, and overall estimate of future revenues.

Gross Operating Revenues. The major divisions of gross operating revenues for all Class I railroads are listed in Table 22-8.

TABLE 22-8

Major Divisions of Gross Operating Revenues
All Class I Railroads

Divisions	1966 ($ Millions)	%	1967 ($ Millions)	%	1972 ($ Millions)	%
Freight	$ 9,281	87.10	$ 9,130	88.08	$12,571	93.74
Passenger*	544	5.11	485	4.68	257	1.92
Mail	304	2.85	264	2.55	94	0.70
Express	67	.63	61	.59	5	0.04
All Other	459	4.31	426	4.10	483	3.60
Total	$10,655	100.00%	$10,366	100.00%	$13,410	100.00%

* As of May 1, 1971, Amtrak assumed most long haul service.

Source: *Yearbook of Railroad Facts* (Washington, D.C.: Association of American Railroads), annual issues.

The profitability of the railroad will depend upon its freight traffic: the composition of the freight, the length of the haul, the traffic density, and the strategic position of the railroad in regard to its freight business. The analyst should study the territory served by the railroad to determine the course and the trends of actual and potential freight tonnage and revenues. Important factors to examine are the mineral resources in the area studied, the agricultural situation, the type and trend of industry and commerce in the area, the volume of traffic developed, population trends, and per capita income trends. A study of the major items carried by the railroad will give insight into its earning power, since those carrying higher freight rate commodities will often be in the most advantageous position. However, certain low-rate commodities such as coal, which can be handled with relatively low labor costs, may also be very profitable. Coal is by far the largest source of income for the Norfolk & Western and Chesapeake & Ohio railroads. The final result of intensive study of these factors should be a projection of railroad revenues by major categories and in total.

Trend of Revenues. The trend of revenues over a period of years should be studied in relationship to the trend of the railroad industry as a whole, the trend of the region, competing roads within the region, and competing modes of transportation such as motor carriers and barge lines.

Carloading analysis. Weekly figures are available on freight carloadings, but it should be remembered that these are quantitative, not qualitative, figures. For any particular railroad, the analyst can estimate the profitability at different levels of freight volume.

Tonnage analysis. Figures for a qualitative as well as quantitative analysis are provided in "Freight Commodity Loading Statistics," a report published by the ICC. Railway freight tonnage figures for each railroad are segregated in these reports into approximately 160 classes. The trend of revenues should be studied for at least one business cycle *for the major items.* A minimum of 10 years should be reviewed, but the cyclical nature of the industry must be considered (for example, 1957-1958, 1961, 1967, and 1970).

Strategic Position of Traffic. The strategic position of the traffic carried is of great importance to the railroad. If the railroad originates traffic, it is in a much stronger position than if it largely handles traffic originated on other lines. If traffic originates on the other lines but must terminate on the line in question, this is also a favorable factor. It is advisable to calculate the percentage of total traffic originated and also the percentage of traffic received from other roads that terminates in its territory.

Trend of Traffic Density. In general, the greater the density of traffic, the greater the net profit. In this connection, fairly diversified traffic is desirable, and it should be determined that the major source of traffic is relatively stable and growing. Roads that connect with important metropolitan areas and traverse densely populated areas generally have a greater traffic density.

Freight traffic density is measured by the net revenue ton miles per mile of road, and passenger density is measured by the number of revenue passenger miles carried per mile of line. Railroads usually have a heavy debt secured by mortgages placed on particular sections of the road. When specific bond issues are being analyzed, analysts must determine the net revenue ton miles per mile of road for the section or division covered by the mortgage, as this indicates the protection available for each dollar of debt.

Ton Miles per Dollar of Debt. The ton miles per dollar of mortgage debt is an important ratio for the section of a railroad covered by a specific mortgage (see Table 22-9). The ratio should generally be at least 40. If it is below 20, charges are usually not being covered on that section of line. Generally, the heavier the traffic density, the more advantageous for the road and for the securityholder. However, it should be noted that a road with reasonable freight traffic density derived from high-rate traffic may be as productive as a road with heavy freight traffic density derived from heavy low-grade freight that is costly to handle.[6]

Other factors must be taken into consideration. For example, if the expense ratio of the railroad is unusually high, the railroad may be in difficulty even if the figure of net ton miles per dollar of debt is up to 100. Some bond analysts calculate the ton miles per dollar of debt required to support adequately a dollar of debt on a particular railroad or a particular division on which the lien rests.

Length of Average Haul. Other things being equal, the longer the average haul for freight carried, the less expensive (on an average per-mile basis) it is to move and the more profitable it is to the railroad. Terminal expenses are major expenses because of high wage costs and the amount of labor costs involved; therefore, the longer the haul, the more these expenses can be allocated on a per-mile basis.[7] The railroads are at a distinct cost disadvantage for hauls of less than 400 miles in competition with motor carriers.

TABLE 22-9
Pertinent Railway Statistics and Ratios, All U.S. Railroads

	1960	1970	1972
Revenue Car Loadings	$ 30,441,415	$ 27,160,247	$ 26,061,246
Revenue Ton Miles (000)	$572,309,000	$764,809,000	$778,137,000
Average Haul—All Ry. Systems	442	493	512
Average Freight Car Capacity (Tons)	55.4	67.1	69.5
Tons Per Car Orig.	44.4	54.9	56.5
Av. Rev. Per Ton	$6.26	$7.08	$8.35
Av. Rev. Per Ton Mile (¢)	1.403	1.428	1.616

Source: *Yearbook of Railroad Facts* (Washington, D.C.: Association of American Railroads), annual issues, and "Statistics of Railroads in the U.S."

Railway Operating Expenses. The major ICC classifications of operating expenses are as follows: (1) total maintenance, (2) maintenance of ways

---

[6] Coal roads, such as Norfolk & Western and Chesapeake & Ohio, are exceptions.
[7] Long haul railroads are Southern Pacific, Union Pacific, and Atchison, Topeka & Sante Fe.

and structures, (3) maintenance of equipment, (4) traffic expenses, (5) transportation expenses, (6) miscellaneous operations (expenses), and (7) general expenses.

Maintenance Expenses. The two major components of maintenance expenses are (1) maintenance of ways and structures and (2) maintenance of equipment. The post-World War II record of maintenance expenditures in total dollar amount and as a percentage of gross operating revenues are presented in Table 22-10. The stability of these expenditures as a percentage of gross revenues should be noted as well as the gradual reduction in these expenses as a percentage of gross revenues. This is particularly significant in terms of the high level of physical maintenance in recent years and the increased costs of labor and modernization. By reducing the percentage of total maintenance expenses by 3% for 1966 versus the 1946-1950 average (32.53% to 29.58%), the savings from the reduction amounted to $320 million. The actual net income of Class I railroads in 1966 would have

TABLE 22-10

Gross Operating Revenues and Maintenance Expenditures
All Class I Railroads

Year	Gross Operating Revenues	Total Maintenance		Maintenance of Ways and Structures		Maintenance of Equipment	
		($ Billions)	% of Gross Revenues	($ Billions)	% of Gross Revenues	($ Billions)	% of Gross Revenues
1946-50 Av.	$ 8.81	2.87	32.53	1.26	14.26	1.61	18.27
1951	10.39	3.42	32.95	1.48	14.23	1.95	18.72
1952	10.58	3.47	32.80	1.52	14.36	1.95	18.46
1953	10.06	3.57	33.44	1.58	14.85	1.98	18.59
1954	9.37	3.08	32.89	1.35	14.43	1.73	18.46
1955	10 11	3.18	31.42	1.39	13.73	1.79	17.69
1956	10.55	3.30	31.25	1.40	13.72	1.89	17.94
1957	10.49	3.34	31.87	1.43	13.64	1.91	18.23
1958	9.56	2.94	30.78	1.22	12.79	1.72	17.99
1959	9.83	3.03	30.88	1.24	12.59	1.80	18.30
1960	9.51	2.95	31.03	1.19	12.53	1.76	18.50
1961	9.19	2.80	30.48	1.12	12.16	1.68	18.32
1962	9.44	2.90	30.07	1.15	12.23	1.74	18.47
1963	9.56	2.91	30.49	1.18	12.37	1.73	18.12
1964	9.86	2.99	30.33	1.23	12.44	1.76	17.89
1965	10.21	3.01	29.49	1.24	12.11	1.77	17.39
1966	10.65	3.15	29.53	1.30	12.23	1.84	17.30
1967	10.37	3.16	30.47	1.29	12.44	1.87	18.03
1968	10.86	3.32	30.57	1.41	12.98	1.91	17.59
1969	11.45	3.50	30.57	1.50	13.10	2.00	17.47
1970	11.99	3.78	31.53	1.61	13.43	2.17	18.10
1971	12.69	4.17	32.86	1.81	14.26	2.36	18.60
1972	13.41	4.31	32.14	1.92	14.32	2.39	17.82

Source: *Yearbook of Railroad Facts* (Washington, D.C.: Association of American Railroads), annual issues, and *Transport Economics—Monthly Comment,* issued monthly by the ICC.

been $582 million instead of the reported $904 million if the percentage had not been reduced. The savings for the 1½% reduction in 1966 versus 1960 was $160 million so that net income for 1966 would have been $742 versus the $904 million actually reported. The percentage was 30.57 in 1968.

In general, the rougher the terrain and the more severe the climate, the higher the maintenance expenses. Of course, there can be undermaintenance or overmaintenance. The investor should examine the trend over the years. Undermaintenance is a factor in estimating future income. Expenditures over a complete business cycle should be analyzed to determine trends and the adequacy of maintenance. Inadequate maintenance is common in depression and recession years; therefore, these business years should be compared with prosperous years.

Maintenance of ways and structures. Maintenance of ways and structures includes repairs of tracks, roadway, tunnels, bridges, stations, shops, buildings, machinery, tools, fences, frogs, switches, culverts, and ballasting. It also includes the depreciation charges against these items.

In general, a railroad should spend a minimum of 13-15% of its gross operating income in maintenance of ways and structures, although the needs will vary somewhat with traffic density and terrain. Depreciation should be approximately 1% per year of the net book value of the assets subject to depreciation, that is, the ways and structures.

Maintenance of equipment. There are two tests for the adequacy of maintenance expenses for equipment: (1) the age and the condition of the equipment, including the percentage of equipment that is unserviceable; (2) the average expenditures for each item of equipment per year and per mile operated.

There is a definite relationship between traffic density and maintenance of equipment expenditures. The denser the traffic, the more equipment required and the heavier the use it gets. An amount of approximately $120 per freight car and $1,500 per passenger car is satisfactory.

It is necessary to trace equipment maintenance expenditures over the period of a business cycle. As a rule-of-thumb guide, maintenance of equipment should represent about 17-19% of gross income. However, if one road is handling only traffic that yields a high revenue per ton, the equipment will not be worked as hard as another handling low-value goods but earning the same gross operating revenues per mile of road. Postponement of necessary expenditures is quickly revealed in the figures of unserviceable equipment.

Traffic Expenses. Included in this category are salaries and wages paid by the road for those who are directly in charge of traffic (such as passenger agents, freight agents, and officers directly in charge of traffic), payments to outside agents handling advertising, and payments for traffic handled by other forms of transportation for the railroad.

These items vary little with amounts of traffic. The traffic expenses are such a small part of total expenses (usually less than 1%) that *analysts generally include them in transportation expenses.*

Transportation Expenses. Transportation expenses include payments made in actually handling traffic; wages of conductors, engineers, station employees, yardmen, and trainmen; fuel and supplies for trains and locomotives; expenses of train dispatchers; telegraph and telephone expenses; and certain other expenses such as the net cost of operating joint yard stations.

Transportation expenses cannot be manipulated by the management as easily as maintenance expenses, since wages are relatively more fixed and fuel prices change according to economic conditions. Transportation expenses also vary with traffic density. For these reasons, transportation expenses frequently have come to mean all operating expenses except maintenance expenses.

For a long period of time, transportation expenses for all Class I railroads have averaged between 38% and 42% of gross revenues. The figure for 1966 was 38.8%; for 1967, 40.38%; for 1968, 40.4%; for 1970, 40.64%; for 1971, 38.52%; and for 1972, 38.8%.

Operating Ratio. The operating ratio is the ratio of operating expenses to operating revenue and consists largely of transportation expenses plus maintenance expenses. It is by far the most important ratio used in railroad analysis. But taken by itself as an indication of operating efficiency, the operating ratio may give a misleading picture, especially if maintenance is being skimped. Lease rentals, together with maintenance policy, may cause wide differences in operating ratios.

The average operating ratios for Class I railroads are shown in Table 22-11 on page 585.

In general, the better railroads will have lower operating ratios than the average. A railroad may have a somewhat higher ratio but have such a relatively low debt in its capitalization that it still will provide a satisfactory coverage of its fixed charges. Therefore, in analyzing a railroad's operating ratios, its fixed charge coverage should be examined simultaneously.

"Other Income." Most railroads derive modest "other income" from interest on their portfolios of short-term government bonds, miscellaneous real estate sales, and dividends on small holdings of stock in other railroads

TABLE 22-11

Average Operating Ratios—Class I Railroads

1954 — 80.2*	1961 — 81.4*	1967 — 79.1
1955 — 75.6	1962 — 78.9	1968 — 79.0
1956 — 77.1	1963 — 78.1	1969 — 79.2
1957 — 78.5	1964†— 77.7	1970 — 80.6*
1958 — 82.2*	1964†— 78.0	1971 — 79.3
1959 — 77.7	1965 — 77.8	1972 — 78.7
1960 — 78.5	1966 — 76.2	

* Business recessions. 1967 was a mini-recession year.

† Class I railroads before 1964, revenues of at least $3 million; beginning 1964, at least $5 million.

(usually acquired for strategic purposes). In numerous instances such income looms large in relation to income derived from railway operations. But in spite of the diversification trend, earnings from railroad operations will constitute the bulk of earnings for most railroads for some time to come. For a few, other income will still be highly significant.

Available for Fixed Charges. The amount available for fixed charges consists of (1) net railway operating income plus (2) other income less other deductions. This is the amount available for all securityholders, and it provides the numerator in calculating the number of times fixed charges are earned as published in ICC statistics. Chapter 9 discussed what should be included in fixed charges and suggested that not only interest on the debt but also contractual lease agreement payments should be considered.

For all Class I railroads the amount available for fixed charges in recent years has averaged about 12.3% of gross operating revenues. The range was from actual deficits to highs for certain roads of 21%, 24%, and 36%.

Times Fixed Charges Earned. The primary test for bonds is the number of times fixed charges are earned. It is calculated by dividing the amount available for fixed charges by the fixed charges. There is a wide range for the number of times fixed charges are earned (see Tables 22-12 and 22-13). The industry average in years of good business is around 3.1x. As with other bonds, the test is also the number of times fixed charges have been earned in recession years—the stability or lack of stability of the figures.

TABLE 22-12

Earnings Record of Class I Carriers, 1948-1972 (Millions of Dollars)

Year	Oper- ating Reve- nues	Avail. for Fixed Charges	Fixed Charges	Fixed Charges Times Earned	Net Income	Cash Divi- dends	Ratios				Gross Profit Margi a
							Mainte- nance	Trans- porta- tion	Oper- ating	Payroll	
1972	13,411	1,106	606	1.82x	500	408	32.1%	38.8%	78.7%	46.9%	7.1%
1971	12,689	985	601	1.64x	354	385	32.9	38.5	79.3	46.4	6.4
1970	11,992	846	589	1.44x	227	421	30.5	40.6	80.6	47.6	4.8
1969	11,450	1,066	521	2.05x	514	487	30.6	40.1	79.2	46.8	6.6
1968	10,855	1,087	484	2.25x	569	515	30.6	40.1	79.0	47.1	6.9
1967	10,366	1,050	460	2.28x	554	503	30.5	40.4	79.1	47.6	7.2
1966	10,655	1.376	426	3.21x	904	499	29.5	38.8	76.2	45.8	11.6
1965	10,208	1,257	401	3.14x	815	471	29.5	39.4	76.9	47.0	11.0
1964	9,778	1,110	376	2.95x	694	457	30.3	39.8	78.5	48.0	9.7
1963	9,560	1,062	368	2.89x	651	379	30.5	39.5	77.9	48.4	10.7
1962	9,439	980	367	2.67x	571	366	30.7	39.8	78.6	49.4	9.3
1961	9,189	798	369	2.16x	382	358	30.5	40.4	79.2	50.3	8.5
1960	9,514	868	374	2.32x	445	385	31.0	40.3	79.5	51.4	8.3
1959	9,826	1,005	375	2.68x	578	403	30.9	39.6	78.4	50.7	10.4
1958	9,564	1,035	380	2.72x	602	372	30.8	40.1	78.9	51.5	10.5
1957	10,506	1,160	369	3.14x	740	426	31.8	39.0	78.4	51.0	11.9
1956	10,551	1,291	364	3.55x	876	432	31.3	38.3	76.8	50.5	13.8
1955	10,107	1,341	367	3.66x	921	447	31.4	37.3	75.6	49.4	15.3
1954	9,370	1,099	382	2.88x	682	374	32.9	38.7	78.8	49.4	11.7
1953	10,664	1,356	405	3.35x	903	382	33.4	36.3	76.3	47.5	15.4
1952	10,581	1,316	442	2.98x	825	338	32.8	36.9	76.1	47.9	16.0
1951	10,391	1,159	420	2.76x	693	329	33.0	38.3	77.4	48.2	14.5
1950	9,473	1,258	428	2.94x	784	312	31.6	36.9	74.5	46.2	17.3
1949	8,580	901	421	2.14x	438	252	33.7	39.8	80.3	48.9	11.1
1948	9,672	1,172	425	2.76x	698	289	31.6	39.5	77.3	46.9	14.9

a—Percentage of Gross Revenues carried through to Net Railway Operating Income before Federal income tax
r—Revised 1964 to date includes 75 Class I roads; 1963 and prior years include the 103 to 106 roads former classified as Class I prior to Jan. 1, 1965. Note the horizontal trend of operating revenues.

Contingent Interest. Only some of the 25 railroads that *were not re- organized* after 1929 have income bonds whose interest is contingent (pay- able if earned). But of the 23 railroads that *were reorganized since 1929,* 18 have income bonds with contingent interest. Any railroad of investment quality will earn its contingent charges *plus* its fixed charges by a satisfactory margin of safety.

Net Income. This is the income available after taxes for all stockholders, both preferred and common. In years of good business for all Class I rail- roads, net income has averaged about 8% of gross revenues. Again there is a wide range. For the better roads it has ranged between 12% and 17%, and 2 railroads show very high percentages of 24.2% and 32.5%. The

TABLE 22-13

Railroad Condensed Income Account (Millions of Dollars)

	1955	1961	1966	1970	1972
Total operating revenues	10,106	9,189	10,655	11,992	13,411
Freight	8,538	7,739	9,281	10,922	12,572
Passenger	743	625	544	420	257
Mail	287	342	304	161	94
Express	118	141	67	22	5
All other revenues	420	342	459	466	482
Total operating expenses	7,646	7,274	8,118	9,660	10,550
Maintenance of way	1,387	1,118	1,304	1,613	1,918
Maintenance of equipment	1,788	1,683	1,844	2,165	2,393
Traffic	235	247	265	285	292
Transportation	3,770	3,711	4,139	4,873	5,209
Miscellaneous	108	77	66	46	12
General	357	438	500	678	727
Total tax accruals	1,080	991	968	1,069	1,143
Payroll taxes	284	364	439	576	622
Federal income taxes	414	242	186	88	114
All other taxes	382	385	343	404	407
Equipment and jt. fac. rents	252	386	523	777	883
Net railway operating income ...	1,128	538	1,046	486	835
Rate of return	4.22%	1.97%	3.90%	1.73%	2.95%
Other income	271	322	399	482	395
Miscellaneous deductions	57	62	78	122	101
Rents for leased roads	60	48	60	62	62
Interest deduction	311	317	360	522	539
Amortization of discount	3	4	5	5	5
Contingent interest	40	47	38	30	24
Ordinary income	927	382	904	227	500

industry figures were only 5.34% for 1967, 5.46% for 1968, and 1.89% for 1970.

Preferred Dividend Requirements. Only 10 of the 25 railroads that were not reorganized after 1929 have preferred stock outstanding, and the preferred dividend requirement is not significant for these roads. For some of the other roads the requirement is as high as 3% of gross revenues and therefore of some significance. For all Class I railroads it averages less than ½ of 1% of gross income.

The protection for preferred stock is measured by the number of times the preferred dividends *plus* all prior charges are earned, that is, the amount available for fixed charges divided by preferred dividends *plus* all prior charges. For most roads with preferred stock, the coverage is only slightly below the coverage for fixed charges.

Available for Common. This is the percent of gross income after taxes and all prior charges including preferred dividends that is available for the common stock. In good years it has averaged about 8% for all Class I railroads. This is a very important figure for the common stock because it indicates the margin of safety for the common stock—how much all expenses and prior charges would need to shrink before there was nothing left for the common stock from the gross revenues.

Available per Share of Common. As with all corporations, this figure is the most important item for common shareholders. The investor must analyze the record and trend over a period of years and make projections for five to six years in the future. The ratio of "other income" is sometimes significant.

Depreciation. This item as a percentage of gross revenues has been particularly significant in recent years after liberalized depreciation was allowed under the 1954 Code and after the reasonable "useful" life of assets, especially equipment, was reduced in the 1962 guidelines. The high depreciation was one of the more significant factors in the reduction of federal income taxes from $242 million in 1961 to $88 million in 1970 and $114 million in 1972. This item has in recent years averaged around 7-8% of gross revenues, or about the same as the amount available for the common stock. Because it is a tax deductible expense, the effect on net income available for the common stock is readily apparent. The investment credit has also been an important plus.

Depreciation as a Percentage of Fixed Charges. Depreciation and net income after taxes are the two major components of cash flow, and of course cash flow provides a margin of safety for fixed charges and debt amortization including serial reduction of equipment debts. For all Class I railroads, depreciation in recent years of good business has ranged between 17.5% and 18.5% of fixed charges. For certain railroads it has been extremely high: Pittsburgh & Lake Erie, 43.4%; Atchison, Topeka & Santa Fe, 60.9%; St. Louis & Southwestern, 83.4%; and Baltimore & Ohio, 92.97%.

Railroad Balance Sheet Analysis

A review of the fluctuations and trends of revenues, costs, and profits (especially the number of times fixed charges are earned, the earnings per share, and the dividends received) as discussed in reference to railroad income statement analysis ordinarily provides a good indication of the prospective quality of a railroad security. However, balance sheet analysis will also provide necessary and useful information.

Working Capital. Railroads have modest working capital requirements because receivables are short term and inventories in the usual sense are not a factor as long as operations are profitable. Working capital for all Class I railroads in recent years has averaged 6-7% of gross revenues, but the company-to-company range has been broad. Fixed charges must be paid out of working capital. In recent years working capital has averaged 1.6x to 2x fixed charges for Class I railroads, but again a wide range is present. The acid-test ratio (current assets less inventories) is used by the Association of American Railways in calculating net working capital. Net working capital has been declining for years as shown in Table 22-14.

TABLE 22-14

Net Working Capital Class I Railroads—January 1, 1972
(Aggregates in Millions of Dollars)

	1955	1963	1966	1969	1972
United States	934	828	477	56	21
Eastern District	263	60	67 def.	140 def.	108 def.
Southern District	191	147	54	120	67
Western District	480	621	356	76	62

Property Account. The major items on the asset side of a railroad balance sheet are investments in roadways and equipment. These items should be analyzed to determine the new equipment added as well as the depreciation charged. There has been phenomenal modernization and improvement for the railroad industry as a whole since 1940, but especially since the end of World War II. The bulk of new capital funds in the railroad industry has gone into equipment, stimulated since 1962 by the "investment credit."

Some analysts question whether railroads can maintain the present volume of capital expenditures, which is needed to exploit and accelerate traffic gains registered in recent years. Railroad capital expenditures had peaks of $1.95 billion, $1.52 billion, and $1.51 billion in 1966, 1967, and 1969, but were down to $1.35 billion and $1.18 billion in 1970 and 1971 and $1.22 billion in 1972. Expenditures for equipment represent about 70% of capital expenditures.

The railroads expanded real estate and other investment activities during the 1960s, and these activities have contributed to railroad income. One important development was the exploitation of downtown air rights in larger cities. Many analysts consider outside investments to be of prime importance in projecting the future of numerous railroads.

Capital Structure Proportions. All Class I railroads have acquired approximately 39% of their funds by means of debt financing and 61% by means of equity financing. Railroad debt has been declining since the 1930s. Generally, debt for an individual railroad should not exceed 40% of total capitalization, and the remaining 60% should consist of preferred stock, capital stock, and surplus. Analysts compute ratios with common at market.

The amount of debt that a railroad can bear is of course determined by the traffic and the level of earnings and, as previously discussed, is measured in terms of the times fixed charges are earned and the adequacy of cash flow to meet debt amortization requirements. The payments required by past indebtedness still pose a serious problem, causing receiverships for some railroads. The biggest railroad to be forced into receivership is the Penn-Central (Pennsylvania Railroad-New York Central).

THE TRUCKING INDUSTRY

The trucking industry (motor freight carrier industry) has two major divisions: private and for hire. The private division comprises all those businesses that provide their own transportation through owned or leased lines. The for-hire division is subdivided into interstate, intrastate, and local. Interstate truckers subdivide further into contract and common carriers, with the former operating under continuing contracts with specific stoppers. Both common and contract truckers are subject to the ICC.

For investment purposes we are concerned with publicly owned interstate ("intercity") common carriers. ICC regulations cover rates, routes, classes of commodities carried, accounting practices, finances, mergers, and acquisitions. ICC requires certificates of necessity that designate the specific routes for each carrier.

There are 1,500 Class I [8] intercity common carriers including the 1,500 truckers subject to ICC regulations. Of these, there were about 55 publicly owned in 1973 which had gross revenues from $30 to $500 million. Standard & Poor in its *Basic Analysis—Trucking* presented financial data for 17 of these companies and included 10 in its composite industry data table and its Trucking Group Stock Index. These carriers enjoy the economies of large-scale operations, modern management techniques, and computer controls,

---

[8] Class I —annual revenues of $1 million or over.
   Class II —annual revenues of $300,000 to $1,000,000. (About 2, 000 carriers)
   Class III—annual revenues under $300,000. (About 11,000 carriers)

thereby benefiting from the fact that rates established by the ICC are based on the *average* costs, including the less efficient truckers. However, even among the 55 large firms or the 17 largest covered by Standard & Poor, there have been wide variances in profitability.

The Industry Record in Brief

In the overall period 1960-1973, the trucking industry showed about the same growth record as real GNP. Reflecting its cyclical nature, it enjoyed somewhat higher growth in the 1962-1965 period and then, because of the decline in the 1969-1970 recession, it experienced a somewhat slower growth in the 1967-1970 years. In accordance with its cyclical nature, the trucking industry should continue to post a satisfactory growth record in the 1970s reflecting, among other factors, the continued geographical dispersion of American industry.

Gross operating revenues of the regulated trucking industry in 1960 were $7.2 billion versus railroad freight revenues of $8.0 billion. However, by 1963 truck revenues slightly exceeded railroad freight revenues. In 1972 revenues of regulated truckers were $16.7 billion, or 37% higher than railroad freight revenues of $12.2 billion. In the period 1960-1971 inclusive, revenues of Class I and Class II motor carriers of property more than doubled from $5.8 to $13.7 billion; tonnage carried rose 70%. Revenue ton miles increased 21% in 1960-1970 inclusive, and increased 15% in 1965-1970 inclusive. Using 1957-1959 as an index base equal to 100, by the beginning of the 1970s the major classifications of motor carrier freight showed the following indexes:

Refrigerated Products	253	Agricultural Commodities	166
Heavy Machinery	243	Refrigerated Liquid Products	165
Motor Vehicles	208	Household Goods	145
Building Materials	181	General Freight	172
Liquid Petroleum Products	178	All Other	197

In 1960 regulated motor carriers received 42% of intercity transportation revenues compared to 49% for the railroads. But by 1963 the truckers' share represented 51% compared to only 41% for the railroads. It is forecast that by 1980 the truckers' share will rise to 61% and the railroads' share will decline to 21%. Furthermore, the truckers have taken the cream of the traffic—the higher rated and the less-than-truckload (and less-than-carload) traffic. In fact, the latter traffic has virtually been taken over by the truckers so that competition for this business is essentially only among the truckers themselves.

The Industry Income Account [9]

We have noted that gross revenues of 15,000 ICC regulated carriers (Classes I, II, and III) rose from $7.2 billion in 1960 to $16.7 billion in 1971. The largest truckers in 1973—the 55 which are publicly owned—had revenues ranging from $30 to $500 million.[10]

Standard & Poor's publishes corporate industry data (see Table 22-15) expressed in terms of its 10-company Group Stock Index for trucking companies, with a base of 1941-43 = 10. In these terms industry sales in 1969 were at 99, or about 10 times the 1941-43 base; and in 1971 industry sales were 13% above the 1969 level. The year 1971 was the first year of recovery after the 1970 recession.

As is the case with railroads, operating expenses represent a very high percentage of revenues, ranging from 93.3% to 96.3%. Therefore, the complementary operating profit margins are low, ranging between 3.7% and 6.7%. The net income percentage was only 1.27% in the recession year of 1970, and then rose to 3.72% in the first recovery year of 1971. The two major factors that produced these results are regulated rates and total labor costs including benefits which absorb nearly 60% of revenues. As wages have risen faster than labor productivity, the truckers have sought and obtained ICC authority to raise rates. The truckers' strong union has obtained periodic wage increases since 1960, far exceeding most other

---

[9] In 1971 the very largest truckers, with gross revenues of over $100 million, had the following revenues:

	Gross Revenues	Net Income
Consolidated Freightways	$480 million	$20.55 million
Roadway Express	305 million	18.13 million
Yellow Freight System	216 million	12.95 million
McLean Trucking	170 million	6.03 million
I.I.N.E.-DC, Inc.	154 million	3.83 million
Transson Lines	110 million	4.96 million
Associated Transport	134 million	0.28 million
Spector Industries	115 million	0.19 million

[10] The operating expense as a percentage of operating revenues for Class I and Class II carriers for selected years is as follows:

	1971	Recession 1970	1968	1965	1962
Transportation	43.0	43.5	44.3	49.4	49.4
Terminal	19.5	19.9	19.0	13.0	12.8
Equipment-Maintenance ..	8.7	9.1	8.8	9.3	9.9
Administration & General .	5.5	5.7	5.3	6.1	6.2
Operating Taxes & Licenses	6.3	6.8	6.7	6.1	6.4
Depreciation	3.8	4.3	4.1	3.9	4.0
Traffic	2.9	2.9	3.0	3.0	2.9
Operating Ratio	93.3	96.2	94.9	94.7	95.8

TABLE 22-15

Corporate Industry Data for Ten Companies, 1969-1971
Expressed in Terms of S&P Group Stock Price Index—Trucking Companies 1941-1943 = 10

		1969	1970	1971
Sales		99.00	96.90	113.61
Operating Income		10.29	8.67	13.91
Profit Margins %		10.39%	8.95%	12.24%
Depreciation		4.17	4.52	4.47
Taxes		2.41	1.50	4.02
Earnings		2.15	1.27	3.72
Dividend		0.85	0.67	0.74
Earnings as a % of Sales		2.17%	1.31%	3.27%
Dividend as a % of Earnings		39.53%	52.76%	19.89%
Price (Stock) 1941-43 = 10	High	52.52	41.96	76.27
	Low	34.46	23.28	41.58
Price Earnings Ratios	High	24.43	33.04	20.50
	Low	16.03	18.33	11.18
Dividend Yield	High	2.47%	2.88%	1.78%
	Low	1.62%	1.60%	0.97%
Bank Value		13.87	14.05	16.49
Return on Equity %		15.50%	9.04%	22.56%
Working Capital		2.95	3.03	3.89
Capital Expenditures		9.92	6.86	6.06

industries. In fact, the three-year contract signed with the industry in 1970 called for a 44% increase in wages over the three-year period.

The second major classification of expenses after direct wage costs are terminal costs, which absorb about 19% of revenues. Maintenance costs absorb another 9% of revenues; operating taxes and licenses absorb 7%.

More important than the rate of net income on sales is the rate of return on total capital invested and on net worth. A strong positive factor for the truckers is the high turnover of capital, 3.4x compared to only 1.8x for "all manufacturing companies" and a mere 0.4% for railroads. The ratio of net income to sales is low for both railroads and trucks. The rate of return on total capital invested for railroads has not been as high as 3% since 1966 or as high as 4% since 1955; it was 1.73% in the recession year of 1970. Return on equity has also been unsatisfactory. However, the high capital turnover for the truckers permits a relatively low rate of return on sales to be translated into a satisfactory rate of return on total capital and on equity except in recessions.

In 1970 truckers' revenues were 5x net worth but, because of the recession, return on equity was only 6.5% (down from 9.2% in 1969). This figure, however, was still far better than the dismal 1.73% on total investment for the railroads. In normal years the trucking industry rate of return on equity averages around 10% but is considerably higher (as much as 20%) for the largest, most efficient truckers.

Another favorable factor is the very low requirement for working capital, a condition similar to that for electric utilities. Truckers generally operate with a working capital sufficient for only 18 to 20 days of cash operating expenses and a current ratio of only 1.1 to 1. This ratio, which excludes current maturities on long-term debt from current liabilities, is calculated in accordance with ICC accounting procedures. The cash throw-off to total funded debt measures the total funded debt that could be paid off in one year if all cash throw-off were used for this purpose. In 1970 it was 48% for Class I and Class II truckers combined.

Accounting Practices in the Industry

The analyst, for comparative analysis, must determine the accounting policies of the carrier. In reporting to stockholders, truckers may report either according to AICPA principles or in accordance with ICC procedures. Under AICPA principles, tax reductions resulting from accelerated tax depreciation and tax credits must be recorded as a deferred federal income tax liability charged to net income. But under ICC procedures this tax liability is not recognized, and tax reduction (savings) flows through to net income. Truckers may *expense* tires and tubes, as well as other prepaid expenses incurred, or may capitalize them and charge them off during their useful life. The method used will affect the current ratio. Finally, the reported financial condition of the carrier will reflect the proportion of assets that are owned versus leased.

Summarized Analysis of a Trucking Company

The analyst should determine the economics of the area served, as well as the past and prospective growth trends of the carrier. He should determine the nature of routes used and the character of restrictions, types of highways, and tax levies. The past financial record should then be analyzed and compared to industry norms and trends in respect to major ratios and items discussed above.[11] Management's record in respect to the industry norms and management's policies toward expenses and mergers and acquisitions should be determined. Finally, the analyst should project revenues and earnings for the next five years. He should recognize the cyclical nature of the industry and be especially alert to opportunities in periods of depressed stock markets, discounting general economic recessions.

THE AIR TRANSPORT INDUSTRY

The air transport industry is regulated by the Civil Aeronautics Board (CAB) which has authority over routes, schedules, rates, services, safety standards, accounting, mergers and acquisitions, and intercorporate agreements. Most industry revenues are generated by four highly competitive CAB certified route carriers. In addition, there are supplemental carriers which generate less than 4% of total industry revenues. Of the certified route carriers, the domestic route carriers plus Pan-American Domestic own about 75% of industry assets and generate 67% of the revenues.[12] The international and territorial operators generate 21% of revenues; local service carriers, 8%; and other certified route carriers, 4%. Three all-cargo carriers (Airlift, Flying Tiger, and Seaboard) generated $252 million operating revenues in 1971. Flying Tiger accounts for most of the revenues and earnings. There have been numerous mergers in the past, but at this writing it does not appear that CAB policy will approve mergers except in the case of dire financial straits of at least one of the partners to the merger.

Industry Balance Sheet

Industry assets as of June 31, 1971, totaled about $13 billion, 82% of which was flight equipment and 11%, building and ground equipment. Operating revenues including supplemental carriers for CAB fiscal year 1971 totaled $9.8 billion, providing a turnover of invested capital of only 75% (somewhat above that for railroads but less than half that for "all manufacturing companies" and only about one fifth that for truckers). Total assets had risen from $2.8 billion in 1963 and revenues from $3 billion.

---

[11] The analyst should always utilize the S&P *Basic Analysis—Truckers* as a major source of comparative data and compare the carrier he is analyzing to industry leaders such as Consolidated Freightways.

[12] About two thirds of industry revenues are generated by the 12 major trunk lines shown below, in millions, for 1971. Delta has for years posted the best industry record.

United	$1,506	Delta	$653	Braniff	$233
American	1,073	Continental	306	Northwest	208
Eastern	822	Western	287	Northeast	117
TWA	791	National	266	Pan-Am Domestic	93

Total capitalization in 1971 was \$9.5 billion, consisting of 67% long-term debt and 33% equity—about the same as in 1963. However, in January, 1966, after several quite profitable years, the debt percentage had been only 54% and the equity 46%. The negative side of the relatively high debt is somewhat modified by the fact that 22% of the debt is convertible. The convertibles, of course, pose the problem of equity earnings dilution. About 30% of the long-term debt is held by banks; 36%, by insurance companies.

Working capital averaged about 9% of total assets from 1961-1965 and was 8% in 1965. It rose to 19% of assets in 1967, but then fell to 7% in 1971. The current ratio of the industry is very low—at about 1.1 to 1.

Industry Growth Record and Income Account

The airline industry has experienced an excellent growth record in the years 1948-1973. In the period 1948-1972 inclusive, total available seat miles have multiplied about 20 times, total assets 18 times, revenue passenger miles and passenger revenues about 16 to 17 times, and gross operating revenues about 15 times. In the same period GNP multiplied about 4 times.

However, in spite of this excellent growth of revenues which also tripled in 1961-1970 inclusive, the net income of the airlines has proved to be highly cyclical. For example, it showed a loss in the 1961 recession and declined from a peak of \$428 million in 1966 and \$415 million in 1967 to a nominal \$53 million in 1969. It again recorded a loss of \$200 million in 1970 and a meager profit of \$15 million in 1971. In the latter year the trunk lines had a total loss of \$32 million.

The major factors which have caused the cyclical volatility of earnings have been the high degree of leverage in operations and financial structure, the direct effect on revenues of economic recessions, the tendency in certain periods to overexpand capacity relative to demand, and the relatively narrow margin between break-even load factors and a load factor which is reasonably attainable in years of good business if capacity has not been increased too rapidly. The use of jet fleets has made lower load factors profitable, especially with the introduction of jumbo jets.

Load Factor and Net Income

A highly important factor in the profitability of airlines is the ratio of passenger revenue seats to available capacity. The expansion of the jet fleets in the 1960s reduced the break-even load factor from around 55% to about 50-51% in 1970 (see Table 22-16). Available seat miles capacity rose from 65 million to 265 million in 1970. It can be noted from this that, as the load factor increased from 1963 to 1965, net income increased and the rate of return on equity rose from a loss in 1961 to 7.7% in 1963 and to 24% in 1965. Then, as the load factor decreased through 1971, the rate of return on equity became a loss in 1970 and was only a nominal plus in the years 1969 and 1971.

TABLE 22-16
Important Financial and Operating Statistics of the Air Transport Industry, 1963-1971

Year	Operating Revenues $ (000,000)	Net Income $ (000)	Net Income % of Revenues	Stockholders Equity $ (000)	Rate of Return on Equity	Industry Load Factor
1963	3759	76.5	2.0	993	7.7%	53.0
1964	4250	223.2	5.3	1192	18.7%	55.0
1965	4958	362.3	7.3	1502	24.1%	55.2
1966	5745	427.6	7.4	2167	19.7%	58.0
1967	6685	415.4	6.2	2682	15.5%	56.5
1968	7762	210.0	2.7	3021	7.0%	52.6
1969	8792	52.8	0.6	3193	1.7%	49.9
1970	9290	−200.5	Loss	3222	Loss	49.7
Fiscal 1971	9473	15.3	0.2	3112	0.5%	48.6

Stock Prices Reflect Earnings Volatility

Investors in 1945-1946 projected exceptional growth for the air transport industry, and the actual record to 1973 has even outstripped the most optimistic projections in terms of gross revenues. However, the earnings of the companies have proved to be quite volatile, with the industry posting actual losses in 1961 and 1970 economic recessions and mediocre earnings in some other years. Based on optimistic forecasts of earnings growth, airline stocks were among the leaders in 1945-1946. However, while the S&P 425 Industrial Index rose about four times from its low 1946 high of 18.53 to its 1961 market peak of 76.69, the airline index at its peak of 32.29 in 1961 had only just recovered to its 1946 high of 32.90. Then, airline earnings had a good record in 1962-1966 so that at its bull market high in 1966, the S&P Air Transport Index at 145.4 was about six times its 1946 low and 4.4 times its 1946 high, compared to the S&P 425 industrials, which was also about seven times its 1946 low and 5.4 times its 1946 high. However, due to the poor earnings record after 1966 at the peak of the 1968 bull market, the air transport index was at 93.8, only 65% of its 1966 high, while the S&P industrials at 118 was 18% above its 1966 high of 100.

Furthermore, because of the cyclically volatile earnings record, the air transport index fell 43% in the 1962 bear market, 42% in the 1966 bear

TABLE 22-17

Revenues and Expenses of Domestic Trunk Lines (Millions of Dollars)

	1963 $	1963 % of Total	1964 $	1964 % of Total	1965 $	1965 % of Total	1966 $	1966 % of Total	1967 $	1967 % of Total	1968 $	1968 % of Total	*1969 $	*1969 % of Total	*1970 $	*1970 % of Total
Oper. Revenues																
Passenger	2,208.4	90.1	2,504.9	89.8	2,908.0	89.1	3,233.1	88.3	3,901.5	88.3	4,451.3	88.3	5,476.0	89.3	5,632.5	89.8
Express	25.2	1.0	27.2	1.0	29.7	1.0	31.6	1.0	30.8	0.7	33.1	0.7	33.3	0.5	31.3	0.5
Freight	116.5	4.7	141.0	5.0	174.2	5.3	201.3	5.5	235.8	5.3	284.7	5.6	387.5	6.3	391.0	6.2
Excess Baggage	16.3	0.7	15.2	0.5	10.7	0.3	5.0	0.1	6.3	0.2	7.8	0.2	10.2	0.2	10.4	0.2
Nontrans. Revenues	12.9	0.5	18.5	0.7	20.9	0.6	27.5	0.8	33.4	0.8	41.5	0.8	49.9	0.8	54.0	0.9
Other	15.9	0.7	22.0	0.8	49.5	1.5	75.6	2.1	112.4	2.5	97.1	1.9	12.1		15.2	0.2
Total Nonmail Rev.	2,395.2	97.7	2,728.8	97.8	3,193.0	97.8	3,574.0	97.0	4,320.2	97.8	4,915.5	97.5	5,969.0	97.3	6,134.4	97.8
U.S. Mail	56.7	2.3	62.1	2.2	70.5	2.2	86.9	2.4	99.2	2.2	123.9	2.5	165.7	2.7	138.4	2.2
Total Operating Rev.	2,451.9	100.0	2,790.9	100.0	3,263.5	100.0	3,660.9	100.0	4,419.4	100.0	5,039.4	100.0	6,134.7	100.0	6,272.8	100.0
Oper. Expenses:																
Flying Operations	626.7	27.0	677.0	27.2	767.9	27.0	869.9	23.8	1,101.5	27.5	1,341.3	28.4	1,690.3	29.2	1,831.0	29.3
Maintenance	464.8	20.0	514.5	20.6	566.3	19.9	596.3	16.3	735.4	18.3	802.8	17.0	908.5	15.7	974.3	15.6
General Services & Admin.																
Passenger Service	179.0	7.8	214.0	8.6	266.3	9.4	311.6	9.7	396.4	9.9	488.6	10.3	600.1	10.4	653.8	10.4
Other Services & Admin.	749.0	32.2	825.8	33.1	949.7	33.3	1,101.9	34.4	1,374.0	34.3	1,607.3	34.1	1,966.0	33.9	2,125.4	34.0
Total	928.9	40.0	1,039.8	41.7	1,216.0	42.7	1,413.5	44.1	1,770.4	44.2	2,095.9	44.4	2,566.1	44.3	2,779.2	44.4
Depreciation & Amort.	302.3	13.0	262.7	10.5	297.3	10.4	327.6	10.2	402.0	10.0	479.2	10.2	624.9	10.8	671.6	10.7
Total Oper. Expenses	2,322.7	100.0	2,494.0	100.0	2,847.3	100.0	3,207.2	100.0	4,009.3	100.0	4,719.4	100.0	5,789.8	100.0	6,256.0	100.0
Oper. Profit (or Loss)	129.2		296.8		416.2		453.7		410.1		320.1		344.9		16.7	
Nonoper. Income	d56.5		d52.2		d46.2		d49.6		d30.7		d105.1		d143.4		d158.3	
Total Income (Bef. Taxes)	72.7		244.6		370.0		404.1		379.4		215.0		201.5		d141.6	
Prov. for Income Taxes	59.6		110.2		148.1		165.5		145.3		88.4		91.1		41.2	
Net Income	13.1		134.4		221.9		238.6		*244.5		126.5		110.4		d100.4	
Ratio of Oper. Rev. to Oper. Expenses		105.6		111.9		114.6		114.1		110.2		106.8		106.0		100.3

* Some intl. routes transferred to domestic 1969. d—deficit.

Source: Civil Aeronautics Board.

market, and 63% in the 1969-70 bear market versus declines of about 27%, 26%, and 36% respectively for the S&P 425 Index. However, in each market recovery the percentage rise in the air transportation index was significantly greater than for the S&P industrials in the first year of the general market recovery. Therefore, those who purchased airline stocks in the low area of major bear markets obtained greater capital gains in the first year of each market recovery from a major bear market than was posted by the general market; but if airlines were held through the next bull market, declines exceeded general market declines.

Summary of Factors in Selection of Airlines

The major factors to consider are the general cyclical nature of the industry; the expected growth rate of the traffic over routes served; the competition on routes served; the past, present, and expected load factor; and the current and expected break-even load factor for the company. The growth of earnings will depend on the traffic growth, the load factor, and the break-even load factor. The particular accounting policies followed by the company in reporting to stockholders must be determined to the extent that they affect reported earnings. The analyst should compare the final data with industry norms and also with the record of the quality companies such as Delta.

QUESTIONS

1. (a) Discuss the relative importance of freight revenues versus passenger revenues in the railroad industry? What is the future of passenger traffic?
   (b) Is capital turnover relatively high or low for railroads? Explain the significance of your answer to this question for investors.

2. Would railroads generally have been classified as quality investment securities prior to 1930? Explain carefully.

3. Would you recommend a buy-and-hold strategy for railroad securities? Support your position.

4. (a) What was the major premise underlying the Transportation Act of 1920? What important factors did this act ignore?
   (b) What important changes were brought about by the Transportation Act of 1958?

5. (a) What has been happening to the relative importance of railroads as a carrier of intercity freight? Why is this of great significance to potential investors?

(b) Discuss the growth record of railroad operating revenues since 1929 in relation to operating expenses and the American economy in general.

6. "The investment community considers that seven railroads represent considerably higher quality than the industry." What factors explain the better-than-average performance of these particular railroads?

7. Discuss recent trends in railroad labor costs and their significance to the investor.

8. What steps might the railroads take to improve future operating results? Do you feel it is likely that significant improvement in operating results will occur during the 1970s? Discuss.

9. (a) What are the important items to examine in an analysis of railroad operating revenues?
   (b) Discuss the importance of (1) length of haul, and (2) traffic density in analyzing a particular railroad.

10. (a) What are the major classifications of railway operating expenses? What is the relative importance of each category?
    (b) How might one judge whether or not a railroad is undermaintaining its property? How would undermaintenance affect the income statement?
    (c) What is the operating ratio as applied to railroad income statements? How might this ratio give a misleading indication of operating efficiency?

11. Contrast growth in the trucking industry with that of the railroad industry.

12. (a) Is the turnover of capital for the trucking industry similar to that of railroads? Of what significance is this comparison to investors?
    (b) The trucking industry is considered quite cyclical in nature. What does this suggest concerning a proper investment approach to this industry? Discuss.

13. Contrast the growth record of airlines to that of the trucking and railroad industries.

14. (a) What factors are mainly responsible for the cyclical volatility of airline earnings that is readily apparent when historical data are reviewed?
    (b) Have airline stock prices reflected this volatility? Discuss.

15. How is "load factor" measured for an airline? What is the significance of this measure?

WORK-STUDY PROBLEMS

1. (a) Prepare an income statement analysis with classifications like those in Table 22-6 for the years 1965-1970 for the Penn Central

Transportation Company and for the Norfolk and Western Railway Company. What significant differences do you observe?

(b) Do the statistics suggest that the difficulties encountered by the Penn Central Transportation Company could have been observed in time to avoid serious loss for an investor who bought the stock in 1965? Discuss.

(c) Would you recommend purchase of Penn Central stock today? That of Norfolk and Western? Support your position briefly.

2. (a) Select and contrast a railroad stock, a trucking stock, and an airline stock in terms of:

    (1) Growth in revenues and operating earnings, earnings after taxes and EPS over the most recent five years.

    (2) Return on total assets and owners' capital over the most recent five years.

    (3) Performance of the price of the stock over the most recent five years.

    (4) Financial strength during the most recent five years.

(b) Which of the three stocks made the most effective use of leverage during the most recent five years? Support your choice with appropriate calculations.

(c) Would you recommend purchase of any of the three stocks currently? Support your position.

SUGGESTED READINGS

Airline Industry Financial Review and Outlook (Irregular, but usually annual). Washington, D.C.: Air Transport Association of America.

American Economic Association. *American Economic Review,* May, 1972.
    (1) Hilton, G. W. "The Basic Behavior of Regulatory Commissions."
    (2) Sampson, R. J. "Inherent Advantages Under Regulation."

American Trucking Association, Inc., Washington, D.C.
    (1) *American Trucking Trends* (Annual).
    (2) *Financing the Motor Carrier Industry.*

Association of American Railroads, Washington, D.C.
    (1) *Yearbook of Railroad Facts* (Annual).
    (2) *Railroad Review and Outlook* (Annual).
    (3) *Statistics of Railroads of Class I in the U.S.* (Annual 10-year record).
    (4) News Releases (Weekly).

Aviation Week and Space Technology (Weekly). New York: McGraw-Hill Book Company, Inc.

Benham, Isabel H. "Railroad Based Conglomerates." *Financial Analysts Journal* (May-June, 1972), pp. 43-45.

Cameron, W. Glenn. "The Railroads—Are They Getting Back on the Track?" *The Institutional Investor* (November, 1971), pp. 62-65.

Civil Aeronautics Board, Washington, D.C.
  (1) *Annual Report.*
  (2) *Air Carrier Financial Statistics* (Quarterly).
  (3) *Airline Industry Economic Report* (Quarterly).
  (4) *Forecast of Scheduled International Air Traffic: U.S. Flag Carriers, 1971 to 1980.*

Davlin, Andrew, Jr. "Trucking Companies: Have They Gained Institutional Standing?" *The Institutional Investor* (February, 1971), pp. 42-45, 67-68.

Douglas, Peter. *Bankers' Analysis of the Motor Carrier Industry.* New York: Chase Manhattan Bank.

Interstate Commerce Commission, Washington, D.C.
  (1) *Annual Report.*
  (2) *Freight Commodity Statistics of Class I Railroads in the U.S.*
  (3) *Transport Economics, Monthly Comment & Statistics.*
  (4) *Transportation Statistics Annual.*

Moody's Transportation Manual (Annual). New York: Moody's Investors Service, Inc.

Railway Age (Semimonthly). New York: Simmons-Boardman Publishing Co.

Standard & Poor's Basic Industry Survey—Transportation. New York: Standard & Poor's Corporation.

Trinc's Blue Book (Annual). Washington, D.C.: Trinc Associates Ltd.

Zuckerman, Stanley. "The Airlines: Can They Convert All the Demand into Earnings Growth?" *The Institutional Investor* (December, 1969), pp. 70-73, 83.

Bank Stocks

The main functions of commercial banks are to receive deposits from other segments of the economy (businesses, individuals, governments, etc.) and to make loans and discounts to industry, commerce, agriculture, and individuals. The nation's commercial banks hold the bulk of the cash assets of individuals, business firms, financial institutions, trust funds, and pension funds, as well as the cash assets of federal, state, and local governments.

During World War II, a large proportion of production was military. Much of this production was financed directly by the government but indirectly by commercial banks, which supplied the United States Government with substantial amounts of funds (deposits). Commercial banks purchased $76 billion of U.S. Government securities between December 31, 1941, and December 31, 1945. In 1945 they held $90.6 billion.

From the end of World War II to the present, the commercial banks resumed their pre-World War II functions of making loans to business and individuals. Also, since the 1960s they have aggressively "purchased" funds from whatever sources were available—savings deposits, commercial certificates of deposit, and sale of debentures and notes, but at rising costs.

STATEMENT OF CONDITION OF COMMERCIAL BANKS

The balance sheet of a commercial bank is better known as its statement of condition. The first part of this chapter will discuss both the assets section and the liability and capital section of the statement of condition of commercial banks.

Assets Section of Statement of Condition

The principal assets and liabilities of all commercial banks are shown in Table 23-1. The assets listed on this statement of condition are discussed in the following paragraphs. Assets of *insured commercial banks* represent 99.5% of assets of *all commercial banks*.

Cash and Balances with Other Banks—Primary Bank Reserves. This item includes cash on hand, cash due from other banks, and cash on deposit as reserves with the Federal Reserve banks. These cash reserves are the primary reserves of the banks. Restructuring of reserve requirements became effective on November 9, 1972, and were expected to reduce required reserves by about $3½ billion.

An examination of Table 23-1 shows the effect of the partial financing of the government in World War II by the commercial banks as well as the decrease in their normal private lending activities. At the end of 1945, the item "Cash and Balances with Other Banks" represented about 22% of the assets of the commercial banks. It remained at the 21%-22% level until 1958, when it began to decline gradually to 15% in 1973. Holdings of U.S. Government securities amounted to 57% of the assets of commercial banks by the end of 1945. Therefore, cash and amounts due from banks plus U.S. Government securities reached 78% of all assets of commercial banks by the end of 1945, and cash plus all security holdings reached 83%. Conversely, by 1945, loans and discounts declined to a low of only 16% of assets. At this point, the banks were *commercial* banks in name only; they were essentially holders (investors) of cash and U.S. Government securities.

U.S. Government Obligations—Secondary Reserves of Commercial Banks. U.S. Government obligations are held by commercial banks primarily for liquidity, although holdings generally have increased in recession years of relatively low loan demand and have declined in expansion years. Banks have a definite minimum amount that they hold in U.S. Government obligations, although the percentage to total assets has rather steadily declined from the peak of 56% of assets in 1945 to 23% in 1960, 16% in 1965, and 9% in 1973 (including U.S. government agencies and corporations, 12%). In terms of the absolute dollar amounts held, the figure was $93.8 billion in 1946, $69 billion in 1947, fluctuated between $69 billion and a low of $53 billion (July, 1966) for the entire period 1947-1973, and $60.0 billion in 1973. Interestingly, in recent years average rates earned on total

TABLE 23-1

Commercial Banks—Major Assets, Deposits, Borrowings (Billions of Dollars)

Dec.	Total Assets	Major Assets	Cash Assets	Total Cash & U.S.	SECURITIES				Loans & Discounts	DEPOSITS				BORROWINGS	
					U.S. Govt.	State Local Govt.	Other Securities	Total Securities		(Non-Inter Bank) Total	Demand	Time	Time % of Total Deposits		Total Capital Accounts
1945	160	159	35	125	91	7.4	2.9	98	26	136	106	30	22	0.2	9.0
1947	155	154	38	107	69	5.3	3.7	78	38	131	96	35	27	0.1	10.1
1950	169	166	40	102	62	7.3	5.1	74	52	141	105	37	26	0.1	11.6
1960	258	252	52	113	61	17.3	3.2	82	118	211	139	72	34	0.2	21.0
1966	403	392	69	125	56	41.0	7.8	105	218	332	173	159	42	4.9	32.1
1969	531	512	90	145	55	59.2	12.2	126	296	408	214	194	49	18.4	40.0
1970	578	555	94	145	52	63.0	12.6	118	313	448	217	231	52	19.4	43.0
1971	640	617	100	165	65	82.4	22.3	170	347	503	231	272	54	25.9	47.2
1972	717	688	98	163	65	89.0	26.0	180	410	562	250	312*	56	39.5	51.2

MAJOR ASSET ITEMS AS % OF TOTAL ASSETS

	Major Assets	Cash Assets	Total Cash & U.S.	U.S. Govt.	State Local Govt.	Other Securities	Total Securities	Loans & Discounts
1945	99.1	21.7	78.2	56.5	2.7	1.3	61.1	16.3
1947	98.9	24.1	68.1	44.5	3.4	2.4	50.3	24.5
1950	98.8	23.9	60.5	36.7	4.3	3.0	44.0	30.9
1960	97.7	20.3	43.9	23.7	6.7	1.2	31.8	45.6
1966	97.0	17.1	31.0	13.9	10.2	1.9	26.0	53.9
1969	96.4	17.0	27.3	10.3	11.2	2.3	23.8	55.6
1970	95.9	16.2	25.1	8.9	10.9	2.2	25.6	54.1
1971	96.7	15.6	25.7	10.1	12.9	3.5	26.5	54.1
1972	96.0	13.7	22.7	9.1	12.4	3.6	25.1	57.1

* As of July, 1972, time deposits = $260 billion; savings deposits, $117 billion (45%); CD's, under $100,000 = $95 billion (37%); other CD's = $42 billion (16%).

securities on a fully taxable basis have equaled or exceeded average rates earned on loans and mortgages.

In order to permit commercial banks to finance business expansion, the Federal Reserve must expand bank credit. This is accomplished primarily by Federal Reserve purchases of U.S. Government securities in the open market. Banks also may increase reserves by discounting eligible paper at their Federal Reserve banks, but open-market operations are the primary source (94%) of Federal Reserve credit.

In the recession of 1969-1970, Federal Reserve bank credit was $64-67 billion, of which holdings of U.S. Government securities previously purchased represented $57-61 billion. The 1961-1969 expansion of the economy was made possible by the expansion of Federal Reserve bank credit from $27.17 billion in 1960 to $64.10 billion in 1969, and increasing U.S. Government holdings by approximately 111%. Largely as a result, insured commercial banks were able to increase their loans and discounts from $117 billion in 1960 and 1961 to $300 billion in 1969, or an increase of 156%.[1] In 1966 and in 1970 the banks sharply reduced their liquidity. The Federal Reserve restricted credit in 1969, 1970, and early 1973 to stem inflation. Because of continued heavy loan demands, the capital markets experienced a near crisis in liquidity in mid-1966 and 1970. However, after each crisis, the Federal Reserve rapidly increased bank credit by heavy open-market purchases of U.S. Government securities, largely Treasury bills. In 1967-1968 demands by business borrowers, individuals, state and local governments, and especially the U.S. Government, were the highest in history. The U.S. Government was incurring heavy deficits to finance the Vietnam War. This demand was a major contributory factor in the rise of bond yields in 1970 to their highest level since the Civil War.

As noted previously, the commercial banks' holdings of U.S. Government obligations, especially those under 1-year maturities, are used largely as secondary reserves.

As shown in Table 23-1, after declining from a peak of $91 billion in 1945 to $69 billion in 1947, government securities tended to fluctuate between $53 and $67 billion thereafter, rising in recessions and declining in expansions. Because of the liquidity function of U.S. Government securities, commercial banks keep 79%-86% of their securities in maturities of 5 years or less. In 1961, at the beginning of the 1961-1969 expansion, commercial bank holdings of U.S. Government obligations totaled $61 billion. These

---

[1] In addition to the increase in Federal Reserve bank credit that resulted from the purchase of U.S. Government securities by the Federal Reserve banks, the commercial banks helped finance expansions by reducing their holdings of U.S. Government securities from $61 billion to $53 billion and by increasing their borrowings from the Federal Reserve bank from $149 million in 1960 to $766 million in September, 1966.

holdings declined to a postwar low of $53.5 billion in October, 1966, rose to $64.6 billion in December, 1968, and fell to $51 billion at the end of the 1961-1969 expansion. A recession occurred in November, 1969, to November, 1970. As normal, in the second quarter of 1970 the Federal Reserve changed its tight money policy to one of credit availability and expansion to combat inflation, but interest rates continued to rise to new peaks to mid-1970. The result of this expansionary policy was a significant increase in bank loans and investments, effecting a general resurgence of economic activity.

Table 23-2 shows the maturity breakdown of the commercial banks' holdings of U.S. Government marketable securities.

TABLE 23-2

Commercial Banks Holdings of U.S. Government Securities
Maturity Classifications

Maturities	December, 1967 %		December, 1968 %		January, 1973 %	
Within 1 year:						
Bills	20.0		17.0		11.8	
Other	15.4	35.4	18.2	35.3	18.2	30.0
1-5 years		50.5		43.3		55.3
0-5 years		85.9		78.6		85.3
5-10 years		12.2		18.8		12.6
10-20 years		.9		1.7		2.0
Over 20 years		1.0		.9		0.1
Total		100.0		100.0		100.0

Approximately 79%-86% of U.S. Government securities held have maturities of 5 years or less, and almost all of the balance have maturities under 10 years. These securities are classed as nonrisk assets,[2] and one analytical test is the ratio of nonrisk assets (cash plus governments) to deposits. The ratio for all commercial banks in January, 1973, was 34%. The converse of this ratio is essentially the ratio of risk assets to deposits.

Other Securities—Largely Tax-Exempt Securities. Investments in "other securities" consist largely of state and local government tax-exempt securities.

---

[2] They are nonrisk only in the sense of the credit risk. However, the decline in the price of U.S. Government securities in 1966, 1967, 1968, 1969, and 1970 shows the substantial market risk inherent in even relatively short-term government issues. The greatest market risk is in long-term issues, but even 5-year issues have real risks.

In 1973 about 78% of other securities were state and local government securities. Of the remaining investments in other securities, about two thirds were federal agency securities and one third were corporate debt issues.

In 1945, at the end of World War II, total security investments of all commercial banks were $106.1 billion, of which $98.5 billion or 93% consisted of U. S. Government securities. Investments in U. S. Government securities declined sharply until 1948 and then leveled off in dollar amount into a horizontal channel of $53-$65 billion, but holdings of "other securities" rose from $7.6 billion in 1945 to $48.4 billion in 1961, of which $40.8 billion consisted of obligations of states and subdivisions. By 1967, total commercial bank investments were approximately $104 billion, of which 53.6% consisted of U. S. Government securities, 39% of state and local government securities, and 7% of other securities. In the case of large commercial banks in 1967 when the total holdings of U. S. Government securities plus state and municipal securities was $52.4 billion, $26.8 billion were U. S. Government securities and $25.6 billion were state and local government securities. In 1972, total investments were $178 billion, of which $60 billion were U.S. Government securities and $118 billion were "other securities."

While holdings of state and local government securities rose steadily after World War II, a decided increase in net holdings came as a result of legislation in 1957 and 1962 that permitted commercial banks to offer rates more competitive with savings banks and savings and loan associations. In the 1960s the banks developed certificates of deposit (CD's), which reached $40 billion in mid-1972 (70% under $100,000 and 30% over $100,000). The commercial banks purchased tax-exempt securities in substantial amounts to provide earnings to meet interest requirements on time deposits and notes which amounted to 46% of their total expenses in 1972. Holdings of tax-exempt securities by 1969 exceeded holdings of U.S. Government securities (see Table 23-1).

Loans and Discounts. The major function of commercial banks is to make loans. When a bank makes a loan, it debits a loan account (an asset account) and credits a deposit account (a liability account).

As noted previously, at the end of World War II, loans and discounts accounted for only 16% of commercial bank assets, while U.S. Government securities accounted for 56%. However, loans and discounts in 1967-1972 leveled off at 54% of total assets, an all-time high, and U.S. Governments were only 9-10%. Analysts also compare gross loans (the risk assets) to total net deposits. The ratio leveled at 64% in 1967-1972.

Table 23-3 furnishes a breakdown of commercial bank loans by type. It is clear from the table that in the period following World War II the

TABLE 23-3

Distribution of Loans—All Insured Commercial Banks (Billions of Dollars)

| Call Date | Total | Commercial and Industrial | Agri-cultural | Real Estate | To Financial Institutions | | For Purchasing or Carrying of Securities | | Other To In-dividuals | Other |
					Banks	Other	To Brokers & Dealers	To Other		
1947 Dec.										
$	38.1	18.8	1.7	9.4	.1	—	.8	1.2	5.7	.9
%	100.0	47.77	4.46	24.67	.26	—	2.10	3.15	14.96	3.3
1966 June										
$	220.7	80.6	8.6	53.9	2.2	13.3	5.8	3.2	47.9	5.2
%	100.0	36.52	3.90	24.42	1.00	6.03	2.63	1.45	21.70	2.36
1967 June										
$	238.9	88.4	9.3	59.5	1.9	12.5	6.2	3.8	51.6	5.7
%	100.0	37.00	3.89	24.90	.79	5.23	2.60	1.59	21.60	2.39
1972 June										
$	348.7	122.1	13.6	89.0	4.8	18.3	8.5	4.0	79.9	8.6
%	100.0	35.0	3.9	25.5	1.4	5.2	2.4	1.1	22.9	2.5

Source: Federal Reserve Bulletins.

major shift in the composition of loans and discounts was a decline in the proportion of commercial and industrial loans to total loans from 48% to 38% and an increase in the proportion of loans to individuals from 15% to 22%. The other important increase was loans to financial institutions other than banks from a less than 1% figure in 1947 to about 5%. The other categories retained roughly the same relative importance.

Liability and Capital Section of Statement of Condition

The liability and capital section of a condensed statement of condition for all commercial banks is shown in Table 23-1. The various items are discussed in the following paragraphs.

Deposit Liabilities. The deposit liabilities of commercial banks are classified under the following headings: business and personal (demand, time, certified checks, etc.), states and municipalities, U. S. Government, and interbank. Table 23-4 shows the total deposits of all commercial banks for various years. The total deposits of all commercial banks, including interbank deposits, rose from $151 billion in 1945 to $555 billion in 1972.

TABLE 23-4

Deposits—All Commercial Banks (Billions of Dollars)

Year	Total All Deposits	Interbank Deposits	U.S. Gov't Demand Deposits	Private Deposits		Time As % of Demand
				Demand	Time	
1945 Dec. 31	151.1	14.1	24.8	80.3	29.9	37.2%
1955 Dec. 31	188.3	15.6	3.7	120.5	48.5	40.2
1960 Dec. 31	229.8	18.9	5.9	133.4	71.6	53.7
1966 Dec. 31	352.3	20.7	5.0	167.8	158.8	94.6
1969 Dec. 31	435.6	27.9	5.1	208.9	193.7	92.7
1970 Dec. 31	480.9	32.6	7.9	209.3	231.1	110.4
1972 Sept. 30	555.5	30.8	9.4	212.7	302.6	142.2

Source: Federal Reserve Bulletins.

Total deposits rose 270% and private demand deposits rose 132% from 1945 to 1972. In 1945, time deposits were 37% of private demand deposits; in 1960, the percentage was 54%. By 1966, however, time deposits finally exceeded private demand deposits and in 1972 were $272 billion versus total demand deposit of $231 billion. The increase in time deposits came about largely as a result of a change in legislation after 1957 that allowed commercial banks to be more competitive in rates paid on time deposits, both savings deposits and certificates of deposit. Corporate treasurers began shifting from demand deposits to interest-bearing certificates of deposit.

There are two major factors in the record of commercial bank deposits since World War II as shown in Table 23-4. First, total deposits in 1972 were twice the deposits in 1960. Second, the ratio of time deposits to demand deposits which was only 37% in 1945 and 54% in 1960 rose to 110% in 1970 and 142% in 1972. As a result, interest cost including interest on capital notes in 1972 represented 46% of all expenses versus 17% in 1956.

Increases in Bank Funds. The 1960s were the beginning of a new era for commercial banks. While commercial banks had required the inflow of substantial funds to finance the post-World War II expansion of the economy, the problem of obtaining funds did not become really crucial until the 1960s. The 1961-1969 economic expansion was the greatest (and longest) in peacetime history, and then the new and even faster rate of expansion, 1971-1973, further increased the problem. Commercial banks were able to meet the challenge only by using a variety of methods to "buy" the needed funds. The following methods were used:

1. Paying increased rates on time and savings deposits .The maximum rates allowed (Regulation Q) were raised in 1957 and several times thereafter.
2. Issuing certificates of deposit. There was an expansion from $1 billion in 1960 to $140 billion in 1972 ($45 billion over $100,000 and $95 billion under $100,000).
3. Borrowing from Federal Reserve banks, borrowing federal funds from banks with excess reserves, and borrowing on notes and through repurchase agreements.
4. Increasing capital accounts through the use of capital debentures. This borrowing through the use of capital debentures increased capital, but not equity capital. The capital debentures are in practice subordinated to the claims of depositors. The term "capital accounts" therefore came to include debentures, while previously "capital accounts" had meant only equity accounts. More and more banks were selling notes in the 1970s.

Increased Rates Paid on Time and Savings Deposits. Beginning in 1957, after pressure by commercial banks to allow them to be more competitive in the battle for savings, the Federal Reserve permitted increases in the maximum rates payable on time and savings deposits (see Table 23-5).

In periods of high interest rates in the capital markets, savers may well withdraw funds from deposit-type institutions to invest directly in government securities. This is called *disintermediation.* In 1965-1966, 1969-1970, and 1973 commercial banks lost deposits to interest-sensitive investors. Large corporations and others tended to shift temporarily surplus funds out of idle (and noninterest-bearing) demand deposit balances into such short-term investments as treasury bills and commercial paper, while longer-term funds gravitated to institutions paying a higher return, including savings and loan associations, and to corporations and governments issuing obligations in capital markets.

Deposits as the main source of bank funds and the expanding role of banks in the credit markets in 1960-1973 reflect a renewed ability of banks to compete for liquid balances. Starting in 1957 and accelerated since 1962, a series of liberalized revisions has increased the maximum rate that insured commercial banks may pay on savings and time deposits. Banks have responded by increasing their rates and by developing new instruments, but earnings have been squeezed. It appears quite probable in 1973 that regulations restricting the rate of interest that can be paid on time deposits (passbook deposits and CDs) will be removed by legislation in 1973 or 1974. This will permit commercial banks, mutual savings banks, and savings and loan associations to compete with the capital markets in periods of high interest rates such as 1965-1966, 1969-1970, and 1973.

Tremendous Expansion of Negotiable Certificates of Deposit. Time certificates of deposit have been the principal medium in the sharpened competitiveness of banks for obtaining funds for expansion. Such certificates

TABLE 23-5

Maximum Interest Rates Payable on Time and Savings Deposits (Percent per Annum)

Rates Jan. 1, 1962—July 19, 1966

Type of deposit	Effective date: Jan. 1, 1962	July 17, 1963	Nov. 24, 1964	Dec. 6, 1965
Savings deposits:[1]				
12 months or more	4	4	4	4
Less than 12 months	3½	3½		
Other time deposits:[2]				
12 months or more	4			
6 months to 12 months	3½	4	4½	5½
90 days to 6 months	2½			
Less than 90 days (30-89 days)	1	1	4	

Rates beginning July 20, 1966

Type of deposit	Effective date: July 20, 1966	Sept. 26, 1966	Apr. 19, 1968	Jan. 21, 1970
Savings deposits	4	4	4	4½
Other time deposits:[2]				
Multiple maturity:[3]				
30-89 days	4	4	4	4½
90 days-1year				5
1 year to 2 years	5	5	5	5½
2 years and over				5¾
Single-maturity:				
Less than $100,000:				
30 days to 1 year				5
1 year to 2 years	5½	5	5	5½
2 years and over				5¾
$100,000 and over:				
30-59 days			5½	(4)
60-89 days			5¾	(4)
90-179 days	5½	5½	6	6¾
180 days to 1 year			6¼	7
1 year or more				7½

[1] Closing date for the Postal Savings System was Mar. 28, 1966. Maximum rates on postal savings accounts coincided with those on savings deposits.

[2] For exceptions with respect to certain foreign time deposits, see BULLETINS for Oct. 1962, p. 1279; Aug. 1965, p. 1084; and Feb. 1968, p. 167.

[3] Multiple-maturity time deposits include deposits that are automatically renewable at maturity without action by the depositor and deposits that are payable after written notice of withdrawal.

[4] The rates in effect beginning Jan. 21 through June 23, 1970, were 6¼ per cent on maturities of 30-59 days and 6½ per cent on maturities of 60-89 days. Effective June 24, 1970, maximum interest rates on these maturities were suspended until further notice.

NOTE.—Maximum rates that may be paid by member banks are established by the Board of Governors under provisions of Regulation Q; however, a member bank may not pay a rate in excess of the maximum rate payable by State banks or trust companies on like deposits under the laws of the State in which the member bank is located. Beginning Feb. 1, 1936, maximum rates that may be paid by nonmember insured commercial banks, as established by the FDIC, have been the same as those in effect for member banks.

Source: *Federal Reserve Bulletin,* October, 1972.

evidence deposits with a bank that bear a stated rate of interest, paid on a specific date or after a required period of notice, with maturities of not less than 30 days and usually not more than 1 year after issue. In certain areas of the United States, time certificates have been issued for many years, largely to individuals by relatively small banks. Many of these time certificates were for relatively small amounts and were typically nonmarketable although legally negotiable.

The circumstance that has made certificates of deposit a significant instrument since 1961 has been the development of a security market that provides liquidity for negotiable CD's, the increasingly attractive yields, and the low reserve requirements applied to time deposits. Through their use, banks have not only retained types of funds that formerly escaped, but have also attracted funds from new sources. Their greatest appeal is to business corporations. The highest denomination in capital markets is $1,000,000, although transactions involving CD's as small as $500,000 are fairly common and there are occasional transactions in denominations of $100,000. In 1960 the total outstanding was only $1 billion, but the entry of large new banks into the market and the willingness of certain investment firms to make a market caused the amount outstanding to rise to $3.2 billion at the end of 1961 and $6.2 billion at the end of 1962. In 1967 the total amount of outstanding certificates of deposit in denominations of over $100,000 issued by large commercial banks was over $19 billion; on January 1, 1969, $24 billion; and in July, 1972, $46 billion.

Commercial Bank Borrowing. In order to finance the great economic expansion of the 1960s, the member commercial banks were more willing to borrow from their Federal Reserve banks than in the past, both at the discount window and through the use of a repurchase agreement covering U. S. Government securities. In December, 1960, borrowing through repurchase agreements totaled $78 million and borrowing through discounts and advances totaled $94 million, a combined total of $172 million. In December, 1966, repurchase agreements totaled $490 million and discounts totaled $570 million, a combined total of $1.06 billion. At the peak of the borrowing in September, 1966, discounts alone totaled $774 million. At all times some banks have excess reserves or "federal funds." There was considerable short-term borrowing (typically for 1 day only) of these funds in the 1960s. At the end of 1965, for example, borrowings by banks deficient in reserves totaled $2½ billion. In 1969, to slow inflation, the Federal Reserve once again instituted a restrictive policy, with the result that by March, 1969, gross borrowings totaled $1.6 billion and net, $1.2 billion. In September, 1972, gross borrowings were $515 million; net, $370 million.

Capital Funds. At the end of World War II, for insured commercial banks the ratio of capital funds (all equity) to deposits was at a low of 6.5% and the total capital accounts were $8.9 billion. In 1960, total capital accounts had risen to $20.7 billion, largely as the result of retained earnings and the sale of capital stock. Capital notes and debentures outstanding totaled only $23 million. By 1972, however, total capital accounts had risen to $50 billion. Capital notes and debentures, used extensively by large commercial banks in the 1960s, had risen to $168 million in 1964, $1.65 billion in 1965, $1.73 billion in 1966, and over $3 billion in 1972.

While the total of capital accounts to deposits had risen from 5.9% in 1945 to 10% in 1960 and fell to 9.4% in 1972, the capital accounts in 1945 contained virtually no notes and debentures while in 1972 they contained $3 billion of notes and debentures compared to $44 billion of equity capital.

The considerable increase in the use of borrowed funds of all types was stimulated by:

1. Tax advantages (interest on borrowed funds are tax deductible).
2. The possibility, through leverage, of greater earnings on the common equity.
3. The absence of dilution of earnings that occurs in the sale of common stock, especially with stock in 1970, 1971, and early 1972 selling at 10-12 P/E's.

Leading specialists in bank securities have estimated that a bank with $10 million in capital and in need of an additional $3 million can over a 10-year period increase per-share earnings 15%-20% more by using debt capital rather than new common stock to obtain additional capital. But by aggressively "buying" funds, the large banks in the early 1970s were experiencing a cost squeeze on earnings from the rising cost of funds and continuously rising "other operating expenses."

SPECIFIC ANALYSIS OF A BANK STOCK

For many years bank stocks were considered in a somewhat different light than other common stocks. Analysis rested on the traditional concepts of *relationship* to book value and the overriding importance of sufficient dividends to allow investors to purchase the group on a yield basis. More recently, as with other stocks, emphasis has been placed on the importance of earning power, both on an absolute basis and on a basis relative to other industries. Analysts have also learned to consider the impact of antitrust legislation; the entry of some banks into mutual funds, credit cards, factoring, leasing, and overseas operations; and the significance of monetary as well as fiscal policies.

Available Data

In order to make informed investment decisions, bank stock investors need financial data reported on a consistent and uniform basis. Such disclosure has come as a result of the passage of the Securities Acts Amendments in 1964. In 1968 and 1969 the American Institute of Certified Public Accountants issued a special report on bank auditing and bank statements, including recommendations to use the "all-inclusive income statement." At the present time shareholders have available a wealth of data on their banks, and further efforts to develop consistent reporting are under way. This is a radical change from the sparse data made available some years ago.

Table 23-6 shows the ratio of earnings, expenses, and dividends of insured commercial banks for various years and percentage breakdowns of current operating earnings and current operating expenses. Table 23-7 shows the compound annual rate of growth of major items of earnings and dividends of insured commercial banks for selected periods.

Since the AICPA strongly recommended the "all-inclusive income statement," analysts have stressed this approach.

Beginning with the year 1969, bank reporting to federal agencies and to stockholders was significantly changed, as noted in this chapter. Income is reported "before taxes and securities gains or losses"; then applicable income taxes are deducted; then income before securities gains or losses; then securities gain or losses net; then net income before extraordinary items; then extraordinary charges or credits net; then less minority interest in consolidated subsidiaries; then net income; finally recoveries, charge-offs and transfers from reserves net. Therefore, data before 1969 are not comparable. Banks traditionally use the net operating earnings approach in reporting to shareholders (recurring revenues less recurring expenses less applicable taxes). Not included are (1) charge-offs and recoveries on loans and (2) losses and gains on securities. The bottom-line method reconciles the changes in capital accounts, tax-paid reserves, and loan loss reserves and should be used by the investor to gauge the long-run performance of his bank and to point up areas where questions should be asked of management.[3]

---

[3] In 1968 the American Institute of Certified Public Accountants published a 171-page study entitled "Audits of Banks," an AICPA Industry Audit Guide, prepared by the Committee on Bank Accounting and Auditing of the AICPA. This was followed in 1969 by an AICPA Opinion that CPA's in certifying financial statements of commercial banks should give only a qualified certification if the income statement was not in the form of an "all-inclusive income statement" but excluded gains or losses on sale of securities, which has been the customary practice in bank reporting. Banks traditionally have used only the "operating performance statement." The "all-inclusive income statement" results in many years in reporting lower earnings, as in most years banks incur losses on transactions in securities. It will be interesting to observe if the banks comply. If listed on the NYSE, their statements must be CPA-certified.

TABLE 23-6

Ratios of Income of Insured Commercial Banks in the United States (States and Other Areas), 1963-1971

INCOME ITEM	1963	1964	1965	1966	1967	1968	1969	1970	1971
Amounts per $100 of operating income									
Operating income—total	$100.00	$100.00	$190.00	$100.00	$100.00	$100.00	$100.00	$100.00	$100.00
Income on loans [1]	64.19	65.13	66.63	68.11	67.24	67.20	69.91	69.05	65.84
Interest on U.S. Treasury securities [2]	16.11	14.91	13.23	11.88	11.95	11.79	9.23	8.87	9.34
Interest on State and local government obligations [2]							7.19	7.55	8.60
Interest and dividends on other securities [2]	6.82	7.22	7.64	7.85	8.74	9.33	2.23	2.42	3.17
Trust department income	4.24	4.19	4.10	3.88	3.77	3.56	3.32	3.26	3.46
Service charges on deposit accounts	5.39	5.20	5.01	4.69	4.53	4.14	3.64	3.39	3.39
Other charges, commissions, fees, etc.	1.84	1.87	1.81	1.81	1.89	1.88	2.25	2.43	2.72
Other operating income	1.41	1.48	1.58	1.78	1.88	2.10	2.23	3.03	3.48
Operating expense—total [3]	71.91	72.53	74.25	74.64	76.00	75.96	78.15	79.47	81.54
Salaries and wages	24.31	23.42	22.37	20.99	20.83	20.02	19.08	19.18	19.81
Pensions and other benefits	3.38	3.27	3.13	3.07	3.07	2.97	2.93	3.05	3.28
Interest on time and savings deposits	25.64	27.21	30.15	32.09	33.88	34.07	31.78	30.20	33.60
Interest on borrowed money [3]	.79	.85	1.13	1.55	1.22	2.08	5.65	5.67	3.79
Occupancy expense of bank premises, net	4.50	4.46	4.35	4.11	4.01	3.81	3.48	3.61	3.88
Furniture and equipment, etc.	2.31	2.41	2.45	2.35	2.45	2.48	2.51	2.62	2.80
Provision for loan losses [3]							1.69	2.03	2.38
Other operating expenses	10.98	10.91	10.67	10.48	10.54	10.53	11.03	13.11	12.00
Income before income taxes and securities gains or losses							21.85	20.53	18.46
Net current operating earnings (old basis)	28.09	27.47	25.75	25.36	24.00	24.04			
Amounts per $100 of total assets									
Operating income—total	4.48	4.57	4.66	4.99	5.12	5.38	5.97	6.38	6.03
Net current operating earnings (old basis)	1.26	1.26	1.20	1.26	1.23	1.29			
Income before income taxes and securities gains or losses							1.30	1.31	1.11
Net income [4]	.71	.69	.70	.69	.74	.72	.84	.89	.87
Amounts per $100 of total capital accounts									
Net income [4]	8.86	8.65	8.73	8.70	9.56	9.70	11.34	11.76	11.68
Cash dividends declared on common stock	4.08	4.03	3.98	4.02	4.08	4.21	4.61	4.94	4.97
Net additions to capital from income	4.77	4.53	4.56	4.46	5.22	5.20	6.71	6.80	6.71
Special ratios									
Income on loans per $100 of loans [1]	5.86	5.82	5.85	6.20	6.35	6.75	7.60	7.95	7.31
Income on U.S. Treasury securities per $100 of U.S. Treasury securities	3.40	3.65	3.74	4.13	4.54	4.88	5.02	5.68	5.67
Income on obligations of States and political subdivisions per $100 of obligations of States and political subdivisions [2]							3.82	4.23	4.19
Income on other securities per $100 of other securities [2]	2.93	2.98	3.09	3.25	3.45	3.64	5.79	6.55	6.34
Service charges per $100 of demand deposits	.46	.46	.47	.49	.51	.49	.49	.50	.49
Interest paid per $100 of time and savings deposits	3.31	3.42	3.69	4.04	4.24	4.48	4.87	4.95	4.78
Number of banks (end of period)	13,291	13,493	13,547	13,541	13,517	13,488	13,473	13,511	13,612

[1] Includes Federal funds sold.

[2] "Interest on State and local government obligations" included in "Interest and dividends on other securities" in 1968 and prior years. Income from securities held in trading accounts is included in "Other operating income."

[3] "Interest on capital notes and debentures," which is included in "Interest on borrowed money" in 1969-1971, and "Provision for loan losses" were not included in "Operating expense—total" in 1968 and prior years.

[4] Because of changes in the form of reporting by banks, figures in 1969-1971 are not fully comparable with those in 1968 and prior years; see table 114 and page 224.

Source: Federal Reserve Bulletins.

TABLE 23-7

Compound Annual Rate of Growth
Major Items of Earnings and Dividends of Insured Commercial Banks

Item	1945-1954	1955-1967	1965-1971
Current Operating Earnings—Gross ...	10.0%	10.8%	13.7%
Current Operating Expenses	10.2	10.1	12.6
Income After Taxes	4.1	8.7	13.0
Cash Dividends on Common Stock ...	8.1	7.6	11.7

Brief History of the Bank

The analyst should review the history of the bank in terms of the previous discussion of the record of the banking industry. The charter of the bank, its operations, and its management should be analyzed and the trends in this respect noted. The major factors to consider are: (1) the nature of the bank's loans and deposits; (2) the growth of the bank's assets, investments, loans and discounts, time and demand deposits separately, and capital accounts including notes and debentures, if any; and (3) most important, earnings per share, past and expected growth, and rate of return on equity.

Distribution of Assets

The analyst should prepare a table showing the major bank asset categories as percentages of total assets for a period of 10 years. The trend should then be compared to that for similar banks over the decade.

Nonrisk Assets. The nonrisk assets are cash and U.S. Government securities. The ratio of these nonrisk assets to total deposits should be calculated and the trend should be determined. The lower the ratio of nonrisk assets to deposits, the higher the ratio of risk assets to deposits. Investments should be analyzed to ascertain the proportion of total investments in U. S. Government securities, in tax-exempt securities, and in other securities; and the maturity schedules and rate of return for each group should be determined.

As previously noted, holdings of tax-exempt securities have increased substantially in recent years and since 1968 have tended to exceed U.S. Government securities. For many banks, they are very considerably in excess of holdings of U. S. Government securities. Analysts should consider the tax rate applicable to a specific bank, for at a given point the addition of tax-exempts has a favorable effect on earnings after tax. Holdings of tax-exempt securities and mortgage investments are related to the proportion of time deposits to total deposits. The higher the proportion, the greater the investment in mortgages and tax-exempt securities that is required to cover the amount that would be paid as interest on time deposits.

The analyst should also prepare a maturity schedule for U. S. Government securities, classifying the maturities under the following headings: within 1 year, 1-3 years, 3-5 years, 5-7 years, 7-10 years, over 10 years, total, and average maturity. The table should include both par value and percent of total for each category.

Risk Assets. Risk assets consist of loans and discounts. If information is available, the analyst should *always* analyze the composition of loans and discounts and their trend. The analyst should prepare a distribution table classifying loans and discounts under the following major headings: commercial loans, industrial loans, total commercial and industrial loans, term loans, installment loans, real estate mortgage loans, and total loans. Both dollar amounts and percentages to total loans should be shown for a period of at least 5 years. The rate of return on loans should also be included. Loan loss provisions in 1970-1971 fell short of charge-offs.

Ratio of Time Deposits to Total Deposits

The analyst will determine the proportion of demand deposits and time deposits to total deposits and their trends and growth rate, especially since 1965. The heavy interest costs of time deposits versus no interest paid on demand deposits are an important factor in the earnings record of the bank. The analyst first should determine the breakdown of time deposits with its major components, especially passbook deposits and certificates of deposit. The higher the amount of certificates of deposit, the more volatile are deposits and the higher is the risk that the certificates may not be renewed when due if competing short-term rates in the open market are more attractive (as in 1966, 1970, and 1973). As noted, the higher the proportion of time deposits, the higher the proportion invested in mortgages and tax-exempt securities. On the other hand, the reserve requirements against time deposits are much lower than the reserve requirements against demand deposits.

Ratio of Capital Account to Risk Assets and to Assets

Prior to the 1960s, capital funds primarily were equity funds representing the stockholders' original investment plus retained earnings. However, beginning in 1963 a number of banks, particularly large banks, increased their capital accounts by selling notes and debentures subordinate in claim to the claim of deposits. Therefore, in reviewing the record over a period of years, the analyst must record the shift for many banks in their capital accounts from pure equity accounts to equity plus debentures.

An important ratio is that of capital account to risk assets. This ratio discloses the amount of a decline in the value of risk assets that could be absorbed by capital funds before any of the deposits would be in jeopardy. The lower the ratio of capital account to deposits, the more pressure there is from regulatory authorities to bring the percentage up to about the 8-10% level and the less chance there is of increasing the payout ratio. Furthermore, if deposits expand, the capital account must be increased to keep the ratio from declining.

Ratio of Capital Account to Deposits

This is also a major ratio as it indicates the cushion of protection for the depositor. Regulatory authorities want to see the ratio at least 9% or better. Considerable pressure was placed on the banks after 1945 to raise the ratio from an average of 6.5% for all banks to the 10% level. By 1960, the ratio was up to about 9-10%, but the tremendous business expansion from 1961 to 1969 and after 1970 caused banks to have great difficulty in keeping the ratio from declining. As noted, many banks sold notes and subordinate debentures to build capital. To the extent that the ratio is low, there is little chance of raising the bank's payout ratio, which for banks tends to be around 50%. If, however, the capital-deposit ratio is really high, the investor can often estimate that the payout ratio could be raised.

Ratio of Market Value to Book Value

For a bank, book value based on the balance sheet value of the assets is of some importance because it can be assumed by the nature of most of the assets that their book value and their economic or liquidity value are quite close.[4] Therefore, analysts may include the ratio of current market

---

[4] Two factors must be considered in respect to book values:
    (1) If interest rates rise sharply (as in 1966, 1970, and 1973), bond prices will decline sharply and thus a bank's cost of bonds (amortized) may exceed

value to book value in their reports. *But while the ratio is of some importance, the value of any common stock rests primarily on its earning power.* Thus, some bank stocks may sell very close to their book value almost always, while other bank stocks of growth banks may sell at 200% or more of book value. In fact, a quick rundown in a table of bank stocks indicating the ratio of market value to book value will generally immediately indicate the relative earnings record of the banks. Those with the highest ratio of market value to book value have generally had the fastest earnings growth.

Income Account

The analyst should review the income account of the bank over a period of at least 5 years. He is interested in the relative contribution of the major income items as well as the importance of the major expense items. Since the mid-1960s, the factor of interest expense on time deposits has become a major item for banks, representing about 46% of total expenses in 1973.

A typical analysis of a bank income account might include the following items calculated as a percentage of gross operating income:

> Gross operating income, 100%
>> Interest on loans
>> Interest and dividends on securities
>
> Major expenses as % of gross operating income
>> Total interest expense on deposits and notes
>> Salaries and employee benefits
>> Other operating expenses
>> Total operating expenses
>
> Balance before income taxes
> Income taxes
> Net operating earnings

Dividends Declared as a Percentage of Net Operating Earnings

At the end of World War II, the average ratio of capital to deposits was 6.5% and the problem was to increase this ratio to the neighborhood of 10%. Good progress was made in this respect up until 1960, but since then the unusual expansion in the economy and in bank deposits has caused a serious capital problem and resulted in the sale of subordinate debentures. For this reason, the payout ratio of the banks since World War II

---

current market value. Banks may take losses in the bond account.
(2) If bank management policy is too liberal regarding loans, the uncollectible loans may be large enough in amount to cause difficulty.

generally has averaged below 50% as contrasted for example with the electric utilities where it has averaged around 70%. If the analyst believes that the capital to deposits ratio is very satisfactory or even somewhat on the high side, he may anticipate an increase in the payout ratio.

The analyst should consider the *relative* price-earning ratio of bank stocks. Since 1955, leading bank stocks have ranged widely on a P/E basis compared with the S&P 425 (at a discount to the S&P in some years and at a premium in others). In the 1962-1966 period of rapid growth of corporate earnings, bank stocks on a P/E basis went to almost an 8-multiple gap to the S&P. In 1970-1971 the 50 largest banks sold at an average P/E of 12.0x. The gap between the S&P 425 narrowed some in 1973.

Bank Holding Companies

In the banking field the merger movement in industry has found reflection in one-bank holding companies. The Federal Bank Holding Company Act of 1956 was amended in 1970. The primary purpose of the act is to separate banking from commerce. Under the act a "bank" is any institution which accepts demand deposits *and* makes commercial loans. A company which does not own or control a "bank" is exempt from the act. Therefore, trust companies which do not make commercial loans do not come under the act, and bank holding companies can expand by acquisition of trust companies in other states. On January 1, 1972, there were 1,567 regulated bank holding companies (including 15 foreign bank holding companies at that time and 21 by mid-1972) controlling one or more banks. There were 2,420 such affiliated banks having 10,832 branches and domestic deposits aggregating $297 billion or 55% of the domestic deposits of all 13,838 insured commercial banks.

The act prohibits the Federal Reserve from approving any application of a bank holding company to acquire or establish a bank in another state unless that state has expressed legislation permitting such entry, which no state had as of 1972. While earnings of domestic banks tended to be flat in 1971-1972, earnings of foreign branches of holding companies rose enough to mask the unsatisfactory domestic situation.

QUESTIONS

1. Briefly indicate the changed composition of bank assets in the 1960s and 1970s versus 1945 and explain the changes noted. Has the pattern that developed in the 1960s continued in the 1970s?

2. (a) Distinguish between primary reserves and secondary reserves.
   (b) What has been the trend in these assets since 1946?

3. Discuss the range in maturity distributions of holdings of U. S. Government securities of commercial banks.

4. What significant change has occurred in the investment portfolios of commercial banks since 1946? Why has this shift come about?

5. (a) Discuss the factors to consider in the analysis of a bank's basic portfolio.
   (b) Note significant shifts in the composition of loans and discounts that have occurred since 1946. What explanations can you offer to explain these shifts?

6. (a) What is a certificate of deposit? What has made them the significant instrument they have been since 1961?
   (b) What is meant by "disintermediation?"

7. (a) What are the important measures to use in assessing a bank's earning potential?
   (b) What is the "bottom line" concept of dealing with bank earnings?

8. Discuss the importance of the ratio of capital account to risk assets.

9. (a) Discuss the importance of the ratio of capital account to deposits.
   (b) How is the nature of a commercial bank's liabilities and capital structure related to potential return on earning assets?

10. (a) Why is the security analyst interested in the ratio of time deposits to total deposits?
    (b) Of what significance is the increased use of subordinated debt during the 1960s by commercial banks to investors in bank stocks?

WORK-STUDY PROBLEMS

1. Data concerning the assets, liabilities, and capital of Bank A and Bank B for a recent year are shown at the top of page 623.

   (a) On the basis of the figures given, calculate for Bank A and Bank B the following ratios:
       (1) Capital funds to deposits.
       (2) Capital funds to risk assets.

	Bank A	Bank B
	(In Millions)	
Cash	$20	$250
Loans	60	300
U. S. Government Bonds	10	100
Municipal Bonds	5	20
Corporate Bonds	1	2
Other Assets	3	68
Total	$99	$740
Deposits	$91	$630
Capital Stock	3	30
Surplus	2	20
Undivided Profits	1	10
Other Liabilities	2	50
Total	$99	$740
Shares	300,000 *	1,000,000 **
Market Average (per share)	$30	$81

* Par value, $10 per share.
** Par value, $30 per share.

(3) Loans to deposits.
(4) Cash and government securities to deposits.
(5) Market value to book value.

(b) Comment on the results of your calculations and compare the ratios with those generally accepted.

2. Choose one of the 100 largest commercial banks and prepare a 5-year analysis based on the procedures described in the text, using the format suggested below. (See *Moody's Bank and Finance Manual*.) For industry comparisons, use tables in the latest annual report of the Federal Deposit Insurance Corporation. Comment on your results.

Bank Analysis

A. Brief history of the bank

Statement of Condition

B. Distribution of assets—trends
  Investments—nonrisk assets (ratio to deposits)
  Loans and discounts—risk assets and their composition (ratio to deposits)
  Deposits—ratio of time deposits to total deposits
  Capital accounts—ratio to deposits and to risk assets
  Book value—ratio to market value

  Assets and liabilities per $100 of total assets
    Assets—total
      Cash and due from banks
      United States Government obligations

Other securities—total
   Tax-exempts
   Other
Loans and discounts
All other assets
Liabilities and capital—total
   Total deposits
      Demand deposits
      Time and savings deposits
   Borrowings and other liabilities
   Total capital accounts

Income Account

C.

	I. In Dollars	II. Ratios— Amount per $100 Operating Revenues of Current
Current operating revenues—total ...		
Interest on securities		
Interest on loans and discounts ...		
Service charges, commissions, and fees		
Trust department income		
Other income		
Current operating expenses—total ...		
Salaries, wages, employee benefits .		
Interest on time and savings deposits		
Interest on borrowed money		
Taxes other than income taxes....		
Depreciation		
Other current expenses		
Recoveries, transfers from valuation reserves, and profits—total		
On securities and loans		
Net income before related taxes		
Taxes on income		
Net income after taxes		
Dividends and interest on capital ...		
Net additions to capital from income		

Also calculate:
   Amount per $100 of total assets and amount per $100 of capital account for each of the items above.

SUGGESTED READINGS

Audits of Banks, An AICPA Industry Audit Guide. New York: The American Institute of Certified Public Accountants.

Bank Stock Quarterly. New York: M.A. Shapiro & Co., Inc.

Bankers Magazine, The (Daily newspaper). New York: American Bankers Association.

Bankers Monthly. Northbrook, Illinois: Bankers Monthly, Inc.

Banking (Monthly). New York: Simmons-Boardman Publishing Co.

Benston, George J. "A Microeconomic Approach to Banking Competition: Comment." *The Journal of Finance* (June, 1972), pp. 722-723; see also in the same issue Eric Brucker, "Reply," pp. 724-726.

Board of Governors of the Federal Reserve System, Washington, D.C.
(1) *Monthly Federal Reserve Bulletin.*
(2) *Monthly Federal Reserve Chart Book.*
(3) *Annual Report.*

Bond, Richard E. "Deposit Composition and Commercial Bank Earnings." *The Journal of Finance* (March, 1971), pp. 39-50.

Bonomo, Vittorio, and Charles Schotta. "Federal Open-Market Operation and Variations in the Reserve Base." *The Journal of Finance* (June, 1970), pp. 659-667.

Bunting, John R., Jr., "One-Bank Holding Companies—A Banker's View." *Harvard Business Review* (May-June, 1969), pp. 99-106.

Dewald, William G., and G. Richard Dreese. "Bank Behavior with Respect to Deposit Variability." *The Journal of Finance* (September, 1970), pp. 869-879.

Federal Deposit Insurance Corporation. *Annual Report.* Washington, D.C.: U.S. Superintendent of Documents.

Federal Reserve District Banks. *Monthly Bulletin* (Each of 12 banks).

Fraser, David A., and Peter S. Rose. "Bank Entry and Bank Performance." *The Journal of Finance* (March, 1972), pp. 65-78.

Frost, Peter. "Banking Services, Minimum Cash Balances and the Firm's Demand for Money." *The Journal of Finance* (December, 1970), pp. 1029-1039.

Garcia, F. L. *How to Analyze a Bank's Statement,* 4th ed. Boston, Mass.: Bankers Publishing Co.

Hendershott, Patrick H., and Frank deLeeuw. "Free Reserves, Interest Rate and Deposits." *The Journal of Finance* (June, 1970), pp. 599-612.

Juncker, George P., and George S. Oldfield. "Projecting Market Structure by Monte Carlo Simulation: A Study of Bank Expansion in New Jersey." *The Journal of Finance* (December, 1972), pp. 1101-1126.

Melnik, Arie. "Short-Run Determinants of Commercial Bank Investment Portfolios: An Empirical Analysis." *The Journal of Finance* (June, 1970), pp. 639-649.

Moody's Bank and Finance Manual (Annual). New York: Moody's Investors Service, Inc.

Nadler, Paul S. "One-Bank Holding Companies: The Public Interest." *Harvard Business Review* (May-June, 1969), pp. 107-114.

National Banking Review (Quarterly). Washington, D.C.: Controller of the Currency, U.S. Superintendent of Documents.

Robinson, Roland L. "The Hunt Commission Report: A Search for Politically Feasible Solutions to the Problems of Financial Structure." *The Journal of Finance* (September, 1972), pp. 765-778.

Valentini, John J., and Lacy H. Hunt, II. "Eurodollar Borrowing by New York Banks and the Rate of Interest on Eurodollars: Comment." *The Journal of Finance* (March, 1972), pp. 130-133.

Vernon, Jack R. "Ownership and Control Among Large Member Banks." *The Journal of Finance* (June, 1970), pp. 651-657.

Insurance Company Stocks

Insurance companies can be divided into two major groups: (1) property and liability insurance companies and (2) life insurance companies. The assets of the former equal only two thirds that of the latter. But premium income of the former represents 90% that of the latter. The characteristics of the two groups, as well as their financial factors, are quite different; consequently, each will be dealt with in a separate section of this chapter. Insurance companies may also be classified as either stock companies or mutual companies.[1]

There are two distinct phases of an insurance company's operations: (1) the underwriting function (writing policies, collecting premiums, paying expenses and losses from premiums) and (2) the investment function (investing available funds to produce an income).

Because of the character of the majority of an insurance company's assets (investments in securities), some investors have assumed that the purchase of an insurance company stock is similar to a commitment in an investment company. However, insurance companies are first and foremost insurance underwriters. Therefore, an analysis as to the profitability of the underwriting phase of the business must *precede* the analysis of the investment aspects. This is especially true of property and liability companies because in quite a number of years the underwriting operations have been unprofitable and these losses have absorbed some of the investment income.

Furthermore, it must be recognized that, although the insurance companies are strictly regulated by the insurance department in each state

---

[1] On January 1, 1972, stock companies had $50 billion in assets, $17 billion in policyholders' surplus; and for 1971, premiums written of $25 billion. Mutuals had $16 billion in assets, $5 billion in policyholders' surplus, and premiums written of $9 billion in 1971. The industry's net new investments averaged $4.4 billion annually from 1970 to 1972.

where they do business, the regulatory authorities consider that their main function is to protect the insured by regulations that will assure the solvency of the insurance companies. The interest of the stockholders is of only secondary concern.

To determine the financial position and solvency of an insurance company, the authorities have jurisdiction over accounting procedures, investments, reserves, rate changes, policy forms, etc. Each calendar year an insurance company must file with its state insurance department a statement of its income and financial condition determined according to the rules prescribed by the department. These statements are designated "convention statements" or "annual statements," and the results reported in the statement are called "statutory results." The statutory net income and the stockholders' equity are not the same as would result from ordinary accounting principles.

PROPERTY AND LIABILITY INSURANCE COMPANIES

Until about 1950, the statutes of many states would not permit casualty companies to engage in the fire insurance business nor fire insurance companies to engage directly in casualty business. Insurance was written through holding companies with separate fire and casualty subsidiaries. This is still being done, but since 1950 many of the subsidiaries have been merged into the parent companies as state laws have permitted the consolidation of the types of business. In any case, subsidiaries are generally 100% owned and the investor does best to work with consolidated statements. The major sources of information on property and liability companies are the annual reports to stockholders, the convention statements filed with the regulatory authorities, Best's insurance publications, and the usual statistical services.

The investor should note the following three important aspects of the business of property and liability insurance companies: [2]

1. The underwriting operations of fire and casualty companies are directly related to the growth of business and capital values in the United States. In fact, with the increased varieties of coverage made available and their wider public acceptance, insurance underwriting has more than kept pace with industrial and commercial growth. Without insurance it would have been impossible for business to have grown so substantially in the face of the risk of loss of assets by fire or other hazards or by liability for acts of employees or others. The existence of insurance has been and will continue to be in line generally with the growth of business and the expansion of insurable values throughout the country.

2. Fire and casualty insurance companies obtain income not only from the investment of their stockholders' funds (capital and surplus), but also

---

[2] "An Aid to Understanding Financial Reports of Fire and Casualty Insurance Companies," (Boston, Mass.: The First Boston Corporation), pp. 7-8.

from the investment of the large reserve funds accumulated out of premiums received from policyholders.

3. Probably of greatest importance, the underwriting operations of fire and casualty companies should be profitable in the long run. This is so because insurance law, recognizing that insurance is an indispensable factor in our economy, requires that insurance companies charge rates that are fair and reasonable and that should assure enough income over a period of years to pay losses and expenses and leave a margin for profit and contingencies. This factor gives the stocks of carefully selected fire and casualty insurance companies a potential advantage, from the standpoint of growth, over stocks of companies in many other industries.

Insurance Accounting

By statute, when policies are written, the premiums received are not taken into the income account but instead are credited in full to the account Unearned Premium Reserve. Later, as the premiums are earned in any fiscal period, the proportionate earnings are taken out of the account Unearned Premium Reserve and are transferred to the income account Net Premiums Earned. Actually, this is in line with sound accounting practices in other lines of business.

However, agents' commissions or other expenses incurred at the time a policy is written cannot be similarly deferred. Such prepaid expenses cannot be carried as an asset as would be the case in other lines of business.

The net result of this accounting procedure is that premium income cannot be taken up as income until it has been earned over the term of the policy, but all expenses (and losses) must be charged immediately against current income as incurred. If a company has a sharply rising premium volume, it will also have sharply rising expenses, including the heavy expense of placing the business on the books. The accompanying rise in income will lag behind the increase in expense, so that net earnings will be understated. Of course, in a period of declining premium volume, the converse is true, that is, earned income falls more slowly than expense. Analysts therefore find it necessary to adjust the reported statutory underwriting results to reflect the true earnings for the fiscal period.

Likewise, stockholders' equity is understated to the extent of the total of expense that should have been deferred beyond the balance sheet date. Consequently, it is customary to adjust stockholders' equity as well as earnings. How these adjustments are made will be explained later in the chapter.

Statutory Underwriting Results

As a result of the accounting procedures required of property and liability insurance companies, the statutory underwriting profits or losses reported to the regulatory authorities and also to stockholders reflect the applicable state laws and not the true picture. A hypothetical example of the effect of statutory reporting will illustrate the problem. Assume that on July 30 a 3-year fire insurance policy is written with a premium of $600. The initial entry on the books would be a debit to an asset account (Cash or Agents' Balances Receivable) and a credit to the Unearned Premium Reserve account. Further, assume an agent's commission of $180 that is charged off immediately as an expense, thus offsetting income.

In each fiscal period (calendar year) during the life of the policy, the proportion of the premium that is earned in the period is transferred from the Unearned Premium Reserve account to the Profit and Loss account. Since the policy was written on June 30 to become effective July 1, at the end of that calendar year one sixth of the $600 premium, or $100, would have been earned. Therefore, by the end of the year, $100 would have been transferred from the Unearned Premium Reserve account with the result that the original $600 premium would have been reduced to $500. Only one sixth of income was available for the first period, while all expenses and losses were charged to the 6-month period income (the fiscal year ended December 31).

Assuming incurred expenses of $180 commission plus office and related expenses of $60, and also a loss of $55 within the first 6 months of the policy's life, the result of this transaction would be as follows:

Net Premiums Written		$600
Increase in Unearned Premium Reserve		500
Net Premiums Earned		$100
Losses Incurred (55% of Net Premiums Earned)	$ 55	
Expenses Incurred (40% of Net Premiums Written)	240	
Total Losses and Expenses Incurred		295
Statutory Underwriting Gain (Loss)		($195)*

* As reported to insurance department and to stockholders.

Adjusted Underwriting Gain [3]

If the investor accepted the statutory underwriting results for a company with continually rising premiums, he would accept a continuous understatement of income. Therefore, he must adjust both the balance sheet figures and the income statement figures to bring them into line with accounting

---

[3] While numerous techniques had been developed by financial analysts for adjusting earnings, it was not until December, 1972, that the AICPA adopted generally accepted accounting principles for the life insurance industry. It is expected that beginning with 1973 Annual Reports, the life companies, especially NYSE-listed companies, will use the newly defined accounting principles. For a number of years some companies followed the adjustment formula recommended by the Association of Insurance Financial Analysts, and for these companies the effect of the switch to the new AICPA principles should be minor. Once companies switch to the new AICPA rules, the work of the analyst in adjusted earnings should be greatly reduced.

practices for other types of companies and to show the true results of the company's operations.

The adjustment of earnings is done because expenses that should have been deferred have been charged to current income. Therefore, the proper way to adjust earnings is (1) to add to net income (subtract from current expenses) the amount of expenses that properly should have been carried over to future years and (2) to subtract from income (add to current expenses) the amount of expenses that should have been deferred from previous years and charged to the current period. Since the expenses being deferred are those related to the premium income that is being deferred in the Unearned Premium Reserve account, it is convenient to express such expenses as a percentage of the deferred premiums. The increase in the Unearned Premium Reserve account represents the excess of premiums written in the current year that are being deferred over the previously deferred premiums that are earned currently. Thus the adjustment for expenses can be calculated by taking the appropriate percentage of the increase in the Unearned Premium Reserve account.

Insurance analysts have traditionally used a standard adjustment percentage of 35%-40%, depending on the lines of business emphasized by the company. It is more logical to use the actual expense experience of the company being analyzed. As will be discussed in a later section, it is usual to calculate the expense ratio for other purposes. This expense ratio can then easily be used as the adjustment percentage to apply to the increase in unearned premiums.

In the previous example, the increase in the Unearned Premium Reserve was $500. Multiplying this increase by the company's expense ratio of 40% gives $200 as the adjustment to reported earnings. The result of this adjustment would be as follows:

Statutory Underwriting Gain (Loss)	($195)
40% of Increase in Unearned Premium Reserve	200
Adjusted Underwriting Gain	$ 5

This adjusted underwriting gain is a more realistic appraisal of company results than is the statutory underwriting loss of $195.

The adjustment made as outlined above ignores the impact of income taxes. If the company had deferred expenses as it would have been justified in doing and reported the income of $5, this income would have been subject to federal income taxes. Consequently, the investor should make an additional adjustment for the effect of income taxes. He might use the actual corporate tax rate for the year. A simpler procedure would be to use a rate of 50%, since this is very close to the actual rate of recent years and is easier to work with. This would give a final adjusted earnings figure of $2.50.

If the company had had taxable income instead of a loss on a statutory basis, the adjustment for income taxes would be deducted from the initial adjustment based on the increase in the Unearned Premium Reserve account. If, in the example, the company had reported a statutory gain of $50, the adjustment would have been as follows:

Statutory Underwriting Gain		$ 50
40% of Increase in Unearned Premium Reserve	$200	
Less Additional Tax Allowance at 50% rate	100	100
Adjusted Underwriting Gain		$150

Adjusted Liquidating Value

Just as the investor must adjust the reported earnings or loss, so also must he adjust the liquidating or book value for the proportion of the Unearned Premium Reserve that is in reality part of stockholders' equity. Liquidating value (or book value) of an insurance company is assumed to be significant because the assets consist largely of security investments. The book value is assumed to approximate actual economic or liquidating value. The adjustment is made by multiplying the total of the Unearned Premium Reserve account at the balance sheet date by the expense ratio and adding the resulting amount to stockholders' equity.

In considering the liquidating value of an insurance stock, not only is a percentage of the Unearned Premium Reserve calculated in respect to the expense ratio added to the stockholders' equity, but certain other adjustments may be considered reasonable. It is advisable, when possible, to adjust the value of security holdings to market value and then to add the excess of market over carrying value to stockholders' equity (or to subtract any excess of carrying value over market value). Also, any voluntary and contingency reserves should be added to stockholders' equity. If the company has loss reserves that are calculated on a required statutory basis, these may overstate the actual liability that the company will have. In such cases, the company will often indicate an estimate of the true liability based on its own experience. The excess of the statutory reserve over the true liability may be added to stockholders' equity.

The tax effect of all the foregoing adjustments must be considered. A deferred tax liability item should be set up (subtracted from stockholders' equity) representing the income taxes that will be payable on realization of the amounts represented by the adjustments. This liability would be equal to approximately 50% of the adjustments for equity in the Unearned Premium Reserve account and for the excess of statutory loss reserves over actual loss liability plus 25% (the corporate capital gains tax rate) of the excess of the market value of securities over their cost. Voluntary reserves have no tax effect. If the market value of the securities is less than their cost, no negative tax liability adjustment is proper because a corporation cannot offset capital losses against other income.

Underwriting Tests

Operating results of different companies may be compared by means of three ratios that are commonly calculated and published for all property and liability insurance companies. The three ratios are: (1) loss ratio, (2) expense ratio, and (3) combined loss and expense ratio which when deducted from 100 represents the profit or loss ratio.

Loss Ratio. The loss ratio is the ratio of losses incurred (including claims expenses) to premiums earned. It is computed as a percentage of premiums earned because losses may occur at any time over the entire length of the contract covered by the premium. It is sometimes called the "loss and loss expense ratio" because expenses *directly* concerned with the loss are included.

The average loss ratios for property and liability insurance companies are given in Table 24-1. It should be noted that between companies the range is wide. For some companies it was in the high 80s or 90s and for others in the 40s and 50s. However, most companies fall within the 60%-75% range. The loss ratio demonstrates the quality of the risk incurred: a low ratio indicates high quality and a high ratio indicates a relatively low quality of risk. It is also an indication of the adequacy of rates. Inadequate rates tend to produce higher loss ratios. The loss ratio usually runs somewhat higher for mutual companies than for stock companies.

Expense Ratio. The expense ratio is usually calculated as the ratio of expenses incurred to premiums written because most expenses in a fiscal period are associated with premiums written rather than with premiums earned. Commissions and the major part of other underwriting expenses are immediately charged to profit and loss accounts when a policy is written rather than being prorated over the life of a policy. The average ratio of expenses incurred to premiums is given in Table 24-1. The expense ratios consistently run somewhere higher for stock companies than for mutual fund companies.

Combined Loss and Expense Ratio. The combined loss and expense ratio is calculated by adding the loss ratio and the expense ratio. It is the third measure of underwriting operations. If the combined ratio is less than 100%, then this *approximately* indicates the underwriting profit margin. If the combined ratio is over 100%, this approximates the underwriting loss. (Table 24-1 shows that the combined ratio for the industry in 5 of the 9 years from 1955 to 1971 inclusive was 99% or higher.) Then the insurance companies are granted rate increases and temporaily, at least, the industry average

TABLE 24-1

Property and Liability Insurance Companies
Loss and Expense Ratios to Premiums Earned and Written, As Indicated

Year	1 Loss Ratio To Prem. Earned	2 Expense Ratio To Prem. Written	3 Comb. Ratio Cols. 1 & 2	4 Under-writing Profit or Loss Ratio To Prem. Earned	5 Loss Ratio To Prem. Earned	6 Expense Ratio To Prem. Written	7 Combined Ratio Cols. 5 & 6 All Stock Cos.	8 Under-writing Profit or Loss To Prem. Earned
1971	66.7	29.1	95.8	2.85	69.1	23.1	95.8	7.0
1970	69.7	29.6	99.5	−0.72	73.3	23.4	99.3	2.4
1969	70.3	30.3	100.6	−2.07	76.5	24.1	100.6	−1.6
1968	68.8	31.2	100.0	−1.17	74.4	24.6	100.0	0.2
1967	67.2	31.7	98.9	0.07	72.7	24.5	98.9	2.1
1966	66.2	31.9	98.1	0.70	70.9	24.2	98.1	4.2
1965	69.2	32.7	101.9	−3.19	73.1	25.0	101.9	1.1
1964	68.0	33.9	101.9	−2.81	73.4	25.9	101.9	0.1
1963	66.3	34.7	101.0	−1.89	71.4	26.5	101.0	0.8
1962	64.5	34.5	99.0	0.02	66.7	25.7	92.4	7.6
1961	64.4	35.0	99.4	0.28	63.6	25.6	89.6	10.4
1960	63.6	34.8	98.4	0.64	64.2	25.6	90.4	9.6
1959	62.5	35.3	91.8	0.74	64.7	25.3	90.9	9.1
1958	63.7	36.3	100.0	−1.05	64.9	25.6	91.3	8.7
1957	66.2	36.7	102.9	−4.33	65.5	25.8	92.3	7.7
1956	63.4	37.1	100.5	−1.75	65.0	26.3	92.1	7.9
1955	58.2	36.7	94.9	3.49	61.3	26.0	87.8	12.2
1954	56.9	36.7	93.6	5.50	59.3	25.3	85.2	14.8
1953	57.2	35.9	93.1	5.00	60.3	24.4	85.9	14.1
1952	58.4	36.0	94.4	3.08	60.5	24.7	86.8	13.2
1951	60.2	36.4	97.1	0.24	61.6	24.8	86.9	13.1
1950	55.5	37.5	93.0	4.00	60.3	22.2	88.4	11.6
1949	50.2	37.4	87.6	9.51	65.6	23.1	84.7	15.3
1948	53.9	37.3	91.2	4.99	61.0	23.7	83.4	16.6
1947	58.4	37.9	96.3	−1.44	58.7	23.8	86.6	13.4
1946	59.6	39.2	98.8	−5.78	61.5	24.3	90.4	9.6

Source: *Best's Aggregates and Averages, Property and Liability,* 1972.

falls below 100%, as, for example, in 1970-1972. Happening after a sharp increase in earnings for two years, they were expected to be flat in 1973. Because of the negative effect of a regulatory lag after two years or more, many states have now adopted a "file and use regulation" which permits companies to file and immediately begin to use a higher premium rate schedule subject to subsequent review by the state commissions. This should tend to reduce or even eliminate the regulatory lag which is mainly responsible for the cycled savings and loans, expense rates, and related savings on earnings.

Investment Income

To a major extent, the assets of insurance companies consist of investments in securities. Balanced against the assets are not only the capital and the surplus of a company but also the various reserve accounts. Thus, the companies' stockholders have a considerable degree of leverage working for them. An important percentage of investments is common stocks, so that the rate of return on investments is considerably lower than for life companies although the rate of return (see Table 24-2) has risen about 1.5% since 1961.

In general, investors in property and liability insurance companies do not expect much in the way of underwriting profits, only wanting the combined loss and expense ratio to be somewhat below 100%, though hopefully in the vicinity of 90-95%. Their major expectation for income and capital gains centers on investment performance and investment income. Therefore, the investor making an analysis of an insurance company must give major attention to the company's investment portfolio and investment results over a period of years. The record from 1946 to 1971 should be reviewed (see Table 24-2).

Investment Policy. Unlike life insurance companies, regulation of investment policies for fire and casualty companies is not severe. Regulations normally require a minimum amount of cash and/or high-grade bonds, with the composition of the balance of the portfolio left to the discretion of management. There is, therefore, a wide range in the composition of portfolios. In general, the stock companies tend to have a noticeably higher proportion of their portfolios invested in equities than do the mutual companies; but even in the case of stock companies, some are quite heavily invested in government securities and high-grade bonds, both corporate and municipals, while others place considerably more emphasis on equities.[4]

---

[4] For mutual companies, equities usually do not exceed a range of 15%-20% of total assets; but in the case of stock companies, it is more usual to have the range 30%-40% of assets.

Most companies have a policy of maintaining cash and high-grade debt instruments equal to their statutory liabilities. The cash balances plus premiums in the process of collection plus new premiums will generally cover the working capital needs, including the payment of expenses and losses. Therefore the remaining assets can be fully invested.

The higher the ratio of capital and surplus to unearned premium reserves, the more justifiable is a large investment in common stock. The investor should always relate the common stock investments to capital funds by calculating what effect a given decline (for example, 25% or 50%) in market value of the common stocks owned by the company would have on capital and surplus.

TABLE 24-2

Property and Liability Insurance Companies
Comparative Investment and Underwriting Record

Year	Investment Income		Investment Profit or Loss (Includes Inv. Income)	Underwriting Profit or Loss Refund Fed. Inc. Taxes	
	$	% Earned on Mean Assets		$	% of Premiums Earned
1971	1,785	3.88	3,417	679.2	2.85
1970	1,439	3.57	1,250	—154.0	—0.72
1969	1,238	3.27	—492	—395.8	—2.07
1968	1,101	3.06	2,279	—210.9	—1.17
1967	987	3.03	2,301	10.4	0.07
1966	896	2.87	—552	102.5	0.70
1965	852	2.78	1,466	—424.5	—3.19
1964	782	2.69	1,821	—347.5	—2.81
1963	721	2.69	2,017	—218.7	—1.89
1962	673	2.62	—230	2.5	0.02
1961	621	2.57	2,516	29.8	0.28
1960	592	2.66	655	65.6	0.64
1959	534	2.55	1,021	70.9	0.74
1958	489	2.57	2,074	—92.7	—1.05
1957	461	2.58	—166	—361.3	—4.33
1956	430	2.45	580	—135.8	—1.75
1955	394	2.38	1,147	255.5	3.49
1954	363	2.46	1,583	385.0	5.50
1953	326	2.37	267	333.2	5.00
1952	294	2.30	549	185.1	3.08
1951	273	2.47	545	13.1	0.24
1950	253	2.52	600	190.8	4.00
1949	215	2.42	528	421.1	9.51
1948	188	2.39	152	199.6	4.99
1947	172	2.44	109	—48.8	—1.44
1946	154	2.38	—11	—151.6	—5.78

Source: *Best's Aggregates and Averages,* 1972.

Investment Results. As noted earlier, underwriting profits have fluctuated considerably over the years, and in numerous years many companies experience underwriting losses. Therefore, underwriting profits when earned are generally not distributed as dividends but are added to surplus. This means that dividends are paid largely or entirely from investment income.

While companies experience both capital gains and losses in their investment portfolios, the gains have exceeded losses over the past three decades. Security analysts generally do not include portfolio gains or losses in calculating annual earnings. This is in line with the usual accounting practice of excluding nonrecurring gains from income. In fact, however, gains on insurance company portfolios recur frequently, so that a case could be made for including such gains as income, perhaps averaging them over a period of years to allow for their variability.

Total Earnings

An insurance company's total earnings consist of the adjusted underwriting gain (or loss) plus net investment income. Analysts often show separate per-share earnings figures for each of these components. The underwriting earnings tend to be quite variable, but investment income does not. Earnings per share should be calculated after income taxes, although for convenience analysts sometimes give a before-tax figure and then income tax per share.

Other Considerations

In addition to the factors previously discussed, it is well for the potential investor in a property and liability insurance company to consider the lines of business that it writes. Preferably, there should be broad diversification both in types of insurance written and in the geographical spread of the risks being underwritten. Heavy concentration in a single line of insurance, especially automobile insurance, should be considered unfavorable.

Investors are sometimes tempted to add a separate value for a company's management or agency force if these seem particularly outstanding. This can lead to overvaluation. The investor should realize that an exceptional agency force shows up in both the quantity and the quality of business being written and needs no separate weight given to it. Likewise, the results of unusually good management are evident in a company's earnings and financial measures, except where substantial management changes have recently occurred.

Value of Insurance Shares

The prices of insurance company stocks are often expressed as a multiple of investment income only. This recognizes the fact mentioned previously that most property and liability companies have a policy of paying dividends only out of investment income. However, it ignores the fact that underwriting gains also benefit stockholders and that underwriting losses are detrimental. It is important to keep in mind that both investment and underwriting operations should be successful. Therefore, it seems preferable to use the combined earnings per share to value insurance company shares, as is done for other companies, with allowances being made for the volatile nature of underwriting earnings.

Liquidating value of insurance company stocks has more significance than book value of most other kinds of companies. The investor may find that the liquidating value is a reasonable price for a property and liability insurer whose underwriting operations are fairly profitable. Less successful companies generally sell below liquidating value, sometimes substantially so. Conversely, unusually profitable companies frequently sell at a premium over liquidating value. Since 1967 numerous property and liability insurance companies have been acquired by noninsurance companies, often by conglomerates, which had the effect of sharply increasing the market price of the shares of the companies being acquired and of others considered to be potential acquisition candidates.

LIFE INSURANCE COMPANIES

The life insurance industry is a major component of the American financial scene. The total assets were about $222 billion in January, 1972, and the gross new loans and investments have approached $70 billion per year in recent years. The net annual flow of savings through life insurance companies ranged between $7 and $8 billion in 1966-1970 and $11 and $12 billion in 1971-1972. Total assets rose about $10 billion annually in 1966-1970 and $14 billion in 1971.

The life insurance industry has traditionally been dominated by mutual companies, which are generally both older and larger than the stockholder-owned companies. But stock companies currently account for 33% of the total assets of the industry, as compared with 28% in 1960. Further gains by stock companies are foreshadowed by the increase in their share of business in force from 40% in 1960 to 49% in 1972. Of the 1,818 life insurance companies in the United States in 1972, 1,664 were stock companies.

Sources of Earnings—Underwriting

There are great differences between the life insurance industry and most industries that investors might consider. The product being sold is not a tangible good, but simply a contract. The differences between insurance and the typical product become even more readily apparent when the investor begins looking at costs and sources of profit. Normally, the investor can take a company's sales for a given period and subtract the costs to arrive at the company's profit. In life insurance "sales," the sales unit referred to is a promise by the company to pay $1,000 at a future time. The amount received by the company is usually no more than a year's premium, which is a very small fraction of this $1,000. It is the premium payment received and not the sale that provides income for the insurance company.

Fixing Premiums. In fixing premiums, the insurance company will calculate the amount that must be received each year so that, with interest earned, the amounts received will just exactly equal the benefits expected to be paid out over the duration of the contracts. This amount per year is called the *net level premium* and corresponds to the cost of goods sold for an ordinary business. To this net level premium the company then adds an amount that it estimates will cover its costs, including commissions, and give it a slight margin of profit. This amount is called the *load* and is the same as the markup for a seller of goods.

Conservative Nature of Reported Earnings. In calculating the profit that a life insurance company will make, it must be emphasized that most of the cost factors are estimates and assumptions for long periods of time in the future. The differences between these estimates and the actual costs that occur are the sources of additional possible profit or loss to the company. Since the estimates and assumptions used have generally been conservative (that is, have tended to overstate the costs), these differences have more often been profits than losses.

Areas of Additional Profit or Loss. There are three areas in which differences between estimated amounts and actual amounts can arise. The first of these is in the load or estimate of expense of administering the contract. This is perhaps the one area that would seem most likely to show a loss rather than a profit, especially during an inflationary period such as has been experienced for much of the past three decades. During such a period, wages, rents, and other costs tend to increase, yet the load on outstanding policies cannot be increased. However, most companies have done an excellent job of meeting these increasing costs with mechanization, automation, and other cost-reducing methods so that the profit has at least remained fairly constant.

The other two areas where differences between estimates and actual amounts can arise are in the assumptions made in calculating the net level premium. The calculations assume that there will be a certain pattern of mortality (based on a given mortality table) and that a specified interest rate will be earned. The mortality table is based on historical experience so that, because of advances in medical science, the actual death rate will generally be less than that shown by the table, although expected improvements in mortality may be taken into account. The most commonly used tables also have a margin of safety built in. This means that not all the amounts set aside as reserves will actually be needed to pay benefits, and the excess is additional profit. But updating has been reducing this factor.

If the insurance company can earn more than the assumed rate (see Table 24-2), this is another source of profit. The rate earned on mean assets rose from 2.52% in 1950 and 2.66% in 1960 to approximately 4% in 1971. The rise in policy loans from 3.6% of assets in 1955 to 4.86% in 1966 and over 8% in 1971 has tended to slow somewhat the rise in the rate of return on investments.

Growth of Life Insurance Industry

The life insurance industry is well known for its continuous and considerable growth over long periods of time. Life insurance in force in the United States increased at a rate of 7.3% in the 1940s, 9.6% in the 1950s, and 9.1% in 1960-1972. However, investors should be wary of attaching too much importance to these figures. Because of the decline in average premium rates and the popularity of lower premium forms of insurance, the growth of premium income has not kept pace with the growth of business in force, rising consistently by 7.82% per year in the 1950s and also in 1960-1972.

Investment income showed an opposite pattern, rising annually 5.5% in the 1940s but 7.9% in the 1950s. From the mid-1940s to the mid-1950s, it increased at less than 7% per year. However, aided by increasing levels of interest rates, investment income climbed 9% per year from 1960 through 1972. Total income advanced at a rate of about 7.2% in the 1940s and 1950s and about 7% in the 1960s. In 1971 premium income represented 78% of income; investment income, 22%.

Earnings of life insurance companies have shown a disappointing slow-down in growth over the past decade compared with the previous one. From 1946 to 1956 the annual rate of growth was over 10%, but it declined after 1956. Part of the decline resulted from the substantial increase in the impact of federal income taxes beginning in 1959. The factors that were cited as affecting premium income seem to account for the balance of the slowdown in growth of earnings.

Growth of the life insurance industry in the 1970s seems likely to be somewhat below that of the years since World War II. Insurance in force should still gain by about 9% per year, but premium income appears likely to grow at a rate of only about 7.8% annually. Growth in earnings could approach that of premium income, but it would not be surprising in view of the increasing competition in the industry to find it falling short of this mark. Naturally, some individual companies will grow more rapidly than this and others less rapidly.

Stability of Earnings

The life insurance industry has a reputation for stability that is not wholly deserved from the investor's point of view. It is true that in only two years in this century, 1932 and 1933, has the amount of insurance in force declined compared with the previous year. However, the investor should realize that this same pattern has not been reflected faithfully in earnings.

Consideration of the capitalization and operating characteristics of life insurance companies makes evident the reasons for instability of earnings in spite of relative stability in other measures of company activity. The tremendous financial leverage in insurance company operations not only magnifies small improvements into substantial benefits for the stockholders, but it also increases the impact of any decline. Coupled with this is a high degree of operating leverage. Net profits amount to only a small percentage of gross revenue. In addition, insurance company costs are relatively inflexible. This means that even a slight reduction in gross revenue, since it will not be accompanied by a proportionate decrease in costs, can have a relatively large effect on the net profit available for stockholders.

Sources of Information on Life Insurance Companies

Life insurance company annual reports, although somewhat improved in recent years, are notoriously uninformative. The usual published sources, such as Moody's and Standard & Poor's services, provide some financial information but not nearly enough for a complete analysis. Best's *Life Insurance Reports* and *Digest of Insurance Stocks,* being oriented specifically to life insurance companies, are somewhat better.

The best source of financial information is the annual statement filed by the insurance company each year with the insurance commissioner or comparable official in each state in which it does business. Most state insurance departments make the statements available for inspection by the investor. Some companies supply copies of their annual statement to analysts.

Determining Companies to Consider

The investor, in contrast to the speculator, should confine himself to well-established life insurance companies. He must therefore determine whether a company can be considered "well-established" before proceeding further. There are many companies, such as Aetna and Connecticut General, that unquestionably fall in this category. A company that has just been organized obviously would not be considered well-established. However, between these two extremes are many other companies that the investor must judge individually.

Two measures that have been used to determine whether a company is sufficiently established to be considered by the investor are the size and the age of the company. Under present conditions, the traditional figure of $100 million business in force does not seem to be adequate. A number of companies in recent years have reached this figure within 2 years after being organized. A company should have at least 5 years of operations behind it simply to give the analyst an adequate basis for judging it. In addition, the company should have shown a profit from operations (before adjusting for increase in business in force) for at least the past 4 years. Since it generally takes a company several years after being organized to show an operating profit, this means that the investor will seldom consider companies less than 7 or 8 years old.

The company should also be sufficiently mature to be getting a reasonable proportion (at least 20%) of its gross income from investment sources. A comparison of first-year premium income with renewal premium income is helpful. The renewal premiums should be several times the first-year premiums collected in order for the company to be considered mature.

Marketability of the stock is another factor usually considered by the investor in deciding on the suitability of the stock for investment. If the stock regularly appears in the quotations supplied to national financial publications by the National Association of Security Dealers, this is evidence that the market in the stock is fairly broad.

Adjustment of Life Insurance Company Figures

As in the case of property and liability insurance stocks, one of the major problems in analyzing life insurance stocks results from the companies' failure to use generally accepted accounting principles. As a result, most analysts adjust the reported earnings of life insurance companies because they feel that these earnings are understated. They also adjust the liquidating value (book value) of life insurance stocks by adding to stockholders' equity the value of business that a company has in force at the end of the year.

Ordinary accounting principles dictate that the cost of assets, such as equipment or any other expenditure expected to result in future income, be allocated over the period in which the income is expected. Since the securing of insurance contracts requires an initial cost analogous to the cost of equipment or other assets, it would seem logical to spread this cost over the period during which the contract is expected to produce a profit. In this way the accounting principle of matching costs with revenues would be followed. However, insurance companies are required by statute to treat the entire acquisition cost of new business as an expense in the period in which the contract is written. This is comparable to a manufacturer charging the cost of equipment and buildings to expense instead of to an asset account. Since the acquisition cost almost always exceeds the first-year premium on the contract, a company finds that its reported earnings are lower than if it were not writing any new business. (See new AICPA rules of December, 1972.)

Basis for Adjustment. It would appear that the investor should adjust life insurance company earnings by eliminating from the year's expense the amount that should be deferred to future periods. This would be possible, though not easy. However, it would also be necessary to determine the amounts from previous years that should be shown as a deferred cost and how much of this previously deferred expense should be charged to the current year. Usually the investor does not have sufficient information to do this, and there is no easy shortcut for the adjustment as in the case of property and liability insurance companies.

However, the investor can approximate the unrecovered cost of life business by an estimated value based on expected future income. This would be difficult to do for an industrial firm, since seldom would the investor have available the needed information on equipment nor could he readily make estimates of future income from it. Life insurance companies are a different case. The investor can secure data with which to make reasonable estimates of a company's future income from its business now in force.

Calculating the Value of Business in Force. Customarily, analysts of life stocks have used a standard figure (such as $20 per $1,000) for the value of business in force. This ignores the fact that the value varies from one company to another.

As suggested previously, the value of a company's business in force can be calculated by estimating the future income from a company's current business in force and discounting this future income back to its present value. The future income can be estimated by projecting year by year the various factors that determine the profit from a particular block of business in force. The discount rate used to find the present value of this future income should be the company's return on equity, but not less than 10%-12%.

The calculations necessary to project income from life insurance policies may seem awesome to one not versed in insurance and are at best tedious, unless a computer is available. However, it is possible to use precalculated tables of values for a wide range of many of the variables to derive the value rather than to calculate it directly.[5]

Values for group, health, and industrial insurance business can be similarly calculated. A higher discount rate is justified for both group and health insurance business because of the greater risk that expected profits from these policies will not be realized.

Making the Adjustments. After calculating the value of the various types of insurance business, the investor is prepared to use these value figures in adjusting earnings and book value. The total calculated value of business in force is added to stockholders' equity. Any increase in this calculated value over the value at the end of the previous year is added to reported earnings for the year. A decrease in the value is subtracted from reported earnings.

Certain additional adjustments may be necessary. Some assets, called "nonadmitted assets," cannot be shown on the company's regular balance sheet. Often these assets should be included by the investor. Similarly, the amounts in voluntary reserve accounts and the mandatory securities valuation reserve should be added to stockholders' equity. (See new AICPA rules.)

Quality in Life Insurance Stocks

In general terms, for a life insurance company to be considered of investment quality, there should be no doubt as to its ability to maintain its solvency indefinitely, and its earnings should be reasonably stable and should be growing. The company's expenses should be moderate. The business that it writes should be of high quality, and the cost of acquiring this business should be low. Finally, return on stockholders' equity should be satisfactory. The following quantitative measures give a good picture of these factors.

---

[5] For such a set of tables, see Reynolds Griffith, *The Valuation of Life Insurance Stocks* (Denton, Texas: Financial Publications, Inc., 1967).

Maintenance of Solvency. Legal reserve life insurance companies seldom fail; however, it is still possible for financial difficulties to develop. One important test is the *stockholders' equity ratio,* which is the ratio of stockholders' equity [6] to total assets. The relative amount of stockholders' equity indicates the cushion available to absorb unusual losses, fluctuations in the value of the company's assets, exceptionally large numbers of surrenders, and other unforeseeable happenings. The permissible level of this ratio for a life insurance company is much lower than for an industrial company or even a utility company. This is because a life insurance company's liabilities are mostly of a long-term nature and its assets are over 90% debt instruments and only 8% in equities. It has been the pattern for life insurance company reserves to be constantly increasing. Premiums collected in any year are sufficient to make all necessary payments in the year without liquidating any of the company's investment portfolio. Assets doubled from 1959 to 1973.

Measures of Stability. The maximum percentage decline in earnings in the past 10 years should be examined. Although the stability of the economy since 1938 has not provided a real test of the ability of life insurance companies to maintain their earnings level under adverse conditions, this percentage will give some inkling of such capability. Companies that had the most unstable earnings during a favorable period can be expected to perform especially poorly in adverse circumstances. This indicator should be calculated on both a reported earnings basis and an adjusted earnings basis. Reported earnings may decline because of a step-up in the rate at which new business is being written, so that a decline in reported earnings unaccompanied by a decline in adjusted earnings need not be viewed as an indication of serious instability.

The number of years in the 10-year period in which earnings declined compared with the previous year should also be considered. Not only is the severity of earnings declines significant, but also their frequency. Obviously, the more years in which earnings declined, the less stable the company is.

Measures of Efficiency. The tests of management in this area, as in other companies, are such measures as the return on stockholders' equity and the growth of earnings. But it will also be helpful to look at specific indicators, especially in the area of expenses. The following two are particularly useful:

Renewal Expense per $1,000 of Old Business in Force. To calculate this measure, renewal expense must first be estimated. This is done by subtracting from general insurance expense the identifiable first-year expenses that are

---

[6] The figure used here should be after all adjustments except for the value of business in force. The value of business is an intangible asset, and it is safer not to include such assets in measures of solvency.

contained in this item. These include medical examination and inspection report fees, advertising, agency expense allowance, agents' balances charged off, agency conferences, first-year compensation to agents other than commissions, and agency supervision. The balance is then allocated between first-year business and renewal business by giving business written a weight of 5 and business at the beginning of the year a weight of 1. To the amount thus allocated to renewal business is added the renewal commissions, producing the total renewal expense. The total renewal expense is then divided by the business in force at the beginning of the year, and the result is multiplied by 1,000 to convert it to the per $1,000 basis generally used in referring to life insurance.

The renewal expense per $1,000, particularly when calculated separately for ordinary business, provides a measure that is suitable for comparison between companies or with a general standard. It largely eliminates the effect of differences in premium levels and of different relative amounts of new to old business.

Investment Yield. Investment yield is the ratio of net investment income to mean assets. This figure measures how well management is investing the assets relative to competing companies. An unusually high yield probably indicates that excessive risks are being taken. The trend of a company's investment yield should be rising in line with the general trend for the industry—2.3% in 1952 and 4% in 1972.

Growth in Earnings. Growth in earnings per share is by far the most important factor to be considered in measuring the growth of a company. The rates of growth of both reported and adjusted earnings should be at a satisfactory level. Any divergence of the two over a period of several years should be investigated.

Quality of Business. The great attention given to growth of business in force and the tendency to measure the success of management by company size can result in concentration by management on selling new business without giving proper consideration to the quality of risks and the return that will accrue to stockholders from the additional business. Tremendous amounts of new business of poor quality will be of little benefit to the stockholder. Consequently, the investor must attempt to measure the quality of the business. The following factors will be of assistance in this effort:

Lapse Ratio. This is the ratio of voluntary terminations (including both lapses and surrenders) to business in force (average of beginning and ending).

The lapse ratio should be calculated by using the amount of business instead of the number of policies; group business should not be included in it.

The lower the lapse ratio, the longer a company's business is remaining in force on the average and the greater is the profit that can be expected. The first-year lapse ratio would be an especially good gauge of how well the company's business is being sold, but unfortunately it is not available because lapses on new business are not reported separately. Some indication of terminations of newer business can be obtained by comparing the amount of surrenders to the amount of lapses. For ordinary life, most policies have a cash value after the second or third year, so that the surrenders approximate the amount of business over 2 years old that is being dropped. Thus it would be desirable for a company not only to have a low lapse ratio, but also to have a large part of the terminations be surrenders rather than lapses.

Composition of Business in Force. The proportion of most profitable lines, particularly ordinary life (whole life and endowment), and the trends are extremely important. Many companies have achieved substantial apparent growth by concentrating on sales of group insurance. This group business generally carries with it a thin margin of profit. Year-to-year fluctuations in mortality have a much greater relative impact on earnings from group business than on earnings from ordinary life because current death claims take a much larger proportion of premium income. Reserves that can benefit stockholders through their leverage effect do not build up to nearly as great an extent on group business as on ordinary business. The group field is highly competitive, and switches of large group cases from one company to another are entirely possible. Investors should prefer life companies that have concentrated on ordinary life rather than group business.

Composition of Premium Income. As with the composition of business in force, the composition of premium income measure should show a substantial proportion of premium income from ordinary life. However, it is even more important to note the proportion of premium income that a company gets from its health insurance business since this class of insurance does not show up in the business in force measure. It is possible for health insurance to be extremely profitable, but most companies have not found it so. With an occasional exception for companies that have shown consistent and substantial earnings from health insurance over a long period of time, dependence by a company on this line for a large part of its premium income should be considered unfavorable.

Acquisition Cost. The business that a company acquires not only must be of high quality, but also must be secured at a reasonable cost. The business is of no net value to the company or its stockholders if it requires an outlay to secure it that will not be recovered together with a reasonable rate of return. The following indicators measure acquisition cost:

First-Year Compensation Ratio. This is the ratio of first-year compensation to first-year premium income. First-year compensation includes, in addition to first-year commissions, the "other first-year compensation" reported by the company, agents' balances that were charged off during the year, and the increase in agents' debit balances. Compensation of agents is the major cost of securing new business. A high first-year compensation ratio not only means that it will take longer for the business written to return net profits to the company, but also it may indicate a relatively poor standing by the company in the industry. An excessive first-year compensation ratio indicates that the company has difficulty in getting agents. The figures for group business should not be included in the calculation of this ratio.

First-Year Expense Ratio. This is the ratio of first-year expense to first-year premium income. The total first-year expense is calculated by subtracting from general insurance expense the renewal expense previously calculated and by adding the first-year compensation figure. Other first-year compensation to agents and agents' balances charged off must then be subtracted and renewal commissions must be added back in order to avoid counting these items twice. This ratio is better when it is calculated separately for ordinary life business. It measures that part of the new premium received that was needed to acquire that premium. However, a first-year expense ratio of less than 1 does not mean that the business was immediately profitable, as it does not take into account required reserves or taxes. It does include the items that are subject to some degree of management control.

Return on Stockholders' Equity. This is the most important single measure of benefit to stockholders in any line of business. It shows how well management is using the funds provided by stockholders and is used for comparison with other companies. It should be calculated using both reported and adjusted earnings and stockholders' equity. The adjusted figures may be more accurate, but a satisfactory return should be indicated by both calculations.

Standards for Quantitative Measures. It is helpful to set specific levels for ratios that should be met by a company in order for it to be considered of investment quality. Table 24-3 presents satisfactory standards that should be applied in the analysis of a life insurance company stock. A company might not be disqualified because it failed to measure up to the standard on a single ratio, but the investor must use his judgment to assess the significance of the shortcoming.

Valuation of Life Insurance Stocks

Valuing the stocks of life insurance companies has seemed especially difficult to investors because of the peculiarities in life insurance accounting and the lack of comparability to other companies in the financial factors. However, the adjustment of earnings as previously discussed largely overcomes the accounting problem. The ratios given in the previous sections can be used to judge life insurance companies as the more traditional ratios are used to judge other companies. Thus the investor, using the methods presented in this chapter, can proceed from this point with the valuation of life insurance company shares as he is accustomed to doing in valuing the stocks of other companies.

TABLE 24-3

Suggested Standards for Ratios for Life Insurance Companies

	Minimum	Maximum
Stockholders' Equity Ratio	8%	
Maximum Decline in Earnings:		
Reported		20%
Adjusted		15%
Years of Earnings Decline in Past 10 Years		3
Renewal Expense per $1,000		$2.50
Yield on Investments	4.5%	5.5%
Growth Rate of Earnings per Share	6%	
Lapse Ratio		8%
Composition of Business in Force:		
Ordinary and Industrial	50%	
Term		30%
Group		30%
Composition of Premium Income:		
Ordinary and Industrial	50%	
Health Insurance		20%
First-Year Compensation		90%
First-Year Expense Ratio		125%
Return on Stockholders' Equity	10%	

Performance of Life Insurance Stocks

Life insurance stocks have enjoyed two periods of extreme popularity in the past 20 years. The first of these was 1946-1955; the S&P Monthly Index of Life Insurance Stocks rose nearly 10 times from 18.6 to 177.7 while the S&P 500 rose only 2.4 times. In the 1956-1960 period the life insurance index moved horizontally, reflecting the uncertainty pending action by Congress to increase the impact of the income tax on insurance companies.

In the strong 1961 market, life insurance stocks were one of the popular groups. The S&P Monthly Index of Life Insurance Stocks went from 146 in the latter part of 1960 to 304 in 1961 or 16 times its 1946 high and 5 times its 1952 high. The index then rose gradually to its all time peak of 365 in 1964. It had bear market lows of 190 in 1966 and 147 in 1970 and then recovered in January, 1973.

QUESTIONS

1. Why should insurance company stocks not be viewed as merely the same as shares of investment companies?

2. (a) Define "statutory underwriting results."
   (b) Discuss the interpretation of statutory underwriting results for a given insurance company, assuming that the company has experienced a sharp rise in premium volume.

3. Discuss the problems of adjusting reported underwriting results to derive a meaningful income figure and a meaningful stockholders' equity figure.

4. What added difficulties are present in estimating the underwriting results for a property and liability insurance company as contrasted to a life insurance company?

5. Discuss the cyclical and long-run characteristics of fire and casualty insurance stocks.

6. (a) What are the three underwriting tests?
   (b) Explain the meaning and the importance of each test.

7. Explain the importance of income from investments in analyzing insurance company stocks.

8. (a) What factors enter into the calculation of the premium that a life insurance company will charge?
   (b) Why should an investor be wary of using the growth in life insurance in force as an indicator of the growth of life insurance companies?
   (c) What are some of the major factors that contributed to the outstanding growth of the life insurance industry?

9. (a) Why do analysts feel that the reported earnings of life insurance companies are understated?

   (b) How would an analyst adjust reported earnings of a life insurance company?

   (c) Could a life insurance company that reported a net loss from operations over the past two years be a better investment than a life insurance company that reported a profit? Explain.

10. Discuss measures useful to the investor in attempting to assess the quality of business that a particular insurance company has in force and is writing.

WORK-STUDY PROBLEMS

1. The following are the important items in the income account and the balance sheets of two fire insurance companies:

	Company A ($ Millions)	Company B ($ Millions)
Net Premiums Written	$ 201	$ 102
Premiums Earned	200	98
Losses Incurred	119	63
Underwriting Expense	95	42
Gain from Underwriting	D4*	D7*
Interest, Dividends & Rents, etc.	22	10
Net Income	18	3
Number of Shares (000)	10,691	1,000
Unearned Premium Reserve	315	76
Capital	53	10
Voluntary Reserves	244	103
Surplus	223	60

   * D = Deficit

   (a) Calculate for both companies:
   1. The loss ratio.
   2. The expense ratio.
   3. The combined ratio.
   4. The liquidating value.
   5. Net earnings per share.

   (b) Assuming that Company A stock is selling at 55 a share and Company B stock at 110, comment on the relative merits of the two companies in the light of the ratios you have derived.

2. Select a life insurance company or a property and liability insurance company and analyze it on the basis of the material discussed in this chapter. Prepare statistical data covering a 5-year period to aid you in your evaluation, including all pertinent data.

SUGGESTED READINGS

An Aid to Understanding Financial Reports of Fire and Casualty Insurance Companies. Boston, Mass.: The First Boston Corp.

Association of Insurance and Financial Analysts, New York: *Final Report of the Committee on Life Insurance Earnings Adjustments,* 1970.

Best, Alfred M. & Co., Morristown, New Jersey.
  (1) *Best's Aggregates and Averages (Annual).* (a) Life; (b) Property & Liability.
  (2) *Best's Insurance Reports,* Property and Liability.
  (3) *Best's Insurance Reports,* Life.
  (4) *Best's Review* (Monthly), Property and Liability.
  (5) *Best's Review* (Monthly), Life Edition.

Economic and Investment Report (Annual). New York: Life Insurance Association of America.

Ferguson, Elizabeth. *Sources of Insurance Statistics.* New York: Special Libraries Association, 1965.

Insurance Advocate (Weekly). New York: Insurance Advocate.

Insurance Bulletin. New York: Insurance Dept., State of New York.

Insurance Magazine (Weekly). New York: Insurance Magazine.

Life Insurance Fact Book (Annual). New York: Institute of Life Insurance.

McGee, John H., and D. L. Bickelhaupt. *General Insurance,* 8th ed. Homewood, Illinois: Richard D. Irwin, Inc. 1970.

National Underwriter, Life Edition (Weekly). Cincinnati, Ohio: National Underwriter.

National Underwriter, Fire & Casualty Edition (Weekly). Cincinnati, Ohio: National Underwriter.

Schott, Francis H. "Disintermediation Through Policy Loans at Life Insurance Companies." *The Journal of Finance* (June, 1971), pp. 719-730.

Spectator (Monthly). Philadelphia, Pa.: Spectator.

Tally of Life Insurance Statistics, The. New York: Institute of Life Insurance.

Investment Company Stocks

Investment companies sell their securities to investors and then invest the funds thus obtained in a diversified portfolio of securities, generally common stocks but in some cases preferred stocks and bonds. The investment company provides the investor with diversification that most investors would otherwise find difficult or impossible to secure. It also provides professional management that should obtain a record of performance superior to that which would be posted by the average investor working on his own. Investment companies relieve the investor of the problems of selection. All dividends and interest income received and all realized capital gains (less operating and management expenses) are normally distributed annually in quarterly dividends, with the final "quarterly" completing distribution.

CLASSIFICATION OF INVESTMENT COMPANIES BY CAPITALIZATION

The three major classifications of investment companies in this category are (1) closed-end funds, (2) dual-purpose funds, and (3) open-end (or mutual) funds.

Closed-End Companies

Closed-end companies have a closed capitalization as do other types of corporations. They do not normally sell additional shares, although some have occasionally had rights offerings. They do not redeem their shares. Of the 24, there are 13 diversified funds of significant interest to investors, and 11 of these are listed on the New York Stock Exchange. Until the late 1940s their unique feature was the existence of senior securities—bank loans, bonds, and preferred stock. But for diversified companies senior capital has almost disappeared. Only five large funds have any leverage, and their leverage effect is insignificant.

The shares of closed-end companies, being nonredeemable, must sell in the market as do other securities. Their prices therefore reflect the supply and demand situation at any particular time. Historically they have usually sold at a discount, sometimes substantial, from the net asset value. The record of discounts and premiums of closed-end funds is given in Table 25-1.

The investor pays a broker's commission when purchasing the stock and another when selling the stock. On the other hand, if he is able to purchase shares of a closed-end fund at a liberal discount, he may more than make up the commissions paid if subsequently the discount narrows. When the investor buys more than one dollar's worth of earning assets for each dollar of market price, he has these extra funds working for him. However, wide discounts may indicate hazards and a poor record, and the investor should investigate carefully.

Dual Funds

Dual closed-end funds first sold in 1967. They have two kinds of shares outstanding—income shares and capital shares—with each group contributing half of the original capital equity. The contract with the income shares resembles a preferred stock contract and calls for stated minimum dividends if earned and accumulation of arrearages if not earned. All net investment is owned by the income shareowners. The contract provides that the fund in a stated number of years (for example, 10) will be liquidated. After payment of original capital investment plus dividend arrearages (if any) to income shareholders, distribution of the remaining assets will be made pro rata to the capital shareowners, who receive no dividends during the life of the corporation. The capital shareowners are simply seeking capital gains, and they are entitled to all accumulated capital gains when the fund is liquidated. Capital shareowners assume all capital risks. The capital shares are capital levered, contributing only half the capital but entitled to all capital gains realized after deductions of any income share dividend arrearages. Similarly, the income shares are income levered.

Since the dual funds are closed-end funds, their shares sell in the over-the-counter market on a demand-supply basis. Through 1969 the capital shares all sold at a discount. At the bear market low in May, 1970, they all sold

TABLE 25-1

Closed-End Investment Companies, Year-End Discounts and Premiums

	1971	1970	1969	1968	1967	1966	1965	1964	1963	1962	1961
Diversified Companies											
*Adams Express	15%	6%	P 6%	P10%	6%	6%	12%	10%	9%	4%	3%
Boston Personal Prop. Trust	7	6	0	P 2	4	11	23	19	17	21	9
*Carriers & General	20	18	14	12	21	19	11	6	8	7	2
Consolidated Inv. Trust	2	2	4	P 1	1	10	21	14	19	18	12
*Dominick Fund	25	18	8	4	5	20	19	12	9	5	4
*General American Investors	12	8	P 8	P14	P 1	11	7	6	3	P 1	10
International Holdings	23	18	10	5	16	25	21	15	19	14	12
*Lehman Corporation	8	P14	P16	P23	P16	9	11	6	P 1	P 4	P 5
*Madison Fund	3	P16	P48	P32	P19	P18	P 2	P 3	P13	P26	P32
*Niagara Share	13	P 5	P12	P 8	11	12	8	0	6	3	P 6
*Surveyor Fund	28	8	P10	P10	13	13	14	16	15	8	P12
*Tri-Continental Corporation	14	5	2	4	16	25	23	24	21	15	13
*U.S. & Foreign Securities	7	3	11	7	17	29	33	26	24	19	16
Diversified Investment Company Average	15	3	P 6	P 7	5	12	14	10	8	4	3
Specialized Companies											
American-South African	P10	P37	15	P54	P77	P12	P 5	10	34	35	39
Diebold Venture Capital Corp.	41	48	25	7	—	—	—	—	—	—	—
Inventure Capital Corp.	52	42	—	7	—	—	—	—	—	—	—
Japan Fund	P 7	P11	P 6	P 5	9	32	27	32	15	34	3
National Aviation	15	12	15	P26	P33	P14	2	10	2	P 2	—
New America Fund	58	47	41	0	—	—	—	—	—	—	—
Petroleum Corporation	14	3	P 4	P 7	3	0	P 6	3	6	5	0
Price Capital Corp.	47	37	34	—	—	—	—	—	—	—	—
SMC Investment Corp.	42	33	32	P 3	—	—	—	—	—	—	—
Value Line Develop. Cap. Corp.	49	36	20	P18	—	—	—	—	—	—	—
Non Diversified Companies											
Allegheny Corporation ‡	33	26	30	18	37	51	38	46	36	10	31
Central Securities	P14	P37	P58	P31	3	P 9	11	P 5	P 5	P 3	P 5
Standard Shares	23	24	13	6	20	21	16	10	8	3	P 1
United Corporation	26	15	14	7	12	20	24	19	12	3	5

* Included in Diversified Investment Company Average.
— Prior to formation of company.
‡ Discounts from net asset values before deducting potential liability for federal taxes on unrealized appreciation.
P Premium.

Source: *Investment Companies, 1972* (New York: Wiesenberger Services, Inc.)

at premiums ranging from 1% to 30%. In January, 1973, they were all sold at discounts between 10% and 41% (see Table 25-2). Initially the capital leverage is 2 to 1; but if capital shares sell at a discount, the leverage may rise, for example, to 4 to 1.

TABLE 25-2

Dual-Purpose Funds—January, 1973

Friday, January 5, 1973

Following is a weekly listing of the unaudited net asset values of dual-purpose, closed-end investment funds' capital shares as reported by the companies as of Friday's close. Also shown is the closing listed market price or the dealer-to-dealer asked price of each fund's capital shares, with the percentage of difference.

	Cap. Shs. Price	N.A. Val.[a] Cap. Shs.	% Diff.
Am DualVest	10¼	13.89	—26.2
Gemini	16¼	21.87	—25.7
Hemisphere	3¾	4.17	—10.1
Income and Cap.	9⅞	15.10	—34.6
Leverage	13½	18.76	—28.0
Putnam Duo Fund	5⅜	8.61	—37.6
Scudder Duo-Vest	8¾	12.55	—30.3
Scudder D-V Exchange ...	32	53.96	—40.7

[a] After giving effect to arrearages, if any, of cumulative dividends and amortization of any difference between original paid-in capital and the redemption price of income shares.

Source: Arthur Lipper Corp., New York.

It is somewhat difficult to appraise the dual funds because management has a dual purpose: (1) to pay the income required annually and at the same time (2) to build capital share values for the capital shareowners. There appears to be a conflict of interest here that may be difficult to reconcile. For example, most professionals on Wall Street believe that the highest income stocks generally have the least capital gains potential, while those with the greatest capital gains potential provide the lowest income and often no dividends. This thinking should not be accepted at face value because the virtue of many out-of-favor stocks is that they provide both above-normal yield and large capital gains opportunities. But most professionals as well as laymen will not operate in out-of-favor stocks. It is therefore unlikely that the management of these dual funds would consider significant investment in out-of-favor stocks. If they did, one would feel much more sanguine about the probability of these funds accomplishing their goals for both classes of investors. It would be difficult to do this with other stocks.

In assessing the probability of a dual fund's meeting the demands of its income shares, it should be remembered that while the income shares contributed only half the capital, they are entitled to all the income (that is, income leverage).

Mutual Funds

The open-end funds are called *mutual funds*. Mutual funds constantly sell new shares and offer to redeem outstanding shares at all times. The two major classifications of mutual funds are (1) load funds and (2) no-load funds. *Load funds* make a sales charge for their shares, while *no-load funds* do not.

The prices of mutual fund shares quoted are: (1) the "bid" or redemption price, which is the net asset value; and (2) the "asked" price, which for load funds is the net asset value plus a "load" or sales charge ranging from 7½% to 8½% of the total payment, or 9.3% of the amount invested.[1]

After 1969 there was a sharp increase in the number of no-load funds with well over 100 in January, 1973, whose combined assets represented about 10% of all mutual fund assets. Fourteen had assets of $100 million or more and 65 had assets of less than $5 million. In general, no-load funds are operated as adjuncts to investment advisory firms with other clients or by brokerage firms. The 1940 Investment Company Act permits them to have only one nonaffiliated director versus 40% in other types of mutual funds. The sales charges for mutual funds cover both the purchase *and* the sale with generally no redemption charge. Brokers and dealers have no incentive to sell no-load funds, and therefore they naturally sell the load funds. They tend to push those with the best performance record, which are the easiest to sell.

While the Investment Company Act of 1940 requires that, for regulated companies, redemption must be made within 7 days of a request, in practice redemption is accomplished the same day. Thus there is no delay such as may occur in the sale of a large block of other types of securities, and furthermore the price is fixed at the net asset value at the time.[2] The price is based on NYSE-closing prices for redemption orders received prior to that closing.

---

[1] The sales charge is usually reduced for large orders, for example to 6% on a purchase of $25,000, to 5% on a purchase of $50,000, to 3% on a purchase of $100,000, and to 1% on a purchase of $500,000 or more.

[2] In 1968 the Mates Fund, because of a heavy commitment in "letter stock" of a company, was forced to request the SEC to permit it to suspend redemption.

Table 25-3 shows the record of gross sales and redemptions of mutual fund shares, the net sales, the redemption rate, the total assets, and the number of funds from 1940 to 1971 inclusive.

Performance Records. The answer as to which mutual fund to purchase should be based, not on whether it is a load fund or a no-load fund, but on the record of management, the fund's performance, and the relation of fund policies to the investor's requirements and goals. Obviously, the fact that there is no load cannot offset a poor performance record. Mutual fund investors should be long-term investors. In the case of load funds with an excellent record, the spreading of the load over a long-term investment period means that the impact of the sales charge is not significant. Of course, if an

TABLE 25-3

Growth of Mutual Funds

Year	Total Net Assets	Gross Sales	Redemptions	Net Sales	Redemption Rate	Shareholder Accounts	Number of Funds
			—000 Omitted—				
1971	$55,045,328	$5,147,186	$4,750,222	$ 396,964	9.3%	10,900,952	392
1970	47,618,100	4,625,802	2,987,572	1,638,230	6.2	10,690,312	356
1969	48,290,733	6,718,283	3,661,646	3,056,637	7.3	10,391,534	269
1968	52,677,188	6,819,763	3,838,682	2,981,081	7.9	9,080,168	240
1967	44,701,302	4,669,575	2,744,197	1,925,378	6.9	7,904,132	204
1966	34,829,353	4,671,842	2,005,079	2,666,763	5.7	7,701,656	182
1965	35,220,243	4,358,144	1,962,432	2,395,712	6.1	6,709,343	170
1964	29,116,254	3,402,978	1,874,094	1,528,884	6.9	6,301,908	159
1963	25,214,436	2,459,105	1,505,335	953,770	6.5	6,151,935	165
1962	21,270,735	2,699,049	1,122,695	1,576,354	5.1	5,910,455	169
1961	22,788,812	2,950,860	1,160,357	1,790,503	5.8	5,319,201	170
1960	17,025,684	2,097,246	841,815	1,255,431	5.1	4,897,600	161
1959	15,817,962	2,279,982	785,627	1,494,355	5.4	4,276,077	155
1958	13,242,388	1,619,768	511,263	1,108,505	4.7	3,630,096	151
1957	8,714,143	1,390,557	406,716	983,841	4.6	3,110,392	143
1956	9,046,431	1,346,738	432,750	913,988	5.1	2,518,049	135
1955	7,837,524	1,207,458	442,550	764,908	6.4	2,085,325	125
1954	6,109,390	862,817	399,702	463,115	7.8	1,703,846	115
1953	4,146,061	672,005	238,778	433,227	5.9	1,537,250	110
1952	3,931,407	782,902	196,022	586,880	5.6	1,359,000	110
1951	3,129,629	674,610	321,550	353,060	11.4	1,110,432	103
1950	2,530,563	518,811	280,728	238,083	12.5	938,651	98
1949	1,973,547	385,526	107,587	277,939	6.2	842,198	91
1948	1,505,762	273,787	127,171	146,616	8.7	722,118	87
1947	1,409,165	266,924	88,732	178,192	6.5	672,543	80
1946	1,311,108	370,353	143,612	226,741	11.1	580,221	74
1945	1,284,185	292,359	109,978	182,381	10.2	497,875	73
1944	882,191	169,228	70,815	98,413	9.2	421,675	68
1943	653,653	116,026	51,221	64,841	8.9	341,435	68
1942	486,850	73,140	25,440	47,700	5.6	312,609	68
1941	401,611	53,312	45,024	8,288	10.6	293,251	68
1940	447,958	†	†	†	†	296,056	68

Data pertain to member companies of the Investment Company Institute. Total net assets at the 1971 year-end are 95% of the combined assets of all mutual funds listed in this book, including 586 regular funds and 24 tax-free-exchange funds. Institute "gross sales" figures do not include the proceeds of initial fund underwritings. In 1972 redemptions exceeded sales for the first time in history. Sales were $4.9 billion and redemptions were $6.6 billion, or an excess of redemptions of $1.7 billion. Funds purchased $1.81 billion in securities and sold $1.62 billion. Purchases of common stock totaled $1.56 billion and sales were $1.42 billion.
　　† Not available.

Source: *Investment Companies,* 1972 (New York: Arthur Wiesenberger Service, Division of Nuveen Corp.)

investor is in and out of mutual funds, which he should not be, then the sales load does become a strongly negative factor.[3]

Special Services of Mutual Funds. The mutual fund industry has developed numerous services and devices to increase the convenience, flexibility, and attractiveness of investing in mutual funds. The principal services are discussed in the following paragraphs:

Accumulative Plans. Because many investors invest in mutual funds as a means of building capital over a period of years, the companies have developed two types of accumulative plans—*voluntary* plans and *contractual* plans.

In 1972 about 40% of the accounts were "accumulation plan" accounts. Under either type the investor makes an application, which together with a check for the initial purchase of shares, puts the plan in operation. He makes subsequent purchases simply by mailing a check to the fund's custodian, and usually he agrees to have all dividends reinvested through this account. Normally no stock certificates are issued, but the shareowner is notified periodically of the balance of shares held in his account.

Voluntary plans. Under a voluntary accumulative plan, the investor makes purchases of fund shares whenever he desires to do so and in any amount that he wishes. Some mutual funds, however, do have minimum amounts for purchases, such as $50, or $100, or $500.

Contractual plans. A contractual plan involves a more formal arrangement (a contract) than other accumulative plans and encourages the investor to follow a specific program to reach a predetermined goal. A contractual plan calls for periodic purchases (usually monthly) of a fixed dollar amount for a stated period of years—anywhere from 5 to 15 years.

The part of the contractual plan that persuades the investor to continue the plan is the procedure for applying the costs—specifically the *front-end load*. Half of the first year's payments are generally deducted for sales charges. The Investment Company Act provides a maximum sales charge limit of 9% and a maximum deduction for these charges of 50% of the first year's installment. But as of 1970, mutual funds are required to agree to rescind within 45 days the entire transaction if requested, or to refund all payments less 15% commission during the first 18 months. Alternatively

---

[3] The difference between no-load funds and growth funds with a sales charge becomes insignificant between a 4- and 5-year holding period based on the mean index for each group. The implication to the investor of this finding is that if he is willing to commit funds for 5 years, then he need not take the load charge of a fund into account. However, if he feels that he might want to pull out of the investment before the end of 5 years, he would be better off in a no-load fund. See Robert J. Crabb, "No-Load Mutual Funds—A Better Buy," *Financial Research, Investment Analysis and the Computer* (Hanover, N. H.: Dartmouth College, 1967).

a plan may charge 20% per year for three years, limited to 64% over the first four years rather than the former plan.

Dividend Reinvestment. Practically all mutual funds make the provision that dividends (both income dividends and capital gains distributions) may be automatically reinvested.

Withdrawal Plans. Many mutual funds make provisions for investors who are no longer accumulating shares but, in fact, wish to gradually liquidate their holdings—usually after retirement. Investment income may be divided evenly into 12 monthly payments, or a level monthly payment may consist of investment income plus a certain percent of capital, or the periodic payments may fluctuate with the current value of the shares in an effort (but not a guarantee) to reduce the risk of exhausting all capital over too short a period of years.

CLASSIFICATION OF INVESTMENT COMPANIES BY POLICIES

Managements of different investment funds follow a variety of policies to suit individual needs. Management must spell out its investment policy in its prospectus. Each investor should clearly define his investment objectives and then select a fund whose stated policy conforms to his individual policies and goals. He should then ascertain whether or not the company in the past has been successful in its stated policy. Stated policies may be quite broad.

The four major bases upon which investment companies are classified according to policies are maximum capital gains, growth, growth and income, and specialized funds. The latter are nondiversified. However, to qualify for special tax treatment of mutual funds, these nondiversified specialized funds come under the same rule for 50% of their assets as opposed to 75% of the assets of a diversified fund. Furthermore, not more than 25% of total assets may be invested in one company.

Common Stock Funds

Of the 610 mutual funds covered in *Investment Companies,* 508 were common stock funds as of December 31, 1971 (see Table 25-4). Usually, these funds are continuously invested 90-95% in common stocks.

Balanced Funds

These maintain at all times a diversified portfolio balanced between bonds,

TABLE 25-4

Classification of Mutual Funds by Size and Type As of January 1, 1972

Size of Fund	Number of Funds	Combined Assets (000 omitted)	% of Total
Over One Billion	13	$20,930,000	36.0
$500 Million—$1 Billion	15	10,385,200	17.8
$300 Million—$500 Million	17	6,383,200	11.0
$100 Million—$300 Million	64	10,746,500	18.5
$ 50 Million—$100 Million	70	4,907,600	8.4
$ 10 Million—$ 50 Million	170	3,984,100	6.8
$ 1 Million—$ 10 Million	191	793,700	1.4
Under One Million	70	29,500	0.1
Total	610	$58,159,800	100.0

Type of Fund	Number of Funds	Combined Assets (000 omitted)	% of Total
Common Stock:			
Maximum Capital Gain	192	$ 8,721,100	15.0
Growth	174	18,419,400	31.7
Growth and Income	130	19,806,400	34.1
Specialized	12	256,900	0.4
Balanced	28	6,695,200	11.5
Income	29	2,353,700	4.0
Tax-Free Exchange	24	1,104,100	1.9
Bond and Preferred Stock	21	803,000	1.4
Total	610	$58,159,800	100.0

Source: *Investment Companies*, 1972 (New York: Arthur Wiesenberger and Company. Typical yield in 1973: growth funds, 1.3%; growth-income funds, 2.3%; balanced funds, 3.0%; and income funds, 5.0%.

preferred stocks, and common stocks with proportions dictated by management's assessment of the probable trend of common prices and interest rates.

Income Funds

Income funds purchase securities primarily for relatively high income by the averages.

Tax-Free Exchange or Swap Funds

Section 351 of the Internal Revenue Code permits tax-free contributions of securities in the formation of a new corporation. First, a new fund must be created; then other requirements of the statute must be complied with. All securities contributed to the new corporation must be held in escrow during the period of organization of the fund. It is a one-deal proposition; there can be no continuous offering of shares as with the regular mutual funds. The first such fund was established in 1960, and by 1973 there were 23 such funds.[4]

The exchange of these securities is assumed to be tax free. Therefore, an individual who owns a portfolio that includes heavy capital gains, often in a relatively few companies, can exchange this portfolio for shares in a widely diversified fund without first selling the portfolio shares and paying a capital gains tax and then reinvesting the remaining funds in an investment company. However, the cost of the new shares in the fund acquired is, for tax purposes, the cost of the original shares exchanged. The capital gains tax has not been eliminated but only postponed.

Generally, the funds have set a minimum contribution of $20,000 and have expressed their policy as one that seeks long-term capital gains and

---

[4] The tax-free exchange funds and their net asset value per share on January 12, 1973, were as follows:

Fund	Net Asset Value 1/11/73	Value 1/4/73	% Change 12 mos. Date *	Fund	Net Asset Value 1/11/73	Value 1/4/73	% Change 12 mos. Date *
Capital Exch	$ 39.85	$ 39.69	+21.25	5th Empire	$ 19.14	$ 19.31	+ 3.07
Congress St	223.53	221.68	+26.87	5th Presidential	40.91	40.96	+12.10
Constitution	71.08	70.47	+29.85	4th Empire	23.21	23.36	+ 6.88
Depositors of Boston	29.46	29.42	+19.60	Industries Exch	16.61	16.51	+11.67
Devonshire St	19.32	19.19	+17.64	Ohio Capital	34.54	34.25	+11.31
Diversification	46.90	46.47	+22.13	Presi Exch	43.37	43.57	+12.57
Empire	25.94	25.79	+13.16	2nd Congress St	46.17	45.67	+26.13
Exchange of Boston	55.01	54.45	+20.60	2nd Fid Exch	41.55	41.25	+20.23
Exeter	55.52	55.52	+ 9.85	2nd Pres Exch	42.20	42.30	+14.72
Federal Street	34.90	34.77	+19.46	6th Empire	18.86	19.01	+ 5.04
Fed Dual-Exch-Cap	25.58	26.04	− 0.53	3rd Empire	10.73	10.96	+ 1.60
Fiduciary Exch	30.45	30.55	+11.96	Average % Change			+14.66

* Includes reinvestment of all capital gains distributions and investment income dividends during the period. **Source:** Arthur Lipper Corp.

income. Management reserves the right to refuse to accept proposed contributions of securities if such securities do not fit the policies of management.

Bond and Preferred Stock Funds

These funds invest only in bonds and preferred stocks, and some of them invest only in tax-exempt bonds so that income paid to shareholders is exempt from income taxes.

Foreign Investments—Canadian and International Funds

Some funds invest only or mainly in foreign securities such as Canadian General Funds, Inc., Canadian Funds, Inc., Japan Funds, and Eurofund. The Japan Fund has had exceptionally large capital gains in 1963-1973.

REGULATION OF INVESTMENT COMPANIES

While investment companies are subject to the state statutes in the state in which they are incorporated and to the state "blue sky" laws in states in which they sell securities, the major protection for investors is afforded by the regulations of the Federal Investment Company Act of 1940. The act resulted from a long and thorough industry study by the SEC. The final legislation as passed was a combined effort by the SEC and the industry. The act provided the basis for the tremendous growth of the mutual fund industry after 1940 and especially after World War II.

Under the 1940 Act, required information about an investment company must be given in full in a registration statement and in summary form in a prospectus. The prospectus must be given to any person to whom the security is offered and to every purchaser. The detailed objectives of the 1940 Act are listed below.[5]

1. Provide investors with complete and accurate information concerning the character of investment company securities and the circumstances, policies and financial responsibility of investment companies and their management;
2. Provide assurance that the investment companies are organized and operated in the interest of all shareholders, rather than in the interest of officers, directors, investment advisers, or other special groups or persons;
3. Prevent inequitable provisions in investment company securities and protect the preferences and privileges of outstanding securities;
4. Prevent undue concentration of control through pyramiding or other devices, and discourage management by irresponsible persons;
5. Assure sound accounting methods;

[5] *Investment Companies,* 1972 (New York: Arthur Wiesenberger Services, Division of Nuveen Corp.).

6. Prevent major changes in organization or business without consent of shareholders;
7. Require adequate assets or reserves for the conduct of business.

Wharton Report—1962

In 1958 the SEC engaged the Wharton School of the University of Pennsylvania to make a study of certain aspects and practices of open-end investment companies. In 1962 Wharton made a 539-page report to the SEC, and the report was also transmitted to Congress at the same time.[6] The study covered the effects of investment company size on investment policies, on corporation performance, and on the securities markets. It also included an analysis of the activities of investment company advisers and their relationship with the funds. The study found little evidence that the size of the funds was a problem and found no instances of violations of legislation or regulation. The report made no specific recommendations for revision of the 1940 Act, although it did raise questions as to the relationship between fund managements and investment advisers and potential conflicts of interest between management and shareholders. For example, it raised the problem of "give-ups" by Exchange members, a practice that was voluntarily canceled by Exchange members in December, 1968.

The SEC stated that the report found that the more important current problems in the mutual fund industry included (1) the potential conflicts of interest between fund management and shareholders already noted and (2) the importance of fund growth and stock purchases on stock prices.

Horowitz and Higgins [7] found a negative relationship between performance and size. A large fund can become so broadly diversified that it cannot hope to show significant better-than-average performance. Also, excessive size can hamper flexibility. A purchase large enough to have a significant impact on total results might drive price up substantially when buying and drive price far down when selling. This fact is important in viewing the future of performance funds, such as the Enterprise Fund, once they reach $1 billion.

Report on Special Study of the Securities Markets—1962-1963

Congress in 1961 ordered the SEC to make a broad study of the securities markets. For this study the SEC engaged a special staff. The study resulted in

---

[6] "A Study of Mutual Funds," prepared for the Securities and Exchange Commission by the Wharton School of Finance and Commerce, University of Pennsylvania. Report of the Committee on Interstate and Foreign Commerce, Pursuant to Section 136 of the Legislative Reorganization Act of 1946, Public Law 601, 79th Congress and House Resolution 108, 87th Congress, 2nd Session, August 28, 1962.

[7] Ira Horowitz and Harold B. Higgins, "Some Factors Affecting Investment Fund Performance," *Quarterly Review of Economics and Business* (Spring, 1963).

the publication in 1962-1963 of a report on the Special Study of the Securities Markets, which, in addition to a broad review of the entire securities industry, covered aspects of the mutual fund industry outside the scope of the Wharton Report. The Special Study focused its attention on sales of mutual fund shares, industry selling practices, special problems raised by the front-end load in the sale of so-called contractual plans, and allocations of mutual fund portfolio brokerages. Neither the Special Study nor the Wharton Report was a report *by* the SEC but was a report made *for* the SEC. Several chapters of the Special Study were related to mutual funds and one (Chapter XI) was devoted entirely to mutual funds.

SEC Report on Investment Companies [8]

After the previous reports were published, the SEC evaluated the probable policy questions that the studies raised and then in 1966 reported its recommendations in a 340-page report. The Staff of the SEC drafted legislative proposals, which were submitted to Congress in 1967, at the same time requesting the industry and others to express their views on the proposed legislation. Hearings on the SEC-sponsored bill occupied much time of the Senate and House Committee in 1967, and the bill became law in 1970. The SEC bill contains many amendments to the Investment Company Act of 1940. The 1970 Act permits any shareholder to institute legal action for a claimed breach of *fiduciary duty*. The NASD has the responsibility to determine that the initial sales load is not excessive.

TAXES AND INVESTMENT COMPANIES

If it were not for Subchapter M of the Internal Revenue Code, investment companies would be taxed as ordinary corporations. If a company complies with the technical term "regulated investment company" as defined in Subchapter M, it has special tax privileges. The requirements in Subchapter M to meet the definition of "regulated investment company" are given in the footnote below.[9] Practically all mutual funds have complied with these requirements in Subchapter M.

---

[8] Report of the Securities and Exchange Commission on the Probable Policy Implications of Investment Company Growth. Report of the Committee on Interstate and Foreign Commerce, 89th Congress, 2nd Session, December 2, 1966.

[9] Requirements to qualify as a registered investment company are:

    1. It must be a domestic corporation (or domestic entity taxable as a corporation), not a personal holding company.

Reporting of Income Taxes by Shareowners

In making distributions, the fund identifies the portion derived from investment income and the portion derived from capital gains. The shareowner reports the income segment as regular income and the capital gains as a long-term capital gain.

Retention of Capital Gains by Investment Companies

Since 1956, a regulated investment company may elect (few do so) to retain all or part of realized long-term capital gains *without a penalty* to shareholders. The fund pays the maximum capital gains tax and notifies the shareowner of his proportionate amount. The shareowner reports this as a *credit* on his return. If his top bracket is less than the top capital gains rate, he in effect receives a refund. The shareowner takes the tax credit and marks up the book cost of his shares by the same amount, as a capital gains tax has been paid on part of the value of his holdings.

Distribution of Capital Gains and Yields

When an investor is calculating yield, he recognizes capital gains distributions. If a fund pays a capital gains distribution equivalent to 20% of net asset value, the value of the shares will decline 20% immediately after the distribution; therefore, in applying dividends paid during the year to the net asset value to determine yield, the investor should use only 80%

---

2. It must be registered at all times during the taxable year under the Investment Company Act of 1940, either as a management company or as a unit investment trust.

3. At least 90% of its gross income for any taxable year must be from dividends, interest, and gains from securities.

4. No more than 30% of its gross income for any taxable year may be derived from sales of securities held for less than 3 months.

5. It must distribute as taxable dividends not less than 90% of its net income, exclusive of capital gains for any fiscal year. Under a 1950 Amendment, such dividends from the earnings of one year may be paid in the following year provided that they are declared not later than the due date of the company's tax return and are paid not later than the first regular dividend date after declaration.

6. At the close of each quarter of the taxable year:
   (a) At least 50% of its assets must consist of cash, cash items (including receivables), government securities, securities of other regulated investment companies, and other securities limited to not more than 5% of its assets in securities of any one issue and not more than 10% of the voting securities of that issue.
   (b) Not more than 25% of its assets may be invested in any one company, or in two or more controlled companies engaged in the same or a similar line of business (20% of voting power constitutes assumed control).

of the dividends received. Otherwise, the yield will appear greater than it actually is because of the reduction in the net asset value of the shares after the distribution.

Keogh Act—Custodial Accounts

The Keogh Act (Self-employed Individuals Tax Retirement Act) was first enacted in 1962 and then amended in 1967 to liberalize the tax advantages. Self-employed individuals may set aside a maximum of $2,500 (10% of business profits or earned income) in custodial accounts for future retirement benefits and may deduct from income for tax purposes [10] the entire contribution up to the $2,500. The act requires the use of trust or custodial accounts as the recipient of the contribution, but the individual still has wide latitude as to how the funds shall be invested. Most mutual funds have arranged for custodial accounts with banks for those desiring to use the fund's shares under the Keogh Act. The individual cannot begin to receive benefits before age 59½ and must begin receiving benefits by age 72½ either in a lump sum or in periodic payments. There is an income tax on all benefits received. Special provisions reduce any annual tax impact for lump sum payments. The peak for plans approved was 100,000 plans in 1968 and again in 1969, but there were only 751 in 1970 and 782 in 1971. Interest picked up again noticeably in 1972.

SELECTING AN INVESTMENT COMPANY

Investors purchasing shares of a fund must decide on their investment requirements, whether to seek to meet all requirements through fund shares, and finally which fund or funds appear best suited to meet these requirements. After considering all factors, the investor should review the record of various funds to select one or several best suited to his requirements. Among the 800-odd existing companies, the diversity of goals and investment policies is sufficient to cover virtually any long-term investor requirements.

Appraisal of Management and Performance

The investor must review the record of management, aware of the fact that past performance is no guarantee of future performance. The problem is how performance is to be measured in such a way as to facilitate comparison of different funds in terms of relative performance. Performance

---

[10] When the individual files his annual income tax return, he deducts his Keogh Act contribution from his total income, attaching IRS Form 2950-SE.

should be measured in terms of the fund's stated objectives and policies. Only funds with similar objectives and policies should be compared in determining relative performance. Much of the discussion that follows applies to an analysis of other portfolios as well as that of investment companies.

Wiesenberger Formula Measure of Performance. The tests of fund performance suggested in *Investment Companies,* the bible of the funds, are: [11]

1. *Combined Capital-Income Formula*

   For mutual funds and for most closed-end investment companies, management results *are based on the history of a single share or its equivalent.* Whether for one year or longer, the formula for a combined capital-income index is as follows: to asset value per share at the end of the period, adjusted to reflect reinvestment of all capital gains distributions, add dividends per share paid during the period from investment income, similarly adjusted; divide the total by the starting per share asset value. The result is the performance, relative to a starting index of 100. Anything over 100 represents a gain; anything under 100 represents a loss, computed by subtracting the figure from 100.

   The formula itself is simple. The major complication in using it is the reinvestment of capital gains distributions and the adjustment of income dividends to reflect the additional shares purchased with capital gains (distributions).

   This process is necessary to avoid distorting the results and to show accurately what management did with the money it had on hand to invest. If, instead, capital gains were treated as if received and retained in cash, the amounts involved would have the same effect as that much cash added to the companies' portfolios. When asset values rise, this assumed but nonexistent cash holding detracts from management's actual accomplishment with the money under its control; when asset values decline, management receives credit for defensive action it did not, in fact, take; no dividends can be assumed paid on this unrealistic cash holding.

2. *Capital Results Alone Formula*

   Capital results alone are obtained by dividing the (latest) . . . year-end asset value, adjusted for capital gains *but not* for income dividends, by that at the start of . . . the period taken (1 year, 4 years, 10 years, etc.). . . .

3. *Income Results Alone Formula*

   Income results (alone are obtained) by dividing the total of the dividends (for the period taken) by the (initial) asset value (at the beginning of the period).

Measuring Fund Performance. In measuring performance it appears best to start with the same dollar amount for each fund being examined to

---

[11] *Investment Companies,* 1972 (New York: Arthur Wiesenberger Services, Division of Nuveen Corp.). Italics and items in parentheses are added for emphasis and clarity. The authors of *Investment Companies* state that, in providing tables for performance comparisons, "mutual funds are grouped according to their major objectives."

arrive at a *percentage* that will express a fund's measure of performance. The following facts should be considered:

1. It is not the total dollar amount of assets of a fund that counts, but the assets per share.
2. The analyst should adhere to the same assumptions as far as reinvestment is concerned when comparing funds with other funds or with a market index.

The four theoretical possibilities concerning eventual reinvestment of proceeds are listed below, but only the first two are actually used.

1. Capital gains reinvested and dividends from income accepted in cash.
2. Both capital gains and dividends from income reinvested.
3. Both capital gains and dividends from income accepted in cash.
4. Capital gains accepted in cash and dividends from income reinvested.

The first of the four assumptions above was used in Wiesenberger's *Investment Companies*. On the other hand, the assumption used in the Wharton School's study [12] was the second one above—both capital gains and dividends from income reinvested—and therefore it is not realistic to compare the Wharton figures with the Wiesenberger figures.

From a practical point of view, the only reasonable procedure for the analyst is to assume that the reinvestment of distributions takes place at the end of the period concerned. Otherwise, the accounting becomes disproportionately complicated so that the results obtained will be somewhat different from those actually obtained by automatic reinvestment on the date of distribution of proceeds. In some cases the difference could be significant. It should be noted that while some funds provide for "automatic dividend reinvestment," which means full shares plus any balance in fractional shares, others make payments in full shares only with the balance in cash rather than optional shares.

Finally, the frequency of the capital gains distributions and the dividend distributions affects the performance record. In a rising market, the more frequently the cash profits are distributed, the lower is the performance, because if the fund had retained the distributions the value would have continued to rise with the market. But in a declining market, the more often a cash distribution is made, the less value is lost in the investment.

---

[12] Wharton Report, *op. cit.* The report stated: "With respect to the performance of mutual funds it was found that, on the average, it did not differ appreciably from that which would have been achieved by an unmanaged portfolio consisting of the same proportion of common stocks, preferred stocks, corporate bonds, government securities and other assets as the comparative portfolio of the funds. About half of the funds performed better and half worse, the same as unmanaged funds. This, in our judgment, in no way implies that the individual with a small nondiversified portfolio could accomplish these results."

Four Factors for Measuring Management Performance. Calculation of performance is equivalent to appraisal of management. Consequently, factors over which the management of a mutual fund has no control, such as taxes payable by the investor and pre-established sales charges, should not be allowed to enter into the measure of capability of the management of a fund as shown by its past results. Only four factors are found that may be used to measure management performance:

1. Net assets per share at the beginning of the period (hereinafter referred to as BA).
2. Net assets per share at the end of the period (hereinafter referred to as EA).
3. Distributions per share from profits realized on sale of securities during the period (hereinafter referred to as DP).
4. Dividends per share from investment income during the period (hereinafter referred to as DI).

Other factors, such as management fees and broker's commissions, do exert an influence on the results achieved by a mutual fund, but only through some modification of one or more of the four basic factors listed above.

Formulas P(1), P(2), and P(3) for Measuring Performance. Standard textbooks describe the following general formula for overall performance, referred to here as formula P(1):

$$P(1) = \frac{EA + DP + DI}{BA}$$

This formula P(1) is an obvious simplification of the following basic formula used in mathematics of finance for overall rate of return or ratio of earnings to investment: [13]

$$\text{Rate of Return} = \frac{\text{Change in the Original Investment}}{\text{Original Investment}}$$

Referring to the difference (EA — BA) as CA, or change in assets, the rate of return as understood above may be expressed by the following formula, hereafter referred to as formula P(2):

$$P(2) = \frac{CA + DP + DI}{BA} = \frac{(EA - BA) + DP + DI}{BA}$$

In explaining how performance is computed, Wiesenberger's *Investment Companies* utilizes in effect formula P(1), but throughout that book the

---

[13] Jerome B. Cohen and Sidney N. Robbins, *The Financial Manager* (New York: Harper and Row, 1966), p. 704.

formula P(2) is used to express the result as a percentage. Obviously, formula P(1) gives results measured in a different scale from formula P(2). For example, assume BA = 100, EA = 150, DP = 25, and DI = 25. Utilizing formulas P(1) and P(2), the results are as follows:

$$P(1) = \frac{EA + DP + DI}{BA} = \frac{150 + 25 + 25}{100} = \frac{200}{100} = 2 \text{ or } 200\%$$

$$P(2) = \frac{CA + DP + DI}{BA} = \frac{(150 - 100) + 25 + 25}{100} = \frac{100}{100} = 1 \text{ or } 100\%$$

The system of disclosure of some funds, as far as figures per share are concerned, suggests for the sake of easy calculation the use of a modification of formula P(1), which will be referred to as formula P(3). Many funds exhibit in their prospectus a 10-year table entitled "Per Share Income and Capital Changes for a Share Outstanding Throughout the Year" in which, among other data, appears a new valuation entitled "Net Change in Realized and Unrealized Profits or Losses on Securities" (hereafter referred to as TCA, or total change in assets). Formula P(3) is expressed as follows:

$$P(3) = 1 + \frac{TCA + DI}{BA}$$

The verification and equivalence of formula P(3) with formula P(1) is easily shown, as follows:

$$P(3) = 1 + \frac{TCA + DI}{BA} = \frac{BA + TCA + DI}{BA}$$

Since TCA is the "Net Change in Realized (DP) and Unrealized (EA − BA) Profits (or Losses) on Securities," we may write:

$$TCA = DP + (EA - BA)$$

and then substitute its value in formula P(3) as follows:

$$P(3) = \frac{BA + TCA + DI}{BA} = \frac{BA + DP + EA - BA + DI}{BA}$$

$$= \frac{EA + DP + DI}{BA} = P(1)$$

Formulas P(1), P(2) and P(3) have the same function. All three formulas give results relative to a starting index of 100. Formulas P(1) and P(3) give 200% for a doubling of the investment, 100% for a no-change situation, and a figure under 100 for a loss. Formula P(2), however, gives 100% for a doubling of the investment, zero for a no-change situation, and a negative figure for a loss. Consequently, care must be exercised in the interpretation of the percentages obtained.

Formula P(2) produces smaller and therefore more manageable figures than those obtained with formulas P(1) and P(3). Formula P(2) is usually preferred because, when long periods of 10 or more years of generally rising markets are considered (for example, 1932-1969, 1942-1969, 1946-1969, 1949-1969, and 1959-1969), it can be expected that the figures for performance should always be over 100%. In fact, for over 3 decades, except for short 1-5 year periods, this has always been the case.

The *distinction* between the formulas and their components (beginning and ending assets, dividends, and distributions from capital gains), while useful to clarify concepts, should not be exaggerated. After all, a mutual fund shareholder may at any time have his shares redeemed by the fund and thus obtain a total in cash without inquiring for its origin, whether income or capital gains. That is why analysis in terms of the original all-inclusive performance measure as expressed by formulas P(1) and P(2) is favored.

Fund Performance and the Averages

Much has been said about using as a comparative measure of performance the record of the major stock indexes (DJIA, S&P 500, and S&P 425). Those outside the fund managements have tended to use such a measure, while some closest to the industry have tended to depreciate such comparisons. First it should be emphasized that funds are sold on two bases—diversification and professional management—with the implication that the average investor will secure better performance with less risk than if he invested directly outside the fund.[14] It is highly debatable whether individuals can secure performance at least equal to the averages, but fund management could buy the averages and secure such performance. Therefore, management must accept the necessity of such a comparative performance analysis.

The Wharton School's study of mutual funds worked extensively with comparisons of mutual fund performance with Standard & Poor's 500 Composite Stock Price Index. *Forbes* [15] uses the same concept in its theory of

---

[14] J. L. Treynor, "How to Rate Management of Investment Funds," *Harvard Business Review* (January-February, 1965). Treynor suggests measuring risk in terms of year-to-year volatility as a consideration in measuring performance along with rate of return.

[15] Beginning with 1956, an annual August issue of Forbes contains a report on mutual funds. One issue stated:

Consistency—Applying a carefully worked-out set of standards to fund performance, our statisticians have graded the funds on a scale ranging from A+ to D—. They have indicated their preferences in both rising and declining markets. Thus Consistency Ratings are based on fund performance in nine distinct periods, four of rising markets and five of declining markets. The four periods of rising markets are (1) Oct. 25, 1957 to Dec. 31, 1959; (2) Sept. 30,

consistency of performance, and Wiesenberger's *Investment Companies* and *Mutual Funds Charts and Statistics* supplies five different acetate lay-on accessories meant to be superimposed on the individual charts of the funds. One acetate lay-on shows the price trend of the Dow Jones 30-Stock Industrial Average on the same semilogarithmic scale as the charts of the performance of the funds. The other four acetate lay-on accessories are adjusted to the charts of the "$10,000 illustrations" and show: (1) Standard & Poor's 500 Composite Stock Price Index; (2) Dow Jones 65-Stock Industrial Average; (3) Dow Jones 50-Stock Industrial Average; and (4) the Cost-of-Living Index.

It would be ideal to compare fund performance with that of the "average individual investor," but the information necessary to appraise the record of the individual investor is simply not available. However, discussions with many qualified professionals with member firms have strongly implied that most individuals, on the average, over any long period of time do not do as well as the averages.

The arguments that comparison with fund performance and the averages is not fair are as follows:

1. The funds keep perhaps 5% in cash or cash items and are therefore not fully invested. This cash reserve is necessary to meet unexpected share redemptions, to take care of dividend needs, and to provide for later purchases of stock when good buying opportunities arise.

2. The funds must incur expenses for management and associated services. One who buys the averages would not require a staff of security analysts, although he would incur some clerical and overhead costs.

3. The funds must incur broker's commissions, etc., in portfolio transactions.

4. Balanced funds keep a substantial portion of funds invested in fixed-value assets, which contribute to safety and stability of principal and income. An investor who has strong constraints in terms of these goals would not keep his entire portfolio in common stocks.

1960 to Dec. 31, 1961; (3) June 30, 1962 to Feb. 9, 1966; and (4) Oct. 7, 1966 to May 8, 1967. The five periods of declining markets are: (1) Jan. 30, 1957 to Oct. 25, 1957; (2) Dec. 31, 1959 to Sept. 30, 1960; (3) Dec 31, 1961 to June 30, 1962; (4) Feb. 9, 1966 to Oct. 7, 1966; (5) Dec. 1968 to May, 1970.

For each "up" period Forbes statisticans asked, Did the fund do better than the averages? Did it merely keep up? Or did it actually fall behind the averages? Funds that managed to keep up with Standard & Poor's "500" stock average in all four of the "up" periods received a B+ for consistency. Funds that kept up three times got a B; twice, a C+; once, a C. Funds that did poorer than the averages in all four periods received a D. A fund that succeeded not only in outperforming the average every time but in outperforming it by 20% or better, rated an A+; by 10% to 19.9%, an A. A fund that was consistently beaten by the averages by a margin of 10% rated a D—. A similar rating system was applied to "down" periods. No ratings have been given when a fund did not exist for at least two up and two down periods.

However, the above factors are not strictly negative factors and certainly they should be overcompensated for by skillful management. While it is true that the average mutual fund investor could not effectively invest in the averages, even the 30 Dow Jones stocks,[16] the funds could so invest if they choose to. If they do not choose to do so, they are implying that they believe they can secure better performance in other ways. The Wharton School study showed that, on the average, funds' performance just about paralleled that of the averages. However, the Wharton School study, the Wiesenberger publications, and the *Forbes* reports all show that some funds post a performance superior to that of the averages, while numerous other funds post an inferior performance.

Some analysts note that a disproportionately large number of investment companies do worse than their group's average performance and that only the relatively few consistently good performers keep the average performance at or above that of hypothetically unmanaged companies. On this basis it is equitable to ask how management has performed versus the averages as well as versus managements for other funds. It is important to recognize that a superior performance has been secured under different portfolio policies. One further note is in order. The spotlight on fund performance has been so glaring in recent years that this has pressured managements to try hard simply to outperform the averages. Some strong doubts have arisen in the minds of numerous professionals and others as to whether this intensive struggle for exceptional performance will, in the long run, work to the advantage of mutual funds' shareowners as a group.

Performance or "Go-Go" Funds

Historically, it was considered the function of a mutual fund to provide a long-term investment vehicle for the individual, offering him the protection of wide diversification and professional management of the portfolio and the opportunity of building capital over the years at a rate somewhat equivalent to the growth of the economy. The emphasis in the sales presentation was on the long-term past record with a strong implication of what the investor could obtain in the future by a long-term investment commitment and by regular periodic additional investments in the fund. Most sales were made on house-to-house calls, and the sales load was admittedly large relative

---

[16] In December, 1968, the DJIA was still slightly below its 1966 high of 995, but the S&P 500 and the S&P 425 were 18% above their 1966 level. In 1972 all indexes made new highs—the DJIA was 4% above 1966 and the S&P indexes were 33% above their 1966 highs.

to brokers' commissions for buying and selling individual stocks listed on exchanges. However, since these investments were considered as long-term investments, the load charge could, in effect, be amortized over a long period and not be either burdensome or inequitable.

As noted earlier, the major reason for the great pressure for performance since 1966 was the exceptional performance of the stock market from 1946-1949 through 1966 when the DJIA (especially representative of major corporations) rose from the 1946-1949 base of 161 to 995 (February, 1966). Mutual funds on the average posted about the same proportionate rise, and mutual fund investors as well as other investors, including owners of pension funds, were quite generally satisfied with the type of performance. For example, $160,000 rose in value to $1,000,000 if it paralleled the rise in the averages from 1946-1949 through February, 1966.

However, the 1966-1971 record was proportionately, for the time period, quite inferior to the 1949-1966 record, as the DJIA by December, 1968, had only recovered to 985 and not until December, 1972, or nearly seven years later, did it go above the February, 1966 high of 995.

After 1966 the experience for well-diversified portfolios was not considered satisfactory by many investors and great pressures for performance developed. To satisfy these demands for performance in the mutual funds field (especially in 1967-1969), there developed the performance or "go-go" funds, called "new type investing."

The portfolio managers of these funds strove for short-term, one-year exceptional performance, that is, performance much better than for the averages. Numerous funds did succeed in securing exceptional performance, usually by investing largely in American Stock Exchange and over-the-counter securities and in companies with a relatively small capitalization and a relatively small floating supply of stock. The emphasis was on such companies, and especially those companies posting a fast quarter-by-quarter growth in earnings. There was a significant amount of short-term trading.

The best records were posted by the relatively small funds, such as $25 million funds at the beginning of a period. These successful funds grew rapidly as a result of these records. For example, Enterprise Fund had a performance record of approximately 123% in 1967 and the fund grew from around $25 million to about $100 million. Then the fund grew to around $1 billion by the end of 1968. Assets declined to $449 million in 1970, and net asset value per share went from $13.63 in 1968 to $6.00 in 1970 and $6.23 in 1971. Analysis of these performance funds shows that the rapid growth attracted substantial new money, which itself contributed to the performance results—success buys success. The new money flowing in for investment contributed heavily to exceptional performance. However, once the funds grew very large ($500 million to $1 billion), it was much more difficult for them to secure exceptional performance because they had to become much more diversified, and diversification historically has made it very difficult to significantly outperform the averages.

One contribution to the performance record of numerous funds was the advantage of "letter stock"—unregistered stock purchased directly from the issuer at perhaps a 33% discount from the current market price. Instant performance could be achieved by carrying this stock at the market price in reporting net asset value the day after it was purchased at say a 33% discount. On the other hand, such letter stock is not liquid, and the Mates Fund was forced to ask the SEC to approve suspension of the redemption privilege of stockholders when one of its large holdings of letter stock was suspended from trading on the Exchange.

Another factor in performance for such go-go funds was the purchase of new issues, many of which rose spectacularly in price the day of issue and for a period thereafter. Many of the performance funds competed in heavy trading activities, buying and selling over very short periods within the year, again violating the long-term investment principle generally assumed to be a basic tenet for mutual funds.

As a fund posted exceptional performance, brokers had shareholders in other "less successful" funds sell and buy into the performance funds. This shifting of fund shares violated a principle of fund investment. In terms of commissions (load fees) it was very profitable to the brokers and very costly to the investors. Of course, if the fund purchased had exceptional performance thereafter, the load charge was not a significant negative factor.

The year 1967 was a boom year for the performance funds just as it was for American Stock Exchange stocks (the latter rising on the average 93% in 1967) [17] and for over-the-counter stocks. However, the year 1968 found that many of the excellent fund performers in 1967 had a record poorer than that of the DJIA.[18] Then came the debacle of 1969-1970 when

---

[17] In 1967 even a large fund that was well diversified in American Stock Exchange stocks could have had a 93% rise; but this was a most exceptional year, and it is highly unlikely that this record would be duplicated in many other years.

[18] The financial record of selected "performance" mutual funds and the DJIA, shown as a percentage increase or decrease, for 1967 and 1968 was as follows:

Fund	All 1967	First 9 Mos. 1968	First 11 Mos. 1968
Manhattan	+39.4%	−3.37%	−1.96%
Ivest	+47.4	−3.39	+2.57

so many of the "go-go" funds did far worse than the 36% decline in the general market, and in the subsequent recovery they did not do well. This was an important reason for the heavy redemption and poor sales of funds in 1970-1973.

The performance game in terms of pressure for one-year performance is, in the judgment of the authors, certainly a relatively speculative, high-risk, fast-trading game in which exceptional success one year can be followed by a poorer-than-the-DJIA record the next. There are no loyalties, and investors (urged on by brokers) shift from one fund to another—from the funds not performing well to the best performing fund at the moment or for the past quarter, 6 months, or year. One notable example of this was the Manhattan Fund, bought out in 1966 by Gerald Tsai, who had gained a notable reputation as a fund manager while with Fidelity Fund. Expecting to sell initially around $50 million of fund shares, the initial sale proved to be over 5 times that amount ($270 million). The fund's capital then rose to around $500 million, but unsatisfactory performance in terms of other much smaller performance funds caused heavy net redemption of Manhattan's shares. In 1968, between January 1 and December 1, redemptions exceeded sales by $64.5 million. O'Neil Fund showed a 115% gain in 1967, but from January 1 to mid-November, 1968, it showed a gain of only 0.25%. There were many other examples of excellent performance one year and relatively poor performance in the next year. The question is how much of such performance was luck—a unique one- or two-year experience—and how much represented superior portfolio management.

The larger a fund grew, the more difficult it became to post unusual gains versus the averages. As a result, redemptions increased and there was a shift to the hot-shot funds of the moment. Then the fund managements, which had been emphasizing their exceptional records, wrote to stockholders telling them that they should be long-term investors and not one-year

Fund	All 1967	First 9 Mos. 1968	First 11 Mos. 1968
Mass. Investors Growth	+29.0	−0.63	+4.39
Fidelity Capital	+32.0	+1.32	+5.33
Diversified Growth	+51.5	−1.25	+5.70
Channing Growth	+47.0	−1.39	+6.93
Fidelity Trust	+34.2	+2.38	+6.97
United Science	+31.2	−0.41	+7.86
DJIA	+15.2	+3.40	+7.87

performance minded [19]—that they should forget the letter of a year ago, which bragged of that year's one-year performance.

In summary, the go-go performance funds are a new type of large-risk, speculative-trading vehicle, operating on principles quite different from the traditional principles of mutual funds. They are distinctly not long-term investment vehicles because not only do they stress short-term time horizons but also, if they are unusually successful, they rapidly grow to such size that they become overdiversified, less flexible, and unwieldy. As their performance record slows down, investors redeem their shares, and this in turn has a negative effect on attempts for performance. A rapidly growing fund with large inflow of new cash has an added positive factor for performance, but conversely a shrinking fund has a strong negative factor.

For investors who are largely attempting to build long-term capital, in the judgment of the authors, this is not the game for them to play. For individuals who are speculators and traders, it has presented another vehicle. Only time will tell whether or not the increasing number of portfolio managers (both mutual fund and pension fund managers) striving for exceptional performance will in fact be able to achieve exceptional performance in the long run. For one thing, there are just not enough "exceptional stocks" to go around. The 1969-1970 bear market was disastrous for these types of funds. "Go-go" funds were called "no-go" funds after 1969.

Competition for Investment Companies

Additional competition for investment companies is provided by the two sources discussed below.

NYSE Monthly Investment Plan. The Monthly Investment Plan (MIP) is the competitive answer of the New York Stock Exchange to investment companies. Under MIP, individuals invest relatively small amounts at regular intervals (usually monthly or quarterly) in a listed stock of their choice. If they follow this procedure over a long period of time, they receive the basic advantages of regular investing plus dollar-cost averaging. both of which are advantages of investing in mutual funds. However, MIP does not provide the two major factors of mutual fund investing: (1) diversification and

---

[19] In November, 1968, Gerald Tsai stated that "shareholders are comparing results of Manhattan Fund with other speculative funds, or even individual securities" and that Manhattan Fund has been unable to satisfy their "extremely ambitious goals." But certainly, at least by brokers who had sold the fund, the stockholders had been sold on expectation of just such "extremely ambitious goals."

(2) professional management and selection of portfolios. These differences are extremely fundamental, and most individual investors will do better by investing in mutual funds. Under MIP there will be a tendency to buy a stock when it is popular but not to stay with it if it temporarily becomes unpopular, thus losing the vital dollar-cost averaging advantage of the plan.

Life Insurance Companies. The first insurance-organized mutual fund came into existence in 1957; however, it was not until 1968 that several insurance companies entered the mutual fund field. At the beginning of 1972, there were 87 mutual funds that had been organized by 64 insurance companies or groups posting total net assets of about $906 million.

However, the bulk of the mutual fund-insurance company association is made up of mutual funds that own or control insurance companies. As of January 1, 1972, some $24.3 billion or 44% of the total net assets of the mutual fund industry was associated in some way with insurance companies.

QUESTIONS

1. (a) Define investment companies.
   (b) Distinguish between the two major types of investment companies.
   (c) Trace the growth of each major type since 1940, and explain any difference in growth patterns.

2. (a) During the major stock market decline (1929-1932) the net asset values of closed-end funds were generally more severely affected than the net asset values of open-end funds. Why?
   (b) Do the same conditions prevail today? Discuss.

3. (a) What is meant by selling at a discount? Can an open-end fund sell at a discount?
   (b) What possible advantages does the investor gain in purchasing the stock of a closed-end fund at a discount?

4. (a) What problems may be solved for the small investor who invests in mutual funds?
   (b) How does a closed-end investment company differ from an ordinary business corporation?

5. (a) What are the two principal distinguishing characteristics of mutual investment funds?
   (b) What costs does the investor incur in acquiring mutual fund shares? Discuss the reasonableness of these costs.

(c) Would you prefer to acquire the shares of a large or a small investment company, other things being equal. Discuss.

6. (a) Would it not be preferable for investors to invest in no-load rather than load funds? How would you arrive at a judgment concerning a no-load as contrasted to a load fund?

(b) What are the advantages and the disadvantages of investing in a closed-end fund as opposed to an open-end fund?

7. What are the objections of the SEC to:

(a) Contractual plans for purchasing mutual fund shares?

(b) The "load" for all funds?

8. What are the highlights of the Investment Company Act of 1940?

9. (a) How are investment companies taxed?

(b) What is a regulated investment company?

10. (a) What are the major types of policies followed by investment companies?

(b) What is a dual fund?

11. (a) Why has the performance of so many mutual funds not been much better than the stock averages?

(b) Why might it be difficult for a mutual fund manager to concentrate on stock representing out-of-favor, low P/E situations?

(c) How may size restrict the performance of an investment company?

12. (a) What are the major tests used by Arthur Wiesenberger Services to measure the comparative performance of investment companies?

(b) What tests are suggested by *Forbes* magazine?

WORK-STUDY PROBLEMS

1. Select three common stock mutual funds and compare their records, using data from the latest edition of Wiesenberger's *Investment Companies* and the latest available reports of each company. Select companies with similar stated policies. Appraise the management and the performance of these three funds by using:

(a) The following Wiesenberger formulas discussed in this chapter:
(1) Capital Results Alone Formula.
(2) Income Results Alone Formula.

(b) Formulas P(1), P(2), and P(3) discussed in this chapter.

(c) Contrast the results you obtained with the rating of the funds chosen in *Forbes* and discuss the results.

2. Select a stock that you believe would have been a good candidate for NYSE Monthly Investment Plan investing 10 years ago.

   (a) Calculate the results over the past 10 years, assuming quarterly investments of approximately $250. (In each case use actual dollar investments that would work out to the nearest even number of shares.)

   (b) Give reasons why you believe that type of stock, considering the industry and the company characteristics, would have been a good candidate for MIP investing.

   (c) Select a stock for MIP investing for the next 10 years and give reasons for your selection.

   (d) Do you believe that investing in this stock by means of MIP investing would be superior to investing in a mutual fund? Discuss.

SUGGESTED READINGS

Barron's (Weekly). *Quarterly Report on Mutual Funds.*

Bleakley, Fred. *The Institutional Investor.*
   (1) "Management Fees, What Happens After the Price Freeze." (October, 1971), pp. 32-35.
   (2) "How Persistence Has Paid Off for T. Rowe Price." (April, 1972), pp. 60-73.
   (3) "Can Mutual Funds Come Back?" (June, 1972), pp. 37-40.

Bogle, John C. "A Wellington (Fund) Whiz Kid Grows Older." *The Institutional Investor* (June, 1972), pp. 62-68.

Forbes. *Annual Survey of Mutual Fund Performance.*

Glenn, Armon. "More Votes for Keogh—Self-Employed Retirement Plans Grow on Popularity." *Barron's* (February 26, 1963), p. 12.

Greely, Robert E. "Mutual Fund Management Companies." *The Institutional Investor* (November, 1968), pp. 72-76.

Investment Companies (Annual). New York: Wiesenberger Service, Inc.

Katona, George, Judith Hybels, and Jay Schmiedeskamp. "Who Owns Mutual Funds?" *The Institutional Investor* (February, 1971), pp. 35-38.

Levy, Robert A. "A Reappraisal: Fund Managers Are Better Than Dart Throwers." *The Institutional Investor* (April, 1971), pp. 46-48.

Mao, James C. T. "Essentials of Portfolio Diversification Strategy." *The Journal of Finance* (December, 1970), pp. 1109-1121.

Mattlin, Everett. *The Institutional Investor.*
   (1) "The Problems of Being the Enterprise Fund." (March, 1970), pp. 25-27.

(2) "New Policies for Insurance Companies: How Connecticut General Is Dealing Itself into the Fund Game." (January, 1970), pp. 53-59.

Mills, Harlan D. "On the Management of Fund Performance." *The Journal of Finance* (December, 1970), pp. 1125-1131.

Mutual Fund Performance (Monthly). The Institutional Investor.

Mutual Funds Forum (Monthly). Washington, D.C.: The Investment Company Institute (National Industry Association for Mutual Funds).

Oberg, Winston. "Make Performance Appraisal Relevant." *Harvard Business Review* (January-February, 1972), pp. 61-67.

SEC Report on the Public Implications of Investment Company Growth. Washington, D.C.: Securities and Exchange Commission. U.S. Superintendent of Documents.

Simonson, Donald G. "The Spectacular Behavior of Mutual Funds." *The Journal of Finance* (May, 1972), pp. 381-395.

Treynor, J. L. "How to Rate Management of Investment Funds." *Harvard Business Review* (January-February, 1965.)

Vickers Associates, Inc. *Vickers Guide to Investment Company Portfolios* (Annual) and Periodic Reports on Individual Mutual Funds.

PUBLIC
SECURITIES

United States
Government Securities

The United States Government is, by a wide margin, the largest single issuer of securities in the world. The market for government securities, therefore, is the largest single securities market and in many ways the most important. Over the past three decades the market for government bonds has undergone dramatic change in both magnitude and character, and it is to a discussion of these changes that this chapter is addressed. At the outset it must be emphasized that the purpose of ownership of government securities is for a combination of liquidity and the highest quality reserves.[1]

FEDERAL DEBT

The federal debt has expanded tremendously since the 1930s. Government spending and debt gained force in the 1930s in an attempt to stimulate an underemployed economy. Spending by the federal government was accelerated out of necessity in World War II. Temporarily, from 1945 until 1952 and then again from 1955 to 1957, the federal debt declined. In both cases, however, the decreases were modest in relation to the increases that took place before and after these periods of budgetary surpluses.[2]

---

[1] This chapter was prepared by Mr. Reese Jones, President, First Valley Bank, Bethlehem, Pennsylvania.

[2] The federal debt (direct and fully guaranteed) in selected years was as follows:

($ Billions)

1917—$ 2.98	1930—$16.19	1945—$285.68	1960—$286.47
1919— 25.48	1940— 42.97	1952— 259.95	March, 1972— 425.54

For current statistics on all Federal Reserve fiscal operations, consult the monthly *Treasury Bulletin* (Washington: U.S. Government Printing Office).

There is little doubt about the upward bias of the federal debt. Debt increases have been closely related to (1) defense and the Vietnam War, (2) the commitment since the Full Employment Act of 1946 to maintain a high level of economic activity and a minimum level of unemployment by augmenting demand in the private sector of the economy when it weakens, and (3) various social and environmental programs.

Federal Debt as an Instrument of Economic Control

During the depression of the 1930s, economists convinced the politicians that government spending could be used to augment private spending and thus ensure a level of demand in the economy that would ensure full employment. One result has been an appreciable expansion of the federal debt and an upward bias in the price level. Ironically, at the very time of debt expansion, rising prices made debt instruments, including government securities, less attractive as an investment vehicle (1933-1939 and 1941-1972).

Quality and Risk of Government Securities

United States Government securities are considered to be the highest quality investment in the world. The investor must be alert, however, to some rather fundamental changes that have taken place from the mid-1950s to the present. Since the mid-1950s, many foreign economies have become much more competitive with the United States economy. Because of this factor, debt issuance and management will have constraints not known since the gold standard. The U.S. balance of payments problems reflect this fact.

Although there is no risk of default, or "crisis at maturity" as it is sometimes called, there are other risks attendant on investing in government bonds. These are the risks inherent in all debt instruments—the interest rate risk and the purchasing power risk.[3] Despite the presence of these two risks (which accompany all fixed-income investments), the credit quality of government bonds makes them "benchmark" securities. Since quality is above reproach, these bonds are used as a bellwether to characterize conditions and changes in both the money and the capital markets. Changes in the government market will be reflected ultimately in all security markets, although the impact will vary among the markets. Government securities set the basic rates and satisfy the basic liquidity needs of the economy.

---

[3] Some U.S. Government securities issued at par sold in the low 60's in 1970 as interest rates reached their highest level on record in May, 1970. In May, 1970, U.S. Government long-term securities sold on the average at 63% of par.

Environmental Changes in the Government Bond Market

Over the past three decades the government bond market has undergone considerable change. The underlying reasons for this change can be seen rather easily during the dramatic changes in the levels of interest rates.

For the greatest part of the 1930s there was an abundance of reserves in the banking system with little investment taking place in the private sector of the economy. Further, state and local governments had curtailed expenditures drastically. In addition, the consumer had retrenched and was hardly in a mood to borrow. The result was that the market for government securities was broad and interest rates were low, with the rate on Treasury bills falling practically to zero by 1938 as overcautious investors (including banks) all tried to crowd into the high-quality securities.

During the early 1940s the United States was engaged in a worldwide war that fully taxed its resources. As part of the total effort, the Federal Reserve System was committed to "peg" the price of government securities, gradually raising their prices and lowering their yields. There was a phenomenal increase in debt and secondary reserves. Inflation was largely curbed by implementation of direct controls over the private economy.[4] In 1946 direct controls were abandoned, but Federal Reserve support of government security prices continued and interest rates hit their low in April, 1946.

In early 1951, approximately 9 months after the start of the Korean War, the United States Treasury and the Federal Reserve System reached an accord that stated that the Federal Reserve would no longer "peg" government bond prices but would act only to insure orderly markets. In the few years subsequent to 1951, government bond yields increased, but it was not until the late 1950s and early 1960s that interest rates began to rise dramatically. In the 1950s, however, the demand for government bonds declined appreciably relative to other investment media. Because of the purchasing power risk inherent in government and other bonds, the investor, both individual and institutional, began to commit more funds to equities as a hedge against rising prices. Also, municipal bonds and corporate bonds were being offered in greater profusion and at attractive rates and were able to attract funds that would normally have gone into government bonds. In short, government bonds had only moderate competition in money and capital markets in the 20-year period prior to the 1950s. After this time, competition for funds became more intense and yields on government as well as other fixed-income securities rose appreciably; but when liquidity

---

[4] Wages and price controls were imposed in August, 1971, in an attempt to curb inflation. As of May, 1972, no controls over interest rates had been put in effect.

and the highest quality of reserves were not required, funds flowed into other investments.

After 1957 another factor became important. Balance-of-payments problems began to plague monetary authorities and economic planners. In deference to the new problem, interest rates were allowed to rise and the bias toward "easy" money and low interest rates was reduced. As a result, yields from government and other bonds increased to levels that had not been reached since the post-Civil War period. Naturally, in the rising yield market, prices of outstanding governments declined sharply, as did other debt instruments.

It can be seen that the government bond market has gone through a complete cycle over the past 30 years. From a position of little competition from other securities and "pegged" prices and no concern for international influences, it has evolved into a relatively free and intensely competitive market with international factors being extremely important. Thus, even securities of impeccable quality can experience vagaries of the marketplace.

GOVERNMENT SECURITIES

Government securities fall into two main categories: nonmarketable securities and marketable securities.

Nonmarketable Government Debt

Nonmarketable government debt includes (1) securities that are not transferable and that are redeemable at fixed prices, such as savings bonds, and (2) "special issues" sold to government trust funds and holdings by foreign governments and central banks. Savings bonds were originally issued to afford the small saver an opportunity to invest in his country with no risk to principal. Yields on these securities have been adjusted upward over the past several years to make them somewhat more competitive with open-market rates and with yields obtainable from other savings media. But the Treasury over the years has had a difficult time selling enough new bonds to offset redemptions. The amount outstanding has held in a narrow range since World War II. The total for savings bonds and notes was $52.1 billion in 1947 and $54.9 billion in February, 1972.

Marketable Government Debt

Marketable interest-bearing government debt is by far the larger part of total Treasury debt and amounted to about $261.2 billion in February, 1972, made up as follows:

Type of Security	Amount ($ Billions)	Percentage
Treasury bonds	50.2	19
Treasury notes	112.9	43
Treasury bills	98.1	38
Total	$261.2	100

Treasury Bonds. Treasury bonds are issues maturing beyond 5 years. They are available in coupon or registered form, and in some cases they can be bought in denominations as low as $50.

As noted earlier, bond issues have been declining relative to other issues because of an aversion by the Treasury to "locking-in" debt at high interest rates and because of the 4¼% restriction on bond issues. As a result, the longer-term market has thinned out and price variation is considerably greater than it was in the early and mid-1950s.[5]

Treasury Notes. Treasury notes have maturities of not less than 1 year and not more than 7 years. Some Treasury notes are available in registered form; other Treasury notes (as well as Treasury bills and certificates of indebtedness) can be obtained only in coupon or bearer form because they are of short maturity and registration would cause more paper work than could be justified by the amount by which the market would be broadened. There are no coupon restrictions on Treasury notes, which accounts for their widespread use in the high interest rate period from 1960 to the present.

Certificates of Indebtedness. Certificates of indebtedness had maturities of 1 year and usually had no coupons because the full amount of interest was payable at maturity. Certificates of indebtedness have been replaced by Treasury bills when the Treasury bill maturities were extended to 1 year. As of March, 1972, no certificates of indebtedness have been outstanding since 1966.

Treasury Bills. Prior to December, 1958, Treasury bills were limited to maturities of 90 to 92 days; in December, 1958, the limit was extended to 6 months; and in April, 1959, the limit was extended to 1 year.

Treasury bills are by far the most important money market instrument.[6] Since their introduction in 1929 they have far outweighed commercial paper,

---

[5] In March, 1971, Congress passed legislation enabling the Treasury to sell up to $10 billion in bonds without the 4¼% restriction. Three bond issues totaling $4.2 billion have been sold under this legislation as of May, 1972.

[6] Since the 1960s, however, the tremendous expansion of commercial certificates of deposit to around $35 billion in May, 1972, caused them to exceed Treasury bills as liquid assets in the corporate treasuries of corporations other than financial institutions.

which had been the prime money market medium prior to that time. Treasury bills are sold at auction every Monday. Bids are opened at the Treasury, and each of the Federal Reserve banks and the highest bidders are awarded the amount of bills on which they bid. Various bond dealers, banks, corporations, and other financial intermediaries participate in this market. Small buyers usually avoid bidding, but they are granted the option of placing orders, up to a prescribed amount, at the average bid price.

Unlike other marketable issues, Treasury bills are appreciation type investments. They have no coupon, but rather are bought at a discount and paid off at face value upon maturity. The difference between acquisition price and face value is equivalent to interest. Under federal income tax laws, Treasury bills are not capital assets and are not subject to the capital gain and loss provisions of the Code; therefore, any appreciation on Treasury bills is always taxed as regular income.

The real rate of interest on Treasury bills is always higher than the rate as usually quoted. There are two reasons for this: (1) bill yields are computed on a 360-day basis, while other issues are on a 365-day basis; and (2) bill yields are computed on acquisition price and not at par. To illustrate, a 60-day Treasury bill with a quoted yield of 4.75% would have a bond equivalent yield of 4.86%. Also, the longer the maturity, the greater the disparity becomes.

Treasury bills were at one time the only medium through which Federal Reserve open-market policy was carried out, and even now they constitute the major instrument. The bill market is ideal for this purpose because of its breadth and resiliency and also because activity in this sector is not disruptive to capital markets. Because short-term yields are much more responsive to change than long-term yields, Treasury bill yields have become the most widely used indicator of conditions in the credit markets.

Maturity of the Marketable Government Debt. In the postwar era, maturity of the marketable government debt decreased from 7 years 11 months to 3 years 3 months in early 1972. From 1946 to 1952 this shortening was intentional in order to maintain greater liquidity in the economy and thus help to stimulate economic activity. From 1960 to 1969 the debt became shorter because of the high cost of issuing longer-term bonds, because of a restriction (dating back to 1917) against issuing bonds with coupons in excess of 4¼%, and because investors largely desire to hold government securities only for liquidity and reserve purposes. As a result, the long-term market for Treasury bonds has become relatively thin, and trading in modest quantities (for these markets) can have an effect on price. Of the total marketable debt of $261.2 billion in 1972, $122.1 billion was due in 1 year (requiring a heavy roll-over pattern) and $93.1 billion was due in from 1 to 5 years, for a total of $215.2 billion or approximately 86% of the federal marketable debt due in 5 years or under and only 18% due in over 5 years. Of this remaining 18%, $26.3 billion was due in 5 to 10 years, $9.5 billion was due in 10 to 20 years, and $10.3 billion was due in 20 years and over.

Investment Features of Government Securities

Treasury securities offer a broad range of maturities to suit the convenience and the needs of virtually any investor in fixed-income securities. Unlike state and municipal securities, Treasury issues are fully subject to federal income tax. They are not, however, subject to any state or local taxes, such as personal property taxes. A number of issues (15 in 1972) are accepted by the government at par for estate tax purposes. When, as in 1970, these issues were selling at deep discounts (some issues as low as 62-63 in May, 1970), it was profitable for an elderly person to purchase these bonds in anticipation of their use by his estate to pay taxes. If a purchaser died immediately after purchase, the estate would receive credit at face value in payment of estate taxes.

Most Treasury issues are not callable. Of a total of about 60 outstanding issues, only 9 are callable. When two years are quoted for an issue, the first year is the maturity year and the second year is the year of first call. Most of the call features are meaningless since they are on issues having very low coupons, with little or no possibility of call for refunding, and usually callable only within 5 years of maturity.

Government Bond Market

The government bond market is made up of a primary market and a secondary market. The former is the market for new issues, while the latter is the market for outstanding issues. Each monthly issue of the *Federal Reserve Bulletin* presents three pertinent tables: (1) dealer transactions, (2) dealer positions, and (3) dealer financing. More complete data appear monthly in the *Treasury Bulletin*.

Primary Market. New Treasury issues come to market either to refund a maturing issue or to raise additional cash to meet increased operating expenses of the Treasury. The Treasury establishes a coupon and yield that it thinks will be attractive and clear the market. In many cases, the Federal Reserve has helped condition the market for new issues by making reserves in the banking system readily available. New issues are offered on either an exchange basis or a cash basis. An exchange basis entitles holders of maturing issues preemptive rights in obtaining the new issue. This often leads to considerable speculation in "rights" and has on occasion led to rather chaotic market conditions, such as in May of 1958 when the 2⅝%s of 1965 were issued [7] during a recession when speculators were "certain" that interest rates were going to decline and bond prices rise.

When a cash refunding takes place, holders of maturing issues have no preemptive rights. They subscribe for new issues on the same basis as anyone else. Usually a cash offering results in oversubscriptions, so that the Treasury must make allotments. In most cases, small subscriptions (up to $100,000 or $200,000) are allocated 100%. The problem for the larger buyer is to guess the allotment and then to oversubscribe to insure getting what he wants. There are some hazards to this procedure, but the investor is left with little choice if he wants the issue.

In 1972-1973 the Treasury began to use an auction method of selling issues for cash or refunding purposes. With an auction, the Treasury announces that it wishes to sell a certain amount of securities and then establishes a coupon and maturity. Then investors bid for a certain amount of securities at a specified price. The Treasury will then accept, beginning with the highest bids, all bids necessary to sell the stated amount of securities. The Treasury has sometimes used a "Dutch" auction where all securities are awarded at the lowest accepted price. The auction method has tended to reduce the new issue concession in the Treasury market.

Secondary Market. The secondary market involves outstanding bonds. Only a few investment dealers and a few commercial banks (dealer banks) make a market in government issues. The market is restricted to few participants because of large capital requirements, the need for very large credit lines, and the relatively low operating margins that necessitate enormous volume. To illustrate this last point, it is not unusual for a government bond dealer to turn over capital in excess of 5,000 times in one year.

It is important to note that dealers in government bonds take positions in or inventory the bonds they offer for sale. Also, they must maintain substantial inventories so that they can offer bonds for sale when called upon to do so. Because of this, the risk is considerable. Sizable losses have been registered sometimes by dealers in the bear market that has prevailed for bonds since 1946 but especially in 1966-1970.

---

[7] For a full treatment of this subject see "Treasury-Federal Reserve Study of the Government Securities Market, 1959" issued in three parts in 1959 and 1960 (issued by the Secretary of the Treasury and the Board of Governors of the Federal Reserve System).

TABLE 26-1

Estimated Ownership of Federal Securities
(Securities Issued or Guaranteed by U.S. Government Exclusive of Guaranteed Issues Held by Treasury—in Billions)

	February, 1946	December, 1950	February, 1972
Total Federal Debt	$279.8	$256.7	$424.1
Held by:			
(a) U.S. Govt. Trust Accounts	$ 28.0	$ 39.2	$106.2
(b) State & Local Governments	6.7	8.8	22.0
(c) Federal Reserve Banks	22.9	20.8	67.7
Total $	$ 57.6	$ 68.8	$195.9
Total % of Federal Debt	20.6%	26.0%	46.2%
Held by Commercial Banks—Total $	$ 93.8	$ 61.8	$ 62.1
Total % Federal Debt	33.5%	24.1%	14.6%
Held by Private Nonbank Investors:			
(a) Individuals			
(1) Savings Bonds			
Series E & H	$ 30.8	$ 34.5	$ 54.3
Other Series	12.5	15.1	0.6
(2) Other U.S. Govts.	20.8	16.7	22.4
Total	$ 64.1	$ 66.3	$ 77.3
(b) Insurance Companies*	24.4*	18.7*	6.5
(c) Mutual Savings Banks	11.1	10.9	2.7
(d) Savings & Loan Assns.	2.4	1.5	13.0
(e) Corporations	19.9	19.7	12.5
(f) Foreign & International	2.4	4.3	48.9
(g) Other Misc. Investors	4.2	4.7	5.2
Total Private Nonbank Investors $	$128.5	$126.1	$166.1
Total % of Federal Debt Held by Private Nonbank Investors	45.9%	49.0%	39.2%

* All insurance companies—life, fire, and casualty. Life insurance companies held $21.6 billion in 1946 and $4.0 billion in 1971.

Source: *Treasury Bulletin,* U.S. Treasury Dept., April, 1972.

Ownership of Government Securities

Table 26-1 shows the changing ownership pattern of U.S. Government securities, the major part of which is owned by government trust accounts, the Federal Reserve banks, and financial institutions. In 1946 government securities represented the largest segment of assets of financial institutions.

In the postwar years, despite the tremendous growth in their assets, all financial institutions except savings and loan associations showed a sharp decline in their holdings of government securities. In all cases, including savings and loan associations, the proportion of government securities to total assets declined precipitously as the institutions shifted to higher yielding investments. Government securities are held only to the extent of requirements for liquidity and other reserves of the highest quality. Such investors desire short maturities, so the average maturity of the debt was 3.25 years in 1972.

Commercial banks are the largest holders of U. S. Government securities, except for Government Trust Accounts. Banks owned $94 billion or

33.6% of the total federal debt in 1946, and these holdings represented about 57% of the assets of the commercial banks. By 1948 their holdings had been reduced to about $65 billion, and from that time until 1972 their holdings ranged between approximately $53 and $65 billion, expanding in recessions and contracting during expansions as banks met heavy load demands. By 1972 these holdings represented only 10.1% of the assets of commercial banks and only 15% of the federal debt.

Holdings of government securities by life insurance companies declined from $21.6 billion or 44% of total assets in 1946 to $4.0 billion or approximately 1.9% of total assets in 1972. Holdings by mutual savings banks declined from $11.1 billion or 63% of assets in 1946 to $2.7 billion or about 3.8% of assets in 1972. Holdings by savings and loan associations did increase from $2.4 billion or about 28% of assets in 1946 to about $13 billion in 1972, but this represented only about 6.6% of their assets. They were the only financial institutions to increase their holdings, and this was only the result of the tremendous increase in their total assets from $10.2 billion in 1946 to $123 billion in February, 1968, and to almost $200 billion in 1972.

Holdings of government securities by individuals totaled $64.1 billion in 1946 ($43.3 billion in savings bonds and $20.8 billion in other governments). However, in 1950, shortly after World War II, holdings of savings bonds rose to $50 billion. From then on, the Treasury was pressed to keep new sales equal to redemptions, because holdings were only $54.9 billion in 1972. Holdings of other governments were $21 billion in 1946, $21 billion in 1965, and $22.4 billion in 1972. Therefore, individual holdings did not increase any significant amount in the postwar years, especially after 1949, except temporarily in certain years of exceptionally high interest rates, as in the 1966-1970 period.

TABLE 26-2

Estimated Ownership of Federal Securities
Net Increase or Decrease, 1972 Versus 1946
(Total Increase in Federal Debt + Net Decrease in Ownership = Net Increase in Ownership)
In Billions

Net Decreases in Ownership		Net Increases in Ownership	
Commercial Banks ..	$93.8 — $62.1 = $ 31.7	U.S. Govt. Trust Accts. .	$106.2 — $28.0 = + $ 78.2
Insurance Companies.	$24.4 — $ 6.5 = $ 17.9	Federal Reserve Banks	$ 67.7 — $22.9 = + 44.8
Mutual Savings Banks	$11.1 — $ 2.7 = $ 8.4	State & Local Govt. Funds	$ 22.0 — $ 6.7 = + 15.3
Corporations	$19.9 — $12.5 = $ 7.4	Individuals	$ 77.3 — $64.1 = + 13.2
		Savings & Loans	$ 13.0 — $ 2.4 = + 10.6
Total Decrease in Ownership	$ 65.4	Foreign & International .	$ 48.9 — $ 2.4 = + 46.5
Net Increase in Federal Debt	$144.2	Other Misc. Investors ...	$ 5.2 — $ 4.2 = + 1.0
Total	$209.6	Total	$209.6

During the 1946-1972 period the Federal Reserve banks, the U.S. Government Trust Accounts, and foreign and international holders were the largest net purchasers of government securities as shown in Table 26-2. The Federal Reserve banks' holdings of government securities increased from $22.9 billion in 1946 to $67.7 billion in February, 1972, or an increase of $44.8 billion. Holdings of U.S. Government Trust Accounts rose from $28.0 billion to $106.2 billion, or an increase of about $78.2 billion. Holdings of Foreign and International rose from $2.4 billion to $48.9 billion. Therefore, these three classes of investors increased holdings from 1946 to February, 1972, by approximately $170 billion. During the same period the federal debt rose from $280 billion to $424 billion, or $144 billion. These three classes of investors not only absorbed amounts equal to the entire increase in the federal debt but, in addition, absorbed $26 billion in government securities sold net by other investors in this period. If it had not been for this acquisition of $170 billion of government securities, the yield on governments would unquestionably have had to rise significantly more than it did from 1946 to 1970. In addition to the increase noted above, holdings in the State and Local Government Funds increased $15.3 billion, holdings by individuals rose $13.2 billion, and holdings in the Other Miscellaneous Investors classification increased $1.0 billion, for a grand total of $209.6 billion by all classes of investors who increased their ownership of government securities during the 1946-1972 period.

On the negative side there were decreases in ownership of government securities by commercial banks, insurance companies, mutual savings banks, and corporations for a total decrease of $65.3 billion. This decrease of ownership of $65.4 billion together with the $144.2 billion increase in the federal debt accounted for the $209.6 billion net increase in ownership of those who did increase their holdings of government securities.

Yield Patterns and Trends for Government Securities

Usually the shorter the maturity of a government debt instrument, the lower the yield; and the longer the maturity, the higher the yield. This is due both to the time preference of investors and to the fact that the farther one projects into the future, the greater is the uncertainty (for example, as to the level of interest rates, the level of commodity and consumer prices, and conditions in the capital markets).

Yield Curves. Yield curves are plotted with the yield on the vertical axis and the maturity on the horizontal axis. Normally, yield curves will be positive and trend upward as maturity is extended. Figure 26-1 pictures such

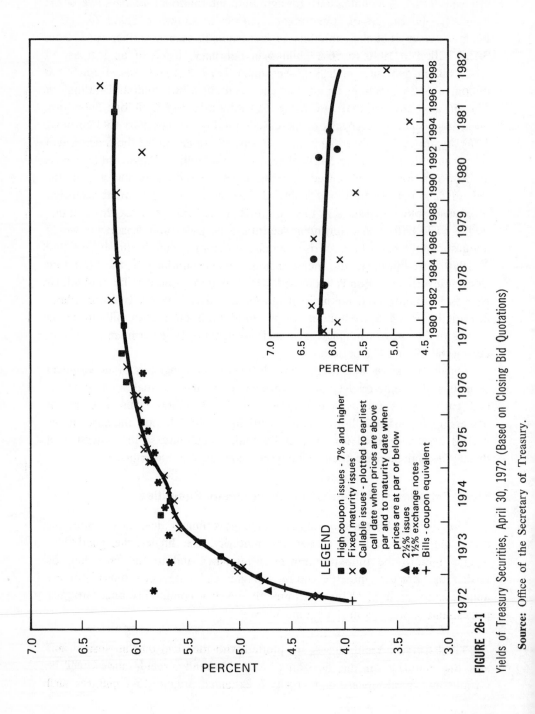

FIGURE 26-1

Yields of Treasury Securities, April 30, 1972 (Based on Closing Bid Quotations)

Source: Office of the Secretary of Treasury.

a yield curve on April 30, 1972. However, at times of credit stringency and tight money in the capital markets as in 1920, 1928-1929, and 1966-1969, the demand for short-term funds in relation to the supply can cause the yields to be relatively higher for the short maturities with an actual downsloping trend for longer maturities. The shortages of liquidity in the banking and business segments of the economy caused such yield curves in the period 1965-1970. Such negative slopes were very common prior to the advent of the Federal Reserve System, as credit crises were not infrequent. Figure 26-2 on page 698 shows yield curves on various dates from June, 1965, to December, 1970.

Predictive Value of Yield Patterns or Curves. There are some who hold that yield patterns or curves have some predictive value. A cursory study of historical yield patterns will show about as much consistency as a technical analysis of the stock market. Yield patterns show the relationship of the independent variable (maturity) and the dependent (yield). Through this relationship some conclusions can be drawn concerning the present state of credit markets. Also, yield curves are helpful in identifying relative values in the bond markets. The investor can quickly ascertain the reward in yield for a given extension of maturities or the absence of reward. But the astute investor relies upon a fundamental analysis of credit markets in making bond decisions and is wary of any ready-made formula whose basis is the configuration of a curve that is dependent on the condition of credit markets.

Secular Trend of Bond Interest Rates. As noted earlier, the secular trend of interest rates has been rising since April, 1946, and especially since Federal Reserve pegging of the market was withdrawn in 1951. In 1951, the yield on long-term government bonds was between 2½% and 2¾%. After the Treasury-Federal Reserve accord, the yield on long-term Government bonds during the 1950s trended upward to a peak of 5% in late 1959. From 1959 through mid-1967, yields fluctuated between 4% and 5%. However, long-term Government bond yields rose sharply from 1967 until they reached an all-time high of 7.59% in early June, 1970, and they have declined irregularly since then until mid-1972. Therefore, despite several interruptions during recessionary periods, the 1946-1972 trend of Government yield has been persistently upward. Investors often overlook secular trends and place more emphasis on cyclical behavior or seasonal patterns. In all areas, government bonds set the base pattern for all yields. The relationship between yields on long-term government bonds, high grade (AA) corporates and AA municipals over the last decade is shown in Figure 26-3 on page 699.

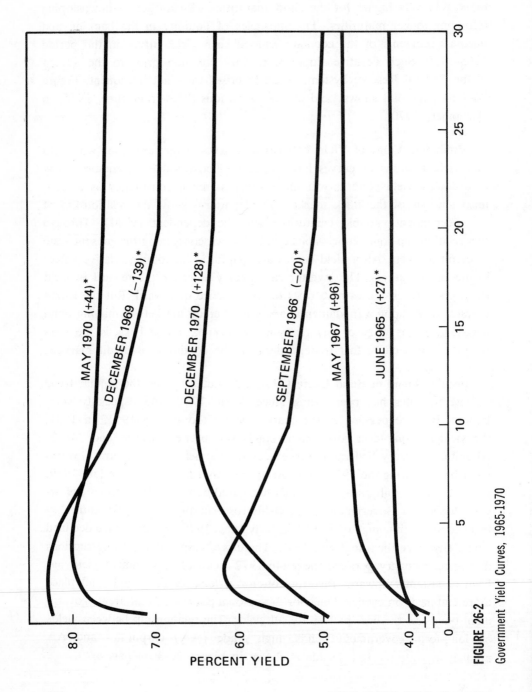

FIGURE 26-2

Government Yield Curves, 1965-1970

MAY 1970 (+44)*

DECEMBER 1969 (−139)*

DECEMBER 1970 (+128)*

SEPTEMBER 1966 (−20)*

MAY 1967 (+96)*

JUNE 1965 (+27)*

PERCENT YIELD

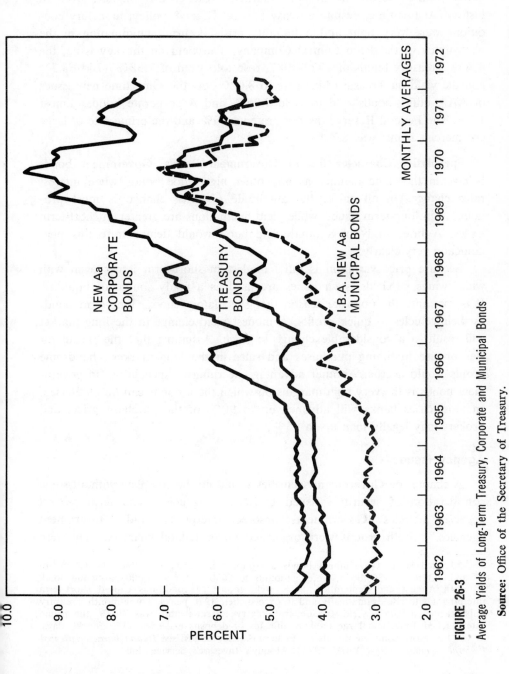

FIGURE 26-3

Average Yields of Long-Term Treasury, Corporate and Municipal Bonds

Source: Office of the Secretary of Treasury.

Highest Yields in History. In May-June, 1970, yields on Government bonds (and all sectors of the bond markets) reached their highest levels in history. At this time, despite an easy Federal Reserve policy, monetary conditions were very tight and a liquidity crisis occurred culminating in the bankruptcy of the Penn Central Company. The yield on the key issue, the 4¼% Treasury bonds of 1972-1987, rose to a yield of 7.58% (Bid 63.2)[8] and the yield on Treasury bills rose to 8.02%. At the same time new issues of AAA utility bonds sold to yield 9.25% and A corporate bonds, almost 10%. The Federal Reserve discount rate was 6% and the prime rate of large commercial banks was 8%.[9]

Speculative Characteristics of Government Bonds. Government bonds behave in the same manner as any other high-grade bonds when interest rates change. In all cases, the amplitude of price change is most pronounced in long-term issues, while yield fluctuations are greater in short-term issues. A brief study of a bond yield book would demonstrate this phenomenon very clearly.

Because price variation is quite modest in short-term issues even with wide swings in yields, such issues are used as a ready source of liquidity. It is for quite the opposite reason that speculators choose long-term bonds as their vehicles to quick profits. A modest yield change in the long market will result in a considerable change in price. Assuming that the speculator was precise in timing purchases and sales in the long markets, handsome profits would accrue. Another advantage accruing to speculators in government bonds is the very high margins on which these bonds can be purchased. In most cases banks will advance up to 90% of the purchase price, and brokers may legally loan up to 95%.

Agency Issues

A chapter on Government securities would not be complete without some consideration of securities issued by federal agencies. The term *federal agencies* includes "Government-sponsored enterprises" and "Government agencies."[9] Both groups were organized under federal charters; they were

---

[8] United States Government bonds are quoted in 32nds, so a bid of 63.2 means 63 and 2/32nds or $63.0625, which amounts to $630.63 for a $1,000 par value bond.

[9] In August and September, 1973, tight monetary conditions caused short-term interest rates to rise dramatically and to exceed their 1970 peaks. Three-month Treasury bills reached a 9.05% yield, the Federal Reserve discount rate was 7½%, the prime rate reached 10%, and large bank certificates of deposits exceeded 11% for 90 days.

[10] For more complete details on Federal Agency bonds, see *Debt Characteristics of Federal Agencies* (New York, 1972), Moody's Investor's Service, Inc.

originally capitalized by the U.S. Treasury; their debt is not expressly guaranteed by the Federal Government and is not included as part of federal debt. The distinguishing characteristic is that "Government agencies" are those in which the public has no ownership interest. Agency issues outstanding in 1972 are shown in Table 26-3 below.

TABLE 26-3

Interest-Bearing Securities Issued by Federal Agencies, February, 1972
(In Billions)

A. *Government-Sponsored Enterprises*

Banks for Cooperatives	$ 1,860
Federal Home Loan Banks and	
Federal Home Loan Mortgage Corporation	7,324
Federal Intermediate Credit Banks	5,660
Federal Land Banks	7,205
Federal National Mortgage Association	17,814
Total	$39,883*

B. *Government Agencies*

Defense Department-Family Housing Mortgages	$ 1,622
Federal Housing Administration	466
Government National Mortgage Association	5,390
Export-Import Bank	1,716
Tennessee Valley Authority	1,685
Federal Home Loan Bank Board	5
United States Postal Service	250
Other	3
	$11,137

* Includes $20 million District of Columbia Stadium Fund Bonds which have an unequivocal guarantee of the U.S. Government.

Source: *Treasury Bulletin,* April, 1972, p. 24.

The relative yield on federal agency issues compared to U.S. Treasury issues as of May, 1972 is shown in Table 26-4. Note that the investor can select a broad range of maturities with uniformly high quality. In many cases, agency issues afford yields of $\frac{1}{8}\%$ to $\frac{1}{2}\%$ higher than direct Treasury issues of comparable quality and maturity. It is for this reason that many investors have substituted federal agency issues for Treasury issues, especially for short-term purposes.

TABLE 26-4

Relative Yields of Treasury and Agency Issues

Issue	Coupon	Maturity	Yield
U.S. Treasury Notes	4¼ %	5/15/74	4.82%
Federal Home Loan Bank Notes	6.35 %	5/27/74	5.14%
U.S. Treasury Notes	6½ %	5/15/76	5.54%
Federal National Mortgage Association ...	5.85 %	6/10/76	5.71%
U.S. Treasury Notes	6 %	11/15/78	5.88%
Federal National Mortgage Association ...	6¾ %	12/11/78	6.25%
U.S. Treasury Bonds	6⅜ %	2/15/82	6.18%
Federal Land Bank Notes	6.90 %	4/20/82	6.64%

QUESTIONS

1. A friend is about to retire. He suggests liquidating all investments he now holds and investing the total in U.S. Government notes with maturities of 3 to 5 years. He desires stable income and minimum risk, and he feels this plan will assure him of both objectives. Comment on his plan.

2. In March, 1959, the Treasury made a new offering of $500 million of 10-year, 4% bonds as part of a $4 billion cash borrowing. This offering served as an important Treasury symbol. Later in the year the Treasury issued the so-called magic fives. Explain the significance of each issue.

3. Over the past three decades the government bond market has undergone considerable change.

   (a) In view of the large demand for funds by the federal government during World War II, how do you explain the relatively low interest rates that prevailed?

   (b) What was the significance and the effect of the Federal Reserve-Treasury "accord" of 1951?

   (c) What factors underlie the dramatic rise in interest rates that took place in the late 1950s and throughout most of the 1960s? Do you anticipate a return to interest rate levels that prevailed during the 1950s? Discuss.

4. The long-term market for Treasury bonds is often spoken of as being "quite thin" during the 1960s.

   (a) What does "quite thin" mean?

   (b) What brought about this condition?

5. (a) Define nonmarketable bonds.

   (b) Discuss the nature of nonmarketable bonds, their relative importance, and to whom they are sold.

6. (a) What was the reason for a downsloping yield curve for Treasury issues in 1969?

   (b) A Treasury bill has no interest coupon attached, nor does the instrument say anything about payment of interest. How does an investor get a return on such an instrument?

7. (a) Name and describe the classes of marketable and nonmarketable U. S. Government issues.

   (b) Indicate the relative importance of each class in reference to total public issues at the end of the most recent fiscal year.

   (c) Discuss the investment characteristics of each type of government security.

8. What special benefits may be derived from Treasury issues in reference to settling of estates?

9. (a) Distinguish between the offering of new Treasury issues on an exchange basis and on a cash basis.

   (b) Who are the dealers in the United States Government securities market? Why is the market restricted to relatively few dealers?

10. (a) List the principal types of owners of United States Government securities and indicate their relative importance. (Use the most current statistics available).

   (b) Why are government securities so attractive to commercial banks?

WORK-STUDY PROBLEMS

1. Assume that an individual has a total portfolio of $250,000. Indicate the amount of U. S. Government securities, including U. S. savings bonds if any, that he should have in his portfolio, the exact type and issues that should be held, and the reasons for your selection.

2. Assume that a commercial bank has total assets of $100 million. Indicate the amount of U. S. Government securities that should be held, the specific issues and their maturities, and the percentage distribution by maturities. Explain your reasons for the selection.

SUGGESTED READINGS

The Federal Budget, Its Impact on the Economy. New York: National Industrial Conference Board, Inc., 1968.

Federal Reserve Bulletin. Board of Governors of Federal Reserve System. Monthly issues.

Handbook of Securities of the United States Government and Federal Agencies. New York: The First Boston Corporation. Biennial editions, even years.

Smith, Warren L. "The Competitive Position of Government Securities," *Debt Management in the United States,* Study Paper No. 19. Materials prepared in connection with the study of employment, growth, and price levels for consideration by the Joint Economic Committee, Congress of the United States, 86th Congress, 2nd Session, January 28, 1960, pp. 61-72.

Treasury Bulletin. U. S. Treasury Department. Monthly issues.

"Treasury-Federal Reserve Study of the Government Securities Market, 1959." Washington: U. S. Government Printing Office, 1959 and 1960. Parts 1-3.

State and Municipal
Securities and
Revenue Bonds

Security issues of state and local governments are commonly referred to as municipal bonds. To simplify matters, they will be so called throughout this chapter, although there are major differences between the two groups. The state group is much more homogeneous than the local government group.[1]

MUNICIPAL BONDS

The principal feature and attraction of municipal bonds is that income from this type of bond is not subject to federal income taxes. This condition derives from the rule of reciprocity established in 1819 in the well-known case of *McCulloch* vs. *Maryland*. Under the rule of reciprocity, it was determined that state and local governments would levy no taxes upon obligations of the United States Treasury and that the Treasury would reciprocate by not taxing obligations of state and local governments.

There has been strong pressure to remove the tax-exempt feature of municipal bonds; but it is realized that to do so would require a constitutional amendment plus an agreement (if the states are to approve the amendment) that the states would receive a federal subsidy equivalent to the higher cost of financing taxable issues. However, the tax-exempt feature was removed for issues of industrial revenue bonds issued after the 1968 amendments to the Internal Revenue Code for all except issues under $5 million.

Aside from the tax-free feature, municipal bonds are essentially the same as other classes of bonds. They have indentures with the usual covenants

---

[1] This chapter was prepared by Mr. Reese Jones, President, First Valley Bank, Bethlehem, Pennsylvania.

pertaining to calls, defaults, security, additional bond provisions, and so forth. For good delivery of a municipal bond, however, it must have a legal opinion from qualified bond counsel stating that the bond has been issued for purposes within the powers of state or local officials and within corporate powers of the issuing body. In recent years, legal opinions have been printed on the bond itself. Older issues, however, were accompanied by a separate legal opinion, and a buyer of such bonds should be certain that a legal opinion is attached.

Classes of Municipal Bonds

Municipal bonds are divided into several subgroupings, as follows:

1. State bonds—full faith and credit obligations.
2. General obligation bonds of political subdivisions of states—full faith and credit obligations.
3. Public housing bonds and notes.
4. Revenue bonds.
5. Industrial revenue bonds.
6. Authority bonds.

State Bonds. State bonds are those issued by the 50 states. These bonds are secured by full faith and credit of the issuing state. State bonds are probably of uniformly higher quality than any other class of municipal bonds. This is evidenced by the fact that Standard & Poor's in 1972 assigned the top "AAA" rating to the direct obligation of 19 states, "AA" to 20 states, and "A" to 2 states. Nine states had no long-term debt issues outstanding at this time.

Because of their high quality, state bonds are more marketable than other classes of municipal bonds. Moreover, marketability is aided by greater recognition of state names, larger volume, and also the fact that state bonds are acceptable for hypothecation while other classes are frequently not acceptable.

In event of default, an individual investor has no legal recourse and must be content to await the state's pleasure in meeting arrearages. The state is sovereign and therefore is in a legal position to refuse to pay its debts, even though legally incurred, simply if it is unwilling to do so. An individual has no standing in court against a state and therefore may not enter suit with the hope of accelerating or obtaining satisfaction of payment unless the state agrees to accept suit. However, as shown in the 1930s, if a state is in default, its credit in the capital markets is zero, so economic pressures are extremely strong to prevent default.

General Obligation Bonds of Political Subdivisions of States. General obligation bonds of cities, counties, or other political subdivisions are secured by full faith and credit or, more succinctly, by taxing power. In most cases, general obligation bonds with ratings of "A" or better enjoy broad markets and trade without much difficulty. In some cases, however, the investor could have trouble disposing of bonds, especially when the issue is of relatively small size. If sale prior to maturity is the intent or a good possibility, the investor should be certain to confine purchases to well-known names and to avoid more obscure issues that may afford some yield concession because of limitations of marketability. Furthermore, no less than $5,000 and preferably $10,000 bonds of a particular issue should be purchased.

Public Housing Bonds and Notes. Public housing bonds and notes are obligations of various housing agencies issued under the 1949 Amendment to the U.S. Housing Act of 1937. Both principal and interest are guaranteed by the federal government. Because of this, these bonds carry "AAA" ratings and afford yields substantially below those of other classes of municipal bonds but higher than direct U.S. Government obligations. Through the end of 1971, $8 billion in public housing bonds had been sold.

Revenue Bonds. Revenue bonds are those with principal and interest payments secured by revenue generated by specific projects such as water systems, sewer systems, electric utilities, toll roads, bridges, and parking facilities. By definition, principal and interest payments are made *solely* from revenues generated by the projects, just as in the case of a private corporate bond which they resemble. Their only factor in common with other tax-exempt issues is their tax-exempt factor. The defaults of such bonds as the West Virginia Turnpike Bonds and Calumet Skyway Bonds highlight the risk factor in new issue, untested revenue bonds—that revenues generated by the project are the sole source of interest and principal payments.

In some cases, the state or municipality in which the revenue project is operating will pledge to make up any deficiencies in amounts needed to service the debt. When this condition obtains, the security is referred to as a "double barrel" obligation and should no longer be classed as a revenue bond but as a full faith obligation issue.

As a general rule, revenue bonds are not as marketable as full faith and credit general obligation issues. Investors usually consider revenue issues as a class to be of lower quality and somewhat below full faith and credit bonds because they are, except for the tax-exempt feature, essentially like a private corporate bond. Many revenue bonds, however, especially those of water and electric systems, are of good quality and frequently are better than those of the municipality in which the system operates. Because analysis of revenue bonds is closely akin to appraisal of corporate issues, it is perhaps easier to identify value in revenue issues than in general obligation issues in which analysis is somewhat more difficult.

Industrial Revenue Bonds. Industrial revenue bonds are issued by agencies or localities for the purpose of financing capital expenditures for private industry. A typical arrangement would be for the authority to sell a bond issue and raise funds and then to erect a plant, which is then leased on a long-term basis to a company. In this manner the municipality attracts industry with its attendant advantages, while the company expands with low-cost funds made possible through the tax-free advantage available to municipalities.

Industrial revenue bonds have been issued since as early as 1936, but it was not until the mid-1960s that they gained prominence and increased appreciably in volume. However, a 1968 amendment to the Internal Revenue Code eliminating the tax-exempt feature on subsequent issues of over $5 million greatly reduced the issuance of additional industrial revenue bonds, as can be seen from Table 27-1. As concern over ecology has grown in the early 1970s, industrial revenue bonds for pollution control in excess of the $5 million limitation have been issued. It appears that this permitted exception will again bring industrial revenue bond issuance to 1967-1968 levels or beyond.

Authority Bonds. *Authorities* are established for the purpose of carrying out functions outside the scope of the municipality or for the purpose of circumventing debt limitations established by outdated charters or constitutions. Authority-type financing has grown markedly since 1950 and, unless constitutional revisions make authorities unnecessary, it is likely that they will continue to grow.

Authority bonds, as a class, are of good quality. However, the investor should exercise caution, especially among the toll road issues. Toll roads have experienced competition in many areas from free highways, and earnings in many cases have suffered. Other authority issues have not met with competition, but in some cases the volume of debt outstanding has mounted to levels at which concern is warranted. Because payments on revenue bonds are made solely on the basis of receipts from the revenue project, they must be analyzed as corporate bonds. The government body that created the authority issue has no responsibility for payment.

Market for Municipal Bonds

Since World War II the market for municipal bonds has been among the fastest growing of all financial markets. The reasons for this growth are:

1. Expenditures by states and municipalities became practically nonexistent during the depression and war years; as a result, there was much catching up to do after the war ended.
2. A greater demand for government services became evident in the postwar years.
3. This country realized an appreciable gain in population in the postwar years.

Immediately after World War II, municipal bonds outstanding amounted to $15 billion. By the end of 1971, the amount of state and local government long-term debt issues had increased to about $143 billion. Not only has volume grown, but also the number of large issues has increased. In 1960 there were only 7 municipal bond issues sold of $100 million or more; in 1971, 45 issues in excess of this amount were sold.

Table 27-1 shows the volume of financing and ownership changes in municipals since 1966. Of the $24.3 billion in long-term bonds issued in 1971, about 24% were for schools, 15% for water and sewer systems, and 11% for highway construction.

The substantial increase in volume of municipal bonds has made them more marketable. As volume increased, ownership became more widespread and markets broadened. Acceptance of municipal bonds has been enhanced by their impressive safety record and by continued high federal tax rates.

Ownership of Municipal Bonds. The principal holders of municipal securities in 1960-1971 are shown in Table 27-2. From this table and Table 27-1 it can be seen that commercial banks are the largest purchasers and the largest holders of state and local government issues. By July, 1972, commercial banks owned approximately 51% of all such issues; individuals, 24%; insurance companies, 14%; and business corporations, 8%. In total these four groups owned 97% of all state and local government issues. From Table 27-1 it can be calculated that these groups also purchased 100% of such issues in the years 1970 and 1971.

In the period 1960-1971 inclusive, commercial banks increased their holdings of municipals from $16.7 billion to $78.0 billion, a rise of 467%. This increase in their holdings was largely the result of the necessity of earning income sufficient, after taxes, to offset costs of the very substantial

TABLE 27-1

State and Local Securities
Net Increase in Amounts Outstanding, 1966-1972 (Billions of Dollars)

	1966	1967	1968	1969	1970	1971	1972*
Gross New Long-Term-Issues ..	11.1	14.4	16.3	11.7	18.1	24.3	23.3
Less Refunding	0.2	0.2	0.1	0.0	0.1	0.2	0.2
Total New Money New Issues ..	10.9	14.2	16.2	11.7	18.0	24.1	23.1
Less Maturities	5.9	6.4	6.9	7.4	7.9	8.4	9.0
Net Increase in Long-Term Debt	5.0	7.8	9.3	4.3	10.1	15.7	14.1
Plus Increase in Short-Term Debt	0.7	1.7	0.1	3.5	3.9	4.5	2.7
Total	5.7	9.5	9.4	7.8	14.0	20.2	16.8
OWNERSHIP:							
Mutual Savings Bank	—0.1	0.0	0.0	0.0	0.0	0.1	0.1
Life Insurance Companies	—0.4	—0.1	0.0	0.1	0.1	0.2	0.1
Fire & Casualty Companies	0.7	1.5	0.9	1.1	1.5	1.9	2.0
State & Local Retirement Funds	—0.1	0.0	—0.1	0.0	—0.4	—0.3	—0.2
Total Nonbanking Investing Institutions	0.1	1.4	0.8	1.2	1.2	1.9	2.0
Commercial Banks	1.9	9.0	8.5	0.6	10.5	13.8	12.5
Business Corporations	1.0	0.7	—0.3	2.2	—0.9	1.6	1.5
Residual Individuals & Misc. ...	2.7	—1.6	0.4	3.8	3.2	2.9	0.8
	5.7	9.5	9.4	7.8	14.0	20.2	16.8
Memorandum:							
New Industrial Revenue Bond Offerings	0.5	1.3	1.6	0.0	0.0	0.2	0.4

* Projected.

Sources: *The Bond Buyer's Municipal Finance Statistics,* Vol. 10 (April, 1972), p. 8; and *Supply and Demand for Credit in 1972* (New York: Salomon Brothers).

increase in total time deposits, including time certificates of deposit. The increase in time deposits was obtained by paying more competitive rates on time deposits after legislation was changed to permit the banks to be more competitive in this area. In 1967, for the first time, private time deposits of commercial banks exceeded private demand deposits. As recently as 1960, private time deposits were equal to only approximately 50% of private demand deposits of commercial banks. As a result of the tremendous increase in time deposits as well as the higher rates paid on such deposits, the total interest paid by commercial banks on time or savings deposits increased from $1.8 billion in 1960 to $10.5 billion in 1970. To meet these costs, the banks substantially increased their holdings of municipals and also of mortgages in the 1960s, especially municipals.

TABLE 27-2

Principal Holders of Municipal Securities, June 30, 1960-1971 (Billions of Dollars)

	1960	1961	1962	1963	1964	1965	1966	1967	1968	1969	1970	1971
Individuals	29.8	31.4	32.4	33.6	35.1	36.5	39.1	38.0	37.0	39.6	39.5	37.0
Commercial Banks	16.7	18.7	23.2	27.8	31.4	36.5	40.6	46.9	52.6	60.1	62.8	78.0
Insurance Companies	11.1	12.2	13.5	14.3	14.6	14.8	15.2	16.4	17.8	18.9	20.1	21.4
Business Corporations ...	2.5	2.4	2.2	2.2	2.4	2.8	3.6	3.3	4.3	5.4	8.8	11.9
Others	8.2	8.5	7.9	7.1	6.4	6.3	5.6	5.6	5.6	5.3	5.5	5.7
Total Outstanding	68.3	73.2	79.2	85.0	89.9	96.9	104.1	110.2	117.3	129.3	136.7	154.0
Long-Term	65.2	69.8	75.5	80.8	85.3	91.5	98.1	103.2	108.9	119.3	123.6	136.1
Short-Term	3.1	3.4	3.7	4.3	4.7	5.3	6.1	7.0	8.4	10.1	13.0	18.0

Source: *The Bond Buyer's Municipal Finance Statistics,* Vol. 10 (April, 1972), p. 17.

Individuals' holdings of municipals increased at a slower pace than the increase for commercial banks, as holdings of individuals rose from $29.8 billion in 1960 to $37.0 billion in 1971. Table 27-2 indicates the pattern of municipal buying by individuals. Typically, individuals buy municipals and sell equities under high-yield, tight money conditions and reverse the procedure during easy money periods.

Holdings of municipals by insurance companies increased from $11.1 billion in 1960 to $21.4 billion in 1971. In 1971, holdings of municipals by life insurance companies were only $3.4 billion, unchanged since 1960. Chapter 32 will explain why tax-exempt issues have lost much of their appeal for life insurance companies, for these issues lost much of the advantages of the tax-exempt features as a result of the Supreme Court decision in the Atlas Case.[2] On the other hand, municipal holdings of fire and casualty companies increased from $7.7 billion in 1960 to $18 billion in 1971. Municipal issues are attractive to fire and casualty insurance companies when their underwriting business is profitable and is subject to the corporate tax rates.

Corporations since 1967 have become large holders of municipal securities. The reason is that with relatively high short-term interest rates, municipals are a productive use for otherwise temporarily idle cash. Virtually all municipal holdings of business corporations are short-term.

Primary and Secondary Markets for Municipal Bonds. Like all marketable securities, municipal bonds have a primary market and a secondary market. The primary market is very similar to that of the corporate bond market. New issues must be sold at competitive bidding. Syndicates are formed for the purpose of bidding on forthcoming issues. The syndicate willing to purchase the issue at the lowest net interest cost is awarded the bonds. If the bond issue fails to sell, which happened especially to some issues in the erratic and difficult capital markets of 1966-1970, then the usual process of price concessions takes place until all the bonds are sold. Yields in 1970 were the highest on record, with The Bond Buyer's Index reaching 7.12% on May 28, 1970.

The marketing of municipal bonds in the secondary market can be accomplished in various ways, but one of the most effective methods is by listing in the Blue List. The Blue List is published daily and reflects the bonds that dealers own and would like to sell. The Blue List shows the bonds by state, the yield basis on which the dealers are offering to sell them, and the dealers who hold the particular bonds.

---

[2] The May 18, 1965, issue of *The Wall Street Journal* had a discussion of the Atlas Life Insurance Case.

Activity in the municipal bond market is also conveyed to the potential investor through financial publications such as *The Wall Street Journal, The New York Times, Barron's, The Daily Bond Buyer,* and *The Weekly Bond Buyer.* Bond dealers also flood potential buyers of municipal bonds with information concerning the calendar of new issues coming to market, secondary market offerings, and pertinent statistics on the municipal market as a whole. Today there are more municipal bonds outstanding, more municipal bond dealers, more financial coverage of municipal markets, and more investors buying and selling municipal bonds than ever before, which implies a growing acceptance of municipal bonds as an investment medium and a broadening market for tax-exempt securities. As a result, the marketability of the $154 billion of municipal obligations has been greatly enhanced.

Improved marketability has broadened the municipal bond market appreciably. Development of an active secondary market with breadth, depth, and resiliency has caused both individual and institutional buyers to substitute municipal bonds for other assets that were used primarily for liquidity purposes. This has been especially true among commercial bank buyers, especially after their exceptional increase in time deposits in the 1960s. With all due respect to municipal bonds, however, the investor should constantly be aware that for purposes of liquidity there is no replacement for short-term government bonds. The "credit crunch" of 1966 and especially the "liquidity crisis" of 1970 demonstrated how vulnerable even short-term municipal bonds can be to tight credit conditions. Sustained selling of municipal bonds by a few major commercial banks resulted in a dramatic decline in price and hence evaporation of any characteristics of liquidity.

Quality of Municipal Bonds

As a class, municipal bonds have a better safety record than any other type of security except U. S. Governments. Municipal bonds fared poorly in the period of reconstruction and were in large part responsible for the financial crisis of 1874. This, however, was a period in which irresponsibility and abuse were rampant in some state and local governments. As a matter of fact, some prejudice still prevails against Southern bonds as a result of practices during the era of reconstruction.

During the depression years of the 1930s, only one state bond defaulted and this was remedied very quickly. There were, however, several thousand municipal bond defaults. Most municipal issues that proved troublesome were those issued for industrial purposes or those issued by municipalities heavily dependent on one or a few cyclical industries or located in largely recreational areas. General obligation issues and revenue issues for water, sewage, and electric facilities have had records of safety that are enviable.

MUNICIPAL BOND ANALYSIS

As in the analysis of any securities, there is no formula that can be followed blindly in the evaluation of municipal credit. The investor must use judgment in assessing the abundance of facts that are at his disposal.

Credit Analysis of Municipal Bonds

The investor must be ever alert to changes in various credits. For example, some major cities such as New York have been suffering an erosion of their socioeconomic bases and have experienced a lowering of their credit rating by the statistical agencies. This has resulted in growing debt burdens and a declining tax base with which to meet the burdens. Extended far enough, this could lead to eventual problems. The investor should remember that no situation is static, even in the unromantic field of municipal finance.

Debt per Capita. Debt per capita is the most frequently used figure in appraising general obligation issues. This ratio is good as a first approximation, but it can be very misleading. It makes no allowance for the quality or the composition of the population and for the source or the nature of the income of the area. Neither does it provide for ability or willingness to pay, which are the two most important factors in any credit. Nevertheless, debt per capita is helpful because it is simple to calculate and can give the investor something to relate easily to other general obligation issues. As a rule of thumb, if debt per capita is below $300, the credit is usually worth further consideration. If debt per capita is in excess of $500, the investor should closely scrutinize the credit before investing.

Debt to Assessed Value and Market Value. Debt to assessed value and debt to market value are also commonly used ratios. Debt to assessed value is not too meaningful because assessments vary among municipalities and counties, and in any event their ability to carry debt burdens depends on the amount and the quality of income generated in the area. Any comparison of debt to assessed value is meaningless unless the basis of assessment is known. Debt to assessed value is important only as some indication of debt in relation to the tax base. Debt to true market value is important in showing whether or not the overall level of debt is becoming burdensome. If debt exceeds 7% of true market value, the investor should investigate other factors thoroughly before investing.

It should be mentioned that assessed value, in combination with millage, gives some idea of latitude remaining to increase taxes to meet any increase in expenditures. If both assessments and millage are high, then little latitude remains, while the reverse is true if either or both are low. This relationship bears close scrutiny, especially at present with debt levels of most major municipalities being at unprecedented levels.

Debt per Capita to Income per Capita. Debt per capita to income per capita is probably as helpful an indicator as exists. This ratio, as much as anything else, will quickly identify the degree of burden of the debt. As a general rule, if debt per capita is in excess of 10% of income per capita, the issue should be avoided. If debt is too high in relation to income, it may become impossible for debt service to be met or the issuance of additional debt may be seriously limited. Many issuers of general obligation debt have reached or will soon reach this level, especially big cities.

Competence of Administration. It is important to have some idea of how well the municipality is administered, but this information is very difficult to ascertain. One indicator is tax collections. If tax collections are poor, then it is reasonable to assume that other areas of administration are lacking. If tax collections are not at least 95% current, the investor has some cause for concern. Also, total debt service costs to total budget give some indication of administration as well as degree of burden of total debt. If debt service costs are in excess of 25% of total budget, the investor should be wary.

Other Factors in Analysis of Municipal Bonds. There are many other factors to consider, but in the interest of brevity only a few will be considered here. The trend of debt is important and should be watched. If the rate of increase becomes too rapid, not only should additional purchases be stopped but any holdings should be considered as candidates for sale. Attention should be given to the industrial and socioeconomic base. Ideally, industry should be diversified so that too great reliance is not placed on one company or one industry. Erosion of socioeconomic base has become commonplace in some cities as a result of high-income groups removing themselves to suburban communities. As a result, there has been a reduction in tax base and an increase in welfare expenses for these cities. Taken to extremes, this could prove burdensome and should be an important item for consideration. Again, New York City is a case in point.

Analysis of Revenue Bonds

The credit of the government body is not pledged and the government body accepts no responsibility for the payment of revenue bonds. Their payment depends *entirely* on revenues generated by the project they financed. Revenue bonds should therefore be analyzed in the same way as corporate bonds. The important factor is size and stability of revenue and its adequacy in servicing outstanding debt. Revenue bonds are issued for purposes such as sewer and water systems, publicly owned electric systems, airports, tunnels, and highways. There are other purposes, but those listed make up the vast majority of revenue bonds.

Of all revenue bonds, water and electric issues, as classes, are considered to be of highest quality. That the market recognizes this is evident from good trading characteristics and lower yields afforded by this type of issue as compared with other revenue bonds. Both water and electric revenue bonds offer a stable stream of income deriving from inelastic demand curves. Because of this, the investor will accept much lower coverage of debt service by revenues from these types of issues than from other revenue bonds. To illustrate market sentiment for water and electric revenue issues, they frequently trade at lower yield levels than general obligation issues of the municipalities in which the systems operate.

Sewer issues also are highly acceptable and trade well in the marketplace. Highway issues supported by some special tax are also well received. Straight toll road issues, however, are different and should be recognized as such. Early toll roads, such as the New Jersey and Pennsylvania Turnpike systems, had several advantages and should be considered apart from the "average" toll road. Older toll roads were financed at lower interest rates and construction costs, which resulted in lower debt service requirements. More recent roads were more costly, and several have experienced serious competition from freeways financed largely by the federal government. Investors in toll road bonds should exercise caution, especially for new roads.

Airport, parking, and seaport revenue issues have grown in volume over the past several years. These issues can be erratic from an earnings point of view, and the investor should recognize that the range of quality is quite wide. In recognition of this, many municipalities have pledged to make up any deficiencies that may arise from inadequate earnings. If the full faith and credit of a municipality is pledged, such bonds are revenue bonds in name only and can be considered to be full faith and obligation municipal issues. Unless there are some unusual circumstances, the quality investor should confine purchases of airport, seaport, and parking revenue issues to those also having the backing of general taxing powers.

Municipal Bond Ratings

As implied throughout this chapter, there is considerable variation in the creditworthiness of municipal bonds. Because of this variation and the heterogeneous nature of this type of bond, two investor services assign quality ratings to municipal issues that are of a certain size: Moody's Investor Service and Standard & Poor's Investor Service.

The question is to what extent the investor should rely upon ratings assigned by these agencies. Since both these services are objective sources of information and because they are well qualified to make judgments on municipal credits, the investor can rely upon their quality ratings as general guides. However, there are wide variations within quality categories and neither rating service makes any guarantee concerning the permanence of a rating. Accordingly, it is incumbent upon the investor to make his own credit analysis. Ratings can be used to make broad judgments, but final decisions should be based on closer investigation.

Market Behavior of Municipal Bonds

Municipal bonds in general behave in the same manner as any other class of fixed-income securities. When interest rates rise, prices of municipal bonds fall; when interest rates decline, prices of municipal bonds rise. There is, however, because of the heterogeneous nature of this market, some variation in the rapidity with which prices change among the various classes of municipal bonds. In the discussion here, attention will be given to price patterns under varying market conditions for premium and discount issues, primary and secondary market issues, and high and lower quality bonds.

Premium and Discount Issues. There is usually some yield advantage to the buyer of premium or discount issues. The reason for this is that institutional investors, especially buyers for trust accounts, show a very strong preference for par or, as they are sometimes called, current coupon bonds. In the case of the trust buyer, this preference is entirely logical, since premium bonds would benefit the income beneficiary to the detriment of remaindermen, while discount issues would have the reverse effect. Other investors, however, have no logical basis to favor current coupon issues.

It would behoove the discerning investor to consider using discount or premium bonds if their net yield is greater than that for par bonds of comparable quality and maturity. Aside from yield advantages, there are other factors to consider. In a rising bond market, discount bonds appreciate faster and by a larger amount percentagewise than other bonds. It is for this reason that speculators in the bond market most often use this medium to realize gains. It should be remembered, however, that discount issues also react more quickly in a falling market. Also, discount issues by virtue of their low coupons are not as subject to call; therefore, the investor usually obtains automatic call protection, a valuable factor in the late 1960s.

Premium bonds, as a general rule, do not show as much appreciation as discount issues in a rising bond market. In a declining market, however, they afford greater protection against downside risk. As the price moves closer to par, the market actually broadens because the amount of the premium is becoming more palatable to those having some prejudice against premiums. It can be seen from this one small example how the astute investor can add to his performance by capitalizing upon prejudices of the market in general.

Market Patterns for Issues of Different Quality. There are definite patterns that evolve under varying market conditions for bonds of high and low quality. During strong markets, the yield spread (differential) between bonds of high and low quality becomes narrow. During weak markets the spread becomes wider. Therefore, the careful investor will upgrade quality when buying into strong markets and will downgrade quality when taking advantage of a weak market.

Patterns on a quality basis are brought on by conditions peculiar to the large institutional investor. Large institutional investors attempt to maintain a given yield level. Since funds for investment are almost continually flowing in, these investors are obligated to buy securities almost without regard to market levels. Accordingly, in strong markets they will sacrifice quality to maintain the given yield level. In weak markets they will upgrade quality to compensate for lower quality bought earlier. An investor without the rigidities peculiar to many institutional investors can improve performance by knowing and making use of these patterns. During strong market conditions, emphasis should be placed on higher quality issues because of little yield advantage in issues of lower quality. During periods of weakness in fixed-income markets, greater stress should be given to bonds of lower quality. In brief, better performance can be realized by following buying practices contrary to those of the vast majority of institutional investors.

Market for Municipals and Free Reserves of Banks. It is important to note that the level of the municipal market closely follows free reserves in the banking system. This is a reflection of commercial bank dominance in the municipal market. Table 27-3 below gives some idea of the closeness of this correlation.

TABLE 27-3

Changes in Free Reserves and Municipal Bond Prices

	No. of Months in Which Free Reserves Increased (plus) or Decreased (minus)		No. of Months in Which Municipals Increased (plus) or Decreased (minus)	
1971	Plus	7	Plus	7
	(minus)	5	(minus)	5
1970	Plus	8	Plus	7
	(minus)	4	(minus)	5
1969	Plus	5	Plus	3
	(minus)	7	(minus)	9
1968	Plus	5	Plus	5
	(minus)	7	(minus)	7
1967	Plus	7	Plus	3
	(minus)	5	(minus)	9
1966	(minus)	12	Plus	6
1965	Plus	2	Plus	9
	(minus)	10	(minus)	3
1964	Plus	11	Plus	8
	(minus)	1	(minus)	4
1963	Plus	12	Plus	10
			(minus)	2
1962	Plus	12	Plus	11
			(minus)	1

Source: *Survey of Current Business,* January editions, 1963-1972.

The year 1965 is atypical because of a large inflow of certificates of deposit into the banking system and considerable buying by commercial banks to offset the increased cost of money. In 1967, Federal Reserve monetary policy changed abruptly from ease in the first half of the year to tightness in the second half, but bank buying of municipals anticipated tighter money by several months. Despite occasional variation, the investor can use free reserves as a rough indicator of market direction and can adjust his buying patterns accordingly.

Yield Patterns in Primary and Secondary Markets. Over the course of an interest rate cycle, some discernible yield patterns evolve in both primary and secondary markets. This being true, it follows logically that there must be a time to avoid one market and to concentrate on the other. In most cases the secondary market is more attractive in rising markets, while the primary market is more attractive in declining markets. This condition obtains because rising prices are usually reflected first in new issues, while upward price adjustments lag in positioned bonds. In declining markets, inventories of municipal bonds are usually mounting and often become burdensome. Therefore, new issues coming to market are priced to sell so that inventory levels do not become more burdensome with additional unsold bonds. At the same time, most dealer houses display some hesitancy in marking down inventoried bonds unless the market shows real evidence of further deterioration.

By using all of the patterns described above, the investor can realize significant yield advantages. The patterns are by no means regular or precise, but they are apparent enough to be highly useful.

QUESTIONS

1. (a) What are the major classifications of municipal bonds?
   (b) What are the major differences between them?

2. (a) Explain the meaning of state sovereignty.
   (b) What is its significance for investors?

3. (a) What is an industrial revenue bond?
   (b) What significant event occurred during 1968 that is of importance to investors considering purchase of industrial revenue bonds? Are any exceptions now available to the restriction imposed in 1968?

4. (a) What has led to the rapid growth experienced in the market for municipal bonds since World War II?
   (b) What explanation can you offer for the fact that commercial banks are the largest holders of municipal bonds?

5. What is the *Blue List*? What is its significance to investors?

6. What determines the investment quality of municipal bonds?

7. (a) Why is the ratio of debt to assessed valuation a rather unsatisfactory measure of the quality of state debts?
   (b) What other comparisons might be more useful?

8. Should an investor in the 70% marginal income tax bracket purchase a corporate bond yielding 8% or a municipal bond yielding 4%, assuming financial risk is negligible in both cases. Why?

9. (a) Why is there likely to be some yield advantage to the buyer of premium or discount issues of municipal bonds?
   (b) What other advantages might the investor gain by investing in discount issues?

10. (a) What market patterns evolve under varying market conditions between municipal bonds of high and low quality. Why?
    (b) What investment policies are suggested?
    (c) When should the investor in municipal bonds buy in the primary market and when should the investor buy in the secondary market? Why?

WORK-STUDY PROBLEMS

1. Assume that a wealthy customer advises his broker that he has been told that the following bond is attractive:

   Miami, Water Revenue Bonds, Series 1953A, 2¾ Serial, due June 1, 1979.

   (a) As his broker, write a memorandum giving him, among other things, the following information:
       (1) Yield to maturity.
       (2) Size of the issue of which it is a part.
       (3) Call provisions.
       (4) Moody's rating and Standard & Poor's rating.
       (5) Collection record and comment.
       (6) Type of obligation.
       (7) Debt per capita compared with median.
       (8) Type of government.
       (9) Maturities.
       (10) Economic aspects:
            (a) Industrial diversification.
            (b) Growth of population.
       (11) Percent of debt to assessed value.

   (b) Assume that this individual has $500,000 in his investment portfolio and that he faces a 50% income tax rate. What is the tax-equivalent yield necessary for him to obtain on a common stock or a U. S. Government bond to make one of these instruments attractive to him? Compare this yield to yields on the DJIA and S&P indexes.

   (c) Would you recommend that your customer buy the bond? Support your recommendation carefully.

2. (a) Take an actual commercial bank and determine the following:
   (1) The actual amount of tax-exempt issues in its portfolio.
   (2) The ratio of tax-exempts to total "other securities."
   (3) The ratio of tax-exempts to holdings of U. S. Government securities.

   (b) Explain the reason for the amount and the ratio of tax-exempt securities in the portfolio of this particular bank.

SUGGESTED READINGS

The Bond Buyer. Monthly issues. (Statistics on state and local government finance.)

Davis, E. H. *Of the People, By the People, For the People—An Informal Analysis of Tax-Free Public Bonds*. New York: John Nuveen Co., 1958.

Industrial Aid Financing. New York: Goodbody & Co., 1965.

Jones, Bethune. *New Trends in State, County and Municipal Government*. Asbury Park, N. J., 1969.

Moody's Municipals and Governments. Annual issues.

PORTFOLIO
POLICIES
FOR
INDIVIDUALS

Financial Planning
and Investment Planning

Every individual should have an overall *financial plan* based on his current financial position and income and on reasonable expectation of future income and financial position. Before an individual invests in securities, he should prepare an *investment plan* that correlates closely with the other segments of his financial plan. The financial circumstances of an individual as well as his psychological temperament establish the perimeter of his financial plan and his investment constraints. Unfortunately, few individuals make such plans except in a very cursory or informal manner.

FINANCIAL PLANNING OF INDIVIDUALS

To show how individuals do invest savings, this chapter will first examine some statistics on the personal savings of individuals and then examine some statistics on financial asset holdings of individuals. Various alternative media for savings will then be discussed. Investment objectives and constraints of the individual will be discussed in Chapter 29.

Personal Savings—National Income Accounts

Table 28-1 presents statistics for selected years from 1929 to 1949 and for all years from 1949 through 1972 for personal income, personal tax payments, disposable personal income, personal outlays (largely consumption expenditures) and the residual figure for savings. Since 1964, personal savings have ranged between 6% and 7% of disposable personal income; but in some years they were higher: 8% in 1970 and 8.2% in 1971. In 1972 they

TABLE 28-1

Personal Income, Disposable Personal Income and Savings—Selected Years 1929-1972
(National Income Accounts in Billions)

Year	1929	1933	1940	1944	1946	1947	1949	1950	1951	1952	1953	1954	1955	1956	1957
Personal income	85.9	47.0	78.3	165.3	178.7	191.3	207.2	227.6	255.6	272.5	288.2	290.1	310.9	333.0	351.1
Less Personal tax and related payments	2.6	1.5	2.6	18.9	18.7	21.4	18.6	20.7	29.0	34.1	35.6	32.7	35.5	39.8	42.6
Equals Disposable personal income	83.3	45.5	75.7	146.3	160.0	169.8	188.6	206.9	226.6	238.3	252.6	257.4	275.3	293.2	308.5
Less Personal outlays (consumption expenditures)	79.1	46.4	71.8	109.1	144.8	162.5	179.2	193.9	209.3	220.3	234.3	241.0	259.5	272.6	287.8
Equals Personal savings	4.2	0.9	3.8	37.3	15.2	7.3	9.4	13.1	17.3	18.1	18.3	16.4	15.8	20.6	20.7
Savings as % of disposable personal income	5.0%	neg.	5.0%	25.5%	9.5%	4.3%	5.0%	6.3%	7.6%	7.6%	7.2%	6.4%	5.7%	7.0%	6.7%

Year	1958	1959	1960	1961	1962	1963	1964	1965	1966	1967	1968	1969	1970	1971	1972
Personal income	361.2	383.5	401.0	416.8	442.6	465.5	497.5	538.9	587.2	629.3	688.9	750.9	806.3	861.4	935.8
Less Personal tax and related payments	42.3	46.2	50.9	52.4	57.4	60.9	59.4	65.7	75.4	83.0	97.9	116.5	116.7	117.0	140.7
Equals Disposable personal income	318.8	337.3	350.0	364.4	385.3	404.6	438.1	473.2	511.9	546.3	591.0	634.4	689.5	744.4	795.1
Less Personal outlays (consumption expenditures)	296.8	318.3	333.0	343.3	363.7	384.7	411.9	444.8	479.3	506.0	551.2	596.2	634.7	683.4	740.4
Equals Personal savings	22.3	19.1	17.0	21.2	21.6	19.9	26.2	28.4	32.5	40.4	39.8	38.2	54.9	60.9	54.8
Savings as % of disposable personal income	7.0%	5.6%	4.9%	5.8%	5.6%	4.9%	6.0%	6.0%	6.4%	7.4%	6.7%	6.0%	8.0%	8.2%	6.9%

Source: Survey of Current Business.

fell back to 6.9%. The figure did skyrocket to 25.5% during the World War II years because of the shortages of consumer goods and the patriotic urge to save.

The percentage that each individual or household can and will save depends upon (1) the disposable personal income available, (2) the size of the household for married individuals, and (3) the psychological intensity of the desire to spend and to save. On the average, the range of 6%-7% of disposable personal income is reasonable and also a median for average families in the $10,000-$25,000 income bracket.

Personal Savings—Increase in Financial Assets

In Table 28-1 we present statistics from the National Income Accounts for personal savings (disposable personal income less personal outlay equals savings) and also savings as a percentage of disposable personal income. In Table 28-2 we present details of the amount and composition of individuals' savings during 1967-1971. Item 44 lists personal savings (flow of funds accounts) and Item 45 lists personal savings (national income and product accounts); Item 46, the difference between Items 44 and 45. Items 44 and 45 are net after deducting increases in debt but include net increase in tangible assets as well as increase in financial assets. Item 1 represents the increase in financial asset holdings of individuals, but it is a gross figure before deducting income in debt.

It is clear from Item 1 that most of the annual increase in financial assets of individuals flows into investment through financial intermediaries (financial institutions such as commercial banks, mutual savings banks, and insurance companies) rather than through direct investment in securities. Furthermore, Items 11 and 12 show direct investment in investment company shares and in other corporate stock. Other than investment in mutual funds, individuals have been net sellers of corporate stock for many years; and even if investment in mutual funds is taken into account, individuals have still been net sellers of common stock and institutional investors have been the net acquirers from individuals even though the total number of individual stockholders has increased substantially.

As of January 1, 1972, households had financial assets of $2,170 billion and liabilities of $526 billion, or net equity of $1,644 billion. Approximately 29% of these financial assets was in the form of currency and demand and savings deposits which, of course, are fixed-value investments. Approximately 48% was in security investments, with 40% of financial assets in corporate stock including investment company shares. The bulk of the remainder consisted of 12.4% in pension fund reserves and 6.3% in life insurance reserves.

TABLE 28-2

Amount and Composition of Individuals' Savings, 1967-1972.
(Annual Increase in Assets, Billions of Dollars)

Line		1967	1968	1969	1970	1971	1972
1	Increase in financial assets	65.8	72.4	62.6	87.1	96.3	124.9
2	Currency and demand deposits	11.2	12.8	3.6	6.3	8.6	12.9
3	Savings accounts	34.8	30.4	6.1	41.5	73.5	75.8
4	Securities	—4.2	3.5	27.3	5.6	—19.2	5.1
5	U.S. savings bonds	.9	.4	—.4	.3	2.4	3.3
6	Other U.S. Treasury securities	—2.9	2.8	8.1	—7.3	—19.3	1.5
7	U.S. Government agency securities	1.1	1.4	4.3	2.6	—5.8	—.5
8	State and local obligations	—1.7	—.2	7.6	2.0	4.9	1.3
9	Corporate and foreign bonds	4.8	4.8	5.7	12.4	7.6	4.9
10	Commercial paper	—2.3	2.0	5.9	—1.8	—3.9	.4
11	Investment Co. shares	2.6	4.7	5.5	2.6	1.3	—.6
12	Other corporate stock	—6.8	—12.3	—9.6	—5.2	—6.5	—5.2
13	Private life insurance reserves	4.9	4.6	4.8	5.1	6.6	7.2
14	Private insured pension reserves	2.6	2.9	2.9	3.3	3.3	4.6
15	Private noninsured pension reserves	6.6	6.4	6.3	7.1	7.3	5.7
16	Government insurance and pension reserves	5.4	6.0	6.6	9.2	9.8	10.5
17	Miscellaneous financial assets	4.6	5.9	4.9	6.0	6.5	3.1
18	Gross investment in tangible assets	116.7	132.5	143.0	140.9	167.7	190.5
19	Nonfarm homes	17.0	21.1	22.0	19.6	25.8	34.3
20	Noncorporate business construction and equipment	25.6	26.7	29.2	30.6	35.8	39.5
21	Consumer durables	73.1	84.0	90.8	90.5	103.5	117.4
22	Inventories	.9	.6	1.1	.1	2.5	—.8
23	Capital consumption (1) allowances	86.9	95.3	104.5	112.2	121.2	130.6
24	Nonfarm homes	7.8	8.3	8.7	9.0	9.4	10.2
25	Noncorporate business plant and equipment	18.4	19.6	21.3	22.6	24.5	26.7
26	Consumer durables	60.7	67.4	74.6	80.6	87.3	93.8
27	Net investment in tangible assets	29.8	37.2	38.5	28.7	46.4	59.8
28	Nonfarm homes	9.2	12.8	13.3	10.6	16.5	24.1
29	Noncorporate business construction and equipment	7.3	7.1	7.9	8.1	11.3	12.8
30	Consumer durables	12.4	16.7	16.2	9.9	16.2	23.6
31	Inventories	.9	.6	1.1	.1	2.5	—.8
32	Increase in debt	33.7	43.3	41.6	32.8	59.6	85.1
33	Mortgage debt on nonfarm homes	10.5	14.9	16.2	12.5	24.5	38.4
34	Noncorporate business mortgage debt	7.0	6.6	6.9	8.0	11.3	13.2
35	Consumer credit	4.6	11.1	9.3	4.3	10.4	19.2
36	Security credit	3.3	2.1	—2.5	—1.9	2.1	4.7
37	Policy loans	1.0	1.3	2.6	2.3	1.0	.9
38	Other debt	7.3	7.4	9.0	7.5	10.3	8.6
39	Individual saving (1 + 27 — 32)	61.9	66.3	59.6	82.9	83.1	99.7
40	Less: Government insurance and pension reserves	5.4	6.0	6.6	9.2	9.8	10.5
41	Net investment in consumer durables	12.4	16.7	16.2	9.9	16.2	23.6
42	Capital gains dividends from investment companies	1.7	2.5	2.5	.9	.8	1.4
43	Net savings by farm corporations	—.1	.0	.0	—.2	.0	*
44	Equals personal saving, flow of funds account basis	42.5	41.2	34.2	63.1	56.5	64.2
45	Personal saving, national income and product account basis	40.4	39.8	38.2	54.9	60.9	49.7
46	Difference (45 — 44)	—2.1	—1.4	4.0	—8.2	4.5	14.4

Therefore, in total these four groups accounted for 96% of the financial assets of all households on January 1, 1972. These percentages had changed only nominally since the mid-1960s.

The question naturally arises why, if individuals have been net sellers of common stock to institutional investors over many years, does corporate stock continue to represent 40% of the total financial assets of individuals (see Table 28-3). The answer is twofold. First, when financial assets of individuals are listed and totaled and the proportions of the items are listed, we are dealing with market values. Secondly, stock prices have risen substantially in the post-World War II years from DJIA lows of approximately 160 in 1946 through 1949 to 1,000 in February, 1966, nearly 1,000 (985)

TABLE 28-3

Households' Financial Assets, January 1, 1972 (Billions of Dollars)

		Assets		Percentage
Demand Deposits and Currency		$ 134.9		6.2
Time and Savings Accounts ...		496.0		22.9
At Commercial Banks	$221.8		10.3	
At Savings Institutions	274.2		12.6	
Savings and Loan Associations	$172.6		8.0	
Mutual Savings Banks	83.3		3.8	
Credit Unions	18.3		0.8	
Life Insurance Reserves		137.0		6.3
Pension Fund Reserves		268.1		12.4
Corporate Stock (Including investment company shares)		878.7		40.4
Other Securities		176.9		8.2
U.S. Government Securities..	77.1		3.6	
State and Local Government Obligations	52.3		2.4	
Corporate and Foreign Bonds *	47.5		2.2	
Mortgages		44.9		2.1
Home Mortgages	13.4		0.6	
Other Mortgages	31.5		1.5	
Other Loans		3.1		0.1
Security Credit to Brokers and Dealers		2.1		0.1
Miscellaneous Financial Assets .		28.8		1.3
Total Assets		$2170.5		
Total Liabilities		525.8		
Net Financial Assets (Financial Assets Less Debt)		$1644.7		100.0

* Foreign bond holdings included are very minor.

Source: *Federal Reserve Bulletin,* June, 1972.

in December, 1968, and again 1,000 in January, 1973. Therefore, if $160,000 in corporate stock had been owned by an individual in a diversified list of common stocks or a large diversified mutual fund and none had been sold, the portfolio would have had a market value of approximately $1,000,000 in February, 1966; December, 1968; and January, 1973. Though some of the individuals sold some of their stock, the total value of the common stock portfolio could still represent say 40% of financial assets in 1973. In the aggregate, individuals each year sold on the average very substantially less in market value than the rise in common stock market values. Therefore, in 1973 common stock in individual portfolios still represented nearly the same proportion of financial assets as it had a decade earlier.

On the other hand, each year the proportion of total common stock market values owned by individuals has been declining. The proportion owned by financial institutions has risen from approximately 5% in the early post-World War II years to approximately 27% in 1973. This is an even more significant rise when we consider that the number of individual shareowners has risen from 6.5 million in 1952 to over 33 million in 1973.

INVESTMENT PLANNING OF INDIVIDUALS

The various media for savings by individuals that are discussed in this section are (1) cash and demand deposits, (2) savings and time deposits, (3) U.S. Government securities, (4) reserve fund, (5) insurance programs, and (6) pension plans.

Cash and Demand Deposits

Individuals' *holdings* of cash and demand deposits represent about 6.2% of total financial assets as was shown in Table 28-3.

Demand deposits (checking accounts) pay no interest so that their purpose is to provide current funds to be used (by check) to pay current bills. The individual deposits his monthly income in these accounts and then draws upon them as current bills are paid. The balance must be sufficient to meet current bills as they come due, which in some months (such as months of federal and local tax payments and insurance payments) may be higher than in others. The more irregular the income, the larger the balance required so that payment needs may be met as bills come due. Many individuals plan for estimated, exceptionally large monthly payments, including vacation expenses, by depositing sums regularly in savings accounts rather than in demand deposit (checking) accounts.

Savings and Time Deposits

Most individuals maintain savings or time deposits or their equivalent (including commercial bank time certificates of deposit) where the funds are safe (through deposit insurance) and immediately available. Balances are maintained to meet unusually large future expenses, unexpected future expenses, and in a large number of cases as a medium for building capital over the years for down payments on homes, for education of children, and simply as a long-term capital fund.[1] In cases where the income tax rate is not significant enough to justify the purchase of tax-exempt bonds and where the total amount involved is less than $100,000, it is suggested that individuals use savings accounts (or certificates of deposit) instead of bonds (either government or corporate). In this way, the risk of market depreciation of bonds (as in 1966-1970 or even 1946-1970) is avoided, no commissions are payable, and interest is earned from date of deposit at a rate sufficient in many years to offset the advantages of bond investment. However, in years like 1967-1970, new AAA corporate bonds yielded over 8% versus 5% on savings accounts. Even with such a yield differential, individuals with less than $25,000 are still advised to place their funds in "fixed-value" assets, that is, in insured savings accounts. But funds in excess of this amount may be used to purchase corporate bonds to take advantage of any wide yield spread advantage over insured savings accounts or to purchase tax-exempt bonds when tax brackets justify their purchase.

That a very large number of individuals view the use of savings accounts or their equivalent in these ways is evidenced by the substantial flow of annual savings into deposit-type institutions, as shown in Table 28-3. Table 28-4

TABLE 28-4

Savings Held by Individuals for Selected Years, 1945-1972 (Billions of Dollars)

Year	Mutual Savings Banks	Savings and Loan Associations	Commercial Banks	Credit Unions	Postal Savings	Total	U.S. Savings Bonds	Total Including Savings Bonds	Holdings of Other U.S. Gov't. Securities	Reserves of Life Insurance Companies
1945	15.3	7.4	29.9	0.4	2.9	55.9	42.9	98.8	21.2	37.5
1950	20.0	14.0	34.9	0.9	2.9	72.7	49.6	122.3	16.7	53.6
1955	28.2	32.1	46.0	2.4	1.9	110.6	50.2	160.8	14.7	73.7
1960	36.3	62.1	66.8	5.0	0.8	171.0	45.6	216.6	20.5	95.8
1961	38.3	70.9	76.7	5.6	0.7	192.2	46.4	238.6	19.5	100.3
1962	41.3	80.2	91.0	6.3	0.5	219.3	46.9	266.2	19.2	105.1
1963	44.6	91.3	102.9	7.2	0.5	246.5	48.1	294.6	20.1	110.4
1964	48.8	101.9	116.6	8.2	0.4	275.9	48.9	324.8	21.1	116.3
1965	52.4	110.3	134.2	9.4	0.3	306.6	49.7	356.3	22.4	122.8
1966	55.0	114.0	146.3	10.3	0.1	325.2	50.3	375.5	24.3	128.4
1967	60.1	124.5	167.6	11.1	. . .	363.3	51.2	414.5	22.8	135.1
1968	64.5	131.6	181.3	12.3	. . .	388.7	51.9	440.6	23.9	141.8
1969	67.1	135.5	177.0	13.7	. . .	393.3	51.8	445.1	29.6	147.5
1970	71.6	146.4	203.4	15.5	. . .	436.9	52.1	489.0	29.8	154.1
1971	81.4	174.5	239.5	18.3	. . .	513.7	54.4	568.1	19.6	164.8
1972	91.6	207.3	273.5	21.7	. . .	594.1	57.1	651.2	17.1	170.7

[1] In fact only about 1 in 5 adult individuals own any corporate or municipal debt securities.

TABLE 28-5

Competitive Yields for Savings Alternatives
Average Annual Yield on Selected Types of Investments (Selected Years)

Years	Savings Deposits in Mutual Savings Banks	Savings Accts. in Savings and Loan Assns.	Time and Savings Deposits in Commercial Banks	Bonds * U. S. Govt.	State, Local Govt. Tax Exempt Bonds	Seasoned Corporate Bonds AAA	BAA
1966	4.45	4.45	4.04	4.66	3.90	5.1	5.7
1967	4.74	4.67	4.24	4.85	3.99	5.5	6.2
1968	4.76	4.68	4.48	5.25	4.48	6.2	6.9
1969	4.89	4.80	4.87	6.10	5.73	7.0	7.8
1970	5.01	5.06	4.92	6.59	6.42	8.0*	9.1*
1971	5.13	5.33	4.78	5.74	5.62	7.4	8.6
1972	5.22	5.40	4.65	5.63	5.30	7.2	8.2

* In 1970 seasoned bonds reached the following peaks: AAA, 8.5%; BAA, 9.4%; and new issue AAA, 9.2%; in 1973, AA, 8.0%; BAA, 9.4%.

Source: *Savings and Loan Fact Book* and *National Fact Book of Mutual Savings Banking,* 1972.

shows the amounts of savings of individuals in various savings media. Table 28-5 shows the competitive yields for alternative types of savings.

U.S. Government Securities

While in some years of high yields in the capital markets individuals have increased their holdings of U.S. Government debt obligations (savings bonds and other government securities), in 1972 individuals' holdings of these securities only totaled 3.6% of total financial assets.

Reserve Fund

A sound financial program should provide a reserve fund for emergencies and for future large expenditures, such as major medical expenses not otherwise covered, temporary cessation of income, education expenses, and unforeseeable contingencies. Today, employment is more stable, unemployment insurance is available, most people have hospital and medical insurance, and constraints on personal borrowing have been reduced considerably. Securities can serve as collateral for a loan, and one can borrow on life insurance policies (other than term). But the stock market can become depressed in price and stay depressed for several years, just at the time when these funds are needed. Therefore, reserve funds should not be invested in equities.

Insurance Program of the Individual

The major purpose of any insurance program is to provide for protection against risks of such magnitude that they cannot adequately be met in any other way. A life insurance program, in addition to providing protection against risks, can also include, within insurance policies, a savings-and-investment element. In some types of life insurance policies the savings-and-investment feature eventually becomes equal to or greater than the strictly insurance protective feature. The annual flow of individuals' savings into private life insurance reserves and insured pension funds ranged around $5 billion in the late 1950s and rose to over $10 billion in 1972.

In planning an insurance program, the individual should decide (1) what risks must be faced that can and should most probably be covered by insurance and (2) what amount of protection is needed in the light of these risks, such as the protection of dependents.

Major Risks Requiring Protection.[2] The major risks that require insurance protection are:

1. Medical risks for the individual and his dependents:
   a. Cost of doctors' services—medical, dental, etc.
   b. Cost of hospital services.
   c. Loss of pay due to illness or accident.

2. Death risks (life insurance)—protection of dependents if the individual responsible for support dies.

The insurance coverage for medical risks is generally provided at least in part by Blue Cross and Blue Shield or similar policies sold by insurance companies and very frequently is provided free by employers. It is frequently supplemented by major medical insurance policies. All individuals are strongly advised to carry such protection.

Most men and many women have dependents who would suffer serious financial hardship if the breadwinner should die. The risk is greatest for men as long as there are dependent children whose education has not been completed. After these dependent children become self-supporting or married, the amount of protection needed decreases. The need for life insurance protection also decreases as the individual builds capital outside his insurance program. However, even after a substantial investment portfolio has been acquired, insurance can still serve the useful purpose of providing funds to cover estate taxes and costs incurred in the individual's last illness, thus

---

[2] In this text, we can only justify touching upon the major factors of insurance within the overall financial plan. The reader may consult specialized books on the subject for further information.

keeping invested capital relatively intact for the beneficiaries of the estate. Life insurance is the only method in the early years, say 20 to 35 or 40, by which most individuals can instantaneously create an estate on death.

It is often quite difficult for young married people in their twenties to save money except for a down payment on a home or for items for the home; therefore, insurance protection needed is very high. Assuming that a family head saves and invests $500 per year from age 30 to 39 and $1,000 per year from age 40 to 65 (an amount of annual savings that is realistic for many individuals), the result at an annual compound rate of 3%, 6%, 7½%, and 9% is shown in Table 28-6.

TABLE 28-6

Results of Accumulating Savings-Investments
At Assumed Compounding Rates Indicated

	3%	6%	7½%	9%
By Age 40	$ 5,904	$ 6,986	$ 7,604	$ 8,289
By Age 50	19,742	26,482	30,380	36,157
By Age 60	38,345	61,397	78,853	102,170
By Age 65	50,921	89,137	120,447	236,123
To create immediate estate of	50,000	90,000	120,000	235,000
Cost of term insurance	298	528	701	1,364

It would not be until age 65 that savings-investments at 3%, 6%, 7½%, and 9% would accumulate to $50,000, $90,000, $120,000 or $235,000. But at age 25, a man could purchase the equivalent amount of term life insurance at the annual costs shown to create the immediate estates indicated.

Minimum Life Insurance Coverage. As a rough guideline, a family head intending to invest outside his insurance program should carry a minimum of life insurance of 5 times his annual salary and a maximum of 10 times his annual salary if he is to invest outside his insurance program.

In recognition of (1) the manner in which most families actually do view insurance protection, (2) the fact that the amount flowing into insurance reserves has been becoming a lower proportion of total savings, and (3) the fact that many individuals do desire to invest outside life insurance, many large insurance companies in the latter 1960s also moved into the mutual fund field (and many mutual fund sales organizations were also selling life insurance).[3]

---

[3] See Chapter 25 on investment companies for more discussion on this point.

Types of Life Insurance. The types of life insurance policies available range from those providing solely protection (term insurance) to those primarily representing an investment vehicle (annuities, and to a somewhat lesser extent endowment policies). For those who may find it difficult to save and invest but who, psychologically, find it easier to be "forced to save" by contracting to pay regular insurance premiums, a case may be made for purchasing insurance policies embodying a savings element and even those with a heavy investment element such as endowment policies. But for others who can and will save and invest outside insurance, their insurance policies should be purchased solely or largely for protection. For the same amount of dollars, much more insurance protection can be purchased if only protection is purchased than if protection is combined with savings. Table 28-7 shows costs of different types of life insurance at various ages.

TABLE 28-7

Relative Costs of Types of Life Insurance for Men
At Ages Indicated—Per $1,000

Type of Insurance	Age 25	Age 35	Age 45	Age 55
Term (10 yr. renewable):				
First $5,000	$ 38.80	$ 52.00	$ 86.20	$161.95
Over $5,000 per $5,000	28.80	42.00	77.20	151.95
Straight Life (paid-up age 95):				
First $2,000	$ 42.54	$ 54.72	$ 75.02	$109.62
Additional $1,000	16.27	22.36	32.51	49.81
Total for $5,000	$ 91.35	$121.80	$172.55	$259.03
30-Payment Life:				
First $2,000	$ 51.94	$ 62.76	$ 80.36	$107.58*
Additional $1,000	20.97	23.37	35.18	48.79
Total for $5,000	$114.85	$132.87	$185.90	$253.95
30-Year Endowment:				
First $2,000	$ 68.14	$ 72.86	$ 85.02	$109.00*
Additional $1,000	29.07	31.43	37.51	49.50
Total for $5,000	$155.35	$167.15	$197.55	$257.50

* Age 54.

Term Insurance. Term insurance premiums purchase only protection. Most group policies are term policies. There is no savings involved, and no reserve or cash surrender values are accumulated.

Term policies are written for a certain number of years, such as 5 or 10 years. No policies should be purchased unless they are automatically renewable at option of the insured without medical examination at the end of each term.[4] The premium rate per thousand dollars of protection rises with each renewal. It becomes expensive when renewed say at age 55 and very expensive when renewed at age 60 or 65. However, the need for insurance protection should have decreased significantly by these ages, as usually the number of dependents declines and capital has been accumulated outside the insurance program. Therefore, on renewal the amount of insurance protection can be reduced, thus compensating at least in part for the higher renewal rates per thousand dollars of protection. The lack of a savings feature and the fact that money cannot be borrowed against a term policy are other disadvantages of such policies.

Because the greatest dollar protection can be purchased at the cheapest cost through term insurance, at least the first $50,000 of life insurance should be of this type for those who expect to invest outside insurance.

Straight Life Insurance. Straight life insurance is also known as ordinary life insurance or whole life insurance. There are numerous subdivisions of straight life insurance policies (such as limited-payment life and one-payment life), but this book will comment only on the major type sold. The insured pays a level annual premium until death or until age 95. The policy may become fully paid up prior to age 95 if the insured allows his dividends to accumulate in reserves.

A part of the annual premium covers straight protection (as in term insurance), but the remainder builds up as a cash surrender value or an amount against which the insured may borrow.

Endowment Insurance. Endowment insurance also includes both protection and savings elements, although the latter is much more important in such policies. There are various types, such as 10-year, 20-year, and 30-year endowment policies. At the end of the specified period, the insured may collect the face amount of the policy.

Annuities. An individual may purchase an annuity policy, which contracts to pay a specified sum beginning at a specified age. Annuity contracts may be based on lump sum purchases or may be paid over a period of years. Because of the inflation of the past three decades, these policies have not

---

[4] A convertible policy is desirable. This policy may be exchanged at some future date, when the insured can better afford it, for other types of permanent life insurance, without medical examination.

been very popular. However, most group pension policies have the characteristics of annuities. The variable type of annuity now available with some pension plans does offer some protection from the purchasing power risk. Annuities may also pay a lump sum at a specific future year.

Pension Plans

Pension plans are classified in two major categories: private pension plans and government pension plans. The first includes plans of individuals and the second includes federal social security programs. In Table 28-8 data are presented on the various types of retirement plans—private and public. Federal social security programs are discussed in the next chapter. Here it is sufficient to say that as a result of 1972 legislation, beginning in 1973 all pretense at amortization and funding has been scrapped; and the federal social security programs have become strictly annual, pay-as-you-go programs, with those who are working paying sufficient taxes annually to balance the annual payments made to the beneficiaries of these programs.

Private Pension Plans. It is estimated that at the beginning of 1973 over 38 million persons were covered by some type of private pension plan. There are two types of private pension plans: insured pension plans and noninsured pension plans. Approximately 12 million persons were covered by insured pension plans.

Insured Pension Plans. Under an insured pension plan, the employer purchases a contract from an insurance company through regular periodic payments. In some cases lump sum payments covering all employees are made each year, while under other contracts deferred annuity payments for each employee are purchased each year. In the early 1960s a number of states—those where the largest insurance companies are domiciled—amended insurance statutes to permit the segregation of insured pension reserves (assets) from other insurance assets. Prior to this, these reserves were commingled, which meant that they were subject to the maximum limitation governing investment in equities, usually 5% of assets. Now the insurance companies can go as high in equities as those who establish and control the pension fund desire. This amendment has permitted the insurance companies to compete more effectively with the noninsured plans.

Noninsured Pension Plans. These plans are either self-administered by the business that establishes the plan or, as is more usually the case, the management of the plan is trusteed under the control of the trust department of a commercial bank. Sometimes a large fund is divided among several banks.

TABLE 28-8

Pension Plan Data, July, 1972

A. Receipts and Disbursements of Private Noninsured Pension Funds
(In Millions)

Receipts		Disbursements	
Employer Contributions	$11,330	Benefits Paid Out	$ 7,070
Employee Contributions	1,110	Expenses and Other Disburse-	
Investment Income	4,080	ments	180
Net Profit on Sale of Assets ..	920	Total Disbursements	7,250
Other Income	90	Net Receipts	10,280
Total Receipts	$17,530	Total Receipts	$17,530

B. Assets of Private Noninsured Pension Funds, Jan. 1, 1972
(Book Value and Market Value End of Year in Millions)

Book Value End of Year			Market Value End of Year		
Cash and Deposits		$ 1,640	Cash and Deposits		1,600
U.S. Gov't. Securities		2,730	U.S. Gov't. Securities		2,800
Corporate Bonds		29,010	Corporate Bonds		26,100
Preferred Stock		1,770	Preferred Stock		2,000
Common Stock			Common Stock		
Own Company	3,500		Own Company	7,600	
Other Companies ..	59,280	62,780	Other Companies ..	77,200	84,800
Mortgages		3,680	Mortgages		3,200
Other Assets		4,800	Other Assets		4,500
Total Assets		$106,410	Total Assets		$125,000

C. Assets of All Public and Private Pension Funds, Jan. 1, 1972
(Book Value in Billions)

Private:

Insured Pension Reserves	$ 46.4
Separate Accounts Included Above Noninsured Pension Funds	106.4
Total Private Funds	$152.8

Government:

State and Local	64.8
Railroad Retirement	4.3
Civil Service	26.0
Federal Old Age and Survivors	33.8
Federal Disability Insurance	6.6
Total Government Funds	$135.6
Total Private and Government Funds	$288.4

Note: Some figures do not add exactly due to rounding.

Source: U.S. Securities and Exchange Commission, July, 1972.

A plan is fully funded, in the strict sense, when the amounts deposited with the trustees are sufficient actuarially to equal 100% of the past service liability plus annual set-asides in the amount of the current service liability. Past service liability arises because no amounts were placed in the fund for past service costs prior to the inauguration of the plan. Any difference between amounts required in the strict sense and those funds that have been set aside are designated as *unfunded pension liabilities*.[5]

In addition to pension funds of private businesses, most public employees and employees of educational and charitable organizations are covered by pension plans.

Variable Annuities. The first substantial variable annuity plan was that of the Teachers' Insurance and Annuity Association (TIAA), which in 1950 [6] added the College Retirement Equities Funds (CREF). Participants may direct that all funds go into TIAA or that a specific percentage up to a maximum of 75% of annual premiums be placed in CREF. All of the funds of CREF are invested in common stocks, and the authors have advised participants to place the maximum permissible in CREF. Over any significant period of time, it is expected that the amount of the investment in common stocks and the income derived therefrom will rise to offset any depreciation in the purchasing power of the dollar.

For several years TIAA was the only major variable annuity plan offered, but since 1968 an increasing number of life insurance companies have made such a plan available. At the beginning of 1972, there were over 110 life insurance companies with variable annuities covering approximately one million persons and representing reserves of $3.5 billion.

Those who participate in a variable annuity like CREF purchase shares (accumulation units) in the fund through contributions of their employers and themselves. This is similar to the purchase of shares accumulated in a mutual fund, and the calculation of net asset value per share is the same as for a mutual fund. At the time of retirement, the *accumulation units* acquired are converted into annuity units. At the date of conversion, the annuity units acquired are shares in the assets of the pension fund purchased at net asset value per unit at the date of conversion.

Each year a certain number of the annuity units are liquidated to pay the retirement income. In determining the number of units to be liquidated, the fund considers the actual and the expected life of the annuitant and the expected rate of return on the remaining units. Each year the annuity units

---

[5] The reader should refer to Chapter 18 for a discussion of the nature and problem of pensions and unfunded pension liabilities in corporate reporting.

[6] DJIA mean: 216 in 1950; 985-995 in Feb., 1966; 975 in Apr., 1969.

are revalued at their net asset value according to the existing level of the stock market. Therefore, the value of the units and the retirement income will change from year to year. It is expected that the value of the units and the income will, over any period of time, rise at least as much as the consumer price level, and the authors of this book believe it will be so.

Federal Social Security Programs. The individual in his financial planning for the future should take into consideration the benefits that he and his dependents will receive under federal social security legislation as it currently stands and as amended in the future. Social security is not solely a retirement system. There are benefits for survivors regardless of the breadwinner's age at the time of his death, and there are benefits for disability regardless of age.

The federal social security system, including the Railroad Retirement accounts, encompasses most employed persons and their dependents and most of the self-employed. Major changes were legislated by Congress in 1972 to become effective in two steps in 1973 and 1974. The 1972 legislation abandons all pretense of an actuarial system or trust fund and adopts fully the annual pay-as-you-go principle. Therefore, each year the government will collect enough social security taxes from employees and employers (equally) to meet current benefit payments. The tax rate has been increased to 5.85% of an annual salary base of $10,800 in 1973 and $13,200 in 1974. The total social security taxes rose approximately $7 to $8 billion in 1973, and in the case of a large number of individuals this tax was greater than their income tax.

The legislation assumes that inflation will continue indefinitely as a way of life and consequently provides that benefits will automatically increase following each 3% rise in the consumer price level. Subsequent increases in benefits will be financed solely by increases in the maximum base to which the tax rate applies but not (under present law) by increases in the tax rate itself.

The relative magnitudes of the receipts and benefit expenditures (the latter assumed to parallel receipts) in the federal budget context are detailed in Table 28-9. By 1974 or shortly thereafter, social security receipts and payments will be double that of corporate federal income taxes and equal to approximately two thirds of individual income taxes.

As noted, the law provides for automatic increases in benefits (and therefore in taxes collected) based on increases in consumer prices (after each 3% rise in consumer prices). Therefore, in the case of a worker aged 39 in 1974 who is earning at least the $13,200 base maximum and whose wages increase in line with the general wage level, and assuming consumer prices rise by 2½% per year, then at retirement age of 65 in the year 2,000 this worker's benefits will be about double the 1973 maximum.

TABLE 28-9

Federal Budget Receipts—Fiscal Years Ended June 30 (Billions of Dollars)

	——Actual——		—Estimated—	
	1970	1971	1972	1973
Individual Income Taxes	$90.4	$86.2	$86.5	$93.9
Corporate Income Taxes	32.8	26.8	30.1	35.7
Social Security Taxes—Total	45.3	48.6	54.2	63.7
Employment Contributions	$39.1	$41.7	$46.4	$55.1
Unemployment Insurance	3.5	3.7	4.4	5.0
Contributions for Other Insurance and Retirement	2.7	3.2	3.4	3.6

Source: Council of Economic Advisers, *Economic Indicators,* January, 1973.

Under the law there are four types of benefits: (1) old-age benefits for retired workers (the basic legislation assumes retirement at age 65 but earlier retirement at age 62 is allowable at lower annual benefits); (2) survivor benefits for dependents of those covered; (3) disability benefits for disabled workers; and (4) medical benefits (Medicare, and Medicaid).

Maximum Benefits. Under the 1972 law the benefits received are based upon the annual earnings that have been subject to Social Security taxes and the number of years used in calculating the average earnings. The calculations cover the following steps:

Step   I. Count the number of years to be used in figuring your average earnings as follows:

    A. Starting or base year
      1. If you were born *before* 1930, start with the year 1956.
      2. If you were born *after* 1929, start with the year you reached age 26.

    B. Number of years—Count your starting year and each year up until but not including:
      1. The year you reach 65 if you are a man.
      2. The year you reach 62 if you are a woman.
      3. The year the worker becomes disabled or dies for disability or death benefits.

Step II. List the amount of the worker's earnings for all years *beginning* with 1951, but only up to the amount of maximum base each year for Social Security (example: 1951-1954 maximum base is $3,600).

Step III. Cross off the list of years of lowest earnings until you reach the number of years calculated in Step I above.

Step IV. Add up the earnings for the years left on your list and divide by the number of years which was the answer to Step I above.

It is obvious that to receive the maximum benefits listed in Table 28-10 the worker must have paid the tax on the maximum earnings in the table, or $9,000; but the maximum did not become the base until 1972. Therefore, no worker retiring in 1971, for example, would have had average earnings (subject to the tax of $9,000). The maximum any worker retiring in 1973 can receive is $266.10 per month or $3,193.20 per year. Under the law the only workers who later have had average earnings subject to the tax of $9,000 for the required number of years will receive the maximum benefits listed in Table 28-10.

TABLE 28-10

Maximum and Minimum Social Security Benefits, 1972
(Maximum Based on Maximum Contributions for Maximum Years)

	Minimum Monthly	Minimum Annual	Maximum Monthly	Maximum Annual
Retired workers 65 or older	$84.50	$1014.00	$354.50	$4254.00
Disabled workers under 65	84.50	1014.00	354.50	4254.00
Wife 65 or older	42.30	760.00	177.30	2127.60
Retired worker at 62	67.60	811.20	283.60	3403.20
Wife at 62, no child	31.80	381.60	133.00	1596.00
Widow at 60	73.30	879.60	253.50	3042.00
Widow or Widower at 62	84.50	1014.00	292.50	3510.00
Disabled widow at 60	51.30	615.60	177.30	2127.60
Wife under 65 and no child	42.30	760.00	265.90	3190.80
Widowed mother and one child	126.80	1521.60	531.80	6381.60
Widowed mother and two children	126.80	1521.60	620.40	7444.80
One child of retired or disabled worker	42.30	760.00	177.30	2127.60
One surviving child	84.50	1014.00	265.90	3190.80
Minimum family payment	126.80	1521.60	620.40	7444.80

Medical Expense Benefits. As noted earlier, an important percentage of employees and also self-employed persons are covered by medical insurance such as Blue Cross-Blue Shield. In 1965 Congress added to the social security legislation the Medicare bill which provided financial aid for medical expenses for those 65 and over.[7] For those already covered by their employment under this social security system, contributions are compulsory under an addition to the social security tax on earnings, and medical benefits are available to all over 65 regardless of financial need. In addition, those not covered by social security can join the medical program voluntarily. Major changes in medicine resulted from the 1972 law. Medicare's hospital insurance and medical insurance will be available to some people under 65 who are disabled, those who have been receiving social security or Railroad Retirement disability checks for 2 years or more, disabled workers, those who have been disabled before age 22, and disabled widows and disabled dependent widowers. The law also provided Medicare coverage to include a wider range of health care services. Persons collecting social security benefits automatically are enrolled under Medicare unless they specifically request that they not be so covered.

SUMMARY OF FINANCIAL AND INVESTMENT PLANNING

Initially this chapter emphasized that individuals, first, should have an overall financial plan and, second, should have an investment plan that would be an integral part of the financial plan. The financial plan covers financial position (balance sheet), income, and distribution of income through expenditures and savings. The individual should follow a financial budget—either a formal one or an informal one. Statistics were presented on how individuals on the average allocate their income to expenditures and the percentage they save and invest. The determination of how income is to be spent and what proportion of income is to be saved is a function of the absolute size of the individual's income and the intensity of the desire to save. It was pointed out that, at least with family incomes below $20,000-$25,000, it would be unusual if annual savings exceeded 6%-8% of income and especially unusual if they exceeded 10%. Statistics were also shown on how savings of $500-$1,000 per year could accumulate by age 65, taking various assumed rates of annual compounding of overall rate of return.

The determination of the amounts to be maintained as cash and demand deposits and the amounts that should be maintained in deposit-type institutions was then discussed. The advantages of the various alternatives available for such savings, including bonds, in periods of historically high interest rates

---

[7] Disability benefits are listed in Table 28-10. The law provides for a waiting period so that disability benefits do not begin until the sixth full month of disability.

were then pointed out. The flow of savings into financial intermediaries where most of the savings flow is channeled into securities was examined in some detail. The financial asset holdings of individuals in total were then reviewed. This review should aid the individual in deciding on the proper disposition of his savings and his financial asset holdings.

The next two chapters will concentrate on investment constraints and realistic investment policies that should be considered by the individual once he has established his overall financial program.

In determining his individual financial program and his financial needs and goals both along the road and for retirement, the individual must not only consider those that result from his own planned savings and investments, but also the advantages and the value of supplemental financial assets produced outside his own direct efforts by his employer (health and disability insurance and pension plans) and by the U.S. Government under the social security program. These adjuncts to the individual's own program financed from his own funds are not only financially valuable, but they reduce in various ways the reserves that he will need along the road and at retirement.

QUESTIONS

1. Many financial considerations should take precedence over security investment for a young family. Discuss the most important of these considerations.

2. (a) Discuss the trends in the number of individual shareowners in the U.S., the relative importance of common stock among the financial assets of individuals and the proportion of total common stock market values owned by individuals. Where patterns seem inconsistent, offer explanations.

   (b) How would you explain the drop in the number of shareowners with household income of under $10,000 from 1965 to 1970?

3. (a) Develop a financial budget appropriate to your circumstances and defend the expenditure pattern programmed by you.

   (b) Develop a tentative budget for a newly married couple (husband 24, wife 22), where the husband will earn $9,000 a year and the wife is not expected to work.

4. What are the major advantages and disadvantages of (a) deposits in banks and savings and loan associations, (b) certificates of deposit, and (c) U.S. Government savings bonds?

5. What total dollar amount would you recommend that an individual hold in deposits and/or U.S. Government savings bonds? Why?

6. (a) What are the major risks best handled by providing insurance protection?
   (b) How are these risks affected by advancing age?

7. Why is it important that investors recognize that various types of life insurance coverage may combine protection and savings elements?

8. What would you recommend as the minimum life insurance coverage that should be carried by the head of a household?

9. (a) What are the advantages and the disadvantages of term insurance?
   (b) Why is term insurance usually considered the most appropriate form for a young head of a household?

10. (a) What is a variable annuity?
    (b) What are the advantages of variable annuities in arranging for retirement as opposed to direct investment in common stocks or mutual funds? Discuss.

11. (a) What are the basic types of benefits available under the current social security programs?
    (b) With a program of social security, life and medical insurance, and private pension plans, is there any need for people to continue to save and invest? Discuss.

WORK-STUDY PROBLEM

Since Chapters 28, 29, and 30 make up a cohesive unit on portfolio policies for individuals, work-study problems for these chapters are presented only at the end of Chapter 30.

SUGGESTED READINGS

"America's Centimillionaires." *Fortune* (May, 1968).

Bellemore, Douglas H. *The Strategic Investor.* New York: Simmons-Boardman Publishing Co., 1962.

Graham, Benjamin. *The Intelligent Investor.* New York: Harper & Rowe, 1954.

Economic Indicators (Monthly). Washington, D.C.: U.S. Government Printing Office.

Economic Report of the President (Annual Statistical Tables on Savings). Washington, D.C.: Supt. of Documents, U.S. Government Printing Office.

"Flow of Funds Tables." (Monthly). *Federal Reserve Bulletins.* Washington, D.C.: Board of Governors of the Federal Reserve System.

"Flying High on Magic Carpets." *Fortune* (May, 1968).

Investment Companies. New York: Wiesenberger Services, Inc.

Lampman, Robert L. *The Share of Top Wealth-Holders in National Wealth.* Princeton, New Jersey: Princeton University Press, 1962.

Life Insurance Fact Book. New York: Institute of Life Insurance.

National Fact Book, Mutual Savings Banking. New York: National Association of Mutual Savings Banks.

Smith, Adam. *Super Money.* New York: Random House, 1972.

Savings and Loan Fact Book. Chicago: U.S. Savings and Loan League.

Investment Objectives,
Constraints, and Taxes

The previous chapter established the perimeters of the individual's financial constraints. The actual amount of the individual's assets and liabilities and net worth, the actual size and stability of his current and expected income and expenses, and the size and regularity of his annual current and expected savings all provide a perimeter of constraints within which the individual can formulate his investment program. Also highly important to the success of investment policy and programs is consideration of the temperament of the particular individual.

INVESTMENT OBJECTIVES AND RISKS

The major investment objectives of individual portfolio policy are those in respect to (1) income, (2) capital appreciation,[1] and (3) liquidity for a portion of the portfolio. In formulating policies to achieve the objectives of income, capital appreciation, and liquidity, there are certain constraints or risks that must be considered and weighed before investment policies and investment commitments are consummated. The investor certainly wishes to attain his objectives while assuming the least risk compatible with these objectives. He wishes to obtain maximum income and appreciation while assuming the least risks. He does not wish simply to minimize risks, because unnecessary conservatism sacrifices the opportunity for larger returns. The investor must attempt to evaluate risks, relate risks to his objectives, and establish portfolio policy accordingly. All too often, optimism towards a

---

[1] The combination of income and capital appreciation provide the "overall rate of return," the most basic concept in security selection and portfolio policy.

potential commitment causes investors to ignore almost completely the potential risks. In other cases, objectives are so unreasonable that to attempt to attain them entails serious risks that make the objectives inappropriate for many investors. Many investors make no effort to evaluate risk.

At this point the reader should review the discussion of investment risks in Chapter 1, the discussion of risks evidenced by the historical behavior of the securities markets in Chapters 3 and 4, and the discussion of strategies for investment in fixed-income securities and common stocks in Chapters 8 and 10. Uncertainties of the future essentially determine risk.

The major risks discussed in Chapter 1 were:

1. Credit or financial risk—the risk that the issuer's credit will deteriorate.
2. Interest rate risk—the risk that interest rates will rise, causing a decline in the market price of limited-income securities.
3. Purchasing power or inflation risk—the risk that an excessive increase in the money supply may cause the purchasing power of money to decline.
4. Market risk—the risk that the market price of all common stocks or individual stocks will decline substantially.
5. Psychological risk—the risk that an investor will act emotionally instead of logically. This is quite closely correlated to market risk.

The potential effects of such risks on the individual's investment objectives of income, capital appreciation, and liquidity will be discussed in this chapter along with a discussion of his ability and willingness to accept risks.

OBJECTIVES AND CONSTRAINTS RELATING TO INCOME [2]

For many and perhaps most individual investors who are *building capital,* current income from a portfolio is not a primary objective and the minimum income required from investments is relatively small. Such investors are not dependent on investment income significantly, if at all, to maintain their standard of living. A high proportion of mutual fund shareowners, as well as other individual investors, reinvest all or most of their investment income, indicating that current income is not a major objective.

However, it is still true that for certain groups of investors, such as retired individuals and widows with portfolios that provide their major income, the income objective may be a very important or the paramount objective. Furthermore, in looking into the future (for example, to retirement) individuals must prepare for a time when investment income will

---

[2] "Income" in the discussion at this point is income in the form of dividend income and interest income and is not the "overall rate of return" that includes expected capital appreciation.

become quite important. Income is also significant for financial intermediaries, such as pension funds, life insurance companies, and investment companies. Earlier discussions of dividends and dividend policy stated that, except for the relatively few rapidly growing companies (annual compound earnings growth of perhaps 12%, 20%, or higher), investors did *expect* dividends and that the slower the company's growth, the higher the dividend payout expected. In this context, then, most investors *expect* a dividend, and dividend yield is important in stock selection. For many years investors over-all have been willing to accept dividend yields of 2½%-3½% in terms of the major stock averages, DJIA and S&P. But this does not mean that dividend *income* is *needed* by most individual investors. They require that stocks purchased provide what they consider to be reasonable dividend yield considering the stock's prospect for growth in earnings. However, the dividend received is often not needed or used in meeting current expenditures but in-stead is reinvested as part of the process of building capital. The greater the ability to accept a decrease in income, the less the constraint in assuming risks that potentially affect income and therefore dividends.

It should be emphasized that while income *per se* (and therefore potential loss of income) is not an important constraint to many individual investors (perhaps most investors in terms of numbers), risk of loss of income cannot be divorced from potential and actual market price depreciation. This is because the reduction of income for any security (default of interest in the case of a bond) will almost always be accompanied by a decrease in its market price if the decline has not already been anticipated by the market. The market will usually reflect a decline in the income of the issuer and its credit rating. Therefore, the risk of decline in income is partly a financial or credit risk. In addition, if market price depreciation is converted into realized losses by actual liquidation, then income is lost in terms of the potential income that would have flowed from the capital if it had not been lost. Finally, a *well-protected* dividend providing an important yield of 4%-6% at current market prices does reduce the downside risk of market depreciation for a common stock. This is an important consideration for buyers of low price-earnings ratio stocks and out-of-favor stocks that are hav-ing some earnings problems. In such cases there can still be a well-protected dividend. In 1973 there were such yields on stock of major companies.

Ability to Risk Loss of Income

In formulating investment policy, the individual should consider and calculate his ability to risk loss of income, either loss of actual current dollars or loss of the purchasing power of income. He should estimate the minimum income that will be satisfactory in terms of his expenditures budget and then establish and follow investment policies that can reasonably be expected to accomplish at least his minimum income objectives. He must estimate his income from sources outside his investment income (either from earned income while working or from sources such as pensions, annuities, and social security after retirement) and then deduct this amount from his total minimum income requirements to establish his minimum investment income requirement. This, in effect, means a projection of (1) the individual's income and expenses, (2) the minimum income expected, and (3) the minimum expenses to maintain a desired level of living.

The larger the amount of the investment portfolio, either current or expected, the lower is the rate of return required to meet a given minimum investment income requirement; and the lower the required rate, the lower is the pressure to assume risks (such as the purchasing power risk) by stressing high-income securities and the more one may reach for growth and capital gains. But the greater the overall yield sought, the greater the risks. Reaching for too great an overall yield contributed to the 1970 and 1973 bear market.

As previously noted, the larger number of individual investors are building portfolios, and their earned income is sufficient not only to meet all their current and expected expenses but also to provide annual savings that can be invested and added to invested capital. But on their longer-term projections, these individuals will have to consider their minimum investment income requirements when their noninvestment income decreases or ceases and will have to calculate the capital that will be required at that time to provide their minimum investment income requirements. They are also interested in the overall rate of return (dividend income plus expected capital appreciation), as this contributes to capital growth. In 1946-1972 this "overall rate" of return averaged between 7% and 8% per year compounded; from 1929-1966, about a 10% rate of return.

For those who have already reached the point where investment income does or must supply a significant proportion or all of their income, meeting the minimum current income requirement is of paramount importance.

Risk of Loss of Purchasing Power of Income—Inflation Risk

All important periods of inflation (loss of purchasing power of the dollar) in our past history have been associated with wars—the Revolutionary War, the Civil War, World War I, World War II, the Korean War, and the Vietnam War. The two most recent instances have been (1) the World War II and Korean War period and (2) the Vietnam War period. The consumer price index (1957-1959 = 100) declined from 59.7 in 1929 to 45.1 in

1933 and then was 48.8 in 1940, and 51.3 in 1941. As a result of World War II and the Korean War, the index doubled from about 49 in 1940 and 51 in 1941 (average 50) to 100.7 in 1958. It then rose slowly to 109.9 in 1965, an increase of only 9.2 points or a compounded annual rate of only 1.25%, at which rate prices would rise somewhat less than 50% in 30 years and would double in 60 years. Then, as a result of intensification of the Vietnam War, the index rose to 113.1 in 1966, 116.3 in 1967. The experience in the 1940-1973 period has made individuals very conscious of the risks of inflation. Those with fixed incomes witnessed a decline in the purchasing power of their income of 50% from 1940 to 1958. Using 1967 = 100, the index rose to 129 in early 1973. Prices had doubled from 1946 to 1973, or risen 2.6% per year. Consumer goods and services which cost 50 cents in 1946 cost $1.00 in 1958 and $1.50 in 1973.

Looking ahead through the 1970s and perhaps the 1980s, the authors are assuming a compound annual rate of increase in consumer prices of from 2% to 4% per year. At a 2% rate, prices would rise 50% in 20 years, about 75% in 27½ years, and 100% in 35 years. At a 3% rate, prices would rise 25% in 8 years, 50% in 14 years; at a 4% rate, prices would rise 5% in 10 years. Assumptions involve all the risks of any long-term projections, and the reader is of course at liberty to use any other assumptions as to the expected rate of future inflation. Only time will verify the reasonableness of the projections. However, it seems reasonable to assume at least some inflation (2%-4%), and the investor must take this into account in formulating his investment policy and in determining his minimum investment income requirements in the future.

Risk of Decrease in Income from Limited-Income Securities

Limited-income securities consist mainly of debt instruments (bonds, notes, and very short-term investments such as U. S. Treasury notes, certificates, and bills) and preferred stocks. Inasmuch as investments in straight nonconvertible investment grade preferred stocks were largely eliminated from consideration for inclusion in portfolios of individuals in the discussion of preferred stocks in Chapter 3, the risk of decline in income from preferred stocks (similar to bond risks) will not be discussed at length in this chapter.

Financial Risk. In an economic environment of only minor recessions such as has existed for over three decades, dividend reductions for preferred stocks rated investment grade have been about as rare as has been the case for high-quality bonds. However, this was not true during the Great Depression of the 1930s. At that time there were numerous dividend reductions or eliminations for preferred stocks that had been rated investment grade in

1928 and 1929 as compared to an exceedingly small number of interest defaults on bonds that had been rated highest grade in 1928 and 1929.

As quality goes down, starting with AAA bonds, it is a truism that the financial risk increases, although very gradually, down to BAA quality. The risk rises more rapidly through the BAA, BA, and B categories. If a portfolio consists solely of AAA, AA, A, or BAA bonds, a few such bonds (say 8 to 12) selected with reasonable care should provide an average income and price history closely correlated to the performance record for the universe of such bonds. On the other hand, as quality moves down to say BA bonds, a large number of separate issues are required in a portfolio to provide reasonable assurance that the record of interest payments (and price action) will parallel the record for the universe of similarly rated bonds. The individual investor will rarely have such a large amount invested in bonds that he can secure the diversification necessary to reasonably assure performance that will be equivalent to the average performance for grade BA or lower.

For the individual investor following the suggested high-quality bond policy, the risk of loss of income in the segment of his portfolio invested in bonds can and should be inconsequential (except for the risk associated with the refunding and maturing of such obligations in periods of low and declining interest rates such as existed from 1930 to 1946). Parenthetically, reserve funds invested in time or savings accounts should be covered by insurance (FDIC or FSLIC), thus eliminating the financial capital risk. Loss of income (except for reductions in rates that occur in periods of low and declining interest rates) will occur only temporarily in the rare situations when the FDIC or FSLIC is forced to take over, and then only for the very short period required by regulatory authorities to accomplish the transfer of funds to another insured financial institution.

The reason that the risk of loss of income in a bond portfolio should be inconsequential is that we recommend that individuals confine their bond investments to AAA, AA, A, or BAA bonds (see Chapter 8). This is especially true if interest rates on short-term bonds remain in their 1965-1973 range, the highest yields since the post-Civil War period. The even higher promised yield obtainable from lower rated issues does not, in our judgment, justify their inclusion in portfolios of individual investors. This is because very few such investors can have the amount of diversification required— the number of issues—to justify their becoming self-insurers as can large institutional investors. The lower the quality rating of investments, the greater is the financial risk and therefore the risk of decline in income. The fewer the issues held in a portfolio, the greater is the risk that their performance will not correlate with the average performance for that grade.[3]

The individual who is selecting bonds *for investment* should not entertain much expectation of capital gains to balance the higher (financial) risk of lower-rated bonds (except for expectation of a decline in interest rates, and he should not attempt to speculate on this factor). This is contrary to the situation for common stocks where there can be the potential of substantial capital gains to balance risks of equities.

Interest Rate Risk Associated with Refunding and Maturity. As previously noted, there is a possible loss of income from the refunding and the maturing of debt issues in periods of low interest rates. This is an interest rate risk. While the risk of default (financial risk) of issues with high quality ratings in 1928-1929 [4] proved to be extremely small in the 1930s, *most of these issues were callable.* Many were refunded, some several times, at lower rates in the 1930-1946 period of declining interest rates and even to 1950. And, of course, issues maturing during these years provided funds that had to be reinvested at the then current low market yield. This risk of income decline is frequently ignored in discussions of risk of income for limited-income securities, but it proved quite serious in the 1930-1946 period. This risk, when combined with the purchasing power risk of 1933-1946 and later, created an extremely serious problem for investors.

---

[3] (a) In Chapter 9 the following three conclusions from W. B. Hickman's *Corporate Bond Quality and Investor Experience* (Princeton, N. J.: Princeton University Press, 1958) were noted: "The principal advantages of high-grade bond portfolios are a low default risk and loss rate and comparative stability of price. (2) The principal advantages of a low-grade bond portfolio are high promised yields and, *if* the list is large, well-diversified, and held over long periods, high realized yields. The principal disadvantages are high default and loss rate and price instability. (3) For small investors, and those seeking liquidity in the bond account, the advantages of a high-grade portfolio frequently outweigh the disadvantages."

(b) Chapter 9 also made the following exceptions to the principle limiting bond investments to grades of A or higher: If a corporation has more than one issue of bonds outstanding, each rated differently, then if any should be purchased (say A or higher), the lower-rated issue may be purchased if the yield spread is significant. This is because none should be purchased unless all are sound investments. This applies especially to many of the convertible bonds, which usually are subordinated debentures and may solely for this reason be rated BAA while other bonds of the same issuer are rated A or higher. But in our judgment BAA rated issues are probably the lowest-rated issues that should be acceptable, and BAA should be intermediate term.

(c) Standard & Poor's bond ratings are: AAA—highest grade; AA—high grade; A—upper medium grade; BBB—medium grade category, borderline between definitely sound obligations and those where the speculative element begins to predominate; BB—lower medium grade with only minor investment characteristics; B—speculative, payment of interest not assured *under difficult economic* conditions.

[4] See W. B. Hickman, *Corporate Bond Quality and Investor Experience* (Princeton, N. J.: Princeton University Press, 1958). Also see F. C. Jen and J. E. West, "The Effect of Call Price on Corporate Bond Yields," *Journal of Finance* (December, 1967).

In summary, while individuals holding high quality rated bonds in 1928-1929 experienced little risk of default in the 1930s, they usually did experience a decline in income from such bond portfolios because of the refunding and the maturing of such obligations so that by 1946-1950 their average income from such portfolios was considerably less (in many cases 50% less) than in 1928-1929.

It is also true that if reserves are kept in insured savings accounts, the financial risk of loss of income by default is practically inconsequential. But there is still the risk that in a period of declining interest rates the rate paid on savings accounts will probably be reduced.

One further comment should be made. Many long-term issues of U.S. Government bonds are not callable until within about 5 years of maturity, which considerably reduces the refunding risk of such issues.[5] However, these securities will usually yield at least ½% less than top quality corporates, and in some years the spread is significantly larger.

Income Position of Bondholders in Recent Years. Long-term interest rates made their lows in early 1946 when they were the lowest since 1900, with long-term U.S. Government bonds yielding about 2.19% and high-grade corporate bonds yielding about 2.5%. Bond yields then rose rather steadily, except for temporary reversals in recessions, to historic highs in 1970 and 1973.

In 1970 investors were able to secure new bond *investments* that offered the highest yields since the post-Civil War period. But practically all issues carried a callable clause permitting the issuer to redeem the entire issue, usually after it was outstanding 5 years. A few issues provided 10-year call protection. For example, Texaco 5¾'s of 1997, rated AAA, actually yielded only 5.75% at issue in 1966, as contrasted to issues with only 5-year call protection that were yielding 6%. In May, 1970, the Texaco issue fell to 71, yielding about 8.05%, while new issues of AAA bonds sold at a 9.2% yield. Therefore, while issues rated AAA carry inconsequential risks of loss of income from default, the risk of a decrease of income from refunding after 5 years is a significant risk.[6] In 1970, AAA utility bonds (new issues) sold temporarily to yield as high as 9.2%.

----

[5] Examples of U.S. Government bonds outstanding in 1973 were:
(a) 4⅛'s — 5/15 — 94-89 — maturity 1994, not callable until 1989.
(b) 4's — 5/15 — 93-88 — maturity 1993, not callable until 1988.
(c) 4's — 8/15 — 92-87 — maturity 1992, not callable until 1987.
(d) 3¼'s — 6/15 — 83-78 — maturity 1983, not callable until 1978.
Furthermore, unless interest rates decline substantially more in the 1970s than is generally expected in the financial community, the risk of these bonds being called appears quite negligible.

[6] Of course, outstanding bonds issued prior to the high yields of the late 1960s declined in price to bring these yields *more* in line with new issues. Still, during tight

In terms of the investment environment of the late 1960s and early 1970s, one other factor is important: the high and widening yield spread in favor of bonds over common stocks that has existed since 1958. Being able to purchase the highest-rated bonds at 7%-8%,[7] the investor could calculate that it was extremely unlikely that any subsequent decline in the overall level of interest rates would cause refunding operations to lower yields on bonds purchased in the early 1970s to anything approximating yields on costs of common stocks, which were yielding on the "Averages" from 2.9%-3.6%. Of course, the investor would probably calculate expected compound annual increase in dividends on common stocks at between 4% and 6% per year. But any reasonable estimate of this compounding rate would still mean that it would take quite a number of years before the dividend income derived from a stock portfolio would be equivalent to the income realized on a bond portfolio.[8] Even when the dividend yield on cost reached the contract yield on the bonds, there was still the factor of compensating for the higher yield on the bonds during the catch-up period for the stocks. Only by viewing the problem in terms of overall rate of return (dividend income plus capital gains) could the purchase of common stocks be justified. The investor had experienced an overall rate of return compounded of 7%-8% annually from 1946-1973.

Risk of Decrease in Dividends

Of the total security holdings of individuals at market value, approximately 83% is represented by common stock investments; the remaining 17% is in debt instruments (7.5% is represented by U.S. Government securities; 5.0% by state and local government securities; and 4.5% by corporate and foreign bonds).

Stability of Income from a Broadly Diversified Common Stock Portfolio. One of the two major advantages of bond investment over common stock

---

money conditions such as existed in 1966-1970, there will be a noticeable spread in favor of the new issues. The new issues must be sold at one time, while only a relatively few bonds of each issue of outstanding bonds may enter the market on any one day so the marketability pressure on the latter is not nearly as severe as for new issues under tight capital market conditions. The reader is referred to the article "The Effect of Call Risk on Corporate Bond Yield," *Journal of Finance,* (December, 1967). The article concluded that "the increase in callable yields on high-coupon bonds is only a 'yield illusion' because the increase is largely offset by a corresponding increase in their call risk."

[7] In March, 1969, 7.4% for new AAA utility bonds with 5-year call protection.

[8] A 3% current yield would rise to 6% at a compounded growth rate of 4% in 18 years; at a rate of 5%, in 15 years; and at a rate of 6%, in 12 years.

investment has always been assumed to be stability of income; the other, stability of principal. Historically, through the years to 1938 the major advantage of income stability assigned to investment bonds versus common stock investment was supported by factual evidence. However, there has been a change since 1938 because of the fact that the economy has enjoyed remarkable stability over the past three decades with prosperity interrupted by only minor recessions. As a result, the advantage of stability of income for a bond portfolio versus stability of income for a *broadly diversified common stock portfolio* (mutual funds and pension funds) has largely been eliminated. This situation should continue *if* the economy maintains the same quality of stability with only minor recessions typical of the 1938-1973 period. Directors set dividends that they believe they can maintain. They have a strong aversion to reducing dividends, knowing the effect on stockholders. Therefore, if directors believe recessions will be mild and short, they maintain dividends even if earnings decline sharply. In most cases, corporations are financially able to maintain dividends during brief and mild recessions.

Substantial Growth in Dividends. In addition to the stability of income of large, widely diversified common stock portfolios since 1938,[9] their dividend income in the year 1972 was approximately 8 times the 1938 depressed dividend income and 6 times the 1937 peak dividends. This increase in dividends provided an excellent hedge against the decreasing value of the dollar. The two factors of dividend stability and substantial dividend growth for broadly diversified common stock portfolios are clearly evident in the dividend figures in Table 29-1. In only five years were dividends reduced for "All U.S. Corporations." In two of these five years, the reductions were insignificant; and even in the remaining three years, the maximum decline was only 4%, a degree of decline sufferable by almost any investor, particularly in the light of the normal compound rate of growth for other years. There was a 9% decline in dividends for the DJIA, a 3% decline for the S&P "500," and an increase of 4½% for "All U.S. Corporations" from 1969 to 1971. But in 1973 all indexes posted new all-time highs.

In this respect, emphasis must again be placed on the decline of income from bond portfolios that occurred as a result of the refunding and the maturing of these obligations in the period 1930-1946 and then the price depreciation that occurred from 1946 to the present.

---

[9] This stability can be viewed in the light of dividends for (a) All U. S. Corporations, (b) the popular market averages—DJIA and Standard & Poor's 500 Composite and 425 Industrial, (c) balanced and diversified common stock investment companies, (d) pension funds, (e) insurance companies, and (f) any other large, well-diversified portfolios. All U. S. Corporations were: 1929, $5.8 billion; 1933, $2.0 billion; 1937, $4.7 billion; 1938, $3.2 billion; and 1972, $26.4 billion. The 1972 figure is 5.6 times the 1937 amount and 8.3 times the 1938 amount.

TABLE 29-1

Dividends Paid—1937-1938 Through 1972

Year	All U. S. Corporations ($ Billions)	S&P 500 † Composite	DJIA †	Year	All U. S. Corporations ($ Billions)	S&P 500 † Composite	DJIA † Cash Only
1937	$4.66	.80	$ 8.78	1955	$10.48	$1.64	$21.58
1938	3.17	.51	4.98	1956	11.28	1.74	22.99
1939	3.77	.62	6.11	1957	11.74	1.79	*21.61
1940	4.02	.67	7.06	1958	*11.57	*1.75	*20.00
1941	4.43	.71	7.59	1959	12.58	1.83	20.74
1942	*4.25	*.59	*6.40	1960	13.44	1.95	21.36
1943	4.45	.61	*6.30	1961	13.77	2.02	*21.28
1944	4.62	.64	6.57	1962	15.18	2.13	22.09
1945	*4.60	.66	6.69	1963	16.45	2.28	23.20
1946	5.57	.71	7.50	1964	17.81	2.50	25.38
1947	6.32	.84	9.21	1965	19.79	2.72	28.17
1948	7.04	.93	11.50	1966	20.77	2.87	30.11
1949	7.24	1.14	12.79	1967	21.39	2.92	*29.84
1950	8.84	1.47	16.13	1968	23.55	3.07	31.34
1951	*8.57	*1.41	16.34	1969	24.33	3.16	33.90
1952	*8.56	1.41	*15.43	1970	24.80	*3.14	*31.53
1953	8.89	1.45	16.11	1971	25.43	*3.07	*30.86
1954	9.28	1.54	17.47	1972	26.42	3.15	32.27

Increase

1966 vs. 1937	....				4.66x	3.59x	3.43x
1966 vs. 1938	....				6.85x	5.63x	6.05x
1972 vs. 1937	....				5.57x	3.94x	3.68x
1972 vs. 1938	....				8.33x	6.18x	6.48x

† Per-share data.   * Year when dividends declined.

Source: *Survey of Current Business,* Dow Jones *Investors Handbook,* and S&P Trade and Statistics.

High Risk of Decrease in Income for a Small Common Stock Portfolio.
A well-diversified portfolio of common stocks—a cross-section of American industry—should provide essentially about as much stability of income as a bond portfolio *if* the overall economy in the future displays as much stability as it has for the past three decades. Therefore, an individual with shares in a well-diversified common stock mutual fund or with a portfolio so large that it can be well-diversified should not have any significant risk of loss of income, perhaps a maximum of 5%-6% in any one year, and only versus the previous year. When income stability and income in terms of purchasing power are important, a well-diversified portfolio must be maintained.

However, the problem is that most individual investors (aside from those holding mutual fund shares) do not have well-diversified portfolios. In the last NYSE survey it was found that the average shareowner had only 3 or 4 separate common stock issues. The record is probably weighted somewhat on the low side by shareowners who own mainly or entirely stock of their employer corporation under one of the employee-ownership or similar plans. *Still, the fact is that most shareowners do not have a large, well-diversified portfolio and therefore cannot rely on the stability of income that is expected in such portfolios. The risk of a decline in income for these shareowners may be quite substantial; and the fewer the stocks held, the greater the risk.*

The risk of income decline from a particular common stock is a function of the financial or business risk. This risk is greatest in small new companies and in those operating in cyclical industries, although it is not limited exclusively to these groups. This risk, therefore, is particularly a function of the industry in which a corporation operates. For example, it would be difficult to find an *operating* electric utility company that has reduced its common stock dividends over the past half century or a large bank over the last three decades. This has also been true for most (although not all) *large* companies operating in industries that provide nondurable necessities and services. In contrast, many corporations operating in cyclical industries—even large, well-established companies—have reduced dividends [10] in periods of general industry or business decline.

Therefore, if stability of dividend income is important to an individual investor and any significant decrease is unacceptable, then he can solve the problem in terms of common stocks only by having an interest directly or through mutual funds in a well-diversified portfolio of common stocks. If an investor is going to hold only a few stocks but still hopes for reasonable income stability, he should concentrate on noncyclical stocks such as utilities, major banks, major can companies, and major merchandisers of the quality of Federated Department Stores, J. C. Penney, or Sears, Roebuck. But the fewer the stocks in the portfolio and the smaller the companies and the more cyclical the industries, the greater is the risk of income decline. The higher the quality of the issues, the less there is risk of income decline; but the number of different issues held is still a major component of the risk factor.

---

[10] The following are examples of DJIA stocks that reduced dividends:

Allied Chemical	1967—1.90; 1968—1.73; 1969—1.20; 1970—1.20
Anaconda	1966—2.50; 1967—2.37½; 1968—2.25; 1969—2.20; 1970—1.90; 1971—0.12½
Bethlehem Steel	1970—1.80; 1971—1.20
Chrysler	1969—2.00; 1970—0.60
International Nickel	1970—1.40; 1971—1.30
Swift & Co.	1967—1.10; 1968—0.90; 1969—0.60
United States Steel	1970—2.40; 1971—2.00.

OBJECTIVES AND CONSTRAINTS RELATING TO PRINCIPAL (CAPITAL APPRECIATION)

The examination of the historical behavior of the securities markets in Chapters 3 and 4 showed that securities fluctuate in price and that, in the case of common stocks, the price fluctuations can be very substantial even in the case of quality stocks. IBM declined from 607 to 300 in six months (late 1961 to mid-1962), and almost all the major chemical and airlines stocks in 1968-1970 sold at least 50% below their previous highs. Furthermore, the stock market averages showed declines of from 20% to 26% numerous times since 1945: 27% in 1962; 25% in 1966; and the largest since 1938, 36% in December-May, 1970. While bonds as a class fluctuate in price, the fluctuations are over a smaller range than common stock fluctuations. Still, in years of sharply rising interest rates (such as 1967-1970), U.S. Government bond price index declined 30% from 81.5 (1967) to 57.4 (1970). There was another bear stock market in 1973.

Ability to Risk Market Depreciation and Realized Losses of Principal

Market depreciation may result in only a "paper loss" from which, more often than not, there is a recovery, especially for quality stocks and bonds. But the loss will become a realized loss if securities are actually sold at low prices. Bond issues may be shifted in loss years for tax purposes.

A number of factors must be considered in determining the individual's ability to risk market depreciation. In many cases, if market depreciation is viewed as temporary, there may not be any problem; the investor merely accepts the paper loss and holds for expected recovery. However, in other cases even a paper loss can cause problems.

Individuals usually have some debts and frequently some contingent liabilities, and some of these may be affected by the market depreciation of the individual's portfolio. If securities are pledged against a loan (a personal loan, a business loan, or a securities loan), market depreciation may require the submission of additional collateral to the lender. If it cannot be supplied, the securities pledged may be sold at depressed prices even though later recovery is expected. Also, if contingent liabilities exist, they may materialize when the stock market is depressed and may require the sale of securities at low prices, for example, the 1973 bear stock market.

If the individual plans to make heavy expenditures in the future (for example, for education of children or for investment in a business) or if specific amounts of gifts are intended in the future, then any important market depreciation may impair the ability to meet these commitments. There is also, in the longer term, the problem of meeting estate taxes and other expenses associated with the final illness and death of the individual. Finally, the older a person becomes, the less time he can count on for a recovery to recoup market depreciation.

Ability to Risk Loss of Principal in Current Dollars

To measure the degree of constraint involved in risking loss of principal in current dollars, the individual should determine the minimum *market* portfolio value that he requires or can accept. As his portfolio grows, this minimum acceptable value may change each year.

Ability to Risk Loss of Purchasing Power of Principal—Inflation Risk

The discussion of the purchasing power risk concentrated mainly on the risk of decline in the purchasing power of income—interest income and/or dividend income. However, there are risks for some investors of a decline in the purchasing power of the principal itself if the latter must at some time in the future be liquidated to secure funds to meet costs that will rise in at least some part as a reflection of a decrease in the purchasing power of the dollar. For example, if capital will need to be liquidated later to meet educational costs, to purchase a business, to purchase a larger and more expensive home, or to meet estate taxes, the risk of a decline in the purchasing power of the dollar must be considered in the management of the capital.

Marketability of Principal

Most investors consider good marketability an important factor in the selection of all types of securities. By proper selection, the individual investor can usually purchase securities that will meet his investment objectives without sacrificing marketability to any great extent. In the case of insured deposits, there is no problem of marketability, as the deposits are, even in the case of savings and time deposits, to all practical purposes available on demand. All issues of U.S. Government securities enjoy excellent marketability. In the case of tax-exempt securities, the issues purchased should be part of an issue that is large enough to assure good marketability, and not less than $10,000 in par amount of each issue (certainly not less than $5,000) should be purchased. Furthermore, the quality grades should not be below A. In the case of corporate issues, again the quality should not be below A (or perhaps below BAA), and the issue should be listed on the NYSE even though most bond transactions are in over-the-counter markets.

There are a sufficient number so listed to provide adequate choice and at the same time to assure reasonably good marketability, although in the case of a few listed bonds the marketability may be limited. In the case of common stocks, marketability can usually be determined by reviewing the market for the issue over a past period in terms of number of transactions and share volume and relate this to market volatility.

OBJECTIVES AND CONSTRAINTS RELATING TO LIQUIDITY

The term "liquidity" means ability to convert rapidly into cash at any time without any significant risk of capital loss. The highest liquidity rests with U.S. Treasury bills. The longer the maturity of debt instruments and the lower their quality, the greater is the liquidity risk. While an important proportion of common stocks enjoy marketability, even the highest quality common stock cannot meet the test of liquidity as properly defined above. Marketability merely implies ability to sell a reasonable block of the issue at or near its current market quotation. Of course, the current market quotation could be substantially below the price paid by an investor when he acquired the security some time previously.

Strength or Weakness of Ownership Position

The strength of the ownership position of the investor is measured by the probability or the necessity of liquidating investments. The stronger the ownership position, the less is the risk that securities, either bonds or equities, will need to be sold in periods of depressed prices. Conversely, the weaker the ownership position, the greater is the risk that securities may need to be sold at depressed prices. Therefore, in determining investment policy, the investor must carefully consider the strength of his ownership position.

Psychological Risk—Temperament of Individual

Probably temperament of investors has been the cause of as many cases of poor portfolio performance as any other reason. Therefore, in establishing investment policies, the individual must make a strong attempt to analyze his own temperament. If he does not have the will to take the time and make the considerable effort to investigate thoroughly before investing, then the individual should probably confine his common stock investments to mutual funds unless his portfolio is of sufficient size to justify the fees of reputable investment advisers. This is also true if he is emotionally activated to follow the crowd in pursuing fads and engaging in speculative activity. If the investor acts under the emotion of greed or fear, he will likely have poor performance. The characteristic of patience coupled with sound analysis has probably caused success for more investors than any other characteristic.

The wild speculation in many issues in 1967-1969 illustrates emotional greed. In April, 1969, the SEC cracked down on the use of corporate names that indicated major activity in certain glamour or scientific industries attractive to investors even though such names were not, in fact, truly indicative of the company's business. This highlights the wild speculation as individuals purchased on the basis of name alone rather than any real analysis of the company and its business and then took large losses in 1970.

TAXES AND INVESTMENT POLICY

Investors who are seeking to ease the impact of federal and state income taxes may: (1) purchase tax-exempt securities (Chapter 27); (2) stress opportunities (in tax terms) for long-term capital gains realized on capital assets held over 6 months where there is an effective maximum tax rate of 25%; and (3) purchase certain stocks entitled to special tax treatment. Dividends paid on such stocks are either tax free in whole or in part (considered a return of capital) or are treated as long-term capital gains.

Capital Gains and Losses

Capital gains (profit on the sale of capital assets such as securities) are accorded separate treatment from other types of income. The law divides capital gains and losses into long-term and short-term transactions according to the holding period of the securities sold or exchanged: short-term if the securities were held for 6 months or less, and long-term if held over 6 months. While all capital gains and losses are recognized 100%, only 50% of net long-term capital gains are taken into account, so that the maximum tax, regardless of the taxpayer's tax bracket on long-term gains, is only 50%. Long-term gains are first matched against long-term losses and short-term gains against short-term losses. If the net short-term gains exceed the net long-term losses, the excess is added to actual income. If the net long-term gains exceed the net short-term losses, the excess is subject to the alternative tax treatment, which in effect sets a maximum tax of 50% on net long-term gains.

If there are both net short-term gains and net long-term gains, the net short-term gains are treated as ordinary income, but only 50% of the net long-term gains are taken into account. If there is a net capital loss, either short-term or long-term, it is fully deductible against a net capital gain in its class, short-term or long-term. If all capital losses exceed all capital gains, the net loss is deducted from ordinary income at the rate of $1,000 per year indefinitely until the loss is all absorbed.

Switching To Employ Capital Loss

A taxpayer may sell securities (stocks or bonds) of one corporation and establish a loss and then purchase securities of another corporation in the same industry, thereby maintaining his interest in the industry but still taking advantage of the tax loss. He may also do this in the case of tax-exempts and in the case of U. S. Governments by selling one issue and buying another. The historically high interest rates in 1966-1970 gave bond investors, both institutional as well as individual, good opportunities in this respect. They could carry unusual losses to future years.

Tax-Free Dividends

There are three main sources of tax-free dividends:

1. When companies sell their holdings of securities or other disposable assets that have book values in excess of current market value, dividends paid from the receipts from such sales are tax-exempt to the recipient, being considered a return of capital and not income.

2. When companies engaged in extractive industries make dividend distributions from depletion "reserves," the dividend distributions are tax-free to the recipient, being considered a return of capital and not income.

3. When companies (many public utilities) distribute dividends not fully earned according to the books kept for tax purposes (usually because tax depreciation has exceeded book depreciation), the portion of the dividends not "earned" for tax purposes is not taxable to the recipient.

It should be noted that tax-free dividends, while not subject to income taxes, must be used by investors to write down the book cost of their investment and any later sale above this adjusted book cost is subject to the capital gains tax. It should also be noted that while income from tax-exempt securities is exempt from income tax, any capital gains received by the later sale or redemption of such securities is subject to capital gains tax, and therefore in calculating yield on securities purchased at a discount this fact should enter into the calculations.

Federal Estate and Gift Taxes

The federal estate tax is a tax levied on the transfer of the net estate of a decedent. Essentially no property is exempt from the tax except that given to charitable organizations, including "tax-exempt foundations." (These foundations have been under serious study and attack by certain members of Congress in recent years.) The tax rates are progressive, rising from 3% on the initial $5,000 of the net estate to 28% of the first $100,000, 37% on $1,000,000, 63% on $5,000,000, and the maximum of 77% on $20,000,000 and over. The taxable estate, or net estate, is the gross estate less the following items: administrative expenses and debts, a specific exemption of $60,000, and the marital deduction. The marital deduction is a deduction allowed on the value of property that is inherited by the surviving spouse.

Certain issues of U. S. Government bonds held in an estate may be used, prior to their maturity, for payment of estate taxes and are acceptable at their par value. When numerous issues selling at discounts are at $680-$720 per bond as in 1969-1970, the advantage of such issues for estate purposes as well as for potential capital gains is significant. (See Chapter 26.)

The federal gift tax was enacted mainly to prevent wholesale avoidance of the estate tax. The gift tax rates are also progressive, but at a less steep scale than the estate tax rates, and they reach a maximum of 57¾ % versus 77% for the estate tax. Also, as gifts may be spread over a number of years, gift taxes would then be paid annually on relatively smaller amounts, enabling the taxpayer to take advantage of the lower rates on the progressive scale. There is an exemption of $3,000 per year to each donee plus a $30,000 lifetime exemption for each donor.

Heirs and Estate and Gift Taxes

When securities are received by gift, the recipient takes the securities on the same basis (cost basis for tax purposes) on which they were legally held by the donor. However, when they are received by an heir of an estate, they are inherited at their current market value (with the option of establishing this value at any time within one year after the decedent's death).

State Estate Taxes

In addition to the federal estate tax, estates are also subject to state estate taxes. However, the amount of taxes imposed by the federal government is adjusted for the amounts imposed by the states and therefore the total estate or inheritance tax bill will not vary materially among the several states, although there is a maximum offset credit allowed against the federal estate tax.

Professional Individual Portfolio Management

If an individual has an investment portfolio of $250,000 or higher, he can afford the substantial fees charged by high quality investment advisers. Only about 1%-2% of the 33 million stockholders have portfolios of this size. The adviser's fee is commonly ½ to ¾ of 1% of the principal, but with a minimum of $2,000-$2,500 per year, which would be 1% of $250,000. They commonly reduce the fee on amounts over $1,000,000, as for example ⅜ of 1% on amounts in excess of $1,000,000. It is true that the individual can secure cheaper advice from the large advisory services, but in effect they do not really provide the highly individualized service furnished by quality investment advisers who charge $2,000 or more. In general, based on our observation, we would advise against these lower-priced services.

This leaves the great mass of individual investors—98%-99% of common shareowners—with only two reasonable choices: (1) they should either train themselves or secure formal educational training to properly manage their portfolios and be willing to devote the considerable time and energy necessary to secure satisfactory performance, or (2) they should invest their common stock portfolios in well-diversified mutual funds. In the case of those who desire to manage their own portfolios, a defensive type of policy will require considerably less time, effort, and skill to obtain satisfactory results than will an aggressive portfolio policy. Selection of a qualified registered representative with integrity is also quite important as such a professional can be helpful.

QUESTIONS

1. What factors should be considered in planning the overall financial program and the investment program for individuals?

2. Why is it stated that aggressive goals are for the "select few"?

3. What differences in investment constraints are likely for an elderly couple just retired, a middle-aged bachelor, and a young married couple?

4. Relate the purchase of out-of-favor, low P/E stocks to the risk of loss of principal.

5. (a) In what way does the refunding of issues and the maturing of issues relate to the income constraint of individual investors?

(b) Why was there little refunding of issues in the late 1960s? Discuss.

6. How does the ability to hold a broadly diversified common stock portfolio affect the investment constraints of an individual? What particular constraints are affected?

7. Discuss the likely effects of inflation on the income constraint of an investor.

8. How could the purchase of common stock be justified during the early 1970s when investors could approximately double current income yields by buying high-grade bonds?

9. What factors would you consider in analyzing the degree of constraint in terms of ability to risk loss of principal for an individual investor?

10. Support the importance of continuous supervision and evaluation of an individual investment portfolio, even when widely diversified.

11. Will a high degree of marketability of securities held offer adequate protection for an individual who has little ability to accept loss of principal? Contrast marketability and liquidity. Discuss.

12. Some investment advisory services and brokerage house recommendations classify certain stocks as "businessman's risk." What does this mean? How would such stocks relate to the investment constraints of individuals?

SUGGESTED READINGS

Babcock, Guilford C. "A Note on Justifying Beta as a Measure of Risk." *The Journal of Finance* (June, 1972), pp. 699-702.

Cheng, Pao, and M. King Deets. "Portfolio Returns and the Random Walk Theory." *The Journal of Finance* (March, 1971), pp. 11-30.

Fama, Eugene F. "Components of Investment Performance." *The Journal of Finance* (June, 1972), pp. 551-567.

Roll, Richard. "Investment Diversification and Bond Maturity." *The Journal of Finance* (March, 1971), pp. 51-66.

Sarnat, Marshall. "A Note on the Prediction of Portfolio Performance from Ex Post Data." *The Journal of Finance* (September, 1972), pp. 903-906.

Schwartz, Eli, and J. Richard Aronson. "How to Integrate Corporate and Personal Income Taxation." *The Journal of Finance* (December, 1972), pp. 1073-80.

Slovic, Paul. "Psychological Study of Human Judgments, Implications for Investment Decision." *The Journal of Finance* (September, 1972), pp. 779-799.

Terrell, William T., and William J. Frazer Jr. "Interest Rate, Portfolio Behavior and Marketable Government Securities." *The Journal of Finance* (March, 1972), pp. 1-36.

Defensive and Aggressive
Policy Patterns

This chapter presents three major topics on investment policy patterns: (1) policies regarding reserves for all individual investors, (2) common stock portfolio policies for conservative investors, and (3) common stock portfolio policies for aggressive investors.

POLICIES REGARDING RESERVES FOR ALL INDIVIDUAL INVESTORS

Before investing in common stock, all individual investors need to have some reserves in fixed-value assets—either in insured deposit accounts or in bonds.[1] It can be assumed from SEC and NYSE surveys that essentially all investors have such reserves. Table 30-1 shows the distribution of financial assets of individuals into various types of reserves and investments.

Insured Deposits

It is recommended that individuals holding reserve funds of $50,000 or less keep these funds in insured deposits where they are available without any decrease in value at all times and where they usually earn interest from the day of deposit. Unlike bond investments, bank deposit capital values do not fluctuate with changes in interest rates. Table 30-1, covering *all* individuals whether or not they own any stocks or bonds, shows that 29% of

---

[1] A review of Chapter 8, "Investment Strategies for Limited-Income Securities," is suggested at this point.

TABLE 30-1

Financial Assets and Liabilities of Households in the United States as of Jan. 1, 1972

Total Financial Assets					$2,170.4	100%
Total Liabilities					525.8	
Net Financial Assets					1,644.6	
Total Financial Assets					$2,170.4	100%
Deposits and Currency					630.9	29
Demand Deposits and Currency			$134.9	6%		
Time and Savings Deposits			496.0	23		
At Commercial Banks	$221.8	10%				
At Savings Institutions	274.2	13				
Life Insurance Reserves					137.0	6
Pension Fund Reserves					268.1	12
Securities					1,055.6	49
Corporate Shares			878.7	41		
Other Credit Market Instruments ...			176.9	8		
U.S. Government Securities *	77.1	4				
State and Local Gov't. Obligations	52.3	2				
Corporate & Foreign Bonds	47.5	2				
Mortgages & Other Loans					48.0	2
Home Mortgages	13.4	.6	44.9	2		
Other Mortgages	31.5	1				
Other Loans			3.1			
Security Credit to Brokers & Dealers ..					2.1	
Miscellaneous Financial Assets					28.8	1

RECAPITALIZATION

Total Financial Assets			$2,170.4	
Deduct Insurance & Pension Reserves ..			405.1	
Balance of Financial Assets			$1,765.3	100%
Deposits & Currency			630.9	36
Securities			1,055.6	60
Corporate Shares	$878.7	50%		
Total Bonds	176.9	10		
Mortgages			44.9	3
Other Loans			4.1	
Miscellaneous			29.7	1

* Including $54 billion of savings bonds.

Source: *Federal Reserve Bulletin,* June, 1972. Figures do not add exactly due to rounding.

financial assets are held in the form of currency and insured deposit accounts. If insurance and pension reserves are deducted from financial assets, then deposits and currency represent 36% of the remaining financial assets.

High-Grade Bond Portfolios

As noted earlier in this book, a policy of high-grade bond investment is advocated for individuals, except that *short-term* BAA may be held.

Advantages of High-Grade Bond Portfolio Policy. In regard to the advantages of a high-grade bond portfolio policy for individuals, the Hickman Study [2] drew the following conclusions:

> The comprehensive record indicates that the principal advantages of a high-grade corporate bond portfolio are a low default risk and loss rate, and comparative stability of prices. . . . For small [individual] investors and those seeking liquidity in the bond account, the advantages of a high-grade portfolio frequently outweighed the disadvantages. . . . Agency [bond] ratings, market ratings, legal lists and other selected indicators of prospective bond quality proved useful guides in ranking bond offerings and outstanding in order of the risk of subsequent default.

The dollar safety of high-grade bonds is provided by the high credit rating of the issuer (coverage), the seniority of the bondholders' position, and the legal strength of the contract. The higher the yield on high-grade bonds when purchased, the smaller is the risk of subsequent price depreciation. For example, risk of price depreciation on bond purchases was comparatively low in 1970 when yields were the highest since the Civil War but was correspondingly high in 1946 when yields were the lowest since 1899. High-grade bonds have much more price stability than equities and therefore more liquidity (convertibility into cash with little risk of loss) than equities, which is why they perform their function as reserves. The shorter their maturities, the lower is the degree of potential price depreciation. For Treasury bills and certificates of deposit the risk is practically nil.

High-grade bonds can serve as general reserves or permanent reserves as well as a temporary haven for funds seeking better investment opportunities later. For the latter purpose we would favor Treasury bills and certificates of deposit. Furthermore, since 1958 high-grade bonds have yielded more than stocks as measured by stock averages, and in 1973 high-grade bond yields were actually double the yields of the stock averages. Therefore, on a strictly current yield basis these bonds offered a major advantage.

Disadvantages of High-Grade Bond Portfolio Policy. The major disadvantage of bonds, including high-grade bonds, is that they provide no protection against inflation. [3] Another disadvantage is that in periods of secular rising interest rates (1899-1920 and 1946-1973), bond prices will decline substantially. The U.S. Government long-term price index declined 45%

---

[2] W. Braddock Hickman, *Corporate Bond Quality and Investor Experience,* a study by the National Bureau of Economic Research (Princeton, N. J.: Princeton University Press, 1958).

[3] One bond authority suggests that the comparison should also include assumed compounding of the rate of return and assumed reinvestment of bond interest and, of course, for stocks, their dividends.

from 112 (1946) to 62 (1970), and in one-year periods such as May, 1969 to June, 1970, it declined as much as 13%.

Another disadvantage of a high-grade bond policy, if it is based on the exclusion of a significant amount of equities, is that a comparison of merely *current* dividend yields with high-grade bond yields is misleading because it does not take into account either the future growth in dividends or the long-term capital appreciation of equities. The overall *expected* rate of return, including capital appreciation, is the major advantage of equities when contrasted to the fixed income from bonds (example, 1937-1938 to 1973).

U.S. Government Bonds. Government bonds are clearly the highest grade of bonds. Of individuals' investments in bonds totaling $177 billion as of January 1, 1972, 43.6% represented holdings of government bonds (including savings bonds), 29.5% was in tax-exempt bonds, and 26.8% was in corporate bonds. Holdings of savings bonds were $54 billion or 70% of holdings of all governments—approximately the same as the holdings by individuals of tax-exempts which were $52.3 billion and 30.5% of all bond holdings. The dollar amount of savings bonds has varied little for many years.

U.S. savings bonds, even at the maximum rate when held to maturity, have consistently yielded less than interest paid on insured savings accounts for many years, and on this basis there is little justification for investment in savings bonds. They have also for quite a long period yielded less than long-term government marketable issues. The only justification for their purchase appears to be the fact that annual interest earned need not be reported until they are redeemed. Therefore, an individual could accumulate these savings bonds during his later working years and not cash them in until after retirement, reporting the total interest earned at that time when presumably he will be in a lower tax bracket.

In most of the post-World War II years the yield spread in favor of long-term government bonds over insured savings accounts has not been sufficient to justify the purchase of the former considering the interest rate risk, especially in instances where reserve funds have been $50,000 or less. On the other side of the coin, the yield spread in favor of high-grade corporates over governments in many years has not been wide enough (for example, only 50 base points) to justify investment in the high-grade corporates except for very large bond portfolios. But in years of very high rates (as in the 1966-1973 period) the yield spread in favor of high-grade corporates widened appreciably until it was as much as 130 base points. Under such conditions a strong case can be made for investing in high-grade corporates for large accounts where the tax factor does not require tax-exempts.

In addition to the quality factor, there is another advantage of government bonds over high-grade corporate bonds. This is the fact that corporates are usually callable 5 years after issue or thereafter, while government bonds if callable at all are usually not callable until within 5 years of maturity. The high yield, as in 1973, can be frozen into a portfolio for a long period in the future—for example, for from 20 to 25 years. The relatively low coupon rate on most long-term government bonds outstanding in 1970 made them essentially noncallable in terms of market yields for the foreseeable future.

There is also a special advantage of certain government issues (21 such issues in 1972). These designated issues are acceptable at par in payment of estate taxes. If they are purchased in periods of historically high interest rates (1970 and 1973) when they are selling at heavy discounts (for example, at $67-$72), they can offer a high yield to maturity and an opportunity for capital appreciation if bond yields decline, plus the opportunity to be accepted for estate tax purposes on the basis of their par value.

An examination of Table 30-2 shows that total holdings of U.S. Government securities by individuals have not changed greatly since 1946 and especially not since 1950.

High-Grade Corporate Bonds (AAA-AA-A). A large number of corporate bond issues enjoy excellent marketability. As previously stated, individuals should purchase issues only in the grade of A or above, and then only if the yield spread in favor of corporate bonds over government bonds is made

TABLE 30-2

Holdings of U.S. Government Securities Fully Guaranteed
By Individuals—Selected Years (Billions of Dollars)

Year	Savings Bonds	Other U.S. Government Securities (Direct Obligations)
1946	44.2	21
1950	49.9	18
1972 (Jan. 1) ...	53.8	23.2

enough to justify investment in corporates versus governments. For maturities up to five years, certain BAA bonds may be purchased.

On January 1, 1972, individuals held $48 billion of corporate bonds (including convertibles), which represented only 4% of the total holdings of securities and 27% of the total holdings of bonds. In general, individuals with reserves of $50,000 or less should keep their reserves in insured savings accounts or in government bonds. For individuals with large portfolios there is usually a tax problem that causes tax-exempts to be more attractive than either governments or corporates.

Tax-Exempt Bonds. The interest from state, municipal, and revenue bonds is exempt from federal income taxes and usually from state income taxes in the state of issue. The higher the tax bracket of the individual, the higher is the effective yield of tax-exempts versus alternate investments— either bonds or stocks. In January, 1972, individuals held $52.3 billion of tax-exempts, significantly higher than their total holdings of *marketable* U.S. governments (including federal agency issues) and equal to their holdings of U.S. savings bonds.

In 1946 tax-exempt bonds were generally attractive only to individuals in tax brackets of 50% or higher, but in 1970 and 1973 their yields made them attractive to individuals in significantly lower tax brackets.

The marketability of blocks of tax-exempt bonds below $10,000 for a single issue and especially below $5,000 is not very satisfactory, and single bonds will usually sell at significant discounts below quoted prices for the issue. Overall, the marketability of tax-exempts is not as good as for governments. There is also a very wide range of quality for tax-exempts, which necessitates careful analysis and selection. However, the standard ratings are reasonably reliable, and if the individual investor confines his purchases to issues rated A or higher, he will probably secure issues of satisfactory quality. If he is somewhat wrong, an A issue can fall to BBB; but if he starts with a BBB issue, the issue may fall to BB as happened to New York City bonds in 1967.

Medium-Grade Bonds

We have advocated that bond purchases by individuals generally be grade A or higher, except for BAA having maturities up to five years. Medium-grade bonds will be discussed here for individuals who wish to purchase BAA or BA issues.

The higher yields on medium-grade bonds reflect lower quality and often lack of institutional demand. Unlike large institutional investors that can, under the principles of the Hickman Study, be self-insurers, individual investors do not have large enough portfolios to secure the insurance protection

TABLE 30-3

Representative Yields on Tax-Exempt and Alternative Investments

						Savings Accounts		
			Corporate Bonds			Savings	Mutual	Com-
	Tax-	U.S. Gov't			Common	& Loan	Savings	mercial
Year	Exempts	Long-Term	AAA	A	Stocks	Assn.	Banks	Banks
1966	3.90	4.66	5.13	5.33	3.40	4.45	4.45	4.04
1970	6.42	6.59	7.84	8.57	3.83	5.06	5.01	4.92
1971	5.62	5.74	7.39	8.02	3.14	5.33	5.13	4.78
1972	5.30	5.63	7.21	7.66	2.84	5.40	5.22	4.65

TABLE 30-4

Approximate After-Tax Equivalents for Tax-Exempt Bonds

	Actual Tax-Exempts	After-Tax Equivalents (Tax Brackets)							
Year	Yields	20%	25%	30%	35%	40%	50%	60%	70%
1970	6.42	8.03	8.54	9.18	9.89	10.72	12.84	16.05	21.38
1971	5.62	7.03	7.47	8.04	8.65	9.39	11.24	14.05	18.71
1972	5.03	6.29	6.69	7.19	7.75	8.40	10.06	12.58	16.75

offered by wide diversification in such issues. Furthermore, it should be observed that in periods of strong business expansion (such as in the 1920s and again in 1960-1973) medium-grade bonds are upgraded in the market, narrowing the yield spread advantage over high-grade bonds and thus reducing their relative attractiveness.

The interest on medium-grade corporate bonds, as with all corporate bonds, is payable before corporate taxes are paid by the issuer. Bondholders enjoy a contractual claim and, even in the case of income bonds, the interest is generally cumulative for a period. These bonds do occupy a senior position to equities and frequently are the senior bond of the issuer. When the medium-grade rating is a reflection of too-heavy debt, management may make strenuous efforts to reduce the debt, thus improving the quality of the bond. Careful analysis and selection can sometimes uncover issues offering a higher degree of protection than is evidenced by the ratings and yields. On this basis, medium-grade bonds offer the best opportunities when treated as "special situations." However, generally we advocate only issues rated A or higher, except for BAA with maturities of five years or less.

Convertible Bonds

Convertible securities offer investors the only debt vehicle that combines the element of relative dollar safety of a fixed-income security (to the extent of the convertible's straight bond value) with the purchasing power protection and growth characteristics of common stocks. Actually the convertible bond is a bond plus a long-term call on the stock.

Advantages of Convertible Bonds. A convertible bond offers full protection of a senior security if purchased at or near its straight bond value disregarding the convertible features. In addition, it provides protection against a decrease in the purchasing value of the dollar. In many cases the convertible bond provides a higher current yield than the current dividend yield of the stock into which it is convertible. Up until 1967-1968 a convertible bond had an added advantage over stock in that commercial banks would generally lend up to 75% of its market value, permitting it to be purchased by speculators on a 25% margin. However, in 1968 the Federal Reserve finalized its margin regulations on convertible bonds. It placed commercial bank loans against convertible bonds (Regulation "U") under the same margin requirements as brokers' margin loans under Regulation "T." Initially the margin requirement was 70%. Margin requirement for stock was 65% in 1973 and for convertible bonds was 50%.

Disadvantages of Convertible Bonds. Convertible bonds, reflecting market enthusiasm for the stock, frequently sell substantially above their value as straight bonds. The higher above the straight bond value that they sell, the less they exhibit the downside protection of a straight bond. Specifically, if a convertible bond has a straight bond value of 100 and it sells at 110 or 115 or perhaps 120, unless overall interest rates rise the purchaser has a downside risk of only 10%, 15%, or 20%, which may be a reasonable calculated risk to assume. However, if this convertible bond sells at 200, it has lost most of the characteristics of a bond but has much of the downside risk of a stock. To secure the downside protection of convertible bonds, individual investors should not purchase convertibles at premiums of over 20% above their straight bond or investment value. In other words, 20% is the maximum that should be paid for the conversion privilege.

In the late 1960s many convertibles [4] were issued by conglomerates. Later, in 1969, many investors (including European investors investing in

---

[4] The amounts (in billions of dollars) of new convertible bonds offered for cash in recent years are listed below. An important proportion in 1965-1968 were issues

American convertibles) learned that many convertible issues had been used as "phony money" by conglomerates in their acquisitions. Price declines in 1969-1970 resulted in severe losses. Coverage of interest was narrow.

COMMON STOCK PORTFOLIO POLICIES AND PATTERNS FOR CONSERVATIVE INVESTORS

There are two major types of common stock investors—conservative investors and aggressive investors. The two groups may be subdivided, but the discussion here will concentrate on the policies and the portfolio patterns by which the two major groups can meet their goals.

Investors should engage in a searching and honest self-appraisal, including among many things their *temperament,* in order to decide whether they should attempt to follow policies and portfolio patterns of conservative or aggressive investors. They should analyze themselves critically with regard to (1) their native ability, (2) their depth of economic and financial education and training, and above all (3) their temperament. Strategy differs widely between these two classes, and misjudgment in choosing the proper classification can lead to failure in reaching goals. Almost all individuals can become successful conservative investors; however, not everyone can be or even desires to be an aggressive investor. Constraints of risk will vary with the financial circumstances of the individual and with his knowledge, skill and judgment, as well as the time and the effort that he spends on security analysis.

Conservative investors have two major portfolio goals: (1) to have total portfolio values post a rate of growth paralleling the rate of growth of the economy and the stock averages such as the S&P 500 Composite, and (2) to reasonably protect both the dollar amount of capital invested and the purchasing power of the portfolio's capital and income. In these respects, policies are defensive in character.

Conservative investors need not spend much time and effort in selecting securities and managing their portfolios, although they must consistently follow sound standards. If they desire to do so, they can simply purchase shares in selected mutual funds, and usually they can accomplish their goals satisfactorily by such investments. However, if investors are going to make their own individual stock selections, the policies and the patterns outlined in the following paragraphs should be followed. Most of these

---

of conglomerates.

1961	$710	1964	$ 425	1967	$4,475	1970	$2,656
1962	445	1965	1,264	1968	3,281	1971	3,644
1963	357	1966	1,872	1969	4,141	1972	2,286

policies and patterns have been developed throughout this book. Conservative investors following these policies and patterns should accumulate substantially more capital over the years than the many investors who, not following sound portfolio patterns and investment policies, will have an unrewarding long-term record except perhaps in highly speculative markets such as 1959-1961 and 1967-1968 (followed by losses in 1969-1970).

Portfolio Patterns for Conservative Investors

Conservative investors can follow one of several portfolio patterns or a combination of them. The following paragraphs discuss the most important patterns: diversification or cross-section-of-American-industry portfolio approach, defensive portfolio approach, and sound-value portfolio approach.[5] As noted previously, the individual can accomplish the goals of a conservative investor by investing in carefully selected mutual funds whose goals are consistent with his goals. In this regard the reader should review Chapter 25, "Investment Company Stocks."

Diversification or Cross-Section-of-American-Industry Portfolio Policy

This portfolio policy may be defined as a policy to develop a well-diversified portfolio composed of stocks of leading companies in the major segments of the economy—a cross-section of the economy.

Basic Assumptions of Cross-Section Policy. The most certain assumption is that the economy will continue to grow as in the past and that a cross-section-of-American-industry approach will result in a compound rate of growth of a portfolio that will parallel the growth of GNP.

A second assumption is that forecasting earnings of particular industries and companies has been shown to involve large risks and uncertainties. Highly regarded industries of one era often turn in disappointing earnings performance subsequently. Managements of companies change, sometimes for the worse. Unforeseen external developments often have unfavorable effects on industries and companies. Shifts from shortages to surpluses within industries, and vice versa, frequently affect earnings and stock values. All these factors result in multiple risks of a selection approach by industries and companies versus cross-section portfolios.

---

[5] It is suggested that the reader review Part 4, Chapters 10-12 inclusive, before reading the rest of this chapter.

A third assumption is that major industries and companies usually manage to solve their problems in time, and yet a selective industry and company approach more often than not tends to direct purchases into industries and companies that appear to have no problems and tends to sell out when problems become apparent. Such a program can lead only to poor portfolio performance, buying at high prices and selling at low prices.

The final assumption is that a *diversified* investment in major segments of industry will develop a portfolio that will reflect the overall growth of the economy and thus lessen portfolio risk and give good long-term results.

Advantages of Cross-Section Policy. A cross-section policy is simple in its application and is really a diversification policy of investing in the averages. It lessens the risk of poor selection if it emphasizes the *major* and generally growing segments of the economy. It lessens the risk as shown by empirical evidence that many managed portfolios post a performance poorer than the averages. This policy minimizes the risk of concentrating on popular issues that currently sell at unduly high P/E ratios. Finally, the policy maximizes the diversification of risk, especially when it is combined with dollar-cost averaging over the years to minimize the timing hazard.

Disadvantages of Cross-Section Policy. This policy certainly minimizes the benefits of analysis and *selection* more than any other policy. It may be argued that while the benefits of selection may have been unimpressive in the past, techniques of selection can be improved to obtain more satisfactory results. A second claimed disadvantage is that the policy may, in order to minimize risk (including the timing risk), fail to emphasize issues that are most favorably situated because of expected growth and other characteristics. Finally, it is argued that the benefits of investing in industries with a favorable earnings trend tend to be canceled out by investments in industries with unfavorable characteristics. Large mutual funds tend to follow this policy.

Potential Adjustments of Cross-Section Policy to Give Superior Results. Instead of a policy of a cross-section of current American industry, the policy can aim at a cross-section of the *prospective* rather than the *current* economy. Holdings can be increased in expanding and dynamic industries. But it must be pointed out immediately that this is a step towards selectivity in favor of "better-situated industries."

Other adjustments can aim at reducing the timing hazard by spreading purchases over a period of time by dollar-cost averaging or by automatically timing purchases under some form of formula timing plan.

Application of Cross-Section Policy. This policy pattern is most suitable for investors who desire to stress diversification much more than selection and whose continuous management of the portfolio is not assured. It is also advocated for the investor unwilling to pay large premiums for investment characteristics highly favored by the market, such as anticipated exceptional growth of earnings, or who does not have time for continuous supervision.

The selection of industries to include in a cross-section portfolio could be based on major industry breakdowns of GNP, or on the relative basis of sales by industries, or on the breakdown of the Federal Reserve Index of Industrial Products, or on the contribution of industries' profits to total corporate profits, or on some other logical basis that would develop a representative cross-section-of-the-economy portfolio.

Defensive Stock Portfolio Policy

This portfolio policy may be defined as a policy to develop an equity portfolio consisting of stocks that are relatively less vulnerable to price declines than stocks on the average *because of their industry characteristics*. It is assumed that in these industries, earnings declines and dividend reductions, if any, will not be serious.

Advantages of Defensive Stock Portfolio Policy. This policy limits the risk in equity investment without assuming the risks of bond investment. It also provides a reasonable rate of current return for lower-tax-bracket investors, plus gradual long-term capital gains. In the past, most institutional investors tended to favor defensive issues that contributed to their price stability. While numerous institutional investors in the late 1960s were still favoring defensive issues, numerous others because of performance pressures were tending to favor performance stocks. But even in the latter cases, because yields on performance stocks were low or nonexistent, many institutions held a proportion of their portfolios in defensive stocks so that the yield advantage could balance the low or zero yields on performance stocks. Defensive stocks are particularly suitable for individuals desiring significant and stable income with some growth. They are also suitable for most investors in periods of historically high stock prices when growth issues are selling at very high price-earnings ratios and very low yields.

Disadvantages of Defensive Stock Portfolio Policy. Defensive stocks give relatively mediocre results in an era of inflation and of rapid growth in the economy. Furthermore, their defensive qualities may be lost if at some time (such as 1961, with the DJIA selling at 23-24 P/E), these stocks also sell at historically high price-earnings ratios and low dividend yields.

Characteristics of Defensive Common Stocks. The relative stability of earnings of defensive common stocks is based on stability of selling prices, stability of sales revenue, and good control over costs. Historically, companies identified in this group have demonstrated an absence of losses that could cut into profits. Finally, the industries and the companies have a good visibility of profits looking ahead over the next 4 to 6 years, that is, there is not too much uncertainty in projections of profits.

The growth element of defensive stocks—generally growth at about the same rate as the economy—increases the assurance of stability of sales and offsets any tendency for profit margins to narrow. Management can also act to secure sales stability and to offset any tendency for profit margins to narrow by changing the product mix to meet changing product demands. However, if there is an absence of sales growth and no significantly improving product mix, there is no element to offset rising costs, particularly in inflationary periods.

To remain defensive, defensive stocks must sell at moderate price-earnings ratios. They cease to be defensive if they sell at high price-earnings ratios. One problem in the past has been that price-earnings ratios of defensive stocks have tended to fluctuate widely, rising to too-high levels and ceasing to be defensive in some periods such as in 1961. This can happen either in rampant bull markets as in 1961 or in other periods when investors—individual and institutional—have fears concerning the future of other groups of stocks.

One factor that has always been considered important for defensive stocks is the relationship of stock yield to bond yield. Except for 1928-1929, until 1957-1958 defensive stocks enjoyed a noticeable yield spread over bonds. But since 1958 yields on defensive stocks have tended to be no higher, and in some periods like 1966-1973 considerably lower, than high-grade bond yields, decreasing the attractiveness of defensive stocks. This was an important reason why electric utility stocks were not looked on with favor by investors in the 1965-1973 period when high-grade bond yields were double average stock yields. The actual yield comparisons in the market at any time tend to reflect investors' evaluation of equities, especially defensive equities.

Other characteristics of defensive common stocks include a large cash flow, a strong liquidity position, and a low dividend payout including good dividend protection.

Defensive Utility and Bank Stocks. Included in the major classes of defensive stocks are electric public utility stocks and bank stocks. It must be emphasized that there are other major classes of defensive stocks, but only these two most important classes will be discussed here.

Electric Public Utility Stocks.[6] There are a number of reasons why it is widely believed that earnings stability of electric public utilities is assured. The industry has shown a pronounced and steady upward *growth* trend in power sales, doubling every 10 years. Revenues have reflected stable selling prices and stable rates. The industry has shown excellent ability to control costs. There is an absence of inventory and receivables losses, except that in severe recessions and depressions (not experienced since the 1930s), there were significant receivables credit losses. Finally, looking to the future, profit visibility is considered to be excellent. The two major risks to future earnings are the risks inherent in relatively high rates of return on investment and threats of public power competition.

The regulatory status of the industry, while not guaranteeing a fair return, has actually provided a fair return on investment for most companies over the years, generally ranging from 5½% to 6½% (in some states up to 7½%). The use since 1954 of accelerated depreciation methods has provided additional cash flow and lower taxes, which have reduced a little the need of the sale of common stock to maintain a balanced capital structure, thus reducing the factor of dilution of earnings.

For some years up to 1961, reflecting to an important extent institutional buying, the price-earnings ratio of electric utilities rose significantly along with the rise in the price-earnings ratio for the DJIA, reducing the defensive element of these stocks. However, in the 1960s the price-earnings ratio fell significantly and remained at an appreciably lower level than the DJIA into 1973, resulting in an increase in the defensive value of these stocks. In 1973 for these stocks, yield appeared attractive for defensive portfolios.

The dividend payout for the industry median has ranged around 70% for many years. Except in periods when price-earnings ratios rose to exceptionally high levels (as in 1960-1961), the result was favorable dividend yields. For investors in relatively high tax brackets, there have generally been some electric utilities that have followed a regular or partial stock dividend policy rather than a fixed cash dividend policy.

Bank Stocks.[7] As a group, based on their long record, bank stocks are considered defensive stocks. Their earning assets have displayed a strong long-term growth trend during all expansions. While fluctuations in interest rates at first might seem to create volatility in earnings, the major shift in the components of assets to longer-term assets (as in the case of consumer loans, mortgage loans, and business term loans) has tended to even out the effect of fluctuating interest rates.

---

[6] The reader should review Chapter 21, "Public Utility Securities."
[7] The reader should review Chapter 23, "Bank Stocks."

Banks have stabilized non-interest cost ratios satisfactorily, largely as a result of automation. Banks are not subject to inventory risks. The closer market price is to net asset value, the less is the risk. The higher the growth rate of earnings, the higher is the ratio of market price to book value. For some growth banks, the market prices have tended to rise to over 200% of book value, largely removing the stocks from the defensive category.

Bank earnings have grown, at a reasonably stable long-term rate, somewhat in excess of the growth rate of the economy, except in the early 1970s. Dividends have generally been maintained at somewhat less than 50% of earnings, thus providing stability and protection because of the low payout. The actual payout ratio for specific banks has depended chiefly on the ratio of capital funds to risk assets, which in the case of growth banks has tended to limit payout ratios to around 40%. Investors in high tax brackets have generally been able to select some bank stocks having at least a partial stock dividend policy. Asset growth has also tended to parallel the growth of GNP against a somewhat faster rate.

Over the years, in spite of significant institutional purchases, price-earnings ratios of most bank stocks (except for a relatively few fast-growing banks) have tended to stay in the reasonable range for defensive stocks; in the 1969-1973 years, at significantly lower P/E's than those of the DJIA and S&P industrial averages. In 1973 the average was 12 P/E and growth banks were only 17x-20x.

The risk element in relation to losses and earnings has not proved significant for the great majority of banks since the 1930s. Most banks have been able to build sizable "hidden" loss reserves, as actual charge-offs have fallen well short of annual charges in the income account in "anticipation" of losses.

Sound-Value Portfolio Policy

This portfolio policy may be defined as a policy of investing in equities whenever specific issues are available at a reasonable multiple of prospective earnings based on earnings projections for 5 or 6 years into the future. This policy is recommended for conservative investors, but it must be recognized that application of the policy requires more research and analysis than is required of the other policies for conservative investors discussed previously. Therefore, many such investors will not wish to expend the time and the effort required to implement this policy successfully.

Basic Assumptions of Sound-Value Policy. One basic assumption is that proper security analysis can make it possible to forecast future earning power with reasonable reliability. As a result, this policy assumes that the price-earnings ratio can provide the chief guide to equity selection. A further assumption is that allowance can properly be made (1) for the quality of earnings by adjusting reported earnings for varying accounting practices that may either overstate or understate earnings, (2) for assets and liabilities that are discovered by analysis but that are not disclosed in the balance sheet, (3) for expected economic and political changes, and (4) for differences in the quality of management. As a result of the above assumptions, the sound-value policy assumes that selection is more important than timing and that market levels can largely be ignored.

Advantages of Sound-Value Policy. Implementation of the sound-value policy compels a thorough analysis of the prospects for industries and companies. Research is centered on specific industries, companies, and securities rather than on economic trends. As a result, the policy lessens the danger of following fads, fashions, and short-term trends.

The potential success of this policy has been aided, especially since the 1930s, by fuller disclosure of corporate developments and by improvement in financial management techniques such as long-term capital budgeting and controls. Also, an SEC ruling in 1973 now permits companies to file and make public their forecast of earnings with the intent of aiding the analysts and the investing public. This has been done for many years in Great Britain. Another favorable factor has been the dedication of the federal government to stabilizing the economy and keeping unemployment at a minimum, which justifies more emphasis on selection and less on timing, that is, less concern about the likelihood of serious recessions or depressions like the 1930s.

The final advantage arises from emphasis on purchasing at medium or low price-earnings ratios. This enables the investor to profit if the issue becomes more fashionable and price-earnings ratios rise. Furthermore, risk is lessened by purchasing at relatively low prices in relation to earnings.

Disadvantages of Sound-Value Policy. The first major disadvantage is that successful results depend especially on the reliability of the projection of earnings. It must be acknowledged that the margin of error on projections may be large and that projections of earnings are usually greatly influenced by the past record, which may not provide a good basis. In addition, investors and analysts do have an emotional bias that influences their judgment and projections. Belief in security analysis favors this approach.

The sound-value policy quite possibly overminimizes the timing hazard and tends to foster a buy-and-hold policy unless equal emphasis is placed on selling individual issues when they are no longer sound values. Those who do not believe that it is possible to determine intrinsic or sound values for particular stocks by security analysis reject the policy for this reason, since the policy does assume that such investment values can be determined.

Application of Sound-Value Policy. A range for sound values must be established for a stock that is being analyzed. Constant reappraisals of prospective earnings and the price-earnings ratio are required. It must be recognized that there have been in the past, and will be in the future, periods of exceptionally high stock market levels in which buying opportunities on the *sound-value* basis may be quite limited. Finally it must be recognized that there will be numerous instances where issues meet a sound-value test but where other issues represent sounder "sound values."

COMMON STOCK PORTFOLIO POLICIES AND PATTERNS FOR AGGRESSIVE INVESTORS

Aggressive investors have one major portfolio goal: to realize substantial long-term capital gains that will result in total portfolio values rising at a rate substantially in excess of the growth rate of the economy and stock averages such as the S&P 500 Composite. A reasonable goal for aggressive investors following sound policies would be a doubling of portfolio values every 5 or 6 years, representing a compound annual growth rate of approximately 12%-14% per year. Aggressive investors must be able to take calculated risks, but more especially they must be able to take the time and the effort to learn investment principles and techniques of analysis and to apply them to specific situations. In this manner they have an excellent potential for long-term capital gains and portfolio performance that will significantly outperform the common stock indexes.

In this book, aggressive investors are separated from intelligent speculators largely on the basis of a time element and the implications of the time element. Under the definitions in this book, speculators are seeking relatively short-term capital gains (defined as under 1 year) while aggressive investors are seeking major capital gains over a longer period (several years). Most investors are restricted in their potentials for securing major capital gains over the short-term. The successful short-term speculator or trader generally has a flair and a natural ability not required for success by the aggressive investor. Of course, successful aggressive investment assumes good judgment.

As noted, the success of an aggressive investor requires training, experience, judgment, and willingness to devote considerable time and effort to review and analysis of securities. Several portfolio policies and patterns for aggressive investors will be discussed in the following paragraphs.

Best-Situated-Industry Portfolio Policy

This portfolio policy concentrates on companies in industries whose *intermediate-term prospects* (2-5 years) are most favorable.

Basic Assumptions of Best-Situated-Industry Policy. The major assumption is that economic and financial analysis can identify industries with *better-than-average* (not the most rapidly growing) outlook more readily than absolute or intrinsic values for particular issues. Furthermore, it is assumed that research and development can lead to favorable intermediate-term prospects. Another assumption is that there is great diversity of industry performance within the business cycle. Some industries will be found to be depression resistant, while others will be found to be prosperity resistant, the latter not reflecting in sales and earnings the conditions of economic prosperity and expansions. A few industries may demonstrate contra-cyclical characteristics. It must also be noted that the relative impact on industries tends to differ at least somewhat in each cycle. No two cycles are exactly the same in their impacts on specific industries.

In general, the best-situated-industry policy ignores the cyclical timing hazard. It justifies a fully invested position in equities at all times. It argues in effect that we have experienced a very long-term secular bull market, at least since 1919 and especially since the 1946-1949 base.

Advantages of Best-Situated-Industry Policy. The record does show that intermediate-range forecasting for industries is usually easier and is more likely to be close to the mark than either short-term or long-term forecasting. The advantage of intermediate-term forecasting for industries is that it gives enough time for the known factors to function and at the same time limits the time for new factors to have any important effect on an industry. It is also claimed that single industry forecasts are often easier and more accurate than forecasts for the entire economy.

Disadvantages of Best-Situated-Industry Policy. The disadvantages are that timing hazards may be ignored and that a buy-and-hold policy may be fostered instead of a best-situated-industry policy. The individual may not sell when the favorable intermediate outlook has been realized or when economic conditions change and the outlook for the industry changes. The relative position in respect to best-situated industries changes, but this factor may be ignored and thus contribute to poor portfolio performance over the long run.

Growth Stock Portfolio Policy [8]

This portfolio policy aims at the selection of equities whose earnings will grow at a significantly higher rate than earnings for the averages and will result in an increase in market value well in excess of the averages. A growth rate of earnings that is at least twice that for the averages is the target—at least 12%-14% per year (example, IBM).

Basic Assumptions of Growth Stock Policy. The most basic assumption is that future growth characteristics and rate of growth for industries and companies can be appraised through careful financial analysis. This policy accepts the thesis that growth is the most desirable attribute of an equity investment because growth can offset adverse developments, thus minimizing risks while taking advantage of the long-term characteristics of equity *investment*. It is also advantageous from the tax standpoint in that expected returns will largely be in the form of long-term capital gains with a maximum tax rate very significantly lower than the rate applied to ordinary income.

The advocates of a growth stock policy state that high price-earnings ratios characteristic in the market for stocks identified as growth stocks are merely an illusion because growth in earnings will reduce the high ratio based on cost; for example, a 40 P/E on cost will be reduced to a 20 P/E on cost in 5 years if earnings double in that period. It is also expected that the price-earnings ratio will continue high in the future as further growth continues to be discounted into the future. This factor is absolutely necessary if major capital gains are to be realized. The advocates of the policy emphasize that it is a dynamic policy, not a static policy, and that a dynamic approach is essential for successful portfolio management.

Types of Growth. There are at least five types of growth, and each will be commented on briefly here. The first is *growth in sales volume,* which is of value to investors *only* if it results in growth in profits and other elements of value. Usually for any extended period there is not a significant

---

[8] The reader is referred to Chapter 14, "Investment Growth Factors and Projections," and Chapter 10, "Investment Strategies for Common Stocks," for a further understanding of the policies described in the remaining sections of this chapter. Numerous skillful and fortunate investors secured very substantial gains in portfolios of growth stocks in the post-World War II years—more than through any other policy— but it is a real question whether most investors can secure exceptional portfolio performance by following a growth stock policy with a diversified portfolio of "growth stocks."

growth trend in earnings if there is not a significant growth in sales, but the latter may occasionally take place for a few years without the former as the result of improving profit margins.

A second type of growth is *growth in asset value* or *net equity per share* of stock. This can reflect growth in fixed assets, growth in tangible natural resource reserves such as oil and gas, and growth in intangibles such as patents, pricing, and brand names. Again, while growth in net equity value per share is usually necessary to produce any extended growth in earnings per share, growth of the former does not assure growth of the latter and there are many instances of such a record. It is expected that growth through reinvestment of earnings will produce a further incremental growth, but this is not always the result.

The third and most important type of growth is *growth in earnings* and in *earnings per share*. Growth in earnings per share is by far the type of growth most commonly sought by those advocating a growth stock policy. But there may be a growth in total net profits without a comparative growth in earnings per share if the element of dilution has been present. One example of dilution is that which sometimes arises from issuing additional common stock in mergers and acquisitions; another results from conversion of convertible securities.

A fourth type of growth is *growth in cash flow*. Cash flow and the uses of cash flow were discussed in earlier chapters, and statistics on cash flow were presented in Table 7-1 in Chapter 7. Cash flow may also be considered in terms of research and development expenses that are considered to be expensed capital expenditures, in terms of other expensed investments such as brand-name buildups through heavy advertising outlays, and finally in terms of expensed research and development costs that many consider to be representative of the equivalent of capital investments or growth in "assets."

The fifth type of growth is *growth in dividends,* which depends on growth in earnings and growth in cash flow. While growth in dividends is primarily dependent upon growth in earnings, the actual annual amount of dividend payments shows a much closer correlation to cash flow than to earnings per share.[9] Except for the relatively few companies exhibiting exceptional growth in earnings, investors consider dividend growth important. Investors recognize that $1.00 in dividends growing at a compound rate of 1% per year will grow to only $1.22 in 20 years, but at 4% it will grow to $2.19 in 20 years and at 6% to $3.21. Therefore, growth in dividends is important, but not for exceptional earnings growth firms.

---

[9] Of course an important component of cash flow is net earnings.

Quality of Growth. There are three principal factors in determining the quality of growth, and each will be commented on briefly here. The first is the *probable growth potential* as indicated by the past record and the present situation of the industry and the company and by a projection of the compound annual growth rate for the next 5 or 6 years. The historical record of growth and the underlying causes for the record are determined by an analysis of research expenditures, capital expenditures, industry pricing, sales, costs, and profits. Interrelated in this analysis is the competitive picture of the industry—past, present, and prospective.

The second factor is the *stability of the growth trend.* Regularity as well as the average annual compound rate of growth is important. A steady rate of growth is far more valuable than a volatile record.

The third major factor in the quality of growth is the *risk factors* present that could slow down or even terminate a favorable growth trend. There are several important factors of risk that may affect future growth. One is that success attracts competition and may also encourage buildup of overcapacity and overproduction in the industry (for example, the paper and aluminum industries in the late 1960s). Another risk factor is that rapid growth may subject a company to antitrust suits (IBM, 1973). Still another risk factor is the extent to which growth is dependent upon patents, for probable expiration of patents can pose a real problem in long-term growth.

Advantages of Growth Stock Policy. There are numerous advantages of a growth stock policy, but only the most important will be mentioned here. A growth stock policy lessens the timing hazard by putting the time factor on the side of the investor. *This is true of no other common stock selection policy.* The policy also benefits from the expected long-term growth of the economy and from government efforts to stimulate growth. The widespread efforts of corporate management to spur growth through research also are an important factor in growth. Our economy is psychologically growth-oriented.

Our tax structure also favors growth companies. It encourages retention of earnings rather than payment of dividends as long as the retention of earnings is "not unreasonable." The tax laws have also contributed to growth by liberalizing depreciation allowances for tax purposes and by providing heavy deductions for tax purposes for research, depletion, and intangible development expenditures.

Another advantage of growth stock policy has been the widening choice of growth issues in recent years. This has been the result of a number of factors, such as the growing emphasis on research and development, the growing ascendency in top management levels of younger growth-minded management, the trend toward diversification, new technological developments, and the ability of numerous new and innovation-oriented companies to grow rapidly in the post-World War II years. Performance-minded investors, both individual and institutional, were seeking these companies in the late 1960s in contrast to the established "blue chip" corporations. In the 1970s there were also many relatively smaller companies available.

Disadvantages of Growth Stock Policy. One of the principal disadvantages of a growth stock policy is the difficulty of selection. If the period of growth has been long, there is no assurance of similar future growth, for the period of rapid growth may be about ending. If the period of growth has been quite brief, growth may be a temporary phenomenon. There is often a tendency for growth companies to get in each other's way as the industry becomes attractive to more companies, and it is difficult to determine which companies will survive. Management (and management-directed research) is always the key factor in growth, and changes in management policies and aging management may lessen the drive for growth. Identification of a growth company before it is widely recognized as such, but while it has good growth prospects for quite a number of years into the future, is not easy. In 1973 numerous growth stocks sold at very high P/E multiples.

Another disadvantage is that a high price-earnings ratio may overdiscount growth. High price-earnings ratios of 50 to 100 times current earnings may overdiscount growth far into the future. If an investor pays 100 times earnings, if earnings double in 3 years, and if the price-earnings ratio 3 years hence remains at 100 times earnings, the investor will have doubled his capital. But if investors in the market 3 years hence forecast that the rate of growth will slow down to a doubling in 6 years rather than 3 years, they may be willing at that time to pay a maximum of say only 50 times earnings, in which case the original investor will have no capital gains. What is worse, if the price-earnings ratio at that time declines to below a 50 P/E multiple (which is probable), the investor will have a capital loss. If it falls to a 25 P/E multiple, he will have a 50% capital loss. Because of the usually very high price-earnings ratio, no other policy places such a premium on the necessity for accurate projections of earnings, especially the minimum growth rate and level of future earnings.

Finally, risks are particularly great in growth industries. By definition, their growth rate is highly abnormal and certainly cannot be continued indefinitely. They are usually the creatures of research and technological changes and may suddenly and unexpectedly become the victims of other research and technological changes outside the company or even outside the industry. However, certain bank and insurance stocks have deserved the designation "growth stocks."

Application of Growth Stock Policy. For a further discussion of growth stock policy and its applications, the reader should refer to Chapters 10, 12, and 14.

Out-of-Favor, Low P/E, Comeback Stock Portfolio Policy

This policy aims at the selection, by careful and thorough analysis, of quality stocks (1) that are in the generally available list of seasoned stocks (major stocks in major industries), (2) that are selling at relatively low multiples of earnings (low relative to the current P/E ratio for the averages), and (3) that can logically be classified in the out-of-favor category. Many major corporations were in this category in 1973.

Basic Assumptions of Out-of-Favor, Low P/E, Comeback Stock Policy.[10] It is assumed that in the future (as in the past) in making selections from a large list of seasoned stocks (important companies, important industries), the *odds* will generally favor investment in low-multiple stocks as vehicles for outperforming the averages by an important margin. This emphasis on selection of low-multiple stocks rests solidly on many studies of a historical record of at least the past three decades. Low-multiple, out-of-favor stocks are the most likely to be undervalued in the market and to provide the best opportunities for relatively safe (because of low P/E ratios) capital

---

[10] In a sense, a price-earnings ratio measures how widely recognized—among the broad spectrum—are the latest expectations given a particular company, a group of similarly related stocks, or the market as a whole. It also indicates the relative price leverage that will be experienced if the expectations *do not* materialize.

Arthur Zeikel (of Standard & Poor's/InterCapital Inc., a new diversified investment management organization) in his article "Coordinating Research Information," *Financial Analysts Journal,* (March-April, 1969), pp. 119-123, states:

> The obvious deserves some comment. It is more likely to see a favorable change develop when stocks are out-of-favor, earnings are depressed, price-earnings relationships are relatively low, expectations are limited, and there is no general interest in the particular industry or stock area. The flow of written research material at this point is usually nil (airlines, chemicals in 1968-69).
>
> On the other hand, negative developments tend to occur when expectations are generally high, stock prices are advancing or have advanced rapidly, price-earnings ratios have been inflated, and the industry or issue continues to gain new investment acceptance on an accelerated basis. Put another way, the odds seem to favor that high price-earnings stocks suffer from unexpected adverse developments and low price-earnings stocks from favorable surprises.
>
> It is not the low multiple by itself which provides the unusual opportunity nor the high evaluations that carry excessive risk, but rather that investment anticipations are low on the one side and high on the other.

appreciation. The opportunities for substantial capital appreciation from this class of stocks will be much more numerous than selections from stocks in the high-multiple class whose recent growth record has been widely recognized in the market as reflected by their relatively high price-earnings record. This is because, on the average, the future earnings growth record of the popular, high-multiple stocks will need to be at least as good as if not superior to their excellent past record if the investor is going to realize substantial capital appreciation over the next three to five years (for example, a growth of 100%).

It is further assumed that careful, sophisticated security analysis can enable the investor to select from the low-multiple stocks those major and seasoned companies whose future earnings' record (a recovery in earnings) will provide the basis for substantial capital appreciation. The very fact that most investors, including most professional investors and institutional investors, find it almost impossible to accept this thesis based on numerous well-documented studies (that selection from a group of companies with problems and *apparently* unexciting potential will provide the best vehicles for substantial capital appreciation) is in itself an important reason why such stocks are available at low multiples and do provide the basis for significant capital appreciation. Lack of patience by most investors and short-term performance pressures add potential opportunities for this policy.

Selection of Out-of-Favor Stocks. In preparing a list of out-of-favor, low-multiple stocks from which they expect to make stock selections, investors should give preference to seasoned, major companies in important industries and to companies that have quality attributes. This is because there are important problems that have caused the industries and the companies to be out-of-favor, and the investor wishes to select companies that have quality factors and that have the financial strength, management experience, and staying power to solve their problems and emerge successfully from the problem period. There are *always* companies available in the low-multiple, out-of-favor group that meet these qualifications, and therefore it is not necessary to assume the risks inherent in newer, unseasoned companies. This concept is highly important for success in following this portfolio policy. Associated with this concept is the need for great patience, which most investors, individual or institutional, do not possess. Only a relatively few will be able, with any consistency to time purchases, to coincide with the beginning of the "turn-around" and "break-out" period.

Advantages of Out-of-Favor, Low P/E, Comeback Stock Policy. Numerous studies in depth, covering long periods of time and including interperiod results as well, have proved that low-multiple stocks of seasoned companies with quality characteristics have significantly outperformed high-multiple stocks. The timing factor, which is in reality the pricing problem of not paying an overvalued price, is greatly lessened by this policy. Recognition of industry and company problems is widespread, and this is reflected in the market price, thus greatly reducing downside risk. In making selections from the low P/E group, the investor should also concentrate on companies that have a well-protected dividend yield that is significantly higher than the yield for the averages and that greatly reduces the downside risk. The investor thus obtains the advantage of relatively high current dividend income as well as the major factor of a large and relatively safe capital gains potential to produce an excellent overall rate of return potential—overall representing dividend return plus capital appreciation. Careful, unemotional analysis and reasonable projections of earnings for the next 5 to 6 years should assure good performance results. It is always a strong advantage to select *undervalued* stocks, and these can most frequently be located in the out-of-favor, low P/E group.

Disadvantages of Out-of-Favor, Low P/E, Comeback Stock Policy. The greatest disadvantage of this policy is that it requires investors to act contrary to what appears logical in their own minds and in the minds of investors in general, that is, to purchase stocks of companies and industries that have problems rather than those that apparently have no problems, current or prospective. This policy also requires an unusual amount of *patience,* which most investors do not possess. If it were possible with any consistency to purchase such stocks in their depressed market levels but *just prior* to recognition by the market (turn-around) that problems were being solved, patience would not be required. Unfortunately, the record does not support the concept that many investors and brokers have the skill to purchase just prior to a turn-around and recovery in popularity. Furthermore, ownership of these stocks has shifted to investors with strong convictions, and they tend to hold the stock for major capital gains so that not much stock is offered during the early stages of recovery. Relatively few investors can purchase significant amounts in the initial turn-around period.

Application of Out-of-Favor, Low P/E, Comeback Stock Policy. Out-of-favor stocks are low-multiple price-earnings stocks. To minimize risks, this portfolio policy should, in the judgment and experience of the authors, concentrate on major stocks in major industries usually when they have declined 45%-50% from their previous highs and are selling at price-earnings ratios below those for the DJIA and at yields above those for the DJIA. In such cases the investor should analyze the industry and the company involved and should make 3- or 6-year earnings projections to determine if such projections justify an expectation that earnings for these major stocks in major industries will recover to their previous levels and therefore stock prices over the next 3 to 6 years. Chemical stocks offered this potential in 1968, and stocks of many major corporations were in this class in 1973.

Special Situation Stock Portfolio Policy [11]

The term "special situation" is used in this chapter to refer to potential capital gains situations arising from *specific corporate action* that is expected to affect the corporation's securities, not the broad term applied by many to any situation that happens to have special favorable attributes. This corporate action is in the administrative area and is related to corporate capitalization (bonds, preferred stocks, and common stocks) rather than to the general operations of the business. The opportunity for capital gains (and therefore the realization of actual capital gains) ends when the specific corporate action is terminated.

Types of Special Situation Stock Policy. One method of classification would be to place true arbitrage situations at one extreme, imperfect arbitrage (for example, uncertainty over the terms and the timing of exchange of securities) in the middle, and situations that cannot readily be termed arbitrage situations at the other extreme. In this book, however, the discussion of types of special situations will be based on the definition that the area situations revolve around corporate administrative actions that affect corporate capitalization. Opportunities exist when the following types of corporate action are present: (1) mergers and acquisitions, (2) tenders, (3) reorganizations, (4) recapitalization, (5) liquidations, (6) spin-offs, and (7) tax refunds.

Advantages of Special Situation Stock Policy. The major advantage of this portfolio policy is that the discount from real value lessens the risk of loss because of faulty timing and selection. The policy also provides significant rewards for skillful if time-consuming analysis. Finally, it provides a yardstick (the discount) to determine the timing for selling as the discount narrows or disappears.

---

[11] Maurice Schiller, *How to Profit from Special Situations in the Stock Market* (Larchmont, N.Y.: American Research Council, 1959).

Disadvantages of Special Situation Stock Policy. The most serious disadvantage is that the policy calls for skillful security analysis of the type not possible by most nonprofessional individual investors. The two major risks are (1) a tendency to evaluate incorrectly the profit potential presented by the corporate action and (2) failure of the corporate action to be consummated. There is also a tendency to downgrade situations and to become less selective if the number of available situations becomes relatively small. A final disadvantage is that timing or consummation may turn out to be much longer than expected. The period of timing is highly important because, for example, a 25% capital gain obtained over a one-year period is only half as profitable as a 25% capital gain in a six-month, one-day period.

Application of Special Situation Stock Policy. Seven applications of this portfolio policy are discussed in the following paragraphs.

Mergers and Acquisitions. The post-World War II years have witnessed the greatest merger movement in history, especially the 1960s. The capital gains opportunities lie in the market's undervaluation of a security in terms of what will result from the exchange of securities or other assets.

Considerations in mergers and acquisitions are: (1) the relative price of shares of the corporation in current and past markets; (2) whether any dividends will be paid during the waiting period that can be included in the capital gains expected; (3) the percentage of stock controlled by directors and other parties directly concerned; (4) the basis and the strength of the opposition, if any; (5) the percentage of outstanding shares that must legally assent to the proposed corporate action; and (6) the proposed period allowed for consideration and approval of the corporate action. In the case of acquisitions, consideration should also be given to whether the shares are to be purchased in the open market or by tender, or whether the proposed acquisition is based on an exchange of securities or a cash payment.

Tenders. There are many instances of tenders by corporations for their own securities and also by other interested parties such as those seeking control or acquisition. Such tenders occurred almost daily in the 1960s.

Reorganizations. When corporations experience financial difficulty and must be reorganized, their securities will frequently sell in the market at substantial undervaluation,[12] as for example in many railroad situations.

---

[12] The Hickman Study discussed earlier in this book found that, on the average, corporate bonds were heavily undervalued in the market at or near default.

Recapitalizations. Corporations may decide to recapitalize in order to effect a change in their capital structure. Special situations arise when the corporation must offer a valuable inducement for securityholders to agree to the recapitalization, as in the case of noncallable preferred stock.

Liquidations. Corporations may be forced by creditors to liquidate or the directors may decide (with the required approval of stockholders) that the corporation should be liquidated because it is worth more dead than alive. Sometimes individuals or groups purchase outstanding stock interests for the purpose of liquidation, especially when working capital is both substantial and liquid and when the market price of the stock is well below *net* working capital book value (that is, below current assets less *all* liabilities).

Considerations in liquidation are: (1) the expected realizable value of tangible assets, (2) the expected realizable value of net working capital, (3) legal problems and contingencies, (4) the tax status of any liquidating dividends, (5) the estimated time period involved and the proposed time schedule of liquidation, and (6) the actual proposed method of distribution of assets.

Spin-Offs. Corporate directors may decide to spin off the securities of certain subsidiaries or affiliates by distributing these securities to the corporate stockholders. The proposed spin-offs may be voluntary or mandatory as required by regulatory authorities or the Department of Justice.

Tax Refunds. Corporations that have losses may carry back these losses and recompute their profits and taxes for the three years previous to the year in which the loss was incurred. Then they are entitled to tax refunds for taxes previously paid on the profits for those years. After carrying back the losses for three years, corporations may carry forward any remaining losses for five years into the future. Stock market prices may not reflect these values.

Factors to Consider in Special Situations. Once a special situation is uncovered by an investor, he must give special consideration to the following:

The Facts. The investor needs to have answers to the following:

1. What is the likelihood that the corporate action will be completed as contemplated?
2. What are the possible legal delays and uncertainties?
3. What are the tax considerations?
4. What are possible contingencies that may delay or prevent the completion of the corporate action, such as opposition to the action by minority stockholder groups?

Length of Special Situation Period. Based on the facts uncovered, the investor should decide how long the special situation period will last before the corporate action is completed. Any long delay reduces considerably the attractiveness of a capital gains situation. This is particularly true when it is realized that such situations generally yield no income.

Timing for the Special Situation. At one extreme in timing is a situation that has not developed sufficiently to a point where there is reasonable expectation that the corporate action will be consummated. At the other extreme is the situation that has developed to such a point that it is generally accepted by investors as a near certainty, thus severely limiting capital gains.

Estimate of Capital Gains Potential. The aggressive investor will need to estimate the value of the security, the value of the security that is to replace it, or the value of assets to be received in exchange for the security at the end of the special situation period. This estimated value, less the current market price (the discount), yields the capital gains potential. Of course, all costs involved must be deducted in determining the estimated capital gains potential.

Estimate of Risk in the Special Situation. Generally, the risk in the special situation is due to the risk that the corporate action may not be consummated. Therefore, the investor should evaluate such risks.

QUESTIONS

1. Briefly discuss the problem of reserves for individuals in relation to their overall financial plan and to total portfolio.

2. How should an individual with reserves of $50,000 or less "invest" these reserves? What are the reasons for your answer?

3. Under what conditions should an individual invest in:
    (a) Government bonds (Discuss savings bonds separately.)
    (b) High-grade bonds.
    (c) Corporate bonds.
    (d) Medium-grade bonds.
    (e) Tax-exempt securities.

4. Distinguish between the conservative investor and the aggressive investor in terms of goals and the requirements for success as a conservative investor and as an aggressive investor.

5. Define for the conservative investor the following portfolio policies and patterns and list the advantages and the disadvantages of each:
   (a) Diversification—cross-section-of-American-industry portfolio policy.
   (b) Defensive stock portfolio policy.
   (c) Sound-value portfolio policy.

6. Define for the aggressive investor the following portfolio policies and patterns and list the advantages and the disadvantages of each:
   (a) Best-situated-industry portfolio policy.
   (b) Growth stock portfolio policy.
   (c) Out-of-favor, low P/E, comeback stock portfolio policy.
   (d) Special situation stock portfolio policy.

7. (a) Explain why the individual investor should select only bonds, corporate or tax-exempt, in the grade classification of A, AA, or AAA. Under what conditions would BBB bonds be acceptable?
   (b) Discuss the advantages and disadvantages of a high-grade bond portfolio.

8. Assume a commercial bank has the option of buying a 20-year AA municipal bond quoted to yield 5% to maturity and an AA corporate bond quoted to yield 8% to maturity. Which bond would you recommend? Why?

9. What should be the policy of the individual investor in respect to including convertible bonds in his investment portfolio? What are the risks?

10. Explain to an individual, who expresses his intention of using all or most of his liquid funds in a trading account, the problems and the risks of such a policy as opposed to the problems and the risks of reaching expected goals by following an aggressive portfolio policy. [See Paul H. Cootner (ed.), *The Random Character of Stock Market Prices* (Cambridge, Mass.: The MIT Press, 1964).]

WORK-STUDY PROBLEMS

(*These problems cover the material in Chapters 28-30 inclusive.*)

1. Assume that the president of an investment counsel firm by which you are employed as an account executive has introduced you to a new client, Mr. A. B. Jones, who is to be assigned to you for management of his portfolio.
   (a) Detail all the information that you would request from the client and also detail the information furnished to you by Mr. Jones:
       (1) In respect to his financial position, including insurance coverage.
       (2) In respect to his family situation.
       (3) In respect to his tax situation.

(4) In respect to his liquid reserves and his investment portfolio, including specifics of each investment (assume a total portfolio of at least $250,000.)

(b) Develop a discussion with Mr. Jones as to his overall financial program and his overall investment program, including his investment goal.

(c) As a result of the above information, outline for Mr. Jones:

(1) Reasonable investment goals, considering his present financial situation, his expected financial situation, and his temperament.

(2) The investment policies to be followed in accomplishing these reasonable goals.

(d) Detail the specific securities and amounts for his recommended portfolio, the income from each, and total income and yield.

You may assume that the firm has a research department that has prepared a list of securities from which you will make your specific selections. Therefore, in each case of a security selection, prepare only a short paragraph giving reasons why that particular security is recommended for the portfolio.

2. Assume that William J. Peters, vice president in charge of research for an investment counsel firm, has asked you, his assistant, to review the list of securities for a client and to submit to him a memorandum outlining an investment program. He gives you the following details concerning the client:

1. Name: Henrietta Jones Lawrence (Mrs. John C.)
2. A recent widow, age 37.
3. Children: boy 17 in high school; girl 12 in grade school.
4. $30,000 home in Scarsdale, New York. No mortgage.
5. Ford station wagon, one year old.
6. Uninvested cash from husband's insurance, $20,000.
7. Cash in savings account at 4¾%, $5,000.
8. All securities have been held over 6 months. (See list below.)
9. She says she needs $10,000 a year, including social security, for living expenses.
10. She has no insurance on her life.

The following are her securities:	*Cost*
$20,000 Maine Turnpike Authority 4% 1989 Serial A	$100
$20,000 Wells Fargo Bank, Convertible 3¼%—1989	100
$20,000 New York Telephone and Telegraph Co. 7%—2009	100
$20,000 New York City 3% 1980	102
$20,000 United States Treasury Bonds 4's-1980, Feb.	99
$10,000 United States Savings Bonds, Series E, due in 6 months	75
$20,000 Federal Land Bank, 5%, January, 1979	89

Number of shares

50	U.S. Smelting and Refining, $5.50 Preferred	90
600	Merck & Co., Inc. Common	85

100	Reynolds Metals Co. 4½% Convertible Preferred	93
500	Santa Fe Industries 5% Preferred.................	8
100	Union Carbide Common (Acquired prior to 9/62) ...	80
20	General Telephone & Electronics Corp. Common	30
10	National Distillers & Chemical Corp. Common	30
100	Kerr-McGee Oil Industries, Inc. Common	40
100	Chrysler Corp. Common	55

Submit a formal memorandum giving: (a) An appraisal of the securities, including the income, the yield, and the future prospects for the industry and the company; (b) Suggestions as to the investment program Mrs. Lawrence should follow; (c) Brief reasons for selling any of the securities held by Mrs. Lawrence; (d) Brief reasons for buying securities suggested as replacements for those sold; and (e) General comments as to total income reasonably expected, including social security benefits, as well as tax implications of changes.

3. Mr. Jones recently retired, and his liquid assets are $250,000. He and his wife are 65 years of age and in sound health. Most of his funds are now invested in U. S. Government bonds and high-quality corporate bonds. He is very disturbed over recent inflation developments and suggests to you that he intends to convert a major portion of his liquid assets into a portfolio of growth stocks.

(a) Comment as to the wisdom of his choice.

(b) Prepare a complete portfolio, including reserves and actual stocks, explaining the portfolio policy that you believe he should follow in respect to common stocks.

SUGGESTED READINGS

Fama, Eugene F. "Components of Investment Performance." *The Journal of Finance* (June, 1972), pp. 551-568.

McDonald, J. G., and A. K. Fisher. "New Issue—Stock Behavior." *The Journal of Finance* (March, 1972), pp. 97-102.

Robichek, Alexander A., and Marcus C. Bogue. "A Note of the Behavior of Price/Earnings Ratios over Time." *The Journal of Finance* (June, 1971), pp. 731-736.

Schwab, Bernard, and Peter Lusztig. "A Note on Investment Evaluation in Light of Uncertain Future Opportunities." *The Journal of Finance* (December, 1972), pp. 1093-1100.

Sharpe, William. "Simple Strategies for Portfolio Diversification." *The Journal of Finance* (March, 1972), pp. 127-129.

PART nine

INSTITUTIONAL PORTFOLIO POLICIES

Commercial Banks, Mutual Savings Banks, Savings and Loan Associations

The portfolio policies for (1) commercial banks, (2) savings banks, and (3) savings and loan associations in this chapter are discussed mainly in terms of the functions, investment constraints, and investment policies of these institutions.

PORTFOLIO POLICIES OF COMMERCIAL BANKS

Certain characteristics of commercial bank operations result in important constraints surrounding the formulation and the activation of commercial bank portfolio policies.

Functions of Commercial Banks

The major functions of commercial banks are to accept deposits and to make loans. In the process of making loans, the banks increase their deposits (secondary deposits) and, in addition, they receive primary deposits not associated with loans. The major divisions of the assets of commercial banks are cash (13%), investments (23%), and loans (57%). The major divisions of the total liabilities and capital of commercial banks are deposits (82%) and capital accounts (7%-8%). Table 31-1 shows the major assets of commercial banks in the United States in various years.

Loan Function. Historically, loans have constituted 50%-55% of the assets of commercial banks. However, as a result of the purchase of approximately $80 billion of U.S. Government securities during World War II

TABLE 31-1

Major Assets of All Commercial Banks in the U.S. (Billions of Dollars)

Type of Asset	December, 1945 $	December, 1945 %	December, 1947 $	December, 1947 %	December, 1959 $	December, 1959 %	January, 1973 $	January, 1973 %
Cash Assets	34.8	21.7	37.5	24.1	49.5	20.2	94.7	13.4
U.S. Govt. Securities	90.6	56.5	69.2	44.6	58.9	24.1	65.4	9.2
Total Cash & U.S.								
Govts.	125.4	78.2	106.7	68.7	108.4	44.3	160.1	22.5
Other Securities*	7.3	4.6	9.0	5.8	20.5	8.4	115.1	16.2
Loans	26.1	16.3	38.1	24.5	110.8	45.3	407.8	57.2
Other Assets	1.5	.9	1.6	1.0	5.0	2.0	29.0	4.1
Total Assets	160.3	100.0	155.4	100.0	244.7	100.0	712.6	100.0

* Other securities consist of 80%-85% of state and local government tax-exempt securities and 13%-15% of federal agency issues. On June 30, 1972, the breakdown of the security investments of commercial banks was as follows:

Other Securities:

Securities of Federal Agencies and Corporations (not guaranteed) ..	16.5%
Obligations of States and Subsidiaries	78.6
All Other Securities	4.9
Total Other Securities	100.0%

Source: Federal Reserve Bulletins.

to finance federal deficit operations, commercial banks held $91 billion of these securities at the end of the war, which constituted 56.5% of their assets. If other securities (4.6% of assets) are added, total securities represented 61% of total assets. Conversely, loans in 1945 represented only 16% of assets, a most exceptional situation. Gradually after the war the business and asset composition of commercial banks returned to normal and in 1973 loans represented 57% of assets, U.S. Government securities about 9%, and total securities about 23%.

In dollar amount, commercial banks' holdings of U.S. Government securities fell from $91 billion in 1945 to $69 billion in 1947 and have fluctuated between this figure and $53 billion since that time. Once this channel was reached, holdings were decreased to meet loan demands in periods of expansion and were increased as loan demands declined in recessions. Commercial bank holdings of U.S. Government securities in selected years of expansion and recession are shown in Table 31-2. (Also refer to related tables in Chapters 23 and 26.)

Holdings of U.S. Government securities increase in recessions when loan demands decline, interest rates are relatively low, and bond prices are

TABLE 31-2

Commercial Bank Holdings of U.S. Government Securities
in Selected Years—Expansions and Recessions (R) (Billions of Dollars)

1948—$62.5	1954—$69.2 R	1959—$60.3	Dec. 1968—$66.0
1949—$66.8	1957—$59.5	1961—$67.2 R	Dec. 1969—$56.8
1953—$63.7	1958—$67.5 R	July 1967—$53.3	Jan. 1973—$65.3

Source: Federal Reserve Bulletins.

relatively high. Holdings are decreased in periods of expansion when loan demands increase, interest rates are relatively high, and bond prices are relatively low. This characteristic of commercial bank operations usually results in additions in the bond account during recessions when prices are high and sales during expansion periods when prices are low in order to meet loan demands. The nature of these operations has led to special provisions in the tax laws favoring commercial banks (losses can be deducted from operating profits) as described later in this chapter.

Deposit Function. Historically, demand deposits have represented nearly three quarters of total deposits, and time deposits have represented the remainder. However, as shown in Table 31-3, as a result of changes in legislation permitting commercial banks to pay higher rates on time deposits to be more competitive, time deposits became increasingly important. By 1969 they had surpassed the total of demand deposits and by 1973 were 56% of total deposits.

TABLE 31-3

Deposits of Commercial Banks (Billions of Dollars)

Year	Total Deposits (Excluding Interbank)	Demand Deposits		Time Deposits	
		$	% of Total Deposits	$	% of Total Deposits
1941—December	$ 60.30	44.35	73.5	15.95	26.5
1945—December	146.16	105.92	72.5	30.24	27.5
1959—December	202.81	136.64	67.4	66.17	32.6
1968—December	406.06	203.55	50.1	202.51	49.9
1972—June	520.64	228.13	43.8	292.51	56.2

As will be noted later in this chapter, the increase in rates paid on savings deposits from 1% in 1945 to 4½% (CD's, 90 days or more, 6¾%; 180

days to one year, 7%; and one year or more, 7½%) in 1973 and shifts in the proportion of total deposits represented by time deposits had important implications for commercial bank investment portfolio policy.

Relationship of Deposit Liabilities to Assets. As with all corporations, assets minus liabilities equals net worth, and the relationship of liabilities to assets and of net worth to assets indicates the leverage factor. The leverage factor is heavy for the commercial banks. In 1973, deposit liabilities were approximately 82% of total assets and together with other liabilities amounted to 93% of total assets, while capital accounts represented only 7.3% of assets and 8.9% of total deposits.

Relationship of Capital Equity Cushion to Assets. Commercial banks have only a thin equity cushion to absorb losses. If total assets should decline 8%, equity capital would be wiped out; if loans (risk assets) should decline 15%, equity capital would be wiped out. If losses impair capital and surplus, a bank is likely to be closed by the supervisory authorities. Bankers must, therefore, pay careful attention to the adequacy of their capital to support the risks assumed in their lending and investment operations.

Regulatory authorities in the past used a rule of thumb that capital should represent approximately 9%-10% of deposit liabilities. In 1945, equity capital was below 6%, but the rate was gradually increased in the postwar years to 8%-9% by the reinvestment of earnings and the sale of common stock. In recent years many banks, usually larger banks, have sold capital debentures. These debentures are subordinate to deposits but are creditor claims and, as such, are ahead of stockholders' claims. Banks and regulatory authorities now use the term "capital accounts" to include the debentures in such accounts in calculating the ratio to deposits; but the ratio so calculated is not the same as the ratio of equity capital to deposits, even though the funds obtained from the sale of debentures protect the deposits because of their subordinated nature.

More recent approaches to the evaluation of capital adequacy relate the equity capital to the particular asset components of each particular bank.[1]

---

[1] The capital adequacy formula of the Federal Reserve Bank of New York is as follows:

Classification	Description	Required Percentage of Assets Backed by Capital
Nonrisk Assets	Cash and due from banks, Treasury obligations due within 5 years, and similar high-grade, short-term instruments.	0%

Capital should be equal to at least the total of the percentage of specific assets listed in the footnote table. In 1945 with nonrisk assets (cash and Treasury obligations) representing 78% of total assets and loans representing only 16.3%, the relatively low level of equity capital (5.6% of deposits and about 5.2% of total assets) was not particularly serious, although regulatory authorities expressed strongly their belief that the equity should be increased to around 9%-10% of deposits. However, while the rate of capital accounts to deposits and to total assets has nearly doubled since 1945, the fact that holdings of U.S. Government securities have declined to about 9% or less of assets and loans have recovered to 56% of assets indicates that the equity cushion in relative risk terms has become thinner.

Investment Portfolios of Commercial Banks

Table 31-1 shows that investments of commercial banks in 1972 totaled 25% of bank assets and that securities were divided about 9.2% U.S. Treasury securities and 16.2% other securities. The classification "other securities" in 1972 was represented by approximately 79% of tax-exempt state and local government issues, by 16.5% of issues of federal agencies and federal corporations not guaranteed by the U.S. Government, and by 4.9% of private corporation issues.

The securities of commercial banks can be subdivided into (1) secondary reserves and (2) the investment in other securities or bond account, which can be considered a tertiary reserve. The functions of, the constraints for, and the policies applied to these two accounts are quite different and therefore they will be discussed separately.

Minimum Risk Assets ..	Government and government-guaranteed obligations due in more than 5 years and loans secured by excellent collateral.	5%
Portfolio Assets	Assets representing the usual banking risks, the remainder of the loan portfolio not adversely classified by examiners, and the remainder of the securities portfolio not classified as substandard.	12%
Substandard Assets	Loans and securities classified as more risky than usual banking risks.	20%
Workout Assets	Stocks, defaulted banks, real estate, and all other assets required by examiners to be disposed of promptly.	50%
Banking House Furniture and Equipment	Real property and physical assets used in conducting the banking business.	100%

Source: Howard D. Cross, *Management Policies for Commercial Banks* (Englewood Cliffs, N.J.: Prentice Hall, Inc., 1962), pp. 169 and 173.

Secondary Reserves of Commercial Banks. Primary reserves [2] and secondary reserves must be adequate to meet the liquidity demands of depositors and also to provide funds to meet seasonal and cyclical demands for loans. Primary reserves provide no earnings, and secondary reserves [3] (usually short-term governments) offer lower yields than other investments and loans. The bank manager must maintain appropriate but not excessive liquidity, which will penalize earnings.

Stability and Liquidity of Principal. As previously noted, deposit liabilities of banks are equal to about 82% of assets, and deposit liabilities are payable either on demand (demand deposits) or on short notice. Banks do experience seasonal variations in loans and deposits that at times result in a seasonal outflow of funds. Because of this fact, plus the relatively small amount of capital to absorb losses, commercial banks must secure a great deal of stability and liquidity in the secondary reserve account. They must be able to convert the secondary reserve into cash immediately at any time and with little loss potential in order to provide for cyclical and seasonal outflows of funds. Large amounts are therefore invested in short-term government securities, which usually yield less than long-term securities.

Need for Income and Stability of Income. Since the outstanding need of the secondary reserve account is stability and liquidity of principal, the income factor for the account is distinctly secondary. In fact, commercial banks invest secondary reserves heavily in short-term Treasury securities. A study by the Federal Reserve Bank of Chicago [4] showed that current operating expenses of Seventh Federal Reserve District Member Banks approximated 77% of total current operating income. Income from sources other than security investments amounted to 68% of *total sources* of income, and investment income represented 9%-10% of total *operating* income. These data suggest that stability and size of investment income is not a crucial factor in managing secondary reserves. In any event, whatever rate of return is current on short-term securities at the time funds are invested in secondary reserves must simply be accepted. This means that income may fluctuate constantly in line with short-term fluctuations in yields on short-term Treasury securities. During and for a time after World War

---

[2] Cash items including cash in vault, balances with Federal Reserve banks, deposits with correspondent banks, and cash items in the process of collection.

[3] Specifically defined as short-term, high-grade, highly marketable securities that can be converted into cash quickly and with little or no loss of principal.

[4] "Operating Ratios of Seventh District Member Banks—1965," Federal Reserve Bank of Chicago.

II, this meant for short-term Treasury securities ⅜ of 1% to ⅞ of 1% even though long-term Treasury securities were yielding over 2%. However, in recent years commercial banks have been fortunate in obtaining yields for short-term securities between 4% and 5% and in 1970 over 6%. But these high yields are fortuitous and banks must accept whatever yields are available, for stability of principal and liquidity must take precedence over income in managing secondary reserves. (See Figures 26-1 and 26-2.)

Period and Strength of Ownership. Because of the demand nature (immediate or short-term) of most liabilities and the need to meet seasonal, cyclical, and other demands of depositors and those seeking loans, strength of ownership of investments by commercial banks is weak. Banks must be able at all times to meet these demands; therefore, as discussed previously, there is an overriding need for stability and liquidity of principal in the secondary reserve account. Of course, final liquidity does rest on the ability of the banks to borrow from the Federal Reserve banks, and during the liquidity crisis of 1966 commercial banks did borrow from them quite heavily. (See Table 31-2.) This was even more true in 1970.

Need for Stability of Purchasing Power. The liabilities of commercial banks (mainly deposits) are payable in dollars regardless of the fluctuating purchasing power of the dollar, and therefore there is no need for the bank to consider stability of purchasing power of the principal invested. As long as the original dollars invested or loaned can be recovered, the bank can meet its liabilities. Bank operating expenses do tend to increase with inflation, but so does bank income. Therefore, even from an income standpoint, commercial banks are not particularly vulnerable to inflation.

Financial Risk. A commercial bank cannot accept any real financial risk in its secondary reserve account, and therefore this account is invested almost entirely in short-term Treasury securities.

Interest Rate Risk. Because the secondary reserve must be available for liquidity at any time with little potential for loss, the interest rate risk (price risk due to increases in interest rates) that is assumed must be kept at a minimum. In the case of the 32% of Treasury securities having maturities of 1 year or less, the interest rate risk is minimal. While bank officers will differ as to the extent to which Treasury securities due in from 1 to 5 years (80% of Treasuries) constitute a secondary reserve, certainly as a practical matter such securities in the earlier maturity range of the 1-to-5-year group could be included. With staggered maturities within this group, many banks will consider a large proportion or even all of this classification as part of the secondary reserve. Many bank officers will include maturities of up to 2 years in secondary reserves as a practical matter. It must be noted that in periods of sharply rising interest rates (such as 1966-1970) Treasury securities with maturities of 5 years may decline in market price as much as 5% within one year (and 20-year maturities 10%). Most writers and bank officers consider only maturities of up to 1 year as the secondary reserve and consider the 1-to-5-year category as a tertiary or third reserve. This, in fact, requires a breakdown of securities into three categories:

1. Treasury securities with maturities of 1 year or less—secondary reserves.
2. Treasury securities with maturities of 1-5 years—tertiary reserves.
3. Treasury securities with over 5-year maturities plus other securities (largely tax-exempts)—investment or bond account.

Table 31-4 shows the breakdown of commercial bank holdings of U.S. Government marketable securities as of September 30, 1972, into the various time categories. The total of U.S. Government securities due within 5 years amounted to 84.5%, while the total due within 10 years was 97.3%.

TABLE 31-4

Commercial Bank Holdings of U.S. Government Marketable Securities
September 30, 1972 (Billions of Dollars)

	Total	Within 1 Year			1-5 Years	5-10 Years	10-20 Years	Over 20 Years
		Total	Bills	Other				
Dollars	44.61	13.41	6.08	7.33	24.53	5.74	0.86	0.07
Percentage	100.0	29.9	13.5	16.4	54.6	12.8	1.9	....

Investment Policies for Secondary Reserves. The preceding discussion considered the constraints within which the secondary reserve accounts of commercial banks must be invested. The smaller the size of the secondary reserve account in respect to deposits, to total assets, to risk assets, and to capital, the greater is the need to invest these funds in the shortest of maturities, that is, 1 year or under. The larger the relative size of the secondary reserve, the greater is the opportunity as a practical matter to extend maturities beyond 1 year, accepting the greater interest rate risk inherent in the later maturities beyond 1 year up to 2 years.

In determining the size of the secondary reserve, the bank must calculate its estimated needs for funds to meet seasonal and cyclical deposit withdrawals and seasonal and cyclical loan demands. Such projections need to be constantly reviewed in the light of changing economic conditions. This point was especially true in the years 1966 to 1973. The more accurately a bank officer can project these needs for funds, the more efficiently he can manage the secondary reserve account.

Investment in Other Securities or Bond Account. In addition to the securities that constitute the secondary reserve account of a commercial bank (U.S. Treasury securities with maturities up to a maximum of 1 year, and according to many bank officers, with maturities up to a maximum of 2 years), the bank will have additional investments that constitute its investment in other securities or bond account and that may be considered as a tertiary reserve, a further line of defense behind the secondary reserve. Investments considered a tertiary reserve should be limited to those Treasury securities not included in secondary reserves but should not include the other investments representing about 16.5% of total assets and 65.1% of total security holdings.

The investment in other securities or bond account consists of all Treasury securities above the maximum maturities considered for secondary reserves plus all other securities. If the very broadest classification of above 5 years is accepted for the Treasury securities in this account, it would include the 14.7% of Treasury securities having maturities of over 5 years (consisting of 12.8% with maturities of 5-10 years and 1.9% with maturities of over 10 years) plus all other securities. As shown in Table 31-1, in 1972 the classification "other securities" in total substantially exceeded Treasury securities, representing 16.2% of total assets versus 9.2% for Treasuries. In 1945 the classification "other securities" represented only 4.6% of total assets. In 1969, of the total other securities, 82.1% represented tax-exempt "municipals," 14.6% represented federal agency and federal corporate securities, and only 3.3% represented private corporate securities. There is no question as to the high quality of the federal agency and federal corporate securities. State and local government securities and private corporate securities are usually limited to the highest quality ratings (AAA, AA, and A), although statutory regulations would permit grades through the fourth classification (BBB). Holdings of all types of bonds are largely kept in the maturity range not exceeding 10 years.

One important question is why "other securities," which represented only 4.6% of total assets and only 7.5% of total security investments in 1945, rose to 16.5% of total assets and 65.1% of total security investments by 1973. From 1946 to 1959, other securities had increased from 4.6% of assets to 8.4% of assets. While U.S. Government securities had declined to 24.1% of assets, these holdings were still about three times the holdings of other securities. Then, as commercial banks substantially increased their time deposits by being permitted to pay more competitive rates, they had to offset the resulting rise in interest costs with earning assets that would earn a high enough return after taxes to make it possible to pay the high rates on time deposits, which by 1973 represented 57% of total deposits. Partly, the choice was between mortgages and tax-exempt securities. As the rate on AAA tax-exempt securities rose to the 6.1% level in 1970 values, these securities became more and more attractive as earning assets. At a 48% corporate tax rate, a 5% yield on tax-exempts is equal to a 5% rate in 1972 on taxable bonds and investments. Essentially, this was the major reason for the substantial absolute and relative increase in holdings of "other securities." In 1973, tax-exempt securities represented 80% of other securities.

The record of net investments in securities by commercial banks from 1963 to 1972 is presented in Table 31-5. On December 31, 1960, commercial bank holdings of Treasury securities were $61.0 billion and in January, 1972, they were $62.8 billion for little net change during the period. However, an inspection of Table 31-5 indicates that commercial banks used their portfolios of U.S. Government securities to adjust to their needs for funds. In the expansion years they decreased their holdings, and in the mini-recession year of 1967 and the recession of 1970, they increased their holdings. Also, in the early stages of recovery, such as in 1971, loan demand was sluggish and consequently banks increased their holdings of government securities.

TABLE 31-5

Net Investment of Funds by Commercial Banks and Affiliates, 1963-1972 (Billions of Dollars)

| | Net Purchases by Commercial Banks | | | | Net Increase in State & Local Govt's. Net Long-Term Financing | |
Year	U. S. Govt. Securities	Federal Agency Securities	State & Local Government Securities	Corp. Bonds		% of Purchases by Commercial Banks
	$	$	$	$	$	
1963	−3.0	0.3	5.2	. . .	6.2	83.9
1964	−0.2	0.6	3.6	0.1	6.0	60.0
1965	−3.1	0.8	5.1	−0.1	7.6	67.1
1966	−3.3	−0.2	1.9	0.1	6.4	29.7
1967	+6.4	3.0	9.0	. . .	8.8	102.3
1968	+2.2	1.3	8.6	. . .	9.9	86.8
1969	−9.2	−0.2	0.4	. . .	8.5	0.5
1970	+5.9	3.5	10.7	0.2	13.9	86.0
1971	+2.3	3.6	13.7	1.3	20.6	61.7
1972E	1.5	3.0	6.7	0.5	15.0	44.7

E = estimated.

Source: *The Investment Outlook* (New York: Bankers Trust Company).

On the other hand, commercial bank holdings of other securities increased steadily year after year. Their net holdings of state and local government securities increased net $46.4 billion from December 31, 1963, to January, 1973. Their holdings of federal *agency* securities increased $12.0 billion in the same period, but their holdings of private corporate bonds remained essentially unchanged.

Investment in Other Securities for Income. Commercial bank investments in other securities (16% of total assets) are considered by some as tertiary reserves as these securities consist of quality investments—17% federal agency issues, 79% tax-exempts, "other" largely corporates, 4%, almost all in the top quality ranges of AAA, AA, and A, with maturities generally not exceeding 10 years. However, even during the greatest economic expansion on record (second quarter of 1961 into the third quarter of 1969), and even during the liquidity crisis and credit crunches of 1966 and 1970, commercial banks in total did not liquidate their net amount of other securities including tax-exempts. However, some banks did liquidate during the tight money period of 1966 to satisfy the needs for funds, and they learned that liquidity and marketability of tax-exempts was not nearly so satisfactory as for Treasury securities.

Stability of Principal. While the investment in other securities or bond account (as opposed to the short-term investment account) may be considered to some extent a tertiary reserve for commercial banks, in total it is not usually used in this manner and therefore the considerations of stability of principal, marketability, and liquidity are not nearly as strong as in the secondary reserve account. The federal agency issues (17% of the bond account) are certainly of high quality and provide relative stability of principal. The tax-exempts, which are invested in the top-quality grade, also provide stability of principal. In both cases, however, marketability is poorer than for Treasury securities.

While the requirement for stability of principal is not as great in the investment in other securities or bond account as it is in the secondary reserve account, it is important because the securities in this account are largely considered as reserves against time deposits and in this respect the thin equity of the bank does require investment in quality issues. It is recognized that the marketability of the tax-exempt securities held is not overall as good as the marketability of Treasury securities, but the problem is not as important as for the secondary reserve account invested in Treasury securities. Generally, in their investment in other securities or bond accounts, the banks follow a policy of wide diversification mainly in tax-

exempt securities, which together with the investment in quality issues keeps
the financial risk to a minimum.

Size and Stability of Income. The major reasons for the very large increase in the investment accounts since 1962, as previously noted, were the
substantial increase in time deposits, which by 1969 exceeded demand
deposits and in 1972 were 56% of total deposits, and the high rate
(4½%-7½%) that had to be paid on these time deposits.[5] There was a need
for income, and the tax-exempts were acquired to provide this income. Tax-
exempts yielded 5.4% on the average in 1969, 6.4% in 1970, and 5.3%
in 1972 which represented the approximate equivalent of 11.5%-12.5% on
investments subject to tax. The high rates paid by banks to attract time
deposits also require stability of income in the bond account. However,
profits have been squeezed in some years.

Interest Rate Risk. In the secondary reserve account there is a need to
keep the interest rate risk to a minimum, and income is distinctly of secondary importance. Whatever yield is available within the maturity classification requirement is accepted. However, in the investment in other securities
or bond account, the need for income is important, and therefore there is
a heavy investment in tax-exempts. Banks minimize the interest rate risk
by heavy short-term holdings in the secondary reserve account and by
diversification by maturities, with the great majority of issues being under
five-year maturity.

Purchasing Power Risk. As with the secondary reserve account and all
other assets of a commercial bank, there is no requirement to consider the
purchasing power of principal because of the nature of the liabilities of the
bank, which are simply claims to stated dollar amounts.

Investment Policies for Investment in Other Securities or Bond Account.
This account should be invested in high-quality issues: federal agency
securities and tax-exempts in the top three quality ratings. It is invested in
longer maturities than is the case with secondary reserve accounts. The
banks will usually stagger the maturities within the maturity range, for the
most part up to 10-year maturities. The interest rate risk (the primary
risk in the long-term investments) is generally handled by spacing maturities
and investing funds as available within this spacing structure. Only a relatively small proportion, if any, of the investment account should be invested

---

[5] Legal maximum: savings deposits, 5%; CD's, 90 days to one year, 5½%;
one year to 2½ years, 6% (1973).

in corporate securities. Financial risk is very small in the investment in other securities and bond accounts because of their high quality.

Certain commercial banks will not entirely ignore the opportunity to post a better-than-average performance by handling all investments within a fairly rigid formula of spaced maturities. Because of the constraints described above, banks do not really have the opportunity to shift portfolios back and forth radically from short to longer maturities in order to secure profits based on changes in the pattern of interest rates. However, with a portion of their portfolios they may attempt to shift the schedule of maturities in line with their expectation of changes in the yield, going out a little longer when they expect rates to decline and shorter when they expect rates to rise. There is a potential for a significant improvement in investment performance if forecasts of interest rate changes are accurate. However, most banks approach this problem cautiously because of the difficulties of managing a portfolio in this manner as shown by long years of experience. The changing pattern of yields in 1966-1973 highlights the risk and the difficulties in this area.

Regulation of Bank Investments

Commercial banks are strictly regulated in their investments. The three federal regulatory agencies have agreed on a uniform regulation governing bank investments, and most state regulatory boards have followed suit. The regulations require that investments be limited to bonds in the top four quality ratings by the rating agencies. However, because relatively few corporate bonds are held in the portfolios and because the tax-exempts held usually are in the top three quality ratings, the regulations do not pose much of a problem. Since the 1930s and the banking debacle that occurred then, commercial banks have almost unanimously been more conservative in the handling of their investment portfolios than the regulations require.

Because bank investments meet the requirements of the regulatory authorities, banks are permitted to *carry their investments at amortized costs rather than at market*. This eliminates the need to reflect changes in market prices such as occurred in 1966-1970 and 1973 when bond prices declined substantially. Amortized cost means cost less systematic amortization of any premium paid above par.

If any substandard bonds or securities are included in the portfolio, they are not valued at current market price but instead are valued at the average of the market price during the previous 18 months. Only half of any depreciation in value so calculated must be charged as a loss of principal against corporate accounts.

Gains and Losses on Security Sales

Typically, commercial banks have funds to increase holdings substantially in recessions when interest rates are low and bond prices are high, and they have the need to sell investments to meet demands for loans during periods of business expansion when interest rates are high and bond prices are low. A special provision in the tax law applying only to commercial banks recognizes the characteristics of their operations and eases the impact of net losses realized in low and declining-price bond markets. Banks are permitted to charge the full amount of losses on securities sold against taxable income and to include only one half of realized capital gains on securities held more than 6 months in taxable income. A bank could realize a capital gain of $2,000, of which only $1,000 would be subject to tax. Assuming a 48% tax rate applicable to the bank, the tax liability would be $480. If these funds were then invested in a new issue that declined $2,000 in price, the bank could realize a loss of $2,000, which would result in a tax saving of $960. This feature does encourage bankers to sell when prices are relatively high in order to realize the capital gain and to repurchase similar issues (or the same issues after 31 days). If the issues acquired in repurchase later decline in price to the original cost of the issues on which the capital gain was realized, the ability to fully deduct the loss from taxable income results in a gain to the bank. But, as with other investors, all losses must first be matched against capital gains, if any, in that fiscal year.

Sophisticated bank management is well aware of the benefits of taking realized losses by making shifts in portfolios to take advantage of the special provision in the tax laws. A bank can maintain its portfolio of securities intact, but by switching issues it can take losses and use these losses to reduce its tax liabilities. Poor bank management considers it a negative factor to show realized losses and tries to avoid taking such losses in spite of the tax advantage. Switching issues to take losses will leave the portfolio in the same basic position while still utilizing the tax advantage of realized losses.

PORTFOLIO POLICIES OF MUTUAL SAVINGS BANKS

Mutual savings banks are the oldest type of savings institution in the United States. They receive deposits and invest the deposits in mortgages and bonds. Essentially all (98%) of their liabilities are time deposits. Being mutual institutions, they have no capital stock. The difference between assets and liabilities is the surplus of the bank. Almost all the mutual savings banks are located in the New England area and in New York and

New Jersey. These banks are chartered by the states and are regulated by state statutes and state agencies. Most mutual savings banks (those holding 87% of the total assets of mutual savings banks) are members of the Federal Deposit Insurance Corporation and are subject to its supervision as well as state supervision. Some belong to the Federal Home Loan Bank System.

Table 31-6 shows the assets of mutual savings banks in selected years. Mutual savings banks do not experience much total volatility in deposits, but they have a rather steady growth in their deposits.[6] Consequently the

TABLE 31-6

Assets of Mutual Savings Banks—Selected Years (Millions of Dollars)

Type of Asset	Dec., 1950		Dec., 1960		Dec., 1968		Sept., 1972	
	$	%	$	%	$	%	$	%
Cash	792	3.5	874	2.2	996	1.4	1,361	1.4
Securities:								
U.S. Governments ...	10,887	48.6	6,243	15.4	3,834	5.4	3,393	3.4
State & Municipals ..	96	0.4	672	1.7	194	0.3	843	0.9
Corporate & Other ..	2,260	10.1	5,076	12.5	10,180*	14.3	21,556	21.9
Loans:								
Mortgages	8,039	35.8	26,702	65.7	53,286	74.9	65,826	66.9
Other	127	0.5	416	1.0	1,407	2.0	3,421	3.5
Other Assets	255	1.1	589	1.5	1,235	1.7	1,992	2.0
Total Assets	22,446	100.0	40,571	100.0	71,152	100.0	98,392	100.0

* In 1968 the corporate securities figure of $10,180 consisted of corporate debt instruments, 80%, and corporate stocks, 20%.

Source: *Federal Reserve Bulletin,* December, 1972.

[6] The annual percentage increase in regular deposits of mutual savings banks was as follows:

1947—5.5%	1952—8.1%	1957—5.5%	1961—5.3%	1965— 7.4%	1969— 3.9%
1948—3.5	1953—7.8	1958—7.4	1962—8.0	1966— 4.9	1970— 6.8
1949—4.8	1954—8.0	1959—3.6	1963—7.9	1967—10.0	1971—13.8
1950—3.8	1955—7.0	1960—3.9	1964—9.6	1968— 7.3	1972—11.2
1951—4.3	1956—6.6				

In certain years like 1959, 1960, 1966, 1970, and 1973, competitive yields in the capital markets, especially in the case of Treasury securities, slowed the deposit growth. Furthermore, there is usually a seasonal decline in April of each year, probably reflecting withdrawals for federal tax payments. In 1971-1972 a major inflow of funds occurred.

banks keep only a small proportion of assets in cash. This proportion has been steadily declining since 1950, from 3.5% in 1950 to 2.2% in 1960 and to only 1.4% in 1968 and 1.4% in September, 1972.

Functions of Mutual Savings Banks

The major function of mutual savings banks is to invest in mortgages. Because mortgage loans were not available in sufficient quantity up to 1946 during World War II, only 25% of assets were invested in mortgages versus 62% in U. S. Government securities and 70% in total securities. However, by 1973 holdings of securities as a percentage of assets had declined to 26.2% of assets. Conversely, holdings of mortgages were 66.9% of total assets in 1973.

Prior to World War II and for a period in the post-war years 1953-1961, holdings of state and municipal securities ranged between 1% and 2% of assets. The dollar amount was reduced from $677 million in 1961 (1.6% of assets) to $190 million (only .3% of assets) in 1969 but rose to $843 million in September, 1972. Corporate and "other" securities rose gradually from 6.6% of assets in 1945 to 10.1% in 1950 and to 22% in 1972.

Investment Constraints of Mutual Savings Banks

The most important investment constraints of mutual savings banks are discussed in the following paragraphs.

Stability of Principal. Mutual savings banks must seek stability and safety of principal because deposit liabilities make up the bulk of the offset to assets. The surplus cushion (general reserves) of mutual savings banks to absorb losses (only 7% of assets in 1972) is somewhat less than the equity cushion of commercial banks, which emphasizes the small margin to offset losses in assets. The fact that the primary reserves of the mutual savings banks (cash) were only 1.4% of assets in 1972 versus about 15% of assets for commercial banks also emphasizes the need for stability and liquidity of principal and inability to risk losses in the securities account.

Finally, the fact that only 22% of assets are invested in securities (only 5.4% in Treasury securities) while 67% of assets are invested in mortgages (risk assets) proves that mutual savings banks have somewhat more at risk than commercial banks. It can be argued that, on the average, there may be less risk with mortgage investments than with large loans other than mortgages; however, this is a debatable point except in the area of government guaranteed mortgages.

Stability and Size of Income. Because 92% of a mutual savings bank's liabilities plus surplus is represented by savings accounts on which interest must be paid, stability of income is required. To meet competition, mutual savings banks have had to increase their rates on deposits. The gap between the rate of income earned on assets and the rate paid on deposits declined from 1.15% in 1951 and 0.87% in 1959 to 0.44% in 1967, but recovered to 1% by 1971. The rate of income earned and the competitive rate paid on deposits are highly important to savings banks.

Table 31-7 shows the rate of return on assets and the rate of return paid on deposits by mutual savings banks over a period of years. It is clear from this table that the gap between interest paid on deposits and the rate earned on assets narrowed and then recovered by 1971.

TABLE 31-7

Rate of Return on Assets and Average Annual Rate of Return
Paid on Deposits by Mutual Savings Banks

Year	Rate of Return on Assets			Average Annual Rate Paid on Deposits	Difference Between Rates Earned on Assets and Rates Paid on Deposits
	Mortgages	Securities	Total		
1955	4.25	2.79	3.33	2.64	.69
1956	4.33	2.88	3.65	2.77	.88
1957	4.39	3.01	3.80	2.94	.86
1958	4.50	3.17	3.90	3.07	.85
1959	4.63	3.31	4.08	3.19	.87
1960	4.75	3.49	4.25	3.47	.78
1961	4.89	3.62	4.41	3.55	.86
1962	5.02	3.76	4.56	3.85	.71
1963	5.13	3.83	4.68	3.96	.72
1964	5.18	3.96	4.70	4.06	.73
1965	5.22	4.07	4.89	4.11	.78
1966	5.30	4.29	5.03	4.45	.58
1967	5.41	4.53	5.18	4.74	.44
1968	5.56	4.94	5.38	4.76	.62
1969	5.77	5.37	5.65	4.89	.76
1970	5.97	5.64	5.88	5.01	.87
1971	6.13	6.00	6.13	5.13	1.00

Source: *National Fact Book, Mutual Savings Banking,* National Association of Mutual Savings Banks, New York.

Purchasing Power Risk. Because of the nature of their business and the fact that offsets to assets are fixed-dollar deposits, there is no requirement to protect the purchasing power of investments in assets.

Tenure of Ownership. Because of the steady and regular annual increase in deposits (except for April of each year), mutual savings banks have a strong tenure of ownership. However, the requirement for income has forced these banks to sell U. S. Government securities year after year and also required a decline in the holdings of state and municipal securities after 1958 and especially after 1961.

Tax Factor and Tax-Exempt Securities. Most mutual savings banks either pay no income taxes or have only very small amounts of their income subject to income taxes. They pay an income tax only on income remaining *after* interest payments on deposits, *after* transfers to surplus accounts, and *after* transfers to loan investment reserves. As long as surplus and reserves amount to less than 12% of deposits, they pay no tax on the income transferred to surplus and reserve accounts. For the industry as a whole, surplus and reserve accounts have historically been considerably below 12% and only in the decade after World War II did they approach the 12% figure. By 1973, the percentage had declined to 7%.

There is, therefore, little advantage to holding tax-exempt securities; in fact, it is a disadvantage, as higher rates can be earned on other investments and on mortgages. There was a sharp drop in these securities held by mutual savings banks from $729 million in 1958 to only $190 million in 1969. A recovery to $843 million had occurred by 1972, but they still amounted to less than 1% of assets.

Investment Policies of Mutual Savings Banks

Security investments of mutual savings banks have gradually been reduced from 70% of assets in 1945 to about 60% in 1950, to about 30% in 1960, and to 26% in 1972 as the pressures to increase income have necessitated the increase in mortgages to 67% of assets. Security investments are limited to U.S. Government securities, 3.4% of assets; corporate securities, 21.9% of assets; and state and municipal securities, 0.9% of assets.

Policy Regarding U.S. Government Securities. Investment policy has considerably reduced mutual savings bank holdings of U.S. Government securities until they represented only 3.4% of assets in 1972. Table 31-8 shows the net reduction in holdings of U.S. Government securities by mutual savings banks. Table 31-9 shows the maturity distribution. Total U.S. governments declined from $11.5 billion in 1946 to $2.4 billion in 1971.

TABLE 31-8

Net Annual Reduction in Holdings of U.S. Government Securities
by Mutual Savings Banks (Millions of Dollars)

1948—$ 475	1953—$252	1958—$313	1963—$244	1968—$ 485
1949— 64	1954— 436	1959— 337	1964— 72	1969— −593
1950— 567	1955— 291	1960— 628	1965— 306	1970— −186
1951— 1050	1956— 481	1961— 83	1966— 721	1971— +183
1952— 388	1957— 400	1962— 313	1967— 445	1972— +105

Source: *National Fact Book, Mutual Savings Banking,* National Association of Mutual Savings Banks, New York.

TABLE 31-9

Holdings of Marketable U.S. Government Securities by Mutual Savings Banks
by Maturity and Type of Issue
Selected Year-End Dates 1946-1972
Percentage Distribution

| Year | Total | Years To Maturity | | | | | Type of Issue | | | |
		Less Than 1	1 to 5	0 to 5	5-10	10 and Over	Treasury Bills	Certificates of Indebtedness	Notes	Bonds
1946	100.0	3.6%	3.5%	7.1%	15.6%	77.3%	. . .	2.2%	1.8%	95.9%
1950	100.0	.9	7.3	8.2	1.0	90.8	.3%	.1	1.3	98.3
1960	100.0	8.1	26.0	34.1	31.1	34.8	2.4	2.4	20.0	75.1
1966	100.0	14.2	32.7	46.9	25.1	27.9	8.8	.6	13.2	77.4
1967	100.0	17.8	36.6	54.4	17.5	28.1	10.9	. . .	22.3	66.8
1968	100.0	19.8	31.8	51.5	20.1	28.4	9.5	. . .	34.4	56.1
1969	100.0	17.1	42.6	59.7	9.0	31.3	5.1	. . .	40.1	54.8
1970	100.0	19.1	42.6	61.7	12.3	26.0	6.2	. . .	45.9	47.8
1971	100.0	15.2	44.5	59.7	18.2	22.1	8.6	. . .	53.5	38.0
1972	100.0	15.3	44.5	59.8	18.2	22.0	6.7	. . .	53.1	40.2

Source: *National Fact Book, Mutual Savings Banking,* National Association of Mutual Savings Banks, New York, and *Federal Reserve Bulletin,* December, 1972.

There has clearly been a shift to shorter-term U.S. Government securities in the postwar years that has accompanied both the substantial decline in holdings of such securities and also the major decline in such securities as a percentage of assets. In 1972, 60% of U.S. Government securities had maturities of 5 years or less compared with only 7.1% in 1946, 11.6% in 1955, and 41.1% in 1965. Conversely, holdings with maturities of 10 years or over have declined from 90.8% in 1950 to 22% in 1972. As holdings of U.S. Government securities have been reduced, it has been judicious to concentrate 60% in the 5-year-and-under category. This compares with 84.5% in the 5-year-and-under category for commercial banks. The difference represents the fact that mutual savings banks have no demand deposits and that, while their deposits are payable immediately in practice if not legally, the volatility of these deposits is much less than for demand deposits in commercial banks. Furthermore, while the proportion in the 10-year-and-over category has been reduced to 22%, it compares to an insignificant 1.9% for commercial banks.

Policy Regarding State and Local Government Securities. As previously discussed, most mutual savings banks pay no income tax; therefore, there is little if any justification for holding tax-exempt securities.

Policy Regarding Corporate and Other Securities. Unlike commercial banks, mutual savings banks hold corporate securities as an important portion of their investment accounts. In 1972, corporate securities amounted to 22% of total assets, or about 6 times the holdings of U.S. Government securities. Corporate securities represent about 83.6% of all types of security investments.

The corporate securities held by mutual savings banks represent a well-diversified list of high-quality securities. In 1972, of the total of $21.6 billion of corporate securities held, about 86% consisted of corporate debt issues and about 14% consisted of corporate stock issues. Therefore, corporate stock issues ($3 billion in 1972) represented about 14% of corporate issues and about 12% of all security investments, including U.S. Government and tax-exempt securities in 1972.

The pressure for income has resulted in the sizable purchase of a well-diversified list of high-quality corporate debt issues, since their yields are higher than the yields of Treasury securities. Holdings of corporate bonds consisted of approximately 45% utility bonds, 6% railroad bonds, and 14% industrial bonds for a total of 65% of total corporate holdings. The balance of 35% consisted mainly of International Bank bonds and Canadian Government bonds, together with other bonds not classified. Even though there is no need to consider the purchasing power risk, mutual savings banks have now invested about 12% of their total securities in equities (essentially stock of commercial banks) and these represent 3.5% of total assets.

Because of the consistent growth of assets and deposits, mutual savings banks can consider investment as permanent and therefore can purchase long-term issues and some equities. Furthermore, these securities need not be as marketable as U.S. Government securities. If they are sold, they are sold in the regular course of portfolio operations, as with other investors, and they are not subject to sudden and forced sale for liquidity purposes.

Regulatory authorities have defined what is legal for mutual fund investors, and portfolio policy must always confine investments to be within these regulations.

PORTFOLIO POLICIES OF SAVINGS AND LOAN ASSOCIATIONS

As with mutual savings banks, the major functions of savings and loan associations are to receive deposits and to invest in mortgages. However, there are some important differences.

Table 31-10 shows the distribution of assets of savings and loan associations. By 1969, savings and loan associations had increased the proportion of their assets invested in mortgages to 84.5%, which compares with 67% for mutual savings banks.

Investment Constraints of Savings and Loan Associations

Savings and loan associations' proportions of assets in cash have been consistently declining, falling to 1% by 1973.

Savings and loan associations normally do not have a *major need* for investment liquidity because of their consistent net growth in savings capital. They do have a heavy turnover ratio, averaging about 30% except for the exceptional years of disintermediation of 1966 (37%), 1970 (39%), and 1973. The consistent growth of net annual savings receipts for savings and loan associations is shown in Table 31-11. Ordinarily, because of the steady net inflow from savings funds and from amortization of mortgages, there is not much call for liquidity.

In certain periods, such as 1966-1967, 1969-1970, and 1973 rates in the capital market were more attractive and savings and loan associations experienced heavy withdrawals. In July, 1969, they had a net loss in savings

TABLE 31-10

Assets of Savings and Loan Associations (Millions of Dollars)

Type of Asset	1944 $	1944 %	1950 $	1950 %	1960 $	1960 %	1971 $	1971 %	Oct. 1972 $	Oct. 1972 %
Cash & Bank Deposits	450	5.1	924	5.5	2,680	3.7	2,783	1.3	2,265	1.0
Investment Securities	2,456	28.1	1,532	9.1	5,208	7.3	18,293	8.9	22,394	9.4
Mortgage Loans	5,521	63.1	13,749	81.4	60,070	84.1	174,385	84.5	200,563	84.4
FHLB Stock	72	0.8	177	1.0	978	1.4	1,550	0.8	1,841	0.8
Real Estate Owned	33	0.4	21	0.1	158	0.2	700	0.3	716	0.3
Other Assets	215	2.5	490	2.9	2,382	3.3	8,592	4.2	9,904	4.2
Total Assets	8,747	100.0	16,893	100.0	71,476	100.0	206,308	100.0	237,683	100.0
Investment Securities	2,420		1,487		4,595		18,293		22,394	
U.S. Gov't. Securities	2,420		1,487		4,595					

Note: Beginning with 1964, "U.S. Govt. Securities" includes other investments previously under "Other Assets."

Beginning with reporting requirements for 1971 classification, "U.S. Govt. Securities" changed to "Investment Securities" which includes U.S. Government and U.S. Agency securities and bankers' acceptances. However, the great majority are U.S. Govts.

TABLE 31-11

Net Savings Receipts of Savings and Loan Associations, 1945-1972 (Billions of Dollars)

1945	$1.04	1951	$2.08	1957	$4.77	1963	$11.07	1969	$ 4.08
1946	1.14	1952	3.08	1958	6.06	1964	10.59	1970	11.02
1947	1.16	1953	3.64	1959	6.60	1965	8.51	1971	28.25
1948	1.15	1954	4.42	1960	7.56	1966	3.62	1972	32.82
1949	1.45	1955	4.89	1961	8.69	1967	10.72		
1950	1.49	1956	5.01	1962	9.51	1968	7.48		

Source: *Savings and Loan Fact Book,* U.S. Savings and Loan League, Chicago, Ill., and *Investment Outlook,* February, 1972, Bankers Trust Co.

capital (total deposits) of $1.1 billion and in January, 1970, a net loss of $1.4 billion. These heavy net withdrawals, together with mortgage commitments that had to be met, caused the savings and loan associations to borrow heavily from their Federal Home Loan banks to offset withdrawal demands. For example, on December 31, 1966, Federal Home Loan advances were $1 billion higher than a year earlier; and these advances rose from $5,259 million on December 31, 1968, to $10,165 million on December 31, 1970. By May, 1972, they were down to $5,825 million but rose to $10.2 billion in May, 1973. In 1966, mortgage loans rose to 100.51% of savings capital and borrowing rose to 6.53% of savings capital, as shown in Table 31-12.

TABLE 31-12

Savings and Loan Associations
Percent of Selected Items to Savings Capital (Deposits), 1966-1972

	1966	1967	1968	1972
Mortgage Loans & Contracts	100.51	97.86	99.36	99.95
Cash & U.S. Govt. Obligations	9.70	10.16	9.49	12.08
FHLB Advances & Other Borrowings .	6.53	3.80	4.31	5.21
General Reserves & Surplus	7.96	7.67	7.83	7.56

Source: *Savings and Loan Fact Book,* U.S. Savings and Loan League, Chicago, Ill., and Federal Reserve Bulletins.

Because of the relatively low percentage of cash to total assets of 1.3% and the relatively low percentage of U.S. Government securities to assets of 7.4% (about half the 3.6% for mutual savings banks), the security investments of savings and loan associations must be of the highest quality with high liquidity and marketability. This fact, together with the 84.6% of assets invested in mortgages and coupled with the low percentage of reserves and surplus savings (deposits) of only 7.6% (somewhat below the 8.8% for mutual savings banks in 1972), emphasizes the inability of savings and loan associations to accept risk in security investments and their need for high quality, liquidity, and marketability.

Investment Policies of Savings and Loan Associations

In mid-1972 the U.S. Savings and Loan League stated:

> The government security and investment portfolio of savings and loan associations represents the second largest asset classification. The third is cash on hand and in banks. While associations can legally purchase many kinds of securities, the bulk of the investment portfolio represents required liquid holdings. Vault cash and demand deposits in banks provide working funds and also count toward liquidity.
>
> Liquidity requirements first were written into the Federal Home Loan Bank Act in 1950. A major amendment in 1968 served to redefine the maturity mix of investments qualifying as legal liquidity.
>
> The FHLB act and the regulations of the FHLB Board determine the composition and maturity of legal liquid investments and specify the required liquidity ratio. This ratio is defined as the percentage relationship between the dollar value of legal liquidity holdings and the total of withdrawable savings account balances and short-term borrowings. Acceptable liquid investments include vault cash, FHLB and commercial bank demand deposits, U.S. government obligations and government agency issues, and bankers' acceptances.
>
> The Board is empowered by law to vary the liquidity ratio between 4% and 10%. The required level of minimum liquidity was changed by the Board on three occasions in 1971. Effective April 1, the overall liquidity ratio for associations was raised from 5.5% to 6.5%. On May 1, it was increased from 6.5% to 7.5% and then cut back to 7% on August 27.
>
> Current regulations require that at least 3% of the total be held in short-term investments. No more than 0.5% of the required 7% can be held in U.S. Government obligations with a remaining maturity of more than seven years.[7]

Due to changed regulations, U.S. Government securities are no longer listed separately; but investment securities, $22 billion or 9% of assets in January, 1973, consisted mainly of 90% U.S. Government securities (see Table 31-13).

Probably as a result of the liquidity crisis of 1966 and 1969-1970 and of bond requirements, savings and loan associations raised the total percentage of U.S. Government securities due in less than seven years to below the 82% figure for commercial banks. On the other hand, while the maturities

---

[7] *Savings and Loan Fact Book,* 1972. (Chicago: U.S. Savings and Loan League, 1972).

TABLE 31-13

Maturity Distribution of Holdings of U.S. Government Securities
by Savings and Loan Associations

	1965		1966		1967		1969*
	$	%	$	%	$	%	%
Due in 1 year or less	1.36	19.3	1.70	22.9	2.58	29.0	26.9
Due in 1 to 5 years	1.98	28.1	2.56	34.5	3.64	40.9	34.7
Due in 0 to 5 years	3.34	47.4	4.26	57.4	6.22	69.9	61.6
Due in 5 to 10 years	2.52	35.8	2.00	27.0	1.51	17.0	22.0
Due in more than 10 years	1.18	16.8	1.16	15.7	1.16	13.0	16.4
Total U. S. Governments ..	7.04	100.0	7.41	100.0	8.89	100.0	100.0

* January. Only marketable debt.
Source: *Savings and Loan Fact Book,* U.S. Savings and Loan League, Chicago, Ill.

due in more than 10 years are negligible for commercial banks, they
represented 16% of U.S. Government securities for savings and loan
associations.

Investments of savings and loan companies in securities other than U.S.
Governments are shown in Table 31-14. These other investments in total
represent only about 1% of total assets of savings and loan associations but
about 12% of total security investments.

TABLE 31-14

Other Investments of Savings and Loan Associations

	1965 %	1966 %	1967 %	1973 %
FHLB Obligations	38.6	38.9	19.0	18.0
Obligations of Other Federal Agencies ..	26.3	33.1	46.6	50.1
Obligations of State and Municipals ...	10.9	8.0	5.6	4.5
Time Certificates of Deposit, etc., Commercial Banks	8.7	10.3	20.2	21.0
All Other Investments	15.4	9.6	8.5	6.4
Total Other Investments	100.0	100.0	100.0	100.0
Other Investments as % of Total Assets	0.6%	0.7%	0.9%	

Source: *Savings and Loan Fact Book,* U.S. Savings and Loan League, Chicago, Ili.

Investment policy towards the other investments have changed significantly since 1965-1967. Holdings of Federal Home Loan Bank obligations declined, while holdings of other federal agency securities rose and holdings of time certificates of deposit, etc., rose significantly. The problem is to hold these investments in high-quality assets but to earn somewhat more on them than on U.S. Government securities.

QUESTIONS

1. Discuss the effects of the functions and the methods of operation of a commercial bank on its investment policy.

2. (a) How does the character of a commercial bank's deposits affect its investment policy?

   (b) What important change occurred in the makeup of commercial bank deposits by 1968? What implications did this have for investment policy?

3. How does the ratio of loans to total assets and to deposits affect the character of the loan portfolio of commercial banks?

4. (a) How would you judge capital adequacy of a commercial bank?

   (b) What has happened to the capital adequacy of commercial banks since World War II?

5. Do commercial banks have a strong investment constraint in terms of need for stability of principal? of income? Explain and distinguish between secondary reserves and the remainder of the investment account in your answer.

6. (a) Is the purchasing power risk a serious problem for commercial banks? Explain.

   (b) How do banks combat the interest rate risk?

7. (a) Explain the rapid rise in relative importance of "other securities" to commercial banks from 1946 to 1968.

   (b) In view of the high tax-equivalent yields offered by state and local securities, why should commercial banks not replace all Treasury securities with these securities?

8. (a) Contrast the investment policies of mutual savings banks with the investment policies of commercial banks. What important differences do you find?

   (b) Discuss the main investment constraints of mutual savings banks.

9. What has happened to the gap between the rate of income earned on assets and the rate paid on deposits by mutual savings banks during

the 1960s? What significance does this have for the investment policies of these institutions?

10. Contrast the investment policies of savings and loan associations with those of mutual savings banks and commercial banks. What important differences do you find?

WORK-STUDY PROBLEMS

1. (a) Determine the legal restrictions on investments in your state of: (1) savings banks, (2) state-chartered commercial banks, and (3) savings and loan associations.
   (b) Compare and contrast the restrictions found.
   (c) Do you believe the restrictions are well-founded? Discuss.

2. Select *one* of the three types of financial institutions in this chapter for the following assignment. Specify the size and the type of financial institution.
   (a) Explain the portfolio policies recommended for your particular financial institution.
   (b) List the major categories and the amounts of financial assets of the institution chosen.
   (c) List the actual securities held by the institution.
   (d) Recommend an actual list of security investments from the security holdings, arranged by maturity distribution.
   (e) Explain why the particular maturity distribution of investments was determined and why each security was placed in the portfolio.

SUGGESTED READINGS

Andersen, Leonall C. "Import of Monetary Policies on the Growth of Banking in the 70's." *The Financial Analysts Journal* (July, 1971), pp. 45-48.

Goldfield, S. M., and D. M. Jaffre. "The Determinants of Deposit—Rate Setting by Savings and Loan Associations." *The Journal of Finance* (June, 1972), pp. 51-55.

Jacobs, Donald P., and Almarin Phillips. "The Commission on Financial Structures and Regulations: Its Organization and Recommendations. *The Journal of Finance* (May, 1972), pp. 319-340.

Jones, L. D. "Some Contributions of the Institutional Investor Study." *The Journal of Finance* (May, 1972), pp. 305-318.

Klein, Michael A. "On the Causes and Consequences of Savings and Loan Deposit Rate Inflexibility." *The Journal of Finance* (March, 1972), pp. 79-88.

Kwon, Jene K., and Richard M. Thornton. "An Evaluation of the Competitive Effect of FHLB Open-Market Operations on Savings In-flows of Savings and Loan Associations." *The Journal of Finance* (June, 1971), pp. 699-712.

Morrissey, Thomas F. "The Demand for Mortgage Loans and the Concomitant Demand for Home Loan Bank Advances by Savings and Loan Association." *The Journal of Finance* (June, 1971), pp. 687-698.

Murphy, Neil B. "The Demand for New York State Mutual Fund Deposits." *The Journal of Finance* (June, 1971), pp. 713-718.

Robichek, Alexander, and Alan B. Coleman. *Management of Financial Institutions, Notes and Cases.* New York: Holt, Rinehart and Winston, 1967. Chapters 5 and 6.

U.S. Savings and Loan League, Chicago, Illinois. *National Fact Book, Mutual Savings Banking, New York National Association of Mutual Savings Banks* (Annual issues), and *Savings and Loan Fact Book.*

Insurance Companies, Pension Funds, and Nonprofit Organizations

There are important differences in the constraints for investment policies of the contractual type of institutions as opposed to the deposit type of financial institutions discussed in the previous chapter. In the latter case the bulk of the assets are offsets to demand liabilities, while in the former case the bulk of the liabilities are long-term liabilities. This has a major impact on portfolio policies in respect to liquidity and marketability.

PORTFOLIO POLICIES OF LIFE INSURANCE COMPANIES

The income of life insurance companies is 75% premium income and 21% net investment earnings, and other income, 4%. Of each dollar of income, approximately 25 cents flows into additions to policy reserve and surplus—21½ cents into additions to special reserves and 3½ cents into surplus funds. This amount of 25 cents of each dollar of income plus receipts from amortization of loans represents the amount available for additional investments. Table 32-1 shows estimates of cash flow for market investment for all United States life insurance companies in recent years.

Sources of Funds of Life Insurance Companies

Table 32-2 shows sources and uses of funds of life insurance companies. For 1972 sources are estimated at $56.3 billion. Benefits, expenses, and taxes absorbed $42.4 billion, leaving $13.9 billion for an increase in assets. All funds received from amortization of loans are available for *reinvestment*. (1972 gross acquisitions were $95 billion including short-term of $59 billion.)

TABLE 32-1

Estimates of Cash Flow for Investment [1]—All U.S. Life Insurance Companies (In Billions)

1962	$13.4	1964	$16.7	1966	$16.9	1968	$17.5	1971	$24.9
1963	15.7	1965	18.2	1967	16.8	1970	16.6	1972	29.9

Source: *1972 Economics and Investment Report,* Life Insurance Association of America, New York, N.Y.

The major offsets to the assets of life insurance companies are the policy reserves, and the minor offsets are the other liabilities and surplus or capital. Of all invested funds, 80% represents reserves of life insurance companies.

Investment Constraints of Life Insurance Companies

The most important constraints that affect the portfolio policies of life insurance companies are discussed in the following paragraphs.

Stability of Principal—Risk of Price Depreciation. With respect to ability to risk potential price depreciation of investments, life insurance companies are in a distinctly superior position to deposit-type institutions. Life insurance companies do not have a liquidity problem in the normal sense. They are long-term investors and usually hold their long-term debt investments (the bulk of their investments) until maturity. While legally the reserves of policyholders are available at least in part on demand in the case of cancellations, cash surrenders, and policy loans, experience shows that these demands are relatively small and therefore there is no liquidity problem with one exception. This exception was seen in 1969-1970 when policy loans rose to $16 billion. Policyholders borrowed at low guaranteed rates and then invested the borrowed funds at a higher rate, as for example in U.S. Government securities. The increase in policy loans was $0.9 billion in 1967 and $1.2 billion in 1968, but $2.5 billion in 1969 and $2.2 billion in 1970. Policy loans were high again in 1973.

These increases in policy loans were not a large demand in terms of cash flow. But companies had miscalculated their cash flow and had made

---

[1] "Cash flow" (for long-term investment) is defined as the net income in ledger assets (reflecting premium payments and investment income, net of expenses), the return flow from existing investments (repayments and sales), and miscellaneous items including temporary bank borrowings. Cash flow available from these sources is reduced by net increases in policy loans and in cash position and by net repayments of bank borrowing in arriving at the total of funds available for investment in securities, mortgages, and real property. "Cash position" is defined to include holdings of cash and short-term securities; thus total cash flow reflects only a change in holdings of short-term issues and excludes the turnover of these securities.

TABLE 32-2

Sources and Uses of Funds—Life Insurance Companies (Billions of Dollars)

	1965	1966	1967	1968	1969	1970	1971	1972 (est.)	1973 (proj.)
SOURCES OF FUNDS									
Income									
Premium receipts	24.6	26.5	28.7	31.1	34.0	36.8	40.7	43.7	47.0
Net investment income	6.8	7.3	7.9	8.6	9.4	10.1	11.0	12.0	13.0
Other income	1.8	2.0	2.1	2.2	2.3	2.1	2.4	2.5	2.5
Total	33.2	35.8	38.6	41.9	45.6	49.1	54.2	58.2	62.5
Outgo									
Benefit payments	18.2	19.8	21.4	23.2	25.4	27.7	29.5	31.8	33.8
Operating expenses, taxes and other	6.0	7.0	7.7	8.7	10.0	10.6	11.4	12.4	13.4
Total	24.2	26.8	29.1	32.0	35.4	38.3	41.0	44.2	47.2
Increase in admitted assets *	8.9	8.9	9.5	9.9	10.2	10.8	13.3	14.0	15.3
USES OF FUNDS									
Investment funds									
Home mortgages	1.1	.6	—.5	—.7	—1.1	—1.4	—1.8	—2.0	—2.3
Multifamily, commercial and farm mortgages	3.8	4.0	3.4	3.2	3.1	3.7	3.1	3.4	4.5
Total mortgages	4.9	4.6	2.9	2.5	2.1	2.3	1.3	1.4	2.2
Corporate bonds	2.4	2.2	3.7	3.7	1.6	1.2	5.4	6.4	5.7
Corporate stocks *	.7	.3	1.0	1.4	1.7	2.0	3.8	3.8	4.2
State and local government securities	—.2	—.4	—.1	. . .	. . .	.1	.1	. . .	.1
Foreign securities	.4	.2	.2	.2	.2	.3	.1	.1	.1
Total	8.2	6.8	7.7	7.7	5.5	5.9	10.6	11.7	12.3
Short-term funds									
Open market paper	. . .	.1	.1	—.1	.8	.8	.6	.5	.7
Policy loans	.5	1.4	.9	1.2	2.5	2.2	1.0	1.0	1.2
Total	.6	1.5	1.0	1.2	3.4	3.0	1.6	1.5	1.9
U.S. Government and agency securities									
U.S. Government securities	—.5	—.3	—.2	—.2	—.3	—.1	—.2	—.1	—.1
Federal agency securities	. . .	. . .	. . .	.1	.1	.1	—.1	—.2	—.1
Total	—.4	—.3	—.3	—.2	—.2	.1	—.3	—.3	—.2
Total funds	8.3	8.1	8.5	8.7	8.7	9.0	11.9	12.9	14.0
Real estate	.2	.2	.3	.4	.3	.4	.6	.5	.6
Cash	. . .	. . .	. . .	.1	. . .	.1	. . .	.2	.2
Other—net	.5	.7	.7	.7	1.2	1.3	.7	.4	.5
Total	8.9	8.9	9.5	9.9	10.2	10.8	13.3	14.0	15.3
MEMORANDUM									
Separate accounts	.2	.4	.5	.9	1.7	1.5	1.8	1.5	2.0

* Net of appreciation or depreciation in market value (Life Insurance Association of America).

Sources: Institute of Life Insurance, Federal Home Loan Bank Board, and Government National Mortgage Association.

large loan commitments. In order to meet these commitments, they were forced to liquidate some securities. In 1969 Treasury securities were reduced $332 million and tax-exempts, $270 million. Only in this respect—policy loans—is there any liquidity problem.

Life insurance companies are largely able to ignore price depreciation under rules of insurance commissioners concerning valuation of securities and valuation reserves for losses on securities. In essence, life insurance companies are permitted to value the bulk of their securities in bonds and preferred stocks (that meet certain standards, and most do) on a "going concern" or cost basis rather than on a liquidation basis. This method of valuation and the valuation reserves in essence permit life insurance companies to ignore fluctuations in market prices of securities in financial statements.[2] While common stocks must be valued at market, this is not a serious problem since such stocks constitute only about 9% of assets.

Income Risk and Need to Maximize Income. The major concern of life insurance companies, unlike deposit institutions, is with maximization of income, not stability and liquidity of principal.

Insurance companies must earn a minimum rate on investments in order to meet their contracts, in recent years a rate of 3¼% to 3¾% on policy reserves.[3] But the contract rate is well below actual rate of return on investments so that this requirement has not been a problem. The very diversification and quality of insurance company portfolios has offered protection against income loss except in the 1930s.

Problems of Maximizing Income. The major problem of widely diversified investments is to maximize the rate of return in competition with other companies. The higher the rate of return on investments, the lower can be the cost of policies offered competitively.

Because the great majority of life insurance investments are debt instruments, the rise in interest rates from 1945 to 1973, together with the shift from U.S. Government securities to other investments, has accounted for the rise in the rate of return shown in Table 32-3. However, only new investments earn the current rate, so the annual rate of return on investments lags behind the long-term secular rise in yields.

---

[2] In the case of corporate stocks, which represent only about 11% of assets on the average for the industry, fluctuations in the market prices must be reflected in asset valuation in annual financial statements as well as be reflected correspondingly in statements of surplus. Holdings of common stocks about doubled from $11.9 billion in 1970 to $21.1 billion in December, 1972.

[3] The rate on new contracts may be changed from time to time, but the average earning rate required for all contracts changes only slightly. Also, life insurance companies have reduced assumed rates on new contracts in the past when faced with a downward trend of average yields on their investments. (See yield tables in Chapter 3.)

TABLE 32-3

Net Rate of Interest Earned on Investment Funds

1951	3.18%	1956	3.63%	1961	4.22%	1966	4.73%	1971	5.44%
1952	3.28	1957	3.75	1962	4.34	1967	4.85	1972	5.59
1953	3.36	1958	3.85	1963	4.45	1968	4.97		
1954	3.46	1959	3.96	1964	4.53	1969	5.12		
1955	3.51	1960	4.11	1965	4.61	1970	5.30		

Source: *Economic and Investment Report,* Life Insurance Association of America, New York, N.Y., annual issues.

Because one third of life insurance assets are invested in mortgages, the average rate of return on mortgage loans of reporting life insurance companies [4] is presented in Table 32-4.

TABLE 32-4

Rate of Income on Mortgage Loans by Reporting Life Insurance Companies

	1955	1960	1965	1970	1971
Gross Cash Income	4.51%	4.99%	5.46%	6.09%	6.36%
Net Cash Income	3.92	4.50	5.02	5.75	6.04

Strength of Ownership Position. Life insurance companies are long-term investors and only rarely find it necessary to liquidate any investments, and then only to fulfill commitments for new investments (and/or loans). Legally, life insurance liabilities are short-term because of the cash surrender and loan provisions of the contracts, but in actual fact the demands from these sources are small in relation to a relatively stable cash flow. The tenure of ownership is strong.

Other Portfolio Constraints. There is little advantage for most life insurance companies in purchasing tax-exempt securities. The Federal Income Tax Code requires life insurance companies to apportion income from tax-exempt securities in the same proportions that income from policy premiums and investment income bear to total income. Specifically, if 75% of total income is derived from premiums and related items and only 25% is derived from investment income, then 75% of income from tax-exempt

---

[4] *1972 Economic and Investment Report* (New York, N.Y.: Life Insurance Association of America).

securities is apportioned to the premium income and is taxed, thus losing the tax advantage. On this basis tax-exempt securities lose much of their attractiveness to investors.

Financial Risks. The fact that policyholders' interests must be completely protected would appear to be a constraint to invest in the very highest type of securities. However, this fact ignores the insurance principle of wide diversification that is followed in the investment policy of life insurance companies, as well as the lack of a liquidity problem and the strong tenure of ownership. About 82% of security investments are debt instruments; therefore, the conclusions of the Hickman Study [5] apply. These conclusions are summarized as follows: A large, well-diversified portfolio of higher-yielding debt instruments, held through all financial difficulties that may develop until they are finally paid off, will yield a higher net return, after absorbing any losses, than a portfolio consisting of only the highest-grade securities. In the case of marketable securities owned—those other than individual private placements—life insurance companies tend to invest in few issues below the Baa range and tend to concentrate in the Baa-A range. But, the very important private placements are not agency rated and therefore are not subject to definite classification. From available reports, life insurance companies are willing and do go below the Baa quality for private placements. Corporate bonds, including private placements, represent about 72% of all security investments for life insurance companies.

Preferred stock represents about 3.5% of total security investments (1.6% of assets) and has a tax advantage in that corporate tax is applied to only 15% of dividends received. Furthermore, these preferred stocks now fall under the present rule of valuation at *cost* rather than market.

Inasmuch as common stocks are widely diversified and represent only about 9% of assets and about 18% of security holdings, and inasmuch as there is no problem of liquidity, the financial risk is minimal. Common stock portfolios will tend to fluctuate in value with fluctuations in the common stock indexes. But common stocks must be valued for statement purposes at *market*. In periods of bear markets, this will require reductions in book values and related charges to surplus reflecting the extent of the market declines. Such charge-offs and valuation reductions are usually kept within reasonable limits.

Wide diversification is the key factor in the portfolio policy of life insurance companies in the case of both debt instruments and equities.

---

[5] W. Braddock Hickman, *Corporate Bond Quality and Investor Experience* (New York: National Bureau of Economic Research, Inc., 1958).

Diversification by industry, by subsidiary groups, and by specific issues within groups reduces overall risk to a minimal figure.

Table 32-5 presents the historical record of life insurance investments. Holdings of U.S. Government securities in 1945 were $20.6 billion, representing 46% of assets. But in 1972 these securities totaled only $4.4 billion (1.8% of assets). Mortgage investments represented 32.6% of assets in 1955 and 32% in 1972. Holdings of industrial debt issues (largely private placements) represented 25.5% of assets in 1972. Public utility bonds rose from 11.6% of assets in 1945 to 16.5% of assets in 1950, but then declined to about 9% of assets in 1972. Private placements on the average yield a higher return than the marketable bonds.

Together, these four groups (U.S. Governments, mortgages, industrial securities, and public utility securities) represent 72.1% of assets and 89% of debt instruments. State, local, and foreign government securities represent only 1.4% of total assets. Stocks (including preferred stocks) represent about 10.9% of assets (common stocks, 8.8%, and preferred stocks, 2.1%). Policy loans represented about 6.0%.

Because stability of principal and liquidity are not problems, life insurance companies hold only about 1.9% of their assets in Treasury (1.6%) and agency (0.3%) securities. They diversify over a broad list of securities as shown in Table 32-5. Investments are considered permanent until they mature, and this is especially true of private placements where there is a low factor of marketability. About 9%-10% is invested in public utility bonds, which are quality securities with excellent marketability but, like other bonds, are subject to the interest rate risk. Life insurance companies have a constant annual flow of additional funds to be invested long-term (see Table 32-1).

Interest Rate Risk. The interest rate risk is the risk that, as interest rates rise, prices of outstanding debt instruments will fall. But insurance companies are permanent investors, basically do not have a liquidity problem, and are little concerned with price fluctuation of their marketable bonds and preferred stocks. There are no price fluctuations for their nonmarketable private placements, although of course they would suffer a loss if these placements were sold in periods of rising interest rates. Funds for investment, including funds received from amortization of debt securities, are invested regularly, usually in long-term securities held to maturity. Because of the constant new additional investments, life insurance companies automatically generate a spaced maturity situation.

Life insurance companies' major concern with price fluctuations and rising interest rates is emphasized in two areas: call protection and deep

TABLE 32-5

Distribution of Assets of U.S. Life Insurance Companies—Selected Years, 1945 -1972 (Billions of Dollars)

Year	Total Assets	U.S.* Gov't & Agencies	Foreign Gov't & Intern. Agencies	State Prov. & Local	Rail-roads	Public Utility	Indus. & Misc.	Mort-gages	Real Estate	Stocks**	Policy Loans	Miscella-neous***
1945	44.80	20.58	1.24	0.72	2.95	5.21	1.90	6.64	.86	1.00	1.96	1.74
1950	64.02	13.46	1.51	1.15	3.19	10.59	9.53	16.10	1.45	2.10	2.41	2.59
1955	90.43	8.58	1.22	2.04	3.91	13.97	18.18	29.45	2.58	3.63	3.29	3.74
1960	119.58	6.53	1.70	3.59	3.67	16.72	26.73	41.77	3.77	4.98	5.23	5.27
1963	141.12	5.95	2.83	3.85	3.37	17.33	33.21	50.54	4.32	7.14	6.66	6.39
1965	158.88	5.29	3.09	3.53	3.31	17.05	38.34	60.01	4.68	9.13	7.68	7.23
1966	167.46	5.16	2.98	3.52	3.39	16.72	41.22	64.61	4.89	8.83	9.12	7.80
1967	177.83	4.91	3.02	3.26	3.44	17.12	44.64	67.52	5.19	10.88	10.06	8.43
1968	188.64	4.75	3.15	3.15	3.55	17.58	47.77	69.97	5.57	13.23	11.31	9.15
1969	197.21	4.51	3.18	3.19	3.61	17.96	49.97	72.03	5.91	13.71	13.83	9.96
1970	207.25	4.57	3.19	3.22				74.38	6.32	15.42	16.06	10.91
1971	222.10	4.46	3.18	3.31				75.50	6.90	20.61	17.07	11.83
1972	238.50	4.35	3.38	3.36				76.68	7.48	26.10	18.05	12.73

Distribution as a Percentage of Total Assets

Year	Total Assets	U.S.* Gov't & Agencies	Foreign Gov't & Intern. Agencies	State Prov. & Local	Rail-roads	Public Utility	Indus. & Misc.	Mort-gages	Real Estate	Stocks**	Policy Loans	Miscella-neous***
1945	100.0	45.9	2.8	1.6	6.6	11.6	4.3	14.8	1.9	2.2	4.4	3.9
1950	100.0	21.0	2.1	1.8	5.0	16.5	14.9	25.1	2.2	3.3	3.8	4.1
1955	100.0	9.5	1.3	2.3	4.3	15.5	20.1	32.6	2.9	4.0	3.6	4.1
1960	100.0	5.4	1.4	3.0	3.1	14.0	22.4	34.9	3.1	4.2	4.4	4.4
1963	100.0	4.1	2.0	2.8	2.4	12.3	23.5	35.8	3.1	5.0	4.7	4.6
1965	100.0	3.2	1.9	2.2	2.1	10.7	24.2	37.8	3.0	5.7	4.8	4.5
1966	100.0	3.1	1.5	2.1	2.0	10.0	24.7	38.7	2.9	5.2	5.5	4.6
1967	100.0	2.8	1.7	1.8	2.0	9.6	25.3	38.3	2.9	5.8	5.7	4.7
1968	100.0	2.5	1.7	1.7	1.9	9.4	25.5	37.2	3.0	6.9	6.0	4.9
1969	100.0	2.3	1.6	1.6	1.8	9.1	25.3	36.5	3.0	7.0	7.0	5.1
1970	100.0	2.2	1.5	1.6				35.9	3.0	7.4	7.3	5.3
1971	100.0	2.0	1.4	1.5				34.0	3.1	9.3	7.7	5.3
1972	100.0	1.8	1.4	1.4				32.2	3.1	10.9	7.6	5.3

* U.S. Government Agency securities: 1957, none; 1960, $101 million; 1966, $236 million; 1972, $650 million.
** Includes preferred stock: 1950, $1.45; 1960, $1.80; 1972, $5. Total corporate debt issues in 1972 was $78.6 billion.
*** Includes cash, which averages just under 1% of assets. "State, Prov. & Local" includes "Foreign Govts." which are largely Canadian (1968 = $1.2 billion).

Source: *Life Insurance Fact Book, 1972* (New York: Institute of Life Insurance).

discounts. In periods of high yields, the companies attempt to secure strong protection against later calls if interest rates should decline below their level at the time of issue. In the case of most new issues of corporate bonds held (largely utilities), there is generally only 5-year call protection and only occasionally 10-year call protection. Private placements which declined after 1965 from 55%-65% of debt issues to 39% in 1972 receive stronger call protection and some contracts effectively prevent call of the issue at any time.

At times, issuers of serial issues sell these securities at deep discounts below the par value that must be paid on call or at maturity. To redeem such issues at par or at call prices near par or above par would cause the issuer to redeem the bonds at a much higher price than was received for the bonds when they were initially sold. Therefore, once such issues are purchased in periods of high interest rates, life insurance companies can feel reasonably confident that they can be kept until maturity.

Conclusions on Investment Policies of Life Insurance Companies

Life insurance companies have liabilities (policy reserves) that are equal to a major portion of total assets, and their surplus reserves are only a small proportion of assets. Therefore, like commercial banks, they have a high degree of leverage. However, *legally* there is a high potential demand for funds, which would imply the necessity for price stability and liquidity in the investment account; but in fact, in the light of experience, this legal liability is not converted into a demand for funds to any significant extent.

Therefore, life insurance companies can be long-term investors, holding issues to maturity, and as such they can ignore market fluctuations. Unlike banks, life insurance companies can act as self-insurers and can purchase lower-quality issues with not too good marketability, as in the case of many industrial private placements.

Furthermore, life insurance companies are permitted to carry debt securities at amortized costs and preferred stock at cost, and their assets are valued on a going-concern basis rather than on a liquidation basis.

Common stock must be valued at market at financial statement dates, but the main limitation to common stock investment is the legal limitation as to the amount of assets that may be invested in common stocks. The percentage varies by states, with the range generally being 3%-5% of unsegregated assets for all equities, including preferred stocks. However, segregated insured pension assets are not restricted, so the percentage of common stocks to total assets rose to 9% in 1972.

PORTFOLIO POLICIES OF PROPERTY-CASUALTY INSURANCE COMPANIES [6]

Unlike the very highly leveraged life insurance companies and commercial banks, property-casualty insurance companies in terms of the ratio of liabilities to assets have a substantial excess of assets over their liabilities and liability reserves. This excess is called policyholders' surplus (for mutual companies) and ranges usually between 40% and 50% of assets. As a result, these companies are in a much stronger position to accept risk of market depreciation of assets (investments) than are life insurance companies and for that matter deposit-type financial institutions. Assets could drop in value for property-casualty insurance companies by 40%-50% before the capital surplus and the voluntary reserves would be eliminated. There is a sizable cushion to absorb losses. Investors in these companies frequently calculate that there should be a minimum of $1 of capital behind each $2 of insurance premiums, perhaps overemphasizing the risk factor of the underwriting business.

In valuing assets for statutory accounting statements, bonds (except bonds in default) are valued at amortized cost; however, both preferred stocks and common stocks must be valued at current market price at financial statement dates.

Sources of Funds of Property-Casualty Insurance Companies

The assets of property-casualty insurance companies are offset 55%-60% by reserves (unearned premium reserves, 25%-26%; loss reserves, 26%-27%; and related liabilities and liability reserves, 6%-7%) and 40%-45% by paid-in capital, voluntary reserves, net surplus, and policyholders' surplus for mutual companies. Table 32-6 shows sources and uses of funds for property-casualty insurance companies.

Investment Constraints of Property-Casualty Insurance Companies

The property and casualty insurance business may be divided into two segments: underwriting and investment. In many years the underwriting business of property-casualty insurance companies has not been very profitable, and in many years the combined operating expense ratio and loss ratio

---

[6] The reader should review Chapter 24, including the discussion of loss and expense ratios, before reading this section of the present chapter. While at one time fire and property-casualty companies were quite separate, most property and casualty insurance is written by multiple-line companies or groups at the present time.

TABLE 32-6

Sources and Uses of Funds—Fire and Casualty Insurance Companies (Billions of Dollars)

	1965	1966	1967	1968	1969	1970	1971	1972 (est.)	1973 (proj.)
SOURCES OF FUNDS									
Unearned premium reserves	.6	.7	.7	.7	1.1	1.7	1.1	1.4	1.5
Loss reserves	1.0	1.2	1.4	1.8	2.1	2.2	2.7	2.4	2.5
Policyholders' surplus *	.3	1.0	.6	.6	.3	1.3	2.4	2.5	2.0
Total	2.0	2.9	2.7	3.0	3.6	5.1	6.2	6.3	6.0
USES OF FUNDS									
Investment funds									
Corporate bonds	.8	.7	.6	1.2	.8	1.5	.3	.8	.5
Corporate stocks **	—.1	.2	.9	.6	.7	1.1	2.5	2.5	2.0
State and local government securities	.5	1.0	1.5	.8	1.1	1.3	3.5	3.5	3.2
Total	1.2	1.9	3.0	2.6	2.6	3.9	6.3	6.8	5.7
U.S. Government and agency securities									
U.S. Government securities	...	.2	—.8	—.1	—.3	...	...	—.5	.2
Federal agency securities	.2	.1	...	.1	...	.1	—.2	—.1	...
Total	.2	.3	—.8	...	—.3	.1	—.1	—.6	.2
Total funds	1.4	2.2	2.2	2.5	2.3	4.0	6.2	6.2	5.9
Cash	—.1	...	...	.1	...	.1	.1	.1	.1
Other—net	.6	.7	.6	.4	1.3	1.0	...	...	...
Total	2.0	2.9	2.7	3.0	3.6	5.1	6.2	6.3	6.0

* Net of appreciation or depreciation in market values.
** Represents net acquisitions.

Source: *Bankers Trust Investment Outlook for 1973,* Bankers Trust Company, New York.

for the industry has been over 100% of premiums written (or premiums earned). The deficit must be absorbed by investment income.

Investment Income—Size and Stability. To cover underwriting losses in loss years and to increase surplus and pay dividends in the case of stock companies, *stability of income* is very important to property-casualty insurance companies.

Unlike life insurance companies, property-casualty insurance companies have no policy reserves on which interest must be earned, for the underwriting contract makes no provision for interest accruals. On this basis, the constraints in respect to income are not as strong as in the case of life insurance companies.

Purchasing Power Risk. The liabilities of property-casualty insurance companies call for payment in fixed dollars, and *in this respect* there are no purchasing power risks and no constraint to protect the purchasing power of investment funds. However, the nature of the property-casualty insurance business is such that the purchasing power of investment funds and the income from those funds is important for the reasons given below.

The size of losses incurred reflects inflation because the current value of property and property replacements rise and liability claims and settlements of all types reflect this. Furthermore, there is a lag between rising claims and settlements and the time when insurance commissions approve major premium rates and when premium income is received. This is a major reason for underwriting loss years. Investment income must absorb the loss in loss years. Furthermore, as total insurance risks (liabilities) rise with the growth of the economy, policyholders' surplus must rise either from investment income or from appreciation in the value of assets. This latter constraint favors investment in common stocks. Property-casualty insurance companies therefore include a substantial amount of common stock in their assets— a higher proportion for stock companies than for mutual companies.

Cash Flow. The net cash inflow of property-casualty insurance companies is neither as regular nor as predictable as with life insurance companies. Premium income for property insurance business reflects premiums paid covering several years rather than the annual contract payment of life insurance companies.[7] Furthermore, claims and settlements made annually are not nearly as regular or as predictable as in the case of life insurance

---

[7] This is not the case with most of the casualty business, such as the automobile business.

companies, and as a result the tenure of ownership for at least a portion of the investment portfolio is not as strong. In the property-casualty field, securities may need to be sold to meet unpredictable requirements for insurance settlements, as for example in severe hurricane years when losses may be especially heavy (see Table 32-6).

Tax-Exempt Securities. If property-casualty insurance companies have profitable underwriting years, there is a distinct advantage in holding tax-exempt securities as in the case of commercial banks. If property-casualty insurance companies have a profit in underwriting, the corporate income tax applies to this income plus investment income. Property-casualty insurance companies are the third largest holders of tax-exempt securities (after commercial banks and individuals). Depending upon the extent to which the underwriting is profitable or heavily unprofitable, the tax rate could vary from the full tax rate all the way down to zero if underwriting losses equaled or exceeded investment income.

Investment Policies of Property-Casualty Insurance Companies

Contrasted to life insurance companies, property-casualty insurance companies invest more heavily in tax-exempt securities and are proportionately larger holders of Treasury securities to meet cash outflow requirements when such requirements exceed cash inflow. Property-casualty insurance companies generally have substantial investments in common stocks compared to the low proportion held by life insurance companies, which is a further reason for holding proportionately more Treasury securities.

Within the property-casualty industry there are much wider variations in portfolio policy than is the case with life insurance companies. Some property-casualty insurance companies have invested over 50% of their assets in common stocks while others have invested below 20%. This variation is the result of three factors: (1) the actual experience and the balance sheet conditions of the respective companies, (2) the degree of aggressiveness or cautiousness of management, and (3) the difference between mutual and stock companies. The stock companies tend to hold a distinctly higher proportion of common stocks than the mutuals.

It is often stated that the larger the ratio of policyholders' surplus to liabilities, the greater is the investment risk exposure that can be tolerated, and vice versa. It is also stated that the larger the absolute dollar amount of assets held, the greater is the overall financial strength and ability to accept investment risk exposure. A simple rule of analysts is that holdings of common stocks should not exceed policyholders' surplus. But the difference in the proportion of common stock holdings to total assets also reflects different concepts of management. Common stock investments are widely diversified and generally represent quality companies.

Property-casualty insurance companies with profitable underwriting experience find it advantageous to invest in preferred stocks because the corporate income tax applies (as with common dividends) to only 15% of dividend income received. But the supply of preferred stocks is limited, and the portfolios of property-casualty insurance companies include only a relatively small proportion of preferred stocks.

State Regulation of Property-Casualty Insurance Companies

State statutes usually require that property-casualty insurance companies hold cash and high-grade bonds at least equal to the total unearned premium reserves and statutory-liability reserves. Bond investments consist largely of Treasury and tax-exempt securities, the latter being rather heavily favored over corporate bonds because of their tax advantage.

Because of statutory requirements and the irregular nature of net cash inflow, holdings of cash and Treasury securities are proportionately much larger for property-casualty insurance companies than for life insurance companies. Treasury securities owned are 10% to 13% of total assets of property-casualty insurance companies as compared to 1.8% for life insurance companies.

Because marketability and liquidity are so important in the bond account, property-casualty insurance companies usually invest in publicly owned marketable securities rather than in private placements when purchasing corporate bonds.

Conclusions on Portfolio Policies of Property-Casualty Insurance Companies

Property-casualty insurance companies are much more aggressive purchasers of common stocks than life insurance companies. Conversely, in the bond account the property-casualty insurance companies are more conservative, as tenure of ownership is weaker and therefore marketability and liquidity are more important. The interest rate risk is also much more important than for life insurance companies because it may be necessary to sell bonds in low bond markets and therefore maturities tend to be shorter. Property-casualty insurance companies must recognize the inflation risk and combat the risk by holdings of common stocks. Finally, property-casualty insurance companies are aggressive purchasers of tax-exempt securities as compared to life insurance companies.

PORTFOLIO POLICIES OF PENSION FUNDS

Private pension funds and government pension funds are discussed separately in this section.

Private Pension Funds

Since World War II, private pension funds have grown at a compounding rate of approximately 10% per year. They may be insured pension funds managed by life insurance companies or the more important noninsured corporate pension funds. The most important reason for the faster growth of the noninsured funds is the fact that, until the 1960s, state statutes required the assets of insured pension funds to be commingled with other assets of insurance companies. This effectively limited common stocks to 4%-5% (as compared to 8% in 1973). By the time the statutes governing life insurance companies were changed permitting the segregation of assets of insured pension funds—permitting an unlimited proportion to be invested in common stocks—a large proportion of corporate pension funds were already trusteed with commercial banks.

Sources of Funds—Noninsured Pension Funds. As shown in Table 32-7, the receipts of corporate noninsured pension funds, estimated at $17.3 billion for 1972 or double the 1965 figure, are derived 68% from employer contributions, 7% from employee contributions, and 25% from investment income. In 1972 benefit payments absorbed an estimated 46% of receipts, leaving 54% of receipts, less expenses, $9.3 billion to be invested.

Employers, under the terms of the contracts, agree to pay retirement income from earnings on the pension fund investments. The payments are based on amounts of the employees' earnings and length of service. Most employees' benefits are either not vested at all until the minimum retirement age or are vested only after a stated number of years of service. However, there is increasing pressure by the unions and even the federal government to have plans fully vested so that employees leaving an employers' service retain rights to retirement benefits accumulated up to the time of leaving the employment.

For 1972 it was estimated that of net sources of funds of $9.3 billion, 72% would be invested in corporate stocks and only 5% in corporate bonds. Of total investment funds of $9.3 billion, it was estimated that 93% would flow into corporate stocks and only 7% in corporate bonds.

In the 1963-1972 period, the noninsured pension funds had net receipts of $61.6 billion, of which $46.1 billion or 75% flowed into corporate stocks

TABLE 32-7

Sources and Uses of Funds—Private Noninsured Pension Funds (Billions of Dollars)

	1965	1966	1967	1968	1969	1970	1971	1972 (est.)	1973 (proj.)
SOURCES OF FUNDS									
Employer contributions	5.6	6.4	7.0	7.7	8.5	9.7	11.3	12.0	13.4
Employee contributions	.7	.7	.8	.9	1.0	1.1	1.1	1.1	1.2
Investment income *	2.4	2.7	3.0	3.3	3.7	4.0	4.2	4.3	4.4
Total receipts	8.7	9.8	10.8	11.9	13.2	14.8	16.6	17.4	19.0
Benefit payments *	2.9	3.5	4.0	4.6	5.4	6.2	7.2	8.4	9.5
Net receipts	5.8	6.3	6.8	7.3	7.8	8.6	9.4	9.0	9.5
USES OF FUNDS									
Investment funds									
Home mortgages	.2	.2	.1	…	…	.1	.1	.2	.2
Multifamily, commercial and farm mortgages	.4	.3	.1	…	.2	…	-.7	-1.0	-.8
Total mortgages	.6	.5	.2	…	.2	.1	-.6	-.8	-.6
Corporate bonds	1.7	2.1	1.1	.6	.6	2.1	-.7	…	.8
Corporate stocks **	3.1	3.5	4.6	4.8	5.4	4.6	8.9	6.8	6.3
Total	5.4	6.1	5.9	5.4	6.2	6.8	7.6	6.0	6.5
Open market paper	…	…	.1	.1	.1	…	…	.2	.3
U.S. Government and agency securities									
U.S. Government securities	-.2	-.2	-.2	.4	.2	…	…	.2	…
Federal agency securities	…	…	-.2	.1	-.2	.3	-.3	.2	.2
Total	-.2	-.2	-.4	.5	…	.3	-.3	.4	.2
Total funds	5.2	5.9	5.5	6.0	6.3	6.9	7.3	6.6	7.0
Cash	.5	.5	.4	.3	…	.2	-.2	…	…
Other—net	…	…	.9	1.0	1.4	1.5	2.2	2.4	2.5
Total	5.7	6.4	6.8	7.3	7.7	8.6	9.3	9.0	9.5
MEMORANDUM									
Insured pension plans									
Premium payments	2.4	2.5	2.8	3.2	3.8	3.9	5.0	4.5	5.0
Increase in reserves ***	2.1	2.1	2.6	2.9	2.9	3.3	5.2	4.0	4.5

* Includes minor amounts of other income and expenses.
** Represents changes in book value of holdings of preferred stock and net acquisitions of common stock.
*** Part of increase in admitted assets of life insurance companies.

Source: *Bankers Trust Investment Outlook for 1973*, Bankers Trust Company, New York.

and $10 billion or 16% into corporate bonds and private placement notes. In all years the amount flowing into corporate stocks exceeded that flowing into bonds, and since 1966 the proportion flowing into common stocks has increased. During the 1963-1972 period, U.S. Government and agency securities were sold net in only four years: 1965, 1966, 1967 and 1971. There were net purchases in the ten-year period of $300 million. By 1972, Treasury and agency securities represented only 2.2% of total assets, or close to that for life insurance companies (1.9%).

Pension funds are fully funded at the point where the value of assets plus an assumed rate of return will produce enough income to meet all present retirement benefit obligations calculated on an actuarial basis. When a fund is initiated, it immediately incurs large obligations based on *past* service costs. The employer will immediately begin to make payments into the fund based on current wage payments *and in addition* must begin to fund obligations based on past service costs. This funding of past service costs may take up to 20 or 30 years, based on the terms of the contract. Government tax regulations do not permit charges against income for tax purposes in excess of 10% annually for unfunded premium liabilities.

Most noninsured pension funds (an estimated 80%-85%) are trusteed with the trust departments of commercial banks, which manage the funds in accordance with the pension fund contracts and the contracts with the banks. Certain large companies have divided the pension fund between several banks, which places more performance pressures on the banks. The better the performance, the lower the pension costs to the company.

The employer payments into the pension funds are a tax-deductible expense for the employer except for funds used for the purchase of its own securities. The income of the fund is nontaxable, and therefore there is no justification for the purchase of tax-exempt securities. Likewise there is no justification for the purchase of preferred stocks versus corporate bonds because the tax exclusion of 85% of dividends received by a corporation is not applicable.

Trustees generally have broad powers to invest under the pension fund contract, but sometimes they are subject under contract to certain limitations. For example, until 1959 the American Telephone and Telegraph pension funds could not be invested in common stocks.

Investment Constraints of Private Pension Funds. The following investment constraints apply to both insured and noninsured private pension funds.

Stability of Principal, Marketability, and Liquidity. It is intended that corporate pension funds will grow annually. Furthermore, inasmuch as only

46% of income from payments into the pension fund (including investment income) is used to pay benefits, 54% of receipts are a net source of funds. The tenure of ownership is strong, and there is no reason for forced sale of securities in low markets.[8]

Liquidity needs are affected by the speed with which pension liabilities are funded, which is a determinant of the cash flow pattern. The less pension liabilities are funded, the less secure are the employees' pension rights and the greater is the need for more liquid investments and avoidance of high-risk investments. But in most cases the trustee usually is not greatly constrained by liquidity considerations on these grounds.

Income Constraints. The amount and the stability of investment income are not of urgent concern as long as the benefit payments are well below total receipts. In such cases, pension fund managers can plan in terms of overall rate of return, including capital appreciation of common stocks. Furthermore, since 1938 there has been a tremendous increase in dividends, and dividend stability in diversified common stock portfolios has been nearly as great as in bond portfolios. The funds are primarily concerned with *long-term overall rate of return,* including investment income and capital appreciation of common stocks. In the really long term, they are concerned with the requirement that investment income in the form of dividends and interest exceed rising benefit payouts.

Purchasing Power Risk. Because benefit payments are actually related to past service costs, at first it might appear that the purchasing power risk is unimportant. However, wage rates rise with price levels. Some plans, under union pressures, have even made retroactive adjustments in which they agreed to raise benefits of workers retired in the past on the basis of current price levels, thus causing a purchasing power risk that must be recognized by portfolio managers.

Assets of Private Pension Funds. As shown in Table 32-8, at the end of 1971 the total book value of assets of private noninsured pension funds was $106.4 billion with a market value of $125.0 billion. Insured pension fund assets at book value were $46.4 billion, so that the total book value of all private pension funds was $152.8 billion. State and local government retirement funds totaled $65 billion at book value, giving a total of $218 billion for all nonfederal funds at book value.

---

[8] Unless the entire pension fund was to be liquidated.

TABLE 32-8

Assets of All Public and Private Pension Funds (Book Value, Billions of Dollars)

	1962	1964	1966	1968	1970	1971
Private	63.5	77.7	95.6	118.0	138.2	152.8
Insured Pension Reserves	21.6	25.2	29.4	35.0	41.2	46.4
(Separate accounts, included above)						
Noninsured Pension Funds	41.9	52.4	66.2	83.1	97.0	106.4
Public	61.4	69.5	80.2	98.6	123.6	135.6
State and Local	24.5	29.7	36.9	46.2	58.0	64.8
Federal (not to increase after 1972)						
Federal Old Age & Survivors Insurance	18.3	19.1	20.6	25.7	32.5	33.8
Federal Disability Insurance	2.4	2.0	1.7	3.0	5.6	6.6
Civil Service Retirement and Disability Program	12.5	14.7	17.0	19.4	23.1	26.0
Railroad Retirement	3.7	3.8	4.1	4.2	4.4	4.3
Total Private and Public	124.9	147.1	175.9	216.7	261.8	288.3

Assets Held by Life Insurance Companies in Separate Accounts. Separate accounts may be invested without regard to the usual investment restrictions (in respect to common stocks) on life insurance company assets (see Table 32-9). While separate accounts have primarily been used to fund individual and group annuities (pensions), the introduction of variable annuities will increase the use of "separate" accounting for insurance purposes (separate accounts, common stock in 1967 = 88%; in 1971 = 85%).

TABLE 32-9

Distribution of Assets Held in Separate Accounts
Life Insurance Companies (Millions of Dollars)

Year	Total	Stocks		Bonds	Mort-gages	Real Estate (Less than 0.5%)	Cash	Other
		Common	Preferred					
1967	1,207	1,055	9	114	14		13	2
1968	2,269	1,915	31	233	20	1	48	21
1970	5,061	3,955	86	878	37	2	69	34
1971	7,523	6,416	83	763	87	24	88	62

Investment Policy. Pension fund managers generally have wide latitude in investment policy. They are not constrained (except as noted previously) by requirements of marketability or liquidity or even by requirements relative to strictly investment income received in the form of dividends or interest as opposed to overall rate of return on investments that includes capital appreciation.

Because of their size, large pension funds can and do practice a policy of very broad diversification. They are relatively long-term investors and, as with insurance companies, they can seek medium-quality, higher-yielding issues in line with the Hickman Study findings.

Unlike life insurance companies, pension funds can and do invest heavily in common stocks and they are the ideal stock investors. The one real disability of common stocks is the factor of wide price fluctuations. However, this disability can be ignored by long-term, permanent investors with broadly diversified investments in common stocks who are not under constraints to liquidate stocks. Furthermore, pension funds are practicing a policy of dollar-cost averaging with the new funds flowing in annually.

With broadly diversified common stock portfolios, large pension funds can expect to have portfolio performance at least paralleling that of the averages. This was very satisfactory through 1966. However, there has been more and more pressure since 1966, with the much slower appreciation of the averages, to secure a performance better than that of the averages.[9] This pressure is being felt strongly by commercial banks acting as pension fund trustees, especially in cases where a pension fund is divided among several banks.

The overall experience with common stocks up to 1966 encouraged non-insured pension fund managers to invest a larger and larger proportion of new funds in common stocks. The almost continually rising dividends on common stocks plus the capital appreciation provided an overall compound rate of return on common stock portfolios in the neighborhood of 9%-10%. Even with the high bond yields on new issues of 1969-1970 and 1973, pension fund portfolio managers were still favoring common stock investments (1972 total was: long-term investments, $7.2 billion, of which $6.7 billion was invested in common stock).

State and Local Government Pension Funds

The growth of state and local government pension funds can be compared to that of private noninsured pension funds in Table 32-10, which shows receipts for net investment of these two classes of funds.

---

[9] The DJIA was 1,000 in January, 1973, versus 995 in February, 1966, the previous all-time peak. Essentially the index moved horizontally from February, 1966, to January, 1973, just as did corporate profits which did not surpass 1966 until 1972.

TABLE 32-10

Annual Net Receipts, State and Local Government Pension Funds
and Private Noninsured Pension Funds (Billions of Dollars)

	1960	1964	1965	1966	1967	1968	1969	1970	1971 (est.)	1972 (proj.)
Private Noninsured	3.9	5.1	5.8	6.3	6.8	7.3	7.7	8.6	8.7	9.3
State & Local Govt.	1.8	3.2	3.4	3.8	4.4	5.1	5.8	6.7	7.6	8.7
% State & Local to Noninsured	46	63	59	60	65	70	75	78	87	94

The state and local government pension funds have been growing at a faster pace than all private pension funds. Their new investment funds totaled 46% of the funds of noninsured pension funds in 1960 but an estimated 94% in 1972. It was estimated that the assets at book value of state and local funds were approximately 61% of the book value of the assets of noninsured pension funds in January, 1972 (48% of total private funds).

Investment Constraints on State and Local Government Pension Funds. The major difference between state and local government pension funds and private pension funds is the stringent restrictions that govern the investment of the public funds. These restrictions on the type of securities that may be purchased at one time limited investments largely or solely to state and local government securities, and many funds still hold a large amount of such securities. Governments are tempted to relieve budget strains by making pension funds captive buyers of the employing government's bonds. This is unfortunate in that these pension funds pay no taxes on income and so at the least would be better to have funds invested in U.S. Government securities. Some statutes limit investments to securities that are legal investments for savings banks and trust funds, while other statutes may detail the type of securities that may be purchased. Also, trustees generally are elected or appointed public officials, and the political process has not insured that professional fund managers fill these posts.

In recent years there has been some relaxation of these legal restrictions. Many state and local government pension funds have actually been selling tax-exempt securities and others have been allowed to purchase common stocks for the first time, as indicated in Table 32-11.

Sources of Funds of State and Local Government Pension Funds. Table 32-11 shows the sources and uses of funds of state and local government

TABLE 32-11

Sources and Uses of Funds—State and Local Governments (Billions of Dollars)

	1965	1966	1967	1968	1969	1970	1971	1972 (est.)	1973 (proj.)
Retirement Funds									
SOURCES OF FUNDS									
Government contributions	2.5	2.8	3.3	3.8	4.3	4.9	5.6	6.4	7.3
Employee contributions	1.7	1.9	2.1	2.3	2.6	3.0	2.4	3.8	4.2
Investment income	1.3	1.5	1.7	2.0	2.3	2.7	3.1	3.4	3.8
Total receipts	5.5	6.2	7.1	8.1	9.2	10.6	11.1	13.6	15.3
Benefit payments	2.1	2.4	2.6	3.0	3.4	3.9	4.4	4.9	5.6
Net receipts	3.4	3.8	4.5	5.1	5.8	6.7	7.7	8.7	9.7
USES OF FUNDS									
Investment funds									
Multifamily mortgages	.7	.8	.5	.4	.6	.8	.3	.2	.2
Corporate bonds	2.1	2.5	3.4	2.5	3.1	3.9	4.4	5.0	5.4
Corporate stocks	.4	.5	.7	1.3	1.8	2.1	3.2	2.9	3.3
State and local government securities	-.3	-.1	-.1	...	-.1	-.3	-.2	-.2	-.1
Total	2.9	3.7	4.5	4.2	5.4	6.5	7.7	7.9	8.8
U.S. Government and agency securities									
U.S. Government securities	.2	-.1	-1.1	-.2	-.5	-.4	-.5	-.1	...
Federal agency securities	.2	-.1	.1	.5	.1	.3	-.3	-.2	-.2
Total	.4	.0	-.9	.3	-.4	-.1	-.8	-.3	-.2
Total funds	3.3	3.7	3.6	4.5	5.1	6.4	6.9	7.6	8.6
Cash	...	.1	.4	.1	...	-.1	-.1	...	.1
Other assets	.1	.1	.1	.5	.1	.2	.1	.1	...
Total	3.4	3.9	4.1	4.7	5.0	6.7	6.8	7.7	8.7
Discrepancy—sources less uses	.1	...	.4	.4	.8	-.1	.9	1.0	1.0
General Funds									
USES OF FUNDS									
Investment funds									
Home mortgages	...	...	...	.1	...	.1	.2	...	.1
Multifamily, commercial and farm mortgages	.2	.1	.1	.2	.1	.4	1.2	1.8	2.4
Total mortgages	.2	.1	.1	.3	.1	.5	1.4	1.8	2.5
State and local government securities	-.1	-.1	...	...	.1	...	...	...	...
Total	.1	...	.1	.3	.2	.5	1.4	1.8	2.5
U.S. Government and agency securities									
U.S. Government securities	1.6	1.3	...	.3	2.2	-.3	.3	3.0	3.5
Federal agency securities	.6	.1	.6	1.3	.5	...	-1.0	.7	1.0
Total	2.2	1.4	.6	1.6	2.7	-.3	-.7	3.7	4.5
Total funds	2.3	1.4	.7	1.9	2.9	.2	.7	5.5	7.0

Source: *Bankers Trust Investment Outlook for 1973*, Bankers Trust Company, New York.

retirement funds. As can be noted, the sources of funds are: government contributions, 46.4%; employee contributions, 28.0%; and investment income, 25.6%.

Investment Policies of State and Local Government Pension Funds. In the 1960-1969 period these pension funds invested $31 billion net. The funds have been net sellers of state and local government securities since 1960. In the 1960-1972 period they sold an estimated $2.8 billion of these securities. For quite a number of years their major purchases have been corporate bonds. In the 1960-1972 period they purchased $36.2 billion of corporate bonds, representing 61% of all net investment funds of $59 billion in the period. Their purchases of mortgage investments of $6.7 billion represented 11.4% of net investment funds.

As shown in Table 32-11, state and local government pension funds have gradually been purchasers of corporate stocks, increasing their annual purchases to $1.8, $2.1, $3.2, $2.9, and an estimated $3.3 billion annually from 1969 to 1973. Purchases of corporate stocks totaled about $17 billion in the 1960-1973 period.

There is no reason except current legal restrictions why state and local government pension funds should not follow the lead of corporate pension funds in investing heavily in common stocks. In fact, these funds should follow policies closely resembling those of corporate pension funds.

PORTFOLIO POLICIES OF NONPROFIT ORGANIZATIONS

There are two major types of nonprofit organizations: (1) college and university endowment funds and (2) tax-exempt foundations.

College and University Endowment Funds

At this writing in April, 1973, the last comprehensive study of these funds was published in 1970 by the Boston Fund. It was announced in 1973 that Vance Sanders & Company, Inc., underwriters of the Boston Fund, would publish in 1973 a less comprehensive study covering 10 to 12 of the largest institutions. The 1970 study was based on 1969 data covering 71 college and university endowments ranging from about $9 million to the Harvard University fund of about $1.16 billion.

The distribution of the 71 funds by size in the abovementioned study is shown in Table 32-12.

TABLE 32-12

Distribution of Endowment Funds, by Size (Boston Fund Study)

Size of Endowment Based on Market Value End of Fiscal Year	Number Endowment Funds	% of Total Value of 71 Endowment Funds
$200,000,000 and over	9	52.9%
$100,000,000 to $200,000,000	13	23.4%
$ 50,000,000 to $100,000,000	12	11.3%
$ 25,000,000 to $ 50,000,000	17	7.8%
$ 10,000,000 to $ 25,000,000	18	4.4%
Under $10,000,000	2	0.2%

Investment Constraints of Endowment Funds. The most important investment constraints and risks that affect the portfolio policies of college and university endowment funds are discussed in the following paragraphs.

Stability of Principal—Risk of Price Depreciation. Protection of principal is of great importance. Unreasonable investment risks that could cause realized losses and a decline in the capital of the fund should not be assumed. On the other hand, these endowment funds are long-term investors that expect the capital of their funds to grow year by year and normally expect to use only income, not capital. In this respect, fluctuations in the market value of securities can be ignored, and therefore endowment funds can judiciously invest heavily in common stocks. Some funds have properly invested 70%-80% of assets in common stocks. However, if projected needs in the foreseeable future assume that some of the capital of the fund may be required for say construction of buildings, then this proportion of the capital should be invested in fixed-value assets of good marketability and generally with maturities of 5 years or less.

Interest Rate Risk. Because of the strength of ownership, the interest rate risk can essentially be ignored except for capital funds expected to be needed for capital budget projects.

Income Risks and Need to Maximize Income. The major objective for endowment funds is maximizing income within the constraints of sound investment policy. In most cases (except for anticipated capital budget requirements) the function of the endowment fund is to provide income for annual operational requirements to supplement tuition and other income.

By far the largest expenditure is for faculty and administrative salaries. This area has been quite competitive, not only because of overall rising salary trends in the economy but also because of a relative shortage of properly trained faculty personnel and, highly important, the need to compete in salaries with rapidly growing tax-supported institutions. Private institutions cannot raise tuition to a level sufficient to meet this salary competition. Endowment income must provide the difference.[10] Therefore, these institutions not only cannot risk loss of income but need consistently rising income, and this directs investment into common stocks. At one time dividend income from stocks was considered to be fluctuating income; but dividend income has been essentially as stable as bond interest for diversified common stock portfolios since 1938 and, in addition, has risen 7 times.[11] Therefore the reasons for investing heavily in common stocks are strong.

Purchasing Power Risk. The major purpose of these endowment funds is to provide endowment income for faculty and other salaries. Therefore, the inflation risk is significant, favoring investment in common stocks.

Investment Policies of Endowment Funds—Empirical Evidence. The major investments of these funds (as shown in Table 32-13) are 60% common stocks and 21% bonds for a total of 81%. The common stock segment has been rising because of great emphasis in new investments and the general rise in stock prices. Furthermore, the distribution for the 9 largest endowment funds was quite similar to that of the 71 funds.[12]

Tax-Exempt Foundations

There was little specific financial data available on tax-exempt foundations prior to the publication of the findings of Representative Patman contained in the report, "Tax-Exempt Foundations and Charitable Trusts: Their Impact on Our Economy." [13] The eighth installment of this report is summarized in the following paragraphs.

The 1972 Patman Report. The Patman Committee's study of the 1968 annual reports of 20,616 private foundations not only contains some revealing statistics on their economic power and operating efficiency but is also

---

[10] Perhaps some tax funds will be channeled to these private institutions.

[11] See Table 29-1 in Chapter 29.

[12] *1969 Study of College and University Endowment Funds* (Boston, Mass.: Boston Fund).

[13] Prepared for the Subcommittee on Domestic Finance of the Committee on Banking and Currency, House of Representatives, 92nd Congress, Second Session, August, 1972.

TABLE 32-13

Summary of College and University Endowment Diversification

	Market Value 71 Endowment Funds	1973 % of Total
Group A Assets		
Cash or its equivalent	$ 356,671,641	4.7%
Bonds	1,595,595,327	20.9%
Preferred stocks	47,025,300	0.6%
Convertible securities	367,627,129	4.8%
Common stocks	4,613,480,907	60.3%
Miscellaneous	67,731,797	0.9%
Total Group A	$7,048,132,101	92.2%
Group B Assets		
Income-producing real estate & mortgages:		
Real estate under long-term net lease	$ 118,920,841	1.6%
Operated real estate	90,810,738	1.2%
Mortgages	186,998,891	2.4%
Other	197,687,220	2.6%
Total Group B Assets	$ 594,417,690	7.8%
Total Assets	$7,642,549,791	100.0%

of great value in determining the effectiveness of the reforms provided in the Tax Reform Act of 1969 as they relate to tax-exempt organizations. The foundations that furnished information for this study reported assets of $29 billion. As astounding as this figure may seem, it in no way reflects the *actual size and wealth* of private foundations. The private foundations that responded represent approximately one half of the total private foundations, and the procedures employed to report assets held by these private foundations fail to take into account the *actual value* of the assets they hold. A recent estimate by the Department of the Treasury places the number of foundations at 42,000 and projects that the total assets of all organizations classified as private foundations will be *approximately $50 billion.* Over 63 percent of all the assets reported were held by one percent of the responding foundations.

Neither the reported asset figure of $29 billion used by the subcommittee nor the more recent $50 billion estimate of the Department of the Treasury accurately reflects the true size of foundation holdings. In many instances the foundations did not seek to determine and report the *market value* of their assets; instead, they reported the value at what their holdings were, as carried on their books (see Table 32-14). Thus, no appreciation was shown on assets, such as privately held corporate stock or real estate holdings, that may have increased many times in value. The undervaluation of assets would also apply to the Treasury Department's $50 billion estimate of

TABLE 32-14

Distribution of Foundation by Size

Foundations	Number	% of Number	Assets (Market Value) [a]	% of Total Assets
$0 to $200,000	14,515	70.4	$ 685,827,089	2.4
$200,000 to $1 million	3,833	18.6	1,733,634,716	6.0
$1 million to $10 million	1,921	9.3	5,773,006,556	20.2
Over $10 million	347	1.7	20,423,839,239	71.4
Total	20,616	100.0	$28,616,307,600	100.0

a Market value of assets is defined as the carrying value of the assets on the foundation's books plus unrealized appreciation on securities (market value less carrying value of the securities). When the market value of securities was not given on the tax return, the carrying value was used.

assets since, at the time of the Treasury Department study, many foundations had failed to obtain the independent appraisal of assets as required by the Tax Reform Act of 1969.

It is difficult to accurately determine the rate of return foundations earn on their investments. The foundations in this study reported total income (gross receipts) of $2.05 billion in 1968, providing an aggregate return (overall gross rate) of 7.17% on $28.62 billion of reported assets (see Table 32-15). The obvious undervaluation of assets as reported ($29 billion) by the foundations grossly distorted the percentage. For instance, if the actual total market value of the reported assets was more likely $40 or $50 billion, the rate of "gross" return would have been 5.1 and 4.1 respectively. These percentages certainly do not compare with the 15% average—overall—rate of return earned by various investment funds for the same year as reported by the Peterson Commission on Foundations and Private

TABLE 32-15

Rate of Return on Foundation Assets by Asset Size

Foundations	Number	Assets (Market Value) a	Income b	Rate of Return (%)	Income Excluding Capital Gains	Rate of Return (%)
$0 to $200,000	14,515	$ 685,827,089	$ 65,726,167	9.58	$ 50,164,424	7.31
$200,000 to $1 million ...	3,833	1,733,634,716	154,619,673	8.92	119,124,050	6.87
$1 million to $10 million	1,921	5,773,006,556	596,749,534	10.34	466,968,597	8.09
Over $10 million	347	20,423,839,239	1,234,471,512	6.04	796,757,739	3.90
Total	20,616	$28,616,307,600	$2,051,566,886	7.17	$1,433,014,801	5.01

a Market value of assets is defined as the carrying value of the assets on the foundation's books plus unrealized appreciation on securities (market value less carrying value of the securities). When the market value of securities was not given on the tax return, the carrying value was used.
b Includes business profits, interest, dividends, rents, royalties, capital gain or loss, and other income.

Philanthropy. (Note that in 1968 the S&P "425" Industrials rose 8%, which together with a dividend yield of 3% gave an overall rate of return of 11%.) The Peterson Commission also determined that the average yearly return of 21 balanced mutual funds in a 10-year period was 9.2%. Once again, 7.17% reported return and the more probable returns of 5.1% and 4.1% fall far below the 9.2% return as determined by the Commission. Nonproductive assets held by the foundations are often in the form of large blocks of corporate stock that pay little or no dividends. There were 593 foundations that owned 5% or more interest in 913 corporations that did not pay a single dividend. The total market value of these holdings was over $6.5 billion, and these holdings produced a dismal average return of 2.6%.

Another significant point revealed was the number of holdings which have (listed) identical carrying and market values. In some instances the dividends received were greater than the estimated values. This confirms the fact that many of the foundations made no attempt to place reasonable values on their assets as required by IRS instructions and supports the contention that the total assets are grossly undervalued. The cost of producing and distributing charitable benefits by private foundations is staggering by any standard. This study revealed that it cost about $1 in administrative expenses for every $2 distributed to charity. The total expenses reported by the responding foundations amounted to more than $715 million. These foundations failed to distribute $1.1 billion of revenue they received in 1968.

For the 20,616 foundations that responded, the average ratio of contributions paid out to gross receipts was 70%. Of the 50 largest foundations that responded, 18 had a lower-than-average ratio of contributions paid out to gross receipts, and 11 of the 50 largest foundations failed to distribute even 50% of their gross receipts.

The Twentieth Century Fund Study.[14] Despite their material resources and multiple activities (see Table 32-16), there has been comparatively little independent research on foundations in the United States. Fixing an accurate value on the wealth of the big foundations is also difficult because the data are elusive.

The Peterson Study found that 94% of all foundation grants were made to established reputable institutions which are officially certified as tax-exempt.[15]

In the case of four of the big 33 foundations (see Table 32-17), the question of voluntary diversification (of assets) did not arise. Vincent Astor,

---

[14] Waldemar A. Nielsen, *The Big Foundations—A Twentieth Century Fund Study* (New York: Columbia University Press, 1972).
[15] *Ibid.*, pp. 274-275.

The conclusion of the 1972 Twentieth Century Fund Study in respect to investment performance was:

> The implications of the foregoing studies can be read in various ways, and because of the wide variations in economic linkages and investment practices among the large foundations, any general conclusions must be drawn with great care. But the evidence *in toto* strongly suggests that the excessive concentration of foundation assets has generally resulted in diminishing income for charity; and if commonly accepted measures of performance are applied to foundation portfolio management, the returns achieved have not been superior to what a totally random selection of securities would have produced.
>
> Manifestly, various private interest considerations have influenced the investment decisions of a great many of the larger foundations. These may consist of the sentimental attachment of the donor's family and other trustees to a particular profit-making company, or the desire of company officers, who are also trustees, to maintain the security of their employment by resisting diversification. Such intentions and others that can readily be imagined are of differing degree of dubiety. But they all cast their shadow over the face of big philanthropy as it functions today. Foundation investment policies may not be serving the selfish interest of those who control them, but in far too many instances they appear to be.[18]

Conclusions on Portfolio Policies of Tax-Exempt Fundations. In summary, tax-exempt foundations and trusts can and do accomplish their purposes by investing heavily in common stocks. As a policy, they hold about 27% of assets in bonds. They could raise the proportion in stocks to 80% of market value of stocks and let the proportion in bonds decline to 10% and still meet all their self-imposed requirements.

Many of the funds when established were solely or largely concentrated in one stock—the basis for the foundation. From the standpoint of a sound investment policy and to assure their purpose of rising assets and rising income, it is probably judicious to diversify widely rather than to hold portfolios heavily committed in one stock in one industry, even though in later hindsight such a commitment might have produced the best results.

QUESTIONS

1. What factors suggest a conservative investment policy and what factors suggest an aggressive investment policy for life insurance companies?

2. (a) Do life insurance companies typically face a strong income constraint?

---

[18] *Ibid.*, p. 290.

(b) Under what conditions might liquidity in the investment portfolio for life insurance companies be important?

3. (a) Are common stocks an important component of the investment portfolios of life insurance companies? Why?

(b) Discuss the appropriateness of common stocks as investment vehicles for life insurance companies, including consideration of legality.

4. Should life insurance companies be large purchasers of tax-exempt securities? property and casualty insurance companies? Explain.

5. How do the conclusions of the Hickman Study apply to life insurance investment policy?

6. Compare the investment portfolios of life insurance companies with those of property and casualty insurance companies. What important differences do you find?

7. (a) Why is stability of income important to property and casualty insurance companies?

(b) Contrast life insurance companies and property and casualty insurance companies in terms of liquidity problems.

8. Contrast life insurance companies and property and casualty insurance companies in terms of the purchasing power risk. Do they face equal degrees of constraint?

9. Analyze the investment constraints on portfolios of pension funds.

10. Criticize the investment portfolios of state and local pension funds, and note any important recent changes in investment policy.

WORK-STUDY PROBLEMS

1. Select *one* of the types of financial institutions discussed in this chapter for the following assignment. Specify the size and the type of financial institution.

(a) Explain the portfolio policies recommended for the particular financial institution chosen.

(b) List the major categories and the amounts of financial assets of the institution chosen.

(c) Recommend an actual list of security investments for that institution, listing specific securities chosen and amounts of each.

(d) Give a brief justification for each selection.

2. Select three life insurance companies and calculate the compounded growth rate of total assets, invested assets, insurance in force, premium income, and investment income for the most recent five- and ten-year

period. Also determine the change that has occurred in policy loans for each company over the ten-year period.

(a) Do the investment policies followed by each of the companies differ? If so, explain in what way.

(b) Do the data you have collected help explain the investment policy of the company? Discuss.

(c) Would the stock of the insurance companies you are studying appear to be interesting purchases based on the data you have gathered? Discuss.

SUGGESTED READINGS

Bassett, Preston C. "Progressive Approach to Pension Funding." *Harvard Business Review* (November-December, 1972), pp. 125-141.

Belliveau, Nancy. "Portrait of the Pru's Prudent Man." *The Institutional Investor* (July, 1970), pp. 48-57.

Bloakley, Fred. "Burt Dorsett-for CREF, A Continuing Faith in Growth." *The Institutional Investor* (January, 1971), pp. 56-60, 86-88.

Dietz, P. O. "Pension Fund Investment Performance." *Financial Analysts Journal* (January-February, 1966).

Ellis, Charles D. "Danger Ahead for Pension Funds." *Harvard Business Review* (May-June, 1971), pp. 50-56.

——————. *Institutional Investing*. Homewood, Illinois: Dow Jones-Irwin, Inc., 1971.

——————. "Let's Solve the Endowment Crisis." *Harvard Business Review* (March-April, 1970), pp. 92-102.

Fiske, Heidi S. "Chase Manhattan's Paper Portfolio Derby." New York: *The Institutional Investor* (March, 1970), pp. 39-42.

Friend, Edward H. "A 1972 Critique on Funding Media for Pension Funds." *Journal of Accountancy* (August, 1972), pp. 29-40.

Fritz, David. "Whatever Happened to the Other Institutional Study?" *The Institutional Investor* (May, 1972), p. 58.

Henke, Emerson D. "Performance Evaluations for Not-for-Profit Organizations." *Journal of Accountancy* (June, 1972), pp. 51-55.

Institutional Investor, The (Editorials).
"A Report on Ten Other State Pension Funds." (February, 1970), pp. 41-47.
"How $125 Million in Pension Money Is Being Spread Around—A Special Survey of Corporate Attitudes." (Number 1970), pp. 32-36.
"Oregon Blazes the Pension Trial." (February, 1970).
"The Problems of Being the Ford Foundation." (November, 1968), pp. 37-41.

McGregor, Douglas A. "Uneasy Look at Performance Approach." *Harvard Business Review* (September-October, 1972), pp. 133-139.

Mennis, E. A. "New Trends In Institutional Investing." *Financial Analysts Journal* (July-August, 1968).

Nielsen, Waldemar A. *The Big Foundations, A Twentieth Century Fund Study*. New York: Columbia University Press, 1972.

Oppenheimer & Co. *The Financial Casualty Insurance Industry*. New York: Oppenheimer & Co. (Member NYSE).

Pension Fund News (Monthly). New York: Communications Channels, Inc.

Schoeplein, Robert N. "The Effect of Plans on Other Relevant Savings." *The Journal of Finance* (June, 1970), pp. 633-637.

Silver, William L. *Portfolio Behavior of Financial Institutions*. New York: Holt, Rinehart and Winston Inc., 1970.

Tax-Exempt Foundations and Charitable Trends: Their Impact on Our Economy (Installments 1-8). Staff Report for the Subcommittee on Domestic Finance of the Committee on Banking and Currency, House of Representatives 88-92nd Congresses, 1968-1972.

TIAA and CREF (Annual Reports).

Wasson, H. C. "Some Investment Policies for Commercial Banks." *Financial Analysts Journal* (May-June, 1966).

Welles, Chris. "Foundations—The Quiet $20 Billion." *The Institutional Investor* (November, 1968), pp. 31-36.

The Computer in
Portfolio Selection

During the past decade, computers have literally revolutionized the techniques of administering business and industry. Many manual operations, such as clerical work of conventional data processing, have been transformed to higher automated functions. Computers not only have speeded up the storage and transmission of information, but also they are actually changing the methods by which things are done. Attempts are being made to create models useful in solving industrial problems that deal in quantified information and also against which various theories can be tested.

Today, the investment field may be on the threshold of a new era in computer application. A group of men in the securities industry are trying to harness the latent potential of the computer into a powerful force for a truly scientific approach to investment management. On the other side of the coin, there are some who feel there is serious danger that analysts will become too enamoured with the information game that can be played on the computer and will overlook the elements that cannot be quantified. In the words of one writer:

> The implication is that the shuffling around of all this information leads to a private solipsistic game which has little to do with the realities of managing money. But it takes a courageous soul to downgrade the effect of the computer revolution. Today computers are screening millions of bits of data for analysts. They are providing managers with models of industries, against which various contingencies can be tested. They are even providing technical analysis and drawing their own charts.[1]

---

[1] Heidi S. Fiske, "The Computer: How It Is Changing the Money Manager," *The Institutional Investor* (April, 1968), p. 23.

One need not own or even lease a computer on a long-term basis in order to use one. Under "time-sharing" plans, computer time can be rented by the hour, the cost varying with the degree of sophistication and the speed of the equipment. An advanced computer is capable of doing in one hour the routine paper work that would require about a day and a half of time with a staff of six or more analysts and portfolio managers. Therefore, the use of computers is not limited to large institutions because of cost factors.

THE "ANALYTICS" SYSTEM

White, Weld & Company has developed a system known as "Analytics" [2] that allows analysts in different institutions to use a computer simultaneously. The system involves time sharing, a data bank, and interrogation by the user in noncomputer financial language to facilitate use by nonprogrammers. A terminal would be placed in the analyst's office connected to a central computer by telephone cable. When the computer receives an inquiry, it works out as much of the answer as it can in about $\frac{1}{10}$ of a second and then does the same for some other user. If there are 20 people on the line, it is back to the first user's problem in 2 seconds. Since it takes more time to print out data than to compute it, there usually will be no noticeable time lag for the user. J. J. Gal, the architect of Analytics, has said:

> The methodology of financial analysis is unclear and that is why it is important to be able to interact with the data. If you know the earnings per share on a stock and all other factors about it, you still don't know what will happen to the stock because you don't know what to multiply or divide by what. So what you want to do is to use your experience and intuition to guess at the relationship, then immediately examine the result of your guess and ask the next question on the basis of it. We designed Analytics to enable the analyst to do this.[3]

White, Weld & Company claims the computer language it has developed for the Analytics system can be effectively learned and applied in less than a day. More esoteric languages, such as Fortran II and IV, can be used on the system, as can BASIC, General Electric's language. BASIC is about the simplest computer language available, but it is not as readily applicable to financial problems as many languages that have been developed.

---

[2] The discussion of Analytics here is based on an article by Penelope Orth, "Will Analytics Ever Fly," *The Institutional Investor* (April, 1968), p. 44. In August, 1968, the Interactive Data Services, Division of White, Weld & Co. (member of NYSE) advertised publicly their Analytics, time-sharing, investor-oriented computer service.

[3] For a more detailed description of "Analytics," see J. J. Gal, "Man-Machine Interactive Systems and Their Application to Financial Analysis," *Financial Analysts Journal* (May-June, 1966).

White, Weld & Company's data bank contains fundamental information from the magnetic tape files of Compustat;[4] technical information (the daily high, low, close, and volume) supplied by Bunker Ramo since January, 1967; and earnings estimates of all the analysts who use Analystics. The latter data offer a way of assessing the aggregate thinking of one's peers in the world of investment analysis. More issues are added to Compustat yearly.

The Analystics service costs from $30,000 to $60,000 a year, but its use avoids the cost of renting or buying a computer, hiring special programmers, and developing the data base. Ira Herenstein, Vice-President of Standard Statistics, has estimated that "to get in this field at all (the computer field) costs from $50,000 to $250,000 a year." Such systems as White, Weld & Company's Interactive Data Services (Analystics) may be much more practical for the user than developing his own computer system.

FUNCTIONS OF THE COMPUTER

The speed and accuracy of the computer in handling masses of data enables it to perform routine repetitive operations, where large volume is involved, efficiently and relatively cheaply. This is already recognized in the investment world as typified in the use of computers to perform many "back office operations" in large brokerage firms. The ability to store, recall, and process mathematically large masses of information suggests even more interesting applications to problems of security analysis and portfolio management. The study of the interrelationships existing among many variables can be facilitated through the use of the computer. More explicitly, the computer can help in the following areas:

1. The many interrelationships studied by the security analyst and useful standards of comparison to facilitate security evaluation can be developed in quantitative form. For example, the computer can be asked to scan the universe of stocks in terms of data derived from the balance sheets and the income statements of many companies to select for more intensive study those companies that meet specified standards in terms of price-earnings ratios, dividend yields, etc. Having selected a limited number of stocks worthy of further consideration, the computer can perform the mathematical calculations necessary to facilitate projections of sales and earnings and, on the basis of these projections, can perform valuation calculations consistent with the assumptions made. Many sophisticated

---

[4] A service developed and sold by the Standard Statistics subsidiary of Standard & Poor's Corporation covering about 60 items of financial statement information for 2,500 companies on an annual basis for the last 20 years (of which, Analystics uses only those on 1,000 companies) and 13 items of quarterly information on 1,000 companies since 1962 (of which Analystics uses 900).

statistical techniques are opened to the analyst, since he is relieved of burdensome calculating work and his horizons are broadened.[5]

2. Many suggested timing devices can be tested on the computer, at least in terms of their usefulness historically. Further, the computer is being increasingly used in economic forecasting, and improvements in these forecasts have meaning to investors. Shiskin's work at the Bureau of the Census is indicative of important work being done in this area.[6] Finally, more effective study of the many techniques suggested by "technical analysis" will be encouraged, and possibly those that prove most consistently useful can be refined on the computer in charting.

3. Existing portfolio management practices can be studied in great depth.[7] Such studies should enable managers to foresee possibilities for improvement. Much bookkeeping, necessary to sound portfolio decisions, can be facilitated. Possibly the most important use in this area will be to study the consequences of different investment strategies under varying assumed economic and institutional conditions. The work of Dr. Markowitz is a well-known effort to analyze alternative investment strategies with given measures of risk acceptability.[8]

The computer will play an important role in utilizing mathematical models to simulate and analyze investment problems. Further study and research in the field of applying mathematical models to the investment decision-making process is urged. To date this work has been largely theoretical.

Screening Processes

Screening processes are widely used so as to select from thousands of stocks and bonds a limited number of securities worthy of extensive analysis. Screening processes are particularly useful to firms too small to cover the entire stock list. Obviously, the computer can only screen stocks on which data have already been gathered and stored in the computer system. For example, a subscriber to the Analytics system could instruct the computer to list all stocks covered by the service that meet the following qualifications: [9]

1. A minimum number of shares outstanding to assure a desired degree of marketability and a minimum daily and/or weekly volume in the recent past.

---

[5] In a study of 100 utility companies, an analyst was able to obtain in approximately one-half hour data that would have taken him about 200 days to compute without the assistance of the computer. As the amount and the timeliness of information gathered increase, the probability of reaching a sound decision also increases.

[6] *Business Cycle Developments,* published monthly by the Census Bureau.

[7] Geoffrey P. Clarkson, *Portfolio Selection: A Simulation of Trust Investment* (Englewood Cliffs, N. J.: Prentice-Hall, Inc., 1962).

[8] Harry Markowitz, "Portfolio Selection," *The Journal of Finance* (March, 1952), and the book by the same author, *Portfolio Selection* (New York: John Wiley & Sons, Inc., 1959).

[9] The list used as an example by Penelope Orth in the article mentioned earlier was paraphrased here.

2. Sales exceeding a given dollar amount.
3. Positive earnings in the last year (also last 2, 3, 4, 5 years, etc.).
4. Earnings changes for each of the last two quarters that are a given percent, such as 5% and 10% respectively, above corresponding quarters of the preceding fiscal year.
5. A price-earnings ratio not to exceed a given multiple defined as last night's close over White, Weld & Company's next year's estimates.
6. A specified payout ratio over the past 5 years. (Miss Orth used less than 50% and a payout of less than 40% in 1967 in her list. This would suggest an emphasis on capital appreciation rather than income in selecting stocks.)
7. An expected yield not less than a stated percentage. (Miss Orth used 2.5%.)
8. Pre-tax and after-tax margins that have increased for each of the last 3 years (also last 4, 5 years, etc.).

Of course, the above criteria could be applied to the Compustat tapes or one's own data bank. Additional criteria could be added, such as return on stockholder's equity and/or total assets and other criteria derived from the list above. Chase Manhattan Bank and Standard & Poor's Corporation have been investigating various hypothesized characteristics of a stock that may cause favorable price movement in an effort to improve the filtering process. Mr. Kisor suggests that companies with *accelerating* earnings growth rates are excellent candidates for further common stock analysis.[10]

Additional information could be asked of the computer in reference to stocks that survived an initial screening. Illustrative of such requests would be the following:

1. Rank the companies in terms of the compound growth rate of sales and/or profits over the last 10 years (or 5 years, etc.).
2. Rank the companies in terms of yield.
3. Rank the companies in terms of price-earnings ratios and earnings yield.

The data developed by Analystics would allow even more complex requests, since forecasts are contained on the tapes. Examples are: [11]

1. Rank the qualifying stocks by the percentage difference between my current year earnings estimate and last year's earnings.
2. Take the average of all user estimates available and divide that figure into last night's closing price to determine a projected price-earnings ratio for each surviving company. Rank the companies on the basis of these projected P/E ratios.
3. Construct a historical P/E ratio by weighting the latest year-end P/E ratio by 4, the previous year-end P/E ratio by 3, the next previous year-

---

[10] Manown Kisor, Jr., "Quantitative Approaches to Common Stock Selection," *Business Economics* (Spring, 1966).
[11] Orth, *op. cit.*, p. 45. Again, questions posed in the article were somewhat changed in the presentation here.

end P/E ratio by 2, and the next previous year-end P/E ratio by 1. Print out the percentage difference between the projected P/E ratio for each company and the historical P/E ratio.

4. Multiply the two P/E ratios determined above by my current year earnings estimate and compare the resultant figure to the current price in terms of percentage difference.

Many additional questions could be raised, thereby greatly extending the horizons of the analyst.

Aiding Stock Valuation Models

Stock valuation models are designed to tell whether a stock is over-valued or undervalued in relation to an intrinsic or fundamental value. Intrinsic value is basically determined by making projections of the growth and the stability of sales, earnings, and dividends and then by applying capitalization factors. Computers can aid greatly in this process by relating an infinite number of variables, far beyond the scope of an individual.

The Program "RETURN." Professor J. Peter Williamson of the Amos Tuck School of Dartmouth has developed several interesting computer programs to aid in stock valuation. The program RETURN can be useful in determining past rates of return experienced on a stock, which may serve as a guide when selecting the appropriate discount rate to use in a present value model of the type discussed in Chapter 11 of this book.

The Program "NICKMOL." The valuation approach suggested by Molodovsky in a number of articles in the *Financial Analysts Journal* is represented by a program called NICKMOL. NICKMOL can be used to calculate intrinsic value, given normalized current earnings per share, dividend payout rates, discount rates, and either a long-term growth rate in earnings continuing indefinitely into the future or a price/earnings ratio forecast for some future point in time. In addition, the program will calculate the time period for which a forecasted growth rate must persist, or the price/earnings ratio that must be achieved at a future point in time to make intrinsic value equal to current market price.

Present value theory suggests that the intrinsic value of a stock is the discounted present value of the stream of dividends the shareholder expects to receive, assuming he holds the stock indefinitely into the future (see Chapter 11). In the NICKMOL model,

$$V = \frac{D_1}{(1+i)} + \frac{D_2}{(1+i)^2} + \cdots + \frac{D_n}{(1+i)^n}$$

where a long-term growth rate in earnings extending indefinitely into the future is assumed, expected cash dividends (D_1; D_2 . . .; D_n) are replaced by expected earnings per share multiplied by the expected payout ratio (P) and growth rate (g). The current period earnings per share estimate (C_o) is in terms of a normalized earnings per share expectation, and a long-term growth rate must also be estimated. The model may be represented by the following formula:

$$V = \frac{C_o(P)(1+g)}{(1+r)} + \frac{C_o(P)(1+g)^2}{(1+r)^2} + \cdots + \frac{C_o(P)(1+g)^n}{(1+r)^n}$$

If a price/earnings ratio expected to be achieved at a future point in time is entered (rather than assume a growth rate continuing indefinitely into the future), or if one wishes to vary the growth rate, the appropriate formula is:

$$V = \frac{C_o(P)(1+g_1)}{1+r} + \frac{C_o(P)(1+g_1)(1+g_2)}{(1+r)^2} + \cdots +$$

$$\frac{C_o(P)\ (1+g_1)(1+g_2)\ \cdots\ (1+g_n)}{(1+r)^n}\quad \frac{C_o(1+g_1)(1+g_2)\ \cdots\ (1+g_n)R}{(1+r)^n}$$

where

C_o = normalized earnings per share
g_1 = assumed growth rate in first holding period
g_2 = assumed growth rate in second holding period
g_n = assumed growth rate in n^{th} holding period
P = assumed dividend payout rate for given year
R = expected price-earning ratio in n^{th} year
r = appropriate discount rate

The user of NICKMOL may forecast growth rates for various time spans in the future and may also forecast periods of adjustment from one growth rate to another, choosing one of three kinds of adjustment: *straight line,* which implies that the rate changes by the same amount during each year of the adjustment period; *fast,* which implies that the adjustment follows a sum-of-the-years digits formula; and *slow,* which implies a reverse sum-of-the-years digits formula.

Developing Probabilistic Models

The computer can also aid in developing forecasts of earnings and dividends necessary to the valuation process. Assume an analyst was trying to project steel demand to form a basis for revenue and profit estimates for a given steel company. He would probably make at least two estimates of how demand would rise or fall, what would happen to the price of steel, and what competition would do, and then he would derive revenue estimates with a limited number of different combinations. With a computer, however, he could consider many estimates of steel demand, domestic and import competition, and many price hypotheses, and he could vary all the possibilities against each other to give a wide range of results in the form of a probability distribution. Also, more sophisticated statistical techniques can be used, such as seasonal adjustment of quarterly data. All this could be done in far less time than it would take an analyst to test a couple of combinations.

Input-output data, discussed in Chapter 14, can be utilized to improve revenue and profit forecasts. First National City Bank, among others, is using computers to construct probabilistic models that give wide ranges of probable sales, earnings prices, etc., under different circumstances. In the 1960s, this bank published a comprehensive computer-based study of the copper industry.

Further, the computer allows the analyst to try many trend-fitting methods to aid in determining past rates of change, pattern of change, and factors underlying those changes. Multiple regression analysis is facilitated. Improved forecasting should lead to sounder future earnings per share, dividend per share, and capitalization figures to be utilized in stock valuation models.

The assumptions involved in such models are tenuous. However, on the basis of tests, Compufund reports that better results were obtained by accepting stocks chosen by a computer model based on fundamentals than by second guessing the computer in terms of subjective evaluating of nonquantifiable data. There is some skepticism in the market as to whether Compufund does allow the computer to have the last word, but an organized and well-thought-out approach to valuation is at the heart of sound security selection. A frequently changing environment requires flexible interpretations that suggest the need of man's independent judgment rather than blind adherence to a model, but the computer can aid in facilitating and improving those judgments.

Testing Timing Techniques

Waltson & Co. and Jesup & Lamont run technical filters on the daily closing tapes to develop timing signals. Jesup & Lamont ultimately bases all its recommendations on fundamentals, but it claims that the technical signals have proved helpful in timing.

Jesup & Lamont uses a computer to calculate figures that are projected as light pinpoints in appropriate positions on a cathode ray tube. A camera photographs the picture formed on the tube and prints the results. O'Neil Fund uses a CalComp plotter with its IBM 360 to draw charts.[12] Computer people suggest that the work involved in preparing charts can be performed more accurately and at lower cost by computer techniques, although admittedly the analyst might gain more insight if he prepared his charts by hand. However, one mutual fund well known for its extensive chart use shuns computer techniques, noting that it would cost about $4 to produce each of its 4,000 or so charts on the computer, whereas it costs a few cents of a clerk's time to update each chart daily; however, this mutual fund does recognize that updating on the computer would be cheaper than generating each chart anew.[13]

Many of the techniques used in technical analysis have not been adequately tested to determine their validity. Computers can be used to test such timing techniques, but precise definitions of each technique must first be developed. In the brief discussion of technical analysis in Chapter 4, the many limitations and ambiguities in the application of techniques were noted. Of course, explicit theories could be developed in a form that could be tested. Intensive research in this area could develop more usable timing tools.

PORTFOLIO BUILDING MODELS

Portfolio building models are not concerned with the relationship of one stock as opposed to another, but rather with developing a process of reasoning from particular investment constraints to conclusions about suitable investment policies and securities that as a group best fit those investment policies and goals. Either of two approaches may be adopted: (1) have the computer analyze and evaluate existing investment management practices, or (2) find a theoretical basis that will improve existing practices and lead to better understanding of the consequences of alternative investment strategies.

Clarkson Model

Clarkson was a proponent of the first approach, which he entitled "heuristic analysis" in his 1962 book.[14] Heuristic analysis requires a particular sequence in approach, since he found that the answer to one question asked by the portfolio manager was part of the information necessary

---

[12] Fiske, *op. cit.,* p. 24.
[13] *Ibid.*
[14] Clarkson, *op. cit.*

to answer a subsequent one.[15] Clarkson determined that the manager, sometimes unknowingly, followed certain rules of thumb, which he then incorporated into a computer program.

F. I. duPont uses the Clarkson technique. This firm has developed a flow chart that first tells the computer to study the portfolio and recommend issues that should be sold. The computer may eliminate issues on the grounds that they are unsuitable in terms of fundamentals or objectives of the portfolio, or to correct overconcentration by issue or by industry, or to correct overdiversification. The computer then recommends stocks to buy with the cash generated. Its selection of stocks is based on a three-part numerical rating scheme. Each issue thus selected is given a score for appreciation possibilities, risk, and income by a single individual after he discusses it with analysts who cover that issue. While admittedly a crude technique, it does demonstrate the usefulness of the computer even when little complex theoretical work is done.

Markowitz Model

The work of Harry Markowitz [16] is a landmark event in the effort to find a theoretical basis that will improve existing portfolio management practices. The basic structure of the Markowitz model, which is called a "covariance variance model," is relatively simple.[17] Markowitz assumes investors prefer larger to smaller returns and that they are "risk averters." [18] Risk is measured in terms of deviation (or variance) from expected portfolio rates of return. Diversification can help minimize deviations from expected rates of return. The adequacy of diversification does not depend solely on the number of securities held but also on avoiding investment in a portfolio of securities with high covariances. Therefore, the portfolio manager asks the model either:

1. To find the group of stocks expected to achieve his target rate of return with the least volatility in the price of the portfolio as a whole. Here the model would seek stocks whose prices tend to move in opposite directions in the same kind of market and whose earnings tend to move in different directions in the same kind of economic climate. The loss in one security would thereby be offset by the gain in the other.
2. To select a group of stocks that will maximize returns with a given degree of acceptable volatility in terms of investment constraints.

---

[15] For example, the amount of securities that the computer indicated would be sold by the manager formed part of the cash available for purchases.

[16] Markowitz, *op. cit.* Results from using the model have not been very satisfactory.

[17] IBM has programmed one approach to the model.

[18] Investors can gain expected return by accepting higher variance in portfolio performance or can reduce variance by giving up returns.

A Markowitz model would determine from numerous possible portfolio combinations of individual securities the most likely expected return from the portfolio (E) and the ranges of deviation likely around the expected return (V). E becomes a weighted average of expected returns in terms of a probability distribution of the expected returns.[19] The variance is measured in terms of the expected deviation of the probability distribution.[20] Let us assume that the portfolios A and B each offered a 9% yield, but the expected deviation of A was 3 and that of B was 4. A would then be the more desirable portfolio. Where expected yields and deviations differ, the decision becomes subjective, depending on the individual portfolio manager's willingness to risk earning a lower rate of return in an effort to achieve a higher rate.

The Markowitz model has not been widely used, largely because of the computational work involved. One writer [21] notes that the number of combinations that must be tested (each time the portfolio is changed) to establish the "covariance matrix" is equal to the square of the total number of stocks in the universe of possibilities, divided by 2, plus the total number of stocks divided by 2. This is about 4.3 million combinations if the universe is the NYSE and the ASE stock lists alone.

Several other criticisms have been levied against the Markowitz approach. Some object to considering variance as the most appropriate measure of risk. Price volatility becomes serious only if an investor must liquidate during a downturn or acts emotionally. If he can wait for an upturn, price volatility does not pose a serious risk. Furthermore, it is questionable whether the margin of error around the assumed return is symmetrical.

Also, a small change in the expected rates of return can lead to massive recommended changes in the portfolio since the elements balance each other. This could lead to excessive churning of the portfolio, unless runs on the computer are infrequent. A major deficiency of the Markowitz model is that it does not allow for transaction costs.

CONCLUSIONS ON USE OF COMPUTERS

There seems to be no doubt that electronic data processing equipment is becoming more prevalent in the financial community. Banks, insurance companies, and brokerage houses are now employing such equipment extensively. The computer not only stores information and does clerical work but has become an important managerial tool in the financial community.

---

[19] $E = p_1 y_1 + p_2 y_2 + \ldots p_n y_n.$
[20] $V = p_1 (y_1 - E)^2 + p_2 (y_2 - E)^2 + \ldots + p_n (y_n - E)^2.$
[21] Fiske, *op. cit.*, p. 27.

The only problem is that both the scholars and the owners of the computers have not yet perfected it to the degree thought possible. All this will take considerable time.

On the Ability to Communicate

The analyst is very much at the mercy of the system and the environment in which he operates. His ability to analyze, to direct, to initiate, and to control depends upon his ability to communicate. Consequently, the computer's greatest impact in the years ahead will be at the level where information is needed. The computer will expand the analyst's horizon by storing and handling masses of data in a timely and informative way, facilitating the testing of hypotheses and broadening the analyst's understanding of the interrelationships in the market and variations in these interrelationships. It will not replace the skillfully creative analyst in his role as a true student of the market. The analyst must have the ability to accept and work with uncertainty. New unknowns in the future will undoubtedly make even more essential the ability to tolerate, analyze, and explore uncertainties.

It is the authors' opinion that as technical and scientific devices become more sophisticated (for example, as the electronic brain plays an ever-increasing role in the financial analyst's decisions), the human element at all levels becomes increasingly significant. Without minimizing the valuable tools that science has placed in our hands, we must not allow ourselves to overlook the fact that the most advanced technical equipment is neither creative nor capable of exercising initiative. The financial analyst must still evaluate and interpret on the basis of his knowledge, experience, and skill the vast accumulation of data and statistics produced at unbelievable speeds by mechanical means. The less skillful and mediocre analyst will find that he may simply make bigger mistakes at a faster rate, with more disastrous consequences than ever before.

On the Ability to Decide

The authors of this book do not agree with those who feel the decision-making process in the investment field can be largely automated. The computer is not a machine to take the place of the human brain. Investment decisions remain as much an art as a science. By sorting, analyzing, and classifying information, the computer can be of great assistance to the financial analyst. Still, the financial analyst must further analyze the facts and the relationships developed with the aid of the computer, in terms of his knowledge and experienced skill, and make investment decisions for his clients. The analyst will still have to cope with and allow for uncertainty in his decision making and the frequently changing environment in which he operates. He never can ignore the psychology of the market environment. The most successful investors still place some reliance on intuition.

This is not to deny that computers can be programmed to behave adaptively and to improve their own programs on the basis of experience. It has been demonstrated that computers can be programmed to solve relatively ill-structured problems by using methods very similar to those used by humans in the same problem-solving situations: "by trial and error research using all sorts of rules of thumb to guide the selection; by abstracting from the given problem and solving first the abstracted problem; by using analogy; by reasoning in terms of means and ends, goals and subgoals; by adjusting aspirations to the attainable." [22] Strongly limiting factors suggest themselves immediately, however, when attempting to use computers to solve ill-structured problems as represented in the investment decision. First, the many complex and interrelated variables important in the investment decision appear to act differently at different points in time. Concern is with the future, not the past or present, and man's judgments are necessary to properly instruct the computer. To date, the authors of this book are unaware of any successful construction of mathematical equations that reflect the relationships among the important variables so as to lead to consistently successful investment performance stemming automatically from utilizing the results of solving such equations. [23] Secondly, the fact that a computer can do something a man can do does not mean the computer should be employed instead of the man. The computer must prove itself in terms of cost. Finally, the information necessary for intelligent analysis is often subjective as well as objective and difficult to come by. (Again, see footnote on pp. 288-289.)

The computer is not the innovator that man is. It is limited by the instructions given it and the data fed it. Man must innovate in terms of new uses and new approaches that completely break with past traditions and understandings. Truly creative thinking by man must accompany the use of the computer if we are to successfully realize its potential.

QUESTIONS

1. (a) What is "Analytics"?
   (b) What advantages might it offer an investor?

[22] Herbert Simon, "The Automation of Management," *Management: A Book of Readings,* ed. Koontz and O'Donnell (New York: McGraw-Hill Book Co., 1964).
[23] In fact, some writers have offered evidence suggesting securities perform a random walk, at least over the short term and perhaps over the intermediate term.

2. What are Standard & Poor's Compustat Tapes? What is the importance of these tapes?

3. How might one use the computer in the investment screening process?

4. In what areas of investment analysis and planning may the computer be of use? Discuss explicitly.

5. "Nickmol can be used to calculate intrinsic value."
   (a) What is Nickmol?
   (b) How is "intrinsic value" defined in Nickmol?
   (c) What limitations do you see in the Nickmol model?

6. What uses might be made of the computer to improve investment timing?

7. (a) Discuss the application by F. I. duPont of Clarkson's heuristic approach to portfolio management.
   (b) What limitations do you see in this approach?

8. (a) How does Markowitz measure risk?
   (b) Discuss the meaning of the (E) variable in the Markowitz model.
   (c) What is meant by high covariance of securities? Of what significance is high covariance to Markowitz?

9. Briefly discuss several of the criticisms that have been levied against the Markowitz model.

10. Can the computer "think"? What limitations surrounding the use of the computer are inherent in this area?

WORK-STUDY PROBLEM

Contact at least three different brokerage firms that have a computer and determine the uses made of the computer by these firms. To what additional areas of investment analysis or portfolio management and general operations would you envisage computer techniques being applied? Are there valid reasons why the brokerage firms you have contacted are not using the computer in these areas? Discuss.

SUGGESTED READINGS

Clarkson, Geoffrey P. *Portfolio Selection: A Simulation of Trust Investment.* Englewood Cliffs, N.J.: Prentice-Hall, Inc., 1962.

Computer Applications in Investment Analysis, The Amos Tuck School of Business Administration. Hanover, N.H.: Dartmouth College, 1966.

Coughtry, Floyd S. "Computers—A Tool in Security Analysis." *Financial Analysts Journal* (November-December 1964).

Eiteman, David K. "A Computer Program for Financial Statement Analysis." *Financial Analysts Journal* (November-December, 1964).

Hodges, Stewart D., and Richard A. Brealey. "Using the Sharpe Model." *The Investment Analyst* (No. 27; September, 1970), pp. 41-50.

Horowitz, Ira. "The Reward to Variability Ratio and Mutual Fund Performance." *Journal of Business* (October, 1966), pp. 485-488.

Institutional Investor, The, April, 1968. The entire issue is devoted to computers, including articles on current and future use of computers.

Investment Decision Making, New Perspectives and Methods. New York: Smith, Barney & Co., Inc. (Member of NYSE), 1968.

"The Investor and the Computer." *Financial Analysts Journal.* (January-February, 1968), pp. 134-158. (Three articles.)

Journal of Financial and Quantitative Analysis, June, 1967. Special issue devoted to portfolio analysis.

Lintner, John. "Security Prices, Risk and Maximized Gains from Diversification." *The Journal of Finance* (December, 1965).

Lorie, James H., and Mary T. Hamilton. *The Stock Market: Theories and Evidence.* Homewood, Illinois: Richard D. Irwin, 1973. Chapters 7, 10, 11 and 12.

Markowitz, Harry. "Portfolio Selection." *The Journal of Finance* (March, 1952).

—————————. *Portfolio Selection.* New York: John Wiley & Sons, 1959.

Martin, A. D., Jr. "Mathematical Programming of Portfolio Selections." *Management Science* (January, 1955), pp. 152-166.

Osborne, M. F. M. "Some Quantitative Tests for Stock Price Generating Models and Trading Folklore" *Journal of American Statistical Association* (June, 1967).

Portfolio Selection: A New Mathematical Approach to Investment Planning. White Plains, N.Y.: International Business Machines Corp., 1962.

Press, S. James. "A Compound Events Model for Security Prices." *Journal of Business* (July, 1967), pp. 317-335.

Sharpe, William F. "A Linear Programming Algorithm for Mutual Fund Portfolio Selection." *Management Science* (March, 1967), pp. 499-510.

Shoolman, Alan R. "The Use of High-Speed Digital Computers in Analysis of Security Values." *Boston University Business Review* (Fall, 1961).

Walter, James E. "A Discriminant Function for Earnings-Price Ratios of Large Industrial Corporations." *The Review of Economics and Statistics* (1959).

Williamson, J. Peter. *Investments: New Analytic Techniques.* New York: Praeger Publishers, 1972. Chapters 1, 4, 5 and 10.

Winkler, Robert. "Quantification of Judgment: Some Methodological Suggestions." *Journal of the American Statistical Association* (December, 1967).

INDEX

beta coefficient, the concept of the characteristic line and the, 290-291
bidding, competitive, 32, 37
blue list, 712
Bluefield Waterworks case, 544
bond indenture, 150-151
bond interest rates, secular trend of, 697
bond investment philosophies and strategies, 210-215
bond portfolio policy, high-grade:
  advantages of, 769
  disadvantages of, 769-770
bond prices:
  and accrued interest on bonds, 164
  brief summary of trends of interest rates and, 86-87
bond rating agencies, 223-225; regulatory restrictions and the legal list for, 225
bond ratings, 223-226:
  a brief empirical review of the basis for, 235
  conclusions on, 226
bond traders, 46
bond yield tables, present value and, 169
bondholders, income position of, in recent years, 754-755
bonds, 149-169:
  adjustment, 152
  authority, 708
  assumed, 162
  baby, 149
  callable or redeemable, 154
  classification of, 152-163
  convertible, 155-156, 774-775; and preferred stocks, 215-220
  coupon or bearer, 153
  defined, 149
  discount municipal, effect of, 169
  general obligation of political subdivision of states, 707
  government, 158
  guaranteed, 162
  high-grade corporate, 771-772
  income, 153-154
  industrial revenue, 708
  leasehold mortgage, 160
  medium-grade, 772-773
  municipal, 705-714
  of nonprofit corporations, 163-164
  perpetual, 156-157
  prior-lien, and receivers' certificates, 152
  real estate mortgage, 232
  refunding of, 152
  registered, 153
  revenue, 707-708
  secured, 158-162
  serial, 155
  sinking fund, 154-155
  state, 706
  subordinated debentures, 157-158
  tax-exempt, 772
  U.S. Government, 770-771
  unsecured, 157
book depreciation and published reported depreciation, 559
book value, 457-458; per share, 497

break-even point, 177
budgets:
  capital, 184-186
  cash, 178-179
bull and bear markets:
  cycles, 104-105
  forecasting of, 105-110
  trend, 104-110
business combinations, goodwill in, 447-448
business in force, composition of, 647
buy-and-hold approach, 260-261

call clause, 154
calls, puts and, 51
capital:
  appreciation, 759-761
  assets, 118
  expenditures, 522, 528
  net working, 461
  working, 177-178, 460-462, 546-547
capital funds, 614; growth of net profits available for all, 494
capital gains:
  and losses, 117-119, 762-763
  and yield, distribution of, 666-667
  retention of, by investment companies, 666
capital markets, empirical evidence in the, 188-189
capital stock, 475
capital stock account, changes in the, 499-502
capital structure, speculative and leveraged, 481-482
capital surplus, 472-473
capitalization, 527-528:
  and actual earnings, 527-528
  of the corporation, 468
  ratios, 481-482, 553-555
  total, percentage of each component to, 482
capitalization structure:
  defined, 182
  variations in, 182-183
cash and cash equivalent items, 463
cash and demand deposits, 730
cash budget, 178-179
cash dividends, 131, 190-197
cash flow, 180-181, 840-841:
  and financial analysis, 448-450
  defined, 830
  differing concepts of, 448-449
  dividends as a percentage of, 489
  the problem of projecting earnings and, 402-404
cash flow analysis, 241
cash flow per share, 498
cash items, 806
cash position, defined, 830
cash ratio, 479
certificates of deposit, negotiable, tremendous expansion of, 611-612
certificates of indebtedness, 689
Clarkson portfolio building model, 871-872

fixed-income securities investments, protection of, 207-209
flat quotations, 164
floor traders, 46
flow of funds, 67-74
forecasting, 313-315; technological, 523-524
foreign investments, 663
formula timing plans, 116-117:
    constant ratio, 117
    variable ratio, 117
freight volume, 499
fund performance, 668-669, 672-674
funds:
    flow of, 67-74
    investment, sources and uses of, 67-72
    performance, 674-678
    supply and demand for, 74
future income, defined, 395

gambling, defined, 6-7
goodwill in business combinations, 447-448
government bonds, 158:
    highest yield in history, 700
    market, environmental changes in the, 687-688, 691-692
    speculative characteristics of, 700
government securities, 688-702:
    investment features of, 691
    ownership of, 693-695
    quality and risk of, 686
    United States, 732
    yield patterns and trends for, 695-700
gross business savings, defined, 59
gross income, 561
gross national product (GNP):
    corporate profits and, 367, 370
    growth rates for, 366-367, 370-371
    projections for, 370-371
gross profit ratio, 484
growth:
    analyzing, 380-393
    and stability ratios and measurements, 493-502
    charting as an aid in analyzing, 380
    common stock, 366
    earnings, management and, 389-390
    industry, 372-373, 378-379
    ingredients of, 265
    life-cycle theory of, 373, 378
    "real," 366
    sales record of, 494
    through mergers, 392-393
growth stock portfolio policy:
    advantages of, 787-788
    application of, 789
    basic assumptions of, 785
    disadvantages of, 788-789
    quality of growth, 787
    types of growth, 785-787
growth stock tables:
    Bauman's, 301-302
    Molodovsky, May, and Chottiner's, 303-304

growth stocks:
    capitalization rate for, 266-267
    price paid for, 266
growth yield formulas and tables, 293-304;
    Guild's, 293-299
    Soldofsky and Murphy's, 299-301
guaranteed bonds, 162

Hope Natural Gas Company case, 544

income:
    bonds, 153-154
    constraints, 846
    funds, 662
    future, 394
    gross, 561
    high risk of decrease in, for a small common stock portfolio, 757-758
    investment, 635-637, 840
    loss of, ability to risk, 749-750
    need for, and stability of, 806-807
    net, 485-490
    objectives and constraints relating to, 748-758
    problems of maximizing, 832-833
    purchasing power of, risk of loss of, 750-751
    retained, 473
    size and stability of, 812, 817
    stability of, from a broadly diversified common stock portfolio, 755-756
income statement:
    all-inclusive, 412
    analysis of items on the, 417-431
    base period analysis, 483-484
    current operating performance, 412
    methods of analyzing, 483-484
    preparation of, 411-417
    projection of, 324-326
    ratio analysis, 482-489
income tax:
    percentages, 485
    reporting of, by share owners, 666
indenture, 149:
    closed, 150
    open, 150
    unlimited, 151
industrial companies, 509:
    stability of, 211
    suggested outline for an analysis of an, 532-535
industrial revenue bonds, 708
industry analysis, 512-519
industry groups, 227-228
industry specialists, qualified, 515-516
inflation, 542:
    and stock prices in Europe, 17-18
    and stock prices in the U.S., 16-17
    defined, 16
    limited-income securities in, 18
information:
    fraudulent and purposely misleading, 404-405

inadequate disclosure *vs.* lack of uniformity of, 405-408
materiality of, 407
sources of, 341-350
input-output coefficient tables, 380
installment sales and receivables, 464
institutional investor performance, 360
insurance:
  accounting, 629
  companies, major groups of, 627
  program of the individual, 733-737
  shares, value of, 638
intangibles, 445-446, 466-468; amortization of, 445-448
interest rates, 75-89:
  and stock yields, 75-79
  brief summary of trends of, and bond prices, 86-87
  historical records of, and prices of debt instruments, 82-84
  rising, 541
  the Federal Reserve and, 84-86
  the structure of, 80-86
interim certificates, 149
Interstate Commerce Commission, 569
inventories, 464-465:
  Fifo and Lifo systems of, 419
  turnover, 480-481
Investment Advisors Act of 1940, 358
investment banker, 13-39:
  advisory service of, to issuer, 32
  as wholesaler and retailer, 32
  investigation of the issuer by the, 32
  other functions of the, 31-32
investment companies:
  appraisal of management and performance, 667-672
  fund performance and the averages, 672-674
  classification of, 653-663
  competition for, 678-679
  regulation of, 663-665
  retention of capital gains by, 666
  SEC report on, 665
  selecting, 667-679
  taxes and, 665-667
Investment Company Act of 1940, 357-358
investment credit, 450-451:
  accounting treatment for the, 451
  amendments to the IRC, 451
investments:
  by financial institutions in equities, 72-74
  economic importance of, 1-2
  funds, sources and uses of, 67-72
  income, 635-637
  long-term, 465
  markets, the two major, 67
  objectives and risks, 747-748
  planning, 730-743
  policy, 635-636; taxes and, 762-765
  productive and unproductive, role of, 2-3
  results, 637
  risks, 10-27; types of, 11-20
  yield, 646
investor protection, market structure, 359

investors:
  conservative, portfolio patterns for, 776
  importance of regulation to, 544
  individual, 7-8; 767-775
  institutional, 3-7, 213-215
  need for philosophy, goals, and policies of, 9-10
  problems of, 8-9
  protection for, 350-361
  security investment and, 3-10
issues:
  call provisions for, 230
  equal and ratable provisions, 229
  junior, 159
  market patterns for, of different quality, 718
  premium and discount, 717-718
  senior or underlying, 159; provisions protecting, 228
  size of, 226-227

Keogh Act (custodial accounts), 667

labor relations, 526-527
lapse ratio, 646-647
lay-off procedure, 34
leasehold mortgage bonds, 160
leases, 469-470; provisions for leasebacks and other, 230
leverage, 149:
  optimum, 187
  trading on the equity and, 148-149
liabilities:
  and capital sections of the balance sheet, 468-474
  current, 462-463
lien position, 231-232
life insurance:
  coverage, minimum, 734
  growth of industry, 640-641
  types of, 735-737
life insurance companies, 638-650, 679:
  adjustment of figures on, 642-644
  assets held by, in separate accounts, 847
  basis for adjustment of earnings, 643
  calculating the value of business in force, 643-644
  conclusions on investment policies of, 837
  determining which to consider, 642
  investment constraints of, 830-837
  making the adjustments in value figures, 644
  portfolio policies of, 829-837
  sources of funds of, 829-830
  sources of information on, 641-642
  stability of earnings of, 641
  underwriting, sources of earnings of, 639-640
life insurance stocks:
  performance of, 650
  quality in, 644-650
  valuation of, 649

limited-income securities:
  cash flow protection for, 241-244
  conclusions on protective features of, 234
  general standards and protective provisions for, 223-234
  investment grade, 205-210
  major advantages of, 206
  risk of decrease in income from, 751-755
  specific quantitative tests for, 234-237
limited open-end mortgage, 159
liquidating dividends, 445
liquidations, 794
liquidity, 42-43;
  and related ratios, 478-481
  objectives and constraints relating to, 761-762
listing, eligibility for, 47-48
load funds, 657
loan function of commercial banks, 801-803
long-term debt, 468-469
long-term earnings projections, 528-529
long-term financing, 182-190; postulates of, 183-184
long-term investments, 465
loss ratio, 633

management performance:
  comparative analysis of, 526
  four factors for measuring, 670
Mann-Elkins Act, 569
margin of buying, 48-49
margin of safety, stability of earnings record and, 210
market and limit orders, 49-50
market price:
  net cash book value of common stock as a percentage of, 497-498
  ratios, 494-496
market ratings, 226
market risk, 18-19
market savings, major, 113-119
market system of the future, 53-54
market value, 456-457: equity per share as a percentage of, 496-497
markets:
  exchange, as auction markets, 43
  over-the-counter, 39-41
Markowitz portfolio building model, 872-873
McCulloch vs. *Maryland,* 705
mergers, 501-502:
  and acquisitions, 189-190, 793
  growth through, 392-393
mortgage:
  closed, 159
  limited, open-end, 159
  open, 159
  priority of the, 160
  types of, 159-160
multiple correlation techniques, 304-305
municipal bond analysis, 714-720

municipal bonds, 705-714:
  classes of, 706-708
  credit analysis of, 714-716
  market behavior of, 717-720
  market for, 709-713
  other factors in analysis of, 715-716
  primary and secondary markets for, 712-713
  quality of, 713-714
  ratings, 717
mutual funds, 657-660:
  accumulative plans, 659
  contractual plans, 659-660
  dividend reinvestment, 660
  performance records of, 658-659
  special services of, 659-660
  voluntary plans, 659
  withdrawal plans, 660
mutual savings banks:
  functions of, 816
  investment constraints of, 816-818
  investment policies of, 818-821
  portfolio policies of, 814-821

National Association of Securities Dealers, 41; automated quotations system, 39
National Bureau of Economic Research, 211
National Railroad Passenger Corporation (AMTRAK), 570
net income, 485-490
net operating margin, 484-485
net savings and investment funds, 59-62
net working capital, 177, 461, 497
net yield to maturity:
  approximating the, 168
  defined, 168
New York (conditional bill of sale) Plan, 163
New York Quotations Company, 48
New York Stock Exchange, 42:
  Board of Governors, 44
  cash purchase, 48
  commissions and transfer taxes, 52-53
  delivery and settlement, 49
  Department of Stock List, 46-47
  exchange members, 45-46
  margin buying, 48-49
  market and limit orders, 49-50
  membership in the, 44-46
  Monthly Investment Plan, 678-679
  odd-lot orders, 50-51
  puts and calls, 51-52
  short selling, 51
  Stock Price Index, 97
  stop-loss order, 50
  trading on the, 48-53
Newmark vs. *RKO General, Inc.,* 356
newspaper prospectus, 37
no-load funds, 657
noncurrent assets, 465
nonprofit organizations, portfolio policies of, 851-859
normalizing method of reporting depreciation, 441-442

stockholders' equity, 645
real estate mortgage bonds, 232
recapitalizations, 794
receivables, 463-464; installment sales and, 464
receivers' certificates, prior-lien bonds and, 152
"red herring," 35, 36, 346, 354
regression analysis and intrinsic value, 304-306
regulatory agencies, major problems of, 359-361
renewal expense, 645
reorganizations, 793
reported earnings, conservative nature of, 639
research:
    and development, 390-392, 523-524
    basic, 391
    product-oriented, 391
    specialized, 391
reserve fund, 732
resistance points, 108-109
restricted securities, defined, 361
restricted (letter) stock, 361
retained income, 473
return on net worth, 528
return on stockholders' equity, 648
revenue bonds, 707-708; analysis of, 716-717
revenue breakdown analysis, 555-557
rights:
    calculation of value of, 136-138
    form of, 136
    market for, 136
    preemptive, 135-136
rights announcement, information in, 136
risk and return, 291-293
risk considerations, 288-293
risks:
    combating, by careful selection based on thorough analysis, 25
    credit or financial, 11-12, 20-21
    defensive policies advocated to combat, 20-26
    financial, 751-753, 807, 834-835
    income, and need to maximize income, 832, 852-853
    inflation, 750-751, 760
    interest rate, 12-13, 21, 753-754, 807-808, 812, 835-836, 852
    investment, 10-27, 747-748
    major, requiring protection, 733-734
    market, 18-19, 22
    psychological, 19-20, 22, 761-762
    purchasing power or inflation, 13-18, 21, 812, 818, 840, 846, 853
    reducing, by intelligent diversification, 25
    systematic and unsystematic, 290
    the problem of, 10-11
    variations in, 288-289
round lot, 44

sales:
    growth, record of, 494; vs. earnings growth, 265
    net income after extraordinary items as a percentage of, 487
    net income before taxes as a percentage of, 485
    other income and other expense as percentages of, 485
sales per dollar:
    of common equity at the market, 492-493
    of total capital funds ratio, 490-492
savings:
    and dissavings, government, 62
    gross, 57-59
    gross business, 59
    in the United States, 57-67
    net, and investment funds, 59-62
    personal, 63-66, 725-730
savings and loan associations:
    investment constraints of, 821-824
    investment policies of, 824-826
    portfolio policies of, 821-826
savings and time deposits, 730-732
secondary market, 692
secondary reserves, investment policies for, 808-809
securities:
    convertible, calculations for, 217-219
    cyclical undervaluation of, 267-268
    highly marketable, 42
    government, quality and risk of, 686
    limited-income, investment grade, 205-210
    listed, trade in, 43-44
    listing of, 46-48
    other, investment in, for income, 811
    other, investment in, or bond account, 809-813
    public offering of, 37
    seasoned, exchange trading in, 43
    tax-exempt, 818, 841
    United States Government, 685-702
Securities Act of 1933:
    liabilities for false registration under the, 354
    registration statement, 350
    the prospectus, 354
Securities and Exchange Commission accounting regulations, 358-359
Securities Exchange Act of 1934:
    provisions controlling and regulating security trading, 355
    regulation of corporate "insiders," 355-356
    regulation of proxies, 356
    regulation of over-the-counter markets, 356-357
securities industry studies, 360-361
securities markets:
    perfect, 187
    report on special study of the, 664-665
security analysis:
    defined, 394
    factors underlying, 396-399

sum-of-the-years-digits method of depreciation, 440
surplus:
  appraisal, 473
  capital, 472-473
  earned, 472-473
  paid-in, 473
system load factor, 564
systematic risk, defined, 290

tax refunds, 794
tax-exempt foundations:
  conclusions on portfolio policies of, 859
  the 1972 Patman Report on, 853-856
  the Twentieth Century Fund Study on, 856-859
tax-free exchange or swap funds, 662-663
taxes:
  and investment companies, 665-667
  and investment policy, 762-765
  federal estate and gift, 764
  heirs and estate and gift, 764
  state estate, 764-765
technological forecasting, 523-524
tenders, 793
term insurance, 735-736
Texas Gulf Sulphur case, 312-313, 356
third market, 53
time and savings deposits, increased rates paid on, 611
timing:
  cyclical, 255-256
  formula, 116-117
  proper, 25-26
timing techniques, 870-871
tombstone prospectus, 36
trading, unit of, 44
trading on the equity and leverage, 148-149
Transportation Act of 1920, 569
Transportation Act of 1958, 570
treasury bills, 689-690
treasury bonds, 689
treasury notes, 689
trucking industry, 590-595:
  accounting practices in, 594
  the record in brief, 591
  the income account, 592-594
Trust Indenture Act of 1939, 151, 357
trustee, functions of, 151
turnover:
  accounts receivable, 480
  inventory, 480-481
  working capital, 479-480

unamortized cost, 436
underwriting, 31; firm, 34
underwriting contracts, 34-37
underwriting spreads, 35-36
underwriting tests, 633, 635
unfunded pension liabilities, 739
unfunded pension reserves, 470-471
United States Government securities, policy regarding, 818-820
unlimited indenture, 151

unsecured bonds—debentures, 157
unsystematic risk, defined, 290
utility common stocks, improvement of, by 1973, 542
utility plant, 547-553

valuation:
  based on earnings, 320-322
  based on projections of earnings for individual companies, 322-328
valuation of common stocks:
  attitudes toward, in the 1920s, 276
  major factors considered in the, 277-278
  methods suggested in the 1930s, 276-277
  procedure, 316-334
  the problem of, 400-402
value, meanings of, 456-457
volume of the market, 109

warrants:
  defined, 136
  stock purchase option, 138
wasting asset companies, 443
wasting assets, 443, 466
Wharton Report (1962), 664
Wiesenberger measure of performance, 668
working capital, 177-178, 460-462, 546-547:
  analysis, 478
  net, 461
  provisions regarding, 229
  position, 478
  turnover, 479-480

year-end tax selling, 110
yield:
  bond, 165-169, 218
  current bond, 165
  curves, 695-696
  dividend, 495-496
  earnings, 495
  investment, 646
  net, to maturity, 168
  patterns in primary and secondary markets, 720; predictive value of, 697
  stock, 165

Alberts, W. W., 189
Alexander, Sidney S., 255
Almon, Clopper, Jr., 325
Anderson, Paul F., 463
Anthony, R. N., 170-171
Atkinson, Thomas R., 211, 215, 224, 243
Baruch, Bernard, 7
Bauman, W. Scott, 301-302
Bing, Ralph A., 287
Blume, Marshall E., 290
Bosland, Chelcie C., 313
Bosse, William D., 471
Boyd, Harmon R. D., 463
Brigham, Eugene F., 286
Briloff, Abraham J., 501, 532
Brittain, John A., 190, 328